HISTORIC U.S. COURT CASES, 1690–1990
AN ENCYCLOPEDIA

AMERICAN LAW AND SOCIETY
Series Editor: John W. Johnson
Volume 2

Garland Reference Library of the Social Sciences
Volume 497

Historic U.S. Court Cases
1690–1990: An Encyclopedia

by
John W. Johnson
Department of History
University of Northern Iowa

GARLAND PUBLISHING
New York & London
1992

Library of Congress Cataloging-in-Publication Data
Johnson, John W., 1946–
    Historic U.S. court cases, 1690–1990: an encyclopedia / by John W. Johnson.
        p. cm. — (Garland reference library of the social sciences; vol. 497.
American law and society; vol. 2)
    Includes index.
    ISBN 0-8240-4430-4
    1. Law—United States—History. 2. Law—United States—Cases. I. Title. II.
Title: Historic US court cases, 1690–1990: an encyclopedia. III. Series: Garland
reference library of the social sciences. American law and society; vol. 2.
KF385.A4J64 1992
349.73'0264—dc20
[347.300264]   91-40175
                                                                        CIP

Printed on 250-year-life, acid-free paper
Manufactured in the United States of America

Design by Marc Shifflet

ABC94

8.11.93

For Matthew and Noah

TABLE OF CONTENTS

PART II: GOVERNMENTAL ORGANIZATION, POWER, AND PROCEDURE

A. Separation of Powers

B. Federalism

PART III: ECONOMICS AND THE LAW

A. Contracts

B. Commerce

G. Natural Resources, Technology, and the Environment

PART IV: RACE AND GENDER IN AMERICAN LAW

A. Slavery

PART V: CIVIL LIBERTIES

C. Freedom of Religion

D. Obscenity and Pornography

FOREWORD

The formal law, its practitioners, and the culture it has engendered pervade the United States. The brilliant nineteenth-century French traveler and writer Alexis de Tocqueville maintained in *Democracy in America* that in this country virtually every political question sooner or later leads to a legal decision. Garland Publishing's American Law and Society series of one-volume encyclopedias, of which the *Historic U.S. Court Cases, 1690–1990: An Encyclopedia* is a part, goes Tocqueville one better. Those of us involved in this series believe that the prism of the law gathers, refracts, reflects, and (not infrequently) blurs American life. At its best, law provides a framework that enables us to make sense out of our physical and intellectual surroundings. At its worst, it confuses, frustrates, and impedes progress. Law has affected and continues to affect virtually everything we do or think about: giving birth, rearing and educating children, marriage, work, travel, business transactions, what we read and see, and, of course, how we get along with one another.

Although studying law in its social context might be a valuable approach to use in grappling with any country's history, it is particularly appropriate for the United States. This is, after all, the country with more statutes and published case law than any in the world. D.H. Lawrence, the great British writer and critic, once referred to America as a nation of "Thou Shalt Nots." The United States now has about 25 times as many lawyers per capita as Japan. Yet Americans are not totally comfortable with the law and those who perform what the legal philosopher Karl Llewellyn once called the "law jobs." For example, the first lawyer who arrived in the Pilgrim colony of Plymouth in the 1620s was quickly driven out of town for being too disputatious. This may have spawned the first American lawyer joke. Perhaps the residents of Plymouth were saying that law is too important to be left to the lawyers.

Historic U.S. Court Cases, 1690–1990: An Encyclopedia is the second number in Garland Publishing's Law and American Society series. Consistent with the philosophy of the series, the 171 essays are written in straightforward prose, unencumbered by technical legal jargon.

John W. Johnson
Series Editor
University of Northern Iowa

PREFACE

The bicentennial of the U.S. Constitution in 1987 and the bicentennial of the Bill of Rights in 1991 have offered splendid civics lessons to the American nation. The spotlight focused on America's founding document and its first ten amendments has generally proven welcome to those of us who teach and write about American law because it has raised the visibility of our field. While we may chafe occasionally at the over-simplifications of important legal concepts (even the Sunday comics section in major newspapers occasionally contains a Bill of Rights feature), most of us welcome the increased interest in the rule of law among students and the public.

The two great legal anniversaries of our time have also whetted the interest of the academic community for specialized writing on American law. Scores of books and articles on law and the Constitution have been pouring out as a result of this increased attention. Publishers, journal editors, and conference program committees seem genuinely more interested in legal topics than they once were. Moreover, general American historians seem to be more willing to adapt legal insights into their syllabi and textbooks than ever before.

The assembly of *Historic U.S. Court Cases, 1690–1990: An Encyclopedia* took place roughly within the 1987–91 period bounded by the two legal bicentennials. Its content and spirit reflect the blend of popular interest and specialized attention recently given to American law. The volume is designed to serve both the student or layperson interested in learning about important American court cases as well as the legal specialist looking for a convenient repository of useful information, analyses, or references.

This is not an "encyclopedia" in the most common sense of the word. Most often when we think of an encyclopedia we think of a volume that offers a comprehensive, exhaustive, or complete compendium of information on a subject. No single volume, no matter how large, could present a comprehensive, exhaustive, or complete treatment of the thousands of U.S. court cases that experts might call "historic." However, there is another level for understanding the term encyclopedia. Dictionaries and thesauruses note that an encyclopedia may also be a volume that offers an extensive, thorough, or sweeping treatment of a subject.

Readers familiar with the old *International Encyclopedia of the Social Sciences* (1968) and the even older *Encyclopaedia of the Social Sciences* (1930) will understand this meaning of "encyclopedia." The essay/entries in the *IESS* and the *ESS* are extensive treatments of important social scientific concepts, written by experts. Obviously not all social science concepts could be defined even in a multivolume set, so the editors of the projects selected some of the most important concepts in the social sciences and commissioned the entries. The results are two sets of volumes that, although now dated, are remarkably readable and provocative. They remain standard reference tools in academic libraries and most public libraries.

It would be arrogant (and erroneous) to compare the *Historic U.S. Court Cases* to the *IESS* and *ESS*. My volume is far less ambitious. But it is fair to say, I believe, that this legal encyclopedia has been strongly influenced by the two well-known reference sets. Like the *IESS* and the *ESS*, it is selective and not comprehensive. The essays are meant to highlight major legal issues and concerns by concentrating attention on selected court cases, not to occupy the entire field of American law. I have employed no single criterion for selecting a case for an essay/entry in this volume. Some cases are obvious choices by virtue of their great impact as precedents in American law. Likewise, some cases are featured because of their fame as important historical events in and of themselves. In addition, some cases have been selected because they are representative of a large body of important litigation. A few cases have been selected for treatment because they are decidedly *not* typical; these cases reveal interesting eccentricities in the American legal past. Other cases have been selected because they raised (or continue to raise) significant legal or historical issues. Finally, a few essays examine cases that showcase the role of a particularly famous jurist, lawyer, or litigant.

Regrettably, there was a handful of cases that I was unable to match with authors, and there were a few potential contributors who never completed their assignments. The volume is poorer due to the absence of these essays. In general, however, I was very pleased with the cooperation of those who did submit their essays. Although I was kept very busy editing, I found it necessary to reject very few essays.

A large number of the essays in this volume probe U.S. Supreme Court decisions. The importance of the U.S. Supreme Court as the final arbitrator for legal disputes in this country is obvious. However, some of the most interesting and important cases in American history were decided in the lower federal courts, the state courts and (in the pre-Constitutional days) in the colonial courts. Some of these important non-U.S. Supreme Court decisions are the subjects of essays in the volume.

As was the case also with the two famous social sciences encyclopedia, the essays in this volume were composed by individual contributors who were not tyrannized by a single lock-step format. The contributors were allowed, within the bounds of stylistic consistency and the number of prescribed words allotted, to express their own voices and stake out their own conclusions. There was no party line or standard of orthodoxy forced upon the authors. If there is a design to the volume it is a result of my charge that the essayists focus on the narrative, dramatic dimension of legal disputes within their larger social and historical context. The recent resurgence of narrative history in the academy is a development that I want, in my small way, to encourage. Hence, the contributors were asked to stress the factual bases of disputes and to emphasize the provocative issues raised by litigation. They were also encouraged to place their case (or cases) within

the broader social context. How they chose to respond to these general suggestions was largely left to their own devices. I provided additional direction when asked. For the most part, the only substantive changes I made as editor in the submissions of the contributors involved the correction of factual errors.

Based on the advice of my advisory board, the suggestions of other senior scholars, and the serendipity of professional and personal contacts, I selected 80 scholars to compose the essays for the volume. As was the case in the assignments for the *IESS* and the *ESS*, every effort was made here to cast the net widely. Because some of the best writing about the law continues to be accomplished by nonlegal experts, I did not want just lawyers or legal historians writing the entries. Thus, I designed the *Encyclopedia* to reflect thoughtful contributions to understanding the law from a variety of scholars and writers.

A bit of prosopography on the 80 contributors is in order. About half (51 percent) qualify as legal experts. These include historians with constitutional or legal specialties (26 percent), political scientists who specialize in public law or jurisprudence (14 percent), and law professors or practicing attorneys (11 percent). The other half—actually about 49 percent—is composed of historians with other than legal specialties (21 percent), unaffiliated scholars (15 percent), other social scientists or humanities professors (10 percent), and academics in governmental service (3 percent). Those knowledgeable about legal scholarship will recognize the names of many distinguished senior legal scholars in the roster of contributors. But there are also many essays by scholars new to the profession; these authors were chosen because of their special interest or expertise on a particular case or area of the law. Of the many people I solicited for contributions to the *Encyclopedia*, most kindly accepted the commission. Those who did not generally recommended others to serve in their stead. Only one individual complained that the payment offered to contributors was insufficient.

Efforts were made to achieve gender and geographic distribution among the contributors to the *Encyclopedia*. Of the individuals who eventually committed to the project, one-fifth

(20 percent) are women. Although this percentage is substantially lower than the size of the female cohort currently in graduate programs in History and Political Science or enrolled in law schools, it is about the same as the percentage of women currently holding academic appointments in History, Political Science, and Law. The greatest number of contributors (41 percent) reside in the South; about an equal number live in the Midwest (25 percent) and the West (21 percent); and the smallest percentage is from the East (13 percent). The preponderance of southern scholars represented is likely a product of my associations while teaching for over a decade in South Carolina. Of the total number of contributors, I am acquainted personally with about two-thirds (69 percent). The other one-third (31 percent) I know only through correspondence and telephone conversations.

The *Encyclopedia* contains 171 essays of varying lengths. Essays on cases deemed to be of monumental importance are about 5,000 words. Cases of medium-level importance are about 2,000 words in length. And a sample of lesser cases are treated in essays of about 1,000 words. The volume is organized into six parts. Part I offers a selection of 15 essays on crime and criminal law in American history. Part II offers 20 essays on governmental organization, power, and procedure. Part III, the longest section, presents 46 essays on economics and the law. Part IV tenders 30 essays dealing with the important issues of race and gender in American law. Part V, on civil liberties, includes 39 essays keyed to some of the most important individual freedoms in the Bill of Rights. And Part VI, on law and critical periods of American history, contains 21 essays focusing on cases that are particularly revealing about controversial periods in the nation's past.

Each part begins with a brief introduction. Each introduction includes a short rationale for the inclusion of this section of essays in a volume on historic U.S. cases. In addition, each introduction provides a synopsis of the cases covered. The introductions do not, however, explain the holdings of the cases or engage in much rhetoric about how the cases fit into their historical context. These tasks the contributors accomplish in their essays: given the story-like composition of most of the essays, extensive editorial commentary would be superfluous.

Within each part of the volume, the essays are arranged in thematic sections according to the chronology of the cases covered. Under the title of each essay is the name and affiliation of the contributor. This is followed by the title of the case(s) discussed in the essay. For those interested in consulting the cases directly, the official legal citations are included (except for cases that were not published in court reports). Finally, the name of the court that decided the case(s) is noted. Each essay is followed by a brief "selected bibliography." Each bibliography reports the sources that the contributor felt to be most useful in constructing his or her entry and in offering relevant information and analysis on the case(s) treated. Many of the authorities cited are books or journal articles that can be found in good academic and public libraries. For legal specialists and others with access to law libraries, there are also numerous references to law review articles.

Who might use this volume and how might it be used? General readers with legal questions should probably begin by consulting the name and subject index. If a case name is known, the *Encyclopedia*'s case index should be the starting point. For someone with a general interest in a broad legal topic, the table of contents or the introductions to the six parts would be the places to begin. Then the focus could be narrowed by reading selected essays or consulting the indexes. Legal specialists might want to enter the volume through any or all of these portals, checking what they already know against the accounts of the cases offered in the essays. For all users, however, the selected bibliographies should be particularly suggestive for additional reading.

Another approach to the *Encyclopedia*—one that might appeal to the informational browsers among us—would be to start paging through the volume, searching for essays on cases that appear interesting. Given the quality of the writing and the inherent drama of historic judicial decisions, I suspect that it will not take the curious intellectual shopper long to find many essays to peruse with care.

John W. Johnson
Cedar Falls, Iowa
December 1991

ACKNOWLEDGMENTS

One of the pleasures of completing a substantial written project is that it presents the author with an opportunity to thank formally those who provided assistance and encouragement. For a volume of one-half a million words, compiled over a period of five years from the contributions of 80 scholars, my list of obligations is long.

First and foremost, the fourscore contributors deserve credit and gratitude for their well-written, substantive, and provocative essays. Despite busy teaching, research, and other employment obligations, they completed their essays in fine fashion—most of them without being prodded. I sincerely thank the contributors for waiting so patiently for the appearance of the volume. I hope that when they see the final product they will feel that the time they devoted to their own essays was time well spent.

I am personally acquainted with about two-thirds of the individuals who wrote essays for the volume. The quality of their work supports the adage that you can always count on your friends. The remaining one-third (25) I have communicated with only by letter or phone; I hope to meet these individuals someday and thank them in person for allowing me to include their work in this volume.

Of the 171 essays in the volume, 170 are original contributions. Only one was published earlier: "Can Nebraska or Any State Regulate Railroads?" in Part III. It appeared in 1973 in *Nebraska History* and is reprinted here in a slightly altered form with the kind permission of the journal's editor.

The members of the informal "advisory board" for the *Encyclopedia*—Kermit L. Hall, David T. Konig, and Paul L. Murphy—merit thanks for helping plan the structure of the volume and for proposing the names of many of the contributors. I trust they will note that I followed their suggestions most of the time and not be too critical of me for foolishly wandering off on my own in a few places.

This project is partly a tale of two institutions—the University of Northern Iowa where I have taught, administered, and snuck in a little time for scholarship since 1988, and Clemson University where I did similar things from 1976 to 1988. I am grateful to the Departments of History at both universities for secretarial help, student assistance, and clerical supplies. Moreover, my former Clemson colleagues and current Northern Iowa colleagues warrant a special measure of gratitude: several offered trenchant advice on legal cases, and others provided the camaraderie that only colleagues who are also friends can render. From my Clemson years I especially want to thank Bernie Duffy, Sue Duffy, Rich Golden, Bob Green, Alan Grubb, Don McKale, Denis Paz, Steve Wainscott, and John Wunder. At Northern Iowa, I have been especially appreciative of the interest and support of Dick Broadie, Jay Lees, Bob Martin, Chuck Quirk, Glenda Riley, Roy Sandstrom, and Don Shepardson.

During the final stages of editing the essays, I was saddened by the death of Mary K. Bonsteel Tachau, longtime professor of history at the University of Louisville. Mary K. was an outstanding legal scholar, a source of sage advice on this volume, and a good friend; I will miss her.

The editorial staff of Garland Publishing, old hands at producing reference volumes, provided exemplary direction and support for this project. Gary Kuris suggested the idea for the *Encyclopedia*, helped me define and revise the prospectus, and had the good judgment to know when to give me a pat on the back and when to deliver a swift kick elsewhere. Chuck Bartelt offered valuable assistance on various computer issues involved in producing the manuscript. Paula Ladenburg and Kevin Bradley provided direction and coordination from a business standpoint. And Paula Grant survived the mind-numbing job of copy editing a 2,000-page manuscript.

Judy Dohlman, the long-time secretary for the Department of History at Northern Iowa, served as a splendid typist, proofreader, and "document converter" for the *Encyclopedia*. She lived with these historic cases for two years, spending hundreds of hours deciphering my eccentric editorial notations and producing letter-perfect pages and properly configured computer diskettes. When she finally finished, the text of this volume required over five million bytes of computer storage. Truly, this project could not have been completed without the unique assistance she rendered.

None of the generous and hard-working individuals named above should be held responsible for the errors and shortcomings in the *Encyclopedia*. As the person whose name appears on the title page, I bear that responsibility.

Finally, I must acknowledge (although not in any way dispatch) my enormous personal debts. Deborah Garland Johnson—despite her busy life as a teacher, mother, and spouse—permitted me the time and space to complete this volume. For her understanding and encouragement I am most grateful. My sons, Matthew and Noah, may not always have understood what was keeping me so long at the office or in the library, but they respected the fact that I was doing something I considered important. This book is for them.

John W. Johnson has served as Professor and Head of the Department of History at the University of Northern Iowa since 1988. He was previously a faculty member at Clemson University (1976–88) and Skidmore College (1973–76). He regularly teaches courses in historical methods, U.S. legal/constitutional history, and recent U.S. history. Among his publications are three books, *The Dimensions of Non-Legal Evidence in the American Judicial Process* (1990), *Insuring Against Disaster: The Nuclear Industry on Trial* (1986), and *American Legal Culture, 1908–1940* (1981). Besides serving as the Series Editor for Garland Publishing's set of volumes on American Law and Society, Johnson is currently working on a book on law and nuclear energy.

HISTORIC U.S. COURT CASES, 1690–1990
AN ENCYCLOPEDIA

PART I: CRIME AND CRIMINAL LAW

PART I: CRIME AND CRIMINAL LAW

INTRODUCTION

It is most appropriate to begin a volume on law with a section on crime. The great jurist and legal philosopher Oliver Wendell Holmes, Jr., in a famous 1897 address entitled "The Path of the Law," counseled: "If you want to know the law and nothing else, you must look at it as a bad man, who cares only for the material consequences which such knowledge enables him to predict." Holmes went on in the speech to emphasize that the bad man's perspective, by itself, is not enough for one to understand and appreciate the place of law in a society. But it is a good starting place.

The 15 essays in Part I offer a sample of cases throughout American history that stem from criminal acts but also illuminate some of the larger issues or problems of their eras. As is true for many essays in this volume, some of the cases are well-known and are themselves important historical events. Other cases, however, are not important *per se*; rather, they offer representative or curious examples of legal issues presented outside of the glare of contemporary publicity.

For the colonial era, the first essay, "Witchcraft and the Law," deals with the most notorious example of the prosecution of the crime of witchcraft in American history. It is followed by two other essays on colonial crimes—"Pirates Walk the Plank in Charleston" and "New York on Fire"—that touch on important historical conflicts, one involving piracy and the other, a racial riot.

For the early national era, there are several essays of historical note. "Treason and the Whiskey 'Insurrection'" presents the first case prosecuted under the definition of treason in the U.S. Constitution. "Congress Should First Define the Offenses and Apportion the Punishment" examines important crimes defined by the so-called federal common law. "John Fries to the Rescue in the Hot Water War" treats another treason case, this one involving the ubiquitous Justice Samuel Chase. "Defective Indictment" discusses the importance of a small technical issue in a state court to the prosecution of a violent crime. And "Federal Common Law of Crimes" examines the leading U.S. Supreme Court case of the period on the federal common law of crimes.

For the mid-nineteenth century there are three essays involving death and/or the death penalty. "A Double Standard of Justice" presents a bizarre Louisiana case involving murder and adultery. "Death for Grand Larceny" examines an early California death penalty case. And "Public Opinion, Expert Testimony, and 'The Insanity Dodge'" probes the criminal trial of Charles Guiteau, the assassin of President James Garfield.

For the late twentieth century, four essays dealing with crime are presented. "You Have the Right to Remain Silent . . ." deals with the well-known "Miranda warning" required since the mid-1960s for police making arrests of individuals accused of criminal acts. "The Death and Resurrection of Capital Punishment" presents a discussion of the two leading U.S. Supreme Court cases on the constitutionality of capital punishment. "Plea Bargaining and the 'Vindictive' Exercise of Prosecutorial Discretion" offers an example of a case from Kentucky concerning the common practice of plea bargaining in the state and federal courts. Finally, "Credibility and Crisis in California's High Court" presents a recent example of what can happen when politics and personalities become enmeshed in a controversial criminal issue.

WITCHCRAFT AND THE LAW

by David Thomas Konig
Department of History
Washington University at St. Louis

Salem Witchcraft Trials (1692) [Massachusetts colonial court]

From the perspective of 300 years, it is hard to comprehend how an entire society—that of Massachusetts Bay in 1692—could plunge into a frenzied fear of the devil. Unable fully to recapture the thinking of the people involved, one tends to see the episode known as the Salem Witchcraft Trials of 1692 as a thinly veiled, cynical mass assault on nonconformists, dissidents, or other powerless groups.

The fact is that the people of New England were no different from good Christians anywhere in the late seventeenth century: they had no doubt of Satan's existence, and they implicitly believed in his relentless assault on the Kingdom of God. According to their beliefs, the former archangel Satan had attempted to usurp God's rule and, for such rebellion, had been flung from heaven. Not content to accept such banishment, Satan had commenced a remorseless campaign to destroy the Kingdom of God denied to him and, as Prince of Darkness, to establish his own rule. Not even New England—and Puritan New England at that, where the saints preserved the holy errand of the Reformation—was immune to the threat. Indeed, the Puritan colony was all the more likely a target. As explained by Reverend Deodat Lawson of Boston (formerly of Salem), God allowed Satan to practice his evil "to serve [God's] own most Holy Ends." The devil's temptations were a test for the believer and a warning to the backslider. "Their Graces are hereby tried," Reverend Cotton Mather said of the New England saints in 1689, and "their Uprightness is made known."

In 1689, God seemed to have good reason to test the faithful. In the minds of many, New England had departed from its original godly purpose. Boston, the holy "Citty upon a Hill" of John Winthrop in 1630, was now a thriving commercial center, with ships traveling all over the Atlantic community. Approximately one in six men took part in the colony's overseas trade; church membership had never approached that figure in the seventeenth century. A once pious holy experiment now seemed given over to Mammon; the Christian communalism now seemed supplanted by a more secular character and an incipient individualism. Worse, many approved of the changes and pushed them forward. Young people, it appeared, had no interest in reformation and used the new openness of society only to go their own way. Parents, complained one minister, were letting their children "have their swinge, to go and come where and when they please, and especially in the night."

How had these changes come about? Many agreed with Cotton Mather in 1689 when he warned, "Go tell Mankind, that there are Devils and Witches; and that tho those night-birds least appear where the day-light of the Gospel comes, yet New-England has had examples of their Existence and Operation."

The message reached a jittery and insecure people all over New England, but it had special meaning for those of Salem, just north of Boston. This small seaport had experienced all of the pervasive social and economic changes affecting the region as a whole. Older even than Boston, Salem was one of the Puritans' first New World settlements and had long held the reputation of being among its most devout communities. But Salem had grown rapidly in the past generation and had become a thriving and worldly commercial center with ties to London and other European cities. The old unity of its founders had faded, and merchants had replaced ministers as the town's leaders.

There were, in fact, two Salems: next to the bustling port (known as Salem Town) was a traditional, and much poorer, outlying parish known as Salem Farms, or Salem Village. The Village encompassed a scattering of homesteads, most of them residences of families who did not share in the wealth or participate in the new ways of life in Salem Town. Humble families barely getting by on their own farm production, they adhered to older notions of communal behavior and religious conservatism.

They also clung to older notions of folk practice, including the use of magic to improve or ameliorate their hard and uncertain lives. For the young, the future held as much fear as promise, and they not infrequently resorted to folk magic to foretell the future and to give themselves some assurances about what to expect from it. Young women in particular looked anxiously to the future, in which the wealth or trade of their husbands would determine their own standing in the community. Largely powerless to control their own lot in life, many young women turned to magic for information or as a way to guide their lives. For a small group of girls in the Salem Village household of Reverend Samuel Parris, the future might be revealed in the white of an egg—much like the image in a crystal ball. But when a murky image resembling a coffin appeared at one of their sessions, it so terrified them that they reacted physically—with violent and uncontrollable contortions. With their hopes turned to horror, they shrank back in fear that they had "tampered with the devil's tools so far that hereby one door was opened [to the devil] to play those pranks."

The anxieties of change in seventeenth-century Salem turned the petty fortune-telling of a few girls into a major crisis for the entire colony. Like nearly everyone at that time, the people of both Salems believed in the reality of Satan and in his never-ending efforts to induce Christians to betray God. The two Salems were as distrustful of one another as any feuding villages ever were, but their resentments were made worse by the wide gap between their two ways of life. After Reverend Parris told others about the "afflictions" of the girls, these tensions erupted into a firestorm of witchcraft accusation when the girls, including Parris's nine-year-old daughter Elizabeth, began to attribute their convulsive torments to the satanic acts of three local women. The effects spread into the neighboring towns in Essex County suffering from the same kind of divisions. Traditionalists at Salem Village believed that the people of Salem Town had sold their souls to the devil in return for their wealth. On the other side, residents of Salem Town feared that their poorer neighbors were enlisting Satan and his tools in revenge for and resentment against their prosperous way of life.

Horror followed shock when it became apparent that some people actually were using magic and witchcraft. Pins and dolls were found in the home of one woman suspected of being a witch. Parris's efforts to overcome Satan's wiles with prayer failed dismally and—more disturbing still—others were turning to magic as a cure for the bewitchments. Parris was aghast to learn that a Village woman had persuaded Parris's West Indian servant Tituba and her husband John Indian to attempt an old English folk remedy by baking a "witch cake." This concoction of ordinary meal and the urine of a victim was fed to a dog (presumably, a "familiar" of the witch), which would then injure the witch and reveal his (or, more likely, her) identity. Parris roundly rebuked this attempt as "going to the Devil for help against the Devil."

But where else could they go for "help against the Devil"? When the first accusations were made in February 1692, the people of Salem found themselves in an odd position because they had no legitimate government from which to seek aid. In 1684, the Crown had revoked the colonial charter of 1629 in its consolidation of all the New England colonies (with New York) into one huge Dominion of New England. For five years New England functioned without its customary legal institutions until, emulating England's Glorious Revolution against King James II, its residents rose in rebellion in 1689 and ousted James's royal officials. Hastily reconstituting their former charter institutions, they attempted to operate government as they had known it until a new charter could bring them the properly constituted legal institutions needed to establish law and order.

Until Governor Sir William Phips arrived with that charter on May 14, 1692, a legal vacuum existed and accelerated the sense of panic. Moreover, war had broken out when Catholic France declared its enmity for the Protestants William and Mary, who now ruled England and its colonies. Salem—exposed on the northern frontier against French Canada— was gripped with fear. Villagers in Marblehead, a few miles away, rioted when colony officials tried to remove that town's cannon for the defense of Boston, and rumors swirled of a combined French and Indian invasion, to be abetted by an uprising of local black slaves.

Helpless against these external threats, the people of Salem begged their acting magistrates to take quick action against the internal threats they perceived around them. They were not alone in panicking amid the insecurity and fear. The provisional Court of Assistants at Boston, sensitive to any imputations against its legitimacy or its capacity to meet violations of the law, had condemned 13 pirates to death in 1689—an unprecedented crackdown that far exceeded the customarily more lenient treatment of felons. Although the reconstituted court pardoned 11 of these men, the sternness of the government had sent an implicit but reassuring message to a frightened people. For those who needed a more explicit message, complained an indignant observer, the assistants ordered the execution of another man "to frighten the people into submission."

The two resident magistrates at Salem, John Hathorne and Jonathan Corwin, found Salem Village rife with accusations on February 29, 1692, when they traveled to its meetinghouse to examine the first three persons accused of witchcraft. Despite having little authority upon which to proceed, they remanded the three— Sarah Good, Sarah Osborne, and Tituba—to Boston gaol. They had still less of a notion of how to proceed, for such examinations had been rare in the colony before 1692. Until that year, only 70 indictments had been handed down in all of New England, but most had been dismissed, and only 11 accused witches (five in Massachusetts Bay, the remainder in Connecticut) had been executed. Even so, Hathorne and Corwin continued to examine and imprison suspects for what they anticipated would be trial

as soon as the new government was established. Martha Corey, Dorcas Good (Sarah's four-year-old daughter), and Rebecca Nurse followed the others to Boston gaol. So widespread were the accusations that the two magistrates had to continue their examinations in Salem Town, with the aid of Deputy Governor Thomas Danforth and four other magistrates (James Russell, Isaac Addington, Samuel Appleton, and Samuel Sewell). From their seats in the Salem Town meetinghouse, they continued to commit suspects to gaols in Boston, Salem, and Ipswich, all three now overflowing with suspects. By the time Governor Sir William Phips sailed into Boston harbor on May 14, probably more than 100 languished under indictment.

Phips confronted a puzzling judicial situation, for, unless he released them all, trials had to be scheduled. According to the new charter, the legislature (but only the legislature) of Massachusetts Bay had the authority to create courts. Before any courts could be established, therefore, elections had to be held, and Phips had expected that no court could thus be set up until January 1693. Such a delay was unthinkable; already, one prisoner (Sarah Osborne) had died from the conditions in Boston gaol, and others were sure to follow in a typical winter under such conditions.

Acting in haste, Phips constituted a special court of a type which, in England, was commissioned to deal with criminal activity, a court of "oyer and terminer" (i.e., to hear and determine). Two problems attached to his decision. First, it created a court without proper statutory authority; in that sense, it rendered all prosecutions legally improper. The other problem was more tangled, for Phips worded his commission ambiguously concerning the court's jurisdiction. Courts of oyer and terminer might be special (i.e., deal with a particular class of crimes in a particular area) or general (i.e., determine all crimes in the area). Phips issued his commission to a "Special Court of Oyer and Terminer," but in the body of the commission he authorized it "to inquire of, hear and determine for this time, according to the law and custom of England and of this their Majesties' Province, all manner of crimes and offenses had, made, done or perpetrated within the counties of Suffolk, Essex, Middlesex, and each of them."

Did this mean that a *special* court had *general* jurisdiction? Phips evaded the question by busying himself with preparations to lead New England troops into battle against the French and Indians. He left the answer to the court, led by Chief Justice William Stoughton (the new lieutenant governor), assisted by John Richards, Nathaniel Saltonstall, Wait Winthrop, Bartholomew Gedney, Samuel Sewall, Peter Sergeant, and the two former examining magistrates, Hathorne and Corwin. Perhaps the answer, when it came, was the product of clerk Stephen Sewall (the judge's brother) or King's Attorney Thomas Newton: either might have prepared the indictments, which were drawn up in advance and specified witchcraft, leaving only the names of the victim and accused to be added. If any crime at all was to be prosecuted before January 1693—that is, if the province was to have any weapon against any form of social disorder—the act would have to involve satanic collusion, and the person named would thus become a witchcraft defendant.

Moreover, the commission had specified trial "according to the law and custom of England and of this their Majesties' Province." Two models—English and local—thus competed for application. The difference was great. If the court followed Massachusetts Bay practice, the Bible would greatly influence the trials. As to substance, the Massachusetts Bay *Laws and Liberties* of 1648 followed the Biblical definition of witchcraft as merely consulting with spirits; it did not require actual harm (*maleficium*) to a victim. In this regard, colonial law matched that of England's, which Sir Edward Coke defined as consulting spirits "for any purpose . . . without any other act or thing."

Despite this agreement in substance, a major procedural difference separated the law of Massachusetts from that of England. New England criminal procedure required two witnesses to any capital crime. A legacy of ecclesiastical law but not a common-law rule, this requirement had been enacted in 1641 and enjoyed a powerful standing in the colony's trial practice. According to the Book of Numbers, "[O]ne witness shall not testify against any person to cause him to die," a point emphasized many years earlier by Reverend Charles Chauncey in answer to Plymouth Governor William Bradford that "God would not put our lives into the power of any one tongue." By contrast, the common-law rule permitted conviction on the testimony of a single witness. (The English requirement of two witnesses was a statutory rule applying only to treason.)

English and local law also differed on the matter of forfeiture of a felon's estate. The common-law rule that a felon's property be confiscated by the state upon conviction was not followed in Massachusetts.

A precise reconstruction of the trials is impossible: no trial records survive, so historians must rely on the pretrial examinations of suspects, the accounts of observers (usually complaints by those opposing the prosecutions), and the petitions of the suspects themselves. Nevertheless, it is possible to reconstruct the trials with some certainty as to how they proceeded. First, it is clear that the court decided to adhere scrupulously to English practice. In part, this decision revealed the overweening ambition of Chief Justice Stoughton, whose political aspirations inclined him to seize every opportunity to impress royal officials with his trustworthiness as lieutenant governor of the province. As it became ever more clear after 1684, the officials who would occupy the highest judicial offices in the colony would be those who conformed to the systems of royal justice and the needs of imperial administration. Stoughton, however, did not have to impose this decision on an unwilling local leadership. No one had forgotten that Massachusetts Bay had lost its charter in 1684 largely because of the colony's many departures from English law. Its rejection of toleration for the Church of England stood as the most serious example of repudiating English law, but other areas also figured in the decision by King's Bench to vacate the charter. The colony's leaders had protested the innocuous nature of their departures from a complicated system "which wee pretend not to a thorow acquaintance with," but their disingenuous claim to unsophisticated provincialism neither convinced the Crown nor gave them confidence for its use in a later conflict. Moreover, Stoughton and Bartholomew Gedney had served on the Superior Court established under the Dominion of New England—a court that adhered strictly to common-law principle and practice—and they would follow that path in 1692.

The oyer and terminer court that convened on June 2, 1692, for the first trial therefore had a strong internally imposed mandate to honor English law. That some measure of uncertainty still remained, however, became clear immediately after the first trial. The first defendant to stand trial was Bridget Bishop, whose case was probably the easiest of all the cases to be tried. Her husband had accused her of witchcraft, the girls of the Parris household had accused her of urging them to sign a covenant with the devil, two women had testified to seeing her with the devil, and workmen renovating a wall in a house she once occupied discovered "several puppets made up of rags and hogs' bristles with headless pins in them." The jury returned a guilty verdict, and she was hanged on June 10. The court's uncertainty was apparent, however, in its prompt adjournment and consultation with the area's ministers on a vital point of law before conducting any more trials.

The court's question concerned "spectral evidence," the acceptance of testimony that described actions by a specter, or devil, in the image of the accused witch. Already, Cotton Mather had urged Judge John Richards not to allow such evidence. Mather's reasoning was hardly modern or secular in the sense of rejecting specters as unnatural and thus impossible. Instead, Mather was acting on a theological imperative; namely, that the devil's powers were so awful that he might, in his horrid dissembling, use the specter of an innocent person to confound God's children and harm anyone. Deodat Lawson agreed, although perhaps as much because his own deceased wife was being accused by such "proof." Warning of immense trouble for innocent persons, Mather argued that if spectral evidence was admitted as conclusive proof, "The Door is opened!"

Phips had sufficient reservation to ask for advice from the local ministry. He did so despite the admissibility of spectral evidence at common law; used in English trials since 1593, it was justified in the widely used handbook for justices of the peace, Michael Dalton's *Countrey Justice*. So convinced of its admissibility was Chief Justice Sir John Holt of King's Bench that he accepted it in English trials *after* those

in Salem, admitting such evidence in trials over which he presided in 1695 and 1696. But would the people of Massachusetts Bay accept trials that used it?

The clergy of the colony answered promptly. Three days later Phips received the "Return of the Several Ministers" with its advice: "exquisite caution, lest by too much credulity for things received only upon the Devil's authority there be a door opened for a long train of miserable consequences. . . ." Squarely confronting the issue, the clergy reported that capital convictions for witchcraft "ought certainly to be more considerable than barely the accused person being represented by a specter unto the afflicted, inasmuch as 'tis an undoubted and a notorious thing that a Demon may, by God's permission, appear even to ill purposes in the shape of an innocent, yea, a virtuous man." It is ironic that this episode, the last ever in which a governor of Massachusetts consulted the clergy for legal advice, saw the ministers taking what would be (for different reasons) the modern position against a secular institution that chose the opposite. Only three ministers (including Parris) disagreed, but Stoughton pressed on against their advice and ordered that spectral evidence be admitted. In protest, a "very much dissatisfied" Judge Nathaniel Saltonstall resigned from the bench.

The acceptance of spectral evidence opened the door for the "long train of miserable abuses" about which the ministers had warned. When the court resumed on June 30, it condemned five more women (Sarah Good, Rebecca Nurse, Susannah Martin, Elizabeth Howe, and Sarah Wildes), all of whom were hanged on July 19. Most shocking—and puzzling to historians— was the case of Rebecca Nurse. A respected member of the community, she was not at all like the mostly poor or obscure defendants so far sent to Gallows Hill. Judge Hathorne's sister and brother-in-law had testified for her as character witnesses, and 39 of her neighbors had petitioned the court on her innocence. In fact, the jury has acquitted her at trial. But no one had yet been acquitted and dismissed; Stoughton, ruling the courtroom with an iron hand, ordered Nurse interrogated about an ambiguous remark she had made in court. Exhausted by her ordeal and hard of hearing, she failed to respond. The jury, sent back to deliberate further, returned with a guilty verdict.

Nurse's acquittal and then conviction turned, perhaps, on a peculiar evidentiary test used at the trials. According to the practice of witch-hunting, a witch might be identified by physical signs of suckling a demon, or a "familiar." As Dalton described what to look for, the court should be watchful for "some big or little Teat upon their body, and in some secret place, where he (the Devil) sucketh them. And besides their sucking, the Devil leaveth other marks upon their body, sometimes like a blew spot or red spot, like a flea-biting; sometimes the flesh sunk in and hollow. . . ." At Salem in 1692, it appears that a jury of women, including midwives, examined suspects for such marks. Given the primitive state of gynecological examination in the seventeenth century (physicians almost never did actual physical examinations of genital areas), it is not surprising that any mark or growth might appear to be the "preternatural excrescence" they were seeking. Under such circumstances, who could definitively say whether a growth was natural?

Nurse made precisely that point at her trial, arguing that what the jury found when examining her was not unnatural; in fact, as she pleaded to the court, one of "the Moaste Antiente skilfull, prudent" women of the examining jury dissented from the others "and Did then declare that she saw nothing in or about yoer Honor's poare pettissioner But what Might arise from a Naturall cause." Nurse's petition apparently convinced the jury, for it returned a not guilty verdict. At that point, however, Stoughton reopened the interrogation and sent the jurors back for more deliberation, whereupon they changed their verdict. Not only Nurse, but all five other women discovered with such marks were executed.

Nurse's treatment was not unusual as the trials reached their peak in the summer of 1692, but it, too, bespeaks the lingering uncertainty attaching to trial procedure. The court preferred a confession above all else, for such an admission of guilt would, in its view, corroborate other flimsier evidence (e.g., the questionable spectral proof). Moreover, a confession might be used as an indication that the accused had repented of the crime and was acknowledging both Christ and the court. Every person who confessed, in fact, was spared upon conviction. Only one confessing suspect, Samuel Wardwell, went to the gallows, but he renounced his confession. For these reasons, the court did everything it could to extract a confession. After all, King James VI of Scotland (later James I of England) had "warmly" recommended torture, even if its purpose was to gain proof for execution.

Torture need not be so brutal, and the court also used a less overtly atrocious method in seeking confessions. "There are numerous instances," reported one opponent of the trials, "of the tedious Examinations before private persons, many hours together; they all that time urging them to Confess (and taking turns to perswade them) till the accused were wearied out by being forced to stand so long, or for want of Sleep, etc. and so brought to give an Assent to what they said; they then asking them, Were you at such a Witch-meeting, or have you signed the Devil's Book, etc. upon their replying, yes, the whole was drawn into form as their confession." Some of these episodes lasted 18 hours and included "most violent, distracting, and draggooning methods."

An adjournment of more than a month, from June 30 to August 5, did not abate the fury of the prosecutions. While the court was in recess, court officials forced the confessions of two men, Richard and Andrew Carrier, tying them "neck and heels" until "the blood was ready to come out of their noses." A third victim of this torture, William Proctor, refused to admit his guilt even though he was tied "neck and heels till the blood gushed out at his nose." Tying "neck and heels" was of dubious legality, though used in both England and New England (and Virginia, where it was legal).

At its August session, the court tried six more defendants and condemned them all, including Reverend George Burroughs, once minister at Salem Village and now serving a parish in Maine. Five of the condemned were hanged on August 19, and only Elizabeth Proctor escaped the gallows. Pregnant, she was able to gain a temporary reprieve until she would deliver her child, on the grounds that her execution would also take the life of an innocent person. (By the time she gave birth, the witch-hunt had ended and all had been reprieved or released.)

Despite (or perhaps because of) the continued popular frenzy, signs of opposition to the trials and sympathy for the accused began to appear among the public. When Burroughs stood before the gallows, his appeal for mercy was so eloquent and his recital of the Lord's Prayer so dramatic that the crowd stirred and seemed ready to demand his release. Escapes became more frequent, and letters of support for the defendants arrived steadily. From Salisbury on August 9, Magistrate Robert Pike wrote to Jonathan Corwin, his Essex County court colleague now serving on the oyer and terminer court, that accepting spectral evidence was succumbing to Satan's trickery. Such a practice, he reported, "do disquiet the country." Later in August, a member of the Governor's Council in Boston complained to Cotton Mather that spectral evidence was so unreliable that anyone accused on that basis ought to have the right of bail, and anyone convicted by it be banished rather than executed.

This trend appears only to have emboldened those pushing the prosecutions forward. At the court's sessions on August 9 and 17, 15 persons were condemned; eight were hanged on August 22. When the court adjourned, it gave no signs of slackening its determination. While in recess, in fact, the court continued to pressure suspects for evidence and confessions. In doing so, it perpetrated the most extraordinary episode of the trials, an event that remains impossible to explain. This was the treatment accorded Giles Corey in what is commonly (though incorrectly) described as an execution. Corey, whose wife Martha had been condemned on September 9 and would be executed on September 22, was brought before the magistrates and asked to plead guilty or not guilty. He pleaded not guilty, but when asked the routine question of how he wished to be tried (the proper answer being, "By God and this court"), Corey balked. Why did he refuse? It is possible that he wished to preserve his estate from forfeiture: if he was not tried, his estate would descend to his heirs. The estates of others had already been confiscated under the common-law rule, but at least one other defendant had made a will, in the hope that New

England practice would obtain. Yet another reason may have operated: Corey was quite possibly entering his own form of protest against the court and its practices. (It is unlikely he was protesting his wife's conviction, since he had offered incriminating testimony against her.) Whatever his reason, the court followed the normal—though rarely invoked—procedure in such cases, the application of peine forte et dure. On September 18, Corey was placed on the ground and heavy stones were placed on his chest, literally to press from him the required plea to be tried by the court. Corey never yielded, and survived ever more weight for another day until he died on September 19. Reputedly, his last words were "more weight."

The accusations of the girls only grew wilder as time went on. Opponents of the trials, such as Nathaniel Saltonstall, found themselves also accused. So, too, did prominent individuals on the Governor's Council. No one was safe from being identified as an instrument of the devil. The girls were being summoned to other villages to identify witches where, it seemed, any illness might be attributable to witchcraft. When the father of a sick child brought the child to Salem for the girls to locate the offending witch, a disgusted Reverend Increase Mather chastised the man and asked "whether there was not a God in Boston, that he should go to the Devil in Salem for advice."

By autumn, popular revulsion against the accusations and the manner of conducting trials finally led opponents to take more assertive action. On October 3, Increase Mather took a more emphatic and insistent public stand against spectral evidence, reading to his ministerial colleagues his statement of *Cases of Conscience Concerning Evil Spirits Personating Men*. Although admitting the reality of witchcraft, Mather lashed out at the reliance on spectral evidence, which the devil himself probably was using to send innocent people to the gallows. "It were better that ten suspected witches shall escape," Mather urged, "than that one innocent person should be condemned."

Governor Phips, beset by doubts from the first, acted soon, too, ordering the court adjourned until further advice might be obtained from England. Before an answer could be received, the legislature in late October called for a day of fasting and counsel from the clergy "so that [we] may be led in the right way as to the witchcrafts." Its purpose, only thinly disguised by this request, was, according to Judge Sewall, "that the Court of Oyer and Terminer count themselves thereby dismissed." By then, 141 persons had been arrested and 26 convicted; 19 had died by the gallows, one by pressing, and two of natural causes while in gaol.

In January 1693, the properly constituted Superior Court of Judicature replaced the oyer and terminer court and began its own trials—but without spectral evidence. Stoughton continued to preside, although the lack of spectral evidence made convictions difficult. No one, in fact, was convicted upon trial by that court: except for three who confessed, all were acquitted. Phips reprieved the three confessors, as well as five persons convicted by the old court. His clemency outraged Stoughton, whose "passionate anger" revealed his frustrated ambition. Soon, all remaining in gaol were freed.

The divided opinion that had existed during the trials continued, although clearly the public had had enough of the trials and wished them over. On one hand, the judges who served on the oyer and terminer court did not suffer politically: all were elected to the Governor's Council later in 1693. On the other hand, a wave of remorse ultimately washed over Salem. Judge Sewall publicly repented at church in 1697, and that same year the jurors admitted to having been "under the power of a strong and general delusion." Asking forgiveness, they repented of "bring[ing] upon ourselves and this People of the Lord the guilt of innocent blood." Anne Putnam, major accuser among the girls, recanted the accusations she had made "ignorantly, being deluded by Satan."

Other steps followed. The Salem Town church revoked its excommunication of several of the convicted, and in 1703 the legislature reversed many of the attainders created by the felony convictions (although only for those requesting it). Confusion continued to the end: the legislature voted to reverse the remaining attainders in 1711, but its list was not complete, and several remain technically in effect today.

Selected Bibliography

Boyer, P., and S. Nissenbaum. *Salem Possessed. The Social Origins of Witchcraft*. Cambridge, MA: Harvard University Press, 1974.

Demos, J.P. *Entertaining Satan: Witchcraft and the Culture of Early New England*. New York: Oxford University Press, 1982.

Fox, S.J. *Science and Justice: The Massachusetts Witchcraft Trials*. Baltimore: Johns Hopkins Press, 1968.

Hansen, C. *Witchcraft at Salem*. New York: G. Braziller, 1969.

Karlsen, C.F. *The Devil in the Shape of a Woman: Witchcraft in Colonial New England*. New York: Norton, 1987.

Konig, D.T. *Law and Society in Puritan Massachusetts: Essex County, 1629–92*. Chapel Hill, NC: University of North Carolina Press, 1979.

Weisman, R. *Witchcraft, Magic, and Religion in 17th-Century Massachusetts*. Amherst, MA: University of Massachusetts Press, 1984.

PIRATES WALK THE PLANK IN CHARLESTON

by Bonnie S. Ledbetter
Clemson, South Carolina

The King v. Bonnet (1718) [South Carolina colonial court]

In the early eighteenth century, the Atlantic Ocean swarmed with pirates. An estimated 1,700 roved the coast of North America. One of the most unusual pirates was Stede Bonnet, who, in middle age, had abandoned a respectable life to become an outlaw on the high seas. A man of education and wealth who had retired as a major in the army, he was a bumbling pirate who knew nothing of the sea. Nevertheless, in 1717, in his ship *Revenge* he plundered ships from New England to South Carolina. In 1718, he formed an alliance with the notorious buccaneer, Edward Thatch, otherwise known as Blackbeard.

Together, Blackbeard and Bonnet terrorized Charleston, taking hostages from ships and threatening to send their heads to South Carolina Governor Robert Johnson if the pirates were not sent supplies. They got their supplies and sailed away after setting the hostages ashore nearly naked.

When word reached Charleston in August 1718, that an unidentified pirate was lurking in the Cape Fear region, South Carolina sent two sloops to raid the pirate den. After a close battle, the victorious South Carolinians were surprised to learn that they had captured the despicable Bonnet. They brought him and his crew back to Charleston for trial before the noted jurist, Nicholas Trott. Judge Trott wrote *The Tryals of Major Stede Bonnet and Other Pirates* (1719), which is the major record of the trials.

Trott had immigrated to South Carolina in 1699 and had held numerous governmental posts, some of them simultaneously, which aggravated some prominent South Carolinians. Trott was a versatile man: the first lawyer in South Carolina, a biblical scholar, the codifier of South Carolina laws, and chief justice at the time of Bonnet's trial. In the political struggles between the supporters of the proprietors and those who wanted South Carolina to become a royal colony, Trott, a strong advocate of proprietary interests, came down on the losing side of the debate. After 1719, his influence declined dramatically.

Although Bonnet had escaped by bribing his guards, the trial of his crew began before the Vice-Admiralty Court as scheduled on October 28. Trott delivered the charge to the jury, a learned historical exposition on the laws against piracy. The attorney general conducted the prosecution. The accused had no lawyers, since the South Carolina bar considered it "a base and vile thing to plead for money or reward." In their defense, the prisoners claimed they had been forced into piracy, but Trott cut them off and denounced them from the bench.

On November 8, 29 men were hung and buried in a marsh below the low watermark. Bonnet was recaptured on November 6 and stood trial before the Vice-Admiralty Court. Once again, Trott showed no patience with the defendant. He not only condemned Bonnet in this life, but consigned him "to the lake that burneth with fire and brimstone" in the next.

Bonnet maintained his dignity and composure until Trott sentenced him to hang. Then he collapsed into a quivering coward, pleading most pitifully with the governor for mercy. Governor Johnson rejected his pleas and set November 10 as the date for his execution. Bonnet was hung and buried with his men below the water line.

Shortly before Bonnet and his men were hung, the South Carolinians had rounded up another group of pirates. During the bloody battle, 24 pirates were captured, most of whom were severely wounded. They were hurriedly tried, so they could be executed before they died of their wounds.

The trial of Stede Bonnet and his fellow pirates marked the beginning of the end of piracy in colonial America.

Selected Bibliography

Hughson, S.C. *The Carolina Pirates and Colonial Commerce, 1670–1740.* New York: Johnson Reprint Corp., 1973.

Johnson, H.A. *South Carolina Legal History.* Spartanburg, SC: The Reprint Co., 1980.

Rankin, H.F. *The Golden Age of Piracy.* New York: Holt, Rinehart & Winston, 1969.

NEW YORK ON FIRE

by Bonnie S. Ledbetter
Clemson, South Carolina

The King v. Hughson (1741) [New York colonial court]

In the spring of 1741, New York City was in turmoil: too many thefts and fires were occurring to be coincidental. While authorities were investigating the thefts, ten fires broke out in a period of three weeks. The first fire began on March 18 at the governor's house in the fort.

The house, chapel, secretary's office, and several other buildings burned to the ground, but the efforts of the citizens passing buckets of water plus a timely shower prevented the fire from spreading beyond the fort to the city. A week later, the roof of Captain Warren's house caught fire. The next week, Mr. Van Zandt's warehouse was destroyed. Three days later, a fire was discovered in Quick's stable. As the people trudged home from that fire, an alarm sounded for a fire at Ben Thomas's house. The next day, a haystack blazed near Joseph Murray's stables, and the following day Sergeant Burns's house burned, Mrs. Hilton's roof caught fire, and Colonel Philipse's storehouse ignited. When the storehouse fire was nearly out, an alarm sounded and most of the fire fighters left to attend to the new fire.

A fire fighter who had remained behind on the roof of Philipse's storehouse had seen a Negro jump from a window of one of the storehouses and leap across several garden fences, evidently in a great hurry to leave the scene. The fire fighter had cried, "A Negro, a Negro!" and quickly a crowd was on the heels of the fleeing black man. They chased him to his master's, dragged him out, and carried him off to the jail. His name was Cuffee and he belonged to Colonel Philipse, whose storehouse had burned.

Inspection of all the sites revealed evidence that looked like arson. By the time a grand jury assembled at the city hall on April 21, many citizens, including the judge who charged the jury to uncover the plot, were convinced there was a conspiracy. The grand jury summoned a 16-year-old servant, Mary Burton, who had hinted to neighbors that she knew of criminal activities at her master's tavern.

Burton claimed that her master, John Hughson, illegally entertained slaves at his tavern near the New York waterfront and that he received stolen goods. In fact, two slaves, Prince and Caesar, had recently brought him items related to the investigation. Moreover, Burton said Hughson presided over meetings of slaves at his tavern where he encouraged them to set their masters' houses on fire and to kill the white people as they tried to extinguish the flames. After killing the masters, she claimed the slaves planned to take the white women for themselves, while Hughson would become king. Burton also implicated Cuffee, along with Caesar and Prince, as ringleaders of this plot. She accused Hughson's wife Sarah and an Irish prostitute, Peggy Kerry, who lived at the Hughson's, of being in on the conspiracy. The grand jury was at first "astonished" and "amazed" that white people would stoop to such villainous activities, but two days later that surprise diminished, because the grand jury maintained the Negroes were not capable of such a plan on their own. Peggy Kerry and the Hughsons were arrested and jailed.

The grand jury met on April 23 with two of the three judges of the New York Supreme Court who would hear the cases, Judges Frederick Philipse and Daniel Horsmanden. Chief Justice James DeLancey was occupied with other business, but joined the deliberations in July. Leading lawyers were invited to advise the judges and grand jury. There was general agreement that they should move swiftly and secretly.

An interesting aspect of the legal procedures in these cases was that the judges were the chief examiners of the accused and the witnesses, and the chief recorders of their depositions. Philipse and Horsmanden began their investigation by questioning Kerry at the jail. Despite hints of a pardon or mercy, she denied knowledge of the fires.

On April 24, Caesar and Prince, Mr. and Mrs. Hughson, and Kerry were indicted and arraigned. They all pleaded not guilty. On May 1, Caesar and Prince were tried on two counts of theft. The prisoners had no legal counsel, and their defense consisted of protests of innocence. Caesar and Prince were found guilty and a week later were sentenced to hang. "They died very stubbornly" on May 11, denying their guilt to the end. Caesar's body was left hanging in chains in a prominent location.

While Kerry and the Hughsons, now joined in jail by their daughter Sarah, waited for their trial, an opportunistic prisoner, Arthur Price, charged with stealing from his master, told a jailer that Kerry and the Hughsons's daughter had confided their guilt to him in jail. Price, whose testimony was taken by a judge, was so skillful in pumping inmates for information that the judges ordered him to be put in the same cell as Cuffee, the slave who fled from the fire at Philipse's storehouse, and allotted "a tankard of punch now and then, in order to cheer up their spirits, and make them more sociable."

Later, Price said Cuffee had told him that Quack, a slave of John Roosevelt, had set the fire at the governor's house. Quack was arrested and tried with Cuffee. At the trial, witnesses said that Quack's wife was a cook at the governor's house, but that the governor had forbidden Quack to come into the fort. On one occasion when a sentry had refused to let him enter, Quack had attempted to push past the sentry but had been clubbed with a gun and thrown from the fort. Two other slaves testified that Quack set the fire and that Cuffee had vowed to burn his master's storehouse. The owners of Quack and Cuffee each spoke in defense of his slave, saying they were not out of their sight when the fires were allegedly set; however, their testimony carried little weight with the jurors. Quack and Cuffee were found guilty and ordered to be burned at the stake the next day, May 30.

The terrified convicts were led to the stakes, where the authorities attempted one last time to extract their confessions. With hints of reprieve, the interrogators told Cuffee that Quack had confessed, and vice versa, which prompted them both to confess. The officials considered postponing the executions until the governor could be consulted, but the sheriff declared he could not move the prisoners through the crowd, which was in a dangerously ugly mood, so the executions proceeded.

In their confessions, Quack and Cuffee confirmed the guilt of several other accused slaves and named seven more. All were arrested that day. The judges tried to examine each of the accused, but each implicated more supposed conspirators, until there were so many that the two judges required assistance from several of the king's counselors to write down the testimony. Ultimately, over 150 people were arrested. Not even Chief Justice DeLancey's Othello was exempt from accusation. Othello was well-known in New York and was considered to have "more sense than the common rank of Negroes." His master "took a great deal of pains with him, endeavoring to persuade him to confess," but Othello stubbornly insisted he

knew of no plot. Nevertheless, he was jailed "some time before any evidence came to light," apparently because he was a leader among the blacks.

On June 10, the governor issued a proclamation offering a pardon to anyone, white or black, who confessed by July 1. In the rush to confess, some were saved from execution, but not Othello. The recorder noted that Othello's confession was "neither voluntary nor free," but that he had behaved "with a great deal of composure and decency, with an air of sincerity which very much affected the recorder." Othello confessed to almost nothing. When the judges decided that he would receive no special consideration because he belonged to the chief justice, he was sentenced to hang. With nothing to lose, he retracted the little he had admitted.

After the central characters—John Hughson, his wife Sarah, and Kerry—were hanged on June 12, attention began to focus elsewhere. England was at war with Spain. Most of the action took place at sea and the previous year, 1740, a captured Spanish vessel was brought to New York as a prize. On board were blacks, claiming to be freemen, but who were nevertheless sold to New York citizens. About six of these Spanish Negroes were among those accused of being accomplices in the plot to burn New York. Depositions began to mention that the conspirators were waiting for the Spanish and the French to attack the city, at which time the blacks were to put the plot into action.

Schoolmaster John Ury, or Jury, had the misfortune to become entangled in this web of fear and suspicion. He had recently come to New York and because he knew Latin and liked to discuss religion, the rumor that he was a disguised Roman Catholic priest was spread. He was arrested, and Burton immediately recognized him as one of the leaders who had attempted to influence the blacks to kill their masters. Numerous blacks also testified that he had led them in mysterious ceremonies.

His defense was significantly undermined by the arrival of a letter from General James Ogelthorpe of Georgia, alerting authorities to watch out for Spanish agents operating as physicians, dancing masters, and the like. Ury defended himself feebly, and he was subsequently sentenced to hang. In his final words at the gallows, he maintained his innocence, forgave his accusers, and exhorted them to confess their "horrid wickedness."

Ury was the last to die in the frenzy surrounding the conspiracy to burn New York City. Between May 11 and August 29, 1741, 13 blacks were burned at the stake, 16 blacks and 4 whites were hung and over 70 blacks and 7 whites were transported to foreign countries. Mary Burton, however, collected a reward.

At the time, there were people who questioned the validity of the charges. Judge Daniel Horsmanden, a participant in the interrogations and trials, found it incredible that anyone could doubt the existence of a conspiracy. To demonstrate what he considered overwhelming evidence, he collected the records of the trials and compiled the eye-witness accounts into a book. Ironically, generations that followed have used his work to condemn his conclusions.

Today, it is difficult to judge the extent of a conspiracy, if there was one. It is not difficult to believe that slaves might want to burn their masters' property and might talk about a combined effort to burn the city. If there was such talk, the record indicates the plot was not well planned: there was no definite timetable; there were no specific tasks assigned, other than each slave was to set fire to his master's house; the fires broke out on various days, which was not an effective method for burning the entire city; and there was no plan for what to do if the plot was successful.

On the other hand, the record speaks loudly of some innocent people having suffered horrible deaths caused by the fears of the white citizens. Even Horsmanden was "moved to compassion" by the pleas of Othello and others, whose sincerity, unfortunately, worked against them: the judges thought it illustrated how crafty slaves could be.

The alleged Negro conspiracy to burn New York demonstrates that a judicial process can go awry under pressures of fear and prejudice. Judging them even by their eighteenth-century standards, there were flaws in the procedure. For example, most of the testimony came from a single witness, Mary Burton, whom even the judges described as having "a warm hasty spirit" and "a remarkable glibness of tongue." To give so much weight to the words of such a young and dubious witness raised questions then and now.

A second white witness, Arthur Price, was a felon and a planted informer. The testimony of slaves was not accepted at colonial law, but in this case the confessions of slaves were used against all of the accused. Suspects were jailed on suspicion without evidence. Liquor was used to loosen tongues. The accused were "prompted" to help them "remember" their part in the plot. Promises of mercy were given to encourage confessions, and after the confessions were made, the promises were discarded. As this case makes obvious, in the name of justice, grave injustices can occur.

Selected Bibliography

Headley, J.T. *The Great Riots of New York: 1712–1873*. New York: The Bobbs-Merrill Co., Inc., 1970.

Hoey, E. "Terror in New York—1741." *American Heritage* 25 (June 1974): 72–77.

Horsmanden, D. *The New York Conspiracy*. Boston: Beacon Press, 1971.

TREASON AND THE WHISKEY "INSURRECTION"

by Mary K. Bonsteel Tachau
Department of History
University of Louisville

United States v. Mitchell, 2 Dallas 348 (1795); *United States v. Vigol*, 2 Dallas 346 (1795) [U.S. Circuit Court of Appeals]

Philip Vigol and John Mitchell were the first to be tried and convicted of treason after the U.S. Constitution had been adopted, with its new and narrow definition of that crime. Their trials set a precedent that soon after led to the convictions of John Fries. Yet it is clear that none of these men had engaged in "levying War against them [the United States] or in adhering to their Enemies, giving them Aid and Comfort," as those words are commonly understood.

Vigol and Mitchell were among the thousands of trans-Appalachian farmer-distillers who strongly opposed the whiskey tax of 1791 because they considered it oppressive and, since it was not uniformly applicable throughout the nation, unconstitutional. Secretary of the Treasury Alexander Hamilton, who had devised the excise, adamantly refused to make substantive changes in the law or to advocate its repeal. When three years of largely peaceful protests punctuated by occasional intimidation of excise officers proved unsuccessful, western Pennsylvanians turned to violence in July 1794. They harassed the U.S. marshal, robbed the mail, and burned the estate of the revenue inspector, a wealthy Federalist slave owner who had been a general during the War of Independence. Until the moderates took control about two weeks later, bands of angry farmers roamed the countryside, frightening those they suspected might cooperate in carrying out the law.

Alarmed, President Washington's administration used force to end the violence and gain compliance. U.S. Supreme Court Justice James Wilson stated that the laws were opposed and their execution obstructed "by Combinations too powerful to be suppressed by the ordinary Course of judicial Proceedings, or by the powers vested in the Marshal." Judicial proceedings had not been tried, nor the powers of the marshal tested, but the declaration gave the president authority to call out the militia under the

Militia Act of 1792. The administration delayed calling out the militia until receiving the report of three appointed commissioners, who were surprisingly successful in gaining 12,950 troops from four states.

Henry Lee was the nominal commander of the militia army, but Washington and Hamilton rode at its head as it proceeded westward in late September. The officers were generously wined, dined, and housed along the way, and farmers waved at the troops. No resistance was encountered; the only indications that the procession was not welcome were a dozen liberty poles and a few taunts in taverns. The president left the army at Bedford to return to Philadelphia for the opening of Congress, where he reported that an insurrection had been suppressed.

A month later, Hamilton reported the arrest of 150 men who were charged with treason—although in No. 84 of *The Federalist*, he had defended the Constitution against critics who wanted a bill of rights by emphasizing the protections already contained in the document. Among those provisions, he specifically named its narrow definition of "treason." As he knew, the framers had intentionally adopted a stringent version of the fourteenth-century English Statute of Treasons, keenly aware of the abuses that had resulted in England from "constructive treason" (broadly construing what constituted treasonous acts).

The prisoners were marched 300 miles to Philadelphia in bitter winter weather and jailed, pending trial. However, in April 1795, grand jurors returned only 48 indictments: one for assault and battery, two for unspecified felonies, 14 for misdemeanors, and 31 for treason. Vigol and Mitchell, among those indicted for treason, were given court-appointed attorneys.

Before the cases were tried in May, William Lewis argued for the insurgents that selection of the jury panel had been illegal under both Pennsylvania and federal laws because the large number summoned from the eastern counties made it highly unlikely that any of the defendants would have a majority of jurors from his own district on his trial jury. Lewis was overruled by Justice William Paterson and District Judge Richard Peters, who composed the federal circuit court bench.

Vigol was charged with high treason for levying war against the United States by trying to prevent the execution of the excise law by force. As "one of the most active insurgents," he had joined in attacking two revenue collectors in their homes and required them to relinquish their offices. He had also been at Couche's Fort, from which the mob had gone to burn the inspector's estate, and he had been among those who had harassed the marshal.

Attorneys Lewis and Moses Levy did not question the law but agreed with the prosecution that the case rested on proof of the overt acts by two witnesses. Paterson ruled that the law arose from evidence and intention. Regarding the former, he said that "the current runs one way"; regarding the latter, that there was not "the slightest possibility of doubt." Lewis and Levy then argued that Vigol had acted under duress and that the indictment was in error regarding the dates of the offenses and the number of participants. Their contention was overruled by Paterson, who instructed the jury that "the crime is proved." Nevertheless, the jury deliberated five hours before reaching its verdict that Vigol was guilty. The court sentenced him to be hanged.

Mitchell was also charged with high treason for having levied war against the United States. He, too, had been at Couche's Fort and, according to one witness, at the attack on the inspector's estate. Moreover, Mitchell had participated in an inflammatory assembly that was said to have threatened Pittsburgh and (admittedly while intoxicated), he had refused to sign an oath of submission to the laws.

U.S. Attorney General William Bradford and federal District Attorney William Rawle asserted that raising a body of men to obtain the repeal of a law by intimidation or violence, or opposing and preventing by force and terror the execution of a law constituted an act of levying of war. Theirs was a doctrine of "constructive levying of war"; it loosely interpreted the narrow meaning of the words that the framers had so consciously adopted only eight years earlier.

Defense counsel Edward Tilghman and Joseph Thomas protested that interpretation of the constitutional language. They contended that while compelling Congress by violence or intimidation to repeal a law might be treasonous, the crimes with which Mitchell was charged were of far less magnitude—at most, arson or a misdemeanor. Finally, they asserted that Mitchell's notorious drunkenness might mark him as "a bad man" but was not sufficient to maintain a charge of high treason.

Bradford and Rawle countered that if the defense attorneys' arguments prevailed, Vigol should have been acquitted and all the prisoners released. Further, they said, if the insurgents' illegal conduct was *intended* to force Congress to repeal the whiskey tax, the excise *would* be suppressed throughout the Union, thus accomplishing the purpose of levying war against the United States.

However strained the prosecution's arguments seem now after the nation has celebrated the bicentennial of the Constitution, they carried weight at the time. Paterson instructed the jury that Mitchell "must be pronounced guilty," and the jury complied. Mitchell, too, was sentenced to be hanged.

After all the arrests, indictments, and a dozen trials, only Mitchell and Vigol were convicted of high treason. Nothing in the records explains why they were singled out from the thousands who had opposed the whiskey tax. Neither owned a still, and both were described as "simple." Soon after their convictions, President Washington received petitions and memorials pleading for mercy. Washington pardoned them in June, and a month later, pardoned all of the other "insurgents."

Mitchell's and Vigol's trials are significant in U.S. constitutional and legal history because of the prosecution's success in establishing the doctrine of constructive levying of war. That precedent was followed in the treason trials of John Fries and Aaron Burr. Only Chief Justice John Marshall's insistence on a strict interpretation of the standard of proof required by the Constitution has obscured the fact that the doctrine has never been overruled. The existence of a "Whiskey Insurrection" has become an accepted fact, although there never was an organized resistance that made war or threatened the government—and even sending an army to western Pennsylvania did not achieve compliance with the law.

Selected Bibliography

Boyd, S.R., ed. *The Whiskey Rebellion: Past and Present Perspectives*. Westport, CT: Greenwood Press, 1985.

Slaughter, T.P. *The Whiskey Rebellion: Frontier Epilogue to the American Revolution*. New York: Oxford University Press, 1986.

Tachau, M.K.B. "George Washington and the Reputation of Edmund Randolph." *Journal of American History* 73 (June 1986): 15–34.

CONGRESS SHOULD FIRST DEFINE THE OFFENSES AND APPORTION THE PUNISHMENT: FEDERAL COMMON-LAW CRIMES

by Yasuhide Kawashima
Department of History
University of Texas at El Paso

United States v. Worrall, 2 Dallas 384 (1798) [U.S. Circuit Court of Appeals]

After the American Revolution, there was a growing sentiment against things English in the United States. The decline in the authority of the common law (i.e., judges' written opinions) was part of this postrevolutionary change in the attitude of the Americans. More specifically, the conviction among Americans that the common law was both uncertain and unpredictable grew stronger, and attacks on common-law crimes became widespread during the 1790s.

The opposition to the common law of crimes, however, occurred at both the federal and state levels. In 1793, Vermont Chief Justice Nathaniel Chipman, in his essay "Dissertation on the Act Adopting the Common and Statute Laws of England," insisted that "no Court, in this State, ought ever to pronounce sentence of death upon the authority of a common law precedent, without authority of a statute." Two years later, Zepheniah Swift, future chief justice of Connecticut, expressed a similar view and challenged the doctrine that "every crime committed against the law of nature may be punished at the discretion of the judge, where the legislature has not appointed a particular punishment." He argued that "no man should

be exposed to the danger of incurring a penalty without knowing it."

The common law of crimes on the federal level generated more heated debates. The common law had always been considered as operating on the local level, "the separate law of each colony within its respective limits" and not "a law pervading and operating through the whole, as one society." The possible establishment of the national government brought the issue into a new dimension. In the Constitutional Convention, George Mason advocated that the common law prevail on the federal level and proposed that the Constitution enact the common law. But the common law, he admitted, "stands here upon no other foundation than its having been adopted by the respective acts forming the constitution of the several States."

The formation of the federal government under the Constitution in 1789 turned this issue into a national constitutional question. *United States v. Worrall* was the first case involving the issue of whether a federal common law of crimes existed. The defendant, Robert Worrall, was charged with attempting to bribe Tench Coxe, the U.S. commissioner of the revenue, who had been authorized to receive proposals and to enter into a contract for building a lighthouse on Cape Hatteras in North Carolina. After submitting his proposal to Coxe, Worrall wrote a letter to him, stating that he, "as having always been brought up in a life of industry, should be happy in serving you in the executing of this job" and upgraded his estimate of profit to £1,400. Worrall also wrote that he had been "always content with a reasonable profit" and that if Coxe would recommend him for the work, he would offer Coxe "one-half of the profit" (£350 on receiving the first payment and the £350 on the last payment when the work was completed). The sum of £700 (Pennsylvania currency) that he proposed to offer Coxe was valued at $1,866.67.

Worrall's letter, dated September 28, 1797, at Philadelphia, was received by Coxe on the same day in Burlington, New Jersey, where he had moved his office due to the yellow fever in Philadelphia. On receiving the letter, Coxe immediately consulted the Pennsylvania attorney general, after which he invited the defendant for a conference at Burlington in order to entrap him in a situation in which he could continue to bribe the commissioner. At this conference, Worrall acknowledged having written and having sent the letter, declared that no one else knew of its contents, and repeated the offer. When he demanded an answer to his proposal, Coxe suggested that Worrall come to his Philadelphia office when it reopened. Accordingly, Worrall called on Coxe when the office was reopened and repeated what he had previously said: that he would give £700 as consideration for Coxe's procuring him the contract.

Worrall was indicted on two counts: (1) offering the bribe in the letter and (2) repeating the offer orally. District Judge Richard Peters and Supreme Court Justice Samuel Chase, sitting together as members of the U.S. Circuit Court for the Third Circuit, tried the case.

Counsel for the defendant argued that it was not sufficient for conviction to prove that the defendant was guilty of an offense. The offense had to be legally defined and had to have been committed within the jurisdiction of the court trying the defendant. Since there was no proof that the letter had been written in Pennsylvania, Worrall's counsel insisted, the first count of the indictment must fail. The proof, instead, was that publication and delivery were at Burlington, New Jersey. Nor could the defendant be convicted, the counsel argued, on the second count, "which is attempted to be supported merely by evidence of recognizing in Philadelphia, a corrupt offer previously made in another place, out of the jurisdiction of the court."

The attorney of the district retorted that the letter being dated at Philadelphia and being mailed at a Pennsylvania post office were sufficient proof that it had been written within the jurisdiction of the court. Accepting the prosecution's argument, the court found that the first count was sufficiently supported and that "no possible doubt" existed as to the second count. The jury accordingly returned a guilty verdict on both counts.

One of the defense lawyers then moved in arrest of judgment, alleging that the circuit court could not have jurisdiction over the crime charged in the indictment. He argued that all the judicial authority of the federal courts should be derived either from the U.S. Constitution or from the acts of Congress made pursuant to the Constitution, but an offer to bribe the commissioner of the revenue was never mentioned as a violation of any constitutional or legislative prohibition.

Nor did the defense attorney tolerate the argument that it was a common-law offense. He pointed out that the Tenth Amendment stipulated that "the powers not delegated to the US by the Constitution, nor prohibited by it to the states, are reserved to the states respectively, or to the people." In relation to crime and punishment, the objects of the delegated power of the United States are enumerated and fixed. Congress, on the other hand, could make all laws that should be necessary and proper for carrying into execution the powers of the general government, but no reference was made to a common-law authority. Congress undoubtedly had power to pass a law making it a criminal offense to offer a bribe to the commissioner of the revenue, he argued, but not having made the law, the crime was not recognized by the federal code, constitutional or legislative.

The prosecuting attorney responded that it was unreasonable to insist that merely because a law had not prescribed an express and appropriate punishment for the offense, the offense, when committed, should not be punished by the circuit court upon the principles of common-law punishment. Coxe, if he had accepted the bribe and betrayed his trust, would certainly have been indictable in the federal court. If he would have been so indictable, the offense of the person who tempted him must be equally indictable before the same judicial authority. The prosecution insisted that this indictment could be supported solely at common law.

The court was divided in opinion. Justice Chase maintained that there was no federal common law of crimes. Although he recognized that the indictment was for an offense "highly injurious to morals and deserving the severest punishment," he insisted that the Constitution was the source of all federal jurisdiction and that the department of the government could never assume any power that was not expressly granted by that instrument, nor exercise a power in any other manner than was there prescribed. Besides, Article I, Section 8, granted power to Congress to create, define, and punish crimes and offenses whenever it shall deem it necessary and proper by law to do so. Although bribery was not among the crimes specifically mentioned, Chase thought it certainly was included in the provision. For him, however, the question at issue arose in the context of the exercise of the power, it did not concern the power itself. The question was whether the federal courts could punish a man for an act before it was declared by a statute to be criminal. He insisted that it was "essential that congress should define the offences to be tried, and apportion the punishments to be inflicted, as that they should erect courts to try the criminal, or to pronounce a sentence on conviction." "It would be improper," he continued, "for a judge to exercise discretion in prescribing punishments."

Chase believed that the United States, as a federal government, had no common law, and, therefore, no indictment could be maintained in its courts for offenses merely at the common law. Reviewing the history of the American colonies, Chase stated that when the colonies were first settled, the English colonists brought

with them as much of the common law as was applicable to their local situation and change of circumstances. But each colony judged for itself what parts of the common law were applicable to its new conditions and adopted some parts and rejected others. He pointed out that the whole of the common law of England had been nowhere introduced because some states had rejected what others had adopted. The common law of one state was, therefore, not the common law of another, but the common law of England was the law of each state as long as each state had adopted it.

If the courts of the United States acquired a common-law jurisdiction in criminal cases, they must have received it from the United States. How then, Chase asked, did the United States come to possess the common law itself, before the government could communicate it to its judicial agents? The U.S. government did not bring it from England, the Constitution did not create it, and no act of Congress had assumed it. Moreover, what was the scope of the U.S. common law? It might be a defect and an inconvenience that the common-law authority dealing with crimes and punishments had not been conferred upon the federal government, but judges could not remedy political imperfection nor correct a legislative omission.

Judge Peters, on the other hand, argued that a federal common law of crimes existed. He maintained that whenever a government had been established, power to preserve itself was a necessary and an inseparable concomitant. The existence of the federal government would be precarious if, to punish offenses of this nature, which tend to obstruct and pervert the administration of its affairs, an appeal had to be made to the state tribunals or else the offenders escape with absolute impunity.

Peters insisted that the United States constitutionally possessed the power to punish misdemeanors, which was originally and strictly a common-law power. It could not only be exercised by Congress in the form of a legislative act but could also be enforced in a judicial proceeding. Whenever an offense attempted to subvert a federal institution or to corrupt its public officers, Peters concluded, it was an offense against the well-being of the United States. It was cognizable, from its very nature, under the authority of the United States and, consequently, was within the jurisdiction of this court by virtue of the eleventh section of the Judiciary Act of 1789.

As Chase and Peters disagreed, it became doubtful whether sentence could be pronounced upon the defendant. The judges and the prosecution wished to put the case into a form that would enable obtaining the ultimate decision of the Supreme Court, but the defense counsel objected to such a compromise.

The court, therefore, after a short consultation, pronounced the sentence, which was declared to have been mitigated in consideration of the defendant's circumstances. The defendant was sentenced to a three-month imprisonment, fined $200, and ordered to stand committed until the sentence was complied with and the costs of prosecution paid.

Francis Wharton, a compiler of early federal criminal cases, suggested that Chase's opinion, which "greatly surprised not only the bar but the community," must have been influenced by the "persuasions" of the "metaphysical" Virginia lawyers, who influenced Chase's belief that the United States had no common law. The oddest part of the case was that Chase, who had expressly denied that there was jurisdiction, "after a short consultation," agreed to impose a sentence of "unequivocally common law stamp." His sudden change of mind is understood to have been the result of his getting, during the "short consultation," the views of his Supreme Court colleagues, who, as it turned out, favored a federal common law of crimes.

The dispute about the federal common law of crimes illuminates early assumptions about the general common law. The question was whether the United States could prosecute crimes under the general common law of crimes or whether a federal statute declaring the conduct to be criminal was necessary for such prosecutions. On the other hand, it became increasingly clear that there was no dispute about the existence of a general noncriminal common law or the ability of the federal courts to apply it. Shortly after they decided *Worrall*, Chase and Peters heard a case involving a negotiable instrument in which they were in perfect agreement on the existence of a general noncriminal common law. They decided the case on general principles of law, and neither questioned the propriety of deciding on that basis.

United States v. Worrall was the first federal case involving a federal common law of crimes. Despite Chase's assertion, the case was finally decided in favor of the federal common law of crimes, confirming the early sentiment of the Supreme Court. The dispute continued, however, and during the first two decades of the nineteenth century, the issue was eventually settled the other way based on the doctrine set forth by Justice Chase in *Worrall*.

Selected Bibliography

Beale, F.H., Jr. "Criminal Attempts." *Harvard Law Review* 16 (May 1903): 491–507.

Caplan, R.L. "The History and Meaning of the Ninth Amendment." *Virginia Law Review* 69 (March 1983): 223–68.

Cooper, E.H. "Attempts and Monopolization: A Mildly Expansionary Answer to the Prophylactic Riddle of Section Two." *Michigan Law Review* 72 (Jan. 1974): 373–462.

Fletcher, W.A. "The General Common Law and Section 34 of the Judiciary Act of 1789: The Example of Marine Insurance." *Harvard Law Review* 97 (May 1984): 1513–77.

Horwitz, M.J. *The Transformation of American Law, 1780–1860.* Cambridge, MA: Harvard University Press, 1977.

Presser, S.B. "A Tale of Two Judges: Richard Peters, Samuel Chase, and the Broken Promise of Federalist Jurisprudence." *Northwestern University Law Review* 73 (March/April 1978): 26–111.

Presser, S.B., and J.S. Zainaldin. *Law and American History: Cases and Materials.* St. Paul, MN: West Publishing Co., 1980.

JOHN FRIES TO THE RESCUE IN THE HOT WATER WAR

by Mary K. Bonsteel Tachau
Department of History
University of Louisville

United States v. Fries, 9 Federal Cases 826 (1799); *United States v. Fries*, 9 Federal Cases 924 (1800) [U.S. Federal District Court]

John Fries, a farmer of German descent, had been a militia captain during both the War of Independence and the Whiskey Insurrection. Like many of his Pennsylvania Dutch neighbors, he believed that the 1798 direct tax on land, houses, and slaves was unconstitutional. The tax was graduated, with the rate dependent on value, which was sometimes determined by counting the number of windows in houses. It was said that when one assessor got too close, a housewife poured a bucket of hot water on him, thus giving the insurgency its original name: the Hot Water War.

Fries's opposition to the tax was expressed by speaking against it when he worked as an auctioneer. In the spring of 1799, a growing tax revolt in southeastern Pennsylvania appeared to be spreading throughout the entire region. Tax assessors and collectors were harassed and intimidated, their records were stolen, and the tax became uncollectible in Bucks, Montgomery, and Northampton counties.

President John Adams, frustrated by continuing French attacks on U.S. shipping and beleaguered by Republicans, ultra-Federalists, Francophiles, and even members of his own cabinet, decided to take action where he could. Mindful of the so-called Whiskey Insurrection five years earlier, he issued a proclamation calling up the militia to suppress "combinations too powerful to be suppressed by the ordinary course of judicial proceedings."

The judiciary responded as quickly as the troops. At the request of William Rawle, federal attorney for the district of Pennsylvania, District Judge Richard Peters issued warrants for the arrest of some of the opponents. The marshal served the papers and took 23 men into custody in Bethlehem, planning to move them to Philadelphia for trial. John Fries, who was not among those sought, led a colorful and dramatic rescue. With his sword at his side and a feather in his cap, he took command of a motley group converging on Bethlehem, some of whom were wearing tricolored cockades (a symbol of the French Revolution). After surrounding the house where the prisoners were held and threatening to free them forcibly, the marshal was persuaded to release them on their own recognizances. Fries was arrested soon after and was charged with high treason for having constructively levied war against the United States under a doctrine established during the Whiskey Insurrection trials of Philip Vigol and John Mitchell. A year later, Fries was brought to trial in Philadelphia.

What is particularly memorable about "the Fries Rebellion" is not the opposition to the taxes or the rescue, but the trials themselves. Federalist William Lewis and Republican Alexander James Dallas volunteered to serve as Fries's counsel. They argued that the trial should be held in Northampton County, where the alleged crimes had taken place, as required for capital cases under the Judiciary Act of 1789. Their motion was opposed by Rawle and Samuel Sitgreaves, who stated that the case should be tried where the indictment had been handed down. Justice James Iredell who, with Peters presided over the court, accepted the prosecution's argument and declined to convene another grand jury in Northampton County to seek another indictment. Further, he said that because the president had declared that the laws could not be carried out in that county, it would be exceedingly unwise to hold the trials there (even though the disturbances had ended months before). In his charge to the jury, Iredell cited the doctrinal precedent established in the trials of the western insurgents.

The jury returned a verdict of guilty in only three hours.

Lewis then moved for a new trial because it was clear that one member of the jury had prejudged the evidence. After having been impaneled but before hearing the evidence, John Rhoad had returned to his boardinghouse and declared that Fries "ought to be hung" and that he himself would not be safe unless that was the fate of all the insurgents. Iredell was persuaded, and Peters reluctantly agreed.

Fries had to wait a year for his second trial because the marshal's commission expired and was not renewed in time to summon jurors for the court's fall term. By the time it was convened, Iredell had died, and Justice Samuel Chase had joined Peters on the bench.

Chase, who had once been an intemperate anti-Federalist, had since become an intemperate Federalist. His conduct during the second *Fries* trial provided the first charge for his own impeachment in 1805 and raised questions about the conventional wisdom that the impeachment was principally a result of political retribution.

Before the trial began, Chase asked Peters for the court opinion that he and Iredell had drafted for the first trial. Chase agreed with its assertion that jurors could decide the facts but not the law (in this case, the doctrine that constructive levying of war fulfilled the constitutional definition of treason), contrary to contemporaneous practice in capital cases. Chase had copies of the opinion prepared and distributed in the courtroom. Lewis was outraged that the court was announcing its decision before the evidence had been presented and refused to cooperate with the proceedings. He and Dallas promptly and eloquently resigned as counsel for the defendant. Chase defended his action as a necessary and useful expedient because the law regarding treason had not changed in the interval since the first trial and 100 civil cases were pending before the court. Although Peters was troubled by the impropriety, he defended Chase's action.

After Lewis and Dallas resigned, Chase offered to protect Fries's rights from the bench, a dubious arrangement that Fries nonetheless accepted. However, when a juror asked to be excused on the grounds that he had frequently spoken of Fries's guilt, Chase refused. Later, he also refused to grant a mistrial when he was informed that another juror had become separated from the others while they were sequestered. The result was predictable: in only two hours, the jury found Fries guilty. He was sentenced to be hanged.

But President John Adams doubted the validity of the doctrine of constructive levying of war, and when he learned about the second trial, he asked the defense attorneys for their account of it. They complied, emphasizing again their conviction that Fries might be guilty of riot and rescue—both misdemeanors—but not of treason. The result was a full pardon for Fries and all others who had been involved in the so-called rebellion.

The doctrine of constructive treason has never been overruled and technically still stands as precedent. Yet Chase's impeachment, although he was not convicted, had a salutary effect on other judges. Their subsequent caution about expanding the meaning of the constitutional language "levying of war" was doubtless reinforced by Chief Justice Marshall's strict interpretation of the standards of proof required for conviction of treason in Aaron Burr's trial in 1807.

That shift in judicial emphasis has obscured the significant error that Chase committed when he circulated the opinion and thus the decision of the court before Fries's second trial even began. Fries, however, was untroubled. Many years later, he called on Chase to thank him for guarding his rights.

Selected Bibliography

Elsmere, J.S. "The Trials of John Fries." *Pennsylvania Magazine of History and Biography* 103 (Oct. 1979): 432–45.

Neeleman, J.R. "Case of Fries: James Wilson, John Adams, and 'Constructive Levying of War' as Treason Under the Constitution." [Unpublished paper, Georgetown University Law School, 1985].

Wharton, F. *State Trials of the United States, During the Administrations of Washington and Adams.* Philadelphia, 1849.

DEFECTIVE INDICTMENT

by Yasuhide Kawashima
Department of History
University of Texas at El Paso

State v. Owen, 5 N.C. 452 (1810) [North Carolina Supreme Court]

John Owen, a cabinetmaker in Wake County, North Carolina, on April 21, 1809, in the city of Raleigh, struck Patrick Conway with a pine stick, causing several mortal wounds. Conway died instantly. The Wake County Superior Court tried the case, and the jury found Owen guilty of murder as charged in the bill of indictment prepared by Attorney General Oliver Fitts.

Owen appealed to the North Carolina Supreme Court on the question of whether sentence of death could be pronounced against him on the bill of indictment. Seawall, Owen's counsel, challenged the validity of the indictment, arguing (1) that the stroke that caused the mortal wounds was laid only by implication and (2) that the indictment did not set forth the length and depth of the mortal wounds.

The attorney for the state, as to the first exception, rejected the notion of implication and argued that the words "then and there" referred the stroke to the time and place of the assault, and the same words following the word "giving" referred the mortal wounds to the time and place of the assault and striking. He interpreted, therefore, that the first allegation of assaulting and striking was carried on throughout the sentence.

As to the second exception, the state maintained that the reason required by law for describing the dimensions of the wound is so that the court might be able to ascertain whether the wound was mortal. Where it was impossible to describe the wound, the description was dispensed with. There were exceptions, but bruises were not mentioned in the enumeration of exceptions. Yet, because bruising came within the reason, it was held to be unnecessary to describe wounds of that nature. The state insisted that wounds caused by sticks were very different from those caused by axes or swords but were very similar to bruises, and, therefore, the description of these wounds might not be necessary.

The supreme court that heard the appeal in 1810 consisted of five judges. The judges were unanimous in their opinion that the first exception taken to the indictment could not be supported. The judge, who delivered the court's opinion, explained that the indictment contained a direct allegation of a stroke accompanied by the necessary terms of art and that since all the sentences were connected by the words "and then and there," in all these respects it bore the strict form of carrying the criminal charge forward from one sentence to another. Further repetition might have obscured but could not have illustrated the charge, the judge stated, nor could it have brought the indictment nearer to the most approved precedents.

In regard to the second exception, the judges were divided. Three judges maintained that the exception was fatal to the indictment and that sentence of death could not be pronounced against the prisoner upon the indictment. Judge Henderson had some doubt about the propriety of requiring the dimensions of a wound charged to be mortal in an indictment, but he could find no authority for a death charged in an indictment to be produced by a wound the dimensions of which were omitted. It was not for the court to determine why this description was required, he reasoned, but it was enough to know that the law required it.

Judge Lowrie added that it was probable that Conway might have come to his death by the strokes stated to have been given, but the dimensions of the wounds, being required, could not be dispensed with. All the exceptions to this rule, he pointed out, were cases in which the wound could not be described, such as where a limb is cut off or the body run through. Judge Hall examined the position of the English common law on this issue at the time it was adopted by the United States and found from all the authorities that whenever death was stated to be produced by a wound, the dimensions of the wound had to be given—it could not now be dispensed with.

The two dissenting judges on the other hand, concluded that wherever death was caused by a cut with a sword, dagger, or other edged instrument, it was necessary to state the dimensions of the wound, but when death was caused by a wound with a club, cudgel, or stick, it was sufficient to state the existence of the wound without the dimensions. They therefore asserted that the exception to the indictment could not be sustained.

By a narrow majority of the court (3–2), the indictment was adjudged insufficient, and the prisoner was remanded to jail to answer the same charge upon another bill of indictment. *State v. Owen* clearly set forth the rule that when death is caused by a wound, an indictment for murder should contain a clear description of the wound's length, breadth, and depth. The omission of such description is fatal to the indictment.

This case established an important precedent in guaranteeing the right of individuals to be fully informed of the charges against them. The court seems to have found a significant implication in this case when it concluded that the "want of the requisite precession and certainty" in the indictment, which might at one time "postpone or ward off the punishment of guilt," might at another "present itself as the last hope and only asylum of persecuted innocence."

Selected Bibliography

"Ninth Annual Survey of North Carolina Case Law." *North Carolina Law Review* 40 (1961–62): 482–602.

"Thompson v. Loyal Protective Ass'n." *Northwestern Reporter* 132 (Aug.–Nov. 24, 1911): 554–58.

FEDERAL COMMON LAW OF CRIMES

by James W. Ely, Jr.
School of Law
Vanderbilt University

United States v. Hudson & Goodwin, 7 Cranch 32 (1812) [U.S. Supreme Court]

The prosecution of common-law crimes in federal courts was one of the most divisive and hotly debated legal issues in the early Republic. The controversy over common-law crimes raised questions about federalism, separation of powers, the role of the judiciary, and the acceptance of English law. Analysis of this issue is hampered by the intensively partisan atmosphere in which prosecution at common law was attempted. Federal jurisdiction over common-law crimes was one of the major issues that divided the Federalists and the Jeffersonians, with the followers of Jefferson opposing such jurisdiction. After decades of public debate, the U.S. Supreme Court in *Hudson & Goodwin* finally ruled that criminal jurisdiction in cases at common law was not within the power of the federal courts.

In England, judges heard prosecution of offenses recognized by common law in the absence of statutes defining the activity as criminal. Many observers reasoned that the newly created federal courts could likewise try persons for common-law offenses. Under Article III of the Constitution, federal judicial power extended to all cases arising under "the Laws of the United States." Similarly, the Judiciary Act of 1789 gave circuit courts jurisdiction over "all crimes and offenses cognizable under the authority of the United States." The dispute over common-law crimes in federal court turned on the meaning of this language.

In 1790, Congress enacted the first federal criminal statute for punishing in federal court a limited range of offenses, such as treason, counterfeiting, and perjury. Nonetheless, federal judges began to instruct grand juries that indictments could be based on common-law without any statutory foundation. Although relatively few cases before the federal courts during the 1790s raised the issue of common-law offenses, most of the judges who considered this question believed in the existence of a jurisdiction over nonstatutory crimes. Initially there appears to have been little public opposition to prosecutions without a statutory basis. Several of the indictments obtained at common law, however, arose from a highly charged political context. For instance, there were several attempts to punish U.S. citizens for breaches of neutrality as the result of activities that aided revolutionary France. As a consequence, many began to question the legitimacy of common-law prosecutions.

The debate over common-law crimes was soon intertwined with emerging political divisions. Anxious to strengthen federal sovereignty, the Federalists argued that the government had inherent powers of self-defense and could punish offenses without criminal statutes. Jeffersonians, on the other hand, saw the doctrine of common-law crime as a political weapon in the hands of federal judges and as a usurpation of power. Aside from partisan struggles, there was sharp division over whether judges or legislators should make law in a republican society. Acceptance of a common-law criminal jurisdiction would have strengthened the federal courts, a result that was not congenial to states' rights adherents.

Following the election of Thomas Jefferson as president in 1800, prosecutions for common-law crimes largely ceased in federal court. Nonetheless, in 1806, the federal district judge in Connecticut invited the federal grand jury to review certain Federalist newspapers in that state. He directed the jurors to consider prosecution for seditious libel as a common-law offense. The grand jury returned indictments in 1807 against several editors, including Barzillai Hudson and George Goodwin of the *Connecticut Courant*, for libelous attacks on President Jefferson. Specifically, Hudson and Goodwin were accused of publishing allegations that President Jefferson and Congress had made secret payments to Napoleon as a bribe to obtain a treaty with Spain. The indictments were

ironic because the Jeffersonians had vigorously opposed both the notion of federal common-law crimes and the trial of seditious libel in federal courts. In fact, the prosecution of Hudson and Goodwin prompted debate in Congress, with both Jeffersonians and Federalists criticizing the doctrine of common-law crime.

There is no evidence that Jefferson instigated the Connecticut indictments, and indeed he directed the prosecutor to dismiss the charges. But *Hudson & Goodwin* was brought to trial before receipt of Jefferson's instructions. The defendants submitted a demurrer to the jurisdiction of the court. After some delays, the two federal judges conducting the trial were divided in opinion concerning the validity of a federal jurisdiction over common-law crimes. Consequently, late in 1808 the matter was certified to the U.S. Supreme Court.

The case came before the Supreme Court in March 1812, the first Term at which there was a Jeffersonian majority on the bench. Consistent with the Jeffersonians' position, Attorney General William Pinckney declined to argue the case on behalf of the government. No counsel appeared for the defendants. Thus, the justices did not have the benefit of a careful argument on this complicated and important question.

The Supreme Court, in a cursory opinion by Justice William Johnson, flatly rejected the doctrine of common-law crimes. Although the case before the Court concerned a prosecution of seditious libel, Johnson addressed the broader issue of whether the federal courts could exercise any nonstatutory criminal jurisdictions. Political considerations bulked large for Johnson. Significantly, he emphasized that in the Court's mind this matter had "been long since settled in public opinion. . . . [A]nd the general acquiescence of legal men shows the prevalence of opinion in favor of the negative of the proposition."

Johnson's opinion was grounded on federalism and strict construction of legislation. Stressing the limited nature of the federal government, Johnson declared that federal power was "made up of concessions from the several States" and that the states reserved all powers not expressly delegated. In his view, lower federal courts could exercise only jurisdiction conferred by statute, and Congress had not granted common-law criminal jurisdiction. Johnson refused to decide whether Congress might confer such a jurisdiction upon the courts. Conceding that a sovereign nation might possess certain implied powers to safeguard its existence, Johnson nonetheless insisted that the federal courts could not punish acts until Congress declared the behavior criminal and fixed a punishment. He did recognize one exception to this general rule—the implied power of federal courts to punish contempt and enforce their orders.

No justice filed a written dissent, but scholars are agreed that the opinion was not unanimous. Justices Joseph Story and Bushrod Washington were likely dissenters, and the position of Chief Justice John Marshall cannot be ascertained with certainty.

Story was particularly upset, believing that *Hudson & Goodwin* was poorly reasoned, inconsistent with past practice, and left the federal government in a weakened position to protect itself against criminal activity. Hence, Story moved on two fronts to limit the impact of *Hudson & Goodwin*. He unsuccessfully urged Congress to enact a statute recognizing common-law crimes as federal offenses. Moreover, Story sought to compel a reconsideration of the issue by the Supreme Court. In a previous case, Story, while on circuit, raised the question of common-law crime in the context of maritime jurisdiction, a subject clearly within the power of the federal courts under Article III of the Constitution. Seeking to distinguish *Hudson & Goodwin*, he argued that the common law merely defined the extent of maritime authority granted by the Constitution. The majority of the Supreme Court, however, was in no mood to reopen the explosive debate over common-law crimes. The Supreme Court abruptly reversed Story, relying on *Hudson & Goodwin*.

Thus, decades of acrimonious debate concerning the prosecution of nonstatutory crimes in the federal courts came to an anticlimactic end. Although the Supreme Court could be faulted for deciding *Hudson & Goodwin* in an offhand manner, the outcome was certainly consistent with democratic notions about a popular voice in the definition of criminal behavior.

Selected Bibliography

Bridwell, R. and R.U. Whitten. *The Constitution and the Common Law*. Lexington, MA: Lexington Books, 1977.

Haskins, G.L., and H.A. Johnson. *History of the Supreme Court of the United States. Vol. II. Foundations of Power: John Marshall, 1801–15*. New York: Macmillan Publishing Co., Inc., 1981.

Levy, L.W. *The Emergence of a Free Press*. New York: Oxford University Press, 1985.

Newmyer, R.K. *Supreme Court Justice Joseph Story: Statesman of the Old Republic*. Chapel Hill, NC: University of North Carolina Press, 1985.

Palmer, R.C. "The Federal Court Law of Crime." *Law and History Review* 4 (Fall 1986): 267–323.

Presser, S.B. "A Tale of Two Judges: Richard Peters, Samuel Chase, and the Broken Promise of Federalist Jurisprudence." *Northwestern University Law Review* 73 (March/April 1978): 26–111.

Preyer, K. "Jurisdiction to Punish: Federal Authority, Federalism, and the Common Law of Crimes in the Early Republic." *Law and History Review* 4 (Fall 1986): 223–65.

Warren, C. *The Supreme Court in United States History. Vol. I., 1789–1835*. Rev. ed. Boston: Little, Brown & Co., 1926.

A DOUBLE STANDARD OF JUSTICE: IS ADULTERY BY A WIFE WORSE THAN MURDER BY HER HUSBAND?

by Marie E. Windell
Special Collections
University of New Orleans

Cortes v. de Russy (1843) [Louisiana Supreme Court]

Between 1843 and 1934 this suit for divorce was hidden in the *Louisiana Reports* behind the cryptic initials, "J.F.C. v. M.E." because the antebellum court reporter considered it too scandalous for normal reporting. The case file contains incriminating letters in a drama filled with accusations of an illegitimate birth, challenges to duels, wife abuse, attempted abortion and suicide, and calculated murder.

It was the only case cited in its category (and still by initials) in the centennial edition of the *American Digest* (1658–1896). In 1934, two Louisiana attorneys, without the benefit of the original documents, identified the litigants but contradicted the record. An accurate and complete history can now be determined from the early manuscript appeals of the Louisiana Supreme Court.

This marital tragedy arose in Natchitoches, an eighteenth-century northwestern Louisiana frontier outpost, which in the 1840s was an important shipping point on the route to Texas and Mexico. The testimony not only illuminates the position of women on the frontier and the social problems of violence and divorce, but also gives insight into the workings of the antebellum Louisiana Supreme Court.

A double standard of justice for husbands and wives has usually been defined for adultery alone: wives received harsh treatment and husbands, forgiveness, for essentially the same offense. According to the 1827 Louisiana law permitting divorce, a single act of adultery by a wife was sufficient grounds for the husband, but she could stake her claim on the same grounds only if her husband kept a mistress in their home or openly and publicly elsewhere. By the law of 1832, flight from an infamous offense was added as grounds, but, in this case

Cortes's attorneys argued that his wife's adultery barred her plea on the grounds of murder by her husband. Which of the two spouses had the morally superior position and thus the stronger claim for divorce?

The suit was brought in March 1842, in the Natchitoches District Court for the husband, J.F.C., after he had murdered his wife's alleged lover and had fled to join the army of Mexico, which was then at war with the Republic of Texas. In 1843, the Louisiana Supreme Court granted a divorce and custody of their small child to the husband on the grounds of his wife's adultery.

In 1934, two Louisiana attorneys published the diary of a Natchitoches lawyer, William Long Tuomey, who referred to the 1842 murder of the alleged lover, James M. Giles. In an explanatory note, the editors, correctly identified the couple, but denied any adultery had occurred on the mistaken assumption that Judge Henry Adams Bullard, writing for the supreme court, had cleared the wife and had given her the divorce.

Out of the original manuscript case file, heard in the supreme court session in Alexandria in 1843, arise several figures preoccupied with honor, control, or endurance, surrounded by a crowd of witnesses. It is remarkable that these manuscript pages survived the Civil War, for the legal archives of the western district were moved about during the war, in part by federal troops, and even shipped to Washington, D.C., before their return to the court a generation later.

Natchitoches was composed of French-speaking Catholics and an increasing number of English-speaking Protestants when John François Cortes and Marie Emilie de Russy were married in 1834. Cortes, then in his early twenties, was the eldest son of a well-to-do merchant and former mayor, who had died while the son was a minor.

Emilie de Russy was the daughter of Major Louis G. de Russy, of the U.S. Army, who was a Whig candidate in 1838 for the state senate. He later served in the Mexican War and was a noted colonel of engineers in the Confederate forces. U.S. Fort de Russy on the Red River was named for him.

Cortes, a steamboat agent, land speculator, and later a director of a local steamboat company, had mutual interests with his father-in-law in U.S. Fort Jesup, 25 miles to the west. In 1839, Cortes had accompanied Major de Russy, a second in the most famous duel in the western district. Eleven men were killed before the chain of honor ran its course in the affair between General Pierre E. Bossier and François Gaiennie. Cortes boasted in 1841 that he had received and accepted challenges to three duels in a single day.

Throughout the seven years of marriage, Cortes drank heavily, abused his wife, and was consumed by bouts of jealousy, followed by moments of remorse, a typical pattern noted in twentieth-century research on violent husbands trying to maintain supremacy in a marriage. At times he was affectionate, at others, so abusive, even in her father's presence, that her uncle once ordered Cortes out of the house.

One of the strongest antebellum controls over married women was the social stigma of divorce. Mrs. Cortes had "long meditated a separation from the plaintiff because of his outrageous conduct," but she hesitated to take "so harsh a step." Had she been able to steel herself to petition for a separation or divorce, she had sufficient grounds based on cruel treatment. For example, in 1837 Cortes threatened his wife with a pistol "if she did not immediately go to bed," and on another occasion she was rescued from being strangled by him while in bed. Also, when they were boarding in a New Orleans hotel, according to a witness in the next room, he dragged her around on the bedroom floor. About two years after the marriage, he pretended to take poison to create the false impression among their friends that she had driven him to this step. In 1838 in New Orleans, he

threw her out of their hotel room into the public hallway after midnight, like a prostitute. A witness, James Waddell, had heard her pleas but was restrained from assisting her by his own wife's caution. Members of Cortes's circle, even his father-in-law, rarely opposed him.

Cortes justified his abuse and violence by accusing his wife of adultery. About 1840, he accused an acquaintance of improper intercourse with her, but later admitted his error and apologized. In 1840 or 1841, his jealousy centered on a young bachelor attorney and neighbor of Mrs. Cortes's aunt, James M. Giles, who lent books to her and her friends in an informal reading circle. Always suspicious, Cortes arranged another scheme to "injure his wife in the good opinion of the public." He invited Giles to accompany his wife to the theater, pretending that his business interfered with his attending. After all were seated, however, Cortes arrived and by "scowling looks" indicated that he was displeased with Giles's attention to his wife.

Cortes, whose emotional problems were compounded by financial embarrassments, was frequently a defendant in lawsuits over debt. His wife often mediated for him with her friends to extricate him from difficulties. Such frustrating episodes must have threatened him with a further loss of control, while his wife demonstrated patience, mildness, and ladylike qualities, which his own witnesses praised.

Her one defiant act described in the testimony took place in 1838 while she was caring for a dying child. When her husband demanded that she leave the child's bedside and come to bed with him (cursing the child—"I wish it was in Hell"), Mrs. Cortes refused.

Following the deaths of her mother and the child, she chose passive resistance by visiting relatives in Texas in 1838, the year of her father's political campaign. Although Major de Russy had never seen his daughter "guilty of light conduct," he gave way to Cortes's insistence that he write a letter urging her to return and adapt more closely to the "disposition" of her husband.

The direct cause of their separation in March 1841, was a ridiculous scene: Mrs. Cortes refused to permit her husband, when drunk, to carry her across a muddy street to a ball. After she escaped for protection to her father's house, Cortes vowed to "crush her and her whole family." Was he jealous of the attorneys and judges who regularly visited the Major at Grande Ecore on the bluff? Cortes refused to acknowledge in writing, as his father-in-law recommended, that his accusations had been groundless. He tore away their young son Edward and confronted the major in a liquor store, pushing and threatening him.

Suddenly Cortes changed his conduct, remained sober, expressed the deepest penitence, and promised to reform. Acceding to pleas by his friends, his wife returned to town in September to live with her aunt, the wife of the deputy clerk of court, Thomas P. Jones. Against her better judgment, she rejoined her husband in October, with the understanding that she would leave permanently if she was mistreated.

Almost immediately, Cortes abandoned his changed conduct, became abusive, and whispered suspicions to his friends that his wife was unfaithful. In December, he deliberately provoked a quarrel with Giles, but was caught in the toils of his own plot. Giles threatened to publish some embarrassing correspondence and was able to extract an abject apology from him. Cortes, humiliated and knowing that his wife, then pregnant, was planning a permanent separation, vowed their utter ruin.

On the night of February 10, 1842, the Cortes family and two slaves, Emma and Emmeline, were at home. A 20-foot passage lay between their house and that of their neighbors, the Fearings, who let a room to John D. Martin. The Fearing household usually retired around 10 p.m.; the Cortes family, not until midnight.

That evening Giles and Benjamin Valcour Cortes, a brother of Cortes and the sheriff, sat drinking in the coffeehouse-tavern of Patrick Shelly. Giles, the last customer, drank alone and left between midnight and 1 a.m., apparently intoxicated.

A little past midnight, Fearing and Martin were awakened by loud talking next door. Shortly after, Cortes walked down the alley and forced open the shutter of his dining room window, which was opposite Martin's bedroom window. Swearing and hitting the sash to open it, he broke the glass, went back inside, and

loud talking resumed inside the Cortes house. The slave Emmeline knocked on Fearing's window and said her master had sent her for a candle. For about an hour the two men watched Cortes walking back and forth in the front room.

Around 1 a.m., a knocking at the Cortes's front door was followed by his voice "in a passion" in French, which the two neighbors did not understand. Apparently the racket was the noisy arrival of Giles, although the two witnesses heard only Cortes, who continued to talk loudly until nearly daybreak, keeping them awake the balance of the night. According to Mrs. Cortes, Giles, who arrived intoxicated, had come at the invitation of her husband to end the quarrel. Cortes shouted for arms and various people, and declared that he had caught his wife and Giles in bed together, which both denied. Giles left, forgetting his hat, cane, and cloak.

Cortes twice sent Emmeline for his brother, the sheriff, but he refused both requests because he thought it was one of the "plaintiff's foolish quarrels with his wife," one of his "foolish frolics." In the meantime, according to Mrs. Cortes, her husband, while awaiting his brother, placed a cloak and pillow wrapped in a lady's shawl on the dining room floor, in order she said to give color to the accusations he had been making against her. A candle, candlestick, and cane lay nearby. A man's hat sat on the pillow. A piece of cloth hung from a nail at the broken window.

Around 4 a.m., Emmeline awakened the jailer, Edward Brenan, and brought him to the house. Cortes showed him the stage set in the dining room and asked him to put the slave Emma in jail and to bring his brother.

The sheriff found his pregnant sister-in-law, wan and passive, in a black dress, in mourning for her mother-in-law. Cortes walked up and down, charging that a lady [her aunt?] had been the cause of her "ruin in this Town." Like many abused and helpless wives, she claimed that "no one was to blame but herself." This attempt to maintain self-respect was interpreted by the sheriff and later by the Supreme Court as an admission of guilt.

When she had somewhat recovered at her aunt's, Mrs. Cortes insisted to her brother-in-law that while appearances were against her, she was not guilty. In cross-examination about this conversation, he admitted that his brother was a jealous man and that Mrs. Cortes's conduct ever since her marriage until this occurrence had always been proper and unreproachable.

Shortly after, Cortes wrote letter No. 3 to his wife: "I must see you, alone . . . it is to *save you* if I *can, Compatibly with my honour* . . . no one shall ever Know it" [emphasis in original]. What violence was he contemplating? Was he implying an abortion to save his "honour?" His wife declined this interview also.

Major de Russy proposed that the two brothers and their friends agree to a future separation for the couple. For this, Mrs. Cortes would return to her husband temporarily until the scandal died down; she would give up her son to Cortes's sister, and write a letter of apology to her husband.

Four years earlier, Major de Russy had written a letter to appeal to his son-in-law. He now composed his daughter's apology, which she copied and signed as her own. Although it was letter No. 4, it was labeled "A" as if in anticipation of Hawthorne's *The Scarlet Letter*: "I find the evidences [circumstantial evidence] against me such as must crush me, my child, my friends." Cortes's avowed goal against his wife had been achieved, and at great cost to her future suit.

Although his efforts had not crushed Giles or his friends, Cortes's erratic behavior frightened them, and the attorney left town. In his absence, Cortes alternated between threats and denials of an attack on Giles, ending with a "sacred promise" in early March to his brother and their friends that he would not undertake violence. Giles, reassured, returned to Natchitoches but never appeared in public alone.

A few days later, March 13, on a Sunday afternoon around 4 p.m., Cortes entered the rooms of Giles and his partner, John E. Rothrock, where they were at dinner, shot and killed Giles in cold blood. Afterwards Cortes calmly walked down the street and "no one pursued of course."

Convinced that his wife would never return, he brought suit for divorce in the Natchitoches District Court, but was persuaded by his friends to flee to Mexico, and his attorneys filed for him. He was defended by seven attorneys from leading local firms. Mrs. Cortes, who had only ten days to file an answer, was apparently unprepared for the suit. After two weeks, Judge James G. Campbell, a friend of the major, issued a judgment by default, and when it was set aside, her ten days had stretched into five weeks.

Her answer summarized the cruel treatment she had received, but the reconciliation had invalidated all her prior evidence on those grounds. She claimed an immediate divorce according to the law of 1832, without the usual delay of two years. Mrs. Cortes also asked for custody of Edward during this suit; a court order for her clothes, "which are withheld from her"; and an allowance for support, since she had "no income whatever." Campbell continued the case until the 1842 November term at Natchitoches, to permit her to collect testimony in and outside the state.

In the meantime, Mrs. Cortes and Mrs. Samuel Kathrens left by steamboat to visit relatives in Kentucky. En route on June 1, Mrs. Cortes leaped from the hurricane deck, and a male child was born that evening. Apparently it was stillborn, for no witness saw it longer than five minutes. Jumping overboard from steamboats was a common method for suicide at the time, but her leap seems rather to have been an attempt to bring about a premature birth. Or, was Mrs. Cortes trying to make the birth seem premature when it actually was close to term (i.e., conceived in September when she was living with her aunt in Natchitoches)? According to Louisiana law, without proof to the contrary, the husband was the father of a child born in a marriage.

During the November term, the plaintiff, the defendant, and her witnesses all were out of the state. Major de Russy, representing his daughter, had located Cortes in Mexico City only two weeks earlier. He hoped to have the suit dismissed because the plaintiff was now a resident of a foreign country or at least to receive a continuance to collect testimony that was vital to his daughter's case.

The district judge for this term was not Campbell, the major's friend, but George R. King, a former district attorney, soon to join the Court of Errors and Appeals in Criminal Matters. He would not grant a continuance and reproached the absent defendant for not having used "even ordinary diligence" to procure witnesses or their testimony by commissions. Without the deposition by Cortes, his wife was left without corroboration of her version of the events, and her defense suffered a fatal weakness during the appeal.

The major question before the district court was the alleged adultery on February 10–11, and as a corollary, the legitimacy of the still-born infant. Cortes's attorneys interpreted her passivity that night as evidence of her guilt, not the exhaustion of a pregnant woman after an all-night vigil. They also interpreted her statement on blame and the copy of her father's letter ("A") written to secure agreement by Cortes to a separation as her admission to the adultery. To prove infidelity, they also dated the reconciliation two weeks later than did her counsel.

Mrs. Cortes's attorney's defense rested on the argument that Martin's and Fearing's testimonies proved that no adultery had taken place on the night of February 10–11 and that the birth was premature. The evidence of four physicians supported her claim: none of them believed that Mrs. Kathrens could determine the age of the newborn "in the dark, wrapped up in a blanket, and for only five minutes."

King instructed the jury to find for a separation from bed and board if not for divorce. An immediate divorce could be granted only on the grounds of flight from justice or proven adultery. The jury, following King's charge, found in favor of a separation and custody for Mrs. Cortes. Having lost the suit, her husband was ordered to pay the costs.

At the same term, Cortes was also a defendant in a case over the bankruptcy of his steamboat company. Unless he won the divorce suit on appeal, his seven attorneys might not be paid. In fact, when he died in Mexico in 1846, his debts in Louisiana exceeded his estate.

During the trial, one juror, Elijah Clark, out of court and against explicit judicial instructions, told witnesses there was insufficient evidence for adultery. Unfortunately for Mrs. Cortes, the comments of the loquacious juror

provided her husband's attorneys with a ground for appeal.

The appeal was heard during the 1843 October term in Alexandria. Cortes's lawyers had to counter his crime and overturn the verdict for Mrs. Cortes. Felix Sherburne, a native of France, argued that adultery was a criminal offense under French law, a primary source for Louisiana civil law. He thereby neatly juxtaposed the husband's crime of murder and the wife's alleged adultery, although the latter was not a criminal offense in the state. If the talkative juror had invalidated the verdict, the decision of unproved adultery could be reversed.

Mrs. Cortes's attorneys, now four, marshaled a convincing argument, supporting her good conduct by witnesses, among others, her brother-in-law and the doctors, all sustaining her point of view. Giles, a longtime friend of the deputy clerk, had lived with his partner Rothrock, opposite the Jones household. Rothrock had once seen the two in the Jones's sitting room in the twilight without a candle, but never in "[C]ircumstances to excite the suspicion of anything wrong." One attorney suggested that Giles had come to visit the slave Emma, who had been (inexplicably) jailed the next morning by Cortes, a jealous man. King's ruling had prevented Mrs. Cortes from acquiring a deposition from her husband, and the two slaves present that night were not eligible witnesses. But as a final authority, her attorneys quoted the *Digest* of Bullard and Curry on infamous crime as grounds for divorce.

Judge Henry Adams Bullard— who co-edited the *Digest*—was a handsome man, noted for his melodious speaking voice and his gift for languages. He had attracted the attention of the learned Reverend Timothy Flint in his travels, and he would become the first professor of civil law in the United States. As a young attorney from Massachusetts, he had participated in 1813 in a disastrous border raid from Natchitoches for Texas's independence, and was one of a few officers to escape the Mexican army ambush of his men. Bullard's pride was easily injured even before the Texas fiasco, and after he retired from the court in 1846 and went into politics, his temper and self-esteem were the butt of newspaper ridicule.

Since 1839, Bullard himself had been involved in a long and acrimonious divorce trial. His wife accused him of adultery with a young neighbor who shared his taste for romantic German poetry. He won a separation on the ground of public defamation, and his wife's appeal was then before his court in 1843. Was Bullard more willing to believe in adultery by Mrs. Cortes and Giles in their reading circle because of his own experience? Moreover, his brother Charles had been a fellow defendant with Cortes in a lawsuit.

Unlike his usual practice, Bullard annotated the Cortes case file with phrases that show he was convinced of her adultery. He misread the testimony on their life after the reconciliation: "[T]here is no evidence that the parties lived unhappily, or that the husband was guilty of any cruelty or outrage." It was not the duty of the court, he said, "to give any analysis of the evidence," and then discarded the jury's verdict. Bullard refused to believe that Cortes, whose letters were filled with references to his honor, could also stoop to dishonorable stratagems. All the circumstances, remarked Bullard, "repel such a charge" despite the pattern of Cortes's schemes to humiliate his wife. The judge's preoccupation with honor surfaces in his description of the murder as "unmanly."

Bullard was also offended by the use of his *Digest* for a woman who, he was convinced, had been surprised by her husband "in his own house, in flagranti delicto" with her paramour. Speaking for the court, he granted a divorce and child custody to Cortes, then a captain in the Mexican army, and ordered his wife to pay the costs in both courts.

The judge had not only ignored Louisiana jurisprudence that required adultery had to be proved and that a spouse's admission was not sufficient proof, but also had denied the evidence of cruelty to Mrs. Cortes after the reconciliation. His rulings on a limitation of divorce actions, reconciliation, and the payment of costs were cited in later Louisiana cases, and they carried this suit into the federal *American Digest* as the classic case of denial of divorce to a wife whose husband had murdered her alleged paramour.

Selected Bibliography

Bonquois, D.J. "The Career of Henry Adams Bullard, Louisiana Jurist, Legislator, and Educator." *Louisiana Historical Quarterly* 23 (Oct. 1940): 999–1106.

Cortes, John François v. Marie Emilie de Russy, Alexandria, 1843. 6 Robinson 135: "*J.F.C. v. M.E.*" Original case file in Supreme Court of Louisiana Collection of Legal Archives, Acc. 106. Archives & Manuscripts/Special Collections Dept., University of New Orleans, New Orleans, LA 70148.

Tuomey, W.L. "A Young Lawyer of Natchitoches of 1836; the Diary of William S. Toumey [sic]." *Louisiana Historical Quarterly* 17 (Jan., April 1934): 64–79, 315–26.

DEATH FOR GRAND LARCENY

by Gordon Morris Bakken
Department of History
California State University at Fullerton

People v. Tanner, 2 Cal. 257 (1852) [California Supreme Court]

The California gold rush, by creating instant wealth and instant cities, provided lawmakers with the challenge of dealing with crime in the streets and vigilance committees operating in lieu of legitimate authority. As part of the legislative effort to stem popular justice and bring statutory law in accord with the culturally accepted penalties for certain crimes, the California legislature provided for the death penalty for grand larceny. George Tanner became the first to appeal his death sentence under this 1851 statute.

The 1851 statute amended the 1850 penal code by giving the jury discretion in robbery cases of setting prison sentences of one to ten years or death. Grand larceny received the same treatment. Petit larceny (i.e., stealing property worth less than $50) had the penalty of "imprisonment in the County jail not more than six months, or . . . fine not exceeding five hundred dollars, or . . . any number of lashes not exceeding fifty upon the bare back, or . . . such fine or imprisonment and lashes in the discretion of the jury." Thus, the legislature put into formal law what the people had been putting into action in the rough and tumble environment of the gold fields.

The narrow legal issue in *People v. Tanner* involved a juror's declaration against the death penalty. The California Supreme Court decided that a juror's declaration of conscientious scruples against the death penalty was sufficient under the current statute to exclude the person from a jury in a grand larceny case. The accused, George Tanner, had stolen 1,500 pounds of flour, six sacks of potatoes, five kegs of syrup, two and one-half barrels of meal, one keg of powder, and one-half barrel of mackerel, thereby running afoul of the 1850 California Penal Code, as amended. The court of sessions jury brought in a verdict of "guilty of grand larceny, punishable with Death." District Judge Gordon N. Mott upheld the verdict with the death penalty, and Tanner appealed to the California Supreme Court.

Chief Justice Hugh C. Murray delivered the opinion for a unanimous court. The statutory challenge of the district judge's order excluding the juror was rejected on statutory interpretation grounds. Legislators had provided that in cases where "the offence charged by punishable with death," a juror would "neither be permitted nor compelled to serve as a juror." Given the fact that the penal statute provided for the death penalty option, the challenge to the juror and the judge's order excluding the juror from service were sustained.

Beyond the narrow ruling on this important issue of criminal justice administration, the court commented on the penal statute and public policy. First, Murray wrote that "it was not" the court's "purpose to discuss the policy of the law." Then he went on to do so, criticizing the legislature's actions "in the face of the wisdom and experience of the present day" and to characterize the death penalty for crimes less than murder as "alike disgusting and abhorrent to the common sense of every enlightened people."

Regardless of its personal distaste for such a penalty, the court recognized that its role was limited. First, the court was to support legislatively defined public policy. This was needed "to correct the administration of the law." Correct administration would, in turn, "secure a due enforcement of the penalties ordained for its violation." Finally, the court was to implement the public policy declarations of the people through their duly elected representatives. "The law has ordained," Murray wrote, "that this offence shall be punished with death, and to allow jurors to sit upon a trial for larceny who declared that they would not impose this penalty, would defeat the intention of its framers, and practically work a repeal of its provisions." Such a result would be "a mockery to justice." It was the court's duty to prevent "the administration of justice from becoming a mockery." The judicial function was to be supportive of the statements of public policy in law regardless of personal philosophy.

Tanner contained several elements common to western criminal cases of the frontier period. The death penalty for property crimes, commonly associated with horse stealing, was broad and part of jury discretion. Justice was often swift. Tanner committed the crime on April 3, 1852, was brought to trial on April 14, 1852, lost his appeal in the district court on April 24, 1852, won a petition for rehearing before the supreme court on May 24, 1852, lost at the hearing on the petition on July 16, 1852, and was executed on July 23, 1852. Finally, western appellate opinions often were communicated to the bar and the populace by the media. On May 16, 1852, the *Alta California*, San Francisco's daily newspaper, published the entire text of the supreme court opinion. In the days before advance sheets and with bound volumes frequently following opinions by many months, western newspapers often informed the people of the developing state of the law.

Selected Bibliography

Bakken, G.M. "The Influence of the West on the Development of Law." *Journal of the West* 44 (1985): 66–72.

Senkewicz, R.M. *Vigilantes in Gold Rush San Francisco.* Stanford, CA: Stanford University Press, 1985.

PUBLIC OPINION, EXPERT TESTIMONY, AND "THE INSANITY DODGE"

by Elisabeth A. Cawthon
Department of History
University of Texas at Arlington

United States v. Guiteau, 1 Mackey 498 (1882) [District of Columbia court]

For a time in the early 1880s, Charles Julius Guiteau was one of the most widely discussed individuals in the United States, and perhaps the world. After attempting to assassinate President James Garfield, Guiteau became a public figure—much to his delight. After the president died, as the central character in the resulting murder trial, Guiteau took on even greater significance. Yet even attentive scholars of late-nineteenth-century U.S. politics often fail to appreciate the furor that surrounded Guiteau's trial. Guiteau is remembered best as a "disappointed office-seeker," whose killing of the president led to calls for civil service reform. That historical understanding of Guiteau's actions, however, does not capture his importance in either a contemporary or a long-term sense. Around Guiteau's rather pathetic persona raged several fundamental legal, medical, and ethical controversies—controversies that, over a century later, still pervade trials at which questions of individual responsibility for criminal acts are decided.

The facts surrounding Guiteau's criminal actions were not much in dispute during his trial for the murder of President Garfield. In front of several witnesses in a Washington, D.C., railway station, on Saturday, July 2, 1881, the unexceptional-looking Guiteau had calmly fired two shots at the president, gravely injuring Garfield. When Guiteau tried to leave the station, a District policeman had detained him; Guiteau's only comments at the scene were that he had shot Garfield and that he expected to go to jail as a result. The president lingered for several months before dying; Guiteau was held in custody during that time. Public interest in Garfield's fate was intense, as was fascination with the background and motivation of the president's assailant.

Some expressions of sympathy for Guiteau during the late summer and early fall of 1881 were related to the widespread hope that the president might recover. If Garfield could regain his health, most commentators thought Guiteau would simply be sent to an insane asylum. That is, many observers postulated that Guiteau must have been insane to have committed such an irrational crime in an unremorseful manner and therefore thought he ought to be institutionalized. But the climate of general opinion on Guiteau altered with Garfield's death. In an effort to make sense of the president's death—who had not been in office long enough to alienate large constituencies—both Garfield's political allies and moralists with other axes to grind began to try to draw lessons from Garfield's death and Guiteau's life. In the wake of Garfield's funeral, Guiteau was cast more as a villain and less as an object of pity who should be locked away in an asylum (which was not the rosiest fate that could befall a defendant in the nineteenth century). Increasingly, Guiteau was described in print, in song, and from the pulpit as a calculating attention-seeker, a legal huckster, a man who had not summoned sufficient moral fiber to rise above an unpromising family history. A brief association by Guiteau's father with the Oneida Community (a nineteenth-century utopian community in upstate New York) was widely discussed, for example, as an indication of a hereditary tendency toward depravity.

Guiteau was formally arraigned on October 14, 1881. His trial stretched over several months in the late fall of 1881, and a guilty verdict was returned (after just over an hour's deliberation by the jury) on January 5, 1881. The major issue of the trial, in the minds of the American public, was Guiteau's character.

The conduct of the trial revolved around a more traditionally legal question: the state of mind of the defendant at the time of the assassination. Since it was apparent that Guiteau had pulled the trigger—he had admitted often and openly that he had meant to kill Garfield—the only substantive question before the jury was whether it accepted the argument by Guiteau's counsel that Guiteau had been acting while "legally insane." Guiteau made his lawyers' position rather tricky. He maintained throughout the trial that he was technically, or legally insane, because he had acted according to God's will in shooting the president. Yet Guiteau's brother-in-law, whose testimony on the Guiteau family history played a key role in the defense, insisted that the family's reputation should not be unduly sullied through evidence that suggested the family's unstable emotional legacy. When Guiteau's lawyers argued that he should be judged not guilty by reason of insanity, they sought, with their case, to make an important clarification in the Anglo-American law on criminal responsibility. Guiteau's trial ultimately became the leading example in the United States in the nineteenth century of the "defense of insanity"—or, as it was popularly known, "the insanity dodge."

The branch of law dealing with the plea of "not guilty by reason of insanity" had been murky in the United States ever since the standards for insanity, the M'Naghten rules, had been formulated by a panel of English judges in 1843. After a series of acquittals of defendants in England in the early 1800s, and a resulting furor over courts' allowing juries to be "lenient" toward criminals, the M'Naghten rules created a relatively simple set of standards that judges could state to trial juries to help them assess the state of mind of accused persons. The gist of the M'Naghten "test" for insanity was whether the accused knew at the time he committed the crime that what he was doing was a crime and was aware of the practical and legal consequences of his actions.

Among legal authorities in England and the United States (where the M'Naghten rules were widely admired, although not uniformly or universally adopted from state to state), the M'Naghten standard for insanity was regarded as a compromise between two earlier "tests" of

criminal responsibility. The M'Naghten test included a requirement that the defendant either had to be acting without reason (as if he were a wild beast, incapable of reason) or must have been unaware that what he was doing was wrong. Furthermore, when a defendant according to the M'Naghten rules wished to argue that at the time of the crime he did not know right from wrong, he also was required to show that his incapacity to distinguish right from wrong resulted from a disease of the mind, rather than from ignorance or mere crankiness. Thus, the M'Naghten rules almost necessitated the use of medical testimony to illustrate the extent to which defendants were diseased rather than simply misguided at the time of the commission of the acts for which they were on trial. Although the guilty verdict in Guiteau's trial settled his case and seemed to indicate some preference in judicial and legal circles for a rather strict (i.e., narrow) legal interpretation of insanity, the insanity defense remained quite controversial in the wake of Guiteau's conviction.

The trial of Guiteau served not only as a legal watershed in the adaptation of the M'Naghten rule to the United States but also as a forum for the airing of a bitter dispute among several groups of professionals interested in the question of insanity and criminal responsibility. Neurologists, psychiatrists and psychologists, criminologists, and state bureaucrats, all of whom served as "expert witnesses" in *Guiteau*, expressed vital disagreements about the causes of crime, the hereditary bases of insanity, the effectiveness of cures for mental disease, and other issues about which they had been battling within their professional journals for years. Among the most vocal expert witnesses in *Guiteau* were John P. Gray, superintendent of New York State's Utica Asylum and editor of the *American Journal of Insanity*, and Edward Spitzka of the New York Neurological Society. Gray and Spitzka were professional antagonists long before *Guiteau* pitted them against each other. In the *Guiteau* trial, Gray's testimony was vital to the prosecution and Spitzka lent valuable assistance to the defense.

Gray held to a narrow definition of insanity, which was compatible with a strict application of the M'Naghten rules. He was unwilling to accept the idea of "moral insanity," which was gaining popularity among some medical professionals, as a way of understanding social nonconformity that had led to criminal actions. To Gray and a number of his colleagues concerned with the supervision of asylums, true insanity was a recognizable but comparatively rare phenomenon; most individuals who fell outside a "wild-beast" test were depraved, sinful, willful, or even momentarily deluded. Although Gray would have admitted that some accused persons who claimed to be insane had come from unfortunate environments that made it more difficult for them to resist temptation, he still would have argued against their being classified for legal purposes as "insane." Gray's observations about his examinations of Guiteau were of great weight during the trial; and the trial itself was an excellent opportunity for him to state his views to a wide audience.

On the other side of the debates about the causation of insanity and its prevalence as a disease were neurologists such as Spitzka. Spitzka, with his grounding in European psychological theory and his respect for the possibilities of anatomical investigation, argued during the *Guiteau* trial for a broader definition of insanity—albeit on the basis of his understanding of insanity as primarily hereditary and organic in origin. Thus, *Guiteau* brought to public attention disagreements that professionals had been airing among themselves, and that continue to rage around the roles that individual choice, environmental influence, and genetics play in criminal behavior. The debate between neurologists (such as Spitzka) and asylum superintendents (such as Gray), however, was not a simple disagreement over nature versus nurture or environment versus heredity. In a larger sense, conflicts among the experts at Guiteau's trial raised in a public forum the issue of how expert testimony should be integrated into a criminal trial—a subject that had not come fully under legal discussion in the United States until *Guiteau.*

Guiteau's conviction and execution (which was carried out on June 30, 1882) also brought into the realm of legal and public discussion quandaries concerning the impact of public opinion on the conduct of trials. During the trial, very few organs of public opinion (from

newspapers to popular songs) expressed much sympathy for Guiteau. In fact, public opinion was distinctly hostile not only to Guiteau but also to anyone who was perceived as too lenient toward him. Judge Walter Cox, who presided at the trial, had decided that Guiteau's jury ought to be given every opportunity to see the defendant's mental state, so he allowed Guiteau some leeway to participate actively in his own defense. That comparative permissiveness caused Cox no end of threatening letters and professional criticism. And when one of Guiteau's regular prison guards, Sergeant William Mason, shot at Guiteau, the less respectable Washington newspapers started a subscription for the expenses of Mason's defense. Several editorial commentators took the opportunity to suggest that lynching Guiteau would be in order, noting that Mason had been merely public-spirited.

In the midst of the heated atmosphere surrounding Guiteau's trial, most newspaper columnists, ministers, and even writers for legal and medical journals argued that the judicial process was being used in a reasonably orderly fashion, which proved that American society was committed to the rule of law. In the months and years following Guiteau's death, however, few writers disagreed that public opinion had played a part in Guiteau's conviction and execution. Had Guiteau killed a less important figure, the argument ran, the insanity defense probably would have been accepted. Guiteau's singing of a strange, childlike song in his last moments, more than any of his odd actions, convinced several sober professionals that he should have been declared legally insane at his trial. And some anatomists made much of autopsy findings that indicated the possibility that Guiteau had syphilis—a disease which, despite its terrible moral connotations, was known to cause insanity in a recognized physiological sense.

Despite the softening of at least professional opinion on Guiteau's physical condition, however, the view of the insanity defense as a "dodge" for crafty defendants and their cunning lawyers persisted as a cherished belief among Americans. For example, in the 1981 trial of John Hinckley, Jr., for the attempted assassination of President Ronald Reagan, a number of parallels to the *Guiteau* trial could be observed: significant portions of the M'Naghten rules were still being invoked as appropriate standards for determining the state of mind of the defendant; public opinion polls indicated that Hinckley's plea of not guilty by reason of insanity was perceived to be calculating and manipulative of the legal process, indeed some members of Congress argued for the elimination of the insanity defense in almost all instances; and an array of expert witnesses testified for each side in the case, often contradicting one another and leaving the jurors confused. The *Hinckley* case, although its outcome was more favorable to the defendant than was the outcome in the *Guiteau* case, showed the extent to which the difficult issues raised in the trial of Charles Guiteau have yet to be resolved by the U.S. judicial system.

Selected Bibliography

Caplan, L. *The Insanity Defense and the Trial of John W. Hinckley, Jr.* Boston: D.R. Godine, 1984.

Clyne, P. *Guilty but Insane: Anglo-American Attitudes to Insanity and Criminal Guilt.* London: Nelson, 1973.

Finkel, N.J. *Insanity on Trial.* New York: Plenum Press, 1988.

Maeder, T. *Crime and Madness: The Origins and Evolution of the Insanity Defense.* New York: Harper & Row, 1983.

Rosenberg, C.E. *The Trial of the Assassin Guiteau.* Chicago: University of Chicago Press, 1968.

Simon, R.J., and D.E. Aaronson. *The Insanity Defense: A Critical Assessment of Law and Policy in the Post-Hinckley Era.* New York: Praeger, 1988.

Walker, N. *Crime and Insanity in England.* Edinburgh: Edinburgh University Press, 1968.

"YOU HAVE THE RIGHT TO REMAIN SILENT . . ."

by B. Keith Crew
Department of Sociology and Anthropology
University of Northern Iowa

Miranda v. Arizona, 384 U.S. 436 (1966) [U.S. Supreme Court]

"You have the right to remain silent. If you give up the right to remain silent, anything you say can and will be used against you in a court of law. You have the right to an attorney, and to have the attorney present during questioning. If you cannot afford an attorney, one will be appointed for you."

Most Americans are familiar with these "*Miranda* warnings" from police shows on television, if not from civics classes or practical experience. After 20 years of routine use, they are an accepted ritual of police work, as much a part of a typical arrest as the placing of handcuffs on the suspect.

The *Miranda* rules can still stir up controversy in those rare cases where an officer's failure to read a suspect his rights allows an apparently guilty person to go free; however, it is difficult now to appreciate the consternation on the part of the public and law enforcement officers that this decision originally sparked.

There are few today who seriously argue that requiring the police to "read them their rights" results in thousands of guilty criminals being released. Nevertheless, *Miranda* still symbolizes to many "law and order" politicians and commentators an allegedly misguided concern about the rights of criminals.

Perhaps no decision has come to symbolize an entire era in Supreme Court decisions to the extent that this case symbolizes the Warren Court's approach to criminal justice. Although it is far from the being the most important or far-reaching decision of that Court, *Miranda* is in many ways the classic Warren Court decision. Chief Justice Earl Warren authored the Court's lengthy opinion, and it contains examples of all the major elements of his jurisprudence. Warren seldom followed a narrow or literal reading of the Constitution. Rather, he felt that the Constitution contained imperative ethical principles, which were progressively realized as society's "standards of decency" evolved. Armed with this evolutionary theory of democratic values, Warren was not bashful about breaking with precedent or imposing new rules on the other branches of government. His opinion in *Miranda* has been criticized precisely because it emphasized substantive issues of fairness and justice over legal reasoning and precedent.

Miranda was the culmination of a series of decisions by the Warren Court, collectively referred to as the "due process revolution." Basically, each of these cases depended on the logic that the Fourteenth Amendment placed the same restrictions on the states' use of criminal law that the Bill of Rights, especially the Fifth and Sixth Amendments, placed on the federal government. Furthermore, the Court repeatedly imposed new rules not specifically mentioned in the Constitution, based on the argument that they were essential to realize the ethical imperatives of the Constitution. For example, in *Mapp v. Ohio* (1961), the Court applied this logic when it extended the exclusionary rule, preventing the use of illegally obtained evidence in court, to the states.

Several of these key due process cases, including *Miranda*, involved extending and defining the right to counsel. In *Gideon v. Wainwright* (1963), the Court extended the right to counsel to noncapital felonies in state courts. In doing so, the Court had articulated the position that, in the complex U.S. criminal justice system, access to legal counsel was essential to assure due process. *Gideon*, however, addressed only the right to be represented at trial. Then, in *Escobedo v. Illinois* (1964), the Court extended the right to counsel to the investigative phase of criminal justice.

Escobedo set the stage for *Miranda*. It provided further illustration of the linkage between the Sixth Amendment right to counsel and the Fifth Amendment protection against self-incrimination. Escobedo had not confessed outright; he had unwittingly incriminated himself in a manner that would have been unlikely had his lawyer been present to advise him. Escobedo had been denied contact with his lawyer while in custody and under interrogation. He had specifically requested that he be allowed to see his lawyer; furthermore, his lawyer was at the police station and repeatedly requested to be allowed to see his client. By limiting its decision to these narrowly defined circumstances, the Court had left open the question of precisely at what point in the investigative process an individual's right to be represented by legal counsel begins.

The *Escobedo* decision created a furor among the nation's prosecutors and police, who complained loudly and often that the Court was "coddling criminals." Law enforcement officials were concerned that the Court was moving toward effectively banning the use of confessions altogether; Justice Arthur J. Goldberg, author of the Court's *Escobedo* opinion, had argued that a "law enforcement system that depends on the confession" was inherently "less reliable and more subject to abuses than a system which depends on extrinsic evidence independently secured through skillful investigation."

In an article for the *New York Times Magazine* published in 1965, former federal prosecutor Sidney Zion summed up the concerns of law enforcement officials as follows: "Does this mean that in the future the Court may rule that all suspects have a right to see a lawyer before the police can talk to them, whether they request counsel or not, and whether they can afford one or not? No one can be sure, but the question itself is enough to turn district attorneys gray. If that should ever happen, most lawyers agree, confessions would disappear, because any lawyer worth his salt would advise his client to remain silent."

In the *Miranda* decision, the Court did precisely what prosecutors feared: it ruled that the right to counsel began with police interrogation. Furthermore, it did away with the existing "voluntariness" standard, under which confessions were usually admissible in court as long as there was no evidence of coercion. Law enforcement officials now had a positive duty to inform any suspect of his rights; any incriminating statements made under interrogation without such warnings would henceforth be presumed to be involuntary and therefore inadmissible as evidence. The Court did limit the new rules to interrogation initiated by investigators; it explicitly excluded the situation where a person "enters a police station and states that he wishes to confess to a crime."

The facts of *Miranda* and its three companion cases are relatively simple. On March 13, 1963, Ernesto Miranda was arrested and taken into custody at the Phoenix, Arizona, police station, where he was identified by the complaining witness. He was then questioned for two hours by police detectives. Miranda had signed a written confession, at the top of which was a typed paragraph stating that the confession was made voluntarily, "with full knowledge of my legal rights, understanding any statement I make may be used against me." One of the interrogating officers testified that he had read this paragraph to Miranda, but apparently only after Miranda had already confessed orally. In a jury trial, Miranda was convicted of rape and kidnapping, and sentenced to 20 to 30 years in prison. In the trial, the written confession and the officers' testimony regarding the oral confession were admitted as evidence over the objections of the defense attorney. On appeal, the Arizona Supreme Court upheld the conviction, emphasizing the voluntariness of the confession and the fact that Miranda did not explicitly request an attorney.

The U.S. Supreme Court reversed the decision of the Arizona Supreme Court. According to the Court's interpretation of the record, Miranda had not been "apprised of his right to consult with an attorney and to have one present during the interrogation." The fact that Miranda had not himself initiated a request for an attorney (as had Escobedo) was deemed irrelevant. Further, his right "not to be compelled to incriminate himself" was not protected in any other manner. The Court did not accept the signed typed statement that the defendant had "full knowledge" of his legal rights as sufficient; the forfeit of a defendant's constitutional rights required proof of a "knowing and intelligent waiver."

This reasoning was applied to similar circumstances in *Miranda*'s companion cases. In each, the Court noted that there was no evidence in the record that the defendant had been apprised of his rights to counsel and against self-incrimination before or during interrogation; hence, the defendants' self-incriminating statements should not have been allowed at trial.

Thus, the Court went well beyond its previous ruling in *Escobedo*. The burden was no longer on the suspect to assert his right to see counsel or to remain silent; now it was the state's duty to establish that a suspect had been fully informed of his rights and the consequences of waiving them. What most galled law enforcement officials was that the police were not accused of violating existing rules of conduct, in any of these cases.

Critics of the legal reasoning Warren used in the *Miranda* decision have focused on two issues in the wording of the Constitution. The first relates to the Sixth Amendment right to legal counsel. Strictly read, the Sixth Amendment seems to establish only a right to have the "Assistance of Counsel" in trials. Obviously, *Escobedo* and *Miranda* extended that right to pretrial phases of criminal prosecution.

Considerably more controversial was the Court's interpretation of the Fifth Amendment clause regarding self-incrimination. The Fifth Amendment states that no person "shall be compelled in any criminal case to be a witness against himself." Much of the ensuing debate revolved around the meaning of "compelled." Traditionally, it was taken to refer only to the use, or threatened use, of physical force. Warren's opinion in *Miranda* stressed the psychological intimidation of the mere fact of being held in custody by the police, particularly if the arrestee is "incommunicado," as were each of the defendants in the instant cases.

To understand why the Court ruled as it did in *Miranda*, as well as the controversy that the decision engendered, it is necessary to place the decision in the context of the history of the police in the twentieth-century United States. The role and image of the police changed drastically between 1920 and 1965. Warren saw his opinion in *Miranda* as contributing to that evolutionary process. Well into the twentieth century, the police were more commonly (and accurately) characterized as at best inefficient and poorly trained, and at worst brutal and corrupt. In 1931, President Hoover's National Commission on Law Observance and Enforcement (commonly referred to as the Wickersham Commission after its chair, George Wickersham) investigated the state of U.S. law enforcement. Various "Wickersham reports" documented the extensive police corruption, brutality, and the use of the "third degree" to extract confessions. Warren cited the Wickersham reports extensively in his opinion in *Miranda*, particularly its comments that reliance on extracting confessions "makes police and prosecutors less zealous in the search for objective evidence" and "brutalizes the police." Worst of all, such conduct by the police was said to reduce public respect for law and order, thus actually leading to more crime.

The Wickersham reports set the agenda for police reform, stressing expert leadership, centralized command, political neutrality, and higher personnel standards. One of its primary authors was August Vollmer, the pioneering chief of police of Berkeley, California, from 1905 to 1932. It is interesting to note that Earl Warren was the district attorney of Alameda County, which includes Berkeley, from 1920 to 1938. Although it is not clear how much, if any, Vollmer may have directly influenced Warren, it is obvious that Warren had first-hand knowledge of the dangers of unchecked police power, as well as an optimistic view of the ability of a professionalized police force to operate within constitutional limits of fair play. As a prosecutor, Warren made his own contributions to the growing reform movement in law enforcement. He expanded and professionalized the district attorney's investigative and legal staff and improved cooperation among local law enforcement agencies. He also established his reputation early by successfully prosecuting several corrupt local police officials.

Nationally, the reforms begun by Vollmer and publicized by the Wickersham Commission began to improve the image and reality of police work. Change was slow, however: older police could not simply be replaced overnight by highly trained, professionally oriented officers. Most big-city police departments were still controlled by local political machines as late as the 1950s, when the next major phase of police reform occurred. In the 1950s, several of the largest police departments were racked by scandals of police brutality and corruption. The typical response to these scandals was to hire a new, reform-oriented chief of police to "clean house." Some of these reformers, such as O.W. Wilson, who became Chicago's chief of police in 1960, were protégés of Vollmer. Ironically, these reformers were among the loudest critics of the Warren Court's due process agenda. The very success of their reforms depended on their demonstrated ability to reform from within. They felt they had shown that the police could police themselves.

Furthermore, the reformers' model of professionalization stressed the law enforcement role of the police. They redefined the main purpose of the police as "fighting crime." Historically, neither the police nor the public had defined the primary function of the police as fighting crime. It was not until after World War II and the introduction of patrol cars, better telephone service, two-way radios, and the use of forensic science to solve cases that the image of police as "crime fighters" began to take hold.

Just as police departments nationwide were successfully portraying their main duty as controlling crime, the United States began to experience an unprecedented increase in the amount of crime. Although the increases, which began in the early 1960s, had more to do with demographic changes than lack of effective police work, the police had raised public expectations about their ability to control crime. The due process decisions of the Warren Court provided a convenient scapegoat.

As far as many prosecutors and police were concerned, as long as they were not beating confessions out of people or threatening to do so, statements by defendants like Miranda were voluntary and should be admissible. They operated on the assumption that no innocent person would "confess"; if a suspect incriminated himself because of ignorance or fear, well, that was the defendant's tough luck and a victory for public safety. To place further restrictions on police interrogation would reduce the number of confessions, thus depriving the police of an important weapon in the fight against crime.

The Court, however, remained skeptical of the utility of confessions. It also saw custodial interrogation as the ultimate test of the rights of individuals against the power of the state. Although the types of abuses documented in the Wickersham reports, such as dangling a suspect by his heels from a fifth-story window, were acknowledged to be the exception rather than the rule, the exceptions were still common enough that Warren could cite several cases he himself had ruled on that involved similar rough treatment of detainees.

Even without brutality, the Court argued, custodial interrogation was designed to intimidate suspects into incriminating themselves. Warren quoted extensively from police manuals to illustrate the point. He noted that the goal of the instructions given to police in these manuals was, quite frankly, to get the subject to relinquish his right to remain silent not to seek legal counsel. Suggested tactics for accomplishing this included isolating the subject, tiring him by questioning nonstop for hours, and even deceit (e.g., giving the suspect false legal advice).

The assumption that only the guilty would confess was dramatically called into question in the case of George Whitmore. Whitmore was a young black man who confessed while in custody to a rape and two murders in New York City in 1964 (shortly after the *Escobedo* decision). Prosecutors pointed to the case as an example of a serious crime that could not have been solved without the confession. Instead, the case turned out to illustrate just the opposite: the unreliability of custodial confessions. Another man was later charged and convicted of the murders; Whitmore's confession was shown to be phony. There was some evidence that the police had beaten Whitmore, but no follow-up investigation was conducted.

The Court also had another model to contrast to the claims of local police and prosecutors that confessions were an essential tool of law enforcement. For years, the Federal Bureau of Investigation (FBI) had downplayed the use of confessions in its investigations, relying on new forensic techniques to solve cases with objective evidence. In fact, the FBI had for years been giving detained suspects warnings very similar to those outlined in the *Miranda* decision.

The Court was also aware of changes in the nature of crime in recent years. Crime was seen to be connected to social conditions, such as urban poverty and racism. The typical defendant who confessed while in custody and without the aid of an attorney was, like Whitmore and Miranda, likely to be undereducated, poor, and a minority. In other words, they were members of social groups who had been discriminated against by other social groups and who had the fewest resources to defend themselves.

A number of studies have been conducted to assess the impact of *Miranda* on law enforcement. Almost uniformly, they show that the impact of this decision, in terms of unsolved cases or lost convictions, has been minimal. The fact that most cases are solved by confessions does not mean that they can only be solved by them. As an example, Ernesto Miranda himself was convicted on other evidence upon retrial, as were each of the defendants in the companion cases. Nevertheless, the symbolic power of the case outweighed by far its actual impact. Richard Nixon made the "liberal" Supreme Court decisions an issue in his 1968 presidential campaign, which featured a heavy appeal to "law and order." He promised to appoint Supreme Court justices who would overturn *Miranda* and other rulings that favored the rights of "criminals" over those of the police. The Supreme Court under Warren's successor, Warren E. Burger, did chip away at *Miranda* in some decisions, but for the most part the police have learned to live with the duty of reading suspects their rights.

Earl Warren did not view his decision as antipolice. It infuriated him that Nixon portrayed it that way in the 1968 election. He was not trying to hamper police work, but to "ennoble" it. Whether his Court's due process revolution contributed to better law enforcement is still a matter of debate. Predictions that suspects would not confess after being informed of their rights have not been borne out, however. Today, the overwhelming majority of felony cases are decided by guilty pleas, which require as a matter of course a confession.

There is an ironic postscript to the case. Miranda was paroled in 1972. In 1976, he was murdered in a fight over a card game. When the police arrested his killer, they dutifully read him his rights, as required by *Miranda v. Arizona*.

Selected Bibliography

Ayres, R. "Confessions and the Court," in *The Ambivalent Force: Perspectives on the Police*. A. Niederhoffer and A.S. Blumberg, eds. Hinsdale, IL: Dryden, 1976.

Grahm, F.P. *The Due Process Revolution: The Warren Court's Impact on Criminal Law.* New York: Hayden, 1970.

Inciardi, J.A. *Criminal Justice.* 2d ed. San Diego: Harcourt, Brace, Jovanovich, 1987.

Manning, P.K. *Police Work.* Cambridge, MA: MIT Press, 1977.

Walker, S. *The Police in America.* New York: McGraw-Hill, 1983.

Wasby, S.L. *The Impact of the United States Supreme Court: Some Perspectives.* Homewood, IL: Dorsey, 1970.

Weaver, J.D. *Warren: The Man, The Court, The Era.* Boston: Little Brown, 1967.

White, G.E. *Earl Warren: A Public Life.* New York: Oxford University Press, 1982.

THE DEATH AND RESURRECTION OF CAPITAL PUNISHMENT

by B. Keith Crew
Department of Sociology and Anthropology
University of Northern Iowa

Furman v. Georgia, 408 U.S. 232 (1972); *Gregg v. Georgia,* 428 U.S. 153 (1976) [U.S. Supreme Court]

The use of capital punishment in the United States peaked during the 1930s. Although most states still had death rows in the 1960s, society appeared to be moving away from capital punishment. The American Civil Liberties Union and the National Association for the Advancement of Colored People, convinced that the death penalty was reserved for poor and black offenders, had been providing legal assistance since the 1950s to virtually every death row inmate, hoping that an appeal would eventually result in the abolition of capital punishment. Executions, which had been declining over the years, actually ceased in 1967, as states anticipated just such a move by the U.S. Supreme Court. In 1972, the Court agreed to decide whether capital punishment, as imposed in the cases of three petitioners, constituted "cruel and unusual punishment in violation of the Eighth and Fourteenth Amendments." The 5–4 decision of the Court in *Furman v. Georgia* effectively abolished capital punishment in the United States by declaring unconstitutional most existing state laws authorizing the death penalty. It was not, however, the Court's final word on the death penalty: four years later, in *Gregg v. Georgia,* the Court upheld new state capital punishment statutes, in effect reviving the death penalty. Infliction of capital punish-

ment resumed shortly after with the execution of Gary Gilmore in Utah in 1977. What accounts for the Court's apparent "about-face" on this most controversial of legal issues? An examination of the opinions of these two cases sheds interesting light on the Supreme Court's task of interpreting the Constitution.

At first, it might be tempting to attribute the Court's turnaround on the issue of capital punishment to a simple change in personnel, since the votes in *Furman* had fallen neatly along ideological lines. The five justices who voted to invalidate existing capital punishment statutes in *Furman* were hold overs from the liberal Warren Court (William O. Douglas, Potter Stewart, Bryon White, William J. Brennan, and Thurgood Marshall); the dissenting votes were cast by the four conservative justices appointed by President Richard Nixon (Chief Justice Warren E. Burger, and Justices Harry A. Blackmun, Lewis F. Powell, and William H. Rehnquist). Each of the Nixon appointees had been nominated to the Court for, among other qualities, their "hardline" positions on crime. Four years later, the liberal Douglas had been replaced by another conservative, John Paul Stevens, who added his vote to the pro-capital punishment side.

Although the shift toward a more conservative Court was certainly real and important, it does not by itself explain the reinstatement of capital punishment. There is more to the story than the pro- or anticapital punishment sentiments of the justices. Indeed, two of the dissenters expressed a personal distaste for capital punishment. Burger and Blackmun each asserted that if they "were possessed of legislative power," they would vote to abolish or at least severely restrict the use of capital punishment. Although the unofficial moratorium on executions from 1967 to 1972 indicates that the country was looking to the Court for moral leadership on the question of the death penalty, *Furman* was decided on grounds other than the morality of capital punishment *per se*. The arguments made in *Furman* set the stage for *Gregg*. Given those arguments, trends in both public opinion and professional debate about crime and punishment in the 1970s made the decision in *Gregg* inevitable, even if the composition of the Court had remained liberal. This is because, in *Furman*, the Court declined to address the constitutionality of the death penalty (except for two opinions) and instead focused on the procedures used to impose it.

In the fall of 1971, the Court agreed to review three death penalty cases to address the issue of whether capital punishment constituted cruel and unusual punishment. The leading case was *Furman v. Georgia*. William Furman, a 26-year-old black man, killed the owner of a home he was burglarizing in the middle of the night. The victim awoke and startled Furman as he was making his escape; Furman tripped, and his gun fired accidentally. The bullet passed through a closed door, striking and killing the victim who was standing on the other side. Here is Furman's version of the murder: "They got me charged with murder and I admit, I admit going to these folks' home and they did caught me in there and I was coming back out, backing up and there was a wire down there on the floor. I was coming out backwards and fell back and I didn't know nothing about no murder until they arrested me, and when the gun went off I was down on the floor and I got up and ran. That's all to it."

The prosecution basically accepted Furman's account of the accidental nature of the shooting. But, because it occurred during the commission of a felony, it met the statutory definition of "premeditated murder," thus making Furman eligible for the electric chair.

In the two companion cases, *Jackson v. Georgia* and *Branch v. Texas*, the defendants were convicted of raping, not killing, their victims. Jackson, a 21-year-old black man, was convicted of raping a white woman. He threatened his victim with a pair of scissors; she was bruised and abrased, but suffered no injuries requiring hospitalization. Branch, a mildly retarded young black man, raped a 65-year-old white widow, holding his arm against her throat. The victim suffered the trauma of the rape, but no injury requiring medical attention.

These three cases contained elements that typified the argument that the death penalty was used as an instrument of racial discrimination. All three defendants were black, and in each case the victim was white. The race of the offenders and their victims was important, because the discriminatory application of the death penalty became the central issue of the Court's decision. Between 1930 and 1967, more than one-half of the 3,859 executions that occurred in the United States were carried out against black defendants.

Discrimination was especially apparent in the imposition of capital punishment for rape. For example, a study by criminologist Marvin Wolfgang and law professor Anthony Amsterdam (who presented part of the argument in *Furman* to the Supreme Court) showed that of defendants convicted of rape in 11 southern states, 13 percent of blacks were sentenced to death, but only 2 percent of whites were sentenced to death. Overall in the United States, 90 percent of the 455 men executed for rape between 1930 and 1967 were members of nonwhite racial minorities.

Furman's case, which did involve a murder, also typified an important issue. One popular assumption about capital punishment is that it is, or should be, reserved for the most extreme crimes. Although any murder is tragic, there was nothing heinous, outrageous, or vicious about it that distinguished it from the hundreds of murder convictions that resulted in less severe punishments—except, that is, that the defendant was black, the victim was white, and the crime occurred in the South.

The Court's decision in *Furman* was unusual in that it was published *per curium* ("unsigned"). The majority could not agree on a single argument to support its decision, therefore each justice published a separate concurring opinion. Only Brennan and Marshall were willing to argue that the death penalty was essentially cruel and unusual. Douglas, Stewart, and White focused on the narrower issue of the wording of the state laws in question and on the effects of those laws on the administration of the death penalty.

In arguing that the death penalty was cruel and unusual punishment, Brennan and Marshall had to overcome several logical pitfalls. The first is that the Constitution implies that capital punishment is permissible: the due process clause of the Fifth Amendment reads that no person shall "be deprived of life, liberty or property, without due process of law," a statement that implies that a person can be "deprived of life" with due process. Previous Supreme Court rulings had restricted only the type of crimes to which capital punishment could be applied and prohibited specifically gruesome or shocking methods of execution.

Nevertheless, Brennan and Marshall felt there were compelling reasons to define capital punishment as cruel and unusual. In *Trop v. Dulles* (1958), former Chief Justice Earl Warren had developed and applied the principle that the constitutional prohibition against cruel and unusual punishments must be interpreted in light of the "evolving standards of decency" of society. Marshall and Brennan felt that the death penalty failed the test of evolving standards of decency. Brennan specified four principles for defining a punishment as cruel and unusual under the evolving standards doctrine: (1) if a punishment is "unusually severe" (by which he meant disproportionate to the crime committed); (2) if there is a likelihood that it is inflicted arbitrarily; (3) if it is inconsistent with social standards of human dignity; and (4) if it serves no penal purpose more effectively than would less severe punishments. Each of Brennan's four principles, implicitly accepted by Marshall, refers to the social effects of the

law as it is actually applied rather than to the logic of the written law.

This line of reasoning reflected a type of "sociological jurisprudence." Sociological jurisprudence is a judicial philosophy characterized by three elements: (1) a distinction between "law in the books" and "law in action" (i.e., a focus on the practical application of law rather than on abstract definitions); (2) a willingness to bring social science data to bear on legal questions; and (3) the assumption of the "living law" (i.e., the idea that the law must be interpreted according to the contemporary norms and values of society). Each of the justices who voted against capital punishment in *Furman* cited sociological data showing that capital punishment was apparently inflicted arbitrarily, that it provided no better deterrent than life imprisonment, and that social support for the death penalty had declined in recent decades.

This latter idea does not mean that the Court should base its decisions on public opinion polls. As Marshall pointed out in his opinion, the public may be misinformed or even misled about the realities of capital punishment. Marshall's usage of the idea of contemporary standards is thus based on what a "reasonable" person must conclude from applying contemporary standards to complete information in a logical manner; this is the job of the judiciary, not pollsters.

Douglas, Stewart, and White also applied the evolving standards of decency approach, but limited their opinions in *Furman* to the arbitrary and thus discriminatory application of the death penalty rather than to the idea of capital punishment. Looking at the evidence provided by criminologists Wolfgang and Reidel and others, the justices concluded that black and poor offenders were disproportionately selected for capital punishment. For these justices, what made the death penalty cruel and unusual was the lack of rational criteria for deciding who was and was not to be executed. The lack of standards or guidelines allowed juries and judges to exercise their prejudices against certain classes of people. Thus, the constitutionality of the death penalty statutes was decided on the basis of their effects (disparities in punishment meted out) rather than on the formal, logical relationship of capital punishment to received constitutional law.

The four dissenting judges rejected the sociological jurisprudence of the majority in favor of a more formalistic or positivist approach. Finding nothing in the wording of the Constitution to imply that capital punishment is cruel and unusual, these justices then turned to previous Supreme Court decisions and other comments on the legal prohibition against cruel and unusual punishments. There were precedents for restricting the use of capital punishment to the most serious crimes; likewise, there were prohibitions against particular methods of execution. However, the Court had repeatedly upheld the use of capital punishment. Furthermore, in a case decided just one year before *Furman*, the Court had upheld the unlimited discretion of juries that the majority now cited as the main reason for abolishing the existing death penalty laws.

The conclusion that it was the lack of guidelines that rendered the death penalty unconstitutional was a new direction for the Court. Barely a year earlier, the Court had held in *McGautha v. California* (1971) that "committing to the untrammeled discretion of the jury the power to pronounce life or death in capital cases" was well within the bounds of constitutionality. *Furman* made that very "untrammeled discretion" grounds for abolishing capital punishment. Yet that logic left the door open for the reinstatement of capital punishment. Several states immediately began rewriting their death penalty statutes in an attempt to meet the standards laid down in *Furman*.

Two strategies were possible for legislatures to pass laws that would meet the *Furman* standards. One was to make the death penalty mandatory for certain types of crimes. For example, Rhode Island had a law mandating capital punishment for murder committed by a prisoner serving a life sentence. The second strategy was to provide juries with guidelines to determine when a person should receive a death sentence.

The approach taken by Georgia and other states was to institute two-stage trials in capital cases. In the first stage, the jury determined the guilt or innocence of the defendant; upon conviction, the jury would then decide on the sentence. At the sentencing stage, the judge is required to instruct the jury about the legal guidelines for inflicting capital punishment: the case must include at least one in a list of "aggravating" circumstances before capital punishment can be recommended. Further, these must be weighed against a list of potentially "mitigating" circumstances. Finally, all cases that result in a sentence of death are automatically appealed to the state supreme court, which must compare each case to other capital cases to determine that the death penalty is not being inflicted in an arbitrary or discriminatory manner.

The Georgia statute was challenged in the case of Troy Leon Gregg. Gregg had been convicted of robbing and shooting to death two men. At the sentencing stage of the "bifurcated trial," the jury considered three aggravating circumstances: (1) whether the offense of murder was committed while the offender was committing another felony; (2) whether the murder was committed for the purpose of receiving money or property; and (3) whether the murder was "outrageously and wantonly vile." The jury agreed that the first and second circumstances were present, and returned four death sentences, two for the murders and two for the robberies.

It is interesting to compare Gregg's conviction with Furman's. Whereas Furman committed murder mainly because of his incompetence as a burglar, Gregg deliberately and "coldbloodedly" shot two men in order to take their property. Although one should be careful about drawing conclusions on the basis of only two cases, this comparison illustrates one intent of the new guidelines: to reserve capital punishment for the most heinous murderers.

On review, the Georgia Supreme Court overturned the two death penalties for robbery. The court noted that capital punishment was rarely inflicted for that crime in Georgia and that the jury could not properly consider the murders as aggravating circumstances for the robberies, after first defining the robberies as aggravating circumstances for the murders. The result for Gregg was the same whether he received one death penalty or several.

The U.S. Supreme Court agreed to review once again whether capital punishment was cruel and unusual and thus in violation of the Eighth and Fourteenth Amendments. Although, as in *Furman*, the Court was unable to agree on a single opinion, by a 7–2 vote it upheld Georgia's capital punishment statute. On the theory that legislatures represent the "will of the people," Stewart, Powell, and Stevens overcame the evolving standards of decency criterion by noting that Congress and 35 states had enacted new death penalty laws since *Furman*. They also suggested that capital punishment is not necessarily "disproportionate" to the crime of murder. Furthermore, they stated that retribution (i.e., vengeance) was a valid purpose of criminal law; thus, there was no need to weigh the deterrent effect of capital punishment against lesser punishments.

Of the *Furman* standards, then, the only remaining question was whether the penalty was inflicted arbitrarily. Given the specific guidelines and automatic review imposed by the new Georgia law, it is difficult to imagine how the "arbitrary" argument could have been made. If the liberals Douglas, Stewart, and White had truly been opposed to capital punishment, they had painted themselves into an ideological corner in *Furman* from which they could not escape. Douglas was no longer on the Court when *Gregg* was decided; Stewart and White joined with the new majority in upholding the death penalty. The four conservatives, joined by Stevens, applied the same formalistic approach as before. Only now, with *Furman* as precedent, the ironic result of that approach was that they voted for the death penalty by invoking arguments that they had rejected as invalid in the previous case.

In effect, the *Furman* decision made the *Gregg* decision inevitable by shifting the debate over the death penalty from substantive to procedural issues. The extent of the dominance of procedural over substantive concerns is further evidenced in *Woodson v. North Carolina* (1976), decided the same day as *Gregg v. Georgia*. In *Woodson*, the Court struck down state laws that had taken the alternative strategy of making capital punishment mandatory for certain types of offenses. The Court ruled in that case that mandatory death sentences merely "papered over" the problem of jury discretion, shifting it to the prosecutor. The result of *Gregg v. Geor-*

gia, then, is that the death penalty is constitutional if it is imposed in a two-stage procedure accompanied by specific guidelines that take into account differences in individual defendants and their crimes.

The terms under which the *Gregg* decision reintroduced capital punishment are consistent with a general trend of reform that dominated criminal justice policy in the 1970s. Disillusioned by the failure of prisons either to rehabilitate or to deter criminals, liberals and conservatives joined forces in calling for a return to fixed or "determinate" sentences. Sentences were to be determined primarily by the nature of the crime, not the offender. This return to a policy of making the punishment fit the crime was supported by the reintroduction of retribution as a legitimate (indeed the main) rationale for punishment. Various states began making retribution official policy by adopting either fixed-sentencing schemes or sentencing guidelines.

Central to both of these approaches is the weighing of punishments for a crime to fit the degree of seriousness of the offense, resulting in a reduction in the discretionary power of judges and juries. Supreme Court rulings on the death penalty since *Gregg* have primarily consisted of a "fine-tuning" of such guidelines. For example, in *Coker v. Georgia* (1977), the Court ruled that the death penalty is excessive for the crime of rape. Following this standard of proportionality, most state laws now permit the death penalty only for crimes that involve the death of a victim. In yet another case from Georgia, *Godfrey v. Georgia* (1980), the Court ruled that the aggravating circumstances contained in death penalty laws must be given fairly specific interpretations.

Opponents of the death penalty may look back on *Furman* as an opportunity lost. Had the other liberals on the Court joined ranks with Brennan and Marshall in declaring the death penalty *per se* to be cruel and unusual under the evolving standards doctrine, it is possible that the challenge of *Gregg* would never have taken place. At the least, the reinstatement of the death penalty would have had to overcome a strong precedent. Instead, the moral and political debate over the death penalty was reframed as an issue of legal formalism. In other words, capital punishment will, for some time to come, be considered legitimate as long as clearly stated rules for its imposition are followed; the question of its moral correctness or practical effectiveness as a deterrent has been rendered a moot point.

Shortly after the *Gregg* decision, executions resumed when Gary Gilmore was killed by a firing squad in Utah in January 1977. Since then, a small, but increasing, number of executions each year indicates that the death penalty will be around for some time to come. In 1990, there were over 1,600 convicts on death row. Any abolitionist movement will have to rely on changing public opinion and legislation rather than on the Supreme Court.

Selected Bibliography

American Friends Service Committee. *Struggle for Justice*. New York: Hill & Wang, 1971.

Bowers, W.J. *Executions in America*. Lexington, MA: D.C. Heath, 1974.

Bowers, W.J., and G.L. Pierce. "Arbitrariness and Discrimination Under Post-Furman Capital Statutes." *Crime and Delinquency* 26 (1980): 563–635.

Hawkins, R., and G.P. Alpert. *American Prison Systems: Punishment and Justice*. Englewood Cliffs, NJ: Prentice Hall, 1989.

Inciardi, J.A. *Criminal Justice*. 2d ed. San Diego: Harcourt, Brace, Jovanovich, 1987.

Martinson, R. "What Works? Questions and Answers About Prison Reform." *The Public Interest* 42 (1974): 22–54.

U.S. Department of Justice. *Capital Punishment 1976*. Washington, DC: U.S. Government Printing Office, 1978.

Wolfgang, M.E., and M. Riedel. "Race, Judicial Discretion, and the Death Penalty." *Annals of the American Academy of Political and Social Science* 407 (1973): 129–48.

PLEA BARGAINING AND THE "VINDICTIVE" EXERCISE OF PROSECUTORIAL DISCRETION

by B. Keith Crew
Department of Sociology and Anthropology
University of Northern Iowa

Bordenkircher v. Hayes, 434 U.S. 357 (1978) [U.S. Supreme Court]

Most criminal convictions are the result of guilty pleas; estimates vary from 80 to 95 percent, depending on the jurisdiction. Many of these guilty pleas are the result of "plea bargains," where a defendant pleads guilty in the expectation of some leniency in sentencing. The central figure in plea bargaining is the prosecuting attorney (i.e., the district attorney, or state's attorney). The prosecutor has virtually unchecked discretion in deciding what charges to bring against a suspect. In 1977, the U.S. Supreme Court had the opportunity to consider one aspect of this discretionary power: the extent to which the state could go to induce a defendant to waive his constitutional right to a jury trial.

Plea bargains usually take the form of "charge bargains." A suspect who has been charged with one or more crimes is offered the chance to plead guilty to fewer charges or to less serious charges (e.g., reducing a charge of first-degree robbery to one of second-degree robbery). In exchange for the reduced charges, the prosecution is assured of a conviction and the state is spared the trouble and expense of a trial. Can the converse occur? In other words, can the prosecutor threaten to increase the charges if the suspect refuses to plead guilty? That was the question facing the Supreme Court in *Bordenkircher v. Hayes*.

In 1973, Paul Lewis Hayes was arrested in Fayette County (Lexington), Kentucky, and charged with a forgery in the amount of $88.30. If convicted, the charge carried a possible sentence of two to ten years in prison. Under Kentucky law at the time, a person with two prior felony convictions could also face the additional charge of being a habitual offender. Upon conviction as a habitual offender, the original sentence could be enhanced to as much as life in prison (with possibility of parole).

Hayes and his attorney attended a pretrial conference with the assistant prosecutor who was handling the case. The prosecutor offered to recommend a sentence of five years in exchange for a guilty plea. With a five-year sentence, Hayes would have been eligible for parole in two years. Instead, Hayes elected to take his chances with a jury trial.

The prosecutor then prepared a new indictment, charging Hayes with the original forgery charge and with being a "persistent felony offender." The jury convicted Hayes on the forgery charge and, in a separate hearing, subsequently added the conviction as a habitual offender. Upon determining that Hayes had been convicted of two prior felonies, the jury sentenced him to life in prison, with possibility of parole.

Hayes filed a petition in federal court for a writ of *habeas corpus* on the grounds that the second indictment was an act of prosecutorial vindictiveness undertaken solely to punish him for exercising his right to trial. The U.S. District Court for Eastern Kentucky upheld the conviction, but it was overturned by the Court of Appeals for the Sixth Circuit, which ruled that Hayes had to serve only the sentence for the original forgery conviction. In its ruling, the Sixth Circuit court of appeals drew a distinction between "concessions relating to prosecution under an existing indictment" and threats to bring more severe charges not contained in the original indictment. Although the distinction between promises by prosecutors to decrease charges and their threats to increase charges may not seem important, it points up two issues that are raised by plea bargaining. The first is the issue of voluntariness. A plea of guilty involves the waiver of constitutional rights: the right to a trial by jury and the right not to be compelled to incriminate oneself. A long series of previous decisions by the Supreme Court, highlighted by *Miranda v. Arizona* (1966), had emphasized that any waiver of constitutional rights places a burden on the state to show that the defendant's decision was volun-

tary and made with full knowledge of the consequences.

The second issue is whether it is fair to punish an individual for exercising a constitutional right. The Court previously ruled that prosecutors could not punish an appellant for successfully attacking an original conviction by either seeking more severe sentences or by filing more serious charges in a new trial. Such actions were defined as impermissible "vindictiveness" on the part of the prosecutor.

The Supreme Court reversed the court of appeals and upheld Hayes' conviction as a habitual offender. In an opinion written by Justice Potter Stewart, the Court ruled that the prosecutor's threats and actions against Hayes did not violate his rights to due process under the Fourteenth Amendment. As long as the prosecutor had probable cause to file the additional charges, his discretion in the selection of charges was not open to challenge.

In overturning Hayes' habitual felon conviction, the court of appeals had argued that the prosecutor's actions violated principles that protected "defendants from the vindictive exercise of prosecutorial discretion." Neither of the cases enunciating these principles, however, arose from the context of plea negotiations.

The Supreme Court asserted that plea bargains were different. Although plea bargains have been a common feature of criminal justice since the nineteenth century, the practice has been openly acknowledged only recently. "Copping a plea" has an unsavory connotation for the public because it implies that a guilty criminal is getting away with less punishment than he "deserves." Legal principles traditionally required that confessions be "free and voluntary," meaning that they are not the result of threats or promises. As plea bargaining became more widely accepted, humorous courtroom charades often occurred: in many states, the judge was required to ask the defendant, for the record, if he had been offered any benefits in exchange for pleading guilty. The defendant was supposed to reply in the negative, but often he would blurt out something like "Yeah, they told me I'd only get two years if I copped a plea!"

The Court had as recently as 1970 in *Brady v. United States* secured the legitimacy of plea bargains. That case did involve direct plea negotiations, however. Brady had changed his plea to guilty after his codefendant pled guilty and was available to testify against him. His lawyer advised him that a jury trial might result in the imposition of the death penalty. The Court merely ruled that the possibility of a jury trial resulting in a more severe sentence, or in any other opportunity or offer of leniency, did not render a guilty plea involuntary. In so ruling, however, the Court acknowledged and accepted the existence of plea bargains, stating that they were justified by the "mutuality of advantage" between the defendant and the state. As long as the plea negotiations were conducted without coercion and the defendant's plea was made with full knowledge of the possible consequences of going to trial, the defendant's Fifth and Sixth Amendment rights were not violated.

Brady left open the question of what rules prosecutors had to follow in plea negotiations. These were developed in subsequent cases. In *Santobello v. New York* (1971), the Court held that prosecutors must keep promises they make during plea negotiations. In *Henderson v. Morgan* (1976), the Court reinforced the idea that to be valid, a guilty plea must be made with the

defendant having "full knowledge of its consequences." *Bordenkircher v. Hayes* can be interpreted as part of this process of defining the acceptable parameters of plea bargains. As such, it put an apparently permanent stamp of legitimacy on the power of prosecutors to use their authority to bring charges to encourage guilty pleas.

In a dissenting opinion in this case, Justice Harry A. Blackmun argued that the prosecutor's only motive for seeking a conviction on additional charges was to "discourage the defendant from exercising his right to trial." The majority opinion held that in the context of plea negotiations, that was a perfectly legitimate motive. The very concept of plea bargains depended on the "mutuality of advantage" cited in *Brady*. The state's advantage was in avoiding the inconvenience of a trial.

Selected Bibliography

Heumann, M. *Plea Bargaining*. Chicago: University of Chicago Press, 1978.

Inciardi, J.A. *Criminal Justice*. 2d ed. San Diego: Harcourt, Brace, Jovanovich, 1987.

Utz, P.J. *Settling the Facts*. Lexington, MA: Lexington Books, 1978.

CREDIBILITY AND CRISIS IN CALIFORNIA'S HIGH COURT

by Brenda Farrington Myers
Fullerton, California

People v. Tanner, 23 Cal. 3d 16 (1978), 24 Cal. 3d 514 (1979) [California Supreme Court]

In February 1977, California Governor Jerry Brown shook up "the good old boys" club by nominating Rose Elizabeth Bird for chief justice of the California Supreme Court. Simultaneously, Brown nominated Wiley Manuel, the first African-American ever proposed for membership on the state's highest court. Manuel won confirmation by the Commission on Judicial Appointments without difficulty; Bird did not. Bird was only 40 years old and had no prior judicial experience or law practice experi-

ence beyond being a public defender. She had served in Brown's cabinet for two years as secretary of the Department of Agriculture and Services, outraging the agribusiness lobby with pro-farmer worker actions. Despite this record, she gained confirmation.

The controversy did not end when Bird took office. Contrary to tradition, she appointed several of her own associates, changed the locks on her office doors, assigned municipal and superior court justices to sit *pro tem* "temporarily," scheduled judicial council meetings in state buildings rather than at resorts, and sold the court's limousine. Bird hoped that these changes would result in a more efficient judiciary; instead they were perceived as arrogant, abrasive, and excessively expeditious. According to Bird, she moved quickly to implement change because she feared that her diagnosed cancer would prematurely end her judicial career.

The campaign to remove her from office began almost immediately. Under California law, supreme court justices appointed by the governor must be approved by the majority of the electorate at the next gubernatorial election. In Bird's case, this was November 1978. The opposition, funded by wealthy agricultural interests, was led by Republican state Senator Hubert L. Richardson's Law and Order Campaign Committee and the Vote No on Rose Bird Committee. The *Los Angeles Times*, probably Bird's most influential supporter, condemned the malicious attempt to unseat her. But on election day 1978, the *Times* ran a carelessly researched front-page story stating that the Bird court had reached a 4–3 decision to "overturn a 1975 law that requires prison terms for persons who use a gun during a violent crime but has not made the decision public." The story inferred that Associate Justice Mathew Tobriner, a distinguished 15-year veteran of the court, was delaying announcement of a controversial decision, *People v. Tanner*, to help Bird win voter approval.

Bird won reconfirmation by a narrow margin of 51.7 percent of voters, but the *Times* story was so damaging that she called for an investigation by the Commission on Judicial Appointments. The purpose of the hearings was to determine whether *Tanner* or any other politically sensitive case was improperly delayed and if any justice had compromised the confidentiality of court deliberations by making improper statements to the press.

Tanner was as bizarre as the appellate decision's course. Around 3 a.m. on January 9, 1976, Harold Tanner staged a "mock armed robbery" of a 7-Eleven convenience store in order to convince the owner to resubscribe to the security service provided by Tanner's employer. Despite Tanner's testimony, the jury found him guilty of first-degree robbery and that he had used a firearm while committing the crime. After reading the lengthy probation report and listening to arguments from the parties involved, the trial judge found Tanner's crime to be one of extraordinary circumstances. The court entered an order striking the firearms-use finding and committed the defendant to the department of corrections for the term prescribed by law, but it suspended the sentence and placed Tanner on five years' probation on the condition that he serve one year in county jail and undertake a program of psychiatric treatment. The prosecution appealed, and the case was argued before the California Supreme Court.

On December 22, 1978, the state high court announced its decision in *People v. Tanner (Tanner I)*. The court ruled against the mandatory prison sentence by a vote of 4–3, which was consistent with the *Times* election-day article. The decision outraged the governor, the legislature, and the public. In an unusual move, the court yielded to public pressure and granted a rehearing, announcing its decision in *People v. Tanner (Tanner II)* on June 14, 1979. Again, the vote was 4–3; however, this time the court upheld the "use a gun, go to prison" statute. Justice Stanley Mosk was responsible for the reversal. Offering no explanation, he merely signed the majority opinion without writing a separate concurring opinion.

In *Tanner II*, Justice William Clark, writing for the majority, rejected "any contention that courts were inherently or constitutionally vested with ultimate authority in fixing sentences or imposing penalty-enhancing factors for conduct made criminal by legislative enactment." He stated that the issue had to be determined by statutory purpose. Applying the rule of statutory construction that a "specific provision concerning a particular subject must govern a general provision to the contrary whenever both provisions apply," the majority held the specific provision relating to the limited power of dismissal for probation purposes prevailed over a general power of dismissal.

Despite its substantive holding, however, the court ruled that the uncertainty of the law had placed such an unusual burden on the defendant that a second incarceration for Tanner would be unjust. At the time of his rehearing, Tanner had met the conditions of his probation, including ; e-year internment at county jail. Bird, Tobriner, and Justice Frank Newman concurred with the majority that Tanner be placed on probation rather than sent to prison a second time. However, each filed a separate dissent from the majority's ruling that the trial court did not have the power to strike the gun-use finding. As in *Tanner I*, Bird presented the issue as one of constitutional separation of powers. In *Tanner II*, she criticized the new majority for its "attempt to carve a compromise of expediency" by making the "defendant a pawn" and exempting him "from the very standard that will be applied to all other defendants."

Meanwhile, Bird hoped that the commission's hearings on *Tanner* would "clear the air" and "restore confidence in the Court." Instead, the testimony revealed the lack of collegiality among the justices, particularly between Bird and Clark. One focus of the "delay allegation" became Clark's *Tanner I* dissent, which included a footnote citing Bird's separate concurring opinion in *People v. Caudillo*, another 1978 California State Supreme Court decision.

In *Caudillo*, Bird found that the legislature could provide that rape *per se* did not always involve "great bodily injury." By law, a finding of great bodily injury provided for an enhanced penalty. During the summer preceding the election, the Law and Order Campaign Committee seized on Bird's *Caudillo* opinion as evidence that she was "soft on crime" and made *Caudillo* the centerpiece of its campaign to oust her. When questioned by the commission as to why he had emphasized the politically charged *Caudillo* citation in his footnote, Clark insisted that he was merely trying to persuade Bird that she was inconsistent.

Bird charged that the *Caudillo* footnote was "politically motivated . . . meant to demean her in the eyes of the public." She thereafter treated Clark and his staff in a "cool, but correct" manner. Clark testified that Bird's "chill" continued for weeks, despite his attempts to exchange simple pleasantries. Rather than delete the *Caudillo* reference, Clark elevated the footnote into the body of his opinion, thereby escalating the tension between Bird and him.

On December 20, 1978, two days before the *Tanner I* decision was announced, Clark composed a memorandum to the chief justice stating, "In conscience, it must be clear to all on the Court that the *Tanner* case was signed up and ready for filing well in advance of November." Outraged, Bird replied the same day: "It is untrue . . . an affront to your colleagues and to the truth." In his testimony, Clark confirmed that he had written this memo; but he was unable to produce evidence to substantiate his claim that *Tanner* "could and should" have been filed. He suspected *Tanner* had been improperly handled, but told the commission that he knew of no impropriety by any of his colleagues in the handling of the case. In fact, the only real evidence of judicial misbehavior was Clark's admission that he was one of two justices who had confirmed the *Times* election-day article.

The other confirming justice, Stanley Mosk, filed a lawsuit to bar his public testimony on the ground that an open investigation was unconstitutional. The court of appeal in Los Angeles ruled in his favor. Ironically, the commission was forced to bring suit against him in the California Supreme Court. Since the justices were subjects of the commission's investigation, they were disqualified and seven substitute justices were chosen by lot. This *ad hoc* supreme court, in *Mosk v. Superior Court* (1979), upheld the court of appeal's ruling and required closed hearings. On November 5, 1979, the commission tersely announced that no formal charges would be filed against any justice. Gagged by the *Mosk* suit, the commission could not disclose the reasoning behind its decision.

Tanner effectively illustrates that the judiciary is not an independent part of the political process. Government—whether the judicial, executive, or legislative branch—derives its power from the governed. When the court's constitutional instincts failed to present the prevailing public perception of what the rule of law should be, the court lost credibility. Political prudence dictated that a rehearing of *Tanner* was necessary, but, again judicial credibility was lost because Mosk switched his vote with no explanation. Rather than for its substantive holding—that the legislature could in fact curtail judicial discretion in sentencing—*Tanner* will be remembered for the unprecedented political turmoil surrounding an unpopular decision.

What happened to the California Supreme Court in the late 1970s is not surprising when evaluated in the larger context of the nation's Watergate crisis. In both Watergate and *Tanner*, investigative reporting played a crucial role. The *Washington Post*'s effort was a journalistic triumph because it painstakingly exposed President Nixon's connection to the Watergate imbroglio; in contrast, the *Los Angeles Times* ran an erroneous story that directly resulted in a full-blown public investigation of nonexistent wrong doing. Although painful, the Watergate hearings were an affirmation that Americans could rid themselves of a dishonest leader— Nixon resigned rather than face certain impeachment and conviction. The *Tanner* hearings, on the other hand, exonerated the justices but failed to end the controversy. Yet in both instances, the results were the same—distrust and disillusionment were extended not only to those under investigation, but also to the high offices they represented.

Selected Bibliography

Kang, K.C. "The Decline of California's Vendetta-Ridden Supreme Court." *California Journal* 10 (Oct. 1979): 343–47.

Kleven, P. "*People v. Barraza*: California's Latest Attempt to Accommodate an Objective Theory of Entrapment." *California Law Review* 68 (July 1980): 776–79.

Medsger, B. *Framed: The New Right Attack on Chief Justice Rose Bird and the Courts.* New York: Pilgrim Press, 1983.

Schrag, P. "The Bird Controversy: California's High Court on Trial." *The Nation* 229 (Dec. 1979): 582–84.

Stoltz, P. *Judging Judges.* New York: Free Press, 1981.

Turner, W.B. "From the *Tanner* Hearings to the Brethren and Beyond: Judicial Accountability and Judicial Independence." *California State Bar Journal* 55 (July 1980): 292–97.

PART II: GOVERNMENTAL ORGANIZATION, POWER, AND PROCEDURE

PART II: GOVERNMENTAL ORGANIZATION, POWER, AND PROCEDURE

INTRODUCTION

The essays in Part II examine cases that have arisen in the United States in the last 200 years concerning the powers of government, most often the federal government. The U.S. Constitution of 1787 provided a grand outline for the new American government, but it would take the courts, generally the U.S. Supreme Court, to add flesh to the constitutional skeleton. Since the Constitution is a living document, its meaning has been evolving since the 1780s. Many of the cases treated in Part II came from the early Supreme Court of Chief Justice John Marshall (1801–35), a great era of constitutional definition. But some essays included here discuss cases decided as recently as the 1980s, thus illustrating that the Constitution can still be stretched and tightened by the judiciary.

A. Separation of Powers

This section presents essays on the separation of powers among the three branches of the federal government. Even before the Constitutional Convention, there was "A Hint of Judicial Review" in a 1784 decision of the New York Mayor's Court. The major case, however, establishing the judicial right to pass on the constitutionality of the acts of a legislature was *Marbury v. Madison*; it is discussed in "The Supreme Court Declares Its Independence." The next essay discusses a twentieth-century case, "The High-Water Mark of Presidential Power," in which the Supreme Court purported to extend a virtually unlimited grant of power to the president in the sphere of foreign affairs. The final essay in this section, "How One Immigrant Shook the U.S. Government to Its Very Core," illustrates how long-enduring understandings of the separation of federal power—

in this case the legislative veto—can be upset and redrawn by modern judicial construction.

B. Federalism

The U.S. Constitution, pursuant to the principle of federalism, permits a sharing of power between the states and the national government. If state and federal laws conflict, however, how should the conflict be resolved? Article VI of the U.S. Constitution (the supremacy clause) stipulates that when federal law and state law come into conflict, federal law is supreme. Two essays in this section, "Judicial Review of State Court Decisions" and "Judicial Review of State Court Decisions: Yet Another Round," illustrate how the Marshall Court first interpreted the supremacy clause. The other essay in this section, "Implied Federal Powers: Pandora's Box?," examines *McCulloch v. Maryland* (1819), the landmark case in which the Marshall Court interpreted the supremacy clause and the important necessary and proper clause of Article I.

C. Judicial Procedure

Over the years, various state and federal court decisions have dealt with technical matters of legal procedure which ultimately had great consequences. Several of the more interesting cases are surveyed in this section. "A Rebuke to the Court" concerns an early Supreme Court case so unpopular that it sparked a constitutional amendment. The second essay, "California Rejects the Mandatory Conciliation Formerly Required Under Mexican Law," provides an example of what can happen in a U.S. state court when the law of another country conflicts with the laws of the United States. The third essay, "Federal Common Law?," deals with two cases, separated by more than a century, in which the U.S. Supreme Court faced the question of whether an early federal statute did or did not permit the establishment of a federal common law for noncriminal matters. The essay "A Leg to Stand On: Taxpayer Lawsuits Against the U.S. Government" presents a modern case dealing with when an individual has standing to sue in a federal court.

The final two essays in this section do not deal directly with the powers of the government. Rather they concern the legality of rules of procedure adopted by private organizations that function in a web of government regulations. "Free Speech and Legal Ethics: The Issue of Lawyer Advertising" concerns the powers of a state bar association to enforce a ban on advertising among its members. And the essay "From Court Side to Courtroom" examines a long-running dispute within the National Collegiate Athletic Association concerning its powers over its member institutions and coaches.

D. Political Questions

Traditionally, U.S. courts have gone to great lengths to avoid deciding cases involving disputes as to the legitimacy of elected governmental officials. In explaining their reasoning, courts have generally avoided entering what judges and justices have termed the "political thicket." In "The *Right* of Revolution vs. the Right of *Revolution*," the mid-nineteenth century U.S. Supreme Court refused to determine which elected government in Rhode Island did in fact have power. But in a series of twentieth-century cases involving legislative apportionment—"The White Primary," "The 'Political Thicket' of Malapportionment," and "From the 'Political Thicket' to 'One Man, One Vote'"—the Court asserted its power over state legislatures, partly for the purpose of promoting equal treatment of the races in state elections.

E. Governmental Scandals

One way to determine the legitimacy of a government is to see how effectively it can deal with alleged corruption or other notorious scandals. American constitutional government, judged by this standard, has been remarkably resilient. One of the first great impeachment trials that occurred under the U.S. Constitution involved the controversial and haughty Justice Samuel Chase, discussed in "Can Intemperate Behavior Be a 'High Crime or Misdemeanor'?" The famous "Watergate Tapes Case" of the 1970s, discussed in "The Court Topples a Presidency," illustrates how well the U.S. system endured and dealt with dishonesty that reached to the very pinnacle of government. Finally, the essay "The Legality of the 'Independent Counsel'" examines the constitutionality of a recently enacted statute that established a mechanism to deal with alleged criminal acts in the federal government.

A. Separation of Powers

A HINT OF JUDICIAL REVIEW

by Robert S. Lambert
Department of History
Clemson University

Rutgers v. Waddington (1784) [New York state court]

One authority has called *Rutgers v. Waddington* "a marker on the long road that led to the ultimate formulation of judicial review."

As a British colony, New York had functioned under the restraints of its charter and the principles of the English common law as interpreted by British authorities in the colony and in England. After independence was declared, the New York Constitution of 1777 stated that colonial acts or British statutes and common-law principles contrary to it were of no force, which, for practical purposes, gave state courts jurisdiction over constitutional questions. The Council of Revision, a panel composed of the governor, the state chancellor, and judges of the supreme court, was given a qualified veto over legislative enactments that did not conform to the "letter and spirit" of the constitution.

Rutgers v. Waddington had its origins in the disputes over property rights that arose because New York City was occupied by the British army during most of the American Revolution. As the British occupation drew to a close, the state legislature enacted laws designed to punish those who had supported the British and to give citizens of the state recourse against persons who had injured them or their property. *Rutgers* was brought under the Trespass Act of March 1783, which allowed persons forced from their property as a result of the occupation to bring suit against those who had occupied, received, or purchased that property during the war. Defendants might not plead "any military order or command whatever of the Enemy" as justification for using the property; and such suits, once brought in any lower court of the state, might not be moved to another court. The act was passed just as the preliminary articles of the peace treaty between Great Britain and the United States arrived from Paris.

Elizabeth Rutgers would seem to have been an ideal person to seek redress under the Trespass Act. When the British captured New York in 1776, she abandoned her property on Maiden Lane, in which she held a life estate, and fled the city. In 1778, under permission granted by the commissary general of the British army, two British merchants residing in the city occupied her property and established a malthouse and brewhouse for the use of the army. The reauthorization to use the property commenced in 1780 and was continued by the British commander in chief until peace was declared in 1783. During the latter period, the merchants paid an annual rent of £150, which went to a relief fund for the city's poor.

When it was known that the British army would evacuate the city, the merchants offered to return the property with improvements to the Rutgers family, but negotiations were broken off when the family demanded the improvements plus £1,200 in back rent. After fire destroyed the brewery and the British army left the city, the merchants once again offered to settle; they were answered in February 1784, by a suit under the Trespass Act brought against Joshua Waddington, their agent, for £8,000 in back rent.

Rutgers v. Waddington drew much public notice because it was tried at a time of intense anti-British feeling in New York, a result of the long occupation of the city and the refusal, in defiance of the treaty of peace, of the British to withdraw from military installations in upstate New York. Its importance is further revealed by the fact that it attracted such established members of the New York bar as Attorney General Egbert Benson for the plaintiff, and Morgan Lewis and Brockholst Livingston for the defense. But two legal newcomers, Alexander Hamilton for Waddington, and John

Lawrence for Rutgers, undertook most of the burden of preparing and arguing the case.

Lawrence's strategy for the plaintiff was clear: the Trespass Act permitted anyone who had abandoned property because of the enemy invasion to "bring an action of Trespass against any Person" who had "occupied" it. But because Lawrence failed to include in his argument the act's clause that forbade the occupier from pleading, "in Justification, any military order . . ., of the Enemy," Hamilton was able to shift the grounds of the argument from those of a simple trespass to the constitutionality of the statute itself.

Hamilton's argument admitted the occupation of the Rutgers property, but on two grounds pleaded justification for it. First, the state constitution made the common law of England, including the law of nations and thus the laws of war, the law of New York. Therefore, the merchants' occupation of the Rutgers property was lawful between 1778 and 1780 under a license from the commissary general of the British army "(as by the laws usages and Customs of nations in time of War he might lawfully do)," and between 1780 and 1783, by authority of the commander in chief, for the same reason. Second, under the definitive treaty of peace between Britain and the United States, the nations agreed that claims by their citizens for "compensation, recompence, retribution or indemnity" as a result of the war were "mutually and reciprocally . . . renounced and released to each other." Lawrence then demurred, citing the Trespass Act's prohibition of "military orders" as a justification.

The trial was held June 29, 1784, before Mayor James Duane, the recorder, and the five alderman who composed the Mayor's Court of the City of New York, a part of the judicial system carried over from colonial times. Counsel for the plaintiff opened by arguing that the court had no power to interpret anything beyond state law; that the law of nations did not apply because the use of land for private purposes, even when authorized by the enemy, did not relate to the war; and that the law of nations was not part of the common law, but only civil law that could not bind a sovereign state. As to the treaty, property rights were an internal matter not covered by the treaty power

under the Articles of Confederation, and New York's ratification of the articles, a simple legislative act, could be rescinded.

Hamilton answered that the Trespass Act violated the law of nations and the law of the state, a power that could reside only in Congress. As to the treaty of peace, the law of nations implied that such agreements carried a general amnesty for injuries incurred in the war, an implication that Congress had accepted and that the states were bound to obey. Finally, if the Trespass Act conflicted with either the law of nations or the treaty, state courts were obliged "to construe them so as to make them stand together" (the only reference to judicial review among Hamilton's notes on the case), and, because the judges could not presume that the legislature intended that British subjects be denied their rights under the law of nations, the Trespass Act must be set aside.

The court's decision was delivered August 27, 1784. The long opinion, apparently the work of Mayor Duane, was, as one scholar has claimed, "essentially a political one"; it picked its way through the issues presented in a way that gave some comfort to both sides but was satisfactory to neither. First, the court found the Trespass Act to be remedial in nature for the benefit of Mrs. Rutgers and that it did apply to Waddington; further, for the period when the merchants occupied the property "under the bare unauthoritative permission of the Commissary General" and paid no rent, their use of it had "no relation to the war" and they were liable. Second, as a result of independence, "the law of nations has become an indispensable obligation" of the United States to protect "a member of a foreign nation" (i.e., the merchants); therefore, "restitution" of rents collected "under the authority of the British Commander, . . . cannot, *according to the law of nations,* be required" [emphasis in original]. Third, the court sustained Hamilton's contention that states could not "abridge" the treaty of peace but held that the omission of an *"express amnesty"* in that treaty made it an insufficient defense for the merchants. Duane did accept Hamilton's point that it could not be presumed that the legislature, in passing the Trespass Act, intended to deprive the defendants of their rights under the law of nations. Finally, although the court felt bound to carry out the express terms of statutes, the separation of powers principle in the state's constitution required that where the terms of statutes were general, "interpretation is the province of the court, and, . . . we are bound to perform it."

On September 2, a jury awarded the plaintiff £791.13.4 in rent and six pence in costs. Counsel for both sides filed writs of error with the state supreme court, but before that court could act, "a voluntary compromise took place" between the parties by which the defendant paid an unrevealed "sum of money," and the suit was dropped.

Local reaction to the decision was swift and hostile, and the legislature passed resolutions denouncing the court for trying to undermine legislative authority. The atmosphere was so charged that most pending suits under the Trespass Act and other anti-Tory laws were settled before coming to trial. Although Hamilton's brilliant defense was an important milestone in his legal and political career, and the legislature later repealed the Trespass Act's prohibition against pleading military orders as justification, he later admitted that "I was never able to get my point established" before the supreme court.

The long-range significance of the *Rutgers* decision is less clear because of what one scholar has called the "studied ambiguity" of Duane's opinion. The court did not declare the Trespass Act to be void but simply "irrelevant" (for the period when the merchants were authorized by the British commander to use the Rutgers property); instead, it found that the legislature could not have intended to violate the law of nations recognized in its own constitution. As for the treaty of peace, although Duane held that state law could not violate it, in this case the treaty did not confer on the defendant any rights not already due him under the law of nations.

The power of courts to set aside legislative acts was not directly addressed, but the right of the judiciary to interpret legislative intent in "general" provisions of statutes was asserted, a position denounced by the state legislature. Although *Rutgers v. Waddington* was hardly a ringing declaration of judicial review, one authority finds that the issue was "well aired" in state courts at the time and that it "may have colored" the views of the framers of the U.S. Constitution.

Selected Bibliography

Barck, O.T. *New York City During the War for Independence.* Port Washington, NY: Ira J. Friedman, Inc., 1966.

Dawson, H.B. *The Case of Rutgers v. . . . Waddington.* Morrisania, NY: Privately printed, 1866.

Goebel, J., Jr., ed. *The Law Practice of Alexander Hamilton: Documents and Commentary.* 5 vols. New York: Columbia University Press, 1964–81.

Morris, R.B., ed. *Select Cases of the Mayor's Court of New York City, 1674–1784.* Vol. 2 of *American Legal Records.* Washington, DC: American Historical Association, 1955.

Syrett, H.C., *et al.,* eds. *The Papers of Alexander Hamilton.* 26 vols. New York: Columbia University Press, 1961–79.

THE SUPREME COURT DECLARES ITS INDEPENDENCE: JUDICIAL REVIEW OF FEDERAL STATUTES

by Herbert A. Johnson
School of Law
University of South Carolina

Marbury v. Madison, 1 Cranch 137 (1803) [U.S. Supreme Court]

Not one of the vast and rapidly growing number of U.S. Supreme Court opinions has occupied such a central place in constitutional law as has Chief Justice John Marshall's majority opinion in *Marbury v. Madison.* Correctly identifying *Marbury* as the case that firmly established judicial review in federal law, scholars differ sharply concerning the political motivations underlying it. They also question the legitimacy of an elite, nonelected body of judges overruling the legislative will of Congress as expressed in federal statutes. On the other hand, the supremacy of constitutional provisions over legislative enactments has never been effectively challenged, nor have critics suggested a practical substitute for the U.S. Supreme Court's judicial review.

Since the American Revolution, and to a degree during the colonial period, government has been viewed as not only derived from the consent of the people, but also as being inherently limited by certain fundamental principles. Those limitations were read into colonial charters and royal or proprietorial concessions; they were incorporated into state constitutions; and, with the ratification of the U.S. Constitution in 1788 and its Bill of Rights in 1791, they became a vital part of federal law. Indeed, the U.S. Constitution establishes a government limited to specifically identified powers. All other political authority is by express constitutional mandate reserved to the states or to the people.

In No. 78 of *The Federalist*, Alexander Hamilton pointed to judicial action as the instrument whereby the legislative and executive branches of government would be restricted to the powers granted to them by the U.S. Constitution. However, the concept of judicial review was not novel. Sixteenth- and seventeenth-century English precedents carried an inference of judicial review, most conspicuously set forth by Sir Edward Coke in 1610 in *Dr. Bonham's Case*. Coke's doctrine—that reason and custom limited the effectiveness of legislative enactments—was brought into American colonial law through James Otis's famous 1761 speech vainly opposing the issuance of writs of assistance in Massachusetts Bay. By 1788, U.S. constitutional thought linked judicial review to limited government and was the basis on which several state legislative programs had been declared unconstitutional by state judges. For the most part, these state statutes involved efforts to seize property without following proper legal procedures or to do so without compensation. In *Hylton v. United States* (1796), a federal tax on carriages was challenged before the Supreme

Court, and the Court gave tacit approval to judicial review by considering the case even though it upheld the constitutionality of the statute. However, it was not until *Marbury* that a congressional statute was declared void on constitutional grounds. Such an exercise of judicial review would not recur until the 1857 *Dred Scott Case* in which the Court nullified the federal statute that embodied the Missouri Compromise of 1820.

There are two forms of judicial review in U.S. constitutional law. The first involves the review of state statutes and court decisions based on the supremacy of the U.S. Constitution and statutes and treaties made pursuant to it. This type of judicial review is essential to the federal union, and it was in fact inherited from similar control exercised by the British Privy Council before the Revolution. The second form, with which *Marbury* was concerned, deals with the power of the state and federal judiciary at all levels to compare legislation with constitutional foundations of governmental power, and to declare legislative enactments null and void when they conflict with the law of the land as embodied in the state or federal Constitution. The first form of judicial review is essential to the maintenance of the federal union, the second functions as a constitutional and political governing wheel to control excessive use of legislative and executive power.

The hectic last weeks of the Adams administration formed the backdrop against which the *Marbury* case took shape. On February 27, 1801, a statute authorizing the appointment of additional justices of the peace for the District of Columbia was passed by Congress and signed by the president. Between then and March 4, 1801, when John Adams was to surrender his office to the incoming Republican president, Thomas Jefferson, the Federalist appointment apparatus was kept running at high speed and some 42 "midnight" justices of the peace were commissioned and placed in office. Assisting President Adams at every step of the process was John Marshall, who continued as secretary of state even after he took office on January 31 as chief justice of the United States. Ironically, it was most likely due to Marshall's administrative oversight that the commission of William Marbury, along with the commissions of Robert Townshend Hooe, Dennis Ramsey, and William Harper, was not delivered. Marshall was not the most orderly of men, and from testimony later presented before the Supreme Court, it appears that these commissions may have been lost when others were hurriedly delivered, enabling their recipients to quiet a pre-inauguration riot in Alexandria.

However the oversight may have occurred, the four commissions were not delivered before the incoming administration took possession of the secretary of state's office. When they were demanded of Jefferson's acting secretary, Levi Lincoln, delivery was refused; Marbury and the three others brought their demand for a writ of *mandamus* directly to the Supreme Court. (A *mandamus* is a court order directing that a public official either perform a given act or refrain from doing so.) Few litigants in U.S. history risked as little as did Marbury and his colleagues. All were prosperous merchants. Ramsey and Harper were former public officials in the city of Alexandria, and Hooe and Marbury were heavy speculators in Washington, D.C., realty. Ramsey had been a pallbearer at George Washington's 1799 funeral, and Harper commanded the artillery company in the procession. In contrast to the claimants' status and wealth, the office of justice of the peace had little monetary or honorific value. District of Columbia justices were to be supported solely by the fees assessed against litigants. Given the wealth of the disappointed judges and their close Federalist connections, it is not surprising that the newly elected administration suspected political motives in their seeking judicial relief.

Receiving Marbury's petition on December 16, 1801, the Supreme Court issued an order directing James Madison, as secretary of state, to show cause why a *mandamus* should not issue and requiring him to surrender the commissions to their recipients. By this point in the litigation, the appointment papers had doubtless disappeared from the State Department office, and Madison, who did not take up the duties of his office until May 1801, may never have seen them. However, neither he nor any member of the Jefferson administration appeared before the Supreme Court, since that might be viewed as acquiescence in the Supreme Court's authority to issue such an order to an executive officer of the government. On the other hand, the new administration did use its majority in Congress to cancel the Summer Term of the Supreme Court scheduled for 1802, postponing any action on the petition until the February Term in 1803.

On February 9 and 10, 1803, the application was argued before the Supreme Court by Charles Lee of Virginia, appearing for the four petitioners. Two State Department clerks were required to testify, and Levi Lincoln, after preliminary objections to the jurisdiction of the Supreme Court, provided the limited information available concerning the commissions. In addition, an affidavit by James Markham Marshall, the chief justice's brother who was a circuit judge for the District of Columbia, was read concerning his effort to deliver commissions during the Alexandria riots.

On behalf of the Supreme Court, Chief Justice Marshall considered three issues in his opinion: (1) did Marbury and his associates have a right to their commissions, (2) if such a right existed and it had been violated, did the laws of the United States afford a remedy, and (3) if they did offer a remedy, was it in the form of a *mandamus* issued by the Supreme Court? He began with a painstaking consideration of the appointment process, concluding that there had been a valid nomination by the president and confirmation by the Senate, and that a commission had been issued bearing the signature of the president and the great seal of the United States. All that remained was for the secretary of state to perform the ministerial act of delivering the commission to its recipient. Concerning the second issue, Marshall recognized that while the "very essence of civil liberty" included the right to protection of the laws, there were certain political acts by executive branch officers that could not be examined by the courts. However, that was not the case where private rights had vested, when the discretion of the executive officer had been exercised, and only a ministerial duty remained in that officer. Observing that the United States was "a government of laws and not of men . . .," Marshall suggested that such a reputation would be undeserved if no remedy was provided for a violation of a vested property right. When an executive officer acts illegally under color of his office, mere possession of the office does not exempt him from legal action or submission to a judgment at law. It was not the office that determined the availability of the *mandamus* writ, but rather the nature of the thing to be done that determined its propriety. Here the thing requested was merely a ministerial act not involving the exercise of discretion. Justice and equity demanded that an executive officer could not "at his discretion sport away the vested rights of others."

Having thus established Marbury's entitlement to his commission, his vested right in the office, and the circumstance that ministerial rather than discretionary executive action was requested, the chief justice asked the critical question: whether federal law provided Marbury with a remedy through Supreme Court issuance of a *mandamus* writ. Article III of the U.S. Constitution conferred both original and appellate jurisdiction upon the Supreme Court. The provision concerning original jurisdiction was quite specific in its grant of powers, but omitted from the provision was any mention of a *mandamus* power. Such authority, if it existed, was based on Section 13 of the Judiciary Act of 1789. Marshall noted that the Constitution was a superior law, paramount to the provisions of an ordinary congressional statute. The federal government existed on the general premise that a statute violative of the provisions of the Constitution was void and should not be obligatory upon judges sworn to uphold the U.S. Constitution. Judicial duty demanded that the statute be ignored and the constitutional provision be upheld. He concluded that "the particular phraseology of the constitution of the United States confirms and strengthens the principle, supposed to be essential to all written constitutions, that a law repugnant to the constitution is void; and that *courts*, as well as other departments, are bound by that instrument [emphasis in original]." In other words, by adding to the original jurisdiction of the Supreme Court, Marshall—speaking for the unanimous Court—ruled that Section 13 of the Judiciary Act of 1789 violated the U.S. Constitution and was thus "unconstitutional."

Public reaction to the Court's opinion in *Marbury* depended on the political affiliation of the commentator. Republican newspapers at-tacked Marshall's reasoning, and his approach to the case was deemed to be clear evidence of his intention to use judicial power to undermine the proposed reforms of the Jefferson administration. The president was particularly agitated at Marshall's chiding him for trampling on vested property rights and for overstepping the bounds of his constitutional authority. For President Jefferson and many others, the full significance of judicial review seems to have been obscured by the heat of partisan politics. It was not until subsequent decisions of the Supreme Court built on the precedent of *Marbury* that the case's true significance was realized.

The legal profession was not slow to challenge *Marbury* in terms of its logic or its approach to the task of judging a constitutional issue. A close historical analysis of the decision suggests that there were a number of grounds upon which the chief justice might have denied relief to Marbury without dealing with the constitutional issue. Denial of the petition on any basis would avoid an embarrassing confrontation between the Supreme Court and the other two branches of the federal government. But denying relief through the exercise of judicial review—through an opinion that disallowed an excessive grant of power to the Supreme Court—not only read judicial review into federal case law, but it did so in a manner that parried any effective Jeffersonian attack.

Marbury provides two valuable insights into the legal thinking of Chief Justice Marshall. First, more than any other opinion written by him, the *Marbury* opinion shows the logical evolution of one issue from another to reach what appears to be an inevitable conclusion. Significantly, before launching into his opinion, the chief justice warned his listeners that he would not treat the issues in the order followed by counsel. Through the sequence in which he discussed the issues, Marshall was able to eliminate all other factors before he focused on judicial review. Unquestionably *Marbury* is one of the best organized opinions to issue from his pen, and scholars have questioned whether it could have been so well constructed during the two weeks between closing argument in the case and his announcement of the opinion. Whatever the circumstances of its preparation, the *Marbury* opinion deserves careful study as the best guide to the chief justice's decision-making process.

The second insight provided by *Marbury* is the way in which jurisdictional and procedural matters were used by Marshall in enhancing the authority of the Supreme Court. In a very real sense, this petition for a *mandamus* instituted a technique that would be used extensively in the remaining years of Marshall's chief justiceship. Assertions or denials of jurisdiction, carefully selected to minimize overt conflict either with the other two branches of the federal government or with the authorities of the various states, were critical to the effective growth of Supreme Court authority and eased political acceptance of the Court as the primary interpreter of the U.S. Constitution.

Marbury is preeminent as the federal Supreme Court decision establishing judicial review. It consolidated much of the received tradition concerning limitation of government through written constitutions, and it initiated the period of Supreme Court growth into the foremost tribunal for constitutional litigation in the United States. It also launched the cre-ative tension between judicial review and legislative supremacy that has remained one of the dominant themes of U.S. constitutional history.

Selected Bibliography

Baker, L. *John Marshall: A Life in Law*. New York: Macmillan Publishing Co., Inc., 1974.

Beveridge, A.J. *The Life of John Marshall*. 4 vols. Boston: Houghton Mifflin & Co., 1916–19.

Bowers, C.G. *Jefferson in Power: The Death Struggle of the Federalists*. Boston: Houghton Mifflin Co., 1936.

Corwin, E.S. *The Doctrine of Judicial Review*. Princeton, NJ: Princeton University Press, 1914.

Crosskey, W.W. *Politics and the Constitution in the History of the United States*. 3 vols. Chicago: University of Chicago Press, 1953–80.

Dewey, D.O. *Marshall versus Jefferson: The Political Background of* Marbury v. Madison. New York: Alfred A. Knopf, 1970.

Faulkner, R.K. *The Jurisprudence of John Marshall*. Princeton, NJ: Princeton University Press, 1968.

Haines, C.G. *The American Doctrine of Judicial Supremacy*. New York: Russell & Russell, Inc., 1959.

Haskins, G.L., and H.A. Johnson. *Foundations of Power, John Marshall, 1801–15*. Vol. 2 of *History of the Supreme Court of the United States*. New York: Macmillan Publishing Co., Inc., 1981.

Warren, C. *The Supreme Court in United States History*. 2 vols. Rev. ed. Boston: Little, Brown, & Co., 1926.

THE HIGH-WATER MARK OF PRESIDENTIAL POWER

by William Lasser
Department of Political Science
Clemson University

United States v. Curtiss-Wright Export Corporation, 299 U.S. 304 (1936) [U.S. Supreme Court]

The constitutional power of the U.S. presidency has ebbed and flowed over the two centuries of the nation's history. Never has that power been given so expansive an interpretation, however, as in the U.S. Supreme Court's *Curtiss-Wright* decision.

The case grew out of international attempts to stop the Chaco War, fought between Bolivia and Paraguay over a strip of land in the plain known as the Gran Chaco. In 1934, several countries, including the United States, agreed to attempt to halt the flow of arms and ammunition into the two countries. President Franklin D. Roosevelt asked Congress for a joint resolution granting him the authority to ban the sale of "arms and munitions of war . . . in any place in the United States to the countries now engaged in that armed conflict" or to any person, company, or association acting on their behalf.

Congress agreed, delegating to Roosevelt the power to ban all such sales if he found that such action "may contribute to the reestablishment of peace between those countries." On the very same day, Roosevelt exercised his power under the resolution and issued a proclamation outlawing arms sales to Bolivia and Paraguay.

The constitutionality of the joint resolution and of the president's proclamation came to the Supreme Court in 1936, after the Curtiss-Wright Corporation was charged with selling 15 machine guns to Bolivia in violation of the president's order. Curtiss-Wright charged that the indictment was invalid for a number of reasons, most importantly because Congress lacked the constitutional authority to delegate to the executive branch the power to make law in such a case. By leaving the decision to ban arms sales to the president's "unfettered discretion . . . controlled by no standard," the company contended, the resolution violated the separation of powers.

Curtiss-Wright thus presented an important test of the "delegation doctrine," as it is known, in the field of foreign affairs. Over the years, the Supreme Court had upheld numerous delegations of legislative power to the executive, dating back to decisions as early as 1813. In 1935, however, just a year before the *Curtiss-Wright* decision, the Court had struck down the National Industrial Recovery Act on the ground that it authorized an unconstitutional delegation of power to the executive branch. Would the Court continue to narrow Congress's power to delegate or would it return to its earlier, broader conception?

The Court did neither. Justice George Sutherland, writing the majority opinion, held that the delegation of legislative power to the executive in the realm of foreign affairs was constitutional because it was superfluous; the president, as the nation's chief executive, already possessed plenary power in this area. "In this vast external realm," wrote Sutherland, "the President alone has the power to speak or listen as the representative of the nation. . . . as [Chief Justice John] Marshall said . . . in the House of Representatives, 'The President is the sole organ of the nation in its external relations, and its sole representative with foreign nations.'"

There was certainly ample precedent to support a broad view of the delegation doctrine, especially in the area of foreign affairs; as Sutherland put it, "practically every volume of

the United States Statutes contains one or more acts or joint resolutions of Congress authorizing action by the President in respect of subjects affecting foreign relations, which either leave the exercise of the power to his unrestricted judgment, or provide a standard far more general than that which has always been considered with regard to domestic affairs." Moreover, a number of such delegations had been explicitly upheld by the Supreme Court. None of these precedents, however, could support Sutherland's sweeping statements pushing Congress into the background in the domain of foreign affairs. These statements are especially curious in light of Sutherland's dim view of executive power in the domestic sphere.

The powers of the federal government in the areas of domestic and foreign affairs, Sutherland began, "are different, both in respect of their origin and their nature." In the domestic sphere, "the primary purpose of the Constitution was to carve from the general mass of legislative powers *then possessed by the states* such portions as it was thought desirable to vest in the federal government" [Sutherland's emphasis]. Such powers were largely given over to the legislative branch.

The power to regulate foreign affairs, however, was different. Sutherland contended that the "powers of external sovereignty" were never vested in the states, but were instead transmitted from the King of Great Britain directly to the Union—first as represented by the Continental Congress, then to the Union under the Articles of Confederation, and finally to the Union under the Constitution. Thus, "the investment of the federal government with the powers of external sovereignty did not depend upon the affirmative grants of the Constitution. The powers to declare and wage war, to conclude peace, to make treaties, to maintain diplomatic relations with other sovereignties, if they had never been mentioned in the Constitution, would have vested in the federal government as necessary concomitants of nationality."

If the foreign affairs power was different in origin from that over domestic affairs, it was also different in nature. "In the vast external realm," Sutherland concluded, "with its important, complicated, delicate and manifold problems, the President alone has the power to speak or listen as a representative of the nation." To avoid any misunderstanding of his position, he later repeated himself: "We are here dealing . . . [with] the very delicate, plenary, and exclusive power of the President as the sole organ of the federal government in the field of international relations—a power which does not require as a basis for its exercise an act of Congress."

Sutherland's argument is subject to logical, historical, and theoretical criticisms. First, his claim that the foreign affairs power of the British Crown devolved directly on the United States without passing through the states would have shocked the members of the Continental Congress. Second, his argument that the president's power in foreign affairs is plenary flies in the face of the Constitution itself, which clearly grants to Congress the power to declare war, define and punish piracies on the high seas and offenses against the law of nations, and ratify treaties. Furthermore, his argument entirely ignores the commonplace view—in the eighteenth century as today—that the powers of the U.S. government were delegated to it by the American people. His argument that the foreign affairs power could not be delegated to the United States because it was never possessed by the states is specious because in conventional American political theory all the powers of government were reclaimed by the people (both in 1776 and in 1787–88) and then redistributed as the people saw fit. Finally, whatever the origins of the foreign affairs power, it is fallacious to argue that such powers automatically devolved onto the executive. Why did they not descend to the legislative branch? In fact, whatever its origin, the power over foreign affairs was clearly divided by the Constitution among both the legislative and executive branches.

The logical deficiencies of Sutherland's opinion notwithstanding, the case remains a favorite of those who would expand presidential power in the realm of foreign affairs. It has been cited with approval by countless presidents and presidential subordinates: in the arguments over the constitutionality of the Destroyers-for-Bases Agreement before World War II, during the Vietnam War crisis, and most recently by Colonel Oliver North and his associates in the "Iran-Contra Affair." Perhaps because of its sweeping character, Sutherland's argument has stood for over 50 years as the theoretical high-water mark of presidential power, though it has never been accepted literally in practice even by the most expansive advocates of executive power. Although used to great effect in the tug-of-war between the legislative and executive branches, *Curtiss-Wright* has never been used by presidents in an effort to ignore Congress altogether.

Lawyers and legal scholars have engaged in endless debates over the precise meaning of *Curtiss-Wright*, and it is possible to read the decision more or less narrowly. Some have argued that the decision speaks only to the question of who *executes* foreign policy and says nothing about who is to *make* foreign policy in the first place. Others have pointed out that most of Sutherland's argument is mere *obiter dicta*, superfluous commentary that does not carry with it the force of law. Still others have tried to read *Curtiss-Wright* as merely permitting a looser delegation of power to the executive in foreign affairs than in the domestic sphere, rather than making an absolute claim of executive supremacy. And commentators have pointed out that later decisions of the Supreme Court—in particular, the "Steel Seizure Case" *Youngstown Sheet and Tube Company v. Sawyer* (1952)—have effectively superseded *Curtiss-Wright*, or at least cast doubt on its authoritativeness.

It remains unclear why the conservative Sutherland, who vehemently opposed Roosevelt and the New Deal, wrote such a sweeping decision in support of presidential power. Some have argued that *Curtiss-Wright* simply shows consistency; they argue that the views expressed by Sutherland in 1936 were views he had long held and expressed, and dated back well before his appointment to the Supreme Court in 1922. In a 1909 article, for example, then Senator Sutherland contended that "national sovereignty inhered in the United States from the beginning. Neither the Colonies nor the States which succeeded them ever separately exercised authority over foreign affairs. . . ." This argument was repeated at length in his book, *Constitutional Power and World Affairs*, written in 1919.

Sutherland's early writings may explain his views on the origins of the foreign affairs power, but they cannot explain his sudden conversion to executive supremacy. Both the 1909 article and the 1919 book stand for the principle that the federal government—Congress and the president together—has plenary power in the field of foreign relations, and that constitutional grants of power must be interpreted as broadly as possible. In effect, Sutherland's early arguments are arguments for national, rather than presidential, supremacy. As he put it in 1909, "Over *external* matters . . . no residuary powers do or can exist in the several States, and from the necessity of the case all necessary authority must be found in the National Government, such authority being expressly conferred or implied from one or more of the express powers, or from all of them combined, or resulting from the very fact of nationality as inherently inseparable therefrom" [emphasis in original]. Neither the 1909 article nor the 1919 book contain anything like the sort of executive aggrandizement found in *Curtiss-Wright*.

Sutherland's conversion to the theory of executive domination in the area of foreign affairs thus remains an enigma, as does the *Curtiss-Wright* decision. On one hand, it is easy to criticize his grandiose claims concerning the origin and nature of the foreign affairs power and to disparage his inflated views of presidential power. On the other hand, one cannot help but be impressed by his prescience—as early as 1909—about the nation's future role in foreign affairs and the necessity for an expansive interpretation of the powers of the national government. Furthermore, while *Curtiss-Wright* has been abused by presidents and presidential advisers who have sought extraordinary powers, its influence is mitigated by the existence of other Supreme Court decisions—such as the decision in the Steel Seizure Case in 1952—which take a diametrically opposite view of presidential power. As Justice Robert H. Jackson put it in the steel seizure case, "Presidential powers are not fixed but fluctuate, depending upon their disjunction or conjunction with those of Congress." In the never-ending debate between the two branches, *Curtiss-Wright* provides a clear, albeit dubious, point of reference.

Selected Bibliography

Levitan, D.M. "The Foreign Relations Power: An Analysis of Mr. Justice Sutherland's Theory." *Yale Law Journal* 55 (1946): 467–97.

Lofgren, C.A. "*United States v. Curtiss-Wright Export Corporation*: An Historical Reassessment." *Yale Law Journal* 83 (1973): 1–32.

Sutherland, G. *Constitutional Power and World Affairs.* New York: Columbia University Press, 1919.

HOW ONE IMMIGRANT SHOOK THE U.S. GOVERNMENT TO ITS VERY CORE

by Barbara Hinkson Craig
Department of Government
Wesleyan University

Immigration and Naturalization Service v. Chadha, 462 U.S. 919 (1983) [U.S. Supreme Court]

There is no doubt that *INS v. Chadha* is a landmark decision. As one congressional scholar has noted, *Chadha* "will profoundly affect how power is exercised and policy made in America for decades to come." When the U.S. Supreme Court handed down its decision in the case on June 23, 1983, it was front-page news nationwide. "Government Power Poised for a Grand Realignment" read headlines in the *New York Times*, and in the *Washington Post*, "Decision Alters Balance of Power in Government." In one fell swoop, the Court had overturned provisions in nearly 200 different statutes, more than it had struck down cumulatively in its entire history. The decision affected issues ranging from war powers and arms sales to budget impoundments and governmental salaries. It also touched on regulations concerning the environment, consumer protection, worker health and safety, and a host of pork-barrel and special interest programs.

Chadha is the extraordinary story of how one immigrant, in his fight to stay in the United States, stumbled into a battle between Titans: ultimately it led to a territorial power struggle that pitted the U.S. Congress in all its might against an equally impressive and formidable foe—the president and the entire executive branch. The issue involved in the case was the constitutionality of the legislative veto, a procedural device invented by Congress to constrain the exercise of power delegated by law to the president, executive branch, or independent agencies. It is a case that will be remembered in history for the power struggle between the branches that it instigated; but it begins with Chadha's own story.

Jagdish Rai Khiali Ram Nathod Ram Chadha is an Indian who was born and raised in Kenya. When Kenya became independent from Great Britain in 1963, all persons born in Kenya prior to that date were automatically made citizens of Kenya—all except those whose parents had not been born there. Since Chadha's father had been born in South Africa and his mother in India, he had to apply for citizenship to become a citizen in the country of his birth. His application, like those of many others similarly situated, was lost in a sea of red tape. And because the new Kenyan government had also placed restrictions on place and type of employment for noncitizens, it was a "Catch-22"—citizenship was not forthcoming and employment was restricted without it.

At the encouragement of some young Peace Corps volunteers who had befriended him, Chadha decided to pursue a college education in the United States. In 1966, traveling on a British nationality certificate and a British passport because his Kenyan citizenship application had not been granted, Chadha came to the United States and entered Bowling Green State University. By December 1971, he had earned a B.A. in business administration and an M.A. in political science and economics. His student

visa was due to expire in June 1972. Chadha wrote to the Kenyan and British embassies to inquire about how he could return home. Kenya said, in effect, "You're not ours anymore." The British said, "It could take years to clear you for a Quota Voucher for employment in England. Why don't you get the United States to regularize your immigration status and stay there?"

The Quota Voucher was Great Britain's response to the flood of Ugandan Indians who held British colonial passports and were fleeing Idi Amin's regime in the wake of his 1972 order for the immediate expulsion of all Asians. It was a time of worldwide recession and the indigenous-employed Britains had risen up to protect themselves against cheaper labor competition.

Chadha was truly a man without a country. He tried to get a job in the United States but employers wanted to see his green card—the prized piece of paper that provides aliens with resident status and the right to work in the United States. Chadha was by then (the summer of 1973) desperate. He went to the U.S. Immigration Office in Los Angeles to see if he could get some document to enable him to work. He was arrested, fingerprinted, photographed for a mug shot, and held well into the evening. He was also presented with an order to appear before an immigration judge on November 1, 1973, to show cause why he should not be deported.

By this time, Chadha was well into the U.S. administrative process—a confusing process involving the three separate branches of the national government: executive, legislative, and judicial. What Chadha was about to experience was a quasi-judicial proceeding that looked very much like (and had powers very much like) a court of law. But it was not a court of law. It was a regional office of an executive branch agency, the Immigration and Naturalization Service, which is part of the U.S. Justice Department. The immigration judge was an employee of the executive branch, not a member of the judicial branch.

After a frenetic search for a lawyer he could afford, Chadha finally found a young, fresh-from-law-school-practitioner who had not even had a course in immigration law. There ensued a series of blunders and misunderstandings of the law by his greenhorn counsel. Finally, due largely to the conscientious actions of an elderly civil servant "immigration hearing judge," Chadha was granted a "suspension of deportation." The immigration judge's decision and the case information were then sent to the attorney general.

The power to suspend deportations in cases in which an alien would suffer "extreme hardship" if deported had been given to the attorney general by Congress in the 1940s and had been regularly renewed since. There was a hitch, however. After determining that the extreme hardship standard was met, the attorney general was required to send the names of individuals granted suspensions and their case information to Congress to remain before it for two years. During that time, if either house voted by majority vote to veto any (or all) of the suspension(s), out he (they) would go. This congressional veto procedure is called "a one-house legislative veto."

Chadha's case was vetoed. On December 12, 1975, Congressman Joshua Eilberg (Democrat from Pennsylvania) introduced a one-house resolution (i.e., a legislative veto resolution) to disapprove Chadha's deportation suspension and that of five others. Without a printed bill; with no hearings, debate, or explanation; with no recorded vote; and under suspension of the rules (i.e., a time when few members are typically on the floor), the resolution was passed. Chadha once again faced deportation.

Chadha did not believe this action could be constitutional based on what he had learned about U.S. law. He had had a hearing, the government had had a lawyer, he had had a lawyer, and a "judge" in black robes had decided his case. How could one house of Congress overturn his hard-won right to stay? It was neither fair nor equitable. And what of due process?

Again Chadha needed counsel. Again he had almost no money. His efforts finally led him to a young immigration attorney, John Pohlmann, who took his case *pro bono* ("without charge"). At last Chadha had counsel who knew immigration law. Unfortunately, that knowledge was not very helpful. The only thing that held any promise—and it was not much—was a constitutional challenge.

The constitutional challenge to the legislative veto that Congress had used against Chadha is based on the principle of separation of powers. In fashioning a government intended to preserve and protect the liberty of its citizens, the founding fathers relied on the principle of separation of powers and the countervailing principle of checks and balances. Power was to be divided among three branches: the legislative power was vested in a Congress made up of two houses; the power to execute the laws passed by Congress was given to the executive, and the power to interpret the laws to the judicial branch. As a check against the possible misuse of power by any one of the branches, each branch was given some power over the others. The Constitution, for example, gives the legislative power to Congress but it also subjects the exercise of that power to the restraint of a presidential veto—a power that is, in turn, restrained by allowing for two-thirds of both houses of Congress to override a presidential veto.

One could argue that the action of the House of Representatives in vetoing Chadha's suspension of deportation and thereby changing a decision made by the attorney general was an unconstitutional intrusion into the domain of the executive branch. In retort, Congress could argue that it was simply trying to correct a mistake made by the executive branch in its interpretation of the intent of the law. In response to this explanation, though, opponents of the legislative veto would argue that the power to determine whether the executive branch has correctly applied a law passed by Congress belongs to the judicial branch, not to the legislature. Separation of powers questions are raised by either effort to explain the legislative veto's function. To determine the constitutionality of the legislative veto in these terms would require a court to balance the core purpose of the separation of powers design against the equally important function of the checks and balances provisions and then to decide whether the intrusion was significant enough to threaten the independence of either the judicial or executive branches.

Another approach to challenging the legislative veto is to question its constitutionality based on the presentment clause in Article I,

Section 7, of the U.S. Constitution; or the incompatibility clause in Article I, Section 6, of the Constitution; or the constitutional requirement of bicameralism. The presentment clause spells out the process for passage of a law: "Every Bill which shall have passed the House of Representatives and the Senate, shall, before it becomes Law, be presented to the President of the United States. . . ." If the president does not sign the bill, Congress can by two-thirds vote in both houses make it law. The framers included the every-order clause to ensure that Congress could not avoid the president's check on the legislative power by calling a bill by another name: "Every Order, Resolution, or Vote to which the Concurrence of the Senate and House of Representatives may be necessary . . . shall be presented to the President of the United States; and before the Same shall take Effect, shall be approved by him, or being disapproved by him, shall be repassed by two thirds of the Senate and House of Representatives. . . ." If the resolution passed by the House of Representatives to veto Chadha's suspension of deportation was in effect a law, it was not passed according to the clear constitutional requirements for passage of a law. Opponents of the legislative veto would extend the logic of this analysis to "prove" the veto's unconstitutionality under a separation of powers analysis as well: if it was not a law, it must be either an effort to execute the law or to interpret it, and these functions belong to the other branches.

Could the House of Representative's actions, without the Senate or the president's involvement, have the constitutional force of law on Chadha? Did not even an immigrant have the right to this most basic of constitutional protections that John Adams, as signer of the Declaration of Independence and the second president, pointed out, ensures that we are "a government of laws, and not of men"? Chadha and his attorney believed that the veto process was wrong and unconstitutional and they prepared to fight.

Throughout 1976 and early 1977, Chadha's attorney appealed through the administrative process and then to the U.S. Court of Appeals for the Ninth Circuit in San Francisco. By April 1977, though, Pohlmann was forced to tell Chadha that he could not go on with the case

much longer. The date for filing the written brief was rapidly approaching, and the complexity of the issues involved required an enormous amount of research time. As a single practitioner with a family to support, Pohlmann could no longer afford to spend so much time for free. If this case were about the plight of one alien, it most likely would have ended here. Chadha would have been just one more of the many aliens deported each year. However, the importance of timing was significant: what was going on in Washington, D.C., during the mid-1970s would work to Chadha's benefit.

In the wake of the Watergate and Vietnam debacles, Congress, with an ever increasing frequency, had attached legislative vetoes to grants of power to the president. In the War Powers Act, Congress had granted to the president the right to use the troops in hostile situations for 60 days, but anytime during that period if the two houses of Congress, by majority vote, ordered him to bring the troops home, he would have to do so. Congress had delegated the power to the president to decide to sell arms to foreign nations, but if both houses voted against the sale, there could be no sale. The president was given the power to impound funds for one year, but if either house passed a legislative veto resolution, he had to spend the funds. There were dozens of other such laws. The president liked the power to act but not the strings of the legislative veto.

The U.S. Justice Department under the Ford, Carter, and Reagan administrations was vehemently opposed to the legislative veto as an unconstitutional intrusion on presidential power to execute the law. If Congress wanted to direct the president, it had to do so through a law and over a presidential veto if he objected. One or two houses acting without the president's involvement had no constitutional power except to impeach, try impeachments, ratify treaties, and advise and consent on appointees. The Constitution, the Justice Department argued, makes this clear.

But there was a problem. How to get a case? The president could not just bring a case to court against Congress—the court would surely call any such attempt a blatant example of a political question. What was needed was a private litigant to bring a case that the Justice

Department could join. Again, there was a problem. What private litigant could pass the court's standing and political question tests when foreign policy and presidential power were the issues? Fate was with the executive (and with Chadha).

Elected to the House of Representatives in the post-Watergate class of 1974 was Elliot Levitas (Democrat from Georgia). Like so many of the "Young Turks," as the freshmen legislators of that year were called by the media, Levitas came to Washington to fight Washington—he was out to get the pointy-headed, overzealous bureaucrats who were the perpetrators of fraud, waste, abuse, and red tape.

To a large extent his frustration, and that voiced by his constituents, was in response to the flood of regulations that was beginning to hit the business and work-world by the mid- to late-1970s. These were the regulations that were putting into operation liberal social policies embraced by Congress. They included dozens of laws that were passed throughout the late 1960s and early-1970s calling for clean air, clean water, safer workplaces, safer products, equal opportunities, and fair advertisement practices. The courts had allowed the broad and often vague delegations of power to the executive branch included in these laws, even though Congress was, in effect, giving away its own law-making power. To overcome separation of powers concerns about these delegations, the courts rationalized that once the power to make regulations was delegated to the executive branch it became executive power—even though those regulations were created like laws, looked like laws, and citizens had to obey them like laws.

As the governmental agencies attempted to implement these congressional goals, the costs of achieving them became very clear to those who now had to pay. And they screamed loudly to their representatives and senators. But what could members do? Surely they did not want to go on record as opposed to admirable goals, such as clean air.

Throughout the 1970s, the Court, as well as Congress, had forced the rule-making process to be more fair and open, more judicial-like. In so doing, Congress had been effectively shut out of influencing the regulatory outcome.

No longer could the committee or subcommittee chair call up the agency head and hint that any action on X ought to take into consideration the effect on Y Company, which just happened to be in the chair's district. The agency head, in most cases, was compelled to keep a full record for possible court review and was likely to be forced to provide a rational connection between evidence gathered during the rule-making process and his final published regulation. It became harder for individual members of Congress to get agencies to respond to their suggestions. If members wanted exemptions or had clear ideas of what they wanted that were not put in the law, they had to go about putting them in another law. But that is not easy to do. A majority in both houses had to support the exemption. The difficulty of accomplishing that task is one of the major reasons why Congress writes vague and ambiguous laws: it endeavors, often successfully, to "paper over" conflict.

Levitas found the tool to get Congress back in on the regulation process—the legislative veto. If Congress adopted a legislative veto over all governmental regulations, most overburdensome, counterproductive, or downright crazy regulations could be stopped before they went into effect.

Washington insiders (members and executive branch actors and the more astute interest groups) quickly saw the legislative veto's real potential—it could be used to stop any regulation for any reason. The legislative veto would allow Congress to narrow the review to a particular regulation: the broad question of whether consumers or the environment should be protected could be avoided. Powerful organized interests, with compelling economic incentives, would be able to gear up lobbying efforts fast, putting them at a distinct advantage. The amorphous "public interest," even when organized, would be at a distinct disadvantage. Spread thinly trying to cover hundreds of potential regulations, with much less financial backing, they would have a much harder time mobilizing within the 30 to 60 days typically allowed for veto reviews. They would win occasionally with the aid of their major ally, the media, but the balance of power would be tipped against them.

Congress took to the legislative veto like a duck to water. This little procedural device of a few sentences at the end of a statute enabled members to continue to delegate broad, vague power to the executive branch, proving to the electorate their concern for the pressing problems of the moment. Congress could come to closure on controversial issues without the necessity of coming to decisions. Majorities could be gathered to support general principles with the promise that if anyone was really disturbed with the particulars, the veto would be available. When the agency proposed a rule, and those who would have to pay (e.g., the businesses that had to convert equipment to make it safe or nonpolluting) complained, Congress would be able to threaten to veto the rule. Members would be able to say, "Look, I'm for clean air, but this rule is too costly, do a better job Mr. Bureaucrat or we will veto your final regulation." And Congress would be under no obligation to say what that better job might be. More importantly, wise executive actors would soon realize the importance of communicating with members (especially members of their oversight committees) during the process of designing their regulations. Many of the troublesome regulations might be altered or stopped before they got to the formal administrative rule-making process and without Congress having even to vote on a legislative veto resolution.

Levitas was quite successful in selling his magic cure-all. In 1976, he came within three votes of getting his legislative veto bill through the House of Representatives. He lost that year on his across-the-board legislative veto proposal, but managed to get numerous veto provisions into individual statutes over the next few years (e.g., safety rules, health and environment regulations, and consumer regulations). And all the while he continued his fight on behalf of what he called his "generic-veto" with a crusader's zeal.

Consumers, environmental protection groups, labor, and minorities who had fought long and hard to get legislation to accomplish their goals were faced with the prospect of losing regulation by regulation, and Congress could claim to be squeaky clean. Not many saw the danger of this eventuality, but one attorney in a position to do something about it did—Alan Morrison, chief litigator for Ralph Nader's legal arm, the Public Citizen Litigation Group.

In 1977, just as Chadha's attorney was ready to give up, Morrison took over Chadha's case. He did so not so much to fight for the right of a single immigrant but to strive for the consumer protection that had been promised in laws passed by Congress. The Justice Department joined in the case on behalf of the immigration service, arguing with Chadha and Morrison that the veto was unconstitutional. Left with no one to defend the veto, and with no case or controversy unless a defender could be found, the appeals court asked Congress to submit *amici curiae* ("friends of the court") briefs in support of the veto's constitutionality. Before long, the two houses of Congress were forced to intervene formally as parties to the case. The real litigants were now clear. The private litigant, Chadha, was much beside the point. This was a case of Congress versus the president.

Chadha v. INS was argued before a panel of three judges of the U.S. Court of Appeals for the Ninth Circuit in San Francisco on April 10, 1978. More than two and one-half years passed before a decision from the appeals court was announced. During that time, both Morrison and the Justice Department were constantly looking for other cases that they might bring (or join) to challenge the legislative veto's constitutionality. Eventually, at least two other cases (both involving challenges to consumer regulations vetoed by Congress) were found, but Chadha's case would be the one that would decide the veto's constitutionality.

On December 23, 1980, the appeals court announced its decision finding the legislative veto in the immigration act unconstitutional. The opinion, written by Judge Anthony Kennedy (who later was confirmed as an associate justice of the U.S. Supreme Court), ruled the legislative veto unconstitutional because "it violates the constitutional doctrine of separation of powers because it is [a] prohibited legislative intrusion upon the Executive and Judicial branches." There was a twofold purpose in the framers' adoption of the separation of powers principle. The first purpose, according to the court, was to "prevent an unnecessary and therefore dangerous concentration of power in one branch"; the second was "to facilitate administration of a large nation by the assignment of numerous labors to designated authorities." The court then proceeded to balance the utility of the legislative veto against its potential for intrusion into another branch's rightful domain, finding the veto to be "an interference with a central function of the Judiciary, and . . . an interference which is both disruptive and unnecessary."

The appeals court decision evidenced considerable judicial restraint, carefully confining its analysis to the situation presented by the immigration law. In that form, however, it was not very useful either to Morrison's effort to rid the regulatory process of legislative vetoes or to the Justice Department's goal of eliminating the bothersome presidential-level vetoes in the budget and foreign affairs acts. In another way, though, the appeals court behaved with considerable judicial activism by stretching far beyond what was necessary to deal with the case at hand. In the summer of 1980, Chadha had married a U.S. citizen and as a spouse of a U.S. citizen he easily could have obtained U.S. citizenship. This should have made the case moot because Chadha no longer stood to lose anything by an adverse ruling. However, the court's willingness to finesse the question of mootness makes it seem that it wanted to reach the question of the legislative veto's constitutionality.

For Morrison and the Justice Department to achieve the results they wanted from the case, they had to appeal the decision to the Supreme Court and hope for a broader ruling. They had a problem, though. Chadha and INS had both already won. How could they appeal a win? In the months following the appeals court decision there were convoluted legal attempts by the Justice Department to enable an appeal, but in the end both the Senate and the House of Representatives saved the day by intervening and appealing in their own attempt to get a favorable court ruling on the legislative veto's constitutionality.

INS v. Chadha was argued twice before the Supreme Court—on February 22, 1982, and again on December 7, 1982. The decision was announced on June 23, 1983. The Court was split 7–2. The split was not a conservative versus liberal one. The majority included Chief Justice Warren E. Burger and Justices Sandra Day O'Connor, Thurgood Marshall, William I. Brennan, John Paul Stevens, and Harry A. Blackmun. Justice Lewis F. Powell wrote a concurrence and Justices Byron R. White and William H. Rehnquist wrote separate dissents.

In what a *New York Times* editorial called a "supremely simple" decision, Chief Justice Burger, "writing like a patient schoolmaster," explained the Court's reasoning in familiar and basic terms. "Remember what we all learned in social studies about how laws are made? Well," the editorial continued, "that's just how it should still work." As Burger had pointed out, the Constitution provides "a single, finely wrought and exhaustively considered procedure" for exercise of the legislative power of the federal government. "Explicit and unambiguous provisions of the Constitution," he went on, "prescribe and define the respective functions of the Congress and of the Executive in the legislative process." Any actions taken by either house, if "they contain matter which is properly to be regarded as legislative in character and effect," must conform with the constitutionality designed legislative process that includes bicameral passage and presentment to the president.

Burger went on to spell out precisely what the Court would consider "legislative in nature." Legislative action is any action that has the "purpose and effect of altering the legal rights, duties, and relations of persons outside the legislative branch." So broad a definition would encompass all the legislative veto provisions on the statute books—from the budget act to the arms sales to all the regulatory acts. The first few lines of Powell's concurrence tells it all: "The Court's decision based on the Presentment Clauses . . . apparently will invalidate every use of the legislative veto. The breadth of this holding gives one pause." Powell's opinion presented a far more narrow analysis, akin to Kennedy's appeals court decision.

In a vehement dissent, White defended the legislative veto as "an important if not indispensable political invention that allows the president and Congress to resolve major constitutional policy differences, assures the ac-

GOVERNMENTAL ORGANIZATION, POWER, AND PROCEDURE

countability of independent regulatory agencies, and preserves Congress's control over law-making." White attacked the majority decision for its lack of judicial restraint. "[T]he apparent sweep of the Court's decision today is regrettable. . . . To strike an entire class of statutes based on consideration of a somewhat atypical and more readily indictable exemplar of the class is irresponsible."

There was no other law with a legislative veto anything like the immigration law veto that gave Congress the power to overturn a quasi-judicial decision of an agency. Nonetheless, the Supreme Court chose *Chadha* to rid the world of the legislative veto. Why? Why did the Court pick so narrow a case to rule so broadly?

The Supreme Court does not explain why it rules, but a fair guess is that it was out of fear of the success of Levitas's campaign. Review of administrative rule-making and order-making (what Chadha was involved with) is today one of the Court's prime functions. Two decades of slow progress toward judicializing (i.e., formalizing) the rule-making process to make it more reviewable by courts was threatened with undoing by behind-the-door, off-the-record negotiations. What would the Court do if faced with a challenge to a rule that had not been vetoed by Congress? Would Congress's failure to veto mean endorsement? Where would that leave the Court in its role to interpret the meaning of laws, since most regulations would not be vetoed? Had Congress used its legislative veto powers with more restraint, perhaps the Court would have exercised more restraint as well. As long as legislative vetoes were applied sparingly and were confined to foreign affairs or special domestic problems like budget impoundments, courts were unlikely to become involved in the interbranch struggle even though the constitutionality of the legislative veto device had long been open to question.

A narrow ruling like Judge Kennedy's or Justice Powell's balancing the due process protections of the individual against Congress's power over law-making and oversight of the executive would not knock out the troublesome vetoes over regulations. The Court would have been inundated with case-by-case challenges.

It was easier to get it over quickly. Still there were two other cases before the Supreme Court by the 1983 Term—a challenge to a congressional veto of a used-car rule intended to protect consumers from devious used-car dealers, *Consumer Union of United States, Inc. v. Federal Trade Commission*, and a challenge to a one-house veto of an incremental gas-pricing rule that had been intended to protect home owners against the increases in gas prices brought about by natural gas deregulation, *Consumer Energy Council of America v. Federal Energy Regulatory Commission*. The only answer to why the Court did not choose one of these more appropriate cases seems to be that neither had yet been argued, and the Court wanted to be done with it. Two weeks after the *Chadha* decision, the Court ruled without argument and without further comment that the legislative vetoes in both these cases to be unconstitutional.

In the years since the decisions invalidating the legislative veto, the debate over the implications and effects of the loss of the veto has continued. So, too, has the debate over the prudence of the Court's involvement in the dispute and the wisdom of the majority's opinion. There is no doubt, though, that *Chadha* has had, and will continue to have, an effect on constitutional law. Dozens of cases have been brought relying on the strict construction of the nature of the legislative power as interpreted by the majority in *Chadha*. *Bowsher v. Synar* (1986), the challenge to the constitutionality of the Budget Deficit Reduction Act (otherwise known as the Gramm-Rudman-Hollings Act) and *Lowry v. Reagan*, a challenge to the president's use of U.S. troops to protect shipping in the Persian Gulf are two examples among many. *Chadha* may have eliminated the legislative veto as a constitutional tool of congressional control over the executive branch, but the incentives for involvement in the regulatory process and the desire to find ways to influence presidential decisions have not disappeared. Congress has been and will continue to be inventive as it searches for constitutional alternatives to the veto. No doubt challenges to the new inventions will one day find there way into the courts as well.

Selected Bibliography

Bruff, H.H., and E. Gelhorn. "Congressional Control of Administrative Regulations: A Study of Legislative Vetoes." *Harvard Law Review* 90 (1977): 1369–1440.

Craig, B.H. *Chadha: The Story of an Epic Constitutional Struggle*. New York: Oxford University Press, 1988.

Fisher, L. "A Political Context for Legislative Vetoes." *Political Science Quarterly* 93 (1978): 241–54.

B. Federalism

JUDICIAL REVIEW OF STATE COURT DECISIONS

by Richard E. Ellis
Department of History
State University of New York at Buffalo

Martin v. Hunter's Lessee, 1 Wheaton 304 (1816) [U.S. Supreme Court]

Between the American Revolution and the Civil War the central constitutional issue in American history was how to distribute power between the federal government and the states. Although the adoption of the U.S. Constitution greatly increased the power of the national government, it did not explicitly provide a clear-cut solution to the problem. During the 1780s, under the Articles of Confederation, various states had adopted laws that circumvented the authority of the federal government. To deal with this threat, James Madison, at the Constitutional Convention in the summer of 1787, had urged that the central government explicitly be given the power to review and negate state laws. But no such provision was included in the final draft of the Constitution. The closest the Constitution came to dealing with the issue was the second paragraph of Article VI, the so-called supremacy clause, which provides: "This Constitution and the Laws of the United States which shall be made in Pursuance thereof, and all Treaties made, or which shall be made, under the Authority of the United States, shall be the Supreme Law of the Land; and the Judges in every State shall be bound thereby, any thing in the Constitution or Laws of any State to the Contrary notwithstanding."

This language, however, did not settle the matter, for it indicated only that federal law should be supreme over state law. It did not clearly indicate what legally constituted body or tribunal should determine when state actions subverted the authority of the federal government. To clarify matters, when the first Congress of the United States adopted the Judiciary Act of 1789, which implemented the judiciary provisions of the Constitution, it in-cluded a provision known as Section 25, which gave the U.S. Supreme Court the power to review all state laws and state court decisions that involved the U.S. Constitution, federal laws, and treaties. Making the Supreme Court the final arbiter in disputes between the federal government and the states proved to be a highly controversial solution. Debate over the constitutionality of Section 25 raged for nearly a century after its adoption. *Martin v. Hunter's Lessee* (1816) is the most important Supreme Court decision to deal with this problem, and is particularly significant because the Court's decision expresses what eventually became the prevailing view about the nature of the federal union and the authority of the Supreme Court.

Martin v. Hunter's Lessee had deep and complicated roots that went back to the Revolution. Involved was the estate of Thomas, Sixth Lord Fairfax, consisting of over five million acres of extremely valuable lands, which had been a kind of proprietary colony in the Northern Neck district between the Potomac and Rappahonnick rivers in western Virginia. Fairfax was a citizen of Virginia, but when he died in 1781 he bequeathed his property to his nephew Denny Martin, a British subject who had never taken up residence in the Old Dominion. When this occurred, Virginia, under the leadership of Patrick Henry, denied the right of an alien to inherit property and passed legislation that removed other special privileges, such as various tax exemptions, that were attached to the land. The state also moved to assume ownership of the waste or unappropriated lands of the estate, and, by 1786, had even begun to sell them. Martin challenged these developments in a number of law suits, arguing the validity of his uncle's will. He also pointed out that the peace treaty of 1783 contained a clause prohibiting the confiscation of loyalist estates.

The state essentially ignored these developments and in 1789 proceeded to sell some of the lands it had confiscated from the Fairfax estate to David Hunter, a speculator. Martin, however, denied Hunter's title to the land, and a lawsuit followed. The state district court at Winchester in 1794 found for Martin, and Hunter appealed the decision to the state's highest court, the court of appeals in Richmond. But before a decision was reached, Martin sold a sizeable portion of his claim to a syndicate of speculators, which included John Marshall and his brother James. Shortly after this, in 1796, the state legislature offered a compromise that had been engineered by Marshall: Martin and the syndicate that purchased the land from him would relinquish title to the undeveloped or waste lands in the Northern Neck in return for clear title to the manor lands that Lord Fairfax had developed for his personal use. This apparently was acceptable to both sides and the compromise was enacted into law. In all probability, this is the way the lands were finally allocated.

This, however, did not end the dispute. The case was never dropped from the docket of the Virginia Court of Appeals, and it was eventually revived by Spencer Roane, Patrick Henry's son-in-law, who in his own right had become a prominent political figure and a member of the Virginia Court of Appeals. He was determined to see the fundamental constitutional issues raised by the case resolved in Virginia's favor. Therefore, after a long delay, in *Hunter v. Fairfax* (1810) the Virginia Court of Appeals reversed the lower court's decision and found for Hunter, who had purchased his land from the state. The Martin-Marshall group responded by appealing the decision to the U.S. Supreme Court on a writ of error, probably signed by Marshall himself, under Section 25 of the Judiciary Act of 1789.

Because of his involvement in the case, Marshall removed himself. The decision in *Fairfax Devisee v. Hunter's Lessee* (1813) was written by Justice Joseph Story, an extreme nationalist, who spoke for a three-member majority with only one justice dissenting. Story reversed the decision of the Virginia Court of Appeals. He rejected the legitimacy of the various statutes under which Virginia had taken custody of the Fairfax lands and argued that Martin's inheritance not only was protected by the common law of descent but also by the anticonfiscation clause of the peace treaty, which had been recently reenforced by a similar provision in the Jay Treaty of 1794. He made no mention of the legislative Act of Compromise of 1796. Story then "commanded" the Virginia Court of Appeals to adopt such proceedings as were necessary to implement the mandate of the Supreme Court.

This was the moment Roane had been waiting for. Under his leadership, the Virginia Court of Appeals decided to respond to what it called "the mandate" handed down by the Supreme Court. To help it deal with the matter, the Virginia court "invited the members of the bar to investigate it," and it was discussed "in a full and able manner." Following this, "it received the long and deliberate consideration of the Court" itself.

The Court's decision in *Hunter v. Martin, devisees of Fairfax* (1815) was handed down shortly after the end of the War of 1812 and was unanimous: Section 25 of the Judiciary Act of 1798—allowing appeals from state courts to the Supreme Court in matters dealing with the Constitution, federal laws, or treaties—was unconstitutional. The four judges delivered their opinions *seriatim* ("in sequence," with no clear "opinion of the Court"), but they said much the same thing. They reiterated the position the state had taken on the origins and the nature of the Union in the Virginia resolutions of 1798 and the Report of the Virginia Legislature in 1799. The Constitution, they argued, was the product of a compact made between the different states in 1787–88. They denied that the Supreme Court was either the exclusive or the final arbiter of constitutional questions, and they argued instead that the states should act as sentinels upon the activities of the federal government. They believed these principles had been validated by Jefferson's election in 1800. They further argued that sovereignty was divided between the states and the national government, and that the latter was one of limited and specifically delegated powers. Since the U.S. Constitution had provided no final umpire on constitutional questions nor specifically granted to Congress the power to bestow such a role on the Supreme Court, the federal and state courts had the right to rule on such questions for themselves, and neither could bind the other on matters before it. In no other way could the states be protected from encroachments by the central government. "No calamity," it was asserted, "would be more to be deplored by the American people than a vortex in the general government, which should engulf and sweep away, every vestige of the state constitutions." In entering judgment, the Virginia Court of Appeals ruled that the U.S. Supreme Court did not have jurisdiction in the case or authority over "this court, and that obedience to its mandate be declined by the Court."

The Supreme Court responded the next year in *Martin v. Hunter's Lessee* (1816). Once again Marshall did not sit, although Story who wrote the majority opinion later indicated he "concurred in every word." The decision was carefully crafted, strenuously argued, and incisive. At the outset Story noted: "The questions involved in the judgment are of great importance and delicacy. Perhaps it is not too much to affirm that, upon their right decision, rest some of the most solid principles which have hitherto been supposed to sustain and protect the Constitution itself." He then proceeded to a nationalist theory about the origins and nature of the Union diametrically opposed to the compact theory offered by the Virginia Court of Appeals: "The Constitution of the United States was ordained and established, not by the states in their sovereign capacities, but emphatically, as the preamble of the Constitution declares, by 'the people of the United States.'"

Story vigorously defended the constitutionality of Section 25 of the Judiciary Act of 1789 and the right of the Supreme Court to review the final judgments of state courts in cases dealing with federal questions. He argued the need for a broad construction of the Constitution that "unavoidably deals in general language," because it was expected "to endure through a long lapse of ages, the events of which were locked up in the inscrutable purpose of Providence." Because of this, Story asserted, the powers of the federal government had been ex-

pressed in "general terms leaving to the legislature, from time to time to adopt its own means to effectuate legitimate objects."

Story further argued that "the Constitution has presumed . . . that state jealousies and state interests, might sometimes obstruct, or control . . . the regular administration of justice." To prevent this, Article II of the U.S. Constitution had given the Supreme Court appellant jurisdiction in all cases involving the Constitution, federal laws, and treaties. Contrary to what the Virginia Court of Appeals asserted, the jurisdiction of the Supreme Court was not limited to cases that came from the lower federal courts but extended to all cases involving federal questions. In other words, it was the issues of the case, not the court from which it came, that gave the Supreme Court its appellant jurisdiction. Story believed this point of view was reenforced by the supremacy clause in Article VI.

According to Story, state prejudice had undermined the central government under the Articles of Confederation, and the state courts could not be allowed to be the final interpreters of the Constitution, for it would lead to different judgments in different states and that "these jarring and discordant judgments" would inevitably destroy the Union. Uniformity, Story was convinced, was absolutely essential for the future well-being of the nation and this could only be assured through federal judicial review of state actions. Not everyone accepted Story's arguments. For example, Thomas Jefferson and Andrew Jackson, who viewed the Supreme Court as the branch of the federal government least responsive to the wishes of the people, agreed with the position taken by the Virginia Court of Appeals. This position was most deftly put by Justice Joseph Cabell, who remarked in *Hunter v. Martin*: "It must have been foreseen that controversies would sometimes arise as to the boundaries of the two jurisdictions. Yet the Constitution has provided no umpire, has erected no tribunal by which they shall be settled. The omission proceeded, probably from the belief that such a tribunal would produce evils greater than those of the occasional collisions which it would be designed to remedy." As a consequence, the issue was to be a source of constant controversy until the Civil War settled it in the nationalists' favor.

Selected Bibliography

Beveridge, A.J. *The Life of John Marshall.* 4 vols. Boston: Houghton Mifflin Co., 1916–19.

Cullen, C., *et al.*, eds. *The Papers of John Marshall.* 5 vols. to date. Chapel Hill, NC: University of North Carolina Press, 1974–91.

Miller, F.T. "John Marshall versus Spencer Roane: A Reevaluation of *Martin v. Hunter's Lessee.*" *The Virginia Magazine of History and Biography* 96 (1988): 297–314.

Newmyer, R.K. *Supreme Court Justice Joseph Story: Statesman of the Old Republic.* Chapel Hill, NC: University of North Carolina Press, 1985.

Warren, C. "Legislative and Judicial Attacks on the Supreme Court of the United States—A History of the Twenty-Fifth Section of the Judiciary Act." *American Law Review* 47 (1913): 1–34, 161–89.

IMPLIED FEDERAL POWERS: PANDORA'S BOX?

by Maxwell Bloomfield
Columbus School of Law
Catholic University of America

McCulloch v. Maryland, 4 Wheaton 316 (1819) [U.S. Supreme Court]

Many Americans in the early nineteenth century hated banks. To some they represented privileged corporations of the sort that had historically oppressed the common folk in England. Others, of a more pragmatic disposition, conceded the utility of a few small banks, but fiercely opposed the creation of large ones. The unsavory practices of one giant institution—the second Bank of the United States (BUS)—caused widespread public anger and demands for political retaliation. In the landmark case *McCulloch v. Maryland,* the U.S. Supreme Court had to determine not only the legality of a national bank, but also the appropriate test to be applied to any federal power not specifically mentioned in the U.S. Constitution. The fallout from this decision is still being felt today.

The roots of the BUS controversy stretched back to the founding period. Alexander Hamilton, the first secretary of the treasury, urged the creation of a national bank as part of a comprehensive program to stabilize the nation's economy. As Hamilton envisaged it, such a bank would be modeled in many ways on the Bank of England and would function as an arm of the federal government. It would receive and hold all federal revenue, facilitate foreign exchange transactions, regulate the practices of state banks through its discount policy, and provide a uniform currency for the entire country. Like other Hamiltonian proposals, the

bank bill aroused strong opposition in Congress, where James Madison and others charged that Congress had no constitutional authority to establish such an agency.

When the bill eventually passed by a sharply divided vote, the debate over its constitutionality shifted to the executive branch. President George Washington, uncertain whether to veto the measure, sought written opinions from Hamilton and from his secretary of state, Thomas Jefferson. The arguments of these men—classic examples of "liberal" versus "strict" constitutional construction—reappeared as major factors in *McCulloch* more than 25 years later. Persuaded by Hamilton's reasoning, Washington signed the bill, and the first BUS came into existence in 1791.

During its 20-year life, the BUS performed much as Hamilton had predicted. Under conservative management, it assisted the federal government in its fiscal operations and helped to create a favorable environment for domestic and foreign investment. It was part of the Federalist party program. However, when the Jeffersonian Republicans came to power after 1800, the bank's days were numbered. When its charter expired in 1811, a Republican Congress declined to renew it. Thus, the nation confronted the severe economic dislocations caused by the War of 1812 with no help from a central bank.

The fiscal confusion of the war years led many to reconsider the advantages of such an institution and strengthened the entrepreneurial wing of the Republican party. With the return of peace came a renewed spirit of nationalism that encouraged the bank's advocates to press for new legislation. This time they were successful. In 1816, Congress chartered a second BUS for another term of 20 years.

Like its predecessor, the new BUS was an immense undertaking. With a capitalization of $35 million, it was by far the largest corporation in the country. In addition to its home office in Philadelphia, it soon boasted of 18 branches in other cities, from Boston and Savannah on the East Coast, to New Orleans, Louisville, and Cincinnati. As before, the federal government owned one-fifth of the bank's stock and named five of its 25 directors. But the president of the United States no longer appointed the head of the bank; this officer was now chosen by the stockholders. The change reflected the increased influence of private banking lobbyists who wanted to minimize federal involvement in the bank's affairs. Although the second BUS still performed valuable services for the government without charge and remained subject (at least in theory) to U.S. Treasury supervision, it operated in most respects like any private corporation. And under the presidency of William Jones, a bankrupt Philadelphia merchant, it engaged in a frantic quest for profits at the expense of the public interest.

Jones encouraged wild speculation in BUS's stock and made no effort to curb the inflationary practices of many state banks. In the Baltimore branch of the BUS, a group of insiders, including the president, a director, and the cashier, James W. McCulloch, loaned large sums of money to themselves and their friends without adequate security, and plundered the bank's assets in other ways that reportedly cost Maryland investors between $1.7 million and $3 million. By the fall of 1818, as the country headed toward the worst depression it had yet known, Congress ordered an investigation of the BUS's affairs.

Several states, responding to popular suspicion and outrage, had already moved against the local branches of the BUS. In February 1818, the Maryland legislature passed a law that required all foreign banks or branches in the state to issue their notes henceforth on stamped paper supplied by the state. The cost of the stamps varied with the size of the notes, and ranged from ten cents to $20. Alternatively, a bank could make a single payment of $15,000 each year to the state or it could go out of business. Noncompliance was costly: $500 for each note issued on unstamped paper, the money to be divided equally between the state and whoever provided the authorities with information against an offending institution. The measure went into effect on May 1, 1818.

A few days later, John James, an informer, visited cashier McCulloch at his office to inquire about some recent unstamped notes that were circulating around Baltimore. McCulloch admitted that he had issued the notes in defiance of the new law. The state promptly brought suit against him in the Baltimore County Court to recover the prescribed penalties. McCulloch was found guilty and fined, and the case was appealed to Maryland's highest court, the court of appeals, on an agreed statement of facts. The pleadings raised two key questions: (1) did Congress have the constitutional power to incorporate a bank? and (2) if it did, was the Maryland land tax law nevertheless constitutional? When the court of appeals predictably upheld the state's taxing power, the case was forwarded to the U.S. Supreme Court on a writ of error.

Oral arguments before the Marshall Court began on February 22, 1819, and lasted for nine days. Aware of the importance of the case and of the intense public interest that it generated, the Court waived its general rule permitting only two counsel to appear on either side. Instead, three prominent lawyers represented each party. Arguing for the BUS were Daniel Webster, the magnetic orator and statesman; William Pinkney, widely regarded as the dean of the American bar; and William Wirt, the genial and erudite attorney general of the United States. Maryland retained equally impressive advocates: the scholarly and incisive Joseph Hopkinson; the brilliant Walter Jones, reputed to be a legal genius; and Luther Martin, the aging but still formidable attorney general of Maryland. Throughout the arguments spectators crowded into the small courtroom in the basement of the Capitol. "The hall was full almost to suffocation," noted Justice Joseph Story at one point, "and many went away for want of room."

On March 6, 1819, only three days after the arguments had concluded, Chief Justice John Marshall delivered the unanimous opinion of the Court. Marshall emphasized at the outset the significance of the case for future federal-state relations and the feeling of "awful responsibility" with which the justices had approached their task. He then turned to the constitutionality of the BUS, noting that its long history of public acceptance could not be "lightly disregarded."

Counsel for Maryland had themselves been somewhat apologetic about reopening the question, but pointed out that it had never been judicially determined. Moreover, they urged, the "necessity" that might have justified the creation of a national bank in 1791 no longer existed in 1816 because state banks were by then capable of providing the same range of fiscal services as a national bank. Since the Constitution did not expressly authorize Congress to create corporations, the only basis for the exercise of that power had to be found in the "necessary and proper clause" of Article I, Section 8. Following a long list of enumerated congressional powers, that clause declares that Congress may make "all laws which shall be necessary and proper for carrying into execution the foregoing powers." Defenders of states' rights and advocates of an expansive nationalism differed vehemently over the meaning of those words.

To the Maryland lawyers, as to Jefferson back in 1791, the necessary and proper clause was restrictive in its effects. Although many means might be appropriate or convenient for carrying out an enumerated power of the federal government, Congress could use only those means that were indispensably necessary to the execution of a granted power. Under the Tenth Amendment, the states retained all sovereign powers that they had not expressly conferred on the federal government in the Constitution. The power to incorporate was one such reserved power, since Congress could implement any of its enumerated powers without the help of federal corporations. As Walter Jones argued for Maryland, "The power of laying and collecting taxes implies the power of regulating the mode of assessment and collection, and of appointing revenue officers but it does not imply the power of establishing a great banking corporation, branching out into every district of the country, and inundating it with a flood of paper money. To derive such a tremendous authority from implication, would be to change the subordinate into fundamental powers; to make the implied powers greater than those which are expressly granted; and to change the whole scheme and theory of the government."

Even if the necessity for a national bank was conceded, there remained the question of the branches. They, too, would have to pass the test of indispensability, and their justification was even more doubtful than that of the parent bank. The charter, it is true, authorized the federal government to establish branches; but Congress had wrongfully delegated this vital legislative power to a small group of private individuals, the directors of the BUS. "Such an exercise of sovereign power should, at least, have the sanction of the sovereign legislature to vouch that the good of the whole requires it, that the necessity exists which justifies it," contended Joseph Hopkinson. "But will it be tolerated, that twenty directors of a trading corporation, having no object but profit, shall, in the pursuit of it, tread upon the sovereignty of the State; enter it without condescending to ask its leave; disregard, perhaps, the whole system of its policy; overthrow its institutions, and sacrifice its interests?"

Marshall rejected all of the state's arguments in his decision, relying instead on Hamilton's famous defense of the first BUS and on additional points raised by the bank's lawyers. To counter the compact theory of the Union advanced by the Maryland advocates of state sovereignty, Marshall briefly traced the history of the founding from a Federalist perspective. The American people, not the states, had created the Constitution, he affirmed. The old Confederation had been a mere "league" or "alliance" of sovereign states, without whose cooperation the central government could not act. But the people, wishing to form "a more perfect Union," had established a new frame of government that effectively divided sovereign power between the nation and the states. The

Constitution had come into existence through the action of popular ratifying conventions that functioned independently of the state governments. "The government of the Union, then," Marshall reiterated, "is emphatically, and truly, a government of the people. In form and substance it emanates from them. Its powers are granted by them, and are to be exercised directly on them, and for their benefit."

Although the federal government was limited in its powers to those enumerated in the Constitution, its authority was supreme within its allotted sphere of action. Article VI specifically declared that the Constitution and laws of the United States were "the supreme law of the land" and must prevail over conflicting state legislation. And in carrying out its prescribed sovereign powers, Congress was entitled to use any appropriate auxiliary powers that accompanied them by implication. The power to coin money thus carried with it the implied power to establish a mint. Such implied powers of execution always resulted from express grants of authority, Marshall suggested, and required no special constitutional justification.

Why, then, did the framers of the Constitution include the necessary and proper clause? Did they intend to limit Congress in the choice of means that would otherwise have been available to it for carrying out its functions? Quite the contrary, Marshall asserted. The clause represents an affirmative grant of power, an addition to the list of broad enumerated powers that preceded it in the same section. Had the framers intended it to be restrictive, they would either have placed it in a different section or phrased it in negative terms. They may well have inserted it, Marshall observed, to "remove all doubts respecting the right to legislate on that vast mass of incidental powers which must be involved in the constitution, if that instrument be not a splendid bauble."

Congress could not use its implied powers to legislate on subjects not entrusted to it by the Constitution. There had to be more than a tenuous or doubtful relationship between a proposed measure and an enumerated power to satisfy constitutional criteria; otherwise the entire federal system would be subverted and a limited government transformed into an all-powerful leviathan state. The necessary and proper clause established the essential guidelines for responsible congressional action.

Marshall denied that "necessary" meant "indispensable." In common usage it had many other meanings, he noted, including "needful," "essential," and "conducive to." The framers understood these nuances, for in Section 10 of Article I, they prohibited states from levying duties on imports and exports, except those that were "absolutely necessary" for implementing state inspection laws. By omitting the qualifying term "absolutely" in the necessary and proper clause, the framers left Congress free to select any reasonable and plainly appropriate means for carrying out its enumerated powers. Such deference to legislative discretion ensured constitutional flexibility, Marshall argued in a famous passage: "This provision is made in a constitution intended to endure for ages to come, and, consequently, to be adapted to the various *crises* of human affairs. To have prescribed the means by which government should, in all future time, execute its powers, would have been to change, entirely, the character of the instrument, and give it the properties of a legal code. It would have been an unwise attempt to provide, by immutable rules, for exigencies which, if foreseen at all, must have been seen dimly, and which can be best provided for as they occur" [emphasis in original].

In the case of the BUS, Congress had chosen to create a corporation to assist the federal government in carrying out its economic powers. The Maryland lawyers strenuously maintained that the power to incorporate was an essential element of sovereignty, a major substantive power that had been retained by the states. Marshall disagreed. There was nothing special about such a power, he insisted; every legislative act represented an exercise of sovereignty. Nor was a corporation ever created as an end in itself; it was simply a means for effecting some other object. While the framers had not directly empowered Congress to erect corporations, they had not forbidden the use of these valuable instruments when appropriate for the execution of some enumerated power. Thus, under its power to "make all needful rules and regulations" concerning the territory of the United States, Congress had established territorial governments, which were corporate bodies.

But was a national bank truly "necessary" for effectuating the fiscal operations of the federal government? Marshall made no effort to demonstrate that it was. He referred at one point to the major economic powers of Congress—to lay and collect taxes, borrow money, regulate interstate commerce, and raise and support armies and navies—but did not relate these powers to any specific functions of the BUS. "The time has passed away when it can be necessary to enter into any discussion in order to prove the importance of this instrument, as a means to effect the legitimate objects of the government," he blandly asserted. None could deny the appropriateness of the BUS, at any rate; and the degree of its necessity was a matter exclusively for congressional determination. By the same reasoning, the branches, too, were constitutional, since Congress had decided they were needed to fulfill the bank's "great duties." Their location was a subordinate matter which Congress had properly left in the hands of the directors.

While upholding the BUS's constitutionality, Marshall made it clear that the Court would strike down any future law that attempted through the necessary and proper clause to deal with a subject not entrusted to the federal government. The guidelines he proposed were carefully drafted and struck an admirable balance between the extremes of states' rights and centralization: "Let the end be legitimate, let it be within the scope of the constitution, and all means which are appropriate, which are plainly adapted to that end, which are not prohibited, but consist with the letter and spirit of the constitution, are constitutional."

The Court's ruling on this phase of the case, although unacceptable to the Maryland attorneys, could scarcely have surprised them, given the prior record of legislative and popular acceptance of a national bank. Of more pressing concern was the issue of the states' taxing power, which the advocates of state sovereignty considered fundamental to the maintenance of the federal system, as they understood it. "This is the highest attribute of sovereignty, the right to raise revenue, . . . without which no other right can be held or enjoyed," argued

Hopkinson. The Constitution expressly prohibited the states from taxing imports and exports or from levying tonnage duties. Otherwise, their taxing power was unlimited and coextensive with that of the federal government. In practice, both Congress and the state legislatures had long exercised a concurrent power to tax such subjects as liquor licenses and land. The BUS claimed immunity from the states' general taxing power on the ground that it was a federal agency; but the Maryland attorneys vigorously denied its public character.

"Strip it of its name," declared Hopkinson, "and we find it to be a mere association of individuals, putting their money into a common stock, to be loaned for profit, and to divide the gains. The government is a partner in the firm, for gain also; for, except a participation of the profits of the business, the government could have every other use of the bank without owning a dollar in it. It is not, then, a bank of the United States, if by that we mean an institution belonging to the government, directed by it, or in which it has a permanent indissoluble interest." Like any other private corporation, then, the BUS was subject to state taxation, just as state banks had to pay a federal tax on the notes they discounted.

Marshall's reply to these contentions evaded troublesome facts through appeals to reason and "principle." The states certainly retained a general taxing power, he agreed, but only with respect to property under their jurisdiction. Federal instrumentalities were created by Congress for the benefit of all the American people, and no state could constitutionally interfere with their operations. In support of this argument, Marshall pointed to a core principle that permeated the entire constitutional structure: "This great principle is, that the constitution and the laws made in pursuance thereof are supreme; that they control the constitution and laws of the respective States, and cannot be controlled by them. From this, which may be almost termed an axiom, other propositions are deduced as corollaries, on the truth or error of which, and on their application to this case, the cause has been supposed to depend. These are, 1st. that a power to create implies a power to preserve. 2nd. That a power to destroy, if wielded by a different hand, is hostile to, and incompatible with these powers to create and preserve. 3d. That where this repugnancy exists, that authority which is supreme must control, not yield to that over which it is supreme."

The Maryland tax on the notes of the BUS, thus, could not stand because it conflicted with the bank's congressional charter, the "supreme law of the land." Marshall did not examine the specific provisions of the tax measure; he did not strike it down because it was overtly confiscatory or discriminatory (although, in fact, the BUS was the only "foreign" bank doing business in Maryland). Instead, he argued that *any* state interference with the functioning of a federal agency was a usurpation of power that could eventually destroy the Union. "The power to tax involves the power to destroy," he intoned, echoing a phrase from Webster's brief. Once the principle of unlimited concurrent taxation is admitted, the states would be encouraged to carry it to its logical conclusion: "If the States may tax one instrument, employed by the government in the execution of its powers, they may tax any and every other instrument. They may tax the mail; they may tax the mint; they may tax patent rights; they may tax the papers of the custom-house; they may tax judicial process; they may tax all the means employed by the government, to an excess which would defeat all the end of government. This was not intended by the American people."

Once again, Marshall ignored the evidence presented by the Maryland lawyers to show that the BUS was essentially a private profit-making corporation rather than a genuine instrument of the federal government. As he had done in the first part of his opinion, he assumed the legitimacy of the BUS's public status without scrutinizing the terms of its charter. He did concede, in a somewhat curious afterthought, that the states might tax the property of the BUS in ways that did not impinge on its daily operations. Thus, a state might impose a nondiscriminatory tax affecting the real property of the BUS, along with all other land located in the state; or it might tax all corporate stock, including shares in the BUS, owned by Maryland citizens. The first example is compatible with the rest of the opinion, since land is a state resource that Congress did not create. But it is difficult to see why the BUS's stock, authorized

by an act of Congress, would not also be considered a means of carrying out a federal power and hence entitled to the same implied immunity from any state tax. In fact, Marshall disregarded his *dictum* in *Weston v. City Council* (1829), in which he struck down a state tax on the holders of federal securities without inquiring whether it was discriminatory.

If the states could not tax the operations of a federal agency, how could Congress claim to tax state banks? The issue had been raised by the Maryland attorneys, and Marshall discussed it at some length, despite its irrelevance. The two situations were not analogous, he maintained. When Congress taxed state banks, it acted with the consent of the representatives of those states, and its taxes had to be uniform throughout the country. But when a state attempted to tax a federal instrumentality, no such political safeguards existed. "The difference," Marshall urged, "is that which always exists, and always must exist, between the action of the whole on a part, and the action of a part on the whole—between the laws of a government declared to be supreme, and those of a government which, when in opposition to those laws, is not supreme."

By the time the *McCulloch* decision was announced, the BUS was under new management and the worst abuses had been corrected. The congressional investigating committee had uncovered evidence of much wrongdoing and issued a report that was sharply critical of the bank's policies. It did not, however, recommend the revocation of its charter. In January 1819, a few weeks before the Supreme Court began its hearing of *McCulloch*, William Jones stepped down from the presidency of the BUS. His successor, Langdon Cheves, was a competent and conservative lawyer from South Carolina, who pressed for immediate reform and a thorough internal housecleaning. A flurry of resignations by BUS officials ensued. According to one estimate, one-half the branch office directors resigned, and some faced charges of criminal misconduct.

In Baltimore, McCulloch, the compliant cashier, was fired, and his cronies—branch president James Buchanan and director George Williams—resigned in disgrace. The BUS subsequently prosecuted them in the Maryland courts for conspiring to defraud its shareholders. Pinkney, who had so eloquently represented the BUS in *McCulloch*, now defended its former employees with equal success. They had merely displayed "the almost universal ambition to get forward," Pinkney explained; and the failure of their speculations had been due to external factors, such as declining foreign investment, which they could not anticipate. Had their BUS stock risen in value, they "would have been looked upon as nobles, as the architects of their fortunes . . . ." Such appeals to the cult of the self-made man, combined with the legal technicalities associated with the common-law crime of conspiracy, won acquittal for Pinkney's clients on two separate occasions. Only one dissenting judge reminded the public that the defendants had in fact "taken from the funds of the office a large sum of money, which they converted to their own use," and had "failed to return to the Bank a cent of their spoil."

Ironically, the BUS's clean-up efforts only made matters worse in the eyes of some states. By tightening credit and requiring specie payments from state banks, the BUS contributed to a rash of bankruptcies and mortgage foreclosures, especially in the South and West. As an immense amount of property in Cincinnati fell into the BUS's hands, the Ohio legislature moved to rid the state of the hated institution forever. In February 1819, the legislature imposed a prohibitory tax of $50,000 on each of the BUS's two branches in the state and directed the state auditor to compel payment by seizing the funds in the branch vaults, if necessary. Ignoring the *McCulloch* decision, state officials ransacked the Chillicothe branch office seven months later and carried off $100,000 in specie for deposit in the state treasury at Columbus. In *Osborn v. Bank of the United States* (1824), Marshall reaffirmed his holding in *McCulloch*, and the BUS controversy died with the return of prosperity. The BUS continued under capable management until 1836, when President Andrew Jackson's bitter hostility led to the nonrenewal of its charter. Thereafter, the nation did without a national banking system until the Civil War era.

The advocates of state sovereignty correctly perceived that Marshall's expansive reading of the necessary and proper clause could legiti-mize extraordinary assertions of federal power in the future. Although *McCulloch* had little impact until the Civil War, it later played an essential role in redefining the scope of national power and justifying the emergence of the modern welfare state. In the late 1930s, the Supreme Court invoked *McCulloch* to sustain the regulatory programs of the New Deal; three decades later excerpts from Marshall's opinion appeared in decisions validating the Voting Rights Act of 1965 and the public accommodations provisions of the Civil Rights Act of 1964. The extreme centralization feared by advocates of states' rights has not occurred, however. Perhaps the two-party system, with its built-in bias toward conservatism and compromise, has done more than any verbal formula to preserve the spirit of moderation advocated by *McCulloch*.

In the area of intergovernmental tax immunity, the *McCulloch* legacy has been less positive. Impressed by Marshall's sweeping *dictum* concerning the destructive power of taxation, later Supreme Courts expanded the principle of implied immunity to encompass a bewildering variety of federal and state activities and personnel. Until the late 1930s, for example, states could not tax the salaries of federal officials; and, conversely, Congress could not tax the income of state authorities. Since *Graves v. New York ex rel. O'Keefe* (1939), however, the Supreme Court has promoted a more "cooperative federalism" by striking down such restrictive precedents; and judges now scrutinize carefully all new claims of immunity. Justice Oliver Wendell Holmes, Jr., anticipated the departure from Marshall's absolutist approach to the immunity question as early as 1928, when he observed in a dissenting opinion: "In those days it was not recognized as it is today that most of the distinctions of the law are distinctions of degree. If the States had any power it was assumed that they had all power, and that the necessary alternative was to deny it altogether. . . . The power to tax is not the power to destroy while this Court sits."

Selected Bibliography

Beveridge, A.J. *The Life of John Marshall.* 4 vols. Boston: Houghton Mifflin Co., 1916–19.

Currie, D.P. *The Constitution in the Supreme Court: The First Hundred Years, 1789–1888.* Chicago: University of Chicago Press, 1985.

Gunther, G., ed. *John Marshall's Defense of* McCulloch v. Maryland. Stanford, CA: Stanford University Press, 1969.

Hammond, B. *Banks and Politics in America From the Revolution to the Civil War.* Princeton, NJ: Princeton University Press, 1957.

Pious, H.J., and G.E. Baker. "*McCulloch v. Maryland*:

Right Principle, Wrong Case." *Stanford Law Review* 9 (July 1957): 710–30.

Smith, W.B. *Economic Aspects of the Second Bank of the United States.* Cambridge, MA: Harvard University Press, 1953.

White, G.E. *The Marshall Court and Cultural Change, 1815–35.* New York: Macmillan Publishing Co., 1988.

JUDICIAL REVIEW OF STATE COURT DECISIONS: YET ANOTHER ROUND

by Richard E. Ellis
Department of History
State University of New York at Buffalo

Cohens v. Virginia, 6 Wheaton 264 (1821) [U.S. Supreme Court]

The constitutionality of Section 25 of the Judiciary Act of 1789 and the right of the U.S. Supreme Court to act as the final arbiter in disputes between the federal and state governments were the sources of constant controversy in the years between the adoption of the Constitution and the Civil War. Although the Supreme Court had forcefully dealt with these questions in *Martin v. Hunter's Lessee* (1816) and *McCulloch v. Maryland* (1819), several states rejected these decisions as dangerously nationalist in their implications and the matter remained unsettled for many years. Despite this opposition, Chief Justice John Marshall refused to back down. When *Cohens v. Virginia* arose, he took the opportunity to restate in very strong terms the High Court's claim to have jurisdiction and to be the ultimate court of appeals in controversies between the central government and the states that involved the powers of the federal government.

The case began when Philip I. and Mendes Cohen were tried, convicted, and fined $100 by the quarter sessions court of the borough of Norfolk for selling lottery tickets in violation of a Virginia law prohibiting the sale of such tickets not authorized by the state. The Cohen brothers appealed the decision to the U.S. Supreme Court under Section 25 of the Judiciary of 1789. They argued that their lottery had been incorporated in Washington, D.C., under an act of Congress, which made it a national lottery not bound by state laws. The case immedi-

ately took on national significance when a number of prominent attorneys issued a public statement in support of the Cohens' claim that national corporations were exempt from state restrictions. Their argument had profound nationalist implications: "It would indeed, be a strange anomaly, if what Congress had created, or authorized to be created, in a valid manner, ... could be considered and treated by a state as the subject of a criminal traffic; ... The power of the union, constitutionally executed, knows no locality within the boundaries of the union, and can encounter no geographical impediments; its march is through the union, or it is nothing but a name. The states have no existence relative to the effect of the powers delegated to congress save only where their assent or instrumentality is required, or permitted, by the constitution itself."

The case raised, once again, the contentious question of the right of the U.S. Supreme Court to review acts of state legislatures and the decisions of state courts. Responding to a summons by Chief Justice Marshall that "cited and admonished" the state to appear before the Supreme Court in *Cohens v. Virginia*, the governor of Virginia, Thomas Mann Randolph, raised the matter in his annual address to the legislature in late 1820. The legislature proceeded to issue a special report and a series of resolutions that denied the authority of the Supreme Court to hear the case. The report restated the principles laid down in the Kentucky and Virginia resolutions: the Constitution was the product of a compact made by the states in 1787–88. It denied that the Supreme Court was either the exclusive or the final arbiter of constitutional disputes. It reiterated the belief, particularly prevalent in the Old Dominion, that the federal and state governments represented distinct and completely separate sovereignties. It argued the position taken by the Virginia Court of Appeals in *Hunter v. Martin, devisees of Fairfax* (1815) that the Supreme Court did not have the power to abrogate the judgments of state tribunals: "The word *'supreme'* is descriptive of the federal tribunal, is relative, not absolute; and evidently implies that the supremacy bestowed upon the supreme court is *over the inferior courts to be ordained and established by congress*; and not *over the state courts*" [emphasis in original].

The case was heard in February 1821. The lawyers for Virginia were instructed by the legislature to confine their arguments exclusively to the jurisdictional question. They asserted Virginia's sovereignty and denied the authority of the Supreme Court to hear the case. They also claimed that the Eleventh Amendment prohibited the federal courts from taking jurisdiction in a case without the state's explicit permission. The attorneys for the Cohen brothers, on the other hand, stressed the precedent established in *Martin v. Hunter's Lessee* and argued that the people not the states had created the Constitution, and that federal judicial control over state encroachments was absolutely necessary if the Union were to be maintained.

Two weeks later, on March 3, 1821, Marshall handed down his decision for a unanimous Court. It was a particularly eloquent restatement and elaboration of the basic principles of constitutional nationalism that had been enunciated in *Martin v. Hunter's Lessee*: "The American States as well as the American people, have believed a close and firm Union to be essential to their liberty and to their happiness. They have been taught by experience, that the Union cannot exist without a government for the whole; and they have been taught by the same experience that this government would be a mere shadow, that must disappoint all their hopes, unless invested with large portions of that sovereignty which belongs to independent

states. Under the influence of this opinion and thus instructed by experience, the American people, in the conventions of their respective states, adopted the present constitution. . . .

"This is the authoritative language of the American people, and, if gentlemen please, of the American States. It marks, with lines too strong to be mistaken, the characteristic distinction between the government of the Union and those of the states. The general government, though limited as to its objects, is supreme with respect to those objects. This principle is a part of the constitution; and if there be any who deny its necessity, none can deny its authority."

Marshall argued that the jurisdiction of the Supreme Court depended on the nature of the cause and not on the particular forum in which it was heard on the lower level. This included all cases in law and equity, under the Constitution, laws of the federal government, and treaties of the United States. "America," he pointed out, "has chosen to be, in many respects, and to many purposes, a nation; and for all these purposes, her government is complete; to all these objects it is competent. The people have declared, that in the exercise of all powers given for these objects it is supreme. It can, then, in effecting these objects legitimately control all individuals or governments within the American territory."

Marshall took explicit issue with Virginia's argument that the federal and state courts were distinct and that no appeal existed from state court decisions to the Supreme Court. Marshall responded that this would lead to chaos. He argued, "[T]he necessity of uniformity, as well as correctness in expounding the constitution and laws of the United States, would itself suggest the propriety of vesting in some single tribunal the power of deciding, in the last resort, all cases in which they are involved." Finally, Marshall dismissed Virginia's claim that the Eleventh Amendment exempted the state from federal jurisdiction in this case. The chief justice pointed out that the present action had been initiated by the state against individuals, not the other way around, and that therefore Virginia could not claim immunity under the Eleventh Amendment.

Having used broad nationalist principles to sustain the jurisdiction of the Supreme Court in *Cohens v. Virginia*, the Court proceeded to hear the case on its merits. The central question was whether the act of Congress authorizing a lottery in the District of Columbia had created a truly national corporation with the power to operate within individual states without their permission. Marshall argued that this raised two basic questions: what was the intent of Congress when it passed the law, and was it constitutional? Marshall, again for a unanimous Court, ruled that no evidence existed to indicate that Congress intended to create a national lottery or to authorize the sale of lottery tickets in states where they had been declared illegal. This was an important sop to Virginia, but it was not entirely satisfactory to the proponents of states' rights. For Marshall had ruled only that the particular act under question had not created a national lottery; he did not confront the more fundamental issue of whether Congress had the constitutional right to use its powers to legislate for the District of Columbia to create national corporations, immune from state regulations, because at this point it was "merely speculative." But the implication was clear: carefully constructed legislation for the District of Columbia could be used to create national corporations. As Marshall observed, "The act incorporating the city of Washington is unquestionably, of universal obligation; but the extent of the corporate powers conferred by that act, is to be determined by those considerations which belong to the case."

The decision was denounced in Virginia. Spencer Roane took the lead. He believed the *Cohens* decision "negated the idea that the American states have a real existence, or are to be considered in any sense, as sovereign and independent states." He attacked federal judicial review of state decisions and the doctrine of implied powers as undermining the concept of true federalism through the idea that the states were subordinate to the national government. He argued, "[I]f this power of decision is once conceded to either party, the equilibrium established by the Constitution is destroyed, and the compact exists thereafter but in name." Strong support for this point of view came from John Taylor, whose book *Tyranny Unmasked*

(1822) denounced the Supreme Court because its decisions consolidated power in the hands of the national government, and because it had become a spokesman for a moneyed aristocracy by defending corporations and special privileges. Thomas Jefferson privately encouraged Roane and Taylor to keep up their assault on the Court and excoriated the *Cohens* decision for being mainly "extra-judicial" in its nationalist pronouncements. The Court, he claimed, could have simply decided the case on its merits and refrained from engaging in its exposition of the origins and nature of the Union. He believed the Court had acted as "an irresponsible body," in order to usurp power from the states and to create a "consolidated government." James Madison, on the other hand, was more restrained, for while he recognized that "the Court had a definite disposition to amplify the authorities of the Union at the expense of the states," he indicated that in matters of conflict between the states and the federal government that the Supreme Court should be the final arbiter, and he declined to get involved in the conflict.

Reacting to these criticisms, Marshall observed, "In Virginia the tendency of things verges rapidly to the destruction of the government . . . ." This was an overreaction by the chief justice. Although Virginia's denunciation of the various nationalist decisions handed down by the Supreme Court in the second decade of the nineteenth century, and especially in *Cohens v. Virginia*, was strident and aggressive, it never threatened to go beyond the level of sharp intellectual debate. It was never suggested that the authority of the federal government should be obstructed or forcibly resisted. Roane, at the beginning of his "Algernon Sydney" essays, which spearheaded the attack on the Court's decision in *Cohens v. Virginia*, stated, "I ask from you no revolutions, but what consists in the preservation of an excellent Constitution. I require from you no insurrection, but that of a frequent recurrence to fundamental principles."

The most basic issue raised in the debate between the proponents of states' rights in the Old Dominion and the Supreme Court was the nationalist claim that the Court should be the final arbiter in conflicts between the federal government and the states. In denying this authority to the Court, Roane, Taylor, Jefferson, and others raised extremely important questions, which even today are not amenable to easy answers. Since this power was not explicitly provided for in the Constitution, where did it come from? Should the Supreme Court be allowed to arrogate this power to itself? What exactly was the relationship of the Court to the will of the people, especially since its members were appointed for life tenure during good behavior and were removable only by resignation, death, or impeachment? Was it proper for the Court to hold its discussions in secret and to hide internal dissent by handing down unanimous decisions? Most important, states' rights advocates doubted the Supreme Court could be an impartial arbiter in disputes between the federal government and the states, since it was a creature of the Constitution and a part of the federal government itself so that, by increasing the powers of the central government, it would be increasing its own powers.

The controversy over Section 25 of the Judiciary Act of 1789 and the Supreme Court's claim to be the final arbiter in federal-state dis-putes was not settled by *Cohens v. Virginia*. The dispute raged on throughout the first half of the nineteenth century, and the matter was finally resolved only when the proponents of states' rights, as well as the South, were vanquished in the Civil War. At this point, Marshall's decision in *Cohens v. Virginia* provided not only a significant precedent but also very important arguments that were used to undergird a nationalist interpretation of the nature of the Union.

Selected Bibliography

Beveridge, A.J. *The Life of John Marshall*. 4 vols. Boston: Houghton Mifflin Co., 1916–19.

Haines, C.G. *The Role of the Supreme Court in American Government and Politics, 1789–1835*. Berkeley, CA: University of California Press, 1944.

Luce, W.R. "The Cohen Brothers of Baltimore: From Lotteries to Banking." *Maryland Historical Magazine* 68 (Fall, 1973): 288–308.

Warren, C. "Legislative and Judicial Attacks on the Supreme Court of the United States—A History of the Twenty-Fifth Section of the Judiciary Act." *American Law Review* 47 (1913): 1–34, 161–89.

White, G.E. *The Marshall Court and Cultural Change, 1815–35*. New York: Macmillan Publishing Co., 1988.

C. Judicial Procedure

A REBUKE TO THE COURT

by Robert S. Lambert
Department of History
Clemson University

Chisholm v. Georgia, 1 Dallas 419 (1793) [U.S. Supreme Court]

This is the first important decision handed down by the U.S. Supreme Court under the newly adopted U.S. Constitution. Reaction to the decision was unfavorable and led almost immediately to the introduction in the Senate of a constitutional amendment to set aside the Court's interpretation of a portion of the federal judicial power granted by the Constitution.

During the American Revolution, agents of the state of Georgia had purchased clothing, blankets, and other items from Robert Farquhar, a merchant of Charleston, South Carolina. Farquhar delivered the merchandise but was not paid for the goods. After Farquhar died in 1784, his executor, Alexander Chisholm of Charleston, acting for a minor heir, sought payment from the Georgia legislature. The legislature rejected Chisholm's claim because the state had already paid its agents for the goods. Unable to collect from the agents, who were dead or bankrupt, Chisholm sought redress in the newly established federal courts.

The Constitutional Convention of 1787 had conferred upon the federal courts jurisdiction over "Controversies . . . between a State and Citizens of another State; . . . and between a State, or the Citizens thereof, and foreign States, Citizens or Subjects." Inserted by its Committee of Detail in its report to the full convention, that body approved the specific provision for jurisdiction between states and citizens of other states with little debate.

In contrast, the laws of the states generally followed the long-established principle in English law of "sovereign immunity" (i.e., that the ruler could not be sued without his consent). Despite their claims of popular sovereignty, and the absence of a king, the states had adopted this doctrine for themselves after independence.

While the states rarely permitted suits against themselves, suits against individual officials were usually accepted by state courts. Nevertheless, proposals to change the jurisdiction of the federal courts were not among the constitutional amendments that the First Congress approved and sent to the states for ratification.

In February 1791, Chisholm sued Georgia (*Farquhar's Executor v. Georgia*) in the U.S. Circuit Court for the District of Georgia to recover the debt—equivalent to $169,633.33 in greatly inflated Continental currency—and damages. The court, consisting of Justice James Iredell of the U.S. Supreme Court and a district judge, rejected the suit on grounds that a state could not be sued by a citizen of another state.

Chisholm then turned to the U.S. Supreme Court, filing an action in *assumpsit* (i.e., a contractual remedy) to recover $500,000 from Georgia. When Georgia was ordered to appear at the August 1792 Term, it refused to attend, and the Court postponed action until its next Term. In February 1793, *Chisholm v. Georgia* was argued before the Court. Although Georgia again refused to appear, the Court handed down its decision two weeks later.

Edmund Randolph, attorney general of the United States, presented the case for the plaintiff. He argued that under the U.S. Constitution and the Judiciary Act of 1789, the Court had jurisdiction over suits by a citizen of one state against another state. The Court apparently accepted this argument, because by a 4–1 margin, in separate written opinions, it found for Chisholm, and ordered the state to show cause at the next Term why the judgment should not be carried out.

The members of the Supreme Court, all appointed by President Washington, had supported the adoption of the Constitution and were adherents of the emerging Federalist party. Chief Justice John Jay of New York was a strong nationalist and critic of state sovereignty; James Wilson, as a member of the Constitutional Convention and its Committee of Detail that framed the judicial article, had advocated greatly increased powers for the central government; and former state judges John Blair of Virginia and William Cushing of Massachusetts were consistent, if less conspicuous, nationalists. Justice James Iredell, a moderate Federalist from North Carolina who had participated in the judgment against Chisholm in the circuit court, was the dissenter.

For Jay, the language of the preamble to the Constitution was sufficient: in "We the people of the United States," he found clear evidence that the United States was a nation of individuals and not a group of sovereign states; and the provision that the new government was to "establish justice" marked clearly for Jay the path of duty for the federal judiciary. It was Wilson's view that after independence was declared, the sovereignty of the Crown had passed directly to the people of the whole country; since the adoption of the Constitution, the states existed merely for certain limited and local purposes. The concurring opinions of Blair and Cushing, while less philosophical and sweeping, also found ample constitutional justification for federal jurisdiction over *Chisholm*.

Iredell's dissent was important because of the subsequent action by Congress to negate the effect of the majority opinion. Although a member of the Constitutional Convention and a supporter of ratification, Iredell certainly was aware that his own North Carolina had only belatedly ratified the Constitution and that state rights' sentiment remained strong there. His opinion took the ground that it was up to Congress to implement the powers granted by the Constitution. But because Congress had failed to give specific authority for the federal judiciary to hear cases against states by outside individuals, the states retained jurisdiction over such suits.

When the *Chisholm* decision was rendered, Georgia was ordered to either appear or be judged in default. Counsel for the state did appear in February 1794, but the Court ruled

unanimously, Iredell absent, that judgment be entered and a jury be impaneled at the next Term to assess damages. Because the issue had entered the political arena, however, the execution of the judgment was postponed each Term until cleared from the Court's docket in 1798.

Congress reacted quickly to the *Chisholm* decision. A constitutional amendment to void it was introduced in the Senate two days after the judgment was delivered, but it was not acted upon in the closing days of the Second Congress. In the nine months that passed before the Third Congress convened, several state legislatures passed resolutions urging their members of Congress to seek a constitutional amendment to negate the decision. Displaying remarkable unity in a period of intense and rising partisanship, the Senate, voting 23–2, and the House of Representatives, 81–9, agreed on a proposed amendment and sent it to the states for ratification. Its language was unequivocal: "The judicial power of the United States shall not be construed to extend to any suit in law or equity, commenced or prosecuted against one of the United States by Citizens of another State, or by Citizens or Subjects of a Foreign State," and was a clear rebuke to the majority in the *Chisholm* decision. Despite the slow communications of that time, within less than a year the legislatures of 12 of the existing 15 states ratified what became the Eleventh Amendment. Some states were slow to certify their action on the amendment, and it did not go into effect until 1798.

This quick overturning of the Court's position showed that the *Chisholm* decision had violated the generally understood role of the states in the federal system created by the Constitution. Ten members of Congress who had been delegates to the Constitutional Convention voted for the Eleventh Amendment. The overwhelming vote against the Court's interpretation demonstrated more than mere sympathy for Georgia; suits by outsiders and foreigners against six other states were awaiting adjudication before the Supreme Court when it handed down the *Chisholm* decision.

The adoption of the Eleventh Amendment had the immediate effect of removing the pending suits against states from the Court's docket.

The prestige of the Court was not enhanced by its obvious inability to enforce its own decisions, although its ruling in *Chisholm* may have energized some states to seek settlements with claimants. The assumption of most state debts by Congress in the early 1790s and agreements made with Great Britain under the Jay Treaty had already sharply reduced the likelihood that further suits would be brought by outside claimants against states in the federal courts.

Nevertheless, the long-term effect of the Eleventh Amendment was less restrictive than might be supposed. First, Iredell's opinion in *Chisholm* merely stated that Congress had failed to authorize the specific contractual remedy sought. More importantly, under the leadership of John Marshall in the early nineteenth century, the Supreme Court rendered several decisions that narrowed the scope of the Eleventh Amendment. In *Cohens v. Virginia* (1821), it held that an individual convicted in a state court did not violate the Eleventh Amendment by removing his case to the Supreme Court in order to challenge the constitutionality of the state law in question. In particular, cases involving state laws adversely affecting private property rights, such as *Fletcher v. Peck* (1810),

might be heard in federal courts if such laws violated the constitutional restriction that "no State shall pass any . . . Law impairing the Obligation of Contracts." And a suit against a state official was allowed in *Osborn v. Bank of the United States* (1824) because, on the record, the state of Ohio was not an actual party in the case.

As for the effort to recover what Robert Farquhar was owed, his son-in-law, Daniel Trezevant, accepted Georgia securities in 1794 as a settlement in full of the claim. However, Trezevant failed to cash all the securities in the time permitted by law, and it was not until 1847 that the Georgia legislature finally redeemed the remainder.

Selected Bibliography

Jacobs, C.E. "Prelude to Amendment: The States Before the Court." *American Journal of Legal History* 12 (1968): 19–40.

Mathis, D. "*Chisholm v. Georgia*: Background and Settlement." *Journal of American History* 54 (1967): 19–29.

———. "The Eleventh Amendment: Adoption and Interpretation." *Georgia Law Review* 2 (1968): 207–45.

Morris, R.B. *John Jay, the Nation, and the Court*. Boston: Boston University Press, 1967.

CALIFORNIA REJECTS THE MANDATORY CONCILIATION FORMERLY REQUIRED UNDER MEXICAN LAW

by David J. Langum
Cumberland School of Law
Samford University

Von Schmidt v. Huntington, 1 Cal. 55 (1850) [California Supreme Court]

Currently, there is a national effort to seek methods of dispute resolution that are alternative to the traditional adversarial trial before court and jury. This is an attempt, first, to relieve overcrowded court dockets and, second, to find less socially costly ways to resolve disagreement and compensate injuries. But there is also the belief that a technique that permits direct input of the disputants themselves, with-

out the direction and control of attorneys, will result in a more psychologically satisfying resolution of disputes, which in turn will result in greater compliance with a proposed resolution than in the case of a court-ordered judgment.

One of the alternative dispute resolution techniques being considered in the United States is mandatory conciliation. In fact, in some jurisdictions and under certain conditions, it has been imposed on litigants. It is ironic in light of this current interest that over 150 years ago a region of the country that was then generally regarded in the United States as backward required formal conciliation before litigation could commence. That region was the Mexican borderlands: an area that was incorporated into the United States through the Treaty of Guadalupe Hidalgo following the Mexican War.

Conciliation is a process often confused with arbitration, but which has its own procedures and history. Arbitration is a referral by disputants to persons or agency, other than a court, to decide a dispute. The full power of the courts, including the processes of execution and garnishment, stand behind an arbitrator's decision as if the decision had been made by a judge.

Arbitrations are sometimes the result of a contractual agreement made before the particular dispute arose and at other times are the result of a submission made by the parties after they find themselves in conflict. Sometimes parties empower arbitrators to make whatever orders seem just and fair to resolve a particular dispute, and at other times the arbitral submission limits the arbitrators to issue only such orders as a judge would compose acting solely under statutes and legal precedent. Although styles and procedures of arbitration vary, the gist of the process is the voluntary submission of a dispute, by the disputants, to an agency or persons other than courts for a final, binding, and enforceable solution to their disagreement.

Conciliation, on the other hand, attempts to avoid litigation by a process designed to induce the disputants to settle their differences voluntarily. As such, a submission to conciliation, as opposed to arbitration, is never final, binding, or enforceable unless, as a distinct and further voluntary step, the parties agree to adopt a conciliation suggestion as their own settlement. Conciliation submissions may be made to agencies selected by a court or to persons selected by the disputants. Even ordinary judges can act as conciliators. If they do, however, it is understood that their suggestions for settlement are recommendations only, since the gist of conciliation is that no forthcoming recommendation for settlement, regardless of who makes

it, is binding or forced on the parties until and unless they voluntarily agree to accept the recommendation.

Since the basis of conciliation is voluntary agreement, at first glance the idea of mandatory conciliation may seem like an oxymoron. But it is not. Mandatory conciliation refers to a legally imposed procedure whereby conciliation is attempted. Under a system of mandatory conciliation the disputants may be required, under threat of various sanctions, to participate in a nonjudicial hearing where third persons listen to the facts of the dispute and then make recommendations for settlement. But if it is to be a true conciliation process and not an arbitration, either of the disputants may refuse the suggestion and demand a formal judicial hearing. After a required conciliation process proves unsuccessful, any party—usually the plaintiff—may then file a formal lawsuit.

Mandatory conciliation was practiced widely in the nineteenth century throughout the Mexican borderlands. It disposed of a large majority of all litigation, perhaps as high as 85 percent. Conciliation had entered the Hispanic world through a statute of the Spanish Cortes in 1812, which was influenced by similar legislation in revolutionary France. When Mexico became independent, its constitution required conciliation as a necessary step before filing a lawsuit. No detailed procedures were spelled out in this 1824 constitution, but a statute of 1837 provided for the steps to be followed. Although very few persons in the borderlands had formally studied law, the lay judges did follow these procedures reasonably well.

When a person had a dispute with another he would first go to the local town judge, called at different times the *alcalde* or the *juez de paz* ("justice of the peace"). The *juez*, or judge, would summon the other party and order both plaintiff and defendant to appear before him at a specified time, under penalty of a fine for nonappearance. He further would order both parties to select and bring with him an *hombre bueno* ("good man") to serve as a conciliator. These *hombres buenos* were not advocates and their function was to provide a community input into the dispute resolution process and not to advance the interest of the parties who had selected them.

The two parties, two *hombres buenos*, and the *juez* would meet to informally discuss the problem. Witnesses could be called into the meeting, but usually it involved only simple explanations by the plaintiff and defendant of their views of the dispute. After each had spoken, the *juez* would make a settlement suggestion. If it was not accepted by either or both parties, the plaintiff and defendant would be asked to leave the room, the statute specifically requiring that, and the *juez* would discuss the case with the two *hombres buenos*.

The two *hombres buenos* were charged with making a recommendation for settlement to the *juez*. The statute then required the *juez* to render a settlement recommendation within eight days that would be most likely, in the words of the statute, "to avoid a lawsuit and obtain the agreement of the parties." Almost always this recommendation was forthcoming immediately, and in perhaps as many as 90 percent of the conciliations, the two *hombres buenos* and the *juez* were unanimous in their recommendation.

The conciliation recommendation was not binding on the parties. Even though they were free to reject it, it was written in the form of a court judgment, so that if the parties agreed to the recommendation it immediately became a court order. If either plaintiff or defendant disagreed, the *juez* gave the plaintiff a certificate stating that conciliation had been unsuccessful. With that certificate in hand the plaintiff could then go to a different judge and file his complaint in a formal lawsuit.

Von Schmidt v. Huntington involved a mining company. The plaintiffs were operating or working members of the company, and the defendants made up the finance committee. The plaintiffs had been expelled from the company, and this action was brought to compel the company to reinstate them and for other orders related to the dissolution of the firm. The defendants pled that the plaintiffs had not produced any conciliation certificate, since no conciliation had been held, and that, therefore, the trial could not proceed. The trial judge overruled this plea and after trial found for the plaintiffs. Defendants appealed to the California Supreme Court on many grounds, including the absence of a conciliation certificate.

International law provides for the continuation of general private law in an area that has been ceded by one nation to another until such time as the new sovereign alters the law. In *Von Schmidt*, the lawsuit was filed in November 1849, after the Treaty of Guadalupe Hidalgo had transferred California to the United States. But Congress had not passed any controlling legislation regarding private law for California, nor had the California legislature yet met. Therefore, the case proceeded on the understanding that Mexican law applied as of the date of the initiation of the lawsuit, November 1849.

The California Supreme Court carefully examined the Mexican statute at length and found that this case was not within the specifically drawn exemptions from conciliation. However, since the time of filing (November 1849) and the date of deciding the appeal (March 1850), the first California legislature had convened. A month earlier (February 1850), the legislature had passed a statute authorizing the supreme court to reverse or affirm trial court decisions as "substantial justice" required and to disregard "formal or technical defects, errors, or imperfections, not affecting the very right and justice of the case."

The California court seized on this statute and declared that the failure to pursue conciliation before the lawsuit was commenced was a technical defect only and could therefore be ignored. The court noted that Hispanic legal scholars placed great importance on conciliation and conceded that it might be beneficial for the Mexicans, but insisted that "amongst the American people it can be looked upon in no other light than as a useless and dilatory formality, unattended by a single profitable result. . . ." The court stated that it went into such an extended discussion so that "the objection for the want of conciliatory measures is, so far as the Court is concerned, disposed of now, and, as we sincerely hope, forever." So much for alternative dispute resolution, circa mid-nineteenth century.

Conciliation was likely given such an off-hand dismissal because it ran against a then prevailing tradition in American jurisprudence. The Mexican requirement of conciliation was an effort to avoid litigation, to reconcile all persons aggrieved, and to heal the tear in the fabric of society caused by the dispute. It operated well within the homogeneous, preindustrial Mexican borderlands. On the other hand, American law in this period had a tone of rugged individualism, more fitting the convulsions of a commercial and industrial revolution. Americans thought disputes should be brought to trial and should be resolved in a clear clash, with the jury declaring a winner and a loser. There is an abundance and wide variety of evidence supporting these contrary traditions of jurisprudence, but the evidence that is most pertinent here is how other American jurisdictions treated conciliation.

By 1850, New York and a few other states had provisions in their constitutions authorizing their legislatures to form conciliation courts. But such experiments were never successfully used. At the New York Constitutional Convention of 1846, one opponent of conciliation argued that such procedures "belonged only to a despotic government, where the people were ignorant, and had a superior class over them, and not for our free Yankee population; who consider they are competent to judge for themselves in such matters."

This individualistic spirit was reflected in a law journal article published in 1866 that suggested conciliation would work only where the litigants "look up to the opinion and advice of the judge as only an ignorant and dependent people can look up." The procedure would never suit the sturdy spirit of even "the least elevated and educated Yankee." These words sound so strange today in the midst of the search for nonlitigious methods of dispute resolution, such as the call in 1985 by the chief justice of the United States for American lawyers to become peacemakers and conciliators.

There were several substantive legal concepts that entered American law through contact with Mexican law in the borderlands. The two most important are community property and the exemption from levy and seizure of the family homestead, livestock, and tools of the debtor's trade. There were also some Hispanic procedural ideas that made their way into American law, but not conciliation. Reception of law from one nation to another is almost always very selective. Yet it is ironic that Americans had the opportunity to embrace, but rejected, a concept for which there is now, 150 years later, an even greater legal need.

Selected Bibliography

Hansen, W.J. *The Search for Authority in California.* Oakland, CA: Biobooks, 1960.

Kirkwood, M.R. "Historical Background and Objectives of the Law of Community Property in the Pacific Coast States." *Washington Law Review* 11 (Jan. 1936): 1–11.

Langum, D.J. *Law and Community on the Mexican California Frontier: Anglo-American Expatriates and the Clash of Legal Traditions, 1821–46.* Norman, OK: University of Oklahoma Press, 1987.

McGinty, B. "Common Law and Community Property: Origins of the California System." *California State Bar Journal* 51 (July/Aug. 1976): 370–73, 419–21; (Sept./Oct. 1976): 478–82, 532–38.

McKnight, J.W. "The Spanish Influence on the Texas Law of Civil Procedure." *Texas Law Review* 38 (Nov. 1959): 24–54.

———. "The Spanish Legacy to Texas Law." *American Journal of Legal History* 3 (July 1959): 222–41; (Oct. 1959): 299–323.

McMurray, O.K. "The Beginnings of the Community Property System in California and the Adoption of the Common Law." *California Law Review* 3 (July 1915): 359–80.

FEDERAL COMMON LAW?

by *F. Thornton Miller*
Department of History
Southwest Missouri State University

Swift v. Tyson, 16 Peters 1 (1842); *Erie Railroad Company v. Tompkins*, 304 U.S. 65 (1938) [U.S. Supreme Court]

A federal or national common law was not expressly established by the U.S. Constitution, yet in 1938 in *Erie Railroad Company v. Tompkins*, it was necessary for the U.S. Supreme Court to strike down a common law that had been developing in the federal courts for 100 years.

In 1798, the Jeffersonian Republicans criticized the Federalists for claiming that the Sedition Acts were an improvement on the English common law. Did that mean there was a federal common law? The Republicans vehemently denied there was. They contended that the common law had been brought from England and had been modified by the statutes of the colonial legislatures and by the colonial court's constructions of the law. There was a common law for each colony, and, after 1776, for each state. But there was no general common law that existed separate from the state governments. The lack of a federal common law was not altered by the U.S. Constitution or by the First Congress in the Judiciary Act of 1789. All federal law was derived from the U.S. Constitution, treaties, and the statutes of Congress. In *United States v. Hudson & Goodwin* (1812), the Marshall Court declared as much. At least on this issue, the Court calmed the Republican states' rights concerns. If there was a national common law, separate from any grant by the Constitution or acts of Congress, the Jeffersonians were afraid that, first, the federal courts could lay claim to a vast jurisdiction, like the English courts, and second, this law would be supreme over state common law in the federal courts in each state.

If there appeared to be agreement on the limits of federal law and courts, a potential ambiguity arose in a relatively new field of the law, which Daniel Webster described as "a system of most admirable utility, certain, complete, and uniform, to a degree of perfection, approaching the end of all that human wisdom may be expected to reach." Based not on statute but rather on practice, precedent, and construction, it had begun only recently, "at the time of what may be called the commencement of the commercial era of the common law." Webster was referring to the customary commercial law, the rules of which were generally followed by all nations engaged in commerce. In England, and the American states, it had become a new and growing part of the common law. Could it be applied in the federal courts?

Section 34 of the Judiciary Act of 1789, which governed common-law trials in the federal courts, stated that "the laws of the several states, except where the constitution, treaties, or statutes of the United States shall otherwise require or provide, shall be regarded as rules of decision in trials of common law in the courts of the United States in cases where they apply." In most legal areas, where the common law varied from state to state, there was no question about how the federal courts were to proceed. But in deciding a question in commercial law, where federal and state judges drew on the same principles, were federal judges to be bound by the decisions of state judges? On a case-by-case basis, the Marshall Court had relied on the generally accepted rules of commercial law, without declaring there was a general or federal common law separate from state law. Justice Joseph Story, believing it would provide a necessary uniformity, was ready to make commercial law the exception.

Swift v. Tyson began as a dispute involving an investment company in New York and land speculators in Maine. Joseph Swift sued George W. Tyson, based on diversity of citizenship, in the Federal Court for the Southern District of New York. At issue was whether a bill of exchange could satisfy a preexisting debt. There was no New York statute relating to the subject. But by the state's common law, there were grounds for restricting payment of a bill of exchange if elements of fraud were involved. The federal district court followed New York law and ruled against Swift. Swift then appealed to the Federal Circuit Court for the Southern District of New York. Again, the court followed New York law. Losing once again, Swift appealed to the U.S. Supreme Court.

Swift's lawyers, including Webster at one point, argued that where there were no relevant state statutes, on cases to be determined by the generally accepted rules of commercial law, federal judges were not bound by state common law. The word "law" in Section 34 of the Judiciary Act of 1789 was to be interpreted as referring only to state statutes and state judicial construction of statutes, and not to common-law rules laid down by a state court. Story, in giving the opinion of the Court, agreed that federal judges were not bound by state law where the general principles of commercial law were used by both them and state judges alike, and where a state had not passed statutes on the subject. He stated that with "contracts and other instruments of a commercial nature, the true interpretation and effect whereof are to be sought, not in the decisions of the local tribunals, but in the general principles and doctrines of commercial jurisprudence. . . . The law respecting negotiable instruments may be truly declared . . . to be in great measure, not the law of a single country only, but of the commercial world." *Swift* established a federal common law specifically in commercial law.

There was no states' rights opposition to *Swift*. It was not unlike many of the Taney Court cases that attempted to strike a balance between the federal and state governments. The Court did not declare a general, federal common law. Indeed, states could pass statutes modifying the commercial law to restrict the actions of federal judges in federal district courts in their state. But it would not be in the interest of a state to have its commercial law different from those of most other states and foreign countries engaged in commerce. To do so could seriously discourage commercial activity within the state. The general acceptance of *Swift* shows that Story was probably correct that a federal, commercial common law well served most state and business interests.

The existence of federal common law did not appear to offend states' rights advocates through the 1840s and 1850s. There was, however, a problem that would develop into a long running controversy. If a general law existed separate from the statutes of Congress and the statutory and common law of the states, would the federal judges show restraint in using it? The Taney Court's attempts to base the new law on the Constitution—so that it would not be a general, unchecked, usurpation of power—only created another problem. Because the Constitution was superior to all state constitutions and law, the new common law could be interpreted as also being superior to state law. The road was thus paved for the Court to move beyond the bounds of state statute. Also, what could prohibit the federal courts from moving beyond commercial law? Story had not intended to create a general, federal common law. But a nationalist Court and Congress during the Civil War and Reconstruction period and pressure from the rising national corporations would press this development toward its logical conclusion.

Congress expanded diversity jurisdiction to include cases in which local prejudice might work against a plaintiff. Creditors and corporations purposely established businesses in far-flung states to secure diversity jurisdiction. Businessmen and their lawyers favored the *Swift* transformation, and the new doctrine was officially endorsed by the American Bar Association. Its development, through several decades of court cases, was completed in *Bucher v. Cheshire Railroad Company* (1887). The Court, viewing the common law as a general law that existed separate from territorial sovereigns, asserted that there was a single American common law. This increased the extent of the jurisdiction of the federal courts in two ways. First, if the general common law was used in both the state and federal courts, because the federal government was superior to the state governments, federal courts were not bound by state statute. The states were only creating problems by maintaining a law different from that of the federal courts. Second, the common law that began as an exception—a commercial law—had now become general. Far from being the rules of how to construe commercial contracts and negotiable paper, this common law encompassed torts, bonds, and over 20 other doctrines.

Because the kinds of law included in the general common-law jurisdiction expanded, and because states enacted statutes to regulate corporations, there was a growing divergence between federal and state common laws. The phenomenon of two common laws in each state allowed for "forum shopping" (i.e., searching for the most favorable courts). Through diversity jurisdiction, corporations could bypass state law. Compared with the states, the federal judiciary tended to support creditors against debtors, and to support corporations against regulation, labor, and liability claims. The conservative Court was thus criticized in the late nineteenth century for political reasons by various groups from Populists to Progressives.

The Court and its now fully embraced *Swift* doctrine were also criticized for legal and constitutional reasons from within the legal profession. For example, Justice Oliver Wendell Holmes, Jr., in one of his classic dissents, contended that each state had drawn on and modified the English common law and had developed its own law through statute and court opinions. He maintained that there had been no law separate from and transcendent to the particular states. Indeed, there was no law in the abstract that existed separate from sovereign governments. Federal judges could not exclusively divine the law from some mystical realm. There was a common law in each state, because it had been established by the legislatures and judiciaries of each state. Holmes argued that neither the U.S. Constitution nor congressional statutes had established a general common law or authorized the Supreme Court to assume that it existed. This assumption in the *Swift* doctrine was, in Holmes's view, fallacious.

Most of the criticism waged against the *Swift* doctrine was for its use by corporations to circumvent state law. But *Erie Railroad Company v. Tompkins* began when an individual used diversity jurisdiction to sue a corporation for a liability claim. In Hughestown, Pennsylvania, Harry James Tompkins was walking on a path alongside a track of the Erie Railroad Company when, he claimed, something extending from a passing train, probably an open door,

struck him. By Pennsylvania common law, he was a trespasser on the railroad company's property and the company was not liable for his injury. Because the company's headquarters was in New York, Tompkins could enter his suit in the U.S. District Court for the Southern District of New York. His lawyers argued that the court should not use Pennsylvania law but rather the *Swift* doctrine's general common law. The court gave judgment in accord with the latter, and the company appealed to the U.S. Circuit Court for the Second Circuit. Tompkins again won, and the company appealed to the U.S. Supreme Court.

In *Erie*, the Court did something it had seldom done before: it declared one of its own decisions unconstitutional. The Court not only ruled against Tompkins, using Pennsylvania common law, but also struck down Story's *Swift* opinion that had established a federal common law. Justice Louis D. Brandeis wrote the majority opinion. Much of it had little to do with Story's original opinion. But the *Swift* doctrine was a logical extension of Story's claim that there was a common law separate from the law of particular governments. Brandeis believed that it was necessary to throw out the opinion to be rid of the doctrine. To have narrowed the doctrine back to Story's specific, commercial common law would have left open the chance of a later Court restoring the *Swift* doctrine. To make the rule clear, Brandeis could not allow Story's exception to stand. There was no federal common law, and that included commercial law.

It is perhaps ironic that Brandeis did not realize the explosion of the federal statute, beginning with the New Deal, would allow the federal courts, through their constructions, to build a common law anew. But it is based on statute, and it is not a general and universal law that transcends all government and has no limits other than those of reason. Brandeis put the constitutionalism back into the jurisdictional boundaries of the federal courts, which it had never been Story's intention to remove.

Select Bibliography

Bridwell, R., and R.U. Whitten. *The Constitution and the Common Law: The Decline of the Doctrines of Separation of Powers and Federalism.* Lexington, MA: D.C. Heath & Co., 1977.

Freyer, T. *Harmony & Dissonance: The* Swift & Erie *Cases in American Federalism.* New York: New York University Press, 1981.

Newmyer, R.K. *Supreme Court Justice Joseph Story: Statesman of the Old Republic.* Chapel Hill, NC: University of North Carolina Press, 1985.

A LEG TO STAND ON: TAXPAYER LAWSUITS AGAINST THE U.S. GOVERNMENT

by Roger D. Hardaway
Department of History
Northwestern Oklahoma State University

Flast v. Cohen, 392 U.S. 83 (1968) [U.S. Supreme Court]

Under the U.S. Constitution, the federal government has the power to tax U.S. citizens and to spend the money collected through taxation "to pay the Debts and provide for the common Defence and general Welfare of the United States." In 1968, the U.S. Supreme Court ruled that taxpayers have a right, under certain circumstances, to sue the federal government to prevent it from spending tax money for unconstitutional purposes.

In the mid-1960s, Congress passed several laws appropriating money to provide educational materials, guidance services, and instructional assistance to children attending private schools, many of which were religiously affiliated. One such law was the Elementary and Secondary Education Act of 1965. Florence Flast and six other taxpayers sued Secretary of Health, Education, and Welfare (HEW) John W. Gardner and the U.S. Commissioner of Education to halt the expenditure of the law's funds for religious schools. The plaintiffs based their claim on the First Amendment, which prohibits Congress from passing any law "respecting an establishment of religion, or prohibiting the free exercise thereof."

A three-judge district court panel in New York City ruled 2–1 in *Flast v. Gardner* that Flast and her fellow taxpayers had no "standing" to sue the U.S. government. Before a plaintiff is allowed to sue a defendant in the United States, the plaintiff must show that he has suffered or will suffer an injury because of the defendant's actions or proposed actions. If the plaintiff cannot prove this injury, his lawsuit is dismissed because he is not a proper party to file suit. He is said to have no standing because there is no controversy between the parties for the court to resolve.

Judge Paul R. Hays of the U.S. Court of Appeals for the Second Circuit wrote the district court's decision in *Flast v. Gardner*. Hays reasoned that Flast's lawsuit was barred by the landmark U.S. Supreme Court case of *Frothingham v. Mellon* (1923). Frothingham had sought to sue the U.S. government for spending tax money for maternal and infant health care. Frothingham charged that such expenditures could be made, under the Tenth Amendment, only by state governments and not by the U.S. government. Thus, in her opinion, the U.S. government was exceeding its constitutional power to spend the taxpayers' money.

The Supreme Court had ruled that Frothingham did not have standing to sue the U.S. government. While admitting that courts had generally allowed taxpayers to sue state and local governments, the Supreme Court decided to draw the line at suits against the U.S. government. The interest any taxpayer had "in the moneys of the [U.S.] Treasury . . . is shared with millions of others; is comparatively minute and indeterminable," the Court said. Thus, the injury endured by Frothingham as a result of the government's expenditure of funds for health care was not a "direct" one but rather a minor one she suffered "in common with people generally." Whether the expenditure was, in fact, unconstitutional, as Frothingham alleged, was not decided.

As for Flast, Hays wrote that she had sustained no "direct dollars-and-cents injury." Like Frothingham, Flast did not possess "the requisite financial interest" in the expenditure of federal funds to allow her standing to sue.

The plaintiffs appealed the district court's decision to the U.S. Supreme Court. By the time the Court issued its opinion in June 1968, Wilbur J. Cohen had replaced Gardner as HEW secretary, changing the name of the case to *Flast v. Cohen*. In an 8–1 decision, the Court distinguished the *Flast* lawsuit from the *Frothingham* complaint and reversed the district court's decision. The Supreme Court's opinion, written by Chief Justice Earl Warren, gave federal taxpayers the right to sue the U.S. government to halt allegedly unconstitutional expenditures under certain narrowly defined circumstances.

Before taxpayers would be granted standing to sue the U.S. government, they would have to meet a two-part test. The first part required the plaintiffs to attack only statutes that created direct spending programs. A suit challenging an "incidental expenditure of tax funds in the administration of an essentially regulatory statute" would not be allowed. Both Flast and Frothingham, the Court said, satisfied the first part of this test.

The second part of the test required the federal spending to violate "a specific [constitutional] limitation upon [Congress's] taxing and spending power." Here, Warren reasoned that the establishment clause of the First Amendment specifically prohibited Congress from spending money for religious purposes. This, he said, was a "specific limitation" on the U.S. government's spending power. Thus, Flast had met the second part of the standard, and she, therefore, had standing to sue the government. Conversely, Frothingham had challenged a law because, in her opinion, it exceeded the U.S. government's general powers to spend; she had

shown no specific constitutional prohibition on the spending involved. Warren concluded by asserting that future taxpayers, in order to have standing to sue the U.S. government, would have to allege that their "tax money is being extracted and spent in violation of specific constitutional protections against such abuse of legislative power."

The Court's decision in *Flast v. Cohen* has been criticized by many commentators. Some, like Justice John M. Harlan in his dissenting opinion, prefer *Frothingham*, which would effectively bar taxpayer lawsuits altogether. Other legal experts agree with Justice William O. Douglas, who filed a concurring opinion in *Flast*. Douglas wanted the Court to overrule *Frothingham* and allow most taxpayer lawsuits to be heard as an effective check upon the actions of Congress. Still other critics have noted that the establishment clause may be the only "specific limitation" on congressional spending in the Constitution.

Certainly, the distinction the Court drew between Frothingham's and Flast's challenges to governmental spending is a legal one that some might find illogical. The *Flast* decision, however, gives U.S. citizens the right, in some instances, to watch over the actions of the U.S. government and challenge unconstitutional expenditures. For this reason, it is an improvement over *Frothingham*.

Selected Bibliography

Kahan, R.L. "Federal Taxpayers and Standing: *Flast v. Cohen*." *UCLA Law Review* 16 (Feb. 1969): 444–55.

Karabus, A. "The *Flast* Decision on Standing of Federal Taxpayers to Challenge Governmental Action: Mirage or Breach in the Dike?" *North Dakota Law Review* 45 (Spring 1969): 353–62.

Tietz, G.F. "Standing—Taxpayers Allowed to Challenge Federal Expenditures." *Temple Law Quarterly* 42 (Fall 1968): 70–81.

FREE SPEECH AND LEGAL ETHICS: THE ISSUE OF LAWYER ADVERTISING

by Roger D. Hardaway
Department of History
Northwestern Oklahoma State University

Bates v. State Bar of Arizona, 433 U.S. 350 (1977) [U.S. Supreme Court]

Critics charged that it would tarnish the image of the profession. Proponents countered that it would help consumers make informed decisions, make services available to a greater number of people, and lower artificially inflated fees. The issue was advertising by attorneys in traditional commercial outlets, such as newspapers. The U.S. Supreme Court addressed the question in 1977.

Attorney disciplinary rules in effect in the United States had traditionally prohibited any form of advertising by attorneys except for brief listings in legal publications and directories. In 1975, the American Bar Association (ABA), which makes recommendations to state entities concerning regulation of the legal profession, suggested allowing attorneys to list fees for initial consultations in telephone book yellow pages. Other forms of attorney advertising were generally forbidden by state regulating bodies. John R. Bates and Van O'Steen, two Phoenix attorneys, decided to challenge Arizona's ban on attorney advertising.

Bates and O'Steen formed a law partnership in 1974, which they termed a "legal clinic." Their plan was simple. They would perform only routine legal matters, such as uncontested divorces and adoptions, uncomplicated bankruptcies, and name changes. They would charge modest fees and count on a heavy volume of business to be profitable. They soon realized, however, that their clients were not sufficient in number to make their experiment succeed. To increase business, they placed an advertisement in the *Arizona Republic*, a Phoenix newspaper, in February 1976, listing their fees for several types of legal services.

The president of the State Bar of Arizona, to which all licensed Arizona attorneys were required to belong, filed a complaint against the two attorney entrepreneurs. The case was referred to a special disciplinary committee, which recommended that Bates and O'Steen be suspended from the practice of law for six months. The state bar association's board of governors, however, reduced the period of suspension to only one week because Bates and O'Steen had advertised in the good-faith belief that the disciplinary rule violated their rights of free speech guaranteed by the First Amendment of the U.S. Constitution.

The lawyers next asked the Arizona Supreme Court to review the bar association's recommendation. The court, in *In re Bates*, upheld the rule prohibiting attorney advertising, but reduced the attorneys' punishment to censure only—a penalty less harsh than suspension. Undaunted (and unsatisfied), Bates and O'Steen attacked the rule in the U.S. Supreme Court.

The Supreme Court issued its ruling on the issue in June 1977, in *Bates v. State Bar of Arizona*. The Court's decision, written by Justice Harry A. Blackmun, first rejected the attorneys' argument that the rule in question violated the Sherman Antitrust Act by its "tendency to limit competition." But the Court, in a 5–4 majority, held that attorneys have a right under the First Amendment to advertise their fees and services, or to engage in what the justices called "commercial speech."

"Commercial speech," Blackmun asserted, "serves to inform the public of the availability, nature, and prices of products and services, and thus performs an indispensable role in the allocation of resources in a free enterprise system. . . . In short, such speech serves individual and societal interests in assuring informed and reliable decisionmaking." Moreover, Blackmun reasoned, the Arizona rule prohibiting attorney advertising "serves to inhibit the free flow of commercial information and to keep the public in ignorance." The justice further noted that studies had shown that commercial advertising reduced the prices of consumer goods, and suggested that the same would be true of services offered to the public by attorneys.

The Court's majority was careful to declare, however, that while attorney advertising was protected by the First Amendment's guarantee of free speech, it could nevertheless be regulated to some degree. Specifically, Blackmun instructed the legal community to promulgate rules that would outlaw "advertising that is false, deceptive, or misleading" as well as that "concerning transactions that are themselves illegal." In addition, disciplinary rules could put "reasonable restrictions on the time, place, and manner of advertising."

The dissenting Court members, led by Justice Lewis F. Powell, Jr., argued that attorney advertising was not protected by the First Amendment and was not in the public interest. Powell noted that it was more difficult to estimate the value of professional services than the value of "tangible products." Moreover, Powell contended that unethical lawyers could use advertisements to mislead the public because legal "services are individualized with respect to content and quality and because the lay consumer of legal services usually does not know in advance the precise nature and scope of the services he requires."

After the Supreme Court's decision was issued, the ABA (which had opposed the Bates and O'Steen advertisement) drafted proposed rules concerning attorney advertising. Today, these regulations, embodied in the *Model Rules*

of Professional Conduct, permit advertisements not only in newspapers, legal periodicals, and telephone directories, but also on television, radio, outdoor signs and in mass mailings to the general public. Each state's legal establishment, however, is free to adopt, reject, or modify the ABA's proposals. Consequently, there currently exists no uniform national standard of conduct for attorneys wishing to advertise their services.

Despite the *Bates* decision, many attorneys remain reluctant to advertise. This is perhaps due to fear of appearing "unprofessional" in the eyes of their peers or simply because of custom. Surveys have shown that most of those who do advertise restrict their activity to the yellow pages of their local telephone books. Other attorneys, however, have advertised in the mass media, and this has apparently been beneficial to consumers. In recent years, the number of legal clinics in the United States has increased steadily, delivering legal services to consumers, in most instances, at reduced prices. This is exactly what Bates and O'Steen had in mind when they fought traditional notions of ethical legal conduct—and won.

Selected Bibliography

Bowers, G.H., and O.H. Stephens, Jr. "Attorney Advertising and the First Amendment: The Development and Impact of a Constitutional Standard." *Memphis State University Law Review* 17 (Winter 1987): 221–62.

Whitman, D., and C.D. Stoltenberg. "Evolving Concepts of Lawyer Advertising: The Supreme Court's Latest Clarification." *Indiana Law Review* 19 (Spring 1986): 497–560.

FROM COURT SIDE TO COURTROOM

by Charles E. Quirk
Department of History
University of Northern Iowa

NCAA v. Tarkanian, 488 U.S — (1988) [U.S. Supreme Court]

"It's never over till its over." This sports adage applies to the lengthy legal battle between Jerry Tarkanian, the highly successful basketball coach at the University of Nevada at Las Vegas

(UNLV), and the powerful National Collegiate Athletic Association (NCAA).

Since the mid-1970s, the NCAA has hounded Tarkanian and UNLV over alleged recruiting violations and academic irregularities. Tarkanian contends that the NCAA is out to get him for a variety of reasons, including his public statements criticizing NCAA procedures and the organization's perception that he exploits black athletes. The NCAA denies any vendetta against Tarkanian and asserts that it is merely doing its job.

On his home basketball court—the 18,500 seat Thomas & Mack Center—the colorful Tarkanian is almost impossible to beat. His Runnin' Rebels are regularly ranked in the nation's "top ten," featuring Tarkanian's characteristic wide-open offense and a full-court pressure defense. In 1989–90, UNLV won the national championship. Tarkanian's teams rely on junior-college transfers, some of whom display remarkable basketball skills but questionable academic abilities. Each year Tarkanian's program nets several million dollars, a figure that includes proceeds from the sale of $1,800-per-seat accommodations for the rich and famous UNLV basketball devotees.

In the courtrooms of Nevada, Tarkanian's record is equally impressive. The NCAA found UNLV guilty of 38 violations, ten of which involved Tarkanian, in August 1977. According to NCAA investigators, Tarkanian improperly provided potential recruits with extra benefits, such as free airfare. Whereas the basketball program received a probation sentence, the governing body of collegiate athletics ordered UNLV to suspend the popular coach for two years. The institution reluctantly followed the demand rather than encounter additional penalties. Adept at the transition game, Tarkanian went on the offensive with a law suit contending that his due process rights had been violated. Eventually he won a permanent injunction in Nevada district court. In May 1979, the Nevada Supreme Court reversed the decision and ordered the case sent back to lower court for another trial. This time the NCAA, as well as UNLV, became a party in the case.

In a legal game that attracted the attention of lawyers and fiercely dedicated UNLV basketball supporters, Tarkanian emerged victorious again in the district court in June 1984. At this juncture, UNLV—an unenthusiastic partner at best—dropped out of the case. The court contended that the NCAA was a "state actor"

and, as such, had deprived the coach of his right to due process. District Judge Paul S. Goldman chastised the NCAA for uncritically accepting the word of its investigators and ignoring sworn statements and physical evidence that supported Tarkanian.

As expected, the NCAA appealed to the Nevada Supreme Court. Three years later, the Nevada high court upheld the judgment of the lower court—the NCAA was a state actor when, in concert with UNLV, it sought to discipline a public employee. Record another win for Tarkanian on his legal home court.

In response to the appeal from the NCAA, the U.S. Supreme Court agreed to review the case. Hearing arguments from the two sides in October 1988, the High Court rendered a 5–4 decision in favor of the NCAA in December 1988.

Was the NCAA acting as a governmental body in pressuring UNLV to suspend Tarkanian? Lawyers for the coach argued yes because it had acted in conjunction with UNLV. Speaking for the majority, Justice John Paul Stevens concluded that, as a private organization, the NCAA was not bound to follow Fourteenth Amendment provisions. Stevens noted that the NCAA is a private body and its members join voluntarily. He also stressed that UNLV had a variety of options, including dropping out of the NCAA. He rejected the contention that the university and association acted together inasmuch as UNLV made every effort to retain Tarkanian.

Justice Byron R. White wrote a brief dissenting opinion, contending that the NCAA acted together with UNLV, thereby becoming a state actor. In the dissent, White stressed that the university suspended Tarkanian because it accepted NCAA rules and had agreed to adopt the findings of the hearings conducted by the association. The big legal game was close, but the NCAA appeared to emerge with the trophy.

But the association found that Tarkanian's legal offense could still generate points. In May 1989, the voluntary, nonprofit organization composed of over 900 colleges, universities, and conferences asked the Nevada Supreme Court to dissolve the injunction barring Tarkanian's suspension. Soon after, UNLV admitted that

NCAA investigators were examining possible recruiting violations that occurred in 1985 and 1986. On September 28, the Nevada Supreme Court lifted the injunction barring NCAA sanctions against UNLV. But it allowed a lower court to rule on the other injunction preventing UNLV from suspending Tarkanian.

Developments in 1990 seemed almost appropriate for a soap opera. Early in the year, widely publicized reports of a compromise between the NCAA and Tarkanian proved inaccurate. In July, the NCAA banned UNLV from defending its title in the 1991 tournament. Then UNLV requested and, surprisingly, received a reconsideration. The university and coach offered four mutually exclusive penalties in exchange for which Tarkanian promised not to launch additional litigation against the NCAA. In response, the NCAA offered two options. UNLV selected the one banning the squad from the 1992 tournament and foregoing television appearances in 1991–92.

The reprieve evoked groans from some basketball precincts and a battery of defensive statements from the NCAA. Athletic officials and coaches at universities where teams had received severe penalties for infractions condemned the compromise. Some expressed surprise that it was apparently possible to negotiate with the NCAA; others expressed their desire for a "multiple choice" penalty system; and one claimed that it was a total farce. Under siege, NCAA officials stressed the uniqueness of the case and denied setting a precedent for future appeals.

An assessment of the compromise requires attention to several complicated issues. One is the pressure placed on the NCAA by legislation introduced in Congress during 1990, which would require the NCAA to give due process during investigations. Another constraint is the availability of the friendly courts of Nevada for Tarkanian and his players to ensure the opportunity to defend their cherished championship. Also, it is true that UNLV served a two-year probation in the late 1970s. In addition, the coach possessed a permanent injunction preventing suspension by his university. Finally, the UNLV basketball program still faces threats from two sources. At the request of the Nevada Board of Regents, the state attorney general launched an investigation into charges of possible fraud related to complimentary tickets to UNLV basketball games. And there is the ever-vigilant NCAA. In December, the NCAA released a list of almost 30 alleged UNLV infractions that occurred during the mid-1980s.

The NCAA is obviously not finished with the highly successful but seemingly improper UNLV basketball program. For his part, the Shark knows how to use and defeat the system as he presides over victories on the road and at the Thomas & Mack Center with his talented Runnin' Rebels.

Selected Bibliography

Bender, L.S. "State Action and the NCAA: Will 'Tarkanian' Sport the Old Look?" *Entertainment and Sports Law Journal* 4 (Fall 1987): 385–409.

Schwartz, M.A. "The NCAA State Action Decision." *Public Interest Law* 201 (Jan., 1989): 3.

Tarkanian, J., and T. Pluto. *TARK: College Basketball's Winningest Coach*. New York: McGraw-Hill Publishing Co., 1988.

D. Political Questions

THE *RIGHT* OF REVOLUTION VS. THE RIGHT OF *REVOLUTION*

by Harry W. Fritz
Department of History
University of Montana

Luther v. Borden, 7 Howard 1 (1849) [U.S. Supreme Court]

In 1849, the U.S. Supreme Court declared the American Revolution unconstitutional. Change in the structure and composition of government, the Court insisted, could occur only with the approval of the existing polity. Since Great Britain clearly did not sanction American independence in 1776, the colonists were forced to secure their goals militarily. They had no *right* of revolution; therefore they asserted the right of *revolution*. And they won. Might made right.

Luther v. Borden did not turn on the American Revolution; indeed, the Court might well have been embarrassed to reflect on the circumstances of the nation's founding. Rather, it arose from a bitter political and constitutional struggle in Rhode Island. There, in the nation's smallest state, a peaceable revolution based on popular sovereignty failed of implementation. A tragicomic effort to impose the revolution by force also fizzled. For the presumptive revolutionaries, both right and might fell short. This was the Dorr War, the Dorr Rebellion of 1842.

The Dorrites—as the followers of the rebellion's leader, Thomas Wilson Dorr, were called—had more than legitimate causes for complaint. The Rhode Island government against which they struggled had no demonstrated popular legitimacy. It had not been properly constituted by accepted revolutionary procedures, either in 1776 or in the aftermath of the U.S. Constitution of 1787. Instead, its origins stretched back to the seventeenth century, to the original Rhode Island charter issued by King Charles II in 1663. Barely adequate at the time of the Revolution, the charter government was hopelessly out-of-

date 50 years later. Four major deficiencies—representation, the suffrage, a bill of rights, and judicial independence—defined it as a curious colonial anachronism in Jacksonian America. Moreover, the charter of 1663 contained no amendatory procedures. And, by the 1840s, it was a bit late to petition the Crown. Several reform efforts, the last spearheaded by Dorr and the Rhode Island Constitutional party in the 1830s, proved futile. But the Rhode Island Suffrage Association, founded in 1840, made up for lost time.

In rapid succession the suffragists called an extralegal constitutional convention, elected delegates, and met in Providence in October 1841. There they drafted an up-to-date document, with expanded suffrage, a reapportioned legislature, an independent judiciary, and a declaration of rights. After setting up their own election procedures, the new people's constitution was ratified in early 1842 by the astonishing vote of 13,947 to 52. The majority amounted to 60 percent of Rhode Island's adult white males, and even included a clear majority of freemen eligible to vote under the charter government. Buoyed by the apparent success of their peaceable revolution, the suffragists abandoned reform for ideological purity. They turned down a palatable constitutional alternative offered by a Freeholders' Convention and approved by the incumbent government. The vote in March 1842 was 8,689 to 8,013 against, with the suffragists incongruously allied with diehard charter supporters in the majority. Both sides geared up for a showdown, but the loss of over 5,000 votes was not auspicious for the Dorrites.

Most charter defenders recognized the need for democratic reform, but they were unwilling to acquiesce in unauthorized, out-of-doors procedures. When their legitimate constitution was rejected by a threatening if declining popular majority, the General Assembly of the standing government got tough. It passed an act, dubbed by both sides the "Algerine Law" for its severity, proclaiming all participants in the proposed new people's government to be traitors. Governor Samuel Ward King sent a delegation to Washington and called on President John Tyler to defend Rhode Island against domestic violence. An aroused law and order coalition contested the gubernatorial elections of April 1842. In the official canvas, King won reelection with 4,781 votes; unofficially Dorr became "people's governor" of Rhode Island. His 6,604 votes represented a further decline in suffragist strength. Undaunted, a people's government convened in Providence in May, and piously awaited formal recognition. Soon the pretenders turned from peaceable to physical revolution. They assembled a ragtag militia and trained two cannons on the state arsenal in Providence. The cannon misfired, the militia disbanded, and the charter authorities remained in power. That was the climax of the Dorr Rebellion.

In the aftermath, the charter government responded with both the carrot and the stick. On one hand, the General Assembly called for a new constitutional convention, extending the vote for delegates to all adult males. Drafted in the fall and ratified in November 1842, the new constitution brought Rhode Island into the modern age. The Dorrites had lost the battle but won the war, even though unscrupulous political practices continued to prevail. On the other hand, the charterites, terrified by a gathering of diehard Dorrites at Chepachet, Rhode Island, imposed martial law on the state. In the longrun, this declaration was even more revolutionary than suffragist agitation. Never before in American history had a standing civil government suspended operations in favor of military rule.

Acting under the new dispensation, a military contingent headed by Luther M. Borden entered the residence of a Dorrite shoemaker named Martin Luther in Warren, Rhode Island, on June 29, 1842. Martin Luther was not at home; already threatened by the Algerine Law, he had moved across the border to Swansea, Massachusetts. Luther Borden's armed militiamen found only Martin's mother, Rachel, her companion, and two hired hands. None suffered physical injury, although Borden sustained a profane tongue-lashing administered by Mrs. Luther, a fervent Methodist. Ultimately Martin Luther sued Luther Borden in federal circuit court under the common-law action of trespass *quare clausum fregit*. Mrs. Luther also sued to test the constitutionality of martial law; the allegations, evidence, and arguments were the same in both cases. The cases were brought before Justice Joseph Story of the U.S. Supreme Court and District Court Judge John Pitman, two ardent charter supporters, in October 1842; they were argued in November and decided one year later.

The outcome was foreordained. At no time did the Dorrites enjoy the support of a significant segment of the U.S. legal or judicial establishment. Although "nine lawyers" had backed the people's constitution early on, many of them subsequently recanted. In an *ex cathedra* opinion, the three judges of the Rhode Island Supreme Court warned in March 1842 that further agitation might be treasonous. Both Dorr and Luther were convicted of treason in Rhode Island. Story and Pitman engaged in a collusive private correspondence in defense of the status quo. The Luthers' arguments, presented by Benjamin F. Hallett, a Massachusetts Democrat, fell on decidedly unreceptive ears.

Hallett rested his case on a spread-eagled defense of popular sovereignty. The people of Rhode Island "had the right to reassume the powers of government, and establish a written constitution and frame of a republican form of government." Lawyers for the defendants, John Whipple and Richard Ward Greene, asserted the integrity of the state's long-existing institutions. Predictably, the court, speaking in the name of Joseph Story, refused to admit the plaintiff's evidence; the jury held for the defendants, and the cases, one on a writ of error and the other by an artificial division of opinion, went to the U.S. Supreme Court.

The *Luther* cases were not argued until 1848, nor decided until 1849. The long delay, due to political considerations and an undermanned Court, rendered the issues in question moot. The Dorrites agreed to demand neither the overthrow of the Rhode Island government nor the installation of the people's constitution. The arguments took on an ethereal tone—an intellectual contest over the meaning of America's abstract self-evident truths.

Once again, Benjamin F. Hallett held forth for the plaintiffs; his rhetorical assault lasted for three days. Since "the People's Constitution was in force in Rhode Island as the fundamental law of the State," the issue was "whether the theory of American free government for the States of this Union is available to the people in practice, that is, whether the basis of popular sovereignty is a living principle, or a theory, always restrained in practice by the will of the law-making power." For Hallett, the "right to establish a written constitution" was "independent of the will or sanction of the Legislature, and can be exercised by the right of eminent sovereignty in the people, without the form of a precedent statute law." Anything else was divine right—"the dogma of *despotism!*" If the people have a right of revolution, "they must also have a right to exercise it peaceably."

The lawyers for the defendants, John Whipple and Daniel Webster, were up to the effort. "All changes must originate with the legislature," Whipple stated flatly. Webster agreed: "When it is necessary to ascertain the will of the people, the legislature must provide the means of ascertaining it." "The Constitution does not proceed on the *ground* of revolution," he added; "it does not proceed on any *right* of revolution; but it does go on the idea, that, within and under the Constitution, no new form of government can be established in any State, without the authority of the existing government" [emphasis in original]. Webster added that any effort to supersede the charter government was illegal; besides, the whole matter was "not of judicial cognizance."

Chief Justice Roger B. Taney agreed with Webster. He affirmed the judgment of the circuit court by denying the validity of the people's constitution. Taney simply refused to consider the arguments of the plaintiffs. Since the charter government never recognized its adversary, neither did he. The case turned on the proper exercise of judicial power. Since the job of recognizing constitutions was the business of "the political department," the Court was "bound to follow the decisions of the State tribunals." Moreover, under Article IV, Section 4, of the U.S. Constitution, "it rests with Congress to decide what government is the established one in a State." Congress, by admitting its senators and representatives, had decided for the charter. Taney summed up: "No one, we believe, has ever doubted the proposition, that, according to the institutions of the country, the sovereignty in every State resides in the people of the State, and that they may alter and change their form of government at their own pleasure. But whether they have changed it or not by abolishing an old government, and establishing a new one in its place, is a question to be settled by the political power."

Justice Levi Woodbury appended a long dissent. He agreed with Taney that the main question was "not properly of judicial cognizance." But he came down hard on martial law, arguing that it could be proclaimed only by armies in actual conflict. Rhode Island had no business suspending civil law over the entire state. Unfortunately, Rhode Island had done just that, and Taney had approved. In "a state of war . . . the established government resorted to the rights and usages of war to maintain itself, and to overcome the unlawful opposition." The decision broadened the American law of emergency powers, allowing states to suppress dissent whenever they defined it as war.

Enhancing governmental power by adding military to civil sanctions was just one outcome of *Luther v. Borden.* The case long provided the classic expression of the distinction between political and justiciable questions. Taney not only refused jurisdiction but also provided job descriptions for the "political department"—Congress and the president. The chief justice rested his arguments on the guarantee clause in Article IV, Section 4, of the U.S. Constitution: "The United States shall guarantee to every State in this Union a Republican Form of Government, and shall protect each of them against Invasion; and on Application of the

Legislature, or of the Executive (when the Legislature cannot be convened) against domestic Violence."

Although Taney confused the separate clauses of this section, *Luther v. Borden* was "the first great turning point in the history of the guarantee clause." Taney's reading divorced the Court from judicial management of domestic issues for over a century. Not until the Court mandated legislative reapportionment in *Baker v. Carr* (1962) did it at last enforce the guarantee.

Luther v. Borden also marked what one historian called the "triumph of institutionalism"—of the sovereignty of government over that of the people. Established political institutions "divested" sovereignty, nullifying the right of the citizenry to exercise power directly. No less "republican" or even "popular," institutionalism recorded American satisfaction with both past and present, even as the determinants of society shifted from voluntarism to coercion.

In bits and pieces, *Luther v. Borden* added up not just to the denial of the Dorrites' version of popular sovereignty but to the absolute

victory of juristic nationalism. When Abraham Lincoln proclaimed martial law in 1861, his attorney general cited Roger Taney's precedent of 1849. In denying his Court's jurisdiction, Taney asserted the sovereign authority of the national legislature; he enhanced federal not local power. His *Luther dicta* allowed Congress to reconstruct the southern states after the Civil War. Six hundred thousand had died to institutionalize the national republic. Like the Dorrites, the Confederates lacked the might to ensure their right of revolution.

Selected Bibliography

Conron, M.A. "Law, Politics, and Chief Justice Taney: A Reconsideration of the *Luther v. Borden* Decision." *American Journal of Legal History* 11 (Oct. 1967): 377–88.

Dennison, G.M. *The Dorr War: Republicanism on Trial, 1831–61.* Lexington, KY: University of Kentucky Press, 1976.

Gettleman, M.E. *The Dorr Rebellion: A Study in American Radicalism, 1833–49.* New York: Random House, 1973.

Wiecek, W.M. *The Guarantee Clause of the U.S. Constitution.* Ithaca, NY: Cornell University Press, 1972.

THE WHITE PRIMARY

by Tinsley E. Yarbrough
Department of Political Science
East Carolina University

Smith v. Allwright, 321 U.S. 649 (1944) [U.S. Supreme Court]

Of all the post-Reconstruction stratagems used to limit black voting, the white primary was undoubtedly the most effective. By the end of the first decade of the twentieth century, the direct primary had become the most common method by which political parties nominated candidates for public office. In the South, where the Republican party—the party of Lincoln and abolition—rarely even fielded candidates, much less won elections, victory in the Democratic primary was tantamount to election. Exclusion of blacks from the primary thus effectively excluded them from meaningful participation in the electoral process.

The Fifteenth Amendment forbids racial discrimination at the polls. The white primary's defenders contended, however, that party primaries were not elections in the constitutional sense, that instead they were simply the private activities of a nongovernmental entity. In support of that position, moreover, they could draw some comfort from *Newberry v. United States* (1921), a U.S. Supreme Court case holding the campaign finance regulations of the 1910 federal Corrupt Practices Act inapplicable to primaries. While the majority opinion in *Newberry* included the assertion that primaries were "in no sense elections for an office," only four members of the five-member majority accepted that contention. Nevertheless, in the ensuing years *Newberry* was widely construed to support the view that primaries were private affairs not subject to federal constitutional or statutory restrictions on the conduct of elections.

Although a common feature of southern politics, the white primary was not used in every section of the South. In Texas, it was required by the rules of the state Democratic party, but in a few areas white factions relied on the black vote in the party's primaries. The San Antonio party faction, which did not benefit from that black vote, lobbied for a state law limiting participation in the primary to white voters only. Bolstered by the *Newberry* decision, the Texas legislature yielded to the pressure and, in 1923, enacted a white primary statute. Its action precipitated over 30 years of litigation, including the Supreme Court's landmark ruling in *Smith v. Allwright*.

Following enactment of the 1923 law, an election judge denied a ballot to Dr. L. A. Nixon, an El Paso, Texas, black. Nixon filed a suit for damages. When the case reached the U.S. Supreme Court in *Nixon v. Herndon* (1927), the Court avoided deciding whether primaries were elections covered by the Fifteenth Amendment's ban on racial discrimination in voting, holding instead that the Texas law was a "direct and obvious infringement" on the Fourteenth Amendment's guarantee to equal protection of the laws. To circumvent the Court's decision, the Texas legislature then repealed the 1923 law and enacted a new one authorizing the executive committee of each party in the state to "prescribe the qualifications of its own members." When the state executive committee of the Democratic party promptly voted to exclude blacks from the party's membership and participation in its primaries, the Supreme Court, in *Nixon v. Condon* (1932), again reversed, terming the executive committee a delegate of the state under the challenged law and thus subject to the requirements of equal protection. The Court refused to decide, however, whether the party itself could exclude blacks. Instead, it merely noted that "[W]hatever inherent power a state political party has to determine the content of its membership resides

in the state convention." At this point, the Texas legislature took no further action. But the state convention of the Democratic party enacted a white primary rule; and in *Grovey v. Townsend* (1935), the Supreme Court unanimously upheld the convention, drawing on the findings of Texas's highest court to conclude that the state's political parties were "voluntary associations," not "creatures of the state." As a private entity, the Court ruled, the Democratic party could exclude blacks from its primaries without violating the equal protection clause, which applied only to state action.

The *Grovey* decision was short-lived, however. By 1940, the Supreme Court's membership had changed considerably. Moreover, its decision in *United States v. Classic* (1941), a federal prosecution for ballot-box stuffing and other notorious incidents of fraud in the conduct of primaries in New Orleans, gave opponents of the white primary a potentially devastating weapon. Rejecting contentions to the contrary, the *Classic* Court concluded that a primary is an election and subject to federal constitutional and statutory commands whenever it is "an integral part of the procedure of choice" or "in fact . . . effectively controls the choice."

The primary was clearly an integral part of Texas's election machinery. State law, for example, required that major party candidates be selected by primary, set the date for the conduct of primaries, required a runoff primary in close races, imposed a poll tax for primaries as well as general elections, and provided for the adjudication of contested primaries in the state courts. Therefore, when poll officials persisted in denying blacks the right to vote in the primary even after *Classic*, a would-be black voter sued Allwright, an election judge, and his assistants. The U.S. District Court for the Southern District of Texas dismissed the case; and the Court of Appeals for the Fifth Circuit, citing the *Grovey* decision, affirmed. But on April 3, 1944, more than 20 years after Texas had first enacted a white primary law, the Supreme Court reversed the lower courts and overturned *Grovey*.

Speaking for the majority, Justice Stanley F. Reed relied heavily on the *Classic* decision and the significant place of the primary in

Texas's election machinery. "When primaries become a part of the machinery for choosing officials, state and national, as they have here," asserted Reed, "the same tests to determine the character of discrimination or abridgement should be applied to the primary as are applied to the general election." Measured by that standard, the Texas scheme was clearly a forbidden state action, though accomplished through an ostensibly private institution. Reed concluded: "The United States is a constitutional democracy. Its organic law grants to all citizens a right to participate in the choice of elected officials without restriction by any State because of race. This grant to the people of the opportunity for choice is not to be nullified by a State through casting its electoral process in a form which permits a private organization to practice racial discrimination in the election. Constitutional rights would be of little value if they could be thus indirectly denied."

Although Justice Felix Frankfurter concurred without opinion only in the Court's judgment, Justice Owen J. Roberts was the lone dissenter. In his majority opinion, Reed had attempted to justify the Court's overturning of *Grovey*, a comparatively recent precedent. "[W]hen convinced of former error," he contended, "this Court has never felt constrained to follow precedent. . . . This is particularly true when the decision believed erroneous is the application of a constitutional principle rather than an interpretation of the Constitution to extract the principle itself."

Roberts was hardly persuaded. Charging his colleagues with assuming a "knowledge and wisdom . . . denied to our predecessors," Roberts attacked their willingness to overturn a unanimous precedent less than a decade old. Such an approach, he complained, brought "adjudications of this tribunal into the same class as a restricted railroad ticket, good for this day and train only." And if *Grovey* had been overruled *sub silento* ("silently") in *Classic*, "the situation" was, to Roberts, "even worse than that exhibited by the outright repudiation of an earlier decision." For no party in *Classic* had suggested that *Grovey* had been wrongly decided, *Grovey* was not mentioned in the opinions filed for *Classic*, and *Classic* involved

no question of a voter's eligibility to participate in a primary. Roberts submitted: "It is regrettable that in an era marked by doubt and confusion, an era whose greatest need is steadfastness of thought and purpose, this court, which has been looked to as exhibiting consistency in adjudication, and a steadiness which would hold the balance even in the face of temporary ebbs and flows of opinion, should now itself become the breeder of fresh doubt and confusion in the public mind as to the stability of our institutions."

Roberts's concerns notwithstanding, the Court's decision in *Smith v. Allwright* was a clear-cut repudiation of the Texas scheme. Even so, campaigns were mounted in several southern states, most notably South Carolina, to circumvent the Court's mandate. Under the *Classic* decision, primaries were held to constitute elections for constitutional purposes if they were integral parts of a state's procedure for choosing government officials *or* in fact effectively controlled that choice. Since the Texas white primary was heavily regulated by state law, however, the Supreme Court based its *Allwright* decision solely on the first prong of the *Classic* rationale, holding the Texas scheme invalid because it was an integral part of the state's election machinery. Seizing on that basis for the Supreme Court's decision, South Carolina Governor Olin S. Johnston convened a special session of the state legislature and proposed that all references to the primary be removed from the state's statute books. "White Supremacy will be maintained in our primaries," Johnston exclaimed. "Let the chips fall where they may!" Although a number of South Carolina politicians and newspapers urged caution, warning that the governor's ploy would leave the conduct of primaries in the state vulnerable to all manner of fraud, Johnston's strategy was quickly adopted. Almost as promptly, however, U.S. District Judge J. Waties Waring, an eighth-generation Charlestonian with impeccable social credentials, voided the scheme in a 1947 ruling. Since 1910, Waring reminded his fellow citizens, every governor, state legislator, and member of South Carolina's congressional delegation had been a nominee of the Democratic party. The Democratic primary thus effectively controlled the election choice and, under *Classic*, was subject to the Constitution's ban on racial discrimination in the electoral process. "It is time for South Carolina to rejoin the union," scolded Waring. "It is time to fall in step with the other states and adopt the American way of conducting elections."

South Carolina politicians were not yet ready to "rejoin the union." After Waring's decision was affirmed by the Court of Appeals for the Fourth Circuit and the Supreme Court declined to review the case, the state Democratic party enacted new rules requiring blacks who wished to participate in the party's primaries to take an offensive oath of support for "states' rights" and racial segregation and opposition to a proposed federal ban on employment discrimination. In 1948, however, Waring struck down that ploy, too. Proposals to follow the South Carolina approach in Florida failed in 1945 and 1947. In Alabama, voters adopted a state constitutional amendment establishing discriminatory voter registration requirements. But a three-judge federal district court composed entirely of native Alabamians struck down that scheme. And in Virginia, years earlier, lower federal courts had invalidated the Old Dominion's white primary.

Fittingly, however, the final judicial blow to the white primary was to be delivered in a 1953 Texas case, *Terry v. Adams*, decided by the U.S. Supreme Court. The Jaybird Association had been formed in Fort Bend County, Texas, in 1889. All whites on the county voting rolls were automatically listed as association members. Before each Democratic primary in the county, the association held its own primary, conducted under the same regulations that governed the party's primary. With few exceptions, winners in the all-white Jaybird primary went on to enter and win with-out opposition the Democratic primary and the general election as well. In *Terry*, the Supreme Court rejected contentions that the association was a "mere private group" whose discriminatory policies were beyond the reach of the Fifteenth Amendment. "The only election that has counted in this Texas county for more than fifty years," Justice Hugo L. Black asserted in an opinion announcing the Court's judgment—an opinion capturing the essence of *Classic* and *Smith v. Allwright*—"has been that held by the Jaybirds from which Negroes were excluded. The Democratic primary and the general election have become no more than the perfunctory ratifiers of the choice that has already been made in Jaybird elections from which Negroes have been excluded. It is immaterial that the state does not control that part of this elective process which it leaves for the Jaybirds to manage. The Jaybird primary has become an integral part, indeed the only effective part, of the elective process that determines who shall rule and govern in the county. The effect of the whole procedure, Jaybird primary plus Democratic primary plus general election, is to do precisely that which the Fifteenth Amendment forbids—strip Negroes of every vestige of influence in selecting the officials who control the local county matters that intimately touch the daily lives of citizens."

Selected Bibliography

Hamilton, C.V. *The Bench and the Ballot*. New York: Oxford University Press, 1973.

Key, V.O., Jr. *Southern Politics in State and Nation*. New York: Alfred A. Knopf, Inc., 1949.

Strong, D.S. "The Rise of Negro Voting in Texas." *American Political Science Review* 42 (1948): 510–22.

Weeks, O. D. "The White Primary: 1944–48." *American Political Science Review* 42 (1948): 500–10.

Yarbrough, T.E. *A Passion for Justice: J. Waties Waring and Civil Rights*. New York: Oxford University Press, 1987.

THE "POLITICAL THICKET" OF MALAPPORTIONMENT

by Tinsley E. Yarbrough
Department of Political Science
East Carolina University

Colegrove v. Green, 328 U.S. 549 (1946) [U.S. Supreme Court]

By the end of World War II, the districts from which members of the U.S. House of Representatives were chosen were badly malapportioned. Population disparities had reached critical proportions in many states. District populations ranged, for example, from 698,540 to 163,561 in Ohio; 534,568 to 195,427 in Maryland; 528,961 to 230,010 in Texas; and 439,895 to 186,831 in Florida. Illinois was the worst: 914,053 persons resided in the most populous district, 112,116 in the smallest. Illinois's districts had been last redrawn in 1901.

While leaving to state legislatures the authority to determine the times, places, and manner for electing representatives and senators, Article I, Section 4, of the U.S. Constitution gives Congress the power to "make or alter such regulations." In the Reapportionment Act of 1911, Congress had stipulated that congressmen be elected in compact and contiguous districts of substantially equal population. But subsequent reapportionment statutes omitted such requirements.

The courts had also taken little action. In *Smiley v. Holm* (1932), one of several suits arising out of redistricting following the 1930 census, the U.S. Supreme Court rejected the contention that state districting statutes were derived from a federal constitutional authority and thus immune from gubernatorial veto. By deciding the case on that narrow ground, however, the Court avoided determining whether the standards of compactness, contiguity, and population equality mandated by the Reapportionment Act were still in force or whether, even if applicable, the extent of a state legislature's compliance with them posed a nonjusticiable "political" question that courts traditionally had declined to resolve. In another 1932 case, *Wood v. Broom*, the Court held that

the standards imposed by the 1911 act had indeed expired, but it did not reach the issue of whether federal courts could impose *constitutional* standards on congressional districting schemes. Justices Louis D. Brandeis, Harlan F. Stone, Owen J. Roberts, and Benjamin N. Cardozo had voted to dismiss the suit, however, for "want of equity."

When Northwestern University political scientist Kenneth Colegrove and other urban Illinois voters challenged the egregious malapportionment in that state's congressional districts in the mid-1940s, it was far from clear how the Supreme Court might react, particularly given its growing solicitude for civil liberties during the late 1930s and the 1940s. Nor, in a very real sense, was the Court's stance to be much clearer when its decision in *Colegrove v. Green* was announced on June 10, 1946. Colegrove and company were denied relief. But only seven justices participated, and one of the four justices in the majority concurred only in the result, declining to join Justice Felix Frankfurter's plurality opinion.

Speaking for himself and Justices Stanley F. Reed and Harold H. Burton, Frankfurter agreed that the three-judge federal district court that had dismissed Colegrove's suit had properly concluded that the standards Congress had imposed on congressional districting in the 1911 statute were not longer applicable. *Wood v. Broom*, he asserted, had settled that issue long ago, and Congress had never challenged the *Wood* Court's judgment. Frankfurter also concurred with the four justices who had concluded in *Wood* that such suits should be dismissed for "want of equity." Such issues, he declared, "must be resolved by considerations on the basis of which the Court, from time to time, has refused to intervene in controversies. It has refused to do so because due regard for the effective working of our Government revealed this issue to be of a peculiarly political nature and therefore not meet for judicial determination."

In Frankfurter's judgment, the appellants were not seeking relief for the discriminatory denial of individual rights. Instead, they were complaining about "a wrong suffered by Illinois as a polity," a wrong courts were not competent to remedy. "Of course no court can affirmatively re-map the Illinois districts," he asserted forcefully, if not prophetically. "At best we could only declare the existing electoral system invalid," leaving the state's congressmen, if its legislature chose not to act, to be selected by at-large elections, despite Congress's long preference for election by district. Instead, the Constitution had clothed Congress with "ample power" to deal with the evils about which the appellants complained "with great zeal." If Congress failed to act, Frankfurter concluded, the "remedy ultimately lies with the people," not the courts. Historically, the congressional apportionment process had been embroiled in politics, and "Courts ought not to enter [that] political thicket."

In a dissent joined by Justices William O. Douglas and Frank Murphy, Justice Hugo L. Black took strong issue with virtually every element of Frankfurter's rationale. First, he challenged his colleague's assertion that Colegrove's suit involved no violation of individual rights. The equal protection clause, he contended, should forbid "the States to pick out certain qualified citizens or groups of citizens and deny them the right to vote at all," or "expressly give certain citizens a half-vote and others a full vote." He saw no difference between such rank discrimination and that perpetrated by a districting scheme in which the votes of certain voters would be "only one-ninth as effective in choosing representatives to Congress as the votes of other citizens." In fact, it seemed to him to be "exactly the kind that the equal protection clause was intended to prohibit."

In Black's view, moreover, the command of Article I, Section 2, that congressmen be elected "by the people of the several states" clearly implied that "state election systems, no matter what their form, should be designed to give approximately equal weight to each vote cast." To him, that provision was intended not merely to eliminate "a nation-wide 'rotten borough' system as between the states," but also to eliminate such discrimination within the states.

Second, Black rejected Frankfurter's conclusion that the suit presented a nonjusticiable "political" question. He agreed that voting and elections were obviously "political," but condemned as a "mere 'play upon words'" Frankfurter's notion that courts have no role in protecting rights relevant to the political process. The appellants were not asking the courts to supervise elections generally; they were asking only that an apportionment scheme be declared invalid. *Colegrove* was thus "exactly" on line with *Smiley v. Holm*, in which the Court was also asked to—and did—invalidate a state apportionment bill. Finally, Black rejected Frankfurter's concern that a decision striking down the existing Illinois system would create undue political difficulties. True, he asserted, at-large elections might be the immediate consequence of the Court's intervention. But such an election had an element of virtue the existing system did not have: "[I]t does not discriminate against some groups to favor others, it gives all the people an equally effective voice in electing their representatives as is essential under a free government, and it is constitutional."

On the authority of *Smiley v. Holm*, Justice Wiley B. Rutledge agreed with Black that the issues raised in the case were justiciable. Unlike Black, however, Rutledge had decided that given the "shortness of time remaining" before the next elections, "effective relief" could not be awarded. At-large elections "might bring greater equality of voting right." But, Rutledge asserted, they would also go against the "prevailing" congressional preference for representation by district. Even if the Court did intervene, he added, it was doubtful it could order extensive reform, given the broad authority of the political branches of government over the election process. "There is not, and could not be except abstractly," Rutledge was convinced, "a right of absolute equality in voting. At best there could be only a rough approximation . . . . And the cure sought may be worse than the disease."

Despite the equivocal nature of Rutledge's controlling opinion in *Colegrove*, it was to be 16 years before the Supreme Court would launch the extended assault on legislative malapportionment it began with *Baker v. Carr* (1962). The Court's unsigned opinion in *MacDougall v. Green* (1948), which denied relief to Henry Wallace Progressives challenging an Illinois law restricting third-party access to the ballot, left it uncertain whether the Court considered such suits nonjusticiable. In refusing to review the constitutionality of Georgia's "county unit" system in *South v. Peters* (1950), however, the Court invoked the "political question" doctrine. Its summary dismissals of a number of reapportionment cases suggested, moreover, that its *South v. Peters* position extended, for the moment at least, to legislative malapportionment.

Selected Bibliography

Baker, G.E. *The Reapportionment Revolution*. New York: Random House, 1965.

Dixon, R.G., Jr. *Democratic Representation: Reapportionment in Law and Politics*. New York: Oxford University Press, 1968.

FROM THE "POLITICAL THICKET" TO "ONE MAN, ONE VOTE"

by Stephen H. Wainscott
Department of Political Science
Clemson University

Baker v. Carr, 369 U.S. 186 (1962); *Reynolds v. Sims*, 377 U.S. 533 (1964) [U.S. Supreme Court]

In the 200-year history of the U.S. Supreme Court numerous cases stand out as milestones in the evolution of U.S. constitutional law. Far fewer cases deserve to be described as revolutionary. In the 1960s, a revolution occurred, but unlike the War of Independence, no blood was shed and no shots were fired. Yet, in certain respects, the "reapportionment revolution" was as significant for the development of representative democracy in the United States as were the conflicts at Saratoga and Valley Forge. The Supreme Court's decision in 1962 to enter the political thicket of legislative apportionment and districting was nothing less than a judicial equivalent of a declaration of independence. Upon his retirement in 1969, Earl Warren described the reapportionment cases as the most important judgments of his 16-year tenure as chief justice.

Like many dramatic court rulings, the reapportionment decisions were rooted in the social and economic developments of previous decades. More specifically, twentieth-century political change in the United States has been largely a by-product of population growth and shift. For example, rapid urbanization helped spawn many demands for political "reform" during the Progressive Era. As early as the 1910 census, rural America was becoming a thing of the past; for the first time in history most Americans were reported as living in areas classified as "urban." It would not be long before these recently transplanted city-dwellers, eager to have a patch of land of their own, would precipitate the creation of a new demographic category, "suburban." By the 1970 census—the first to follow the reapportionment decisions of 1962 and 1964—70 percent of the nation's population occupied two percent of the nation's land.

As late as World War II, few Americans fully comprehended the problems and dislocations that would result from these vast shifts from the countryside to the city and from farm to factory. Also, few were able to contemplate the enormous new demands that would be placed on government at all levels for services ranging from pollution control to mass transit systems.

Urban America inherited its share of problems and tensions, yet when city folk brought their claims to the public arena, they discovered that population shifts had not been accompanied by a migration in political power. Across the country, halls of government, especially legislatures, had a distinctly rural tilt. Congressional malapportionment was particularly evident in Georgia where, as of 1950, there was a population disparity of more than 500,000 between the largest and smallest districts.

However, rural domination was especially flagrant in state legislatures, with Florida's providing an excellent case study in malapportionment. Between 1950 and 1960, Florida experienced a population growth of nearly 80 percent, most of which occurred in the southeastern coastal counties and in the retirement communities of the southwestern Gulf region. Even so, the state legislature was dominated by a coterie of lawmakers, known as the "Pork Chop Gang," who represented the rural counties of the northern part of the state. In fact, a majority of the seats were held by members whose districts accounted for less than 15 percent of the state's population. An example of the policy effects of Florida's malapportionment can be seen in the disbursement of revenue from state-operated race tracks. The Pork Chop Gang saw to it that the receipts were equally distributed to the state's 67 counties, with the effect that Dade County (Miami) got 20 cents per person while tiny Liberty County received in excess of $61 per person.

In many respects, malapportionment had a characteristically, though not exclusively, southern flavor. Georgia demagogue Eugene Talmadge, in bragging that he never campaigned in a town large enough to have a streetcar, seemed to echo a widely shared feeling that cities breed sin and that country people have a superior talent for public service. Also, it was part of the southern anti-urban prejudice that big cities had ample sums of cash stashed away in secret accounts and, thus, did not deserve the financial largesse of state government.

During the 1920s, Illinois became the setting for the first significant challenges to state and federal apportionment arrangements. With a heavily urban population, Illinois was a hotbed of constant conflict between rural "downstate" interests and the political empires of Cook County (Chicago). For years, the state legislature, a bastion of downstate power, had rejected demands for reapportionment. In 1925, the Cook County Board of Commissioners voted to withhold state taxes collected and even threatened to secede from the state if the lawmakers in Springfield continued to ignore the matter of reapportionment.

In 1930, John Keogh, a Chicago businessman placed on trial for federal income tax evasion, contended that Illinois's failure to reapportion the state legislature had deprived the state of its constitutional guarantee of a republican form of government, thereby absolving Keogh of any obligation to pay taxes. Later, during a foreclosure suit involving one of his businesses, Keogh claimed that the state courts had no legal standing in view of legislative malapportionment. When the court ruled against his motion for dismissal of the case, Keogh shot and killed the prosecuting attorney and fired errant shots at the judge. Upon his arrest for the shootings, Keogh stated that the death of the prosecutor was an unfortunate but necessary sacrifice in the crusade for reapportionment.

In the mid-1940s, the issue of apportionment resurfaced, this time centering on the matter of Illinois's congressional districts. Kenneth Colegrove, a political science professor at Northwestern University, on behalf of several other academicians and Chicago lawyers, filed suit in federal district court challenging the validity of the state's congressional districts, which ranged in population from 112,000 to 914,000. Colegrove, a resident of the largest district, sought a court order enjoining the state from conducting the 1946 congressional elections under the existing districting arrangement. He further requested an order for the election of U.S. representatives at-large.

The plaintiffs contended that the enormous disparity in the populations of the state's congressional districts was in conflict with certain requirements of the federal Reapportionment Act of 1911 and with the Fourteenth Amendment's guarantee of equal protection of the laws. The suit also argued that the existing apportionment violated the provision of Article I that U.S. representatives be allocated to the states "according to their respective numbers" and that they be elected "by the people of the several States."

Colegrove v. Green was argued before the U.S. Supreme Court in March 1946. On its face the case appeared to turn on the question of whether Colegrove and other residents of more populous districts had been discriminated against. However, before the Court could consider the case on its merits, it had to wrestle with more vexing questions of jurisdiction and other procedural matters.

From one perspective, the Court could have taken the position that it lacked jurisdiction entirely, since Article I, Section 4, permits states to determine the manner of electing congressional representatives. On the other hand, some justices, including William O. Douglas, felt that the case presented questions of equal protection and due process of law over which the Court could legitimately exercise jurisdiction. A third alternative was that while the Court possessed jurisdiction, it could decline to exercise it. Supporting the latter approach was a long-standing notion of jurisprudence that held that the Court should refuse to hear cases deemed to be of an inherently "political" nature. Viewed by some as a dodge, the "political questions" concept, properly understood, is intended to extricate courts from controversies in which judicial authority lacks guidance or is incapable of fashioning reasonable and appropriate solutions.

During the time that *Colegrove* was docketed in the Supreme Court, Justice Robert H. Jackson was serving as prosecutor at the Nuremburg war-crime trials. And, less than a month after the Court heard oral arguments in the case, Chief Justice Harlan F. Stone suddenly died of a heart attack. Thus, it was a seven-member Court that split 4–3 in rejecting Colegove's suit seeking the invalidation of Illinois's congressional districts. Relying heavily on his interpretation of Article I, Section 4,

Justice Felix Frankfurter's majority opinion summarily dismissed the suit for lack of jurisdiction. But he went a step further. Deciding *Colegrove* on its merits, he said, would require the Court to embroil itself in "party contests." "It is hostile to a democratic system to involve the judiciary in the politics of the people," he wrote. The courts "ought not enter this political thicket."

Although the *Colegrove* ruling legally applied only to congressional districting, the case sent a loud and clear message throughout the U.S. judicial system that reapportionment was a matter for legislatures, not courts, to decide. The posture of judicial nonintervention was especially evident in state courts. In the rare instances in which they claimed jurisdiction, state courts seldom ruled in favor of plaintiffs, and when they did, rulings merely invalidated existing arrangements without providing remedies.

In 1960, Dr. C. G. Gomillion, dean of Tuskegee Institute in Alabama, filed suit challenging the validity of the city's elections. At the time, nearly 80 percent of Tuskegee's population was black. The all-white state legislature, fearful that blacks might soon enjoy a majority of the city's registered voters, passed legislation transforming city boundaries into the shape of a sea horse. The effect of the gerrymander was the exclusion from municipal elections of all but five of the city's black voters. Ruling in Gomillion's favor but determined not to disturb the precedent of *Colegrove*, the Court ducked the Fourteenth Amendment issue of equal protection and instead declared the racial gerrymander to be violative of voting rights guaranteed by the Fifteenth Amendment. Although the issues presented in *Gomillion v. Lightfoot* were only tangentially related to reapportionment, the case nonetheless led the Court back to the edge of the political thicket.

Despite the Court's *Gomillion* ruling and other foreshadowings of shifting judicial opinion, successful challenges to apportionment schemes were virtually impossible throughout the 1950s. Adding to the frustration of plaintiffs was that few state constitutions required legislative apportionment on an equal population basis. Tennessee was different. The state's constitution, drafted in 1870, called for both houses of the legislature to be apportioned among districts "according to the number of qualified electors in each." Under this seemingly clear directive, the legislature was reapportioned in 1881, 1891, and 1901. Six decades would pass before reapportionment would occur again. The existence of a clear legal mandate for reapportionment and the state's persistent refusal to do so made Tennessee a logical setting for an assault on *Colegrove.*

In many ways, Tennessee was typical of twentieth-century growth trends across the nation. In 1960, only 11 percent of the state's work force was employed in agriculture, compared with 33 percent in 1940. Between 1950 and 1960, the four principal cities (Knoxville, Memphis, Nashville, and Chattanooga) experienced a population gain of 30 percent. The so-called urban fringe bordering these metropolises grew 135 percent during the same period.

The forces of industrialization and urbanization had clearly put Tennessee in the forefront of the "New South," but politically the grip of Old South tradition remained strong. By unspoken custom, the governor almost always hailed from a small town, and the state legislature was an antediluvian assembly of rural potentates. State senate district populations ranged from 25,000 to 132,000. Twenty of the 33 senate members were from counties that accounted for barely one-third of the state's population. Had legislative apportionment been based on population, Shelby County (Memphis) would have been allotted 20 members of the General Assembly; instead, it had nine. Inequalities in the legislative halls of Nashville led to disparities in Washington as well. As of 1960, the congressman from the ninth district (Memphis) represented 170,000 more constituents than the legislators from two neighboring districts combined.

Breaking the stranglehold of rural power seemed virtually impossible. Tennessee, like most other southern states, had witnessed occasional skirmishing between progressive-minded governors and recalcitrant state legislatures, but few state executives had dared to make reapportionment a top priority of their administrations. Compounding the frustrations of reapportionment advocates was the fact that Tennessee's constitution—which, until 1953, was the oldest unamended state constitution in the nation—contained no provision for popular initiative or referendum. With legislative pathways effectively blocked, complainants would be forced to go to court, an unappealing alternative in view of the long shadow of *Colegrove.*

Charles Baker was mayor of Millington, Tennessee, a burgeoning suburb of Memphis. From the end of World War II, the greater Memphis area felt the impact of two migration flows: blacks from the cotton fields of western Tennessee and northern Mississippi, and white professionals and business managers transferred by their companies from places farther north. As chairman of the Shelby County Quarterly Court, a legislative entity that sliced the financial pie of the state's fastest growing metropolis, Baker experienced firsthand the pressures of new people and new demands. In trying to cope with the problems of urban growth, he got little help from Nashville, where the legislative mindset reflected the sentiments of house floor leader Jim Cummings: "I believe in collecting the taxes where the money is—in the cities—and spending it where it's needed—in the country." Baker believed that until the legislature was forced to reapportion, the Cummings brand of populism would continue to rob his county of its just financial due. So he decided to sue.

Baker v. Carr was argued before the Supreme Court in April 1961 and again in October of that year. Baker and his coplaintiffs contended that the Tennessee legislature had violated the state constitution by its unwillingness to reapportion. Voters in overpopulated areas, Baker's brief asserted, were deprived of meaningful representation and, therefore, were denied their fair share of state revenues. Entitlement to due process and to equal protection of the laws under the Fourteenth Amendment required that legislative districts be of equal population. The appellants sought invalidation of the state constitution's antiquated apportionment provisions and substantive relief in the form of a court order requiring at-large elections until the General Assembly acted to equalize state legislative districts.

As in *Colegrove*, procedural rather than substantive issues dominated the Court's attention in *Baker v. Carr*. At the outset, the Court was concerned with whether the federal courts possessed the jurisdiction to hear claims of Fourteenth Amendment violations stemming from state legislative apportionment. Second, the Court sought to determine whether Baker and the other appellants were individually affected by an alleged wrongdoing and, therefore, had standing to bring suit. Finally, the Court's decision had to clarify the question of justiciability (i.e., whether there existed, regardless of the merits of the complaint, a "judicially discoverable and administrable remedy").

The Court's *Baker* decision was announced on March 26, 1962. Justice William J. Brennan, writing for a six-member majority, declared that the Court would confine its ruling to the matters of jurisdiction, standing, and justiciability. The Court would not pass judgment on the merits of the complaint of malrepresentation. A leading critic of Warren Court activism in the area of reapportionment observed that the Court's approach in *Baker* can be likened to a "three-legged stool with a crucial fourth leg left for future construction."

Somewhat cavalierly, the Court settled the question of jurisdiction. Unless the complaint was so frivolous as to be absolutely devoid of merit, the mere fact that the case presented a Fourteenth Amendment claim was sufficient to convince Brennan that the Court had jurisdiction.

With similar ease the Court established consensus on the question of standing. The only justice to demur was Frankfurter, who reminded his colleagues that the *Colegrove* case involved not a private wrong but an incidence of alleged public malfeasance. Dismissing this objection, Brennan's opinion stated that, as registered voters in overpopulated legislative districts, the plaintiffs were entitled to claim that they had been personally as well as collectively disadvantaged. Furthermore, they had standing to sue regardless of the merits of their allegations.

As expected, the question of justiciability proved to be much thornier, for it required a reexamination of the doctrine of political questions. Brennan held that several criteria were essential to a finding of a nonjusticiable political question. Among these criteria were (1) a "textually demonstrable constitutional commitment of the issue to a coordinate political department" or (2) "a lack of judicially discoverable and manageable standards for resolving it." Cases involving foreign relations, time limits for ratifying constitutional amendments, and guarantees to states under Article IV (e.g., a "republican form of government") are examples of political questions imposing reasonable constraints on the federal judiciary, Brennan stated.

At considerable length, Brennan's opinion attempted to differentiate between *Baker* and past cases the Court had judged to be of an inherently political and, therefore, nonjusticiable nature. In *Baker*, "[W]e have no question decided, or to be decided, by a political branch of government coequal with this court," he claimed. Then, in a brash assertion of judicial power, Brennan held that judicial standards necessary for resolving the dispute "are well developed and familiar" and indeed had been available since the ratification of the Fourteenth Amendment. Perhaps sensing his colleagues' unease with such a broad claim, Brennan used the Court's decision in *Gomillion* to show that challenges to certain state governmental arrangements could be construed as justiciable under the Fifteenth Amendment.

The majority opinion was greeted by a stirring dissent by Frankfurter, who contended that except in matters of racial discrimination, mandates under the equal protection clause for judicial intrusion into "matters of state government" were not as self-evident as Brennan seemed to imply. Frankfurter rejected the appellants' contention that their individual votes had been "diluted" as a result of alleged malapportionment. Such a claim, Frankfurter argued, was "circular talk," since the value of a vote was indeterminate. He noted that representation based solely on population was not universally practiced by the states at the time the Fourteenth Amendment was ratified. He summarized his objections by stating that the Court was being asked "to choose among competing bases of representation—ultimately, really, among competing theories of political philosophy" in an ill-advised and misguided effort to devise a preferred system of state elections. In presuming to prescribe an apportionment system suitable for Tennessee or any other state, the Court's majority, in Frankfurter's view, had not only entered the political thicket; it was wallowing in it.

Frankfurter's dissent was somewhat overwrought, for the Court's decision avoided establishing a standard for state legislative apportionment. Instead, the case was remanded to the federal district court in Nashville for trial on its merits.

Reaction to the Court's *Baker* decision was swift. Editorial support came forth from most of the major metropolitan newspapers. The American Municipal Association, the U.S. Conference of Mayors, and major labor unions also expressed approval. Attorney General Robert Kennedy, who would soon represent the government in a Georgia reapportionment case, called *Baker* "a landmark in the development of representative government." And, in sharp contrast to President Eisenhower's posture of detachment from the Court's school desegregation decision in 1954, President John Kennedy professed unqualified approval of the *Baker* ruling.

However, the decision was not without its critics, especially in the South. In Tennessee, a state representative drew a parallel between the Court's desegregation rulings and the recent reapportionment decision: "Apparently [the Court's] formula is more Negroes and less money for rural areas." Georgia U.S. Senator Richard Russell accused the Court of no less than setting out to destroy the American system of checks and balances.

Although the Supreme Court did not specify precise standards for reapportionment, the practical implication was that at least one house of a state's legislature had to be apportioned on the basis of equal population districts. In the flood of state and federal court litigation that ensued, the mere demonstration of population inequalities was sufficient in most instances for plaintiffs to win decisions invalidating existing apportionment systems.

As an example of Warren Court activism, it is tempting to compare the historic *Baker v. Carr* decision to the Court's decree in *Brown v.*

Board of Education (1954). Although similarities exist, the differences are more striking. First, unlike *Brown*, which was the capstone of the Court's increasing willingness to strike down racial barriers in public accommodations, *Baker v. Carr* was a dramatic reversal of two decades of precedent. More important, in contrast to the desegregation decision, which met with considerable resistance and noncompliance, the impact of the reapportionment decision was immediate. Within a year of the ruling, 36 states were involved in litigation. By the end of 1963, at least one house of 24 state legislatures had been ruled unconstitutional by either a federal or state court.

"Round Two" of the reapportionment revolution began in March 1963, when the Supreme Court took up arguments in *Gray v. Sanders*. At issue was the validity of Georgia's "county-unit" system for nominating the governor, U.S. senators, and other statewide officers. Under this system, each of Georgia's 159 counties was assigned six, four, or two "units," awarded on a winner-take-all basis to the candidate receiving a plurality of the county popular vote. Defenders of the system argued that it was equivalent to the electoral college system of presidential election. However, unlike the electoral college, wherein the allocation of electors to states is adjusted decennially according to population changes, the allotment of units to Georgia's counties had remained static since 1917. To illustrate the inequity implicit in this system, Fulton County (Atlanta), with a 1960 population of 500,000, had six units, compared with Echols County's (population 1,800) two units. Thus, to offset a single popular vote in Echols, a candidate would have needed to receive 99 in Fulton.

In *Gray v. Sanders*, the justices ordered that simple-majority at-large nomination be substituted for the county-unit system, which was held to be unconstitutional under the equal protection clause of the Fourteenth Amendment. Writing for the majority, Justice William O. Douglas declared that the "conception of political equality. . . . can mean only one thing—one person, one vote." Although the decision did not involve questions of legislative apportionment or districting, the catchphrase "one person, one vote" became the guiding force in future reapportionment cases.

In February 1964, the Court handed down another sweeping decision involving Georgia. At issue in *Wesberry v. Sanders* was the apportionment of the state's congressional districts. As of 1960, one of every five Georgians lived in the district encompassing Atlanta. Yet, with a population three times that of the state's smallest district, Atlanta had only one of Georgia's representatives. This time the Court's majority opinion was written by Justice Hugo L. Black, who stated that "as nearly as is practicable, one man's vote in a congressional election is to be worth as much as another's."

Having mandated equal population districts for purposes of congressional representation, it was but a matter of time before the federal courts would apply the same principle to state legislatures. In *Reynolds v. Sims* (1964), a case in which challenges to legislatures in six states (Alabama, Colorado, Delaware, Maryland, New York, and Virginia) were joined, the reapportionment revolution finally unfolded.

Few were surprised that the Alabama case would provide the framework for the principal arguments in *Reynolds v. Sims*. Like many of its neighbors, the state was a classic case study in southern political pathology, the dominant symptom of which was the suppression and disfranchisement of Alabama's black population.

The origins of Alabama's reapportionment wars date back to 1901 when, after considerable factional infighting, the all-Democratic legislature adopted a new state constitution. Largely conceived as an instrument for eliminating blacks from the political process, the constitution was an unqualified triumph for the conservative alliance of industrial "Big Mules" and "Black Belt" planters. Over the objections of northern Alabama lawmakers who, true to their populist heritage, advocated state spending policies favorable to their have-not constituencies, the reapportionment plan, while ostensibly based on population, guaranteed each of the state's 67 counties at least one seat in the House of Representatives. Respecting the integrity of county boundaries, single-member Senate districts comprised one or more whole counties.

The constitution of 1901 required reapportionment decennially according to census enumerations, but this mandate was regularly ignored. In the 1940s and 1950s, Governor James ("Kissin' Jim") Folsom, a populist hillbilly with a sympathy for blacks that eventually led to his political demise, tried unsuccessfully to circumvent the legislature's inaction by assembling a constitutional convention. The apportionment formula devised in 1901 remained unchanged until the 1960s, when the first volleys were fired in *Reynolds v. Sims* (1964). Consistent with the provisions of the antiquated constitution, population variances among the state's single-member Senate districts were as great as 40 to one. In the House of Representatives, Bullock County, located in the heart of the Black Belt (where blacks were counted for census purposes despite being denied voting rights), had one representative for its population of 13,000. Jefferson County (Birmingham), with a 1960 population of 600,000, had just seven representatives and, like Bullock, a single senator.

On August 12, 1961, Charles Morgan, a young Birmingham attorney, filed suit in federal district court alleging that he and his five coplaintiffs were deprived of free and equal elections guaranteed by the Fourteenth Amendment. Noting the failure of the legislature to reapportion for 60 years, the suit claimed that less than 23 percent of Alabama's voters elected more than one-half of the state legislators. Personally motivating Morgan, a white liberal with ties to the national Democratic party leadership, was a belief that racial justice would not come to Alabama until power were wrested from the Black Belt.

A month later, the U.S. Court of Appeals for the Fifth Circuit, headquartered in New Orleans, assigned the case to a three-member panel chaired by Alabama federal judge Frank M. Johnson. Appointed by President Eisenhower, Johnson was one of the "fifty-eight lonely men" (i.e., federal judges crosspressured between their southern loyalties and their sworn duty to carry out the civil-rights decisions and orders of the Supreme Court). In 1965, Johnson, a law school classmate of George Wallace, locked horns with the governor when the judge dissolved an executive order banning the Selma-to-Montgomery voting-rights march.

After considering two alternative reapportionment schemes, both of which had received the tentative acceptance of the state legislature, the Johnson panel fashioned a compromise calling for a 106-member House of Representatives apportioned according to population provided that each county be guaranteed at least one seat. And, in a plan that differed only slightly from the existing arrangement, 35 single-member Senate districts were proposed. Finally, the panel made it clear that its order was temporary pending enactment by the state legislature of a judicially acceptable apportionment system.

The appeal of the Johnson ruling to the U.S. Supreme Court was most curious. The state probate judges who were originally named as defendants in the suit presented predictable arguments laced with states' rights rhetoric and asked the Court simply to acknowledge its error in *Baker v. Carr* and to reinstate the *Colegrove* rule of nonjusticiability. Morgan's brief, a short one, applauded Johnson's compromise and requested that the final details of reapportionment be remanded to the district court. However, a group of three of the victorious plaintiffs presented a separate brief contending that the Johnson ruling did not go far enough because it guaranteed every county, regardless of population, one House member.

Oral arguments in *Reynolds v. Sims* were held intermittently from November 1963 to April 1964. In his presentation before the justices, Alabama Attorney General Richmond Flowers, nominally a defendant in the case, conceded that state legislative apportionment under the 1901 constitution was grossly inequitable. Realizing the unlikelihood that the Court would turn back the clock to the pre-*Baker* era, Flowers argued that "to some extent," population-based apportionment would be essential for both houses of the state legislature.

On June 15, 1964, the Court announced its decision in *Reynolds v. Sims* and the five companion cases. In an opinion remarkable for its simplicity—though critics have called it politically naive—Chief Justice Earl Warren spoke for a six-member majority in establishing population as the only legitimate and constitutionally defensible basis of apportionment. "Legislators represent people, not trees or acres," nor economic interests, he pronounced. Warren rejected the defendants' claim that inexactness among Alabama's state legislative districts was no different from the equal representation of states in the U.S. Senate. At the federal level, the chief justice responded, representation was the result of historical necessities and was forged by "compromise and concession indispensable to the establishment of our republic." Dismissing the federal analogy as specious and unparallel, Warren concluded that the Fourteenth Amendment "requires both houses of a bicameral state legislature to be apportioned on a population basis."

Though the Court's decision was couched principally in equal-protection reasoning, Warren could not resist drawing on two decades of precedent-setting in the Fifteenth Amendment area of voting rights. Surely, if the Court could void a law permitting some citizens to cast ten votes, it could bar antiquated state legislative apportionment systems that produced the same effect.

Justice Harlan, the lone dissenter in all six cases, echoed the sentiments of his former colleague Felix Frankfurter in characterizing the decision as an exercise in "venturesome constitutionalism." Acting as an instrument for political reform, the Court had taken it upon itself to amend the Constitution, Harlan said.

Political reaction to the Court's decision was mixed. As expected, southern legislators vilified the decision as yet another judicial intrusion into the affairs of the states. Arizona Senator Barry Goldwater, eager to win southern support for his presidential candidacy, denounced *Reynolds v. Sims* as a prime example of the Court's disrespect for limited government. Predictably, liberal Democrats praised the decision as the capstone of recent civil and voting rights rulings. However, many moderate Democrats, including President Johnson, who had generally approved of the Court's ruling in *Baker*, wondered if the justices had gone too far in *Reynolds*.

Regardless of one's appraisal of the Court's wisdom, there was universal agreement that a constitutional milestone had been reached. *The New York Times* commented that the reapportionment decisions of 1964 easily surpassed the 1954 desegregation ruling as the most sweeping judgment of the Warren Court. Indeed, there was considerable truth in the editorial assessment of *Reynolds* as the most momentous decision since *Marbury v. Madison* (1803), in which the Court established the power of judicial review. One legal expert, while regarding the Court's reasoning as constitutionally untidy, nonetheless proclaimed the reapportionment decisions, especially those of 1964, to be as significant for the "theory and practice of representative democracy as the equally bloodless Glorious Revolution of 1688." In *Baker v. Carr*, the Supreme Court took a bold step in indicating its willingness to enter Justice Frankfurter's political thicket. In *Reynolds v. Sims*, the thicket was cleared.

Selected Bibliography

Cortner, R.C. *The Apportionment Cases.* Knoxville, TN: University of Tennessee Press, 1970.

Dixon, R.G., Jr. *Democratic Representation: Reapportionment in Law and Politics.* New York: Oxford University Press, 1968.

Graham, G. *One Man, One Vote:* Baker v. Carr *and the American Levellers.* Boston: Little, Brown, 1972.

Hanson, R. *The Political Thicket.* Englewood Cliffs, NJ: Prentice-Hall, 1966.

Hardy, L., A. Helsop, and S. Anderson, eds. *Reapportionment Politics: The History of Redistricting in the 50 States.* Beverly Hills, CA: Sage Publications, 1981.

Jewell, M. *The Politics of Reapportionment.* New York: Atherton Press, 1962.

Key, V.O., Jr. *Southern Politics in State and Nation.* Knoxville, TN: University of Tennessee Press, 1971.

Polsby, N.W., ed. *Reapportionment in the 1970s.* Berkeley, CA: University of California Press, 1971.

Rigdon, L. *Georgia's County Unit System.* Decatur, GA: Selective Books, 1961.

Taper, B. Gomillion versus Lightfoot: *The Tuskegee Gerrymander Case.* New York: McGraw-Hill, 1962.

E. Governmental Scandals

CAN INTEMPERATE BEHAVIOR BE A "HIGH CRIME OR MISDEMEANOR?"

by Richard E. Ellis
Department of History
State University of New York at Buffalo

The Impeachment Trial of Samuel Chase (1805) [U.S. Senate]

The trial of Samuel Chase in 1805 was one of the earliest and most dramatic examples of the implementation of the impeachment clause of the U.S. Constitution. The framers of the Constitution had provided for the removal of federal judges, who held their offices for "life tenure during good behavior," if they committed "treason, bribery, or other high crimes and misdemeanors." This removal could be accomplished through a process whereby the House of Representatives, by a majority vote, could impeach a judge and require him to stand trial before the U.S. Senate, where a two-thirds majority vote was necessary for the judge's conviction and removal. Chase's trial was the first *cause célèbre* involving this mode of removal, and it raised fundamental questions about what constituted "good behavior" for judges and how far Congress could go to make members of the federal judiciary amenable to popular opinion, as well as what meaning a change of administrations had for how the Constitution was to operate.

Samuel Chase was an extremely bright, aggressive, and difficult personality. During the 1760s and 1770s, he played an important role in the revolutionary movement in Maryland. He also signed the Declaration of Independence and served as a member of the Continental Congress from 1775 to 1778. He left the Congress in disgrace in 1778 after Alexander Hamilton denounced him for using privileged information to speculate in commodities. Returning to Baltimore, Chase pursued a variety of business interests, practiced law, and reentered politics. He was an important anti-Federalist leader in the struggle over the ratification of the Constitution in 1787–80, but once it was adopted, for reasons that remain a mystery, he became an ardent nationalist and supporter of the Federalist party.

During this time, Chase was appointed to several important political posts in Maryland. As a state judge, his career was fraught with controversy. He developed a reputation for being not only partisan, combative, and insensitive to others, but also for being extremely energetic and knowledgeable about the law. In 1795, he was nominated to the U.S. Supreme Court. Although President George Washington was reluctant to appoint him, because Washington had trouble filling the post, he finally offered it to Chase.

Chase proved to be an important and enthusiastic member of the Supreme Court during the pre-Marshall period. His decisions in *Ware v. Hylton* (1796), *Hylton v. United States* (1796), and *Calder v. Bull* (1798) are able and learned. At the same time, however, he became increasingly committed to the Federalist cause. He used his charges to grand juries to make political speeches, taking sides in electoral contests and commenting on controversial issues.

Like many of his contemporaries, Chase refused to recognize the legitimacy of the Jeffersonian opposition, viewing it as subversive, intending to overthrow the government created by the U.S. Constitution. While it is clear, in retrospect, that Jefferson and Madison did not intend this, the Federalist point of view had a certain logic to it, since its adherents had participated in or observed the overthrow of English rule in America and the discarding of the Articles of Confederation. Their view was further strengthened by the fact that the overwhelming majority of anti-Federalists (i.e., opponents of the adoption of the Constitution) had moved into the Jeffersonian opposition.

Federalist concern led in 1798 to the adoption of the sedition law, which made it a crime, punishable by fine and imprisonment, to obstruct the execution of a federal law or to prevent an official of the national government from performing his duties, and to aid or participate in "any insurrection, riot, unlawful assembly, or combination." It also made it a crime to "write, print, utter, or publish . . . any false, scandalous, and malicious writing" against the government or its officers "with intent to defame . . . or to bring them . . . into contempt or disrepute; or to excite against them . . . the hatred of the . . . people . . . or to stir up sedition."

Incensed by Jeffersonian attacks on John Adams and the Federalist-dominated Congress between 1798 and 1800, and lacking a judicious temperament, Chase decided when he covered the middle circuit from April through June of 1800 to enforce the Sedition Act with a vengeance. The initial trial was of an English immigrant editor, Thomas Cooper, who was indicted under the Sedition Act for attacking Adams and his supporters. Overall, Chase conducted the trial fairly, but when he charged the jury he made clear his belief that Cooper was guilty. He asserted that what Cooper had published was untrue and seditious. He concluded his charge by observing, "[T]his publication in all its parts . . . is the boldest attempt I have known to poison the minds of the people. . . . This publication is evidently intended to mislead the ignorant, and inflame their minds against the president. . . ." A short time later, the jury brought in a guilty verdict.

Chase next proceeded to Philadelphia, where he presided over the trial of John Fries, a minor militia officer who had led a group of Pennsylvania Germans in a rebellion against the federal tax collector. Fries had previously been tried, convicted, and sentenced to death, but the discovery that a juror had expressed a bias had resulted in a new trial. The political implications of the trial became clear when two leading Jeffersonian attorneys who were members of the Philadelphia bar, William Lewis and Alexander Dallas, volunteered their services for Fries's defense. Conceding the facts of the

case, Lewis and Dallas's strategy was to argue that the facts did not fit the legal definition of treason. After the jury had been impaneled, Chase, faced with a full docket and eager to expedite the trial, precipitously handed down a ruling confining the defense to the facts. Angered by this development, Lewis and Dallas denounced the ruling as politically motivated and withdrew from the case. Recognizing that he had acted impetuously and erroneously, Chase offered to withdraw his ruling. But Lewis and Dallas insisted on withdrawing. This left Fries without counsel, and he was again convicted and sentenced to death, although he was eventually pardoned by President Adams.

Most spectacular of all was Chase's actions in the sedition trial of James T. Callender, a particularly scurrilous newspaper man. Chase had been openly critical of Callender during the trial and frequently expressed his desire to see him convicted. Moreover, since the trial was being held in Richmond, Virginia, where almost all the leading members of the bar believed the Sedition Act to be unconstitutional, Chase considered the trial a personal test of strength. He was determined to teach a lesson to the Jeffersonian lawyers who had rallied to Callender's defense. Before a packed courtroom, Chase began by refusing to grant a continuance of the case and denouncing the defense for requesting it. The confrontation continued with a struggle over how prospective jurors were to be examined and the questions they were to be asked. Chase also required a juror to serve who was allegedly hostile to Callender, and he required the defense to reduce to writing the questions it intended to ask of its key witness, John Taylor of Carolina. After studying these questions, Chase refused to allow Taylor to testify. He also interrupted, attacked, and embarrassed the defense counsel so often that they finally abandoned the case. Convicted, Callender was sentenced to pay a fine of $200 and to spend nine months in prison.

Next stop on the circuit was Newcastle, Delaware. When Chase learned that the grand jury there planned no indictments under the sedition law, he used his address to warn that a treasonable newspaper was being published in Wilmington and ordered the U.S. attorney to search the newspaper's files. He also refused a request from the jurors to be discharged, but he was forced to relent the next day when the federal prosecutor indicated that his investigation had revealed nothing seditious. By this time, Chase's activities were receiving considerable public attention, and this episode was carefully noted by the judge's enemies, who were rapidly increasing in number and on the road to victory in the election of 1800.

Thomas Jefferson's assumption of the presidency in 1801 and his party's capture of both houses of Congress raised important and complex constitutional and ideological questions, for it was the first time an opposition party had come to power under the U.S. Constitution. Would it involve only a change in the personnel and the policies of the new government, or would it lead to changes in the government itself? To what extent was the Jeffersonian victory a popular mandate for the new administration to do whatever it wanted? Or would it be wiser for the new administration, after an especially bitter campaign, to try to accommodate the interests of the defeated minority? Not all Republicans agreed on how to answer these questions. Some, led by John Randolph, viewed Jefferson's victory as only a means to an end and favored fundamental alterations to the Constitution. Others, led by Madison, who, more than anyone else, had created the Constitution, were opposed to these kinds of changes.

Although Jefferson sympathized with the concerns of those who wanted basic changes made, he nonetheless opted for a policy of reconciliation and moderation. He indicated this in his inaugural address, observing, "We are all Republicans; we are all Federalists." Jefferson simply refused to go along with a direct assault on the Constitution itself, although he did introduce reforms: he reduced the size of the army and the navy, repealed all internal taxes, established a program to pay off the national debt completely, reduced government spending, and introduced policies to encourage settlement of the national domain. But these reforms were all done within the framework of the Constitution.

Nonetheless, Jefferson had a particularly difficult time dealing with the national judiciary. It had been totally dominated by the Federalists in the 1790s. Since its members held their office for life tenure during good behavior, the federal judiciary was not subject to popular control, and it emerged from "the Revolution of 1800" without a single Republican member. Even more infuriating to Republicans, after the election results were known, the Federalist-dominated lame-duck Congress had passed the Judiciary Act of 1801, further expanding the power of the national courts and increasing their personnel by creating a system of circuit courts. Moreover, before he relinquished his office to Jefferson, Adams made sure that all the appointments under the new law went to Federalists. At the same time, he also appointed John Marshall, whom Jefferson did not like, chief justice of the U.S. Supreme Court.

Republicans favoring changes in the Constitution argued that these developments justified a thorough overhauling of the national judiciary. But Jefferson pursued a more moderate course. He simply brought about in 1802 a repeal of the Judiciary Act of 1801, returning the national court system with minor modifications to the way it had existed throughout the 1790s under the Judiciary Act of 1789. Many Federalists denounced these proceedings. They argued that the repeal was unconstitutional because federal judges could be removed from office only when found guilty of high crimes or misdemeanors. They took the matter to the U.S. Supreme Court, but that Federalist-dominated body, wary of further provoking the Jeffersonians, refused to declare the repeal of the Judiciary Act of 1801 unconstitutional. At the same time, under Marshall's leadership, the High Court handed down its famous decision in *Marbury v. Madison* (1803), declaring a part of the newly revived Judiciary Act of 1789 unconstitutional. But *Marbury* was in many ways an extremely ambiguous decision. While the Court claimed for itself the right to oversee the Constitution, it did not claim that its power to do so was either exclusive or final. Moreover, the Marbury holding worked to the advantage of Jefferson's administration, for the Court turned down the request of disappointed Federalist appointees for a writ of *mandamus* ordering the secretary of state to hand over to them their commissions as justices of the peace, signed by Adams, but still undelivered when the new administration took office. The decision in *Marbury* later took on enormous significance as the first example of the Supreme Court declaring a part of an act of Congress unconstitutional, but at the time it was handed down it was considered, if anything, a defeat for the more belligerent members of the Federalist party and a conciliatory gesture on the part of the Supreme Court toward the Jefferson administration.

It is clear that in early 1803 both Jefferson and Marshall hoped that the controversy over the national judiciary would abate. Chase, however, was unhappy with these developments. He had vigorously, if unsuccessfully, campaigned behind the scenes for the Supreme Court to declare the repeal law unconstitutional, and he remained adamant in his opposition to the Jeffersonians. "Things," he stated, "must take their natural course, from *bad* to *worse*" [emphasis in original]. Refusing to alter his partisan behavior, Chase continued to attack the Republican party and its principles.

At this point, developments in New Hampshire revived and further polarized the question of continued Federalist control of the national judiciary. Jefferson received word about the activities of John Pickering, a Federalist district court judge there who was engaging in bizarre and partisan activities on the bench. Closer examination revealed that Pickering was both insane and an alcoholic. Jefferson, at first, tried to persuade prominent New Hampshire Federalists to pressure Pickering into resigning. But they refused to do this unless Jefferson guaranteed that Pickering would be replaced by someone of their own choosing. Jefferson, therefore, reluctantly asked for Pickering's impeachment.

The trial that followed was a mess. Impeachment required a conviction for "high crimes and misdemeanors," but if evidence indicating Pickering's insanity were admitted, it would not be possible to find the demented judge guilty on these grounds. As required by the Constitution, the case was tried before the U.S. Senate with the vice president as presiding officer. Members loyal to the administration, with Jefferson's support, conspired to prevent any discussion of the judge's mental condition. Although Pickering was convicted, it was an

unpleasant and partisan business, and some of the more moderate Jeffersonian senators absented themselves from the final balloting. The outcome, however, was a victory for the more extreme Jeffersonians, since the impeachment clause of the Constitution had been successfully used to remove a federal judge from office.

Pickering was the first federal judge to be removed under the impeachment clause of the Constitution. Because of the special circumstances under which he had violated the trust of his office, because the Federalists would not cooperate in obtaining his resignation, and because neither the Constitution nor the existing laws provided an adequate remedy, the Jefferson administration was forced into the uncomfortable position of giving a very liberal definition to the clause in the Constitution defining impeachable offenses. As one observer noted, "[T]he process of impeachment is to be considered in effect as *a mode of removal*, and not as a charge and conviction of high crimes and misdemeanors" [emphasis in original]. Support for this interpretation of the meaning of the impeachment process came from eighteenth-century English and American colonial precedents in which impeachment had been used to remove one's political opponents from office. Nonetheless, it went counter to the Jefferson administration's earnest desire to reduce partisan tensions and to the feelings among many of the president's closest political supporters—feelings that had found muted expression during the Pickering trial—that impeachment should be narrowly defined and likened to a criminal prosecution.

The implications of all this were fully understood by the Republicans who wanted to cleanse the Supreme Court of Federalist influence. William Branch Giles, a U.S. senator from Virginia, argued that "[r]emoval by impeachment was nothing more than a declaration by Congress to this effect: you hold dangerous opinions and if you are suffered to carry them into effect, you will work the destruction of the Union. We want your offices for the purpose of giving them to men who will fill them better." John Randolph went even further, implying that alterations to the Constitution were necessary by arguing that the provision in the Constitution that the judges shall hold their offices during good behavior was intended to guard them against the executive alone, and not by any means to control the power of Congress.

What all this meant became clear on the day the Senate convicted Pickering, which was also the day that Randolph moved and the House passed a resolution to impeach Chase. At first Jefferson appeared to sympathize with this development. He was furious over a charge Chase had delivered to the federal grand jury in Baltimore in 1803. In it, Chase had denounced the repeal of the Judiciary Act of 1801 as unconstitutional and attacked Jeffersonian activities on both the national and state levels. To a Maryland congressman Jefferson wrote "ought the seditious and official attack on the principles of our Constitution . . . to go unpunished?" Since most conversations about Chase invariably turned to the issue of impeachment, and because this Maryland congressman was a close ally of Randolph and one of the prosecutors for the House of Representatives in the proceedings against Pickering in the Senate, the president seemed to be giving his consent to having Chase removed. Despite this, it is a mistake to think of the Chase impeachment as an administration-sponsored measure. In fact, when it became clear that Randolph and his allies intended to redefine the impeachment process so that it would be a way of removing political opponents from office as opposed to a means of removing public officials who had engaged in criminal activities, Jefferson began to back away from the issue and quietly withdrew his support. Chase's impeachment was a direct assault on the independence of the federal judiciary as provided for in the Constitution; for if Chase were convicted, it is highly likely that other members of the Supreme Court would have been similarly removed from office.

The driving force behind Chase's impeachment was Randolph, who from the beginning of Jefferson's administration had been openly critical of its moderate course. Because of this Randolph was never on close terms with the president. Moreover, Randolph had an abrasive personality and an acid-tongue, which made him unpopular with many of his colleagues. "His insolent, haughty, overbearing disposition know[s] no bounds," commented one observer. Consequently, the administration and many Republican congressmen not only wished to see Randolph's influence curbed, but were taking steps to have this done. There are strong indications that it was a combination of this attack on his influence, combined with a desire on Randolph's part to force the administration to adopt a more aggressive attitude toward the Federalist-controlled judiciary, that spurred Randolph to take the initiative and move the impeachment proceedings against Chase. It is doubtful that Randolph made his motion either at the request or with the consent of the president. Still, although there was opposition in the House of Representatives from moderate Jeffersonians as well as from Federalists, in the spring of 1804 Jeffersonian antagonism toward Chase was greater than toward Randolph; so the motion passed.

Jeffersonian divisions deepened in the months between Chase's impeachment and the beginning of his trial. By far the most important battle concerned the Yazoo compromise. The problem had its origins in 1795 when a corrupt Georgia legislature had been bribed by land speculators to sell, for one and one-half penny an acre, over 35 million acres of Indian land in the Yazoo territory, located in what are today parts of Alabama and Mississippi. The next year, an irate citizenry elected a reform-minded legislature, which rescinded the sale. But in the intervening time much of the land was sold to out-of-state speculators who had no knowledge of the fraud involved and many of whom had resold it to parties even further removed from the original contract. The federal government became involved in 1802 when Georgia relinquished all claims to the land west of it with the proviso that the national government was to assume responsibility for satisfying the claims of various second-, third-, and fourth-party purchasers of Yazoo land. To this end, Jefferson appointed a special commission, which included the leading members of his administration. Although the commission found against the claimants, it strongly urged for reasons of "tranquility" and because of "equitable considerations" a compromise whereby five million acres of land would be set aside to satisfy the claimants.

When the matter came before the House of Representatives, Randolph bitterly attacked the commission's report. He argued that the original act was so evil that any compromise with it should be out of the question. In this fashion, Randolph succeeded in preventing Congress from legislating on a matter that the administration considered of great significance. It was a major setback for both the administration and the moderate Jeffersonians. Equally important, it went a long way toward convincing them that Randolph was a more formidable and dangerous opponent than Chase, whose influence on the Supreme Court had been circumscribed by Marshall.

Randolph had crossed the Rubicon. Up to this point most Republican members of the House, while quietly expressing their dislike for him, had generally accepted his leadership. Now they were openly critical of him. One Federalist noted that Randolph had "resigned his office of ruling the majority of Congress, for the substantial reason that he finds they will no longer be ruled by him. . . . One thing is certain the party at present seem broken and divided, and do not act with their usual concert." The significance of this was clearly recognized by a member of the House of Representatives, who observed: "The unanimity of the majority is broken. . . . The Samson Randolph is shorn of his locks, and as to any . . . influence . . . is become as weak as another man. Indeed, I believe for him to be very zealous in support of a question, would be a very ready way to lose it if the decision was confined exclusively to the Democratic party."

During all this, Chase quietly contrived to prepare his defense. His actual trial began on February 4, 1805. Aaron Burr, as vice president, was the presiding officer at the trial and had made the necessary preparations. He looked to England for precedents and was particularly influenced by the recent "theatrical" proceedings against Warren Hastings. As a result, the Senate chamber was arranged to look more like a stage than a courtroom. Burr had his chair placed in the center against a wall. Benches covered in crimson cloth were extended along each side for the senators. Directly in front of them were two enclosed areas. The House managers, led by Randolph, occupied one, Chase and his lawyers, the other. Behind the senators, in three tiers of benches draped with green cloth, sat members of the House of Representatives. Above, in specially built semicircular galleries, also covered with green cloth, sat the rest of officialdom. Further back, and open to the public, was the permanent gallery where over 1,000 people were present. The Senate, one of its members commented, was "now fitted up in a style beyond anything which has ever appeared in this country."

The trial began with Chase's response to the charges against him. He extensively analyzed the eight articles of impeachment. In less capable hands the reply could have been extremely tedious, but it had been prepared by some of the best lawyers in the country; moreover, most of the senators were themselves lawyers, perfectly capable of appreciating the technical arguments involved. Chase's answer revealed that the defense's strategy was to deny that any of his actions were indictable offenses under either statute or common law. Chase challenged the legal appropriateness of the articles of impeachment that accused him of misconduct in the trials of Fries and Callender by raising complicated, subtle, and even moot legal questions. They included the binding quality of local customs in federal courtrooms; the reciprocal rights and duties of the judge, jury, and defense counsel; the legality of bad manners in a courtroom; the rules for submission of evidence; and the problems involved in proving criminal intent. Chase denied outright that whatever mistakes he may have made in procedure at the *Fries* and *Callender* trials were impeachable offenses as defined by the Constitution. To those articles that accused him of misconduct in charging a grand jury and refusing to release it at Newcastle, Delaware, in June 1800, Chase replied that he had only done his duty by directing that body to investigate an alleged offense, and that he had dismissed its members when they refused to make any presentments or indictments. Finally, in response to the article that accused him of misconduct in charging a grand jury in Baltimore in 1803, he denied making any seditious statements and gave a brief history of jury charges to demonstrate that he had acted according to custom. Chase concluded by defending his right as a citizen to speak on political topics. Throughout, he referred to the unwillingness of the prosecution to seek impeachment of the district judges who had presided with him at the different trials and who had concurred in his actions. The implication was clear: Chase was being tried for his political convictions.

Randolph did not reply effectively to Chase's carefully crafted defense. Since he was the author of the articles of impeachment, it was only natural for him to try to refute the arguments the defense had raised against them. Randolph could, under the right circumstances, be an effective and moving speaker, but against the intricate legal arguments of Chase's response, his primarily moral and emotional appeal was not persuasive. In the days that followed, Randolph's lack of legal training quickly became apparent as he failed to substantiate the charges against Chase. It also soon became clear that in a legal sense, the articles of impeachment had been poorly constructed.

Randolph concluded for the prosecution on February 27. It was an embarrassing performance. He began by announcing that he had lost his notes. Then, instead of refuting the defense's interpretation of impeachment, he denounced it. Instead of using logic, he damned his opponents. A member of the House of Representative described Randolph's performance in these terms: "He began a speech of about two hours and a half, with as little relation to the subject matter as possible—without order, connections or argument; consisting altogether of the most hackneyed commonplaces of popular declamation, mingled up with panegyrics and invectives upon person, with a few well-expressed ideas, a few striking figures, much distortion of face and contortion of body, tears, groans, and sobs, with occasional pauses for recollection, and continual complaints of having lost his notes."

The Senate met shortly after noon on March 1, 1805, to vote on the articles of impeachment. Each article was read in its entirety, and the question was put to each senator whether Chase was guilty or not guilty,

as charged, of a high crime or misdemeanor. This took two hours, and throughout that period the chamber, filled with spectators, remained hushed. After the last senator voted and the votes were tabulated, Burr announced that there had not been a constitutional majority (a two-thirds vote) against Chase on any count, and, therefore, he was acquitted. The vice president then permanently adjourned the court.

All nine Federalists in the Senate voted not guilty on every article of impeachment. Six Jeffersonians joined them. The highest vote for conviction was 19 on the article accusing Chase of misconduct for delivering a partisan charge to the grand jury in Baltimore. Not a single vote was cast against him on one of the articles alleging procedural mistakes at the *Callender* trial, and only four votes were cast against him on another article. This was a clear repudiation of Randolph's attempt to broaden the interpretation of what the Constitution intended to be impeachable offenses. Fewer than one-half of the senators voted guilty more than four times. Even the meaning of those guilty votes is not altogether obvious. For example, a Tennessee senator who had voted against Chase seven times privately admitted that he was glad the judge had been acquitted because it "would have a tendency to mitigate the imitation of party spirit." Thus, Jeffersonians as well as Federalists were responsible for Chase's acquittal.

Any explanation of Chase's acquittal must stress the fact that Randolph did not make an effective case against the judge. Despite this, some scholars have argued that Chase's behavior was not simply reprehensible, but also illegal and therefore impeachable and that he deserved to be convicted, and that he would have been convicted if the prosecution had been placed in more capable hands. There is some evidence for this point of view. At least two important members of the federal judiciary were critical of Chase's blatant political behavior and his often arbitrary rulings. Richard Peters, a particularly able district court judge in Pennsylvania, who often sat with Chase in the circuit courts, noted that he never did so without some embarrassment. Chase, "was forever getting into some intemperate and unnecessary squabble." Moreover, Chief Justice Marshall, testifying during the impeachment trial, questioned the judge's conduct in a number of matters.

But it is also clear that Chase's actions were by no means unique. Several important Jeffersonians realized this. For example, Speaker of the House Nathaniel Macon, a political ally and friend of Randolph, had been unenthusiastic about Chase's impeachment because he knew that other judges, including many Jeffersonians on the state level, had used their positions for partisan purposes. He warned: "[I]t deserves the most serious consideration before a single step can be taken. Change the scene and suppose Chase had stretched as far on the other side, and had praised where no praise was deserving, would it be proper to impeach, because by such conduct he might lull the people to sleep while their interest was destroyed?" And George Clinton, vice president elect at the time of Chase's trial, a leading anti-Federalist and no friend of either a strong or active central government nor a Federalist-controlled national judiciary, explained Chase's acquittal in the following way: "The members who voted for his acquittal had no doubt but that the charges against him were substantial and of course that his conduct was improper and reprehensible, but considering that many parts of it were sanctioned by the practice of the other judges ever since the commencement of the present Judiciary systems and that the act with which he was charged was not prohibited by any express and positive law they could not consistently with their ideas of justice find him guilty of high crimes and misdemeanors. It was to such refined reasoning of some honest men that he owed his acquittal." Another Jeffersonian senator, noting that he and a colleague had voted with the Federalists for Chase's acquittal, observed, "[W]e did so on full conviction that the evidence, our oaths, the Constitution, and our consciences required us to act as we have done."

For the highly politicized generation of revolutionary Americans, no clear-cut definition of proper judicial behavior, especially in political trials, existed. Like the contemporary debate over the proper construction of the constitutional impeachment process, where competing definitions clamored for attention, so too the role of the early nineteenth-century judiciary in cases involving political and partisan questions was by no means a settled matter. It, therefore, cannot be said that Chase had clearly violated established judicial procedures, or, that what he did was singular, especially in a period of American history when lawbooks, treatises, and judicial codes generally did not have wide circulation. In other words, what was considered proper in legal theory often did not have any relationship to what was going on in the courtroom. The significance of the Chase trial seems to be that its results supported the views of those who argued that impeachment should be a criminal process and that judges should refrain from political activities. Since the Chase trial, impeachment for political purposes has been eschewed, at least where federal judges have been concerned. Notwithstanding his acquittal, from the time of his trial until his death in 1811, Chase refrained from engaging in political controversies. And, since his impeachment, members of the federal judiciary have come to be thought of as having ideological philosophies (states' rights or nationalist before the Civil War, liberal or conservative after 1865) but not as spokesmen for particular political parties.

Beyond this, any meaningful explanation of Chase's exoneration must also take into account the struggle within the Republican party. Randolph recognized this when, after the trial, he complained: "[T]he *'whimsicals'* advocated the leading measures of their party until they were nearly ripe for execution, when they hung back. Condemned the step *after* it was taken, and, on most occasions, affected a *glorious neutrality*" [emphasis in original]. President Jefferson was the most important member of the group who "affected a glorious neutrality." In the year preceding Chase's trial, he neither commented on the impeachment proceedings nor discussed them in his private letters. When the subject was raised at the numerous dinner parties to which he invited congressmen, the president remained silent. Had he not vigorously favored Pickering's removal, the insane judge probably would also have been acquitted. Jefferson's unwillingness to enforce party regularity on the Chase impeachment must be included as an important factor contributing to the final verdict.

Chase's acquittal delivered so serious a blow to Randolph's prestige and influence among Jeffersonians that he never recovered from it. His lack of preparation and inept handling of the trial put him in an especially bad light, since he "had boasted with great exaltation that this was *his* impeachment—that every article was drawn by *his* hand, and *he* was to have the whole merit of it" [emphasis in original]. Even his friends were disgusted with him. Randolph's loss of influence was made clear the same day Chase was acquitted. Angered by the verdict, he delivered "a violent phillipic" that afternoon in the House, denouncing both Chase and the Senate. Randolph concluded by moving an amendment to the Constitution giving the president the authority at the request of a majority of both houses of Congress to remove any federal judge. If it had been made before Chase's trial, the proposed amendment might have received considerable support and serious attention. Precedents for it existed in several of the state constitutions. But coming as it did at the culmination of the intense struggle that had taken place within the Republican party over the judiciary and constitutional reform, it simply gave Randolph's opponents another opportunity to embarrass him. The administration, it was noted, "disapproved of this extreme measure." By a large majority, the House referred the resolution to a committee and postponed its consideration. Observing these proceedings, Chase wrote, "I have always said that my enemies are as great fools as knaves."

Chase's impeachment trial represented the culmination of four years of struggle between Jeffersonians over the meaning of the Revolution of 1800. Viewed in this light, the acquittal was more a vote against Randolph and what he represented than one for Chase. In many ways the outcome of the impeachment trial constituted not so much a defeat for the Jeffersonians, as it has so often been portrayed, but a victory for the policy of moderation and conciliation that the administration wanted to see implemented. At the end of Jefferson's presidency, the U.S. Constitution remained unimpaired. Perhaps the most important result of Chase's acquittal was the enormously significant legacy of constitutional stability that has so marked American history.

Selected Bibliography

Berger, R. *Impeachment: The Constitutional Problems.* Cambridge, MA: Harvard University Press, 1973.

Ellis, R.E. *The Jeffersonian Crisis: Court and Politics in the Young Republic.* New York: Oxford University Press, 1971.

Haw, J., *et al. Stormy Patriot: The Life of Samuel Chase.* Baltimore: Johns Hopkins University Press, 1981.

Hoffer, P.C., and N.E.H. Hull. *Impeachment in America, 1635–1805.* New Haven, CT: Yale University Press, 1984.

Presser, S.B. "A Tale of Two Judges: Richard Peters, Samuel Chase, and the Broken Promise of Federalist Jurisprudence." *Northwestern Law Review* 73 (March–April 1978): 26–111.

Turner, L. "The Impeachment of John Pickering." *American Historical Review* 54 (April 1949): 485–507.

THE COURT TOPPLES A PRESIDENCY

by Richard R. Broadie
Department of History
University of Northern Iowa

United States v. Nixon, 418 U.S. 683 (1974) [U.S. Supreme Court]

Few would disagree that without the discovery of the White House tapes the case against President Richard M. Nixon would not have resulted in his resignation from the presidency on August 9, 1974. Without this revelation, the Nixon presidency, although noticeably weakened by the allegations against it, would probably have survived to limp across the finish line at the scheduled end of its second term in January 1977. The tapes, key segments of which were obtained after more than one year of prodding and litigation, provided investigators with the so-called smoking gun, irrefutable evidence that Nixon had participated in the cover-up of the Watergate break-in of June 17, 1972. The culmination of the legal efforts to obtain the tapes was the unanimous U.S. Supreme Court decision of *United States v. Nixon*.

Richard Nixon was not the first U.S. president to tape White House conversations. For example, it is now known that similar recordings were made during the Kennedy administration. Historians and political scientists have learned much about high-level decisionmaking during this presidency by listening to the conversations of the Kennedy brothers responding to various crises. In proceedings reminiscent of the Watergate hearings, Congress sought to obtain various personal documents—notes, journal entries, even presidential scribblings—from President Ronald Reagan to assess more accurately his role in the "Iran-Contra Affair." But never has this type of information been as crucial to an on-going criminal investigation involving a sitting president as it was in the year prior to Nixon's resignation.

The Watergate investigation went on for some time before the existence of the tapes was discovered. The burglars, arrested at the time of the break-in, were indicted in September 1972 and went to trial in January 1973. Soon after they pled guilty, and former Central Intelligence Agency (CIA) agent E. Howard Hunt and one-time Federal Bureau of Investigation (FBI) agent and White House "plumber" G. Gordon Liddy were found guilty, a Senate select committee under the chairmanship of Democratic Senator Sam Ervin of North Carolina was established to investigate the Watergate affair and to make recommendations for a new set of campaign regulations.

Despite promising to cooperate with the investigation, Nixon insisted that, as a matter of "executive privilege," neither he nor members of his staff would be willing to testify. Accounts detailing involvement of White House staffers continued to surface, however, and by April 1973, federal prosecutors became convinced that the administration was involved in a cover-up. Presidential counsel John Dean's testimony late that spring strongly supported this view, but without further documentation it remained Dean's word against Nixon's that the president had been involved in the Watergate cover-up.

By their own account, *Washington Post* investigative reporters Bob Woodward and Carl Bernstein—who originally helped to break the Watergate story—"had gotten lazy" by the time the senate Watergate hearings began in May 1973. Instead of vigorously pursuing their own leads, they began to rely on the information coming out of the committee for their stories. There was one "unchecked entry" on both their lists, however, and sometime that month Woodward asked a committee staff member if Alexander Butterfield, listed as a deputy assistant to the president and an aide to chief of staff H. R. Haldeman, had been interviewed. Early in the investigation, they had discovered that Butterfield "supervised internal security and the paper flow to the president," and both were curious as to what this meant. After Woodward pursued this with another staff member, it was agreed that the committee's chief counsel, Sam Dash, would be asked to interview Butterfield.

Dash put off the interview on at least one occasion, but on July 13, 1973, he had a lengthy discussion with Butterfield. The next day Woodward and Bernstein learned that Nixon had "bugged himself"—recorded all presidential conversations since February 1971. After some initial concern that the tapes might be a set-up—recorded after-the-fact by Nixon to clear himself—it was soon concluded that the tapes were legitimate and the best hope of finding the smoking gun for which they had been looking.

Events of the next 13 months centered around the efforts of the Ervin committee, the special prosecutor, and the House judiciary committee to obtain these tapes. When the committee voted unanimously in April 1974 to subpoena 42 additional tapes, including a key July 23, 1972, conversation between Nixon and Haldeman, it set in motion a chain of events that led to the president's resignation. Within two weeks, the Nixon White House released edited transcripts of 43 conversations, including portions of 20 of the conversations that were subject to subpoena. In a speech the next day, Nixon told the American people that "these materials will tell all." Public reaction to the speech—not the first in which the president was less than truthful—was decidedly negative. About the same time, the House judiciary committee discovered that key transcripts differed significantly from the original tapes in the committee's possession. Therefore, Special Prosecutor Leon Jaworski continued to press for the tapes and in time demanded several more. Nixon responded by moving to quash the subpoena accompanied by a formal claim of privilege.

The district court that ruled on the case concluded that the special prosecutor had made a sufficient showing to rebut the presumption that the tapes were privileged and satisfied the requirements of Rule 17 (c) of Federal Rules of Criminal Procedure, under which the subpoena was issued. The court thereafter denied the president's motion to quash and ordered delivery for *in camera* ("private") inspection of the "originals of all subpoenaed items along with an index of these items and tape copies of those parts of the subpoenaed recordings for which transcripts had already been released to the public. . . ."

The president promptly appealed this ruling to the Court of Appeals for the D.C. Circuit and the district court stayed its order pending appellate review. Sensing that the legal process might serve as an effective means of presidential "stonewalling," delaying a final resolution of the matter for months or even years, the special prosecutor filed in the U.S. Supreme Court a petition for a writ of *certiorari* before judgment. "Because of the public importance of the issues presented and the need for their prompt resolution," the Court granted the special prosecutor's petition and agreed to an expedited briefing schedule. The case was heard on July 8, and the decision handed down on July 24. The Court ruled unanimously that Nixon had to surrender the subpoenaed material. It rejected all the president's assertions, including his most significant, the claim of executive privilege.

The Court, in its opinion written by Chief Justice Warren Burger, first disposed of jurisdictional issues and then considered whether the special prosecutor had satisfied the requirements of Rule 17(c) of the Federal Rules of Criminal Procedure. On the former, the Court held that the "order of the District Court was an appealable order" and "the appeal from that order was therefore properly 'in' the Court of Appeals, and the case is now properly before this court . . . ." On the latter, it was decided that the production of the tapes would not be "unreasonable or oppressive," and the special prosecutor had shown the tapes to be relevant, admissible, and specific. Thus, the Court refused to say that the district court had "erred in authorizing the issuance of the subpoena. . . ."

Tougher issues for the Court to resolve—indeed, those most crucial to understanding what was significant about the ruling—were Nixon's claims concerning justiciability and executive privilege. The administration took the position that the matter was an intrabranch dispute between the president and the special prosecutor and thus not subject to judicial resolution. According to this view, the dispute did not present a "case" or "controversy" that could be adjudicated in the federal courts. Instead, the administration argued that it was a jurisdictional dispute within the executive branch between a subordinate and a superior officer. Turning the matter over to the courts would, therefore, be an improper intrusion of one branch into the affairs of another based on the doctrine of separation of powers. Nixon's lawyers conceded that the president had delegated certain powers to the special prosecutor, but they insisted that this did not include the final authority over what evidence could be used in a criminal trial.

The Court ruled that "Congress has vested in the Attorney General the power to conduct the criminal litigation of the United States government." In turn, the attorney general delegated authority to represent the United States to a special prosecutor who subpoenaed the tapes while operating within the scope of his authority. While the Court agreed that it is possible for the attorney general to "amend or revoke the regulation defining the special prosecutor's authority," it pointed out that he had not done so. The Court ruled that the regulation remained in force and the president was bound by it. The Court also found that "the demands of and resistance to the subpoena . . ." were indeed a "controversy" in the constitutional sense, which "means the kind of controversy the courts traditionally resolve." It was, therefore, justiciable.

The final point made by Nixon's lawyers was the claim of executive privilege, defined by one legal scholar as "the president's claim of constitutional authority to withhold information from Congress." According to this scholar, the concept of executive privilege as used by Nixon went back no further than the 1950s, when the Eisenhower administration staked out a claim of "uncontrolled discretion" to withhold information from Congress in response to the "bullying tactics" of Senator Joseph McCarthy. But during the Nixon administration, executive privilege had "become a shield for executive unaccountability . . . an iron curtain which shut off critical information from Congress and the people."

The bulk of the opinion is devoted to an analysis of the concept of executive privilege as it is relevant to this case. The president, for example, had contended that it was inconsistent with the public interest to produce confidential conversations between a chief executive and his close advisers. While accepting that "human experience teaches that those who expect public dissemination of their remarks may well temper candor with a concern for appearances and for their own interests . . . ," the Court concluded that "neither the doctrine of separation of powers nor the generalized need for confidentiality . . . can sustain an absolute, unqualified, Presidential privilege of immunity from judicial process under all circumstances. Absent a claim of need to protect . . . [national] . . . secrets, the confidentiality of Presidential communications is not significantly diminished by producing material for a criminal trial under the protected conditions of *in camera* inspection."

Chief Justice Burger was willing to concede a presumptive privilege for presidential communications. But he insisted that this privilege could not become absolute because the need to "develop all relevant facts in an adversary system [of criminal justice] is both fundamental and comprehensive." To deny the courts full access to relevant matters in a criminal investigation under anything less than extraordinary circumstances would "cut deeply into the guarantee of due process of law and gravely impair the basic function of the courts."

While the subpoena was ruled appropriate, Burger was adamant in insisting that "the public interest requires that Presidential confidentiality be afforded the greatest protection consistent with fair administration of justice." In fact, the Court ruled that any conversation found to be irrelevant or inadmissible in the criminal prosecution be returned under seal to its lawful custodian.

The tapes, released after *United States v. Nixon* was handed down, did indeed contain the smoking gun that doomed the Nixon presidency. In a conversation between Nixon and Haldeman held on July 23, 1972, six weeks after the break-in, Nixon can clearly be heard ordering Haldeman to tell the CIA to fabricate a national security operation to keep the FBI off the case. This was proof that the president had conspired to obstruct justice and had lied about his Watergate involvement.

While Nixon lost what he valued most—his presidency—it is not clear at all that the ruling in *United States v. Nixon* is a complete victory for those who forced him from office. Nixon opponents, and those like Raoul Berger who claimed that executive privilege is a myth, must surely be disappointed that the Supreme Court accepted the notion of an executive privilege not to divulge certain confidential communications and that "an absolute instead of a qualified privilege may exist where there is 'a claim of need to protect . . . national security secrets.'"

In fact, in one view, *United States v. Nixon* is "a quite limited precedent without great doctrinal importance." It raised as many questions as it answered and was decisive only in that it compelled the president to turn over the tapes. Given the likelihood of continued conflict between the branches of government—indeed, exacerbated by the recent trend of Republican presidents and Democratic congresses—the issues raised in this case are certain to surface again.

Selected Bibliography

Berger, R. *Executive Privilege: A Constitutional Myth.* Cambridge, MA: Harvard University Press, 1974.

Bernstein, C., and B. Woodward. *All the President's Men.* New York: Simon & Schuster, 1974.

Cox, A. "Executive Privilege." *University of Pennsylvania Law Review* 122 (June 1974): 1383–1438.

Kutler, S.I. *The Wars of Watergate: The Last Crisis of Richard Nixon.* New York: Alfred A. Knopf, 1990.

THE LEGALITY OF THE "INDEPENDENT COUNSEL"

by Donald E. Boles
Department of Political Science
Iowa State University

Morrison v. Olson, 487 U.S. 654 (1988) [U.S. Supreme Court]

Following the Watergate scandals, the impeachment proceedings, and subsequent resignation of President Richard Nixon, the Ethics in Government Act was passed in 1978. Among other things, it required the judiciary to appoint an independent counsel to investigate and prosecute top executive branch officials accused of criminal misconduct. The statute was premised on the political reality that it was effectively impossible to expect the attorney general, who is appointed by the president, to prosecute vigorously either the president or members of his inner governmental circle for criminal acts they allegedly committed. In the late 1980s, the law became the target of constitutional challenge as an increasing number of former Reagan officials fell within its reach.

Legal scholars also saw a broader issue raised. They perceived attacks on the law as part of a larger effort to reestablish firm boundaries between legislative and executive authority pushed by groups unhappy with the growing power of independent regulatory commissions. By the 1980s, regulatory agencies, such as the Environmental Protection Agency, were being attacked by right-wing critics for merely existing, and from forces on the left and center for not using energetically enough the powers granted them by Congress.

In *Morrison v. Olson*, Alexia Morrison was appointed independent counsel by a special division of the U.S. Circuit Court of Appeals for the District of Columbia. She was to investigate allegations that former Assistant Attorney General Theodore Olson, of President Ronald Reagan's Justice Department, had lied in testimony before a House subcommittee in 1983.

From the outset, it seemed clear that this case—along with the much more publicized cases involving Reagan's top aide Michael Deavers, and the "Iran-Contra Affair" involving Lieutenant Colonel Oliver North—was likely to go to the U.S. Supreme Court. The Justice Department, therefore, began issuing back-up appointments to some special prosecutors involved in ongoing cases, in effect giving them a second home in the executive branch's Justice Department. This was done to protect the independent counsel's work in the event the authorizing law was held unconstitutional as an invalid invasion by the legislative branch into the jurisdiction of the executive branch.

Morrison refused to accept such an appointment because she felt it would place her under the political influence of the presidential-controlled Justice Department, which was exactly the situation the independent counsel law sought to prevent. When the case came to trial, a federal district court found Olson guilty of contempt for not honoring subpoenas issued by independent counsel, Morrison.

The Court of Appeals for the District of Columbia, however, struck down the independent counsel act on the three grounds. First, it violated Article II, Section 2, Clause

3—the appointments clause—of the U.S. Constitution. Second, it violated the limitations placed on the federal judiciary by Article III of the Constitution. Third, the law was an unconstitutional violation of the separation of powers doctrine.

The issues in the case go to the heart of the American constitutional system and involve the almost inherent clash between the principle of separation of powers on one hand, and the principle of checks and balances on the other. The separation of powers doctrine results from the founding fathers' attempt to prevent the growth of an authoritarian form of government by dividing into three branches the basic powers necessary for a government to function. On its most elemental level, the legislative branch was assigned the duty of passing the laws, the executive branch had the duty of enforcing the laws, and the judicial branch was given the responsibility of interpreting the laws.

There was, however, a fundamental problem with the separation of powers concept, as the founding fathers knew from their study of world history. It was that, standing by itself, nothing prevents the separate branches of government from becoming so alienated from each other because of political or policy differences that a stalemate would occur, and anarchy could result from prolonged governmental inaction.

To prevent such a gridlock, the founders added another principle of government to the Constitution—checks and balances. It was designed to ensure a working cooperation between the three branches by requiring each branch to share some basic responsibilities of the other two branches—thus preventing them from becoming too separate. For example, the executive branch shares some legislative power through its veto over legislation and exercises judicial power in its appointment of federal judges. The legislative branch, in turn, exercises executive powers (e.g., in confirming executive appointments) and judicial power through the enactment of legislation governing the creation and jurisdiction of federal courts. The Supreme Court, through its power of judicial review, involves itself in both legislative and executive activities.

The result is a somewhat untidy situation where the line between the function of separation of powers and the checks and balances principle is, at best, imprecise. Historically, the Court has taken a broad view of the scope of checks and balances. Such an approach has permitted Congress to experiment with various governmental forms, such as independent regulatory commissions, to meet unique contemporary problems that did not readily submit to solution solely within the domain of one branch.

In the 1980s, however, the Court put a damper on such innovations. By ignoring checks and balances and relying exclusively on the separation of powers principle, it struck down the legislative veto in *Immigration and Naturalization Services v. Chadha* (1983), and portions of the Gramm-Rudman-Hollings Act in *Bowsher v. Synar* (1986). It was widely feared that the Court would also use this narrow view of the constitutional system to strike down the independent counsel law.

Morrison advanced the check and balances argument before the Supreme Court, urging that although law enforcement is typically an executive function, "there is no absolute prohibition on legislative restrictions that circumscribe presidential discretion or insulate decision-making from the normal chain of command."

To the surprise of many observers, Chief Justice William H. Rehnquist, the leader of the Court's right wing, spoke for the majority in upholding the constitutionality of the independent counsel statute. First, he explained that the law did not violate the appointment clause of the Constitution, since the independent counsel was an "inferior" officer within the constitutional provision. That clause states: "[T]he Congress may by Law vest the Appointment of such inferior Officers, as they think proper, in the President alone, in the courts of Law, or in the Heads of Departments." He went on to note that while the counsel might not be subordinate to the attorney general and the president, since she possessed a degree of independent discretion, the fact the act authorized her removal by the attorney general indicated that she was "inferior" in rank and authority. Moreover, the independent counsel had only limited duties, had limited jurisdiction, and had a "temporary" tenure limited to the accomplishment of a single task. All of this demonstrated that it was an "inferior" office.

The Court next rejected the argument that the appointment clause did not permit the appointment of an inferior officer by any branch other than the executive. These positions are sometimes called interbranch appointments. The history of the constitutional provision, as the Court saw it, seemed clearly to give Congress significant discretion to determine whether it is "proper" to vest the appointment of executive officials in the "courts of law." This seemed particularly appropriate in situations at which the independent counsel law was aimed. There conflicts of interest could arise when the executive branch is called on to investigate its own high-ranking officials. Furthermore, the statute provided that judges of the special division who make the appointment are ineligible to participate in any matter relating to an independent counsel they have appointed.

The Court next rejected the argument that the statutory provision vesting appointment power in a special division of the federal courts violated Article III, under which executive or administrative duties of a nonjudicial nature may not be imposed on judges receiving their power under Article III. No such violation could occur, the Court explained, since the authority to appoint independent counsels came from the appointment clause of Article II, which is a source of authority for judicial action that is independent of Article III. Moreover, when Congress creates a temporary "office," such as this, where the nature and duties will vary with the factual circumstances giving rise to the need for the appointment in the first place, the Court found that Congress may vest the power to define the office's scope in the Court as an incident to the appointment under the appointment clause.

Next the Court held that Article III did not absolutely prevent Congress from vesting certain miscellaneous powers in the special division of the federal courts as the law provides. Rehnquist stated that Article III's broad prohibition on the courts' exercise of executive or administrated duties of a nonjudicial nature was designed to provide a separation necessary to ensure that judges did not encroach upon the execution of legislative tasks that are more properly accomplished by those branches. What is involved in this case are miscellaneous powers, such as the passive power to receive, but not act upon, various reports of the independent counsel. Since the Court is given no supervisory power over the independent counsel, the Court held that the functions involved are not "executive," but are analogous to functions that federal judges perform in other contexts.

The opinion concluded that the special division's power to terminate an independent counsel's office when the task was completed is, to a degree, "administrative" in nature, but the degree is insignificant as far as Article III limits are concerned. In the Court's view, this was because the law's termination provision did not give the division anything approaching the power to remove the counsel while an investigation or court proceeding was underway. That power rested solely in the attorney general who was part of the executive branch.

Nor was the independence of the federal judiciary jeopardized by the law, since the special division's members were prohibited from participating in "any judicial proceeding concerning a matter which involves such independent counsel" while counsel was serving in that office. Thus, the Court felt that there was no risk of partisan or biased adjudication of claims regarding the independent counsel by that court.

Finally, and probably most important, the Court found that the law did not violate the separation of power doctrine by impermissibly interfering with functions of the executive branch. Limiting the attorney general's power to remove the counsel only for "good cause" could not be considered a congressional invasion of executive authority, said the Court. The Court had long held that congressional provisions spelling out removal grounds did not involve an exclusive executive function as long as it did not interfere with the executive's power to "faithfully execute the laws" as required by Article II. Here, the Court observed, Congress considered the setting out of the grounds for removal an essential element to ensure the necessary independence of the office of independent counsel.

Even though the law empowered certain members of Congress to request that the attorney general apply for the appointment of an independent counsel, the attorney general was not required to comply with the request. Beyond this requirement, the Court emphasized that Congress's role under the law is limited to receiving reports. Thus, even though the counsel is freer from executive branch supervision than other federal prosecutors, the law gives the executive branch sufficient control over the independent counsel to ensure that the president is able to perform his constitutionally assigned duties.

It is difficult to square the narrow, almost procrustean application of the separation of powers approach followed in *Chadha* and *Bowsher*, to the broader employment of the checks and balances principle enunciated here. The *Morrison* doctrine, in short, permits Congress to experiment with innovative mechanisms to cope with problems defying solutions through traditional means. *Chadha* and *Bowsher* make such experimentation constitutionally difficult, if not impossible. While it is too early to know which of these sharply conflicting doctrines will prevail, it is not too early to hope that it will be the *Morrison* approach if the nation is to deal effectively with the increasingly complex problems of a technological age.

Selected Bibliography

Carter, S.L. "The Independent Counsel Mess." *Harvard Law Review* 102 (1988): 105–41.

Krent, H.J. "Separating the Strands in the Separation of Powers Controversies." *Virginia Law Review* 74 (1988): 253–323.

Robinson, G.O. "Public Choice Speculation on the Item Veto." *Virginia Law Review* 74 (1988): 403–22.

Stith, K. "Rewriting the Fiscal Constitution: The Case of the Gramm-Rudman-Hollings Act." *California Law Review* 76 (1988): 593–668.

PART III: ECONOMICS AND THE LAW

PART III: ECONOMICS AND THE LAW

INTRODUCTION

Every day courts are called on to resolve disputes that involve money or other financial concerns. Therefore, it should come as no surprise that the longest section of this volume surveys cases concerning law and economics. For the last two generations, the leading scholarly orientation in U.S. legal history has been the so-called Wisconsin School, identified with James Willard Hurst and his former students. The focus that Hurst and his disciples placed on the intersection of law and economics is reflected in most of the essays in this part.

A. Contracts

Article I of the U.S. Constitution contains a "contract clause" that prohibits states from "impairing the obligation of contracts." Given the importance of contracts in commercial transactions, particularly in a rapidly expanding national economy, it was reasonable to expect the contract clause of the Constitution to be tested by litigation in the early national period. One of the first contract clause cases to come before the Supreme Court involved an attempt by Virginia to reserve the power to amend a state charter. Whether this was permitted is discussed in "The Power to Amend Corporate Charters." Two of Chief Justice John Marshall's greatest decisions involved "loose interpretations" of the contract clause: these are examined in "When a Contract Obtained by Fraud Is Still a Contract" and "Balancing Private Good and Public Good." The relationship of bankruptcy to contracts is considered in "Justice Story, Bankruptcy, and the Supreme Court."

Perhaps the greatest Supreme Court contract clause decision involved a dispute between two Massachusetts bridges; it is discussed in "Abridging Vested Interests: The Battle of the Massachusetts Bridges." The last contract essay in this section, "'An Innocent Sort of a

Duck'," involves a dispute on the Minnesota iron range in the waning years of the nineteenth century.

B. Commerce

Paralleling the stark language of the contract clause in the U.S. Constitution is the equally blunt commerce power in Article I, which bestows on Congress the power "to regulate Commerce . . . among the several States." The first commerce clause Supreme Court case, another one of Marshall's great decisions, is featured in "A More Perfect Union: The Steamboat Case." The steamboat case appeared to extend to Congress plenary power to regulate commerce. But opinions of the Taney Supreme Court, such as the one discussed in "An Omen of Change: State Power to Regulate Commerce," seemed to reserve considerable power to the states.

Late in the nineteenth century, as discussed in "When Monopoly Mattered," the Supreme Court held that manufacturing was not commerce. However, two years later, as examined in "Regulation in the Public Interest," the Court discussed how two recently passed federal laws—the Interstate Commerce Act and Sherman Antitrust Act—impinged on the commerce clause.

In the twentieth century, federal courts have generally interpreted the commerce clause liberally. For example, as discussed in "Commerce and National Police Powers," lottery tickets fall under the commerce power. Other commerce clause issues were resolved in Supreme Court decisions of the 1930s as discussed in Part VI. Finally, even recent civil rights legislation, as examined in the essay entitled "Mandate for Social Change," has been ruled constitutional pursuant to the commerce power of the federal government.

C. Labor

Trade unions have been an important feature of American life since the nineteenth century. Three essays in this section examine disputes involving labor unions. "The Legitimacy of Labor Organization" discusses one of the earliest labor disputes in American history. "'An Injury to One Is an Injury to All'" scrutinizes the role of the famous labor leader Eugene Debs in the Pullman strike. And "Can Children Under 14 Legally Hold Full-Time Jobs?" examines the constitutionality of a congressional attempt to do away with child labor.

D. Miscellaneous Governmental Regulation

The eight essays in this section probe a miscellaneous series of historically interesting legal disputes concerning state and federal economic regulations. "Copyright Law: Limiting Literary Monopolies" reviews one of the earliest copyright cases in American law; ironically, this decision involved the literary rights to Supreme Court opinions. "Corporate Growth vs. States' Rights" deals with an important banking case of the Jacksonian Era. "The Scope of Admiralty Jurisdiction" treats one of the U.S. Supreme Court's most important opinions on the law of the seas. "'A Sore Grievance' to the Traveler" concerns the legal power of eminent domain. "Destructive Creation" discusses a California case that touches on a number of interrelated economic issues. "Politics vs. Precedents" provides an account of the great income tax cases of the late nineteenth century. "National Police Powers: The Oleomargarine Case" offers an example of a legal situation in which national regulatory powers were supported. And "State Legislative Power and Municipal Trusts" offers an example of where state power over municipal trusts was upheld.

E. Substantive Due Process

The eight cases in this section confront an issue in American law that occupied hundreds of thousands of hours of judicial time and took almost a century to resolve. The question was whether a court could use its own standards of "reasonableness" in determining whether particular economic legislation violated the "due process" of an individual or group even though the law was not prohibited by explicit constitutional language. An early presentation of this matter is discussed in "Prohibition and the Due Process Clause."

Most of the leading cases in the line of substantive due process were based on the due process clause of the Fourteenth Amendment, ratified in 1868. "The Fourteenth Amendment Receives Its First Judicial Construction" concerns the complicated *Slaughterhouse Cases* from Louisiana, cases that would also be important in the sphere of race relations. Three essays probe the spread of economic substantive due process in the late nineteenth century : "The Court Enters the Age of Reform," "A 'Right' to Make Cigars," and "Can Nebraska or Any State Regulate Railroads?" The temporary conversion of the U.S. Supreme Court to the conservative doctrine of substantive due process came in *Lochner v. New York* (1905) and is discussed in "'Mere Meddlesome Interferences': The Apogees of Substantive Due Process."

The retreat from substantive due process is probed in the essay on *Muller v. Oregon* in Part IV, "The Law Recognizes 'Women Are Different'," and in "Minimum Wages and Maximum Hours for Women." "The Chambermaid's Revenge" profiles the 1937 case that finally buried economic substantive due process.

F. Negligence and Tort Law

A tort is a private or civil wrong or injury, other than breach of contract. The usual remedy for a decision in tort law is a monetary award. The apportionment of damages through tort litigation can have significant economic implications, particularly in large industries where thousands of individuals are potentially affected by legal precedents.

Many industrial tort actions of the nineteenth century involved the engine of economic development—the railroad. "Fellow Servants Beware," "Contributory Negligence as a 'Brake' on Suits Against Railroads," and "Railroad Development and the Nuisance Law" deal with three such cases. One of the great tort law cases of the nineteenth century, however, involved an unfortunate attempt of two men to come between their fighting dogs. This dispute, which proved to be a breakthrough in the development of negligence case law, is profiled in "The Great Dog Fight Case."

In the twentieth century, some of the leading tort decisions came from the pen of New York Court of Appeals Judge Benjamin Cardozo. Two of Cardozo's greatest decisions are discussed in "The Origins of Consumer Rights in Tort Law" and "Negligence Theory at Its Zenith." The final essay in this section, "The 'Nuking' of American Civilians," deals with a modern class action suit involving the untoward consequences of atomic testing.

G. Natural Resources, Technology, and the Environment

Court decisions involving the natural resources or the environment can also have substantial economic consequences. The cases in this section illustrate this economic reality.

The first five essays examine the controversial area of water law, which had distinctly different doctrinal histories in the East and the West. "Riparian Doctrine: A Short Case History for the Eastern United States" and "Conflict Over Water Power in Massachusetts" discuss leading nineteenth-century cases in the Northeast and the South. And "A Law for Water in the West," "Dividing the Rivers: Rule of Law in an Arid State," and "The Hydraulic Society of the Colorado River" examine nineteenth- and twentieth-century cases that arose out of western water litigation.

The final three essays in this section present cases that concern the country's most exotic and expensive modern technology—nuclear energy. "Controversy Over a Fast-Breeder," "The Atomic Energy Commission and the Environment," and "Insuring Against Nuclear Plant Accidents" examine cases dealing with the legal, environmental, and economic impact of the commercial atom.

A. Contracts

THE POWER TO AMEND CORPORATE CHARTERS

by *Yasuhide Kawashima*
Department of History
University of Texas at El Paso

Currie's Administrators v. Mutual Assurance Society, 4 Va. 315 (1809) [Virginia Supreme Court]

In 1819, the U.S. Supreme Court held as an unconstitutional impairment of contracts New Hampshire's action in terminating the powers of the trustees of Dartmouth College under a royal charter and in making them appointive by the governor. The New Hampshire act would have changed the fundamental nature of the college and appropriated its control to the political decision of the state, but the Supreme Court said such is not the American scheme. If, however, a power was reserved for the purpose of subsequently amending the charter, it would be quite another matter. Virginia was one of the states that had already enacted such reservations. *Currie's Administrators v. Mutual Assurance Society* involved the first Virginia law with the reserved right of amendment.

In 1794, the Virginia legislature passed an act authorizing the establishment of an insurance corporation, the Mutual Assurance Society, to protect buildings against fire. The benefits of the institution were clearly and expressly confined to citizens of the state. Houses in the country and in towns were mutually assured: every member of the Assurance Society, whether residing in town or country, became an insurer for every other member.

Under this act of incorporation, the Assurance Society was authorized to adopt rules and regulations for its government. It further provided that the Society would be at liberty, from time to time, to alter and amend such rules and regulations as it judged necessary and that the Society agreed on the premiums to be paid. Dr. James Currie subscribed to and became one of the initial members of the Society.

Within a few years, experience revealed that the losses in the country bore no relationship to those in towns. Thus, the legislature, on January 29, 1805, at the insistence of a majority of the members of the Assurance Society either personally present or represented by members of the General Assembly, passed another act. This act separated the interests and risks of the inhabitants of the country from those of the towns so that the countryman was no longer liable for losses by fire occurring in towns, nor was the townsman for losses occurring in the country. It also declared that there "shall be in future only three directors, out of whom a president shall be chosen," providing that the society should not be prevented from "appointing more than three directors," if necessary.

Shortly after, Alexander McRae was elected president of the board of directors, and on the same day three other persons were appointed directors. Previously, the president had not been chosen from the directors, out of whom he was to be chosen, but rather was elected by the same electoral body that chose the directors.

After the election of the president and directors, a resolution was adopted on February 25, 1805, at the meeting of the Society's board of directors, calling on the town members, but not on the country members, for one-half a quota (i.e., a premium). Currie, who held a building in a town insured by the Society, refused to pay his required quota of $291.73 on two grounds. First, the requisition was made not under the original charter, but rather under a subsequent act that attempted to increase his risk without his consent. Second, the president of the board of directors was not chosen out of the directors, as the law of 1805 required, and consequently there could be no legal call of a quota.

The district court gave judgment in favor of the Mutual Assurance Society, and Currie appealed to the Virginia Supreme Court of Appeals. Since Currie died pending the appeal, the case came to be reviewed in the name of his administrators. The court that reviewed the case consisted of two judges, the third having declined to sit in the case.

The Virginia supreme court rejected the appellants' contention that the legislature could not lawfully increase Currie's risk without his consent because the demand for a quota was not made to the whole Society but only to a part of it, thus impairing the obligation of the contract set forth in the original act of 1795. The court maintained that Currie had been fully apprised of the power of the Society when he became a member, the power to alter and amend "the rules and regulations as they may judge necessary," and, therefore, had no just ground of complaint. The Society soon came to realize that the risk was unequal between the town and country subscribers, in favor of the former, and felt it necessary to separate their interests. This change, the court stated, was essential to equalize the risks. A majority of the Society, on a representation to the legislature, procured an act of the General Assembly, passed in 1795, separating these two interests. Furthermore, the court pointed out, the appellants' principal had less reason to complain because any member had the right to withdraw from the Society. It is better for an inconvenient member to be lopped off than for the whole corporate body to perish.

With regard to the election of McRae as president, the court upheld its validity by accepting the argument of the counsel for the Society. The clause, "there shall be in future only three directors, out of whom a president shall be chosen," the court insisted, should be construed as "there shall be in future only three directors, one of whom shall be president." Here the court failed to recognize the possibility for a different composition of the board and a different president that a different order of election might produce. The court instead simply concluded that there would be no utility in requiring an unnecessary circuity of proceeding. Since a previous election as director was not required by the act, there was no objection to the Society's husbanding its time by appointing a president and director at one ballot.

The court, thus, affirmed the judgment of the district court and established an important three-part precedent. First, the General Assembly has power, from time to time, to annul or alter acts of incorporation. Second, a member of the Mutual Assurance Society against fire loss is bound by an act of the General Assembly varying the terms of the original act of incorporation passed at a legally constituted meeting of the Society even though that individual member was not present at the meeting. And third, when an act provides that there shall be "three directors, out of whom a president shall be chosen," it is sufficient if the president be elected by a legally constituted meeting, and at the same time with the other directors, without having been previously appointed a director.

Selected Bibliography

Gibson, G.D. "The Virginia Corporation Law of 1956." *Virginia Law Review* 42 (May/June 1956): 445–87, 603–26.

Vagts, D.F. "Reforming the 'Modern' Corporation: Perspectives From the German." *Harvard Law Review* 80 (Nov. 1966): 23–89.

WHEN A CONTRACT OBTAINED BY FRAUD IS STILL A CONTRACT

by Harry Fritz
Department of History
University of Montana

Fletcher v. Peck, 6 Cranch 87 (1810) [U.S. Supreme Court]

In 1803, John Peck, of Newton, Massachusetts, sold 15,000 acres of land in Mississippi Territory to Robert Fletcher of Amherst, New Hampshire. In a feigned or collusive case, deliberately designed under the diversity of citizenship rule to bypass the Eleventh Amendment, to bring the case in federal courts and to test a number of disputed issues, Fletcher sued Peck in the U.S. Circuit Court of Massachusetts. The land in question, he claimed, was not Peck's to sell. Seven years later, in an opinion of the U.S. Supreme Court, Chief Justice John Marshall decided for the defendant: the land sale was legal. Therein lies a story.

Fletcher v. Peck arose from the tangled state of Georgia land claims—as had *Chisholm v. Georgia* (1793). In 1795, the state of Georgia sold 35 million acres of its western lands to four land companies for $500,000—about 1.4 cents per acre. Sixteen of the 17-member legislative majority that made the sale received either cash or shares for their votes. In the following year, on February 13, 1796, Georgia repealed the sale act. Its citizens either rose in righteous indignation against the suborned legislature or they had received a better offer. These two Georgia measures—the land sale of 1795 and its recision in 1796—are the chief ingredients of *Fletcher v. Peck*.

The "Yazoo Land Fraud" (Georgia's western lands were collectively named after the Yazoo River, a tributary of the Mississippi River) quickly became one of the great, epic domestic battles of early American history. Three factors fueled the explosion. First, on the same day as the Georgia repeal act was enacted, 11 million acres of the Yazoo claims were sold to the New England Mississippi Land Company, a third, or "innocent" party, or $1,138,000, or 10.3 cents per acre. Land speculation was profitable. Second, in 1798 Georgia ceded its western lands to the federal government, and Congress created the vast Mississippi Territory. The Yazoo issue went national. Third, most of the investors in the New England Mississippi Land Company were northern Federalists, who sought a national verification of their claims, while supporters of the Georgia repeal were states' rights Republicans. Yazoo became a sectional and a partisan issue.

Under President Thomas Jefferson, who assumed office in 1801, the Republicans backed a compromise solution. Negotiated by three administration heavyweights—Secretary of State James Madison, Secretary of the Treasury Albert Gallatin, and Attorney General Levi Lincoln—the deal seemingly satisfied everyone. It paid off Georgia to the tune of $1,250,000, thus quieting the state's shrill insistence on the legality of its 1796 repeal. It set aside 5 million acres to satisfy the claims of innocent purchasers, now expanded in number and increasingly bipartisan. It allowed these claimants, the "New Yazooists," to take either land or money. All that remained to close the deal was a congressional appropriation of $5 million to compensate the money claimants. A bill to this effect was introduced in Congress in 1804.

The bill failed. It failed again in 1805, 1806, and 1807. It failed due largely to the inveterate opposition of Congressman John Randolph of Virginia, the self-styled defender of the "old republican" principles of 1798. Randolph's magnetic oratory rallied the South, the states' righters and the Georgia repealers against the North, the Federalists, and the moderate Republicans in his own party. Though the votes were close, Randolph and his quondam allies continued to deny a powerful array of investors their legislative right to federal largesse. Increasingly, the Yazoo claimants leaned toward a judicial solution.

Fletcher v. Peck was held in abeyance in the Massachusetts circuit court for three years. These were the years when the entire federal judiciary reeled under the onslaught of the Jeffersonian attack. The case was finally tried before a jury in late 1806. The jury's verdict on the legality of the original sale was noncommittal, but the two federal judges who constituted the court, Supreme Court Justice William Cushing and District Judge John Davis, rewrote the history of Georgia: the Yazoo land sale of 1795 was binding and had not been undone in 1796. Robert Fletcher, the putative loser, asked the U.S. Supreme Court for a writ of error; it was granted and the case was argued before the Court early in 1809. John Quincy Adams and Robert Goodloe Harper, no mean talent, appeared for the defendant, Peck; Fletcher was represented by the volatile Luther Martin of Maryland. Reversed on a technicality, *Fletcher v. Peck* was not remanded to the Massachusetts circuit court but continued for another Term and was reargued in 1810. Joseph Story, a Massachusetts congressman and Yazoo lobbyist, replaced John Quincy Adams as counsel for Peck. The deck was now carefully stacked.

Rarely in American constitutional history has a decision of the Supreme Court been so foreordained. Every legal and constitutional precedent, every personal and political prejudice, every national and ideological tendency pointed to the reasoning and decision found in Marshall's opinion of March 16, 1810. *Fletcher v. Peck* was not only managed litigation, carefully crafted to raise every pertinent issue, but it was also deliberately designed to ensure favorable rulings on every disputed point.

Article I, Section 10, of the U.S. Constitution states: "No state shall . . . pass any bill of attainder, ex post facto law, or law impairing the obligation of contracts." This is the "contract clause," the key to Marshall's decision. Prior to 1810 it had not been broadly interpreted; it protected, the founders agreed, only private business transactions from state intervention. But there were early signs of its broader potential significance. The U.S. Circuit Court for Rhode Island voided a state debtor-relief law in 1792, citing the constitutional prohibition against impairment of contract. In 1795,

the Circuit Court for Pennsylvania, Justice William Paterson presiding, invalidated a state law fixing the ownership of property. The act was unconstitutional, Paterson declared in *Vanhorne's Lessee v. Dorrance*, because it impaired the obligation of a contract and was, thus, contrary to Article I, Section 10, of the Constitution.

More to the Yazoo point were specific legal opinions. As early as 1796, the Federalist congressman from South Carolina and ardent Yazooist Robert Goodloe Harper had argued that the 1795 Georgia sale constituted a contract that could not be broken by one of the parties. Harper's opinions were echoed by Alexander Hamilton, who cited the U.S. Constitution against the Georgia repeal and maintained that "the revocation of the grant by the act of the legislature of Georgia, may justly be considered as contrary to the constitution of the United States, and, therefore null." These views found their way into *Derby v. Blake* (1799), a decision by the Massachusetts Supreme Judicial Court, which, in the first instance of a state court holding another state's laws unconstitutional, declared the Georgia repeal of 1796 void.

The rigged case of *Fletcher v. Peck* raised each of these issues. Georgia owned the land it legally sold in 1795, and the sale had not been "constitutionally or legally impaired" by the repeal act of 1796. Chief Justice Marshall took up these points in prescribed order.

Marshall quickly disposed of legal niceties. Georgia possessed title to the Yazoo lands, and nothing in its constitution of 1789 restricted the legislature's power to dispose of them. But since the legislators were "unduly influenced" by shares and promises, was the sale act "a nullity?" He wrote: "That corruption should find its way into the governments of our infant republics, and contaminate the very source of legislation, or that impure motives should contribute to the passage of a law, or the formation of a legislative contract, are circumstances most deeply to be deplored." On the other hand, he submitted: "If the title be plainly deduced from a legislative act, which the legislature might constitutionally pass, if the act be clothed with all the requisite forms of a law, a court, sitting as a court of law, cannot sustain a suit brought by one individual against another founded on the allegation that the act is a nullity, in consequence of the impure motives which influenced certain members of the legislature which passed the law."

Marshall, thus, abandoned the ancient common-law theory of contract, which held that courts might pry into the circumstances of a bargain. Instead, he articulated the modern "will theory": a deal was a deal, despite the conditions under which it was struck. But he was not through reinterpreting the nature of a contract. Was Peck's title "constitutionally and legally impaired, and rendered null and void" in consequence of the Georgia recision act of 1796? No, for three reasons. First, subsequent purchasers of the Yazoo lands did not participate in the original transaction, however fraudulent. "They were innocent." They "were not stained by that guilt which infected the original transaction." Second, no conceivable legal reasoning could justify the Georgia legislature's pronouncing its own deed invalid. It was "a mere act of power." Courts of equity, not legislative parties, are the proper tribunals; even they cannot set aside "the rights of third persons." Third, "if an act be done under a law, a succeeding legislature cannot undo it. The past cannot be recalled by the most absolute power."

Here Marshall reached the nub of the matter. A law conveying property "is in its nature a contract," and "when absolute rights have vested under that contract, a repeal of the law cannot devest those rights." "[I]f the property of an individual, fairly and honestly acquired, may be seized without compensation," there are no limits to legislative power. But the Georgia legislature is constrained by two bounds. First, it merely prescribes the rules; "the application of those rules to individuals" is "the duty of other departments." Second, Georgia cannot act alone. It is not "a single sovereign power." "She is a part of a large empire; she is a member of the American Union; and that union has a constitution the supremacy of which all acknowledge, and which imposes limits to the legislatures of the several States."

What constitutional limits does the Yazoo repeal transcend? "In considering this very interesting question, we immediately ask ourselves what is a contract? Is a grant a contract?" Marshall asked. He defined a contract as "a

compact between two or more parties," either "executory" or "executed." Georgia sold the Yazoo lands under an executory contract, which, when the sale was made, became executed. An executed contract is a grant. A grant contains binding obligations and implies a contract. By this somewhat circular reasoning, Marshall, with the aid of the English treatise writer William Blackstone, was able to declare that "a grant is a contract executed." Its obligations continue. The Constitution does not distinguish between executory and executed contracts. Therefore the Georgia recision, "annulling conveyances between individuals" despite their grant/contract, is "repugnant to the Constitution."

One final hurdle remained. Are state grants (i.e., state contracts) excluded? Does the Constitution prohibit the impairment only of private, not public contracts? Marshall answered in the negative, "The words themselves contain no such distinction. They are general, and are applicable to contracts of every distinction."

Marshall thus formulated, in *Fletcher v. Peck*, three fundamental constitutional doctrines: a state grant is a contract, public contracts are no different from private, and a state-attempted repeal of a grant constituted an unconstitutional impairment of contract. *Fletcher v. Peck* both broadened the meaning of contract and, for the first time, invalidated a state law under the Constitution. The case is the federal equivalent of *Marbury v. Madison* (1803), in which Marshall declared a national law unconstitutional. As if that were not enough, Marshall added that the repeal was a bill of attainder, an *ex post facto* law, and contrary to "the general principles of our political institutions." He summed up: "It is, then, the unanimous opinion of the court, that, in this case, the estate having passed into the hands of a purchaser for a valuable consideration, without notice, the State of Georgia was restrained, either by general principles which are common to our free institutions, or by the particular provisions of the Constitution of the United States, from passing a law whereby the estate of the plaintiff in the premises so purchased could be constitutionally and legally impaired and rendered null and void."

It was a unanimous opinion, but Associate Justice William Johnson appended a concurring statement. Johnson was not quite sure that all Indian title to the Yazoo lands had been quieted—a point passed over by Marshall. Johnson was no advocate of unlimited private property rights, for the state must retain the power of repossession "when necessary for public uses." He stopped short of Marshall's unequivocal defense of executed contracts. But he supported the decision on a "general principle" that differentiated between "the right of jurisdiction and the right of soil." The "national sovereignty" could in no way part with the former, but the latter are unnecessary to political existence and may always be conveyed. And "[w]hen the legislature have once conveyed their interest or property in any subject to the individual, they have lost all control over it."

In the short run, *Fletcher v. Peck* greased the wheels for the passage, in 1814, of the long-sought $5 million compensation bill. Randolph's absence from Congress helped; the opposition, now led by Georgia Representative George M. Troup, could not carry the day. Passage was also aided by the desire of Mississippi for statehood and the need to secure land claims there, as well as a strong political sentiment to placate New England Republicans.

In the long run, *Fletcher v. Peck* elevated the contract clause of the Constitution, and the private property rights it protected, into a strong national mechanism for promoting economic development and restraining state regulation. Marshall's definition of contract reduced the state to the status of a private party and allowed freely contracting agents to set the rules for entrepreneurial activity in a market economy. Courts interpreted contracts strictly, to protect business interests against what Marshall called the "violent acts" and the "sudden and strong passions" of the people. For the rest of the nine-teenth century the contract clause was a frequent roadblock to state interference with business and to public regulation of enterprise.

Marshall made quick use of his new contract doctrine. In *New Jersey v. Wilson* (1812), he overturned a state law repealing a tax exemption attached to a land grant. In *Dartmouth College v. Woodward* (1819), he ruled that a colonial charter constituted a contract and was thus immune for state regulation. In *Sturgis v. Crowninshield* (1819), he protected creditors in bankruptcy proceedings, and in *Green v. Biddle* (1823), the Court upheld private land titles in Kentucky. "Contract" assumed a dimension beyond the intent of the framers but one that was conducive to order, speculation, growth, and national power.

Beyond constitutional doctrine, property rights, and economic advancement lay an even higher value enshrined by *Fletcher v. Peck*: individual liberty. The natural law doctrine of vested rights began with the individual. Contractarian ideology reduced each participating agent to a private citizen, the ultimate republican. The free, autonomous individual—free to acquire and use property, to enter into agreements with others, to participate in business and society—represented the highest ideal in early America. *Fletcher v. Peck* swept aside the sordid tangle of Yazoo land claims, interested speculators, and political bargaining, and enshrined that ideal in the U.S. Constitution.

Selected Bibliography

Margrath, C.P. *Yazoo: Law and Politics in the New Republic: The Case of* Fletcher v. Peck. Providence, RI: Brown University Press, 1966.

Wright, B.F., Jr. *The Contract Clause of the Constitution.* Cambridge, MA: Harvard University Press, 1938.

BALANCING PRIVATE GOOD AND PUBLIC GOOD

by Francis N. Stites
Department of History
San Diego State University

Dartmouth College v. Woodward, 4 Wheaton 518 (1819) [U.S. Supreme Court]

In 1819, the Supreme Court met for the first time in its new basement room in the Capitol. The surroundings, dark and inconvenient, offered no hint that this was the nation's most important tribunal. At 11 a.m. on February 2, Chief Justice John Marshall and his associates entered, donned their black robes, and took their seats behind the raised bench while the marshal announced the opening of the Court. Then the chief justice, with three associates sitting on each side, began to read the Court's opinion in *Dartmouth College v. Woodward*.

Few decisions have been as important as precedent. Here the Court was wrestling with some of the early republic's most vexing uncertainties about the implications of the American Revolution, the meaning of the Constitution, and the manner of balancing private and public interests. Yet, because too much is attributed to Supreme Court decisions and they are read backwards from the present, more is known about the case as precedent than as the product of real controversy.

The roots of the case trace back to the eighteenth century when one of the Great Awakening's prominent preachers, Eleazar Wheelock, established a pastorate and a school in Lebanon, Connecticut, to teach Indians and English youth dedicated to working as Indian missionaries. Chronic money problems led Wheelock to seek incorporation under a college charter. Colonial colleges were intimate parts of their communities, and their charters generally placed college government in the hands of independent and self-perpetuating boards of trustees, which included prominent community persons and government officials who would, hopefully, preserve the colleges against factional influence on the legislatures, and would protect the donors by giving the trustees the supervisory power to prevent the misuse of funds.

In 1769, the governor of New Hampshire issued a royal charter incorporating the trustees of Dartmouth College—the namesake was Lord Dartmouth, secretary of state for the colonies and a prominent English donor to Wheelock's school. The charter named Wheelock founder and president and gave him the right to appoint his successor in his will, subject to approval by the trustees. Like most colonial college trustees, those at Dartmouth had the legal right but not the energy to govern, and so they acquiesced in old Wheelock's enlightened if despotic management of the small college on the Connecticut River at Hanover, New Hampshire. They could replace him; they could not displace him.

The republican enthusiasm unleashed by the Revolution helped shape the background to the decision in 1819. Few things were as important to the revolutionary generation as the shaping of future citizens. Americans wanted, paradoxically, freedom, competition, and a uniformly republican government with complementary institutions like colleges. These goals required political leaders to respond to rapidly changing circumstances by balancing government power and individual liberty. Only an educated citizenry could sustain self-government, civic virtue, and the generation of wealth in response to the opportunities the government created. For these reasons, Americans prized voluntary associations and lavished attention on such problems as the relation of the state to education, how much to spend on education, and what to teach that would secure the blessings of liberty. "The business of education," said Benjamin Rush, "has acquired a new complexion by the independence of our country. The form of government we have assumed has created a new class of duties to every American." With an intimate connection existing between education and the other facets of society, political differences usually reflected policy disagreement over means to consensual ends.

This was the context at Wheelock's death in 1779 when his son, John, assumed the presidency of the college with trustee approval. Although the new president had an imperious manner, his devotion to the college and his hard work at managing its always precarious finances brought trustee cooperation. Gradually, however, the board always began to change as new, less tractable members replaced old ones. Wheelock began both to suspect a conspiracy to deprive him of control and to notice the real power that the board had always had but had not exercised. These suspicions governed Wheelock's angle of vision on everything as he finagled for control. By 1810, when the trustees refused to appoint one of his friends to a language professorship, things looked bleak.

In 1811, a quarrel between Wheelock and the local church in Hanover brought an open break at the college. Dartmouth's classics professor and a supine Wheelock friend had been the pastor of the church since 1787. In 1804, the trustees had appointed a new divinity professor—part of whose job was the pastorate at the Hanover church, thereby displacing Wheelock's friend. Wheelock insisted that his friend stay in the pastorate; the congregation resisted; and, when Wheelock appealed to the trustees for support, they determined to remain neutral. Wheelock saw this as further evidence of a conspiracy. Repeated efforts at compromise failed, and in 1811 the congregation finally split with Wheelock and his friend and adopted Congregationalism. Wheelock and a small band of followers in Vermont remained Presbyterian. The trustees refused to sanction a church dependent on the college and insisted that their authority as trustees gave them no power over matters of conscience. The long-smoldering feud between president and trustees was now in the open. The board was formally opposed to Wheelock. Over the next several years, trustees began removing some of his duties and prerogatives. Wheelock was determined to fight and he petitioned the legislature. He wanted the state to intervene to strengthen his position.

This quarrel, given college-community ties, was essentially a small civil war. Wheelock initiated a pamphlet assault as a prelude to his request for legislative assistance. After arousing public interest with an anonymous 80-page polemic accusing the trustees of forming a Federalist-Congregationalist conspiracy dangerous to the public welfare, he joined forces with New Hampshire Republicans. These partisans joined the fray eagerly because they had long been concerned with education. The trouble at Dartmouth was, they said, a matter for public concern because the state had liberally supported the institution and because education ought to be every citizen's concern.

Republicans exploited Wheelock's allegations during the state elections of 1816. When the trustees ultimately fired Wheelock, the Republicans traced the animus to the college's royal charter provision that the trustees be self-perpetuating. The absence of accountability was, they said, more congenial to monarchy than to the spirit of free government. They warned that the future of popular government in New Hampshire demanded state control of Dartmouth. After capturing the legislature and the governorship in 1816, the Republicans converted the college into a state university by changing the corporation's name to Dartmouth University, enlarging the number of its trustees, and adding a board of overseers. Old Wheelock got lost in the enthusiasm.

Stunned, eight of the 12 trustees (known ever after as the Octagon) quickly rallied and resolved not to accept the legislative changes they interpreted as confiscation. Two of the lawyers on the board (there were five lawyers among the eight) drafted a careful pamphlet response to Wheelock's anonymous charges. They argued that a corporate charter was a grant of private property rights, that the state constitution prohibited the legislature from deprivation of property without judicial trial, and, because grants were contracts, that the 1816 legislation violated the contract clause, Article I, Section 10, of the U.S. Constitution.

The 1816 legislation reverberated beyond New Hampshire. The number of colleges had grown with the nation, and there had been a movement since the 1740s to make them more responsive to public needs by bringing them under governmental control. The widespread concern generated only a confusion of voices. Everyone apparently wanted colleges to ensure the promise of the Revolution, but uncertainty about the nature, rights, and obligations of the colleges brought only fumbling legislative creations or remakes of colonial colleges. The struggle at Dartmouth was but the latest in this long series. With the legal status of educational corporations still uncertain, the 1816 legislation looked ominous. The 1780 Massachusetts constitution contained a provision reaffirming the traditional legislative power to change government at Harvard University, and demands there for change in institutional government had been continuous since 1800. There were rumors that New Hampshire's success was stimulating Kentucky Republicans to challenge Presbyterian domination of Transylvania College. Those anxious to prevent such changes urged the Dartmouth trustees to "[h]old on till the last finger is cut off, and to protest the legality of the measure and if necessary carry that protest to the Supreme Court of the United States." That is what they did.

Wanting the fullest judicial examination as rapidly as possible, the trustees sought tactical advice. Lawyers, including members of the Octagon, urged them to begin their action in the state court. Even so, because the 1816 elections had also placed Republican justices on the New Hampshire superior court, the advisers told the Octagon not to expect final resolution until they had appealed the contract question to the U.S. Supreme Court. The trustees also engaged the services of Jeremiah Mason and Jeremiah Smith—two of the legal giants of the early nineteenth century—and Daniel Webster, junior counsel and Dartmouth alumnus. In 1817, they sued the former college treasurer who had deserted to the university, William H. Woodward, for the college records and the college seal.

In the New Hampshire Superior Court, college counsel emphasized the private nature of the corporation, its property, privileges, and rights, and raised an argument based on separation of powers. They used English precedents

to show that there were two classes of corporations: civil and eleemosynary. Civil corporations were for purposes of government, trade, or commerce; they might be called public, and the legislature could control them to a certain extent. Eleemosynary, or charitable, corporations were private and immune from interference. Originating in private gifts, they shared nothing with civil corporations. Hospitals, colleges, and schools had at English common law always been private eleemosynary ones.

Mason turned to the state constitution and asked whether the legislature's power resembled Parliament's before the Revolution. Parliament, he noted, could have abolished the corporation because it was omnipotent, but the king could not do so until he determined it had "become forfeit." For corporations, at least, Mason said, the legislature was the successor to the king. So, there were general limitations on the legislature's power and specific ones (notably Article 15 of the New Hampshire bill of rights, which provided that no one should be "deprived of his property, immunities, or privileges" without due process of law). One held the right of property, then, under the constitution and not at the will of the legislature. This was not a denial of state power over private corporations, only over legislative power. Mason believed it was a settled principle that it was the judiciary's responsibility to protect the rights and enforce the duties of these private eleemosynary corporations. What was true for the state was also true for the national constitutions in which Mason found protection in the contract clause.

The 1816 legislation was a "bold experiment," which, unless checked, would set a precedent that would stifle freedom by keeping colleges subservient to state legislatures. Smith said that political men were unfit to manage an "academical institution." He likened the alliance of politics with education to that of state and church and insisted that he preferred in either case for the government to "stand neuter." Who better to enforce such a stance than the judiciary?

New Hampshire's attorney general, George Sullivan, and Ichabod Bartlett, attorneys for the university, tried to show that Dartmouth had always been a civil or public corporation by pointing to its object of serving the public and to the state's contributions since 1769. Because legislatures granted corporate charters only when there was an expectation of public good resulting, they argued that it was a reasonable inference that every charter—even one for a private corporation—contained an implicit agreement that the state might alter the charter for the public good. The college charter, they insisted, was not the sort of contract the framers of the 1787 Constitution had had in mind when they drafted the contract clause.

In November 1817, the New Hampshire court unanimously upheld the legislation. Chief Justice William M. Richardson's able opinion addressed the future of the college and the burning policy question of state control of corporations. Corporations, he said, were of two classes. Private corporations—banks, insurance, and manufacturing companies—were created by individuals for their private benefit. Their property stood on the same legal ground as the property of individuals; their charters were contracts protected by the Constitution. Public corporations were those the state created for public purposes. The legislature had the power to regulate them, Richardson argued, without limitation by the contract clause. Because the education of future generations was a matter of the highest public concern, Dartmouth College was a public corporation and subject to the kinds of alteration the state had undertaken in 1816. That Richardson mentioned business corporations separately from educational ones shows that he was primarily concerned with the relation between education and the state. The Octagon used Section 25 of the Judiciary Act of 1789 and appealed to the U.S. Supreme Court on a writ of error.

The Court at Washington heard three days of argument in the case near the end of the 1818 Term. Opening for the college on March 10 and repeating the points of Mason and Smith, Daniel Webster gave one of the most famous performances in the Court's history. For four hours, he asserted the inviolability of private corporate rights under general principles, English common law, and the state constitution. Turning, at last, to the contract clause, he cited the Court's opinion in *Fletcher v. Peck* (1810) to contend that a grant of corporate rights was as much a contract as a grant of land. Like his colleagues in the New Hampshire court, Webster stressed that the Court's ruling would affect "all the literary institutions of the country" and the future of the nation. Everything about him—the flashing eyes, resonant voice, and dramatic gestures—held spellbound the small audience as he paused, then turned to the chief justice and delivered an emotional summation. "Sir, I know not how others may feel, but, for myself, when I see my Alma mater surrounded like Caesar in the senate-house, by those who are reiterating stab upon stab, I would not, . . . have her turn to me, and say, . . . And thou too, my son!"

John Holmes, the university counsel, and William Wirt, U.S. attorney general, could match neither Webster's forensic skill nor his points. Feebly, they rehashed Judge Richardson's argument that the contract clause did not restrain the states in the government of their internal affairs, including public corporations. Joseph Hopkinson, Webster's associate, presented a closing statement for the college with a persuasive argument against state monopolies over education.

Marshall informed counsel that the Court would give the matter all the consideration due an act of a state legislature but warned that an immediate decision was unlikely. The next morning he announced that because the justices were divided, the Court would continue the case to 1819.

The continuance gave both sides time to strengthen their causes. The trustees arranged three additional cases in the federal circuit court to bring before the Supreme Court a more complete review of the 1816 legislation. *Woodward* had presented only the contract clause question. The larger issue the Octagon wanted to raise through the cognate cases was whether the "general principles of our governments" restrained the states "from divesting vested rights" (i.e., the due process question). To bring cases in circuit court it was necessary that the parties be from different states. So, college counsel and the trustees made arrangements to lease some college lands in New Hampshire to citizens of Vermont and then, in the spring of 1818, to bring three actions in ejectment—an old form of trying land title. In ejectment cases, the plaintiff was always a lessee seeking damages resulting from an ouster; recovery involved establishing the lessor's title to the property. This established method of suit regularly involved fictitious lessors and lessees and offered the surest and most convenient way to bring the college questions into circuit court on diversity of state citizenship grounds.

The Octagon hoped the circuit court would act quickly to get these cases before the Supreme Court by the 1819 Term. Supreme Court Justice Joseph Story, from Massachusetts, had long been hoping to hear these cases because he did not think that *Woodward* presented all the important contract clause questions. That the cases would come on his circuit aided and encouraged the trustees.

Both the college and the university hurried to gather whatever ammunition they could to persuade the Supreme Court of the correctness of their respective positions on the validity of the New Hampshire legislation. Webster circulated printed copies of his argument. The university retained the redoubtable William Pinkney, flamboyant leader of the federal bar, to reargue the main case during the 1819 Term and to get some new information before the Court. The university proved inadequately prepared. Cyrus Perkins, a university adviser, approached the 1819 Term believing that if the institution could not persuade the Court that Dartmouth was a public institution, it would lose the case.

When the Court reconvened in 1819, the chief justice pulled an 18-page opinion from his sleeve and shattered the university's hopes. Dartmouth College, he said, was "an eleemosynary, and [as] far as respects its funds, a private corporation." Private corporations could acquire property as could natural persons. The charter was a vested right of the trustees of Dartmouth College, and the corporation was to be governed by them and their successors forever. Its charter as a private eleemosynary corporation was a contract within the meaning of the Constitution; the New Hampshire legislation was unconstitutional. Justices Story and Bushrod Washington filed concurring opinions. William Johnson concurred in Marshall's opinion; Justice Henry Brockholst Livingston concurred in the opinions of Marshall, Story, and Washington. Justice Thomas Todd was absent,

and Justice Gabriel Duvall dissented without giving an opinion.

Dartmouth College climaxed Marshall's expansion of the contract clause into a mighty instrument for the protection of the private property right—understood as the dynamic right to acquire goods. In *Fletcher v. Peck*, he had invalidated a Georgia repeal act on both natural law and constitutional grounds. That ambiguity was gone in 1819. Charters of incorporation, he proclaimed unequivocally, were contracts, "the obligation of which cannot be impaired, without violating the constitution of the United States." The contract clause extended to "contracts respecting property under which some individual could claim a right to something beneficial to himself," and a private corporation was one "endowed with a capacity to take property, for objects unconnected with government, whose funds are bestowed by individuals on the faith of the charter." No stronger judicial defense of property was put forth in the early nineteenth century. Chancellor James Kent, the eminent New York jurist, called the decision the most important step in securing rights derived from a governmental grant. He believed it made inviolable the "literary, charitable, religious and commercial institutions of our country."

Marshall had immunized private education against state legislative tinkering. Although he believed education a fit subject for governmental attention, he could not accept Richardson's view that education should be "altogether in the hands of government" because experience had taught him that American education had suffered from the fluctuating policy and repeated interferences of state legislatures. "Does every teacher of youth become a public officer, and do donations for the purpose of education necessarily become public property?" Marshall thought "the interest which this case has excited" proved that these questions were of "serious moment to society." For him, sound policy to preclude sectarian battles for legislative power required that "private" institutions, especially denominational colleges, have "security and permanence" through federal constitutional protection.

There was a sizable body of judicial experience with colleges by 1819 that supported

Marshall's conclusion. The chief justice had been a lawyer for Virginia in *Bracken v. Visitors of William and Mary College* in 1790 and 1797, and Harvard had made Story a member of its board of overseers in 1818. Justice Livingston's experience with problems between college and state was the most extensive. He had been working for decades to keep Columbia University out of the hands of the New York legislature. In 1810, this contest had prompted Chancellor Kent's comment in an opinion for the New York Council of Revison that it was "a sound principle in free governments that charters of incorporation, whether for private or local, or charitable, or literary or religious purposes, were not to be affected without due process of law, or without the consent of the parties concerned." In 1795, during a contest at Yale University, Zepheniah Swift, Connecticut's future chief justice, first articulated the distinction between private and public corporations that proved decisive in *Dartmouth*. The North Carolina legislature had funded a state university in 1789 and granted it property. In 1800 the legislature repealed the grants, and in 1805 the North Carolina court declared the repeal unconstitutional, in part because it violated the due process clause of the state constitution.

Marshall's 1819 opinion revealed not only his familiarity with the history of English common law governing private colleges' relation to the state but also a talent that had contributed to his success as an appellate lawyer in Virginia (i.e., the ability to sort through precedents and pick from them the points necessary to win). He did not parade this knowledge in citations to English and state precedents because this was a constitutional opinion, and he was aware of their shortcomings and limited applicability under the Constitution. He relied on the general principles of the common law but preferred to ground these constitutional opinions solely in the Constitution. As he said in *McCulloch v. Maryland*, the other great case of 1819: "We must never forget it is *a constitution* we are expounding" [emphasis in original].

The Court had clarified the meaning of "business of education" that percolated through the early republic. Colleges, some called them "nurseries of power and influence," were to be as important as business to American develop-

ment. Although business and commercial corporations were not his principal focus, Marshall's sweeping statement covered the growing number of business corporations even if he simply assumed that the contract clause covered them. Personal and professional connections with the development of business corporations in Virginia had made Marshall a keen observer of their nominal and actual relation to the state. "Banks, canal companies, and numerous associations of similar description, are formed on the principle of voluntary subscription," he had said in his argument in *Ware v. Hylton* (1796). "The nation is desirous that such institutions should exist." Ultimately, the *Dartmouth College* rule became one of the principal weights in the balancing of government and the economy in the nineteenth century.

In 1819, however, Marshall considered corporations important only as a species of private property. He noted early in the opinion that the parties in this case differed less on general principles than on the application of them to this case. Even Richardson for the New Hampshire court had admitted that *Fletcher v. Peck* left little room to doubt that some corporate charters were constitutionally protected contracts. But Marshall rejected Richardson's standard that a public interest in the objects (i.e., the uses) of private property was sufficient to justify state regulation. Such a standard, he believed, would generate blanket state meddling with private rights. Only by protecting the property, either of individuals or groups of individuals, could the government encourage the productive labor necessary to open the continent and develop the national economy. Such a change as the New Hampshire legislature had made, he said, "may be for the advantage of this college in particular, and may be for the advantage of literature in general; but it is not according to the will of the donors, and is subversive of the contract on the faith of which their property was given."

The question of what individual rights were involved in this case caused Marshall "real difficulty." That was because what he had to demonstrate was that the contract clause protected the charters of privately founded charitable institutions. His answer was another impressive example of his pragmatic, undoctrinaire approach to the Constitution's fundamental principles. Although "an artificial being, invisible, intangible, and existing only in contemplation of law," the corporation was the instrument for perpetuating the design of the original donors. It stood in their place. Corporate rights, then, were equivalent to private individual rights. As in *Fletcher*, the chief justice conceded that the framers did not have such contracts as these in mind when in 1787 they had drafted the Constitution's contract clause. But, he asserted, the framers were also not so imprudent as to attempt to provide specific rules for problems they could not have foreseen. A constitution had to be flexible and adaptable to circumstances. The language of the Constitution did not exclude this particular interpretation, and the "case being within the words of the rule, must be within its operation likewise."

Story attempted to bring business corporations within the embrace of the decision. His lengthy concurring opinion noted, among other things, that the contract clause should protect all state grants of funds to hospitals and colleges, whether the grants were for "special or general purposes, for public charity or particular beneficence." He then said that the clause reached all contracts concerning immunities, dignities, offices or franchises, or other rights deemed valuable in law, including contracts for the exercise of mere authority. "Each trustee has a vested right, and a legal interest, in his office, and it cannot be divested but by due process of law." And he would have found such rights protected both by the general principles of free government and the specific contract clause of the Constitution. Clearly, he wanted to broaden that clause into a general due process clause to protect both public and private institutions.

This broad application prompted Justice Washington to write a separate opinion limiting the ruling to corporations similar to Dartmouth College. Washington, like Marshall, was primarily concerned with the immediate issue of education and what it suggested about the balancing of private and public good.

There remained the cognate cases. Discussions between lawyers for both sides and the Court produced an agreement that the Supreme Court should remand the cases to the circuit for more discussion on the facts. There was more maneuvering, but Story's concurring opinion in *Woodward* covered all the points the cognate cases would have raised and so accomplished what college planners had been hoping for all along. When the cases were at length heard at Boston in May 1819, Story delivered another learned opinion covering all the questions again and ruling for the college. Counsel for both sides agreed to let this opinion stand unless the university could produce some decisive new information by June 10. On May 27, the University presented the new facts, but Story did not find them persuasive, and the Court gave its final judgment in the college controversy on June 10 as both parties had agreed.

Isaac Hill, editor of the New Hampshire *Patriot* and a determined Wheelock partisan and ferocious Republican, commented when he learned that the new information would not alter the Court's judgment: "Thus ends the third act of the drama." The first had been the Octagon's firing of Wheelock; the second had been the action by New Hampshire's legislature and court (the "people"). In the third act, Hill said, a "foreign power," the federal courts, had supported the few, the trustees, as opposed to the people. "The fourth act," he concluded, "is yet to come—*the drama is not* ended" [emphasis in original]. But it was. The college had already dispossessed the university. This, plus a burdensome debt and the improbability of state assistance, prompted it to acquiesce. Thus ended not only its existence, but the "drama" of the college controversy.

The *Dartmouth College* decision, however, did not end argument about the relation between corporations and the state, between private rights and public needs. Educational corporations appear to have benefited. Private denomination colleges proliferated throughout the midnineteenth century using the decision as their legal base, and the Court's separation of school and state had guaranteed the academic freedom of trustees, faculty, and students. Business corporations prospered, and, by the late nineteenth century, burgeoning corporate power had become the central political-economic issue. Then commentators began reading backwards to the 1819 case to discover there, rather than in subsequent judicial balancings and circumstances, the source of corporate invincibility. This, however, yanked the case out of context and substituted notoriety for significance.

The Court in 1819 had only balanced these competing interests. Only state legislatures could grant corporate charters, and at the moment of the grant the states were free to set whatever limits they deemed appropriate. Marshall's prohibition on subsequent alteration without consent was an admonition to the states to exercise more caution in their grants. Moreover, he suggested the idea, later known as the state police power, when he said that the framers of the Constitution did not intend to restrain the states in the regulation of civil institutions adopted for internal government. Story observed that a state could amend corporate charters by reserving the authority to do so in the original grant. Reservation clauses had already become common in college charters by the 1790s and by the late 1820s were common in business corporation charters. Improvident legislative grants, more than the *Dartmouth College* rule that corporate charters were contracts protected by the Constitution, robbed states of regulatory power. As in *Fletcher v. Peck*, Marshall insisted that the wisdom of legislative action was beyond the Court's purview. In a 1934 opinion, reminiscent of Marshall and Story

in 1819, Chief Justice Charles Evans Hughes noted that the history of the Court's contract decisions showed a "growing appreciation of public needs and of the necessity of finding ground for rational compromise between individual rights and public welfare."

Selected Bibliography

Baxter, M.G. *Daniel Webster and the Supreme Court.* Amherst, MA: University of Massachusetts Press, 1966.

Beveridge, A.J. *The Life of John Marshall.* 4 vols. New York: Houghton Mifflin Co., 1916–19.

Campbell, R.A. "*Dartmouth College* as a Civil Liberties Case: The Formation of Constitutional Policy." *Kentucky Law Review* 70 (1981–82): 643–706.

Herbst, J. *From Crisis to Crisis: American College Government, 1636–1819.* Cambridge, MA: Harvard University Press, 1982.

Newmyer, R.K. *Supreme Court Justice Joseph Story: Statesman of the Old Republic.* Chapel Hill, NC: The University of North Carolina Press, 1985.

Richardson, L.B. *History of Dartmouth College.* 2 vols. Hanover, NH: Dartmouth College Publications, 1932.

Shirley, J.M. *The Dartmouth College Causes and the Supreme Court of the United States.* St. Louis: G.I. Jones & Co., 1879.

Stites, F.N. *Private Interest and Public Gain: The Dartmouth College Case, 1819.* Amherst, MA: University of Massachusetts Press, 1972.

White, G.E. *The Marshall Court and Cultural Change, 1815–35.* New York: Macmillan, 1988.

JUSTICE STORY, BANKRUPTCY, AND THE SUPREME COURT

by Craig T. Friend
Lexington, Kentucky

Sturges v. Crowninshield, 4 Wheaton 122 (1819) [U.S. Supreme Court]

Occasionally, Supreme Court justices abstain from ruling on cases in which they have personal interest. During the Marshall years (1801–35), however, such a precedent had not been established, and justices participated fully in such cases, even when they had much to gain (or to lose) from the result. Such a decision to participate was made by Justice Joseph Story

when *Sturges v. Crowninshield* came before the Supreme Court in 1819.

In 1811, the state of New York passed a bankruptcy law that freed debtors from obligation upon relinquishing property and listing creditors. Richard Crowninshield used the law to escape his business debts, but Josiah Sturges, who had loaned Crowninshield over £1,000 less than a week before the law's passage, refused to accept the minimal compensation. In October 1817, he filed an action of *assumpsit* in the federal circuit courts.

Sturges had sufficient reason to believe he could regain his money. In 1814, Justice Bushrod Washington had decided on his circuit that bankruptcy laws could not be retroactive. Earlier in 1817, Justice Brockholst Livingston confused the issue. On circuit court in New York, he dissented from Washington's opinion and, in a separate case, ruled that such laws could be retroactive. At the October term of the Massachusetts' circuit court when Sturges's case was to be heard, Justice Story was on the bench.

Story's interest in economics was well-known. His political reputation had been built on his understanding of economic issues. In 1802, President Thomas Jefferson had offered Story a position as commissioner of bankruptcy in Massachusetts. The national Bankruptcy Act of 1801 was repealed before Story could accept the offer, however, and the position was eliminated. After President James Madison nominated him to the Court in 1811, Story remained interested in the national economy.

Even though Sturges may have hoped for Story to rule against the state law, he also had reason to worry. Story had close political ties with the Crowninshield family. In 1808, the Crowninshields had assisted him in gaining one of Massachusetts's seats in the House of Representatives and he had chosen alliance with the Crowninshields over several old friendships. His dedication to the Crowninshields appeared unquestionable.

On circuit court in 1817, Story realized the implications of Sturges's suit, especially if it were decided by the U.S. Supreme Court. Story was convinced that bankruptcy legislation was a power reserved to the federal government, and a favorable decision by the Marshall Court would establish that power. Story had begun work on a national bankruptcy bill, and the path should be cleared for its passage.

Story and the district judge disagreed on the decision, largely due to Story's manipulation to have the case decided by the Supreme Court. Directing the case to the Marshall Court enabled Story to avoid an official decision on

the circuit; the circuit court's decision would be made after the justices' collective opinion was heard. Thus, in 1818, when *Sturges v. Crowninshield* came to the Supreme Court, Sturges was certain that Washington would decide for him, Livingston would decide against him, and Story could be the deciding factor.

By February 1819, Marshall had brought the justices together and had written a unanimous opinion. Marshall united his Court through a twofold examination of the case. The first issue was the Constitution's grant for Congress "to establish . . . uniform laws on the subject of bankruptcies throughout the United States [Article I, Section 8]." Washington and Story argued that only the federal government could legislate on bankruptcy. Justices Livingston, William Johnson, and Gabriel Duvall, however, debated that states could pass bankruptcy laws if the federal government had not done so. Marshall persuaded Story and Washington that the latter interpretation still recognized federal authority.

Overcoming division on the first issue, Marshall turned to the second issue of *Sturges v. Crowninshield*. The constitutionality of New York's law was resolved, but its retroactive nature was not. Marshall, applying the contract clause rationale that he had firmly established in *Fletcher v. Peck* (1810), reasoned that the retroactive law impaired Crowninshield's obligation to Sturges and was, therefore, unconstitutional.

The decision in *Sturges v. Crowninshield* satisfied Story. Even though his national bankruptcy bill was not accepted, the justice remained involved in economic legislation, helping Daniel Webster draft the Bankruptcy Act of 1841. The decision also provided the states with a method to deal with bankruptcy following the Panic of 1819. Yet, the laws that were passed did not provide for retroactive insolvency.

Marshall, however, had not been clear in his written opinion. Many inferred from his words that states were prohibited from passing bankruptcy laws. His eagerness to resolve the division within the Court had left his resolution of the first issue ambiguous. Others interpreted the decision as allowing bankruptcy laws that could impair subsequent contracts. Eight years later, Marshall would have the opportunity to clarify his words in *Ogden v. Saunders* (1827).

Selected Bibliography

Newmyer, R.K. *Supreme Court Justice Joseph Story.*

Chapel Hill, NC: University of North Carolina Press, 1985.

————. *The Supreme Court Under Marshall and Taney.* Arlington Heights, IL.: Harlan Davidson, Inc., 1968.

White, G.E. *The Marshall Court and Cultural Change, 1815–35.* New York: Macmillan Publishing Co., 1988.

ABRIDGING VESTED INTERESTS: THE BATTLE OF THE MASSACHUSETTS BRIDGES

by Elizabeth B. Monroe
Department of History
Indiana University—
Purdue University at Indianapolis

Charles River Bridge v. Warren Bridge, 11 Peters 420 (1837) [U.S. Supreme Court]

This "Tale of Two Bridges" shows how increasing demands on legislatures to grant charters to banking, transport, and manufacturing endeavors raised the issue of whether the public interest was better served by fostering new opportunities in the marketplace or by securing existing ones. The two bridges and their corporations represented technologically identical improvements, over the same line of travel, designed to benefit the community by providing ready access between Boston and Charlestown and to secure a financial return on private investment. The proprietors of the bridges clashed over whether priority was to be given to community rather than to private vested interests.

In the early nineteenth century, public demands for transportation facilities forced national and state legislatures to consider governmental support for roads, bridges, canals, and river improvements. Legislative decisions hinged on whether government could intervene, and, if so, to what extent. Congress limited federal intervention to construction of a few projects of national scope, such as the Cumberland Road and improvements of the Ohio and Mississippi rivers. Most governmental provision for transportation development in the first half of the nineteenth century took place at the state and local levels. Support took two forms: direct aid, by which government built the improvement and maintained it; and indirect aid, by which government provided positive legal and economic mechanisms (e.g., corporation charters and public subsidies) for entrepreneurs who built and maintained improvements for the benefit of the community.

By the mid-1820s the phenomenal success of the state-built Erie Canal and the increasing prosperity of New York City forced competing Atlantic seaports and the states of which they were a part to challenge New York's superior transportation facilities. Boston merchants and investors compelled the Massachusetts legislature to consider improving local transportation in the immediate Boston area and developing a major line of travel from Boston to the eastern terminus of the Erie Canal at Albany, New York. How the Massachusetts legislature acted on these proposals raised important legal questions about the ability of the state to promote public benefit by means of grants to corporations.

With regard to the demand for better transportation facilities between the increasingly interdependent suburbs and the Boston peninsula, the legislature considered chartering a second company to build a bridge connecting Charlestown and Boston. Proponents of the new bridge charged that the proprietors of the existing Charles River Bridge had grown wealthy at the expense of the public. Tolls collected over its 40-year history far exceeded construction costs and maintenance. Promoters of the new bridge couched their scheme in terms of the development of Boston's suburbs and offered to donate their bridge to the state after they had recovered their initial investment.

After weighing the investors' risks to provide this public service against the extent of their rewards, the Massachusetts legislature chartered the proprietors of the Warren Bridge. But the indirect costs of this action met with marked resistance outside the legislature. The proprietors of the Charles River Bridge believed that the corporate charter for the new Warren Bridge would infringe directly on their earlier corporate grant by creating a competing bridge along the same line of travel and indirectly by destroying their property in tolls. Investors in other corporate improvements shared the Charles River Bridge proprietors' concerns. Claims of infringement of one bridge charter by another immediately led to litigation and threatened the favorable legal and economic climate that the legislature had created to lure scarce capital to needed projects.

The *Charles River Bridge* suit underscored the inadequacies of surviving colonial solutions to public transportation problems. Yet the successors of the almost 200-year-old franchise looked to the state to maintain their exclusive commitment until its expiration in 1855. The initial grant to provide public transport at the site of the Charles River Bridge dated from 1640, when the colonial legislature had authorized the newly established Harvard College to operate a ferry between Boston and Charlestown. For the remainder of the seventeenth century, the college had provided public transportation between these two villages on the banks of the Charles River. In 1701, the college began to lease its ferry rights to concessionaires. By the end of the revolutionary era, the college found it necessary to complete extensive repairs to its boats and ways in anticipation of increased postwar traffic and resulting rent increases. But complaints about ferry service continually reached the legislature. Responding to pleas for better service from communities north of the river and to proposals to build toll bridges, the Massachusetts legislature in March 1785 granted a charter to Charlestown and Boston bridge promoters.

The Charles River Bridge proprietors were incorporated to build a bridge in place of the ferry, to collect tolls for its use, and to indemnify the college for its lost revenue at the rate of £200 per year. At the end of 40 years, the bridge was to revert to the state. By 1792, the success of the Charles River Bridge had encouraged other promoters to request charters for similar projects, which led the Charles River Bridge proprietors to protest that the proposed bridges would capture some of the Boston-Charlestown traffic and, therefore, reduce their expected revenues. As a result of this protest, the new charter for the West Boston Bridge (connecting Boston to Cambridge) compensated the proprietors of the earlier bridge by extending their charter an additional 30 years.

In the first two decades of the 1800s, the Massachusetts legislature chartered four more bridge companies in the Boston area without providing additional concessions to the Charles River Bridge proprietors. General prosperity and rapid population growth greatly increased the use and therefore the revenue of Boston's oldest bridge. By the 1820s, its proprietors could claim a steady income of $20,000 per year on property valued at $280,000. The value of stock had risen over 300 percent since the original charter was granted. But such success led inevitably to direct challenge; beginning in 1823 Charlestown merchants proposed a new free bridge between Charlestown and Boston that would provide additional access between the two points and break the Charles River Bridge monopoly. The legislative contest between the sponsors of the competing bridges lasted for the next five years.

Legislative issues included the necessity of a competing bridge, the legislature's ability to authorize one, and its potential effect on future investments in the state. The promoters of the new Warren Bridge claimed that public necessity and convenience could not be accommodated by the old bridge and its approaches. The Charles River Bridge proprietors countered that the proposed charter included a clause to the effect that if the Charles River Bridge was surrendered to the state, a new bridge would not be built. Such a surrender clause, they pointed out, demonstrated the specious character of arguments based on increased traffic.

The second issue related to the state's ability to charter a new bridge that would directly compete with the older one. The Warren Bridge developers avowed that the legislature had an "equitable right" to intervene in the public interest to eliminate the burdensome tolls of the Charles River Bridge and to remedy a "public injustice." The Charles River Bridge proprietors felt otherwise, and they cited specific constitutional provisions to back their viewpoint.

Invoking the Massachusetts bill of rights, the proprietors pointed to the clause that guaranteed enjoyment of "life, liberty and property." Authorization of the Warren Bridge meant effective destruction of the Charles River Bridge toll receipts, since traffic would divert to the free bridge. According to the proprietors, destroying their property in tolls by the indirect means of chartering a free bridge company violated the Massachusetts constitutional guarantee just as surely as physically destroying the bridge. Even if public interest required the expropriation of the Charles River Bridge, its proprietors believed the state had to comply with the Massachusetts Constitution by offering reasonable compensation. Further, the contract clause of the U.S. Constitution prevented state impairment of contracts, and a legislative charter was recognized as a form of contract. The proposed Warren Bridge, by competing with the Charles River Bridge's monopoly along a line of travel, would violate the U.S. Constitution as well as the state's.

The bridge controversy also underscored the policy clash between those who wanted to provide immediate public benefits and stimulate growth with new corporate grants and those who wanted to protect already ventured capital and maintain a predictable investment environment by denying new competing grants. Differences between the two groups involved attitudes toward the state's role in encouraging private initiative for public benefit, as well as the relative importance of the rights of the community and private property rights.

An Act to Establish the Warren Bridge Corporation passed the Massachusetts legislature and was signed by the governor in March 1828. It authorized the new proprietors to build a bridge between Boston and Charlestown and to collect tolls for its use until they had been reimbursed for the cost of construction plus five percent interest, as long as the term of toll collection did not exceed six years. The Warren Bridge would then revert to the state and become free. Until reversion, the Warren Bridge proprietors were required to pay one-half of the Charles River Bridge's annuity to Harvard College.

The Warren Bridge proprietors immediately began purchase of the site, and in June the Charles River Bridge proprietors filed for an injunction to halt construction of the new bridge. The preliminary request was denied, construction continued, and the Warren Bridge opened to public traffic on Christmas Day. Both bridge companies filed supplemental bills and spent much of the following year taking depositions, gathering evidence and preparing arguments. In October 1829, the Massachusetts Supreme Judicial Court heard arguments on the merits of the case.

The arguments of counsel for each bridge interest raised points similar to those raised during the prolonged legislative controversy, although the major conflict before the court centered on the terms of the 1785 charter to the Charles River Bridge proprietors. The Charles River Bridge lawyers argued that Harvard College's exclusive ferry privileges over the line of travel had been transferred implicitly to the bridge company and therefore the Warren Bridge grant impaired the contract between the Massachusetts legislature and their clients. Such an impairment violated both the Massachusetts and U.S. Constitutions. The Warren Bridge lawyers contended that there had been no explicit grant to the Charles River Bridge and, therefore, the legislature had acted within its rights in authorizing the new bridge.

Both sides placed their arguments within the context of public policy. According to the Charles River Bridge attorneys, an adverse decision would halt public improvements because private capital would be unable to trust the government to honor its contracts. The Warren

Bridge counsel argued that public interest demanded an end to monopoly grants that retarded the legislature's ability to meet public needs for improved transportation. A decision adverse to their clients would inhibit the "free course of legislation" and free competition in the marketplace.

In January 1830, the supreme judicial court dismissed the complaint so that the Charles River Bridge proprietors could appeal to the U.S. Supreme Court (the Supreme Court could hear appeals only if the state courts sustained state laws challenged as violating the U.S. Constitution). In their opinions, the four Massachusetts justices split evenly over the validity of the 1828 legislative grant to the Warren Bridge. Justices Marcus Morton and Samuel Wilde rejected the claims of the Charles River Bridge proprietors; Justice Samuel Putnam and Chief Justice Isaac Parker upheld them. Morton's opinion emphasized the community's needs for material improvements and accepted the defendant's argument that the 1785 charter to the Charles River Bridge proprietors had not been exclusive. While the new bridge admittedly diverted tolls from the old one, the damages to the old bridge were merely consequential. In Morton's opinion, public grants were to be strictly construed. Broad construction and recognition of implied rights and privileges would impede business and community interests; better transportation would be blocked because all such improvements potentially diminished earlier grants. Wilde agreed with Morton.

On the other hand, Putnam's decision found for the complainants by resorting to the "spirit" and "substance" of their charter. According to Putnam, the spirit of the legislature's contract with the Charles River Bridge proprietors was the grant of exclusive privileges, and its substance the right to collect tolls. The subsequent charter of the Warren Bridge had effectively destroyed the Charles River Bridge's property in tolls, thereby impairing the earlier contract. The latter grant was therefore unconstitutional. Parker agreed with Morton that the college's exclusive right to the line of travel had not been transferred to the Charles River Bridge proprietors and, like Morton, he indicated his concerns about technological progress.

But he found for the Charles River Bridge proprietors because the state had destroyed their property by enfranchising another bridge in the immediate area. Therefore, the first proprietors were entitled to compensation from the state. Since the 1828 law creating the Warren Bridge did not provide such an indemnity, it was unconstitutional. Immediately following the Massachusetts decision the Charles River Bridge proprietors applied to the U.S. Supreme Court for a writ of error, and the case was placed on the Court's calendar.

The Supreme Court, in January 1831, was composed of seven justices, a majority of whom had served together for 20 years and had acted in concert on many of the important constitutional controversies of the period. Chief Justice John Marshall, the dominant figure of the Court, exerted enormous influence over his colleagues. In his 30-year tenure Marshall had written almost one-half of the Court's decisions and had rarely dissented from a majority opinion. In 1831, new appointments to the bench were only beginning to affect the consolidated views of the Marshall Court. Six of the justices heard the arguments in *Charles River Bridge*, and five days later announced their inability to reach a decision.

Failure to reach a decision depended as much on shifting views of public contracts and public policy as on personnel. While the earlier decisions of the Marshall Court had invariably interpreted the contract clause to give primacy to property interests, in the last decade of the Marshall era decisions broadened the scope of state powers at the expense of consistent protection of property rights. In two cases decided the year before the *Charles River Bridge* arguments were heard, the Marshall Court restricted corporate charter rights to those powers specifically conferred, and protected government taxation power from implied immunities in corporate charters.

The Court had become increasingly aware that corporations initially designed to serve the public interest could threaten the state's subsequent ability to supply community needs. Yet, in many instances, protection of vested property interests remained the most efficient means to secure public goals. The justices' divergent views on these issues, together with illnesses and vacancies on the bench, led to delay in resolving the *Charles River Bridge* dispute. Finally, in 1837, the case was reargued before a transformed Court.

Arguments commenced January 19 and continued for six days. Daniel Webster and Warren Dutton, both of whom had appeared in 1831, again represented the Charles River Bridge proprietors. The Warren Bridge proprietors had new counsel, John Davis and Simon Greenleaf. All four attorneys were prominent members of the Massachusetts bar, Davis and Webster were U.S. senators, and Greenleaf was Royall Professor of Law at Harvard College. Public comment acknowledged the learning and skill of their arguments, while, according to Justice Joseph Story, "it was a glorious exhibition for old Massachusetts."

Webster and Dutton reiterated their presentations to the state court and to the Supreme Court six years before: the Charles River Bridge had succeeded to the ferry rights held by Harvard College; the ferry had exclusive rights to the line of travel; the bridge assumed the same rights; and the subsequent grant to the Warren Bridge violated the state's contract obligation when the free bridge destroyed the proprietors' property in tolls, which was the essence of their original grant.

Resorting to familiar vested rights and contract clause arguments, the Charles River Bridge counsel insisted that to protect property interests from capricious actions of legislatures, public charters should be liberally construed. According to Dutton and Webster, the interests of the public demanded security of title and full enjoyment of property rights, for "[n]othing is reasonable but the fulfillment of the contract."

Davis and Greenleaf refuted their adversaries by a different line of reasoning: the ferry had always been subject to the state; the ferry rights had never passed to the bridge, but had been resumed by the state after compensating the college; and neither ferry nor bridge had exclusive rights to the line of travel. When the Charles River Bridge proprietors accepted the extension of their charter in 1792, they acknowledged the state's authority to make competing grants. Therefore, the subsequent grant to the Warren Bridge was within the legislature's authority.

The Warren Bridge attorneys argued that liberal construction of Charles River Bridge charter would impede governmental provision for the needs of the community, particularly in the area of transportation. In the case before the Court, the legislature, as the representative of the people, had assessed their needs and granted the Warren Bridge charter. According to Davis and Greenleaf, the public interest had been served by curtailing private rights that threatened future economic growth.

The Court that heard arguments in 1837 had been transformed during the intervening six years by the deaths of the chief justice and one associate justice and the resignation of another associate justice. These vacancies on the bench had provided President Andrew Jackson the opportunity to make the Court more "democratick." Diverging judicial views on protection of vested property rights, which had been discernible at the first *Charles River Bridge* hearing, became more marked with the new appointments. In 1837, three justices heard the case for the first time; given the deadlock after the previous hearing, the new justices' opinions would be decisive.

The justices' attitudes toward the state's role in the economy reflected the fundamental partisan differences of the period. Jacksonian Democrats encouraged new entrepreneurs' attacks on older capital privilege. Since the legislative and executive branches responded most readily to public demands, they should determine the role of government in the economy. Jackson's opponents, soon to coalesce as the Whigs, believed that private capital could only be coaxed into public action when vested rights were protected from the potentially capricious legislature and the potentially despotic executive. Consistent interpretation of charters based on precedent and determined by the courts should determine the role of the government in the economy.

The arguments of counsel in *Charles River Bridge* also reflected partisan positions. Legislative battles over both the bridge controversy and the proposal to build the east-west railroad had served as catalysts for the resurgence of political parties in Massachusetts in the 1820s. At that time, the promoters of the Warren Bridge had resorted to popular rhetoric, insisting that the Charles River Bridge "monopolists" had received "exorbitant compensation" from "heavy tolls." They consistently portrayed the struggle over whether to charter the Warren Bridge as one between the workers and tradesmen of Charlestown and the rich proprietors of the Charles River Bridge. While counsel for the opposing interests for the most part eschewed the political rhetoric and bombast of the legislative debates, their arguments had appealed to the political attitudes of the time.

Less than three weeks after hearing the arguments, the Court announced its decision. Chief Justice Roger B. Taney and three other Jackson appointees to the bench confirmed the decision of the Massachusetts Supreme Judicial Court and upheld the Warren Bridge charter. The other Jackson appointee voted for dismissal for lack of jurisdiction, while the two pre-Jackson members of the Court dissented from the majority opinion.

Taney's majority opinion and Justice Joseph Story's dissent presented contrasting views of legal principles, governmental responsibility, and economic progress. The two justices disagreed on matters of judicial interpretation of charters and contracts, the powers of the states, and the relative importance of the rights of the community and the rights of the individual. Their opinions placed the local dispute between two bridge companies in the broader arena of the power and purpose of government.

The new chief justice agreed with the Warren Bridge attorneys that the ferry's franchise had ended with the legislature's charter for the Charles River Bridge. Comparing the legislature's action to a royal grant, Taney found authority for construction in the grantor's favor. The legislature, representing the sovereign power of the people, had granted to the Charles River Bridge proprietors the privilege to build a bridge and collect tolls. Taney reasoned that, like royal bounties, the grant of legislative largess should be construed narrowly to protect the benefactor. In the present case, such narrow construction in the public interest disposed of any implied exclusive rights to the line of travel. Therefore, the legislature's later authorization of a competing grant did not amount to destruction of the proprietors' property in tolls. Since the state had not taken private prop-

erty, compensation by eminent domain proceedings was not required.

The Charles River Bridge proprietors had presumed too generous a legislative grant. While the chief justice declared that the "rights of private property must be sacredly guarded," nonetheless in his eyes the rights of the community were paramount. According to Taney, "[T]he object and end of all government is to promote the happiness and prosperity of the community by which it is established; and it can never be assumed, that the government intended to diminish its power of accomplishing the end for which it was created." For private property in the form of a legislatively granted privilege to be protected, it would have to be explicitly conferred.

Story's dissent followed a different line of reasoning. Instead of viewing the Charles River Bridge charter as analogous to a royal grant, Story insisted that it was a form of contract for valuable consideration. The proprietors had offered to build the bridge at their own expense to further the public good. In return they had received from the legislature the right to collect tolls. Where valuable consideration was received, public contracts were construed in favor of the grantee. Story's broad construction of the bridge charter inferred an exclusive grant to collect tolls along the line of travel. The subsequent legislative charter to the Warren Bridge, by indirectly destroying property in tolls, impaired the earlier contract.

According to Story, it was "to the dishonour of the government that it should pocket a fair consideration, and then quibble as to the obscurities and implications of its own contract." Taney was mistaken, Story maintained, in defining the Charles River Bridge charter as a bounty and in justifying the legislature's action as in the public interest. "If the government means to invite its citizens to enlarge the public comforts and conveniences, . . . there must be some pledge that the property will be safe; . . . and that success will not be the signal of a general combination to overthrow its rights, and to take away its profits." Justice demanded that the legislature abide by the consequences of the earlier agreement.

Both Taney and Story favored public policies that encouraged investment and fostered economic progress. Both recognized that if states chose not to build transportation facilities at their own expense, private capital must be tempted to supply community needs. Taney emphasized broadened entrepreneurial opportunity; Story relied on security of title and the full enjoyment of its benefits.

Their opinions in *Charles River Bridge* also point out their differing attitudes toward the roles of the state and national governments in the American federal system. Taney's opinion shied away from federal involvement in what he saw as a state matter. His reliance on strict construction endorsed the charter to the Warren Bridge proprietors and, therefore, the Massachusetts legislature's determination of the public interest. For Taney, strict construction served the twofold purpose of limiting judicial interpretation and avoiding federal encroachment on state powers. On the other hand, Story, as an avid supporter of the constitutional nationalism of the Marshall era, used the more conservative doctrine of contract to maintain both judicial interpretation of state contracts and a superior role for the federal government.

Two other important Supreme Court decisions in 1837 complemented *Charles River Bridge*. Story dissented in these as well. In *New York v. Miln*, the Court qualified Marshall's broad hints at an exclusive national commerce power by acknowledging that a state law affecting incoming passengers was not a regulation of commerce but an exercise of state police power. And in *Briscoe v. Bank of Kentucky*, the new Court tempered Marshall's denial of state power to emit bills of credit by accepting that currency issued by a corporation of the state did not violate the Constitution. Taken together, the three decisions broadened areas of state action and narrowed the nationalism of the Marshall Court.

For all Story's despair at the end of the Marshall era, the Court's decision in *Charles River Bridge* did not overturn Marshall's authoritative statement in *Dartmouth College v. Woodward* (1819) on nature of state charters of incorporation. The 1837 opinion merely held that such a charter would be strictly construed. While this decision represented a departure from Story's concept of contract law, it followed Marshall's own reasoning in *Providence*

Bank v. Billings (1830), in which he refused to let exemption from state taxation pass by way of implication. In the *Charles River Bridge* decision, Taney extended Marshall's narrow construction of the Providence Bank charter to the Charles River Bridge charter without damaging the earlier definition of contract in *Dartmouth College*.

Corporations were not slow to grasp the implications of *Charles River Bridge*. As early as 1831, the promoters of the east-west railroad in Massachusetts had demanded not only an explicit monopoly along the line of travel, but also the ability to set rates (previously established by charter) and eminent domain powers. Concessions to the Boston and Worcester Railroad's investors reflected the extent to which railroads had captured the public imagination and the legislative concern that the pending Charles River Bridge suit threatened to discourage investment in state-chartered enterprises. The already volatile climate of railroad promotion was further agitated by the Supreme Court's decision. To coax private investment into railroad ventures, state legislatures expanded charter privileges by expressly granting route monopoly, ratemaking, eminent domain and, in some cases, tax-exemption provisions.

The doctrinal impact of *Charles River Bridge* was felt almost immediately. Within a few months, a New York court endorsed the decision when it refused to halt construction of a railroad bridge adjacent to a chartered toll bridge. The doctrine of strict construction achieved particularly telling results in state courts in disputes between different transportation technologies, since earlier charters had not barred later railroad development. But the Supreme Court restricted its use of the doctrine because strict construction supporting expressly granted corporate privileges might be turned against the public interest. Strict construction of legislatures' reserved powers of charter amendment might also be adverse to the interest of the community. Ambiguity in these cases would be construed in favor of the corporation. While the courts generally used the doctrine to strike down outmoded and obstructionist interests in order to sustain new interests that benefited the community, strict construction was a two-edged sword.

In *Charles River Bridge*, that sword had been used in the interest of progress. Although the two bridges were virtually identical and technological development was not at issue in the case, Taney's opinion and the earlier opinions of Massachusetts justices Morton and Parker recognized that the search for speed, dependability, and economy would lead to increased demand for and rapid adoption of new technologies. All three judges were concerned with the potential obstruction of new transportation improvements by older ones. Taney envisioned older corporations "awakening from their sleep and calling upon this court to put down the improvements which have taken their place." Fearing this threat to the millions of dollars already invested in new enterprises, and recognizing the magnitude of the problem that a decision in favor of the older interests would create, Taney fashioned his opinion to justify creative destruction.

Creative destruction of one form of property in order that another might prosper placed a higher social value on new uses of capital than on maintenance of old uses. The Court's decision in *Charles River Bridge*, like legislative ac-tion to subsidize improvement corporations, served as an instrumental alliance of law with anticipated technological advances. The decision allowed residents of Massachusetts "to avail themselves of the lights of modern science, . . . which are now adding to the wealth and prosperity, and the convenience and comfort of every other part of the civilized world."

Selected Bibliography

Binford, H.C. *The First Suburbs: Residential Communities on the Boston Periphery, 1815–60.* Chicago: University of Chicago Press, 1985.

Horwitz, M.J. *The Transformation of American Law, 1780–1860.* Cambridge, MA: Harvard University Press, 1977.

Kutler, S.I. *Privilege and Creative Destruction: The* Charles River Bridge *Case.* Philadelphia: J.B. Lippincott Co., 1971.

Newmyer, R.K. *Supreme Court Justice Story: Statesman of the Old Republic.* Chapel Hill, NC: University of North Carolina Press, 1985.

Salsbury, S. *The State, the Investor, and the Railroad: The Boston and Albany, 1825–67.* Cambridge, MA: Harvard University Press, 1967.

Warren, C. *History of the Harvard Law School and of Early Legal Conditions in America.* New York: Lewis Publishing Co., 1908.

"AN INNOCENT SORT OF A DUCK": IRON RANGE PIONEERS CHALLENGE JOHN D. ROCKEFELLER

by David A. Walker
Department of History
University of Northern Iowa

Rockefeller v. Merritt, 76 F. 909 (1896) [U.S. Circuit Court of Appeals]

The Mesabi Range in northeastern Minnesota once contained America's richest iron ore deposit. Its initial development in the early 1890s was the result of the efforts of a remarkable group of pioneer residents—the Merritt family of Duluth. Following the initial discovery of high-grade ore, the Merritts assumed tremendous financial obligations in order to construct a railroad from the mining range to ore docks on Lake Superior.

Led by brothers Alfred and Leonidas, the Merritts left the comfort of local banking circles and entered the realm of high stakes, eastern financiers. They contacted officials of the American Steel Barge Company, a New York corporation engaged in shipbuilding and transportation on the Great Lakes. John D. Rockefeller had invested substantially in the barge company, thus forming the first, indirect link between the head of Standard Oil and the Duluth family.

The Merritts seemed poised for spectacular growth. Then, the nationwide Panic of 1893 struck, and the ensuing severe depression years accelerated the replacement of the individual entrepreneur with the merged corporation. Burdened by mounting debt, the Merritts secured a $1 million loan from Rockefeller. But even that sum failed to relieve their deteriorating financial condition. Reopened negotiations with the head of Standard Oil resulted in the formation of Lake Superior Consolidated Iron Mines, a large-scale combination of iron mining interests. The two sides later presented conflicting views of the nature of this alliance. Rockefeller claimed that the Consolidated preserved and allowed for the completion of the Merritt railroad, opened the mines, and carried the brothers successfully through the panic. Members of the family portrayed a well-planned conspiracy to wrest control of their Mesabi enterprises.

Unfortunately, the country's depressed economy forced the Merritts to sell their Consolidated stock, but they were unable to do so at even 10 percent of its par value. Desperately seeking to regain the family's financial standing, Alfred filed suit against Rockefeller in the local district court, attempting to recover $1,226,400 in damages. By the time the jury trial opened on June 5, 1895, both sides had agreed to transfer the proceedings to the U.S. district court in Duluth.

Alfred alleged that Rockefeller knowingly inflated the value of the stocks and bonds he contributed to the Consolidated and falsely assured the Merritts that the companies were solvent and prosperous and that their presence in the merger would enhance its value. In response, Rockefeller spokesmen denied that any deception or fraud had been perpetrated. One of the eastern financier's strongest lines of defense was the fact that the Merritts had approached him to purchase their railroad and mining stock, thus initiating the financial relationship. The Merritts had access to the appropriate financial records, and there was nothing to prevent their representatives from examining these documents.

On June 13, after more than five hours of deliberation, the 12-member jury drawn from throughout Minnesota awarded Alfred $940,000. Reacting quickly, the Rockefeller forces noted that regional sentiment favored the Merritts, pointing out that the family owed substantial sums of money to many Duluth residents and, according to one spokesman, "public sentiment was not averse to the circulation of some Rockefeller money." A local newspaper editor counterattacked, writing that "the Standard Oil octopus . . . would be able to swallow and digest the Merritts. . . . Rockefeller is a financial cannibal who eats men every day." For their part, the Merritts alleged that important documents had been stolen, which prevented them from presenting an even stronger case. Their most virulent attacks were aimed directly at Rockefeller, proclaiming that his absence from the Duluth courtroom was indicative of his disdain for the proceedings.

After weighing several alternatives suggested by counsel and wanting to avoid a new trial in Duluth, Rockefeller took the dispute to the U.S. Court of Appeals for the Eighth Circuit. This three-judge tribunal accepted the case on a writ of error that the lower court had "refused to permit" him to show the actual value of the Consolidated stock, and that the presiding judge had improperly instructed the jury on how to determine the amount of Alfred's loss.

Meeting in St. Louis on November 9, 1896, the appeals court held that "the true measure of the damages suffered by one who is fraudulently induced to make a contract . . . is the . . . loss which he has sustained, and not the profits which he might have made by the transactions." The judges ruled that the damages recovered "far exceeded the just measure of full compensation for this injury. . . . In other words, they were speculative rather than compensatory damages." The appeals court then reversed the lower court's decision, charged Alfred $1,040.35 in costs, and remanded the case to the district court in Duluth.

The Merritts saw this as the final "staggering blow" in their struggle against eastern financiers. Within a few months, however, the two sides negotiated an out-of-court settlement whereby Rockefeller paid his former business associates $525,000; in turn, 20 members of the Merritt family signed a statement retracting all charges of fraud. Although reluctant to exonerate their combatant, the Merritts accepted the settlement to relieve the family from "their destitution and absolute poverty." More than a decade later, Alfred testified before a congressional committee and admitted, "I was a kind of an innocent sort of a duck."

On the surface, it seems puzzling that Rockefeller would have agreed to such a large payment, but experience had provided him with little faith in local juries. In addition, protracted litigation would be costly in time and money.

Rockefeller now controlled an extensive deposit of high-grade iron ore and a railroad linking the mines with Lake Superior ore docks. In 1902, this empire formed an essential cornerstone in the creation of the United States Steel Corporation.

Selected Bibliography

Gates, F.T. *The Truth About Mr. Rockefeller and the Merritts.* New York: Knickerbocker Press, 1911.

Nevins, A. *John D. Rockefeller: The Heroic Age of American Enterprise.* 2 vols. New York: Charles Scribner's Sons, 1940.

Walker, D.A. *Iron Frontier, The Discovery and Early Development of Minnesota's Three Ranges.* St. Paul, MN: Minnesota Historical Society Press, 1979.

B. Commerce

A MORE PERFECT UNION: THE STEAMBOAT CASE

by *Francis N. Stites*
Department of History
San Diego State University

Gibbons v. Ogden, 9 Wheaton 1 (1824) [U.S. Supreme Court]

The link between the U.S. Constitution and the steamboat began in Philadelphia in the summer of 1787. Delegates to the Constitutional Convention were so alarmed about commercial problems that the commerce clause (Article 1, Section 8) slipped virtually without discussion or clarity into the Constitution. The interstate tariff war, raging between Connecticut, New Jersey, and New York while they met, was a reminder of the importance of commerce to a more perfect union. It seemed clear that only an energetic national government with power "to regulate commerce with foreign nations, among the several States, and with the Indian tribes" could remove such impediments to the free flow of commerce. The steamboat, the instrument that would revolutionize commerce, also made its first consistent appearance in American waters on the Delaware River out of Philadelphia in August 1787. Some of the framers rode on it, and its developer John Fitch noted, many more came by to look at it. Fitch's steamboat left in its wake an enlarged possibility both for national commerce and for commercial rivalry between the states. Years later, the promise of the steamboat and the ambiguity of the commerce clause would come together to produce the U.S. Supreme Court's first interpretation of the commerce power of the national government in the "Steamboat Case" of *Gibbons v. Ogden*.

The factual background to the case commenced when Robert R. Livingston and Robert Fulton obtained from the New York legislature in 1807 a steamboat monopoly. It depended on their success in getting a boat to operate at a stipulated speed within two years. In August 1807, these two successfully launched their steamboat, known popularly as the *Clermont*, in New York City for its maiden trip up the Hudson River to Albany. In 1808, New York granted a 30-year monopoly on steam navigation in state waters to Livingston and Fulton or their assignees. In separate legislation, the state also empowered the monopoly to seize the boats and equipment of unlicensed operators.

Fulton, unlike Fitch and other early steamboaters, had a talent for duplicating success. So, he shortly had several boats plying New York waters on regularly scheduled runs. Like Fitch, though, Livingston and Fulton envisioned a national network of steamboat lines, moving upstream and downstream and able to carry more goods and passengers farther, faster, and cheaper than other forms of transport, and they would all be under their control. Accordingly, they took the customary step of petitioning state and territorial legislatures (Virginia, Kentucky, Tennessee, Ohio, Indiana, Upper Louisiana, Mississippi, and Orleans) for monopolies like New York's. All but the Orleans Territorial legislature rejected their petitions. Orleans, in April 1811, awarded them an 18-year monopoly on the lower Mississippi. By January 1812, one Livingston-Fulton boat, the *New Orleans*, had completed an epic run down the Ohio, over the falls at Louisville and, during the great earthquake at New Madrid in 1811, down the Mississippi to New Orleans. The transportation revolution creating a national market had begun. So had the reaction against special privilege.

The commercial potential in steam navigation whetted the appetites of speculating entrepreneurs, whose boats quickly challenged the monopoly. From the start, the monopoly had to contend with arguments that the commerce power of the national government was exclusive and precluded state laws like New York's.

That argument came with a major challenge in 1811 when John Van Ingen and other Albany businessmen launched rival boats, *Hope* and *Perseverance*, on the Albany-New York run. The monopolists retaliated by asking the New York Court of Chancery to grant an injunction. When the court ruled against the monopoly, Livingston and Fulton appealed. In 1812, the New York Court of Errors, the highest state court, upheld the monopoly.

In this case, *Livingston v. Van Ingen*, the most important and impressive opinion was that of Chancellor James Kent, one of the outstanding jurists in the early nineteenth century. The key question was the relation between the state law and the commerce clause. Was the commerce power exclusive? Could states act if Congress was silent?

Kent reasoned that the power to grant monopolies inhered both in sovereignty and in the English common law. That New York had already granted monopolies to banks, canals, and turnpike companies established an unquestioned legislative power to make grants. The only limits to this power were the state constitution, the fundamental principles of all governments, or the external limit imposed by the national Constitution. Kent ruled that the states' delegation of a commerce power to the U.S. government in 1787 did not preclude the states from exercising the same power. The commerce power, like the taxing power, he asserted, was not exclusive but concurrent. The Constitution did not prohibit it to the states, and the Tenth Amendment proclaimed that powers not delegated still remained.

The "possible contingency of a collision" between state and national laws did not trouble Kent, because the supremacy clause of the U.S. Constitution (Article VI) settled such conflicts conclusively in favor of the United States. There could be no conflict, however, until Congress acted. As long as Congress remained silent, there was room for the states to regulate. His "safe rule of construction" was that if any given power was originally vested in this state, if it had not been exclusively ceded to Congress, or if the exercise of it had not been prohibited to the states," the state could exercise the power "until it comes practically in collision with the actual exercise of some congressional power."

He could find no national law in conflict with New York's laws.

Livingston v. Van Ingen ended only one of many legal challenges to the monopoly. Livingston and Fulton were less successful in Louisiana, where they had to contend with unsympathetic courts, hostile public opinion, and, worse yet, superior competition. Their monopoly there collapsed, and the dissatisfaction became epidemic. New Jersey, Connecticut, and Ohio in 1818 and 1822 banned Livingston-Fulton steamboats from their waterways. Massachusetts, New Hampshire, Vermont, and Georgia retaliated by conferring their own monopolies. The steamboat seemed hopelessly snagged on states' rights, and the promise of free trade in an expanding national market seemed about to dissolve in a commercial civil war.

The monopoly tried co-opting its competition either by purchasing their boats or selling them franchises. One purchaser was Aaron Ogden, a former New Jersey governor, who tried for several years to defy the monopoly by operating a steam ferry from Elizabethtown, New Jersey, to New York City. Ogden was aided by friendly legislation from the New Jersey legislature and a federal coasting license. By 1815, however, Ogden had surrendered and purchased a license from the Livingston assignees (both Fulton and Livingston were dead by this time).

Ogden's entrance into a partnership with the cantankerous and independent Georgian, Thomas Gibbons, marked the beginnings of *Gibbons v. Ogden*. The testy partnership collapsed in 1818 when Gibbons used the formidable talents of the unscrupulous young Cornelius Vanderbilt to run an unlicensed steamer on Ogden's route. Ogden sued for an injunction in the New York courts in 1819. Ultimately, the New York Court of Errors upheld Kent's *Van Ingen* opinion and granted a permanent injunction against Gibbons in 1820.

Gibbons appealed to the U.S. Supreme Court. Using the arguments he had used in the New York courts, he claimed that the New York monopoly, under which Ogden was operating, conflicted with the federal Coasting Act of 1793, under which he held a license to "navigate the waters of any particular state by steamboat," and with the commerce clause of the Constitution. There were numerous technical delays, but finally, in 1824, the Court got its first opportunity to discuss and to clarify the meaning of the commerce clause.

Steamboat entrepreneurs and judges were not the only ones debating the meaning of the commerce clause. After 1815, nationalists and states' righters had been at odds over proposals to have the national government pay for internal improvements, such as turnpikes and canals. Presidents James Madison and James Monroe had vetoed bills on the strict constructionist grounds that the commerce clause did not authorize a positive federal program of internal improvements.

During the argument in *Gibbons*, Congress was debating a bill to provide a federal survey of road and canal routes. The political and constitutional implications of both the debate and the case troubled southerners who were increasingly aware of their region's minority status and sensitive to any potential threat to the security of their "peculiar institution." The Missouri debates in 1820 brought criticism of broad construction. Senator Philip Barbour of Virginia urged the "necessity of restraining the Federal Government within the prescribed limits, to guard against encroachments on the authority of the States, and thereby prevent a consolidation." A Massachusetts congressman noted that Congress could have no power claimed to restrict slavery in the new states unless it "be constructive." In the General Survey debates, John Randolph warned that if Congress possessed broad power over commerce, "they may *emancipate every slave in the United States*" [emphasis in original]. Similar southern opposition to the commerce power appeared in the debates on the tariff of 1824. There was, too, the continual fulmination about repealing Section 25 of the Judiciary Act of 1789, which authorized appeals from the highest state tribunals to the U.S. Supreme Court. The monopoly's steamboat also carried this load into the Supreme Court.

Chief Justice John Marshall was aware of the case's political dimensions. After all, he and the Court had been under vigorous attack from Virginia and other states for the ringing endorsements of national power and broad construction in the decisions of 1819–21. Southerners saw the link between broad construction

and commerce in his statement in *Cohens v. Virginia* (1821) that in war, peace, in "all commercial relations, . . . [and] [i]n many other respects, the American people are one." Those decisions and criticisms did not mean, however, that the Marshall Court was centralizing.

Regularly, Marshall and his brethren tried to negotiate a path through the divided sovereignty of the American federal system. In *Dartmouth College v. Woodward* (1819), he had said that the framers had not intended "to restrain the states in the regulation of their civil institutions." *McCulloch v. Maryland* (1819) had presented "in truth, a question of supremacy," but Marshall pointed out later in essays answering the trenchant states' rights criticism of Spencer Roane and the Richmond Junto that "supremacy" did not mean despotism and that "national" was not synonymous with "consolidated." In the superheated context of 1824, negotiation was probable.

The throng of congressmen, reporters, and Washington ladies spilling into the aisles of the Court's chambers in the basement below the Senate reminded all that "the great steamboat question from New York" was no ordinary case. Both sides had retained eminent counsel: Daniel Webster and Attorney General William Wirt, two of the giants of the bar, for Gibbons; Thomas J. Oakley, New York attorney general, and Thomas Addis Emmet, the brilliant Irish expatriate and veteran Livingston-Fulton attorney, for Ogden. Wirt predicted that it would "be a great combat." He was right. After Marshall had sharpened the nib of his quill pen, pulled up the sleeves of his robe, and nodded, counsel began an argument that lasted five days and examined every aspect of the controversy.

Webster probed the commerce clause to decide whether New York had the power to pass the laws. He concluded that because the commerce power was to a certain extent exclusive to the national government, it could not be a concurrent state power. Webster had the good sense to recognize what Kent had pointed out: that the states had already regulated much interstate commerce with monopolies on banks and turnpikes, and that this regulation could not be undone. He tried to mark out some territory for the states, but he would not do it through the silence of Congress. If Congress did not legislate on a subject, Webster took that as evidence of congressional intent that the subject be left free and unregulated. Existing state regulations of things involved with commerce were not regulations of commerce, Webster said, and hence were not traceable to a commerce power. They were "police power" actions. Webster also saw a conflict between Gibbons's coasting license under the 1793 law and the state law. For him, the 1793 law gave Gibbons the right to "navigate freely" all the waters of the United States.

Oakley, who was thoroughly familiar with the arguments in the New York courts, spent over one day arguing for a concurrent state power over commerce that resembled Kent's in *Van Ingen*. The states, ran this argument, had reserved a part of the commerce power and could share it unless there was a conflict between state and national law.

Emmet followed Oakley with a detailed examination of the commerce clause. He stressed the connection between slavery and the commerce clause to support state concurrent power. States, he noted, had legislated to ban the importation of slaves, and the Constitution treated slaves as articles of commerce. So, a national law of 1803 punishing the importation of slaves into states that had banned their admission was a congressional recognition of a state concurrent power over commerce.

Wirt closed with a powerful argument for Gibbons. Some branches of the "complex, multifarious and indefinite" subject of commerce, he said, "might be given exclusively to Congress; the others may be left open to the states." So, only some national powers over commerce are "exclusive in their nature; and among them, is that power which concerns navigation." Wirt did not think it was necessary in this case to decide the whole commerce power question. The specific issue was navigation. Once Congress "legislated concerning a subject on which it is authorized to act, all State legislation which interferes is absolutely void." The Coasting Act of 1793 was such a congressional action; the New York law was, therefore, invalid.

In an eloquent peroration, Wirt told the Court that it faced a "momentous decision." As in 1787 when the framers were drafting the Constitution, Connecticut, New Jersey, and New York were "almost on the eve of war." If the Court did not mediate and "extirpate the seeds of anarchy which New York has sown, you *will* have civil war. . . . Your republican institutions will perish in the conflict. Your constitution will fall. The last hope of nations will be gone" [emphasis in original]. Justice Joseph Story called it a speech of "great splendour and force."

Three weeks passed before the Court delivered a decision. The reason was that the 69-year-old Marshall had tripped over the cellar door at the justices' Washington boardinghouse, dislocated his shoulder, and bruised his skull.

On March 2, 1824, the chief justice appeared with his arm in a sling and in a feeble voice read his opinion striking down the New York monopoly. He began by expounding the commerce clause with a broad construction in the style of *McCulloch*, where he had referred to the "great" power to regulate commerce. Strict construction of this and other enumerated powers would, he said, cripple the national government. The meaning of those powers was intimately connected to the purpose for which they were conferred; the framers of the Constitution "must be understood . . . to have intended what they said." Freedom of commerce among the states was a primary purpose of the Constitution, prerequisite to Union and to national economic growth. Marshall asserted that the rule for construing the extent of powers was to take the "language of the instrument" that conferred the powers "in connection with the purposes for which they were conferred."

What meaning would this broad, nationalist interpretation give to the words "regulate," "commerce," and "among the several states?" Commerce, Marshall proclaimed in the classic and still-quoted definition, was more than buying and selling. "Commerce, undoubtedly, is traffic, but it is something more; it is intercourse. It describes the commercial intercourse between nations, and parts of nations, in all its branches." It embraced, then, navigation, and "every species of commercial intercourse," including steamboats. The power to regulate was the power "to prescribe the rule by which commerce is to be governed" and had no limits other than those "prescribed in the constitution." Commerce that was "among the states" could not stop at the external boundary of each state but might be introduced into the interior.

That meant that Congress could regulate commerce wherever it existed or, by extension, whatever form it might take from pipelines to telecommunications. Marshall based this definition not just on logic but on precedent by analogy. Since 1787, he noted, the United States had experienced exactly what the framers had intended, a broad and flexible interpretation of commerce that extended beyond the commerce clause proper. Moreover, said Marshall turning to the phrase "among the several states," "among" meant intermingled with. "A thing which is among others is intermingled with them. Commerce among the states cannot stop at the external boundary line of each state, but may be introduced into the interior." The power of Congress to regulate would accompany the introduction.

It was this sweeping definition of the national commerce power, verging ever so close to exclusive national power, that had alarmed Randolph and the other states' rights critics of broad construction of enumerated powers. So, although his opinion strongly intimated exclusive national power, the chief justice was reluctant to declare it. Sensitive to the practical difficulties of the federal system—what in *Gibbons* he called "genius and character of the whole government"—Marshall struggled to negotiate a formula that would accommodate state regulation of local problems and the demands of free trade for an expanding national economy.

Formally repeating the point of his 1819 *McCulloch* opinion, the chief justice emphasized that national power was not plenary. The framers would not have enumerated "foreign nations, among the several States, and the Indian tribes" in the grant of power "had the intention been to extend the power to every description." It did not extend to those concerns "which are completely within a particular state, which do not affect other states, and with which it is not necessary to interfere for the purpose of executing some of the general powers of the government." So, the "completely internal commerce of a state, then, may be considered as reserved for the state itself." He did not, however, say what was "completely" internal commerce that did not "affect other states."

This selective exclusiveness approach enabled the Court to allow states to enact inspection, health, and pilotage laws that might affect interstate commerce. Marshall simply would not admit that such legislation was an exercise of a concurrent commerce power (the word "concurrent" did not appear in the Constitution until the Eighteenth Amendment). He preferred to call it, as had Webster, the state police power. Congress could enter this area, too, if the national interest required it.

And what of Webster's point that the silence of Congress indicated congressional intent that a subject was to be free of regulation? Marshall did not give an explicit answer, but he did say Webster's argument had "great force" and that he was not satisfied "that it has been refuted." By implication, then, the Court would have the responsibility of deciding the extent of permissible state activity in the future on a case-by-case basis.

The one point on which all parties had agreed was that national law took precedence over state law in case of conflict. Marshall used this agreement and the conflict between the federal Coasting Act of 1793 and the New York laws to resolve the steamboat controversy. The 1793 law required only the licensing of vessels engaged in the coastal trade so as to give U.S. vessels an advantage. Marshall turned it into an implicit guarantee of free navigation on the waterways of the United States. He interpreted the coasting act to have conferred a license or a "right" to trade. It was, then, a federal regulation of interstate commerce. Because the New York laws impeded free navigation and the right to trade, they conflicted with this national law and were, therefore, unconstitutional.

In the manner of his earlier constitutional decisions, Marshall had again used the case to expound the meaning of the Constitution. This course was "unavoidable," he said, because "powerful and ingenious minds" always used strict construction to "explain away the constitution of our country, and leave it a magnificent structure indeed, to look at, but totally unfit to use." He was as much interested in the health of the union as in the New York monopoly.

The decision was unanimous. The recently appointed Justice Smith Thompson was absent because of his daughter's death. Justice William Johnson, Jefferson's first Supreme Court appointee who had just determined to speak his own mind in constitutional cases, wrote a powerful concurring opinion asserting what Marshall had not—that congressional power over commerce "must be exclusive" and that the grant of this power carried with it "the whole subject, leaving nothing for the state to act upon."

The explosive issue of slavery was partly responsible for Johnson's vigorous concurrence. In June 1822, Charleston, South Carolina, had learned of a planned slave uprising led by the free black Denmark Vesey. After brutally punishing the alleged conspirators (there is substantial debate among historians as to whether there was an active conspiracy), South Carolina enacted a Negro seamen law reflecting its belief that free black sailors on ships in Charleston harbor had incited the unrest and requiring that all such sailors be jailed until their ships departed.

A Charlestonian and a strong libertarian, Johnson had publicly attacked the high-handed, summary trial and execution of the conspirators. Then Henry Elkisson, a black sailor and British subject, petitioned Johnson's circuit court for a writ of *habeas corpus*. In *Elkisson v. Deleisseline* (1823), Johnson boldly ruled the Negro Seamen Act unconstitutional because it violated a treaty with Great Britain and the "paramount and exclusive" power of Congress to regulate foreign commerce. Johnson asserted that the grant to Congress had to have "swept away the whole subject" and "left nothing for the states to act upon." Otherwise, the Union would become like the old Confederation—a "mere rope of sand." A wave of indignation swept through the South. South Carolina defied this decision using an exclusive national power to threaten the "peculiar institution." More ominous was the threatening talk of states' rights, secession, and forcible resistance.

After reading Johnson's opinion in the *National Intelligencer*, Marshall thought it had unnecessarily fueled the fire at which states' rights extremists would "roast the Judicial Department." The chief justice was more circumspect. He had had a similar case, *Wilson v. United States*, on his Richmond circuit in 1820, but he

had more prudently chosen to avoid the commerce question and to avoid being snagged "in a hedge composed entirely of thorny State-Rights." Because it was not "absolutely necessary" to consider the constitutional question of the commerce clause, Marshall, unlike Johnson, "escaped on a construction of the act." He was "not fond," he wrote Justice Joseph Story, "of butting against a wall in sport."

Gibbons showed Marshall's talent for avoiding the practical difficulties of constitutional questions and for "escaping" both commerce and slavery by construction. He dismissed the latter in one paragraph by noting that the constitutional ban on slave trade action until 1808 was exceptional because it allowed states some power to act on that subject only during that time. State laws enacted after that would be invalid, he said.

Most of the nation applauded *Gibbons* for hastening the demise of a hated and obnoxious monopoly. Some have called it the first antitrust decision in U.S. history. Newspapers in New York and elsewhere, which had scarcely noticed the *Clermont*'s 1807 voyage, reprinted the full opinion. This "masterpiece of judicial reasoning concerns every citizen," ran a typical comment, because "unlimited scope is now afforded to enterprise and capital in steam navigation." For once, it seemed, a Marshall decision had articulated popular aspirations. A Missouri paper chided New York for its restive reception of the decision. New Yorkers, it continued, "may rest assured that it is a decision approved of in their sister States, who can see no propriety in the claim of New York to domineer over the waters which form the means of intercourse between that State and others, and over that intercourse itself."

Realizing the benefits the success of steamboat operation would bring to transportation and to his personal fortune, Henry Wheaton, Court reporter, published a separate pamphlet report of *The Case of Gibbons Against Ogden* in October 1824. Others, like Randolph, remained unhappy and alarmed. Randolph knew it was fashionable to praise the opinion, but confessed to one correspondent that he was not noted for being a fashionable man. He thought the opinion "unworthy" of Marshall because it contained a "great deal that has no business there, or indeed anywhere."

Gibbons, unfortunately, left everything about as unsettled as before. One could read the decision equally as expanding national power in the tradition of *McCulloch* or as admitting limits to the reach of national power. Marshall had used the "sense of the Convention" to reject an exclusive national bankruptcy power in *Sturges v. Crowninshield* (1819). For him a "mere grant of power to Congress did not imply a prohibition on the States to exercise the same Power." In *Gibbons*, he said that "the sovereignty of Congress" had always been understood to be "limited to specific objects" though it was "plenary as to those objects." By holding only that an undefined exclusive power existed and had been used in 1793 regarding steamboats, Marshall had invalidated the interstate operation of the New York monopoly. But what of the monopoly within New York?

The *Gibbons* opinion did not offer much help to New York courts as they wrestled with that question in subsequent litigation. The range of opinions about what Marshall had actually said offers compelling evidence of its ambiguity. Ultimately, the New York courts used *Gibbons* to invalidate the monopoly's intrastate operation.

One result of that contemporary confusion has been a persistent confusion about Marshall's opinion—a tendency to call it a commerce clause decision even though it was a conflict of laws decision. Nevertheless, the expansive interpretation of commerce has become the controlling legacy of the decision. Marshall stands as the progenitor of the flexible and centralized national power that now governs the United States. Congressmen and judges among others have sprinkled the magic phrases from *Gibbons* through their justifications for expanding national power. As late as 1942 in *Wickard v. Filburn*, the Supreme Court cited *Gibbons* and the commerce clause as the constitutional foundation for virtually unlimited national power. *Wickard* upheld federal regulation of wheat grown for on-farm consumption. It is doubtful that such regulation was the sort that Marshall had intended as commerce "among the states" in 1824.

Commerce questions were not about to diminish. In 1827 and again in 1829 the Marshall Court had to deal with the questions first raised in *Gibbons*. In *Brown v. Maryland* (1827), the Court asserted an exclusive national power to regulate foreign commerce, but on the thorny question of state concurrent power to regulate commerce, Marshall would only grant a state police power as he had in 1824. The same question came up again two years later in *Willson v. Blackbird Creek Marsh Company*, the last commerce case of the Marshall years. Once more the chief justice used selective exclusiveness. This time, however, his pragmatism caused him to rule for the state and to neglect the same 1793 coasting law he had used to such good effect to "escape" in *Gibbons*.

Marshall's commerce clause cases showed how carefully he could preserve the principles of a "truly federal" union by both enlarging national power through broad construction and preserving a measure of power for the states. This practice, first used in *Gibbons*, represented a shift from states' rights to concurrent power as the basis of state sovereignty. Such a shift preserved the states by recognizing, not challenging, federal supremacy. This negotiation served the Court and the union well by accommodating the times and winning public acceptance for the decisions. Marshall attempted no more good than the people could bear because he knew full well that the Court could not enforce its opinions and had to rely on persuasion. His comprehensive definition of the national commerce power had made it possible for Congress to act, but it remained to be seen whether and to what extent social, economic, political, and sectional pressures would allow it to do so.

Selected Bibliography

Baxter, M.G. *Daniel Webster and the Supreme Court*. Amherst, MA: University of Massachusetts Press, 1966.

———. *The Steamboat Monopoly: Gibbons v. Ogden*. New York: Alfred A. Knopf, 1972.

Beveridge, A.J. *The Life of John Marshall*. 4 vols. New York: Houghton Mifflin Co., 1916–19.

Currie, D.P. *The Constitution in the Supreme Court: The First Hundred Years, 1789–1888*. Chicago: University of Chicago Press, 1985.

Frankfurter, F. *The Commerce Clause Under Marshall, Taney, and Waite.* Chapel Hill, NC: University of North Carolina Press, 1937.

Newmyer, R.K. *Supreme Court Justice Joseph Story: States-man of the Old Republic.* Chapel Hill, NC: University of North Carolina Press, 1985.

White, G.E. *The Marshall Court and Cultural Change, 1815–35.* New York: Macmillan, 1988.

AN OMEN OF CHANGE: STATE POWER TO REGULATE COMMERCE

by Craig T. Friend
Lexington, Kentucky

New York v. Miln, 11 Peters 102 (1837) [U.S. Supreme Court]

One important characteristic of the U.S. Supreme Court is its adherence to precedent. Sometimes, however, justices find it hard to cling to precedents as social conditions change and new justices come to the bench. The 1837 decision of *New York v. Miln* demonstrated both of these features of Supreme Court decisionmaking.

In 1824, the Supreme Court decided *Gibbons v. Ogden*, the first great commerce clause case. Chief Justice John Marshall's nationalistic philosophy prevailed here as it would throughout most of his tenure. Yet even after Marshall died in 1835, his influence remained in the form of his judicial precedents and his friend, Justice Joseph Story.

Marshall's successor was Roger B. Taney, a man who did not share many of Marshall's legal views. As a Jacksonian Democrat, Taney opposed strong centralization of the federal government. Prior to his appointment as chief justice, Taney served as U.S. attorney general, a position that made him a key figure in Jackson's decision to veto the Bank of the United States. Supporters of Marshall's nationalistic philosophies, therefore, did not greet Taney's appointment to the Court's center seat with much enthusiasm.

One of the earliest decisions by the Taney Court was *New York v. Miln*, a case continued from 1834. The argument concerned a New York statute requiring captains of vessels arriving in New York to submit a list of all passengers within a day after docking. The purpose of the law was the regulation of indigents, for whom the city could not provide. This reasoning provided the state with its surest defense—the state's right to exercise "police power." Even the great nationalist, John Marshall, when he wrote the opinion in *Gibbons v. Ogden*, had referred to the police power as a power through which the welfare of citizens could be protected. The present statute, however, appeared to interfere with interstate commerce. If all the justices had been present in 1834 when the case first came before the Court, Marshall would have probably seen the dispute as an occasion for another nationalistic opinion. As it was, however, several justices missed the session and the decision was postponed. It reappeared on the docket in 1837.

The Court of 1837 faintly resembled that which Marshall had known. The election of Andrew Jackson to the presidency had initiated an evolution of thought within the federal government that reached into the judiciary. The death of Marshall and two other justices provided Jackson with the opportunity to mold the Court as he desired. Only Joseph Story and Smith Thompson survived as reminders of the Marshall years. They were joined by five Jacksonian appointees, all Democrats: Justices John McLean, Henry Baldwin, James Moore Wayne, Philip Pendleton Barbour, and Roger Taney. The Court's new composition essentially foretold the demise of Marshall's nationalistic precedents.

Story had reason to be concerned over the changes on the bench. During his previous 26 years as a justice, he had, at times, appeared more of a nationalist than Marshall. Although his role in *Gibbons* is unknown, Story concurred with Marshall's opinion, which did not expressly exclude states from exercising power over interstate commerce, but clearly permitted Congress to claim supremacy through legislation. Indeed, *Gibbons* seemed extremely similar to *New York v. Miln*. Both cases centered around state regulation of shipping; and the state claimed policing rights in both instances. To Story, the resolution was clear.

To the other extreme was Wayne who, as mayor of Savannah, Georgia, had sponsored similar state laws. During his administration, restrictions were placed on immigration, and the purchase of bonds was required to assist the city in providing health measures for sickly passengers. As Story surely noted, Wayne would support New York's claim as a policing agent.

Yet, Story attempted to convince the justices of his interpretation of the law. He believed that the case could be resolved in point with Marshall's *Gibbons* opinion. Congress had been regulating passenger ships since 1819, and Story understood a clear conflict between federal and state powers in the New York statute. His fellow justices, however, disregarded his argument.

Barbour produced the written opinion for the majority. Barbour had previously demonstrated his states' rights ideals in 1821. As counsel for the defense in *Cohens v. Virginia*, he argued zealously before the Supreme Court that the federal judiciary had no power to review decisions made in state courts. Barbour's reasoning was lost in the increasingly nationalistic ideology of the Marshall Court. His opportunity to reverse that tide came with *New York v. Miln*.

In this, his only major Supreme Court opinion, Barbour wrote that "a state has the same undeniable and unlimited jurisdiction over all persons and things, within its territorial limits . . . where that jurisdiction is not surrendered or restrained by the constitution of the United States." Although the statement echoed

Marshall's *Gibbons* opinion, there were two specifics that made Barbour's opinion decisively different. Initially, he emphasized that the justices "shall not enter into an examination of the question whether the power to regular commerce, be or be not exclusive of the states, because . . . we are of opinion that the act is not a regulation of commerce, but of police." Second, Barbour supported his first premise by noting that the ships in question were transporting persons, not goods, and that persons were not the subject of commerce. The opinion was read in conference the evening before the Term ended and a majority agreed. Only Story dissented, with "the consolation to know that I had the entire concurrence, upon the same grounds, of that great constitutional jurist, the late Mr. Chief Justice John Marshall."

Barbour's logic established an exclusivity for the states that was, to that point in American history, unprecedented. The concept of internal policing powers had been implied in several previous cases, but Barbour's interpretation created a realm of state power beyond the restrictions of the Tenth Amendment of the Constitution. The other justices accepted Barbour's ideas and served notice to supporters of Marshall nationalism. The Term ended the following day and *New York v. Miln* appeared to be resolved.

Twelve years later, however, the decision haunted the Taney Court when it confronted the *Passenger Cases*. New York and Massachusetts had placed taxes on immigrants. Once again Taney supported the internal police power of the states, but his opinion was that of the minority. The majority noted that the levies were in conflict with the commerce clause; Justice Wayne concurred in a separate opinion. He stated that persons could be commerce and that the present statutes were unconstitutional. Wayne then proceeded to question whether Barbour's statement in 1837 that persons could not be commerce had actually been presented to the justices when the decision was read. Justice Baldwin agreed with Wayne and recalled that he noticed the sentence after the Court's adjournment, too late for a modification.

Barbour had died in 1841, unable to respond to Wayne's accusation. Taney took up the gauntlet, however, and replied that the statement had been clear and agreed on. He then expounded on the dangers of dismissing precedent. If one phrase of an opinion could be so easily overlooked, he implored, the public's confidence in the Court itself could be jeopardized. Wayne did not respond to Taney's exhortation and the debate thus ended.

New York v. Miln left the distinction between regulation of commerce and a state's police powers more ambiguous than before. As an early decision of the Taney Court, *New York v. Miln* demonstrated that Marshall's influence was waning less than two years after his death. Story clung tenaciously to the nationalistic precedents of former Court decisions. But Taney, Barbour, and the rest of the Court embraced a new interpretation of the conflict between state and federal governments. Paralleling the change in the Supreme Court was an increasing frag-

mentation within it. The unity of the Marshall Court, which usually produced only one opinion per case, dissolved so that by 1849 when the *Passenger Cases* were decided, several justices offered their own opinions to supplement the majority and minority decisions. The significance of *New York v. Miln*, therefore, was as an omen of change, not only for the Court but for the nation as well.

Selected Bibliography

Frankfurter, F. *The Commerce Clause Under Marshall, Taney, and Waite.* Chicago: Quadrangle Books, 1937.

Newmyer, R.K. *Supreme Court Justice Joseph Story: Statesman of the Old Republic.* Chapel Hill, NC: University of North Carolina Press, 1985.

———. *The Supreme Court Under Marshall and Taney.* Arlington Heights, IL: Harlan Davidson, Inc., 1968.

WHEN MONOPOLY MATTERED

by Robert Stanley
Department of Political Science
California State University at Chico

United States v. E.C. Knight Company, 156 U.S. 1 (1895) [U.S. Supreme Court]

Business corporations stood at the heart of the process of industrialism that fractured and refashioned American society after the Civil War. Among the first to recognize the social power to be gained from increased size and reduced competition, large corporations began during the 1870s to experiment with several new forms of combination: pools, trusts, and holding companies. At the same time, farmers, workers, merchants, and urban consumers united around an old radically democratic tradition that called for the removal of barriers, private or governmental, to a more equitable pattern of economic power. Antimonopoly sentiment collided with corporate combination throughout the 1880s, and by the depression of the 1890s social struggle had been channeled into constitutionally charged conflict.

In *United States v. E.C. Knight Company*, the U.S. Supreme Court faced for the first time

the broad political question of how to apportion antimonopoly authority within the still-diffuse "American state." A specific legal question directly provoked the contenders: whether, through its control of 98 percent of the refining capacity in the United States, the widely hated Sugar Trust had run afoul of the newly minted Sherman Antitrust Act of 1890. The Court's emphatically negative answer infuriated antimonopolists, left with the states a legal load they proved unwilling to carry, and generated a formalistic view of interstate commerce that remained influential until the depression crisis of the 1930s. Yet for all its infamy, the *Knight* decision proved to be less determinative of the future paths of combinations and commerce than emblematic of the rapidly fading antebellum economic and legal conceptions on which it relied. Engulfed in an onrushing tide of corporate gigantism and cooperative governmental centrism, *Knight* looked resolutely and hopefully backward.

The key to understanding the evident paradox of *Knight* lies in Gilded Age conceptions of the corporation. Lawmakers viewed the business corporation as a legal creation dependent for its existence and power on the state legislative charter that gave it life. From the perspective of any single state, for example Pennsylvania, regulatory problems might arise over domestic corporations—those chartered by the Pennsylvania legislature—or with "foreign" corporations—those chartered by other states and doing business in Pennsylvania.

Through the corporate charter, each state legislature enjoyed power to promote and to regulate business activity. The charter could specify the size and purpose of the corporation, prescribe whether it might combine with others, and guarantee the propriety of its activities. When the corporation acted against any limitations established in the charter, court-approved doctrines of *ultra vires* and *quo warranto* empowered state officials to invalidate their transactions or dissolve their charters. Through the charter and its enforcement devices, the state therefore possessed legal power to control corporate pools, trusts, and holding companies at their organizational roots.

Without additional authority to prevent foreign corporations from engaging in activities forbidden to domestic corporations, however, these devices to protect the public interest would have been useless. An effort by Pennsylvania to prohibit the establishment of a domestic holding company in the sugar refining business, for example, would have been superfluous if a foreign corporation could enter and make just such a move with impunity. But in their early efforts to control foreign corporations within their jurisdictions, the states faced challenges raised by the interstate commerce clause of the U.S. Constitution.

The Supreme Court chose to allow the freest possible trade among the states without, at the same time, opening the gates so widely that they would be unable to control foreign corporate activity that might undermine their own domestic business policies. Viewing the problem in categorical terms, as it had in labor and taxation cases, the Court developed two distinct lines of doctrine. And, to achieve its delicate policy balance, it rigidly policed the frontiers. Whether a state's foreign corporation law violated the commerce clause would depend on the Court's definition of what constituted "commerce" among the states, and here the Court drew a distinction between marketing and nonmarketing acts of corporations.

In the first line of cases the Court overturned state laws that impeded the marketing of foreign products on a parity with local goods. Following the leading case *Welton v. Missouri* (1875), the Court struck down state laws that laid discriminatory taxes on foreign goods or required licenses of out-of-state salesmen not also required of locals. The Court feared, in such legislation, a reenactment of the interstate tariff wars that had preceded the adoption of the Constitution and were understood to have led to the drafting of the commerce clause itself.

The second line of cases represented the Court's insistence that the states be empowered to control the nonmarketing acts of corporations within their jurisdictions. If the commerce clause protected *only* marketing, juridical room would exist for the states to regulate other kinds of foreign corporate activity. Here the leading case was *Paul v. Virginia* (1869), which sustained Virginia's foreign corporation law against a challenge by a New York insurance company. Between 1888 and 1903, the Supreme Court approved several state foreign corporation laws prohibiting the local exercise of franchises by foreign corporations. Most significantly, it did so by holding that such processes as manufacturing and mining did not constitute interstate commerce. Pursuant to this line of cases, state legislatures might exclude, license, or otherwise regulate foreign corporations consistently with their domestic corporate policies. The states, therefore, held formal legal authority under their own charter grants to dictate to domestic corporations what their form of organization would be, and under the Court's *Paul* line, could apply that authority to foreign corporations wishing to do business within their jurisdictions.

Faced with the economic pressures that foreign corporations brought to bear in the late nineteenth century, state officials rarely used their disciplinary power. But, beginning in the late 1880s, prompted by antimonopolist anger at newly forming trusts in oil, whiskey, and sugar, several states brought successful *quo warranto* proceedings challenging the legal power of corporations to reorganize themselves under their charters.

For a brief moment it seemed that the states might combine legal authority and political will to overcome concentrated private economic power. Yet, at virtually the same time, New Jersey in 1889 enacted a law that permitted all of its domestic corporations to acquire control of foreign firms. In 1890, the Sugar Trust took advantage of the law to reorganize itself as a New Jersey corporation. By the end of the century, all of the trusts dissolved by the states in their moment of control had done the same, as had some 270 other large combinations. In the wake of this development, a political firestorm broke out in the administration of Grover Cleveland, forcing Attorney General Richard Olney to bring the first Sherman Antitrust Act prosecution against the hated Sugar Trust. Drafted with sensitivity to state authority over corporations and adopted in 1890 at the peak of state antimonopoly activity, the Sherman Act made illegal contracts or combinations "in restraint of trade or commerce among the several States," and monopolies in "the trade or commerce among the several States." The act relied for its authority on the interstate commerce clause of the Constitution.

Given the Court's determination to preserve for state corporate regulatory purposes a categorical conception of interstate commerce, poorer facts for the government's challenge could hardly have been invented than those at issue in *Knight*. The Sugar Trust refineries were all in the single state of Pennsylvania, its products were distributed by independent wholesalers, and the contracts creating the holding company provided only for the standard transfer of stock. The government argued that the contracts created a combination in restraint of trade and that the company constituted a monopoly. And it sought to break the combination back into its constituent parts—one of which was the Knight Company. The government boldly interpreted the act in economic terms familiar to twentieth-century sensibilities, arguing that

control over the manufacture of sugar meant a practical monopoly over a basic necessity for which interstate commerce was required. Control over manufacture yielded, in practical fact, control over interstate commerce.

Chief Justice Melville W. Fuller's opinion for the majority (only Justice John Marshall Harlan dissented) framed the issue as "whether, conceding that the existence of a monopoly in manufacture is established by the evidence, that monopoly can be directly suppressed under the act of congress in the mode attempted by this bill." Fuller relied for his negative answer on the distinction between the state police power, which exclusively governed locally chartered corporate activities, and Congress's equally exclusive power over interstate commerce, which supported the Sherman Act. Since *Gibbons v. Ogden* (1824), Fuller argued, "that which belongs to commerce is within the jurisdiction of the United States, but that which does not belong to commerce is within the police power of the state." The key question raised by the government was whether the control over the manufacture of refined sugar that the contracts gave to the Sugar Trust fell within interstate commerce. Fuller said no. "Commerce succeeds to manufacture," he contended, "and is not a part of it." Thus, the contracts that aimed to control manufacturing remained outside the formal conception of commerce, and therefore beyond the reach of the Sherman Act, despite the acknowledged practical link to eventual interstate sale.

The distinction was "vital" for Fuller. While the commerce power "furnishes the strongest bond of union," the state police power "is essential to the preservation of the autonomy of the states as required by our dual form of government." To call manufacturing a part of commerce would give Congress "to the exclusion of the states . . . power to regulate not only manufactures, but also agriculture, horticulture, stock-raising, domestic fisheries, mining; in short, every branch of human industry." Such a result would mean that "comparatively little of business operations and affairs would be left for state control."

Fuller understood that to have ruled otherwise would have undermined the *Paul* line of cases and vastly expanded *Welton*'s scope, leaving the states unable to prevent foreign manufacturing corporations from exercising franchises within their borders and rendering useless their charter-based control over domestic corporations, since they could simply reorganize as newly untouchable New Jersey corporations and avoid *quo warranto* dissolution. To call manufacturing a part of commerce was to deny the states their traditional control over the roots of corporate organization and activity, and to hand to Congress virtually complete authority over the economy.

But the Sugar Trust's escape from the Sherman Act did not mean a free hand for corporate combination, since "the relief of the citizens of each state from the burden of monopoly . . . was left with the states to deal with." Under existing state law, as long as firms chartered outside of New Jersey were denied the power in their charters to become members of larger combinations, their efforts to do so could be met with state prosecution. Further, under *Knight*, whether or not chartered in New Jersey, foreign corporations could still be met with Court-approved regulation through *Paul*. The relief called for by the government in *Knight* was already available in the Pennsylvania courts, and was a far more direct procedure—*quo warranto* prosecution based on a charter violation—than determining under the Sherman Act whether a restraint or monopoly existed.

Knight proved immediately significant for the social conflict between corporations and their critics for the broad question of authority to regulate combinations and for the meaning of the interstate commerce clause. In the longer term, its power over the trust problem quickly diminished and its influence as a commerce power benchmark slowly disintegrated. As the first symbol of the fitful course of antitrust law, it remains both prominent and problematic today.

For antimonopolists, the case speedily conjured up their worst nightmare: a shadowy and abstraction-fixed Court was in the pocket of big business stripping the national government—the only power with the size to make a difference—of the ability to stop the onward rush of dangerous combinations. Subsequent progressive commentators, eager to destroy the last impediments to the New Deal of the 1930s,

likewise too quickly assumed that a weakened Sherman Act meant that trusts would escape regulation altogether.

Relying on a long history of state control over the organization of corporations, the decision contemplated state regulatory success. Yet, while the legal tools existed to do the job, the political will was rapidly routed by their practical economic influence. The states simply found it lucrative in terms of jobs and revenue to permit domestic corporations to join New Jersey combinations and to relax foreign corporation laws.

Fuller's conception of the distinction between manufacturing and commerce, so tenuous in economic and social terms, so removed from the realities of business intentions, was nevertheless critical to his conception of federalism. The formal line had to be drawn to protect state autonomy. Its implications for the commerce clause frustrated those whose vision empirically forecast a future of huge interstate combinations, obsequious state legislatures, and a crippled Congress. From *Knight* until the 1930s, Fuller's contention that commerce was a logical, categorical concept limited the ability of the Congress to regulate certain kinds of economic activity. Notoriously, for example, in *Adair v. United States* (1908), the Court struck down on interstate commerce grounds a congressional attempt to ban yellow-dog labor contracts in railroads, ruling that no "legal or logical connection" existed between membership in a labor union and interstate commerce.

Considered in the longer term, *Knight*'s significance took on a different shape. Its hold on the trust problem was brief, in large part because its facts were so peculiarly narrow. Almost immediately, the same Court began to support the government in its own half-hearted efforts to bring the combinations under some control. The Court soon sustained Sherman Act prosecutions of pools and associations designed to control the pricing of pipe, railroad rates, and beef. It also upheld prosecutions of holding companies engaged in railroading and oil refining.

Knight's influence in the commerce clause context was more pronounced, in large part because Fuller's clearly defined antebellum position permitted the Court to hold important activities beyond the pale of commerce. Yet, within a few years, two alternative styles of analysis linking local business activity to interstate commerce had emerged which took into account the economic realities of the business process and the failure of the states to meet the challenge. In 1905, the Court announced through Justice Oliver Wendell Holmes, Jr., that local business activity might be reached by the Sherman Act if it occurred in the "current of commerce." In the *Shreveport Rate Case* (1914), the Court held that local activities directly "affecting commerce" could be prosecuted. The spirit of *Knight* flared for the last time in *Schechter Poultry Corporation v. United States* (1935) and *Carter v. Carter Coal Company* (1936), but was quickly interred as the New Deal triumphed in *NLRB v. Jones & Laughlin Steel Corporation* (1937) and *Wickard v. Filburn* (1942). Empirical commerce analysis dramatically expanded congressional power, and Fuller's prediction came true.

By 1985, the top 15 percent of corporations were collecting 85 percent of corporate receipts. The largest one-tenth of one percent of industrial firms accounted for 70 percent of all industrial sales. The wealthiest corporation, Citicorp, and the largest industrial firm, Exxon, controlled as much wealth as all of the nation's ten million proprietorships combined. Under these circumstances it seems at best irrelevant to label as a failure a decision that in retrospect could not have solved the problem of corporate

combination had it gone the other way. If the Court's tenacious commitment to a formalistic antebellum resolution of the issue seems at this date mannered and quaintly antique, the confident progressive antitrust program called for by its critics—empirical, brashly functional, statistical, and "modern" to the core—has hardly proven more effective as a public counterweight to private economic concentration. *United States v. E.C. Knight Company* stands finally as the first dramatic embodiment of the persistent and perplexing failure of the radical democratic tradition to develop juridical concepts and social strength adequate to the task of creating the more equitable sharing of economic power called for by antimonopolists a century ago.

Selected Bibliography

Arnold, T.W. *The Folklore of Capitalism.* New Haven, CT: Yale University Press, 1937.

Hurst, J.W. *Law and Markets in United States History: Different Modes of Bargaining Among Interests.* Madison, WI: University of Wisconsin Press, 1982.

———. *The Legitimacy of the Business Corporation in the Law of the United States, 1780–1970.* Charlottesville, VA: University Press of Virginia, 1970.

Letwin, W. *Law and Economic Policy in America: The Evolution of the Sherman Antitrust Act.* New York: Random House, 1954.

McCurdy, C.W. "The Knight Sugar Decision of 1895 and the Modernization of American Corporation Law, 1869–1903." *Business History Review* 53 (Autumn 1979): 304–42.

Paul, A.M. *Conservative Crisis and the Rule of Law: Attitudes of Bar and Bench, 1887–95.* New York: Harper & Row, 1960.

REGULATION IN THE PUBLIC INTEREST

by Robert A. Waller
Department of History
Clemson University

United States v. Trans-Missouri Freight Association, 166 U.S. 290 (1897) [U.S. Supreme Court]

During the late nineteenth century, the United States came to grips with the issue of private gain versus national regulation through the actions of Congress, the courts, and the new independent regulatory commissions. Through the legislative, judicial, and administrative pro-

cesses, the relationship between railroad empires and the public interest was established. Among these responses was the decision of the U.S. Supreme Court regarding the conduct of the Trans-Missouri Freight Association, a voluntary pooling arrangement for rail traffic west of the Missouri River. This case is a subject of great controversy in achieving balance between companies and consumers.

The congressional expression of the relationship between the nation's major businesses and the consumers' needs took a principal form in the Interstate Commerce Act of 1887. In this early legislation, proponents established the need to accomplish three essential goals: (1) to prohibit charging more for the short haul than for the long haul, (2) to publish the interstate commerce carriers' rates and forbid charging more or less than the published schedules, and (3) to prohibit pooling of services by competing railroads. The administration of these principles was placed in the hands of a commission, but enforcement was the province of the courts. It was expected that publicity would deter the transportation giants from practices inimical to the consumer's interest. The five-person commission proceeded to enforce the act vigorously, but soon judicial roadblocks were encountered, for compliance was not always forthcoming without resort to the court procedures provided in the law.

The companion legislation, the Sherman Antitrust Act, was passed by Congress in 1890. In response to public resistance to monopoly practices, the law forbade businesses, in very general and sweeping terms, from engaging in unfair practices. This legislation prohibited every contract, combination, and conspiracy in restraint of trade in both interstate and foreign commerce. Here again, the provisions were to be enforced by judicial process through the federal courts. Wittingly or unwittingly, the administrative and legislative prerogatives were surrendered to still a third branch of government. Problems were to arise.

The issue became the interpretation of both pieces of legislation. Were these acts intended to prohibit all restraints of trade or only those deemed to be unreasonable? The U.S. Supreme Court first dealt with these alternatives in *United States v. Trans-Missouri Freight Association* in 1897. In a 5–4 decision, the majority held that the Sherman Act prohibited all restraints of trade in interstate or foreign commerce, without exception, not just those that were deemed unreasonable at common law.

The case arose when the federal government brought suit to dissolve an association of midwestern railroads formed for the purpose of fixing rates. For the majority on the Court, Justice Rufus W. Peckham wrote: "A contract . . . that is in restraint of trade or commerce is by the strict language of the act prohibited even though such contract is entered into between competing common carriers by railroad, and only for the purpose of thereby affecting traffic rates for the transportation of persons and property." Peckham rejected the contention that rate agreements were authorized by the Interstate Commerce Act. "It may not in terms prohibit [an agreement of this nature], but it is far from conferring either directly or by implication any power to make it." Ostensibly, there was no conflict between the Interstate Commerce Act and the Sherman Act.

Justice Edward D. White and three others dissented. The minority opinion argued that the act prohibited only unreasonable restraints of trade. Utilizing the concept of a "rule of reason," White argued that "[t]he plain intention of the law was to protect the liberty of contract and freedom of trade. Will this intention not be frustrated by a construction, which, if it does not destroy, at least gravely impairs the liberty of the individual to contract and the freedom of trade? If the rule of reason no longer determines the validity of contracts upon which trade depends and results, what became of the liberty of the citizen or of the freedom of trade?" This interpretation became the majority opinion in *Standard Oil Company v. United States* (1911) and allowed a distinction between "good" and "bad" trusts. For the time, however, the signal being sent by the nation's highest court was unclear if not chaotic in its result.

The definition of "public interest" frequently lies in the eyes of the beholder. In American experience, boards or commissions have been principal vessels to navigate the narrow channel of quasi-administrative, quasi-legislative, and quasi-judicial function. The Interstate Commerce Act was a major national effort to reconcile competing interests using the commission approach as typified the late nineteenth-century progressive desire for informed, disinterested administration. In the school of trial and error to achieve that balance, *Trans-*

Missouri Freight was a temporary setback. Subsequent legislation in the form of the Hepburn Act of 1906 rectified that interruption.

Selected Bibliography

Harbeson, R.W. "Railroads and Regulation, 1877–1916: Conspiracy or Public Interest?" *Journal of Economic History* 27 (June 1967): 230–42.

Martin, A. "The Troubled Subject of Railroad Regulation in the Gilded Age—A Reappraisal." *Journal of American History* 61 (Sept. 1974): 339–71.

McGraw, T.K. "Regulation in America: A Review Article." *Business History Review* 49 (Summer 1975): 159–83.

COMMERCE AND NATIONAL POLICE POWERS

by Fred D. Ragan
Department of History
East Carolina University

Champion v. Ames, 188 U.S. 321 (1903) [U.S. Supreme Court]

Dubbed "the Lottery Case," *Champion v. Ames* reflected the growing willingness of the U.S. Supreme Court at the beginning of the twentieth century to sustain Congress's use of its delegated powers to remedy social and economic ills. All parties fully realized the significance of the case, and the justices scheduled arguments on no less than five occasions. At issue was a 1895 statute prohibiting interstate transportation of lottery tickets to safeguard public morals. If the Court sustained Congress's power, it would take an important step toward creating federal police powers to protect the health, welfare, safety, and morals of the national community.

The government charged Charles F. Champion and his companions with conspiring to ship, by Wells Fargo Express Company, Paraguayan lottery tickets from Texas to California. Arrested in Chicago to assure appearance at trial in Texas, Champion sued for a writ of *habeas corpus*.

The defense, led by the distinguished advocate William D. Guthrie, developed three lines of argument. First, lottery tickets were not commerce within the meaning of the Constitution, since they had been used for "worthy" public purposes before drafting the Constitution and since. The Constitution, Guthrie argued, meant today what it did when it was adopted. He also compared lottery tickets to insurance policies because both were essentially tickets of chance. Second, Guthrie asserted that

Congress's power to regulate commerce did not include the power to prohibit; for if Congress had such a power, it would convert the "limited power to regulate commerce, [into] the unlimited power to regulate all intercourse, including public morals." Finally, he conceded that the power to prohibit existed but not at the national level. If states desired to exclude "noxious articles," the power was "absolute." This police power knew only two limitations: a state could not prohibit articles of commerce; nor could it prohibit importation of noxious articles when they remained in the "original package." But when the states had not acted, Guthrie recognized no limitation on the right of his client. Although he won a minority of four justices to his position, Guthrie failed to convince the majority.

Justice John Marshall Harlan delivered the majority opinion. After a review of commerce cases, Harlan embraced former Chief Justice John Marshall's sweeping language to define commerce and Congress's power over it. Commerce encompassed "navigation, intercourse, communication, traffic, the transit of persons and the transmission of messages by telegraphs." Congress's power over commerce "is plenary, complete in itself"; and in determining the nature of regulations, Congress has a "large discretion," which is not limited because the courts, in their opinions, do not think the "best or most effective" method has been employed. Guthrie's comparison of lottery tickets to insurance poli-

ECONOMICS AND THE LAW

cies found little sympathy with Harlan. He contended that the "tickets were the subject of traffic; they could have been sold; and the holder was assured that the company would pay to him the amount of the prize drawn." Consequently, the tickets were commerce and "subjects of commerce, and the regulation of the carriage of such tickets . . . by independent carriers is a regulation of commerce among the . . . states."

Next Harlan addressed the argument that Congress could regulate but not prohibit commerce. Drawing on *McCulloch v. Maryland* (1819), Harlan emphasized that Congress must be allowed a choice of means, especially involving this "particular kind of commerce." If the state governments can take into view the nature of the evil to be suppressed, why could Congress not ensure that commerce among the states "shall not be polluted"? Congress "no doubt shared" with the Court the view that the "suppression of nuisances injurious to public health or morality is among the most important duties of government." To the argument that such power denied Champion his Fifth Amendment liberty, Harlan emphasized the limits of such liberty. It meant the right to be free to live and work where one desired, to earn a livelihood by lawful means, and to follow interest by engaging in all contracts that may be proper. Liberty did not include the right to "introduce into commerce . . . an element that will be confessedly injurious to the public morals."

Also, Harlan rejected Tenth Amendment arguments. The issue here, he countered, was the use of a power "expressly delegated to Congress." Congress had not interfered with lotteries conducted "exclusively within the limits of any state. . . ." But since a "state may, for the purpose of guarding the morals of its own people, forbid all sales of lottery tickets . . ., so Congress, for the purpose of guarding the people of the United States against the 'widespread pestilence of lotteries' and to protect the commerce . . . may prohibit" the lottery traffic. Somewhat defensively, Harlan main-

tained that Congress only "supplemented" the action of states trying to protect public morals. "We should hesitate long before adjudging that an evil of such appalling character, carried on through interstate commerce, cannot be met and crushed by the only power competent to that end." After so sweeping a statement, Harlan hedged. Conceding that Congress could not use its power in an arbitrary manner, he nevertheless refused "to lay down a rule for determining in advance" every case that may arise.

The dissent, written by Chief Justice Melville W. Fuller for himself and Justices David J. Brewer, George Shiras, Jr., and Rufus W. Peckham, drew heavily from defense counsel arguments. Fuller feared for the traditional division of power within the Union. If Congress could prohibit lottery tickets, he asked, what were the limits to its power? Adopting a position "inconsistent with the views of the framers," Fuller asserted that the majority had taken a "long step in the direction of wiping out all traces of state lines, and the creation of a centralized government."

All parties recognized the importance of this case. Fuller, expressing his reverence for the existing federalism, bitterly attacked the decision because it created national police powers. Harlan and the majority seemed to recognize the need for an enlarged role for Congress if problems of an increasingly complex industrial society were to be effectively managed. Certainly, these men could not have foreseen that later generations would find in the commerce clause the power to prohibit individuals from growing food crops and discriminating against one another. Coupled with *McCray v. United States* (1904), the majority opinion in the Lottery Case gave the national government broad new regulatory police powers under the guise of the tax power and the commerce clause.

Selected Bibliography

Semonche, J.E. *Charting the Future: The Supreme Court Responds to a Changing Society, 1890–1920*, CT: Greenwood Press, 1978.

MANDATE FOR SOCIAL CHANGE

by Robert T. Barrett
Clemson, South Carolina

Katzenbach v. McClung, 379 U.S. 294 (1964) [U.S. Supreme Court]

Ollie's Barbecue and the Heart of Atlanta Motel, both located in Birmingham, Alabama, had much in common following passage of the Civil Rights Act of 1964. They were operating in violation of Title III of the act, which prohibits racial discrimination in places of public accommodation. Their interests would become further identified through separate legal actions that turned defiance of the law into a major constitutional test of this key provision of the act.

During the summer of 1964, however, it was far from clear that Ollie's Barbecue and the Heart of Atlanta Motel would find their legal fortunes so closely bound. The owners of Ollie's Barbecue, Ollie McClung, Sr., and Ollie McClung, Jr., brought suit against the government in federal district court. They claimed that Title III of the Civil Rights Act was unconstitutional and requested that the government be prohibited from enforcing it against their restaurant and others.

Title III was considered by legal scholars to rest solidly on the commerce clause (Article 1, Section 8) of the U.S. Constitution and it was drafted in unambiguous language: "All persons shall be entitled to the full and equal enjoyment of the goods, services, facilities, privileges, advantages, and accommodations of any place of public accommodation, as defined in this section, without discrimination or segregation on the ground of race, color, religion, or national origin." Restaurants were specifically defined as places of public accommodation if their operations "affect commerce or are supported by state action." They also came under this provision if they served or offered to serve interstate travelers or if a "substantial portion" of the food they sold "moved in commerce."

There was no doubt that the McClungs discriminated against blacks in the operation of their restaurant. Since opening in 1927, blacks had been refused seating in their dining room and could purchase food only through a take-out service. Less obvious was the relationship between Ollie's Barbecue and interstate commerce. Located 11 blocks from the nearest interstate highway and further removed from rail and bus terminals, it served a local clientele and made no effort to attract interstate travelers. There was an indirect link with interstate commerce through the purchase of meat from a local wholesaler. This accounted for approximately 46 percent of the restaurant's food supplies, which were obtained by the supplier from sources outside the state.

The McClungs contended that their business had only a remote connection to interstate commerce and that this was not sufficient for Congress to regulate their customer practices. The strength of their arguments can best be gauged by the government's reaction. Rather than face a challenge to the act from Ollie's Barbecue, the government moved for dismissal. There had been no threat of enforcement against the McClungs and they claimed no injury; the suit was, therefore, premature.

The U.S. District Court for the Northern District of Alabama did not agree and decided the case on its merits. It found no support for Title III in either the Thirteenth or Fourteenth Amendment and concluded that no significant relationship existed between discrimination in a restaurant and the flow of food in interstate commerce. Congress had exceeded its commerce powers and an injunction was granted barring the government from enforcing Title III against the plaintiffs.

As expected, the decision gained national attention and, in a presidential election year, the issues were intensified. Senator Barry Goldwater, the conservative Republican candidate for the presidency who had voted against the law in Congress, declared it unconstitutional. Those who sought to cast the decision in partisan political terms were disappointed. The three-judge district court was headed by Judge Walter P. Gerwin, a Kennedy appointee, who was joined by Judges Seybourne H. Lunne and H. H. Grooms, appointees of Presidents Truman and Eisenhower.

It was in the middle of the presidential campaign that the case came before the U.S. Supreme Court on appeal by the attorney general. The first Monday in October begins a new Term for the Court and is usually a brief, formal affair. But, at the Court's request arguments in *Katzenbach v. McClung* were scheduled for opening day of the 1964–65 Term. It became obvious that the Court was prepared for a definitive test of the new law when it suggested that the case concerning the Heart of Atlanta Motel also be scheduled for opening-day arguments. A three-judge federal district court in Atlanta had upheld Title III as it applied to hotels and motels and ordered the Heart of Atlanta Motel to comply with the law.

The constitutional challenge by the Heart of Atlanta Motel was considerably weakened by the nature and range of its business. It advertised its accommodations nationally and nearly 75 percent of its guests were from out of state. The Court, it was thought, would not find it difficult to conclude that racial discrimination in such places of public accommodation has a disruptive effect on interstate commerce. The McClungs' case could not be so easily decided. *Amicus curiae* ("friend of the court") briefs had been submitted by the National Association for the Advancement of Colored People's Legal Defense and the Educational Fund on behalf of the federal government and by North Carolina on behalf of the McClungs. Powerful arguments had been submitted in the lower court, but for the past 27 years the Supreme Court had consistently upheld the power of Congress to regulate interstate commerce.

The Supreme Court announced its decisions on December 14, 1964. As expected, the Court upheld the decision of the lower court in the Heart of Atlanta Motel. The government's arguments to dismiss *McClung* as premature were rejected. The Court clearly saw these as "companion cases" that met an urgent need in deciding the constitutionality of Title III.

In *Katzenbach*, Justice Tom C. Clark delivered the unanimous opinion of the Court, which reversed the district court ruling and upheld the constitutionality of Title III of the Civil Rights Act of 1964. In reaching this decision, the Court referred to testimony given before Congress concerning the effect of racial discrimination in restaurants on the flow of interstate commerce. Clark noted that there was sufficient testimony to demonstrate that racial discrimination not only artificially depressed the sale and purchase of interstate goods, but that it obstructed interstate travel as well. Referring to a series of cases, the Court reaffirmed the power of Congress to regulate interstate commerce, which includes restaurants, "which directly or indirectly obstruct interstate commerce." Clark also observed that Ollie's Barbecue had an insignificant effect on interstate commerce, but when considered as representative of many other restaurants, the effect was considerable.

The decision of the Court cleared the way for full-scale enforcement of the Civil Rights Act and it also gave Congress a broad mandate in the field of social legislation by finding that discrimination itself placed a burden on interstate commerce.

Selected Bibliography

Cohn, R. Case Notes. *Alabama Law Review* 17 (Spring 1965): 338–43.

Greenawalt, K. *Discrimination and Reverse Discrimination.* New York: Alfred A. Knopf, 1983.

C. Labor

THE LEGITIMACY OF LABOR ORGANIZATION

by William M. Wiecek
Department of History
Syracuse University

People v. Fisher, 14 Wendell's Reports 9 (1835) [New York Supreme Court of Judicature]

Shoemakers pioneered tactics of labor organization in the United States, partly because their trade was one of the first to experience the wrenching differentiation of management from worker and capital from labor. *People v. Fisher* loomed large on the legal landscape as a monument to this separation and to American jurists' determination that workers must not be allowed to explore the possibilities of collective action.

In 1833, a journeyman shoemaker (i.e., an employee of a master shoemaker) known as "Fisher" and an unspecified number of his unnamed fellow-workers organized what Chief Justice John Savage of the New York Supreme Court of Judicature called a "club"—a proto-union. They drew up bylaws prohibiting members from making men's boots for master shoemakers for less than $1 a pair. They also agreed that they would not work for any master who employed a journeyman for a rate less than $1 a pair. When a master named Lum employed a journeyman at the rate of 75 cents a pair, Fisher and others walked off the job. For this, Fisher was indicted for violation of a New York statute making it a criminal conspiracy "to commit any act injurious to . . . trade or commerce."

In his defense, Fisher claimed that since it was not illegal for him and any of his fellow journeymen to refuse to work for less than a specified rate as individuals, they could not be prosecuted for doing the same thing in concert. To refute this argument, Savage relied on two arguments: Anglo-American common-law precedent, and policy.

Drawing on vague and imprecise English precedents, Savage held that concerted labor actions were "against the spirit of the common law." The doctrinal problem confronting Savage was this: at common law, a conspiracy was criminal if organized for an illegal objective or to accomplish a legal objective by illegal means. Savage conceded that from the viewpoint of the individual worker, the objective of higher wages was not illegal. So, if he was to conclude that a conspiracy existed, he was forced to find the means illegal. Though he did not cite them directly, two prominent American precedents, the *Philadelphia Cordwainers' Case* (1806) and the *New York Cordwainers' Case* (1810), provided the support he needed. Both had upheld conspiracy convictions of shoemakers who had struck for higher wages or a closed shop. Because Fisher was being prosecuted for violation of a statute, not the common-law crime of conspiracy, Savage was able to hold that the mere act of conspiring together, even if for a legal end, was indictable, because the means were declared illegal by statute (i.e., concerted employee action, including a strike, was "injurious . . . to trade or commerce," in the terms of the statute).

To prove this latter point, Savage turned to policy arguments, demonstrating that union organization interfered with the workings of a *laissez-faire* market economy. The major portion of his opinion was a tract on the free market. He argued, for example, that "it is important to the best interests of society that the price of labor be left to regulate itself, or rather be limited by the demand for it." Because "competition is the life of trade," he went on, the "officious and improper interference" of the journeymen with the natural workings of the market created "a monopoly of the most odious kind."

Fisher was in the mainstream of American precedent in labor cases; the law stood as a formidable lion in the path of union organization. For that reason, the great case *Commonwealth v. Hunt* (1842) has been called "the Magna Carta of labor" in the United States. Decided by Chief Justice Lemuel Shaw of the Massachusetts Supreme Judicial Court, the *Hunt* decision held that labor organization is not, of itself, a criminal conspiracy indictable at common law. Shaw acknowledged the considerable precedential weight of *Fisher*, but distinguished it on the ground that the New York decision turned on the construction of a statute, while the Massachusetts case involved only the common law. Finding that neither the objective nor the means used by the Massachusetts bootmakers were unlawful, Shaw held that "we cannot perceive, that it is criminal for men to agree together to exercise their own acknowledged rights, in such a manner as best to subserve their own interests." Shaw thus rejected Savage's basic assumption. *Hunt* did not legitimate all union activity, however. It merely removed the stigma of criminality that automatically attached to collective action under the *Fisher* holding.

A change in the law, represented by the shift from the New York to the Massachusetts rule, did not endear labor organization to employers, especially as industrialization drastically altered the terrain of labor-management relations in the late nineteenth century. With conspiracy a dulled and rusting weapon after *Hunt*, corporate employers sought more effective instruments to bludgeon unions. Between 1870 and 1900, they found such weapons in two places: the labor injunction and the antitrust laws. The labor injunction bore no relation to the *Fisher* doctrine; it permitted judges to enjoin some union activity, such as organizing a strike, and then to hold workers disobeying the order in contempt of court, whereupon the judge could impose fines and jail sentences without the inconvenience of having to submit the case to a jury. Prosecutions of unions and labor organizers for violation of the Sherman Antitrust Act of 1890, on the other hand, hearkened back to the theory of *Fisher*, for such judicial assaults on labor proceeded on the premise that union organization and strikes were in restraint of trade, the pivotal point of Savage's opinion. This revival of an early nineteenth-century assumption proved to be protean and long-lived, being reburied only by the labor policies of the New Deal in the 1930s. *Fisher* thus had a lingering influence long after its specific doctrines had become obsolete.

Selected Bibliography

Nelles, W. *Commonwealth v. Hunt. Columbia Law Review* 32 (1932): 1128–69.

Sayre, F.B. "Criminal Conspiracy." *Harvard Law Review* 35 (1928): 393–427.

Witte, E.E. "Early American Labor Cases." *Yale Law Journal* 35 (1926): 825–37.

"AN INJURY TO ONE IS AN INJURY TO ALL"

by Wayne K. Hobson
Department of American Studies
California State University at Fullerton

In re Debs, 158 U.S. 564 (1895) [U.S. Supreme Court]

Does a labor union have the right to obstruct interstate commerce while pursuing otherwise legitimate aims? Do federal courts have jurisdiction to issue injunctions against unions in such cases? Is it legitimate for federal officials and officers of struck corporations to coordinate their strategies so that the government acts as an agent of the corporations against the striking union? Does it strain reason to extend the provisions of a law enacted by Congress to restrict monopolistic business practices to labor unions engaged in conflicts against such businesses? Will labor organizing be confined to the "bread and butter" aims of skilled craft workers, or will the labor movement speak for a broader range of workers and seek a more radical restructuring of the America's society and economy? If courts and the political system seek to block radical labor, what strategies will labor adopt in reply?

These were major questions in the dramatic Pullman strike and ensuing court battles of 1894–95, which culminated in a unanimous U.S. Supreme Court decision upholding the contempt convictions of Eugene V. Debs and other American Railway Union (ARU) officers. Debs's union had ignored a federal court injunction ordering it to cease supporting a massive railroad strike. The injunction had been issued by federal judges William A. Woods and Peter S. Grosscup at the request of U.S. Attorney General Richard Olney, who was acting in concert with the railroads. The Pullman strike had begun in early May 1894 among workers in the Pullman Company's sleeping-car manufacturing plants. These workers had endured a 33 percent wage cut since the previous summer with no corresponding reduction of food prices, rents, or utilities. Workers in Pullman, a "model" company town, already deeply resented the company's paternalistic and autocratic control of their lives. In late June, as their situation became more desperate, the Pullman strikers appealed to the recently formed ARU, led by Debs. This union represented a major departure for organized labor in the railroad industry. Four railroad brotherhoods organized along craft lines had long dominated labor organizing in the industry. The brotherhoods were cautious, serving their members more by their insurance programs than by advocacy of workers' interests against the railroad companies. The ARU, on the other hand, was an industrial union committed to confronting employers and welcoming as members all white nonmanagement employees who served the railroads in any capacity. Even coal miners, longshoremen, and car builders, if in the employ of a railroad, were invited to join.

ARU leaders recognized a boycott was very risky. The nation was in the midst of an economic depression. There was good reason to believe either the state or federal government, or both, would intervene on the employers' side, and the railroad companies were powerful and well organized. Twenty-four railroads with terminals in Chicago formed a tightly knit organization, the General Managers Association (GMA), which coordinated the companies' economic and labor practices. The GMA was a formidable opponent for organized labor. In fact, Debs's decision to create the ARU was a deliberate response to the organized power demonstrated by the GMA in labor disputes in 1893. Organization, Debs believed, had to be met with counter organization.

Despite their leaders' resolve to be cautious, the ARU's national convention, meeting in nearby Chicago, voted to support the Pullman workers by boycotting trains connected to Pullman cars. Delegates had visited the community of Pullman and were moved by the desperate conditions there. They could also plainly see that without outside support, the strikers' cause was hopeless. ARU delegates had come to Chicago with mounting grievances against the railroad companies, which were systematically reducing wages and using blacklists and other devices to break the new union. The delegates were convinced a crisis was building in their industry as the organized power of the GMA threatened to obliterate workers' power. Unity and solidarity on the one side had to be met with unity and solidarity on the other.

On June 26, ARU members began refusing to handle Pullman cars. The boycott quickly paralyzed railroad traffic coming to and going from Chicago. When the GMA responded by firing workers who refused to handle Pullman cars, the boycott against Pullman cars became a strike against the railroads. But the conflict was not destined to be a test of power between only the GMA and ARU; the federal government became the third and decisive actor in the drama. On July 2, Attorney General Olney, working in conjunction with railroad lawyers, devised a strategy to crush the strike. Olney, a former Boston railroad lawyer, appointed Edwin Walker, a leading Chicago corporate lawyer, as a special U.S. attorney. He directed Walker to seek an injunction against ARU leaders for obstructing the passage of the mails. The injunction was quickly issued. In fact, the issuing judges assisted Walker in drafting his request. ARU leaders decided to ignore the injunction. Even before labor's response was clear, President Grover Cleveland sent 2,000 troops to Chicago to ensure that mail would be transported. This order came over the strong objection of Illinois Governor John Altgeld and despite the fact that the ARU had deliberately relaxed its boycott so that there would not be any serious obstruction of the mail. Clearly, the administration's aim in calling out troops was to break the strike. These federal troops soon became violent participants in the conflict, escalating the situation well beyond what it had been. Their presence, however, did break the strike. By July 13, all rioting ended and trains were running on schedule. On July 20, the strike formally ended and attention shifted to the courts, where both criminal and civil actions were initiated against Debs and other ARU leaders.

Injunctions are an equitable remedy giving courts the power to diminish a nuisance or to prevent irreparable damage to private property that could not be adequately compensated in an action at law, and they were unusual in labor disputes in 1894. The first major use of this device against organized labor was during the nationwide railway strike of 1886–87. Several appellate court decisions were rendered shortly thereafter, but the *Debs* case was the first U.S. Supreme Court test.

Debs's lawyers did not dispute that he had defied the injunction. The issue was whether the injunction had been legitimate. Judge Woods, in December 1894, found Debs guilty of contempt. Woods's 40-page decision relied heavily on the Sherman Antitrust Act of 1890, ruling that Section 4, which authorized the government to seek injunctions against conspiracies in restraint of trade, applied to labor unions. Woods sentenced Debs to six months in jail and his fellow national officers to three months.

Olney was not entirely pleased with the ruling of the federal circuit court. Although he was satisfied that the injunction he had sought was upheld and that Debs was to pay for his defiance, Olney was troubled by Woods's heavy reliance on the Sherman Act, seeing it as an opening for unnecessary government limitations of economic freedom.

The ARU's appeal was argued before the Supreme Court on March 25 and 26, 1895. Debs's lawyers made four points. They argued, contrary to Woods's reading, that the Sherman Act did not apply to unions. Furthermore, they maintained, the defendants had done nothing unlawful by urging ARU members to quit their employment. In any case, the government had

no right to apply for an injunction to restrain interference with the private property of the railroads; the federal government could apply for injunctions only to protect public property. Finally, Debs's attorneys argued that if he had done anything unlawful, he should have been subjected to prosecution in the criminal courts rather than in civil tribunals. In fact, the government had initiated a criminal conspiracy charge against Debs, but it had a hard time making a convincing case before a jury, since the evidence pointed as fully to a government-employer conspiracy as to a union conspiracy. When a juror became ill in February 1895, the criminal trial was suspended and never resumed.

The government's case was argued by Olney, one of only two times he appeared before the Supreme Court during his tenure as attorney general. He had a particular purpose in mind: he sought to shift authority for the injunction from the Sherman Act to some other basis. In oral argument, he declared both the Sherman Act and the federal obligation to protect the mails unessential to the government's case. He did not deny the validity of those arguments, but he invited the Court to issue a far broader ruling than had Woods. Olney insisted that the key basis for the federal government's jurisdiction was its general constitutional power to regulate interstate commerce, deriving both from the Constitution and from the Interstate Commerce Act of 1887. This act, Olney asserted, gave Congress full and complete authority over the nation's railroads and denied such power to the states. If the states had no right to interfere with the operation of railroads, how much less right had mere citizens, such as Debs, to interfere with their operation? Olney contended that the federal government had the power to act as a trustee of the railroads. Furthermore, the ARU boycott produced a massive blockage of railroad traffic. The federal government was the only entity with sufficient authority to end that chaos.

Two months later the Supreme Court ruled, in a unanimous vote, to uphold Debs's contempt conviction. Justice David J. Brewer wrote the decision, taking Olney's arguments and making them the opinion of the Court. Brewer agreed that the federal government had power to prevent anyone from interfering with interstate commerce. He cited numerous past instances where the federal government had used this constitutional power to deny state government interference with interstate commerce. Echoing Olney, Brewer argued that if it could exercise such power vis-à-vis a state, it could certainly do so vis-à-vis a mere voluntary association of individuals. Brewer ignored Woods's reliance on the Sherman Act as the basis for the federal government's authority until the opinion's final paragraph, in which he stated that he was not necessarily overturning the circuit court and not necessarily affirming it. He preferred, instead, to rest the judgment on a broader ground—the federal government's constitutional right to regulate interstate commerce.

Brewer's opinion, as he acknowledged, extended federal equity jurisdiction substantially. He went well beyond the traditional view of injunctions by sanctioning their use even in the absence of an irreparably threatened property interest and extending their application from the traditional one of protecting the rights of private parties to the novel one of preserving public rights and punishing public wrongs. What remained to be determined were the limits on the use of this new weapon against labor. Brewer's decision, construed narrowly, applied only to federal injunctions against obstructions of interstate commerce.

The next several decades were to see a greatly expanded use of injunctions against labor unions. Since many labor disputes did not involve interstate commerce, it was up to state courts to decide them. Leading experts on these decisions maintain that the key question that quickly emerged was the legitimacy of the ends sought by a union in a particular dispute. It was always easy to get an injunction against unlawful activity, such as destruction of property. But most strikes, including the Pullman strike before federal troops intervened, were not destructive. Could an injunction be obtained against such legal activities as picketing or leafletting? Could it be argued that such activities interfered with commerce or represented a conspiracy in restraint of trade? In most jurisdictions it became settled that if the purpose of the strike was to gain higher wages, shorter hours, or improved working conditions, an in-

junction could not be granted as long as the union was not engaging in criminal activity. However, when the aims of the strike were less obviously directly beneficial to the members, such as a strike for a closed shop or to obtain the reinstatement of a discharged employee, courts were much more willing to sanction injunctions. In such cases, the specific behavior of the union was a major determinant of court action. Brewer's *In re Debs* opinion had implicitly invited this activist state effort to limit the scope of labor union activity.

The *Debs* decision was one of three major Supreme Court decisions in 1895. The other two were *United States v. E.C. Knight Company*, restricting the Sherman Act's applicability as a weapon against monopolistic practices, and *Pollock v. Farmers' Loan & Trust Company*, invalidating a federal income tax. These decisions, taken together, decisively marked the emergence of a new era in which the Supreme Court would take a more activist role as one of the shapers of public policy in national affairs. Although the majority of justices from the 1890s to the late 1930s adhered to a *laissez-faire* ideology hostile to governmental regulation of business, their decisions in most areas are now seen by Court historians as conservative and pragmatic rather than as dogmatically ideological. One major exception is labor law. Here the Supreme Court, until the late 1930s, consistently issued decisions against labor unions and against economic legislation to protect workers. In doing so, it relied not only on a formalistic *laissez-faire* ideology, but it also evidenced a class-based and often ethnically based hostility toward organized labor. In this sense, it was significant that, whereas the Court was divided in the *Pollock* and *Knight* decisions, Brewer spoke for a unanimous Court in *Debs*.

In the broadest sense, the Pullman strike and *Debs* decision dramatized where the balance of power lay between the forces of labor and capital in the United States in the 1890s. The episode taught Americans on all sides what the underlying social, economic, and political realities of power were. Certainly that was the lesson Eugene Debs drew. His ARU did not survive the strike's failure. Rank-and-file railway workers dropped affiliation with the union, in part from disappointment with its failure to defeat the companies, but also because the railroads established a severe and effective blacklist to deny employment to union supporters and activists. Railway workers, convinced that major obstacles to interstate commerce would be suppressed by the federal government, hesitated for years to engage in strikes or boycotts of any significance. Debs emerged from six months in jail at Woodstock, Illinois, to announce that the combined forces of capital and government were too strong for traditional union activities to prevail. He was abandoning economic struggles, switching from reliance on strikes to reliance on politics and the ballot. Debs also announced his conversion to socialism and soon became the leader and perennial presidential candidate of the Socialist Party of America.

Within the labor movement, the failure of the Pullman strike helped swing the balance toward Samuel Gompers's brand of unionism. Gompers, president of the American Federation of Labor, favored a conservative approach, concentrating on craft unions and "bread and butter" issues of wages, hours, and working conditions. He had seen the ARU as a threat and had discouraged Chicago trade unions from participating in an ARU-sponsored general strike in Chicago called for July 10, 1894, to protest government intervention. The general strike's failure helped seal the fate of the ARU and with it the hopes of those who saw militant industrial unions as the best challenge to capitalist domination of American workers.

Both Debs and Gompers recognized that the Pullman strike marked the emergence of a new era in labor-capital relations. All elements of the federal government were now clearly aligned on the side of capital and were willing to countenance the use of force to compel an outcome favorable to that side. The two working-class leaders drew different conclusions about how to respond to this situation, but they did agree that industrial unionism was not a viable basis for labor organization until the attitude of the federal government altered. That did not happen until the 1930s.

For outside observers, the meaning of the Pullman strike and its legal aftermath seemed both clear and menacing. If the strike cemented an alliance between government and capital, it also stirred middle-class concerns about the rising power of big business. The U.S. Strike Commission, for example, spoke for many. This three-member body had been appointed by President Cleveland to investigate the broader issues revealed by the Pullman strike. The commission interviewed over 100 witnesses and issued a report condemning all sides in the dispute. Debs and the ARU were criticized for admitting nonrailway workers, such as the Pullman car builders, into their union. They were also criticized for not seeing the inherent futility of their boycott-strike in a time of widespread unemployment. George Pullman was criticized for his stubborn refusal to deal with the union representing his employees and for not arbitrating the issues in the dispute. The GMA was excoriated for its unsavory policies, especially for its arrogance in refusing to deal with the ARU and for its monopolistic control over the industry. Despite the fact that the commission had been appointed by President Cleveland, his Justice Department and attorney general were criticized for their close relationship with the railway companies, especially for permitting loyal railroad employees to be sworn in as deputy U.S. marshals. In essence, these railway workers became federal officers paid, armed, fed, and housed by the GMA. In private correspondence, Carroll D. Wright, the chair of the commission, called the strike a "pigheaded affair all around."

The commission implicitly rejected the view of labor-capital conflict that the major actors had shared: a battle to the death between rival conceptions of industrial America. Instead, the commission took the view that industrial disputes were matters that reasonable men could resolve if they would only adopt a conciliatory attitude. Specifically, the commission called for arbitration as an alternative to strikes. This plea for industrial peace went unheeded. Capital had no incentive to give up its newly won injunction weapon or its renewed alliance with the federal government. Labor was too divided against itself and was unwilling to accept the wound to dignity and manhood that an unequal conciliation with capital would entail.

Selected Bibliography

Beth, L.P. *The Development of the American Constitution, 1877–1917.* New York: Harper & Row, 1971.

Eggert, G.G. *Railroad Labor Disputes: The Beginnings of Federal Strike Policy.* Ann Arbor, MI: University of Michigan Press, 1967.

———. *Richard Olney; Evolution of a Statesman.* University Park, PA: Pennsylvania State University Press, 1974.

Frankfurter, F., and N. Greene. *The Labor Injunction.* New York: Macmillan, 1930.

Lindsey, A. *The Pullman Strike—The Story of a Unique Experiment and of a Great Labor Upheaval.* Chicago: University of Chicago Press, 1942.

Salvatore, N. *Eugene V. Debs—Citizen and Socialist.* Urbana, IL: University of Illinois Press, 1982.

Semonche, J.E. *Charting the Future: The Supreme Court Responds to a Changing Society, 1890–1920.* Westport, CT: Greenwood Press, 1978.

CAN CHILDREN UNDER 14 LEGALLY HOLD FULL-TIME JOBS?

by Philippa Strum
Department of Political Science
City University of New York

Hammer v. Dagenhart, 247 U.S. 251 (1918) [U.S. Supreme Court]

During the late nineteenth and early twentieth centuries as the United States became industrialized, the country gradually changed from one with an economy based largely on family farms and small businesses into one in which many people worked for huge, impersonal corporations. In addition, successive waves of immigrants brought to the country large numbers of people anxious to establish themselves economically and ready to accept whatever jobs were available. With such an extensive labor supply, employers in mills, factories, mines, and other workplaces were able to set whatever terms they chose regarding wages, hours, and conditions of employment.

The conditions of employment, by today's standards, were appalling. Men, women, and children all worked for as many as 12 hours a day and for as many as seven days a week on premises that were frequently unsafe and unsanitary. Wages were low; and federal laws had not yet been promulgated to regulate minimum wages, maximum hours, working conditions, or to provide unemployment insurance, disability insurance, social security pensions, and medical care for the poor.

The situation produced a labor union movement that was viewed by employers and most politicians as threatening the traditional American way of life—as well as corporate profits. Unions insisted that individuals were no longer in a position to negotiate with prospective employers on a one-to-one basis, as had been possible in the days of individually owned and small businesses, and that the only hope of bettering the working conditions of laborers was collective demands made through organizations sufficiently strong to challenge the financial power of employers. The translation of financial power into political power was evident in the treatment of unions by the state and federal governments. In general, government believed that unions threatened the *status quo* not only by demanding a more equitable distribution of wealth, but also by asking if the American society was really one in which any individual who worked hard enough could be economically successful.

The union movement was hampered by the existence of the federal system, which left most economic matters in the hands of the states. Thus, if workers became too bothersome in a particular state, employers had the option of moving their businesses to other states that were harsher in their treatment of unions. And states, recognizing that more businesses meant a bigger tax base, additional jobs, and the revenue from the purchases made by workers—in short, economic prosperity—competed with each other to attract businesses by being increasingly less responsive to the demands of workers.

There were members of the middle and upper classes who responded to the workers' complaints of exploitation, and a reform movement with the purpose of bettering workers' conditions gradually came into existence. It focused not only on how long and for how much pay laborers worked, but also on who worked, and particularly on the situation of women and children in the work force. As a result, by 1916 every state in the Union had established a minimum age for child labor. The regulations varied widely, however, as states attempted to balance the demands of the reform movement with their competition for corporations. Child labor laws were most stringent in the northern industrial states where labor was most powerful; southern states, by comparison, had relatively weak laws. North Carolina, for example, prohibited only children under 12 from working. The leniency of the southern regulations had the effect of making the northern labor laws milder than they might have been, for the northern states realistically feared the movement of factories—particularly in the textile industry—to the South. Thus, there was a growing sense of frustration not only among unions and within the reform movement but, where such matters as child labor were concerned, among increasingly large numbers of voters.

Clearly, many felt, the only effective remedy would be enactment of federal regulation. Congress, therefore, decided to discourage the hiring of small children by passing a law affecting producers, manufacturers, dealers, mines, mills, canneries, factories, and workshops that employed children younger than 14 or employed children aged 14 through 16 for more than 8 hours a day, more than 6 days a week, or before 6 a.m. or after 7 p.m. The federal Child Labor Act of 1916 decreed that products from any such workplace could not be shipped in interstate commerce until 30 days after use of such child labor was ended.

In passing the law, Congress relied on the power given to it in the Constitution, Article I,

Section 8, to "regulate commerce among the several states." The U.S. Supreme Court had interpreted that clause as meaning that Congress could regulate the movement of goods across state lines. The Supreme Court had earlier ruled that interstate commerce involved transportation, but not production of goods. Production, the Court said, could only be regulated by the states.

The Court derived its interpretation from a theory known as "dual federalism," which held that in their respective spheres, Congress and the states were sovereign and their power could not be interfered with by another body. The Constitution gave Congress sovereign power over foreign policy, for example, and the states could not act in that area. Similarly, the Tenth Amendment, which reserved to the states all powers not specifically given to the national government, thereby gave the states sovereign control over the "police power"—the power to regulate health, welfare, safety, and morals—and Congress could not constitutionally act in *that* sphere. This meant that while Congress could control interstate commerce, it had no right to regulate intrastate commerce (i.e., commerce within one state), including the terms for which labor was performed. Thus, the labor leading to production of cotton in a North Carolina mill, which constituted intrastate commerce, could be regulated only by North Carolina.

The Court had, however, made exceptions. In *Champion v. Ames* (1903), it had upheld an 1895 federal act making it unlawful to transport lottery tickets into a state from another state; in *Hipolite Egg Company v. United States* (1911), it upheld the Food and Drug Act of 1906, which excluded impure food and drugs from interstate commerce; in *Hoke v. United States* (1913), it validated the Mann Act of 1910, which forbade the transportation of women in interstate commerce for the purpose of prostitution; and in *Clark Distilling Company v. Western Maryland Railway Company* (1917), it legitimized the Webb-Kenyon Act of 1913, which outlawed interstate commerce in intoxicating liquors. The Court had held that Congress might well consider each of these forms of commerce undesirable, and opponents of child labor hoped the Court would interpret the clause similarly when dealing with the employment of children.

It did not. In fact, it took the occasion to issue the strongest possible statement of dual federalism.

The question reached the Court when the North Carolina child labor law was challenged by Roland H. Dagenhart, father of Reuben and John Dagenhart, all of whom worked in a Charlotte, North Carolina, cotton mill. Reuben was under 14 and John was between 14 and 16; both worked longer work weeks than those permitted by the federal statute. Mr. Dagenhart claimed that the act was not a true regulation of interstate commerce, that it violated the Tenth Amendment, and that it also violated the due process clause of the Fifth Amendment by depriving his sons of their liberty to work. Scholars have suggested that Mr. Dagenhart was induced by his employers to bring the suit as a way of eliminating the restriction on child labor, since assertions of violations of rights must be made by those possessing them (or, in the case of minors, by their parents) and the employers could not sue on behalf of the children. In any event, after the trial court agreed with Mr. Dagenhart and enjoined the federal government from enforcing the act, the government appealed to the U.S. Supreme Court.

Justice William R. Day wrote the opinion for the 5–4 majority (himself, Chief Justice Edward D. White, and Justices Willis Van Devanter, James McReynolds, and Mahlon Pitney), upholding the lower court's ruling. He said that not only was commerce in the articles involved in the earlier cases harmful, but that interstate transportation was necessary to the accomplishment of the harmful results Congress wished to avoid. In this case, however, there was nothing harmful about the goods the cotton mill wished to ship, as indicated by the fact that they could move into interstate commerce 30 days after the mill ceased using the proscribed child labor. The law was not a real regulation of commerce, the Court said, but rather an attempt to regulate the employment of children. Day added that child labor had nothing to do with commerce among the states. Regulation of child labor was a matter reserved for the police power of the states by the Tenth Amendment.

In so holding, Day said that powers "not expressly delegated to the national government" are reserved to the people and the states. This is a misstatement of the Tenth Amendment, which does not use the word "expressly" but says only, "The powers not delegated to the United States by the Constitution, nor prohibited by it to the States, are reserved to the States respectively, or to the people." In fact, the records of the First Congress, which formulated the Bill of Rights, show that it had specifically rejected inclusion of the word "expressly" in the Tenth Amendment. And Chief Justice John Marshall, in *McCulloch v. Maryland* (1819), had held that omission of the word "expressly" from the Tenth Amendment meant that the question of whether a particular power had been delegated by the Constitution to Congress had to be decided by looking at the entire document. There, Article I, Section 8, Paragraph 3, gives Congress the "Power . . . to regulate Commerce . . . among the several States," and Paragraph 18 gives it the "Power . . . to make all Laws which shall be necessary and proper for carrying into Execution the foregoing Powers." Thus, whether exclusion of the products of child labor was within Congress's power depended on whether one considered such exclusion either necessary or proper, or both, for the carrying out of the power to regulate interstate commerce. For Day, however, the answer was not given in the Constitution but depended on a value judgment. His opinion, therefore, indicated his and his four fellow justices' distaste for governmental regulation of child labor rather than an interpretation that was mandated by the Constitution.

Day acknowledged that "all will admit" that "there should be limitations upon the right to employ children in mines and factories" and that North Carolina's prohibition on the employment of children under 12 was an indication that it opposed employment at too early an age. Other states had set the age minimum higher, but it was North Carolina's right to choose the age it considered appropriate. Uniform child labor laws might be desirable public policy but, however noble Congress's purpose, it could not force such laws upon the states. To do so would be to violate the "essential" constitutional principle that gave the states power "over matters purely local."

Addressing the argument that the desire to attract businesses had led some states to pass more "lenient" laws that gave the business establishments in those states an unfair advantage over their competitors in other states, Day replied that Congress had no power to rectify the situation. Some states, he noted, had passed laws limiting the hours that could be worked by women or fixing minimum wages for them, but Congress had no more right to force other states to follow their example than it did to achieve the same result indirectly by keeping goods produced by women out of interstate transportation.

Day was concerned not only about the *Hammer* case but about its wider implications—what he called the "far reaching result of upholding the act." Were the Court to do so, he argued, Congress would be able to regulate virtually any local activity simply by prohibiting the movement of goods in interstate commerce. The prospect of such a phenomenon distressed Day. Not only did it imply to him that "all freedom of commerce" would end; worse still, the power of the states over local matters would also be eliminated, "and thus our system of government [would] be practically destroyed."

The Court's decision was in keeping with its general attitude toward laws dealing with governmental control of business. Interpreting the Constitution as giving business as much freedom as possible, the Court tended to read statutes regulating hours of work, minimum wages, and other limitations on employers as unconstitutional. This approach was challenged, however, in the dissenting opinion that Justice Oliver Wendell Holmes, Jr., wrote in the case for himself and Justices Joseph McKenna, Louis D. Brandeis, and John H. Clarke. Holmes began by stating that which "no one is likely to dispute—that the statute in question is within the power expressly given to Congress if considered only as to its immediate effects," which is to keep goods out of interstate commerce, and that if it is invalid there must be some reason. But Holmes could find no such reason. Congress's power over interstate commerce is "given . . . in unqualified terms," he stated, and "the power to regulate" includes "the power to prohibit." This was made clear by the decisions

listed above, holding it constitutional for Congress to prohibit such things as impure food and drugs from being transported in interstate commerce.

Since Congress had the undoubted right to prohibit products of child labor in interstate commerce, the question then became whether the regulation was unconstitutional because of its effect on the states. But the Court itself had made clear that a congressional regulation of interstate commerce was not unconstitutional simply because it interfered with the domestic policy of a state. Holmes pointed to Court decisions upholding federal interstate regulations that "interfered" with things that states normally would control. These included the manufacture of oleomargarine, state banking policies, and businesses within a state that have branches in other states as well. Indicating outrage that the Court would uphold Congress's right to prohibit transportation of "strong drink" but not "the product of ruined lives," he reminded the justices that "if there is any matter upon which civilized countries have agreed—far more unanimously than they have with regard to intoxicants . . . it is the evil of premature and excessive child labor." So, even if the Court permitted Congress to prohibit transportation in interstate commerce of some articles but not others (a power Holmes thought the Court had no right to exercise), it could not claim that Congress was acting irrationally in attacking child labor.

As for the argument that the motivation for Congress's action had been a desire to wipe out child labor rather than a concern about interstate transportation as such, Holmes cited earlier decisions in which the Court stated that the purpose of a law forbidding an article in interstate commerce was irrelevant as long as the power exercised was legitimate. "It is enough," he stated, "that in the opinion of Congress the transportation encourages the evil."

The case was a crucial one because it severely limited the ability of the federal government to use the interstate commerce clause as a means of dealing with social problems ignored by the states. The Court would later hold that Congress could not use the spending and taxing power clause to regulate child labor. Together, these cases made federal regulation of child labor impossible. Thus, what might appear to be an obscure argument about the interpretation of the commerce clause was actually the reflection of a clash among the justices about the way in which society should be organized and about approaches to constitutional interpretation. Reflecting the dissension within society, members of the Court were divided about which group should be given greater governmental protection: corporations, which benefited from the competition among the states and from an absence of uniform national legislation regulating the workplace, or the workers, whose terms of employment might be bettered if Congress was permitted to legislate. In addition, Day's method of constitutional interpretation was challenged by that of Holmes, who believed that the Constitution had been designed to be adjusted to the "felt necessities" of different historical eras and that the Court should interpret it so as to permit Congress to respond to changing societal conditions unless some provision of the Constitution specifically prohibited it from doing so. The majority of the Court could accept federal regulation when it dealt with morality or health, but not when it affected traditional economic arrangements—and the Court saw no implications for either morality or health in conditions of labor.

Neither the disagreement about which economic groups should be given governmental protection nor that about constitutional interpretation would be resolved until the 1930s and 1940s, when Supreme Court justices appointed by President Franklin D. Roosevelt decided decisively in favor of governmental protection of labor and a flexible interpretation of the Constitution. Congress passed the Fair Labor Standards Act of 1938, regulating child labor, and in 1941 a unanimous Court said in *United States v. Darby Lumber Company* that it was constitutional and that Day, in *Hammer v. Dagenhart*, had misread the Constitution. The answer to the question of whether children under 14 could be employed became a resounding "No."

Day's gloomy prognostication about the effects on government and American life if such regulations as that in issue at *Hammer* were upheld was not entirely wrong. Since the ad-vent of the New Deal, Congress has indeed used the interstate commerce clause, as well as the taxing and spending and the "necessary and proper" clauses, to minimize state control not only of production and labor but also of many other governmental functions supposedly left to it by the Constitution. These include education, police, health, agriculture, and economic welfare. Extensive funding has been made available to the states by Congress for such functions, on condition that the states follow specific policies laid down by Congress. This has turned the states into something far more equivalent to administrative agencies for the federal government than the sovereign bodies favored by Day and, perhaps, by the framers of the Constitution. Nonetheless, the decision to do so has been ratified repeatedly by U.S. citizens in elections that have returned to office those politicians responsible for creating a welfare capitalist state in which the central government accepts responsibility for a minimum level of individual well-being.

It is this system that has replaced a central government practicing *laissez-faire* policies along the lines favored by Day. In fact, the early twentieth-century system, by passing tax laws that encouraged the growth of large businesses and by refusing to give legal sanction to workers' organizations, actually had the effect of empowering the interests of business over those of individuals.

The political system with a relatively weak central government favored by the founding fathers toward the end of the eighteenth century has been altered greatly in the last 200 years due to shifts in American values and changing technology. The Court was asked in *Hammer* to help speed along the process of change through constitutional interpretation. It declined to do so, but society ultimately rejected its decision. Mr. Dagenhart won his case, and the view of Justice Day and his supporters on the Supreme Court triumphed temporarily. But it was Justice Holmes's vision of a constitutional system that responded to the changing desires of the electorate in different historical eras that has become the basis for more recent decisions of the Supreme Court and for the constitutional jurisprudence now practiced in the United States.

Selected Bibliography

Semonche, J.E. *Charting the Future: The Supreme Court Responds to a Changing Society, 1890–1920.* Westport, CT: Greenwood Press, 1978.

Wood, S.B. *Constitutional Politics in the Progressive Era: Child Labor and the Law.* Chicago: University of Chicago Press, 1968.

D. Miscellaneous Governmental Regulation

COPYRIGHT LAW: LIMITING LITERARY MONOPOLIES

by Maxwell Bloomfield
Columbus School of Law
Catholic University of America

Wheaton v. Peters, 8 Peters 591 (1834) [U.S. Supreme Court]

Advocates of republican government in the late eighteenth century always insisted that its survival depended on a well-informed and responsible citizenry. As one means of public improvement, the framers of the Constitution, in Article I, Section 8, empowered Congress to "promote the progress of science and the useful arts, by securing for limited times to authors and inventors the exclusive right to their respective writings and discoveries." The First Congress acted to protect literary property by passing a copyright law in May 1790; its provisions were supplemented by further legislation in 1802. Pursuant to these statutes, an author who followed certain prescribed notification procedures could enjoy complete control over the publication and sale of a book or map for 14 years. No writer tested the limited of copyright protection until 1831, when a court reporter sued his successor for copyright infringement. The case established the foundations of modern American copyright law and, incidentally, revealed some major contradictions in the republican value system.

Court reporters were the legal drudges of the early republic. Underpaid and overworked, they found their own real compensation through the sale of their published reports, for which they claimed monopoly rights under the copyright laws. Henry Wheaton, who served as the third reporter of the U.S. Supreme Court from 1816 to 1827, brought out 12 volumes of *Reports* before he resigned to become *chargé d'affaires* to Denmark. Wheaton planned to renew each copyright as it expired by issuing a new edition; he hoped in this way to secure a steady annual income of $2,000 for many years.

But his successor, Richard Peters, had other plans. Citing the high cost and relative inaccessibility of the previous 25 volumes, Peters proposed to publish an inexpensive set of *Condensed Reports* in only six volumes. These would comprise all Supreme Court decisions down to 1827, leaving out the accompanying arguments of counsel and other material supplied by the original reporters. The series would then continue with the publication of Peters's ongoing *Reports* each year, enabling him to profit both from his own labors and from the work of his predecessors. Such a project appealed to the competitive entrepreneurial spirit of the Jacksonian age, and Peters had no difficulty in lining up 900 advance subscribers. Despite Wheaton's outraged protests, the several volumes of *Condensed Reports* appeared as promised between 1830 and 1834, at a cost to the public of only $25 per set.

As soon as he saw "his" cases back in print, Wheaton sought an injunction to restrain Peters from further publication and to compel him to account for any profits he had already made through copyright violations. Wheaton's attorneys appealed both to the federal statutes and to Anglo-American common law, which in their view gave authors perpetual and exclusive control of their literary works.

In response, Peters's lawyers denied that he had violated any law. Wheaton's rights depended solely on congressional legislation, they argued, and he had not performed one of the essential conditions prescribed for establishing those rights. Moreover, they argued, no one could obtain a copyright in judicial opinions that were as much the law of the land as legislative acts, and hence fell within the public domain.

Wheaton v. Peters forced the federal judiciary to choose between two basic components of republican ideology: the promotion of competition and democratic access to markets and knowledge, on the one hand; and an equally strong commitment to the sanctity of private property on the other. In the federal circuit court at Philadelphia, Judge Joseph Hopkinson ruled against Wheaton. Hopkinson's learned and persuasive opinion was later adopted in large part by a majority of the U.S. Supreme Court, which heard the case on appeal early in 1834.

The arguments and opinions fill 108 pages in Peters's *Reports*. Justice John McLean, speaking for four of the six participating justices, disposed first of Wheaton's common-law claims. There is no common law of the United States, McLean flatly declared. Each colony was settled at different times and under different conditions; and the settlers adopted only those parts of the English common law that were suited to their varying needs. In addition, the English common law of copyright remained undeveloped and confused down to the eve of the American Revolution; it could not have provided a coherent body of principles which the early settlers of Pennsylvania—or, by implication, any other colony—might have brought with them. Wheaton therefore could look only to the federal copyright laws for the protection of his literary rights.

Since those congressional statutes did confer temporary monopolistic privileges, McLean reasoned that their provisions should be strictly construed in the public interest. The record did not provide sufficient proof that Wheaton had deposited one copy of each volume with the secretary of state, as required by the act of 1790. Accordingly, McLean ordered the case remanded to the circuit court so that a jury might determine the facts.

Although Wheaton may have taken some small comfort from this part of McLean's opinion, the faulty state of federal recordkeeping made it extremely unlikely that he could prove to a jury's satisfaction that he had complied with the law. And McLean's final words effectively demolished any lingering dreams of future enrichment he may still have entertained: "It may be proper to remark that the court are unanimously of opinion, that no reporter has or can have any copyright in the written opinions delivered by this court; and that the judges thereof cannot confer on any reporter any such right." In other words, Wheaton's copyright, if it existed, extended only to his supplementary notes, not to the decisions themselves.

As a result of *Wheaton v. Peters*, American authors today can claim only the copyright protection afforded them by statute. And judicial opinions continue to belong only to the public. They must always be available "for the free and unrestrained use of the citizens of the United States," one of Peters's lawyers urged, because "knowledge of them is essential to the safety of all."

Selected Bibliography

Baker, E.F. *Henry Wheaton*. Philadelphia: University of Pennsylvania Press, 1937.

Newmyer, R.K. *Supreme Court Justice Joseph Story: Statesman of the Old Republic*. Chapel Hill, NC: University of North Carolina Press, 1985.

White, G.E. *The Marshall Court and Cultural Change, 1815–35*. New York: Macmillan Publishing Co., 1988.

CORPORATE GROWTH VS. STATES' RIGHTS

by Eric Monkkonen
Department of History
University of California at Los Angeles

Bank of Augusta v. Earle, 13 Peters 519 (1839) [U.S. Supreme Court]

The cases coming together in *Bank of Augusta v. Earle*, known as the Alabama, or Comity, Cases, have had a continuing, though changing, significance in American constitutional and economic history. The decision handed down by Chief Justice Roger Taney marked the end of a legal conflict that raged during the Panic of 1837; the decision also marked the beginning of the Court's stand on foreign corporations, the beginning of economic nationalism, and the beginning of the peculiar American attitude toward control of economic forces.

The case arose out of Joseph Earl's refusal in Mobile, Alabama, to pay a bill of exchange to the Bank of Augusta. Earle contended that out-of-state banking corporations were forbidden by the Alabama Constitution, which gave the state bank a monopoly. Earle also tried the same trick on the New Orleans and Carollton Railroad Company, a banking corporation. The Bank of Augusta brought suit in circuit court, and newly appointed Justice John McKinley of Huntsville decided in favor of Earle. His decision was based on two points: first, he agreed with Earle that the Alabama Constitution prohibited out-of-state banks from doing business within the state; second, he argued that the international legal theory of comity (i.e., respect for the laws of another jurisdiction within one's own territory) did not apply and that corporations cannot operate outside the jurisdiction of the legislative body that created them (the so-called restrictive theory of corporations).

Not too surprisingly, given the loophole offered by McKinley's decision, a man named William Primrose refused to honor a bill of exchange on the Bank of the United States, a bank operating under a charter from the state of Pennsylvania. Since most banks, including the Bank of Augusta, suspended payment during the Panic of 1837, a legal basis for refusing to pay on bills of exchange would have been a boon to cotton factors and merchants. The panic

ended quickly, however; "flush times" returned; and Earle's device was no longer needed. The case went to the Supreme Court on a writ of error, Justice Joseph Story noting that McKinley's decision had "frightened half of the lawyers and all the corporations of the country out of their proprieties."

The Court considered these cases together. Although touching on McKinley's first point—the language of the Alabama constitution—the focus of the arguments and of Taney's decision was the question of comity and the related problem of the "restrictive" theory of corporations. This theory holds that the corporation has no extraterritorial existence; it is created as a legal entity and cannot exist beyond the jurisdiction of its creating authority. This theory had evolved in the seventeenth and eighteenth centuries as a corollary to the special, privileged nature of corporations. The competing "liberal" theory of corporations, on the other hand, holds that once chartered, the corporation may move from the area of jurisdiction in which it was created. Proponents of this theory, which is implicitly accepted today, admit its somewhat illogical basis—for it amounts to extraterritorial legislation—but point to its practicality. In 1839, the terms "liberal" and "restrictive" were not applied this way, but the arguments before the Court accepted and even defined these concepts.

Daniel Webster, arguing for the Second Bank of the United States, took the liberal point of view, contending that once created a corporation was free to move about and was, in fact, a citizen under the Constitution. This entitled corporations to the benefits of the privileges and immunities clause (Article IV, Section 2) of the U.S. Constitution: "The Citizens of each State shall be entitled to all Privileges and Immunities of Citizens in the several States." Charles Jared Ingersoll argued, for James Earle, the "restrictive" theory: "Corporations are creations of municipal law, having no existence or power to contract whatever, until enabled so to do by a law, or other legitimate permission of the sovereignty wherever acting. Especially is this conservative principle indispensable as an undelegated right of these United States. Otherwise the smallest member of this union may legislate for and govern all the rest." The other arguments before the Court ran along the same lines, the major variation being the argument of attorney David B. Ogden, who claimed that comity was an implicit binding principle between states. The principle of comity, though used in conjunction with the liberal theory of corporations, was really an independent argument that did not consider corporate law.

In his decision, Taney took advantage of the principle of comity to avoid confronting a choice between the restrictive and liberal theories. He denied that corporations were citizens and agreed that laws, including corporate charters, did not have extraterritoriality. But he held that comity was implicitly accepted by every state, and unless it was explicitly repudiated, the Court had to assume its existence.

Interpretations of the meaning of his decision have varied greatly due to its avoidance of issues and inherent ambiguity. After all, Taney rejected the liberal practice. This has led one recent commentator to plead for a revision of the theory and for an end to the deplorable difference between theory and practice. Other commentators see Taney's decision as a brilliant acceptance of the liberal theory of corporations and his conceding to states the right to repudiate comity as a sensible approach to corporate regulation. At the time of his decision, Alabamians saw it as an encroachment upon their rights; Justice John McKinley, in his dissenting opinion, saw the Court as imputing national power to the states. The old Federalists saw the decision as a boon to corporations; Justice Story congratulated Taney on the decision and said it did "honor" to Taney and the Court—no doubt thinking of the Federalist Marshall Court. Recent writers have seen the case as laying the foundations for the nonregulatory state after the Civil War, while some see it as a causal factor in the growth of corporate capitalism. Finally, some see it as a concession to the *status quo*, neither retarding

nor creating institutional, economic, or legal change.

But the most significant impact of the case is in its legitimizing and institutionalizing of the concept of positive regulation. This position was hinted at by McKinley in his dissenting opinion: "[The] Court having . . . conceded that Alabama might make laws to prohibit foreign banks to make contracts, thereby admitted, by implication, that she could make laws to permit such contracts. I think it would have been proper to have left the power there, to be exercised or not, as Alabama, in her sovereign discretion, might judge best for her interest or comity." In other words, McKinley sketched two approaches to regulating corporations: one gave the state the power to forbid, the other gave the state the power to permit. Put another way, one required positive effort on the part of the state to regulate, the other having implied regulation, required positive effort to allow corporate action. The first is the concept of positive regulation, the other, negative regulation. By approving the concept of positive regulation, Taney set the stage for continuing efforts of the state to police corporations, with laxness on the part of the state often allowing dangerous corporate freedom. Had the negative regulation concept been sanctioned, the corporation would be required to ask permission for all actions, a change that would put the state automatically in control of corporate action. Thus, the implications and long-range effects of this case are still being felt, even though these effects change with the economy. And what was once a regulatory and egalitarian point of view has become an antiregulatory and privileged position.

There are three levels of cultural context within which to view *Bank of Augusta v. Earle*: (1) the integrated commercial-political structure of Alabama as the participants themselves viewed it; (2) the nature of institutional growth and change in the period from today's perspective; and (3) the broader patterns of economic growth and change, again seen from today's point of view.

The best, and most entertaining, way to find how the actors perceived their own environment may be to review the writings of the southwestern humorist, lawyer, and legislator,

Joseph G. Baldwin. Widely known and appreciated by his fellow Alabamians for his wit and insight, Baldwin saw the economic world as one of "humbug" and deception, with paper money and corporations at its false base. Also, William Garrett, the secretary of state of Alabama, later described the carnival atmosphere connected with bank affairs, thus corroborating Baldwin's views.

More attention has been devoted to the second level of explanation. It describes, from a modern point of view, the institutions of the period, especially those of corporations. It emphasized the lack of banking facilities in Mobile (there were two), and this created difficulties for the merchants and factors in the busy cotton-exporting port. Until 1836, corporations, as governmental agencies, were chartered mainly for public services, schools, and hospitals "to facilitate the growth, prosperity, and welfare of the community." The pace of incorporation speeded up in 1836, and a state bank was finally chartered in hopes of stopping currency drain and loss of profits to other states. The bank's key role in public policy indicates its political, economic, and public importance, a role approximated by that of Alabama's state-owned bank. It is small wonder, then, that Alabama felt threatened by out-of-state banks. The Bank of Augusta, with one-sixth of its stock reserved for the state, was a good source of income for Georgia, although even it had to suspend payments in the Panic of 1837.

The third level of explanation provides a description of broad movements in the economy and attempts to measure the effects of government intervention. Quantitatively, little money was spent by government agencies in the nineteenth century (about 2.4 percent of gross national product in 1839). This small amount was highly significant in causing economic growth because of the way in which it was spent—in specific and direct support to selected industry; in risk-taking, innovation, and bottleneck removing; and in creating a favorable economic climate and thereby raising the expectations of the private sector.

Because southern cotton was the major American export, fluctuations in its price caused fluctuations in the American economy and, when the fall of cotton prices in 1837 was joined by the drop in western land sales, a major depression set in. Interregional and international trade depended on money transfer through bills of exchange. Because of these factors, Taney's decision could have easily wrecked the American economy had it been against the plaintiff. One cannot claim Taney's decision caused the corporate and economic growth of the nineteenth century, but certainly it provided the foundation of federal policy and legitimized the basis of the American economy.

It will remain unclear whether *Bank of Augusta* was the result of James Earle just trying to pull a slippery maneuver during the Panic of 1837 or whether the case represented the result of a long struggle in Alabama. The national importance of the case has obscured its origins and, if it were not for the broader patterns described above, the case would seem almost like a random occurrence. The accounts of Garrett and Baldwin make clear that the panic of 1837 was perceived as a result of Andrew Jackson's fiscal policies. Perhaps Earle's maneuver was viewed as another attempt to fight back against the false paper corporations. Clearly, the panic and the following depression caused some desperate economic behavior in the West, and westerners were not reluctant to try any expedient. Possibly the most important aspect of this case is its relationship to the attempt of Alabama to control corporations in its local economy, from the state bank chartered by the constitution in 1822 to the state's obvious lack of control over various external factors in 1848. If the experience of Pennsylvania is at all typical, most states lost control of their quasi-public corporations; the image that emerges is of the states holding a tigerish economy by the tail.

Perhaps one of the most significant elements in this case was the newly appointed justice, John McKinley. McKinley, a native of Culpepper County, Virginia, was a Huntsville resident who distinguished himself first in the U.S. Senate and later in the House. "He was," in the words of his only biographer, "a man of high and noble aims, possessed of remarkable force and energy. In appearance he was tall and commanding, with a countenance that exhibited great strength of character, and wore an habitual benevolent expression. . . ." His dissent in *Bank of Augusta v. Earle*, essentially a recasting of his circuit court opinion, remains a fitting monument to his life. Upholding the restrictive theory of foreign corporations and the rights of Alabama, McKinley's decision radically ignored the dependence of the national economy on bills of exchange. He perceived a difference between Jacksonian principles and contemporary practice and opted in favor of principles.

All of the lawyers who argued this case before the Court were well known in their day, but, with the exception of Daniel Webster, their significance seems to have faded. The name of Charles Jared Ingersoll, Philadelphia poet, playwright, historian, and lawyer, was once a rallying standard for the enemies of large corporations, money powers, and other unpopular causes. Described to his grandson as "sharp and incisive as a hatchet," he was noted for his enmity toward John Sergeant and his eccentric penchant for wearing costumes of the Revolution. Little fame remains of this once controversial and eccentric character.

Daniel Webster was an archetypal lawyer, and there is more material on him than on anyone else involved in this case. In his published letters, the only reference Webster makes to the Court before which he argued this case is blasé, "the business before the court is not now great, nor is the court itself what it has been." His main concern was over his upcoming European trip. Yet, one Webster biographer claimed that this case was one of Webster's "most important banking and corporation cases."

Representing the Second Bank along with Webster was John Sergeant, the Second Bank's chief legal political adviser and Ingersoll's enemy. Somewhat surprisingly, David B. Ogden, who represented the Bank of Augusta with a states-sovereignty-comity argument, was a well-known Federalist. In a famous argument, he once said, "We deny . . . there is any such thing as a sovereign state." Little is known about William J. Vande Gruff, the lawyer who defended Primrose, except that his last name was likely spelled Vandergraff. Nineteenth-century Supreme Court reporters frequently misspelled the names of litigants.

The composition of the Supreme Court in 1839 was truly Jacksonian: only Story, appointed by President Madison, and McKinley, appointed by President Van Buren, were not Jackson appointees. The key to understanding the Court of Jackson appointees is Chief Justice Roger B. Taney. For five generations, the Taney patriarchs had purchased plantations for their sons, but in Roger's generation this was no longer feasible or profitable; thus he went to college and became a lawyer, a sign of changing times and a changing economy. Taney apparently distinguished carefully between "great moneyed corporations," which he hated, and "normal" corporations, if still very large, which he could abide.

In *Bank of Augusta v. Earle*, Taney steered a middle course between polar positions, denying a corporation's extraterritorial existence, yet circumventing this by implied consent through comity.

The best criticism of Taney's decision came in McKinley's dissenting opinion. Using the restrictive theory of corporations, McKinley claimed, "This is the first time since the adoption of the Constitution of the United States, that any federal Court has, directly or indirectly imputed national power to any of the states of the Union." Governor Bagby of Alabama seconded McKinley's reaction. The Court's decision, he claimed, was a "palpable and direct encroachment upon the sovereignty of Alabama."

Two remarks in letters written by Story stand as evidence of the fear McKinley's decision created and the relief of Taney's decision. Story, in a letter to Charles Sumner, of June 1838, writes, "My brother, McKinley, has recently made a most sweeping decision in the Circuit Court of Alabama which has frightened half of the lawyers and all the corporations of the country out of their proprieties. . . . What say you to all this? So we go!" In a letter to Taney after the case, Story writes, "Your opinion in the corporation cases has given very general satisfaction to the public; and I hope you will allow me to say that I think it does great honor to yourself as well as the court." The only personal reaction on the losing side of the case, other than in McKinley's dissenting decision, is a letter written to Ingersoll by a Mr.

Gilpin in which Ingersoll "was told in reply that he should not be worried at his inability to defeat a corporation, when the whole country had to bear them, as Sinbad had his burden."

Many scholars see in Taney's decision the foundations of corporate growth in the nineteenth century. In one view, this decision and Taney's other corporate decisions demonstrated how "law lent its weight to the thrust of ambitions" in the nineteenth century. Another author claims that the decision encouraged the "commercial harmony" of the country while the long-range result "was decidedly to encourage corporate expansion." Finally, another scholar of the period claims that *Bank of Augusta v. Earle* laid the "legal foundation" of the "promotional, non-regulatory state of post-Civil War America." On balance, the legacy of Taney's implied comity doctrine, which introduced the concept of positive regulation, has been responsible for the continuing difficulty in governmental control of corporate behavior. Thus, corporate behavior is implicitly sanctioned, while regulation has become, at best, a rear-guard attempt to follow the economy.

Selected Bibliography

Baxter, M. *Daniel Webster and the Supreme Court.* Amherst, MA: University of Massachusetts Press, 1966.

Hurst, J. W. *Law and the Conditions of Freedom in the Nineteenth Century United States.* Madison, WI: University of Wisconsin Press, 1967.

Swisher, C.B. *The Taney Period, 1836–64.* New York: Macmillan, 1974.

THE SCOPE OF ADMIRALTY JURISDICTION

by James W. Ely, Jr.
School of Law
Vanderbilt University

Propeller Genesee Chief v. Fitzhugh, 12 Howard 443 (1851) [U.S. Supreme Court]

A nighttime collision between two ships on Lake Ontario afforded an opportunity for the U.S. Supreme Court to reconsider the scope of federal judicial authority under the admiralty clause of the U.S. Constitution. The result was a significant extension of admiralty jurisdiction to encompass navigable fresh water lakes and rivers.

Admiralty jurisdiction in England was limited to waters within the ebb and flow of the tide. An acceptance of this doctrine in the United States would have precluded an exercise of federal admiralty power in the Great Lakes and the extensive chain of inland rivers. Dissatisfaction with the traditional rule mounted as the country grew in size, and commerce on western lakes and rivers increased rapidly. Yet shipping on lakes and rivers was governed by a patchwork of often inconsistent state laws, and cases were tried in state courts. Anxious to promote trade on the interior waterways, Congress enacted a statute in 1845 extending the jurisdiction of the federal courts to certain cases arising on the Great Lakes and rivers connecting them. The constitutionality of this measure was soon put to a test.

In May 1847, the steamboat *Genesee Chief* hit and sank the *Cuba*, a schooner engaged in transporting wheat. The owners of the *Cuba* filed an action for damages in the U.S. district court. They alleged that the accident was caused by the negligence of the *Genesee Chief*'s crew. Their lawsuit was instituted under the 1845 act. The owners of the *Genesee Chief* blamed the mishap on the *Cuba*. More important, the owners also argued that the collision occurred within New York waters and, consequently, the federal court had no jurisdiction over the case.

The district court judge ruled in favor of the owners of the *Cuba* and the owners of the *Genesee Chief* appealed to the circuit court. When the tribunal affirmed the decree, the owners of the *Genesee Chief* carried their case to the Supreme Court. The attorneys for the

Genesee Chief advanced a states' rights position. They argued that the 1845 act was unconstitutional because there was no basis for admiralty jurisdiction. Further, the statute did not purport to regulate commerce between the states and, thus, could not be upheld by virtue of the commerce clause.

Chief Justice Roger B. Taney skillfully led the Supreme Court to sustain the validity of the 1845 act and thereby enlarged federal admiralty jurisdiction. In a blow to states' rights sentiment, Taney first concluded that the statute dealt with the reach of judicial authority and could not be upheld as a regulation of commerce. He then turned to the thorny issue of federal admiralty jurisdiction. The Constitution simply provided that the judicial power should extend "to all cases of admiralty or maritime jurisdiction." The crucial question was the extent of this authority.

The Supreme Court, in the *Thomas Jefferson*, an 1825 opinion by Justice Joseph Story, had adopted the traditional English rule restricting admiralty jurisdiction to tidal waters. To undercut this precedent, Taney began his analysis by stressing the differences between England and the United States with respect to maritime commerce. In England, there were no major rivers or lakes beyond the ebb and flow of the tide, so courts might naturally equate tidewater with navigation. Such a restrictive definition was entirely unsuitable in the United States with its "thousands of miles of public navigable water, including lakes and rivers in which there is no tide." Taney characterized the Great Lakes as "in truth inland seas." According to the chief justice, admiralty jurisdiction depended on "the navigable character of the water, and not upon the ebb and flow of the tide."

Taney then explained that the 1825 decision was rendered "when the commerce on the rivers of the west and on the lakes was in its infancy, and of little importance. . . ." The chief justice also stressed that Congress had recognized a broad scope for admiralty jurisdiction by enacting the measure under review. He proceeded to overrule the earlier decision on the ground that it "was founded in error," and he thus upheld the constitutionality of the 1845

act. Turning to the facts of the pending case, Taney found that there was evidence of carelessness on the part of the *Genesee Chief*'s crew. Consequently, the decree of the circuit court was affirmed.

Only Justice Peter V. Daniel dissented. An ardent champion of states' rights, he maintained that the admiralty power of the federal courts was determined by the English practice at the time the Constitution was adopted. Moreover, Daniel expressed sharp disagreement with Taney's method of analysis, declaring that the Constitution could not be enlarged "according to the opinions of the judiciary, entertained upon their views of expediency and necessity."

It is difficult to exaggerate the significance of the *Genesee Chief* decision for American commerce and navigation. Indeed, Charles Warren observed that "few decisions had ever produced so revolutionary a change in Federal jurisdiction. . . ." Technically, the Supreme Court concluded only that the 1845 act was within the constitutional grant of admiralty power, but the rejection of the tidal waters doctrine had wider implications. As a result of *Genesee Chief*, shipping on inland lakes and rivers was regulated by uniform federal admiralty principles. This, in turn, encouraged the extension of commercial activity throughout the country.

The decision in *Genesee Chief* offers valuable insights into the workings of the Supreme Court under Taney's leadership. Although supposedly less nationalistic than his predecessor, John Marshall, Taney was prepared to greatly extend federal power in appropriate circumstances. Moreover, Taney demonstrated that he was no blind adherent to the principle of *stare decisis*. His opinion in *Genesee Chief* was apparently only the second Supreme Court opinion to overrule a prior constitutional ruling.

In addition, Taney was willing to accommodate legal doctrine to the emergence of new technology. The invention of the steamboat revolutionized travel on inland waterways and rendered the restrictive tidal rule obsolete. Indeed, Taney observed that "until the discovery of steamboats, there could be nothing like foreign commerce upon waters with an unchanging current resisting the upward passage." Like his opinion in *Charles River Bridge v. Warren Bridge* (1837), *Genesee Chief* exemplified the impact of technology on the growth of law.

Selected Bibliography

Conover, M. "The Abandonment of the 'Tidewater' Concept of Admiralty Jurisdiction in the United States." *Oregon Law Review* 38 (Dec. 1958): 34–53.

Currie, D.P. "The Constitution in the Supreme Court: Article IV and Federal Powers, 1836–64." *Duke Law Journal* 1983 (Sept. 1983): 695–747.

Lewis, W. *Without Fear or Favor: A Biography of Chief Justice Roger Brooke Taney*. Boston: Houghton Mifflin Co., 1965.

Swisher, C.B. *History of the Supreme Court of the United States. Volume 5: The Taney Period, 1836–64*. New York: Macmillan Publishing Co., Inc., 1974.

Warren, C. *The Supreme Court in United States History. II, 1836–1918*. Rev. ed. Boston: Little, Brown & Co., 1926.

Wiecek, W.M. *Liberty Under Law: The Supreme Court in American Life*. Baltimore: Johns Hopkins University Press, 1988.

"A SORE GRIEVANCE" TO THE TRAVELER

by Elizabeth B. Monroe
Department of History
Indiana University—
Purdue University at Indianapolis

West River Bridge Company v. Dix, 6 Howard 507 (1848) [U.S. Supreme Court]

In 1842, Joseph Dix and 54 other petitioners of Brattleboro and Dummerston, Vermont, spoke of "a sore grievance" to the traveler to describe the nearby toll bridge over the West River. In their petition, Dix and his fellow-citizens requested that the county court follow the procedures of a recent state statute that provided for public takeover of "any real estate, easement, or franchise" when "the public good requires a public highway." According to the statute, courts could take such private property providing the owner was compensated for the loss. In answer to the petition, the Windham County Court appointed a commission to examine the matter. In May 1843, the commissioners reported that the bridge should be taken for public use and that the towns of Brattleboro and Dummerston should pay the West River Bridge Company $4,000 for the bridge, tollhouse, two acres of land, and the franchise. Both of the towns and the bridge company filed objections to the commissioners' findings. In November, the county court heard arguments but accepted the commissioners' report and assessed the two towns for payments to the bridge company.

In 1844, the Vermont Supreme Court reviewed the constitutional issues of the case. Attorneys for the bridge company stated that their client had received its charter from the Vermont legislature in 1795 and that this charter was a contract. Their client had agreed to build and maintain the bridge at its own expense, and, in exchange, the legislature had granted it the privilege of collecting tolls for 100 years. The bridge company had fulfilled its obligations and conformed to all of the requirements of the charter. The attorneys argued that according to the Vermont Constitution, revoking their client's charter required specific action by the legislature or by a jury trial at common law. Since the 1839 statute did not provide for either of these procedures, it appeared to violate the state constitution. Because the statute infringed on the bridge proprietor's charter, it also appeared, on its face, to violate the U.S. Constitution, which proscribed state impairment of contractual obligations. The defendants' attorneys contended that the statute was constitutional and that the county court proceedings had conformed to the statute. The Vermont Supreme Court decided in favor of the defendants: it ruled that the statute was valid for the purpose of revoking the franchise in order to create a free public highway; and it held that the proceedings were a lawful exercise of the eminent domain authority of the state. Therefore, the state supreme court held that the statute did not violate either the Vermont or U.S. Constitution.

Eminent domain had been used during the colonial period to condemn private property for public highways, ferry-ways, and bridges. In the early national period, eminent domain continued to be used for state takings of private property for public use. Public demand for better transportation facilities also compelled state legislatures to grant corporate charters to investors who agreed to meet public transportation needs in exchange for the ability to collect tolls for a period of years. But, by the second quarter of the nineteenth century, many corporations had collected tolls far in excess of their construction and maintenance costs. Other corporations had charters conferring long-term monopolies along important lines of travel. As a result, by the 1830s the public perceived outstanding charters as burdens and impediments to future transportation development and demanded the termination of extensive privileges. State legislatures soon invoked their powers of eminent domain to condemn existing charter rights in order to create free access to transportation improvements and to expedite replacement of old technologies with new ones.

The bridge company appealed to the U.S. Supreme Court and retained Daniel Webster and Jacob Collamer as counsel. Samuel S. Phelps represented the defendants. The Court heard the arguments of the two sides in early 1848. Webster and Collamer contended that the power of eminent domain reached only real and personal property. According to these legal luminaries, a corporate franchise was not property, but was "pure franchise." Therefore, it was not available for taking. Even if eminent domain could reach franchises, the contract clause (Article I, Section 10) of the U.S. Constitution barred such action. On the other hand, Phelps argued that eminent domain was an indispensable attribute of sovereignty, limited only in its application by "public use" and "just compensation" restrictions. The county court's expropriation of the West River Bridge and the company's charter complied with these restrictions. There remained only the question of the superiority of the contract clause. According to Phelps, every grant from the state was subject to eminent domain. While the contract clause protected the grantee from legislative bad faith, it could not protect private property from the sovereign power to provide for public purposes.

Justice Peter V. Daniel wrote the opinion for the Supreme Court. He accepted the view that the charter was a contract, but he declared that it contained implicit as well as explicit terms. Among the former was the state's power of eminent domain, for "it cannot be justly disputed, that in every political sovereign community there inheres necessarily the right and the duty of guarding its own existence, and of protecting and promoting the interest and welfare of the community at large." Eminent domain was "paramount to all private rights vested under the government" and "in no wise interfere[d] with the inviolability of contracts." According to the Court, the internal improvement policy of the country rested on this power which condemned private property for public use. Franchises were merely one form of property, and there was "nothing peculiar to a franchise which can class it higher or render it more sacred than other property." Vermont's exercise of eminent domain to extinguish the West River Bridge franchise did not violate the U.S. Constitution.

Daniel recognized that government must continue to meet changing public needs, even at the expense of private property. In *West River Bridge Company v. Dix*, he found the state power of eminent domain superior to the constitutional protection of private property by the contract clause. By the late nineteenth century, when public concern shifted to the need to regulate private property "affected with a public interest," courts returned to Daniel's reasoning in *West River Bridge* to uphold state exercise of reserved police powers.

Selected Bibliography

Frank, J.P. *Justice Daniel Dissenting: A Biography of Peter V. Daniel, 1784–1860*. Cambridge, MA: Harvard University Press, 1964.

Scheiber, H.N. "The Road to *Munn*: Eminent Domain and the Concept of Public Purpose in the State Courts." *Perspectives in American History* 5 (1971): 329–402.

DESTRUCTIVE CREATION

by Gordon Morris Bakken
Department of History
California State University at Fullerton

California v. Gold Run Ditch and Mining Company, 66 Cal. 318 (1884) [California Supreme Court]

Gold mining in the American West pushed the creative fervor of technology to ecologically destructive ends. Hydraulic mining quickly developed with a gospel of efficiency to produce more gold more quickly than by other methods. Huge supplies of water were appropriated and channeled a great distance into high pressure nozzles aimed at the gold-bearing hillsides of the motherlode country of California. These monstrous streams of water slashed away dirt, sand, grass, trees, gravel, and a little gold. They also created floods of mud slopping into sluices. Gold was rapidly obtained and the topography was brutally altered. Profit was obtained, but downstream the mud cascaded into channels of trade and onto fertile agricultural fields.

The hydraulic mining caused the channels of the American and Sacramento rivers to begin to fill. The filth fouled Suisun Bay and swirled into the San Francisco Bay and San Pablo Bay. The bed of the American River oozed up ten to 12 feet, and the Sacramento ascended by six to 12 feet. The river channels widened and the spring floods invaded the rich farm lands of the delta, destroying more acreage every year. Deep-draught-river steamers could no longer navigate to Sacramento City except during the spring flood season. Commerce and agriculture were clearly impaired, and victims looked to the law for recourse. Ultimately, on behalf of many victims, the state sued the mining company.

The California Supreme Court in *California v. Gold Run Ditch and Mining Company* took judicial notice of the navigation of the Sacramento River as "a great public highway." As a public highway, the people had "paramount and controlling rights" including "a right to use the water flowing over it, for the purposes of transportation and commercial intercourse." The law provided that "an unauthorized invasion of the rights of the public to navigate the water fouling over the soil is a public nuisance; and an

unauthorized encroachment upon the soil itself is known in law as a purpresture." The law of the case was based on English law (particularly on Sir Edward Coke's *Institutes of the Laws of England*) and state cases decided in the eastern states.

The court also dispensed with the defendant's argument regarding identifying the company's debris amid the turbid waters. Why should one hydraulic mining operation be stopped when the pollution is the aggregate product of many hydraulic miners and the forces of nature? The court reminded counsel that it had recently decided that in equity proceedings involving an action to abate a public or private nuisance, "all persons engaged in the commission of the wrongful acts which constitute the nuisance may be enjoined, jointly and severally." It was the nuisance that would be enjoined if it were found to be destructive of public or private rights in property.

The mining company also argued that it had gained a right to pollute by custom, by prescription, and by the statute of limitations. The law protected enterprise regardless of the impact of the operations on businesses. It was quite clear that it had been the custom of miners from the earliest days to use water in placer mining and to allow the debris to fall where it may in the process. Based on these customs, many mining corporations had invested heavily in the process of hydraulic mining. They deserved the protection of the law in the pursuit of profit. The *Gold Run* court clearly rejected the implications of the argument and turned the essence of the common law on its claimants. "But a legitimate private business," the court wrote, "founded upon a local custom, may grow into a force to threaten the safety of the people, and destruction to public and private rights; and when it develops into that condition, the custom upon which it is founded becomes unreasonable, because it was dangerous to public and private rights, and could not be invoked to justify the continuance of the business in an unlawful manner." An enterprise, creative and positive in inception, thus, could become destructive of economic development after many years of operation.

Further, the government could not absolve itself of its duty to protect a public trust. While government could authorize uses of the waters and regulate them, it could not alienate the right of the people in their public waterways. Even more certainly, an enterprise could not gain the same position by prescription. There was no right to continue a public nuisance acquired by prescription. The court ordered a perpetual injunction.

Although California's Supreme Court helped end one of mining's greatest environmental abuses, the fight continued across the West. Colorado's supreme court issued a similar injunction as late as 1935, and the fight with the Homestake Mining Company in South Dakota continued into the 1930s. The balanc-ing of enterprise and environment became the focus of the twentieth century, replacing the contest of enterprises of the nineteenth century. Public nuisance and public trust doctrines developed in prior centuries and became increasingly important as environmental interests attacked the threats to ecology posed by mining. As the environmental awareness of the nation increased, the federal government offered legislation to strengthen the law's hand in keeping the government's promise to protect the public trust.

Selected Bibliography

Bakken, G.M. "American Mining Law and the Environment: The Western Experience." *Western Legal History* 1 (1988): 211–36.

Kelley, R.L. *Gold vs. Grain: The Hydraulic Mining Controversy in California's Sacramento Valley*. Glendale, CA: Arthur H. Clark, 1959.

Smith, D.A. *Mining America: The Industry and the Environment, 1800–1980*. Lawrence, KS: University of Kansas Press, 1987.

POLITICS VS. PRECEDENTS: THE INCOME TAX CASES

by Maxwell Bloomfield
Columbus School of Law
Catholic University of America

Pollock v. Farmers' Loan & Trust Company, 157 U.S. 429 and 158 U.S. 601 (1895)
[U.S. Supreme Court]

Judicial decisions seldom pulse with emotion. Especially in the late nineteenth century, when judges professed to be objective scientists, they wrote opinions that aimed at a dry-as-dust technical precision. On occasion, however, cases arose that tore away the judicial mask and revealed the nonrational aspects of decisionmaking. One such episode occurred in 1894, when Congress passed an income tax law that threatened to redistribute the nation's wealth in a significant way. The resulting litigation raised important, and still unresolved, questions concerning the separation of powers and the limits of judicial review.

Congress imposed the first income tax in 1861, at the start of the Civil War, and followed it with eight other income tax measures within a decade. Graduated rates were in effect during wartime; by 1865 they ranged from five percent on incomes of $600 to $5,000 up to 10 percent on incomes above $10,000. Although postwar Congresses lowered the rates and abandoned the graduation principle, they continued to enact new income tax laws until 1870. Opponents challenged this legislation four times in federal courts; but the U.S. Supreme Court in each instance upheld congressional power, except for taxes levied on the salaries of state officials.

In 1872, a revenue surplus enabled conservative critics to block further income taxation. Thereafter, the federal government relied exclusively on tariffs and domestic duties on consumer items to meet its financial needs. This regressive tax system severely burdened lower income groups, and contributed to a climate of continuing economic instability that culminated in the Panic of 1893. The following year, in the wake of massive unemployment and farmer protest, a coalition of Democrats and Populists from the Midwest and South pushed through Congress a new income tax law as part of a tariff reform package.

The Wilson-Gorman Tariff Act of 1894 proposed to make substantial reductions in existing tariff rates, and to compensate for the resulting revenue loss by imposing a tax of two percent on all personal income above $4,000. Corporations would be taxed at the same rate on any profits they made beyond operating expenses. Although protectionists in the Senate managed to restore most tariff cuts through multiple amendments, Republicans and conservative Democrats were unable to defeat the income tax provisions of the bill. In this mutilated form, the measure became law on August 28, 1894, without the signature of President Grover Cleveland, who was deeply disappointed at the failure of tariff revision.

Frustrated in their legislative efforts, opponents of the income tax now sought to prevent its collection with the help of the courts. At first, however, their chances of obtaining an early judicial hearing appeared negligible. An 1867 statute prohibited any advance interference with the collection of a federal tax; only after a person had paid such a tax under protest could he challenge its constitutionality in a lawsuit. Despite this prescribed procedure, ex-Senator George F. Edmunds of Vermont launched a test case in the District of Columbia in mid-December. Edmunds's client, taxpayer John G. Moore, sought an injunction from a federal district judge to restrain the collector of internal revenue from collecting an allegedly unconstitutional tax.

Correctly perceiving that Edmunds's frontal assault was unlikely to succeed, a shrewd New York attorney devised a more subtle strategy for striking down the income tax before it could affect any pocketbooks. William D. Guthrie, at 35 already a partner in a prestigious Wall Street firm, proposed to evade statutory restrictions by raising the tax issue in a private suit that did not directly involve tax collecting. Guthrie first persuaded the boards of directors of two major New York trust companies to announce that they were setting aside funds to pay the tax. He then found two stockholders willing to pose as plaintiffs in actions to restrain their respective companies from paying an unconstitutional tax. Finally, he arranged with Lawrence Maxwell, the solicitor general of the United States, to expedite the passage of the cases through the federal courts.

The income tax law went into effect on January 1, 1895. Guthrie filed his suits in a New York circuit court on January 19, and Maxwell promptly entered demurrers (i.e., formal declarations that the facts as alleged did not create a legal cause of action). On January 24, the court sustained the government's position without opinion, and the cases were ready for appeal to the U.S. Supreme Court. Four days later Maxwell performed his last friendly service for Guthrie. Without consulting either the president or Attorney General Richard Olney, he induced the Court to revise its calendar so as to hear opening arguments in all three pending tax cases on the first Monday in March. When Olney learned of this arrangement, which left the government with little time to prepare its case, he reacted with a furious outburst that sparked Maxwell's immediate resignation.

Contemporary observers were generally aware of the collusive—some called it conspiratorial—nature of these proceedings. Perhaps to reassure the public that both sides would be fairly represented, the indefatigable Guthrie persuaded the Continental Trust Company, one of the defendants, to employ James C. Carter as its counsel. Carter, a leading New York practitioner, was a past president of the American Bar Association and an advocate of unquestioned integrity. He joined Attorney General Olney and Assistant Attorney General Edward B. Whitney, both hardworking and competent lawyers, in defending the constitutionality of the income tax.

To challenge the law, Guthrie assembled an even more impressive team. Besides himself, this included Clarence Seward, the distinguished head of his law firm, George Edmunds, and—at a reportedly extravagant fee—Joseph Hodges Choate, the most famous legal orator and trial lawyer of the time. Popular interest in the fate of the tax ensured that the approaching litigation would receive nationwide press coverage.

On March 7, oral arguments began before an eight-member Supreme Court (Justice Howell E. Jackson did not participate because of serious illness) headed by Melville W. Fuller, a former corporation attorney. Spectators, including congressmen, lawyers, and the general public, crowded into the courtroom in the Capitol—once the Senate Chamber—to listen to the debate, which lasted five days.

At issue was the meaning of several key tax provisions in the Constitution. Article I, Section 8, gave Congress the power "to lay and collect taxes, duties, imposts, and excises, to pay the debts and provide for the common defense and general welfare of the United States." But in exercising this sweeping authority, Congress had to follow prescribed procedures. A "capitation, or other direct tax" had to be apportioned among the states on the basis of population, while duties, imposts, and excises had to be "uniform throughout the United States." The briefs raised two questions that dominated the oral arguments: (1) was an income tax a direct tax? and (2) if not, did the exemptions provided in the Wilson-Gorman Act violate the principle of uniformity?

In response to the first question, the defenders of the income tax could rely on an unbroken chain of supportive judicial precedents and legislative practices that stretched back to the beginnings of the Republic. From *Hylton v. United States* (1796) to *Springer v. United States* (1881), the Supreme Court had consistently maintained that the only direct taxes were those levied on lands or persons—subjects found in every state and capable of assessment according to census figures. The *Springer* precedent was particularly relevant, since in that case a unanimous Court had upheld a similar income tax after hearing exhaustive arguments from counsel. Moreover, Congress had always followed these judicial guidelines. It had imposed direct taxes on three occasions—in 1798, 1812, and 1861—to meet wartime emergencies; and each time it had taxed only land and its fixtures. To overturn a constitutional exposition almost coeval with the Constitution itself, urged Olney, would "set a hurtful precedent and go far to prove that government by written constitution is not a thing of stable principles, but of the fluctuating views and wishes of the particular period and the particular judges when and from whom its interpretation happens to be called for."

Since an income tax was not a direct tax, it had only to be assessed in a uniform way to meet constitutional criteria. The term "uniform," argued Olney and his associates, referred to geographical uniformity. Congress could not tax a commodity at one rate on the East Coast and at a different rate in the West. Similarly, Congress had to tax all persons within a particular class of taxpayers at the same time. In establishing categories of taxpayers, however, or in exempting certain classes from the payment of taxes, Congress could claim broad discretionary power under the Constitution. As long as a legislative classification might be reasonably related to a public purpose, Carter insisted, the legislature's action "cannot be reviewed by the judicial tribunals." Thus, when Congress exempted mutual savings banks and other cooperative institutions from the coverage of the Wilson-Gorman bill, it did not act arbitrarily, since it may have wished to promote habits of thrift and self-reliance among a mass of small investors. The wisdom of such a policy was a matter for Congress alone to determine; and Carter warned the Court not to engage in judicial lawmaking over the income tax: "Nothing could be more unwise and dangerous—nothing more foreign to the spirit of the Constitution—than an attempt to baffle and defeat a popular determination by a judgment in a lawsuit. When the opposing forces of sixty millions of people have become arrayed in hostile political ranks upon a question which all men feel is not a question of law, but of legislation, the only path of safety is to accept the voice of the majority as final."

The opposing lawyers split the issues neatly between them for purposes of argument.

Guthrie and Edmunds concentrated on the uniformity question, while Seward and Choate elaborated a new theory of direct taxation that became the controlling element in the Court's decision. In Guthrie's view, a uniform tax had to fall equally on all persons or types of property. "The requirement of approximate equality inheres in the very nature of the power to tax," he maintained; "and it exists whether declared or not in the written constitution." Since the Wilson-Gorman Act, through its arbitrary exemptions, placed the tax burden on less than two percent of the population, it clearly failed the constitutional test. In a more emotional presentation, Edmunds appealed to the Court to strike down this monstrous piece of class legislation by applying the equal protection principle found in the Fourteenth Amendment.

The arguments of Seward and Choate invited the Court to engage in more radical judicial revisionism. The time had come, Seward declared, to correct a century of error by reexamining the meaning of direct taxation, as understood by the founding fathers. In a scholarly analysis that drew upon eighteenth-century dictionaries, economic tracts, and state records, as well as the debates in the Federal Convention, he sought to show that the framers had used the term "direct tax" in a precise way that had later been misunderstood by the courts. When asked by one justice how he could advocate overturning so many precedents, Seward replied: "There is a tradition in the legal profession that once when a suggestion was made to Mr. Lincoln that a judicial decision settled a question, he responded with some firmness that in this country nothing was settled until it was settled right."

Choate's presentation, which closed the arguments, did not disappoint his admirers. With ingenuity and verve he linked the tax issue to states' rights, past and present. Less than two percent of the population paid four-fifths of the income taxes assessed under the 1870 law, he noted; and these wealthy taxpayers all lived in four eastern states—New York, Pennsylvania, Massachusetts, and New Jersey. Using historical sources, he argued that the framers had inserted the direct tax provisions expressly to prevent the exploitation of property owners in a few states through the combined political power of the rest. In a stirring peroration he called on the justices to stand firm in the defense of private property and equality before the law: "If it be true, as my learned friend said in closing, that the passions of the people are aroused on this subject, if it be true that a mighty army of sixty million citizens is likely to be incensed by this decision, it is the more vital to the future welfare of this country that this Court again resolutely and courageously declare, as Marshall did, that it *has* the power to set aside an act of Congress violative of the Constitution, and that it will not hesitate in executing that power, no matter what the threatened consequences of popular or populistic wrath may be" [emphasis in original].

The arguments ended on March 13. During the next three weeks the newspapers speculated at length on the probable outcome of the litigation, analyzing for readers the personal and philosophical backgrounds of the justices. On April 8, Chief Justice Melville W. Fuller announced the opinion of the Court. Speaking for a six-member majority, Fuller reinterpreted the meaning of "direct taxes" in light of the historical data supplied by Seward and Choate. Taxation and representation were inseparably linked in the minds of the framers, he argued. At the Federal Convention, the seaboard states ultimately made enormous tax concessions to the federal government. They gave up their right to tax imports and interstate commerce, and granted Congress concurrent power over all other forms of taxation. In return, however, they sought to safeguard the property of their citizens from despoilment at the hands of political majorities from poorer states. Their chief instrument for this purpose was the direct tax, with its apportionment requirement, which guaranteed that any federal tax on property would fall "upon the immediate constituents of those who imposed it." According to Fuller, the framers anticipated that direct taxes would be imposed only in national emergencies. At all other times, the private property of citizens would fall, as a practical matter, within the exclusive purview of state authority.

But what exactly did the framers mean by a direct tax? Here Fuller read back into the historical record an economic definition that attained popularity only in the nineteenth century. A direct tax, he asserted, was any tax on an individual's property whose burden could not be shifted to a third party; that is, any tax other than a tax on consumption. Such a definition had never been accepted by the federal courts; but Fuller avoided overruling earlier precedents by distinguishing them on narrowly technical grounds, as Choate had suggested. Thus, he pointed out that the *Springer* Court had not considered some of the specific sources of taxable income identified in the Wilson-Gorman Act; hence their constitutionality remained open to question.

Two such undecided issues involved congressional efforts to tax the rents or income from real estate and the income from state or municipal bonds. There was no difference in principle, Fuller maintained, between a tax on land, which everyone agreed was a direct tax, and a tax on the income from land. He ignored the fact that the proposed tax was a general one levied on a person's net income, which was derived from many different and commingled sources. A tax on the income from municipal bonds was also unconstitutional, though for different reasons. It represented an illegal interference with the borrowing power of states and their instrumentalities. The doctrine of intergovernmental tax immunity was well established in the jurisprudence of the late nineteenth century. Just as the Marshall Court had declared in *McCulloch v. Maryland* (1819) that states could not tax the operations of the federal government and its agencies, so the Supreme Court in the decades since the Civil War had applied the same rule to the federal government. Even the dissenting justices in the income tax cases conceded this point. (Only recently, in *South Carolina v. Baker* (1988), has the Rehnquist Court overruled this part of the *Pollock* decision by holding that Congress may impose a nondiscriminatory tax on the income from state bonds.)

Up to this point in Fuller's opinion it seemed that the Court was going to strike down the entire income tax law in a piecemeal fashion. But suddenly the chief justice revealed that the majority's consensus had shattered over three remaining questions: (1) did the elimination of the tax on income from land invalidate the rest of the law? (2) was a tax on the income from personal property also a direct tax? and (3) were other provisions, although not direct taxes, nevertheless invalid for lack of uniformity? On these issues the justices divided 4–4, leaving most of the income tax law still in effect.

Fuller's opinion was studiously dispassionate and "scientific." Crammed with citations to other court decisions, it conveyed none of the intense emotionalism that the income tax proposal aroused in liberals and conservatives alike. Much more revealing in this regard was the concurring opinion of Justice Stephen J. Field, whose individualistic philosophy had been forged in the antebellum years. Field denounced the entire income tax as unconstitutional class legislation, concluding with an apocalyptic vision of America's future that might have been lifted from one of the period's popular dystopian novels: "The present assault upon capital is but the beginning. It will be but the stepping-stone to others, larger and more sweeping, till our political contests will become a war of the poor against the rich; a war constantly growing in intensity and bitterness." Such visceral fears may well have influenced other members of the majority as well, despite the resolutely "objective" tone of Fuller's opinion.

The two dissenting justices, while avoiding strident rhetoric, emphasized their profound disagreement with the majority's position. Justice Edward Douglass White, a moderate traditionalist, provided a thorough and penetrating critique of Fuller's logic and methodology. White particularly condemned the majority for ignoring its own controlling precedents in its dubious pursuit of the original intent of the framers. If such judicial activism were legitimate, he warned, "then every question which has been determined in our past history is now still open for judicial reconstruction." Justice John Marshall Harlan, the Court's leading liberal, argued in a brief concurrence that the Court should have refused to hear all three suits, since they violated the jurisdictional guidelines established by Congress.

The decision in *Pollock v. Farmers' Loan & Trust Company*, as the income tax cases were collectively designated in the official reports, pleased neither side. Within a week, Guthrie petitioned the Court for a rehearing on the remaining issues. In reply, the attorney general requested that if a rehearing were granted, it should cover all of the legal and constitutional questions previously argued. The government, he explained, had not expected the direct tax to become a major issue and had not researched the question as carefully as it otherwise would have done. The Court granted both petitions, and set May 6 as the date for reargument. Justice Howell E. Jackson, although far from well, agreed to participate in the rehearing, to prevent any further tie votes.

This time the arguments were more restrained, as each side sought to buttress its position with copious historical data on the nature of eighteenth-century taxation. Only two lawyers were permitted to represent the respective parties. Guthrie and Choate again appeared for the antitax forces, while Olney and Whitney presented the government's case. The Court's first opinion set the parameters of debate in both the briefs and the oral arguments. Olney labored valiantly to convince the Court that a tax on rents was not a tax on land, and that the inclusion of rents with other sources of income did not convert a general income tax into a direct tax. The realty provisions of the law were essential, he believed, to its effective operation, since without them the government would lose a major share of its anticipated revenue. William Waldorf Astor, the wealthiest New York landlord, would, for example, reportedly save $108,000 in taxes if the Court's original decision concerning landed income were not reversed. "Unless the Court can be induced to reconsider that question," Olney informed a legal associate, "what remains of the law is hardly worth preserving."

Although Olney's presentation was lucid and forceful, it was again eclipsed by the artful pleading of Choate. Treating the Court's first decision as fixed and irrevocable, Choate now invited the justices to take the next logical step by declaring that a tax on the income from personal property, like that on the income from realty, constituted a direct tax on the property itself. Alternatively, he urged that the Court's prior invalidation of the tax on rental income required that the rest of the law should be struck down as well, since Congress had not intended

that the remaining taxpayers should bear the full burden of taxation. "The biggest fish," he observed, "have got out through the rent that Your Honors have made in the meshes of the law. Will you allow the little fish to be alone made the victims?"

The arguments went on for three days, ending on May 8. On May 20, the Court handed down its decision before a hushed and expectant audience, many of whom had been waiting for hours for the courtroom doors to open. Once the justices had taken their seats, the chief justice leaned forward and, without any preliminary comment, began to read in a low voice the final majority decision in *Pollock*.

"Whenever this Court is required to pass upon the validity of an act of Congress as tested by the fundamental law enacted by the people," he began, "the duty imposed requires in its discharge the utmost deliberation and care, and invokes the deepest sense of responsibility. And this is especially so when the question involves the exercise of a great governmental power." With this perfunctory nod in the direction of judicial self-restraint, Fuller proceeded to reaffirm the questionable revisionism of his first opinion. Again he insisted that direct taxes were those that fell squarely and inescapably upon property; that the states alone had levied such taxes prior to the Federal Convention; and that the founders expected that the states would continue to meet their revenue needs through direct taxes, while the federal government would rely primarily on tariffs and other indirect taxes on consumption. A land tax was clearly a direct tax, he reiterated; and a tax on the income from land was equally direct, and must be apportioned among the states.

The argument to this point was familiar enough; but Fuller now moved beyond *Pollock I* by ruling that a tax on the income from personal property, including corporate stock, was also a direct tax on the property itself. This conclusion required a leap of creative imagination, since it defied both history and common sense. In the past, Congress had levied direct taxes on land; but it had never attempted to tax personal property directly, even in wartime emergencies. On the other hand, it had passed an early excise tax on carriages, over the strong objections of many who considered it a direct tax requiring apportionment. In *Hylton*, a unanimous Supreme Court had sustained this carriage tax. Justice William Paterson, who had participated in the Federal Convention, explained in his opinion the origins of the direct tax: "The provision was made in favor of the southern States. They possessed a large number of slaves; they had extensive tracts of territory, thinly settled and not very productive. A majority of the States had but few slaves, and several of them a limited territory, well settled, and in a high state of cultivation. The Southern States, if no provision had been introduced in the Constitution, would have been wholly at the mercy of the other States. Congress in such case, might tax slaves, at discretion or arbitrarily, and land in every part of the Union after the same rate or measure; so much a head in the first instance, and so much an acre in the second. To guard them against imposition, in these particulars, was the reason of introducing the clause in the Constitution, which directs that representatives and direct taxes shall be apportioned among the States according to their respective numbers." Fuller attempted to dismiss *Hylton* as involving solely the definition of "excises," but his analysis was as unconvincing as the spurious law-office history concocted by Seward and Choate to explain the "original" meaning of direct taxes.

With the two principal sources of anticipated revenue nevertheless invalidated, the chief justice turned to the remaining tax provisions. While the proposed tax on income from state and municipal bonds could not stand because of intergovernmental tax immunity, taxes on the income from business, professions, or employment were in the nature of excises, and therefore constitutionally permissible. These indirect taxes were minor and dependent parts of a general revenue system, however; without its major props—the realty and personalty provisions—the entire structure must fall. Otherwise, Fuller observed, paraphrasing Choate, "what was intended as a tax on capital would remain in substance a tax on occupations and labor."

As Fuller finished his opinion and looked up from the manuscript, there was perfect stillness in the crowded chamber. Then a few spectators began to clap, until silenced by a gesture

from the marshal. Several reporters squeezed out of the room to get the news to the wire services: the income tax was dead, and there was no possibility of any further legislation, since it would be impossible to apportion such a tax equitably among the states. If two states, for example, had approximately equal populations, each would be assessed the same amount of tax. But if 100 persons with incomes over $4,000 lived in state A, while only 10 persons of such wealth lived in state B, the wealthy residents of state B would have to pay ten times more in incomes taxes than their counterparts in state A. Such pragmatic considerations led the *Hylton* Court to reject the argument that carriage taxes were direct taxes.

The majority in *Pollock II* was even smaller than that in *Pollock I*. Supporting the chief justice were Associate Justices Field, David J. Brewer, George Shiras, Jr., and Horace Gray; while Justices Harlan, White, Jackson, and Henry B. Brown dissented. Each of the dissenters read an opinion. Substantively, their analyses added little to the critique made by White in *Pollock I*; but collectively they testified to the deep concern that each felt over the Court's aggressive activism and its potential consequences for the future.

Harlan's performance was by far the most dramatic. His voice cracking with barely suppressed anger, he assailed the majority for depriving the national government of a vital economic power. What particularly incensed him was that the Court had struck down only the income tax sections of the Tariff Act, although the entire law was intended to form a comprehensive revenue system. As a result, Americans of modest means would continue to pay most of the government's operating expenses through high taxes on consumer goods. "The practical effect of the decision to-day," Harlan concluded, "is to give to certain kinds of property a position of favoritism and advantage inconsistent with the fundamental principles of our social organization, and to invest them with power and influence that may be perilous to the portion of the American people upon whom rests the larger part of the burdens of the government, and who ought not to be subjected to the dominion of aggregated wealth any more than the property of the country should be at the mercy of the lawless." The other three dissenters, although less vehement, were equally outspoken. Brown referred to "the surrender of the taxing power to the moneyed class"; Jackson called the decision "the most disastrous blow ever struck at the constitutional power of Congress"; and White predicted that if Congress should ever attempt to levy an income tax through apportionment, "the red spectre of revolution would shake our institutions to their foundations."

The amending process proved the only practicable way of overturning *Pollock II*, and it took 18 years to accomplish that result. Meanwhile the gap between rich and poor steadily widened, and the federal government experienced novel financial needs as it began to construct the institutions of the modern welfare state. The Sixteenth Amendment, which took effect on February 25, 1913, at last authorized Congress "to lay and collect taxes on incomes, from whatever source derived, without apportionment among the several States, and without regard to any census or enumeration."

In broader terms, the income tax cases point up the political nature of the Supreme Court's work, and the impossibility of neatly separating "legal issues" from the personalities and ideological presuppositions of the justices. Jackson was supposed to be the swingman in *Pollock II*; but his vote had no effect on the outcome of the case, because one of his associates switched sides during the rehearing. The identity of this "vacillating jurist" remains a mystery, although commentators have expended enormous energy and ingenuity in efforts to flush him out. What

matters is not the man but his behavior, which seems to have been motivated more by fear than by reason or logic. Indeed, the same charge might be leveled against the other members of the *Pollock* majority, who took it upon themselves to rewrite the law in conformity with their *laissez-faire* convictions. Judges in any age may sometimes confuse their personal predilections with the mandates of constitutional law. When they do, as *Pollock* demonstrates, no effective institutional remedy exists, apart from the amendment procedure. That procedure Fuller aptly described as "a slow and deliberate process, which gives time for mere hypothesis and opinion to exhaust themselves, and for the sober second thought of every part of the country to be asserted."

Selected Bibliography

Eggert, G.G. "Richard Olney and the Income Tax Cases." *Mississippi Valley Historical Review* 48 (June 1961): 24–41.

Farrelly, D.G. "Justice Harlan's Dissent in the *Pollock* Case." *Southern California Law Review* 24 (Feb. 1951): 175–82.

King, W.L. *Melville Weston Fuller*. New York: Macmillan Co., 1950.

Paul, A.M. *Conservative Crisis and the Rule of Law: Attitudes of Bench and Bar, 1887–95*. Ithaca, NY: Cornell University Press, 1960.

Ratner, S. *American Taxation: Its History as a Social Force in Democracy*. New York: W.W. Norton & Co., 1942.

Swindler, W.F. *Court and Constitution in the Twentieth Century: The Old Legality, 1889–1932*. Indianapolis, IN: Bobbs-Merrill Co., Inc., 1969.

Westin, A.F. "The Supreme Court, the Populist Movement and the Campaign of 1896." *Journal of Politics* 15 (Feb. 1953): 3–41.

NATIONAL POLICE POWERS: THE OLEOMARGARINE CASE

by Fred D. Ragan
Department of History
East Carolina University

McCray v. United States, 195 U.S. 27 (1904) [U.S. Supreme Court]

As the twentieth century began, the U.S. Supreme Court was struggling with cases arising from the enlarged role Congress had begun to play in the economic and social aspects of national life. With *Champion v. Ames* (1903), *McCray v. United States* was prominent in recognizing and expanding national police powers. This expansion came when Congress responded to pressure from dairy interests and in 1902 enacted an excise tax intended to drive a competing product, oleomargarine colored to resemble butter, from the market.

Developed in France during the Napoleonic wars, margarine underwent numerous improvements before being introduced into the United States during the 1870s. Confronted with problems of overproduction and falling commodity prices, agricultural interests fought the unwelcomed competitor. Although an early producer labeled his product "artificial butter," others were less scrupulous and fraud and deception soon plagued the marketplace. In 1877, New York began state regulatory efforts when it passed legislation to protect its farmers from "deception in the sale of butter." Other states followed the example of the Empire State, but consumption continued to increase.

Demanding a national solution to their problem, dairy farmers prevailed on Congress to enact legislation in 1886 designed to control and regulate the oleomargarine industry. The law required a license for manufacturers, wholesalers, and retailers and placed a production tax of two cents per pound. The statute, however, did not address the fundamental reason for oleomargarine's growing popularity: the practice of coloring it to imitate butter in appearance.

Beginning in 1888, the U.S. Supreme Court handed down a series of decisions that arbitrated margarine's destiny. The first rejected Pennsylvania's attempt to prohibit the sale of oleomargarine produced in the state; six years later, the court conceded that although oleomargarine was a legitimate article of commerce, a state could forbid importation of colored oleomargarine, since the intent of coloring was to deceive consumers. Two years later, the Court upheld the 1886 act. Ending its first decade of decisions, the Court concluded that a state could neither bar the sale of oleomargarine delivered and sold in its original package nor require that it be colored pink.

Even as Congress responded to dairy interest demands with the 1886 act, New Jersey and New York enacted legislation to ban the sale of colored oleomargarine. After the Court found the approach acceptable in 1894, other states rapidly followed it. By 1902, 32 states prohibited the sale of colored margarine. Others required that the product be "branded," while still others insisted that diners in hotels and restaurants be informed when served the product. Production and consumption of oleomargarine increased, nonetheless, setting a record in 1902.

That reality set the stage for Congress to reexamine the 1886 law. By this time, however, agricultural interests had become sharply divided. Preferring to have the product prohibited, the National Dairy Union endorsed a tax increase to ten cents per pound on colored oleomargarine as an acceptable method of limiting consumption, since the lard-white appearance of uncolored margarine had no consumer appeal. Defenders included cotton and cattle producers, because they had found a new market for their oils. Dairy interests, however, controlled the day, and Congress amended the 1886 law to tax colored oleomargarine at ten cents a pound, about one-half of the retail price, while at the same time, reducing the tax on the uncolored product to one-quarter cent a pound. The act also substantially reduced the cost of a license for wholesalers and retailers.

Almost immediately the law was challenged. Leo W. McCray, a retail dealer in Ohio, bought a shipment of colored margarine and paid the one-quarter-cent rather than the required ten-cents tax. The government sued for a penalty and the tax. McCray, represented by noted attorney William D. Guthrie, argued that the margarine color came from "natural" ingredients, since the manufacturer, the Ohio Butterine Company, had used creamery butter to produce the yellow color. Consequently, the margarine was not artificially colored within the meaning of the law. McCray also argued that the tax was repugnant to the Constitution. Since butter was colored by the same process as margarine during all seasons of the year except spring, the tax on margarine constituted discriminatory treatment of an industry in favor of a competitor. Moreover, the tax made it impossible to produce and sell margarine in competition with butter, thereby destroying an otherwise legitimate business. Such action violated McCray's Fifth Amendment rights by depriving him of property without due process of law. Finally, the defense argued that Congress had overstepped its authority and invaded the police powers reserved to the states.

In a 6–3 decision, Justice Edward D. White of Louisiana wrote for the Court upholding Congress's use in this circumstance of the tax power. White found that McCray should have paid the ten-cents tax, since the oleomargarine he purchased "was not free from artificial coloring," regardless of the fact that its color was derived from butter that had itself been artificially colored. Rejecting Guthrie's argument that a valid tax must be reasonably related to

raising revenue, White refused to inquire into Congress's motives and held that its power to impose excise taxes was "completely established." When the power of tax is exercised oppressively, the responsibility is that of Congress and not the courts. If dissatisfied with the exercise of that power, the remedy "lies, not in the abuse by the judicial authority of its functions, but in the people, upon whom . . . reliance must be placed for the correction of abuses . . . of a lawful power." Finally, White dismissed Fifth and Tenth Amendment arguments. Neither of the amendments diminished "the grant of power to tax. . . ." If the tax destroyed the industry, it "cannot be said that such repression destroys rights which no free government could destroy"; and consequently, no ground exists to justify intervention by the judiciary "save such rights from destruction."

Although the move was a hesitant one, the Court, with *Champion v. Ames*, allowed Congress to expand the means it could use when responding to national problems traditionally associated with state police powers. When the justices agreed with the ends sought by Congress, they sanctioned the use of the taxing power as a police power. But dual federalism did not quickly fade from the scene. In *Bailey v. Drexel Furniture Company* (1922), the Court rejected the child labor law and held, as it refused to do in *McCray*, that a tax must have a natural and reasonable relation to the raising of revenue.

Selected Bibliography

Cushman, R.E. "The National Police Power Under the Taxing Clause of the Constitution." *Minnesota Law Review* 4 (March 1920): 247–81.

Riepma, S.F. *The Story of Margarine*. Washington, DC: Public Affairs Press, 1970.

STATE LEGISLATIVE POWER AND MUNICIPAL TRUSTS

by Sondra L. Gould
Anaheim, California

Monterey v. Jacks, 203 U.S. 360 (1906) [U.S. Supreme Court]

This case pitted David Jacks, a shrewd Scotsman, against the board of trustees of the city of Monterey, California. The U.S. Supreme Court affirmed the judgment by the California State Supreme Court, settling a land grant dispute that began in 1848 with the Treaty of Guadalupe Hidalgo and ended over half a century later. The dispute focused on the authority of Monterey, as the successor of the pueblo of Monterey, to dispose of lands held in trust. The U.S. Supreme Court held, on December 3, 1906, that pueblo lands were a municipal trust, and not a proprietary trust, and since Monterey was a municipality it was "a creature of the laws of the state and subject to the state." Consequently, this ruling affirmed state control over municipal trusts and has been cited, as recently as 1955, in defense of that control.

The city of Monterey was originally established on June 3, 1770, as the Presidio of Monterey, a Spanish military outpost. On June 23, 1813, under the decree of the Cortes, Monterey was incorporated and became the capital of the Province of Upper California. Although the original land records confirming the Spanish grant of pueblo lands to Monterey were lost, the city was consistently referred to in this case as the former "pueblo of Monterey." But unlike most pueblos, and by special concession from the Spanish Crown, Monterey was entitled to more than the four square leagues of land generally allocated to the pueblos. It was this large grant of land that became the focal point for this dispute. After the independence of Mexico, the constituent Congress authorized municipal authorities of the towns to retain their pueblo lands for common use or to dispose of them, as long as their actions would benefit the town and the town's inhabitants. Authority over the pueblo lands was transferred to the United States, on July 4, 1848, following ratification of the Treaty of Guadalupe Hidalgo. This treaty provided for ceding the territory of California to the United States whereby the United States agreed to honor and ratify all legal Mexican land grants conferred to the ranchos, missions, and pueblos residing within the boundaries of the territory.

However, for most recipients of Mexican land grants, including the town of Monterey, their title was not clear and their boundaries were not certain. In addition, the promise by the U.S. government to ratify all grants proved to be difficult to fulfill. To dispose of fraudulent claims and to quiet title to legitimate grants, the U.S. Congress passed the Land Act of 1851. This act established definitive guidelines a claimant had to follow to obtain a land patent and authorized the formation of the Board of Land Commissioners to adjudicate these claims.

On March 22, 1853, the city council of Monterey resolved to petition the Board of Land Commissioners for confirmation of the pueblo grant to the city of Monterey. Participating in this resolution were Delos R. Ashley and David Jacks, future owners of the pueblo lands. Ashley was a local attorney who served as a city alderman and as the city attorney. Jacks, a Scotsman who moved to Monterey from San Francisco in 1849, was the city treasurer. In this resolution the council directed Ashley, as attorney for the city of Monterey, to present the pueblo land titles to the commissioners.

Title to the pueblo lands was confirmed to the city of Monterey by the Board of Land Commissioners on January 22, 1856. A subsequent appeal of this confirmation by the U.S. government was dismissed in 1858. Following the confirmation, and presumably at the request of the board of trustees of the city of Monterey (the city council was replaced by trustees in 1853 by state statute), the California legislature authorized the trustees to sue for the recovery of property of the city and, in order to pay for the expenses of prosecuting the title of the city, to sell and transfer any property for such price as they may deem reasonable.

On January 24, 1859, the trustees reconvened for the first time in almost six years. This new board received Ashley's claim of $991.50, for attorney's fees and expenses in successfully prosecuting the title of the pueblo lands. The board resolved on the following day that since the city's treasury was broke, to pay Ashley's claim by auctioning the pueblo lands of Monterey on February 9, 1859.

The auction notice was published in the *Pacific Sentinal* for the next two weeks and on February 9, 1859 one bid was received: a joint bid from Jacks and Ashley for $1,002.50. This was the exact amount required to settle the city's debt with Ashley and to pay $11.00 for the public notice in the *Pacific Sentinal*. On February 12, 1859, the city of Monterey conveyed the pueblo lands to Jacks and Ashley, with the conveyance being recorded on June 11, 1859.

Immediately following the conveyance, the first of several surveys were initiated to establish the legal description of the pueblo lands. However, because of several serious disputes over the interpretation of the original land grant, the final survey was not recorded until 1890. This long period in establishing the boundaries was an unfortunate delay for Jacks.

A new, hostile, board of trustees were elected on June 5, 1865. Shortly thereafter, this board declared the initial sale unauthorized and illegal. It ordered that notice be served "that the Board is ready to negotiate for the relinquishment, by Jacks and others, of any and all claims that he or they may have to the pueblo lands."

Jacks's first apparent response was on April 2, 1866, when the California legislature amended the act to incorporate the city of Monterey. This act ratified and confirmed all sales and conveyances made by the board of trustees since February 8, 1859 (one day before the public auction). It also corrected a possible defect in the deeds to Jacks and Ashley whereby the city may not have been previously authorized to convey the lands. It is this act, and the associated authority assumed by the California legislature both to ratify the conveyance of municipal trust lands and to ratify a possible unlawful transaction, that the city would later question.

On November 19, 1891, with the final survey having been recorded the previous year, the city of Monterey was issued a Patent of the United States to pueblo lands. The lands documented encompassed a region "from the mouth of the River of Monterey in the sea to the Pilarcitos; thence running all along the Canada to the Laguna Seca, which is in the high road to the Presidio; thence running along the highest ridge of the mountains situated towards the Mission of San Carlos unto Point Cypress further to the north and from said point following all the coast unto the said mouth of the River of Monterey." This patent covered four tracts consisting of 29,698.53 acres and was the last step necessary to provide clear title to the pueblo lands. Jacks was now the legal owner following the ratification of the conveyance by the state legislature in 1866 and with the previous purchase of Ashley's interest in the pueblo lands in 1869.

However, the city maintained that both the purchase and the ratification were illegal. Consequently, the city filed suit against Jacks in the Superior Court of the County of Monterey on December 19, 1891. In the initial complaint, the city of Monterey, as the plaintiff, alleged that it was the owner of Lot No. 2 of the pueblo lands and that the defendant's claim was an estate or interest adverse to the city. A second complaint, filed on November 17, 1896, against Jacks alleged that additional property, consisting of the sum total of tracts one through four, was owned by the plaintiff.

The court found on September 25, 1899 that the plaintiff, the city of Monterey, was a municipal corporation, that plaintiff was not entitled to any relief, that Jacks was the owner of the land described in the complaint, and that Jacks was entitled to recover his costs. Subsequently, the city requested and was denied a new trial.

The city of Monterey filed a notice of appeal with the California Supreme Court on April 3, 1900. The contention was that (1) the former trustees did not have the authority to sell or to convey the pueblo lands, (2) the former trustees were never officially trustees for the city,

(3) the act of April 2, 1866 did not ratify the sale, and (4) the legislature did not have the power to ratify the transaction.

On July 11, 1903, the California Supreme Court issued its ruling. The court agreed that the question "is not what power the pueblo or the city of itself had over the pueblo lands, but what power or control the legislature had over them." Additionally, the court observed that there is a significant difference "between lands which are held by a municipality in trust for public municipal purposes, such as pueblo lands, and lands acquired by a municipality through purchase or special grant, and held in proprietary right." The court held that the pueblo lands were previously a municipal trust subject to the authority of the Mexican government, that the state of California succeeded to the sovereignty previously exercised by Mexico, and therefore the state had authority both to authorize and confirm the sale of these pueblo lands. In addition, the court ruled that the legislature's power extended over all of the pueblo lands, that the act of April 2, 1866, ratified and confirmed all defects in the sale and cured an alleged defect in the conveyance, and that the trustees who signed the deed were at least *de facto* trustees for the city of Monterey.

Following this ruling, the city appealed to the U.S. Supreme Court. The question presented to the Court was whether "the California Legislature could enact the act of April 2, 1866, ratifying conveyances made by the corporate authorities of the city of Monterey of pueblo lands confirmed to that city by the United States, and afterwards patented to it, its successors and assigns."

Jacks, however, did not place all his faith in receiving a favorable Supreme Court ruling. Concurrent with the city's appeal, and again presumably through his efforts, Congress passed an act designating the city of Monterey as trustee of the pueblo lands and confirming the land to the city as patented. This act, passed on June 15, 1906, effectively eliminated the city's argument that it did not have legal title to the pueblo lands, and therefore could not legally convey title to them.

On December 3, 1906, Justice Joseph McKenna delivered the opinion of the Supreme Court, which affirmed the judgment of the lower court. The Court held that "if the United States was, as contended, a paramount sovereign, and, as such, possessed the power to direct the trust to which pueblo lands were subject, it did not do so, but conveyed land to the 'city of Monterey, its successors and assigns.'" Therefore, "the conveyance was made to a municipality of the state of California, a creature of the laws of the state and subject to the state."

This case is significant because of its confirmation of state authority to rule municipal trusts. As late as April 1955, it was cited in support of that position. In *Mallon v. City of Long Beach* (1955), the Supreme Court of California held that the city of Long Beach was still subservient to the state when trust property was placed under its management. Justice Roger Traynor, one of California's leading jurists, did not dispute the precedent cited in the *Monterey v. Jacks*. Consequently, the power of the legislature to control municipal trusts was preserved.

Monterey v. Jacks represents both an affirmation of the authority of the state over municipal corporations and the critical role of legislation in the resolution of land title disputes. Fortunately, Jacks lived to see the resolution of a dispute that spanned nearly one-half century.

Selected Bibliography

Bakken, G.M. *The Development of Law in Frontier California: Civil Law and Society, 1850–90.* Westport, CT: Greenwood Press, 1985.

Beck, W.A., and D.A. Williams. *California: A History of the Golden State.* Garden City, NY: Doubleday, 1972.

Bestor, A.E., Jr. *David Jacks of Monterey, and Lee L. Jacks His Daughter.* Stanford, CA: Stanford University Press, 1945.

Gates, P.W. *California Ranchos and Farms, 1842–62.* Madison, WI: The State Historical Society of Wisconsin, 1967.

E. Substantive Due Process

PROHIBITION AND THE DUE PROCESS CLAUSE

by *William M. Wiecek*
College of Law and Department of History
Syracuse University

Wynehamer v. People, 13 N.Y. 378 (1856) [New York Court of Appeals]

Two powerful forces of antebellum America clashed in state courtrooms during the 1850s: the drive to outlaw "demon rum," and the development of higher-law doctrines. Each profoundly impacted on the other when the New York Court of Appeals determined that the State's Act for the Prevention of Intemperance, Pauperism, and Crime of 1855 violated the New York Constitution's prohibition against taking property without due process of law. This holding anticipated the doctrine of substantive due process that was to dominate turn-of-the-century American jurisprudence, and it set the stage for the later campaign to secure national Prohibition by constitutional amendment.

The issue in *Wynehamer* and its companion case, *People ex rel. Mathews v. Toynbee*, was straightforward. James G. Wynehamer, a Buffalo barkeep, and Thomas Toynbee, a Brooklyn hotelier, were convicted of selling rum, brandy, gin, wine, whiskey, "strong beer," and champagne to their customers after the state had banned the retail sale of intoxicating beverages. In what amounted to test cases, both men challenged the constitutionality of the recently enacted New York Prohibition law on the ground that it conflicted with various provisions of the federal and state constitutions. The court of appeals, New York's highest court, focused on the sibling clauses of the New York Constitution providing that "no member of this state shall be disfranchised, or deprived of any of the rights or privileges secured to any citizen thereof, unless by the law of the land or the judgment of his peers" and that "no person shall be . . . deprived of life, liberty, or property without due process of law; nor shall private property be taken for public use without just compensation."

The court thus confronted one of the most determined reform movements of the antebellum years, the crusade to make America alcohol-free. Americans during the first half of the nineteenth century drank more alcohol per capita than at any time before or since. Reformers who were worried about the social and economic costs of alcoholism in the bibulous Republic reacted by promoting "Temperance" (which is quite different from Prohibition). Like its contemporaneous counterpart, the early effort to encourage the manumission of slaves, Temperance relied on suasion rather than legal force. Temperance reformers sought to persuade alcohol consumers to reform themselves by drinking only in moderation and by setting a moral example for others. This early phase of the movement was dominated by middle-class leaders, many of them industrial or agricultural employers who wanted a sober work force, and by evangelical Protestant ministers.

The Temperance reformers represented a moderate, gradualist phase of the effort, and they became frustrated when confronted with the intransigence of liquor interests and the hostility of the drinking public. The movement responded by turning toward more radical ends and means. Moderate drinking and voluntary abstinence gave way to teetotalism; suasion to political action; and moral example to legal coercion. A Portland, Maine, businessman, Neal Dow, labored uncompromisingly for enactment of a state law that would ban outright the sale of alcohol for beverage purposes. His effort was rewarded in 1851 with the passage of the so-called Maine Law, a Prohibition statute copied in the next four years in 12 other states and territories. Prohibition lobbyists touted the Maine Law prototype as a remedy not only for alcoholism but for broader social ills: as the title of New York's statute declared, Prohibition was the solution to vice, poverty, immorality, madness, and deviance.

The New York statute, which Justice George M. Comstock labeled a "fierce and intolerant proscription," banned the sale and possession for sale of alcohol and provided for seizure and destruction of existing liquor stocks—the fatal flaw of the measure, in the eyes of the court. The statute contained exceptions for medicinal, chemical, and sacramental uses.

When *Wynehamer* and *Toynbee* reached the court of appeals, five of the eight judges found the statute unconstitutional. Although Comstock considered a variety of possible grounds for voiding the measure—including natural law and separation of powers—he passed them by in favor of the due process and law-of-the-land clauses. In doing so, he relied on the second great force implicated in *Wynehamer*: the expansion of higher-law jurisprudence in the United States.

In the landmark 1798 case *Calder v. Bull*, Justice Samuel Chase of the U.S. Supreme Court acclimated the natural-law tradition to U.S. jurisprudence, arguing that "there are certain vital principles in our free republican governments which will determine and overrule an apparent and flagrant abuse of legislative power. . . . The legislature cannot . . . violate . . . the right of private property." Chief Justice John Marshall endorsed this approach in *Fletcher v. Peck* (1810), and it received the persistent support of Justice Joseph Story throughout his career.

But Marshall and a majority of the justices of the Supreme Court grew uneasy about the vagueness of formulations like "vital principles of free republican governments," coming to agree with Chase's *Calder* colleague Justice James Iredell that a standard so vacuous can mean nothing more objective than the policy preferences of the individual judge applying it. Accordingly, in *Dartmouth College v. Woodward* (1819), Marshall abandoned the higher-law formula in favor of requiring that a statute be shown to violate a specific provision of the U.S. Constitution (e.g., the contract clause of Article I, Section 10) in order for the Court to hold it unconstitutional.

But the higher-law tradition did not disappear; it lingered on in state-court jurisprudence, as the highest courts of Maryland, North Carolina, Delaware, Connecticut, Alabama, and New York developed various formulas embodying the idea that state laws might be void for incompatibility with some vague standard of republicanism or natural law. However, the state judges also looked for some textual basis in their state constitutions for voiding a statute, especially as the movement to elect judges attracted popular support. The state judges realized that vague declarations about republican principles provided a flimsy basis for voiding popular laws, and they too turned to the firmer ground of specific provisions in their states' constitutions.

It was because of this search that *Wynehamer* was so significant in its time, for no court before then had used the due process clauses of the state or federal constitutions, or their law-of-the-land analogues, as a basis for holding a statute unconstitutional on substantive grounds. Before 1856, the due process clauses had an exclusively procedural connotation, mandating that life, liberty, or property could be taken only in the course of a common-law trial and only by compliance with various traditional safeguards, such as jury trial, indictment, and so on. This accounted for the pathbreaking quality of Comstock's opinion. He began by demonstrating that extant stocks or liquor were property and thus entitled to whatever protection the law afforded any other sort of property. Comstock insisted that if the legislature's claim that liquor was dangerous to individual health or civic virtue "can be allowed to subvert the fundamental idea of property, then there is no private right entirely safe, because there is no limitation upon the absolute discretion of the legislature, and the guarantees of the constitution are a mere waste of words." He acknowledged that in popular governments "theories of public good or public necessity may be so plausible, or even so truthful, as to command popular majorities. But," he intoned, "there are some absolute private rights beyond their reach." The due process clauses thus for the first time took on substantive significance.

Thus, the enduring contribution of Prohibition litigation, especially *Wynehamer*, to constitutional development was the identification of a specific textual touchstone—property as protected in the due process clause—to replace the nebulous generalities of higher-law doctrine. This extended the life of natural law at a time when it had matured to the point of expiration. Thus reinvigorated, higher law retained its hold on the judicial imagination for the next two generations. The contribution of the substantive due process doctrine to liquor control, by contrast, was to submerge the political development of Prohibition for the time being, and in the long run to divert it to constitutionally more drastic channels.

The New York Court of Appeals was not alone in groping toward a substantive concept of due process as a means of protecting property rights. In the same year, Justice Benjamin R. Curtis of the U.S. Supreme Court stated in *dicta* in *Murray's Lessee v. Hoboken Land and Improvement Company* that the due process clause of the Fifth Amendment "is a restraint on the legislative as well as on the executive and judicial powers of the government." In 1854, Chief Justice Lemuel Shaw of the Massachusetts Supreme Judicial Court held in *Fisher v. McGirr* the Massachusetts version of the Maine Law void on various grounds, among them as a violation of the state constitution's law-of-the-land clause, construed in a procedural sense. And in 1856, the Vermont Supreme Court in *Beebe v. State* struck down its state's prohibition law on natural-law grounds.

The most extraordinary support for New York's innovative reading of the due process clause came from U.S. Supreme Court Chief Justice Roger B. Taney in his 1857 *Dred Scott* opinion. Taney held that a congressional statute excluding slavery from the territories "deprive[d] a citizen of the United States of his liberty or property, without due process of law, merely because he came himself or brought his property into a particular territory of the United States . . . [and] could hardly be dignified with the name of due process of law. . . ." Though the rest of Taney's opinion was repudiated in the course of the Civil War, his suggestive reading of the Fifth Amendment's due process clause attracted little attention. In 1870, his successor, Chief Justice Salmon P. Chase, relied on the clause in *Hepburn v. Griswold* to hold unconsti-

tutional Congress' declaration that paper money should be legal tender for paying preexisting debts.

As a political matter, *Wynehamer* was a stunning blow to the Maine Law and the Prohibition movement. While Prohibition statutes survived judicial scrutiny in two states—Connecticut, which upheld its statute against a takings clause challenge; and Vermont, which sustained it against a law-of-the-land clause attack—the Prohibition movement itself collapsed. It had been strikingly sectional, being limited to northeastern United States and to a handful of midwestern states and territories peopled by migrants from New England and New York, and even there its support dwindled. Elsewhere Prohibition had always been a nonstarter.

But the two great issues implicated in *Wynehamer*—Prohibition and substantive due process—were far from dead. In a different social environment, Prohibition was revived by the Women's Christian Temperance Union and the Anti-Saloon League during the last two decades of the nineteenth century, and grew in appeal until its great but short-lived triumph in the Eighteenth Amendment. Substantive due process fared better. The U.S. Supreme Court, after first rejecting it in the *Slaughterhouse Cases* of 1873, accepted it during the 1890s and exalted it to the status of dogma in such landmark cases as *Lochner v. New York* (1905) and *Adkins v. Children's Hospital* (1923), where it served as a vehicle for the Court's hostility to labor organization and state legislative efforts to ameliorate the conditions of labor. State courts also embraced the innovative doctrine to the same ends. Historians and other constitutional scholars, seeking to understand the origins and expansion of so potent a doctrine, rediscovered *Wynehamer*, attributing to it and to *Dred Scott* a doctrinal significance little noticed in their own time.

Selected Bibliography

Haines, C.G. *The Revival of Natural Law Concepts*. Cambridge, MA.: Harvard University Press, 1930.

Mott, R.L. *Due Process of Law*. New York: Da Capo Press, 1973.

Tyrrell, I.R. *Sobering Up: From Temperance to Prohibition in Antebellum America, 1800–60*. Westport, CT: Greenwood Press, 1979.

THE FOURTEENTH AMENDMENT RECEIVES ITS FIRST JUDICIAL CONSTRUCTION

by Donald G. Nieman
Department of History
Clemson University

Slaughterhouse Cases, 83 U.S. 36 (1873) [U.S. Supreme Court]

When they reached the U.S. Supreme Court in 1870, the *Slaughterhouse Cases* did not seem to be the stuff of which epic constitutional decisions are made. They were brought by disgruntled butchers who challenged a Louisiana law regulating the slaughtering of livestock in the New Orleans metropolitan area. Yet the cases attracted considerable attention because the plaintiffs challenged the statute as a violation of the recently ratified Fourteenth Amendment. Thus, in ruling on the butchers' claim, the nation's highest court would offer its first interpretation of a new constitutional provision that defined citizenship, expanded national protection for individual rights, and promised to make dramatic changes in the balance of power between the states and the national government. Moreover, when the Court rendered its decision in 1873, it cast a long shadow into the future, giving the amendment a narrow reading and thus minimizing its effect on the American federal system.

The cases originated in the Byzantine world of Reconstruction-era Louisiana politics. In 1869, the Louisiana legislature passed a bill incorporating the Crescent City Stock Landing and Slaughter House Company and authorizing it to build a stockyard and slaughterhouses south of New Orleans. The law gave the company a monopoly: after June 1, 1869, all livestock entering New Orleans and the three surrounding parishes for sale or slaughter were to be sent to the company's stockyards, where they would be examined by state inspectors. Moreover, all slaughtering in the three parishes was to be done in the company's slaughterhouses. Independent butchers might rent space there at reasonable rates, but they would have to close their shops in other parts of the city and slaughter and prepare meat for sale in the Crescent City Company's facilities.

In passing this measure, legislators invoked the police power, a venerable constitutional principle that allowed states to restrict individual liberty and property rights in order to promote the public health, safety, and welfare. The law, legislators contended, would make the city more sanitary and protect the public health by requiring inspection of livestock and concentrating slaughtering in one location outside the city. In adopting the slaughterhouse statute, Louisiana was following the lead of several northern states. Concern about urban public health had already prompted legislatures in New York, Massachusetts, Wisconsin, and California to enact similar regulations for rapidly growing cities in their jurisdictions.

More than concern for public health lay behind the Louisiana law, however. The entrepreneurs who formed the Crescent City Company saw substantial profits to be made from controlling the stockyards and slaughterhouses that supplied meat to a bustling city of 200,000. With the vast cattle herds of Texas nearby and the promise of refrigerated ships and railroad cars in the offing, they believed that New Orleans would become a major supplier of fresh meat to the entire nation. And they were confident that the slaughterhouse monopoly would enable them to dominate this lucrative business. Indeed, in 1869, a great fortune (which Chicago packers such as Swift and Armour would soon realize) seemed within the grasp of members of the Crescent City Company. Driven by these visions of grandeur, they turned to politics to secure the legislation that would enable them to dominate livestock shipping and slaughtering in New Orleans, bribing legislators and other politicians whose support for the measure was critical.

In May 1869, shortly before the statute was to take effect, a series of suits and countersuits began, as opponents and defenders of the monopoly each looked for protection to state judges who were friendly to their respective causes. A group of about 400 small, independent butchers, who had formed the Butcher's Benevolent Association two years earlier, struck first. They retained John A. Campbell, who had resigned from the U.S. Supreme Court in 1861 to serve the Confederacy, and J.Q.A. Fellows, a prominent local attorney. Appearing in a state district court, Campbell and Fellows won an injunction blocking the Crescent City Company's monopoly from taking effect. The company launched a counteroffensive, engaging a group of distinguished local attorneys led by Christian Roselius, the head of the University of Louisiana (now Tulane) School of Law. Roselius and his colleagues went before a different state judge and obtained an injunction against the association, barring it from harassing the company with lawsuits aimed at blocking implementation of the law.

While these cases went forward, matters became even more complicated. Substantial livestock dealers, fearing that the monopoly would destroy them, formed the Live Stock Dealers' and Butchers' Association. In defiance of the monopoly, the association promptly acquired land south of New Orleans and began constructing stockyards and a slaughterhouse there. This group also retained Campbell, who won an injunction against Crescent City prohibiting it from blocking his client's plans. Louisiana Attorney General Simeon Belden then entered the fray and obtained an injunction against the Live Stock Dealers' Association.

In January 1870, after the lower courts had rendered contradictory decisions in these cases, appeals were taken to the Louisiana Supreme Court. In a 4–1 decision announced in April, the state's high court sustained the law, dissolving the injunctions against the company and sustaining those against the butchers and livestock dealers. But the monopoly's opponents had not exhausted their remedies. In state court they had contended that the monopoly statute violated the Thirteenth and Fourteenth Amendments to the U.S. Constitution. Consequently, to win a hearing before the nation's highest court, Campbell and Fellows used a provision of federal law permitting appeals from the highest court of any state to the U.S. Supreme Court in cases involving the Constitution, federal laws, or treaties.

While the appeals awaited consideration by the Supreme Court, the Crescent City Company and the state attorney general instituted new suits aimed at breaking opposition to the monopoly. In June 1870, the company obtained an injunction against the sale of meat prepared outside of its facilities, and the metropolitan police immediately seized $20,000 worth of fresh meat, which quickly spoiled in the early summer heat. At about the same time, Attorney General Belden moved to have his injunction against the Live Stock Dealers' Association enforced.

The butchers and livestock dealers turned to the federal circuit court, then in session in New Orleans, seeking an injunction barring the Crescent City Company and the police from further action against them pending the outcome of the appeal to the Supreme Court. Their motion was heard by William Woods, the circuit judge, and U.S. Supreme Court Justice Joseph P. Bradley, who served as circuit justice for the Deep South. In a lengthy opinion, which offered the first extended judicial interpretation of the Fourteenth Amendment, Bradley held that the law establishing the monopoly denied the butchers rights protected by the amendment. However, a 1793 federal statute prohibited federal courts from issuing injunctions to stop proceedings in state courts. Therefore, while Bradley enjoined Crescent City from bringing new suits against the butchers, he declined to bar state courts from acting in suits that had already been instituted.

This proved a hollow victory. Most of the independent butchers, stung by the police's action and aware that the injunction against the sale of meat prepared in violation of the slaughterhouse statute was still in force, moved into the Crescent City Company's slaughterhouses. However, the appeal pending in the Supreme Court meant that the butchers and the livestock dealers might still prevail. Indeed, at least one member of the Court had unequivocally supported their claims. The situation was thus ripe for a compromise, and in March 1871, members of the Crescent City Company reached an agreement with the leaders of the

Live Stock Dealers' Association. The latter promised to drop its appeal, while the Crescent City Company agreed to purchase the association's slaughterhouse, give it a block of shares, and place several of its members on Crescent City's board of directors. Although the parties believed that members of the Butchers' Benevolent Association would follow the lead of the livestock dealers, they refused to compromise the suits to which they were parties and kept the matter before the Supreme Court.

In January 1872, the Court heard two days of arguments in the cases, but failed to render a decision. Justice Samuel Nelson, who was ill, did not participate, and the other eight justices divided evenly. A tie vote would have allowed the holding of the Louisiana Supreme Court to stand, but would have offered no clear resolution of the important constitutional issues involved. Therefore, the justices ordered the cases reargued the following Term, hoping that a reconsideration before the full court would produce a clear-cut decision.

The justices were so sharply divided because they confronted a new constitutional provision that had the potential to alter the federal system. Prior to the Civil War, states enjoyed almost complete freedom to define the rights of individuals. In *Barron v. Baltimore* (1833), the Court had ruled that the Bill of Rights had been adopted to allay fears of a powerful central government and that its provisions did not apply to the states. Thus, neither Congress nor the federal courts could prevent states from denying their citizens rights enumerated in the first eight amendments.

Moreover, the Constitution itself imposed only a few explicit restrictions on the states, prohibiting them from enacting *ex post facto* laws, bills of attainder, and laws impairing the obligation of contract. The privileges and immunities clause of Article IV, Section 2 ("The Citizens of each State shall be entitled to all Privileges and Immunities of Citizens in the several States.") held out the prospect of more meaningful federal protection of individual rights. Some judges, legal writers, and politicians had argued that it guaranteed citizens the rights essential to freedom and barred the states from impairing these rights. However, most observers had contended that it merely guaranteed a citizen of one state who entered another state the rights enjoyed by the citizens of that state, whatever they might be. This left states free to define the rights their citizens possessed, but not to deny these rights to citizens of other states. Since neither Congress nor the Supreme Court had resolved this dispute before the Civil War, the clause's meaning had remained unclear and it had offered little protection for individual rights.

The events of the Civil War and Reconstruction had led Republican Congresses to adopt measures designed to expand federal power to protect individual rights. To defend wartime emancipation from constitutional challenge, Congress had adopted the Thirteenth Amendment in 1865. Declaring slavery and involuntary servitude illegal and giving Congress power to enforce the ban on them, the amendment had destroyed states' authority to sanction slavery and had expanded Congress's authority over individual rights. In the months following the war, presidentially reconstructed state governments in the South had enacted the black codes, imposing harsh restrictions on the freedmen and sharply curtailing their freedom. Congressional Republicans believed that the Thirteenth Amendment empowered them to sweep aside such vestiges of slavery and to guarantee blacks the rights essential to freedom. In early 1866, they had enacted the Civil Rights Act, guaranteeing blacks equal rights in state law and imposing penalties on persons who denied blacks equality before the law.

Concerned about potential challenges to the constitutionality of the Civil Rights Act, congressional Republicans had also adopted the Fourteenth Amendment. The first section of this amendment overturned the Supreme Court's holding in *Dred Scott v. Sandford* (1857) that blacks were not entitled to U.S. citizenship. All persons born in the United States, the amendment declared, were citizens of the United States and of the state in which they resided. Other parts of Section 1, reflecting awareness of the plight of former slaves, provided sweeping guarantees against state denial of individual rights. States were forbidden to abridge the "privileges and immunities" of U.S. citizens, to deprive any person of life, liberty, or property without due process of law, or to deny any person "equal protection of the laws." Although the courts could protect these rights in the absence of congressional action, the amendment gave Congress authority to enforce them by "appropriate legislation."

How much the amendment increased federal authority to protect individual rights was unclear. After all, what were the privileges and immunities of citizens of the United States, and what did due process of law entail? Debates on the amendment in Congress had not clarified the meaning of these sweeping, but vague, phrases. John A. Bingham, the Ohio Republican who drafted Section 1, had commented that they included "the inborn rights of every free person," but this offered little in the way of specific guidance. Senator Jacob Howard, a leading Republican and a member of the committee that had proposed the amendment, had admitted that these rights could not be defined precisely, but had maintained that they included at the very least the rights enumerated in the Bill of Rights. Yet the debates had not indicated whether most Republicans shared this view. When the amendment was ratified and took effect in 1868, it was left to Congress and the courts to grapple with its meaning and to determine its effect on the federal system.

In his appearances before the U.S. Supreme Court on behalf of the butchers, Campbell exploited this ambiguity, pressing for an interpretation of the amendment that would substantially increase national authority to protect individual rights. He began by emphasizing that the law creating the monopoly was not a legitimate exercise of the state's police power. Protection of the public health might justify confining slaughterhouses to one section of the city, but it did not extend to granting one firm an exclusive right to establish and operate slaughterhouses. According to Campbell, the legislature's real aim had been to confer special privilege on a few, not to promote the public health. Although states might have been free to enact such oppressive legislation before the Civil War, Campbell argued, the Fourteenth Amendment had removed individual rights from their previous dependence on state law. By making national citizenship primary and prohibiting states from denying the privileges and immuni-

ties of U.S. citizens, it had created one people who enjoyed fundamental rights guaranteed by the Constitution. He admitted that the amendment did not define these rights precisely, but maintained that the right to pursue a lawful occupation was so essential to personal liberty that it was protected by the privileges and immunities clause.

Campbell also claimed that the slaughterhouse monopoly violated other Fourteenth Amendment guarantees. He asserted that because it unreasonably prohibited the butchers from operating their own shops, it denied them liberty without due process of law. He also contended that the law gave one group a right—to establish and operate slaughterhouses—that others were denied, thus depriving the butchers of equal protection of the laws.

Finally, Campbell asserted that the statute creating the monopoly violated the Thirteenth Amendment. Reminding the Court that the amendment did not mention race and made involuntary servitude as well as slavery illegal, he contended that it went far beyond abolition of Negro slavery. It banned anything that established and maintained personal servitude, including laws that discriminated between classes of persons and compelled one group to serve another. The Louisiana statute, he asserted, gave to a privileged few an exclusive right to own and operate slaughterhouses and compelled the city's butchers to pay them a toll for the privilege of pursuing their craft. Like feudal laws requiring peasants to use the mills, wine presses, and ovens of their lords, Campbell concluded, the slaughterhouse monopoly established a personal servitude in violation of the Thirteenth Amendment.

In the High Court, Campbell was opposed by a new team of lawyers representing the Crescent City Company. Charles Allen, who had distinguished himself as attorney general of Massachusetts, and Thomas Jefferson Durant, a prominent Louisiana Republican and an early advocate of black suffrage, prepared briefs for the company. Senator Matthew Hale Carpenter of Wisconsin, a leading civil rights advocate and one of the most eloquent members of the Supreme Court bar, joined Durant in presenting the company's oral argument.

Crescent City's lawyers emphasized that the law creating the monopoly was a legitimate exercise of the state's police power. By restricting slaughtering to one location and by providing for inspection of livestock, they contended, the law promoted sanitation and helped to prevent the spread of disease. They also defended the Crescent City Company's exclusive right to operate landing and slaughtering facilities. The monopoly did not, they argued, deny the butchers the right to practice their craft: any butcher had the right to rent space from the Crescent City Company at reasonable rates. Moreover, the courts had consistently maintained that legislators, not judges, had the authority to determine the means best calculated to promote the public good. Thus, they concluded, if the Louisiana legislature believed that the most effective way to control disease and odors was to concentrate meat preparation at one great slaughterhouse and preferred to have the facility built with private capital rather than state funds, nothing prevented it from doing so.

Durant, Carpenter, and Allen also maintained that the Thirteenth and Fourteenth Amendments did not affect the police power. They argued that the public debates on these measures demonstrated that they were designed to eradicate Negro slavery and to guarantee former slaves the same rights that whites enjoyed. The framers of the amendments had sought to secure freedom and equal rights for blacks and had no intention of eroding the states' power to promote the public health and welfare. To interpret their work otherwise would undermine states' rights and carry out a constitutional revolution that the amendment's framers had not intended.

The Court heard the reargument February 3–5, 1873, and announced its decision on April 14. Before the reargument, Justice Nelson, whose absence had left the Court deadlocked 4–4 a year earlier, had resigned and had been replaced by Ward Hunt. A former chief judge of the New York Court of Appeals, Hunt was a firm supporter of the police power. While on the New York court, he had written an opinion upholding a state law requiring New York City butchers to move their slaughterhouses outside the metropolitan district. With the other justices remaining evenly divided, Hunt's support

for the police power was decisive, and the Court rejected the butchers' plea, 5–4.

Justice Samuel F. Miller of Iowa, a conservative Republican who was nonetheless sympathetic to the congressional civil rights program, wrote the opinion for the majority. Miller began by asserting that the Louisiana law was unquestionably a legitimate exercise of the state's police power. By concentrating the obnoxious and potentially hazardous activity of slaughtering livestock in one small area outside the city, it clearly attempted to promote the public good. Miller also found unexceptionable the legislature's decision to give a private corporation exclusive rights to operate a slaughterhouse. Although some might deny the wisdom of this decision, choosing the best means of protecting the public health was a matter of policy that legislators must decide. Moreover, he flatly rejected Campbell's claim that the statute destroyed the butchers' right to pursue a lawful occupation. While it restricted their freedom in order to promote the public good, the law guaranteed them the right to practice their occupation in the Crescent City Company's facilities at reasonable rates.

Admitting that the recent amendments might have placed restrictions on the police power, Miller next addressed the butchers' claims under the Thirteenth and Fourteenth Amendments. He began by asserting that the amendments could be properly understood only in light of their historical origins. Congress had passed them in order to bring an end to the conflict over slavery, which had driven the nation into a bloody civil war, and to guarantee substantive freedom to the slaves, who had fought valiantly on behalf of the Union. In enacting the amendments, Miller concluded, Congress had intended to eradicate Negro slavery, guarantee the freedmen equality before the law, and give the national government adequate authority to secure freedom and equality for blacks. However, he argued, Congress had not intended to concentrate in the federal government all power to define and protect individual rights.

After these preliminary remarks, Miller discussed specific provisions of the amendments, devoting most of his attention to the Fourteenth Amendment's privileges and immunities clause.

He pointed out that the amendment clearly recognized a dual citizenship, expressly stating that Americans were both citizens of the U.S. and of the states in which they resided. Consequently, he asserted that they possessed two separate and distinct sets of rights, one deriving from U.S. citizenship and the other from state citizenship. Because the Fourteenth Amendment forbade states to abridge the privileges and immunities of U.S. citizens, he concluded, it protected only those rights that attached to U.S. citizenship. Rights that derived from state citizenship were not protected by the amendment.

What were the privileges and immunities of U.S. citizens? According to Miller, they constituted a small group of rights "which owe their existence to the Federal government, its national character, its Constitution, or its laws." These included the right of *habeas corpus*, the right to assemble and petition the government for redress of grievances, the right to protection from the government on the high seas and in foreign lands, the right of access to navigable rivers and ports in the United States, and the right to travel to the nation's capital. Thus he rejected the notion that the privileges and immunities clause protected all of the fundamental rights necessary to freedom, suggesting instead that it secured a modicum of rights that were of limited importance to Americans in their day-to-day lives.

Miller justified this narrow interpretation by pointing out the revolutionary consequences of Campbell's contention that the privileges and immunities of U.S. citizens included all of the fundamental rights of citizens. Such a ruling would make the Fourteenth Amendment a grab bag of rights and the federal courts "perpetual censors" of the states, passing judgment on the myriad provisions states established to regulate individual rights. This would not only swamp the federal courts with a case load they were ill-prepared to handle, but would also deprive the states of the authority they needed to govern themselves.

There was another danger, according to Miller: Congress possessed authority to enforce the Fourteenth Amendment's guarantees by enacting "appropriate legislation." He warned that if the privileges and immunities of U.S. citizens were broadly defined, Congress, under the guise of legislating to protect these rights, might establish a code of laws minutely defining the rights of Americans. This would transfer from the states to the federal government authority to make the laws governing contracts, property, family relations, crime and punishment, and the like.

Speculating on what the framers of the amendment had intended, Miller asserted that Congress would not have taken such revolutionary action by simply declaring that no state shall abridge the privileges and immunities of U.S. citizens. Had it intended to make sweeping changes in the federal system, it would have stated its intention clearly and would not have left the matter in doubt.

Deeply concerned about preserving federalism's delicate balance between state and national power, Miller produced a badly strained argument. The sweeping consequences that he imagined would result from a broad interpretation of the privileges and immunities clause actually shed no light on the question of the framers' intent. Indeed, many of the framers had clearly believed that the amendment substantially increased the power of the federal government to protect individual rights. Moreover, he greatly exaggerated the consequences that would result if the Court accepted a broad interpretation of the privileges and immunities clause. If the privileges and immunities of U.S. citizens included rights that were truly fundamental—such as those enumerated in the Bill of Rights—the results would have been much less disruptive than Miller suggested. States would have continued to regulate individual rights to make contracts, hold property, conduct business, marry, and the like. However, the federal government would have possessed authority to guarantee that in doing so they did not abridge such rights as freedom of speech or protection against self-incrimination. Finally, the rights that Miller listed as being among the privileges and immunities of U.S. citizens were, for the most part, rights that had been subject to federal protection prior to ratification of the amendment. Thus he came close to arguing that the privileges and immunities clause was meaningless verbiage added to the Constitution.

Miller dispensed with Campbell's other constitutional claims in short order. The context in which the Thirteenth Amendment was adopted, he asserted, suggested that the framers intended it to root out Negro slavery. They had prohibited involuntary servitude as well as slavery in order to destroy any subterfuges—such as peonage or apprenticeship—that states or individuals might use to keep blacks in bondage. However, they had not intended the amendment to prevent the states from imposing such restrictions on liberty as were necessary to protect the public health. He also rejected the butchers' claims under the Fourteenth Amendment's equal protection clause, explaining that it was clearly intended to prohibit laws, like the black codes, which discriminated on the basis of race.

Finally, Miller argued that the concept of due process of law was familiar in American law, but that the courts had never given it the interpretation Campbell had suggested. Although he did not elaborate, his meaning was clear. Campbell had contended that the clause established a right to have the courts determine whether a measure that deprived a person of life, liberty, or property was, in substance, fair and equitable. But due process, as traditionally understood, had a procedural meaning, requiring government to follow certain procedures when it deprived persons of life, liberty, or property. In criminal proceedings, for example, due process guaranteed that the accused was informed of the charges, enjoyed protection against self-incrimination, had the right to counsel, and received a jury trial. Read as a procedural rather than a substantive guarantee, due process offered no basis to challenge the legitimacy of the Louisiana statute.

Miller's opinion was greeted by sharp dissent. Justice Noah H. Swayne, a staunchly antislavery Republican who had been President Abraham Lincoln's first appointee to the Court, charged that the majority fundamentally misunderstood the Fourteenth Amendment. Its framers, he argued, had been aware of the shortcomings of the antebellum federal system and had intended to make significant changes in it. They had believed that the greatest threat to liberty came from the states and had sought to empower the national government to protect the fundamental rights of its citizens, regardless of race. By assuming that the amendment was limited in its scope, Swayne concluded, the majority established limitations that the framers had not intended and transformed "what was meant for bread into a stone."

Two other dissenting opinions offered more detailed analyses of the amendment. Justice Stephen J. Field, a California Democrat who served on the Court from 1863 to 1897 and became its most vigorous advocate of conservative judicial activism, wrote a passionate dissent that was joined by Chief Justice Salmon P. Chase and Justices Swayne and Bradley. While Miller refused to probe the legislature's motives and judgment, Field subjected them to careful scrutiny. He indicated that the state might legitimately restrict individuals' use of their property, holding that those provisions of the act that limited slaughtering to areas below the city and required inspection of livestock were legitimate exercises of the police power. However, he argued that the slaughterhouse monopoly did not really promote public sanitation, but merely conferred special privileges on the Crescent City Company at the expense of its rivals. In a thinly veiled reference to the political corruption that had produced the slaughterhouse statute, Field concluded: "The pretense of sanitary regulations for the grant of the exclusive privileges is a shallow one."

While Field admitted that the antebellum Constitution had offered no protection against such obnoxious legislation, he contended that the Fourteenth Amendment had supplied a remedy. The amendment made national citizenship primary and, by demanding that states confer citizenship upon all national citizens residing within their borders, made state citizenship derivative and subordinate. According to Field, individuals possessed the fundamental rights of free persons as U.S. citizens, and the Fourteenth Amendment's privileges and immunities clause protected these rights. Nothing was more fundamental, he concluded, than the freedom to pursue a lawful occupation without interference from special-interest legislation. The slaughterhouse monopoly, he asserted, was a "most barefaced and shameless" violation of the Fourteenth Amendment.

Justice Bradley, who had ruled in favor of the butchers while on circuit, issued a third dissent. Clearly appalled by the chicanery by which the monopoly was established and enforced, he penned a sharp denunciation of the law. Much of his opinion followed Field's, maintaining that national citizenship was paramount and that the privileges and immunities clause protected fundamental rights, including the right to protection against legislation conferring special privileges. However, Bradley also urged that the slaughterhouse monopoly violated the Fourteenth Amendment's due process clause. Creating a monopoly was not necessary to protect the public health, he argued, and was an "unreasonable, arbitrary, and unjust" measure adopted to promote the interests of "a few scheming individuals." Thus, the Louisiana statute deprived New Orleans butchers of their liberty to pursue a lawful occupation and the intangible property that they had in their occupation without due process of law in violation of the Fourteenth Amendment. In making this argument, Bradley moved from a procedural to a substantive definition of due process. Laws must be reasonable and just to pass constitutional muster, he argued, and the courts should decide these very subjective matters.

The opinions in the *Slaughterhouse Cases* were of considerable significance. The Fourteenth Amendment's privileges and immunities clause had the potential to permit the federal government to protect a wide range of fundamental rights—including those enumerated in the Bill of Rights—against infringement by the states. Miller's opinion for the majority, however, held that the privileges and immunities clause protected only a few rights that were not of much consequence to most Americans. Combined with subsequent rulings that interpreted the amendment's due process clause narrowly, it signaled that the Court rejected making major changes in the federal system by expanding significantly national protection for individual rights.

Indeed, the *Slaughterhouse Cases* dealt the privileges and immunities clause a blow from which it never recovered. In the 50 years after *Gitlow v. New York* (1925), the Court decided a series of cases holding that states may not violate selected provisions of the Bill of Rights.

And since *Griswold v. Connecticut* (1965), it has held that persons have a right to privacy that states may not violate. In deciding these cases, however, it has relied on the Fourteenth Amendment's due process clause and has not rehabilitated the privileges and immunities clause.

It is easy to exaggerate the role of the case in signaling the Court's retreat from Reconstruction and its abandonment of blacks. To be sure, by limiting the rights protected by the Fourteenth Amendment the case made it more difficult for Congress and the federal courts to check repressive state action against unpopular minorities. However, the main problem confronting blacks in the 1870s was not direct state action denying them rights, but private acts of discrimination and violence. Even if the minority had prevailed in the *Slaughterhouse Cases*, the decision would have been of limited value in protecting blacks from these threats. Moreover, one must remember that Miller insisted that the Reconstruction amendments had been adopted to guarantee full freedom and genuine equality for blacks. His language clearly offered Congress and the federal courts broad authority under the Thirteenth Amendment and the Fourteenth Amendment's equal protection clause to deal with racially motivated discrimination. If in subsequent cases the Court did not fully exploit this analysis, the outcome was not dictated by Miller's *Slaughterhouse* opinion.

The outcome of the cases also indicated that the Court would permit states to engage in economic regulation under the police power. The Court clearly refused to read the Fourteenth Amendment as a measure protecting private property from state interference. It also refused to probe behind the action of legislatures, scrutinize their motives, and determine whether police regulations they enacted were fair and reasonable. Four years later, in the *Munn v. Illinois* (1877), the Supreme Court confirmed this, upholding state legislation setting railroad and warehouse rates. Thus, during the 1870s, the Court demonstrated a consistent concern for maintaining a decentralized federal system in which states not only retained broad authority to define individual rights but possessed adequate power to cope with the problems that rapid economic growth presented. It did not, as scholars have sometimes suggested, strip the Fourteenth Amendment of its capacity to protect the rights of blacks and transform it into a bulwark of private property.

The dissents of Field and Bradley also proved influential. They offered to make the amendment a vehicle to protect property and to authorize courts to determine whether restrictions on property rights were equitable and reasonable. This vision of the amendment would ultimately triumph and be used by the Supreme Court to protect capital from legislation aimed at protecting the rights of workers and consumers. However, this did not occur until the early years of the twentieth century, long after the *Slaughterhouse Cases* had been decided.

Selected Bibliography

Connor, H.G. *John Archibald Campbell, Associate Justice of the United States Supreme Court, 1853–61.* Boston: Houghton Mifflin, 1920.

Franklin, M. "The Foundation and Meaning of the Slaughterhouse Cases." *Tulane Law Review* 18 (Oct., Dec. 1943): 1–88, 218–62.

Hyman, H.M., and W.M. Wiecek. *Equal Justice Under Law: Constitutional Development, 1835–75.* New York: Harper & Row, 1982.

Kaczorowski, R.J. *The Politics of Judicial Interpretation: The Federal Courts, Department of Justice and Civil Rights, 1866–76.* New York: Oceana Publications, Inc., 1985.

Nelson, W.E. *The Fourteenth Amendment: From Political Principle to Judicial Doctrine.* Cambridge, MA: Harvard University Press, 1988.

Palmer, R.C. "The Parameters of Constitutional Reconstruction: Slaughter-House, Cruickshank, and the Fourteenth Amendment." *University of Illinois Law Journal* (1984): 739–70.

THE COURT ENTERS THE AGE OF REFORM

by Richard R. Broadie
Department of History
University of Northern Iowa

Munn v. Illinois, 94 U.S. 113 (1877) [U.S. Supreme Court]

Prior to the last third of the nineteenth century, reform movements arose, more often than not, in response to moral and social dilemmas. Abolitionists, prohibitionists, feminists, and various utopian crusaders all tackled tough problems, but concluded that finding solutions to them did not necessarily require governmental coercion. Individuals were often encouraged to "take the pledge"—to give up strong drink, free their slaves, be born again—because most reformers did not expect the state to assume a direct role in remaking the world according to their own image.

Economic problems were thought by many to be caused by forces over which people (and their government) have little control. As economist Lester Thurow has pointed out, preindustrial agricultural economies are often strong or weak depending on the whims of nature: it is too hot or too cold, too wet or too dry. What can the politicians in Washington or the various state capitals do to fine-tune the economy at this level of economic development? And even if government wants to provide direct aid to those battered by the forces of nature—give them welfare, to use twentieth-century lingo—from whom can the funds to finance these programs be expropriated? Societies where little surplus wealth is created simply cannot afford compassionate government.

During the first decade after the Civil War it became apparent that the subsistence farmer was no longer the linchpin of the U.S. economy. Industrial growth was far outpacing any increases in wealth derived from land ownership or crop production. The farmers who were able to hang on were increasingly vulnerable to the fluctuations of the market and what they perceived to be the machinations of various middlemen from whom they bought what they needed and sold what they produced. It is not necessary for one to accept the view held by some historians that farmers felt victimized by villains acting in a conspiratorial manner to acknowledge that they were able to spot those segments of the evolving market economy which did not have their best interests at heart.

As it was clear that government had already taken a hand in promoting economic growth—protecting infant industries, financing railroads and canals, administering western lands—it was perhaps inevitable that some would conclude that the state should be used to regulate the market economy and aid those considered losers in the new economic arrangement.

According to the early twentieth-century historian Justus Buck, the Granger movement of the 1860s and 1870s was "a movement for agricultural organization for the advancement of farmers in every possible way—socially, intellectually, politically and economically—by concerted effort." As times on the farm became worse in the 1870s, the emphasis shifted from the social and intellectual to the political and economic. The so-called Granger laws—passed mostly in the 1870s in the midwestern states of Illinois, Iowa, Minnesota, and Wisconsin—were early attempts at economic regulation. Generally, this legislation sought to limit the prices railroad companies could charge for transporting or storing grain. Farmers felt that the railroads were "gouging" them. It is incorrect to suggest that the Grange itself was behind this legislation—the organization was officially apolitical. It would also be a mistake to believe that the more radical elements of the Grange wrote the Granger laws. Rather, the Granger railroad laws were "prepared by lawyers with the aid of merchants and shippers and sometimes with the aid of railroad officials." Regulations put on the books by the Granger laws often roughly corresponded to the farmers' interests, but they often did not and were routinely criticized for not going far enough by the more vocal members of the Grange.

In Illinois, a bill passed the state house of representatives as early as 1861 (six years before the Grange was formed) that aimed to "prevent and punish any fraudulent discrimination by railroad companies." The Illinois state senate and governor rejected this approach and the bill did not become law. The cause did not die, however, and a bill regulating railroad rates

was passed in 1869. The law provided no adequate provision for enforcement and was described by one historian as a "mere encumbrance on the statute books."

Led by a coalition of reformers, which included elements of the Grange, the voters of Illinois ratified a new constitution in 1870. It contained provisions granting authority to regulate railroads, public elevators, and warehouses for the storage of grain. The sections relating to railroad and warehouse regulation proved to be extremely popular with voters, which created a strong impetus for reform in the next legislative session. This, coupled with the fact that unusually high numbers of farmers pledged to support regulation were elected to the Illinois legislature that convened in 1871, led to the passage of many of the Granger laws during the year that followed.

While most Granger laws in Illinois and elsewhere attempted to regulate railroads, there were exceptions. Considerable time and effort were also devoted to leashing other middlemen whose practices—in particular, pricing their goods and services—farmers found objectionable. Illinois enacted a statute in April 1871 that regulated "public warehouses and the public inspection of grain." This law classified public warehouses according to how the grain was stored—mixed together or segregated by farmer—and the size of the city in which the warehouse was located. "Class A warehouses," for example, were defined as "all warehouses, elevators and granaries in which grain is stored in bulk, and in which the grain of different owners is mixed together, or in which grain is stored in such a manner that the identity of different parcels cannot be accurately preserved. . . ." In addition, a Class A warehouse must be located in a city of at least 100 inhabitants—a requirement that only Chicago met in 1871. And finally, the law required all Class A warehouses to procure a license and set rates based on the length of time the grain had been stored.

Most companies technically complied with the provisions of the railroad and warehouse acts but officially denied the validity of these laws and declared all of their rights to be reserved. Others, such as Munn and Scott of Chicago, "managers and lessees of a public warehouse known as the Northwestern Elevator," defied the statute. In 1872, a suit was instituted against Munn and Scott for failure to take out licenses required by law and charging in excess of the rates established in January 1872 under the provisions of the statute.

After a brief delay caused by the Chicago fire, the defendants were found guilty by the Criminal Court of Cook County and fined $100. This decision was later affirmed by the Illinois Supreme Court but rose on appeal to the U.S. Supreme Court. A decision on *Munn v. Illinois*, and several other Granger cases, was issued on March 1, 1877.

The decision in *Munn* was placed first, according to George Miller, because Munn and Scott was a partnership rather than a corporation, thus "its suit, free of all complications resulting from corporate charter provisions, permitted a more direct confrontation with the basic issues raised by the plaintiffs counsel." The Court's majority opinion, written by Chief Justice Morrison R. Waite, rejected the arguments of plaintiffs counsel on all counts, thus upholding the Illinois statute by a 7–2 margin.

The court in *Munn*, and in others such as *Chicago, Burlington and Quincy Railroad Company v. Iowa*, established several propositions that collectively laid the legal foundation on which early reform legislation was based. With them—and several others going back to 1867—the Court entered what political scientist Robert G. McCloskey called the "second great period of constitutional history," during which the major interest of the Supreme Court became the relationship between government and business.

The *Munn* decision established that a state may, under its police power, regulate, to the extent of determining maximum rates, any business that is public in nature or has been "clothed with a public interest." Warehouses and railroads were considered of a sufficiently public nature as to permit their regulation. And, although a railroad charter is a contract, the Court held that the Constitution does not interfere with the right of a state to regulate charges unless it contains a direct stipulation to that effect.

Waite established two other principles that were later overturned or significantly modified. First, the majority concluded in *Munn* that lack-

ing federal legislation, states were permitted to regulate interstate commerce so far as its citizens are affected by it. In 1886, the Court reversed itself by ruling that "national commerce must be nationally controlled, if it is to be controlled at all."

Perhaps even more crucial for understanding *Munn v. Illinois* was how the Court settled the issue of procedural versus substantive due process—a debate that would reappear in many significant decisions involving the relationship between business and government for the rest of the nineteenth century. The attorneys for Munn and Scott had argued that certain sections of the Illinois statute were repugnant to the first section of the Fourteenth Amendment, which ordains that no state shall "deprive any person of life, liberty or property without due process of law, nor deny to any person within its jurisdiction the equal protection of the law." The Court's response to these points, though clearly making the job of the regulators easier, left plenty of room to maneuver.

Waite's majority opinion provided for a narrow procedural construction of the due process clause of the Fourteenth Amendment. According to the Court, the Fourteenth Amendment could not be used to interfere with state regulatory initiatives as long as the property had become "clothed with the public interest." This occurs, according to Waite when it is used in a manner "to make it of public consequence, and affect the community at large." If a business, such as a railroad or a warehouse standing in "the very gateway of commerce," is involved in an activity in which the public has an interest, it "grants to the public an interest in that use, and must submit to [control] . . . for the common good." As long as a business was deemed to be affected with a public interest, the substantive regulations (e.g., in *Munn*, the storage rates set by the statute) were placed outside the scope of judicial review. If property owners were not given reasonable compensation—the power to regulate could be abused, Waite acknowledged—the proper recourse was at the polls, not in the courts.

Legal scholars have detected a loophole in Waite's opinion in that he seemed to concede some of what Justice Stephen J. Field had argued in his minority opinion. Waite was careful to say that "under some circumstances" a statute may deprive an owner of his property without due process of law. Waite, however, did not make clear when and under what circumstances future courts would be justified in handing down rulings limiting governmental regulation of business. Within roughly ten years, Waite's views were abandoned in favor of Field's substantive due process position, which sought to safeguard private property from what conservatives termed "arbitrary and unreasonable" regulatory schemes. In addition, the reach of the Fourteenth Amendment was extended by later courts, establishing that a corporation is legally a person and cannot be deprived of its property without due process. A far cry, indeed, from the Court's position in *Munn*.

Thus, it can be argued that the *Munn* decision was a false start—favorable to reform but severely gutted in later decisions. To a point, this is a reasonable conclusion. But it would be unfortunate to conclude that *Munn v. Illinois* was of no value to later reformers. In it, the Court established principles, such as the propriety of government regulation under the state's police powers, that were never over-turned. The pace of reform was slow during the remainder of the century but in all probability this was a result of more than simply a recalcitrant Court. When political majorities began to demand reform during the Progressive Era, the politicians found a way to put new regulations on the books.

In spite of what the Court did in the next two decades to back away from *Munn*, the fundamental principles of the Granger cases still stood. In 1913, historian Justus Buck pointed to the "voluminous restrictive railroad legislation of the last 40 years" as the legacy of the Granger cases. The Court, though never wild about the "schemes" of many reformers, had become a willing partner in the age of reform. There was no turning back.

Selected Bibliography

Buck, J.S. *The Granger Movement: A Study of Agricultural Organization and Its Political, Economic, and Social Manifestations, 1870–80*. Cambridge, MA: Harvard University Press, 1913.

McCloskey, R.J. *The American Supreme Court*. Chicago: University of Chicago Press, 1960.

Miller, G.H. *Railroads and the Granger Laws*. Madison, WI: University of Wisconsin Press, 1971.

A "RIGHT" TO MAKE CIGARS

by Melvin I. Urofsky
Department of History
Virginia Commonwealth University

In re Jacobs, 98 N.Y. 98 (1885) [New York Court of Appeals]

Today's apartment dwellers would properly object if their neighbors ran noisy industrial machines or manufactured noxious products. And they would be able to call upon the law to put an end to the nuisance. Even though a person's home is pertained to be his castle, most people assume that the power of the state can and should be used to prevent one person's use of property from infringing on the right of others to enjoy theirs. In fact, one of the most oft-quoted of the old common-law maxims is *sic utere tuo ut alienum non laedas* ("use your own property so as not to injure the property of others").

But today's sense of how one may properly use his property is quite different from that held a century ago, a period when initial efforts of the state to exercise its police powers ran headlong into a prime tenet of prevailing legal thought: the sanctity of property and the right to use it for gain. This difference between today's views and those of the latter nineteenth century is evident in this famous case of the tenement cigar maker.

Although industrialization affected nearly every aspect of the American economy after the Civil War, some trades remained labor-intensive and immune from the need to cluster workers around machines in giant factories. In many American cities, workers in such trades as garment manufacturing labored in lofts, storefronts, and often in their own homes. Individuals contracted with wholesalers to do piecework, and they did the work in the crowded tenements where immigrants who composed the bulk of these labor forces lived.

One such trade was cigar making, which remained essentially an individual hand-rolling operation, the worker wrapping tobacco leaves into shape. One needed no special machinery, nor did the laborer have to go to a factory; only a chair and a table were required. In the mid-1880s, the bulk of the nation's cigars were produced in New York tenements, and reformers concerned about the possible health risks involved sought legislation to move the noxious weed out of living quarters and into regular commercial space. In May 1884, the Empire State legislature passed an act "to improve the public health" by prohibiting cigar making in New York City and imposed criminal penalties of up to $100 and/or six months in jail for violation of the law.

Two days after enactment of the law, the police arrested Peter Jacobs, who with his wife and two children lived in a New York tenement. The Jacobs family enjoyed a relatively spacious seven-room flat, occupying an entire floor of the building. In one room, Jacobs prepared tobacco leaves and made cigars, and according to the police report, there was no smell of tobacco in any room in the flat except that one.

Jacobs had plainly violated the law, and the local magistrate committed him to prison for trial. He appealed to the state supreme court (which, in New York, is the lowest court of record in the state judicial system). The court ordered him released and declared the cigar act unconstitutional. The prosecuting attorney then appealed to the state's highest tribunal, the court of appeals, which heard the case on December 17, 1884. A month later, on January 20, 1885, Judge Robert Earl spoke for a unanimous court in declaring the act unconstitutional, since it had deprived Jacobs of his rights to property, in this case the right to labor at a lawful trade, without due process of law.

The case must be seen in light of a debate going on at the time between defenders of the new industrial system and those who sought through reform to mitigate its more harmful effects. For the latter, the state's nascent police powers could be used to regulate property in order to protect the health and safety of the people. Conservatives admitted that the state had this power, but took a very narrow view of its extent. Influential legal writers, such as Christopher Tiedeman and Thomas M. Cooley, argued that the government should do no more than provide police protection against criminals who would injure life or property.

To erect a legal barrier against the police power, conservative jurists in state and federal courts adopted the doctrine of substantive due process, which invested property, including the right to pursue any lawful trade, with safeguards against interference by the state. The doctrine did not win the approval of a majority of the U.S. Supreme Court until *Allgeyer v. Louisiana* (1897), but it captured the approval of many state courts well before then. The conservative New York Court of Appeals was one of the first to adopt the idea of substantive due process to strike down reform legislation.

The cigar law, according to Judge Earl, bore no relation to health or safety, but interfered "with the profitable and free use of his property by the owner . . . and arbitrarily deprives him of his property and some portion of his personal liberty." This liberty, according to the court, "means the right, not only of freedom from actual servitude, imprisonment or restraint, but the right of one to use his faculties in all lawful ways, to live and work where he will, to earn his livelihood in any lawful calling." Any laws, of whatever type, that restricted this liberty, violated constitutional protection.

While admitting the broad reach of the police power, the court noted that the legislature could not, under the guise of the police power, trammel basic constitutional rights. The courts had the obligation to protect those rights, and therefore it would be the final arbiter of whether the statute was a reasonable exercise of the police power. Thus, the court arrogated to itself not only the relatively narrow role of determining if a specific power existed, but also the broader authority to pass on the wisdom of the statute.

In re Jacobs quickly became one of the most cited state court decisions of its time, quoted approvingly by both state and federal jurists for its defense of property rights, as well as its expansive view of judicial power.

Selected Bibliography

Corwin, E.S. *Liberty Against Government*. Baton Rouge, LA: Louisiana State University Press, 1948.

Paul, A.M. *Conservative Crisis and the Rule of Law: Attitudes of Bar and Bench, 1887–95*. Ithaca, NY: Cornell University Press, 1960.

Urofsky, M.I. "State Courts and Protective Legislation in the Progressive Era: A Reevaluation." *Journal of American History* 72 (1985): 63–91.

CAN NEBRASKA OR ANY STATE REGULATE RAILROADS?

by Eric Monkkonen
Department of History
University of California, Los Angeles

Smyth v. Ames, 169 U.S. 466 (1898) [U.S. Supreme Court]

The celebrated late nineteenth-century U.S. Supreme Court case *Smyth v. Ames* concerns one of those rare instances in which what seems to be a purely local conflict takes on national importance. In *Smyth*, the Court declared unconstitutional the Newberry Bill, which Nebraska Populists had enacted in 1893. This bill was an attempt to force railroads to lower their shipping rates by almost one-third, bringing them more in line with neighboring Iowa, and relieving some of the economic hardships that Nebraska farmers had been suffering. Not only did this bill have bread-and-butter importance, but its passage heralded a symbolic victory for Populists nationwide; finally the embattled farmers had achieved concrete legislative action. But then, in *Smyth v. Ames*, the Supreme Court in essence said that states could control railroad rates only within a limited range of options to be set by the Court. The constitutional issues suddenly made Nebraska's problems symbolize those of a nation going through an awkward economic transition, and the solution to these problems became national policy for the next 50 years. Thus, *Smyth* was not merely the Supreme Court overturning state legislation. It represented a solution—and not necessarily a just one—to an economic, politi-

cal, and legal crisis that had come to a head with the Nebraska legislature's passage in 1893 of the bill named for its sponsor, Fred Newberry, a farmer from Aurora, Nebraska.

In the 1890s, state regulatory agencies had begun to wield their power vigorously and somewhat inconsistently, while at the same time federal regulatory agencies, such as the Interstate Commerce Commission, began to gain power. For corporations with national operations, the state regulation seemed to be a kind of guerilla war, and the milder, more consistent, and flexible federal control appeared to be the lesser of two evils. For the midwestern farmer, the combination of fluctuations in the international wheat market, severe drought in the early 1890s, and a depression in 1893 made the economic outlook seem grim. As a result, there were sporadic agrarian movements to lower and regularize the costs of the elements of the national economy that affected the farmer most: the railroads and various warehousing concerns. Known as Populists, these farmers gained power in the Nebraska legislature and after a two-year struggle passed the Newberry Bill, which cut intrastate railroad freight rates 29.5 percent. The railroads obtained an injunction against the enforcement of the act and challenged its constitutionality under the due process clause of the Fourteenth Amendment. Thus, *Smyth v. Ames* was composed of economic, political, and legal causes. But, as it came before the Supreme Court, most people saw the complex issue in terms of bad or good. As one railroad president put it, "Another effect of a decision in favor of the Nebraska law would be the bad example which it would set to other states where the Populists and demagogues of other kinds are strong."

After a U.S. circuit court decision by Justice David J. Brewer of Leavenworth, Kansas, who held the statute to be unconstitutional because it deprived the railroads or property (i.e., profit) without due process of law, the case was appealed to the U.S. Supreme Court by Constantine J. Smyth. Smyth was a poor Irish immigrant who had ridden the rails to Nebraska in 1876, sold Omaha newspapers, worked for the Union Pacific, studied law, and later became attorney general of Nebraska from 1897 to 1901. Both the arguments before the Court and Justice John Marshall Harlan's decision revolved around two accepted legal concepts: (1) the common-law doctrine that requires reasonable compensation for goods and services and the right of the public to pay a reasonable rate; and (2) the due process clause of the Fourteenth Amendment (i.e., "nor shall any State deprive any person of life, liberty, or property, without due process of law," person meaning corporation as well as human). The disagreement involved the meaning of "reasonable" and the meaning of the due process clause.

Several leading Nebraskans presented the arguments for the appellants. The state's previous attorney general, Arthur S. Churchill, and John L. Webster, a prominent Omaha lawyer since 1869, pointed out that at common law "reasonable" compensation does not include compensation for high costs due to bad management and inefficiency. Thus, the plaintiffs should have been required to show that the railroads were prudently managed. Further, they argued that reasonable compensation should mean only that which is necessary to pay operating expenses—anything above is a legislative question. William Jennings Bryan, also for the appellants, argued essentially the same point, claiming that courts can suspend only state rates

that do not pay operating expenses. He noted that profit should be computed on the basis of reproduction cost; otherwise overcapitalization, stock watering, and poor investment would be rewarded.

The various railroads making up the appellees (Ames, one of the appellees, was a railroad president) had both locally and nationally known legal counsel. James M. Woolworth was probably the most prominent lawyer in Nebraska; though he had tended to avoid political office, he was well known as a pioneer businessman and investor in Omaha. Woolworth argued that there were two ways of determining whether the new rates would allow the railroad reasonable compensation: (1) the new rates could be tried out or (2) the effect of the rates could be retrodicted (i.e., calculated for previous years). Only the second method was feasible, he claimed, because the results of the first were unpredictable and perhaps destructive. He calculated that the Nebraska rates would not have paid operating expenses for the previous years. He further argued, citing *McCulloch v. Maryland* (1819), that because the Union Pacific had been chartered by Congress, Nebraska was interfering with the federal government. James C. Carter, a well-known New York lawyer, also appeared for the appellees. First, he said that if no return on investment was yielded, the result would be practical destruction of property. Second, he appealed to the principles of *laissez-faire* economics (and here is a paradox of *laissez-faire* in the late nineteenth century: Adam Smith's hidden hand needed the protection of the Supreme Court). The railroad charges, he said, should be determined by "laws of free competition: Should an unwise policy (never followed in present times) tempt the imposition of high rates, it would speedily be baffled by the appearance in the field of new roads and new competitors."

Justice John Marshall Harlan delivered the decision, upholding Brewer's circuit court decision. Harlan pointed out that it had been settled that a state cannot deprive a railroad of just compensation without due process; the Fourteenth Amendment protects railroads even within the states. Harlan admitted that a commission of experts might more easily determine what compensation a railroad is "entitled to receive," but he then modestly took that task upon himself: "The court cannot shrink from the duty to determine whether it be true, as alleged, that the Nebraska statute invades or destroys rights secured by the supreme law of the land." He calculated, in a series of impossible-to-follow operations, the effect the proposed rate reductions would have had on the railroad in the years before the act was passed. He concluded that only four of the companies involved would have made a profit, which made the statute unconstitutional.

Confessing that just compensation would always be an "embarrassing question," Harlan, at the end of his decision, set up standards for determining just compensation: "The basis of all calculations as to reasonableness of rates . . . must be the fair value of the property being used by it [the company] for the convenience of the public. And in order to ascertain that value, the original cost of construction, the amount expended in permanent improvements, the amount and market value of its bonds and stock, the present as compared with the original cost of construction, the probable earning capacity of the property under the particular rates prescribed by the statute, and the sum required to meet operating expenses are all matters for consideration." These points quickly became the criteria used by the Interstate Commerce Commission and other state commissions to determine all public rate charges; Harlan's guidelines were thus used by commissions to avoid constant court cases.

Smyth not only set guidelines for rate regulation, but effectively stopped further state legislative attempts at controlling railroads. The door to state regulation of railroad rates opened by the Granger decisions in 1876 had been closing ever since. *Smyth* locked it. In many ways the issues posed by specific application of the case were to be insignificant within the next 40 to 50 years. The growth of truck transportation furnished real competition for the railroads, and they suffered—their privileged position perhaps had encouraged inefficiency. Finally, Harlan's decision marked the judicial acceptance of the doctrine of substantive due process, the "limitation upon the right of legislatures to regulate private property in the interests of the public welfare."

The farmers' calls for rate regulation have had continuing interest for historians, beginning in the 1870s with the Illinois Granger laws, which set maximum grain elevator rates and were upheld by the Supreme Court in 1877. The regulation movements of the late nineteenth century are often seen as the beginning of Progressive and New Deal regulation; thus, the whole subject of regulation is linked to various turn-of-the-century reform movements. By the mid-1950s, historians began to portray the regulation movement as being pro-business, essentially a rationalization of industrial capitalism. This interpretation contrasted with the earlier version of various control attempts as being essentially anticapitalist and antibusiness. Lee Benson has shown how all of the major participants in the economy came to realize "that the positive use of state power was an indispensable supplement to private, self-policing agreements." As James C. Carter's argument in *Smyth v. Ames* ironically illustrates, *laissez-faire*, the economic theory that insists on the freedom of economic activity from state interference, needed the Supreme Court's assistance.

It is interesting to note that Henry Lee Higginson, a Boston banker and railroad director named in one of the suits decided in *Smyth*, had had many discussions with Theodore Roosevelt on the subject of governmental regulation. Roosevelt once wrote Higginson that he thought railroad problems were self-inflicted and said, "Unquestionably there is loose demagogic attack upon them in some of States, but not one particle of harm has come to them by Federal action." If the federal government left the railroads alone, "[i]t would result in a tidal wave of violent State action against them throughout three-fourths of the country," Roosevelt continued.

Contemporary reaction to the Newberry Bill was divided. As far as newspapers were concerned, "the opinion that the bill was unfair seemed to prevail throughout the state, if the press expressed the public opinion." As historians have often pointed out, the press represented village opinion, not farmer opinion. Yet

House Chaplain B. F. Diffenbacher of Hay Springs, Nebraska, predicted that traitors who were against the bill would end up in a "moral volcano" complete with "lurid lava" and the "muttered thunder of hidden forces."

Nationally, newspaper editors breathed a sigh of relief at the Court's *Smyth* decision. The press quit writing about the upcoming war in Cuba and rejoiced at the victory in the Court. One midwestern newspaper called the decision "one of the most important of recent years," seeing it as one of "extreme fairness." Another was even more laudatory, claiming that the "landmark" decision rested on "fundamental equalities" and the "impregnable bulwarks" of the Constitution, preserving "orderly liberty and material and social progress." The *Chicago Tribune*, in discussing the decision, commented on the Populist legislation: "But they overdid the business, and this particular law, like so many others the Populists have enacted, could not stand a judicial test." And the *New York Tribune* quoted a member of the Joint Passenger Committee, meeting at the Waldorf-Astoria Hotel, who said, "The decision was one of the most far-reaching in the land, inasmuch as it proved that Populistic tendencies were by no means apparent in the framers of the Constitution." The paper also quoted Chauncey Depew, president of the New York Central Railroad: "If the Supreme Court had upheld the Nebraska law," Depew stated, "I feel certain that we would have had a panic, worse than anything we have experienced." Thus, the Supreme Court's decision, coming so long after the excited passage of the Newberry Bill, after William Jennings Bryan's defeat in 1896, and in a period of better farm prices, seems almost to have been a final crow of all those who had opposed the Populists.

The legal significance of *Smyth* is to be found not so much in terms of abstract principle as for giving the established common-law principle of reasonableness a modern operational meaning. This meaning has been important because soon after the decision it functioned as the guidelines for federal commission rate setting. Thus, although the social, political, and economic meanings of the case related to the power of states to regulate, the power of oppressed groups to control business through legislation, and the shape of business-government relations, the legal meaning of the case is much more specific and narrow.

An early legal analysis that included *Smyth v. Ames* and the legal economic issues connected with it traced three stages of rate regulation under the Fourteenth Amendment. In the first stage—*Munn v. Illinois* (1877)—reasonableness was considered a legislative question; in the second stage—*Stone v. Farmers' Loan and Trust* (1886) and *Minnesota Rate Cases* (1913)—it was decided that the Court could review rates set by states for "the power to regulate is not a power to destroy"; and in the third stage, state-set rates were considered invalid unless they yielded a reasonable return. The difference between *Smyth* and earlier cases was its consideration of investments and earnings as evidence; and the Court was criticized for doing a poor job in its calculations based on the evidence.

After the early Progressive criticism of the *Smyth* decision, legal opinion on the case seems to have been quiescent. Curiously, the case drew legal criticism again during the Depression of the 1930s, with critics claiming it was no longer relevant. One critic in 1932 focused on the application of the rate-setting guidelines established by Harlan. Not only had Harlan's guidelines been used for public transportation, but public utilities, too, had come under the same rules; however, the critic claimed that by the late 1920s, reproduction cost was no longer used except as a theoretical reference. Thus, it was argued that *Smyth* was "no longer applicable" and the whole concept should be forgotten.

Apparently the Supreme Court paid little attention to its critics in the law journals, for 15 years later a persuasive argument was presented to show how commission rate making no longer used *Smyth*. Harlan's doctrine in *Smyth* was declared obsolete by this critic for three other reasons: (1) a situation of transportation competition existed between rail, truck, and air freight, thus ending many railroad monopolies; (2) rate regulation through charters and contracts had grown; and (3) railroad rate regulation had become promotional, often with subsidies. The conclusion: rates should be administrative or legislative, due process should be procedural, and if rates were too high—too bad. So 50 years after the decision had been handed down, this modern argument paralleled that of

Webster and Churchill for Ames of Nebraska with no outburst of protest from the railroads. Perhaps the one area in which the case's importance is uncontested is in its completing "the evolution of substantive due process," an evolution the result of industrialization and urbanization, "social issues of basic consequence to America's destiny." This shift from procedural to substantive due process meant a shift from "nor shall any State deprive any person of life, liberty, or property, without due process of law" to "nor shall any State deprive any person of property."

Although today one can criticize Harlan's decision overturning the Nebraska legislation and especially his judicial rate calculating, one need no longer fall prey to the partisan arguments that the case aroused in the past. With community control becoming more and more a critical issue, one should be able to understand the passion and fears on both sides of the issue that was finalized in *Smyth v. Ames*. Whether one is on the side whose established rights are being invaded and destroyed (as Harlan, the Court, and the railroad owners felt theirs were) or on the side that decides the time has come to seize power from those who ap-

pear to be oppressors (as the Nebraska farmers felt they were doing), one can certainly empathize with the involvement of both sides. This case represents a legal-economic aspect of the repressive attitudes of those in power in the late nineteenth century. While the labor unions were beaten down in the East, blacks denied their civil rights in the South, and women continually ignored in their struggle to get the vote, the Nebraska farmers lost in their attempts to control the economic environment of their own state. And although railroad rates may no longer be a crucial issue, the larger questions raised in this case are still felt: can and should a group of people control their economic destiny? And if so, how?

Selected Bibliography

Adams, A.D. "Reasonable Rates." *Journal of Political Economy* 12 (Dec. 1903): 79–97.

Benson, L. *Merchants, Farmers, and Railroads: Railroad Regulation and New York Politics, 1850–87.* Cambridge, MA: Harvard University Press, 1955.

Blachly, F.F. "*Smyth v. Ames* in Federal State Regulation." *Virginia Law Review* 33 (March 1947): 141–77.

Lewin, T. "*Smyth v. Ames* in the Supreme Court." *St. Louis Law Review* 17 (1932): 163–76.

"MERE MEDDLESOME INTERFERENCES": THE APOGEE OF SUBSTANTIVE DUE PROCESS

by Fred D. Ragan
Department of History
East Carolina University

Lochner v. New York, 198 U.S. 45 (1905) [U.S. Supreme Court]

It is rare to have an advocate of legislative reform change his position and call on the U.S. Supreme Court to undo his handiwork. When Henry Weismann, former baker and union leader, appeared before the Court in 1905, he insisted in the name of freedom of contract that Court overturn his work as a union leader.

As the twentieth century dawned, a divided Supreme Court struggled to implement old values amid the new realities of the industrial

era. In its desire to protect property from the rising tide of state regulatory legislation, a position often urged upon the Court by some of the most influential members of the bar, the Court developed the due process clause of the Fourteenth Amendment into an instrument, much as the Supreme Court of the early nineteenth century had used the doctrine of vested interest and the contract clause, that would permit it to determine whether states acted in an appropriate, direct, and reasonable manner when regulating business. If the state overstepped its authority, the Court struck down the law as arbitrary and unreasonable. Employing this new weapon of substantive due process, the Court took upon itself the responsibility to balance rights claimed by business against the traditionally recognized right of a state to protect the health, safety, and welfare of its people under the police powers.

The Depression of the 1890s inspired and intensified efforts by reformers to improve conditions of employment and the working environment. Although lacking a unity of motives, goals, and methods, the Progressive reformers at the state level tried to humanize industrial plants by limiting child labor, establishing maximum hours and minimum wages, and aiding organized labor. Their efforts ran into judicial opposition. To counter state regulations, especially those concerning hours of work and wages, courts further developed the doctrine of freedom of contract, which held that governmental interference with free market forces constituted the exception to the rule of untrammelled liberty of contract. This doctrine, discovered in the liberty protected by the Fourteenth Amendment and a legal extension of *laissez-faire* economic thought, protected a right not enumerated in the Constitution, one created by judicial fiat. Unless convinced of the danger of an occupation, judges struck down state interference with what the courts viewed as a worker's right to contract freely for a work day and wages he thought acceptable. The doctrines of economic substantive due process and freedom of contract, in the eyes of critics, made the Supreme Court into "a superlegislature," writing its own views into law unrestrained by the balancing of power with the other two branches of government.

The judicial opposition to the reformer's efforts, however, was not absolute. *Lochner v. New York* began in 1901 when a New York court convicted Joseph Lochner of violating a state statute limiting bakers from working more than ten hours a day or 60 hours a week. When the U.S. Supreme Court struck down the law four years later, reformers cried foul, painting the Court as a bastion of economic conservatism. Recently writers have revised that long-

accepted view of the courts, especially the U.S. Supreme Court, as a major obstacle to Progressive Era reforms. If no longer universal, most authorities have continued to question the Court's *Lochner* decision and its use by the later Courts of the 1920s and 1930s.

The "shorter hour" movement for bakers in New York began in earnest after passage in 1868 of federal legislation regulating the hours of labor on public works projects. Two years later, New York adopted a statute modeled after the national act. At the time, bakers, a trade dominated by German immigrants, had not organized themselves into trade unions. According to one source, they earned $5 for a 60 hour week, while plasterers in the building trades, who were organized, earned $4.50 for a 48-hour week. Over the next few years, bakers, chiefly those in New York City, began to unionize. Objecting to long hours and especially to Sunday work, a labor paper reported improvements by 1883. It complained, nonetheless, that lack of strong unions meant "eight dollars for ninety hours" of crushing labor which continued to produce "so many coffins. . . ."

The next year, the Journeymen Bakers Union, a recently organized group trying to promote concerted action among New York City bakers, called for meetings to plan a strategy for achieving shorter work days. Although the union insisted that the "yellow-dog contract" (i.e., an agreement many workers were forced to sign as a condition of employment, promising that they would not join a union) be outlawed, their principal goal was for the ten-hour day with additional pay for overtime. The union's representative on the Central Labor Union of New York City took the lead in drafting a bill for introduction at the next session of the legislature. Success in that arena did not come quickly, however.

The 1880s were a decade of turmoil for organized labor. The eight-hour day became a major long-term goal, and in 1885 labor groups formed the National Eight Hour Association in Chicago. Amid a new sense of enthusiasm and confidence, a reinvigorated trade union movement sponsored demonstrations and adopted resolutions demanding shorter work days. Few tangible improvements grew from the activities, however. The 1886 Chicago

Haymarket violence not only added a nail to the coffin of the Knights of Labor but also temporarily stymied the eight-hour movement. Increased agitation did produce, however, new strategies for furthering baker union goals. Adopting the example of the cigar makers union, New York City bakers began using the union label. More effective, however, was their use of the "strike boycott," a device that contributed to significant improvement for members of baker's union. By the late 1880s, many New York City bakers had won the ten-hour work day for themselves. Those not members of unions, especially the recently arrived Italian and Jewish bakers, continued to work long hours. According to a New York State factory inspector report, the recent immigrants worked "12, 13, or 14 hours a day. . . ."

Other developments during the 1880s also helped to further the interests of labor. The establishment of state and national agencies that gathered information on working conditions represented one important advancement. While not replacing the often vague and generalized humanitarianism upon which many reformers acted, agency reports anchored the impulse upon a more realistic view of industrial life. The reports helped to publicize workers' problems and mobilize union members and sympathizers. When presenting their reports or testifying before legislative committees, agency officials also served as an informed lobby against industrial abuses.

Recognizing the necessity of mobilizing their own rank and file and galvanizing public support, labor publications issued calls for action. For bakers, the *Baker's Journal*, first published in 1887 in both English and German, served as a forum for grievances and a vehicle for motivating supporters. Probably the *Journal's* most important role after Henry Weismann assumed leadership in 1890 became that of advocate for legislation to improve working conditions.

A baker in his native Germany prior to coming to San Francisco, Weismann successfully led California bakers before moving to New York. His leadership seemed to energize the Journeymen Bakers Union, as he agitated for legislation and recruited the support of influential reformers, especially religious leaders who helped lobby the state legislature. An endorsement from the Church Association for the Advancement of Labor gave his cause a significant boost. Only three years after his arrival, Weismann could boast of a measure of success. In 1893, the legislature made it illegal for bakers to be "required or permitted to work" more than "sixty hours in any week or more than ten hours in any one day," unless to reduce Sunday work. Along with regulation of hours of work, the law, An Act to Regulate the Manufacture of Flour and Meal Food Products, also established standards for plumbing, construction, storage of flour and meal, hygiene facilities, and sleeping quarters for bakers. Placing enforcement of the statute under the state factory inspector, the 1893 law failed to provide penalties for violation, prompting Morris Hillquit, a leading socialist and labor advocate, to label it a "purely platonic" exercise.

Having achieved a partial victory, the campaign continued to add penalties to the law. Pointing out the law's deficiencies in the *Journal*, Weismann also rallied allies. He reported the lack of compliance with sanitation provisions by some establishments while urging local baker's unions, community leaders, and leaders of national labor organizations to renew their efforts to strengthen the law. Yielding to the continuing pressure, the 1895 legislature amended the law and established penalties. For first offenders, fines ranged from $20 to $50; for a second violation, fines could be not less than $50 nor more than $100 and imprisonment could be for no more than ten days; and for a third offense, fines of not less than $250 and jail terms of no more than 30 days could be imposed. When the 1897 legislature reorganized its laws, the baker's law joined other acts regulating employee hours, sanitation, and working conditions in a section entitled The Labor Law.

The excitement of victory and hope for the dawn of a new day soon turned into frustration. Many bakery shops simply ignored the law. Fear of being fired made employees reluctant to report violations; when an employer was indicted and tried, workers made poor witnesses. Also, since the statute provided no flexibility for emergencies or for workers who desired to work beyond the ten-hour day for additional pay, some in both groups seemed to have resented the law.

To combat the growing influence of the Journeymen Bakers Union, owners organized the Master Bakers Association when legislation first appeared in the early 1890s. With their ranks composed of middle-class entrepreneurs, many of whom had moved from worker to owner, their association prevented the inclusion of penalties in the 1893 legislation. Defeated in 1895, however, master bakers felt trapped between the growing power of labor with its demonstrated ability to influence the legislature on the one side and the new competitive challenge presented by large commercial bakery factories on the other. To survive in this environment, master bakers simply required more from their workers and often refused to comply with the law's provisions.

As the century drew to an end, bakery workers concluded that the hours law could be made effective only where a strong union existed. The *Baker's Journal* reported a survey that revealed over one-third of bakeries worked their employees either more than the ten-hour day or in excess of the 60-hour week. A practice thought to be on the decline—work through Saturday night—the *Journal* now found to be a common requirement in at least one-third of the bake shops. Only in bakeries with a strong and effective union did the *Journal* find that the provisions of the law were respected. Drawing a clear message from its findings, the *Journal* acknowledged the law's usefulness but concluded it could not rely on the state for enforcement. To make the ten-hour day a reality, the union had to organize the nonunion bake shops. If it could do that, the union, not the state, would force compliance with the law using the strike and boycott. With that goal, the union launched a major organizing effort not only in New York City but also in upstate communities.

In a period of general increase in union membership, the Journeymen Bakers Union achieved significant success with its organizing effort. Increasingly New York City bakeries fell in line, recognizing the union and honoring the ten-hour day. Resistance increasingly came from upstate bakers. To combat the unionization effort, the Master Bakers Association de-

veloped a two-prong attack. First, it created company unions, retaining for itself control over the workplace and allowing the company unions to maintain the open shop and reject the union label on their products.

Their second line of attack came in the form of court challenges to the constitutionality of the hours law. To further its organizing campaign, the Journeymen Bakers Union recruited community supporters, who informed state authorities when they found noncompliance with the law. In Utica, the state charged that Joseph Lochner, the operator of a nonunion bake shop, "permitted and required" Aman Schmitter to work more than the 60 hours allowed under the statute. This was Lochner's second time before the court, having been convicted in 1899 of the same offense. Refusing to defend himself and raising no arguments against the law, the Oneida County Court convicted him in 1901. After Lochner's conviction, the Master Bakers Association appealed his case on constitutional grounds.

The law failed the test of constitutionality on several grounds, it argued. Although the state described the act as a health statute, it was not, and for that reason it was not a legitimate exercise of the state's police powers. What the law was, the Master Bakers Association argued, was special class legislation that discriminated against all those excluded from its protection. It also violated the liberty guaranteed by the Fourteenth Amendment of the U.S. Constitution. Conceding that liberty was not absolute, it could only be abridged when the state acted on compelling reasons. In this case, the state had no such reasons.

The Appellate Division of the New York Supreme Court rejected Lochner's arguments by a split vote of 3–2. The Master Bakers Association then appealed to the Court of Appeals, New York's highest court. Again, a divided court, 4–3 this time, ruled against Lochner. For the court's majority early in 1904, Chief Judge Alton B. Parker, later that year the Democratic presidential candidate, conceded the difficulty of defining the extent of the state's police powers. The real test, he maintained, was whether the statute had a "reasonable relation" to public health, welfare, and safety. Although some justified the practice, the courts should not, he argued, "substitute their judgment for that of the Legislature." The health problems of bakery workers, chronic bronchitis, pulmonary diseases, and "dust-laden air," convinced the majority that the "occupation of a baker or confectioner is unhealthy, and tends to result in diseases of the respiratory organs."

The dissenters rejected the majority's judicial restraint. They viewed the law as arbitrarily depriving workers of their liberty, the opportunity to work longer than a ten-hour day. Rejecting the contention that the law was a health measure, Judge Denis O'Brien, employing a bit of judicial logic popular during the period, maintained that a loaf of bread baked by one who worked more than ten hours was no more "unwholesome" than a loaf baked by a person working only ten hours. To the majority view that the court must not substitute its judgment for that of the legislature, the dissenters countered that the courts "must determine for themselves whether in any given case the legislation which is claimed to be an exercise of the police powers is what it is claimed to be."

After defeat in the New York courts, the Master Bakers Association appealed to the U.S. Supreme Court. To present its arguments, it recruited Henry Weismann, the former editor of the *Baker's Journal*, secretary of the journeymen's union, and probably the individual most responsible for enactment of the ten-hour law. Weismann abruptly resigned his union positions in the fall of 1897. Later, other union officials charged that while being paid to represent the union's interest, he fraternized with their enemies. "The truth," Weismann later explained, was that he had "never been in sympathy with the radicals in the labor movement." After his departure from the union, Weismann became a bake-shop owner, but the enterprise soon failed. He later entered politics and became the chief deputy to the clerk of King's County. While in that post, Weismann studied law and passed the New York bar examination as Lochner's case worked its way through the state's court system. His appeal to the Master Bakers Association appears obvious: as a former baker who opposed the law, he would help respond to Justice Henry Brown's sharp rebuff of employers who argued for freedom of contract for their employees. The argument "would cer-

tainly come with better grace and greater cogency," the justice asserted in *Holden v. Hardy* (1898), if it came from the workers. Weismann just might provide that "grace" and "cogency." Also, Weismann had come to "recognize the injustice" the law created. This strongly held conviction, one story has it, prompted him to study law to attack the constitutionality of the hours law. After the Court's decision, however, Weismann acknowledged that he supported the ten-hour law, opposing only the inability of a "man to work an hour or so overtime for extra compensation if necessity arises and he needs the money and is willing to do the work."

The Supreme Court granted Weismann special permission to argue before it, since his brief law practice had not made him eligible for membership at the Court's bar. Joined by Frank H. Field, Weismann's brief repeated arguments addressed in the court of appeals. He argued that the law denied "certain persons" in the baking trade the "equal protection of the law," since it limited protection to a special group; for example, it did not cover the housewife, the "real artist in biscuits, cake, and bread, not to mention the American pie." For his main argument, he accepted the validity of police powers but challenged their use in this case. Granted, it was "difficult to define" the extent of those powers, Weismann acknowledged, but that difficulty cannot be used to allow a legislature to "sweep away the most cherished rights" of Americans. When laws interfered with contracts, property, and the "freedom to exercise a trade or calling," the Court should, he emphasized, scrutinize them closely and resolve doubts in favor of individual liberty; for to do otherwise "would lead to absurd conclusions . . . more consistent with autocratic" states than this Republic.

Endorsing the Court's decision in *Holden v. Hardy*, which upheld a Utah law limiting miners to an eight-hour day because mining was a "hazardous and unhealthful" occupation, Weismann contended no more danger existed in the bakery trade than a wide range of unprotected employment. This law, which recognized no circumstances where an emergency might legitimately require work beyond the ten hours, in contrast to Utah's act, was "purely a labor law." As such, the Court should strike it down because it constituted an unreasonable use of state police powers.

New York's attorney general, Julius M. Mayer, argued the state's case. Questioning whether Lochner should be allowed to raise constitutional issues, since he raised none at the initial trial, Mayer defended the act as a reasonable exercise of police powers. Those powers, "necessarily elastic," allowed the state to respond to "new and changing conditions" of industrial life. Determining where to draw the "line" to protect workers and the public, he argued, was "eminently a matter for the Legislature. . . ." Mayer also addressed the controversial wording of the statute, making it illegal for workers to be "required or permitted" to labor in excess of 60 hours a week. The legislature used that language to prevent employers from arguing that they had not "orally or in writing *required* [emphasis in original]" employees to work additional hours but did so by "inference and acquiescence." Mayer also raised the issue of the state's interest in protecting "certain classes of men" to have them healthy and available "at its command" when a need might arise. For reasons of internal security and national defense, he argued, the state has a "profound interest" in the "vitality" of its citizens.

The appointees of Presidents Benjamin Harrison and Grover Cleveland dominated the Fuller Court in 1905. Cleveland appointed three members, two who make up part of the *Lochner* majority—Melville W. Fuller of Illinois and Rufus W. Peckham from New York, the author of the majority opinion. Peckham's dissent, while a member of the New York Court of Appeals, in the turn-of-the-century case *People v. Budd* telegraphed his views on the use of state police powers. Following the lead of the Supreme Court in *Munn v. Illinois* (1877), the state fixed maximum charges for grain elevators, but Peckham saw the law as an invasion of rights of property and liberty of contract that was "not only vicious in its nature, communistic in its tendency . . . but illegal." The third Cleveland member of the Court, Edward Douglass White of Louisiana, dissented. Harrison contributed two to the majority, David J. Brewer from Kansas, nephew of Justice Stephen J. Field, and Henry Billings Brown, author of the *Holden v. Hardy* (1898)

decision. President William McKinley made one appointment, Joseph McKenna of California, who joined the majority. President Theodore Roosevelt added two who dissented, Oliver Wendell Holmes, Jr., of Massachusetts and the Ohioan, William R. Day. President Rutherford B. Hayes appointed the senior member of the Court in 1877, John Marshall Harlan of Kentucky, a dissenter.

Hearing arguments over a two-day period in late February 1905, a majority of the Court during conference initially agreed to sustain the lower court decision. Harlan accepted the task of writing that opinion. Peckham led four dissenters. In a situation reminiscent of *Pollock v. Farmers' Loan and Trust Company* (1895), someone abandoned Harlan's majority and joined Peckham, creating a new majority. Since Harlan, White, Day, and Holmes dissented and Peckham, Brewer, and Fuller were the strongest advocates of liberty of contract, either Brown or McKenna is left as the probable switcher. In the past, both had upheld broad construction of state police powers. Although it is impossible to identify the "vacillating jurist," that individual, nonetheless, must bear much of the responsibility for the attacks on the Court that followed.

Writing for a sharply divided Court, Peckham addressed the central question of which should prevail, the power of the state legislature or the "right of the individual to liberty of person and freedom of contract." Court observers that day must have recognized from the outset that the law was in trouble. Noting that the statute lacked provisions for "special emergencies," Peckham reviewed instances in which the Court had sanctioned the use of police powers to interfere with the "right of contract" but emphasized the limits to the "valid exercise" of such power. To pass the constitutional test, a law must be "fair, reasonable and appropriate," Peckham contended.

Arguments of internal security and national defense failed to impress Peckham. If the Court sustained this law based on the need for a "strong and robust" population, almost any interference could be justified. "Not only the hours of employees, but the hours of employers, . . . doctors, lawyers, scientists, all professional men, as well as athletes and artisans, could be forbidden to fatigue their brains and bodies. . . ."

Denying that it was a question of substituting the Court's judgment for that of the legislature, Peckham, nonetheless, argued that the Court must determine for itself not only whether the act fell within the scope of a legislature's powers but also the motives for passing it. To sustain this act, it must be as a health law. But such a law cannot have only a "remote" relation to the ends of the legislation but must have a "more direct" effect on the public's or the baker's health. If a connection existed, Peckham felt it "too shadowy and thin" to warrant interference with liberty of contract. Acknowledging that bakers faced a greater danger to health than some occupations, the justice concluded, that "common understanding" never regarded baking as unhealthy labor. It seemed incredible to Peckham that hours of work could be construed as a public health issue; "wholesome bread does not depend upon whether the baker works but ten hours per day or only sixty hours a week." To be a health measure, the protection must be for the general public and extend beyond the worker in a bakery. The law then raised "at least a suspicion" that factors other than the "public health and welfare" motivated the legislature. The "real object and purpose" he found in the legislature's desire "simply to regulate the hours of labor between the master and his employees (all being men, *sui juris*)" engaged in a business not dangerous to any substantial degree. Such acts, regulating "grown and intelligent men," are "mere meddlesome interferences with the right of the individual. . . ."

Harlan, joined by White and Day, vigorously dissented. Echoing Justice Brown in *Hardy v. Holden*, Harlan emphasized that employees did not stand on an equal footing with their employers and that it was unrealistic to argue that employees voluntarily agreed to work for hours the legislature deemed harmful to their health. Unless the legislature's determination clearly went beyond reasonable bounds, the Court should not interfere. Citing medical evidence used by New York, Harlan agreed that the legislature had a reasonable basis for its judgment, and this use of police powers should be sustained.

If Harlan's dissent is read as the reverse side of the judicial standards applied by the majority, Holmes virtually dismissed both Harlan and Peckham for being outside the proper role of the judge. "It does not need research to show," Holmes maintained, that this statute did not "infringe fundamental principles as they have been understood by the traditions of our people and our law." Underlying the majority view, Holmes found "an economic theory which a large part of the country does not entertain." Whether he agreed or disagreed with that theory had "nothing to do with the right of the majority to embody their opinions in law." After listing examples, "ancient" and "more modern" of police powers that had been permitted, he noted that "liberty of the citizen to do as he likes so long as he does not interfere with the liberty of others to do the same" had been a "shibboleth of some well-known writers. . . ." The Fourteenth Amendment had not enacted "Mr. Herbert Spencer's Social Statics." Some Court approved laws "embody convictions or prejudices which judges are likely to share. Some may not. But a constitution is not intended to embody a particular economic theory. . . . It is made for people of fundamentally differing views. . . ." To Holmes, "liberty in the Fourteenth Amendment" had been "perverted" when "held to prevent the natural outcome of a dominant opinion" unless a "rational and fair man" concluded that the law violated "fundamental principles" of law and tradition. Peckham's majority thought that was exactly what the New York law did.

Although the press reported a threatened strike immediately after the Court's decision, it never occurred. New York bakers gradually came to question the impact of the ruling. The *Baker's Journal* continued to find that the ten-hour day prevailed where unions were strong. Continuing to attack the Court for its philosophy, labor leaders emphasized anew the need to organize the nonunion bakeries.

If the effect of the ruling was limited among bakeries, it did not affect workers outside that industry, leading one authority to label it as an "aberration." Prior to its ruling in *Lochner*, the Court had upheld state legislation limiting hours for public workers. Nor did the Court reverse *Holden v. Hardy*, limiting hours for occupations considered dangerous. Railroad workers were also accepted as legitimate subjects for protection. After its 1908 *Muller v. Oregon* decision limiting the working hours of women and children, men—unless employed by the state, the railroads, or in dangerous work—constituted the only group not generally protected. But even there, protection increased. New Jersey, for example, revised its ten-hour bakery law in 1912, providing that bakers could work overtime for additional pay during emergencies. By 1917, when the Court upheld in *Bunting v. Oregon* a law that limited the work hours of all factory employees, the majority *sub silentio* ("silently") seemed to overrule *Lochner*. But since it had not done so explicitly, a new Court majority in *Adkin's v. Children's Hospital* (1923) prohibited Congress from authorizing a commission to establish minimum wages in the District of Columbia and revealed a majority unmoved by the arguments that a relation existed between "low wages and long hours and low morals. . . ." Not until *West Coast Hotel v. Parrish* (1937) did the Court finally turn its back on *Lochner* and the impulse to substitute its judgment of the proper relation between management and labor for that of the state legislature.

After the Court's retreat from *Lochner* in 1937, it rejected, as its critics insisted it must, the creation of economic constitutional rights and superimposing its own view of wise social and economic policy for those of the legislature. Justice Hugo L. Black in *Ferguson v. Skrupa* (1963) summarized the Court's position: "The doctrine that prevailed in *Lochner* . . . and like cases—that due process authorizes courts to hold laws unconstitutional when they believe the legislature has acted unwisely—has long since been discarded. We have returned to the original constitutional proposition that courts do not substitute their social and economic beliefs for the judgment of the legislative bodies, who are elected to pass laws. . . . We refuse to sit as a superlegislature to weigh the wisdom of legislation. . . ."

Critics of recent Supreme Court decisions have detected, or in some cases desired, a return to *Lochner*. One defender of economic liberties argues that the Court has an obligation to protect those freedoms in order to promote a "free, humane, and plentiful society." The

Court's abdication of its role as protector of economic liberties, signaled in Justice Harlan Fiske Stone's famous footnote number four in *United States v. Carolene Products Company* (1938), has failed to produce, he argues, the results critics of economic substantive due process expected. What it has done, as one expert maintains, is turn the "economic marketplace" over to regulations and regulators who have "frequently and frivolously" wielded enormous power harmful to the nation's welfare. The regulators, often individuals whose only "expertise" consisted of winning a local election or of support for a winning candidate, have "critical power" over the economy. In light of what presently exists, it is "difficult to believe that *Lochner* would have harmed so many so often."

Other critics have struck at the Court for more telling reasons. They have criticized it for creating new "fundamental" rights, like "liberty of contract," regardless of whether they have a connection with any constitutional value marked as "special." In *Griswold v. Connecticut* (1965), Justice William O. Douglas held unconstitutional a law prohibiting married couples from using contraceptives because it violated their right to privacy. The Court, in *Roe v. Wade* (1973), significantly enlarged that right when it applied it to an unmarried pregnant woman who wanted an abortion. Although *Lochner* and *Roe* are "twins," they are "not identical," asserts constitutional scholar John Hart Ely. Finding *Lochner* a "thoroughly disreputable" decision, Ely worries that *Roe* "may turn out to be the more dangerous precedent." While Justice Peckham balanced the state's interest against the liberty of the individual, Justice Blackmun established a "compelling" interest test for the exercise of those state powers. Using the balance of interest test, *Lochner* sowed the "seeds" of its own destruction because it argued that long working hours are not reasonably related to the promotion of the ends of health and safety. In *Roe*, the Court made no convincing attempt "to trace its premises to the charter from which it derives its authority." Certainly with *Lochner*, the Court took an issue, raised it to constitutional principle, was overly influenced by counsel, and intruded where it had "no business."

Selected Bibliography

Ely, J.H. "The Wages of Crying Wolf: A Comment on *Roe v. Wade.*" *Yale Law Journal* 82 (June 1973): 920–49.

Groat, G.G. "The Eight Hour and Prevailing Rate Movement in New York State." *Political Science Quarterly* 21 (1906): 414–33.

Semonche, J.E. *Charting the Future: The Supreme Court Responds to a Changing Society, 1890–1920.* Westport, CT: Greenwood Press, 1978.

Siegan, B.H. *Economic Liberties and the Constitution.* Chicago: University of Chicago Press, 1980.

Stephenson, D.G., Jr. "The Supreme Court and Constitutional Change: *Lochner v. New York* Revisited." *Villanova Law Review* 21 (1975–76): 217–43.

Tarrow, S.G. "Lochner Versus New York: A Political Analysis." *Labor History* 5 (1964): 277–312.

Urofsky, M.I. "State Courts and Protective Legislation During the Progressive Era: A Reevaluation." *The Journal of American History* 72 (June 1985): 63–91.

MINIMUM WAGES AND MAXIMUM HOURS FOR WOMEN: VICTORY WITHOUT DECISION

by Fred D. Ragan
Department of History
East Carolina University

Stettler v. O'Hara, 243 U.S. 629 (1917) [U.S. Supreme Court]

Decided on the eve of America's participation in World War I, the U.S. Supreme Court settled, albeit temporarily, the question of minimum wages and maximum hours for women factory workers. At issue were minimum wages established pursuant to a 1913 Oregon law. The act, based on police powers, provided for protection of the "lives and health and morals of women and minors" and created the Industrial Welfare Commission, charged with establishing a minimum wage sufficient to maintain them in "good health." It set a wage of not less than $8.64 for a 50-hour week.

Louis B. Brandeis, successful before the U.S. Supreme Court in *Muller v. Oregon* (1908), which upheld a ten-hour law for women, argued *Stettler v. O'Hara* and a companion case in December 1914. In what had become his typical approach to such problems, Brandeis tried to convince the Court that the facts of modern industrial life made the statute reasonable. The legislation, he asserted, was only enacted after Oregon found a large number of women employed at wages insufficient to support an adequate standard of life. That situation resulted in a significant portion of the population being ill-fed and ill-housed, and it depressed their productivity. These victims of the industrial order often gave birth to unhealthy children; and some, forced by their circumstances to supplement their meager income, took "contributions from 'gentlemen friends.'" Viewed broadly, below-subsistence income for women threatened the well-being of the community. To correct the situation, Oregon could have waited for the gradual effects of education, but it chose the direct and positive step of adopting legislation patterned after that in the Australian state of Victoria, which had been successfully followed in New Zealand and Great Britain.

In the final quarter of his brief, Brandeis discussed the constitutionality of the statute. The test, he argued, should not be whether the act is wise or unwise but whether the legislature had a "reasonable" basis for believing that the statute would have the desired effect on the health, safety, or morals of women earning subsistence wages. Concluding, Brandeis urged the justices not to close the door on social experimentation. Nothing, he thought, could be more revolutionary because the Constitution, "perhaps the greatest of human experiments," surely does not preclude a modest effort to "reconcile the existing industrial system with our striving for social justice and the preservation of the race."

Brandeis could not, however, convince a majority of the Court. The majority probably included Chief Justice Edward D. White and Justices Willis Van Devanter, Joseph R. Lamar, Mahlon Pitney, and James C. McReynolds. Oliver Wendell Holmes, Jr., probably persuading Justice Charles E. Hughes, Joseph McKenna, and William R. Day, prepared and circulated a dissent. Taking a position similar to that in *Lochner*, Holmes attacked the practice of using the Fourteenth Amendment to deny states the opportunity to conduct "social experiments . . . upon a limited scale." The expansion by the Court of liberty in the due process clause from "platitude into the dogma of liberty of contract is extravagant and mistaken." After enumerating restrictive statutes upheld by the Court, Holmes argued that if there was to be a criterion for limiting the state, it should be "whether the law is one that a reasonable man could believe to be for the public good." The dissent, however, was never needed.

For whatever reason, the justice assigned to write the majority opinion found it impossible to complete his draft in the spring of 1915 before the Court Term ended. During the summer, Justice Lamar became ill and never returned to the Court. He died in January 1916. President Wilson nominated none other than Louis D. Brandeis to replace Lamar, but Brandeis was not confirmed by the Senate until June 1916, the same month Hughes resigned to accept the Republican nomination for president. John H. Clarke took the seat vacated by Hughes. Chief Justice White restored *Stettler v. O'Hara* to the docket the same month for reargument, although it was clear Brandeis could not participate in the decision.

Felix Frankfurter followed Brandeis as counsel and reargued the issues in January 1917.

He emphasized that the Oregon statute justified limiting freedom of contract because society had to supplement low-wage earners with welfare and that amounted to a subsidy for the employer as well as giving the employer a competitive advantage over firms that paid a fair wage.

Decided on April 9, 1917, Frankfurter won *Stettler* and the companion case, *Bunting v. Oregon*. In *Stettler*, the victory came because the Court divided evenly, and consequently sustained the Oregon Supreme Court ruling upholding the law as a valid exercise of state police powers. Justice John H. Clarke joined Holmes and those favoring the Oregon law. Brandeis replaced Lamar, thus depriving those who wanted to hold the statute unconstitutional of a majority. While most commentators viewed the 5–4 decision as favoring the minimum wage, since Brandeis's position was well known, the victory was short-lived. Six years later, in *Adkins v. Children's Hospital* (1923), the Court found a District of Columbia minimum wage statute unconstitutional. That decision stood for 15 years before the Court finally retreated from the position of economic supervisor of the nation.

Even after the Supreme Court "revolution" of the late 1930s, the Court did not relinquish the power acquired over the years when it acted as the ultimate arbitrator of the American political system, wielding its sword of substantive due process. It simply shifted from economic supervision to other important aspects of American national life.

Selected Bibliography

Bickel, A.M., and B.C. Schmidt, Jr. *The Judiciary and Responsible Government, 1910–21*. New York: Macmillan, 1984.

THE CHAMBERMAID'S REVENGE

by C. Herman Pritchett
Department of Political Science
University of California, Santa Barbara

West Coast Hotel Company v. Parrish, 300 U.S. 379 (1937) [U.S. Supreme Court]

Elsie Parrish was employed at the Cascadian Hotel in Wenatchee, Washington, as a chambermaid at $12 for a 48-hour week. Under the state minimum wage law, adopted in 1913, she should have received $14.50. Rejecting the hotel's offer of a $17 settlement, she sued for $216.19. The state supreme court supported her claim, but the hotel appealed. On March 29, 1937, the U.S. Supreme Court agreed with the state court and upheld the minimum wage law by a vote of 5–4.

There was a distinguished audience in the Court chamber the morning the decision was announced, for it was widely anticipated that the justices might rule on the constitutionality of the National Labor Relations Act, a highly controversial New Deal statute. They did not. But Parrish's case was a worthy substitute, for it not only resolved the Court's long uncertainty about the constitutional rights of women in industry, but also signaled the surrender of the Court to President Roosevelt's New Deal.

Chafing under a series of rebuffs by the Court during his first term, Roosevelt had sent his so-called Court-packing plan to Congress on February 5, 1937. He proposed that the president be authorized to appoint one additional justice to the Court for every sitting justice over the age of 70, up to a limit of six new justices. His argument was that over-age justices (five of the nine were 70 or over) had slowed the efficient dispatch of judicial business. The proposal set off an uproarious national debate. Even those who had opposed the Court's conservative course rejected this assault on the judicial tradition. Realizing that his initial approach had been a blunder, on March 4, Roosevelt made a radio address charging that the real problem was the Court's assumption of the powers of a policy-making body. In rebuttal, Chief Justice Charles E. Hughes, on March 20, presented to the Senate's judiciary committee an effective document arguing that the Court was fully abreast of its work.

The *Parrish* decision, approving in dramatic fashion significant regulatory legislation, came down nine days later, with Hughes writing the opinion. The shock effect of the ruling was heightened because only a year earlier the Court in *Morehead v. New York ex rel. Tipaldo* (1936), also by a vote of 5–4, had declared a similar New York minimum wage law unconstitutional. The reversal was due to the change of position by Justice Owen J. Roberts between the two cases, an action promptly characterized in the nation's press as "the switch in time that saved nine."

In fact, it appears that Roberts had not been happy with his vote in *Morehead* and that he had "switched" before Roosevelt's Court-packing message. According to Hughes's biographer, Justice Roberts had disclosed to Hughes in a private conversation his intention to vote to sustain the Washington law. Hughes was delighted with the prospect of a majority to reverse *Morehead*. But when *Parrish* was argued, Justice Harlan F. Stone was absent due to illness, and the result was a 4–4 division. If this vote had been allowed to stand, the state law would still have been upheld by reason of the state court's favorable vote. But Hughes held up announcement of the decision until Stone returned (possibly at the urging of Roberts), and a 5–4 vote was assured. In the meantime, however, Roosevelt had proposed his Court-packing plan. So in order not to seem to be acting under pressure from the White House, Hughes withheld announcement of the Court action until March 29.

By 1937, the Court had had 30 years of experience with laws protecting women in industry, and its record was mixed. In 1908, the Court had upheld a ten-hour law for women workers in *Muller v. Oregon*. It was in this case that a Boston lawyer, Louis D. Brandeis, so impressed the Court by a brief that contained only two pages of legal arguments and over 100 pages of extracts from reports of official committees, bureaus of statistics, commissioners of hygiene, and factory inspectors—all of which demonstrated the evil effects of long working hours on women. In its decision, the Court took "judicial cognizance of factors that make women the weaker sex" and held that "she is properly placed in a class by herself." Legislation "designed for her protection could be sustained even when like legislation is not necessary for men and could not be sustained."

Indeed, the Court in *Lochner v. New York* (1905) had rejected a New York law limiting bakery employees (presumably all male) to a ten-hour day or a 60-hour week. This famous case was decided by a 5–4 vote. The law, said Justice Rufus W. Peckham for the majority, could be upheld only as a measure "pertaining to the health of the individuals engaged in the occupation of a baker." Did the health of bakers need protection? Peckham thought not, and he gave two reasons. First, "to the common understanding the trade of a baker has never been regarded as an unhealthy one." Second, statistics regarding trades and occupations show that although "the trade of a baker does not appear to be as healthy as some other trades, [it] is vastly more healthy than still others." In the absence of special health hazards about baking, to permit bakers' hours to be regulated would be to permit general legislative control of hours in industry. This was so unthinkable to Peckham that it clinched his argument. "Statutes of the nature of that under review, limiting the hours in which grown and intelligent men may labor to earn their living, are mere meddlesome interferences with the rights of the individual." Unless the Court called a halt, he asserted, we would all be "at the mercy of legislative majorities."

Justice Oliver Wendell Holmes, Jr., dissented from the *Peckham* opinion with some of his best known rhetoric: "This case is decided upon an economic theory which a large part of the country does not entertain. . . . The Fourteenth Amendment does not enact Mr. Herbert Spencer's Social Statics. . . . I think that the word liberty in the Fourteenth Amendment is

perverted when it is held to prevent the natural outcome of a dominant opinion, unless it can be said that a rational and fair man necessarily would admit that the statute proposed would infringe fundamental principles as they have been understood by the traditions of our people and our law."

Did the decision in *Muller* override the *Lochner* doctrine of *laissez-faire*, or did it merely classify women as exceptions to the *Lochner* rule and as such, entitled to special treatment? At first it appeared that *Lochner* had been fatally weakened. In *Bunting v. Oregon* (1917), the Court approved a ten-hour law for both men and women in industry without even mentioning *Lochner*. As Chief Justice William Howard Taft said subsequently, he had assumed that *Lochner* had been overruled *sub silentio* ("silently") by *Bunting*. But in *Adkins v. Children's Hospital* (1923), the *Lochner* ruling was resurrected to strike down a District of Columbia minimum wage law for women.

For the five-justice majority in *Adkins*, Justice George Sutherland's opinion was a paean to freedom of contract in its purest form, with no nonsense about the special needs of women or inequality of bargaining position. The District of Columbia law was "simply and exclusively a price-fixing law, confined to adult women . . . who are legally as capable of contracting for themselves as men." Sutherland considered that the standards set by the statute to guide the administrative board in fixing minimum wages were vague and fatally uncertain. The sum necessary to maintain a woman worker in good health and protect her morals, he submitted, is not precise and unvarying. It will depend on her temperament, habits, moral standards, and independent resources. It could not be determined "by general formula prescribed by a statutory bureau." Moreover, the law was invalid because it took account of "the necessities of only one party to the contract," compelling the employer to pay the minimum wage whether or not the employee was worth that much to him.

Chief Justice Taft, dissenting, argued that *Adkins* was controlled by *Muller*. He could see no difference in principle between regulating maximum hours and minimum wages. Holmes agreed. "The bargain is equally affected whichever half you regulate." He had supposed that *Lochner* "would be allowed a deserved repose." Sanford also dissented, but Brandeis disqualified himself because his daughter worked for the minimum wage board.

Following the *Adkins* decision, many states assumed that a minimum wage law that did take into account the value-of-service-rendered principle would be constitutional and, therefore, enacted statutes including such provisions. A New York law of this type came before the Supreme Court in *Morehead v. Tipaldo*, in the midst of the Court's furious battle with the New Deal. But the four surviving members of the *Adkins* majority—George Sutherland, Pierce Butler, Willis VanDevanter, and James C. McReynolds—joined with Roberts to invalidate the New York law. Butler dogmatically restated the *Adkins* objections in these words: "The State is without power by any form of legislation to prohibit, change, or nullify contracts between employers and adult women workers as to the amount of wages to be paid."

This bland reiteration in 1936 of a position, which had had little enough support in 1923, was one of the great mistakes in Supreme Court history, and it did more to destroy the country's confidence in the Court as then constituted than some of its more publicized anti-New Deal decisions. The ruling earned the dissent of as distinguished a foursome as ever sat on the high court—Chief Justice Hughes and Justices Brandeis, Benjamin N. Cardozo, and Harlan F. Stone. The chief justice wrote a long opinion, which was a devastating refutation of the unreality of the majority's "free bargaining" assumptions.

Morehead was all the more surprising in that the Court had already begun to give way on issues of price control. In *Nebbia v. New York* (1934), a 5–4 majority had accepted the validity of a Depression-born state law regulating milk prices, with none other than Roberts writing the opinion. Yet in *Morehead*, Roberts's vote returned the *Nebbia* foursome to a minority position, though—as it turned out—only briefly.

It was only ten months after *Morehead* that *Parrish* was decided, with Roberts joining the *Morehead* dissenters to form a 5–4 majority. Chief Justice Hughes wrote the Court's opinion. First, he accepted as valid the stated purposes of the Washington law: prevention of employment of women and minors "under conditions of labor detrimental to their health and morals" or at wages "not adequate for their maintenance." To achieve these purposes, the statute had created a commission directed to establish wages and conditions of labor that were reasonable, not detrimental to health and morals, and "sufficient for a decent maintenance of women."

Second, the *Adkins* precedent had to be disposed of or explained. The Washington supreme court, Hughes said, had "refused to regard the decision in the *Adkins* case as determinative and has pointed to our decisions both before and since that case as justifying its position. . . . This ruling of the state court demands on our part a reexamination of the *Adkins* case."

Beginning this process, Hughes first stressed the prestige of the *Adkins* dissenters, including that of Chief Justice Taft. But more important was Hughes's rejection of the *Adkins* conception of liberty of contract: "The Constitution does not speak of freedom of contract. It speaks of liberty and prohibits the deprivation of liberty without due process of law. In prohibiting that deprivation the Constitution does not recognize an absolute and uncontrollable liberty. . . . The liberty safeguarded is liberty in a social organization which requires the protection of law against the evils which menace the health, safety, morals and welfare of the people. Liberty under the Constitution is thus necessarily subject to the restraints of due process, and regulation which is adopted in the interests of the community is due process."

Continuing, the chief justice then rehearsed all the cases, going back to *Holden v. Hardy* (1898) and *Muller v. Oregon* (1908), where the Court had approved legislative restrictions on freedom of contract. He stated: "This array of precedents and the principles they applied were thought by the dissenting Justices in the *Adkins* case to demand that the minimum wage statute be sustained. . . . We think that the views thus expressed are sound and that the decision in the Adkins case was a departure from the true application of the principles governing the regulation by the State of the relation of employer and employed. . . . Our conclusion is that the case of *Adkins v. Children's Hospital* . . . should be, and it is, overruled." Nothing was said about *Lochner v. New York*, but one can assume, with Taft, that this time it had been overruled *sub silentio*.

Hughes then undertook to explain the Court's apparent reversal of *Morehead* and, incidentally, Roberts's switch between the two cases. The explanation was technical. In deciding *Morehead*, Hughes explained, the New York Court of Appeals had concluded that the New York statute was in no material respect different from the District of Columbia statute in *Adkins*. Consequently, *Adkins* had to be followed by the state court as a matter of respect for the Supreme Court. In turn, Roberts in the *Morehead* appeal to the Supreme Court concluded that the state court's views of the statute had to be respected. On that basis, the only issue for Roberts was whether *Adkins* was distinguishable. But counsel for the state had not raised that issue. Apparently reluctant to ask for the overruling of *Adkins*, they had only contended in state court that the statutes in the two cases were distinguishable and that the state court had held that they were not. Given this ruling, the only way the Supreme Court could have upheld the New York law was to overrule *Adkins*. But counsel for New York had not asked the Supreme Court to overrule *Adkins*. In this dilemma, Roberts took the incredible position that the Supreme Court could not overrule its own decision in *Adkins* because counsel had not asked the Court to do so.

Whatever one may think of Roberts's reasoning in *Morehead*, his reconsideration and vote in *Parrish* gave the New Deal one of its major constitutional victories. The Washington law had been passed in 1913 and enforced continuously thereafter. Like the District of Columbia statute condemned in *Adkins*, it contained no value-of-service standard and so seemed more in defiance of the *Adkins* ruling than that of the New York law. But Hughes completely ignored that issue. He constructed his majority opinion from quotations of Taft and Holmes, asking questions such as: "What can be closer to the public interest than the health of women and their protection from unscrupulous and over-reaching employers?" In fact, as a contemporary scholar pointed out, Hughes's opinion "spoke more about the justice of minimum wages than about the right to enact them without judicial interference."

Justice Sutherland wrote for the dissenters. He argued that the *Adkins* and *Morehead* majority opinions were "a sufficient answer" to all that Hughes had said, but nevertheless he thought it well to restate the reasons and conclusions of the minority. His emphasis was on the personal nature of the judicial obligation. He rejected the recent and widely quoted warning by his colleague Justice Stone, who, in *United States v. Butler* (1936), had written that "the only check upon our own exercise of power is our own sense of self-restraint." Such a view, Sutherland retorted, was "both ill-considered and mischievous." Sutherland, facing these New Deal statutes, could not "subordinate his convictions . . . and keep faith with his oath or retain his judicial and moral independence." Self-restraint "belongs to the domain of will and not of judgment." The only restraint on the judge should be that "imposed by his oath of office, by the Constitution, and by his own conscientious and informed convictions."

The Supreme Court's blessing on minimum wage legislation provided legal and political support for Congress in adopting the Fair Labor Standards Act in 1938. On the constitutional foundation of the commerce clause, the act provided for a minimum wage of 25 cents per hour for employees engaged in interstate commerce or in producing goods for commerce. It also required payment of 50 percent more for overtime for all hours worked over 44 per week. Known as the Wages and Hours Act, it was unanimously upheld in *United States v. Darby Lumber Company* (1941). Justice Stone wrote: "Since our decision in *West Coast Hotel Company v. Parrish* [1937], it is no longer open to question that the fixing of a minimum wage is within the legislative power and that the bare fact of its exercise is not a denial of due process under the Fifth more than under the Fourteenth Amendment. Nor is it any longer open to question that it is within the legislative power to fix maximum hours."

The constitutional support that *Parrish* provided for the Fair Labor Standards Act was its most immediately significant role. However, the decision quickly became a standard citation in all decisions involving freedom of contract, price control, and other statutory ventures in state or federal regulation of the economy. In fact, on the day that the decision was handed down, Justice Hugo L. Black invoked it in upholding the Railway Labor Act, saying: "The Fifth Amendment, like the Fourteenth, see *West Coast Hotel Co. v. Parrish*, decided this day . . . is not a guarantee of untrammeled freedom of action and of contract."

From 1937 to 1980, *Parrish* was cited 41 times by the Supreme Court, in 46 rulings by the federal courts of appeals, and in 68 federal district court decisions. Typical is *Bass Plating Company v. Windsor* (1986), involving a municipal requirement concerning disposal of industrial wastes: "A government regulation that does not impose on fundamental rights, that is adopted in the interests of the community and is not arbitrary or discriminatory does not violate due process so long as there is a reasonable relationship between it and the legitimate end it seeks to further." In *Long Island Lighting Company v. Cuomo* (1987), where the issue was exclusion of the cost of a nuclear power plant from the rate base, a federal judge wrote: "Since the Supreme Court's landmark decision in *West Coast Hotel Co. v. Parrish*, the federal courts have consistently refused to limit the scope of the police power of the states in addressing perceived social and economic problems through economic legislation if that legislation does not impinge upon fundamental personal rights, and have been extremely deferential in assessing the reasonableness of actions taken pursuant to that police power."

The authors of a 1984 *Stanford Law Review* article awarded *Parrish* a key position in the development of American legal thought: "Since 1800, America has experienced at least three different phases of legal thought, each of which has responded in some way to [the] need to regard adjudication as a rational process. Up to the mid-nineteenth century, there was wide acceptance of a broadly instrumental approach to law; judges decided cases by overt reference to policy considerations. Around 1860, there began a discernible, if tentative, shift away from this broad conception of the legal process. By the 1890s, this transformation was completed. The legal community had fallen victim to the classical contagion. Judges claimed to resolve disputes by the rigorous application of rules alone. This train of legal thought—commonly known as conceptualism—flourished for a couple of decades or more, reaching its zenith by the mid-1920s. Its subsequent decline was swift and dramatic. If the triumph of conceptualism was *Lochner v. New York* in 1905, its official death knell was *West Coast Hotel Co. v. Parrish*."

Selected Bibliography

Baer, J.A. *The Chains of Protection: The Judicial Response to Women's Labor Legislation.* Westport, CT: Greenwood Press, 1978.

Hutchinson, A.C., and P.J. Monahan. "Law, Politics, and the Critical Legal Scholars." *Stanford Law Review* 36 (Jan. 1984): 199–245.

Leonard, C.A. *A Search for a Judicial Philosophy: Mr. Justice Roberts and the Constitutional Revolution of 1937.* Port Washington, NY: Kennikat Press, 1971.

Mason, A.T. *Harlan Fiske Stone: Pillar of the Law.* New York: The Viking Press, 1956.

Pusey, M.J. *Charles Evans Hughes.* New York: The Macmillan Co., 1951.

F. Negligence and Tort Law

FELLOW SERVANTS BEWARE

by *John W. Johnson*
Department of History
University of Northern Iowa

Farwell v. Boston and Worcester Railroad Corporation, 4 Metcalf 49 (1842) [Supreme Judicial Court of Massachusetts]

From 1835 to late 1837, Nicholas Farwell worked as an engineer for the Boston and Worcester Railroad Corporation. He earned $2 a day, a relatively high industrial wage for the time. In fact, it was substantially more than what Farwell had earned in his previous position as a machinist. On October 30, 1837, while Farwell was operating one of his company's engines, his train barrelled through a switch that was "left in a wrong condition" by Whitcomb, another employee of the railroad company. The engine was derailed and the train's wheels crushed Farwell's right hand. He sued the railroad to recover damages for his injury. These are the simple and uncontested facts in one of the most famous state court decisions in American legal history: its impact on American industrialization would be hard to overemphasize.

Farwell presented the first occasion for a Massachusetts appellate court to rule on whether an employer should be held liable for damages stemming from the injury of one of its employees caused by the carelessness of another employee. But it was not the first Anglo-American court to confront this issue. Two other "fellow-servant" cases were brought by attorneys for Farwell and the railroad to the attention of the Massachusetts court: *Priestly v. Fowler,* an 1837 case from the British Court of the Exchequer, and *Murray v. South Carolina Railroad Company,* an 1841 decision of the South Carolina Court of Errors. In both cases, the courts found that a employer was not liable for an injury to an employee caused by the carelessness of another employee. Thus, the "fellow-servant rule" was born.

The *Farwell* opinion was handed down by the Massachusetts Supreme Judicial Court. In the mid-nineteenth century, this highest appellate court of the Commonwealth of Massachusetts was one of the most prestigious judicial bodies in the United States; some legal historians have argued that it was more renown than the U.S. Supreme Court. The Massachusetts court's reputation derived mainly from the legal erudition and powerful writing style of its chief justice, Lemuel Shaw. Shaw was a legal giant in what historians have called "golden age of American law." He was certainly one of the most brilliant and prolific jurists in American history, serving as chief justice of the Supreme Judicial Court from 1830 to 1860. During his tenure on the bench, Shaw wrote over 2,000 opinions. His opinion for a unanimous court in *Farwell* may have been his best known decision; it was certainly one of his most controversial.

Any decision emanating from the pen of Lemuel Shaw demanded attention from the American legal community. Shaw's reputation and the prestige of his court gave his rulings great persuasive value in other state courts. But *Farwell* was not just any decision. It was a decision involving industrial accidents at just the time that America was industrializing. Whatever Shaw decided would be studied very closely by judges, lawyers, and corporate leaders across the United States. Shaw, never one to downplay his own significance, knew that he was deciding a case that would alter the course of American industrial and legal history. In a careful and powerfully phrased opinion, he followed and extended the holdings in the English and South Carolina cases, thus denying recovery to the injured plaintiff.

Shaw began his opinion by discussing a general principle of tort liability known as *respondeat superior.* This maxim holds that masters are responsible for the negligent acts of servants causing injuries to clients or strangers as long as the servants are operating within the normal course of their duties for the master. But Shaw declared that a situation involving two persons in the same service or employment is different from one involving a company's agents and the general public. The employer, he said, is liable to the public for the tortious acts of its employees, but he is not liable to one of his employees for the carelessness of another employee: thus, a case involving fellow servants falls outside of the general principle of *respondeat superior*.

Chief Justice Shaw based his opinion in favor of the railroad on three grounds. First, he concluded that an employee such as Farwell "takes upon himself the natural and ordinary risks and perils" of his employment. If the job is dangerous, Shaw maintained, the employee does not have to accept it or continue in it. But if he takes the job or remains in it, he assumes the risks. Moreover, dangerous jobs usually carry wages commensurate with the danger. After all, Farwell the railroad engineer commanded a higher wage than Farwell the machinist. The "implied contract" between employer and employee compels the employee to accept the risks of his employment or find another job. This became known as the "assumption of risk" doctrine.

The second ground for the decision was what Shaw termed one of "policy." Safety of employees is best promoted, Shaw contended, when employees are expected to be responsible for their own conduct and that of fellow employees. A single employee can observe the conduct of his fellow workers. If one worker is behaving so as to endanger the safety of others, an employee should bring this to the attention of the careless worker so that he can correct his actions. If the careless worker fails to respond to constructive suggestions, the employer can then be notified so he can then act accordingly. In this way, employee safety is best encouraged by placing the responsibility for safety on the workers. By contrast, Shaw pointed out, the best policy to promote the safety of railroad passengers or others not employed by the railroad who might be injured through the care-

lessness of an employee is to make the company liable.

The final ground for the decision addressed a concern of Farwell's attorney, who maintained that the facts in the Massachusetts case were distinguishable from those in the English and South Carolina fellow-servant rule cases. In both of the other situations, the injured employee and the employee whose carelessness led to the injury were working in the same contained working place. In the English case, both were on a butcher's van; and in the South Carolina case, both employees were in the cab of a railroad engine. Loring, the attorney for the injured Farwell, argued that because Whitcomb and Farwell worked in different divisions of the railroad and had no reasonable way of monitoring each other's work, this case was legally different from its predecessors.

Shaw acknowledged that Farwell and Whitcomb worked in different divisions of the railroad. But the important factor in their job situations was that they shared a common employer. The chief justice stated that it would be "extremely difficult to establish a practical rule" governing what does and does not constitute a separate division. Should it depend, Shaw asked rhetorically, on the distance that the employers are apart? Or should there be some other rationale for determining when two employees are sufficiently separated so that they could not be said to be in close enough proximity to monitor each other's carefulness? Shaw could not envision a workable rule. Furthermore, Shaw submitted, the argument of Farwell's attorney presupposes "an assumed principle of responsibility which does not exist." The chief justice maintained that the "implied contract [between the employer and employee] . . . does not extend to indemnify the servant against the negligence of any one but himself." Shaw, therefore, rejected the "different division" argument and found for the defendant railroad corporation, thus extending the fellow-servant rule to apply to complex industrial situations in which an injured worker might have no close contact with another worker whose carelessness might lead to his own injury.

Shaw closed his opinion with a caveat. He admonished lawyers and judges reading his decision not to venture "any hasty conclusion as to the application of this rule to a case not fully within the same principle." He cautioned that his opinion did not say that there were no implied warranties arising out of the relationship between employer and employee. If the engine had been defective, or if the track had been bad, or if the railroad had not employed a switchman who was generally deemed competent, Shaw intimated that the resolution of the case might have been different. But mere employee negligence was not enough to justify an employer's liability.

In the generation following the *Farwell* decision, the fellow-servant rule was adopted by virtually every state court that was called on to confront the issue. For example, when the highest court of Wisconsin favorably received the fellow-servant rule in 1861, it commented that the doctrine had been "sustained by almost unanimous judgments of all the courts both of England and this country." And the holding in *Farwell* became the fellow-servant rule case most prominently cited by jurisdictions faced with suits mounted by employees alleging management liability for injuries caused by worker carelessness.

There were several reasons that the Massachusetts precedent was a stronger one for employers to cite than either *Priestly v. Fowler* or *Murray v. South Carolina Railroad Company*. First, the English case offered scant quotable language, and the South Carolina opinion came with several dissents that muddled the precedent. Second, the *Farwell* precedent extended the fellow-servant rule into complex industrial situations. By contrast, the English case dealt with a fact situation involving a preindustrial individual proprietorship, and the South Carolina case concerned an engineer and a fireman in the same cab of an engine. What the *Farwell* decision told the industrial community was that the impersonality of the industrial environment did not make an employer any more liable for the consequences of employee negligence than would be the case in a small business where all the employees are regularly in close contact. It was a ready tool to be used by lawyers defending corporations against suits by employees. Finally, the *Farwell* opinion had more precedent value than the previous fellow-servant rule decisions because of the prestige of Lemuel

Shaw and the Massachusetts Supreme Judicial Court.

The decision in *Farwell* and the fact that most courts in the country followed in its wake helped to place the unintended but tragic costs of industrialization on the working poor. As a result, employers did not have to bear the costs of most industrial accidents. If the decision had gone the other way, the costs to businesses might have put a brake on economic development in the crucial early stages of America's industrial revolution.

Some legal historians have found Shaw's *Farwell* opinion to be a clear example of the antilower class bias of the nineteenth-century judiciary. In the words of one historian, decisions like this threw "the burden of economic development on the weakest and least active elements in the population." It is clear that the sweat of the working poor helped to fuel the American industrial revolution, and certainly the fact that businesses did not have to absorb the cost of industrial accidents also helped industrialization to gain momentum, but *Farwell* should not be taken as a sign of Shaw's hostility to labor. Only about a week after handing down the *Farwell* decision, Shaw was the author of *Commonwealth v. Hunt*, a decision recognizing the right of a labor union to exist. The *Hunt* decision has been referred to as the "Magna Charta of American trade unionism." Historians who maintain that Shaw was hostile to the working class have a tough time reconciling the *Farwell* and *Hunt* decisions. A more likely philosophical basis for the chief justice's position in *Farwell* is that Shaw had a special place in his legal heart for the railroad. During his tenure on the Massachusetts high court, scores of railroad cases were decided. Although Shaw generally upheld the state's right to place regulations on railroads, in disputes between railroads and individuals—passengers, highway travelers, and railroad employees—the railroads invariably emerged victorious. Shaw was well aware that had he ruled in favor of Farwell, a great burden would have been added to the New England railroads which were, at least in 1842, struggling to survive.

In the 60 years after *Farwell*, industrial accidents in the United States increased in severity and frequency. By 1900, it was estimated that each year 35,000 deaths and two million injuries occurred on the job. Sympathy for injured and killed workers led some courts to fashion exceptions to the fellow-servant rule. For example, the "vice principal rule" permitted a worker to recover damages from his employer if his injury was caused by the negligence of another worker who was in a supervisory position and thus could be said to be more than just another fellow servant. Also, some courts fashioned a "safe place rule" that allowed an injured employee to recover damages if he could demonstrate that his injury was the result of a hazardous working environment that might have compounded the negligence of a fellow employee. Furthermore, by 1900, a number of lawyers were willing to accept clients on a contingent fee basis. This provided many poor men and women with the opportunity to retain an attorney and no doubt stimulated thousands of lawsuits in which injured employees attempted to affix their employers with financial responsibility.

In 1885, a Connecticut court commented that the tendency in nearly all jurisdictions was to "limit rather than enlarge" the coverage of the fellow-servant rule. Spurred on by reformers appalled by the untoward consequences of industrialization, Congress and many state legislatures moved to restrict the ambit of the fellow-servant rule. In 1908, Congress enacted the federal Employers Liability Act, which abolished the fellow-servant rule for interstate railroads. And by 1911, 25 states had laws modifying or completely dispensing with the fellow-servant rule for railroads wholly within their state boundaries.

To provide compensation for victims of industrial accidents, states in the early twentieth century began to adopt "workmen's compensation statutes." These laws abolished the fellow-servant rule and the assumption of risk doctrine. Furthermore, they established sched-

ules of compensation for injuries and took the responsibility for settling any disputes involving the amounts of employee claims away from courts and placed them in the hands of administrative agencies. In 1911, Wisconsin was the first state to have its workmen's compensation laws survive a constitutional test. Mississippi, in 1948, was the last state in the union to adopt a compensation law. In addition, in the twentieth century, many labor-management contracts have established compensation schedules for employees in industries affected by collective bargaining.

Payments to injured employees under workmen's compensation were (and are) seldom large enough to indemnify an injured person for the total costs and long-term consequences of industrial accidents. But they do provide a systematic means of recovering some damages and they remove one large class of disputes from the court system. If Nicholas Farwell had sustained his injury today, he would not only have received better medical care and a guaranteed amount of compensation, but he would also not have been victimized by the fellow-servant rule.

Selected Bibliography

Friedman, L.M., and J. Ladinsky. "Social Change and the Law of Industrial Accidents." *Columbia Law Review* 67 (1967): 50–82.

Horwitz, M.J. *The Transformation of American Law, 1780–1860.* Cambridge, MA: Harvard University Press, 1977.

Hurst, J.W. *Law and the Conditions of Freedom in the Nineteenth-Century United States.* Madison, WI: University of Wisconsin Press, 1967.

Johnson, J.W. "Creativity and Adaptation: A Reassessment of American Jurisprudence, 1801–57 and 1908–40." *Rutgers-Camden Law Journal* 7 (Summer 1976): 625–47.

Levy, L.W. *The Law of the Commonwealth and Chief Justice Shaw: The Evolution of American Law, 1830–60.* New York: Harper & Row, 1967.

White, G.E. *Tort Law in America: An Intellectual History.* New York: Oxford University Press, Inc., 1980.

CONTRIBUTORY NEGLIGENCE AS A "BRAKE" ON SUITS AGAINST RAILROADS

by Paul M. Kurtz
School of Law
University of Georgia

Haring v. New York and Erie Railroad Company, 13 Barbour's Supreme Court Reports 9 (1852) [New York Supreme Court]

Professor Lawrence Friedman, in his *History of American Law*, states that in the 1800s, almost "every leading case in tort law was connected, mediately or immediately, with [the railroads]." Friedman states that the railroad "was the key to economic development. It cleared an iron path through the wilderness. It bound cities together, and tied the farms to the city and the seaports. Yet, trains were also wild beasts; they roared through the countryside, killing livestock, setting fire to crops, smashing passengers and freight. Railroad law and tort law grew up, then, together. In a sense, the two were the same."

Several tort doctrines were, therefore, created by the courts, which had the effect of protecting the burgeoning industrial mechanism from potentially ruinous lawsuits. Perhaps the most important was the adoption of a negligence standard requiring that before a plaintiff could recover in tort for injuries caused by the defendant, the plaintiff would have to show that the defendant's behavior failed to measure up to a standard of reasonableness. Rather than impose absolute liability for "accidents" caused by defendants, the courts denied recovery unless the defendant was acting unreasonably under the circumstances.

A natural concomitant of a rule of law requiring proof of defendant's negligence is a rule disqualifying a culpable plaintiff. This doctrine has come to be known as contributory negligence. Under the doctrine of contributory negligence, no recovery could be obtained if the plaintiff's unreasonable behavior contributed in any way to the injuries he had suffered at the defendant's hands. While some cases described this as a defense that could be offered by the defendant, in other cases it was stated that the plaintiff had the affirmative obligation to show

that the defendant's behavior was the "sole cause" of the injuries suffered. The doctrine was first enunciated by an English court in 1809, but was rarely used in the United States before the 1850s. One of the earliest American cases to use contributory negligence to deny a plaintiff recovery was *Haring v. New York and Erie Railroad Company*, an 1852 railroad case arising in New York.

In *Haring*, the plaintiff's husband was riding on a sled across a railroad track and was struck by the engine, thrown from the sled and killed. It is apparent that the railroad was negligent through its failure to abide by a statute that required the use of a bell to warn pedestrians of the train's approach. The plaintiff's wife sued the railroad company in what would be described today as a wrongful death action.

The trial court, however, after hearing the plaintiff's evidence refused to allow the jury to even consider the case and granted the defendant's motion for a nonsuit, which today would be called a directed verdict. The court noted the sled was traveling at 12 to 15 miles per hour at the time of the crash, the decedent knew trains passed the intersection hourly and, because of a high embankment at the side of the track, the decedent was unable to see the oncoming train. The court described the decedent's behavior as gross carelessness and stated that the "law, while it imposes duties upon the railroad companies, also imposes duties upon the citizens. . . ."

The New York Supreme Court upheld the trial court's action. The court wrote that where the plaintiff "has defeated his claim by his own misconduct, there can be no propriety in requiring the jury to pass upon the evidence." The court revealed its fear of allowing suits by citizens against railroads to go to a jury by stating: "We can not shut our eyes to the fact that in certain controversies between the weak and the strong—between a humble individual and a gigantic corporation, the sympathies of the human mind naturally, honestly and generously, run to the assistance and support of the feeble . . . and that compassion will sometimes exercise over the deliberations of a jury, an influence which, however honorable to them as philanthropists, is wholly inconsistent with the principles of law and the ends of justice." Thus, Haring's widow was left without relief because of her late husband's negligence.

The opinion in *Haring* was particularly striking in that it approved of removing the case from the jury's consideration. It is one thing to allow a jury to consider the possibility that the plaintiff was negligent in deciding a case, it is much more drastic to find contributory negligence as a matter of law and refuse to allow the jury to even consider the case. *Haring* was one of 12 reported appellate cases between 1850 and 1860 to approve of a nonsuit against a plaintiff on the ground of contributory negligence. In the 1860s, 31 such cases were reported; in the 1870s, there were 58. As Friedman has written, "The doctrine of contributory negligence kept pace with crossing accidents."

Selected Bibliography

Friedman, L.M. *A History of American Law.* New York: Simon & Schuster, 1973.

Malone, W.S. "The Formative Era of Contributory Negligence." *Illinois Law Review* 41 (July/August 1946): 151–82.

RAILROAD DEVELOPMENT AND THE NUISANCE LAW

by Paul M. Kurtz
School of Law
University of Georgia

Hentz v. Long Island Railroad Company, 13 Barbour's Supreme Court Reports 646 (1857) [New York Supreme Court]

The transformation of the United States from agrarian nation to industrial giant is an oft-told story. This epic tale, however, consists of many small chapters; one of the most interesting is a series of cases in which single landowners challenged the operation of railroads, particularly during the nineteenth century. The main legal weapon that these landowners attempted to use was that of nuisance. The English common law of nuisances, adopted by the colonies and eventually the states, was a strict one, imposing absolute liability on those who interfered with another's use of property. Unlike modern concepts under which liability depends on a defendant acting in a culpable or negligent fashion, the common law was expressed in the stern command of the legal maxim, *sic utere tuo ut alienum non laedas* ("use your own so as not to

injure others"). The story of how courts refashioned nuisance law reflects what some experts call the instrumental use of law—the use of law to achieve a desired societal goal, which, in this case, was an efficient industrial economy.

Hentz v. Long Island Railroad Company is a paradigmatic case for witnessing a part of this refashioning of the law. The plaintiff was a landowner in the New York village of Hempstead who objected to a railroad track that had been constructed in front of his dwelling house and store on Main Street. He complained that the trains were responsible for obnoxious smoke, odors, and noise that constituted a "danger, nuisance and inconvenience." He filed suit against the railroad company, seeking $2,000 in damages and, more broadly, an injunction prohibiting the operation of the railroad in front of his house altogether. In *Hentz*, the plaintiff had previously obtained an emergency order forbidding the operation of the railroad and the New York Supreme Court (then as now a trial court) was asked to make the order permanent.

The plaintiff offered three theories to justify the relief he sought: (1) a claim that the defendant had violated the New York legislative authorization for the laying of its tracks; (2) a claim that the railroad had taken his land without just compensation in violation of the state constitution; and (3) an assertion that the railroad's operation in front of his house and store constituted a public nuisance, particularly injurious to him. All three claims were rejected by the trial court judge on the basis of an examination of the pleadings and affidavits filed in the case. There apparently was no hearing.

With regard to the first claim, Hentz did not complain about the laying of most of the defendant's tracks but instead asserted that the Hempstead station was in an inappropriate place and, thus, the portion of the track in front of his property leading to that station was also inappropriate. The court, however, pointed out that the legislation permitted the company to establish a branch road into the village and to construct the railroad on "the most practicable route." Clearly reflecting its pro-railroad bias, the court said that the choice of route would not be disturbed unless the company management had "*clearly* erred. . . . If a mere difference of opinion between (the railroad operators) and those whose immediate interests might be affected . . . should be allowed to annul their proceedings, but few of them could be sustained . . ." [emphasis in original].

The court pointed out that wherever the tracks might have been laid there would be the same smoke, danger of fire, "exposure of human life," and obstacles to passage through the streets complained of by the plaintiff. While the court might declare, therefore, that all railroads within villages were nuisances, it felt powerless to do so in light of the "action of both the legislative and judicial departments of this state." What the court was describing here is what has been called the statutory authorization defense for railroad placement; as long as the railroad

was complying with the legislative mandate, its very existence could not be found to be actionable.

To bolster its conclusion of state authorization, the court pointed out that when the track was originally laid 14 years earlier there had been very little objection, that a number of local property owners (including, incredibly enough, Hentz) had lent the company money to construct the tracks, and that there had been a public meeting approving the re-laying of the track just a year before Hentz brought his action. At this point in the opinion, therefore, the court concluded the railroad was not liable for laying the tracks where it did because it was merely doing what the state (and the public) had authorized. It reserved until later the question of whether the particular way the railroad was being operated constituted an actionable nuisance.

As for the second theory of recovery, the plaintiff argued that the railroad had taken a portion of his property without paying for it in violation of the state constitution. Interestingly, this assertion was based not on the claim that the smoke, noise, risk of fire, etc., interfered with his peaceable enjoyment of his house and store, but on the narrower argument that the railroad tracks in the middle of Main Street were on his property. Hentz said his property extended to the middle of Main Street and that a portion had been taken by the laying of the tracks.

In dealing with this, the court conceded that compliance with the legislative authorization to lay track could not justify an action that otherwise would constitute a taking of plaintiff's land. The court, however, found no such taking for several reasons. First, in a very careful reading of the complaint, the court noted that the plaintiff had alleged he had possessed the property, but not that he had title to it. Only the owner would be entitled to compensation for a taking, and the court was suggesting that the plaintiff might not even be the owner.

The court went on to point out that Hentz had alleged possession of the Main Street land for only the past five years. Thus, said the court, even if he was alleging ownership, he had alleged it for only five years. The track had been originally laid 14 years earlier. Again, there would be no valid claim by a property owner who had purchased the property nine years after the tracks had been laid. As the court said, "If the land was subsequently conveyed to the plaintiff, as it probably was, he took it . . . with the railroad upon it."

As if these two conclusions were not enough to defeat the plaintiff, the court further observed that even if there had been a taking an injunction would be inappropriate. The court asserted that if there had been a taking without compensation, it would be appropriate to seek compensation when the property was first taken, but the court would not be "doing justice to the public to allow him to stop the cars until he might coerce the company to pay him an exorbitant amount. . . ." The court concluded a plaintiff ought not be allowed to wait until an injunction would be "seriously injurious" before seeking relief. Again, the court was showing its bias in favor of allowing industrialization, once begun, to continue.

Hentz's final theory was nuisance. Perhaps the statute authorized the laying of the tracks here and perhaps his property on Main Street had not been taken, but certainly the operation of the trains with the risk of injury, noise, odors (the court noted that "manure and merchandise" were carried on the trains), and smoke constituted an interference with plaintiff's use of his house and store. Unfortunately for Hentz, the court did not agree.

The court began its analysis by listing other cities in which the legislature had authorized the operation of railroads and other cases that had rejected the claim of nuisance. It then asked, "Is there any thing peculiar to Main-street, or in the management of the defendants, which makes the railroad where it passes the plaintiff's house a nuisance?" The court found the railroad did not constitute an impediment to other travel on the street, the rails were not "badly laid down," and many other residents of the village and the street had sworn in depositions that the street had actually been improved as a "passway" by defendant's "works upon it."

As for the claim that the steam locomotive's operation in front of plaintiff's house was particularly noxious, the court found nothing in the railroad's charter or the statute prohibiting this and decided to "leave the matter to the good sense of the (railroad's management)." The plaintiff had alleged no serious accidents and, as for the smoke, while it must "undoubtedly be annoying to some extent," it was no more "disagreeable or prejudicial than what may proceed from many lawful establishments in the village. . . ."

While the court purported to be simply examining the facts of *Hentz* to determine whether this defendant was operating a nuisance, its language makes clear that it was painting on a much broader canvas. Thus, in minimizing the risks to the plaintiff, the court wrote: "Accidents to children, or to adults who are not grossly careless, from the locomotives when passing through our most populous cities, are very rare. The times of their passage are generally known, and the noise made by the movement over the rails, and the engineer's whistle, give timely notice of the approach of the train. When the usual precautions are practiced the danger is very slight, and when there is any carelessness or mismanagement the company and its officers are very properly held to a rigid accountability."

The court went on to conclude that the "evils of which the plaintiff complains are by no means peculiar to himself. They are the necessary concomitants of this species of locomotion, whether in the city or in the country. They cannot be prevented without an entire suspension of one of the greatest improvements of modern times." In summarizing its rejection of the plaintiff's claim, the court wrote: "[T]here are some useful employments which endanger the lives of human beings which cannot and *ought not* to be prohibited. Lives are sometimes destroyed by an omnibus, a carman's cart, a stage or a steamboat, but so long as they are not imminently dangerous they cannot be prohibited. We cannot enjoy our private rights, nor can we avail ourselves of the many advantages resulting from modern discoveries, without encountering some risk to our lives, or our property, or to some extent endangering the lives or injuring the property of others" [emphasis added].

Interestingly, while the case ostensibly involved only the question of whether an injunction should be issued, the court in passing stated that if the "injury or danger to others" from a legitimate pursuit was "inevitable," there would be "no remedy either by way of *indemnity* or prevention" [emphasis in original]. The court was clearly suggesting that damages would also be inappropriate in this and similar cases.

The *Hentz* court, through its treatment of the plaintiff's claim, was making it clear that the traditional law of nuisance that had been received from a preindustrial England had to make way for the urbanization and industrialization of the United States. Both its attitude and its language revealed a pro-development bias. While it did not overtly use a balancing approach weighing the advantages to society against the harm to the individual (a test that would become commonplace later in the century), it was obvious that the strict law of nuisance was a matter of legal history by the time this case was decided.

Selected Bibliography

Bone, R.G. "Normative Theory and Legal Doctrine in American Nuisance Law: 1850 to 1920." *Southern California Law Review* 59 (Sept. 1986): 1101–1226.

Brenner, J.F. "Nuisance Law and the Industrial Revolution." *Journal of Legal Studies* 3 (June 1974): 403–33.

Coquillette, D.R. "Mosses From an Old Manse: Another Look at Some Historic Property Cases About the Environment." *Cornell Law Review* (June 1979): 761–821.

Kurtz, P.M. "Nineteenth Century Anti-Entrepreneurial Nuisance Injunctions—Avoiding the Chancellor." *William & Mary Law Review* 17 (Summer 1976): 621–70.

Scheiber, H.N. "Public Economic Policy and the American Legal System: Historical Perspectives." *Wisconsin Law Review* (1980): 1159–89.

———. "State Law and 'Industrial Policy' in American Development, 1790–1987." *California Law Review* 75 (Jan. 1987): 415–44.

THE GREAT DOG FIGHT CASE

by Kermit L. Hall
Department of History and College of Law
University of Florida

Brown v. Kendall, 6 Cushing 292 (1850) [Supreme Judicial Court of Massachusetts]

Until the middle of the nineteenth century, the term "tort," which has emerged as the most protean legal concept of the twentieth century, had no well-defined legal meaning. Instead, wrongs that are covered by the concept today were treated in this earlier era in a piecemeal fashion. There were such archaic actions as trover, deceit, slander, assault, and the various forms of trespass. The last of these was the most important because it provided the basis on which most personal injuries were covered.

The various kinds of trespasses were lumped into two separate legal actions: trespass and trespass on the case (or, as it was often simply termed, "case"). Trespass actions were based on direct contact between a plaintiff and defendant. If one person struck another with a stick, for example, the suit would have been for trespass, and all that was necessary as proof to secure damages was to show that the injury was direct. Case, on the other hand, treated indirect contact. Hence, if a person left a stick in the street and someone tripped over it through no negligence of his own, the action that applied was "trespass on the case." Under this theory, an injured party had to prove not only that the stick belonged to the person who left it in the street but that tripping over it was the fault of that same person. Hence, the critical difference between trespass and trespass on the case was proving negligence. In the first instance, the person hit by the stick had only to prove that the other person wielded it. In essence, that person was strictly liable, even it he was not negligent. But with action on the case, the injured person had to prove that the other person had acted negligently in leaving the stick in the street, a difficult matter at best.

While legal historians agree about the broad outline of the distinction between trespass and case, they sharply disagree about how significant the differences were, the contribution of *Brown v. Kendall* to the establishment of modern tort law, and the acclaim to be credited to the author of that opinion, Lemuel Shaw, chief justice of the Massachusetts Supreme Judicial Court and the most influential state judge of the mid-nineteenth century. On one side is Charles O. Gregory, whose research and writing in the 1950s stressed the distinction between trespass and case sketched above. Gregory and others have given high marks to Shaw for essentially giving birth to modern tort law through his opinion. On the other side is Morton J. Horwitz, whose revisionist writing departed radically from that of Gregory. Horwitz, for his part, claimed that there is no evidence that American judges ever accepted either the pleading distinction between trespass and case or that trespass was based on strict liability and case on negligence. Horwitz insists that at the time of *Brown*, the negligence action already had begun to flower and that Shaw merely added the force of his intellect to developments already well underway. That is, even if the distinction had once existed in American law between strict liability for trespass and negligence for case, that distinction had collapsed by the time Shaw penned his opinion for a unanimous court in Brown. The historiographical dispute notwithstanding, *Brown* remains of special importance precisely because a judge of Shaw's reputation lent his prestige to the proposition that where unintentional acts were involved, there could be no liability without fault.

As is so often true in American legal history, the facts surrounding *Brown* were mundane. Kendall and Brown were both residents of Boston, and their dogs fell into fighting on a city street. Kendall attempted to separate them by hitting the animals with a four-foot stick, but his efforts proved unavailing and, as the snarling dogs moved closer to him, he continued to retreat toward Brown. As Kendall raised the stick over his back to strike the dogs, he accidentally hit Brown, who was standing behind him, doing serious damage to Brown's eye.

Brown sued Kendall for damages in a Boston trial court. Kendall's attorney asked the judge to instruct the jury to find for his client because Kendall was using "ordinary care" and because Brown had himself contributed to his own injury by failing to get out of the way of Kendall and the fighting dogs. Kendall insisted that the burden of proof was on Brown to prove that he had done wrong; it was not up to Kendall to show that he had not done wrong. Brown's attorney pressed an opposite line of argument, one that the trial judge incorporated into his jury charge. Brown's attorney claimed that Kendall was responsible for the injuries, unless Kendall was "doing a necessary act" or was under a "duty" to separate the dogs. Since Kendall could prove neither of these conditions, the jury found against him and awarded damages to Brown.

Kendall then appealed to the Massachusetts Supreme Judicial Court. In the time between the jury verdict and the argument on appeal, Kendall died. Under the common law his death would have ended the action, but Massachusetts had provided by statute that actions in trespass survived, and Kendall's wife stood in his place during the oral arguments on appeal.

Shaw's opinion began by brushing aside many precedents that would have supported Brown and turned instead to the writing of Simon Greenleaf, a prominent treatise writer whose two-volume work on the law of evidence was widely available to lawyers. Shaw relied on Greenleaf for the rule that a plaintiff must present evidence to show that the defendant was at fault or that the defendant's intentions were unlawful. Shaw, therefore, placed the burden of proof in the case squarely on the plaintiff (Brown) in direct opposition to the action of the trial judge. Since Kendall had acted lawfully, the key question became whether he had exercised "ordinary care" in attempting to separate the fighting animals. Shaw went on to define "ordinary care" as "that kind and degree of care, which prudent and cautious men would use, such as is required by the exigency of the case, and such as is necessary to guard against probable danger." Only a negligent person, therefore, could be held responsible for unintentionally inflicted harm on another. "If, in the prosecution of a lawful act," Shaw concluded, "a casualty purely accidental arises, no action can be supported for an injury arising therefrom."

But Shaw did even more. In addition to spelling out the requirement for the plaintiff to show the defendant's negligence, Shaw also enunciated another doctrine—contributory negligence. Under this theory, an injured party cannot recover from a negligent defendant if the injured party was even slightly responsible for the accident. "[I]f the defendant was chargeable with some negligence," Shaw observed, "and if the plaintiff was also chargeable with negligence, we think the plaintiff cannot recover without showing that damage was caused wholly by the act of the defendant, and that the plaintiff's own negligence did not contribute as an efficient cause to produce it."

Whether or not Shaw intended to do so, the upshot of his decision was to provide an indirect stimulus to emerging industries during the last half of the nineteenth century. Well into the twentieth century, courts regularly freed railroads, trolleys, and other forms of transportation from paying damages in accidents because their attorneys were able to show that the plaintiffs had contributed to the accident. State legislatures sometimes circumscribed the full impact of this common-law doctrine by passing legislation that made railroads and other

businesses strictly liable for some facets of their conduct (spewing sparks and such) without regard to the plaintiff's negligence.

Shaw overturned the jury verdict in favor of Brown and ordered a new trial. His opinion articulated a modern theory of liability for unintentionally caused harms and a theory of contributory negligence. While historians disagree about the extent to which Shaw was a legal innovator in this case, there is little doubt that his opinion successfully adapted the common law to the demands of a thriving and expanding society and laid the cornerstone upon which the modern concept of liability rests.

Selected Bibliography

Adlow, E. "Chief Justice Lemuel Shaw and the Law of Negligence." *Massachusetts Law Quarterly* 42 (Oct. 1957): 55–74.

Friedman, L.M., and J. Ladinsky. "Social Change and the Law of Industrial Accidents." *Columbia Law Review* 67 (1967): 50–82.

Gregory, C.O. "Trespass to Negligence to Absolute Liability." *Virginia Law Review* 37 (April 1951): 359–97.

Horwitz, M.J. *The Transformation of American Law, 1780–1860.* Cambridge, MA: Harvard University Press, 1977.

Schwartz, G.T. "Tort Law and the Economy in Nineteenth-Century America: A Reinterpretation." *The Yale Law Journal* 90 (July 1981): 1717–75.

THE ORIGINS OF CONSUMER RIGHTS IN TORT LAW

by G. Edward White
Department of History and School of Law
University of Virginia

MacPherson v. Buick Motor Company, 216 N.Y. 382 (1916) [New York Court of Appeals]

It is not too much to say that the rights of consumers to recover against manufacturers for injuries caused by defective products originated in *MacPherson v. Buick*. The decision, issued by the New York Court of Appeals (that state's highest court) in 1916, was an example of a prescient judge seizing on a fortuitous moment to recast the legal rights and responsibilities of

countless persons. The judge was Benjamin Cardozo, in only his third year on the Court of Appeals. The time was the 1920s, which was witnessing the rise of the most dramatic and influential symbol of modernized America, the motorcar. The persons affected were all those who purchased products under the emerging system of American merchandising, now taken for granted but then a revolutionary development, under which consumers of products did not buy them directly from the persons who made them.

Everything came together in *MacPherson*: the transportation, merchandising, and legal relationships of the future and the legal doctrine of the past. The injury that spawned *MacPherson* had been caused by a wheel that suddenly broke off a Buick Model 10 Runabout. It was the kind of injury that was likely to occur again as more and more Americans turned to the motorcar as a means of transportation. The suit in *MacPherson* was not against the dealer that had sold the car, Close Brothers of Schenectady, New York, but against the Buick Motor Company of Detroit, Michigan, which had assembled the automobile and sold it to Close Brothers. The principal legal issue in the case was not whether Donald C. MacPherson, the driver of the Model 10, could recover against Close Brothers, but whether he could recover against Buick, with whom he had no contractual relations. And on this point the New York Court of Appeals' decision in *Torgeson v. Schultz* (1908), handed down eight years before *MacPherson*, seemed clear: persons not in contractual relations with the manufacturers of defective products could not recover in tort against those manufacturers. Yet MacPherson won his case, and a new era in the law of consumer rights began.

The *MacPherson* case began when MacPherson purchased the Buick with the defective wheel from Close Brothers in 1910. Close Brothers had bought the car from the Buick Motor Company a year earlier. Buick assembled cars from its own parts and parts supplied by other manufacturers: the wheels on the Model 10 had been made by the Imperial Wheel Company of Flint, Michigan. The Model 10 was a two-seater with a rumble seat; its horsepower was 22, and it could go 50 miles per hour. MacPherson used the car in the summer and fall of 1910, put it up on blocks for the winter, and began using it again in May 1911.

On July 25, 1911, MacPherson, who lived in Galway, New York, was on his way to Saratoga Springs to take John E. Carr, also a resident of Galway, to the Saratoga Springs Hospital. He was driving the car, Carr was riding in the front passenger seat, and Charles E. Carr, John's brother, was seated in the rumble seat. As the MacPherson car approached Saratoga Springs, one of its hind wheels ran into a rut. MacPherson turned off the engine and twisted the steering wheel to the left so as to stabilize the car. He then turned the engine back on and turned back toward the right-hand side of the road, where he had been traveling. As he turned a cracking sound occurred, and the rear left-hand side of the car began to collapse, eventually resting at a spot six to eight inches off the ground, with the axle scraping on the road. The front end of the car began to swing to the right, approaching a telephone pole, and as MacPherson turned the steering wheel to the left to avoid the pole, the right side of the car's frame caught the pole, twisting the car completely around until it faced in the opposite direction. MacPherson was thrown from his seat and pinned under the hind axle of the car. He suffered injuries in the process.

Testimony in the trial court established that MacPherson was traveling only about 15 miles an hour at the time of the accident, when the spokes of the left rear wheel had broken out. Testimony also established that many of the spokes were not of first-quality wood and that the manufacturer could have performed tests to determine the quality of wood in the wheel. Nevertheless, the trial court found for the Buick Motor Company at the close of MacPherson's presentation. The court obviously believed that the fact that MacPherson had no contractual relations with Buick made it impossible for him to recover.

MacPherson appealed to the Appellate Division of New York's court system, an intermediate court. That court reversed the judgment of the trial court. Its decision rested on three factors: (1) the fact that Buick Motor Company knew that the automobiles it sold to Close Brothers in Schenectady might be used in a wide radius around Schenectady, including Galway and Saratoga Springs; (2) the fact that the car was represented as capable of going 50 miles an hour and thus needed wheels to withstand such speed; and (3) the fact that Buick had the ability to submit the wheels of its cars to pressure tests. These factors, in the view of a majority of the judges on the Appellate Division, made a car with a defective wheel an "inherently dangerous" product, which under a line of New York cases resulted in liability extending from the producer of such products to remote purchasers injured by them. One judge of the Appellate Division dissented from this characterization of the case, preferring to reverse on the ground that MacPherson had made out a *prima facie* case of negligence against the Buick Motor Company by showing that it had failed to inspect the wheels on Model 10 Runabouts. All of the judges agreed that MacPherson was entitled to a new trial.

Before that trial could take place, however, the Buick Motor Company appealed to the court of appeals. The issue in *MacPherson* had always been doctrinal, not factual: Buick conceded that it had not inspected the wheel to determine whether the spokes were in good condition or could withstand the pressure of a 1,800 pound car traveling at up to 50 miles per hour. Buick was likely negligent, then, but negligent to whom? An old English case, *Winterbottom v. Wright* (1842), which held that a supplier of mail coaches to the English postmaster general was not liable to persons injured while riding in them, suggested that "privity of contract" was the controlling doctrinal principle: liability ran only as far as contractual relations. There were policy justifications for this doctrinal proposition as well: to extend liability for injuries for defective products beyond contractual relationships ran the potential risk of very extensive manufacturer liability. In an industrializing society, the ramifications of defects in products used in commerce could be very significant, raising the specter that growing industries might face crippling losses from lawsuits.

On the other side, there were policy justifications for extending liability in the *MacPherson*-type situation. The exception to the "privity" principle for "inherently dangerous" products suggested that there should be disincentives for manufacturers to put products on the market that had the capacity to do severe harm. Poisons, explosives, and products that gave off toxic fumes were examples: public policy suggested that the liability of manufacturers of such products should not be confined to persons in contractual relations with them. While the social utility of such products sug-

gested that they should remain on the market, their capacity to do harm suggested that those who made profits from their manufacture should be accountable to those injured by them, assuming the injuries could be prevented by ordinary care. *MacPherson*, then, resolved itself into an exercise in doctrinal conceptualization. If an automobile was treated as an inherently dangerous product, liability beyond privity might ensue; if it was treated like a stagecoach, liability would remain confined to privity.

The genius of Judge Cardozo's opinion for the court of appeals's extending liability was that he made an automobile seem more like a poison bottle than a stagecoach. In an artful synopsis of the precedents governing inherently dangerous products in New York, Cardozo suggested that the "principle" of protection to remote purchasers from injuries caused by dangerous products had long been part of New York law. In actuality the inherently dangerous line of cases had been a limited exception to the English rule of *Winterbottom*. Cardozo ignored *Winterbottom* throughout his opinion, however, concentrating on the evolution of the inherently dangerous cases to include products such as coffee urns and scaffolds. That evolution, he suggested, meant that "inherently dangerous" did not simply refer to the product's nature, but to the potential risks created by the product when negligently made. Coffee urns could blow up if placed too near heat; scaffolds could collapse if the wood used to construct them was inferior. In the scaffold example, Cardozo revealed how he was conceptualizing the Model 10 in *MacPherson*: a wheel with spokes made from inferior wood was as "dangerous" as a scaffold. He then dismissed *Winterbottom*: "Precedents drawn from the days of travel by stagecoach do not fit the conditions of travel today." Buick was liable to the consumers of its motorcars if it could be shown to have been negligent in their manufacture or their inspection.

So stated, the principle of *MacPherson* was potentially vast: any product could be dangerous if manufactured in a way so as to create risks, and any person might come within the ambit of the manufacturer's liability. A manufacturer of a component part might ship a defective batch; the batch might not be discovered by the assembler on inspection; in a subsequent accident caused by the defect an onlooker, not even the purchaser of the product, might be injured. But the *MacPherson* opinion was firmly rooted in negligence theory. The same tests that subjected the manufacturer to potential liability could be used to limit it. Manufacturers were not liable for defects that could not be discovered on reasonable inspection for products that had been altered in the chain of distribution or for products not used in a reasonably foreseeable manner. Manufacturers could show that, on balance, it was more expensive for them to prevent injuries than to permit an occasional one. If their cost of prevention exceeded the expected seriousness and frequency of injuries caused by their products, they were not supposed to be held liable.

The doctrinal structure created by *MacPherson*, in fact, proved insufficient to compensate the victims of defective products. While *MacPherson* expanded in the two decades after its appearance to cover nearly any product, by the 1940s an alternative theory of liability had surfaced to afford greater protection to the consumer. Under this theory—traditionally referred to as "strict" liability—manufacturers of defective products were deemed liable to injured consumers whether or not they could have discovered or prevented the defect through reasonable care. They were liable simply because they had put the product on the market and were in a better position than the consumer to bear the costs of its defectiveness. Among the grounds cited for the installation of strict liability in the defective products area was the tendency of negligence theory to *prevent* recovery by injured consumers.

MacPherson was thus revolutionary only in a historical sense. As Cardozo said, the decision wrested products liability of contract and put it "where it belongs"—"in the law," by which he meant tort law. This was still a significant achievement, marking a shift in the modern law of products from a regime dominated by contract principles and damages to a regime dominated by the negligence principle. The shift implicitly conceded that in industrialized societies most persons injured by defective products were not likely to have any on-going relations with the persons who had made the products. The tests and standards of negligence law were those of hypothetical "reasonable" men and women, not the subjective standards of bargained-for transactions. Contract was in a sense out of place in the standard modern products liability suit; *MacPherson* recognized this. But negligence can be out of place as well, and most jurisdictions have gone beyond *MacPherson*. Nonetheless the modest, almost pastoral accident of MacPherson and his companions was a major event in twentieth-century American law.

Selected Bibliography

Posner, R.A. *Cardozo: A Study in Reputation.* Chicago: University of Chicago Press, 1990.

Seavey, W. "Mr. Justice Cardozo and the Law of Torts." *Harvard Law Review* 52 (1939): 372–404.

White, G.E. *Patterns of American Legal Thought.* Indianapolis: Bobbs-Merrill Co., Inc., 1978.

———. *Tort Law in America: An Intellectual History.* New York: Oxford University Press, 1980.

NEGLIGENCE THEORY AT ITS ZENITH

by G. Edward White
Department of History and College of Law
University of Virginia

Palsgraf v. Long Island Railroad Company, 248 N.Y. 339 (1928) [New York Court of Appeals]

In law classrooms all over the United States, countless "hypothetical" cases are posed. The hypothetical cases are designed to show the workings of legal doctrine in unusual situations: the bizarre facts of the hypotheticals demonstrate how the meaning of legal rules can never wholly be separated from the fact situations to which those rules are applied. *Palsgraf* is an example of a real case that has served professors better than nearly any hypothetical. The wonder of *Palsgraf* is that it not only arose out of a million-to-one series of events, it also arose at precisely the time when legal scholars and judges believed that legal doctrine in the law of torts had reached a stage where no set of facts, however bizarre, could remain ungoverned by a legal rule. But the rule chosen to govern *Palsgraf* collapsed on application, and with it a whole structure of tort doctrine. *Palsgraf* was thus both the culmination and the end of an era in the intellectual history of American tort law.

The *Palsgraf* case began at 10:00 a.m. on August 24, 1924, when 40-year-old Helen Palsgraf was standing on the platform of the East New York station of the Long Island Railroad. With her were two of her three children, Elizabeth, aged 15, and Lillian, aged 12. August 24 was a Sunday, a very hot day, and Mrs. Palsgraf and her daughters were planning to spend the day at the beach. They bought their tickets to Rockaway Beach and proceeded to the platform to wait for a train. Many other persons had the same idea: the platform was crowded with people carrying bundles. As the Palsgrafs were waiting for their train, Mrs. Palsgraf asked Lillian to buy a Sunday newspaper, and Lillian went off to a newsstand on the platform.

The next train to come into the East New York station was the *Jamaica Express*. Herbert Gerhardt, a resident of Brooklyn who was also waiting for the Rockaway Beach train, testified as to what happened as the Jamaica train pulled into the station. "Two Italians came up," he said, "and they wanted to make this here *Jamaica Express* . . . and the two of them come, and one of them had a bundle under his arm . . . and just then the train was starting off and this fellow who had the bundle was last, the other fellow was already on the train and the train was in motion and the guard inside [the Jamaica train] was trying to help the fellow on, and the platform man was trying to help him on from the outside . . . [The second Italian] had a bundle in his right hand; the platform man pushed his arm and the bundle fell between the platform and the train . . . and about

a second later, why, everything went in a black smoke and explosion."

Subsequently, Gerhardt revealed that the bundle that "one of the Italians" had been carrying was about 18 inches in diameter and wrapped in a newspaper. He also indicated that after the guards had succeeded in assisting "the second Italian" onto the train, the platform guard waved the train on, and the train, after a momentary pause, pulled out of the station. As it did the explosion occurred. At trial, neither "the Italians" nor the railroad guards were present, but it was stipulated that the bundle that had exploded contained fireworks and that the bundle had been dislodged when one of the guards assisted the second Italian onto the Jamaica train.

Mrs. Palsgraf then gave an account of what happened next. She and Elizabeth had taken a position on the platform next to a weighing scale, which was about as high as her head. The scale had a glass front. On the other side of Mrs. Palsgraf was the wall of the station; the spot where the Palsgrafs stood was about 30 feet from the place where the explosion occurred. Lillian was not standing at that spot when the bundle exploded; she was returning from the newsstand. When the explosion occurred Mrs. Palsgraf heard "fireworks shooting," and then "a ball of fire came, and we were choked in smoke." She told Elizabeth to turn her back, and then the glass of the scale broke, sending glass flying through the air, and the scale toppled over on its side. On its way down, the scale fell against Mrs. Palsgraf, striking her on her left arm and thigh. She remembered Lillian crying, "I want my mama," her holding onto Elizabeth's wrist, and the crowd pushing away from them. Subsequently, a police officer arrived and led Mrs. Palsgraf and the children to a bench by the newsstand, and eventually assisted her down to the waiting room, where several ambulances eventually came and an "ambulance man" examined her. About one-half hour later, she and the girls took a taxi home to 238 Irving Avenue in Ridgewood, Kings County.

Mrs. Palsgraf testified at her trial that as a result of the accident, she had suffered from nervousness and stammering, which her doctor, Karl A. Parshall, diagnosed as traumatic shock. She had worked as a janitor before the accident, making about $420 a year and receiving $10 a month deducted from her rent. (Her yearly rent amounted to $168 with the deduction.) After the accident, she had been less able to work, and in 1926 had stopped work altogether, being supported by her children. She also testified that she was married, but her husband clearly did not live with her or provide any support.

At the trial, the Long Island Railroad put no witnesses on the stand. Its lawyers, Joseph F. Keany and William McNamara, contented themselves with cross-examining Mrs. Palsgraf and the two doctors who testified in her behalf. The trial judge charged the jury that if it found that the railroad's guards acted in a negligent manner in assisting the second Italian onto the train, and thereby causing the package to fall, and that their negligence resulted in the injury to Mrs. Palsgraf, they should find the railroad liable to Mrs. Palsgraf. The jury brought in a verdict for Mrs. Palsgraf of $6,000, to which was added $142.45 for court costs.

The railroad appealed, and the jury verdict was sustained by the five-judge Appellate Division, New York's intermediate appellate court, by a 4–1 margin. Judge Albert H. Seeger wrote the opinion for the majority. He noted that the jury had found that the railroad's guards had been negligent and that their actions had caused the bundle to explode. He added that Mrs. Palsgraf was a passenger of the railroad and was thus owed "the highest duty of care required of common carriers." The dissenter, President Judge Edward Lazansky, agreed that the guards were negligent but believed that their negligence was not a "proximate cause" of Mrs. Palsgraf's injuries. "Between the negligence of defendant and the injuries," Lazansky argued, "there intervened the negligence of the passenger carrying the package containing an explosive . . . . The explosion was not reasonably probable as a result of defendant's act of negligence." The 4–1 decision of the Appellate Division meant that the trial court's verdict was upheld, and the railroad appealed once more to the New York Court of Appeals, that state's highest court.

The 1928 *Palsgraf* case in the court of appeals represented a consummate test of two of the leading doctrines of twentieth-century negligence theory—duty and proximate causation. The concept of a "duty" owed by each person to take care not to injure his neighbor was perceived by early twentieth-century scholars to lie at the very core of tort law. Negligence amounted to the breach of such a duty, and before negligence could be found the existence of a duty had to be shown. In many instances, such a showing could easily be inferred from a defendant's conduct, but in *Palsgraf* the existence of a duty was more problematic. If the guards owed a duty not to jostle persons in assisting them on trains, or perhaps not to assist them onto moving trains at all, they most likely were responsible for injuries to those persons or their property. If the second Italian had surfaced and demanded compensation for his damaged fireworks, he might have recovered against the railroad, or at least he would have been able to demonstrate that the guards owed a duty either to refrain from assisting him or to assist him more carefully. But he was not suing the railroad; Mrs. Palsgraf was. Did the guards owe a duty to her?

If the railroad, through its guards, owed a duty of care to all its passengers, perhaps Mrs. Palsgraf could anticipate protection from injury while a passenger. But what did that duty amount to? It certainly included a duty of safe passage on the train and perhaps a duty to maintain train platforms in a safe condition. But did that duty extend to protection against unseen dangerous objects in bundles carried by passengers? If the second Italian had dropped the bundles himself, would Mrs. Palsgraf have been able to recover against the railroad? That seemed unlikely. But why did it matter that the guards, and not the second Italian, had dislodged the package when the guards had no notice that it contained fireworks? How far, in other words, did the duty of the guards extend?

That the concept of duty did not extend to cover all situations where an injury could be factually traced to a careless act on the part of the dutyholder was another central proposition of early twentieth-century tort law. The way in which spatial and temporal limits on the scope of duties was represented was through the concept of proximate causation. "Proximate" the term in "proximate causation" was designed to distinguish those causal connections between breaches of duty that were "too remote" in time and space to permit recovery from those that were close enough to be labeled "proximate." Mrs. Palsgraf's injury was remote in space and, to some extent, in time. She had been injured by a scale felled by the explosion; she was standing about 30 feet from the spot where the bundle exploded. She was on the scene and a passenger of the railroad, to be sure, but she was nowhere near the guards who had assisted the second Italian onto the *Jamaica Express*. It was only because of a freakish connection between the explosion and the scale, and because of her proximity to the scale, that Mrs. Palsgraf was injured more severely than the wife of Mr. Gerhardt, who had been jostled by the second Italian just before he attempted to board the *Jamaica Express* and who subsequently fainted when she heard the explosion and saw the smoke.

In one sense, Mrs. Palsgraf's injuries were a proximate result of the guard's having dislodged the bundle, and in another sense they were not. The case was truly a close one in terms of the ordinary language of proximate causation. Perhaps for this reason, and perhaps because he and other jurists had grown increasingly skeptical about the usefulness of the concept of proximate cause, Cardozo persuaded the court of appeals to adopt a different approach in *Palsgraf*. He grounded the decision on duty, as measured by the foreseeability of a person in the position of the defendant. "The risk to be perceived," he said, "defines the duty to be obeyed." Risk was determined by "relation": it was "risk to others within the range of apprehension." This meant that the conduct of the guards was not a "wrong" to Mrs. Palsgraf, because Mrs. Palsgraf was not in the range of persons whose safety the guards might reasonably fear if they dislodged a bundle carried by someone in their immediate vicinity. "The law of causation," Cardozo concluded, was "foreign" to the *Palsgraf* case. Before inquiries about causation could be made, inquiries about negligence needed to be satisfied, and the guards were not negligent with respect to Mrs. Palsgraf.

Cardozo's solution to *Palsgraf* and similar "unforeseeable plaintiff" cases was thus to subsume questions of causation in questions of negligence. Duty, risk, and relation controlled "proximate cause" cases: the reasonable foreseeability of the defendant determined the scope of the defendant's duty. Saying that an injury was the proximate cause of a defendant's conduct was another way of saying that the plaintiff's injury was something that a reasonable person in the position of the defendant should have foreseen. *Palsgraf* was, thus, intended to be the end of proximate causation as a doctrinal force in tort law, and the elevation of the negligence principle, with its focus on duty and foreseeability, to an all-encompassing status.

Cardozo's solution was premature. In the dissent in *Palsgraf*, Judge William S. Andrews brushed aside elevated talk of duty and foreseeability and conceptualized the case as a proximate cause case where the label "proximate" could be arbitrarily attached in favor of or against liability. Andrews's approach has come to be the way in which the case is presently understood. A universal conception of "duty" also guided Andrews's dissent: he spoke of "negligence in the air," such as recklessly driving down a street without yet having injured anyone. Cardozo sought to displace this idea of duty in the abstract with the more relational theory of *Palsgraf*, in the hope that foreseeability of risks would become the guiding principle of negligence theory. That hope has not panned out. There still exist cases, like *Palsgraf*, where one could not have imagined the scenario of an accident in one's wildest dreams, and yet one still is confronted with an injured person and some strange causal connection between that injury and a defendant's careless act. The archetypal proximate cause case is thus still present, and no amount of doctrinal rearrangements will make it go away. *Palsgraf* remains a compelling case not for Cardozo's attempted doctrinal solution, but for its strange combination of circumstances. That Cardozo's solution ended up taking away Helen Palsgraf's $6,000 verdict, and imposing court costs of $350 (nearly a year's healthy wages) on her should, at a minimum, make one pause before accepting it.

Selected Bibliography

Noonan, J.T., Jr. *Persons and Masks of the Law*. New York: Farrar, Straus & Giroux, 1976.

Posner, R.A. *Cardozo: A Study in Reputation*. Chicago: University of Chicago Press, 1990.

White, G.E. *Tort Law in America: An Intellectual History*. New York: Oxford University Press, 1980.

THE "NUKING" OF AMERICAN CIVILIANS

by Howard Ball
Department of Political Science
University of Utah

Allen v. United States, 816 F. 2d 1417 (1987) [U.S. Court of Appeals]

From 1951 to 1963, the United States detonated atomic weapons on the American continent. In December 1950, President Harry S. Truman approved a proposal by the Atomic Energy Commission (AEC) that the United States develop an atomic testing facility on the continent in order to maintain nuclear superiority over the Soviet Union. The reasons for the AEC's proposal seemed plain at the time; among them was the fact that U.S. military and political leaders had recently been angered and shocked by the exposure of a Soviet spy operation that had been passing secrets about the atom bomb to the Soviet Union since 1944.

In the summer of 1950, Julius and Ethel Rosenberg had been arrested and charged with conspiracy to pass secrets to the Soviets—a violation of the 1917 Espionage Act. Also, in June 1950, the Cold War suddenly turned very hot as Americans became involved in the "police action" in Korea. For the commissioners of the AEC, concerned about the maintenance of security as well as the difficulties in sustaining an operational research and development facility thousands of miles away from U.S. scientific laboratories at their Pacific Ocean test facility site, it was imperative that they locate an atomic test facility in a fairly remote section of the continental United States.

They chose an old World War II gunnery range in the Nevada desert for the test site. The AEC viewed the government-owned land as "virtually uninhabitable" and therefore no threat to the health and safety of significant numbers of Americans. In making that assessment, it took into account the fact that some radioactive fallout would drift off-site and deposit radioactive particles on the tens of thousands of U.S. citizens living in Nevada, Utah, and Arizona, to the east and north of what has been called the Nevada Test Site (NTS) by the government since 1954.

A review of the AEC commissioners' "top secret" minutes clearly indicates that they knew of the human risks of the atomic testing on the continental United States. However, they insisted that while the risk to the people of St. George, Utah, for example, existed (St. George "always gets plastered," said one of the commissioners), the much greater risk was allowing the Soviets to gain the upper hand in the race for nuclear superiority. Using a benefit-cost analysis, the AEC concluded that the testing had to go on at the NTS. Nothing would stop the testing, said another commissioner in 1957. All told, there were over 120 atomic shots in the desert air north and west of Las Vegas, Nevada. Over 80 of these atmospheric shots deposited radioactive debris off-site, or downwind, of the test site.

There is no question that the pathological and genetic dangers of ionizing radiation were well known to the nuclear scientists working at the NTS as well as to the AEC administrators. The AEC's Division of Biology and Medicine scientists and doctors, responsible for the safety and health of persons coming into contact with the testing program, knew of the dangers to persons exposed to radioactive fallout. Engaged in bureaucratic struggles with the AEC's Division of Military Application scientists and Department of Defense administrators, however, they always seemed to lose to those responsible for producing the fissionable materials and conducting the research and development of atomic weapons. From the beginning of the AEC's history in 1946, it was given a contradictory task: develop atomic weapons in order to maintain nuclear superiority over the Soviets but develop these weapons in a safe environment. When these two stipulations clashed, weapons development was always primary. Eugene Zuckert, chairman of the AEC from 1952 to 1954, put it starkly: the atomic weapons testing program was characterized by a "lack of balance between the safety requirements and the requirements of the program. . . . [When there was a] conflict, the balance was apt to tip on the side of the military programs."

In 1978, reporters used the Freedom of Information Act to uncover documents held in AEC files since the late 1950s and early 1960s disclosing that the "downwinders" had been exposed to unsafe levels of radioactivity. Furthermore, the documents indicated that early AEC and the Public Health Service medical reports had informed the AEC of the dangers but that the AEC did little to warn those who were exposed to the fallout. A deputy director of the AEC justified not informing the downwinders in this way: "Well, look, we've told these people all along that it's safe and we can't change our story now, we'll be in trouble." The documents also revealed that the AEC officials were negligent (i.e., did not take adequate safety precautions as mandated by the 1946 Atomic Energy Act) when they implemented the program.

After a rebuff from the Department of Energy, a group of petitioners, which would number almost 1,200 by 1980, sought remediation in federal court from the government for injuries to and deaths of—primarily caused by cancers and leukemia—their children, spouses, and parents due to exposure to the fallout from the atomic tests over the Nevada desert in the 1950s. Using the 1946 Federal Tort Claims Act (FTCA), legislation passed by Congress that enables citizens to sue the government and governmental agents under certain circumstances, is difficult under even ordinary circumstances (e.g., when a person suffers an injury from being hit by a U.S. mail truck).

This was not an ordinary case, however. First, *Allen* involved the AEC's implementation of a major governmental policy involving national security (atomic testing), and the FTCA contains an exception (called "discretionary function") that disallows persons from suing the government if the injury occurs as a consequence of a governmental agent using judgment to implement such a policy. Additionally, the *Allen* litigation charged that the governmental negligence during the testing period led to nontraditional injuries. That is, due to the detonation of the atom bombs in the 1950s, years—even decades—later, biological injuries occurred to plaintiffs and to their progeny.

The lawyers representing the downwinders in the suit against the U.S. government had to meet and overcome two legal burdens. First, they had to convince the federal judge that the federal agents who implemented the testing policy at the NTS in the 1950s were not immune from a tort liability suit under the FTCA. If they could not persuade the federal judge in the trial court that the discretionary function exception did not apply in their case, the case would be over before reaching the substantive issue. Second, assuming that they made the case for jurisdiction, the lawyers for the plaintiffs in *Allen* had the very difficult burden of showing that the cancers and leukemias, discovered in the 1960s and 1970s, were "more likely than not" caused by the negligence of the government when it exploded atom bombs over the Nevada desert in the 1950s.

The federal judge who heard the case, Bruce S. Jenkins, grew up in Utah. He was appointed to the federal district court in Utah in 1978 by President Jimmy Carter. A year later, he was assigned the *Allen* case. Living in Salt Lake City, he was familiar with the media reports about the activities of the AEC personnel at the NTS during the 1950s. Jenkins was, from the beginning, leery of the government's arguments that (1) there was absolute immunity from any FTCA suit brought by petitioners due to the discretionary function exception, (2) there was not a "scintilla" of evidence that plaintiffs could present at trial to show that the government acted negligently or carelessly when it detonated the atom bomb, and (3) there was no way to prove scientifically that the cancers and leukemias contracted by the persons who lived downwind of the NTS were caused by the radioactive fallout produced by the atomic testing at the NTS.

Three times between 1979 and 1982 the government's lawyers asked Jenkins to summarily dismiss the suit on the grounds of the discretionary function exception. Three times he turned aside their request. The last rejection occurred during the trial. Jenkins, in rejecting the government's petition, stated that the jurisdiction issue was so important and so intertwined with other issues that he could rule on it only after hearing the evidence presented at trial.

The trial lasted three months. Thousands of documents were introduced into the record. Dozens of witnesses—former AEC employees, Department of Energy bureaucrats, medical epidemiologists, nuclear physicists, oncologists, and the downwinders themselves—testified before Jenkins. In December 1982, he took the case under advisement and then spent the next year and one-half—with a law clerk who he kept on the payroll for eight months after his clerkship had expired—crafting his opinion. The judge and the clerk, Russell Kearl, toiled away in the document room, the "Theoretical Physics Division, U.S. District Court," as they called it, until the opinion was ready to be handed down. In early May 1974, *Allen* was announced.

On the jurisdictional issue (i.e., whether the government was immune from tort litigation), Jenkins ruled that the local agents at the NTS and the AEC monitors working in the local towns that dotted the deserts and the valleys of the Southwest were not immune from tort action under the FTCA. They were responsible for carefully administering a discretionary policy. For Jenkins, the manner in which the tests were conducted, carefully or carelessly, was also a matter of choice, but was not a matter of discretion because such operational conduct was subject to a standard of due care. The downwinders were owed a duty by the AEC to act with due care. These governmental personnel, according to Jenkins's review of the facts, did not provide certain safety activities: they did not provide adequate warnings, adequate measurements of the fallout or adequate edu-

cational programs. "Jurisdiction is proper," Jenkins announced in *Allen*, because the carelessness and negligence of the AEC local officials were not immunized by the FTCA. The AEC provided a reasonable standard of care and the AEC personnel in the field could be held accountable if that standard was not met. Furthermore, Jenkins found that the personnel clearly breached their responsibility to act with due care.

Having established jurisdiction and determining that the AEC showed a lack of due care to the downwinders, Jenkins then turned to the very difficult question of causation. Did the AEC's negligence and breach of duty more likely than not cause the petitioner's illnesses and deaths? In any tort action for damages, Jenkins wrote, the plaintiffs have the burden of showing that the injury suffered was "a result of the defendant's conduct, at least in part" and must "demonstrate factually that there is a reason why this particular person is the defendant."

In the downwinders suit, the factual connection was "in genuine dispute" due to the lengthy latency of the diseases that petitioners claimed were caused by the careless AEC testing of atomic devices. Proving causation-in-fact in this type of "indeterminate causation" litigation was difficult, admitted Jenkins. Therefore, he said in a burst of creative adjudication, the "court must use its own best judgments, experience and common sense in light of all the circumstances." Accordingly, he ruled that the difficulty that the downwinders had in proving that the government caused their cancers did not mean that the government did not, "in fact," cause the damage.

To assist in the search for justice, Jenkins "fashioned" a "remedial framework" to determine the causation question. He held that if the AEC created a radiological hazard for an identifiable group and members of that group contract "a biological condition which is consistent with having been caused by the hazard to which [they have] been negligently subjected, a federal judge "may reasonably conclude that the hazard caused the condition absent persuasive proof to the contrary offered by the defendant."

Jenkins then reviewed the circumstances of each of the 24 plaintiffs in the *Allen* litigation in light of the remedial framework: were they exposed to excess amounts of radiation, were they living downwind of the NTS at the time of the above-ground testing program, and did they succumb to a type of cancer or leukemia that was radiogenic (i.e., caused by radioactivity)? In ten of the cases, he found for the plaintiff: the cancers and leukemias that had killed them were the consequence of AEC "risk taking conduct" and therefore liability was imposed on the government by the federal judge. The award totalled almost $3 million. The remaining 14 plaintiffs, Jenkins concluded, did not show that the government was more likely than not the cause of their cancers.

The response to Jenkins's ruling was predictable: the government immediately criticized his judgment as inconsistent with precedent in the area of tort law and filed an appeal in the U.S. Court of Appeals for the Tenth Circuit in Denver. For the Reagan Administration's Justice Department, Jenkins's opinion was an "outrageous new theory of liability [created by an] activist judge engaging in social engineering."

The court of appeals handed down its judgment nearly three years later. On April 20, 1987, a three-judge panel overturned Jenkins's decision. The panel concluded that the AEC activities were immune from tort liability actions under the FTCA by virtue of the presence of the discretionary function exception. All the actions of even the most local of AEC operatives "also fall within the discretionary function exception." The opinion concluded that the government was "immune from liability for the failure of AEC administrators and employees to monitor radioactivity more extensively or to warn the public more fully than they did." If there is any justice to be dispensed in the issue, they said, it is for the Congress and not the federal courts to so apportion. Until Congress acts, said a concurring judge, "we have no choice but to leave them uncompensated."

The downwinders then took the case to the U.S. Supreme Court, hoping that the Court would grant *certiorari* and review the issue on the merits. However, the Court, without a single publicly announced dissent from the denial of *certiorari*, refused to hear the *Allen* case. The court of appeals's overturning of Jenkins's *Allen* opinion was affirmed. A month after Jenkins handed down his *Allen* opinion, the Supreme Court handed down an opinion that maintained the narrowly drawn scope of the FTCA as developed by the Court as early as a 1953 case. This may explain why the Court did not grant *certiorari* in *Allen*.

In the shortterm, the only remediation for the downwinders is legislation passed by Congress. The legal remedy is no longer available to these plaintiffs. While the law of torts may eventually change to take account of the dilemma of the nontraditional tort injury, unless Congress responds to the pleas of the downwinders, there will be no remedy for the people placed at risk by agents of the U.S. government.

Selected Bibliography

Ball, H. *Justice Downwind: America's Atomic Testing Program in the 1950's*. New York: Oxford University Press, 1986.

Titus, A.C. *Bombs in the Backyard: Atomic Testing and American Politics*. Reno, NV: University of Nevada Press, 1986.

G. Natural Resources, Technology, and the Environment

RIPARIAN DOCTRINE: A SHORT CASE HISTORY FOR THE EASTERN UNITED STATES

by *William F. Steirer, Jr.*
Department of History
Clemson University

Omelvanny v. Jaggers, 2 Hill 634 (1835); *White v. Whitney Manufacturing Company* 60 S.C. 254 (1901) [South Carolina Supreme Court]

East of the thirty-first parallel in the United States, the doctrine governing the uses of surface water is called riparian. Today that doctrine generally holds that owners of land contiguous to watercourses possess the right to use that water provided the use is reasonable and kept within the basin's boundaries. Riparian doctrine developed in Europe and by-passed the normal channels whereby legal doctrines were imported to the United States from England. A 1793 Connecticut decision is apparently the first case decided on riparian principles in the United States, but gradually during the next four decades most of the northeastern states embraced riparianism. The rejection of prior appropriation tenets (i.e., the idea that the first proprietor on a stream possessed a superior right) remained incomplete in the East until well into the nineteenth century. As late as 1821, the Massachusetts Supreme Judicial Court was still applying prior appropriations remedies to water use conflicts.

The 1835 South Carolina case *Omelvanny v. Jaggers* provided a point of definition for riparianism in the Southeast where, even more than in the northeastern states, the spread of riparian doctrine was both steady during the last half of the nineteenth century and unchallenged in court and custom. *Omelvanny* came at a time when attitudes about property and entrepreneurial opportunities were shifting dramatically toward the individualization of society known to historians as "Jacksonian democracy."

Historians, generally, understand Jacksonian democracy to have been the celebration of the individual in society, that individual effort took priority over a sense of collective responsibility, that what an individual wanted was at least equal to the community's wants and needs, and that all inhabitants of society deserved equal access to the exploiting of natural resources. *Omelvanny* reflected the Jacksonian credo in opening the rights to water use to all comers on an equal basis regardless of prior claims. Quoting New York's Chancellor James Kent, the court observed in *Omelvanny*, "Every proprietor of lands in the banks of a river, has naturally an equal right to the use of the water which flows in the stream adjacent to his lands, as it was wont to flow . . . without diminution or alteration. No proprietor has a right to use the water to the prejudice of other proprietors above or below him, unless he has a prior right to divert it, or a title to some exclusive enjoyment. He has no property in the water itself, but a simple use of it while it passes along."

In these words, the South Carolina Supreme Court articulated in 1835 the early version of riparian doctrine known as the natural flow theory. H. & W. Omelvanny erected a mill a short time after Elisha Jaggers built his mill one-half mile downstream on the Rocky Creek. There had been a mill on the Jaggers site from 1794 to 1814, so Jaggers had a prior claim to the water in Rocky Creek. In 1833, it was discovered that the defendant's dam raised the water at the plaintiff's mill by four and one-half feet, sufficient for the wheels not to turn.

The lower court held that Jaggers possessed a prior right to use the water, and "to deprive the first occupant of this privilege at the pleasure of the owner above, would be giving one owner an unreasonable advantage over the other, which might be exercised capriciously and unjustly."

The supreme court's majority overturned the lower court's application of prior appropriation's doctrine. In spite of an unfortunate misquoting of Kent (stating "reasonably" where "unreasonably" appeared), the point was clear. Claims based on prior occupancy or use are "opposed to the weight of reasoning and authority." The natural flow of a watercourse may not be interrupted to the injury of other riparian proprietors in spite of claims to prior occupancy.

With the abundance of surface water available, few conflicts over water rights needed to be resolved in eastern state courts during the nineteenth century. South Carolina saw only three riparian cases reach its supreme court before 1900. Shortly after, the supreme court rendered the definitive decision in *White v. Whitney Manufacturing Company* (1901), rejecting the natural flow theory in the process. Instead, the court held that a riparian proprietor had a right to use the water in a stream in a "reasonable way." In *White*, the defendant's right to use the water even though it interfered with the natural flow of Lawson's Fork Creek was upheld. The court stated: "But as between different proprietors on the same stream, the right of each qualifies that of the other, and the question always is not merely whether the lower proprietor suffers damage by the use of the water above him, nor whether the quantity flowing on is diminished by the use, but whether, under all the circumstances of the case the use of the water by one is reasonable and consistent with a correspondent enjoyment by the other."

The court carefully observed that "[s]treams of water are intended for the use and comfort of man, and it would be unreasonable and contrary to the universal sense of mankind" to prevent a riparian proprietor from using the water in ways "conformable to the usages and wants to the community, . . . and not inconsistent with a likewise reasonable use by the other proprietors of land on the same stream above and below." Determination of reasonable use, the court said, should be left to the jury in each case.

Flexibility and freedom from administrative strictures and costs continue in the late twentieth century to be the advantages of maintaining riparian principles. Whether those advantages will suffice in the face of perceived shortages of surface water and apparent conflicts in water uses in South Carolina and other eastern states is problematical. Already, Florida, Kentucky, and Mississippi have turned toward administrative solutions for allocating water. Pressures are building everywhere to devise some kind of administrative remedy, but to date the precedents established in cases like *Omelvanny* and *White* prevail.

Selected Bibliography

Cox, W.E., ed. *Legal and Administrative Systems for Water Allocation and Management.* Blacksburg, VA: Virginia Water Resources Research Center, 1978.

Dewsant, R.L., and D.W. Jensen, eds. *A Summary—Digest of State Water Laws.* Arlington, VA: United States Government Printing Office, 1973.

CONFLICT OVER WATER POWER IN MASSACHUSETTS

by James W. Ely, Jr.
School of Law
Vanderbilt University

Cary v. Daniels, 49 Mass. 466 (1844) [Supreme Judicial Court of Massachusetts]

Access to waterpower was crucial for industrial technology in the nineteenth century. The heavy demand for waterpower required lawmakers to reconcile the conflicting interests of riparian landowners in the use of rivers and streams. Indeed, litigation over water rights increased rapidly in antebellum America. A dispute between two mill owners on the Charles River raised the difficult question of which operator was entitled to priority in water use and allowed the Massachusetts Supreme Judicial Court to reformulate water law.

Before 1833, William H. Cary was one of several tenants in common who owned two mills on the Charles River. While the mills were under common ownership, a practice developed of opening the gate on the lower mill dam to relieve the upper mill from backwater. In 1833, the co-tenants conveyed the upper mill and adjacent land to a third party, who in turn transferred the property to Cary in 1837. The lower mill and surrounding land were conveyed several times. Finally, in 1838, Albert Daniels became the sole owner. The lower mill dam was carried away by the river, and so Daniels built a new and larger dam. The new dam raised the water level above its usual height and caused the river to flow back upon Cary's mill wheel. This hampered Cary in the use of his mill.

Cary then brought a lawsuit against Daniels, alleging two counts of unlawful interference with his rights. First, Cary charged that Daniels had improperly obstructed the use of Cary's mill. Second, Cary asserted that Daniels had interfered with his right to enter the lower mill property and open the gates on the lower dam. The case was tried before a jury and resulted in a verdict for the plaintiff on both counts. Cary was awarded $300 in damages on the first count, and $100 on the second. Thereafter, the supreme judicial court heard legal arguments on whether judgment should be entered upon the verdict.

Water law in the United States was in the process of evolution during the antebellum era. Eminent jurists, such as Joseph Story and James Kent, fashioned riparian rights on their understanding of English common-law principles. They formulated the reasonable use doctrine under which every landowner along a river or stream, by virtue of such ownership, enjoyed a right to use the water in its natural flow. Thus, all riparian owners had equal rights to use the water and none could lawfully cause injury to landowners above or below him.

The reasonable use doctrine posed several problems. One was the obvious difficulty of determining reasonable use under a variety of circumstances. Another was that the reasonable use doctrine tended to inhibit the most productive uses of water by preventing any riparian owner from heavy consumption. Yet to allow one riparian owner to reduce the flow of water for his own benefit could destroy the value of the other mill sites.

In his *Cary* decision, Chief Justice Lemuel Shaw sought to adjust the reasonable use doctrine to the need of mill operators to harness waterpower. Stressing the commercial value of waterpower, Shaw declared that in the United States "one of the most important" uses of a watercourse "is its application to the workings of mills and machinery; a use profitable to the owner and beneficial to the public." Qualifying the reasonable use doctrine with novel considerations, Shaw explained that "each proprietor is entitled to such use of the stream so far as it is reasonable, conformable to the usages and wants of the community, and having regard to the progress of improvement in hydraulic works. . . ."

Although in the abstract each riparian owner was allowed reasonable use of streams and rivers, Shaw's analysis moved toward the doctrine of prior appropriation. He asserted that "the proprietor who first erects his dam for such a purpose has a right to maintain it, as against the proprietors above and below; and to this extent, prior occupancy gives a prior title to such use." In short, the first appropriation of a watercourse for mill purposes was a property right. Consequently, the damages caused by backwater from a previously established mill dam were a mere inconvenience and did not constitute a legal injury.

Applying these principles to the case before the court, Shaw ruled that Daniels received the lower parcel of land subject to the prior appropriation of the Charles River by plaintiff's upper mill dam. Thus, Daniels had no right to erect a new dam that was higher than his old one. The court accordingly upheld the jury verdict for obstruction of plaintiff's mill. How-ever, the court disallowed the second count, holding that once the properties were separated, the owner of the upper estate had no right to enter the lower mill parcel.

As a result of *Cary*, courts began to view the use of water for mills and machinery as requiring special considerations. Judicial recognition that the first proprietor who built a mill dam had a right to maintain it facilitated industrial use of waterpower. This desire to encourage efficient use of water undercut the notion of equal distribution that was at the heart of the reasonable use doctrine.

Selected Bibliography

Clark, R.E., ed. *Waters and Water Rights*. Indianapolis: Allen Smith Co., 1967.

Horwitz, M.J. *The Transformation of American Law, 1780–1860*. Cambridge, MA: Harvard University Press, 1977.

Lauer, T.E. "The Common Law Background of the Riparian Doctrine." *Missouri Law Review* 28 (1963): 60–107.

A LAW FOR WATER IN THE WEST

by Gordon Morris Bakken
Department of History
California State University at Fullerton

Irwin v. Phillips, 5 Cal. 140 (1855) [California Supreme Court]

The flood tide of humanity that followed the lure of gold to California in 1849 brought with it concepts of law that found immediately popular application in the gold fields. People from all walks of life found themselves toiling in the mines of the mother lode country and quickly developed laws to regulate their enterprise. Forming local mining districts, the early miners wrote down these rules and regulations, created institutions to enforce the laws, and carried these early district regulations from place to place as they searched for gold. All of this activity took place in the public domain without federal legislative direction. Part of these local mining district regulations involved the use of water.

Water was critical to the mining industry. To work a claim successfully, a miner had to have water to wash gravel and sand away to reveal the glitter. First in the humble pan, then in sluice boxes and "long toms," and finally in elaborate timbered edifices, the miners brought the gold-laden gravel and sand in contact with water. Water cleansed metal of its common medium, but water was too often a scarce commodity. Conflicts over its use arose in the mining districts and were manifested in lawsuits.

The question before the California Supreme Court in 1855 went beyond mining district regulations because it involved water and the English common-law concept of riparian rights. The riparian proprietor gained rights in water by ownership of the stream bank. The rights included the quantity and quality of stream flow along the property abutting the stream. Owners of land on the stream above a riparian were "upper riparian proprietors" and those below were "lower riparian proprietors." All had rights to the quantity and quality of water undiminished by reasonable use of the other riparians. In *Irwin v. Phillips*, a canal company had diverted water from the natural watercourse for the purpose of supplying water to miners. This diversion took place prior to miners staking claims to the bank of the stream as lower riparians. The lower riparians wanted the diversion stopped to assure their common-law right to a water supply.

Justice Solomon Heydenfeldt, after noting the fact that the parties were on the public domain, looked to the history of mining to find legal authority. He noted that by 1855 neither the state government nor the federal government had exhibited any intent to regulate the business of mining on the public domain. Rather, a system had "been permitted to grow up by the voluntary action and assent of the population, whose free and unrestrained occupation of the mineral region has been tacitly assented to by the one government, and heartily encouraged by the express legislative policy of the other."

The history of federal land policy had been one of spending land for the public benefit and specifically for mineral lands, encouraging rapid exploitation by private parties. The rough and tumble mining camps had, in turn, written rules and regulations that protected the interests of the first arrives in the name of entrepreneurial liberty.

Heydenfeldt viewed the mining district regulations as "crude and undigested," yet having legal force. Despite the nature of these regulations, "there are still some [rules] which a universal sense of necessity and propriety have so firmly fixed as that they have come to be looked upon as having the force and effect of *res judicata*" ("matters settled by judgment"). He found two principles to be clear in the regulations. First, the miners were to be protected

in their locations. A miner who staked a claim in accordance with the district regulations had a location at law and that location was to be protected by law. Second, the regulations protected "the rights of those who, by prior appropriation, have taken the waters from their natural beds, and by costly artificial works have conducted them for miles over mountains and ravines, to supply the necessities of gold diggers." This latter right must be accorded legal protection because, without the water companies, "the most important interests of the mineral region would remain without development." Beyond the public policy basis for the encouragement of enterprise, the legislature had more than tacitly recognized the district regulations by reference in statutes. Canals and water races were property subject to taxation. The property of canal companies liable for assessment and taxation included "dams, . . . canals, or other works for mining purposes." Regardless of the fact that the enterprise was on the public domain, it was property and it had received "recognition from the sovereign power."

Miners seeking mineral wealth on the public domain took claims subject to prior interests. The priority principle, devised by miners, known to miners, and recognized by statute, informed any subsequent claimant that if water had "been already diverted, and for as high, and legitimate a purpose as the one he seeks to accomplish, he has no right to complain. . . ." The doctrine of prior appropriation of water had received judicial recognition and would become the leading principle of resource allocation in water for the arid West.

Selected Bibliography

Bakken, G.M. "American Mining Law and the Environment: The Western Experience." *Western Legal History* 1 (1988): 211–36.

Paul, R.W. *Mining Frontiers of the Far West*. New York: Holt, Rinehart, & Winston, 1963.

Pisani, D.J. *From the Family Farm to Agribusiness: The Irrigation Crusade in California and the West, 1850–1931*. Berkeley, CA: University of California Press, 1984.

Smith, D.A. *Mining America: The Industry and the Environment, 1800–1980*. Lawrence, KS: University of Kansas Press, 1987.

DIVIDING THE RIVERS: RULE OF LAW IN AN ARID STATE

by M. Catherine Miller
Department of History
Texas Tech University

Lux v. Haggin, 69 Cal. 255 (1886) [California Supreme Court]

Lux v. Haggin was one of the most controversial cases to confront the California Supreme Court in the nineteenth century. At issue was the meaning of California's law of waters and, to many, the future of the state's arid lands. In 1850, the California legislature adopted the common law as the rule of decision in the state. Presumably, it had received the common law of waters, riparian rights, which viewed water as "part and parcel" of the land through which it flowed. But as miners transported water away from streams to wash fortunes from the auriferous hills, the doctrine was ignored. Most miners were trespassers on the public lands. With the federal government making no effort to protect its rights as a riparian owner, judges settled rival claims to water as they had those to land: first in time, first in right. While riparian rights were not abrogated, in 1872 the legislature codified rules governing this appropriation of water.

In *Lux v. Haggin*, the state supreme court was asked to decide which of these doctrines governed the water rights of privately owned agricultural land. Underlying this request were conflicting views of the role of law and the judiciary. Advocates of riparian rights called on the court to apply traditional principles. The proponents of prior appropriation demanded that it be flexible and democratic, recognizing regional differences, encouraging entrepreneurial activity, and accepting the will of the people as expressed in public opinion and local custom. In 1886, the California court insisted that it must uphold rule of law and declared in favor of riparian rights, a decision that to this day continues to be assailed as inappropriate to the needs of the state.

Lux v. Haggin was a clash between Titans. On one side were the cattlemen Henry Miller and Charles Lux. Former rivals, these immigrant butchers had formed a partnership that dominated the San Francisco meat industry. They purchased hundreds of thousands of acres of land in California, Oregon, and Nevada, on which they raised cattle, sheep, and hogs. Much of their land was riparian, bordering rivers that could irrigate pastures and water stock. James Ben Ali Haggin and his partners, Lloyd Tevis and William Carr, were likewise wealthy and politically powerful. All had been connected with the Southern Pacific Railroad, and Carr was the railroad's political boss in the state legislature. Together and individually they had invested in large-scale financial and mining ventures and owned a million acres of western land.

Both of these groups sought control of the Kern River, located in the county of the same name in the southern end of California's rich Central Valley. Flowing past expanses of high desert, the river ultimately dwindled into Buena Vista Slough and the swamplands it fed before terminating in a shallow inland lake. In the 1850s, federal largesse and the connivance of state land officials attracted speculators to the swamplands at the lower end of the river. Some 90,000 acres of Kern County land were granted to a group proposing to develop irrigation and transportation canals that would link the region with San Francisco and its lucrative markets. When this scheme failed, in the 1860s cattlemen took up the overflowed lands. Miller and Lux acquired 40,000 acres along Buena Vista Slough. They excavated a canal to drain the wetlands and irrigate the reclaimed acres and, with large herds pastured in the region, began fencing their ranges.

Haggin and his partners arrived in Kern County with the opening of the Southern Pacific line in 1874. Holding options on railroad land, they bought up the numerous canals that small farmers had scratched out further upstream. Haggin also acquired thousands of acres north of the river, much of this through fraudulent use of the Desert Land Act. Promising to expand irrigation systems and to subdivide his holdings, Haggin and his money were welcomed by local boosters as the leavening needed for rapid economic development. In fact, as he achieved control of land and canals, the area under irrigation grew sevenfold.

In 1877, the Central Valley suffered a profound and costly drought. Little water reached Buena Vista Slough, and the cattlemen helplessly watched their pastures wither and their cattle die. Banding together, they blamed Haggin for the severity of their losses. Haggin had recently opened the Calloway Canal, which irrigated his desert lands. This diversion, they charged, had stolen water that should have flowed to their fields in even the driest years. After an unsuccessful attempt to negotiate a division of the river, Miller and Lux and their allies filed 78 suits against Haggin and other upstream water users. Asserting that they were riparian owners and thus entitled to use the full flow of the stream, Miller and Lux asked the court to restrain Haggin's interference with their rights and property.

In responding, Haggin denied that Miller and Lux were riparian owners. After the cattlemen established their title to land and the extent of the damages, Haggin countered that possession of these wetlands did not convey water rights. This factual contention occupied the greater portion of the 49-day trial. Parading forth a dreary stream of engineers, surveyors, and friends, he alleged that the slough was not a watercourse as required by law. Lacking defined banks and a steady flow, it was merely part of the swampy morass that Miller and Lux were obliged to reclaim. In addition, having allowed the Kern Valley Water Company to erect a dam at the head of the sough, the cattlemen had cut off both the flow of water and their entitlement. Besides, Haggin pointed out, he had initiated his appropriation of water in 1875, three years before Miller and Lux received the final patents to their land; thus, any water rights they might have were subject to his prior claims.

More important to the history of the case was Haggin's attack on the riparian doctrine itself, both in the arguments of his attorneys and in his funding of a public antiriparian campaign. Citing decisions recognizing prior appropriation in the mining districts, Haggin's forces insisted that riparian rights had been abolished. To bolster this reasoning they appealed to public policy: the common-law doctrine should not (and could not) be accepted in California because it did not serve the needs of arid regions. By binding water to the land through which it flowed, riparianism gave a monopoly to cattlemen like Miller and Lux who contributed little to the development of the state. Vast stretches of land that when irrigated would support thousands of families would lie in waste and be held hostage to this few. In contrast, under the doctrine of appropriation these lands could produce the bountiful harvests that would secure the state's future.

William Stewart, former senator from Nevada, author of the federal mining code of 1866 which recognized prior appropriation on the public domain, and friend of Haggin, marshaled a kind of popular sovereignty to resolve the seeming conflict of law inherent in California's recognition of two water doctrines. Geography and climate dictated which doctrine suited, he argued, riparianism for humid parts of the state, appropriation for the arid; and local judges and juries with their knowledge of the community should decide which applied in a given case. The usages and customs of reasonable men, not precedent or statute, must determine law, which if it reflected local standards would set the stage for rapid economic growth and development.

Benjamin Brundage, the land agent and recently elected Kern County judge who tried the case, accepted this reasoning when he ruled against Miller and Lux. During the hearing, he had denied the cattlemen's request to enter additional evidence rebutting Haggin's assertions that there was no watercourse through the swamplands and that the diversion into the Calloway Canal antedated their acquisition of land. He then decreed that the swamplands possessed no riparian rights and were subject to Haggin's appropriation. Behind this law was a belief that only such a ruling protected the future of the community. Irrigation was a natural want, and the opening of Haggin's canal had transformed wastelands into vineyards, orchards, and gardens. To recognize Miller and Lux's claims would deprive these lands of water and render them once again "utterly barren, desert, and worthless."

Similarly, when the cattlemen appealed Brundage's decision, three of the seven members of the state supreme court rejected riparianism as inappropriate to the needs of the state and denied that it had been received as part of the common law. Erskine M. Ross, the only justice from Southern California, argued that the state and federal governments had nullified riparian rights when they recognized prior appropriation on the public lands. Even the common law, he insisted, did not countenance riparianism in an arid state: the two most important qualities of the common law were flexibility and rationality; but it was a perversion of human reason to require that California's waters, its very "lifeblood," continue to flow in natural channels to be wasted in the sea.

However, in 1884, the four-member majority tersely rejected these entreaties. To them the law was "plain enough": the common law of waters had never been revoked, riparian rights were part of property in land, and riparian owners were entitled to the continued flow and benefit of the stream. The chief problem in *Lux v. Haggin* lay instead in arriving at the facts, and Brundage's decision was overturned because he had not allowed the cattlemen to present rebuttal evidence essential to determining if they had valid claims to water. However, acknowledging the crescendo of antiripariamism, the court agreed to rehear the appeal and to entertain arguments from others interested in the issue of water rights. The reargument changed no minds. In 1886, still divided 4–3, the California Supreme Court again threw out Brundage's verdict and ordered a new trial. Now the court issued a 200-page decision, the longest in its history, directing that broad color of title be given to assertions of riparian rights.

The essence of this opinion lay in a heartfelt commitment to rule of law and to protecting vested rights. Property, including that in water, could be taken only by following established eminent domain procedures and paying compensation. While Brundage had seized on every insinuation of weakness to strike down

the cattlemen's claims, the court's majority presumed their title was good. Only convincing and conclusive proof, which had not been provided during the earlier trial, not inference, justified the rejection of the traditional privileges of ownership. Similarly, the majority denied that the recognition of prior appropriation had stripped land along the state's rivers of riparian rights. While Haggin argued that in accepting appropriation the legislature had bestowed its waters on all the people, the court saw this statute as a limited "concession" to those fulfilling its requirements. With this exception, state-held lands retained their attached water rights, both because the same statute protected existing riparian interests and because it did not explicitly donate them to the public. At the same time, federal lands and those in private hands, even if title had not been perfected, retained water rights: the state could not give away what it did not own.

Throughout, the court rejected an activist role. Once law was settled, in this instance by the adoption of the common law in 1850, courts could not annul it but must apply it as consistently as possible. The majority found no legal principle negating riparian property rights in the Spanish and Mexican codes that had earlier governed California and dismissed as preposterous the notion that geography or public policy should deter the application of established rules. Though eschewing a concern with policy, the court did evaluate Haggin's argument that prior appropriation nourished economic democracy, concluding that on the contrary it spawned water monopoly. Only in accepting irrigation as a use of riparian waters did the court depart from traditional doctrine. However, while this was an accommodation to local needs, the court perceived the ruling as a natural application of precepts of reasonable use found in decisions of judges such as Lemuel Shaw of Massachusetts. Like many other jurists in the late nineteenth century, the four here upholding riparian rights denied that courts made law. Rather, in applying the rules of law to each circumstance, the judiciary provided certainty, stability, and security, protecting individual freedoms (and property) from all threats, especially threats with popular support.

An outcry of protest, much of it funded and organized by Haggin and Carr, greeted this decision. The governor was induced to call a special session of the legislature to overturn the ruling and to oust the justices who had supported it as old men out of step with the times. Quickly branded a threat to judicial independence, the proposed restructuring of the court failed, and efforts to revise the water code foundered with it. During the next regular session in 1887, lawmakers adopted the Wright Act, a seminal bill providing for popularly organized irrigation districts with the power to tax and to employ eminent domain. The legislature also rescinded the portion of the 1872 water code that acknowledged riparian rights. However, with riparian rights recognized as vested under the common law, this last action was an empty, symbolic gesture. Meanwhile negotiations, not the second trial provided for in *Lux v. Haggin*, settled the original conflict. In 1888, Miller and Haggin signed a contract partitioning the waters of the Kern between them; and with control of the river secured, both the riparian and the appropriator continued to amass land within the county.

Though the bitter refrain of antiriparianism continued to reverberate through the legislature, public debate, and legal briefs, *Lux v. Haggin* was not overturned. Irrigation expanded rapidly, most often under the favored doctrine of appropriation; but where riparian owners asserted their rights, they were successful. Henry Miller used *Lux v. Haggin* as a powerful weapon, repeatedly suing those who infringed on his claims to rivers such as the San Joaquin, the second largest in the state. In the mire of subsequent litigation, the divided decision of 1886 hardened into rigid doctrine. Riparian owners were entitled to the full flow of the stream even if they squandered water that upstream appropriators might put to beneficial use. Such broad prerogatives were only limited, and at that timidly, with the amendment of the state constitution in 1928. Following *Lux v. Haggin*, succeeding jurists treated water as a part of land, not as a separate resource to be governed by independent principles. They accepted boundaries set by four men who had rejected all serious consideration of water policy out of a belief that only the strict rule of law could protect property rights.

Selected Bibliography

Freyfogle, E.T. "*Lux v. Haggin* and the Common Law Burdens of Modern Water Law." *University of Colorado Law Review* 57 (1986): 485–525.

Miller, G. "Shaping California Water Law, 1781–1928." *Southern California Quarterly* 55 (1973): 9–42.

Miller, M.C. "Riparian Rights and the Control of Water in California, 1879–1928: The Relationship Between an Agricultural Enterprise and Legal Change." *Agricultural History* 59 (1985): 1–24.

Pisani, D. *From the Family Farm to Agribusiness: The Irrigation Crusade in California and the West, 1850–1931.* Berkeley, CA: University of California Press, 1984.

Shaw, L. "The Development of the Law of Waters in the West." *California Law Review* 10 (1922): 444–60.

Wiel, S.C. "Public Policy in Western Water Decisions." *California Law Review* 1 (1912–13): 11–31.

THE HYDRAULIC SOCIETY OF THE COLORADO RIVER

by Gordon Morris Bakken
Department of History
California State University at Fullerton

Arizona v. California, 373 U.S. 563 (1963) [U.S. Supreme Court]

Construing the Boulder Canyon Act of 1928 to evidence a congressional intent to create a federal scheme of water apportionment, the U.S. Supreme Court in *Arizona v. California* decided a multistate dispute over the division of water from the Colorado River among its claimants and launched a new era of increased federal involvement in the evolving hydraulic "society" of the American West. The Court held that Congress intended to authorize the Secretary of the Interior to apportion and to regulate water flowing from federally financed Colorado River projects in California, Arizona, and Nevada. Prior to this decision, multistate water rights disputes had been settled only by interstate compacts and federal court decisions. Now the Court held that Congress had decided the exact amounts of water that each state would receive and, in a far-reaching element of decision, determined that the Secretary of the Interior had the authority to apportion surplus waters and to regulate water allocations in periods of shortage. This authority extended beyond decisions relating to states to individual water users within the state.

This case grew out of decades of litigation and multistate disputes over the use of water in the Colorado River basin. Water law prior to federal statutory intervention had been the province of state and territorial law. One of the federal government's first ventures into the field was the Carey Act of 1894, a statute that authorized the Secretary of the Interior to donate up to one million acres to arid states, provided the states improve, irrigate, and reclaim tracts. Individual settlers could occupy and eventually own improved parcels of 160 acres. State finances hindered the success of the plan, and by 1899 only Wyoming had actually developed land under the statute. The Reclamation Act of 1902 continued the expansion of the hydraulic

society, but now the federal government was the administrator of the law. The statute set aside land-sale receipts for the construction of reservoirs in the arid states, authorized the Secretary of the Interior to survey and construct such facilities, and designated the Reclamation Service as administrator of the program. More acres received water from bigger and bigger projects. Litigation by the states was increasingly replaced by interstate compacts dividing the waters.

With the infusion of federal reclamation dollars into the region and with increased water demand due to urbanization, industrialization, and intensive irrigation, competition for water and federal money increased among the states. In 1922, Congressman Phil Swing and Senator Hiram Johnson, both of California, introduced the Boulder Canyon Bill, calling for the construction of a dam in the Boulder Canyon of the Colorado. The dam would create a huge storage reservoir for irrigation and hydroelectric power generation.

That same year, the U.S. Supreme Court held that the rule of prior appropriation in water law applied to interstate streams and controversies. The ruling denied Colorado's argument that it alone possessed the right to waters arising within the state's borders. Clearly, agreements among the states appeared to be a means to resolve the growing volume of water controversies in the arid West.

One such attempt at resolution was the Colorado River Compact of 1922. On November 24, 1922, the Colorado River Commission, chaired by Herbert Hoover, issued the compact document making allocations by basins and settling use priorities. California, Colorado, Nevada, New Mexico, Utah, and Wyoming ratified the compact within five months, but Arizona balked, precipitating six years of bitter haggling leading up to the Boulder Canyon Act of 1928.

The Boulder Canyon Act's implementation positioned Southern California for tremendous growth. The Hoover Dam was completed in 1935, and hydroelectric power arrived in California the next year. In 1941, water flowed into Southern California and Los Angeles, and the Imperial Valley started converting desert into crops, cash, and condominiums.

California's growth based on Colorado River water and power was at the expense of Arizona. Arizona responded with law suits; it went to the U.S. Supreme Court arguing that the Boulder Canyon Act was unconstitutional. In a 1931 decision, the Court rejected the state's claims and held that the statute was a "valid exercise of Congressional power." Three years later, Arizona mounted another legal stratagem: it asked the Court to "perpetuate" some oral testimony that was intended for use in future litigation to prove that one million acre-feet of water under the compact was intended for Arizona. On May 21, 1934, the Court unanimously ruled that the proposed testimony was not relevant and could never be relevant because Arizona had refused to ratify the compact. In November 1935, Arizona went back yet a third time. Now it asked the Court to determine Arizona's equitable share of the water. In 1936, the Court explained an elementary concept of jurisdiction to the state's attorneys. To come before the Court, the state would have to allege and prove that a "justifiable controversy" existed. The state could only show such a controversy if it could demonstrate that it was being harmed in some way. The Court noted that there were millions of acre-feet of water flowing down the Colorado unused. The jurisdictional hint was that Arizona would be hard pressed to show harm under the circumstances. The Court also noted that the United States should have been made a party to the suit. Not doing so was an equally fatal jurisdictional error.

Arizona's losses in the federal courts turned it to negotiation. In 1944, the state ratified the compact. Then the state went to Congress. Arizona's senior U.S. senator, Carl Hayden, started a campaign for a federal project to bring water to the interior of the state, particularly to Phoenix and Tucson. From 1947 on, Hayden was successful in getting the Senate to approve the billion-dollar Central Arizona Project. Every year the California delegation in the House of Representatives blocked the legislation, arguing that there was simply not enough water. The reason there was not enough water was California's excessive use.

Thwarted in Congress, Arizona went back to the Supreme Court in 1952. The suit lasted 11 years, necessitated the services of a special master, cost nearly $5 million, recorded the testimony of over 300 witnesses, and demanded the services of over 48 attorneys. In *Arizona v. California*, Arizona finally emerged victorious. It was awarded 2.8 million acre-feet of water. In addition, native Americans water rights received important legal recognition. Indian water rights (which were measured by irrigable acreage rather than use) dated from the creation of the various reservations, were superior to subsequent non-Indian use, and were not subject to abandonment rules for nonuse. The decision put Indian tribes, particularly the Navajo, into the irrigation and water rights litigation business. Law suits regarding the extent and nature of native Americans continue to be a feature of western water development.

Congress put Arizona into the hydraulic society business with this 1963 decision. The Colorado River Basin Project Act of 1968 gave the state the Central Arizona Project. The federal government built Parker Dam, creating Lake Havasu and a network of pipes, channels, and aqueducts servicing Phoenix and Tucson. The water started to flow in 1985. The Colorado River, as historian Donald Worster has so aptly put it, "had been transmogrified into an industrial artifact, an almost perfectly realized expression of the new imperial West." The federal government's money and the U.S. Supreme Court made it possible for the Colorado to become the West's leading river of empire.

Selected Bibliography

Bakken, G.M. *The Development of Law on the Rocky Mountain Frontier: Civil Law and Society, 1850–1912*. Westport, CT: Greenwood Press, 1983.

Hundley, N., Jr., *Water and the West: The Colorado River Compact and the Politics of Water in the American West*. Berkeley, CA: University of California Press, 1975.

Worster, D. *Rivers of Empire: Water, Aridity, and the Growth of the American West*. New York: Pantheon Books, 1985.

CONTROVERSY OVER A FAST-BREEDER

by George T. Mazuzan
History Office
National Science Foundation

Power Reactor Development Company v. International Union of Electrical, Radio and Machine Workers, AFL-CIO, 364 U.S. 889 (1960) [U.S. Supreme Court]

Few judges are qualified to determine the safety of a technology. They are qualified, however, to determine if the established legal procedures used to influence the safety of the technology are correct. In so doing, judges shape the direction the technology takes. The federal courts did this in the *PRDC* case.

The commercial application of nuclear energy was in its infancy in the mid-1950s, when different types of reactors were being proposed for a new American nuclear power industry. The revised federal Atomic Energy Act of 1954 gave regulatory power over construction and operation of privately owned nuclear facilities to the Atomic Energy Commission (AEC). The act also established a two-step licensing procedure for each nuclear plant and required adherence to a statutory standard of assuring "public health and safety." A company planning to build a plant first had to apply to the AEC for a construction permit and submit detailed plans as to how the facility would be constructed to assure public health and safety. Once constructed, the company could apply for an operating license to run the plant. To promote the development of this new industry, the AEC implemented new regulations under the act. The agency also used its already established Advisory Committee on Reactor Safeguards (ACRS), a part-time group of highly respected reactor experts, for advice on the safety of any proposed facility.

Taking advantage of the revisions under the 1954 act, a group of privately owned power utilities and industrial corporations, led by Detroit Edison, formed a consortium, the Power Reactor Development Company (PRDC), to build and operate an advanced-design fast-breeder power reactor at Lagoona Beach, about 30 miles south of Detroit, Michigan. Fast-breeder technology, showing great promise, was nonetheless still fairly experimental compared with the more developed light-water reactors

that were adopted by many utilities and which would become the mainstays of the American nuclear power industry. But in this incubation stage of the industry, the AEC encouraged development of different reactor types.

The PRDC submitted its application to the AEC for a construction permit in early 1956. In a letter to the commission dated June 6, 1956, the ACRS, after reviewing the PRDC application, unfavorably commented on the company's plan. The experts suggested that a construction permit not be issued until more characteristics of the dangerous fast-breeder technology could be determined through an ongoing AEC experimental program. The letter concluded that "there is insufficient information available at this time to give assurance that the PRDC reactor can be operated at this site without public hazard." The letter, not publicly issued but "leaked," became the catalyst for a series of events. The commission, despite the misgivings of the ACRS, granted a construction permit to the PRDC on August 4, 1956. Agency officials felt that during the lengthy construction period, the technical problems underscored by the ACRS could be worked out so that a license eventually could be issued for safe operation of the facility.

Three labor unions of the American Federation of Labor-Congress of Industrial Organizations (AFL-CIO)—the International Union of Electrical, Radio and Machine Workers; the United Paperworkers of America; and the United Automobile, Aircraft, and Agricultural Implement Workers of America—each of which had substantial memberships in the Detroit area, soon submitted intervention petitions to the AEC for a hearing on the PRDC construction permit. The AFL-CIO, while a supporter of development of a nuclear industry, was also concerned about the way the AEC appeared to be disregarding its obligation to assure public health and safety. The petitions to intervene were the first to be directed against the agency.

A protracted public hearing and commission review drew considerable media interest. The talented general counsel of the machinists' union, Benjamin Sigal, represented the unions; the PRDC retained W. Graham Claytor, Jr., a senior partner in Covington and Burling; and the AEC established a "separated" legal staff to represent the agency. On December 10, 1958, the AEC issued its long-awaited initial decision. It continued the construction permit and dismissed the unions' charge that the AEC had failed in its obligation to assure public health and safety. After allowing time for filing of exceptions, the commission issued a final decision on May 26, 1959, reiterating its decision of December. The unions, as expected, petitioned for review by the U.S. Court of Appeals for the District of Columbia.

A three-member appeals court panel heard oral arguments on March 23, 1960. Sigal argued, as he had done before the commission, that the AEC had not met the requirements of the 1954 law establishing the two-step licensing procedure and the implementing regulations. Citing the legislative history of the act, Sigal said that the Congress intended that an applicant who received a construction permit should also have assurance that he would receive a permit to operate the reactor as long as he constructed it according to the conditions of the construction permit. Therefore, the essential finding with respect to safety had to be made at the time the construction permit was issued and that that finding would also be made at the time of the granting of an operating license. This protected the paramount interest of the public in safety.

The commission's brief countered by drawing a clear dichotomy between the standards applicable to construction permits and those applicable to operating licenses. The implementing regulation carried out that distinction, the commission argued. It prescribed safety standards for construction permits on the "basis of the developmental nature of nuclear power technology, of which Congress was aware." The commission had issued the PRDC construction permit on that acknowledgement.

On June 10, 1960, the panel, in a 2–1 opinion, upheld the unions by declaring the PRDC construction permit illegal. Circuit judges Henry W. Edgerton and David L. Bazelon formed the majority; Judge Warren E. Burger wrote a dissenting opinion. In deciding for the unions, Edgerton's majority opinion found that the AEC had an obligation to use the same standards in judging a construction permit application as it did for a subsequent operating license. On the basis largely of a detailed review of the 1954 act, Edgerton concluded: "It seems certain that if the Act did not require, as a condition to the issuance of a construction permit, a finding that the proposed facility can be operated without undue risk to the health and safety of the public, the Act would not require the issuance of a license when the permitted construction permit is carried out." His opinion went on to find inconsistencies in the commission's findings in this case. Taken together, they implied that while it seemed reasonable that scientific research would eventually establish that the PRDC reactor could be operated safely, the evidence currently available did not establish the fact. The court disliked the existing uncertainty.

In his dissent, Burger wrote that in a technological area such as the development of nuclear energy in which so much scientific uncertainty prevailed, the AEC must be allowed to proceed on a step-by-step basis. He suggested that his colleagues, in their majority opinion, were "undertaking to assume responsibilities which Congress vested in the Commission." They were, in effect, telling the agency it had made an unwise decision. The majority assumed, Burger charged, that once the commission had "permitted PRDC to invest its millions in the plant, they are 'bound' or 'likely' to relax their notion of what is safe or dangerous in order to bail out the investors." Burger refused to believe that the AEC would act "to make a finding of safety which is not supported by substantial scientific evidence."

Reactions, naturally, were mixed. The unions were highly pleased. A United Automobile Workers spokesman said the decision showed "that no one, the AEC especially, should brush aside the opinions of atomic scientists who serve on the Advisory Committee on Reactor Safeguards." The ruling stunned officials at both the AEC and PRDC. At the agency, the commission started the wheels in motion to overturn the decision through an appeal. To not do so would jeopardize construction permits issued to other companies. In addition, the whole licensing scheme that the agency had developed would be undermined. After being denied by the appeals court for a rehearing *en banc*, the AEC and the Justice Department filed a petition for *certiorari* with the U.S. Supreme Court asking it to review the court of appeals record. On November 19, 1960, the Supreme Court issued a writ granting the review and placed the case on its docket.

The High Court agreed to consider two main questions and a subsidiary one. One was whether the AEC had the legal authority to license a power reactor near a large city without showing compelling reasons for the location, and the other was whether the 1954 act permitted the AEC to license the construction and operation of nuclear power plants in two steps. The subsidiary question related to the latter one: had the commission really addressed the safety issues as required by its own regulations or were its findings as ambiguous as the court of appeals had found?

Two aspects of the Supreme Court proceeding are noteworthy. First, the justices avoided the question of whether the PRDC reactor could be proved to be sufficiently safe. Although a main issue on which the commission originally granted a hearing was the sufficiency of information available to provide assurance that the reactor could be operated without undue risk to the health and safety of the public, the High Court would not resolve that matter. But the second issue that the unions pressed—that the AEC violated its own regulations in initially issuing the construction permit—the Court decided to review.

On June 12, 1961, the Supreme Court announced a 7–2 vote in favor of the AEC and the PRDC. Justice William J. Brennan, Jr., wrote the majority opinion, while Justice William O. Douglas filed a dissent.

Brennan wrote that the main question before the Court was whether the AEC in issuing a construction permit must make the "same definitive finding of safety of operation" as it would have to make before it issued an operating license. After reviewing the 1954 act and the AEC regulations, the Court determined that Congress "contemplated a step-by-step procedure." Second, the Court found that before licensing the operation of a reactor, the commission "will have to make a positive finding that operation of the facility will 'provide adequate protection to the health and safety of the public.'" But the statute did not make it clear, and so it became "the center of controversy in this case" whether the commission "must also have made such a finding when it issued PRDC's construction permit."

Brennan reviewed the AEC regulation that elaborated on and described the step-by-step procedure contemplated by the statute. The Court found that the regulation "was a valid exercise of the rule-making power" granted to the AEC. And it required that "some finding as to the safety of operation be made before a provisional construction permit is granted." The real question, Brennan wrote, "is whether the first finding must be backed up with as much conviction as to the safety . . . as the second, final finding must be." Brennan and the majority thought the weight of the argument permitted the AEC "to defer a definitive safety finding until operation is actually licensed." Brennan offered common sense reasoning for this: "For nuclear reactors are fast-developing and fast-changing. What is up to date now, may not, probably will not, be as acceptable tomorrow. Problems which seem insuperable now may be solved tomorrow, perhaps in the very process of construction itself." Based on that, the Court held that the AEC had complied with the statute and its own regulations fully.

Douglas's short dissenting opinion found the AEC's interpretation that "safety findings can be made after construction is finished" to be socially irresponsible. The commission's interpretation was, Douglas wrote, "a lighthearted approach to the most awesome, the most deadly, the most dangerous process that man has ever conceived."

The *New York Times* highlighted the decision as "an important test case for the atomic energy program." Indeed it was, for had the AEC not been sustained by the Supreme Court, it would have meant, at the very least, significant delays in the civilian nuclear power program while Congress and the agency developed new procedures to license private power reactors. The decision did not resolve any of the safety questions raised by the ACRS. By implication, the decision of the Court affirmed that it lacked the technical expertise to evaluate such issues. The law gave that responsibility to the AEC, and if the Court had attempted to answer safety questions, it would have been second-guessing the commission. The justices correctly avoided that role because they did not view it as a judicial function.

Although the AEC "won" the case, the manner in which it handled the early proceedings undermined public confidence in its judgment on safety issues. The whole proceeding contributed to the beginning of a credibility problem over the agency's role as a regulator while also acting as a promoter of nuclear power.

Selected Bibliography

Fuller, J.G. *We Almost Lost Detroit*. New York: Reader's Digest Press, 1975.

Mazuzan, G.T. "Atomic Power Safety: The Case of the Power Reactor Development Company Fast Breeder, 1955–56." *Technology and Culture* 23 (July 1982): 341–71.

Mazuzan, G.T., and J.S. Walker. *Controlling the Atom: The Beginnings of Nuclear Regulation, 1946–62*. Berkeley, CA: University of California Press, 1984.

Morrisson, J.L., and B.J. Garrick. "What We Learned from the PRDC Case." *Nucleonics* 17 (July 1959): 60–63.

THE ATOMIC ENERGY COMMISSION AND THE ENVIRONMENT

by J. Samuel Walker
History Office
U.S. Nuclear Regulatory Commission

Calvert Cliffs Coordinating Committee, Inc. v. United States Atomic Energy Commission 449 F. 2d 1109 (1971) [U.S. Court of Appeals]

During the latter half of the 1960s, the decline of environmental quality in the United States took on growing urgency as a public policy issue. A series of controversies over the effects of substances such as DDT, asbestos, mercury, and phosphates; of ecological disasters such as a huge oil spill off the coast of California and fish kills in the Mississippi River; and of easily visible evidence of foul air and dirty water fueled public alarm about the deterioration of the environment.

At the same time that the environmental crisis commanded increasing attention, questions about the availability of electrical power triggered deepening concern. Since the early 1940s, the use of electricity had expanded by an average of seven percent per year, which meant that it roughly doubled every decade. Utility and government planners found no indications that the pace of growth was likely to slow in the near future.

The growing public concern with environmental quality and the continually increasing demand for electricity put utilities in a quandary. Electrical generating stations were major polluters. Fossil fuel plants, in particular, which provided over 85 percent of the nation's electricity in the 1960s, annually spewed millions of tons of noxious chemicals into the atmosphere. The concurrent demands for sufficient electricity and clean air created, in the words of a leading environmental group, "a most vexing dilemma: How do we protect the environment from further destruction and, at the same time, have all the electricity we want at the flick of a switch?"

After the mid-1960s, utilities increasingly viewed nuclear power as the answer to that dilemma. It promised the means to produce electricity without fouling the air, and environmental concerns were a major spur to the rapid growth of the nuclear industry. Officials of the

U.S. Atomic Energy Commission (AEC) actively promoted the idea that nuclear power provided the answer to both the environmental crisis and the energy crisis. Under its statutory mandate, the AEC was responsible both for encouraging the use of atomic energy for peaceful purposes and for regulating its safety. The AEC saw the energy/environment dilemma as an opportunity to enhance the attractiveness of nuclear power. Chairman Glenn T. Seaborg declared in 1966, that in light of expanding demand for electricity and deteriorating air quality, "we can be grateful that, historically speaking, nuclear energy arrived on the scene when it did."

Within a short time, however, some environmental groups, members of Congress, and other governmental agencies were suggesting that nuclear power plants, while reducing air pollution, threatened water quality by discharging large quantities of heated water used to cool the steam that drove the turbines to produce electricity. This incited a major controversy over the effects of "thermal pollution" and eventually over the general issue of the impact of nuclear power on the environment. Much of the debate centered on the role of the AEC in requiring nuclear plants to meet environmental standards, and differing perspectives and priorities inevitably led to court.

The AEC was reluctant to regulate environmental hazards other than radiation. It asserted that it sympathized with efforts to curb environmental abuse, but that it had no authority to take action against thermal pollution or other nonradiological environmental effects. The AEC's position elicited sharp criticism from those who thought it should do more to combat thermal pollution. The agency's legal claim received support, however, from the U.S. Court of Appeals for the First Circuit, which agreed in a January 1969 ruling that the AEC lacked the statutory jurisdiction to regulate the thermal effects of its licensed plants. The court denied the petition of New Hampshire, which asserted that the AEC had the obligation to force the Vermont Yankee plant, under construction across the Connecticut River, to meet water quality standards. Nevertheless, the court expressed "utmost sympathy with the appellant" and urged Congress to grant the AEC the necessary authority over nonradiological environmental effects.

Congress appeared to fulfill that request when it passed the National Environmental Policy Act (NEPA) in December 1969. NEPA gave federal agencies a broad mandate to weigh the environmental impact of their activities and to take corrective measures when necessary, though it left unclear the precise boundaries of their authority and responsibilities.

The AEC took a narrow view of its jurisdiction under the new law. Although NEPA clearly expanded its responsibilities, the agency was cautious and restrictive in applying its environmental mandate. It was particularly concerned that an expansive interpretation of its authority would cause unwarranted delays in licensing new plants. The flood of orders for plants had already increased the time required to review applications, and the AEC worried that NEPA would cause a "quantum leap" in the length of the process. If this occurred, it would aggravate the shortage of electrical power, which the AEC considered a more serious and immediate threat to public welfare than the environmental consequences of operating nuclear plants. It attempted to strike a balance between environmental concerns and energy needs in writing its regulations to carry out NEPA.

In December 1970, the AEC published the final version of its environmental regulations. The regulations required that applicants for licenses submit a detailed statement on the environmental impact of proposed plants. The statement would become a part of the licensing process and could be challenged in licensing hearings. The AEC would not make an independent appraisal of the anticipated environmental effects of nuclear plants, but would instead rely on the evaluations and standards of other federal and appropriate state agencies. On questions of water quality, the AEC would follow the provisions of the Water Quality Improvement Act, passed three months after NEPA, which required that applicants for federal licenses present certification from appropriate state or interstate agencies (or, in the absence of adequate state regulations, the secretary of the interior) that the proposed facility could meet existing standards. Once again, the AEC would accept the judgment of certifying agencies without undertaking an analysis of its own. The AEC's regulations also specified that environmental issues under NEPA could not be raised in licensing proceedings for which a notice of hearing was published before March 4, 1971. This was done, it explained, "to avoid unreasonable delays in the construction and operation of nuclear power plants."

The AEC's regulations went further than ever before in accepting responsibility for nonradiological effects of nuclear plants, but they met stern opposition from environmentalists. Within a few days after they were issued, three groups—the National Wildlife Federation, the Sierra Club, and the Calvert Cliffs Coordinating Committee—challenged the rules in a suit filed in the U.S. Court of Appeals for the District of Columbia Circuit. The litigation focused on the twin Calvert Cliffs nuclear plants under construction by the Baltimore Gas and Electric Company on the Chesapeake Bay. The suit not only called on the AEC to consider immediately the environmental costs of the plants and to halt construction if necessary, but also disputed its entire approach to NEPA. The petitioners' brief, written by Anthony Z. Roisman, a 33-year-old Harvard Law School graduate who had recently joined with two other young attorneys to establish a public interest law firm, argued that the AEC's regulations fell far short of full compliance with NEPA. It emphasized that the agency had failed to carry out the purposes of the act because it planned to rely on the standards of other agencies in evaluating environmental issues. This would "foreclose any examination of adverse environmental effects which will occur even when the standards and requirements are met." The petitioners also strongly objected to the AEC's deferral of consideration of NEPA issues until after March 4, 1971.

The AEC responded that it was attempting to take a "balanced approach" to environmental and energy needs, and it stressed that its policy on NEPA was necessarily influenced by the serious shortage of power that the nation faced. It pointed out that the major environmental effects of nuclear plants—radiation emissions and thermal discharges—were covered by statutes other than NEPA, which made the petitioners' charge that the AEC was ignoring environmental problems "hyperbole." It further suggested that to rely on the judgment of other agencies on NEPA matters was "wholly reasonable," since its own expertise focused heavily on radiological health and safety.

The AEC's brief made the strongest possible case for its plan to implement NEPA, but staff lawyers feared that the arguments would not fare well in court because they emphasized policy considerations rather than legal precedents. The concerns arising from the frailty of the AEC's legal position were heightened by revelations of the identity of judges on the panel selected to decide the case. They seemed likely to give the environmentalists a sympathetic, or at least an open-minded, hearing. "The luck of the draw was with us," Roisman commented later.

The court's decision, handed down on July 23, 1971, was a crushing defeat for the AEC. Not only did the ruling categorically reject the agency's arguments, but it did so in language that was extraordinarily harsh. Judge J. Skelly Wright, who wrote the opinion, faulted the agency for not doing more to consider environmental issues in its licensing process. In his most widely quoted phrase, he declared: "We believe that the Commission's crabbed interpretation of NEPA makes a mockery of the Act." He further submitted that the law required the AEC to conduct independent evaluations of the environmental effects of proposed plants rather than solely relying on the standards of other agencies. He agreed that their views should be solicited, but he denied that NEPA authorized a "total abdication to those agencies." Wright sharply reproached the AEC for its plan to postpone consideration of NEPA requirements. He described it as "shocking," and added: "Whether or not the specter of a national power crisis is as real as the Commission apparently believes, it must not be used to create a blackout of environmental consideration."

The court's ruling did not come as a surprise to those who had followed the case, but the tone of Wright's language and the totality of the AEC's defeat were unexpected. Once it recovered from its initial shock, the AEC acted promptly to comply with the decision. Within a month, it decided not to file an appeal and drafted new regulations that broadened its approach to carrying out NEPA. Ironically, in light of the AEC's efforts to prevent NEPA from causing licensing delays, the Calvert Cliffs decision led to a *de facto* licensing moratorium of several months to allow time to rewrite regulations, revise environmental impact statements, review applications, conduct hearings, and train new staff members. The ruling had a decisive impact on both the substance and the process of nuclear regulation. It thrust the AEC, grudgingly, into an era of environmental awareness and anxiety in which full consideration of the impact of power plants on their natural surroundings was an absolute imperative.

As a result of *Calvert Cliffs*, other federal agencies assumed the same obligations as the AEC in applying NEPA. Although later decisions modified or bypassed *Calvert Cliffs*, as the first comprehensive judicial ruling on NEPA it was the landmark that established the broad-ranging effects of the law and the responsibilities of the federal government to carry out its purposes.

Selected Bibliography

Liroff, R.A. *A National Policy for the Environment: NEPA and Its Aftermath.* Bloomington, IN: Indiana University Press, 1976.

Melosi, M.V. *Coping with Abundance: Energy and Environment in Industrial America.* Philadelphia: Temple University Press, 1985.

Walker, J.S. *Containing the Atom: Nuclear Regulation in a Changing Environment.* Berkeley: University of California Press, 1992.

INSURING AGAINST NUCLEAR PLANT ACCIDENTS

by John W. Johnson
Department of History
University of Northern Iowa

Duke Power Company v. Carolina Environmental Study Group, Inc., 438 U.S. 59 (1978) [U.S. Supreme Court]

It is not often that a private citizen with a complaint is able to convince the U.S. Supreme Court to devote a major decision to its resolution. But for Gayl Waller, a diminutive southern woman who did not want to see a nuclear power plant built next to her lake home, this is exactly what happened.

In the early 1970s, Waller joined a handful of environmentalists near Charlotte, North Carolina, in an attempt to stop the local utility, Duke Power Company, from embarking on an ambitious program of nuclear construction in the Carolina Piedmont. Their efforts sparked confrontations with Duke Power and the federal body charged with regulating nuclear power in the United States, the Nuclear Regulatory Commission (NRC).

Waller and her fellow activists called themselves the Carolina Environmental Study Group (CESG). Taking advantage of volunteer legal assistance, they sought in various ways to stop Duke Power from building nuclear plants in the Western Carolinas. Yet, every issue they raised was eventually thrown out by regulatory panels or the federal courts—save one. The claim that allowed the CESG to have its day in court was a challenge to the constitutionality of an important but little known law, the Price-Anderson Act.

The Price-Anderson Act limits the liability of licensed nuclear power plant operators to the American public in the event of catastrophic nuclear accidents. It was passed by Congress in 1957, has been amended several times over the last 30 years, and is still in force. The Price-Anderson Act's most important provision establishes a scheme to compensate the public for damages from a serious nuclear accident, such as a reactor core melt—the often mentioned "China Syndrome." When the CESG brought its lawsuit in the mid-1970s, the act provided that the total available compensation pool would be $560 million.

At first $560 million might appear to be adequate compensation. However, the $560 million is a ceiling amount, no matter how many individuals—50 or 50,000—suffer injury to person or property. Furthermore, government-sponsored studies of the potential damages from a serious nuclear plant accident have estimated that damage claims for the consequences to lives and property could run into tens of billions of dollars. It was because of estimates such as these that companies interested in owning and operating nuclear power plants insisted on the establishment of a statutory scheme to limit their liability to the public in the event of serious accidents. These companies continue to demand such protective legislation. The present liability limits under the 1988 amended version of Price-Anderson are more than ten times higher than they were in the 1970s, but not high enough to suit those critical of nuclear power.

Admittedly, the chances of a serious accident taking place at a single location are minuscule, but the NRC has estimated that there exists almost a 50 percent likelihood of the occurrence of a core melt at one of the approximately 112 licensed American nuclear reactors before 2000. The Three Mile Island accident in 1979 and the Chernobyl accident in 1986 demonstrate that serious nuclear accidents happen. Although the accident at Three Mile Island did not result in the release of a significant amount of radiation into the atmosphere, if the core melt had continued for another hour or so, the containment structure might have been breached and the health and financial consequences could have been catastrophic. The Chernobyl accident did lead to a substantial release of radiation. The West will probably never know the full health and financial consequences of Chernobyl, but rough preliminary estimates place the total damages at more than $3 billion.

For the United States, supporters and critics of nuclear power agree: without the Price-Anderson Act, there would be no commercially generated nuclear power. Therefore, the CESG challenge to the constitutionality of the act was not only a device to test the legality of one aspect of nuclear power regulation, it was also an assault upon America's large and powerful nuclear industry. Thus, *Duke Power Company v. Carolina Environmental Study Group* holds an important place in American business, economic, and legal history.

The main legal argument the CESG raised against Price-Anderson's limitation on liability clause was that it denied "property" of CESG members. This claim was based on the Fifth Amendment to the U.S. Constitution, which protects individuals against the deprivation of life, liberty, or property without due process of law or the taking of private property for public use without just compensation. The CESG, represented in federal court by attorneys employed by Ralph Nader's Public Citizen Litigation Group, maintained that, if a catastrophic accident occurred, Price-Anderson's ceiling on liability made it likely that some of the individuals residing near the defective reactor would not be fairly compensated for their losses. The arbitrarily low ceiling amount, the Nader lawyers stressed, violated the Fifth Amendment. Also, the CESG attorneys argued that those living near reactors faced greater financial dangers from nuclear power than other groups in the population because of the Price-Anderson limitations. This, they maintained, offended the equal protection feature of American law gleaned from the Fourteenth Amendment.

These claims were interesting, but few legal scholars gave the CESG much chance to have its case heard on the merits in federal court. No accident had occurred to damage the CESG plaintiffs in North Carolina and South Carolina. In fact, the plants that Waller and her friends were worried about were years from completion when the lawsuit was initiated. Thus, Duke and the NRC argued that the plaintiffs lacked "standing" (i.e., that they had not suffered any measurable loss) and that the case was not "ripe" for decision (i.e., that because no accident had taken place there was no need to decide the legal questions advanced).

However, one federal district judge, James B. McMillan of the Western District of North Carolina, found the CESG's arguments worthy of consideration and scheduled a hearing in 1976 to test their validity. McMillan, a 1968 appointee of President Lyndon Johnson, was the first federal judge in the country to order busing to achieve racial balance in a public school district. His ruling was upheld in the landmark U.S. Supreme Court decision *Swann v. Charlotte-Mecklenburg Board of Education* (1971).

For a week in September 1976, McMillan listened to witnesses and accepted exhibits from the CESG, Duke Power, and the NRC relating to the constitutionality of the limitation of liability feature of the Price-Anderson Act. Because of the fundamental relationship between the liability statute and the existence of commercial nuclear power in the United States, it can be justifiably said that the country's nuclear industry was on trial in McMillan's courtroom. Evidence was submitted and witnesses testified on all aspects of nuclear energy—scientific, engineering, environmental, financial, and social. Appearing along with health physicists, NRC staff members, actuaries, Duke Power executives, and nuclear engineers were Waller and selected CESG members.

During the pretrial skirmishing and at the hearing itself, it was clear that McMillan was uncomfortable with aspects of the Price-Anderson Act. Just how uncomfortable was not revealed until he issued his decision in 1977. In his 50-page opinion, distinguished as much by well-turned phrases and literary allusions as by legal analysis, McMillan not only ruled that the CESG had satisfied the standing and ripeness tests for having its claims adjudicated in court but he also found the limitation of liability clause of the Price-Anderson Act unconstitutional. Although he was unwilling to speculate as to the chances of a nuclear accident at an American plant (he said "the court is not a bookie"), he did conclude that the likelihood of an accident causing damages above the Price-Anderson ceiling was "not fanciful but real." Thus, the plaintiffs had standing and the case was ripe for decision.

In his discussion of the merits of the CESG's suit, he found the Price-Anderson Act wanting on several points. In terms of due process and just compensation, he concluded that the amount of compensation authorized by the statute was not rationally related to the possible upper level of damages (he cited a 1975 NRC estimate of $17 billion for a major nuclear

accident). He also found some of the technical features of the act wanting. For example, he criticized the mechanism for disbursing compensation in the aftermath of an accident because of the delays built into the law. He also cited what he felt was the unfairness of the Price-Anderson Act absorbing the entire pool of insurance money wagered on nuclear accidents, thus making it impossible for property owners to purchase individual nuclear liability insurance policies. In terms of "equal protection," the judge ruled that the act placed an unreasonable burden on those living close to nuclear power plants.

The CESG and other antinuclear groups greeted McMillan's decision with resounding approval. The attorneys for the plaintiffs said that the decision went beyond the wildest hopes. But Duke Power and the rest of the nuclear industry found it very disturbing. Although the decision technically had validity only in the western third of North Carolina, the major organizations in the nuclear industry (e.g., the Atomic Industrial Forum, nuclear construction and engineering firms, and licensed nuclear utilities) recognized that if the Supreme Court affirmed McMillan's ruling, the Price-Anderson Act would no longer protect licensed reactors anywhere in the country. So the industry quickly mounted a campaign to overturn the decision. The leading groups in the nuclear industry met several times in 1977 under the rubric of a "Price-Anderson Appeal Project" to coordinate appellate strategy and to draft *amicus curiae* ("friend of the court") briefs for submission to the Supreme Court on behalf of Duke Power and the NRC. Ultimately, the major nuclear industry groups submitted seven long briefs.

The case was argued before the Supreme Court in March 1978. On June 25, 1978, the Supreme Court handed down its decision. As predicted, the Court reversed Judge McMillan and upheld the constitutionality of the Price-Anderson Act. Surprising to many legal experts, however, was the fact that a majority of the Court—six justices—voted for reversal on the merits. That is, they felt that the CESG had satisfied the legal requirements for standing and ripeness. Even without a showing of appreciable physical damage to the plaintiffs and in the absence of a serious nuclear accident, the Court held that this was the time to pass muster on the constitutionality of the Price-Anderson Act. The Court quoted with approval McMillan's aphorism, "the time to put on the roof is before it starts raining."

The opinion of the Court in *Duke Power Company v. Carolina Environmental Study Group* was written by Chief Justice Warren E. Burger. The chief justice's main point in support of the constitutionality of the Price-Anderson Act was that McMillan did not accord the law the appropriate presumption of constitutionality. The attorneys for the CESG had tried to convince the Supreme Court that the Price-Anderson Act should be evaluated as a law affecting the rights and liberties of individuals and thus seen as "suspect" for its arbitrary liability limit. The Supreme Court disagreed. Relying on a line of cases reaching back to the New Deal, Burger submitted that courts must respect the validity of congressional enactments relating to the economy as long so there is "a reasonable basis" for the legislation. Studies citing the infinitesimal chances of a serious nuclear accident that McMillan had criticized, the Supreme Court found reasonably well-founded.

Reactions to the opinion were predictable. Nuclear industry and most general business publications supported the decision, while antinuclear and environmental organizations were critical. Much of the law review commentary on the case focused on the surprising willingness of the Court to brush aside procedural barriers and rush to the merits of the case. Because of the case's complexity and because it was decided in the shadow of the *University of California Regents v. Bakke* (1978) decision on affirmative action, it did not receive as much media coverage as perhaps might have been expected given the momentous issues involved in the litigation.

In June 1978, when the *Duke Power* decision was issued, the justices and most of the public believed that the chances of a serious nuclear accident were remote. Within nine months after the decision, however, the NRC had discredited a crucial section of one of its safety studies for underestimating the chances of a nuclear accident and, shortly following that, the accident at Three Mile Island took place,

significantly souring the American public's view of nuclear energy. If the High Court had been faced with the CESG suit against Duke Power in the spring of 1979 rather than the spring of 1978, would the Court's majority have been so confident in the safety of nuclear power upon which the limitation of liability features of Price-Anderson is predicated? Several law review commentators and some of the principals in the CESG suit have expressed doubt that the decision would have been the same.

When the Supreme Court decided *Duke Power* in 1978, a myriad of financial problems were just beginning to afflict the nuclear industry. In fact, it has been over 13 years since an American utility has placed an order for a nuclear reactor. And over 100 orders have been cancelled since the *Duke Power* decision. In the early 1980s, a number of bills were introduced in Congress to amend, extend, or otherwise refine the Price-Anderson Act. The intensifying controversy over nuclear power in the United States frustrated hopes of easy compromise over nuclear liability legislation. And the 1986 Chernobyl accident further polarized and prolonged the debate over nuclear power legislation. Finally, in 1988, Congress passed amendments to the Price-Anderson Act that extended the limitation of liability feature into the early twenty-first century. Although the constitutionality of Price-Anderson is now settled law, the wisdom and policy implications of the limitation on liability remain controversial.

Selected Bibliography

Green, H.P. "Nuclear Power: Risk, Liability and Indemnity." *Michigan Law Review* 71 (Jan. 1973): 479–510.

Johnson, J.W. *Insuring Against Disaster: The Nuclear Industry on Trial.* Macon, GA: Mercer University Press, 1986.

Maleson, D.C. "Historical Roots of the Legal System's Response to Nuclear Power." *Southern California Law Review* 55 (March 1982): 597–640.

Mazuzan, G.T., and J.S. Walker. *Controlling the Atom: The Beginnings of Nuclear Regulation, 1946–62.* Berkeley, CA: University of California Press, 1985.

Meek, D.W. "Nuclear Power and the Price-Anderson Act: Promotion Over Public Protection." *Stanford Law Review* 30 (Jan. 1978): 393–468.

Nichol, G.R. "*Duke Power Company v. Carolina Environmental Study Group.*" *Santa Clara Law Review* 20 (Spring 1980): 381–404.

Varat, J.D. "Variable Justiciability and the *Duke Power Case.*" *Texas Law Review* 58 (Feb. 1980): 273–327.

PART IV: RACE AND GENDER IN AMERICAN LAW

PART IV: RACE AND GENDER IN AMERICAN LAW

INTRODUCTION

Despite the stirring affirmations of equality in the Declaration of Independence and the U.S. Constitution, thousands of legal disputes in the history of the American colonies and the United States have involved inequalities of race and gender. The general tendency over three centuries has been for American courts to extend incrementally, albeit at a glacial pace, the rights to racial minorities and women that most white men enjoyed from the beginning of American history.

Most experts would agree that the American courts have been more sympathetic to the rights of women and minorities than have this country's legislative or executive bodies. Courts, in other words, have been the focus and the fora for the most significant advances in the legal rights of the people whom the "founding fathers" (an appropriate term for 55 white males who attended the 1787 Constitutional Convention in Philadelphia) largely left out of the great democratic experiment.

A. Slavery

By any quantitative or qualitative standard, the greatest injustice to a racial minority in U.S. history was the chattel slavery of African-Americans. It is important to emphasize that slavery was a legally protected institution from the earliest colonial times until well into the nineteenth century in virtually all jurisdictions of North America. "The End of Slavery in Massachusetts" presents a discussion of an early set of cases that helped extinguish slavery in New England.

The other five essays in this section deal with the vexing legal issues presented when slaves were taken out of the American South. "Emancipation of Slaves in Transit" describes a famous ruling in which a Massachusetts court held that any slave, except a fugitive, becomes free the moment he enters a free jurisdiction.

The fugitive slave exception is covered in "Upholding the Fugitive Slave Law of 1793." The landmark *Dred Scott Case*, sometimes called the U.S. Supreme Court's "greatest self-inflicted wound," is examined in "They Have No Rights." Efforts by northern states to resist fugitive slave laws on the eve of the Civil War are discussed in "Slavery, Freedom, and Federal Judicial Power" and "Slaves-in-Transit and the Antebellum Crisis."

B. African-Americans Since 1865

The advancement of African-Americans from slavery to freedom has taken over a century. And the process is still not completed. The essays in this section chart the ebb and flow of legal rights of American blacks. The retreat from black civil rights in the Reconstruction is discussed in "No 'Right' to Vote" and "Civil Rights or Last Rites?" The essay "Separate But Equal Approved" presents a discussion of the case that provided the inglorious justification for the segregation of blacks from whites.

"Race, Law, and Gender in South Carolina" and "Justice Vindicated: The Case of William Harper" probe two little-known but revealing state cases involving black defendants in the inter-War years. Perhaps the most notorious example of racism in the southern courts of the Jim Crow years is discussed in the essay "The Scottsboro Cases."

The appointment of Earl Warren as chief justice of the U.S. Supreme Court in 1953 proved to be one of the most important events in the modern American civil rights movement. Warren, as discussed in "Separate Education Is Not Equal Education," was able to craft a unanimous opinion in 1954 striking down school segregation. The effort to desegregate schools and other public facilities has still not been completed. Two important cases in the continuing history of desegregation are discussed in "The

Little Rock Crisis" and "The School Busing Case."

C. Native Americans

Native Americans have been involved in several significant U.S. court cases over the last two centuries. The first essay in this section, "The Cherokee Cases," deals with the attempt of one Indian tribe to have its status as a "nation" respected by American law. Although the Cherokee people did technically win certain legal rights before the Supreme Court, the momentum of white migration and executive policy forced the Cherokee nation to suffer the brutal "trail of tears."

The next two essays in this section, "The Death Knell of the Nations" and "Why Native Americans Can No Longer Count on Treaties With the U.S. Government," illustrate how the Supreme Court in the post-Civil War era allowed Congress to override stipulations in Indian treaties. However, a recent spate of Indian land claim litigation has reversed the pattern of legal defeat by native Americans. One of the leading cases is profiled in "Native American Land Claims: The Indians Finally Win."

D. Other Racial Minorities

Although African-Americans and native Americans have been the parties to most of the important U.S. court cases involving racial discrimination, there is a handful of historically important cases growing out of disputes involving other racial minorities. In "Chinese Laundries and the Fourteenth Amendment," the late nineteenth-century U.S. Supreme Court uncharacteristically ruled in favor of a Chinese litigant. However, in "The Japanese Internment Cases," an essay focusing on a set of cases that tested the legality of the imprisonment of over 100,000 Americans of Japanese background (most of whom were U.S. citizens) during World War II, the Court found against the Japanese-American plaintiffs. "How Should We Pay for Our Schools?" discusses a 1973 case involving public school financing and the Fourteenth Amendment in which the plaintiff children were Mexican-American.

The last essay in this section, "Affirmative Action: Can a White, College-Educated Male Be a Victim of Discrimination?" examines the leading Supreme Court case on affirmative action, the most controversial dimension of civil rights public policy today.

E. Women

Although not a minority throughout most of the country's history, American women have enjoyed fewer rights and privileges than their male counterparts. Many legal experts would argue that women have been forced to suffer a pattern of discrimination similar to that of racial minorities.

The essays in this section provide a glimpse of some of the leading cases on women's rights. "Should a Woman Be Admitted to the Bar?" discusses a leading state case of the nineteenth century in which the then typical practice of excluding women from the highest paying and highest status professions was upheld. In the early twentieth century, some state legislatures passed "protective" or "compensatory" legislation, allegedly for the benefit of women. "Aberration in the Movement Toward an Eight-Hour Day" discusses a state case in which a protective maximum hours law for women was struck down. But in "The Law Recognizes 'Women Are Different'," the U.S. Supreme Court, benefiting from the pioneering "Brandeis Brief," upheld the constitutionality of another state maximum hours law.

The next three essays—"A Supreme Court 'First': Equal Protection Applied to Women," "Sex Discrimination: Reasonable or Suspect?" and "'Benign' Favors to the 'Weaker Sex' Are Not Discriminatory Toward Men"—provide leading illustrations of how the modern Supreme Court is attempting to struggle with state statutes that allegedly deny women equal protection of the laws under the Fourteenth Amendment.

The final essay in this section, "Law Upheld Guaranteeing Right to Return to Work After Childbirth Leave of Absence," discusses a recent case in which a California pregnancy leave statute was upheld by the U.S. Supreme Court.

A. Slavery

THE END OF SLAVERY IN MASSACHUSETTS

by David Thomas Konig
Department of History
Washington University at St. Louis

Walker v. Jennison (1781); *Jennison v. Caldwell* (1781); *Commonwealth v. Jennison* (1783)
[Massachusetts state courts]

As the Revolutionary generation in Massachusetts looked back on its accomplishments, the abolition of slavery seemed one of its most tangible achievements. The federal census of 1790 listed no slaves in Massachusetts because, claimed opponents of slavery, the Declaration of Rights in the state constitution of 1780 stated that "all men are born free and equal." According to a belief widespread in Massachusetts at the turn of the nineteenth century, the state's highest court had cited that provision in declaring slavery unconstitutional in the 1780s when a black man, Quock Walker, successfully challenged his alleged owner's property rights in him. In truth, the Walker litigation (known collectively as the "Quock Walker Cases") did not establish any constitutional principle and did not end slavery in Massachusetts. Nonetheless, the episode did have a significant impact, and it stands as a landmark in the legal attack on slavery.

Quock Walker was nine months old in 1754 when he and his 19-year-old mother, Dinah, were sold to James and Isabell Caldwell of Barre, Massachusetts. According to Walker, James Caldwell promised him his freedom at the age of 24 or 25, while Isabell spoke of manumission at age 21. Unfortunately for Walker, James died in 1770; three years later Isabell died, leaving Walker to her second husband, Nathaniel Jennison. Just short of his twenty-first birthday, Walker learned that Jennison had no intention of honoring the Caldwells' promise.

Walker patiently worked for Jennison until 1781, when he finally abandoned any hope of manumission and fled to Seth and John Caldwell, younger brothers of his former owner. Presumably, they would corroborate James's promise and convince Jennison to manumit him.

To Walker's disappointment, Jennison reacted angrily. Brushing aside the Caldwells' assertion that their brother had, indeed, promised Walker his freedom by 1778, Jennison confronted the alleged runaway working for the Caldwells. With the help of several servants, Jennison whipped Walker, returned him to the Jennison farm, and locked him in a barn for several hours. As soon as he could, Walker sought out a county justice of the peace and entered a trespass complaint against Jennison, seeking damages for injuries suffered in the whipping. Lacking jurisdiction, the local justice referred the complaint to the Worcester County Inferior Court of Common Pleas.

At the county court, Jennison entered his own complaint, too, suing the Caldwells in trespass upon the case for luring away his employee and depriving him of services. Jennison's and Walker's actions were both heard at the June 1781 session of the court before a three-judge bench. Like most county judges, the three men were not trained lawyers but respected local leaders: the merchant Moses Gill, and farmers Joseph Dorr and Samuel Baker.

In the first action, *Walker v. Jennison*, the defendant produced a bill of sale to argue that Walker was his slave and that as owner he had the right to discipline a runaway. The jury, thus, had a straightforward and simply framed factual question: was Walker Jennison's slave? Its verdict was equally clear: it reported that plaintiff "was a Freeman, and not the proper Negro slave of the Defendant," and it awarded Walker £50 in damages. The sum was less than the £300 demanded, but more important, the jury had established Walker's freedom. Jennison, frustrated in his attempt to regain Walker as his slave, nevertheless gained a small measure of recompense in the other action, *Jennison v. Caldwell*, where the jury, finding that Jennison had lost the services of an employee, awarded him the sum of £25.

A powerful array of legal talent had taken up Walker's and the Caldwells' causes. Jennison had capable counsel, too, in John Sprague and William Stearns, but they lacked the stature of those pleading for his opponents. Levi Lincoln, who argued Walker's case, was probably the most eminent attorney in the county and later served as attorney general of Massachusetts. For the second cause, Lincoln was joined by Caleb Strong, a member of the state convention that had drafted the constitution of 1780 with its Declaration of Rights; Strong later served as governor of the Commonwealth.

To gain Walker's freedom in *Walker v. Jennison*, Lincoln did not raise any constitutional issues. Rather, he chose an increasingly common antislavery device, the "freedom suit," which drew on the jury's power in eighteenth-century Massachusetts to interpret the law as it saw fit. In eighteenth-century Massachusetts, juries often acted, in effect, to settle legal issues by treating the question as a factual matter within their authority. During the Revolution, for example, accused violators of the hated Navigation Acts had charged customs officials with trespass for wrongful use of force in arresting them and seizing cargoes; juries hostile to Crown regulation would then return verdicts finding that the men making the seizures were not customs officials and awarding damages to the complainants. From this tactic grew the antislavery freedom suit, which Walker, like many other slaves, was using against his master. Walker sued Jennison in trespass for wrongful use of force—wrongful because Walker was not his slave. The freedom suit bypassed any larger question of whether slavery was legal; instead, it put to a jury a simple question: was this particular plaintiff free? Even in the case he had won at the county court, Jennison had established only that the Caldwells had deprived him of service; he could have recovered in any such action involving a free man.

Although *Walker v. Jennison* decided only Walker's freedom and did not touch the status of other slaves in Massachusetts, it served an important larger purpose. Through this case

and others like it, judges, lawyers, and jurors were stating unequivocally that they would not permit the machinery of the law to support a system of which they disapproved. For this reason, John Adams could recollect in 1795, "I never knew a Jury by a Verdict to determine a negro to be a slave—they always found them free." Walker's case therefore encouraged other such suits and reinforced the message that slave owners would have difficulty maintaining a distasteful system.

Appeals were necessary, however, for the verdict in *Jennison v. Caldwell* might appear to contradict that of *Walker v. Jennison*, and Jennison was a contentious individual unwilling to let the matter rest. Moreover, the Massachusetts legal system until it was reformed in 1859 allowed trial de novo ("trying the matter anew") on appeal, thus making lower court decisions precarious and in many instances merely an elaborate form of pretrial discovery. The losing parties in the two cases therefore appealed to the Massachusetts Superior Court of Judicature, which heard the cases at its Worcester session in September 1781.

The trespass case, *Walker v. Jennison*, was on the docket first, but Jennison defaulted. Why he did so is unclear; perhaps he wished to have all the issues settled in one case, *Jennison v. Caldwell*, which he had won at the lower court. Whatever the reason, Levi Lincoln was well prepared for Jennison. Aware of the larger significance of freedom suits and eager to strike a blow for more than just Walker's freedom, Lincoln embellished his argument. In addition to arguing that Walker was free by James Caldwell's promise of manumission, he brought in the question of whether slavery was legal under natural law and the law of God. "Is it not a law of nature that all men are equal and free?" he asked. "Is not the law of nature the law of God? Is not the law of God then against slavery?" Although he raised the constitutional question, too, only in passing did he argue that the Massachusetts Declaration of Rights had made slavery unconstitutional by declaring all men "free and equal."

The bench, with Judge Nathaniel Peaslee Sargent presiding, did not rule such arguments out of order. Although he and the other superior court judges hearing the case were, unlike their counterparts on the county bench, professional lawyers, they were receptive to the moral dimensions of the case. In any event, the jury was to decide, not they, and both sides addressed the broader question of slavery's legality. Sargent, an opponent of slavery, not only permitted Lincoln to plead natural, divine, and constitutional law, but he, too, raised the constitutional issue when he mentioned the "free and equal" clause of the state constitution in his jury instructions. The jury responded by reversing the lower court verdict: the Caldwells were not guilty of enticing Walker from Jennison and depriving him of services. Yet it is still unclear why they so decided. They may have responded to the natural law argument or they may have believed, as other juries did, that slavery was morally repugnant. It is possible, too, that they may have merely regarded the matter as settled by appellant's default in *Walker v. Jennison*; with that judgment affirmed (namely, that Walker "was a Freeman"), the jury may have decided that Walker was neither the servant nor the slave of Jennison. Nothing exists in the record to indicate the grounds for its verdict.

Uncertain of the outcome of the Caldwell's appeal, however, and before it came to trial at the superior court, opponents of slavery obtained a criminal indictment of Jennison for beating Walker. When the appellate jury verdict in *Jennison v. Caldwell* seemed to assure Walker's freedom, *Commonwealth v. Jennison* did not go to trial. But when the litigious Jennison refused to accept defeat and in June 1782 petitioned the legislature to order the defaulted *Walker v. Jennison* reopened, abolitionists saw to it that *Commonwealth v. Jennison* would be tried. At the April 1783 term of the supreme judicial court (successor to the superior court) both sides once again debated the legality of slavery—"as far as their fancy would lead them," recalled the court clerk when asked about the case in 1798, "although not directly on the point."

More directly to the constitutional question, however, and the reason that historians for so long mistakenly viewed this case as having abolished slavery in Massachusetts, was the charge to the jury prepared by Chief Judge William Cushing. In the final draft of his charge,

Cushing wrote that the state constitution declared that "*every subject* is *entitled to liberty*" [emphasis in original]. He saw no need to construe the unconstitutionality of slavery or to address the factual question of whether James or Isabell Caldwell had promised manumission. Rather, he wrote, "slavery is in my judgment as effectively abolished as it can be by the granting of rights and privileges wholly incompatible and repugnant to its existence. The court are therefore fully of the opinion that perpetual servitude can no longer be tolerated in our government. . . ."

It is not clear that Cushing ever delivered this charge, nor is it apparent that the jury followed it if he did. For the record, the jury only "found the master guilty," recalled the clerk in 1798, and nothing of the charge or legal argument was committed to the record. Because the jury technically had decided only the facts at issue, the clerk explained, "nothing could be recorded to distinguish this case from any other common assault and battery."

Judge Cushing's charge nevertheless remains powerful evidence of the antislavery attitudes that prevailed among Massachusetts judges, lawyers, and jurors. Although Walker's cases produced no judicial decision that could operate as determinative constitutional law, they stood as three more highly visible demonstrations that slavery would have little legal protection in Massachusetts. Jennison, in fact, had to remove his slaves (one of whom was Walker's brother Prince) to Connecticut in order to sell them. Meanwhile, whites continued to hold slaves in Massachusetts after 1783, but Jennison's failures discouraged many other slave owners from contesting the legal efforts that slaves might exert to gain their freedom. In that limited but important regard, they signaled the death knell for slavery in Massachusetts.

Selected Bibliography

Cushing, J.D. "The Cushing Court and the Abolition of Slavery in Massachusetts: More Notes on the 'Quock Walker Case.'" *American Journal of Legal History* 5 (April 1961): 118–44.

Davis, D.B. *The Problem of Slavery in the Age of Revolution.* Ithaca, NY: Cornell University Press, 1975.

O'Brien, W. "Did the Jennison Case Outlaw Slavery in Massachusetts?" *William and Mary Quarterly* 17 (April 1960): 219–40.

Spector, R.M. "The Quock Walker Cases (1781–83)—Slavery, Its Abolition, and Negro Citizenship in Early Massachusetts." *Journal of Negro History* 53 (Jan. 1968): 12–32.

Wiecek, W.M. *The Sources of Antislavery Constitutional-*

ism in America, 1760–1848. Ithaca, NY: Cornell University Press, 1977.

Zilversmit, A. "Quock Walker, Mumbet, and the Abolition of Slavery in Massachusetts." *William and Mary Quarterly* 25 (Oct. 1968): 614–24.

EMANCIPATION OF SLAVES IN TRANSIT

by Paul Finkelman
Brooklyn Law School

Commonwealth v. Aves, 18 Pickering 193 (1836) [Supreme Judicial Court of Massachusetts]

Commonwealth v. Aves was the first important northern state case to determine the status, under common law, of a slave brought into a free state. In *Aves*, Chief Justice Lemuel Shaw of the Massachusetts Supreme Judicial Court ruled that any slave, except a fugitive, became free the moment he entered a free jurisdiction. By 1860, all but four northern states had adopted the *Aves* precedent through court decisions, statutes, or both. The legislatures in New Jersey, Indiana, and Illinois explicitly rejected the *Aves* precedent through statutory law, while a California court adopted a modified version of the *Aves* doctrine.

Chief Justice Shaw's holding in *Aves* can be understood only in the context of three prior developments in law and society: the 1772 English case *Somerset v. Stewart*, the ending of slavery in the North, and the growth of a revitalized northern antislavery movement after 1831.

James Somerset was the slave of Charles Stewart, a British customs officer living in the American colonies. In 1769, Stewart returned to England and took Somerset with him. In 1771, Somerset escaped from Stewart, but was captured and consigned to a sea captain named Knowles, with directions to transport the troublesome slave to Jamaica and to sell him there. Somerset was confined to the hold of Knowles's ship, but before the ship sailed the great English abolitionist Granville Sharp convinced Lord Chief Justice Mansfield of the Court of King's Bench to issue a writ of *habeas corpus* in order to test Somerset's status.

Mansfield initially suggested that Stewart manumit Somerset in order to moot the case. Stewart stubbornly pursued the case, and after five hearings Mansfield ruled that while English courts would uphold contracts for slaves in the colonies, the actual practice of slavery was contrary to the common law of England. "The state of slavery is of such a nature," Mansfield wrote, "that it is incapable of being introduced on any reasons, moral or political; but only positive law [statutory law], which preserves its force long after the reasons, occasions, and times itself from whence it was created, is erased from memory; it's so odious, that nothing can be suffered to support it, but positive law."

The narrow holding of this case was that an alleged slave could not be forced out of England against his will. The decision meant that there was no law that would maintain slavery in England. Slaves could claim their freedom and no law could intervene. Although *Somerset* did not lead to an immediate end to slavery in England, most people in America thought it did.

The *Somerset* precedent for American purposes meant this: if a master brought his slave into a free jurisdiction, the slave could refuse to return to a slave jurisdiction, and no law could intervene to aid the master. On the contrary, the law would side with the slave.

In 1772, there were no free jurisdictions in the American colonies: at the outbreak of the Revolution all of the 13 colonies allowed slavery. This began to change during the struggle for independence.

Between 1780 and 1804, all the northern states took steps to end slavery within their jurisdiction. In 1780, Massachusetts adopted a constitution that declared all people were "free and equal." Quickly this clause was interpreted to mean that no slavery could exist in the state. New Hampshire and Vermont (the fourteenth state) similarly abolished slavery in their constitutions. By 1800, no slaves were living in any of these places. In 1780, Pennsylvania adopted a gradual emancipation statute, under which the children of slaves would be born free. Connecticut (1784), Rhode Island (1784), New York (1799), and New Jersey (1804) followed Pennsylvania's lead. Although slaves could be found in some of these states well into the nineteenth century, by 1804 the "North" had defined itself as those states that had either ended slavery outright or set it on a course of ultimate extinction.

The northern assault on slavery was led by a group of abolition societies that formed during and immediately after the Revolution. This first wave of abolition societies concentrated on four goals: the end of slavery in the North, the end of the African slave trade, the amelioration of conditions for free blacks in the North, and the protection of free blacks from kidnapping. By 1810, these societies had made a great deal of progress toward the first two goals and some progress toward the other two. However, by this time their leadership had died out and the societies began to lose their vigor. With the exception of various charitable projects—such as schools and orphanages for blacks—these societies ceased to have any impact on northern life.

In the early 1830s, a new antislavery movement emerged around the leadership of William Lloyd Garrison in Boston, the Tappan Brothers in New York, and Theodore Dwight Weld and James G. Birney in Ohio. This movement called for the immediate end to slavery everywhere in the United States. Abolitionists in Massachusetts were particularly active in seeking ways to attack slavery. In 1836 such an opportunity arose.

In May 1836, Mary Aves Slater, the wife of a New Orleans slave owner, returned to her native Boston to visit her father. Slater brought with her a six-year-old slave girl named Med. In July, Slater became ill and left Boston for a short time. While out of the city she left Med with her father, Thomas Aves.

At this point, the Boston Female Anti-Slavery Society obtained a writ of *habeas corpus* for Med. In August, the case came before Chief Justice Shaw. Although he had been on the bench for only a few years, Shaw was already emerging as one of the most important state jurists in the nation. The case was argued by two distinguished lawyers. Benjamin R. Curtis, who would eventually serve on the U.S. Supreme Court, where he would write a vigorous antislavery dissent in *Dred Scott v. Sandford* (1857), represented Aves. Ellis Gray Loring, who would devote much of his life to antislavery, but who would also serve as a member of the Harvard Corporation, presented the case for Med's freedom on behalf of the Boston Female Anti-Slavery Society. After reading the arguments in the case, Supreme Court Justice Joseph Story commented to Loring: "I have rarely seen so thorough and exact arguments as those made by Mr. B. R. Curtis and yourself. They exhibit learning, research and ability of which any man may be proud."

Curtis argued that Massachusetts should grant comity (i.e., respect) to the law of Louisiana, under which Med was held as a slave. He argued that there was no reason not to give a "qualified effect" to Louisiana law. He argued that Aves could hold Med in his custody without bringing into Massachusetts all of the "consequences" of slavery. Curtis pointed out that under the fugitive slave clause of the U.S. Constitution the judges of Massachusetts were bound to recognize the slave status of fugitives captured within the state. He argued that recognizing Med's status, for the purpose of preserving interstate harmony, would not overly burden Massachusetts.

Loring's main argument centered on the immorality of slavery. He argued that for the people of Massachusetts slavery "offends their morals" "contravenes their policy," and "offers a pernicious example." Equally important, he argued that any slavery in the state "violates a public law." Loring further argued that *Somerset* was part of the common law of Massachusetts, and under it Med had to be set free. He answered Curtis's arguments about the fugitive slave clause by asserting that the clause was "a barter of conscience, a violation of the express law of God" to which the North had unfortunately agreed, but that this compromise did not affect slave transit. Loring finished his argument with a poetic and emotional plea: "Let not the accursed system thrive amongst us. If we are to be restrained from attacking the giant trunk—if we have even consented to let a single bough shoot over us, to taint our air—I trust by the blessing of Heaven we have yet strength and virtue enough to lop its luxuriance. God forbid that the deadly branches should bend over and strike root, to become in their turn, a parentstock, growing up on the soil of Massachusetts."

Shaw stated the legal issues concisely: "The Precise question presented . . . is, whether a citizen of any one of the United States, where negro slavery is established by law, coming into this State, for any temporary purpose of business or pleasure, staying some time, but not acquiring domicil here, who brings a slave with him as a personal attendant, may restrain such slave of his own liberty during his continuance here, and convey him out of this State on his return, against his consent."

Shaw expressed surprise that this was a novel issue. He thought it the common belief of all lawyers in the state that slaves became free when brought into Massachusetts. This was so, "not so much because his coming within our territorial limits, breathing our air, or treading on our soil, works any alteration in his *status*, or condition, as settled by his domicil, as because by the operation of our laws, there is no authority on the part of the master, either to restrain the slave of his liberty, whilst here, or forcibly to take him into custody in order to his removal" [emphasis in original].

After reviewing English and American cases, on this subject, including *Somerset*, Shaw concluded that this was in fact the law of his jurisdiction, even though no case on the subject had previously arisen. Shaw was also pleased to note that cases in Louisiana and Kentucky had also held that a slave gained freedom when brought to a free state.

Shaw carefully distinguished this case from one of fugitive slaves, pointing out that Massachusetts had an obligation to return runaways. The logic of this distinction was clear to Shaw. A master could choose whether to bring a slave into Massachusetts, but a master could not control a runaway slave. Thus, "it is only when they [slaves] escape, without the consent of their owners, into other States, that they [masters] require the aid of other States, to enable them to regain their dominion over the fugitives."

Although Shaw's opinion set a precedent followed by most other northern states, beginning in the 1830s some southern states rejected the concept that slaves gained their freedom by living in free states. However, not until the 1850s would this become a major political issue. In *Strader v. Graham* (1851) and *Dred Scott v. Sandford*, Roger B. Taney chief justice of the U.S. Supreme Court, ruled that slaves brought to free jurisdictions did not necessarily become free. By 1860 most southern states would no longer recognize the *Somerset-Aves* principle that slavery was a status based on local law, and once the slave was taken from the locality, the status disappeared. However, the Supreme Court had not yet decided if the free states had the right to emancipate slaves brought into their jurisdiction. A case that might have raised this question, *Lemmon v. People*, was making its way through the New York courts in the 1850s. However, the election of Lincoln and the Civil War prevented a final decision on the question of slave transit in the North.

Selected Bibliography

Finkelman, P. *An Imperfect Union: Slavery, Federalism, and Comity.* Chapel Hill, NC: University of North Carolina Press, 1981.

Levy, L. *The Law of the Commonwealth and Chief Justice Shaw.* Cambridge, MA: Harvard University Press, 1957.

Wiecek, W.M. *The Sources of Anti-Slavery Constitutionalism in the United States, 1760–1848.* Ithaca, NY: Cornell University Press, 1977.

Zilversmit, A. *The First Emancipation.* Chicago: University of Chicago Press, 1967.

UPHOLDING THE FUGITIVE SLAVE LAW OF 1793

by Paul Finkelman
Brooklyn Law School

Prigg v. Pennsylvania, 16 Peters 539 (1842) [U.S. Supreme Court]

Prigg v. Pennsylvania was the first decision by the U.S. Supreme Court interpreting the meaning of the fugitive slave clause of the U.S. Constitution (Article IV, Section 2, Clause 3) and the validity of the federal Fugitive Slave Law of 1793. In a complicated decision, with seven separate opinions, the Court upheld the validity of the 1793 law.

The case began with an alleged fugitive slave named Margaret Morgan. Margaret was the daughter of two slaves who had once been owned by a Marylander named Ashmore. Ashmore had allowed these two slaves to live as if they were free, and he had never exerted a claim over Margaret, who lived her life as if she were free. Margaret eventually married a free black named Jerry Morgan. In 1832, the couple moved to Pennsylvania.

When Ashmore died his estate went to his niece, a Miss Ashmore. In 1837, she hired Edward Prigg, a professional slave catcher, to seize Margaret and bring her back from Pennsylvania. Miss Ashmore claimed Margaret as a slave because Margaret's mother had been her uncle's slave, and, since neither Margaret nor her mother were formally manumitted, Margaret had never been legally free. This was in fact a correct understanding of Maryland law.

Because Margaret had always lived as a free person, she made no attempts to hide her whereabouts. Prigg easily found her and seized her as a fugitive slave. At the time that Prigg acted, the seizure of a fugitive slave in Pennsylvania was regulated by both the federal law of 1793 and a state act of 1826. The state law was one of many "personal liberty laws" passed in the North throughout the antebellum period. This law, An Act to Give Effect to the Provisions of the Constitution of the United States Relative to Fugitives From Labor, for the Protection of Free People of Color, and to Prevent Kidnapping, had been adopted to fulfill the state's obligation to aid in the rendition of fugitive slaves and also to protect the state's free black population from kidnapping. Complying with the law, Prigg applied to Justice of the Peace Thomas Henderson for an arrest warrant. Acting under this warrant, Prigg arrested Margaret and brought her back to Henderson to obtain a certificate of removal, which was required by both the 1826 law and the federal act of 1793.

At this point Henderson "refused to take further cognizance of the case." Why he acted this way is unknown, although three explanations seem likely. He may have been offended by the notion that a woman who had lived her entire life as a free person could now be seized as a slave. He may also have objected to the seizure of Morgan's youngest child, who had been conceived and born in Pennsylvania and, thus, was a free person under Pennsylvania law. Finally, it is quite likely that Prigg was unable to produce the documentation necessary to prove Ashmore's title to Margaret. The evidentiary requirements under the Pennsylvania law were far more exacting than those of the federal law.

Prigg was probably not really interested in following all the procedures of the 1826 law because, among others, the law provided for a formal trial of the status of an alleged fugitive. Instead, Prigg simply forced Margaret back to Pennsylvania. For this act, a York County (Pennsylvania) court soon indicted Prigg for kidnapping. In 1839, Maryland extradited Prigg following an agreement that, if convicted, no sentence against Prigg would be enforced until after the case had been heard by the U.S. Supreme Court. The agreement furthermore stipulated an expedited appeals process in Pennsylvania. This allowed for Prigg's trial and conviction, which the Pennsylvania Supreme Court upheld. The contrived nature of the supreme court case is illustrated by the fact that Prigg's counsel also represented Maryland.

In reversing Prigg's conviction, Justice Joseph Story's opinion made four major points. First, Story held that the federal law of 1793 was constitutional. This conclusion rebuffed those who argued that the text of Article IV of the Constitution clearly indicated that fugitive slave rendition was strictly a state issue and Congress was incompetent to act under the cause. Second, Story held that the power to regulate the rendition of fugitive slaves was exclusively within the prerogative of Congress. This meant that the Pennsylvania personal liberty law of 1826 (and similar statutes from other states) was unconstitutional because it interfered with the enforcement of the federal law by placing additional (and stricter) burdens on masters seeking a fugitive slave. Story's opinion, however, allowed the continued existence of state laws that did not add new steps or requirements to the rendition process. Third, Story asserted that state officials had a moral obligation to help enforce the Fugitive Slave Law of 1793, but Congress could not require any state official to act. This stemmed from the prevalent notions of Federalism that state officials might not interfere with federal law enforcement, but that the federal government could not force any state official to take a particular action. Finally, Story found that the fugitive slave clause of the Constitution guaranteed slave owners a common law right of self-help in capturing their runaway slaves. This meant that under the Constitution "the owner of a slave is clothed with entire authority, in every state in the Union, to seize and recapture his slave." Because this right "may be properly said to execute itself," Story's opinion meant masters or kidnappers could remove from a free state fugitive slaves (or kidnapped free blacks) without any judicial supervision, as long as it could be accomplished "without any breach of the peace, or any illegal violence."

Story's opinion jeopardized the liberty of all blacks, both free and fugitive, in the North. Most personal liberty laws, which had been designed to protect free blacks, were now void. The North could still pass antikidnapping laws, but these laws could not be used to prevent the surrender of fugitive slaves. Thus, any free black

who was seized would have to be able to prove his freedom quickly in order to get the state to interfere in a rendition. Without state supervision, any free black might be seized under the federal law and claimed as a fugitive slave. Even more dangerous to free blacks was Story's assertion that anyone who could seize a black without a "breach of the peace" could remove that person to the South and sell him as a slave. This was an open invitation to kidnapping, if it could be done secretly and quietly. Without any judicial superintendence no black could rest secure.

While not a "holding" in the case, part of Story's rationale for his opinion was critical to the evolving antebellum crisis. Story's notion of a common-law right of recaption for slave owners implied that slavery was a national institution. Story stated this clearly, declaring that "the owner must, therefore, have the right to seize and repossess the slave, which the local laws of his own state confer upon him as property; and we all know that this right of seizure and recaption is universally acknowledged in all the slaveholding states." This, in effect, nationalized slavery. It applied the law of the slave states to the free states. The *Philanthropist*, an abolitionist paper, complained that this decision "establishes slavery as the law of the whole Union, on the ruins of state sovereignty, habeas corpus, and the jury trial." In the opinion, Story argued "that it cannot be doubted that" the fugitive slave clause "constituted a fundamental article, without the adoption of which the Union could not have been formed." Story based this analysis on Madison's *Notes of the Federal Convention*, even though those *Notes* show that unlike all of the other slavery-related compromises at the Convention, the fugitive slave clause was added near the end of the Convention without any debate or even a recorded vote. This assertion by Story, even though based on a faulty analysis of the Convention, nevertheless gave slavery a protected status within the constitutional and political framework of antebellum America.

At the same time that Story's opinion undermined the liberty of free blacks, it may also have undermined the ability of owners to capture legitimate fugitive slaves. Although the Pennsylvania personal liberty law toughened the evidentiary standard necessary for the return of a fugitive slave, the law also involved some state officials in the rendition process. Under Story's ruling, most of the existing personal liberty laws were unconstitutional, and, thus, most states no longer had valid legislation directing state officials to aid in the rendition process. States could pass such laws, and Story urged them to do so. But Story's opinion noted that the states could not be required to do so.

Only Justice John McLean of Ohio dissented from this result. The rest of the Court agreed with the result of the opinion and most of its ramifications. However, Chief Justice Roger B. Taney wrote a long concurrence in which he clearly misrepresented and bitterly attacked Story's opinion.

Taney did not like that aspect of Story's opinion that held Congress could not require state officials to enforce the federal law. Taney claimed that under this holding "all laws upon the subject [of fugitive slaves] passed by a State, since the adoption of the Constitution of the United States, are null and void, even although they were intended, in good faith, to protect the owner in the exercise of his property rights, and do not conflict in any degree with the act of Congress." He complained that under Story's ruling "no State, since the adoption of the Constitution can pass any law in relation" to the return of fugitive slaves.

Taney made this point and misstated Story's opinion for one apparent reason. He wanted to stress the importance of state cooperation in the return of fugitive slaves. He argued that under the "police powers" of a state, it was permissible for a state to order "the arrest and confinement of the fugitive in the public prison . . . until he could be delivered to his owner."

This portion of Taney's opinion totally misrepresented Story's opinion. Story held unconstitutional only state laws that conflicted with the act of Congress by adding additional requirements to the rendition of fugitive slaves. In fact, Story explicitly asserted that "to guard, however, against any possible misconstruction of our views, it is proper to state that we are by no means to be understood in any manner whatsoever to doubt or to interfere with the police power belonging to the States by virtue of their

general sovereignty. . . . We entertain no doubt whatsoever that the States, in virtue of their general police power, possess full jurisdiction to arrest and restrain runaway slaves, and remove them from their borders and otherwise to secure themselves against their depredations and evil example, as they certainly may do in cases of idlers, vagabonds, and paupers." Furthermore, he asserted that "the operations of this police power . . . may essentially promote and aid the interests of the owners."

Taney's real complaint was Story's assertion that state officials could not be required to enforce the 1793 law. The chief justice wrote that "if a State could not authorize its officers, upon the master's application, to come to his aid, the guaranty contained in the Constitution was of very little practical value." Taney decried the fact that under the Court's opinion, the "State officials are absolved from all obligation to protect this right." This again misrepresented Story who, in fact, urged states to help enforce the law.

Taney took this extreme position because he feared that under Story's opinion states would decline to help in fugitive slave cases. With few federal judges and marshals in the nation, rendition might prove impossible.

Ironically, Taney's scathing concurrence provided ammunition for northerners who did not want to enforce the 1793 law. Some northern legislatures explicitly prohibited state officials from aiding in the rendition process in any way. Some northern judges, who refused to hear fugitive slave cases, cited Taney's assertion that they lacked jurisdiction in such a case. It is quite possible that if Taney had not drawn attention to the ability of northerners to opt out of the enforcement process, fewer northerners would have done so. But Taney's opinion did draw attention to the antislavery possibilities of the case and various northerners acted on them. Taney, in fact, so misrepresented Story's opinion that he may have led some northerners to believe that they were in fact not permitted to enforce the 1793 law. Northern noncooperation with fugitive slave rendition after *Prigg* led to intensified southern demands for a new and stronger fugitive slave law. This was achieved in 1850 with a law that created a system of federal enforcement through commissioners,

U.S. marshals, and, if necessary, the army and navy.

Selected Bibliography

Cover, R.M. *Justice Accused: Antislavery and the Judicial Process*. New Haven, CT: Yale University Press, 1975.

Finkelman, P. "*Prigg v. Pennsylvania* and Northern States Courts: Antislavery Use of a Proslavery Decision." *Civil War History* 25 (March 1979): 5–35.

———. *Slavery in the Courtroom*. Washington: Government Printing Office, 1985.

Leslie, W.R. "The Pennsylvania Fugitive Slave Act of 1826." *Journal of Southern History* 18 (Nov. 1952): 429–45.

Morris, T.D. *Free Men All: The Personal Liberty Laws of the North*. Baltimore: Johns Hopkins University Press, 1974.

Newmyer, R.K. *Supreme Court Justice Joseph Story: Statesman of the Old Republic*. Chapel Hill, NC: University of North Carolina Press, 1985.

Nogee, J. "The Prigg Case and Fugitive Slavery, 1842–50." *Journal of Negro History* 39 (Jan. 1954): 27–42.

Wiecek, W.M. "Slavery and Abolition Before the United States Supreme Court." *Journal of American History* 65 (June 1978): 34–59.

———. *The Sources of Antislavery Constitutionalism in the America, 1760–1848*. Ithaca, NY: Cornell University Press, 1977.

"THEY HAVE NO RIGHTS"

by Kermit L. Hall
Department of History and College of Law
University of Florida

Dred Scott v. Sandford, 19 Howard 393 (1857) [U.S. Supreme Court]

Only a handful of U.S. Supreme Court cases can claim the designation of true landmarks, points along the path of U.S. history that genuinely separate one constitutional epoch from the next. Although scholars agree that *Dred Scott* fulfills this definition, they have differed about why. Until the 1960s, most scholars tied the case to the coming of the Civil War, arguing that had it not been for the Court's decision war might have been averted. Cast in this light, the Court seemingly suffered a self-inflicted wound that diminished its authority to shape the great constitutional controversies of the war and later Reconstruction. Since the 1960s, however, a new generation of scholars, molded by events of the "Second Reconstruction" and the Supreme Court's constitutional revolution in civil rights, has adopted a different perspective on *Dred Scott*. These scholars have stressed that what the justices did in the case was not only racist but that it involved an unprecedented usurpation of power by the High Court. They discounted the case's importance in bringing on the war and emphasized that the judicial power remained in tact throughout the war and Reconstruction. These scholars insisted that

Dred Scott was especially critical in establishing the authority of the justices to review acts of Congress on constitutional grounds. The case, they cogently observed, was only the second instance before the Civil War—the first was in *Marbury v. Madison* (1803)—in which the High Court struck down a federal law.

The litigants who began the case in the mid-1840s had little idea that their dispute would eventually assume such monumental proportions. Scott was a Missouri slave who, along with his family, accompanied his owner, Dr. John Emerson, an army officer, to his various duty posts. The most significant of these travels involved prolonged stays at military posts in Illinois and in federal territory at Fort Snelling, in what is now Minnesota. Both Illinois and Minnesota territory were on free soil, the latter above the line 36° 30' where the Missouri Compromise of 1820 had banned slavery in the Louisiana Purchase. There is no evidence that Scott ever demanded his freedom while residing in either place, and he and his wife, Harriet, returned with Emerson to Missouri.

After leaving the military in 1842, Emerson made a fitful attempt to establish a private practice in St. Louis. In the spring of 1843 he moved to Davenport, Iowa, territory, where he died at year's end. The attending physician listed the cause as consumption, but Emerson most likely succumbed to the late stages of syphilis. Emerson's will bequeathed almost all of his estate, including Dred Scott and his family, to his wife, whose maiden name had been Eliza Irene Sanford. Some historians have argued that Emerson actually left his estate to his daughter and designated his wife only a trustee with limited powers. The truth is that Mrs. Emerson enjoyed a life estate that included authority to diminish the principal of her inheritance and that gave her full control over Scott and his family.

Emerson also designated John F. A. Sanford, his brother-in-law, executor of the will. Sanford was a prominent St. Louis business-man connected by marriage to the upper rungs of that city's social elite. Despite his designation as executor, Sanford played only a marginal role in the disposition of Emerson's estate, which involved lands in Missouri and Iowa, and slaves (the Scotts) in Missouri. Rather, Mrs. Emerson assumed control over the property, including the slaves, with a minimum of legal fuss.

Three years after Emerson's death, Scott and his wife filed separate suits for freedom in the state circuit court in St. Louis against Irene Emerson and not John Sanford. They did so only after Mrs. Emerson refused to allow them to purchase the family's freedom. Why she refused is unclear. By 1846, the Scotts were middle-aged slaves for whom Mrs. Emerson had little personal use. Perhaps she doubted her legal authority to grant the request; perhaps the terms offered by the Scotts (partial payment with security for the remainder) were unsatisfactory, especially with the value of slaves rising. Perhaps she simply wanted to maintain the income they produced when hired out.

The Scotts' suits were typical of actions brought by slaves in Missouri. The laws of that state, as with most other southern states, had long embraced the rule that slaves who traveled into free territory and set up residences were emancipated. The circuit court judge quite predictably granted them leave to sue. The Scotts' declarations charged that Mrs. Emerson had "beat, bruised and ill-treated" them and had falsely imprisoned them. They sued not only for their freedom but damages of $10.

The trials dragged on for more than four years, during which time Mrs. Emerson continued to hire out the Scotts. After an abortive first trial, which the Scotts lost on a legal technicality, a second trial commenced in January 1850. Thanks to a highly favorable charge from the presiding judge, the jury found in favor of the Scotts. The counsel for Mrs. Emerson promptly appealed to the Missouri Supreme Court. Lawyers on both sides agreed that this and other appeals would be based on Dred's case alone, with the findings applying equally to Harriet. What had been two cases became one, and the Scotts, with a judgment in their favor, remained enslaved while they waited for a decision from the state's highest court.

Until 1850, *Dred Scott* attracted little attention beyond the immediate circle of litigants. It had no political implications and the legal precedents were clearly in Scott's favor. Against the unfolding sectional crisis of the 1850s, however, the case assumed increasingly momentous proportions. Events conspired to propel Scott's case into the national spotlight and to rob him and his wife of their earlier courtroom victory.

Until the 1830s, American judges had fashioned a seemingly workable legal compromise over what to do with sojourning slaves, but it was a compromise that departed significantly from the nation's English common-law inheritance, which favored the slave. The celebrated 1772 British case *Somerset v. Stewart*, for example, had held that slavery was a local institution and that a slave who came to free territory became free. Following independence American judges refused to follow *Somerset* exactly. Masters were able to sojourn with their slaves into free territory and return with them to the slaves states without interference by free-state authorities. Slave state courts, at the same time, accepted the general principle that slaves domiciled in free states became forever free. This tacit arrangement began to collapse in the 1830s under the weight of growing antislavery agitation. Several northern states passed personal liberty laws that withdrew the longstanding privilege of masters to maintain their slaves while sojourning. The Supreme Judicial Court of Massachusetts added insult to injury when, in *Commonwealth v. Aves* (1836), it abandoned the domicile requirement altogether and held that a slave other than a fugitive from justice became free the moment he set foot on free soil.

The highest appellate court of Missouri was also in the process of hardening its position, although in a completely different direction from that of Massachusetts. The appeal taken by Emerson's counsel to the Missouri Supreme Court required two years to decide, just long enough for the political cast of Missouri politics to change dramatically in reaction to the growing controversy over the expansion of slavery into the western territories. Missouri was peculiarly exposed to the cross currents of sectional wrangling. Three free states bordered on it and Democrats who were moderates on the slavery expansion question, such as Senator Thomas Hart Benton, were constantly assailed by a small but articulate band of antislavery advocates. These antislavery pressures pushed moderates in the Democratic party increasingly into the slaveholders' camp, a development that was reflected in the composition of the popularly elected Missouri Supreme Court. By a vote of 2–1 in 1852 that Democrat-dominated body overturned the jury verdict in favor of Scott. The majority did so through a dramatic rejection of legal precedent, holding that the state could no longer enforce the antislavery law of other jurisdictions against Missouri's citizens. In short, the fact that Scott had once been on free soil had no effect on his slave status in Missouri.

Normally, the next step should have been an appeal by Scott's counsel to the U.S. Supreme Court, but such a course of action was blocked by the justices' actions. By 1850, the climate of opinion, especially in the border states, had shifted against slaves bringing freedom suits, and the High Court's opinion in *Strader v. Graham* (1851) acknowledged as much. This Kentucky case involved slave musicians who were taken briefly into Ohio for performances and later fled from Kentucky to Canada. Their owners sued several men who had allegedly aided the escape. Counsel for the defendants argued that the slaves had been freed as a result of their travel in free territory (and

hence the defendants had committed no crime), but the Kentucky Court of Appeals rejected that argument. So, too, did the U.S. Supreme Court with Chief Justice Roger B. Taney, a slave-state Democrat from Maryland, writing a unanimous opinion.

Taney concluded in *Strader* that the Court lacked jurisdiction to decide the case, and his opinion saved the justices from entering directly into the growing sectional dispute over slavery. On close examination, however, the decision was more than an exercise in judicial self-restraint, since its holding meant that each state supreme court alone could decide whether a slave became free upon entering free territory. Amid growing sectional rancor over the peculiar institution, a slave-state judge had no incentive to find that slaves from his state had become free as a result of sojourning on free soil. The High Court's holding in *Strader* meant that once a slave reentered a slave state from free territory, he reverted to slave status and that the federal Supreme Court had no authority even to hear the case let alone find for the slave.

The Court's *Strader* decision prompted Scott's lawyers to adopt a new strategy. A direct appeal from the Missouri Supreme Court to the justices in Washington would not bring relief. Instead, they initiated an entirely new law suit for freedom in the federal circuit court for Missouri against John F. A. Sanford, who had moved to New York. Since the case would begin in a federal rather than a state court, the *Strader* precedent would not apply.

Sanford's exact legal relationship to Scott is unclear. There is much evidence to indicate that Sanford handled some of his sister's business dealings and that he may have acted as her agent in the previous *Scott* litigation. There is even some additional evidence, although inconclusive, that by this time Sanford actually owned Scott. An earlier generation of scholars lavished great attention on the question of ownership because they believed that the suit against Sanford was part of some grand conspiracy, although they disagreed on the exact line up of conspirators. Some insisted that abolitionists manufactured a counterfeit suit, especially since Mrs. Emerson in 1850 married Calvin Chaffee, a Massachusetts antislavery congressman.

Chaffee, however, publicly and privately disavowed any knowledge of such a scheme. Others argued that the suit was part of a pro-slavery plot that succeeded. Since the historical evidence is shaky on several key points, a conclusive answer to the ownership question will remain elusive. It is largely irrelevant in any case. Whether Sanford owned Scott was immaterial to the slave's bringing suit in federal court. All that mattered was that Sanford had authority over Scott and that in keeping with the requirement for diversity of citizenship, he resided in a state other than Missouri. So began the case of *Dred Scott v. Sandford* (with Sanford's name misspelled in the official record).

The federal suit for freedom was a customary form of an action of trespass. Scott's declaration asserted that he was a citizen of Missouri and complained that Sanford, a citizen of New York, had assaulted and wrongfully imprisoned him, his wife, and his children. The suit also sought damages of $9,000. The case was brought before Judge Robert W. Wells, a slaveholding ex-Virginian and former attorney general of Missouri, who did not suffer the same sectional hubris that had infected the justices of the state supreme court.

Until the case reached Wells's court the principal issue had been how Scott's previous travel on free soil affected his status as a slave in Missouri. But the decision of Scott's counsel to proceed in federal court raised an entirely new and very explosive issue: could a slave be a citizen? If Scott was not a citizen, he would be barred under the diversity of citizenship provision of the Constitution from bringing suit. Sanford's counsel attacked Scott's claim of citizenship by filing a plea in abatement, a procedural device that contended that since Scott was not a citizen, the federal circuit court lacked jurisdiction to hear the case. Scott was incapable of suing, the plea asserted, because a Negro, descended from slaves of "pure African blood," could never be a citizen, either of Missouri or of the United States. The cost to Scott's counsel of proceeding in the federal court was that this strategy invited the slave regime to advance racist arguments to attack a seemingly technical jurisdictional question.

Wells sustained Scott's demurrer to the plea and ruled that for purposes of bringing a suit in federal court, citizenship implied only residence in a state and the legal capacity to own property. Wells's ruling was quite narrow. He did not, for example, sketch any comprehensive grounds upon which to rest Negro citizenship, such as the privilege and immunities clause of Article IV, Section 2 of the U.S. Constitution. A Negro was enough of a citizen to be covered by the diversity of citizenship clause but it did not follow that he was a citizen in any broad, general sense. The rights of citizenship, in sum, were entirely contextual. On the merits of the case, however, Wells instructed the jury that established Missouri law should hold, and that once Scott had returned to that state his fate depended entirely on its laws and not on any residence on free soil. The jury quickly returned a verdict in favor of Sanford.

Scott then appealed to the U.S. Supreme Court on the basis of a writ of error, charging that Wells had improperly instructed the jury. The case was first argued in February 1856 before a Court composed of five southern Democrats, two northern Democrats, one northern Whig, and one Republican. This time it was Sanford's counsel who dramatically altered its strategy by introducing the claim that Scott had not become free in federal territory because the law forbidding slavery there (the Missouri Compromise) was unconstitutional. Such an argument further fueled the surging sectional conflict that had already inflamed national politics. The Kansas-Nebraska Act of 1854 and the ensuing struggle over "Bleeding Kansas" had already ignited a new round of constitutional debate about the authority of Congress over slavery in the territories and had given birth to the Republican party.

Many scholars have argued that the Kansas-Nebraska Act mooted the issue of the Missouri Compromise's constitutionality in *Dred Scott*. Such was not the case. The 1854 act repealed only part of the Missouri Compromise and applied only to Kansas and Nebraska. What Sanford's counsel wanted was to extend the principle of that legislation to all of the territories and, in so doing, to open vast new stretches of formerly slave-free territory to slaveholders. The seemingly limited jurisdictional question actually offered, as the most recent scholarship has concluded, an opportunity for the slave power to plead an expansive view of masters' rights before the nation's highest court.

The justices disagreed sharply about how to dispose of the case after first hearing arguments in early 1856. With the sectional crisis at fever pitch and the presidential campaign underway, several of them sought shelter in the seemingly safe technical question of whether the Court could review a plea in abatement. They ultimately decided to buy time by directing counsel to reargue the case, and the new proceedings began on December 15, 1856, after James Buchanan had been elected president but before his inauguration.

The Court's call for reargument only heightened political expectations, and the Washington press corps and members of Congress lavished great attention on it. The oral arguments consumed 12 hours spread over four days. Montgomery Blair and George T. Curtis, the brother of sitting Justice Benjamin R. Curtis, presented Scott's case; Henry S. Geyer and Reverdy Johnson furnished counsel for Sanford. The courtroom struggle, however, was drawn almost entirely between Blair and Geyer. The former argued that the *Strader* precedent did not apply in *Dred Scott* because the case had begun as a matter of original jurisdiction in the federal courts and that Scott, while not a complete citizen, was, as Judge Wells had concluded, sufficiently endowed with citizenship to sue in a federal court. The latter asserted that Congress had no authority to exclude slaveholders' property from the territories and that Scott, as a black who had never been naturalized, could not claim citizenship and therefore could not sue in a federal court.

A majority of the Court decided in the initial conference to skirt the larger issues and draw as heavily as possible on the *Strader* precedent. Justice Samuel Nelson, a New York Democrat, composed a brief draft of approximately 5,000 words that kept Scott a slave and sidestepped the constitutionality of the Missouri Compromise. Nelson's draft, however, immediately encountered resistance, both from the southern Democrats on the Court, notably Justice James Moore Wayne, and from the two northern antislavery justices, Curtis, of Massachusetts, and John McLean, of Ohio. Not surprisingly explanations of why the Court abruptly

changed direction paralleled political sentiments. Wayne subsequently explained that public expectations were so high that the justices simply decided that they could not leave the issue unresolved. But it was Wayne who made the vital motion to abandon Nelson's draft, to explore the issues fully, and to have Chief Justice Taney write the opinion. Justice John Catron offered another explanation of events. He charged, in a confidential communication to about-to-be-inaugurated President Buchanan that Curtis and McLean were prepared to issue dissents from Nelson's opinion that would discuss all of the issues raised in the case. The southern Democratic wing, in this view, had no choice but to respond.

Whatever the reason for the reversal in the Court's behavior, President Buchanan was kept well informed. When he learned from Catron that the Court would decide the broad constitutional issue in a way favorable to the South, he included a reference in his inaugural address that urged Americans to abide by the justices' ruling without saying what it would be. The Court's opinion followed two days later, on March 6, 1857.

Although Taney spoke officially for the Court, every other justice wrote an opinion and only one, Wayne, concurred with the chief justice in every particular. Despite this jumble of opinions, one result was clear: Scott lost. Moreover, the welter of opinion writing should not obscure the fact that a majority of the Court fully agreed with Taney. On the critical issue of excluding Negroes from citizenship, a majority of the justices joined Taney, and seven of the justices (Curtis and McLean were the exceptions) concluded that as a matter of law Scott was still a slave. Taney devoted more than 40 percent of his opinion to the question of citizenship. He ruled not only that slaves were not citizens but neither were free blacks. Any person of African descent, he explained, was "regarded [by the founding fathers] as beings of an inferior order, and altogether unfit to associate with the white race." "[T]hey have no rights," the chief justice continued, "which the white man was bound to respect," and the framers of the Constitution had intended "that the negro might justly and lawfully be reduced to slavery for his benefit." Taney's excursion into history was clearly wrong. Free blacks had not, as a matter of law, been reduced to slavery; to the contrary, they had enjoyed a modest guarantee of rights in some states and, in any case, their ranks were regularly swollen by slaves who either purchased their freedom or were manumitted by their masters. But the correctness of Taney's argument was less important than its purpose, and that purpose was to place blacks—all blacks—in an inferior legal position.

Republicans at the time and many historians subsequently blasted Taney's discussion of the constitutionality of the Missouri Compromise as mere *obiter dictum*. That is, what he had to say did not hold as a matter of law. Once having settled the citizenship question, the argument runs, Taney should have avoided any discussion of Congress's constitutional authority over the territories. His choice to discuss it, therefore, was not part of the Court's holding—it was just so much speculation by the chief justice. This argument had particular appeal to moderate Republicans because it permitted them to blast Taney's opinion and thereby sustain one of the main planks in their platform (i.e., that Congress could keep slavery out of the territories) without making a radical attack upon judicial authority. But correctly understood, Taney's discussion of the Missouri Compromise was not *obiter dictum*. It was a central part of the Court's holding, a holding that the chief justice designed to be comprehensive and, therefore, definitive. Having concluded that Scott could not be a citizen because he was a Negro, the chief justice fortified that position by demonstrating to a majority of the Court's satisfaction that Congress could not interfere with the rights of slaveholding citizens in the territories. Some scholars have argued that Taney rested this portion of his decision on the due process clause of the Fifth Amendment, which required compensation for the taking of property (in this instance, the property of slaveholders). But the due process argument was weakly stated and buried in the middle of his opinion. In the end, Taney simply did not provide any coherent explanation for why the Missouri Compromise was invalid. Nonetheless, his ruling was authoritative and not mere *obiter dictum*.

The decision had powerful political implications. It meant that the Republican party, which strongly advocated congressional control over slavery in the territories, had been organized on an unconstitutional premise. It also struck a powerful blow against the northern wing of the Democratic party and Stephen A. Douglas, the apostle of popular sovereignty. Douglas and his followers had maintained that each territory should be allowed to decide whether it would accept slavery. Taney's opinion slammed the door shut on that option; according to Taney, Congress could not authorize a territorial legislature to prohibit slavery. But this portion of Taney's opinion was *dictum*. The chief justice was absolutely determined to cover all of the possible bases in providing judicial protection to slavery. McLean and Curtis responded in kind. They insisted on the constitutionality of the Missouri Compromise and denounced Taney's blanket rejection of Negro citizenship.

Their dissenting opinions added grist to the Republican and antislavery propaganda mills, and an earlier generation of scholars gave great credence to this rhetoric by maintaining that the decision actually precipitated the Civil War. In the light of more recent historiography, however, this exercise in causation lacks merit. There is no doubt that the majority's decision contributed to rather than soothed already frayed sectional nerves. The decision also drove a wedge between the Douglas and southern wing of the Democratic party, snapping the last threads of bisectional party cooperation. Radicals in the South assumed that the decision meant that the federal government could pass a territorial slave code. Yet, given the strong Negrophobic cast of the Republican party, it seems doubtful that the decision either enhanced Republican recruiting or that it added much in the way to the election of Abraham Lincoln.

The constitutional effect of the decision was even more modest. As an unsuccessful candidate for the Senate in 1858 and as the successful presidential standard bearer for the Republican party in 1860, Abraham Lincoln asserted that he was not bound by the *Dred Scott* decision. The Court, Lincoln insisted, simply lacked authority to act unilaterally on a matter of such constitutional breadth. Lincoln's position was at least partly expedient; he did not suggest that the Court could not settle these matters, only that it had to wait for the proper time to do so. Lincoln knew that Republican justices were likely to reach positions different from Taney and his southern Democratic brethren. As president, Lincoln proceeded as if the decision had never been rendered. Attorney General Edward Bates in 1862 issued an official opinion holding that free men of color born in the United States were citizens of the United States. Congress, in the same year, abolished slavery in all the federal territories. The Thirteenth Amendment (1865), which invalidated slavery, and the Fourteenth Amendment (1868), which, among other provisions, extended citizenship to newly freed slaves, completed the burial of Taney's handiwork.

Recent scholarship has argued persuasively that Taney's opinion is best understood as a powerful demonstration of judicial review and a model of sorts for the modern development of a policy-directed, end-oriented form of judicial authority. Taney went much beyond what Chief Justice John Marshall had done in 1803 in *Marbury v. Madison,* offering no explicit reason why the federal law at issue was unconstitutional. Yet one should not be too quick to cast Taney and his Court in entirely modern judicial garb. Taney clothed his political and racial proclivities in rhetoric that stressed the inherent limitations of judicial power as an appropriate means of adjusting the Constitution to a world that was quickly rejecting human slavery. Despite the 55 pages of text, Taney's message was simple: Dred Scott remained a slave because the framers had "constitutionalized" slavery and subsequent generations could do nothing through the judicial process to alter that fact.

Furthermore, Taney's opinion invoked the traditional departmental theory of constitutional adjudication. This theory, which had precedent in the debates of the founders and in early state judicial proceedings, held that each department—branch—of government could construe the Constitution where its powers were involved. Constitutional interpretation was a defensive and preserving practice in which the judiciary's authority to act was strictly limited.

Courts and judges could not do anything that they wanted. "No one supposes," Taney wrote, "that any change in public opinion . . . should induce the court to give to the words of the constitution a more liberal construction . . . than they were intended to bear when the instrument was framed. . . . Any other rule of construction would abrogate the judicial character of this court, and make it the mere reflex of the popular opinion or passion of the day." The Constitution, in Taney's view, might change, but the justices could not change it; they could only interpret those values constitutionalized by the framers, one of which was slavery. "If any of its provisions are deemed unjust," Taney wrote, "there is a mode prescribed in the constitution itself by which it may be amended."

Some scholars have refused to accept Taney's assertions at face value, preferring to see in the opinion an example of the new, policy-making scheme of review that first appeared in the 1890s and has become a controversial feature of the present constitutional era. Taney, these scholars suggest, simply read his values into the Constitution. In one sense, this was true. Taney and his pro-slavery colleagues certainly understood that they were making social choices, and their willingness to decide the case—quite apart from the opinion itself—indicated that the Court had moved toward embracing what has become the modern, liberal conception of judicial review.

Yet this argument explains too much. Taney's opinion, despite its innovation in legal doctrine, was an exercise in strict construction. In this context, the invocation of more power culminated in less authority for the Court. Taney was no modern-day jurist exalting his special knowledge over that of Congress. Taney could not, and did not, seek to legitimate his invalidation of the Missouri Compromise based on his own will. Rather, he is better understood as the agent of jurisprudential values that were themselves undergoing rapid change and of political forces that had thrust upon the Court the responsibility for deciding an issue that neither Congress nor the president wished to resolve. That the collapse of the departmental theory was underway seems certain; it seems equally plausible that Taney's *Dred Scott* opinion was rooted as much in a traditional as in a modern conception of the role of appellate judges.

Dred Scott was the first case in which the public had to consider the consequences of judicial review of a federal law. Marshall's *Marbury* opinion was self-liquidating and altogether defensive of the Court's authority. *Marbury* required no executive enforcement, and it placed no inhibition on Congress (and thus on the exercise of popular will). *Dred Scott* did both. For the principals in the case, the verdict of the Court made little difference. John Sanford died in an insane asylum two months after Taney read his opinion. Dred Scott was soon manumitted, but he lived only 16 months as a freeman before succumbing to tuberculosis.

Selected Bibliography

Ehrlich, W. *They Have No Rights: Dred Scott's Struggle for Freedom.* Westport, CT: Greenwood Press, 1979.

Fehrenbacher, D.E. *The Dred Scott Case: Its Significance in American Law and Politics.* New York: Oxford University Press, 1978.

Hall, K.L. *The Supreme Court and Judicial Review in American History.* Washington, D.C.: The American Historical Association, 1985.

Morgan, D.G. *Congress and the Constitution: A Study in Responsibility.* Cambridge, MA: Harvard University Press, 1966.

Potter, D.M. *The Impending Crisis, 1848–61.* New York: Harper & Row, 1976.

Swisher, C.B. *The Taney Period, 1836–1864.* New York: Macmillan, 1974.

SLAVERY, FREEDOM, AND FEDERAL JUDICIAL POWER

by Thomas D. Morris
Department of History
Portland State University

Ableman v. Booth, 21 Howard 506 (1859) [U.S. Supreme Court]

Neither Benammi S. Garland nor Joshua Glover could have known that when Glover fled Garland's farm outside of St. Louis in 1852 that he would set in motion a series of events that led to one of the more important jurisdictional rulings by the Supreme Court in the nineteenth century. Sherman M. Booth, a hot-tempered abolitionist newspaper editor in Milwaukee, Wisconsin, could not have known it either. In March 1854 these three, along with others, had a violent meeting.

Glover, a runaway slave, was playing cards with two black friends in a cabin on the outskirts of Racine, Wisconsin, where he had fled earlier. On March 10, 1854, Garland, two U.S. deputy marshals, and four other men captured Glover. There was a struggle, Glover was badly hurt, manacled, and taken to a jail in Milwaukee. When Booth heard that the runaway was in jail "all bruised and bloody," he rode a horse through the city, stopping at each street corner, yelling "To the rescue! Slave catchers are in our midst! Be at the court-house at two o'clock!" That evening a mob gathered to listen to an impassioned speech by Booth, and then it demanded the release of Glover. When that was refused, the mob broke into the jail, took the battered slave out, and put him aboard a steamer bound for Canada. Glover was free at last, but for Booth the legal drama had just begun.

On March 15, 1854, Booth was arrested for aiding the escape of a fugitive in violation of the federal fugitive slave law. He was arrested by U.S. Marshal Stephan V. R. Ableman. Shortly after, Booth's case became a *cause célèbre* among abolitionists, and a test of the constitutionality of the Fugitive Slave Law of 1850. That statute had been a clear victory for the South. It provided for the appointment of fugitive slave commissioners by lower federal judicial officials. They would sit throughout the North and hear claims by slave owners and grant certificates authorizing the removal of the alleged runaways. These commissioners could also summon the aid of bystanders, a *posse comitatus*, to help in the recovery of fugitives. A commissioner would hear the proofs offered by the slave owner or his agent. The testimony of the alleged fugitive would not be admitted, and once a certificate of removal was granted it was conclusive evidence of the right to remove the person and would "prevent all molestation . . . by any process issued by any court, judge, magistrate, or other person whomsoever." What this meant was that the basic presumption of freedom that underlay the law of the free states and of states whose laws were designed to secure the personal liberty of free men could not be used to defeat a claim that a person was a slave, whether it was true or false. If anyone obstructed a claimant making a seizure "with or without" a legal process or rescued a runaway, he would be guilty of a federal offense. Finally, antislavery people in Congress had tried, without success, to require that an alleged slave would be granted the right to a writ of *habeas corpus* and the right to a trial by jury.

Although Booth and the others had violated this law, the question remained, was the law constitutional? Ultimately, the question was, who shall decide? On May 27, 1854, by which time Glover was safely in Canada, Booth, who was still in jail, asked Associate Justice Abram D. Smith, of the state supreme court, to issue a writ of *habeas corpus* and free him on the ground that the fugitive law was unconstitutional. Byron Paine, Booth's counsel, delivered a searing indictment of that law and of the federal judicial power that had affirmed a duty and power in the federal government to provide for the return of runaways.

Paine contended that the so-called fugitive slave clause of the U.S. Constitution (Article IV, Section 2, Clause 3) was addressed not to the federal government but to the states. "The trampling of the gathering hosts is already heard," Paine intoned, "the murmuring of the rising storm is wafted upon every gale. The North is snapping asunder the bands that have bound it in subjection to the slave power, as

Sampson broke the withs of tow! The last link that binds it, is the judicial sanction that power has received! Let that be broken, and the people are free!" What Paine received in 1854 was a favorable state judicial decision. But it ultimately led to another judicial sanction of the slave power and of federal judicial power.

Associate Justice Smith, at the end of May, freed Booth on the ground that the federal law was unconstitutional in that it denied trial by jury to alleged fugitives and it took their liberty without due process of law. Upon the request of the federal marshal, Smith's ruling was heard by the full state supreme court, which upheld his decision on July 19, 1854. The marshal, Ableman, appealed this decision to the U.S. Supreme Court. While this appeal was pending, Booth was rearrested in January 1855. He was tried by a jury in a trial presided over by U.S. District Judge Andrew Miller. Miller was determined to uphold the federal law and its enforcement for fear of a serious erosion of order and stability. Booth was found guilty, sentenced to serve one month in jail, and fined $1,000. Once again he appealed to the Wisconsin Supreme Court for release on the ground that he was held under an unconstitutional federal statute.

On February 3, 1855, the Wisconsin court again freed Booth. It ruled that he was illegally confined under an unconstitutional law and that a state was empowered to protect its citizens. Without this authority, "the state would be stripped of one of the most essential attributes of sovereignty." This decision was also appealed to the U.S. Supreme Court.

Booth's original idea was to present a vigorous defense before the U.S. Supreme Court in an argument made "in behalf of liberty." Booth sought the help of Charles Sumner, the powerful U.S. senator from Massachusetts, to argue the case on his behalf. Although he did not agree to serve as Booth's attorney, Sumner did write to Paine that "it were well that the self-defensive power of the States should be recognized." The Wisconsin Supreme Court began to obstruct the process in May 1855. It ordered its clerk to make no return whatsoever to the writ of error issued by the U.S. Supreme Court. The clerk, however, had already handed over a certified copy of the record to the federal district attorney. On March 6, 1857, the same day that it handed down one of the most significant decisions in its history, *Dred Scott v. Sandford*, the Court granted the motion of the U.S. attorney general to file the copy of the record despite the order of the state court. The earlier appeal was consolidated, and the two cases were decided two years later, March 7, 1859.

The only argument presented was that of Jeremiah S. Black of Pennsylvania, the U.S. attorney general. No one appeared to present an argument "in behalf of liberty." Among the more critical points Black raised were that the Fugitive Slave Law of 1850 was constitutional, that a judgment of a federal court was conclusive of all questions of constitutional law or statutory construction, and that no state court could free a man on a *habeas corpus* when he was held by a federal court of exclusive jurisdiction.

The power of a state court under its *habeas corpus* jurisdiction was controversial at that time. A leading treatise on the writ, for instance, held that a state court could free a person if he were illegally detained, even if that might involve "questions of the constitutionality of acts of Congress, or of the jurisdiction of a court of the United States."

In a very brief and unanimous opinion for the Court, Chief Justice Roger B. Taney flatly rejected this notion. It was an opinion of considerable importance in terms of federal judicial power, which in one sense, reads like a brief essay in arcane jurisdictional law. But it involved more than disembodied technicalities; it upheld national supremacy and fed the raging fires of controversy over slavery. One scholar called Taney's opinion in *Ableman v. Booth* "the most powerful of all his notable opinions." Another observed that it was "thoughtful, measured, and disciplined to the last degree." Whatever its ultimate significance, it ought not to be wholly abstracted from the context within which it was decided. It was the affirmation not so much of national supremacy in general as it was of federal judicial supremacy at a time when the federal judiciary was prepared to diminish federal legislative power in the interests of the institution of slavery, as in *Dred Scott*.

Taney began his opinion with the assertion that the Wisconsin Supreme Court had claimed far too much; it had claimed that the state courts were supreme over the courts of the nation. What it had actually claimed was that the state must possess the authority to protect its citizens on its own soil from being jailed under an unconstitutional law. Broadly stated, this harkened back to the position of Thomas Jefferson and James Madison in the Kentucky and Virginia Resolutions adopted to undermine the enforcement of the Sedition Act, an act that directly threatened civil liberty. The Wisconsin court claimed only that it had authority to protect personal liberty; it did not claim a general supervisory power over all federal legislation.

Still, the sweeping and controversial claim made by the Wisconsin court, Taney reasoned, could lead to chaos. There would be conflicting decisions throughout the country and decisions would be affected by "local influences." Under such a situation, federal supremacy could not be maintained peacefully unless there were a federal "judicial power equally paramount in authority to carry it into execution." Taney did admit that a state court could use its *habeas corpus* jurisdiction to inquire into any and all imprisonments. However, once it was informed that the person was held under federal authority, the case would end. *Habeas corpus* authority did "not pass over the line of division between the two sovereignties." This was the heart of the decision.

Although it was not necessary to the judgment in *Ableman v. Booth*, the Court, without full argument by counsel or discussion by the Court, announced that the Fugitive Slave Law of 1850 was "fully authorized by the Constitution of the United States." The Court's assertion about the fugitive law seems to have escaped the notice of many scholars, but it did not escape that of some contemporaries. When Byron Paine, Booth's counsel, was elected to the Wisconsin Supreme Court, Charles Sumner wrote to him that "[t]rial by Jury, *habeas corpus*, and the other safeguards of the rights of all . . . will again become realities." The Wisconsin legislature, moreover, condemned *Ableman v. Booth* as an "arbitrary act of power" that abrogated the writ of *habeas corpus*, and left the liberties of the people defenseless beneath "unlimited power."

Federal officials in Wisconsin obviously confronted a rather delicate situation, and they moved with less than dispatch. In the spring of 1860, they finally acted. Booth, who had a little bit of John Brown in him, was rearrested. Booth considered himself a martyr and refused to pay the fine that had been levied against him. A little over a year after his arrest, after war had broken out, the Wisconsin Supreme Court, with a new set of jurists, ended the case against him when it upheld a judgment against his printing press to cover his fine.

Perhaps a more telling conclusion to the matter came the following year. In a minority report of a special legislative committee of the Wisconsin legislature, the remarks of G. W. Hazelton made clear what was at stake in the jurisdictional battle represented by *Ableman v. Booth*. Jurisdiction is power, the power to decide, but one should not forget that the substantive issues involved are also important. Hazelton did not forget. The federal government, in his view, had long been under the control of pro-slavery elements. But, with the secession and the outbreak of war, it had "passed from the grasp of the slave power," and it would never be repossessed by that power. Because freedom and not slavery now controlled the institutions of the nation, the "true interests of freedom are to be developed in our nation, not . . . by States acting in their individual spheres . . . but by the whole body of the people operating through a national organization."

Buried deep within jurisdictional law are often issues of profound significance. In *Ableman v. Booth*, the issues were the relationship between federal and state judicial power and the issue of freedom or slavery. Caught in between were the free blacks whose liberty might be protected by the states or who might fall victims to claims that they were slaves. Also intertwined, but not expressed in the opinion, were the divergent moral perceptions of the North and South: one side held that the ownership of human beings was proper and defensible, and the other that it was not. There was no way that a judgment, such as that in *Ableman v. Booth*, could resolve the division. As important as the case was for the affirmation of a nation and of a federal judicial supremacy, the case was but one more element in the deterioration of the relationships between the sections. In the end, it was not federal judicial supremacy that resolved that problem. Despite Taney's hope, the sectional divisions could not be resolved peacefully.

Selected Bibliography

Bestor, A. "State Sovereignty and Slavery: A Reinterpretation of Proslavery Constitutional Doctrine, 1846–60." *Journal of the Illinois State Historical Society* 54 (Summer 1961): 117–80.

Hagan, H.H. "Ableman vs. Booth." *American Bar Association Journal* 17 (Jan. 1931): 1–20.

Hyman, H.M., and W.M. Wiecek. *Equal Justice Under Law: Constitutional Development, 1835–75.* New York: Harper & Row, 1982.

Schafer, J. "Stormy Days in Court—The Booth Case." *Wisconsin Magazine of History* 20 (1936): 89–110.

Swisher, C.B. *History of the Supreme Court of the United States: The Taney Period, 1836–64.* New York: Macmillan Publishing Co., Inc., 1974.

SLAVES-IN-TRANSIT AND THE ANTEBELLUM CRISIS

by Paul Finkelman
Brooklyn Law School

Lemmon v. People, 20 N.Y. 562 (1860) [New York Court of Appeals]

In 1852, Jonathan and Juliet Lemmon prepared to move from Virginia to Texas. At that time the easiest way to make such a move was to travel by steamboat to New York City and then board a steamboat going directly to New Orleans. On November 5, 1852, the Lemmons arrived in New York City and rented a hotel room while awaiting passage for New Orleans. They expected to stay in New York for only a few days. Along with their baggage and other property, the Lemmons had eight slaves. They locked these slaves in a hotel room.

On November 6, a black man named Louis Napoleon secured a writ of *habeas corpus* on behalf of "eight colored persons lately taken from the steamer City of Richmond." The Lemmons responded that the eight people were slaves owned by Juliet Lemmon and that she "never had any intention of bringing the said slaves or persons into the State of New York to remain therein, and that she did not bring them into said State in any manner nor for any purpose whatever, except *in transitu* or transit from the State of Virginia . . . through the port or harbor of New York. . . ." The Lemmons essentially argued that as citizens of one state, they had a right to travel unmolested with their property through another state. This argument did not impress Judge Elijah Paine of the New York Superior Court. On November 13, Judge Paine discharged "the colored Virginians." While the Lemmons prepared their appeal to a higher court, the eight former slaves quickly disappeared.

The Lemmons felt that they had suffered a great injustice, and that the position of Judge Paine threatened the Union. The Lemmons had not wanted to establish slavery in New York. They had not even allowed their slaves to leave their hotel room. All they sought was to exercise their rights, under the U.S. Constitution, to travel from one state to another, through a third state.

Judge Paine acted under a New York law of 1841, which amended earlier statutes dealing with slavery. In 1810, New York adopted legislation allowing visitors and transients to bring slaves into the state for up to nine months. In 1841, the legislature repealed this nine-month exemption. The statutes of New York now read that any slave (except a fugitive) entering the state became instantly free. Judge Paine, the first New York jurist to construe this repeal, interpreted it literally, and freed the slaves before him.

The Lemmons were especially depressed by this result because their slaves constituted most of their property. The *New York Journal of Commerce* immediately began a fund to recompense the Lemmons, and in the process showed Southerners that not all Northerners were abolitionists. The newspaper soon raised $5,000, far more than the five slave children, two women, and one adult man were worth. Before returning to Virginia with this large sum of money, the Lemmons formally manumitted their slaves, so that the outcome of any litigation would not turn on the actual fate of the eight "colored Virginians," who by this time had become "colored Canadians."

Although the Lemmons no longer had a personal stake in the case, the state of Virginia felt obliged to appeal Paine's decision, and employed the distinguished New York attorney and prominent Democrat Charles O'Conor. Meanwhile, the New York legislature appropriated special funds to William Evarts and Chester A. Arthur as special counsel. Governors in both states declared their determination to vindicate the rights of their state. The 1857 decision of the U.S. Supreme Court in *Dred Scott v. Sandford* exacerbated this increasingly politicized situation. That same year the New York Supreme Court upheld Paine. Finally, in 1860, the state's highest court, the New York Court of Appeals, reached the same conclusion.

Speaking for the New York Court of Appeals, Judge Hiram Denion conceded that under the commerce clause Congress might have the power to regulate the interstate movement of slaves. But until Congress passed such a law, he asserted the state was free to act. Denion argued that New York was in full compliance with the privileges and immunities clause of the U.S. Constitution because Virginians could "hold property by the same titles by which every other citizen may hold it, and by no other." Denion argued that if the right of transit with slaves was constitutionally protected, "it would naturally be supposed that . . . [this right] would be adjusted in connection with the provision [in the Constitution] looking specially to that case instead of being left to be deduced by construction from clauses intended primarily for cases to which slavery had no necessary relation." Absent such a clause, no right existed.

In dissent, Judge Thomas Clerke asked, "Is it consistent with this purpose of perfect union, and perfect and unrestricted intercourse, that property which the citizen of one State brings into another State, for the purpose of passing through it to a State where he intends to take up his residence, shall be confiscated in the State through which he is passing, or shall be declared no property, and liberated from his control?" He pointed out that under international law, New York's action might lead to war. But "relations of the different States of this Union . . . are of a much closer and more positive nature . . . war between them is legally impossible." He condemned his judicial brethren for "forgetting that the compact, by which" the states were governed and thus undermining the Union.

Lemmon was the last important slavery-related case to be decided by a northern state supreme court. The election of Abraham Lincoln and the Civil War prevented the Supreme Court from hearing the case. Given its proslavery biases, it is quite likely that the Taney Court would have overturned the New York decision and ruled that all Americans had a constitutional right to travel with their property through other states. *Lemmon* was probably the "next Dred Scott" case that Abraham Lincoln predicted in his "House Divided Speech." In the late antebellum period, Lincoln and other Republicans feared that *Lemmon* would lead to a nationalization of slavery. Lincoln's election and the outbreak of the Civil War made this speculation moot.

Selected Bibliography

Finkelman, P. *An Imperfect Union: Slavery, Federalism, and Comity.* Chapel Hill, NC: University of North Carolina Press, 1981.

———. *Slavery in the Courtroom.* Washington: Government Printing Office, 1985.

Foner, E. *Free Soil, Free Labor, Free Men.* New York: Oxford University Press, 1970.

Hyman, H.M. and W.M. Wiecek. *Equal Justice Under Law: Constitutional Development, 1835–75.* New York: Harper & Row, 1982.

Wiecek, W.M. *The Sources of Antislavery Constitutionalism in the America, 1760–1848.* Ithaca, NY: Cornell University Press, 1977.

Zilversmit, A. *The First Emancipation.* Chicago: University of Chicago Press, 1967.

B. African-Americans Since 1865

NO "RIGHT" TO VOTE: THE RECONSTRUCTION ELECTION CASES

by Robert M. Goldman
Department of History-Political Science
Virginia Union University

United States v. Reese, 92 U.S. 214 (1876); *United States v. Cruikshank*, 92 U.S. 542 (1876)
[U.S. Supreme Court]

By some accounts the slaughter was reminiscent of the worst Civil War massacres. On April 13, 1873—Easter Sunday—at least 105 blacks and three whites were brutally murdered by a force of white Democrats in and around the Grant Parish courthouse in Colfax, Louisiana. Almost half of those killed had been shot after they had surrendered, and some of the bodies were mutilated and robbed.

The Grant Parish Massacre (or Colfax Riot) was one of the worst of many instances of violence and intimidation directed against the recently emancipated slaves in the South after the end of the Civil War. To protect the civil and political rights of the freedmen, Republicans in Congress had passed the Civil Rights Act of 1866 and added the Fourteenth Amendment to the Constitution. When those proved insufficient to guarantee that blacks in the South would be allowed to participate in the political process of Reconstruction in that section, Republicans passed and ratified the Fifteenth Amendment in 1868.

Under the Fifteenth Amendment, "The right of citizens of the United States to vote shall not be denied or abridged by the United States or by any State on account of race, color, or previous condition of servitude." A second section gave Congress authority to enforce the provisions of the amendment "by appropriate legislation."

It quickly became evident that the amendment alone was not enough. Reports poured into Congress from throughout the South of continued terrorism directed against blacks attempting to vote or to participate in political activities. Often the acts were committed by organized groups of southern white Conservatives, most frequently the Ku Klux Klan. In response, Republicans in Congress passed a series of three acts in 1870–71 known as the Enforcement Acts. These measures defined in great detail a wide variety of crimes directed against potential voters, and provided the machinery for the federal government and Justice Department officials to counteract them.

Prosecutions were begun in the South under the Enforcement Acts, and during the first two years they achieved some success in protecting civil and voting rights. What was not yet clear was whether the Supreme Court would find these measures constitutional, and appeals were brought by defendants convicted under the acts in the federal courts. In one early lower court ruling, Circuit Court Judge William B. Woods of Alabama upheld a series of indictments brought under the acts. Judge Woods used the privileges and immunities clause of the Fourteenth Amendment to affirm the conviction of a group of white Alabamians accused of breaking up a political rally of blacks.

On the basis of extensive federal investigations, District Attorney James R. Beckwith of New Orleans used provisions of the May 1870 Enforcement Act to bring indictments against 97 men who had participated in the Grant Parish Massacre. Only nine of those indicted, however, were brought to trial. That trial lasted from February 23 to March 16, 1874, and resulted in the acquittal of one defendant and a mistrial for the eight others. A second trial was held in which William J. Cruikshank and two others were eventually found guilty of conspiracy. Following a division over the constitutional issues raised, the presiding judges on the circuit court, Supreme Court Justice Joseph P. Bradley and Judge Woods, certified the case for appeal to the U.S. Supreme Court.

An impressive array of legal counsel, including former Attorney General Reverdy Johnson, and David Dudley Field, brother of Supreme Court Justice Stephen J. Field, argued the defendants' case before the Court in March and April 1874. Attorney General George Williams and Solicitor General Samuel Field Phillips represented the federal government.

In their briefs and oral arguments before the Supreme Court, the defendants' attorneys argued that the primary issue was whether Congress had the power to protect individual rights from infringement by private individuals. Using what one historian has called a "states rights view of American federalism," defense counsel insisted that Congress had no such power, and that the Enforcement Acts were an unconstitutional infringement on state authority. Murdering a group of black men may have been a denial of their rights, but it was a denial that could only be protected by the states. The attorney general and the solicitor general confined their arguments to the narrowest possible grounds, arguing that the defendants were properly accused and convicted of a crime, that of conspiracy, cognizable under federal law.

While *United States v. Cruikshank* was making its way through the courts, federal officials brought another case involving prosecutions under the Enforcement Acts that dealt even more directly with the scope of the Fifteenth Amendment. The case began during the municipal elections in Lexington, Kentucky, in January 1873. A state law required voters to pay a $1.50 "capitation tax" and present a receipt for the same to election officials before being allowed to vote. Two Lexington officials, Mathew Foushee and Hiram Reese, were indicted by a federal grand jury for refusing to allow William Garner, a citizen "of African descent," to vote. They claimed he had failed to present the required receipt. Upon a division of opinion among the circuit court judges reviewing the indictments in December 1873, the case was docketed for review by the Supreme Court shortly thereafter.

United States v. Reese was not argued before the Court until January 1875. Representing the defendants were two prominent Democratic attorneys: Henry Stanbery and B. F. Buckner of Kentucky. Attorney General Williams and Solicitor General Phillips again presented the government's case. Buckner and Stanbery contended that Sections Three and Four of the 1870 Enforcement Act were unconstitutional under the Fifteenth Amendment because there was no allusion in those sections to discrimination "on account of race." Foushee and Reese had prevented Garner from voting, but the indictment did not allege that the refusal had been because of his race. Williams and Phillips, on the other hand, argued that the act was constitutional inasmuch as the Fifteenth Amendment had given Congress broad affirmative powers to prevent any racially motivated interference with voting rights. The Enforcement Act made race an element of all its provisions, they insisted, and while the sections being reviewed "have a much wider application" than was necessary for the defendants in the case, they certainly covered the crimes that were committed.

At the time both cases were argued before the Supreme Court, the chief justice was Morrison R. Waite, an Ohio Republican appointed by President Ulysses S. Grant. Serving with Waite were Republican appointees Joseph P. Bradley, Samuel F. Miller, William Strong, Noah H. Swayne, Ward Hunt, and David Davis, along with Democrats Nathan Clifford and Stephen J. Field. The Supreme Court had already rendered one significant decision on the scope of the Reconstruction amendments in the *Slaughterhouse Cases* (1873). In that case, the Court had limited the meaning and scope of the privileges and immunities clause of the Fourteenth Amendment. But the *Slaughterhouse* decision involved a Louisiana butcher monopoly law: *Reese* and *Cruickshank* presented questions that dealt directly with the post-War amendments as they related to the protection of the rights of blacks in the South.

After initial hearings, the Court continued the cases for further argument in October 1875. A month later, the Court agreed to affirm the lower court judgments in each case, thus overturning the convictions of both sets of defendants. They also agreed to keep the grounds of the decisions so narrow as to "not have any intimation in the opinion upon the constitutional questions" raised. The chief justice assigned Justice Clifford to write the opinion on that basis. On November 20, the Court rejected Clifford's draft, and Waite himself assumed responsibility for preparing the final opinions. Three months later, the Court approved Waite's version, and the decisions were announced together on March 27, 1876.

In *Reese*, the Supreme Court declared Sections Three and Four of the May 1870 Enforcement Act unconstitutional. The key issue confronted by the Court's opinion was whether the two sections went beyond the "appropriate legislation" necessary to enforce the provisions of the Fifteenth Amendment. Waite did not deny Congress's power to provide for such legislation. On the contrary, he stated, "Rights and immunities created by or dependent upon the Constitution of the United States can be protected by Congress. The form and the manner of the protection may be such as Congress, in the legitimate exercise of its legislative discretion shall provide."

The problem, according to Waite, was that the Fifteenth Amendment "does not confer the right of suffrage upon anyone." What it does do is prevent the states from discriminating or "giving preference" in the exercise of franchise rights on account of race or color. The statutes in question had gone beyond that protection and were so "general" in their import as to be beyond both the intention and the powers of Congress. They encroached upon the traditional right of states to determine voter qualifications for their own citizens. Given the generality of the statutes, it might have been possible for the Court itself to limit their meaning and scope by reading racial motivation into them, as the government's attorneys had suggested. This Waite declined to do, since it would "substitute the judicial for the legislative department of government." Having decided that Congress had not as yet legislated against the crimes charged in the indictments (i.e., discrimination based on race), the lower court was correct in finding the indictments faulty and giving judgment for the defendants.

In a lone dissenting opinion, Justice Hunt pointed out that the majority had ignored the constitutional issues at stake and based its opinion on a narrow and inaccurate reading of the statutes. The purpose of the Enforcement Act as a whole, insisted Hunt, was to protect blacks against violations of their right to vote. This purpose was clearly set forth in the first two sections of the act, which made explicit reference to race as the basis for the crimes set forth. While Sections Three and Four did not specifically mention race, the crimes listed concluded with the words "as aforesaid," referring back to the first two sections in which race and the Fifteenth Amendment were mentioned. In other words, the majority had seen fit to throw out part of an act as a way of notifying Congress that "unless it crossed every 't' and dotted every 'i' the Court would not sustain its civil rights legislation."

Waite's opinion in *Cruikshank* reached an even more narrow conclusion than did the *Reese* opinion. The Court reversed the convictions of the defendants, without voiding the relevant sections of the Enforcement Act. Waite admitted that the right to assemble peacefully was an attribute of national citizenship which Congress, under the Fifteenth Amendment, was empowered to protect from infringement on account of race. Congress in fact had done this in Section Six of the Enforcement Act under review.

The crucial issue was whether the indictments under which defendants had been prosecuted were sufficient in law to the extent that they set forth the same elements of the crimes committed as the crimes proscribed in Section Six of the act. The Court ruled that they did not, since the indictments failed to allege that the murders in Grant Parish were committed because of the victims' race. "We may suspect that race was the cause of the hostility," Waite concluded, "but it is not so averred." For the Supreme Court, this flaw was fatal to the indictments. Moreover, the omission was one of substance and not form, making the indictments so "defective" as to be useless in supporting a conviction based on them.

Court fears of negative public and congressional reactions to the decisions proved groundless. Northerners who had condemned the Grant Parish Massacre made no outcry, and the Republican press actually approved of the way the Court reached its decision. Southerners and Democrats praised the decision and went so far as to compare the recently appointed Waite with the great chief justices of the past, such as John Marshall and Roger B. Taney.

Most twentieth-century constitutional scholars have concluded that the decisions left the federal laws "almost wholly ineffective to protect the Negro. . . ." The two cases were part of a series of Supreme Court rulings in the late nineteenth century that limited the effectiveness of the Fourteenth and Fifteenth Amendments in protecting the civil and political rights of Southern blacks. Moreover, by placing strict limits on federal authority, the Court signaled Southern states, by now back in the hands of the Democratic party, that they were essentially free to do what they would with their own citizens. For Southern states, this meant the establishment by law of "Jim Crow" segregation and the virtually complete disfranchisement of black voters.

A careful reading of the opinions and their immediate impact suggests an alternative view. In one case, only two sections out of a comprehensive body of legislation were voided, and in the other case only the indictments were dismissed by the Court. This hardly constituted a total rejection of national authority. Furthermore, prior to the Court's announcement of the decisions, Congress incorporated both sections voided in *Reese*, along with the rest of the Enforcement Acts, as part of the new federal revised statutes. The new sections were more specific than the original ones, but were still based on the Fifteenth Amendment. In 1883, Virginia Circuit Court Judge Hugh Bond upheld a conviction based on these statutes. A year later, the Supreme Court upheld a series of convictions based on the same laws and, in the process, the Court issued a strong affirmation of federal authority to protect voters in federal elections. Until most of the legislation was repealed by Congress in the 1890s, federal Justice Department officials continued to bring prosecutions in the South under these statutes.

The Supreme Court's decisions in *Reese* and *Cruikshank* represented an attempt to "preserve federalism" as it had come to be understood by the 1870s. On one hand, this meant acceptance of a strong national authority, confirmed by the Civil War and Reconstruction, while at the same time it also meant recognition of the limits of that power in deference to state authority and the political realities necessary for sectional reconciliation. The price was high, for it meant that those like the perpetrators of the Grant Parish murders and Hiram Reese went unpunished. The "heritage of sanctioned congressional power" to protect the voting rights of blacks in the South would remain dormant for another 90 years, to be revived with the struggles and achievements of the civil rights movement of the 1950s and 1960s. In that sense, it is not surprising that the sections of the Enforcement Acts reviewed by the Supreme Court in 1867 could be found in almost identical wording and form in the opening sections of the Voting Rights Act passed by Congress in 1965.

Selected Bibliography

Benedict, M.L. "Preventing Federalism: Reconstruction and the Waite Court." *The Supreme Court Review* (1978): 39–79.

Cummings, H., and C. McFarland. *Federal Justice: Chapters in the History of Justice and the Federal Executive.* New York: The Macmillan Co., 1937.

Fairman, C. *Reconstruction and Reunion, 1864–88, Part Two.* New York: The Macmillan Co., 1987.

Goldman, R.M. "A 'Free Ballot and a Fair Count': The Department of Justice and the Enforcement of Voting Rights in the South, 1877–93." Ph.D. dissertation, Michigan State University, 1976.

Kaczorowski, R.J. *The Politics of Judicial Interpretations: The Federal Courts, Department of Justice and Civil Rights, 1866–76.* New York: Oceana Publications, 1985.

Magrath, C.P. *Morrison R. Waite: The Triumph of Character.* New York: The Macmillan Co., 1963.

Warren, C. *The Supreme Court in United States History.* Vol. 2. Boston: Little Brown & Co., 1922.

CIVIL RIGHTS OR LAST RITES?

by Jonathan Lurie
Department of History
Rutgers University at Newark

Civil Rights Cases, 109 U.S. 3 (1883) [U.S. Supreme Court]

The several cases decided together under the collective title of the *Civil Rights Cases* represent an epilogue to the Civil War era. The 1883 decision concerned the constitutionality of the Civil Rights Act of 1875, the last civil rights statute of the Reconstruction. Understanding its significance requires discussion of events between 1861 and 1883.

The Civil War began in 1861 as an attempt to prevent an illegal act: secession on the part of several Southern states. By 1865, however, the conflict had become one of freedom for the slave, as well as restoration of the Union. President Abraham Lincoln had not intended this result. "I claim," he wrote, "not to have controlled events, but confess plainly that events have controlled me." After four years of internal carnage, the intangible goal of a permanent Union merged with the very tangible aim of abolitionism.

The North strongly supported freedom for the slaves as reflected in the Thirteenth Amendment. Yet, the issue of exactly what this freedom involved represented (and remains) a much more difficult challenge. For many Northerners, racial antipathy toward blacks seemed fully compatible with their strong pro-Union and antislavery sentiments. In no way did they envisage abolition as providing social equality within a newly integrated society. Nor did the great majority believe that the traditional operation of federalism, with the states assuming "local control of the character of daily experience" would change with a Union victory. This strong belief in traditional federalism, coupled with a very real and deep-seated streak of Northern racism represented a truly potent obstacle toward new national efforts at racial integration. Given the rapidly shifting political currents after 1865, a variety of motives—reconciliation, revenge, restoration, reconstruction, racism, and republicanism—was in evidence.

It is unclear how Lincoln would have handled the awesome challenge of integrating the ex-slave into the American polity; although there is no doubt of his racial conservatism. It is clear that his sudden death deprived the Union of consummate political leadership—skills notably absent in his successor Andrew Johnson, a southern Unionist with a traditional racial bias. Others in the Republican party, especially Massachusetts Senator Charles Sumner, took a much more radical stand, calling for total racial equality in public facilities, including public schools. To be sure, Sumner and his supporters were always in the minority. But he persisted, much to the discomfiture of the Republican party as a whole. From 1867 until his death seven years later, Sumner continually sought to have a civil rights act providing for such equality enacted into law. The fact that such a statute was not passed while he lived indicated the racial ambivalence of the Reconstruction era.

This ambivalence was also reflected in the Fourteenth Amendment, sent to the states by Congress for ratification in 1866. Although intended to provide some federal protection for the ex-slave, the first section of the amendment (and the only section of major constitutional significance) made no mention either of equality or of political and civil rights. It forbade the states from making any law "which shall abridge the privileges and immunities of citizens of the United States," and it further held that no state could "deprive any person of life, liberty, or property, without due process of law; nor deny to any person within its jurisdiction the equal protection of the laws." Another section gave Congress power to enforce, "by appropriate legislation," the provisions of the new amendment.

The Supreme Court first interpreted this amendment in 1873 in the famous *Slaughterhouse Cases*, a dispute that appeared in no way to involve ex-slaves. For a bare majority of the Court, Justice Samuel F. Miller held that the amendment protected only federal privileges and immunities of U.S. citizens, and that these did not include what was usually referred to as "civil rights or liberties." For protection of these rights, one had to look to the state for relief, as had been primarily the case since adoption of the federal Constitution. In other words, the majority was unwilling to hold that American federalism had itself been fundamentally reconstructed during the Civil War era.

The decision gravely troubled politicians, like Sumner, who had assumed that the new amendment provided protection to the former slaves from improper state, and possibly even private, action. One possible solution to the problems posed by the interpretation of the Constitution in the *Slaughterhouse Cases* might be a federal statute that would specify the rights that states had to protect. Here, Sumner confronted the racial ambivalence of members of his party, many of whom did not favor legislation that named specific rights as, for example, public school integration. But some members of Congress were equally unwilling (by voting against such a measure) to indicate support for segregation. The ideal solution from their point of view was to do nothing. Against such pragmatic prejudice, Sumner's eloquence was inspirational but ineffectual.

In 1872, Sumner argued that emphasis on separate facilities was in reality a fake substitute for equality, a "contrivance by which a transcendent right, involving a transcendent duty is evaded." There can be, he insisted, "no substitute for equality; nothing but itself. Even if accommodations are the same, as notoriously they are not, there is no equality. In the process of substitution the vital elixir exhales and escapes. It is lost and cannot be recovered; for equality is found only in equality."

More than the racial ambiguity noted above explains Sumner's failure to gain this legislation he considered so vital. By 1872, the Republican party had split over the issue of a second term for President Ulysses S. Grant, under whose leadership the presidency had evolved, according to Henry Adams, to a level that would have upset even Darwin. Sumner and other "liberal Republicans" had supported a third-party candidate in 1872, with issues focusing on budgets and corruption, not on blacks and civil rights. Soundly trounced in the election, Sumner's wing had even less influence within the party after 1872 than the little it had enjoyed before. To make matters worse, the Democrats, who as a national party were even more opposed to racial progress than the Republicans, won enough congressional seats in the mid-term elections of 1874 to control the House—something that had not happened since before the Civil War.

Given these facts, one might have expected that the lame-duck session of Congress that convened in December 1874 would do nothing in the area of civil rights. In fact, their congressional defeat may have galvanized the Republicans into a belated if not final attempt to gather support on behalf of Southern blacks. Moreover, Sumner's death in March 1874 could now justify as a memorial tribute the legislation to which he had devoted the last years of his political career. Finally, Republicans, while far less sympathetic to issues of integration than Sumner had been, had to admit that there was a need for some sort of federal statute. Benjamin Butler noted, for example, that the Supreme Court's decision in *Slaughterhouse* "allowed the nation to protect American citizens anywhere in the world except in the states." Thus, for a variety of reasons, the Republicans tried to enact a civil rights law.

The result, accomplished only through traditional political methods of compromise, all-night sessions, and lengthy partisan wrangling was far from what Sumner had sought. It held that "all persons were entitled to the full and equal enjoyment of public accommodations in inns, transportation facilities, and places of public amusement." The statute made no mention of public schools, and thus in reality was more a mockery than a memorial to Sumner. Indeed, "the widely understood assumption that the measure would never operate effectively was the reason the bill had passed." Accepted by the Senate without change, President Grant signed the bill into law on March 1, 1875, without comment.

Contemporary reaction to the new statute confirmed that little positive value was to be expected from it. According to the *Baltimore*

Sun, the law "represented buncombe, pure and simple." *Harper's Weekly* observed correctly that shorn of application to public schools, the bill "indirectly sanctioned the very prejudice it was intended to combat." The *Southern Law Journal* commented "that such a law can be practically enforced . . . no intelligent person of either race or color believes." The *Mobile Register* called the statute "infamous, tyrannical, malicious, insolent," and added for good measure that it was unconstitutional as well. Privately, Supreme Court Justice Joseph P. Bradley agreed.

He drew a distinction between protecting one's privileges as a citizen—an appropriate area for federal intervention—and matters of social preference—an inappropriate area for federal legislation. Between 1875 and 1876, Bradley recorded his thinking on the 1875 statute. He stated: "Surely Congress cannot guarantee to the colored people admission to every place of gathering and amusement. To deprive white people of the right of choosing their own company would be to introduce another kind of slavery. The civil rights bill [of 1866] had already guaranteed to the blacks the right of buying, selling and holding property, and of equal protection of the laws. Are not these the essentials of freedom?"

For Bradley, and probably the vast majority of white Americans, to ask such a question was to answer it. He insisted further that "[it] never can be endured that the white shall be compelled to lodge and eat and sit with the negro. The latter can have his freedom and all legal and essential privileges without that. The antipathy of race cannot be crushed and annihilated by legal enactment. The Constitutional amendments [referring to the Thirteenth, Fourteenth, and Fifteenth Amendments] were never intended to aim at such an impossibility." Bradley concluded his statement by emphasizing that "surely it is no deprivation of civil rights to give each race the right to choose their own company." Thus, Bradley had formulated his own distinct viewpoint about the inappropriateness if not unconstitutionality of the 1875 law, soon after it was enacted. His views should be kept in mind, for what he wrote privately would later appear publicly as the opinion for

the Court in the *Civil Rights Cases,* handed down in 1883.

It is not clear why the Supreme Court waited until 1883 to consider the Civil Rights Act of 1875. There is no doubt that the longer it waited, the more sentiment in favor of racial integration dissipated. A desire for national reconciliation and growing Northern willingness to concede that Southern attitudes toward blacks were not very different from their own seemed more important. Moreover, the famous "Compromise of 1876" that ensured the election of Republican Rutherford Hayes in 1877, also ensured white control of the Deep South and reinforced the view that the era of active involvement by the federal government in protecting the civil rights of black Americans had ended.

The *Civil Rights Cases* that the Court decided in 1883 actually consisted of five separate suits. Four were the result of federal criminal indictments, while one was an action brought by a black plaintiff for damages against a Southern railroad because she had been refused access to the "ladies" car. Perhaps reflecting an assumption that the statute was constitutionally insignificant, the defendants in the criminal cases did not even bother to file briefs before the Court. Such was not the case for the federal government, nor for the plaintiff against the Memphis and Charleston Railroad.

In separate briefs, both the U.S. government and its solicitor general asserted the constitutionality of the 1875 civil rights statute. The "business to be carried on [in theatres and hotels] is quasi public in its nature, and for the general accommodation of the people." Because it was thus a public right, appropriate federal legislation "may be raised to meet the necessities of the particular right to be protected." Freedom from racial discrimination by private owners serving the public had become a "right" of federal citizenship, and "what the United States had the right to give, it necessarily has the right and duty to preserve and protect."

The solicitor general emphasized that the conduct of innkeepers and passenger carriers was frequently "a mere reflection of the views of the community." Their action "testifies to and at the same time tends to enlarge, a particular current in *public opinion*, and this in its

turn is fruitful of *public, i.e. State* institutions."
A problem could arise if this opinion was contrary to the national will as reflected by Congress. *"Is it not a mere matter of legislation discretion to decide upon the stage of growths at which it will be best to suppress such vegetation?"* [Emphasis in original brief.]

The counsel for the black passenger noted that his case "involves the rights of a citizen of one State travelling [via public carrier] through another State, for the purpose of reaching a place in a third State." Existing constitutional authority, such as the interstate commerce clause, "leave[s] very little room for argument." In other words, this attorney did not feel it necessary to rely on the Fourteenth Amendment as the constitutional basis for the 1875 statute. Rather, he insisted that it could be justified by well-established legal precedents. He added, however, that the civil rights law did give the right to "the full and equal enjoyment" of the *"very same"* [his emphasis] accommodations enjoyed by other persons similarly circumstanced.

By a vote of 8–1, the Supreme Court, speaking through Justice Joseph P. Bradley gutted the 1875 statute. Bradley based his opinion on a disarmingly simple proposition, one that Justice John Marshall Harlan in dissent described as "a subtle and ingenious verbal criticism." It was "state action of a particular character that is prohibited" by the Fourteenth Amendment. Congress could indeed adopt legislation to correct "the effects of such prohibited state laws and state Acts," but that was the full extent of congressional authority. "And so . . . until some state law has been passed or some state action through its officers and agents has been taken, adverse to the rights of citizens . . . no legislation of the United States under [the Fourteenth Amendment] . . . can be called into activity."

Bradley conceded that Congress did indeed possess the power to redress conditions of slavery or servitude, but he insisted that "the refusal to any persons of the accommodations of an inn or a public conveyance or a place of public amusement, by an individual and without any sanction or support from any state law or regulation" did not "inflict upon such persons any manner of servitude, or form of slavery, as those terms are understood in this coun-

try." Therefore, Congress had no authority on which to enact this statute. Well reflecting the racial realities of 1883, which Bradley strongly supported, the justice claimed that "it would be running the slavery argument into the ground, to make it apply to every act of discrimination which a person may see fit to make as to the guests he will entertain, or as to the people he will take into his coach or cab or car, or admit to his concert or theatre, or deal with in other matters of intercourse or business."

Almost 20 years after the end of the Civil War, Bradley concluded that "there must be some stage in the process of the [ex-slave's] elevation when he takes the rank of a mere citizen, and ceases to be a special favorite of the laws. . . ." In truth, many free blacks "were not admitted to all the privileges enjoyed by white citizens," yet they possessed "all the essential rights of life, liberty and property." Because private discrimination was not barred by the Fourteenth Amendment, no congressional power had existed on which to construct the 1875 law. Hence, it was unconstitutional.

Justice Harlan, a former slave owner, found Bradley's conclusions unwarranted, unconvincing, unfortunate, and inaccurate. He emphasized that it was state approval if not state action through issuance of a license that enabled an innkeeper or theatre proprietor or railroad operator to function in the first place. Such private property when affected with a public interest ceased to be purely private property. Here, Harlan quoted Chief Justice Morrison R. Waite in the famous case *Munn v. Illinois* (1876). When one uses his property for a purpose in which the public has an interest, "he, in effect, grants to the public an interest in that use and must submit to be controlled by the public for the common good to the extent of the interest he has thus created." Bradley, it might be noted strongly supported *Munn*, and indeed had aided Waite in formulating this argument.

Since there could be no doubt that such private enterprises as inns, theatres, and railroads were thus clothed with a public interest, they were legitimate subjects for state regulation. Furthermore, if Congress had the power to abolish slavery, why could it not also forbid private discrimination "based merely upon race or color" in public conveyances, inns, and places of public amusement? For Harlan, Bradley's insistence on state action as the required trigger for federal intervention was more than fulfilled by the obvious fact that proprietors of these types of businesses could not operate without state sanction, either in the form of a corporate charter (common to the railroads,) or a state license (common to inns and places of public entertainment).

Harlan, no less a child of his era than Bradley, also conceded that government "has nothing to do with social, as distinguished from technically legal rights of individuals. . . . Whether one person will permit or maintain social relations with another is a matter with which government has no concern." Indeed, "for even upon grounds of race, no legal right of a citizen is violated by the refusal of others to maintain merely social relations with him." But the actions involved in these cases were from individuals or corporations "wielding power under state authority for the public benefit or the public convenience." They were far from mere social relations.

Finally, Harlan emphasized a point made by federal attorneys in the briefs submitted to the Court. Under the Fourteenth Amendment, Congress had an affirmative power to intervene to "guard, secure and protect" a constitutionally protected right. Unlike Bradley, Harlan saw both affirmative and prohibitive provisions within its mandate. It was "a grave misconception to suppose" that the enforcement section "has reference exclusively to express prohibitions upon state laws or state action."

Harlan may have had the better argument, but Bradley had the votes. Harlan spoke alone, and for the most part contemporary reaction to the decision strongly supported Bradley's position. Perhaps this was because the 1875 statute had had virtually no effect on existing discrimination. The *Chicago Tribune* had called the measure harmless, but unnecessary; while the *Nation* had described it as both "amusing," and an example of "tea-table nonsense." In 1883, the *Nation* observed that the "calm" with which the country accepted Bradley's conclusions revealed "how completely the extravagant expectations . . . of the war have died out." The great majority of those who voted for the law "knew

very well," according to the writer, "that whenever it came before the Supreme Court it would be torn to pieces." Actually, it may be that the law was never effectively enforced at all, even between 1875 and 1883.

The *Civil Rights Cases* and the weakened statute that inspired them illustrate that law is frequently an accurate reflection of the society from which it comes. A logical corollary to Bradley's reasoning would be to permit a state requirement of separate but equal facilities, while denying that such action violated the Fourteenth Amendment. The Court took this step in *Plessy v. Ferguson* (1896). Again, Justice Harlan dissented, and again he spoke alone. *Plessy*, however, was unanimously overruled in 1954. On the other hand, two problems raised in Bradley's 1883 decision continue to plague American public policy in the late twentieth century.

In terms of civil rights, American constitutional doctrine still confronts the twin challenges of affirmative action and state action. To what extent does the Constitution permit private discrimination based on race? To what extent can the legal order use the force of law to affirmatively redress such discrimination? Indeed, does the public community have any obligation to pursue affirmative action as a matter of public policy? Or must it merely correct discrimination that has already occurred? Where does one draw the line between private discrimination and discrimination somehow sanctioned by state action? Much U.S. constitutional history since 1883 has focused on these questions. If one seeks the ways in which American society has answered them, one only has to look around.

Selected Bibliography

Brown, B.W. "The Civil Rights Act of 1875." *Western Political Quarterly* 18 (1965): 763–75.

Donald, D.H. *Charles Sumner and the Rights of Man.* New York: Alfred A. Knopf, 1970.

Fairman, C. *Reconstruction and Reunion, 1864–88, Part Two.* New York: The Macmillan Co., 1963.

Gillette, W. *Retreat From Reconstruction.* Baton Rouge, LA: Louisiana State University Press, 1979.

Hyman, H.M., and W.M. Wiecek. *Equal Justice Under Law: Constitutional Development 1835–75.* New York: Harper & Row, 1982.

Kelly, A.H. "The Congressional Controversy Over School Segregation." *American Historical Review* 64 (1959): 537–63.

Lurie, J. "Mr. Justice Bradley: A Reassessment." *Seton Hall Law Review* 16 (1986): 343–75.

———. *Law and the Nation, 1865–1912.* New York: Alfred A. Knopf, 1983.

McPherson, J.M. "Abolitionists and the Civil Rights Act of 1875." *Journal of American History* 52 (1965): 493–510.

SEPARATE BUT EQUAL APPROVED

by Robert P. Green, Jr.
Department of Elementary and Secondary Education
Clemson University

Plessy v. Ferguson, 163 U.S. 537 (1896) [U.S. Supreme Court]

On June 7, 1892, Homer Adolph Plessy, a light-skinned black, boarded an East Louisiana Railway train and took a seat designated for whites. When asked by the conductor to move to the "colored" car, he refused and was immediately arrested. Tried before Judge John H. Ferguson of the Criminal District Court for the Parish of New Orleans, Plessy was found guilty of violating an 1890 Louisiana statute entitled An Act to Promote the Comfort of Passengers. Plessy's appeal of Ferguson's decision ended up before the U.S. Supreme Court, where, in 1896, the High Court's decision profoundly influenced judicial application of the Fourteenth Amendment to the Constitution, permitting the practice of racial segregation in "separate but equal" facilities.

The Louisiana statute under which Plessy was tried stated that "all railway companies carrying passengers in their coaches in this State, shall provide equal but separate accommodations for the white, and colored, races, by providing two or more passenger coaches for each passenger train, or by dividing the passenger coaches by a partition so as to secure separate accommodations." Passengers who refused to cooperate with railroad officials charged with implementing the statute faced a possible $25 fine or a sentence of up to 20 days in jail. Before Ferguson, Plessy argued that this law denied his privileges and immunities and violated the equal protection clause of the Fourteenth Amendment. Ferguson rejected this argument, as did, on appeal, the Louisiana Supreme Court. The Louisiana chief justice, however, granted

Plessy's petition for a writ of error, allowing his case to be heard by the U.S. Supreme Court. The Court's opinion in *Plessy v. Ferguson* culminated a process that for over 20 years had chipped away at the original meaning of the Fourteenth Amendment.

Proposed in June 1866 and ratified in 1868, the Fourteenth Amendment was an attempt to ensure the basic rights of U.S. citizenship to the newly freed slaves. Mainly designed as a response to the development of the infamous "Black Codes" in the South after the Civil War (i.e., state laws that returned freedmen to virtual slave status), the first section of the amendment declared: "All persons born or naturalized in the United States, and subject to the jurisdiction thereof, are citizens of the United States and of the State wherein they reside. No State shall make or enforce any law which shall abridge the privileges or immunities of citizens of the United States; nor shall any State deprive any person of life, liberty, or property, without due process of law; nor deny to any person within its jurisdiction the equal protection of the laws."

The historical record clearly shows that the Fourteenth Amendment was adopted to protect the civil rights of freedmen. Proposed during the height of tension between Congress and President Andrew Johnson over Reconstruction, the amendment was designed to remove questions of constitutionality raised by acts like the Civil Rights Act of 1866. That act, passed over the president's veto, recognized the citizenship of persons born in the United States, guaranteed them certain rights and privileges, and provided penalties when any person, because of color or race, was deprived of those protected rights. Many believed, as did President Johnson, that acts like the Civil Rights Act infringed upon state sovereignty and were unconstitutional. Johnson, for example, argued that such measures would lead to "an absorption and assumption of power by the general government which, if acquiesced in, must sap and destroy our federative system of limited powers and break down the barriers which preserve the rights of the states." Proponents of the Fourteenth Amendment and potential enabling legislation, such as John A. Bingham of Ohio, believed that the amendment's language would resolve any constitutional issue. Through it, they believed, the national government would become the protector of individual civil rights. That, however, would prove not to be the case.

Almost from the beginning, the Supreme Court's interpretation of the Fourteenth Amendment undermined its original intent. In the *Slaughterhouse Cases* (1873), Justice Samuel F. Miller, writing for the Court, drew a distinction between United States and state citizenship as treated in the amendment. The first sentence, he argued, clearly gave citizenship to the freedmen, but in the second sentence, "the distinction between citizenship of the United States and the citizenship of a State is clearly recognized and established. . . . It is quite clear, then, that there is a citizenship of the United States, and a citizenship of a State, which are distinct from each other. . . ." Despite the obvious history of the amendment, Miller argued that it was "not the purpose of the Fourteenth Amendment . . . to transfer the security and protection of . . . civil rights . . . from the states to the federal government." Rather, the intent had been to place national rights under the protection of the federal government, and "those fundamental civil rights for the security and establishment of which organized society is instituted" under the care of the state. What, then, were the rights the amendment was designed to protect? They were such rights as the right to vote in federal elections, the right to go to the seat of government and gain access to federal buildings, and the right to petition the federal government for redress of grievances.

Even that paltry list of rights was soon undermined by the Supreme Court. For example, Chief Justice Waite argued for the Court in *United States v. Cruikshank* (1876) that "the right of suffrage is not a necessary attribute of national citizenship" and that the Fourteenth Amendment protected only individual rights— life, liberty, privileges, immunities, due process of law, and equal protection of the laws—when a state deprived citizens of those rights, not when citizens deprived other citizens of those rights. The fact that the state had failed to guarantee the rights of one group of its citizens against another remained an issue for the state. It was not a matter for the federal courts.

The reasoning in *Cruikshank* was reinforced a few years later in the *Civil Rights Cases* (1883). In the face of a growing number of reported instances of discrimination against blacks, Republican leadership pushed the Civil Rights Act of 1875 through Congress. Given the understanding that John Bingham and Charles Sumner (who had died in 1874) had of Section 5 of the Fourteenth Amendment, stating that "Congress shall have power to enforce, by appropriate legislation, the provisions of this article," the Civil Rights Act would seem to have been an appropriate action on the part of the national government. Section 1 of that act declared that "all persons within the jurisdiction of the United States shall be entitled to the full and equal enjoyment of the accommodations . . . of inns, public conveyances on land or water, theaters and other places of public amusement; subject only to the conditions and limitations established by law, and applicable alike to citizens of every race or color." In the *Civil Rights Cases*, the Court reviewed a number of discrimination cases originating in violations of this law. Writing for the Court, Justice Joseph P. Bradley argued that the Civil Rights Act exceeded the authority of Congress under the Fourteenth Amendment and was thus unconstitutional. The Fourteenth Amendment, he argued, was designed to address state deprivations of rights and was not meant to encompass individual acts of discrimination.

Why had the Court retreated from defense of the freedmen? Evidently the nation had tired of the turmoil surrounding Civil War and Reconstruction. Its attention had shifted to other matters, and the Court reflected that trend. Many of the older "Radical Republicans" had passed from the political scene, and concern over such issues as economic growth and government reform captured the attention of those who remained. Popular pseudo-scientific theories purporting to explain racial differences—to the discredit of anyone of non-Teutonic stock—tended to reinforce doubts concerning the assimilation of blacks into the broader society. Social theory based on these and other "scientific" ideas suggested that government should avoid involvement in society and allow the "fittest" to succeed and survive. These changes were reflected in the Court's decision in the *Civil Rights Cases* when Bradley argued that the time had come when the black American no longer needed to be "a special favorite of the law" and instead should take on the "rank of a mere citizen." Unfortunately, this decision came at the very time when Southern politicians were beginning to rediscover and exploit racial fear and the call for white supremacy in shaping electoral majorities.

It was in this atmosphere that Louisiana passed its statute to provide for the "comfort of passengers" on its railways. In the early 1890s, however, blacks refused to be cowed by their losses, and the black community in New Orleans—composed of many men and women of culture and learning—decided to challenge the new state statute. Evidence suggests that the Plessy incident was planned in advance, with the cooperation of the East Louisiana Railway. In any event, the black community sought a test case over the issue, and *Plessy* provided just such a vehicle.

Plessy's case was argued before the Court by attorney Albion Tourgee, a well-known novelist who, as a carpetbagger, had been a leader of the North Carolina Radical Republicans during Reconstruction. Tourgee argued that the law in question was incompatible with the Fourteenth Amendment. Pointing out that it served only to perpetuate distinctions "coincident with the institution of slavery," Tourgee rejected the argument that the concept of "separate but equal" was, indeed, equal and impartial. Rather, he argued, "the object of such a law is simply to debase and distinguish against the inferior race. . . . Its object is to separate the

Negroes from the whites in public conveyances for the gratification and recognition of the sentiment of white superiority and white supremacy of right and power. . . ." Decrying the obvious intent of the law, he declared in an oft-quoted passage, "Justice is pictured blind and her daughter, the Law, ought at least to be color blind."

The Court did not render its decision until 1896. In the interim, the pace of "Jim Crow" legislation quickened in the South as conservatives, frightened by Populist gains built in part upon black and poor white political solidarity, more frantically exploited racial fears. They were soon joined in the practice by their erstwhile white opponents. The segregation, disfranchisement, and lynching of blacks spread. The Supreme Court's decision in *Plessy* acquiesced in these developments.

On May 18, 1896, Justice Henry Billings Brown delivered the opinion of a near-unanimous Court. Focusing on interpretation of the Fourteenth Amendment as central to the issue, Brown cited the distinction that the Court had earlier made in the *Slaughterhouse Cases* between "the rights and immunities of citizens of the United States, as distinguished from those of citizens of the States" and sought to clarify the kinds of rights protected from hostile state legislation. He concluded: "The object of the amendment was undoubtedly to enforce the absolute equality of the two races before the law, but in the nature of things it could not have been intended to abolish distinctions based upon color, or to enforce social, as distinguished from political equality, or a commingling of the two races upon terms unsatisfactory to either. Laws permitting, and even requiring, their separation in places where they are liable to be brought into contact do not necessarily imply the inferiority of either race to the other, and have been generally, if not universally, recognized as within the competency of the state legislatures in the exercise of their police power."

In support of this new distinction between political and social rights, Brown cited cases that protected the political rights of blacks (like the right to sit upon juries) and those (both judicial and legislative) that ostensibly recognized or sustained segregation. The case, then, developed to a question of the "reasonableness" of the Louisiana action. But, in determining the question of reasonableness, argued Brown, the legislature "is at liberty to act with reference to the established usages, customs and traditions of the people, and with a view to the promotion of their comfort, and the preservation of the public peace and good order." Gauged by that standard, Brown opined, "[W]e cannot say that a law which authorized or even requires the separation of the two races in public conveyances is unreasonable. . . ."

Adding insult to injury, Brown came to an incredible—and from today's perspective, disingenuous—conclusion: "We consider the underlying fallacy of the plaintiff's argument to consist in the assumption that the enforced separation of the two races stamps the colored race with a badge of inferiority. If this be so, it is not by reason of anything found in the act, but solely because the colored race chooses to put that construction upon it."

Brown's opinion for the Court ignored the historical origin of the Civil War amendments and the political atmosphere under which segregation laws were passed. He cited cases as precedent that had only the most superficial relationship to the issue at hand. For example, in support of his point concerning the common nature of the state sanction of segregation, he cited the Massachusetts Supreme Judicial Court case *Roberts v. Boston* (1849). That case arose when, in the late 1840s, the family of a black child, Sarah Roberts, argued that city maintenance of a separate school for blacks violated her rights under the state constitution. Attorney Charles Sumner argued for the plaintiffs that not only was the school inferior to those maintained for whites, but also that the segregation of black children "branded a whole race with the stigma of inferiority and degradation." Segregation based on some reasonable relationship to the educational endeavor—by age, sex, intellectual capacity—might be justifiable, but segregation by race was not. Such discrimination stigmatized the minority while it "hardened" the hearts of the white children. Despite Sumner's eloquence, Chief Justice Lemuel Shaw upheld the city's discriminatory policy. While the case was cited as precedent in many later decisions, its relevance to *Plessy* was questionable at best because it was decided before the

Fourteenth Amendment became part of the Constitution. Other "precedents" cited by Brown had little or nothing to do with the issue of equal protection under the Fourteenth Amendment.

The lone voice of dissent to the majority opinion in *Plessy* was that of John Marshall Harlan of Kentucky, the "Great Dissenter." Harlan, who had ironically once been a slave owner, argued that the Louisiana statute at issue was clearly a violation of the Civil War amendments. Accepting the reasoning of Tourgee and rejecting the idea that the law was not discriminatory because it applied equally to both races, he wrote, "Every one knows that the statute in question had its origin in the purpose . . . to exclude colored people from coaches occupied by or assigned to white persons. . . . The thing to accomplish was, under the guise of giving equal accommodation for white and blacks, to compel the latter to keep to themselves while traveling in railroad passenger coaches. . . . The fundamental objection, therefore, to the statute is that it interferes with the personal freedom of citizens. . . ." He continued eloquently: "Our constitution is color-blind, and neither knows nor tolerates classes among citizens. In respect of civil rights, all citizens are equal before the law. The humblest is the peer of the most powerful. The law regards man as man, and takes no account of his surroundings, or of his color when his civil rights as guaranteed by the supreme law of the land are involved. . . . We boast of the freedom enjoyed by our people above all other peoples. But it is difficult to reconcile that boast with a state of law which, practically, puts the brand of servitude and degradation upon a large class of our fellow citizens—our equals before the law. The thin disguise of 'equal' accommodations for passengers in railroad coaches will not mislead any one, nor atone for the wrong this day done."

With a great deal of prescience, Harlan predicted that "the judgment this day rendered will, in time, prove to be quite as pernicious as the decision made by this tribunal in the *Dred Scott* case. . . . The present decision, it may well be apprehended, will not only stimulate aggressions, but will encourage the belief that it is possible, by means of state enactments, to defeat the beneficent purposes which the people of the United States had in view when they adopted the recent amendments of the Constitution. . . ." As the sad history of race relations in the United States attests, it would be nearly 60 years before the Court would begin to undo the "pernicious" effects of its decision in *Plessy v. Ferguson.*

Selected Bibliography

Kluger, R. *Simple Justice: The History of* Brown v. Board of Education *and Black America's Struggle for Equality.* New York: Alfred A. Knopf, 1975.

LaMorte, M.W. *School Law: Cases and Concepts.* Englewood Cliffs, NJ: Prentice Hall, 1982.

Lurie, J. *Law and the Nation, 1865–1912.* New York: Alfred A. Knopf, 1983.

Woodward, C.V. *The Strange Career of Jim Crow.* 3d ed. New York: Oxford University Press, 1974.

RACE, LAW, AND GENDER IN SOUTH CAROLINA

by H. Lewis Suggs
Department of History
Clemson University

South Carolina v. Lowman (1927) [South Carolina state court]

There is a fine distinction between murder and lynching. For an act of violence to qualify as a lynching, several factors must occur in concert. First, a group of three or more must have participated and the group must have acted under the pretext of service to justice, race, or tradition. Moreover, the victim's body must have been found or other legal evidence must prove that the victim was killed.

Based on the above characteristics of a lynching, the event that resulted in what became known as "the *Lowman Case*" in South Carolina in the late 1920s was clearly a lynching. It was not unusual for a southern mob in the 1920s to lynch a black male accused of a capital offense such as rape or murder. But the *Lowman Case* is different for two reasons. First, a black woman was lynched. Therefore, re-marked, black intellectual W.E.B. DuBois, "there can be no mention of the usual crime." He characterized the lynching as "a black stain upon the American South . . ." And inasmuch as DuBois at the time was editor of the *Crisis*, the official organ for the National Association for the Advancement of Colored People (NAACP), his opinion probably mirrored that of other black intellectuals. Next, unlike other lynchings, the perpetuators of the violence did not go unnoticed. The governor of South Caro-

lina and other high officials not only condemned the lynching but also used their power to pursue a grand jury indictment.

The facts leading to this uncharacteristic resolution commenced on April 25, 1925, when Aiken County Sheriff Henry Howard and deputies Nollie Robinson, A. D. Sheppard, and Robert McElheney visited the home of Sam Lowman, a black tenant farmer, to investigate charges of bootlegging. As the sheriff approached Lowman's home on foot, he observed Lowman's wife, Annie, age 55, and her daughter Bertha working in the backyard. Annie was making soap in an iron pot; Bertha was sweeping the yard with a home-made brush broom.

When Bertha observed four white men in "civilian dress" approaching the house, she reflected on an incident two weeks earlier in which her brother Demon had been severely beaten by several robed and hooded Klansmen. She quietly alerted her mother to the presence of the armed and unfamiliar men in civilian dress. As Bertha and her mother attempted to retreat to their farm house, the men drew their weapons and ran toward the house. Sheriff Howard stopped Bertha within a few feet of the back door and began to pistol whip her as he ordered her to "stand back." Meanwhile, Annie hit him with an ax handle. In retaliation for the attack on Howard, Deputy Sheriff Nollie Robinson, "emptied his gun into Annie Lowman's body."

As Annie "crumpled" to the ground in what Walter White, the executive director of the NAACP, later termed, "a lifeless heap," her son Demon and her nephew Clarence arrived on the scene. An exchange of gunfire occurred between the Lowmans and Sheriff Howard and his deputies. Within seconds, Annie and the sheriff lay dead. Bertha was seriously wounded by shots in her breast and abdomen. Her brother Demon and her cousin Clarence lay gravely wounded as well.

Almost immediately, Bertha, Demon, and Clarence were arrested and housed in the Aiken County jail. Sam Lowman, the father, who was away at a local mill when the shootings occurred, returned home to find himself a widower and his two children and his nephew seriously wounded. Three days later, three-fourths of a quart of liquor was found buried in the yard of the Lowman home. Sam Lowman was arrested, tried, and sentenced to two years on the chain gang. Meanwhile, rumors persisted that the Ku Klux Klan was going to lynch the Lowman children. For their safety, although seriously injured, Bertha and Demon were transferred to the state prison in Columbia, South Carolina.

Approximately 200 Klansmen in full regalia attended Howard's funeral on April 25, 1925. And when the Lowman's trial began on May 12, 1925, an atmosphere of fear pervaded the courtroom and the Aiken community. And like the more famous Scottsboro cases of the 1930s, an "ugly mood" permeated the daily crowd outside of the courtroom.

The outcome of the trial of Bertha, Clarence, and Demon was never in doubt. The defense attorneys asserted that they were "assigned" to defend the Lowmans, and Judge H. F. Rice apologized to the jury for the defense attorneys. "Don't hold it against them because they defended these Negroes," Rice stated. "They were ordered by the court to take the case; the ethics of their profession force them to defend a man when the courts assign them such a task," he continued. "None of them wanted to do it."

The jury found Demon and Clarence guilty

of murder, and Price sentenced them to die on June 12, 1925. Although Bertha was found guilty of murder, Price sentenced her to life imprisonment because the jury had recommended mercy for her.

Meanwhile, in Columbia, South Carolina, newspaper accounts of the trial angered black attorney N. J. Frederick. He was outraged after examining the court's procedure and decided to appeal the Lowmans' convictions to the South Carolina Supreme Court. Inasmuch as South Carolina did not have an NAACP chapter until the mid-1930s, it is safe to assume that he consulted on strategy with Walter White, Executive Director of the NAACP, and NAACP officials in New York.

Frederick had three objectives. First, he wanted to save the Lowmans from execution. Next, he wished to use this travesty of justice to highlight inequities in the South's judicial system and, at the same time, to encourage a more palatable social and political atmosphere for what black journalist P. B. Young called "the South's proscribed people." A final objective was to exploit the case to organize an NAACP charter in Columbia, South Carolina. Even though the organization of an NAACP chapter seems inconsequential in the 1990s, in 1925 the NAACP was regarded as a subversive organization in communities throughout the South. NAACP chapters in Virginia, for example, were forced to use oral communication only to announce meetings. The NAACP met under the guise of the "Helping Hand Club" or some other fictitious or innocuous organization. The speaker was often a prominent minister from the North or an official of the NAACP.

Although a South Carolina black newspaper, *The Palmetto Leader*, dutifully reported the *Lowman Case*, there was no attempt to organize a defense fund or to sponsor a mass meeting in support of the Lowmans. Frederick, the Lowman's attorney, shouldered most of the burden of the defense, both personally and financially.

As the South Carolina Supreme Court deliberated on Frederick's motion for a new trial, the Klan held "a great celebration" on April 25, 1926, the anniversary of Sheriff Howard's death. The *State* newspaper reported that 1,500 people attended; eyewitnesses estimated the crowd at

4,000–5,000. Within days after the "great celebration," the state supreme court reversed the Lowmans' conviction and ordered a new trial on the grounds that the warrant was improperly drawn and executed. The court also rebuked Judge Rice for his unethical conduct and hostility to the prisoners in the first trial.

On October 6, 1926, the *State* newspaper headlined: "New Trial Opens in Lowman Case." The black attorney Frederick and L. G. Southard, a white attorney, whose grandfather had been a Confederate army general, presented the Lowmans' defense. Interestingly, the defense did not petition the court for a change of venue. When the trial began, attorneys Frederick and Southard hammered away at the prosecution's attempt to introduce evidence that the Lowmans had conspired to murder Howard. The defense also questioned the legality of the warrants and charged that Howard had trespassed on the property of a peaceable, law-abiding family. Besides, argued Frederick, "A man's home is his castle." The Lowmans, he continued, had every legal and human right to repel invaders of that home. Accordingly, one day after the trial began, the defense petitioned for a directed verdict of not guilty for the three defendants on the ground that the state had failed to prove an act of conspiracy.

On October 7, 1926, the state judge in the *Lowman Case* directed a verdict of not guilty against Demon, the principal defendant, but denied the petitions of Bertha and Clarence. Demon was immediately rearrested on a charge of assault and battery and was returned to the Aiken County Jail along with Bertha and Clarence. Although both court and law enforcement officials had assured South Carolina Governor Thomas McLeod, who called several times during the trial, that there was "no danger of any violence," they were wrong.

On October 9, 1926, the *State* headlined: "Negro Prisoners Lynched at Aiken." Apparently, several Aiken County whites felt a need to avenge Howard's death. Also, Howard's detractors were angered by the presence and the cross-examination of witnesses by black attorney Frederick. An embarrassed and angry Governor McLeod lamented, "I regret it exceedingly more than I can express." The prosecutor

and the jury foreman demanded a thorough investigation.

Upon his ascendancy to the governorship in 1927, John G. Richards termed the Lowman lynching "a miscarriage of justice." He promised to stand for the "majesty of the law." And in his inaugural address of January 1927, he promised the South Carolina electorate that "if it lies within my power, the Aiken Lynchers shall be brought to justice." The governor's remarks were applauded by the Commission on Interracial Cooperation, a liberal southern organization, and by white editors in South Carolina who expressed anger over the Aiken lynching. In scathing editorials, white publishers demanded that the lynchers be tried and convicted for what the Columbia (South Carolina) *Record* called, "one of the most bestial crimes that has ever happened in our state." The Spartanburg *Herald* called the lynching a "murderous defiance of the law by a few men," while the Charleston *News and Courier* urged Governor Richards "to defend the state's honor."

Vigilant NAACP publicity efforts kept the story of the Loman lynching before the South Carolina public. In particular, black newspapers carried numerous stories about this "typical Southern tragedy." Nevertheless, justice was not served. Although several lynchers were identified and ordered before an Aiken grand jury, no true bill of indictment was returned against any of the accused.

In March 1927, a man whom the Palmetto *Leader* characterized as "a man of sorrow," left for Philadelphia, Pennsylvania. Sam Lowman had served all but 72 days of his sentence on the charge of bootlegging. But his real crime was that he was the father of Demon and Bertha. When asked why he was leaving the South, Lowman replied: "I can't live among these people."

Selected Bibliography

Brown, R.M. *Strain of Violence.* New York: Oxford University Press, Inc., 1975.

Smith, L. *Killers of the Dream.* New York: W.W. Norton & Co., Inc., 1949.

Suggs, H.L. *The Black Press in the South, 1865–1979.* Westport, CT: Greenwood Press, 1983.

Zangrado, R.L. *The NAACP Crusade Against Lynching, 1909–50.* Philadelphia: Temple University Press, 1980.

JUSTICE VINDICATED: THE CASE
OF WILLIAM HARPER

by H. Lewis Suggs
Department of History
Clemson University

Virginia v. Harper, (1931) [Virginia state court]

One of the most unusual cases in Southern legal history is that of William L. Harper. Like the much more publicized cases of the same era involving other defendants—the Scottsboro Nine, Angelo Herndon, and Claude Neal—Harper involved a black man accused of raping a white southern woman. All record the failure of the South's criminal justice system. Each provoked intense national indignation and became a rallying point for the struggle to push antilynching and civil rights legislation through Congress. What distinguished *Harper* is that the defendant was acquitted by a southern trial court.

Harper began on January 7, 1931, when Dorothy Skaggs, a young white resident of Portsmouth, Virginia, claimed that she was raped in Upton Lane in the city of Norfolk. The following day, William Harper, a Negro arrested on an unrelated misdemeanor, confessed to the crime. In his original confession, Harper acknowledged that he had waited for Skaggs in Upton Lane, "hit her in the stomach," and started "messing with her." He also admitted that he took $1.50 from her pocketbook. At the time, the Norfolk police described Harper's crime to a reporter from the Norfolk *Virginian-Pilot*, who was present during Harper's interrogation, as one of "the most daring and brutal acts" in Norfolk's history. The Norfolk paper later reported that Skaggs was "hysterical" and confined to bed with a badly bruised body.

Harper's family had retained W. H. Land, a black Norfolk attorney to defend Harper on the assault charge. Land noted that Harper was "not of normal mentality" and asked the court for a "continuance" and for time to investigate. However, after Harper's confession and indictment for rape, Land withdrew from the case, and the court appointed a white attorney, William H. Starkey, to represent Harper. Starkey later emerged as one of Harper's strongest defenders; however, at the time, he indicated that he was "not anxious" to defend a Negro and that he would not oppose Harper's scheduled trial date of January 15, 1931.

Harper was declared "sane" by three court-appointed physicians on January 12, 1931. When his trial finally began on Wednesday, January 28, 1931, spectators were prohibited from attending. The Norfolk *Journal and Guide*, a black weekly, was the black community's only source of information on the trial. The judge instructed the jurors to find Harper guilty if they determined that he possessed the capacity to distinguish morally right and wrong and understood the nature, character, and consequences of his act. Apparently, the jury was convinced of Harper's guilt, for they found him guilty on Thursday, January 29, 1931, and fixed his punishment at death. The case might have slipped into obscurity had it not been for the efforts of Harper's white attorney, Starkey, and P. B. Young, Sr., publisher of the *Journal and Guide*. Because of their interest, the Harper-Skaggs controversy became one of the most historic and celebrated cases in Norfolk and tidewater Virginia.

Shortly after Harper's trial, Starkey immediately introduced a motion for a new trial on the basis of "after discovered evidence." Starkey presented to the Norfolk court affidavits from Rex and Virginia Rogers, who maintained that they were knowledgeable of Skaggs's "habits and customs" and that it was impossible for her to have been in Norfolk between 6:30 and 6:45 on the night of January 6, 1931. The Rogers's affidavits called Skaggs testimony "false, perjured, without foundation, and wholly and completely designed to injure Harper." On the strength of the affidavits, Judge Allan R.

Hanckel, "set aside" Harper's conviction and ordered a new trial.

During the interim period, the Norfolk branch of the National Association for the Advancement of Colored People (NAACP) and the *Journal and Guide* began organizing a defense fund for Harper. The national NAACP saw *Harper* as an excellent opportunity to resurrect its dormant Norfolk chapter, to increase black Virginians' lackadaisical support of the NAACP, and to enhance the struggle for blacks to serve on juries in Virginia.

Young had organized the Norfolk chapter of the NAACP in 1917. But, by 1925, it was inactive due to internal bickering and a lack of confidence in Young's leadership. Young and his friends saw *Harper* as a unique opportunity to unite a divided black community, to reestablish Young's reputation as an "able and safe" Negro leader, and to enlarge the circulation of the *Journal and Guide.*

Although it was not unusual in the South for a black man "without friends or funds" to receive a death sentence for sexually assaulting a white female, many whites were skeptical of the charge. And after Harper was found guilty by an all-white jury, the white citizens of Norfolk and Portsmouth, in the words of Young, "revolted at the prospect of a legal lynching." They were concerned because an innocent man was being sent to the electric chair. John Jordan, a Portsmouth native, and former editor-in-chief of the *Journal and Guide*, recalled that in an unusual display of interracial cooperation, both whites and blacks labeled Harper's case "a frame-up" and supported the *Journal and Guide*'s call for "a careful inquiry" and a new trial.

In an action virtually unprecedented in the South between the two World Wars, the Virginian legal system acceded to pressure brought by those outraged with the conviction of a black man on the charge of raping a white woman. A new trial was ordered, which began on March 5, 1931. At this trial, white citizens in the vicinity of Upton Lane testified that they neither saw an attack nor heard cries for help during the time of the alleged assault. A strong point for the defense was the testimony by the police, which noted that on the night in question, Upton Lane was patrolled three times between

6:30 p.m. and 11:00 p.m., and "no victim was laying there." Furthermore, it was proved that Skaggs was a woman of questionable character. Several whites testified that at the time of the alleged attack, Skaggs was with her lover at the Caroon Dance Hall in Elizabeth City, North Carolina. Even her lover, W. P. Kidd, testified that he accompanied her to North Carolina the night of January 6, 1931, and returned at 6:00 a.m. the following day. Skaggs's landlords, Rex and Virginia Rogers testified that Skaggs "suffered from delusions," drank heavily, and once claimed that she had been "kidnapped." D. K. Howard, a prominent white physician, testified that he found "no bruises" or other evidence that Skaggs was "attacked or roughly handled." In fact, more than 100 defense witnesses eventually came forward to testify on Harper's behalf.

Meanwhile, Skaggs sat beside her Navy husband and frequently dabbed tears from her eyes with a handkerchief. The prosecution characterized her as "an example of a fine Southern woman" who was "wantonly attacked by an imbecilic black brute." And when Skaggs took the stand to describe how Harper, who was only 5 feet, 6 inches tall, had assaulted her, spectators were again barred from the courtroom.

Later, the trial judge reminded the jury that they were not bound to consider the evidence as "equally balanced." Moreover, he noted, the credibility of a witness was "exclusively" the duty of a jury to decide, and that a jury had the right to determine from the appearance of witnesses "their candor and fairness." More important, the judge explained that Harper was presumed to be innocent, and the burden of proof was upon the state. Also, he continued, if reasonable doubt existed, Harper must be acquitted. The judge asked the jury to take into account Harper's mental capacity, the embarrassment occasioned by his arrest and confinement, and the prospect of execution or a long term of imprisonment.

After 35 minutes of deliberations, on Thursday, March 5, 1931, an all-white male jury found Harper not guilty. The *Journal and Guide*, which maintained reporters inside the courtroom throughout both trials, called the judge "absolutely fair" and Harper's acquittal an act of "justice vindicated." Harper was released from police custody and Starkey was later paid $25 from Norfolk's treasury.

Had the *Harper* case ended at this point, it would have been only an anomaly in Southern justice. However, it did not. Within a few weeks, it evolved into one of the most complicated cases in Virginia' judicial history.

Shortly after Harper's acquittal, Skaggs was indicted by an all-white male grand jury for perjury. At the same time, Harper was indicted for robbing Skaggs of the $1.50 in her pocketbook. In June 1931, Skaggs was tried in Norfolk's Corporation Court No. 1. During the trial, Catherine Ketchum, a white female Portsmouth resident, testified that Skaggs arrived at her home on January 6, 1931, at 11:00 p.m. and remained until the next day. Ketchum's testimony was rebutted by numerous white witnesses who observed that Skaggs had arrived the following morning, January 7, 1931, about 7:00 a.m. Skaggs was found guilty and sentenced to five years in prison. Interestingly, within weeks of Skaggs's conviction, Ketchum was indicted for perjury. After a week of testimony, the *Ketchum* case went to the jury. But the jury could not agree on a verdict and a mistrial was declared. On the second day of the Ketchum trial, Starkey, who had defended Harper in the first trial, announced his candidacy for the state Senate at the suggestion of "a number of personal friends."

The second trial of Skaggs for perjury began on September 15, 1931, in Norfolk. But unlike the first perjury trial, the jury was empaneled from Norfolk instead of Newport News. Verbal clashes and intense heat marked the Skaggs's second trial. Men were forced to keep on their coats "to preserve dignity in the temple of justice." Spectators listened intensely to testimony that many had heard four times before. Harper's confession was deemed "irrelevant." Interestingly, the defense did not call Skaggs to testify. After one full week of testimony, Skaggs was acquitted of perjury. Shortly after, the state prosecutor dropped robbery charges against Harper and indicated that he would not prosecute Ketchum again.

Thus, one of the most curious legal battles in southern history came to a close. The Harper-Skaggs legal controversy opened a new chapter in the administration of southern justice by alerting whites to the dubious nature of what the *Journal and Guide* called "Negro-Did-It" crimes.

Selected Bibliography

Bardolph, R. *The Civil Rights Record: Black Americans and the Law, 1849–1970.* New York: Thomas Y. Crowell Co., 1970.

Buni, A. *Robert L. Vann of the Pittsburgh Courier: Politics and Black Journalism.* Pittsburgh: University of Pittsburgh Press, 1974.

Carter, D. *Scottsboro: A Tragedy of the American South.* New York: Oxford University Press, 1969.

Ely, J.W. Jr. *Ambivalent Legacy: A Legal History of the South.* Jackson, MS: University Press of Mississippi, 1984.

McGovern, J.R. *Anatomy of a Lynching: The Killing of Claude Neal.* Baton Rouge, LA: Louisiana State University Press, 1976.

Martin, C.H. *The Angelo Herndon Case and Southern Justice.* Baton Rouge, LA: Louisiana State University Press, 1976.

Suggs, H.L. *Black Press in the South, 1865–1979.* Westport, CT: Greenwood Press, 1983.

———. *P.B. Young Newspaperman: Race, Politics, and Journalism in the New South, 1910–62.* Charlottesville, VA: University of Virginia Press, 1988.

THE SCOTTSBORO CASES

by Robert F. Martin
Department of History
University of Northern Iowa

Powell v. Alabama, 287 U.S. 45 (1932); *Norris v. Alabama*, 294 U.S. 587 (1935)
[U.S. Supreme Court]

Early on the morning of March 25, 1931, a freight train pulled out of the railroad yards of Chattanooga, Tennessee, and wound its way westward out of the mountains toward Memphis. Like many other freights of the Depression era, it carried not only the usual load of raw materials and manufactured goods but also an illicit cargo of unemployed men and women in search of opportunity and adventure. As the train moved through the hills of northern Alabama, a fight broke out among some of the black and white youths on board. During the struggle, the black combatants forced most of the whites to leap from the gondola car in which they had sought shelter from the chill of the March wind.

By the time the train pulled into the station at Paint Rock, Alabama, news of the fight had reached the authorities there and they immediately began searching the cars for unauthorized personnel. The police rounded up 12 people, nine of whom were black youths ranging in age from 13 to 20. Two of the three whites discovered on the train were young white women from Huntsville who had reportedly been seeking work in the textile mills of Chattanooga and were now returning home. Victoria Price and Ruby Bates related a story that transformed a relatively inconsequential brawl among hoboes into a culturally and constitutionally significant incident.

Price and Bates charged that after having driven all but one of the white males from the gondola, their black companions had raped them. On the basis of this testimony, the authorities jailed the nine accused rapists—Haywood Patterson, Olen Montgomery, Clarence Norris, Willie Roberson, Andrew Wright, Ozie Powell, Eugene Williams, Charley Weems, and Leroy Wright—in Scottsboro, county seat of Jackson County.

As news of the alleged rapes spread throughout the county, a lynch mob bent on punishing those who had violated the virtue of the white women of the South gathered outside the jail. The courageous and determined efforts of the local sheriff, assisted after a few hours by a small contingent of Alabama national guardsmen, prevented the mob from seizing the prisoners. On March 31, less than a week after the arrests, a special session of the Jackson County grand jury indicted the nine black youths. Judge Alfred E. Hawkins appointed all seven members of the Scottsboro bar as council for the defense. Within a few days, however, all but one had excused themselves from service. Meanwhile, P. A. Stephens, a black physician of Chattanooga, read with concern newspaper accounts of developments in Scottsboro. Since four of the Alabama defendants were from Chattanooga, Stephens had little difficulty persuading the city's black ministerial alliance to assist in obtaining counsel for "the Scottsboro boys," as they were called by both their supporters and critics. The alliance secured the services of Stephen R. Roddy, a local attorney of modest ability who had represented members of the city's black community on several occasions.

Roddy appeared in Scottsboro on the morning of Monday, April 6, shortly before the trial began. Although he had been in town a few days earlier for the grand jury hearing, he had not previously met with his clients and was unfamiliar with both the details of the case and Alabama law. He was reluctant to assume responsibility for the defense of the nine youths until a 69-year-old Scottsboro attorney, Milo Moody, agreed to assist him.

The state chose to try Clarence Norris and Charley Weems first. In a tension-filled courthouse protected by Alabama national guardsmen, Roddy and Moody attempted to defend their clients by questioning the character and undermining the credibility of Price and Bates. Their tentative efforts were complicated by the dramatic testimony of Price and by the fact that Norris testified that while he had not been involved, he had seen the other eight defendants attack the two white women. The jury deliberated scarcely an hour before returning a verdict of guilty with the recommendation that the defendants be sentenced to death.

Patterson's trial was already underway when the jury reached its decision in the *Weems-Norris* case. The judge excused the *Patterson* jury from the courtroom while the verdict in the initial trial was rendered. However, the reaction of the spectators in the courtroom and that of the crowd waiting outside was so loud and enthusiastic that the *Patterson* jury could not escape hearing it. Roddy hoped to turn the unruly behavior of the spectators to the advantage of his client. Charging that the atmosphere surrounding the proceedings was so hostile and intimidating that Patterson could not receive a fair trial, he asked the judge to declare a mistrial. Hawkins denied the request and the trial proceeded, going to the jury at 11:00 a.m. the next day. Within a quarter hour later, the trial of Powell, Roberson, Andrew Wright, Williams, and Montgomery began. Less than 25 minutes later, the *Patterson* jury concluded its deliberations, and the proceedings were halted long enough for the court to hear the verdict of guilty with the recommendation of the death penalty.

The third trial resumed after lunch and went to the jury at 4:20 p.m. The remaining Scottsboro defendant, Leroy Wright, was only 13. Under Alabama law he could be tried only in a juvenile court unless the state brought waiver proceedings. Solicitor H. G. Bailey offered Roddy a deal. In exchange for a guilty plea, he would ask only for life imprisonment rather than the death penalty. Roddy refused, knowing that a guilty plea would mean forfeiture of the right of appeal. He did, however, agree to make his defense brief. Within an hour, this case too went to the jury. In his summation, Bailey asked for life imprisonment in view of the defendant's youth. The juries were unable to reach a decision until the next day. On Thursday morning, Powell, Robertson, Andrew Wright, Williams, and Montgomery were all

found guilty with the recommendation that they be sentenced to death. The jury in (Leroy) *Wright* was unable to reach a verdict, since seven of the 12 members wanted the death penalty in spite of the state's request for life imprisonment. Therefore, Hawkins declared a mistrial in the (Leroy) *Wright* case. Then, only four days after the trials had begun, he sentenced the remaining eight defendants to death.

The events that transpired in the Scottsboro courthouse in the spring of 1931 were merely the first scene of an ideological, cultural, and legal drama that unfolded before the nation throughout the remainder of the decade. During the late 1920s, the Communist party had begun laying plans to woo the black masses of the South. The leaders of the International Labor Defense (ILD), the legal arm of the party, recognized the potential value of the *Scottsboro Cases*. The ILD temporarily won the backing of the black ministers of Chattanooga and secured the services of George W. Chamlee, an able southern Tennessee lawyer, to represent the *Scottsboro* defendants.

The National Association for the Advancement of Colored People (NAACP), which might have been expected to take up the boys' cause, moved rather slowly. The association lacked reliable information about developments in Jackson County and was reluctant to risk its reputation by becoming involved in a sordid rape case. However, when NAACP Secretary Walter White learned of the ILD's involvement in the cases, he moved swiftly to thwart what he believed were Communist efforts to capitalize on the situation. The battle for control of the Scottsboro defense that followed was heated, bitter, and public. The NAACP charged that the ILD was merely using the Scottsboro boys as pawns in an ideological struggle for the hearts and minds of the South's black population. The ILD countered with the accusation that the NAACP was a reactionary tool of the white capitalist class and out of touch with the black masses.

The inexperienced, poorly educated defendants were confused and uncertain about who should represent them in the appellate process. During the summer and fall of 1931, they vacillated between the ILD and the NAACP. Although White engaged such able attorneys as

Clarence Darrow and Arthur Garfield Hays to help in the presentation of the case before the Alabama Supreme Court, by late 1931 the ILD had won the confidence of the defendants and their families and had gained control of the defense. The Alabama Supreme Court heard the Scottsboro appeals in early 1932. ILD attorney Joseph Brodsky, with the assistance of George Chamlee, presented the defense's case before the court. The two lawyers contended that the mob atmosphere surrounding the trials, the exclusion of blacks from the jury, the speed with which the verdicts were reached, and the lack of adequate counsel combined to deny the defendants a fair trial.

Attorney General Thomas G. Knight, son of one of the Alabama Supreme Court justices, responded to the defense case. He paid little attention to allegations of inadequate counsel or systematic exclusion of Negroes from jury service. Rather, he concentrated on the charge that the atmosphere surrounding the trial had been detrimental to the defendants. Brodsky had cited Oliver Wendell Holmes's dissent in the 1915 Leo Frank case (*Frank v. Mangum*) in which he had declared that a trial conducted in the midst of mob pressure was invalid. In responding to this reference to the eminent jurist, Knight declared, "I have the deepest reverence for Justice Holmes, but I wonder if he had lived a little closer to the South whether he would have written these decisions, had he known how jealously we have striven to uphold our rights and protect our womanhood."

The court's ruling on March 24, 1932, surprised no one. The majority of the justices upheld the sentences of seven of the eight defendants. They granted Williams a new trial on the ground that he had been a minor at the time of his conviction. The justices commended the speed with which the *Scottsboro* court had proceeded. They argued that the presence of Alabama guardsmen had guaranteed the defendants a fair trial. Contending that within limits, Alabama had the right to fix qualifications for jury service, the justices rejected the charge that the exclusion of Negroes from Jackson County juries had violated the Fourteenth Amendment or had in any way been detrimental to the defendants. Only Chief Justice Anderson dissented. He could find no single legal basis on which to ground a reversal but concluded that the weight of the collective evidence suggested that the ends of justice had not been served. After the ruling of the Alabama Supreme Court, the ILD retained Walter Pollak, a nationally known constitutional lawyer, and prepared to take the case of the Scottsboro defendants to the U.S. Supreme Court. Following a preliminary hearing on May 27, 1932, the High Court agreed to hear the appeal. The arguments presented five months later were much like those made before the Alabama high court with one notable difference. Pollak stressed the exclusion of Negroes from Alabama juries since the days of Reconstruction.

On November 7, 1932, the Supreme Court handed down its ruling in *Powell v. Alabama*. Justice George Sutherland, one of the most conservative of the justices, read the majority opinion. The Court did not address the socially volatile matter of the exclusion of blacks from Alabama juries. It concentrated instead on whether the defendants had been denied the right of counsel and if they had, whether this denial constituted a violation of the due process clause of the Fourteenth Amendment. Most of the justices considered the way in which counsel had been provided for the defendants to be unacceptable. It quickly became clear as Sutherland read the majority opinion that the Court was going to reverse the convictions on the ground of inadequate counsel, but the constitutional basis for the ruling was not immediately apparent.

The Sixth Amendment guaranteed the right to counsel, but the Supreme Court in *Hurtado v. California* (1884) had held that the defendant's right to due process in a state court did not necessarily include protections of the first eight amendments to the Constitution. The *Hurtado* Court described due process in vague terms and suggested that the people could establish new procedures as long as these were in "furtherance of the general public good." The Supreme Court was the ultimate judge of what constituted "furtherance of the general public good," and in *Gitlow v. New York* (1925), it had already begun to undermine the *Hurtado* ruling by extending the application of the First Amendment to the states. In *Powell v. Alabama*, it went a step further. After an extensive review of precedents, Sutherland asserted that the right to counsel had been so accepted by the states that it was now an integral part of due process. He maintained that the "right to have counsel appointed when necessary is a logical corollary from the constitutional right to be heard by counsel." Therefore, on the grounds that the Scottsboro defendants' guarantee of due process had been violated, their convictions were reversed and their cases remanded to the lower courts. For almost 50 years, the Court had used the due process clause of the Fourteenth Amendment to protect property rights and to obstruct state and federal economic regulatory efforts. Now, however, the justices were interpreting the Fourteenth Amendment in a way that was consistent with its original intent: protecting the civil rights of black Americans.

Justices Pierce Butler and James C. McReynolds dissented, arguing that the defendants had received a fair trial. Butler, who wrote the minority opinion, declared that even had there been a miscarriage of justice the Court's ruling marked "an extension of Federal authority into a field hitherto occupied exclusively by the several states." Legal authorities later maintained that *Powell v. Alabama* was indeed the first time that the U.S. Supreme Court had set aside a state criminal conviction on any grounds.

While many moderates hailed the Court's decision, radicals condemned it. The Communists charged that the Court had provided Alabama authorities with the means by which to engage in legal lynching. Some Socialists complained that the Court had avoided the socially significant issues raised by the case and had based its opinion on narrow legal grounds. Most white Southerners regarded the ruling as an unwarranted intrusion into their region's race relations.

As preparation for the new trial began, the ILD hired Samuel S. Leibowitz, an eminent criminal lawyer, to handle the Scottsboro defense. Leibowitz had little interest in the ideology of the ILD and tried to distance himself from the Communists, but he believed that the civil rights of the Scottsboro boys must be protected. ILD attorneys obtained a change of venue and the new trials were held in Decatur, Alabama, about 50 miles west of Scottsboro. The atmosphere there was not markedly different from that in Scottsboro. Nevertheless, the defense, although somewhat disappointed, hoped that the relocation of the proceedings would be beneficial to their clients.

When the first of the new trials, that of Patterson, began, Leibowitz tried to discredit the testimony of Price by questioning her character and revealing inconsistencies in her story. Leibowitz's treatment of Price as little more than a common prostitute was probably a mistake, because he failed to recognize the degree to which she had become a symbol of white southern womanhood. In spite of the contradictions in her testimony and the doubt that Leibowitz cast on her character, the jury and spectators remained convinced of the defendant's guilt. Patterson was convicted with a recommendation of the death sentence. However, the presiding judge, James Edwin Horton, Sr., had serious misgivings about the verdict. Discrepancies in Price's testimony, questions about the accuracy of the statements of some of the witnesses, and the fact that one of the doctors who had examined the two women told the judge privately that he doubted their story so troubled Horton that on June 22, 1933, he set aside the verdict and granted a new trial.

Attorney General Knight immediately announced that the state would retry Patterson as soon as possible. In November 1933, a new trial began. Horton had been removed from the case and replaced by Judge William Washington Callahan. From the outset Callahan appeared prejudiced against Patterson and the other defendants. He made it difficult for Leibowitz to challenge either the credibility or character of Price and Bates. The judge's bias was evident in his instructions to the jury. He initially failed to include the form for an acquittal. The judge's oversight was inconsequential, since the jury required little time before reaching a verdict of guilty with a recommendation of the death penalty. The trial of Norris was equally swift and his fate was the same as that of Patterson. Leibowitz asked for a postponement of the remaining trials, and a weary Callahan granted the request. The ILD appealed the Patterson and Norris convictions, but in June 1934, the Alabama Supreme Court refused to set aside the lower court's decisions.

During the summer of 1934, the ILD was caught attempting to bribe Price to change her testimony. When Leibowitz, who had been unaware of the effort, learned of it he was furious and accused the organization of having "assassinated" the Scottsboro boys. Leibowitz's public criticism of the ILD caused it to drop him from the defense on the grounds that he was inexperienced in constitutional appeals. Leibowitz then attempted to seize the case from the ILD. There followed another complicated tug-of-war over the Scottsboro boys. During October and November 1934, the frightened and confused young men changed their minds about whom they wished to represent them no less than five times. In October, a group consisting primarily of New York supporters of Leibowitz established the American Scottsboro Committee to champion the cause of the nine youths.

In early 1935, the Supreme Court agreed to hear appeals in the *Patterson* and *Norris* cases. To avoid undermining the defense, Leibowitz and the ILD worked out a compromise. Leibowitz and George Chamlee, who had now broken with the ILD, would represent Norris, while ILD attorneys Osmond Fraenkel and Walter Pollak would represent Patterson.

On February 15, 1935, Leibowitz appeared before the Supreme Court to begin presenting his case. He contended that his client had been denied a fair trial because, although Alabama law did not actually exclude Negroes from jury duty, they were in fact denied the right to serve. He charged that the roll books had been fraudulently altered to make it appear that Negroes were indeed eligible for jury service. Attorney General Knight argued that the small number of blacks serving on Alabama juries was not the result of discrimination but the consequence of a careful selection process.

In 1880, the Supreme Court ruled in *Strauder v. West Virginia* that any systematic exclusion of Negroes from jury service constituted a violation of the equal protection and due process clauses of the Fourteenth Amendment. Over the years, however, in several decisions the Court had emasculated this guarantee. On April 1, 1935, in *Norris v. Alabama*, the Court issued a dramatic reversal of the stance that had evolved over the previous half century.

Chief Justice Charles Evans Hughes delivered the majority opinion. The justices ruled that the exclusion of Negroes from jury service deprived a black person of equal protection of the law guaranteed by the Fourteenth Amendment. The Court contended that Alabama was guilty of systematic exclusion of black people from jury service and that local officials had attempted to conceal this fact by fraudulently tampering with the jury rolls. They rejected the contention of Alabama officials that there were no qualified jurors in Morgan County. Therefore, Norris's rights under the equal protection and due process clauses of the Fourteenth Amendment had been violated, and they overturned his conviction.

Patterson's case presented the Court with a problem. Although the point was debatable, the Alabama high court had ruled that the defense's bill of exceptions in the *Patterson* case had not been filed within the 90 days required by state law. The Supreme Court rarely overturned lower court decisions that were technically correct, but in this instance it was possible that, because of a technicality, one person might go free and another be executed on the same evidence. Without actually overturning the decision, the Court strongly suggested that the Alabama Supreme Court review its judgment in *Patterson*. Following the U.S. Supreme Court's ruling, yet another struggle for control of the Scottsboro defense developed between the ILD and the American Scottsboro Committee. Out of this contest eventually emerged a new, somewhat more stable and effective organization. On December 19, 1935, representatives of the NAACP, ILD, League for Industrial Democracy, American Civil Liberties Union, and Methodist Federation for Social Service established the Scottsboro Defense Committee, representing a broadly based coalition of individuals and groups interested in the fate of the nine black prisoners. Leibowitz, whose intemperate remarks about Alabama's system of justice had alienated many of the state's residents, continued to act as chief counsel but agreed to remain in the background while a prominent southern attorney played the primary role in the courtroom.

On November 13, 1935, a Jackson County grand jury consisting of 13 whites and one

Negro returned another indictment against the nine defendants. Judge Callahan announced that a new trial would begin on January 20, 1936. Patterson was tried first. As expected, the jury found him guilty but, to the surprise of everyone including the prosecution, recommended 75 years in prison. Although the defense was disappointed, the verdict represented something of a victory since it was rare, if not unprecedented, for a black man in the South to be convicted of raping a white woman and to escape the death penalty. The trial of the other eight defendants was postponed due to the illness of one of the state's witnesses.

During 1936, Alabama showed signs of a willingness to compromise on the *Scottsboro Cases*. In October, Governor Bibb Graves suggested that the youths plead guilty to the less serious charge of miscegenation. While the defense rejected this proposal, the attorneys were heartened that the state appeared willing to ask for less than the death penalty. On October 13, 1936, Clarence Watts, the southern lawyer retained by the Scottsboro Defense Committee to assist Leibowitz, met with Attorney General Carmichael and attempted to have all charges against Montgomery, Roberson, Williams, and Andrew Wright dropped. Watts indicated that if the state agreed to this proposal, the committee would then be willing to have the remaining five defendants plead guilty to a lesser charge, with the understanding that they would serve relatively short sentences. Carmichael told Watts that he would accept nothing less than a sentence of 20 years on a charge of rape for each of the youths.

Over the Christmas holidays of 1936, Knight and Carmichael visited Leibowitz in New York. They proposed to release some of the defendants if Norris, Patterson, and several others would plead guilty to rape. Leibowitz declined the offer, declaring that the defendants had told him on a number of occasions that they would rather die in the electric chair than confess to a crime they had not committed. Leibowitz offered to have the boys plead guilty to vagrancy or to the fight on the train. This compromise would enable the state to have a conviction while resulting in a minimal penalty for the boys.

In a later meeting in Washington, Leibowitz and Carmichael reached an agreement. Patterson's appeal was to be withdrawn. Powell would be tried only for assault on the deputy sheriff whom he had attacked. Weems, Andrew Wright, and Norris were to plead guilty to some form of assault. They would then receive sentences of less than five years. Eventually Patterson would be released so that his term in prison would be no longer than that of Weems, Andrew Wright, and Norris.

The Scottsboro Defense Committee was not happy with the compromise and threatened to reject it. Leibowitz did not like the arrangement either but warned the committee that the alternative might be death or life imprisonment, since the defendants' grounds for appeal were running out. The committee therefore agreed that it would neither endorse nor oppose the compromise.

However, for reasons that are not entirely clear, Alabama authorities seem to have had a change of heart. Judge Callahan announced that he intended to proceed with the trial of the remaining defendants, and in the summer of 1937 they found themselves in court again. In mid-July, Norris was tried for a third time. After only two and one-half hours of deliberation, the jury found him guilty and recommended the death penalty. When the trial of Andrew Wright began, there were hints that a compromise might still be in the offing. The prosecution announced that the state would not seek the death penalty. The proceedings were brief and the jury found Andrew Wright guilty and recommended 99 years in prison. In the subsequent trial of Weems, the state again failed to ask for the death penalty. Once again the jury convicted the defendant and sentenced him to a lengthy prison term. Powell was to be tried next, but the state announced that it was charging him not with rape but only with assault on a deputy sheriff, the penalty for which was 20 years. Powell pled guilty and received the maximum sentence.

Then, to the surprise of many observers, charges against Montgomery, Leroy Wright, Roberson, and Williams were dropped. The state contended that the fact that Roberson had a severe case of venereal disease and that Montgomery was nearly blind cast serious doubt on their guilt. Price's identification of them was apparently a matter of mistaken identity. In the case of Williams and Leroy Wright, one of whom was 12 and the other 13 at the time of the alleged crime, the state argued that the six and one-half years they had served in jail was sufficient punishment and agreed to release them on the condition that they leave Alabama and never return.

On October 26, 1937, the U.S. Supreme Court refused to review the conviction of Patterson. Defense attorneys knew that they had no better grounds on which to appeal the verdict in the *Norris*, *Weems*, and (Andrew) *Wright* cases and decided not to do so.

The Scottsboro Defense Committee hoped to persuade Governor Graves to pardon the remaining prisoners. Graves appeared sympathetic to the idea but indicated that he wished to allow the appeals process to run its course before taking any action. In mid-June 1938, the Alabama Supreme Court upheld the death sentence of Norris and the prison terms of Weems and Andrew Wright. Graves then commuted Norris's sentence to life imprisonment but made no move to free any of the Scottsboro boys. In August, the Alabama Parole Board met and refused to grant paroles to any of the prisoners. There was now considerable support in the Alabama press for clemency, and Governor Graves appeared ready to grant pardons in the fall. However, after a meeting with the Scottsboro boys during which they were quarrelsome and one was found to be carrying a homemade knife, the governor refused to pardon them. He reportedly concluded that the character and level of intelligence of the prisoners were such that they would be an embarrassment to all those who had come to their defense. This unfavorable impression may well have determined Graves's final decision, but some members of the Scottsboro Defense Committee also felt that he had begun to worry about the unfavorable political ramifications of a pardon for the controversial prisoners.

Over the next few years, negotiations continued between Alabama officials and those working on behalf of the Scottsboro boys. On several occasions, apparent compromises failed to materialize. Finally, on November 7, 1943, the Alabama Board of Pardons and Paroles released Weems, and in January also freed Norris and Andrew Wright on the condition that they would not leave the state. After working for some time for an Alabama lumber company for $13 a week, Norris and Andrew Wright fled the state, violating their parole. Allan Knight Chalmers, chairman of the Scottsboro Defense Committee, persuaded them to return to Alabama, believing that the state would give them another chance. However, the two young men were returned to prison. In late 1946, Powell was released and Norris was granted a second pardon. The parole board judged Patterson to be incorrigible and refused to parole him. In the summer of 1948, Patterson slipped away from a work gang and made his way north. Remaining in hiding for two years, he was finally arrested in Detroit. Michigan Governor G. Mennen Williams refused to extradite Patterson, and Alabama dropped extradition proceedings. In May 1950, the parole board unanimously agreed to grant Andrew Wright another pardon.

With Wright's release on June 9, 1950, a saga of injustice that had begun almost two decades earlier came to a rather anticlimactic end. The decision of nine young black southerners to catch a west-bound freight train on a cool spring morning in 1931 had a devastating impact on their lives but a salutary effect on the constitutional law of the United States. The experiences of the Scottsboro boys led the Supreme Court to substantially expand the scope of the due process clause of the Fourteenth Amendment and to challenge the *de facto* exclusion of blacks from the juries of the South.

Selected Bibliography

Carter, D.T. *Scottsboro: A Tragedy of the American South*. Rev. ed. Baton Rouge, LA: Louisiana State University Press, 1979.

Klehr, H. *The Heyday of American Communism*. New York: Basic Books, Inc., 1984.

Norris, C., and S.D. Washington. *The Last of the Scottsboro Boys*. New York: G.P. Putnam's Sons, 1979.

Record, W. *Race and Radicalism: The NAACP and the Communist Party in Conflict*. Ithaca, NY: Cornell University Press, 1964.

Zangrando, R.L. *The NAACP Crusade Against Lynching, 1909–50*. Philadelphia: Temple University Press, 1980.

SEPARATE EDUCATION IS NOT EQUAL EDUCATION

by Robert P. Green, Jr.
Department of Elementary and Secondary Education
Clemson University

Brown v. Board of Education, 347 U.S. 483 (1954) [U.S. Supreme Court]

On May 17, 1954, the U.S. Supreme Court issued a decision that many have described as its most dramatic and far-reaching of the twentieth century. In a unanimous opinion, the Court held that separate educational facilities were inherently unequal, that "in the field of public education the doctrine of 'separate but equal' has no place." With that decision, the Court overturned *Plessy v. Ferguson* (1896) and set the stage for further dramatic developments in the field of civil rights. The decision in *Brown v. Board of Education* was a moral victory in the realm of American ideals; it was a victory for black Americans in their attempt to promote racial justice; but more particularly, it was a legal victory for a bright and persevering group of black lawyers who convinced the Court to do what it is most hesitant to do, overturn long-standing precedent. The road to that victory, however, was both long and tortuous.

In *Plessy v. Ferguson*, the U.S. Supreme Court had reviewed a Louisiana statute requiring "separate but equal" accommodations in railway cars. Dismissing the argument that such legislation violated the equal protection clause of the Fourteenth Amendment, Justice Henry Billings Brown, writing for the Court, drew a distinction between "laws interfering with the political equality of the negro and those requiring the separation of the two races in schools, theatres and railway carriages." While the former clearly violated Fourteenth Amendment rights, the latter did not. Legislatures, he argued, are at "liberty to act with reference to the established usages, customs and traditions of the people, and with a view to the promotion of their comfort, and the preservation of the public peace and good order." In that context, the Louisiana law was not unreasonable and did not violate the rights of the minority. Reflecting the racial attitudes of his day, Justice Brown

went on to argue that "legislation is powerless to eradicate racial instincts or to abolish distinctions based upon physical differences. . . . If the civil and political rights of both races be equal one cannot be inferior to the other civilly or politically. If one race be inferior to the other socially, the Constitution of the United States cannot put them upon the same plane." In a lone voice of dissent, Justice John Marshall Harlan decried the "pernicious" nature of the majority decision and predicted that it would "stimulate aggressions, more or less brutal and irritating, upon the admitted rights of colored citizens, [and] encourage the belief that it is possible, by means of state enactments, to defeat the beneficent purposes which the people of the United States had in view when they adopted the [Civil War] amendments of the Constitution."

Justice Harlan could not have been more prescient, for the next three decades saw a litany of abuses—ranging from the "irritating" to the "brutal"—against the rights of black Americans. This was a period when racism ran rampant, fueled by pseudoscientific theories concerning racial differences. From popular cultural expressions such as Thomas Dixon, Jr.'s *The Clansman* (the basis for the 1915 movie, *The Birth of a Nation*) to academic tracts such as those from the pens of historian Ulrich Bonnell Phillips (*American Negro Slavery*) and political scientist William Graham Sumner (*Folkways*), racial stereotypes were abetted, blacks and their roles in and contributions to American society were disparaged. "Jim Crow" legislation flourished: separate railcars were followed by separate streetcars, restaurants, boardinghouses, public washrooms and water fountains, separate neighborhoods, and even separate ballparks. Discrimination spread to the workplace as blacks were retained in the most menial positions, in part because of their poor education (separate but equal was anything but equal) and in part because even the union movement discriminated against them.

But the darkest aspect of the story of the first quarter of the twentieth century was the sheer brutality that blacks frequently faced. Race riots (whites rioting against blacks) and lynchings claimed the lives of many innocent victims. The true flavor of the times can be captured only with a realization of the barbarisms to which blacks were periodically subjugated. Richard Kluger recounted one such incident: "[T]he South's ongoing disfigurement of the Negro as a human being reached the zenith of heartlessness during the summer of 1911 when one of the more barbaric lynchings of the era was literally staged in Livermore, Kentucky. A Negro charged with murdering a white man was seized and hauled to the local theater, where an audience was invited to witness his hanging. Receipts were to go to the murdered white man's family. To add interest to the benefit performance, seatholders in the orchestra were invited to empty their revolvers into the swaying black body while those in the gallery were restricted to a single shot. And so it happened. . . ."

Black educational opportunity was a particular victim of segregation and discrimination, a development that seemed to be fostered by Supreme Court decisions in the decades after *Plessy*. A series of decisions during the period saw "separate but equal" entrenched, but in a way that was both unequal and particularly discriminatory. In the late 1890s, Richmond County, Georgia, maintained three high schools: one for white boys, one for white girls, and one for blacks. When the student population at the black elementary school outgrew the accommodations there, the school board converted the black high school into another elementary institution, leaving black high school students without a school. Advised by the school board that they should send their children to church-sponsored schools, the protesting parents of the black high school students instead took their case to court, arguing that the white high school should be closed down as long as there was no black high school available. While the case appeared to be a clear violation of the

Plessy separate but equal doctrine, the courts treated only the demand of the plaintiffs that the white high school be closed. Thus, in *Cumming v. Richmond County Board of Education* (1899), the U.S. Supreme Court upheld the school board: "While all admit that the benefits and burdens of public taxation must be shared by citizens without discrimination against any class on account of their race, the education of people in schools maintained by state taxation is a matter belonging to the respective states, and any interference on the part of Federal authority with the management of such schools cannot be justified except in the case of a clear and unmistakable disregard of rights secured by the supreme law of the land. We have here no such case to be determined." Not only was segregation recognized in the *Cumming* decision, but clearly unequal facilities (in fact, the absence of facilities) were condoned.

Even more disturbing, however, was the Court's decision in *Berea College v. Kentucky* (1908). Berea College, a private institution, had held racially mixed classes since its incorporation in 1859. During the height of racist mania, however, Kentucky passed a law stating that an institution could teach members of both races at the same time only if classes were held separately at least 25 miles apart. Berea College sued, but the Court upheld the state, thus establishing a further precedent: not only did the states have the right to establish separate educational facilities, they also had the right to prohibit mixed facilities in institutions they had chartered—even when those institutions were private.

Finally, in *Gong Lum v. Rice* (1927), any question over the state's right to segregate "colored" children in its schools seemed ultimately put to rest. When Gong Lum, an American of Chinese descent living in Bolivar County, Mississippi, challenged the placement of his daughter in the county's obviously inferior black school by the white superintendent, the courts again upheld the school system. Lum had challenged his daughter's classification as "colored," but Chief Justice William Howard Taft, citing as precedent *Plessy* and *Cumming*, among other cases, wrote for the Supreme Court: "The right and power of the state to regulate the method of providing for the education of its youth at public expense is clear." Again, the federal courts would not intervene.

Inequities in educational policy simply mirrored inequities in other aspects of life. Just as blacks were segregated socially, even before the *Plessy* decision at least in the South, they were disfranchised politically. As the basic civil rights of blacks—tenuous at any time—eroded further, it was no wonder that resentment in the black community grew. Ray Stannard Baker captured some of that sentiment when he interviewed blacks for his *Following the Color Line* (1908): "How would you feel, if with our history, there came a time when, after speeches and papers and teachings, you acquired property and were educated, and were a fairly good man, it were impossible for you to walk the street (for whose maintenance you were taxed) with your sister without being in mortal fear of death if you resented any insult offered to her? How would you feel if you saw a governor, a mayor, a sheriff, whom you could not oppose at the polls, encourage by deed or word or both, a mob of 'best' and worst citizens to slaughter your people in the streets and in their own homes and in their places of business? Do you think that you could resist the same wrath that caused God to slay the Philistines and the Russians to throw bombs? I can resist it, but with each new outrage I am less able to resist it."

Yet even as resentment grew, blacks were beginning to address these ills. At the same time that oppression was greatest, changes were taking place in the black community. Traditionally a rural phenomenon, black communities were growing in urban areas of the South and the North. Like so many others seeking a better fate, blacks were driven from the land by hardship and drawn to the cities by perceptions of economic opportunity. In these urban, black communities, a new middle and professional class appeared, educated and ready to do battle against an unjust system. Here was the "Talented Tenth" for which W.E.B. DuBois had called.

From the black middle class, the backbone of the National Association for the Advancement of Colored People (NAACP) would be drawn. Formed in 1909 by both white sympathizers and black leaders like DuBois, the NAACP would play a leading role in the civil rights struggle ahead. Recognizing the need to support blacks in legal proceedings, the NAACP began early to take part in court cases involving Fourteenth and Fifteenth Amendment issues. During the 1920s, the NAACP's efforts met with mixed success, but more importantly during the period, bright young black lawyers became more and more involved in the association's work. Principal among these was Charles Houston, an Amherst Phi Beta Kappa and graduate of Harvard Law School, who was appointed dean of the Howard Law School in 1929. In the mid-1930s, Houston was appointed chief legal counsel in the NAACP's desegregation efforts. In that position, Houston attracted a number of sharp minds to the association's cause: William Hastie, later to become the nation's first black federal judge; James Nabrit, successor to Houston as dean of law, then president of Howard University; Ralph Bunche, later U.S. delegate to the United Nations; Spotswood Robinson, III, later a federal judge; and most significant of all, Thurgood Marshall, later to become the first black justice of the U.S. Supreme Court.

While throughout its early life, the NAACP had, in essence, been fighting a holding-action, a singular development in the 1920s provided the organization with funds to go on the offensive. In 1922, Charles Garland, son of a Boston millionaire, had devoted a substantial share of his inheritance to a fund for liberal causes. In 1929, the directors of that fund provided a grant of $100,000 to the NAACP to initiate a campaign "to give the Southern Negro his constitutional rights." Educational equality—obviously lacking in the most segregated states, where funding for black schools ranged from one-half to one-tenth that of white—was to have been a particular emphasis of the effort. In 1931, attorney Nathan Margold created a plan that would form the basis for the NAACP's effort over the next two decades. In essence, the Margold Plan called for a series of suits that would focus on the inequalities of facilities in segregated schools in the South, especially where they were habitually so, emphasizing, in particular, the absence of statutory requirements in the several states that such schools be equal. The Court, reasoned Margold, operating under the doctrine of separate but *equal*, would certainly force states to equalize funding for black schools.

The Margold Plan was conservative—it attempted only to enforce the principle of *Plessy*, not to challenge separation—but still had drawbacks. To address some of these shortcomings, Houston modified the plan to focus at first on graduate and professional schools. At that level, evidence of inequality was obvious. State-supported, black graduate and professional schools were nonexistent in the segregated states. Since the students involved were adults, white "sensibilities" would be least offended by black legal victories. Finally, Houston hoped that each victory would build on the next, establishing a series of precedents from which broader action might be pursued. During the next 15 years, the NAACP pursued the Margold Plan as modified by Houston, first under the direction of Houston himself, then, increasingly, through the efforts of Thurgood Marshall.

In February 1935, Donald Murray, a fully qualified black, was refused admission to the University of Maryland Law School on the grounds of his race. Maryland had a segregated system of higher education, but it had no law school for blacks. Rather, it had established partial scholarships for black students who wanted to pursue programs not offered by Maryland's black schools. In *Murray v. Maryland* (1936), Houston demonstrated that the partial scholarships were inadequate and that they would fail to provide a comparable education to that provided at the university. The Maryland Court of Appeals upheld a lower court ruling that Murray be admitted to the university's law school.

In a similar case in Missouri, Lloyd Lionel Gaines was rejected by the University of Missouri Law School. Missouri officials argued that he should apply to the state's institution of higher education for blacks, Lincoln University, where a black law school would, given his application, in time be established. Furthermore, a legal education equivalent to that offered at the University could be pursued by black students through an out-of-state tuition supplement. On appeal in *Missouri ex rel. Gaines v. Canada* (1938), the U.S. Supreme Court rejected the state's argument and ruled that Gaines be admitted to the university: "The basic consideration is not as to what sort of opportunities other states provide, or whether they are as good as those in Missouri, but as to what opportunities Missouri itself furnishes to white students and denies to Negroes solely upon the ground of color. The admissibility of laws separating the races in the enjoyment of privileges afforded by the State rests wholly upon the equality of the privileges which the laws give to the separated groups within the State. . . . By the operation of the laws of Missouri a privilege has been created for white law students which is denied to Negroes by reason of their race."

Early success in forcing equality within separate facilities laid the foundation for a broader argument against segregation, but roadblocks remained. In *Sipuel v. Oklahoma State Board of Regents* (1948), Marshall began to attack segregation itself: "Segregation in public education helps to preserve a caste system which is based upon race and color. It is designed and intended to perpetuate the slave tradition. . . . the terms 'separate' and 'equal' cannot be used conjunctively in a situation of this kind; there can be no separate equality." In *Sipuel*, however, the Court approved a jerry-built "law school" for the plaintiff.

Thus stimulated to further effort, Marshall consolidated earlier gains in *Sweatt v. Painter* and *McLaurin v. Oklahoma State Board of Regents*, both decided by the U.S. Supreme Court in 1950. In each case, the Court reviewed makeshift accommodations for the professional and graduate education of blacks. In *Sweatt*, the University of Texas Law School had denied admission to Herman Sweatt on the basis of race, but, to provide "equal" facilities, the state had created a "law school" in the basement of a downtown Austin office building. In *McLaurin*, George W. McLaurin was admitted to the University of Oklahoma to work on a doctorate in education, but he was segregated from the rest of the students: he was required to sit outside the regular classrooms, assigned a segregated desk in the library, and even required to sit at a separate table and dine at a different time in the university cafeteria.

Again, Marshall used the cases in an attempt to broaden the attack on segregation. In

Sweatt, Marshall called on Professor Robert Redfield, a distinguished University of Chicago anthropologist, to testify that modern anthropology had discarded the old arguments concerning racial differences, and that where they did exist they might readily be attributed to such factors as segregation itself. When the relevance of this line of testimony was challenged by the state's attorney, Marshall's thinking became apparent: "[W]e have a right to put in evidence to show that segregation statutes in the state of Texas and in any other state, actually when examined—and they have never been examined in any lawsuit that I know of yet— have no line of reasonableness. There is no understandable factual basis for classification by race, and under a long line of decisions by the Supreme Court, not on the question of negroes, but on the Fourteenth Amendment, all courts agree that if there is no rational basis for the classification, it is flat in the teeth of the Fourteenth Amendment." Later, when *Sweatt* was appealed to the Supreme Court, Marshall arranged for an *amicus curiae* ("friend of the court") brief on the part of the plaintiff by a coalition of law professors. That brief directly attacked the principle of separate but equal: "Laws which give equal protection are those which make no discrimination because of race in a sense that they make no distinction because of race." In *McLaurin*, Marshall's challenge to segregation was implicit in the case itself: McLaurin had been admitted to the white school, so on the face of it the facilities were equal. All that remained was the question of his segregation within the school.

Yet a unanimous Court took a narrow stand on both cases. Chief Justice Fred M. Vinson wrote, "Broader issues have been urged for our consideration, but we adhere to the principle of deciding constitutional questions only in the context of the particular case before the Court." Given the efforts of Texas to provide separate but "equal" facilities for Sweatt, Vinson wrote, "we cannot find substantial equality in the educational opportunities offered white and negro law students by the state." He continued: "What is more important, the University of Texas Law School possesses to a far greater degree those qualities which are incapable of objective measurement but which make for greatness in a law

school . . . reputation of the faculty, experience of the administration, position and influence of the alumni, standing in the community, traditions and prestige. It is difficult to believe that one who had a free choice between these law schools would consider the question close." Sweatt was ordered admitted to the University of Texas Law School. Given the restrictions placed on McLaurin, restrictions that clearly impaired "his ability to study, to engage in discussions and exchange views with other students, and, in general, to learn his profession," Vinson wrote: "State imposed restrictions which produce such inequalities cannot be sustained." Oklahoma had to remove such restrictions. The Court, however, refused to step beyond the confines of *Plessy*. Marshall and his colleagues had gone as far as they could with Houston's modification of the Margold Plan—separate facilities had clearly to be equal—but bolder legal action would be needed to attack segregation itself.

The time was ripe for bolder action. Despite continued outrages against the rights of blacks in many parts of the country, the nation was slowly moving away from old prejudices. In part, this movement was due to a new-found political power among black Americans. Black, urban communities had begun to wield some political power—albeit of a local nature—in the late 1920s, but during the 1930s black Americans became an important part of Franklin D. Roosevelt's coalition. In part it was due to two chief executives, Roosevelt and Harry Truman, who sympathized with black efforts for racial justice, and, through actions and appointments, began to move the vast federal machinery in their support. In part it was due to World War II. Black soldiers and sailors contributed to the military effort. Black industrial workers played an important role on the home front, increasing both economic and political power. But more important, the war was fought for democracy, against German totalitarianism and racism. The all-too-obvious contrast between America's ideology and the nation's treatment of black citizens spurred reform. And, finally, this movement was reinforced by developments in the social sciences showing that intelligence and educational performance were related much more closely to environmental factors than they were to race. Scientific research was undermining old racial stereotypes.

These changes were accompanied by a broad range of NAACP successes in the courts and dramatic moves on the part of the White House. In *Mitchell v. United States* (1941), the Supreme Court applied the principle achieved in *Gaines* to the railroads, requiring equality of facilities; in *Smith v. Allwright* (1944), the Court threw out the all-white election primary; in *Morgan v. Virginia* (1946), the Court struck down segregation on buses operating across state lines; and in *Shelley v. Kraemer* (1948), the Court held that while restrictive housing covenants were in themselves not illegal, such covenants could not be enforced by the state. At the same time, President Harry Truman aggressively pushed civil rights, asking Congress for action on a broad range of issues: antilynching laws, poll taxes, segregation in interstate transportation, discriminatory hiring practices, and, on the positive side, creation of a permanent civil rights commission. Requests for legislation were followed by executive orders ending racial discrimination in federal employment and in the armed forces. The time was indeed ripe for a bolder move against segregation in schooling, and, in 1950, Marshall announced that NAACP legal efforts would reflect just such a shift in emphasis.

The shift away from equalization within *Plessy* to an attack on the fundamental principle of *Plessy* was not without risk. Important precedents had been achieved with *Sweatt* and *McLaurin*, and clearly the Court would have to extend those principles to elementary and secondary education. Furthermore, the Court had repeatedly reconfirmed *Plessy*, had approved the state's "right" to classify students by race. The Supreme Court was exceedingly averse to overturning clear precedent, and if the Court chose not to overturn *Plessy*, black America's struggle for equality might set back for years. Marshall was quite aware of the risks he was taking and at times had second thoughts, but by late 1950 the die was cast. In a series of cases, the NAACP would challenge *Plessy*.

Four cases pursued by the NAACP would ultimately be decided by the Supreme Court in the decision known to history as *Brown v. Board of Education* (a fifth would also be included in

the decision, but it was not an association case). In each case, Marshall's strategy was twofold: first, the NAACP would attempt to show that segregated schools clearly were, and historically had been, unequal. Second, and more importantly, the association would argue that race was not a reasonable basis for the classification of students, that racial separation caused severe psychological damage and antisocial tendencies, and that segregation was, in fact, discriminatory and therefore in violation of the Fourteenth Amendment. The first element of the strategy was conservative, relying on *Sweatt* and *McLaurin*, the second challenged *Plessy* directly. In a controversial but most significant attempt to buttress that second element of the strategy, the NAACP in each case introduced the testimony of social scientists concerning the adverse effects of segregation. Holding out little hope for success at the state or district court level, the strategy was designed to build cases for appeal to the U.S. Supreme Court.

There was no clearer example of inequality in educational opportunities than that in Clarendon County, South Carolina. During the 1949–50 school term, the average expenditure for white students was $179; for blacks, $43. The valuation of 61 black schools (often no more than wooden shacks) housing 6,531 student was $194,575, that of 12 white schools (brick and stucco) housing 2,375 students was $673,850. The county provided no transportation for the black students, while busing was provided for whites. The average salary for white teachers was two-thirds more than that of blacks. There was also no clearer example of the racial prejudice that lay behind such inequality: the black minister/teacher who, in the late 1940s, had begun the effort for equal treatment that would ultimately end before the Supreme Court was fired from his job (along with his wife, two of his sisters, and a niece), physically threatened, sued, and convicted on trumped-up charges; he saw his house burned down and church stoned; and he was finally chased out of the county. Other blacks involved in the case received similar treatment. Undaunted, black plaintiffs, backed by the NAACP, sought an injunction abolishing segregation.

Briggs v. Elliott, the South Carolina case, was the first in which Marshall pursued his new strategy. The evidence of inequality was overwhelming, but the heart of the black case was the attack on *Plessy*. In support of that effort, Marshall introduced the testimony of witnesses such as social psychologist Kenneth Clark. Clark's ground-breaking research with "projection tests" using dolls suggested a detrimental effect of school segregation on personality development, the essence of which, according to Clark, was "a confusion in the child's concept of his own self-esteem—basic feelings of inferiority, conflict, confusion in his self-image, resentment, hostility towards himself, hostility towards whites. . . ." Nevertheless, the court denied the plaintiff's plea for an injunction. Judge John Parker wrote for the court: "[W]hen seventeen states and the Congress of the United States have for more than three quarters of a century required segregation of the races in the public schools, and when this has received the approval of the leading appellate courts of the country including the unanimous approval of the Supreme Court of the United States . . . it is late in the day to say that such segregation is violative of fundamental constitutional rights." However, the decision did require the school district to "promptly" provide equal educational facilities for the black students. It was an empty victory, and Marshall appealed.

Meanwhile, in Topeka, Kansas, black citizens sued to have their children enrolled in white grammar schools. The first name on the list of plaintiffs was that of Oliver Brown, so the case was entitled *Brown v. Board of Education*. Again, the NAACP attorneys pursued Marshall's strategy. Again, data suggesting inequality were presented (although to a much lesser degree than in the South Carolina case), and expert witnesses testified that "separate but equal" was a contradiction in terms. Again, the district court deferred to *Plessy*. This time, however, since the physical facilities of the white and black schools were deemed comparable, no relief was given the plaintiffs. Despite the loss, an important step was taken in the attempt to build a case for the Supreme Court. One of the "findings of fact" attached to the court's opinion was the following: "Segregation of white and colored children in public schools has a detrimental effect upon the colored children.

The impact is greater when it has the sanction of law; for the policy of separating the races is usually interpreted as denoting the inferiority of the Negro group. A sense of inferiority affects the motivation of a child to learn. Segregation with the sanction of law, therefore, has a tendency to retard the educational and mental development of Negro children and to deprive them of some of the benefits they would receive in a racially integrated school system." For the first time, a court had questioned Justice Henry Billings Brown's incredibly callous statement in *Plessy*: "We consider the underlying fallacy of the plaintiff's argument to consist in the assumption that the enforced separation of the two races stamps the colored race with a badge of inferiority. If this be so, it is not by reason of anything found in the act, but solely because the colored race chooses to put that construction upon it."

The third case that would finally appear before the Supreme Court began as two cases, *Belton v. Gebhart* and *Bulah v. Gebhart*, in Wilmington, Delaware. The first case revolved around inferior facilities for blacks and the second around the absence of transportation. Like the earlier cases, expert witnesses testified as to the impact of segregation. Psychiatrist Frederick Wertheim, for example, reported on Delaware children he had studied: "Most of the children we have examined interpret segregation in one way and only one way—and that is they interpret it as punishment." Unlike the earlier two cases, however, Delaware's court of chancery, Chancellor Collins Seitz presiding, found in favor of the plaintiffs and ordered the immediate admission of their children to the previously all-white schools. Yet Seitz avoided *Plessy*: "I do not believe a lower court can reject a principle of United States Constitutional law which has been adopted by fair implication by the highest court of the land. I believe the 'separate but equal' doctrine in education should be rejected, but I also believe its rejection must come from that Court." The defendants appealed to the Supreme Court.

The fourth case, *Davis v. County School Board*, came from Prince Edward County, Virginia. There, conditions comparable to Clarendon County, South Carolina, prevailed. A series of events that included a student boycott of classes at an inferior, black high school led to a suit requesting that the Virginia law requiring segregated schools be struck down. By this time, the other cases had been tried, and the Virginia legal establishment was familiar with the NAACP's approach. For the first time, expert witnesses were challenged—albeit weakly—by experts testifying for the defense, and the state argued that attempts to provide equal facilities were moving forward. In words that seem incredible to modern eyes, the state even claimed that its segregation policy had benefited Virginia blacks. Defense counsel Justin Moore argued that "in these eighty years. . . there has been an outstanding piece of work done in building up the Negro in every way—socially, politically and economically—where today he occupies a position of importance in economics and politics, in many ways, all due to the opportunities that have been given to him in this land in which we live and love. . . ." The district court panel, composed of three Virginians, found that segregation was neither prejudiced nor capricious and rejected the plea of the plaintiffs. The court required merely that district and state plans for equalization of facilities continue apace. The NAACP appealed.

The final case considered under *Brown* came from the District of Columbia. There, in *Bolling v. Sharpe*, black parents represented by James Nabrit sued District of Columbia school officials. The plaintiffs argued that their Fifth Amendment rights were violated by the practice of segregation in the nation's capital, and that the burden was upon school officials to prove any reasonable basis for segregated schools. The district court threw out the suit, arguing that the constitutionality of segregation itself was at issue, and on that issue the precedents were clear. The plaintiffs appealed.

The Supreme Court scheduled the oral argument in the five cases dealing with segregation for December 1952. In the interim, South Carolina attempted to strengthen its position before the Court. Governor James F. Byrnes had pushed through a bond issue which, the state argued, would go a long way toward equalizing black facilities (the district court had approved those efforts), and the state had retained the services of John W. Davis, ex-presidential candidate and perhaps the most distinguished

constitutional lawyer in the country. Davis was confident of victory. The lines were clearly drawn: given the equalization efforts of the segregationist states, the legal issue devolved to the reasonableness of segregation. The legal precedent, thought Davis, was clearly on the side of segregationists. Furthermore, the current Court was not distinguished by civil libertarian decisions.

By the same token, the NAACP legal staff was concerned. Criticism from the black press reminded them of their precarious position if the Court decided that *Plessy* must stand. In the light of that possibility, the association's brief tried to make a case for deciding the segregation issue outside *Plessy*. *Plessy* itself had dealt with transportation, not education, and many of the precedents—including *Gong Lum*—did not deal directly with the question of the reasonableness of segregation in education. On the other hand, the Court had clearly denied race as a basis for classification in other circumstances. In *Nixon v. Herndon* (1927), for example, Justice Oliver Wendell Holmes, Jr., had argued that color could not be "made the basis for a statutory classification" with regards to qualifications for participation in primary elections. Marshall and his team hoped that with this line of reasoning, they might give the Court a way to decide in the plaintiff's favor without dealing directly with *Plessy*.

In any event, however, it was clear that the Court recognized what was at stake. Probing questions by Justice Felix Frankfurter, for example, revealed that the justices were troubled. Overturning precedent was a weighty matter. Other issues were also significant: given the clear resistance among southern whites to desegregation, what might be the impact of a desegregation decision—especially if the Court, as it seemed to be—was badly divided on the issue? Were the efforts to equalize facilities promoted by southern leaders like James Byrnes legitimate? What was the position of the incoming Republican presidential administration of Dwight D. Eisenhower? In fact, the issue was so troublesome that the Court decided to postpone a decision until several issues were pursued in greater depth. In June 1953, the five segregation cases were restored to the Court's docket for reargument in October. At that time, the parties to the litigation would be invited to discuss a series of questions ranging from the original intent of the authors of the Fourteenth Amendment to the extent of judicial power to abolish segregation in schools and, given that abolition, the best means to achieve it. Also, the new administration was invited to file a brief in the cases.

The summer's delay was significant. Marshall organized an intensive research effort on the part of historians and social scientists to solidify the NAACP's interpretation of the original intent of the amendment's authors. The evidence was cloudy, but a strong case was made for a broad, equalitarian purpose. In the fall, the administration's brief was filed, calling for desegregation but requesting a transitional period. Finally, and most significantly, in September Chief Justice Fred M. Vinson—perhaps the staunchest proponent of *Plessy*—died. In his place, President Eisenhower appointed Earl Warren of California.

Chief Justice Warren was a shrewd politician whose personality and tact soothed a fractious Court, and he felt that segregation was wrong. Reargument in early December (after yet another postponement), convinced Warren and a number of other justices that the issue of public school segregation could be avoided no longer. Consequently, Warren argued in conference, "I don't see how, in this day and age, we can set any group apart from the rest and say that they are not entitled to exactly the same treatment as all others. To do so would be contrary to the Thirteenth, Fourteenth, and Fifteenth Amendments. They were intended to make the slaves equal with all others. Personally, I can't see how today we can justify segregation based solely on race." By staking the high moral ground, Warren, for all practical purposes, shifted the justices' debate from what to do to how to do it. As Justice Robert H. Jackson argued, "Our problem is to make a judicial decision . . . [and find] a judicial basis for a congenial political conclusion."

Thus, the problem remained: how could the Court, in the face of precedent, reverse itself? The Court's greatest advocate of judicial restraint, Frankfurter, had earlier grappled with the question and seemed to resolve it in his own mind. In notes to himself before the 1952

conference, he wrote that respect for earlier decisions did not mean that the reasoning and principles upon which they were based could not be reexamined: "The equality of laws enshrined in the Constitution is not a fixed formula defined with finality at a particular time. It does not reflect as a congealed formulation the social arrangement and beliefs of a particular epoch. . . . It is addressed to the changes wrought by time and . . . must respond to transformation of views as well as to that of outward circumstances. The effect of the change in men's feelings of what is right and just is equally relevant in determining whether discrimination denies the equal protection of the laws." Frankfurter's thoughts portended the direction the Court would take.

On May 17, 1954, Chief Justice Warren read his opinion for a unanimous Court, an opinion described by historian Alfred H. Kelly as "remarkable both for its simplicity and for the extraordinary fashion in which it avoided all legal and historical complexities." Warren recognized that there was "little in the history of the Fourteenth Amendment relating to its intended effect on public education" and dismissed as inconclusive the arguments dealing with the intent of its authors. Rather, in order to consider the "effect of segregation itself on public education," Warren argued that the Court could not "turn the clock back to 1868 when the Amendment was adopted, or even to 1896 when *Plessy v. Ferguson* was written. We must consider public education in the light of its full development and its present place in American life throughout the Nation." That place was central, and where educational opportunity was provided by the state, it was "a right which must be made available to all on equal terms." Did segregation based on race deprive minority children of equal educational opportunities? Yes, argued Warren. Alluding to the social science evidence suggesting the detrimental impact of segregation on children, Warren argued for the Court: "We conclude that in the field of public education the doctrine of 'separate but equal' has no place. Separate educational facilities are inherently unequal."

Marshall and his associates had won their biggest case. The constitutional foundation for segregation in education had been destroyed. Yet the Court did not order immediate desegregation. Rather, recognizing the complexities inherent in desegregation under a "great variety of local conditions," the Court postponed implementation until it could hear recommendations from the parties involved. A year later, in a supplementary decision, the Court ordered desegregation carried out under local federal court direction "with all deliberate speed."

Although it would be years before meaningful desegregation would come to many schools in the country, the decision in *Brown* set the stage for important developments in black America's struggle for civil rights and, ultimately, the rights of other groups suffering from unreasonable classification. Under Warren, the Court became a major player in those developments as it continued to strike down racial segregation in its variety of forms: on public beaches and in municipal parks, public buildings, housing, transportation, and eating facilities. By 1963, the Court would declare: "It is no longer open to question that a State may not constitutionally require segregation of public facilities." The nation was beginning to redress the "brutal and irritating aggressions" so accurately predicted by John Marshall Harlan.

Selected Bibliography

Graglia, L.A. *Disaster by Degree: The Supreme Court Decisions on Race and the Schools*. Ithaca, NY: Cornell University Press, 1976.

Kluger, R. *Simple Justice: The History of* Brown v. Board of Education *and Black America's Struggle for Equality*. New York: Alfred A. Knopf, 1975.

LaMorte, M.W. *School Law: Cases and Concepts*. Englewood Cliffs, NJ: Prentice Hall, 1982.

Schwartz, B., with S. Lesher. *Inside the Warren Court*. New York: Doubleday, 1983.

Wilkinson, J.H., III. *From* Brown *to Bakke: The Supreme Court and School Integration*. New York: Oxford University Press, 1979.

THE LITTLE ROCK CRISIS: STATE INTERPOSITION AGAINST THE SUPREME COURT

by F. Thornton Miller
Department of History
Southwest Missouri State University

Cooper v. Aaron, 358 U.S. 1 (1958) [U.S. Supreme Court]

The *Cooper v. Aaron* litigation was, in general, typical of the slow, gradual, and, for the most part, orderly process of the racial desegregation of the public schools of the South in compliance with *Brown v. Board of Education* (1954). The significance of *Cooper* lies elsewhere. Beyond the schools and school boards, extreme segregationists and politicians, such as Orval E. Faubus, Arkansas's incumbent governor running for reelection, wished—or felt it was necessary for their political survival—to tap the potential popularity of a strong segregationist stand. The attempt by the Arkansas state government to prevent desegregation caused a constitutional crisis.

The burdensome task of implementing the *Brown* decision fell on the federal district judges. It had been the practice for presidents to defer to a state's U.S. senators for appointments of district judges in that state. The appointees were generally from the area and shared in the community's ideas and values. Most white southerners and southern federal district judges, alike, had doubts about the propriety of the *Brown* decision. But the judges and many moderates believed that the decision was the law of the land, as determined by the highest court, and it would have to be carried out. They hoped that it could be done gradually and with the least public disturbance. They knew that extreme segregationists would attempt to create problems every step of the way. The judges were caught between their duty to carry out a law of desegregation and their place in a society where segregation was fully entrenched.

In the late 1950s and early 1960s, a pattern emerged in the implementation of *Brown*. The National Association for the Advancement of Colored People (NAACP) would organize attempts by black parents to register their children in racially segregated public schools, the students would be turned away, and then, on their behalf, the NAACP would bring a suit against the school district in federal district court. The federal judge would follow a course of studied vacillation, delay, and compromise, giving the school districts time to draft plans to gradually desegregate their schools. The school boards were relieved to have court-ordered plans to follow, because they could tell extreme segregationists that they were only complying with the law. Long after the original *Brown* case, through years of tokenism and phases of implementation from elementary to high school (or vice versa), racial segregation in the public schools of the South was virtually completed.

In its early stages, *Aaron v. Cooper* seemed to fit this pattern. The Little Rock school board in the mid-1950s was dominated by moderates who did not like, but were willing to carry out, the *Brown* decision. Indeed, they voluntarily agreed to a plan—called the "Blossom Plan," prepared by Virgil Blossom, the district superintendent—for the gradual desegregation of Little Rock's public schools, beginning with Central High School. The local NAACP believed the plan was inadequate, because desegregation would begin in only one school, and much of the timing of the phases was left indefinite. After black parents tried to enroll their children in another public high school and were turned away, a suit was filed by the NAACP in the U.S. District Court for the Eastern District of Arkansas on behalf of John Aaron and 32 other students against William G. Cooper, president of the school board, and other officers of the board and the school district. The case went before Judge John E. Miller, a native of Arkansas. He thought the *Brown* opinion was wrong and sympathized with local dislike for it,

but believed he was duty bound to carry it out as the law of the land.

The attorneys for the Little Rock school board argued that the only issue was whether the board had, in good faith, devised a reasonable plan to carry out the *Brown* decision. The counsel for the NAACP argued that the actions of the board had complied with Arkansas law, which was segregationist and unconstitutional. Miller, ruling in favor of the board, decided that the Blossom Plan was not based on state segregation laws and was a reasonable attempt to comply with federal law. He maintained jurisdiction in the matter, however, to assure that the board continued, in good faith, to implement its plan, and that the time schedule in the plan was made definite. After an NAACP appeal, the U.S. Court of Appeals for the Eighth Circuit upheld Miller's decision. At this point, the *Cooper* litigation was similar to many others that were part of the slow process of desegregation in the courts and the schools. It became different and highly significant when the U.S. Supreme Court had to deal with forces, beyond the control of a school board, that, in effect, created a situation in which no plan of desegregation could, in good faith, be carried out.

Southern moderates and extremists disagreed over whether they should comply with the Supreme Court's *Brown* decision; they agreed, however, in raising serious objections to it. The separate but equal doctrine had been accepted as constitutional by the Supreme Court, Congress, and the states for decades. If the doctrine had not been in line with the original intention of the framers of the Fourteenth Amendment, it had since become an accepted part of constitutional law. Southerners thought the Supreme Court would need ample grounds to alter it. The Court's agreement with sociological arguments in *Brown* was disturbing, because the whole issue along those lines was debatable. Segregation had been ingrained in southern society and law since the late nineteenth century. Social upheaval in reaction to the implementation of the *Brown* decision was to be expected. The chance that desegregation could weaken more than strengthen the public school system in the South had to be taken into account. Moreover, by what authority could the Court act in an area that most white southerners in the 1950s believed was outside the proper sphere of the federal government? Public education was the domain of the states. Southerners seriously questioned the Supreme Court's constitutional authority to make the *Brown* decision.

The moderates believed the decision was unwise but hoped that Congress or the Court would later correct the mistake and prayed, in the meantime, that change would be gradual and peaceful. But the extremists wished to take their stand against what they saw as a misguided attempt by the federal government to intervene in their internal affairs. Against this threat to their racially segregated society by a "foreign" court, they brushed off and invoked the old states' rights doctrine of interposition.

Interposition went back to Thomas Jefferson's and James Madison's Resolutions of 1798 when the Kentucky and Virginia legislatures voiced their opinion that the Alien and Sedition Acts were unconstitutional. A question was raised, at the time, whether the states could constitutionally challenge federal law. Later, in the Nullification Crisis of 1832, John C. Calhoun and South Carolina proposed that a state could challenge and, indeed, nullify federal law within its jurisdiction. Secession carried this line of reasoning to its logical conclusion, and the Civil War determined that a state could not defy federal law. But could a state government, drawing on the original and milder Madison/Jefferson model, declare its opinion on the constitutionality of a Supreme Court decision? For awhile, Arkansas officials merely voiced their disagreement with the *Brown* decision. They appeared ready to carry it out. Yet, when Governor Faubus and the majority of the Arkansas legislature tried to thwart the action of the lower federal courts, the further ramifications of interposition became clear: Arkansas crossed the line from the Madison/Jefferson model of the doctrine, as a statement of constitutional opinion, to the Calhoun/nullification model, as an act of direct opposition by a state to the enforcement of federal law within its jurisdiction. This state challenge would have to be met by the Warren Court.

After desegregation was set to begin in the Little Rock school district in the fall of 1957, Governor Faubus placed the Arkansas National Guard at Central High School, he claimed, to keep order. Afraid that the troops would be used, instead, to prevent the black children from entering the school, the federal district court ordered them removed. Faubus did so, and, after desegregation began, disturbances forced the Little Rock mayor to call on President Eisenhower for federal assistance. Eisenhower, instead of relying on federalized national guard and U.S. marshals, sent in the 101st Airborne paratroopers. This heavy-handed federal action allowed nine black students to attend Central High School. But it made Faubus even more popular. Ironically, it proved he had been right in claiming that the federal courts' actions were leading to social unrest and that the National Guard troops had been necessary to keep order. The governor's "secret orders," however, and his subsequent public actions brought about a constitutional crisis.

A report by the Federal Bureau of Investigation, made available to the federal district court, charged that Faubus had given orders to the National Guard not to allow black students to enter Central High School. This maneuver, if factual, was a clear violation of a federal court order. With federal regular troops in Little Rock outraging extreme states' rights segregationists and demoralizing the moderates, the legislature passed, and Faubus signed into law, a bill authorizing the governor to close all public schools that had come under federal court order to desegregate. This state law stipulated that the schools remain closed until the voters could decide whether to reopen them. The state had now crossed that line between making public its constitutional disagreement with the federal government and placing its own state law counter to federal law. Arkansas was directly challenging the uniformity and enforcement of American constitutional law. Chief Justice Earl Warren called the Supreme Court into a special session.

The appeal of *Cooper v. Aaron* from the U.S. Court of Appeals for the Eighth Circuit had been on the docket, but there was no urgency in deciding the case until Faubus and the Arkansas legislature acted to prevent desegregation. The school board's plan was not the issue. No school board could possibly continue a plan of desegregation given the actions of the state government. The onus rested on Faubus and the legislature. The main issue was interposition. Could a state government interpose itself between its citizens and the national government in order to prevent the implementation of a decision of the Supreme Court?

Cooper answered this question clearly and resoundingly in the negative. The Warren Court was unanimous in its decision. Justice William J. Brennan wrote the majority opinion. Justice Felix Frankfurter wrote a concurring opinion. As stated by the Court, the major question at issue was of the "highest importance to the maintenance of our federal system of government. It squarely presents a claim by the Governor and Legislature of a State that there is no duty on state officials to obey federal court orders resting on this Court's deliberate and considered interpretation of the United States Constitution." The Court would not allow any southern state to prevent directly the implementation of *Brown*. *De jure* ("legal") segregation of the public schools had to end.

Cooper was but one case in the desegregation story in southern public schools. Desegregation was brought about through a combination of forces, with hesitancy, vacillation, and postponement occurring at every level and in every branch of government. In the courts, there were continuous motions made, hearings, and appeals. After *Cooper* was finally decided by the Supreme Court, the Little Rock NAACP was still at work in the federal district court trying to get a desegregation plan implemented. The process continued, and some success could be claimed. But there resulted a concurrent development of private schools for whites. Through either public neighborhood or suburban school systems or private schools, the mission of *Brown*, that separate was inherently unequal, would still be thwarted. Also, the accomplishment of the law in bringing about desegregation was mixed. Going through a gradual, legal process had the advantage of making desegregation possible with minimum public disturbances, though it also allowed *de facto* ("actual") discrimination and inequality to continue. But the significance of *Cooper* is its prevention of *de jure* segregation in the public schools by states resorting to the old constitutional doctrine of interposition.

Selected Bibliography

Freyer, T. *The Little Rock Crisis: A Constitutional Interpretation.* Westport, CT Greenwood Press, 1984.

Huckaby, E. *Crisis at Central High: Little Rock, 1957–58.* Baton Rouge, LA: Louisiana State University Press, 1980.

Peltason, J.W. *Fifty-Eight Lonely Men: Southern Federal Judges and School Desegregation.* New York: Harcourt, Brace & World, Inc., 1961.

THE SCHOOL BUSING CASE

by Robert P. Green, Jr.
Department of Elementary and Secondary Education
Clemson University

Swann v. Charlotte-Mecklenburg Board of Education, 402 U.S. 1 (1971) [U.S. Supreme Court]

While *Brown v. Board of Education* (1954) was a significant victory in the battle for black Americans' civil rights, it was not a complete victory. Declaring "that in the field of public education the doctrine of 'separate but equal' has no place," the U.S. Supreme Court in *Brown* struck down legally segregated school systems. At the same time, however, the Court postponed implementation of its decision. In fact, full implementation of the *Brown* decision in the South would require nearly 20 more years of legal struggle. The Court's decision in *Swann v. Charlotte-Mecklenburg Board of Education*, endorsing busing as a tool for desegregation, played a major role in that struggle.

During the Supreme Court's deliberations in *Brown*, two issues of particular concern arose.

First, the justices were aware of the potentially explosive nature of the impact of an antisegregation decision on an unwilling, white South. "It will take all the wisdom of this Court to dispose of the matter with a minimum of emotion and strife," argued Chief Justice Earl Warren. The Court recognized that while border states might desegregate relatively quickly and without friction, white resistance in the Deep South might be violent. A good deal of sentiment appeared to exist among the justices for a decree flexible enough to allow different handling of the decision in different places. A second issue, closely related to the first, was the question over the degree to which the Supreme Court should involve itself in shaping the details of plaintiff's relief. Several of the justices wanted to avoid Supreme Court entanglement in enforcement, yet some guidelines for lower courts were obviously necessary. Given the divisiveness of these two issues, and in order to achieve a unanimous opinion on the overriding issue of segregation, Chief Justice Warren agreed to postpone a decision on implementing the Court's ruling in *Brown*. Thus in 1955, over a year after the first decision of *Brown v. Board of Education (Brown I)*, and after hearing further arguments from interested parties, the Supreme Court issued its relief decree in a second decision titled *Brown v. Board of Education* (generally known as *Brown II*).

Brown II reflected a compromise designed to impose the constitutional principles enunciated in *Brown I* in a way that would give school districts and states time to adjust. The Court recognized that "full implementation of these constitutional principles" might require varied solutions, so local school districts were given the primary responsibility for "elucidating, assessing, and solving" particular problems that might arise as they desegregated. District courts were given the task of considering "whether the action of school authorities constitutes good faith implementation" of the constitutional principles. The district courts were directed to "require that the defendants make a prompt and reasonable start toward full compliance," but once such a "good faith" start had been made, "the courts may find that additional time is necessary to carry out the ruling in an effective manner." Such extension of time might be based

on a variety of problems, ranging from those related to administration and transportation to the need for "revision of local laws and regulations." The Supreme Court thus remanded the original *Brown* cases to the district courts to ensure that black students were admitted to public schools on a "racially nondiscriminatory basis . . . with all deliberate speed."

Taken together, *Brown I* and *Brown II* held that certain constitutional rights were being violated, but that these violations need not be fully and immediately redressed. While such conceptual ambiguity might have been good politics, it was not good law. Furthermore, leaving the burden of review to district judges—judges closest to, sometimes products of, and certainly more subject to, sanctions from the white communities that so disliked the High Court's decision—invited problems. While the intent of the Supreme Court in *Brown I* had been to end dual school systems, the lower courts often interpreted the decision in a way far short of that goal. The influential Circuit Judge John J. Parker, for example, interpreted *Brown I* narrowly: "What [*Brown*] has decided, and all that it has decided, is that a state may not deny to any person on account of race the right to attend any school that it maintains. . . . The Constitution, in other words, does not require integration. It merely forbids discrimination." Supreme Court ambiguity and the consequent lack of aggressiveness on the part of lower court judges combined to form an open invitation to southern delay. In fact, the history of litigation from *Brown* to *Swann* became a history of ever more specific guidelines from the Supreme Court, guidelines designed to combat southern intransigence.

Southern intransigence took a number of forms. In some areas, schools were closed or blacks, attempting to enroll in previously white schools, were intimidated. More typically, southern states adopted complicated pupil-placement laws, which provided for assignment of students to schools according to nonracial factors ranging from the pupil capacity of the various schools to level of a pupil's academic preparation or characteristics of a pupil's home environment. If dissatisfied with a particular assignment, a student had to pursue a detailed administrative procedure in order to request a change. The net effect of all of this was to inhibit large-scale desegregation.

At first, as black plaintiffs challenged the pupil-placement laws, the courts upheld such statutes. In a 1956 case, for example, Circuit Judge Parker declared North Carolina's pupil-placement statute constitutional "upon its face." That is, pupils were enrolled in schools based on factors other than race. In *Shuttlesworth v. Birmingham Board of Education* (1958), the U.S. Supreme Court endorsed a lower court ruling on the Alabama pupil-placement law: "The School Placement Law furnishes the legal machinery for an orderly administration of the public schools in a constitutional manner by the admission of qualified pupils upon a basis of individual merit without regard to their race or color. We must presume that it will be so administered."

The presumption that these laws would be administered without racial bias, however, was obviously inaccurate. Under the North Carolina law approved by Judge Parker, there were only three blacks in Charlotte "white" schools in 1957, four in 1958, and one in 1959. Records indicate that during the period under the Alabama statute considered in *Shuttlesworth*, only one black was assigned to a "white" Alabama school, and that student transferred under pressure after only a few weeks. By the early 1960s, it was clear that if the Supreme Court were to foster enforcement of the principles in *Brown I*, more active judicial measures were necessary. A series of rulings over the next decade demonstrated that the Court was tired of delay, and that more precise direction would be given the lower courts in desegregation cases.

In June 1963, the Court decided two desegregation cases that signaled the changes to come. In *McNeese v. Board of Education*, the Court ruled that plaintiffs challenging failure to desegregate need not exhaust unpromising state administrative remedies before bringing suit in federal court. The same day, in *Goss v. Board of Education*, the Court ruled against a provision of the Knoxville, Tennessee, desegregation plan allowing students to transfer from a school that had previously served the other race, or where their race was in a minority. The decision clearly noted that nine years from *Brown I* and eight after *Brown II*, the Court's patience with southern delaying tactics was running out.

The message from the Court became clearer over the next few years. One of the original defendants in *Brown*, Prince Edward County, Virginia, rather than desegregate under a circuit court order, had closed its public schools and provided tuition grants to white families who sent their children to private schools. In *Griffin v. County School Board* (1964), the Court declared that such a device deprived the black students of equal protection of the laws. More importantly, however, the Court argued, "There has been entirely too much deliberation and not enough speed in enforcing the constitutional rights which we held [had been denied] in *Brown v. Board of Education*." Furthermore, for the first time, the Supreme Court gave lower courts more specific administrative guidelines. Not only was the district court called to enjoin the county from giving tuition grants and tax credits to families sending their children to private schools; it was also to "require the Supervisors to exercise the power that is theirs to levy taxes to raise funds adequate to reopen, operate, and maintain without racial discrimination a public school system in Prince Edward County." *Griffin* was followed a year later by *Bradley v. Richmond School Board* (1965). In *Bradley*, the Court prohibited further delay in desegregating facilities. Reflecting the language in *Griffin*, the Court argued, "more than a decade has passed since we directed desegregation of public school facilities 'with all deliberate speed.' . . . Delays in desegregating school systems are no longer tolerable."

As it became apparent that the pupil placement laws of southern states would no longer meet the Supreme Court's criteria for desegregation, many southern systems adopted "freedom of choice" plans. On their face, freedom of choice plans allowed students to choose freely the schools they wished to attend. In practice, very little desegregation took place. For example, New Kent County, Virginia, maintained two schools: one traditionally white and one traditionally black. In theory, under a freedom of choice plan instituted in 1965, students could choose to attend either school. In the absence of a choice, students remained in the school in which they were currently enrolled. As a result of this policy, all of the white students in the county attended the traditionally white school, and 85 percent of the black students attended the traditionally black school. Only token desegregation took place.

In *Green v. New Kent County School Board* (1968), such tokenism was challenged and found inadequate. Writing for the Court, Justice William J. Brennan, Jr., declared that "a plan that at this late date fails to provide meaningful assurance of prompt and effective disestablishment of a dual system is . . . intolerable. . . . The burden on a school board today is to come forward with a plan that promises realistically to work, and promises realistically to work *now*" [emphasis in original]. To foster real desegregation, district courts were directed to evaluate desegregation plans "in practice" and "retain jurisdiction until it is clear that state-imposed segregation has been completely removed." Finally, Brennan suggested positive steps, such as pairing or geographic zoning, that the school board might pursue to aid desegregation.

Green was a turning point in the history of school desegregation in the South. It marked the Supreme Court's transition from the passivism of *Brown II* to a new activism characterized by specific guidelines and positive suggestions. This new activism was extended in *United States v. Montgomery County Board of Education* (1969), in which the Court endorsed the use of numerical goals in faculty desegregation, and *Alexander v. Holmes County Board of Education* (1969), in which the Court reversed a Fifth Circuit Court delay in implementation of a desegregation plan and reasserted its position that desegregation take place immediately. It was in this atmosphere of activism that the Court considered *Swann*.

Swann began as a result of black dissatisfaction with a desegregation plan proposed for the Charlotte-Mecklenburg school system, a unified system composed of largely black, inner-city schools in Charlotte and predominantly white schools in what formerly had been the Mecklenburg County system. The plan entailed the closing of a number of traditionally black schools, the creation of geographic attendance zones (which would leave a great majority of

blacks in separate schools), and a watered-down freedom of choice provision. Arguing that the plan placed the burden of desegregation on black students and thus perpetuated a dual system, black plaintiffs brought suit in January 1965. When, however, a federal district court approved the plan and, a year later, that decision was affirmed in circuit court, the plaintiffs decided to appeal no further. The 1968 *Green* decision, however, suggested that by that time the Supreme Court might not accept Charlotte-Mecklenburg's plan. In September 1968, the *Swann* plaintiffs reopened the case.

The reopened case was tried before District Judge James B. McMillan. Judge McMillan found that a large majority of the school system's black students attended schools in which the enrollments were either totally or more than 99 percent black. Influenced by the *Green* decision, he ordered the school board to devise a new plan. The board delayed but finally came up with a weak plan in July. McMillan approved that plan on an interim basis, but ordered the board to file another plan that would desegregate the schools "to the maximum extent possible" for the 1970–71 school year. In November, the school board filed for an extension of time, but McMillan, influenced by *Alexander*, denied the request. The board then presented another unsatisfactory plan. Recognizing that he was getting nowhere with the board, McMillan, in December, appointed an educational consultant to the court to develop a satisfactory desegregation plan. In February 1970, McMillan adopted the consultant's plan.

The consultant's plan was comprehensive in nature. It desegregated all of Charlotte-Mecklenburg's schools by pairing and clustering groups of white and black schools so that enrollment in each school would roughly reflect the white-black ratio in the system at large. Attendance zones were shaped like "wedges of a pie," extending from the black, urban center out into the suburban and rural areas of the county. Through the use of busing, black, inner-city students would be transported to predominantly white suburban schools, and white students from the suburbs would be transported to the inner city. Thus, roughly a quarter of the busing in Charlotte-Mecklenburg would be solely for the purpose of desegregation.

The school board appealed McMillan's order, and the Court of Appeals for the Fourth Circuit, in a mixed vote, affirmed those portions of the plan dealing with secondary education but overturned those portions affecting elementary students. In turn, the black plaintiffs appealed the circuit decision to the U.S. Supreme Court.

The Supreme Court that heard *Swann* was no longer the Warren Court. Upon the retirement of Earl Warren in 1969, President Richard Nixon had appointed Warren E. Burger as chief justice. Court watchers expected the Burger appointment, in keeping with the president's conservative political philosophy—which promoted the idea of neighborhood schools and rejected busing to achieve racial balance—to move the Court to the right. Indeed, Burger's position in the *Swann* conference was that McMillan's remedies were too sweeping. Despite indications that his view was in the minority, Chief Justice Burger ignored Court precedent and assigned himself the responsibility for writing a draft opinion. Court supporters of McMillan's order, however, led by Justices William J. Brennan, Jr., and John M. Harlan, were able to influence a final, unanimous opinion affirming the district judge.

The key elements of the opinion revolved around the specific remedies prescribed by McMillan: the use of ratios as beginning guidelines for desegregation; the remedial altering of attendance zones through gerrymandering, clustering, or grouping schools in noncontiguous areas; and the use of bus transportation. While rejecting the idea of mathematical ratios as inflexible requirements, the Court argued that "awareness of the racial composition of the whole school system is likely to be a useful starting point in shaping a remedy to correct past constitutional violations." With regard to the manipulation of attendance zones, the Court pointed out that in the absence of a constitutional violation, "there would be no basis for judicially ordering assignment of students on a racial basis." However, in the presence of a history of segregation, and when "school authorities present a district court with a 'loaded game board,' affirmative action in the form of remedial altering of attendance zones is proper to achieve truly nondiscriminatory assignments." Finally, while recognizing that objections to busing might be valid when "the time or distance of travel is so great as to either risk the health of the children or significantly impinge on the educational process," such was not the case here, and "the remedial techniques used in the District Court's order were within that court's power to provide equitable relief."

Thus, nearly 17 years after *Brown*, the Supreme Court outlined specific measures that might be required in order to desegregate school systems that had, by law, previously been segregated. Those measures included the use of ratios as beginning guidelines for desegregation, the remedial altering of attendance zones, and busing.

Selected Bibliography

Graglia, L.A. *Disaster by Decree: The Supreme Court Decisions on Race and the Schools*. Ithaca, NY: Cornell University Press, 1976.

LaMorte, M.W. *School Law: Cases and Concepts*. Englewood Cliffs, NJ: Prentice-Hall, 1982.

Schwartz, B. *Swann's Way: The School Busing Case and the Supreme Court*. New York: Oxford University Press, 1986.

Wilkinson, J.H., III. *From* Brown *to : The Supreme Court and School Integration*. New York: Oxford University Press, 1979.

C. Native Americans

THE CHEROKEE CASES

by John R. Wunder
Department of History
University of Nebraska at Lincoln

Cherokee Nation v. Georgia, 5 Peters 1 (1831); *Worcester v. Georgia*, 6 Peters 515 (1832)
[U.S. Supreme Court]

A-ni-tsa-la-gi'—the Cherokee people; Ge-wa-ne:-ga—They are near the horizon walking away. Such were the circumstances after the fateful decisions of the U.S. Supreme Court in 1831 and 1832 and the subsequent refusal of Andrew Jackson's administration to prevent the ultimate outcome of these cases, the "Trail of Tears." Perhaps at no other time in American history has the failure of law been so evident. Here a people, A-ni-tsa-la-gi', were forced to walk from their homelands in the Appalachian foothills of North and South Carolina, Georgia, and Tennessee to new lands in Indian territory, or Oklahoma. It was a forced migration fraught with great hardships, including the lack of food and clothing and of brutal winter travel. Some estimates suggest as high as 10,000 Cherokees perished. What were the legal circumstances that led to this tragedy?

The Cherokee nation is one of the largest native American nations in North America. By the time of the Cherokees first contact with British traders in the seventeenth century, they probably numbered at least 20,000. They lived as hunters and farmers in five regions along the eastern edge of the Appalachian Mountains. These five regions contained at least 60 independent towns. The regions extended from the northernmost point on the upper Little Tennessee River where the Overhill towns were located to the southernmost point on the Keowee River in southwestern South Carolina.

The Cherokees by 1700 had begun to spread their influence beyond their traditional Appalachian homelands. They had moved as far north as Kentucky and Virginia and as far south as Georgia and Alabama. They controlled over 70 million acres of rich lands. It is not known specifically how the Cherokees came to this point, that of a significant nation of North America. In the Cherokee oral tradition, they are said to be the people of the fire. It is conceivable that their migration may have occurred in concert with volcanic eruptions of an earlier period.

The Cherokee history prior to the constitutional crisis of the Jacksonian era had three stages. The initial stage was the "frontier contact," 1540–1785. During this time the Cherokee first met Europeans, the introduction being to Hernando De Soto's expedition. This period also witnessed: the encroachment of Cherokee lands by British, French, and Spanish colonials; the introduction of more sophisticated weaponry and horses; and the destructive forces of a fur trade economy. The challenge to the Cherokees was to develop a national consensus to combat the serious pressures before them. Moving from independent city-states to a nation state was an extremely difficult and delicate process. This era closed with the first treaty, the Treaty of Hopewell, signed with the new nation, the United States. The agreement guaranteed Cherokee hegemony over Cherokee homelands.

The second stage for the Cherokees was the "rise of white ascendancy," 1786–1828. White ascendancy took various forms. It included attempts by Caucasians to take Cherokee lands, to end Cherokee cultural practices, and to destroy Cherokee legal institutions. It also signified the increase of the power of mixed-bloods in the Cherokee political system, the creation of the Cherokee Republic, and the acculturation attempts of many Cherokee to adapt Cherokee traditions to European institutional forms. For example, the Cherokees developed their own syllabary, they published their own newspapers, they set up a constitutional convention which adopted a republican form of government, and they selected a national capitol site at New Echota, near present-day Calhoun, Georgia.

The Cherokee cases occurred during the third stage, the "tribal dislocation," 1829–46. During this stage, all of the Cherokee attempts to adapt to U.S. political and legal institutions were attacked. The Jackson administration encouraged this hostility by passing Indian removal acts and by sanctioning Georgia's extension of Georgia law over the Cherokee nation. The Cherokees were not the only Indian nation under these pressures, but they were the only Indian nation to fight for cultural survival and retention of their homelands through the American court system. This resulted in two landmark decisions, both written by Chief Justice John Marshall, *Cherokee Nation v. Georgia* (1831) and *Worcester v. Georgia* (1832).

The immediate evolution of *Cherokee Nation* began with U.S. efforts to come to grips with the theory and reality of native American sovereignty. From its beginning, the United States had negotiated treaties with Indians that treated each "tribe" as an independent nation. Land title, boundaries, and legal rights punctuated these treaties. Nevertheless, actual practice provided for the abrogation of these treaties when lands were "sold" and Indians were forced to move away from homelands.

The U.S. Supreme Court first began to consider this conflict in *Fletcher v. Peck* (1810). In this case, Chief Justice Marshall decided an issue that attracted little attention compared with other aspects of the dispute. Georgia, according to Marshall, held a fee simple interest (absolute title) in lands occupied by Indian nations. This interest emerged as a complete right once lands were obtained by the United States from native Americans. Thus, states had specific realty interests that could not be extinguished.

In 1823, the Marshall Court once again looked into an Indian sovereignty matter.

Marshall decided in *Johnson v. McIntosh* that Indians held a peculiar place within the U.S. legal system: Indians possessed rights of occupancy and concurrent rights of dependency. The United States had the ultimate right to the soil, but native Americans could occupy the soil and sell it, but only to the United States. Where the state fit into this equation was not explicitly noted.

The basic inconsistency of the theory and practice of U.S.-native American relationships came under the glare of national consciousness in the 1820s when southern tribes refused to sign any more treaties that required them to cede land. In addition, the Cherokees took as a model the United States and created their own democratic institutions. This process allowed them to claim absolute sovereignty within their homelands. Georgia chose to react.

To meet this diplomatic and domestic dilemma, Georgia adopted laws that placed Cherokee lands within organized Georgia counties. Georgia law was to be enforced in these counties, and Cherokee law was to be rendered void. Other legal restrictions on Indian rights were also passed. The laws were not enforced at first while Georgians waited to see how the new administration in Washington would react. They were not disappointed. President Jackson made it clear that Cherokees and other Indian nations had only two choices: move to western lands to be set aside for them or live under state law.

The Cherokees did not plan to let this matter end. They petitioned Congress to protect their rights. They traveled throughout the Northeast encouraging memorials on their behalf. And they hired a respected Washington, D.C., attorney, William Wirt, to begin planning for a Supreme Court challenge. In spite of this lobbying effort, a removal law was passed in 1830. This law went further than previous removal laws, because it lessened the requirement of native American permission before removals could be ordered.

Once the removal law was passed, it became imperative that Wirt challenge Georgia's aggressive anti-Cherokee behavior in court. Wirt first publicly offered the governor of Georgia, George Gilmer, a mutual opportunity to appear before the Supreme Court to settle any differences. Gilmer refused. Wirt then composed an extensive legal brief arguing that the Cherokees were a foreign nation. He attempted to prove that they were sovereign against the world, except that they could sell their lands only to the United States and they could have diplomatic relations with no other nation than the United States. He reasoned that the Georgia laws were unconstitutional because they impaired the obligation of contracts, violated existing treaties, and constituted a violation of a legislative sphere exclusively reserved for the federal government. This argument was published in newspapers that John Marshall and Andrew Jackson no doubt read.

Even so Wirt was cautious. While he remained confident about the constitutional arguments on behalf of the Cherokees, he was worried about how to achieve standing before the U.S. Supreme Court. He thought he had only two possible avenues to the Court: either through a suit to be instituted by Chief John Ross against a Georgia officeholder in a lower federal court or by means of a direct appeal by the Cherokees to the Supreme Court based on original jurisdiction. He was least confident about the latter, but it was this road he chose to take.

In many ways the Cherokees had no choice. While they were considering their legal options, Georgia acted. A Cherokee, George Tassel, was convicted of murder in Cherokee country by a Georgia court. Even though this conviction was appealed to the U.S. Supreme Court, Georgia executed Tassel in January 1831. Such belligerent action necessitated an immediate response.

By January 1, 1831, the Cherokee nation served notice on the officials of the state of Georgia asking them to appear before the U.S. Supreme Court. A hearing was to be held to determine if Georgia should be prevented from any further attempts at enforcement of Georgia law in Cherokee country. When, on March 5, 1831, Wirt appeared before the Supreme Court justices to present the Cherokee nation's case, Georgia refused to answer the motion or to participate in the argument.

The Supreme Court was composed of seven justices in 1831. Chief Justice John Marshall presided. Also sitting were Federalist Joseph Story, Jeffersonian antagonist William Johnson, and the relatively new justices Smith Thompson, Henry Baldwin, and John McLean. Gabriel Duval could not attend.

Wirt asked for an injunction to prevent further actions by Georgia. He predicated this request on the basis that the Cherokees were a sovereign nation, and as such were entitled to the original jurisdiction of the Supreme Court, the exclusive right to their territory, and the exclusive right of self-government within their territory. To hold otherwise would be to violate the treaties made between the Cherokee nation and the United States. In addition, Wirt argued, if the Court did not prevent Georgia from further outrages, the Cherokees would be forced either to move to western lands where their "progress" toward Christianity and "civilization" might be lost or "to arm themselves in defence [sic] of these sacred rights, and fall sword in hand, on the graves of their fathers."

The Supreme Court did not rule in favor of the Cherokees even though it clearly expressed sympathy for their position. In *Cherokee Nation*, the majority opinion was, not surprisingly, penned by Marshall (the great chief justice wrote over one-half of all the Court opinions during his long tenure). However, there were three other opinions submitted, including a dissent. This was a most remarkable situation, because Marshall simply did not tolerate a great deal of diversity of opinion on his Court. Rare were the occasions on the Marshall Court when four separate opinions were officially published.

On March 19, 1831, Marshall began to read his opinion by letting his audience know his agony. "If courts were permitted to indulge their sympathies," Marshall wrote, "a case better calculated to excite them can scarcely be imagined." But Marshall would never reach the merits of the case. Instead, he chose to discuss whether the Supreme Court had jurisdiction.

For the Supreme Court to even consider this matter, the Cherokees had to be officially considered a "foreign state." Marshall then embarked on a historical survey of the relationship of the Cherokees to the United States, finding that the Cherokees and all other Indians had a unique relationship with the United States. Their treaties put them under federal protection. They allowed the United States to have the right to regulate their trade agreements, and they could send a deputy to the Congress not to vote but to observe. On the other hand, Indians, according to Marshall, had the unquestioned right to the lands they occupied unless that right had been voluntarily extinguished by the United States. Only the United States could negotiate with native Americans over this matter.

Marshall then set in stone three words that have come to characterize the relationship of the United States to American Indian peoples. He decided that native Americans should be considered under American law "domestic, dependent, nations." This was a typical Marshallian move. He combined the meaning of three contradictory words to denote a new legal concept. "Domestic" signified internal, "dependent" suggested subordinate, and yet "nation" implied sovereign independence.

He then went on to clarify his meaning. "They," referring to the Cherokees and all other Indians, "are in a state of pupilage." To Marshall, native Americans were the wards of their guardian, the United States. Marshall had accepted the myth of the Indian as child that was shared by many educated Americans during the nineteenth century.

Thus, an Indian tribe could not be a foreign nation, because it was both not foreign to the United States and, like a child, it lacked complete sovereignty. Even the U.S. Constitution, according to Marshall, did not use words to imply that native Americans were members of foreign nations. The commerce clause stated that Congress could "regulate commerce with foreign nations, and among the several states, and with the Indian tribes." Marshall suggested that had the framers thought of Indians as foreign nations, they would not have added them to the clause.

Marshall, therefore, had disposed of the case before he could reach the merits. Since the Cherokees were a domestic, dependent nation, they could not sue for an injunction under the original jurisdiction of the Supreme Court. Any rights to be asserted by the Cherokees would have to be brought into another court first. Still, Marshall had carved out a third, new position for the Cherokees. They were not at the total mercy of Georgia, nor were they released from federal control. This third dimension remained to be devised.

After Marshall announced his opinion, Justices Johnson and Baldwin read theirs. Marshall's six pages paled when compared with Johnson's 12 and Baldwin's 20. Johnson was well-known as a dissenter from Marshall. Johnson, after all, had been Thomas Jefferson's man on the Court. In his concurring opinion, Johnson stressed a much stronger view toward the Cherokees. He set up the same questions as Marshall, but he answered them with a decidedly anti-Cherokee stance.

As to whether the Cherokees were a state, Johnson intoned that "to a people so low in the grade of organized society as our Indian tribes most generally are," no statehood could be imagined. Johnson did grant that the Cherokees had improved, but he found that this new development had not been in place long enough to know whether it was simply a fleeting moment. Johnson also disputed Marshall's notion of occupancy. He wrote that Indians had never been recognized as holding any form of sovereignty over their occupied territory. They had never been known to any other nations except the United States, and in any agreements they made with the United States, they gave up every attribute of sovereignty they might once have had.

Having disposed of the foreign nation argument with verve, Johnson then turned to the practical implications of any other decision. He worried that if Indians were ever recognized as foreign nations, even as domestic, dependent nations, this would overburden the family of nations. It would constitute a folly of a few people holding onto a few acres that would disrupt and make needlessly complex all foreign relations of the United States. Johnson then noted that the U.S. Constitution specifically referred to Indians not as nations but as tribes. Thus, he concluded that the law of nations would interpret this declaration as seeing native Americans as what Johnson thought they truly were: "wandering hordes, held together only by ties of blood and habit, and having neither laws or government, beyond what is required in a savage state." Johnson's hostility was clear to all. He agreed with Marshall only in the chief justice's results. To Johnson, the Cherokees were under the jurisdiction of Georgia, and if the merits were reached under a future case, that is how he would hold.

Baldwin took an even stranger tact. He agreed with Marshall's result, but he found that there was no plaintiff in the suit. To Baldwin, Indians could never sue in federal court as Indians. They could only come to court as U.S. citizens or citizens of a particular state, such as Georgia. Even so Baldwin felt compelled to address the same issue Marshall and Johnson confronted. Baldwin went on for many pages trying to decide if, as a matter of debate, Indians were independent nations or "tribes of savages." The histories of the Iroquois Confederation, the Catawbas of South Carolina, and other native Americans were interpreted by Baldwin to demonstrate lack of sovereignty.

Perhaps Baldwin's most novel point was that since the treaties signed with the Cherokees by the United States did not use the word "nation," the Cherokees were not in fact a nation. This led Baldwin to discuss whether the treaties signed were really treaties. He decided that even though the word "treaty" was mentioned in these agreements, they were not treaties because Indians were not nations. Thus, a treaty was not a treaty even if it called itself a treaty, but Indians were not nations because the treaties did not specifically delineate them nations. Baldwin declared that these "treaties" should instead be termed, "indentures of servitude."

Baldwin next turned to belittle Johnson. Baldwin thought it useless to consult legal theorists or the Federalist Papers. This kind of exercise was pointless to Baldwin, although very important to Johnson. Plain reasoning was all that Baldwin needed, and he found it in previous Supreme Court cases, such as *Sturges v.*

Crowninshield (1819) and *Cohens v. Virginia* (1821).

Baldwin concluded as if he anticipated some action by Marshall. Baldwin could see no means of denying the sovereignty of Georgia over the Cherokees, and he could not contemplate any action by the Supreme Court that might change matters. "Foreign states," warned Baldwin, "cannot be created by judicial construction; Indian sovereignty cannot be roused from its long slumber, and awakened to action by our fiat."

No further opinions were announced that day. One has the sense that Marshall was probably not happy with the outcome. He, no doubt, found much to dislike in the concurring opinions. This can be discerned from the fact that Marshall set about to encourage Justices Thompson and Story to write down their objections. They did so, and they were later printed with the other three opinions.

As author of the dissent, Thompson strongly rejected the reasoning of all three opinions, but especially Baldwin's and Johnson's. Thompson stated at the beginning of his dissent that the Supreme Court had jurisdiction and that he was going to address the merits of the Cherokee claim. In so doing, he considered the issue all of the previous opinions had (i.e., whether the Cherokees were a competent party before the Court). Once he handled this matter, he then went on to determine if a sufficient case had been made to warrant court action and whether an injunction was the appropriate form.

It was the first issue that mattered. Thompson set up several criteria to determine what constituted a foreign nation, relying heavily on Emmerich Vattel, noted international law theorist. To Thompson, a group of people constituted a nation if (1) the people governed themselves, albeit under any possible form, and (2) if the people were without any significant dependence on a foreign power. Under this second requirement, the key interpretation hinged on a stronger state. Thompson explained this matter by citing a maxim: no weak state that for its safety places itself under the protection of a strong state can lose its right to self-government or sovereignty.

Thompson, once he had set up a model for the determination of a foreign nation, sought to apply the Cherokees to the model. Not surprisingly, he concluded that the Cherokees were a foreign nation. They had a form of governance that provided them with a basic political entity, and they were powerful enough to exercise control over a significant area of land. Moreover, once they became weakened, they signed treaties protecting themselves with a stronger nation, the United States, but this did not lessen their sovereignty.

In recent times, Thompson noted, the Cherokee government had changed in form. It now more closely resembled that of the United States. Thompson reasoned that, for him at least, progress made in national governance by the Cherokee should not be allowed to destroy their national character. Indeed, he seemed to tie this recent development to the treaty guarantees of which the United States was a party. To attack Cherokee sovereignty was to attack Cherokee progress, and this in turn was attacking the very fundamentals of the American constitutional experience.

This brought Thompson to confront the nature of treaties, a topic Baldwin had dwelt on earlier. Thompson found treaties to be contracts between national sovereigns. The subjects of treaties included war, prisoners, territorial cessions, and peace. The United States, according to Thompson, entered into treaties with native Americans, and these agreements contained all of the normal components found in treaties. Thus, the Cherokee agreements had to be honored if the United States was to be a member of the family of nations. In particular, Thompson cited Article 12 of the Treaty of Hopewell between the United States and the Cherokees. This contained language that recognized the sovereign and independent character of the Cherokee nation, and it allowed them to send a representative to the Congress to make known their positions. Thompson, perhaps stretching his argument, said it made no difference whether such a representative was called a minister, such as an ambassador; or a deputy, such as a territorial delegate.

Thompson's last important point in his 30-page dissent pertained to citizenship. The Cherokees could not be sovereign if they were citizens of Georgia. If they were not sovereign, they could not be a foreign nation and appear before the Supreme Court. If Georgia was to claim jurisdiction over Cherokee lands, as both Johnson and Baldwin had agreed to (although Baldwin also suggested a slavery-type analogy), those persons within that jurisdiction would be citizens. But Georgia does not wish that to be the case nor do the concurring opinions. Consequently, Thompson concluded that Cherokees were not citizens of Georgia, and that was because Georgia could not exercise jurisdiction over the Cherokees. It was circular reasoning of a spectacular nature.

Once Thompson had found the Cherokees to be a foreign nation, it was a simple matter to dispose of whether an injunction could be issued. Thompson, and his fellow dissenter, Story, agreed that an injunction should be brought against Georgia prohibiting it from any further attempts to erode the sovereignty of the Cherokees. Domestic, dependent nationhood did not concern Thompson, nor did wards and guardianships. Those concepts were Marshall's alone.

Given Marshall's discomfort and the strength of the Thompson-Story dissent, the majority decision in *Cherokee Nation* was tenuous at best. It had been a marriage of strange bedfellows, and Marshall wanted out. One year later the opportunity presented itself. Thompson's dissent and Marshall's *dicta* encouraged Wirt and the Cherokees to find another case to attempt to resolve the constitutional status of native Americans.

In March 1831, Samuel A. Worcester and several other whites were arrested after church services in Cherokee country by the Georgia militia. Worcester was a white Congregational missionary who was backed by the American Board of Commissioners for the Foreign Missions, one of the most powerful mission organizations in the United States. Moreover, Worcester was the postmaster for New Echota, capital of the Cherokee nation.

Worcester had deliberately violated Section 7 of a Georgia statute that prohibited "all white persons [from] residing within the limits of the Cherokee nation . . . without a license or permit from his excellency the [Georgia] governor...." Violation of this section constituted the commission of a high misdemeanor and a punishment of not less than four years in the penitentiary at hard labor.

To prevent Worcester from claiming he was a federal employee, the Georgia governor had President Jackson fire Worcester as postmaster of New Echota. Worcester and his friends were then rearrested, recharged, and tried before a Georgia state court in September. Worcester and the others were found guilty and sentenced to four years in the penitentiary. Worcester appealed, and the Supreme Court accepted the case.

Politics were even more interwoven into the Georgia-Cherokee confrontation this time than in the case decided the previous year. The Cherokees' attorneys were especially active in anti-Jackson forces. One was running as vice-president in the election of 1832 on the Whig party ticket. Wirt was the presidential candidate of the Anti-Masonic party. President Jackson was also the subject of many rumors, the most antagonistic being that he would never allow Worcester to leave prison without serving his term. Cherokee leaders toured nationwide seeking support for their cause. They even met with Justice Story, who later mentioned that he was most impressed with the Cherokees' understanding of the legal issues.

On February 20, 1832, the Supreme Court heard arguments in *Worcester v. Georgia*. Wirt and his co-counsel once again argued for the Cherokee nation, and Georgia once again stayed away. The composition of the Court had not changed since the *Cherokee Nation* decision, but this time Duval was present and Johnson was ill. The delicate balance of the Court on this issue could easily be altered, and it was.

The missionary's attorneys argued that the Georgia act asserting jurisdiction over Cherokee country was void. It was void because it was repugnant to various U.S.-Cherokee treaties, the contract and commerce clauses of the U.S. Constitution, and the sovereign national authority of the Cherokees. The strategy was to suggest indirectly to the justices that the Cherokees were a foreign nation, and that the protec-

tion of their sovereignty necessitated the declaration of Georgia's laws unconstitutional.

In *Worcester v. Georgia*, Marshall, joined by Story, Duval, and Thompson, wrote the majority opinion. Justice McLean added a concurring opinion. Baldwin dissented, and he wrote down his views, but they were not included in the official printed reports. It was assumed that Justice Johnson agreed at least in part with Justice Baldwin. The Court had moved from a split decision denying the Cherokees access to the Supreme Court in *Cherokee Nation* in 1831 to a clear 5–1 decision in favor of Worcester and the Cherokees in 1832.

Since it was Marshall who had changed his mind and now gathered a clear majority, it fell to him to attempt to write a majority opinion that dealt with the *Cherokee Nation* precedent. Just as Justice Robert H. Jackson did with *West Virginia State Board of Education v. Barnette* (1943), when the Supreme Court found it wanted to reverse the recent precedent of *Minersville School District v. Gobitis* (1940), Marshall more than rose to the occasion. In his opinion, he simply refused to acknowledge or even mention *Cherokee Nation*.

Marshall began his decision by looking at the Court's jurisdiction. "It behooves this court," wrote Marshall, "in every case, more especially this, to examine into its jurisdiction with scrutinizing eyes...." Citing *Martin v. Hunter's Lessee* (1816) and *McCulloch v. Maryland* (1819), Marshall appeared to poke gently at the previous concurrence of Baldwin from *Cherokee Nation*. Since Worcester was a citizen of Vermont and since he was appealing the action of another state, Georgia, he easily came within the ambit of the Supreme Court's diversity jurisdiction.

Marshall then turned to the merits of Worcester's position, which required examining the constitutionality of the Georgia statute. To determine constitutionality, Marshall chose to look at the effect of the statute. In so doing, he brought up the nature of the Cherokees as a nation through a discussion of the history of the Indian-British and then U.S. relations. Many treaties were surveyed. Throughout Marshall emphasized what he called "the language of equality." Indians, to Marshall, were viewed in the treaty process and within the treaties themselves as if they were similar to European nations.

Marshall borrowed heavily from Thompson's dissent in *Cherokee Nation*. For Marshall, as it had to Thompson, one nation asking for the protection of another power in a treaty did not imply the destruction of sovereignty. It was simply a basic part of the nature of nations. Some were stronger than others. Furthermore, to agree on safety did not mean that self-government was necessarily surrendered. That, Marshall noted, would be "a perversion of their necessary meaning," and, by looking at the effect of such an interpretation, it would convert a peace treaty into "an act annihilating the political existence of one of the parties." This was not intended nor desired.

It was at this point that Marshall essentially divorced himself from his own opinion in *Cherokee Nation*. He concluded that the Cherokees were a nation, a nation able to negotiate basic national issues, such as maintaining peace or war or setting boundaries. This was recognized in the Treaty of Hopewell. Additional pledges of support from the United States came in the Trade and Intercourse Act of 1802 and subsequent laws. Moreover, the Constitution itself recognized Indians as special foreign nations. The Georgia act clearly was unconstitutional.

Thus, from treaties, U.S. statutes, and the Constitution, Marshall derived a conclusion he had specifically rejected in *Cherokee Nation*. Indian nations, according to Marshall were always "distinct, independent political communities, retaining their original natural rights." An Indian nation was "a people distinct from others." It should be viewed like "other nations of the earth." This was a significant distance from the "domestic, dependent nation" of Marshall's creation just one year previously. In essence, he constructively reversed *Cherokee Nation*'s majority opinion. Worcester, decided the majority, should be released, and the Georgia lower court decision was reversed.

McLean, who had agreed with Marshall in *Cherokee Nation*, felt compelled to concur and to set his views apart from the "new" Marshall.

McLean spent a significant part of his concurring opinion on procedural matters, but then he turned to a discussion of the nature of the Cherokee nation. McLean did not disassociate himself from his *Cherokee Nation* views. McLean wrote that the Georgia statute under consideration was unconstitutional because it violated treaties and federal powers, but Indians were not like other nations of the earth. "[I]t is equally clear," determined McLean, "that the range of nations or tribes, who exist in the hunter state, may be restricted within reasonable limits." Such restrictions included amounts of land they could claim, areas over which native Americans could travel, and hunting and fishing rights.

McLean concluded by noting that Indians never held full sovereign power over their lands and that native Americans did not constitute a foreign state. McLean continued to believe that Indians were to be treated under American law as domestic, dependent nations. Moreover, they were also wards of the guardian United States. "The humane policy of the [federal] government towards these children of the wilderness," observed McLean, "must afford pleasure to every benevolent feeling." This was a subtle hint to Marshall. He could still derive his moral sympathies from McLean's views without creating international legal confusion by declaring native Americans to be foreign nations.

McLean also worried about the implications of *Worcester*. What if President Jackson refused to back the Supreme Court's pronouncement? In strong language, McLean warned the president, "It is in vain, and worse than in vain, that the national legislature enact laws, if those laws are to remain upon the statute book as monuments of the imbecility of the national power." If the executive refused to enforce a declaration by the Supreme Court of unconstitutionality, "the existence of the federal government is at an end."

Because of the crucial element of the timing, the need for specific papers, and the lack of cooperation from Georgia, the Supreme Court was not in a position to obtain Worcester's release. Wirt realized this, and he attempted to have new laws drafted so that the problems presented by this specific case could be resolved. Such laws would make it difficult for a state to resist a federal court's mandate. The United States was not yet ready for this major constitutional change, and President Jackson was not about to use force to make Georgia comply, although later he would need to do so in South Carolina because of the nullification controversy. Worcester eventually served out his sentence, and the Cherokees were forced to move to Oklahoma.

The importance of these two cases to Indian law cannot be overstated. Marshall's opinion in *Cherokee Nation* came to represent the fundamental basis by which Native Americans were to be regarded in American law. This is somewhat ironic in that this opinion was never shared by more than two out of seven justices at any one time, and the author himself repudiated it one year later. Nevertheless, the legal concept of an American Indian domestic, dependent nation has endured.

After *Cherokee Nation* and *Worcester*, Indian law went through a series of evolutionary attempts to interpret the meaning of "domestic." Post-World War II revivals of civil rights plus the creation and implementation of the Indian Claims Commission led to notions of Indian home rule and a greater focus on the word "nation" in U.S. governmental relations with native Americans.

These recent developments in federal Indian law no doubt would have been positively received by Chief John Ross and the Cherokees. It might have made their attempts to preserve their homelands and nationhood in the early nineteenth century more meaningful to them. Nothing can blur the memories of the Trail of Tears and the inability of America's greatest legalist John Marshall to win a resolution to the legal place of native Americans within the geopolitical confines of the United States; nor should it.

Selected Bibliography

Burke, J.C. "The Cherokee Cases: A Study in Law, Politics, and Morality." *Stanford Law Review* 21 (Feb. 1969): 500–31.

McLoughlin, W.G. *Cherokee Renascence in the New Republic.* Princeton, NJ: Princeton University Press, 1986.

———. *Cherokees and Missionaries, 1789–1839.* New Haven, CT: Yale University Press, 1984.

Perdue, T. *The Cherokees.* New York: Chelsea House Press, 1988.

Reid, J.P. *A Better Kind of Hatchet: Law, Trade, and Diplomacy in the Cherokee Nation During the Early Years of European Contact.* University Park, PA: Pennsylvania State University Press, 1976.

THE "DEATH KNELL OF THE NATIONS"

by *Thomas Burnell Colbert*
Department of History
Marshalltown Community College

Boudinot v. United States, 11 Wallace 616 (1871) [U.S. Supreme Court]

Mixed-blood Cherokee Elias Cornelius Boudinot was often embroiled in controversy. Indeed, he created many enemies among his native American brethren with his "progressive" views and actions. Ironically, though, it was his conflict with the federal government over taxing tobacco manufactured in the Cherokee nation that not only propelled him into advocating legal absorption of Indians into white society but also, and more importantly, led to a change in federal policy toward Indian treaties.

The seed of the legal imbroglio was sown in 1867 when Boudinot and his uncle Stand Watie established a tobacco factory in the Cherokee nation. They made a deal with the owners of a factory in Missouri to move the operation into the Cherokee nation, not far from the Arkansas border, near Maysville, Arkansas. The Missourians would receive $5,000 for their machinery and expenses. However, Boudinot lacked cash, so he offered them two-thirds of the profit.

The site of the factory, only 100 yards west of the Arkansas state line, received the name Boudyville. Tobacco would be purchased in Missouri, and farmers in Arkansas of the Cherokee nation would be encouraged to grow the plant. Furthermore, Boudinot could undersell white competitors because of the Cherokee Treaty of 1866. Article 10 of the treaty stated that a citizen of the Cherokee nation "shall have the right to sell any products of his farm . . . or any manufactured products, and to ship and drive the same to market without restraint, paying tax thereon, which is now or may be levied by the United States on the quantity sold outside of the Indian Territory."

The business was so successful that Boudinot expanded his operations in 1868. By then, he had erected two two-story frame buildings and several one-story log-and-frame houses. He also owned state-of-the-art hydraulic equipment and employed several workers.

However, Boudinot feared that tobacco manufacturers in St. Louis might use their political influence to hinder his endeavors. Therefore, on May 8, 1868, he asked Deputy Commissioner of Internal Revenue John R. Risley for an opinion on the legality of Boudinot's selling his tobacco outside of Indian territory. Risley answered that "under *existing* laws, no tax can be legally assessed and collected upon tobacco manufactured at such a factory, whether it be sold in the Cherokee country or elsewhere in any of the United States" [emphasis in original]. But he cautioned that he did not feel able to remark on how a new revenue bill under congressional consideration would affect the situation.

On July 20, 1868, the new law was enacted, and Section 107 of the legislation provided for collecting taxes on liquor and tobacco produced within the "exterior boundaries of the United States." Boudinot concluded, though, that the Cherokee Treaty of 1866 exempted his goods from coming under this statute. But apprehensive nonetheless, in November he informed James Marr, the supervisor of Internal Revenue for the region, that he was a Cherokee by birth and the owner of a tobacco factory in the Cherokee nation and that tobacco sold in the Cherokee nation was exempt from taxation if produced there. He further stated that he did sell some tobacco outside of the Indian territory and did pay taxes on it when the tobacco was sold, not before. He asked to be allowed to continue this practice.

Marr referred Boudinot's request to the Office of Internal Revenue, recommending that officials "be instructed to assess and collect this tax upon requiring Major Boudinot to report all tobacco to them that he intends offering for sale in this state [Missouri]." Thomas Harland, the acting commissioner of Internal Revenue, replied that although Boudinot did not have to pay on tobacco sold in the Cherokee nation, he had to affix revenue stamps before selling it in the states. He could do so, however, by purchasing stamps at the nearest collection point before selling his product. Consequently, on January 4, 1869, Marr informed E. A. Rollins, the new commissioner of Internal Revenue, that under instructions from Harland, Boudinot could "go on with his business without molestation."

In February 1869, Boudinot communicated with Rollins. After reminding the commissioner of Article 10 of the treaty and noting that there was not much of a market for tobacco in the Cherokee nation, he conveyed his desire to sell outside of the Cherokee nation. "No one manufacturing tobacco in the nation," he wrote, "can pay taxes on the same until he gets into a market where he can anticipate the proceeds on the sale of the same." In fact, he contended, to pay such taxes while his tobacco was still at the factory, as the law stipulated, would violate the treaty. Therefore, he asked to be allowed to put the tobacco he intended to sell outside of the Indian territory in the custody of revenue collectors until he had a buyer. Then he would pay the tax. Rollins, who agreed that the treaty held precedence over statutory law, gave Boudinot permission to ship his tobacco to specified towns, "provided that the packages indicate . . . the place of manufacture, the name of the manufacturer, and [are] shipped to the care of the collector of the district." Boudinot would have to inform the collector of where and when the tobacco would be sold and to pay the tax before removing it.

Less than a month later, Columbus Delano replaced Rollins as Commissioner of Internal Revenue, and under Delano's leadership, Internal Revenue authorities decided to take action against those who sold unstamped tobacco. In turn, Boudinot engaged his old friends Albert Pike and Robert W. Johnson as his attorneys. They contacted Delano, who stated that the government did not intend to tax goods made and sold in the Cherokee nation, only products shipped into the United States from there.

Regardless of Delano's remarks, on December 20, 1869, two officials from the Revenue Service, John McDonald and John A. Royce, arrested Boudinot and seized his factory. On January 1, 1870, Boudinot, in a signed statement, confirmed that he had purchased thousands of pounds of leaf tobacco in Missouri and Arkansas and that he had sold thousands of pounds of processed tobacco in the Indian territory, paying taxes only to the Cherokee nation. He also declared that he had affixed stamps to only 200 pounds, which he had sent to James E. Trott in Fayetteville, Arkansas. That was all he had sold outside of Indian territory. Nonetheless, he did admit that he had not complied with the revenue act of 1868.

Pike and Johnson demanded that Delano return Boudinot's property. When the commissioner refused, they argued that arresting Boudinot was an illegal act for it violated Article 10 of the Cherokee Treaty. As for Boudinot, he was released, but he refused to post bond, declaring that his arrest had been done illegally. He publicly contended that McDonald refused to acknowledge the Cherokee nation as a legal entity and that he served the interests of Missouri tobacco manufacturers.

Many years later, McDonald asserted that he had received instructions "to investigate gigantic frauds which it was reported were being perpetrated by tobacco manufacturers in the Indian Territory." He claimed that President Ulysses S. Grant told him to proceed "without fear." Eventually, McDonald confiscated four factories. And, although Delano ordered him several times to release the property, he refused, believing that he had good cases against the offenders. As for agent Joyce, he remembered officials concluding that "the Indians were simple figure-heads for the brains and capital of cunning white men."

Whatever prompted the actions of McDonald and Joyce, Boudinot did not waste time speculating about their motives. He needed to save his property. First, he tried without success to draw the attorney general into the conflict. Boudinot then announced in Washington that he was an escaped prisoner from Arkansas, for he had not given bail. He wanted to be arrested in that city so he might test the case under *habeas corpus* law. The Treasury Department, however, refused to call for his arrest. Next, he offered to compromise with Delano, saying that he would "conform strictly hereafter . . . with all regulations respecting collection of tax on tobacco in the United States" and would also "pay the . . . tax on all tobacco . . . hitherto sold unstamped whenever the courts shall determine that such tax is due."

The Treasury Department, however, was already taking stronger steps to enforce tax collection in Indian territory. In fact, the day before Boudinot made his plea to Delano, a tax assessor and a collector had been appointed for Indian territory. A few days later, Treasury Secretary George Boutwell informed Boudinot that "the action taken by Mr. Delano in the matter [confiscating the tobacco factory] was after consultation with me." In desperation, through Senator Alexander McDonald of Arkansas, Boudinot begged Delano to allow him to continue doing business. The commissioner rejected his request in mid-February 1870.

In May, Boudinot's case was tried in the U.S. District Court for the Western District of Arkansas. Judge Henry C. Caldwell decided against Boudinot. Although Caldwell believed that Boudinot had acted in good faith, he concluded that the revenue law of 1868 abrogated Article 10 of the Cherokee treaty. Boudinot's factory and tobacco were declared forfeited, and his only recourse lay in appealing to the U.S. Supreme Court.

By now, Boudinot lacked money to pursue the case, but fortunately the Cherokee National Council authorized the hiring of lawyers to represent him. Not only was Boudinot a Cherokee citizen, but more important, the case involved "great principles of international law and rights of foreign nationality vital to the interests and security of the Cherokee Nation and people."

In April 1871, the Supreme Court heard the case. The lawyers for Boudinot included himself, A. H. Garland, Albert Pike, Robert Johnson, and Benjamin F. Butler. Boudinot sued the government on writ of error, offering several points in his argument. It was pointed out that as a Cherokee, he was not a citizen of the United States and not represented in Congress. Therefore, Congress had no right to tax him. Then, too, Delano officially extended Internal Revenue authority in Indian territory after the arrest of Boudinot. Furthermore, not only did Article 10 of the Cherokee treaty have precedence over an act of Congress, but also the Court had earlier opined that "all provisions of

laws and treaties in regard to the Indians shall be construed most favorably to that people." And finally, the attorneys argued that Boudinot was on "impregnable ground" under the rule of construction. That is, there was no indication that Congress intended the internal revenue law to cover Indian territory.

Attorney General Amos Akerman presented the government's side. He argued that the United States and the Cherokee nation were not equals and that the federal government had the power to levy and collect taxes in Indian territory under proper legislation, such as the revenue act of 1868.

The six sitting justices voted 4–2 against Boudinot. Justice Noah H. Swayne, delivering the majority decision, said that the language in the law was quite clear, and if the legislation caused an injustice, it was a political matter. Congress, not the Court, would have to resolve that conflict. Justice Joseph P. Bradley, in dissent, maintained that it was clear Congress had not intended for the law to affect Indian territory and that the case reflected on the honor of the federal government to uphold the integrity of Indian treaties.

In effect, the Supreme Court destroyed the supposed binding power of a treaty. The ruling, Boudinot informed Stand Watie, "is the Death Knell of the Nations." In fact, though, partly due to the effect of Boudinot's case, earlier, in March 1871, Congress had attached a rider to the Indian Appropriations Act, declaring that no new treaties would be made with Indian tribes and tribal concerns would be controlled by the federal government. Indian tribes would no longer be considered independent powers. Although existing treaties were to be honored, the decision on the tobacco case brought new fears. The Grand Council of Indian Territory declared that Indian treaties "are now dependent wholly upon the forbearance of the government for we are powerless to enforce their fulfillment." The federal government could, if it desired, abrogate a treaty, and then the tribe would be at the mercy of government policy without the safeguard of another treaty.

As for Boudinot, he now became an arch-proponent of territorial government for Indian territory. He concluded that the Indian, especially an enterprising one such as himself, needed legal protection—citizenship—and personal ownership of his real property, not merely use of land held in common by the tribe. Had he been protected by the Constitution in an official territory of the United States, Boudinot reasoned, he would not have lost his property. He spent much of the next 20 years lobbying Congress and making speeches across the nation promoting his views—much to the chagrin of most Cherokees and other Indians.

With regard to his tobacco factory and his losses, Boudinot memorialized Congress for compensation. Eventually, Congress voted to dismiss civil proceedings against him, and upon the request of the House Judiciary Committee the attorney general withdrew the criminal counts. And in 1880 Congress allowed Boudinot to sue in the court of claims for damages against the United States.

The court of claims acted on Boudinot's petition in 1883. Boudinot asked for $175,000. The court awarded him only $3,272.25. This amount covered the tobacco lost, damage to his property, and his legal expenses, for the buildings and machinery had been returned to Boudinot. And in rendering this decision, the court offered the following commentary: "In no instance, probably, in the history of this court has a special act authorizing a party to sue the United States here, been couched in terms so liberal to the claimant. . . . It removes any ground for questioning the right of an Indian to sue in this court, and gives jurisdiction to this tribunal, which it would not otherwise have, of a claim against the Government based on an alleged tort committed by its officers. . . . and

declares an act done by the internal revenue officers . . . which had been sustained by a verdict of a jury and . . . affirmed by a solemn judgment of the Supreme Court . . . on a grave constitutional question, to have been 'a *wrong* done' to the claimant" [emphasis in original]. Certainly, Congress's allowing Boudinot to receive damages was a testimony to his influence in Washington, and, thus, after 14 years of controversy, the court of claims finally ended Boudinot's case.

Boudinot's financial claim, however, was ultimately of secondary importance. The specific issue in *Boudinot* was whether Boudinot had violated the internal revenue act of 1868, but the ramification of the Supreme Court's verdict was far-reaching. The case did deal with a "grave constitutional question," and the Court's ruling gave Congress the power to override stipulations in existing Indian treaties through legislation. At the same time, the concerns raised by the case even before the Supreme Court heard it prompted Congress to reverse its long-time policy of making treaties with Indian tribes. Congressional Indian policy would hereafter be more authoritarian, and it could be so with the concurrence of the Supreme Court.

Selected Bibliography

Colbert, T.B. "Prophet of Progress: The Life and Times of Elias Cornelius Boudinot." Ph.D. Dissertation. Oklahoma State University, 1982.

Heimann, R.K. "The Cherokee Tobacco Case." *Chronicles of Oklahoma* 41 (Autumn 1963): 299–322.

WHY NATIVE AMERICANS CAN NO LONGER COUNT ON TREATIES WITH THE U.S. GOVERNMENT

by *John R. Wunder*
Department of History
University of Nebraska at Lincoln

Lone Wolf v. Hitchcock, 187 U.S. 535 (1903) [U.S. Supreme Court]

Lone Wolf v. Hitchcock is to the Kiowa people and native Americans what *Plessy v. Ferguson* (1896) is to African-Americans and *United States v. Ju Toy* (1902) is to Chinese-Americans. It represented a direct legal attack on the fundamental basis governing U.S.-Indian relationships—the treaty. After *Lone Wolf*, treaties of the past were not perceived within the American legal system as inviolable instruments of law until the decisions of the Indian Claims Commission during the 1950s and 1960s began the long legal road back.

Approximately 12,000 years ago, the first ancestors of the Kiowa people migrated from Asia to North America. These ancestors were hunters, who eventually resided in the forests of what is today Canada. Approximately 9,000 years ago, the forests that predominated in much of North America began to die out due to a change in climate. The Great Plains region became an area characterized by lush grasslands, and native Americans began to move onto the Plains. It is here that the Kiowa settled.

Although explanations of Kiowa migration are mostly theory, most Kiowa believe that their nation began on the northern plains of western Montana. Their neighbors were the Flatheads, the Crow, and the Sarci. The Sarci are an Apachean people, and the Kiowa and Sarci lived and traveled together. During the seventeenth century, the Kiowa moved to the Black Hills, where they obtained the horse, a significant cultural, technological, and military breakthrough.

By the beginning of the eighteenth century, the Kiowa controlled much of the area around the Black Hills. However, this military hegemony was not to last. A new nation entered what the Kiowa considered their homelands. This nation, the Comanche, launched wars against the Kiowa from the south. At the same time, the Shoshone attacked the Kiowa from the west; the Cheyenne with their Arapaho allies put pressure on the Kiowa from the north; and the Sioux, the Kiowa's greatest threat, menaced them from the east. These military pressures plus a smallpox epidemic in 1781 weakened the Kiowa and forced them to evacuate the Black Hills. They moved south and encountered French traders, Spanish settlements, and the Comanche.

The Kiowa were known to other Plains Indians as the diplomats of the Great Plains. A relatively small nation, the Kiowa relied on their diplomatic skills to survive in a volatile region. The move onto the South Plains necessitated making agreements with the Comanche, which the Kiowa successfully pursued. This alliance, made around 1790, continues today. It also was through a diplomatic approach that the Kiowa met the new nineteenth-century invaders of the Great Plains, the United States.

Kiowa foreign policy relationships officially began with the United States in 1835. The Kiowa and other Plains Indians listened to a proposed treaty of peace and friendship with the United States. Some tribes agreed to share a common hunting territory and to allow U.S. citizens safe passage through the southern Plains. They also promised to pursue peaceful relations with Mexico. Although the Kiowa were interested, they chose not to sign the treaty. This did not deter the United States. Two years later, the United States and the Kiowa formally entered into a similar agreement. Both nations claimed that their peoples had been attacked and injured by the other, and these past disputes were forgiven. A treaty proclaiming peace and friendship was signed.

During the next 30 years, the southern Great Plains proved to be a very unstable area. Numerous wars were conducted by many participants, ranging from Mexico, an independent Texas, and the United States, to the Comanche, Ute, and Kiowa. Attempts by all parties to bring stability to the region were unsuccessful. The Civil War brought a respite for the Kiowa, but after the war the United States turned its attention to the full military capitulation of all Indian tribes on the Great Plains.

In the fall of 1867, the United States again tried to make another treaty with the Kiowa and other southern Plains tribes. The Treaty of Medicine Lodge Creek was the result. Ten Kiowa chiefs signed the document, which created a reservation between the Canadian and Red Rivers in southwestern Oklahoma. Two provisions of this treaty would prove important in the future. One allowed heads of Indian families to select up to 320 acres of reservation land to own if they so desired. The second provision of significance was Article 12, which stated, "No treaty for the cession of any portion or part of the reservation herein described [the Kiowa-Comanche Reservation], which may be held in common, shall be of any validity or force as against the said Indians, unless executed and signed by at least three fourths of all the adult Indian males occupying the same. . . ." Because he did not trust the United States to keep its word, young Chief Lone Wolf did not sign the treaty.

Many Kiowa continued to range beyond the reservation lands because of the scarcity of buffalo. This did not sit well with U.S. settlers or military leaders. Before long, war broke out again on the southern Plains, with both sides violating the terms of the Medicine Lodge Creek Treaty. The U.S. Army was particularly effective. Winter campaigns were very destructive and the message to the Indians was: cease fighting and remain on the reservation or face annihilation. Shortly after the Battle of the Washita, Lone Wolf and another chief delivered a message from the Indian agent assigned to the Kiowa to General George Armstrong Custer. The message stated that the Kiowa had not taken part in the battle. The two chiefs who were carrying a white flag of truce were immediately seized, and the rest of the Kiowa fled.

After the army threatened to hang Lone Wolf and the others under custody, the Kiowa returned to the fort.

Life on the reservation was not easy. The land in southwestern Oklahoma was not particularly conducive to economic activities within the range of Kiowa experiences. Governmental officials in charge sought to alter Kiowa cultural values in ways particularly punitive rather than to place a positive emphasis on farming and ranching training. White settlers tried to invade the reservation to occupy lands, and they sought long-term leases to the valuable grasslands on the reservation. Lone Wolf and other Kiowas tried to resist these attacks.

Perhaps the greatest force to threaten Kiowa culture came from the General Allotment Act (or Dawes Severalty Act) of 1887. This law allowed reservation lands to be divided into separate units that were distributed or allotted to individual Indians who were to farm or live on their allotments. After each person from a tribe received a plot, the remaining lands were sold. The money from the sale of this land was to be held in trust for the particular Indian tribe.

From the beginning, the Kiowa, like many other reservation Indians throughout the country, strongly opposed allotment. The tribe's chief, Lone Wolf, notified Washington that his people would go to war if allotment was forced on them. Nevertheless, non-Indians wanted the reservation lands, and in 1889 Congress set up a three-member committee to negotiate allotment with all 20 Indian reservations in Oklahoma. The delegation, known as the Jerome Commission after its chairman, David Jerome, arrived at Fort Sill in September 1892.

At the Fort Sill hearings, many Kiowa expressed their opposition. They did not want allotment. They cited the Medicine Lodge Creek Treaty as binding. Jerome persisted, offering each member of the three tribes on the Kiowa-Comanche Reservation 160 acres each plus the payment of $2 million for the surplus lands. Lone Wolf and others were opposed. Lone Wolf noted: "Look on Quanna's [Quanah Parker was the primary negotiator for the Comanche] people, they are Indians; look on Lone Wolf's people and Whiteman's [leader of the Kiowa-Apache] people, they are Indians;

they are not educated, they do not know how to till the ground. They do not know how to work. Should they be forced to take allotments it means sudden downfall for the three tribes." Even though most Kiowa had objections and Lone Wolf feared that the worst danger was losing tribal lands, Parker succeeded in persuading Lone Wolf and others to sign the document. They realized that no one could return to the way things were and that they had to accept change. Lone Wolf, himself, favored building schools and houses.

Lone Wolf and others thought that Parker's proposals were a part of the original agreement. These included payment for two sections in every township that were set aside for education, 320 acre allotments, payment of up to $2.50 per acre for leftover lands, and retention of mineral rights to the reservation lands. Soon after the Fort Sill meeting, however, it became clear that Jerome did not believe the agreement included these provisions. Opposition developed, and Lone Wolf now opposed the agreement, which he considered to be based on fraud. For Congress to begin assigning Kiowa-Comanche Reservation lands, three-fourths of all tribal members had to sign the agreement. This was based on the provision in the Medicine Lodge Creek Treaty. With the collusion of the Indian agent, whites were added to tribal roles and Indians were deleted. The commission certified that there were 562 eligible signers, but in reality that figure was closer to 725. The commission claimed they had 456 signatures, but many of the 456 who had signed it originally did so under false pretenses and they wished their names dropped from the document. Nevertheless, the commission presented the document to Congress.

It took seven years, but the agreement was accepted by Congress on June 6, 1900. Lone Wolf and other Indians had spent a great deal of time lobbying against ratification, but their efforts were to no avail. Secretary of the Interior Ethan A. Hitchcock was charged with implementing the allotments. Shortly after the bill had been passed by Congress, representatives of three tribes met with President William McKinley. He refused to modify the bill. This split the tribes, with some refusing to acknowledge defeat. Lone Wolf was among those who vowed to fight on in the courts.

In June 1901, Lone Wolf went to Washington and retained former congressman and federal judge William Springer as the tribe's attorney. Springer encouraged the Indian Rights Association, a private, humanitarian, reform group that organized during the late nineteenth century, to help with the case, and it did. Unfortunately, Springer was not a very good attorney, was short of funds, and was looking for an easy case. He demanded funding from the Department of the Interior, and he was refused. The Indian Rights Association was also alerted to what were perceived to be Springer's shortcomings.

Springer, however, pushed ahead, filing a complaint for Lone Wolf in the federal district court in the District of Columbia. Secretary Hitchcock was named as the defendant. Lone Wolf's suit sought an injunction to prevent the Secretary of the Interior from allotting the Kiowa-Comanche Reservation. The brief argued that the Jerome Commission report ratified by Congress was unconstitutional because it was contrary to the provisions of the Treaty of Medicine Lodge Creek and, if the allotment was allowed, it constituted a taking of property without proper due process. Two weeks later, Springer added seven more plaintiffs who had been named representatives of the three tribes by a general council held back on the reservation.

The district court ruled against Lone Wolf. It denied the injunction and the assertion that property would be taken without due process of law. The judge, A. C. Bradley, ruled that the allotment procedures were "the usual process," and he held that it did not make any difference if misunderstandings or deceptions were involved. He did not see irregularities as relevant, because Congress had spoken. Springer appealed the decision to the court of appeals, but by the time the court met in August 1901, the Kiowa-Comanche Reservation had been divided and opened for settlement.

On December 4, 1901, the Court of Appeals for the District of Columbia rejected Lone Wolf's appeal. The appellate judges held that treaties with Indians by the United States were not a proper judicial subject for scrutiny. Instead, this was a policy matter that was the sole function of the legislature. Moreover, they found that "lands and reservations are held by the Indians subject to the control and dominion of the United States." Indians, according to the appellate court, had no title in reservation lands. They were simply occupants, subject to the will and whim of the federal government.

The appellate opinion caused great consternation among groups favoring Indian rights as well as the Indians themselves. The Indian Rights Association concluded that an appeal had to be made in order to overturn the extremely damaging appellate opinion. The association hired Hampton L. Carson, professor of law at the University of Pennsylvania, to argue the case. Springer's competence was subject to question by the association, and, now that the case had gone this far with an unmitigated disaster near at hand, more experienced and stronger counsel was needed. Meanwhile, Lone Wolf and 200 others refused to accept the first land payment.

Lone Wolf's attorneys had a challenging argument to make. Recent U.S. Supreme Court decisions had moved steadily toward rendering U.S. treaty agreements with Indians unenforceable. Indians under American law were being reclassified from members of sovereign nations to dependent wards of the federal government. For example, in *United States v. Kagama* (1886), the Supreme Court ruled that crimes committed by Indians on reservation land were subject to federal criminal jurisdiction because Indians were now wards of the federal government. *Kagama* was interpreted by lower courts to mean that Congress had total authority to do as it wished even if it disregarded specific provisions of Indian treaties.

Oral arguments began on October 23, 1902, before the Supreme Court. Carson presented the bulk of Lone Wolf's case. Those present at the hearing remarked that Carson's presentation was outstanding. Representing the Department of the Interior was Assistant Attorney General Willis Van Devanter, a lawyer from Wyoming and a future Supreme Court justice. Pro-Lone Wolf partisans reported that Van Devanter's argument was dull and unexciting and that the justices did not pay much attention to it.

Lone Wolf argued that the allotment act passed by Congress dividing up the Kiowa-Comanche Reservation was unconstitutional for three reasons. First, the agreement violated the Medicine Lodge Creek Treaty because fewer than three-fourths of the adult Indian males on the reservation had signed it. Second, those who did sign were fraudulently misled by the commission. And third, the agreement allowed only $1 per acre for surplus lands reimbursement, which was significantly below the value of real estate and also abrogated the $2.50-per-acre promise. Thus, the attorneys concluded that the allotment act violated Kiowa and Comanche property rights and deprived them of due process of law.

Van Devanter, for Secretary of the Interior Hitchcock, relied on recent cases to conclude that Indians were wards of the U.S. government and, as such, they were totally dependent on Congress. Thus, when Congress acted, treaty obligations might be revised or voided. Indian legislation was essentially a political matter, not a judicial issue.

Justice Edward D. White wrote a near-unanimous opinion for the Court. White's holding agreed with the appellate court and Van Devanter, but he went even further. White decreed that Congress was to have unlimited power over Indian property, regardless of treaty guarantees. He reached the conclusion that Indian treaties were not valid legal instruments if they conflicted with congressional action. Indians were dependent on the federal government, White maintained, and, therefore, they had no power or ability to function outside a guardianship relationship. Congress also might need to dispose of Indian land in an emergency, so it could not afford to be inhibited by Indian consent. White quoted an 1877 case involving a claim of reservation status on disputed lands, where the Court ruled, "It is to be presumed that in this matter the United States would be governed by such considerations of justice as would control a Christian people in their treatment of an ignorant and dependent race." Finally, White reasoned that the Resolution of 1871, a law whereby the United States was prevented from making any future treaties with native American nations, should be interpreted as meaning that past treaties were revokable by Congress at any time and for any reason.

Thus, the Court found that Congress had total control over Lone Wolf and the Kiowa because Indians were a dependent, racially inferior group incapable of challenging congressional power. Such a challenge might be rendered in a treaty, and therefore treaties as legal contracts were no longer enforceable once Congress acted. With this holding, it made no difference whether fraud or deceit was used by the Jerome Commission. In essence, the allotment act nullified the Treaty of Medicine Lodge Creek. All the judicial branch could do was presume that Congress would act in good faith. Any remedy the Kiowa might seek had to occur within the legislative branch, not with the judiciary.

Lone Wolf v. Hitchcock was a devastating opinion for native Americans. The only protection Indians had traditionally had for individual and tribal rights was their treaty agreements, and now treaties were no longer given credence. With one stroke of the pen, a new doctrine was articulated authorizing the unilateral termination of treaties. It would take over 50 years before this new doctrine began to fade, although it has never been overruled.

In the interim, the Kiowa-Comanche Reservation was divided and abolished. The Kiowa concentrated in seven communities in the northern portion of Caddo and Kiowa counties of southwestern Oklahoma. The descendants of Lone Wolf settled in the most isolated and westward of the communities and named the settlement after the prominent chief. Awarded $2 million by the Indian Claims Commission in 1960 for past treaty abrogations, the Kiowa nation today strives to overcome the legacy of rural poverty and the destruction of its land base that was its heritage from *Lone Wolf v. Hitchcock*.

Selected Bibliography

Barsh, R.L., and J.Y. Henderson. *The Road: Indian Tribes and Political Liberty*. Berkeley, CA: University of California Press, 1980.

Hagan, W.T. *United States-Comanche Relations: The Reservation Years*. New Haven, CT: Yale University Press, 1976.

Wilkinson, C.F. *American Indians, Time, and the Law: Native Societies in a Modern Constitutional Democracy*. New Haven, CT: Yale University Press, 1987.

Wunder, J.R. *The Kiowa People*. New York: Chelsea House Press, 1989.

NATIVE AMERICAN LAND CLAIMS: THE INDIANS FINALLY WIN

by John R. Wunder
Department of History
University of Nebraska at Lincoln

Joint Tribal Council of the Passamaquoddy Tribe v. Morton, 528 F.2d 370 (1975)
[U.S. Court of Appeals]

An old Passamaquoddy tale concerns the scarcity of tobacco. A young Passamaquoddy sees his grandmother smoking and he wants to smoke with her. She says that she will share the tobacco, but she worries because tobacco is very rare. He says he will get some tobacco, and she tells him he must go to an island. The boy journeys to the island, but he confronts a woman who tries to prevent him from obtaining any tobacco. A struggle ensues between the boy and the woman, and the woman changes into a crow. The boy becomes a large bird, and the two fight in the air. Eventually the crow/woman drops the tobacco she has in her claws. The bird/boy swoops down and seizes it. Then he brings it to his grandmother and says, "Ho'k'mi yut, t'ma'wei kwuskwe'sul (My grandmother, here is the tobacco)." His grandmother wisely replies, "Ndege'k'ma'jehan (You'd better go your way); k'dunlogo'kw (she will be after you)."

This story certainly applies to the Passamaquoddy's relationships with other nations over time and with Maine and the United States in particular. These relationships have taken a variety of twists, the most recent resulting in a significant, path-breaking federal court decision, *Joint Tribal Council of the Passamaquoddy Tribe v. Morton*, which forced an unusual federal-state legislative package, the Maine Indian Claims Settlement Act and the Maine Implementing Act.

The Passamaquoddy are an eastern woodlands people who have lived in Maine for at least 3,000 years. The earliest evidence of occupation by descendants of the Passamaquoddy is found around Passamaquoddy Bay on what is today the U.S.-Canadian border. There is no evidence of agricultural cultivation. The Passamaquoddy lived a semi-nomadic life of hunting and fishing, migrating up and down the St. Croix River basin. In the summer, they raised corn, beans, and tobacco. Linguistically, the Passamaquoddy spoke the Algonquian language. They shared a dialect with their neighbors, the Maliseets, and they were related linguistically and culturally to other neighbors, the Micmac and the Penobscots.

The first major European contact with the Passamaquoddy occurred in the early seventeenth century. The French established missions in Passamaquoddy country, and they involved the Indians in the fur trade. Unfortunately for the Passamaquoddy, many pressures built up by the mid-seventeenth century. Disease took its toll; British and French rivalries required northern New England tribes to choose sides; and the League of the Iroquois became a power to the west that threatened the very existence of eastern tribes. A combination of British atrocities and French diplomacy led to the Passamaquoddy becoming French allies. Moreover, a confederation of Algonquian-speakers was formed among the Micmac, Maliseets, Penobscots, and Passamaquoddy termed the Wabanaki, or "People of the Dawnland." The Wabanaki Confederacy remained at war with the British from the end of

King Philip's War in 1677 to the end of the American Revolution in 1781. In 1700, the Wabanaki Confederacy made peace with the League of the Iroquois. Even though the Iroquoian-speakers remained staunch allies of the English, this did not cause a breach in the peace. In 1749, the Great Council Fire began between the two confederacies. Such diplomacy established the basis for Indian-European relations on the eastern American continent for two centuries.

The victory of the British over the French in 1759 caused a strain in the Wabanaki Confederacy. The Passamaquoddy and others concluded that they had to make peace with the British. They did so in 1760, but they did not give up their autonomy or swear loyalty. At first the British tired to protect Passamaquoddy lands. But the Proclamation of 1763 and other promises could not hold off white settlement. By 1764, the Passamaquoddy were complaining to the governor of Massachusetts that whites were illegally taking land on islands in Passamaquoddy Bay, selling alcohol, and committing trading frauds. The British ignored the Passamaquoddy.

Thus, it was an easy choice for the Passamaquoddy and the Wabanaki Confederacy when war broke out between the patriots and loyalists in 1776. The Passamaquoddy and Maliseets signed a treaty of alliance with the patriots in 1777 at Aukpaque. The patriots promised trade, supplies, a priest, payment for military service, and a beaver monopoly to the Indians. The alliance was further secured when the French joined the patriot cause in 1778. During the war, the Passamaquoddy helped repulse a British naval attack at Machais, but when the negotiations were begun and concluded with the Treaty of Paris in 1783, Passamaquoddy interests were neither represented nor protected. This oversight occurred even though John Allan, George Washington's agent on the eastern frontier, reported to the Continental Congress in the spring of 1783 that the Wabanaki Confederacy had been crucial to the holding of Maine for the patriots. Allan stated, "These Indians, particularly St. John's [Maliseets] and Passamaquoddy are very tenacious of their liberties; delegacious and subtle people and may be very dangerous if not attended to; their zeal in the cause and their virtue in persevering through many difficulties throughout the war with the attachments and affections the subscriber has experienced himself commands attention . . . ."

The boundary agreed to by the British and Americans was the St. Croix River, but both parties did not agree as to where that river was. The British, before the treaty was formally signed, confiscated the Passamaquoddy summer camps, and the Americans allowed this. The final determination of the Maine boundary did not occur until the Webster-Ashburton Treaty of 1842. Still, by choosing the St. Croix River, the Wabanaki Confederacy was divided with the Passamaquoddy and Penobscots plus one band of Maliseets living in Maine and the rest of the Maliseets and Micmacs residing in Canada.

In 1790, the United States enacted the first Indian Trade and Intercourse Act (which many courts and historians have incorrectly labelled the Nonintercourse Act). This law was designed to prevent confusion over Indian land cessions and to establish federal control over Indians within the United States. Section 4 of the act provided: "That no sale of lands made by any Indians, or any nation or tribe of Indians within the United States, shall be valid to any person or persons, or to any state, whether having the right of pre-emption to such lands or not, unless the same shall be made and duly executed at some public treaty, held under the authority of the United States." The act was further strengthened in 1793 when it was provided that no representatives of state governments could negotiate for Indian land sessions. The burden was placed on a state to stay out of these negotiations. Nevertheless, states ignored the Trade and Intercourse Act. They made tribes subject to state law. In 1794, Massachusetts concluded a treaty with the Passamaquoddy whereby the Passamaquoddy ceded all of their lands except 27,000 acres, located at two reservations on the Canadian border. When Maine became a state in 1820, Massachusetts gave Maine $30,000 to use as a trust fund for taking on the responsibilities of providing for Indians in the new state.

From 1820 to 1964, the Passamaquoddy land base was nibbled away, and the conditions of the Passamaquoddy deteriorated significantly. Maine assumed complete power over the Passamaquoddy without federal interference. The Maine legislature gave out 999-year leases to whites on Passamaquoddy reservation lands, sold timber rights, and granted railroad, highway, and utility rights-of-way over Passamaquoddy lands without consultation or compensation. A portion of the Passamaquoddy lands was used for German internment during World War II. After the war, the federal government returned control of the reservation land to the state, and Maine sold the land to whites.

Maine simply hoped that the Passamaquoddy would go away. At first the state dealt directly with the Passamaquoddy Council and the two reservation chiefs or governors. But in 1927 Maine stopped dealing directly with the Passamaquoddy and placed all state activity with them in the Forestry Department. This lasted until 1933, when Maine shifted Passamaquoddy affairs to the Health and Welfare Department. Then, in 1965, Maine created a Department of Indian Affairs. The funds in the state trust fund were not used for Maine Indians. Maine decided who could be a Passamaquoddy, and it restricted hunting, fishing, and trapping rights. Maine went so far as to declare the Passamaquoddy no longer an Indian tribe. Beginning in 1823, the Passamaquoddy chose a nonvoting representative to the Maine legislature. The state abolished the position, however, in 1941. In 1953, Maine became the last state to allow Indians the right to vote, and the Passamaquoddy finally achieved the franchise for state legislature elections in 1967. The Passamaquoddy had to pay all state taxes but the property tax, and they paid federal income taxes. They could be drafted, but they could not receive Veteran Administration benefits.

By 1964, the Passamaquoddy had two reservations, which had come to provide them with a strong sense of community and continuity. One was at Pleasant Point, or Sebayick, a 100-acre treeless and barren tract between Eastport and Perry on Passamaquoddy Bay. This is the second most easterly point of the United States. In 1964, nearly 400 Passamaquoddies resided at Pleasant Point. The other reservation was located at Indian Township, or Medakinegook, a 17,000-acre, heavily wooded, undeveloped estate near Princeton. Fresh water streams and lakes dot Indian Township as well as shoreline on the St. Croix River. Two Indian towns, Peter Dana Point and Indian Strip, contained most of the 300 Passamaquoddy living in Indian Township. The rest of the Passamaquoddy, some 500, lived off the reservations. Both reservations border on Canada, and both are in Washington County, the poorest county in all of the New England states. The average annual income for the Passamaquoddy in the 1960s was approximately $430. Part-time work existed in logging operations and sardine factories, and the Passamaquoddy had seasonal opportunities in potato picking and blueberry raking. Nearly one-third of all Passamaquoddy were unemployed. The Passamaquoddy had a 99.5 percent dropout rate in high school. Some scattered welfare programs reached the reservations, and Maine spent some funds on food and health programs for the Passamaquoddy. Still, the reservation settlements had no running water, electricity, or sewage disposal. Only two pay telephones were on each reservation; there were no home telephones.

Given these very difficult conditions, the Passamaquoddy still had not proven to be disruptive to Maine authorities prior to 1964. In part, this was because of a cultural taboo on criticism. Most people accepted authority without questioning unless a group consensus reflected a need for change. There was a strong, mutual sense of loss—the loss of land, self-sufficiency, and aspects of Passamaquoddy culture. These losses combined with the physical conditions of Passamaquoddy life and the cultural traditions of consensus made for a near national depression.

The motions of change were set in place for the Passamaquoddy in a poker game in February 1964. William Plaisted, a white man, held a 999-year lease on property in Indian Township between Lewey's Lake and U.S. Route 1. On this property, Plaisted had built some tourist cabins. In the poker game, Plaisted won the rights to a 999-year lease held by a neighbor. The next morning Plaisted set out stakes around the adjoining land in order to put in a new road, and he hired some Passamaquoddies to cut down trees. This property was also inhabited by a Passamaquoddy named George

Stevens, and he did not like what was happening. He flagged down his brother, John Stevens, who was on his way to his job at the Georgia-Pacific Corporation paper mill. John Stevens was the Passamaquoddy tribal governor for the Indian Township Reservation. He had served in the Korean War and had spent some time off the reservations, and he had been encouraging his people to stand up to white confiscation of Passamaquoddy lands. Moreover, Stevens's wife's great-aunt, Louise Sockabesin, had earlier shown him several documents she had been keeping in a shoebox. Among the documents were letters from George Washington to the Passamaquoddy during the American Revolution and the original copy of the 1794 Passamaquoddy-Commonwealth of Massachusetts Treaty. Stevens discovered disparity of 6,000 acres and several islands between the lands guaranteed by the treaty and the lands actually held by the Passamaquoddy. Stevens had tried to find a Maine lawyer to look into this matter, but he had been unsuccessful.

The next evening, Stevens called a meeting of the Indian Township Tribal Council at Peter Dana Point. Everyone already knew about Plaisted's plans. The hall was packed with angry Passamaquoddies, who recalled many other instances of white takings of Passamaquoddy property. The council decided to go see Maine Governor John Reed and ask for his help. Governor Reed did not take the Passamaquoddy seriously. The council returned and called another meeting. Now the Passamaquoddy identified Maine as the primary problem, and they decided to block construction of Palisted's planned road. Seventy-five Passamaquoddy took up positions the next morning. After a standoff for several hours, five men, including George Stevens, and five women remained. The men were arrested by a Princeton policeman, who took them to Woodland where he released them. However, the five women were arrested by state troopers and taken to Calais, where they were booked and charged with trespass and put in the city jail. That afternoon, Stevens bailed the women out. He then sought legal counsel.

The suit against the women was eventually dismissed, but in the process the attorney and Passamaquoddy leaders decided to look into the loss of Passamaquoddy land. At first the strategy was to find a means of obtaining the missing 6,000 acres by upholding the Massachusetts 1794 treaty. But after a change in legal counsel, the Passamaquoddy turned to a young attorney, Thomas Tureen, who had only recently finished law school and who was working with the Indian Legal Services Unit of Pine Tree Legal Assistance, a program funded in Maine by the federal Office of Economic Opportunity. First, Tureen helped the tribe set up corporations so it could receive grants from federal agencies. In this process, he discovered that the Passamaquoddy were never recognized by the federal government. This led him to see that the federal government had attempted to protect the Passamaquoddy and other tribes with the 1790 Indian Trade and Intercourse Act. The act prohibited the private sale of Indian lands; and if it was still in force, it superseded the Massachusetts treaty. Thus, the Passamaquoddy might well be entitled to several million acres because their title to land in Maine had never been extinguished. In 1970, Tureen began to plan a suit to recover these lands for the Passamaquoddy. Other eastern tribes watched the litigation closely because they believed they could recover land by making the same arguments regarding their own claims.

Because the Passamaquoddy could not sue Maine, they needed the assistance of the Department of the Interior. This would be a problem because they were not a federally recognized tribe and, after an initial contact with several Washington constituencies, it became obvious that the Department of the Interior was not very interested. The delays from the Department of the Interior took on an even greater significance when Tureen and the Passamaquoddy discovered that Congress on July 18, 1966, had passed a statute of limitations on damages Indians might sue for, which meant that any suit the Passamaquoddy wished to file had to be made by July 18, 1972. They were eight months from the total expiration of their claim, and the Department of the Interior appeared to be deliberately stalling.

After a great deal of frantic research, on June 2, 1972, Tureen filed a suit for the Passamaquoddy against Secretary of the Interior Rogers C. B. Morton in federal district court at Portland, Maine. The Passamaquoddy sought a declaratory judgment that they were protected by the Indian Trade and Intercourse Act of 1790. They also wanted an injunction to order the Department of the Interior to file a court action for monetary damages and return of acreage against Maine. The district court judge, Edward T. Gignoux, held two hearings. After the first hearing, Gignoux ordered the Department of the Interior to decide within a week whether it would voluntarily file suit. The Department of the Interior appeared one week later and said it would not file voluntarily, and Judge Gignoux ordered it to do so. In late June, the Department of Justice presented Judge Gignoux with a $150 million damage suit against Maine on behalf of the Passamaquoddies. Two weeks later, the Penobscots and the Houlton Bank of Maliseets also joined the suit. All of Maine's Indians were now represented, and they had beat the deadline by one day. Ironically, Congress then extended the deadline for Indian law suits.

In the winter of 1973, Judge Gignoux heard argument on the substantive issues raised by the Passamaquoddy suit. The plaintiffs argued that the Indian Trade and Intercourse Act of 1790 must be applied to the Passamaquoddy and that it created a trust relationship for all Indians with the new nation, the United States. The defendants, which now included Maine, urged the judge to hold that no trust relationship existed because the Passamaquoddy had never been officially recognized. On January 20, 1975, Judge Gignoux issued his opinion which found that the Indian Trade and Intercourse Act applied to the Passamaquoddy even though there had never been federal recognition of the tribe, that a trust relationship was created by the act, and that there existed a right on the part of the Passamaquoddy to use the courts to attain land and damages based on the holding. The defendants appealed.

The three-judge panel of the U.S. Court of Appeals for the First Circuit heard arguments from all parties beginning in September 1975. The Passamaquoddy reiterated their district court position, and Maine offered several refinements of its basic arguments. Each side agreed that there were three issues: (1) whether the Indian Trade and Intercourse Act of 1790 applied to the Passamaquoddy; (2) whether the Indian Trade and Intercourse Act of 1790 created a trust relationship between the United States and the Passamaquoddy; and (3) what remedies, if the first two issues were decided in the affirmative, were afforded the Passamaquoddy. Circuit Court Judge Levin H. Campbell wrote a unanimous opinion for the panel in favor of the Passamaquoddy.

The opinion began with a history of the Passamaquoddy's relationship to the United States and to Maine. The court seemed particularly impressed with the supportive role the Passamaquoddy played in the American Revolution and the legal relationship the tribe had with Maine and the United States. Maine, since its statehood, had passed nearly 350 laws relating to the Passamaquoddy, whereas the United States only dealt with the Passamaquoddy briefly during the 1820s when it supported the bringing of education to the Passamaquoddy reservations.

The circuit court then identified what it considered the basic issue of the case: whether the United States had a trust relationship with the Passamaquoddy. To determine this, the court asked three questions. First, given the Indian Trade and Intercourse Act of 1790, were the Passamaquoddy to be considered a tribe within the meaning of the act? The act referred to "any tribe of Indians." Maine argued that a tribe included only those officially recognized by the federal government. Even if the Passamaquoddy were a tribe in a sense of a racially and culturally separate entity, Maine argued that when it assumed statehood, the United States, by ignoring the terms by which Maine took over the administration of the Indians in Maine, simply agreed tacitly not to recognize Passamaquoddy tribal status. The court rejected this contention, finding that the word "tribe" in the act was to be broadly defined and that it applied to all groups of Indians regardless of whether they were recognized by the federal government. (Eventually the U.S. Department of the Interior would issue guidelines for the determination of tribal status.) In addition, the court ruled that the act was designed so that the federal government protected the right of Indians to occupy lands that they claimed or were agreed on by U.S.-native

American treaties. No Maine-Massachusetts agreement could extinguish the federal responsibilities under the act.

The second question probed whether the United States had a specific trust relationship with the Passamaquoddy. Since the court had held that the Indian Trade and Intercourse Act of 1790 did apply to the Passamaquoddy, it was relatively simple to reason that a federal duty existed to investigate and protect Passamaquoddy interests, even if Congress were to recognize the Passamaquoddy as a tribe in the future. The third question then asked whether time or Passamaquoddy-Maine relationships precluded any trust relationship. The court reasoned that no action on the part of Maine or neglect on the part of Congress could mitigate or deny federal responsibility. Even Maine's argument that an old judicial ruling that the Passamaquoddy were not an Indian tribe was dismissed by the court. The federal government, stated Judge Campbell, was under no obligation to react to a state court's opinion.

Thus, the Passamaquoddy had won an important decision. Even though the circuit court refused to discuss how the Passamaquoddy might go about seeking a remedy, an important precedent had occurred. Moreover, neither side sought to appeal, and the decision stood as law. By this point there was much political fallout in Maine and in Washington. What would the Passamaquoddy want? Would they desire lands already occupied? What would other eastern tribes affected by the 1790 act do? It was a time of great political passion and negotiation.

The governor of Maine, James Longley, and his political rival, Attorney General Joseph Brennan, sought to score political points at the expense of the Passamaquoddy. Maine's Washington delegation was also caught up in the hysteria, particularly after Ropes & Gray, a Boston law firm and legal adviser to New England municipal bond companies, refused to give unqualified approval to municipal bonds to be issued in Maine's disputed area. Only Senator William Hathaway tried to assist the Passamaquoddy in receiving a fair settlement, but he lost reelection to the Senate to Congressman William Cohen.

After much maneuvering, Maine passed legislation approved by the Passamaquoddy. The Indians agreed that serious crimes committed by Indians on reservations would be tried in state courts, that Indians who lived on reservations and made their living on reservations would pay state income taxes, and that Maine's environmental laws would apply to the reservations. Maine agreed not to regulate tribal membership; that all reservations now fell under the Indian Trade and Intercourse Act, thereby preventing any land losses without congressional action; and Indians could regulate fishing, hunting, and trapping on reservation lands without state interference.

Senators George Mitchell and Cohen then introduced the Maine Indian Claims Settlement Act in the Senate. The Passamaquoddy agreed not to press claims for occupied lands. Instead, timber lands would be obtained from lumber companies, and they agreed to set aside a maximum of 200,000 acres for sale. After several hearings, it was approved and sent to the House, which also approved it. President Jimmy Carter signed the settlement act on October 10, 1980, and he signed an appropriations bill on December 12, 1980, after being defeated by Ronald Reagan. This act established the Maine Indian Claims Settlement Trust Fund of $27 million to be administered by the Department of the Interior. The Maine Indian Claims Land Acquisition Fund was also created ($26.8 million each for the Penobscots and the Passamaquoddy plus $900,000 for the Houlton Band of Maliseets). This fund could be used to purchase up to 300,000 acres. The tribes were officially recognized by the federal government and, as such, could receive the benefits afforded other recognized tribes. Since then, the Penobscots have purchased 150,000 acres in five large tracts. The Passamaquoddy have been more deliberative. They acquired a 5,000-acre blueberry farm and 4,000 acres previously taken away in Indian Township.

Joint Tribal Council of the Passamaquoddy Tribe v. Morton and the accompanying legislation proved to be a most important step in the evolution of U.S. Indian law. It demonstrated the importance of negotiations with court action. No settlement would have been possible without federal participation. In a sense, the courts acted as a catalyst. The federal courts ruled that the Indian Trade and Intercourse Act applied to all Indian tribes. This case led to others and to determinations concerning tribal status. In a 1978 case, a jury decided the Mashpees were not a tribe; this was upheld later with specific applications of tribal qualifications. The Mashpee setback did not deter the Narragansets from gaining federal recognition and $3.5 million to purchase 900 acres through the Rhode Island Claims Settlement Act of 1978. A 1981 case led to the Mashantucket Pequot Indian Claims Settlement Act of 1982 in Connecticut. The Gay Head Wampanoags of Massachusetts, the Schaghticoke and Mohegans of Connecticut, and the Catawbas of South Carolina have also pressed claims.

In the aftermath of the Maine litigation and the settlement acts, it is important to recognize that land is viewed by the Passamaquoddy as a means of self-identity. It was not necessarily seen as an economic entity. There is a Passamaquoddy trade song that explains the court case and legislation. A Passamaquoddy goes to the wigwam of another person. Near the entrance he sings a song. He then enters continuing to sing the song and begins to dance. At the end of the song he points to an object in the room he wants to buy and offers a price. The owner is then obliged to sell the object selected or to barter something of equal value. The Passamaquoddy for thousands of years have lived on the northern coast of Maine. Although they had lost most of their homelands, they were patient but firm. When the opportunity was presented, when the courts allowed them to sing and dance in Augusta, Maine, and in Washington, they were reasonable people. The Maine Indian Claims Settlement Act became the result and a reality, and it enhanced the life of the Passamaquoddy and many other native Americans.

Selected Bibliography

Axtell, J. *The Invasion Within: The Contest of Cultures in Colonial North America.* New York: Oxford University Press, 1985.

Brodeur, P. "Annals of Law: Restitution." *The New Yorker* 58 (Oct. 11, 1982): 76–155.

———. *Restitution: The Land Claims of the Mashpee, Passamaquoddy, and Penobscot Indians of New England.* Boston: Northeastern University Press, 1985.

Paterson, J.M.R., and D. Roseman. "A Reexamination of *Passamaquoddy v. Morton.*" *Maine Law Review* 31 (1979): 115–51.

Tureen, T.N., and F.J. O'Toole. "State Power and the Passamaquoddy Tribe: 'A Gross National Hypocrisy?'" *Maine Law Review* 23 (1971): 1–39.

Vollmann, T. "A Survey of Eastern Indian Land Claims: 1970–79." *Maine Law Review* 31 (1979): 5–16.

Wallace, H.B. "Indian Sovereignty and Eastern Indian Land Claims." *New York Law School Law Review* 27 (1982): 921–50.

D. Other Racial Minorities

CHINESE LAUNDRIES AND THE FOURTEENTH AMENDMENT

by John R. Wunder
Department of History
University of Nebraska at Lincoln

Yick Wo v. Hopkins, 118 U.S. 356 (1886) [U.S. Supreme Court]

In the summer of 1885, Yick Wo and over 150 other Chinese residents of San Francisco deliberately violated two ordinances in order to challenge an infringement on what they considered a basic right: the right to engage in economic activity. The San Francisco county and city ordinances, passed in May and July 1880, placed restrictions on laundry operators that were applied to prevent Chinese laundries from functioning. This challenge eventually was resolved by the U.S. Supreme Court in a unanimous decision, *Yick Wo v. Hopkins*.

The period from 1820 to 1882 was a time of free Chinese immigration, and hundreds of Chinese moved to California. By 1870 over 49,000 Chinese lived in California, and that number increased to over 75,000 by 1880. This amounted to nearly 10 percent of California's population. Approximately 40 percent of all Chinese in California lived in the six counties of the San Francisco Bay area.

Many Caucasian and Hispanic Californians did not like this influx of Chinese. As a result, laws were passed that discriminated against them. The first California anti-Chinese law passed was the Foreign Miner's License Tax Act of 1853, which required a head tax of $4 per month to mine. In 1860, a Foreign Fishing License Tax Act of $4 per month was passed, and two years later the Chinese police tax covered those not engaged in mining with a monthly $2.50 fee charged.

The legal assault on Chinese living in San Francisco became especially acute in the 1870s. The city and county passed such ordinances as the "Queue Ordinance" of 1876, which required the hair of Chinese prisoners to be cut and the "No Special Police for Chinese Quarter Ordinance" of 1878, which singled out the Chinese

to deny them police protection for their homes and businesses. Also, an 1876 ordinance required all hand laundries with horse-drawn delivery vehicles to pay a new license fee of $2.25 per month.

Outright banning of the Chinese from certain economic activities also started in the 1870s. In 1879, Chinese were prohibited from working for state, county, or city governments. This provision was placed in the new California Constitution. The next year the California legislature made it a misdemeanor to employ Chinese workers by any corporation chartered in California. Thus, these state laws and local ordinances made life extremely difficult for the Chinese in California. One historian concluded that "so severe and strident were the local laws that sought to banish the Chinese people from American life that in some ways they equaled the slave ordinance of the South."

Anti-Chinese feeling manifested itself nationally in 1876 when a committee of California legislators memorialized Congress to restrict Chinese immigration. Six years later, Congress successfully passed the first of several exclusion acts aimed at halting Chinese from coming to the United States. These laws were enforced, and Chinese immigration was significantly curtailed.

Simultaneously, political agitation and violence struck California. In 1877, Denis Kearney led the Workingmen's party in protests against the Chinese in San Francisco. This group eventually took over the California Democratic party, which embraced anti-Chinese rhetoric and actions. It was this group that played an important role at the California Constitutional Convention by inserting anti-Chinese sections into the new constitution. It also took over local San Francisco government with the election of Isaac Kalloch as mayor of San Francisco in 1879. Political agitation eventually led to the expulsion of the Chinese from Eureka and Truckee and the first organized massacre of Chinese at Rock Springs, Wyoming.

Federal and local laws and anti-Chinese violence caused many Chinese to abandon rural areas and to congregate in Chinatowns in urban areas. The Chinese were also forced to leave farming, mining, manufacturing, railroading, and the professions for self-employment in marginal and noncompetitive occupations. In 1881–82, a Trades' Assembly labor census was taken in San Francisco. Chinese labor was concentrated in four areas: cigar making (8,500 Chinese, or 97 percent of all persons working at this occupation), boot and shoe making (5,700 Chinese, or 84 percent), clothes making (7,510 Chinese, or 88 percent), and laundry operation (5,107 Chinese, or 89 percent).

The Chinese did not go into laundry work by choice. It was a difficult job, which caused social isolation from the Chinese community because the laundry owner had to do business primarily with hostile non-Chinese customers. Chinese laundries were not liked by many whites as well. Missionaries believed them to be centers of moral perversion. Visions of white females captured by Chinese and forced into prostitution headquartered at Chinese laundries were readily propagated. Such was the fear and loathing that California mobs began attacking isolated laundries in the 1870s. Even so, the laundry business attracted many Chinese. It afforded a modest and steady income. Few skills, little capital, and minimal English-speaking skills were needed. To some degree, the outreach to selected portions of the white community cushioned the violence of the anti-Chinese era.

Most laundries were family operations and three kinds evolved. The hand laundry with one or two persons was most common. The other two types required specialization and a greater investment: shirt-processing firms specialized in ironing only, and wet-washing firms only washed clothes. All of these laundries required back-breaking labor, and they operated throughout the day and night.

Yick Wo knew this life. He had been in the laundry business for 22 years prior to his arrest. He had arrived in California in 1861 and never became a U.S. citizen, a process which in the 1860s and 1870s would have been most difficult for him. As the owner of a laundry, Yick Wo was quite familiar with the ordinances monitoring laundry operations in San Francisco. He had a license dated March 3, 1884, from the board of fire wardens certifying that his stoves, irons, and washing machines were safe. He also had a certificate from the health officer that his laundry was sanitary and that it drained properly. His city license to operate his laundry was to expire on October 1, 1885.

To comply with local law, Yick Wo, on June 1 1885, applied to the Board of Supervisors for renewal of his general license to operate his laundry. The board rejected his request on July 1. The ordinance that allowed the Board to grant laundry licenses was first passed in 1880. This local law provided that all persons who established a laundry within the San Francisco city limits had to obtain the consent of the Board of Supervisors. Violation of the ordinance would result in a misdemeanor conviction and a fine of up to $1,000, a county jail sentence of not more than six months, or both. The ordinance also prohibited certain scaffoldings. Laundries found in brick buildings did not need the license, whereas laundries in wooden buildings did. This allowed the Board of Supervisors to claim that the ordinance was necessary as a fire protection measure.

Yick Wo was not the only Chinese laundry owner who was denied a license by the board. The petitions of 200 other Chinese owners had also been denied. Eighty laundry licenses had been granted, all but one to non-Chinese owners. The only exception was a permit given to Mary Meagles, and no doubt this exception had missed the board's attention. The lack of permits issued to Chinese laundry owners did not seem to be correlated to the structure of the buildings. Of the 320 laundries listed for San Francisco in 1880, 310 laundries were in wooden buildings. Chinese owners constituted approximately 240 laundries. By 1885, 200 of the 240 Chinese-owned laundries were denied licenses to operate.

Shortly after his license request was denied, Yick Wo was arrested for operating a laundry without a license. He was taken to a San Francisco police court, where he was found guilty and fined $10. Yick Wo refused to pay the fine, and he was jailed for ten days. He then petitioned California's highest court, the California Supreme Court, for a writ of *habeas corpus*. When his petition was denied, he appealed to the U.S. Supreme Court, naming Sheriff Hopkins in his suit.

Yick Wo had a difficult case. He knew that San Francisco would argue that the ordinances in question were designed to protect the health and safety of its residents. Yet clearly the result of enforcing this law was discriminatory. Thus, he had to address this twofold problem in his argument.

In a masterful defense, Yick Wo's attorneys, led by prominent San Francisco Republican Hall McAllister, conceded that the state and city had the right to regulate certain businesses that posed potential health and safety problems. Laundries fell under this framework. However, laundries were not dangerous or unhealthy *per se*, and therefore they could not be prohibited. They argued that the best evidence for this conclusion was the ordinances themselves, which regulated rather than banned laundry operations. The purpose of the statutes was to ensure the health and safety of San Francisco's residents *and* the continued operation of laundries.

The plaintiff next cited the results from the enforcement of the ordinances. What had in effect happened was the curtailment of the laundry business through a blatant discriminatory practice of not granting licenses to Chinese laundry owners. Statistics presented to the Court showed that, of the 280 license petitions received by the Board of Supervisors, 80 were granted. Only 25 percent of the laundries in San Francisco could operate, and only one of the 201 Chinese applicants was granted a license. Thus, in a bold move, pre-Brandeis brief and pre-*Brown v. Board of Education* (1954) statistical evidence was presented before the Court.

Having proven the discriminatory result of the administering of these ordinances, Yick Wo then claimed this state action violated China's 1880 treaty with the United States and the Four-

teenth Amendment. More specifically, he argued that the due process clause of the Fourteenth Amendment had been abrogated by the ordinances and their enforcement.

San Francisco claimed it was only practicing a traditional right of every governing body: the duty to protect the health and safety of its citizens. This police power, it argued, was "indestructible and inalienable," and it had been granted at the beginnings of American governance. Thus, to the defendant, it was too late to question the existence of the police power, even with the Fourteenth Amendment. The police power was sufficiently strong so as to allow discriminatory interpretations.

It was a haughty argument. San Francisco virtually dared the Supreme Court to limit the police powers of state and local government. It tried to force the Court to choose between abolishing police power and ratifying any police power. If the Court could find a middle ground, it would have to adopt a position never before taken—extending the Fourteenth Amendment to prevent discriminatory municipal actions, and this is precisely what it did.

On May 10, 1886, Justice Stanley Matthews read the unanimous opinion of the Court. He began by dismissing the issue of the plaintiff's imprisonment, his jail term having expired. The Court might have stopped here, but Matthews asserted that the "meaning of the ordinances" of San Francisco had attracted the Court's concern.

The Court found that the ordinances were so vague as to vest a power broader than police power in the Board of Supervisors. This power constituted "a naked and arbitrary power to give or withhold consent, not only as to places, but as to persons." Thus, the Court saw this power as discriminatory, a form of class legislation prohibited by the Fourteenth Amendment.

To reach this conclusion the Court specifically noted that the Fourteenth Amendment applies to all persons, citizens and aliens alike. Moreover, Matthews developed a test for legislation to see whether it was prohibited by the Fourteenth Amendment. Legislation must specifically regulate an economic activity in terms of safety and health practices, and such laws must be applied fairly. For Yick Wo, the San Francisco ordinances failed both tests, but the

Court was most offended by the discriminatory application by the Board of Supervisors. Wrote Matthews, "The very idea that one man may be compelled to hold his life, or the means of living, or any material right essential to the enjoyment of life, at the mere will of another, seems to be intolerable in any country where freedom prevails, as being the essence of slavery itself." Thus, the Court ruled the ordinances unconstitutional. The actions of the Board of Supervisors were discriminatory and violated the due process clause of the Fourteenth Amendment.

The significance of this case was especially important to the evolution of constitutional law and to the Chinese. The Court in its opinion expanded the Fourteenth Amendment. In one motion of the pen, Matthews limited state police powers, activated the due process clause to prohibit discriminatory action, broadly construed the coverage of the Fourteenth Amendment to include aliens, and placed state and local governments on notice that the Fourteenth Amendment would be applied to actions not previously associated with slavery and the Civil War.

The effect of this case on the anti-Chinese movement in California and throughout the West was profound. The Supreme Court answered the question posed by Yick Wo's attorneys: "That it [the enforcement of the ordinances] does mean prohibition, as to the Chinese, it seems to us must be apparent to every citizen of San Francisco who has been here long enough to be familiar with the cause of an active and aggressive branch of public opinion and of public notorious events. Can a court be blind to what must be necessarily known to every intelligent person in the State?" The Supreme Court was not blind, and by condemning the official actions of the city of San Francisco, it placed public officials on notice that the anti-Chinese agitations of Californians and

other westerners would no longer be tolerated. One reason why the anti-Chinese movements lessened in the next decade can be attributed to the stand taken by the *Yick Wo* Court.

Yick Wo v. Hopkins did not, however, achieve an immediate end to discrimination, nor did it activate the Fourteenth Amendment. Shortly after 1886, the Supreme Court's composition changed and the new Court saw the Fourteenth Amendment more as a vehicle to prevent broad social change. It extolled property rights, and attempts by states and localities to use regulatory powers to restrict property rights and economic activities were thwarted. The Fourteenth Amendment became a haven for substantive economic theory protected by the due process clause. *Yick Wo* would reassert itself in the twentieth century when the Fourteenth Amendment was reactivated to destroy the "Jim Crow" system of discrimination against blacks that had been erected in the border states and the South after the Civil War.

Selected Bibliography

Barth, G. *Bitter Strength: A History of the Chinese in the United States, 1850–70.* Cambridge, MA: Harvard University Press, 1964.

Cheng-Tsu W., ed. *"Chink": A Documentary History of Anti-Chinese Prejudice in America.* New York: World Publishing Co., 1972.

Konvitz, M.R. *The Alien and the Asiatic in American Law.* Ithaca, NY: Cornell University Press, 1946.

Kung, S.W. *Chinese in American Life: Some Aspects of Their History, Status, Problems, and Contributions.* Seattle: University of Washington Press, 1962.

Miller, S.C. *The Unwelcome Immigrant: The American Image of the Chinese, 1785–1882.* Berkeley, CA: University of California Press, 1969.

Saxton, A. *The Indispensable Enemy: Labor and the Anti-Chinese Movement in California.* Berkeley, CA: University of California Press, 1971.

Shih-shan, H.T. *The Chinese Experience in America.* Bloomington, IN: Indiana University Press, 1986.

Steiner, S. *Fusang: The Chinese Who Built America.* New York: Harper & Row, 1979.

THE JAPANESE INTERNMENT CASES

by Paul Finkelman
Brooklyn Law School

Hirabayashi v. United States, 320 U.S. 81 (1943); *Yasui v. United States*, 320 U.S. 115 (1943); *Korematsu v. United States*, 323 U.S. 214 (1944); *Ex parte Endo*, 323 U.S. 283 (1944)
[U.S. Supreme Court]

In 1941, approximately 112,000 Japanese-Americans, about three-quarters of whom were U.S. citizens, lived on the West Coast of the United States. At the beginning of World War II, civilian and military officials expressed concern about their presence. General John L. DeWitt, head of the Western Defense Command, very quickly began to argue for military control of aliens and citizens of Japanese ancestry. He added to a growing hysteria by constantly—and always erroneously—reporting acts of sabotage and military actions off the coast of California by the Japanese Navy.

In late 1941 and early 1942, newspaper columnist Walter Lippman urged a relocation of all Japanese-Americans in California. Another columnist, Westbrook Pegler, declared "to hell with *habeas corpus*" in arguing for "concentration camps" for Japanese-Americans. Politicians, including California Attorney General Earl Warren, demanded federal action against the Japanese-Americans. In January 1942, for example, Congressman Leland Ford, a California Republican, wrote to Secretary of War Henry L. Stimson, urging that "all Japanese, whether citizens or not, be placed in inland concentration camps." Ford argued that a U.S. citizen of Japanese ancestry would prove he is "patriotic" and "make his contribution to the safety and welfare of this country . . . by permitting himself to be placed in a concentration camp. . . ." Noting that such an enterprise "presents a very real problem," Stimson suggested that Ford make his views known to the attorney general.

Attorney General Francis Biddle resisted a mass evacuation of U.S. citizens on the ground that such a procedure would violate their constitutional rights. However, in cabinet-level discussions, Biddle was outmaneuvered by his own assistant attorney general, Tom C. Clark (later a U.S. Supreme Court Justice), who favored an internment, and by a former corporate lawyer,

Assistant Secretary of War John J. McCloy. According to Major General Allen W. Gullion, the provost marshal general of the Army, when Biddle made it clear that the Justice Department would not support military evacuation of civilians who were not charged with any crimes, McCloy, told the attorney general, "You are putting a Wall Street lawyer in a helluva box, but if it is a question of the safety of the country [and] the constitution . . . why the constitution is just a scrap of paper to me."

Despite Biddle's protests, on February 19, 1942, President Franklin D. Roosevelt signed Executive Order No. 9066, which empowered the Secretary of War and various military commanders to create "military areas" from which civilians might be excluded. Roosevelt issued the order under authority granted to him by the Espionage Act of 1918 and various acts passed in 1940 and 1941. Acting in his capacity as commander-in-chief, Roosevelt declared that "the successful prosecution of the war requires every possible protection against espionage and against sabotage to national defense material. . . ." Thus, Roosevelt authorized "the Secretary of War and the Military Commanders who he may from time to time designate . . . to prescribe military areas in such places and of such extent as [they] . . . may determine, from which any or all persons may be excluded and with respect to which, the right of any person to enter, remain in, or leave shall be subject to whatever restrictions the Secretary of War or the appropriate Military Commander may impose in his discretion." Roosevelt ordered the Secretary of War "to provide for residents of any such area who are excluded therefrom, such transportation, food, shelter, and other accommodations as may be necessary. . . ."

Roosevelt further authorized the Secretary of War to take "such other steps" as he might deem "advisable" to enforce this order in designated military areas "including the use of Federal troops and other Federal Agencies, with authority to accept assistance of state and local agencies." All other executive departments and federal agencies were also ordered "to assist the Secretary of War or the said Military Commanders in carrying out this Executive Order, including the furnishing of medical aid, hospitalization, food, clothing, transportation, use of land, shelter, and other supplies, equipment, utilities, facilities, and services." Finally, Roosevelt declared that this order superseded any authority of the attorney general or any other agency of the government over civilians or U.S. territory in areas designated "military" under the order, with the exception that the Federal Bureau of Investigation (FBI) was still empowered to investigate "alleged acts of sabotage." The attorney general was still authorized to regulate "the conduct and control of alien enemies" in nonmilitary areas.

On March 18, the president issued Executive Order No. 9102, establishing the War Relocation Authority for the purpose of relocating persons named in Executive Order No. 9066. On March 21, Roosevelt signed a law that Congress had unanimously passed to implement these orders. The Japanese internment quickly followed.

There were five stages to the internment process. First, a curfew was imposed on all persons of Japanese ancestry living in designated areas of the West Coast. Second, Japanese-Americans living in those areas were forbidden to leave the areas in which they lived. Third, Japanese-Americans were prohibited from remaining in the designated areas. Thus, they could neither leave nor stay in their homes. Instead, they had to comply with the fourth stage of the process, which required them to report to an assembly center, or civilian control center as they were officially called. From the assembly center the fifth stage began: the evacuation of the Japanese-Americans to "relocation centers" or "relocation camps."

On March 24, General DeWitt imposed an 8:00 p.m. to 6:00 a.m. curfew on all enemy aliens and persons of Japanese ancestry on the West Coast. Gordon Hirabayashi refused to obey this curfew, and his conviction for this unlawful act was upheld by a unanimous Su-

preme Court. DeWitt's proclamation of March 24 also declared that at all other times these persons were not permitted to be more than five miles from their homes. On March 27, DeWitt issued a new proclamation prohibiting Japanese-Americans from moving away from where they lived. Starting on March 24, and continuing through May, DeWitt issued a series of Civilian Exclusion Orders for various parts of the West Coast. Under these orders, Japanese-Americans were required to report to civilian control centers, from which they were, virtually without exception, removed to relocation camps. Fred Korematsu was convicted of failing to report to such a center.

The internment camps were surrounded by barbed wire, guarded by soldiers carrying weapons, and located in isolated parts of the country. Except for the men who were drafted, virtually all the Japanese-Americans sent to these camps were forced to remain in them until 1945. Except for a few personal items and some clothing, those sent to camps were forced to abandon almost all of their possessions. Many sold their homes, farms, and businesses for a fraction of their real value. Many who boarded up their property or left it in their neighbor's care lost their possessions to thieves and vandals.

Four major internment cases reached the U.S. Supreme Court: *Hirabayashi v. United States* (1943), *Yasui v. United States* (1943), *Korematsu v. United States* (1944), and *Ex parte Endo* (1944). In the first three, the Supreme Court upheld convictions for violating the laws surrounding the internment. In the last case, the Court ordered the release of the plaintiff and set the stage for a dismantling of the internment camps.

In the spring of 1942, both Gordon Hirabayashi and Minoru Yasui refused to obey the curfew orders issued by DeWitt. Hirabayashi, a U.S.-born citizen of Japanese ancestry, was a senior at the University of Washington. He violated the curfew imposed on Japanese-Americans and failed to report to a civilian control center, where his presence was required as "a preliminary step to the exclusion from that area of persons of Japanese ancestry." Hirabayashi disobeyed the curfew and exclusion orders because he believed if he submitted to these "he would be waiving his rights as an American citizen." A jury found him guilty on both counts, and the court sentenced him to two concurrent three-month sentences.

Yasui was also born in the United States of Japanese immigrants. In 1941, he was a member of the Oregon bar and a second lieutenant in the U.S. Army Infantry Reserve. When the war broke out, he immediately left his job at the Japanese consulate in Chicago. In mid-January, he reported for active duty at Camp Vancouver in Washington State. Upon arrival there, he was told to go home and await further orders—orders that never came. Yasui returned to his native Oregon. When the first curfews were put in place, he informed the FBI that he would violate the curfew in order to test its constitutionality. At 11:00 p.m. he went for a walk, in violation of the curfew. A policeman ordered him to return home, but refused to arrest him. Yasui later recounted: "I had to go on down to the Second Avenue police station and argue myself into jail." The district court in Oregon ruled that the act of March 21, implementing Roosevelt's two executive orders, could not be constitutionally applied to U.S. citizens. But, the court also ruled that by disobeying the law, Yasui "must be deemed to have renounced his American citizenship." The court then imposed the maximum sentence of one year in prison and a $5,000 fine.

Both Hirabayashi and Yasui appealed their convictions. Both cases were argued on May 10 and 11, 1943, and both were decided on June 21, 1943.

The Supreme Court first dealt with Hirabayashi. He had appealed both his conviction for curfew violation and his conviction for failure to report to a civilian control center or assembly center. However, because of the concurrent sentences, the justices ruled that if they upheld one conviction—the curfew violation—they would not have to consider the constitutionality of the order to go to the assembly center.

Speaking for the Court, Chief Justice Harlan F. Stone gave a detailed legislative history of the curfew and the military situation in 1942 in order to justify the constitutionality of the curfew. Stone argued that under the "power to wage war successfully," Congress and the president had the right to delegate authority to military commanders. Furthermore, it was clear

that a curfew was a reasonable and constitutional act under that authority. The big question, however, was whether a single group of people—Japanese-Americans—could be singled out for the curfew.

Stone noted that Japanese aliens were ineligible for citizenship in the United States, that U.S.-born citizens of Japanese parents were considered, under Japanese law, also citizens of Japan, and that "social, economic and political conditions" in the nation had, over the years "intensified their solidarity and have in large measure prevented their assimilation as an integral part of the white population." He pointed out that large numbers of Japanese-American children had been "sent to Japanese language schools outside the regular hours of public schools" and that some of these schools were "generally believed to be sources of Japanese nationalistic propaganda. . . ." There had, the chief justice observed, "been relatively little social intercourse between them and the white population."

Stone found that "Congress and the Executive could reasonably have concluded that these conditions have encouraged the continued attachment of members of this group to Japan and Japanese institutions" and that it was reasonable for "those charged with . . . the national defense" to "take into account" these factors in "determining the nature and extent of the danger of espionage and sabotage, in the event of an invasion or air raid attack." Stone declared that the Court "cannot reject as unfounded the judgment of the military authorities and of Congress that there were disloyal members of that population, whose number and strength could not be precisely and quickly ascertained."

Stone acknowledged that "racial discriminations are in most circumstances irrelevant," but he argued that "in dealing with the perils of war, Congress and the Executive" were not "precluded from taking into account those facts which are relevant to measures for our national defense . . . which may in fact place citizens of one ancestry in a different category from others."

Stone declared, "We cannot close our eyes to the fact . . . that in time of war residents having ethnic affiliations with an invading enemy may be a greater source of danger than those of a different ancestry." In essence, Stone and the Court refused to question the authority of the military. In reaching this decision, on the narrow question of the curfew, Stone specifically declared that the Court was not considering whether more drastic measures "differing from the curfew order" would be permissible.

Although a unanimous decision, not all the judges agreed to share in Stone's opinion. Justices William O. Douglas, Wiley B. Rutledge, and Frank Murphy qualified their support and sought to narrow the scope of the opinion. In fact, Murphy's concurrence reads more like a dissent. He noted that this "is the first time . . . that we have sustained a substantial restriction of the personal liberty of citizens of the United States based on the accident of race or ancestry. Under the curfew order here challenged no less than 70,000 American citizens have been placed under a special ban and deprived of their liberty because of their particular racial inheritance. In this sense it bears a melancholy resemblance to the treatment accorded to members of the Jewish race in Germany and in other parts of Europe. . . . In my opinion this goes to the very brink of constitutional power."

Having decided the constitutionality of the curfew in *Hirabayashi*, the Court had little problem disposing of *Yasui v. United States*. The Court reversed the ruling of the district court that the curfew was unconstitutional when applied to citizens and also reversed the ruling that Yasui had effectively renounced his citizenship. His conviction remained, and the case was remanded for resentencing. On remand, U.S. District Judge James A. Fee reduced the one-year sentence he had previously imposed to time served and removed the $5,000 fine. After about eight months in jail, Yasui was removed to a relocation camp.

The shaky unanimity of *Hirabayashi* disappeared in *Korematsu*. Like Hirabayashi and Yasui, Fred Korematsu was a U.S.-born citizen of Japanese ancestry. However, Korematsu did not resist the relocation out of constitutional conviction. Korematsu had lived all his life in Alemeda County, in Northern California. When the war began, he volunteered for military service but was rejected for health reasons.

He then obtained a job in a defense industry, after first using his own funds to learn welding. On May 3, 1942, the day Japanese-Americans in the Alemeda County were required to report to an assembly center, Korematsu had a good job and a non-Japanese girlfriend unaffected by the relocation orders. He had no reason to want to leave his home or to think he was a threat to the nation, and he had many good reasons for staying.

Rather than report to an assembly center, Korematsu moved, changed his name, and attempted to avoid arrest by claiming to be of Mexican ancestry. He was now in violation of a new order, for after May 9 it was no longer legal for Japanese-Americans to remain in the area where Korematsu lived. On the other hand, it was also illegal for him to leave the area where he lived. As Justice Robert H. Jackson noted in his dissent, "Korematsu . . . has been convicted of an act not commonly a crime. It consists merely of being present in the state whereof he is a citizen, near the place where he was born, and where all his life he has lived." How did he get into this situation? Because, as Jackson wrote, an "unusual . . . series of military orders . . . forbid" Korematsu "to remain, and they also forbid him to leave." In his dissent, Justice Owen J. Roberts explained the problem in greater detail: "The predicament in which the petitioner thus found himself was this: He was forbidden, by Military Order, to leave the zone in which he lived; he was forbidden, by Military Order, after a date fixed, to be found within that zone unless he were in an Assembly Center located in that zone. General DeWitt's report to the Secretary of War . . . makes it entirely clear . . . that an Assembly Center was a euphemism for prison. No person within such a center was permitted to leave except by Military Order."

Faced with this dilemma, "that he dare not remain in his home, or voluntarily leave the area, without incurring criminal penalties, and that the only way he could avoid punishment was to go to an Assembly Center and submit himself to military imprisonment, the petitioner did nothing." On June 12, he was arrested and charged with violating the orders excluding all Japanese-Americans from the area. Once convicted, the trial court sentenced him to five years in prison and then immediately paroled him. He was then taken to an assembly center and from there to the internment camp at Topaz, Utah.

As a major case in constitutional law, *Korematsu* is remembered for the assertion in Justice Hugo L. Black's majority opinion that "all legal restrictions which curtail the civil rights of a single racial group are immediately suspect" and should be given "the most rigid scrutiny." Significantly, this case is the only one in which the Supreme Court has applied the "rigid scrutiny" test to a racial restriction and still upheld the restrictive law.

As in *Hirabayashi*, the Court in *Korematsu* never questioned the assertion of the military that the Japanese on the West Coast posed a special problem for the nation. Black wrote: "Like the curfew, exclusion of those of Japanese origin was deemed necessary because of the presence of an unascertained number of disloyal members of the group, most of whom we have no doubt were loyal to this country. It was because we could not reject the finding of the military authorities that it was impossible to bring about an immediate segregation of the disloyal from the loyal that we sustained the validity of the curfew order as applying to the whole group. In the instant case, temporary exclusion of the entire group was rested by the military on the same ground. The judgment that exclusion of the whole group was for the same reason a military imperative answers the contention that the exclusion was in the nature of group punishment based on antagonism to those of Japanese ancestry." Thus, Black upheld the exclusion order "as of the time it was made and the petitioner violated it."

In reaching this conclusion, the Court turned a blind eye to what was really happening. Korematsu argued that if he had gone to an assembly center or relocation center, as ordered, he would have been immediately shipped to a relocation camp. These arguments did not impress Justice Black, who asserted that "[h]ad the petitioner here left the prohibited area and gone to an assembly center we cannot say either as a matter of fact or law that his presence in that center would have resulted in his detention in a relocation center." In fact, this is what

happened to virtually every Japanese-American who went to such a center.

Black blithely asserted that reporting to an assembly center could be separated from being forced to go to a relocation camp. Since Korematsu was charged only with failing to report to the assembly center, Black and the majority of the Court would not examine the constitutionality of the military forcing people into relocation camps. Black asserted, "It will be time enough to decide the serious constitutional issues which the petitioner seeks to raise when an assembly or relocation order is applied or is certain to be applied to him, and we have its terms before us." In other words, Korematsu could only litigate the constitutionality of the internment after he had been incarcerated in a camp.

Finally, Black bristled with indignation at the assertion by counsel for Korematsu and the dissenting justices that this decision was based on racism and that the relocation centers were concentration camps. In his concluding paragraph, Black declared: "It is said that we are dealing here with the case of imprisonment of a citizen in a concentration camp solely because of his ancestry, without evidence or inquiry concerning his loyalty and good disposition toward the United States. Our task would be simple, our duty clear, were this a case involving the imprisonment of a loyal citizen in a concentration camp because of racial prejudice. Regardless of the true nature of the assembly and relocation centers—and we deem it unjustifiable to call them concentration camps with all the ugly connotations that term implies—we are dealing specifically with nothing but an exclusion order. To cast this case into outlines of racial prejudice, without reference to the real military dangers which were presented, merely confuses the issue. Korematsu was not excluded from the Military Area because of hostility to him or his race. He *was* excluded because we are at war with the Japanese Empire, because the properly constituted military authorities feared an invasion of our West Coast and . . . decided that the military urgency . . . demanded that all citizens of Japanese ancestry be segregated from the West Coast temporarily . . ." [emphasis in original].

Justices Owen J. Roberts, Frank Murphy, and Robert H. Jackson found Black's reasoning and analysis unacceptable. In dissent, they argued that the requirement of reporting to a relocation center differed substantially from the constitutionally permissible curfew approved in *Hirabayashi*. Furthermore, they had little patience for Black's fine distinction between the exclusion order and the internment. As Justice Roberts remarked, "The Government has argued this case as if the only order outstanding at the time the petitioner was arrested and informed against was Exclusion Order 34 ordering him to leave the area in which he resided. . . ." But, the justice noted: "We cannot shut our eyes to the fact that had the petitioner attempted to . . . leave the military area in which he lived he would have been arrested and tried and convicted under Proclamation No. 4. The two conflicting orders, one which commanded him to stay and the other which commanded him to go, were nothing but a cleverly devised trap to accomplish the real purpose of the military authority, which was to lock him up in a concentration camp. . . . We know that is the fact. Why should we set up a figmentary and artificial situation instead of addressing ourselves to the actualities of the case?"

Justice Murphy, meanwhile, challenged Black's blind support for military expertise and his denial of racism. He pointed out that the internment was not based on any military analysis, but rather "[j]ustification for the exclusion" was based "mainly upon questionable racial and sociological grounds not ordinarily within the realm of expert military judgment." He found no compelling evidence that tied the Japanese-American community to sabotage or espionage. He charged, "The main reasons relied upon by those responsible for the forced evacuation . . . appear . . . to be largely an accumulation of much of the misinformation, half-truths and insinuations that for years have been directed against Japanese Americans by people with racial and economic prejudices—the same people who have been among the foremost advocates of the evacuation. A military judgment based upon such racial and sociological considerations is not entitled to the great weight ordinarily given the judgments based upon strictly military considerations."

Murphy argued that the Japanese-Americans should have been treated "on an individual basis" through "investigations and hearings to separate the loyal from the disloyal, as was done in the case of persons of German and Italian ancestry." He noted that the first exclusion order was not issued until "nearly four months elapsed after Pearl Harbor" and that "nearly eight months went by until the last order was issued; and the last of these 'subversive' persons was not actually removed until almost eleven months had elapsed." Concluding that "[l]eisure and deliberation seem to have been more of the essence than speed," Murphy undermined the claim of military necessity. Thus, Murphy dissented "from this legalization of racism."

The Court's majority in favor of the government disappeared in *Endo*. On the same day it upheld Korematsu's conviction, the Court ordered the release of Mitsuye Endo, who at the time was held in a war relocation center in Topaz, Utah. Endo, a U.S. citizen of Japanese ancestry, had complied with all of the relocation orders. In July 1942, shortly after she was removed to the Tule Lake Relocation Center, she petitioned for a writ of *habeas corpus*. When a U.S. district court rejected her petition, the relocation authorities moved her to Utah. This transfer was designed to frustrate her legal efforts and to punish her for her attempt to gain freedom. From Topaz, she appealed to the circuit court of appeals and then to the U.S. Supreme Court.

Endo asserted that she was a "loyal and law-abiding citizen of the United States, that no charge has been made against her, and that she is being unlawfully detained, and that she is confined the Relocation Center under armed guard and held there against her will." The United States did not deny her loyalty, nor did the government claim a right "to detain citizens against whom no charges of disloyalty or subversiveness have been made for a period longer than that necessary to separate the loyal from the disloyal and to provide the necessary guidance for relocation." Rather, the government argued that the whole purpose of the program was to determine which Japanese-Americans were loyal and to relocate them beyond military areas. The government argued it needed more time because "a planned and orderly relocation was essential to the success of the evacuation program" and an immediate release of Endo and others in the camps would lead to "a dangerously disorderly migration of unwanted people to unprepared communities," which would result in "hardship and disorder." The program's success "was thought to require the knowledge that the federal government was maintaining control over the evacuated population except as the release of individuals could be effected consistently with their own peace and well-being and that of the nation. . . ."

Speaking for a unanimous Court, Justice William O. Douglas rejected these arguments, asserting that the exclusion orders were for the "single aim" of "protection of the war effort against espionage and sabotage." Douglas found that Executive Orders Nos. 9066 and 9102 and the legislation supporting them authorized the military only "to formulate an effectuate a program for the removal" of the Japanese-Americans. Douglas would not say that detention was unconstitutional *per se*, but only that it was unauthorized by statute. Thus, since no one doubted Endo's loyalty, there was no reason or statutory authority to incarcerate her. The Court ordered her release.

Within a month after the *Endo* decision the military allowed about 50,000 internees to return to their homes. Some 20,000 remained interned, mostly in Tule Lake, the camp designated for troublemakers and those suspected of disloyalty. Some remained scattered in other camps until after the war ended.

In 1948, Congress passed the Japanese-American Evacuation Claims Act, which authorized compensation to internees who could prove property losses by records. Claims under this law totaled $148 million, but because of the strict proof requirements, the Treasury Department paid out only $37 million. As one scholar noted: "[T]he Federal Reserve Bank had estimated the Japanese Americans lost $400 million in property. Losses of earnings and profits from businesses and farms sold in 1942 under distress conditions, and compensations for deprivations of constitutional rights, were not covered by the 1948 law."

In 1980, Congress established the Commission on Wartime Relocation and Internment of Civilians to make recommendations on restitution for the victims of the internment and their heirs. During the commission hearings, Wall Street lawyer John J. McCloy, who, as Assistant Secretary of War had been the most forceful high-level government advocate of the plan, admitted that the internment had been a "retribution for the attack that was made on Pearl Harbor." Thus, almost 40 years after the internment began, the man who helped bring it about admitted what lawyers for Hirabayashi, Yasui, Korematsu, and Endo had always argued: it was not "stern military necessity" that forced the internment, as the army and government had argued before the Supreme Court; rather, it was racism that allowed the white majority to punish U.S.-born citizens for the actions of people of the same ethnic background but from another country. These hearings revealed that the FBI and the Office of Naval Intelligence consistently opposed the internment because both intelligence organizations believed the Japanese-Americans were fundamentally loyal and, as a group, posed no threat to the nation's security. The hearings showed that while the internment was being planned and carried out, lawyers in the Justice Department branded as "lies" the assertions of the War Department that the Japanese posed a threat to the nation. The hearings revealed that the alleged incidents of sabotage and espionage by Japanese-Americans were fabrications or fantasies of General DeWitt and his staff. In 1983, the commission concluded that the internment was a "grave injustice."

The manipulation of facts by governmental lawyers in the internment cases, revealed by the commission hearings and private investigations by lawyers and scholars, made it clear that the internment cases were wrongly decided. In the first three cases, the Court had deferred to military judgments based on lies and incomplete information. For example, an Oregon power outage at the beginning of the war was blamed on Japanese sabotage; the government knew it was caused by cattle scratching their backs on power lines. Similarly, the military asserted that Japanese farmers were using flashlights to guide enemy planes at night, although the FBI had established that in the areas in question flashlights were used at night by people going to their outhouses. Information like this was suppressed during the internment cases.

In January 1983, Hirabayashi, Korematsu, and Yasui reopened their cases in federal district court in San Francisco. In November, Korematsu's conviction was overturned. In February 1986, a federal court reversed Hirabayashi's conviction. Meanwhile, numerous Japanese-Americans began receiving checks for back pay for federal, state, and local government jobs they held at the time the interment began, on the ground they were illegally fired. However, an attempted reparations suit for $24 billion failed because the courts ruled that a six-year statute of limitations had expired. The plaintiffs argued that because the government concealed vital evidence in the internment cases, the statute of limitations should not have begun until after the plaintiffs discovered the illegal activity of the government. In August 1988, Congress passed a law, which the president signed, establishing a $1.25 billion trust fund to pay $20,000 in reparations to each survivor of the internment or their families.

In 1945, Professor Eugene V. Rostow wrote an article entitled "The Japanese American Cases—A Disaster." Also that year, Nanette Dembitz wrote "Racial Discrimination and Military Judgment: The Supreme Court's *Korematsu* and *Endo* Decisions." The titles of each aptly sum up the High Court's response to these cases.

When the Court heard these cases, it was clear that there had been no espionage or sabotage by the Japanese-Americans on the West Coast. In the Hawaiian Islands, which were significantly closer to the Pacific war and where Japanese-Americans made up a much larger percentage of the population, there were no mass arrests, evacuations, or internments. Yet, there was also no sabotage or espionage perpetrated by members of the Japanese-American community. In Europe, the "Nisei brigade," made up entirely of Japanese-Americans, was on its way to becoming the most decorated military unit in U.S. history. The Court ignored these facts. Nor did it even question the "facts" of sabotage presented by the government. Instead, the Court accepted, without hesitation, the assertions of military necessity.

During the congressional hearings in 1983, McCloy defended the internment, in part, because the Supreme Court had upheld it. In *Endo*, the Court did not uphold interning people; it did, however, uphold the curfew, the evacuation, and the right of the government to force citizens to leave their homes based solely on their race and ethnicity. The 1943–44 Supreme Court, in essence, agreed with McCloy that, at least for Japanese-Americans during World War II, the Constitution was "just a scrap of paper."

Selected Bibliography

Daniels, R. *Concentration Camps USA*. New York: Holt Rinehart, Winston, 1971.

Dembitz, N. "Racial Discrimination and the Military Judgment: The Supreme Court's *Korematsu* and *Endo* Decisions." *Columbia Law Review* 45 (March 1945): 175–239.

Irons, P. *Justice at War: The Story of the Japanese Internment Cases*. New York: Oxford University Press, 1983.

Rostow, E.V. "The Japanese American Cases—A Disaster." *Yale Law Journal* 54 (June 1945): 489–533.

Tateishi, J. *And Justice for All: An Oral History of the Japanese American Detention Camps*. New York: Random House, 1984.

HOW SHOULD WE PAY FOR OUR SCHOOLS?

by John R. Wunder
Department of History
University of Nebraska at Lincoln

San Antonio Independent School District v. Rodriguez, 411 U.S. 1 (1973) [U.S. Supreme Court]

On March 21, 1973, five members of the U.S. Supreme Court issued a directive in *San Antonio Independent School District v. Rodriguez*. Their opinion placed a clamp over the hemorrhaging school litigation released after *Brown v. Board of Education* (1954), decided nearly 20 years earlier. But in *Rodriguez*, the children were Mexican-American, not black; the primary issue was whether education was a fundamental right under the U.S. Constitution, not whether separate-but-equal facilities were inherently unequal; and the legal threat was to school finance systems nationwide, rather than to segregated southern school districts. Clearly, the stakes were high, and the Court, led by Chief Justice Warren E. Burger, had an agenda it was ready to place in motion.

Demetrio Rodriguez was one of several Mexican-American parents who sent their children to Edgewood Independent Schools, an urban district in San Antonio, Texas. Their descendants had been in Texas since the late seventeenth century, and in 1718 they had founded San Antonio de Bexar, a mission outpost to East Texas. By 1820, 2,500 Texas-Mexicans, or Tejanos, lived in three settlements, one being San Antonio. The next year, Texas officially became a part of the Mexican nation.

The Anglo migration to Texas that occurred during the next 15 years was so significant that by the Texas revolution of 1836, Anglos outnumbered Tejanos. At that time, Anglos began to assert political control over county and local governments—except for San Antonio, which developed a tradition of Tejano political activity.

The Mexico-United States War increased local racial tensions in Texas. During the 1850s, Anglo lynchings of San Antonio Tejanos occurred. After the war, hostility also took the form of legal discrimination, especially against the use of the Spanish language. Laws could not be officially printed in Spanish, Spanish could not be used in Texas courts, and in 1870 Spanish was officially banned in the schools.

By 1900, many Tejanos wanted to be educated. At first, they gravitated toward Catholic parochial schools, but they were expensive and Catholic officials refused to integrate. That left the public schools—also segregated but much cheaper. San Antonio's first public school started in 1875, and it included several wealthy Tejano children. After the push for education, two schools (of limited quality) were established in the barrio for Mexican-Americans; but this would not prove sufficient.

The twentieth century brought a huge migration of Mexicans to their lost province. These new immigrants added burdens to their Tejanos relatives. They rarely spoke English; they were extremely poor; they had few skills; and they came in large numbers. By 1930, the number of school districts designated Mexicano in Texas had doubled from 20 (in 1920) to 40. Mexican-American children represented 13 percent of the Texas school population. Only 40 percent of the Texas school districts maintained separate "Mexican schools." In San Antonio, at least 11,000 Mexican-American pupils were attending elementary schools.

The 1940s witnessed World War II, a strong Mexican-American participation in the U.S. war effort, and the beginnings of a significant Mexican-American organized attack on separate-but-equal education. As early as 1929, with the founding of the League of United Latin American Citizens (LULAC), Mexican-Americans had challenged segregation. LULAC, centered in San Antonio, was joined in 1948 by the G. I. Forum, organized by Mexican-American veterans in Corpus Christi, Texas. The forum, which investigated education in Texas, concluded, "We, as Veterans, did not fight a system like the Nazi Socialist system in order to come back to our own state and live and tolerate such humiliation and suffering of our own children and the children of those soldiers who died fighting for the rights and privileges of our great Democracy." Until *Brown v. Board of Education*, Hispanic organizations kept up pressure to eliminate discrimination.

Although education in Texas was to be integrated for Mexican-Americans by 1948, a Texas court that year struck down Mexican-American segregation. The next year, Attorney General Price Daniel issued an opinion forbidding the segregation of Mexican-American children in public schools by race, but language discrimination was still acceptable. Thus, no changes were made. Culture became the discrimination tool of Texas school districts.

Nevertheless, most Texas districts ignored these legal pronouncements until after *Brown*. By the early 1960s, integration was piecemeal, and Mexican-American expectations had gone beyond wanting an integrated education to expecting quality public education. Quality education, however, would be elusive. *Brown* may have helped end segregated schools, but it did not solve long-term educational economic disparity.

By 1960, San Antonio was the second largest U.S. city in terms of Hispanic population. Within ten years, its Hispanic population had increased to over 40 percent of the city's population of nearly 250,000. Most Chicanos were very poor and uneducated. Annual income averages for Mexican-Americans in San Antonio in 1960 was $968; for Anglos, $2,047; and other nonwhites, $1,044. Thirty percent of Mexican-Americans lived in deteriorated houses. San Antonio had the highest rate of tuberculosis of any U.S. city. Fewer than 10 percent of Mexican-Americans finished high school, and one-half of all Chicanos in San Antonio had only a fifth-grade education.

These conditions and the restlessness they generated led to the organization of a more activist group, the Political Association of Spanish-Speaking Organizations (PASSO). At first, PASSO was rapidly successful, its most highly visible achievement being the political takeover of Crystal City, Texas, in 1963. One of the first centers of controversy in Crystal City came with the firing of teachers who had exhibited overt racist behavior. In PASSO, however, factions evolved that disagreed over moderate versus militant approaches to social change. Those desiring more immediate change channeled their activity into the Mexican American Legal Defense and Education Fund (MALDEF). MALDEF, much like the legal arm of the National Association for the Advancement of Colored People (NAACP), began to file civil rights law suits. Its primary goal was to eliminate discrimination in public education in Texas and to stop the assimilationist thrust of the public schools. Thus, MALDEF sought to reinforce Mexican culture through traditional U.S. philosophical and political forms.

Brown v. Board of Education, the 1961 election of San Antonian Henry Gonzalez to Congress, the civil rights legislation of the 1960s, and the 1968 Bilingual Education Act all encouraged Mexican-Americans to seek remedies for their educational problems. MALDEF decided to challenge the Texas finance system for public education. As one political figure observed, Texas was notorious "for providing the least amount of public education for Mexican Americans while fiercely defending its record of inferior and separate schooling." On behalf of Demetrio Rodriguez, several San Antonio parents, and other minority or poor families in Texas, MALDEF sued Texas.

The original 1968 suit filed by MALDEF charged that the Texas school finance system was unconstitutional under the equal protection clause of the Fourteenth Amendment. However, the system was complex: it provided for a redistribution of funds and a collection of taxes based both on ability to pay and on per capita enrollment. The Minimum Foundation Program required every school district to pay a set amount into a common state fund based on ability to pay. This money was then redistributed to school districts, and it constituted up to 80 percent of a school districts operating budget. In addition, each district was expected to pay the remaining 20 percent. If it could afford additional taxation, an even greater amount could be devoted to local education.

At the time of the suit (1968), Rodriguez lived in the Edgewood School District, a poor San Antonio district without a high property tax base. No factories or significant stores were in the district. Ninety percent of Edgewood's students were Mexican-American, and 6 percent were black. In 1968, the school district contributed $26 per pupil, the Texas Minimum Foundation Program gave $222 per pupil, and federal funds contributed $108 per pupil, for a total of $356 per pupil available to the Edgewood School District.

Across the city was Alamo Heights School District—the richest district in San Antonio with over 80 percent Anglo, 18 percent Mexican-American, and 1 percent black pupil population. In 1968, Alamo Heights raised $333 per pupil locally. It received $225 per pupil from the Texas Minimum Foundation Program and $36 per pupil from federal funds. Thus, Alamo Heights had $594 per pupil to spend; Edgewood had $356—a significant disparity.

At the time of this case, litigation attacking state public school financing was occurring throughout the country. The argument accepted by those who wished to equalize educational funding centered around the principle of fiscal neutrality; that is, the quality of public education must be a function of the wealth of an entire state rather than that of a community. Thus, a state had an obligation not to discriminate against poor school districts.

Tying this principle to the U.S. Constitution was another matter. Those who wished for state intervention to rectify educational disparities argued that state educational laws fell under a "strict scrutiny" test. If a state policy created a class of people or if it restricted a fundamental right, the state had to show its policy was necessary for a compelling purpose. The onus was on the state to defend its educational laws. If it could not, the equal protection clause of the Constitution was abrogated and the state policy was unconstitutional. Three phrases were important to this test: class of people, a fundamental right, and compelling purpose. *Brown* established race as one category of class. Certainly race was evident in *Rodriguez*, but so was wealth. *Brown* found that integrated education was a fundamental right guaranteed in the Constitution, but *Rodriguez* plaintiffs went further. They argued that quality education is a fundamental constitutional right. In *Brown*, the Supreme Court found that separation of the races was not a legitimate compelling interest to justify the basic violations of the Fourteenth and Fifth Amendments. MALDEF fought a deter-

mination that state aid to education, because of an expanded class and a fundamental right to quality education, had to be fiscally neutral.

Between the time *Rodriguez* was filed in 1968 and the time a three-judge panel convened by the federal district court rendered its opinion (1972), two cases challenging other state educational finance systems were resolved. Both would affect the outcome of *Rodriguez*.

In Illinois, the federal courts held that the state's financial system did not violate the Fourteenth Amendment. An Illinois district court ruled that the proper constitutional test in this kind of case is the "rational basis" test. Here, in the absence of special circumstances (e.g., blatant racial discrimination), the burden was on a plaintiff to prove that state policy caused an unequal treatment not rationally related to a legitimate purpose. Differences in school district funding allocations were constitutional if the overall goal was legitimate. In reaching the conclusion that Illinois had acted responsibly, the court decided that the Fourteenth Amendment did not require a state to base expenditures only on need, that funding levels were not the sole measure of a student's opportunities in public education, and that no standards could be applied that might be manageable on a national scale. Thus, there was no constitutional mandate for change, and even if there was, no constitutional remedy existed to implement change.

A 1971 California decision held otherwise. Here the state relied almost exclusively on local property taxes to fund public education. In that case, the federal district court ruled that this system was not fiscally neutral, that education was a right guaranteed by the U.S. Constitution, and that California's method unfairly discriminated against poorer school districts. Thus, the district courts were divided. Illinois, which channeled most funds through the state, when subjected to the rational basis test, was found constitutionally compatible. On the other hand, California, which left school districts to fund local education mostly from local sources, when held against the strict scrutiny test, was constitutionally deficient. Texas's system was somewhere in the middle.

Shortly after these cases were decided, the West Texas judicial panel ruled in favor of

Gonzalez, other parents, and MALDEF. It accepted the California district court's rationale, and by holding the Texas school financial system to the strict scrutiny test, the court found the Texas system to be unconstitutional. Texas appealed.

Was Texas's system of public school finance unconstitutional? How should one measure the constitutionality of state public school financial systems? What tests and remedies should be applied? These issues were paramount when the U.S. Supreme Court agreed to hear arguments in *San Antonio Independent School District v. Rodriguez* in October 1972. This was a very significant legal issue. At stake was the fundamental basis by which most U.S. primary and secondary education was financed.

At oral argument, Charles Alan Wright, noted Texas conservative constitutionalist, articulated the positions of Texas: the Texas financial system could not pass the strict scrutiny test, but that test should not be applied. Nowhere, posited Wright, did Texas single out a suspect class, nor did Texas suppress a fundamental right. Given acceptance of this twofold argument, the only test to be applied was the rational basis test, which Texas's educational finance system met. The issue was not quality education, but basic education. Moreover, if the Court found differently, Wright noted that the effect would be to throw U.S. schools into disarray.

MALDEF countered these arguments by relying on the findings in the California district and by showing the financial disparities within the Texas school system. The class of the poor was deemed a suspect class, and education was termed a fundamental right under the Constitution as it related to the rights of free speech and voting. Unfortunately for San Antonio's Mexican-American community, the U.S. Supreme Court did not agree with its argument.

In a 5–4 split opinion, the Court held for Texas, reversing the lower court. Justice Lewis F. Powell, Jr., wrote the majority opinion. He was joined by Chief Justice Warren E. Burger and two other justices, Harry A. Blackmun, and William H. Rehnquist. Justice Potter Stewart concurred, helping to put together the slim majority. Justices William J. Brennan, Jr., Byron R. White, and Thurgood Marshall wrote dissenting opinions, which were joined by Justice William O. Douglas.

Powell accepted the arguments of Charles Alan Wright. He found that the strict scrutiny test could not be applied because no class was being implicitly discriminated against; that wealth, or lack of it did not constitute a suspect class in noncriminal cases; and that education, as important as it is, was not a fundamental right protected by the Constitution. Moreover, Powell stressed that basic, not quality, education was the requirement. Powell also worried about limits. If education was elevated as a fundamental right, what else might the Court find to set aside? And if the Texas system was struck down, where would the funding come from for all of the school districts? How could the Court supervise local chaos that Powell saw as inevitable? Powell then had to deal with the California district court ruling. He noted that the Supreme Court had not heard the case, but that quite possibly the lower court holding would not stand up. Nevertheless, he seemed to suggest that California needed to take a long look at its school financing system, and it needed to do so with an eye to the new *Rodriguez* precedent.

Marshall's 37-page dissent castigated Powell's majority opinion. Marshall accused the majority of adopting a "rigidified approach to equal protection analysis" and of arguing with "labored efforts." He pointed to numerous elevations of fundamental rights requiring the strict scrutiny test, and he noted the dangerous precedent that appears to be law—that education as a right was not constitutionally guaranteed. Marshall sarcastically concluded, "The Court seeks solace for its actions today in the possibility of legislative reform. The Court's suggestions of legislative redress and experimentation will doubtless be of great comfort to the school children of Texas's disadvantaged districts, but considering the vested interests of wealthy school districts in the preservation of the status quo, they are worth little more."

What Marshall recognized was the end of an era. Had this case been heard in 1968, the four justices of the majority opinion would have been practicing rather than interpreting law. In that short time, Earl Warren, Abe Fortas, Hugo L. Black, and John Marshall Harlan were replaced by the signers of the *Rodriguez* majority opinion: Powell, Burger, Blackmun, and Rehnquist.

Perhaps this case more than any other symbolizes the emergence of the Burger Court and the end of the Warren Court. The breadth of *Brown v. Board of Education* was now limited. Only basic education would be monitored by the Supreme Court. In addition, matters regarding educational finance and other school issues became the focus of state, not federal, courts. There, some state courts ruled their educational finance systems violated their constitutions (Connecticut, New Jersey, West Virginia, Wyoming), but others upheld their systems (Ohio, Oregon). A polyglot quilt, matching the variety of traditions of the states, emerged with no sense of a national educational system.

In Texas, continuity continued in educational finance. During the post-*Rodriguez* years of the 1970s and 1980s, predominantly Mexican-American schools received three-fifths of the appropriations given to predominantly

Anglo schools. In San Antonio, Chicano districts received less state funding than did the Anglo districts. The landmark *Rodriguez* decisions clearly placed limits on any attempts to alter fundamental aspects of U.S. education.

Selected Bibliography

Acuña, R. *Occupied America: A History of Chicanos.* 3d edition. New York: Harper & Row, 1988.

Alexander, K., and M.D. Alexander. *The Law of Schools, Students, and Teachers in a Nutshell.* St. Paul, MN: West Publishing Co., 1984.

Cortes, C.E., ed. *Education and the Mexican American.* New York: Arno Press, 1974.

DeLeon, A. *They Called Them Greasers: Anglo Attitudes Toward Mexicans in Texas, 1821–1900.* Austin, TX: University of Texas Press, 1983.

Madsen, W. *The Mexican-Americans of South Texas.* New York: Holt, Rinehart & Winston, 1964.

San Miguel, G., Jr. *"Let All of Them Take Heed": Mexican Americans and the Campaign for Educational Equality in Texas, 1910–81.* Austin, TX: University of Texas Press, 1987.

Shockley, J.S. *Chicano Revolt in a Texas Town.* South Bend, IN: University of Notre Dame Press, 1974.

Strahan, R.D., and L.C. Turner. *The Courts and the Schools.* London: Longman, 1987.

AFFIRMATIVE ACTION: CAN A WHITE, COLLEGE-EDUCATED MALE BE A VICTIM OF DISCRIMINATION

by Mike Healy
Monona, Iowa

Regents of the University of California v. Bakke, 438 U.S. 265 (1978) [U.S. Supreme Court]

Allan Bakke was raised in Minnesota; his father was a postal carrier and his mother was a teacher. After graduating with honors from the University of Minnesota in 1962 with a B.S. in mechanical engineering, he entered the Marines to fulfill his ROTC commitment and eventually served a tour of duty in Vietnam. In 1967, he was hired by the National Aeronautics and Space Administration as a research engineer, at the same time he continued graduate work at Stanford University, earning an M.S. degree in mechanical engineering in 1970.

Despite Bakke's apparent success as an engineer, he had a further goal. He wanted to become a physician. To this end, he attended night school to complete needed undergraduate science courses and performed volunteer work in a hospital emergency room. In 1973, Bakke applied for admission to the University of California—Davis Medical School (UCDMS). He was turned down.

In 1973, UCDMS had 2,464 applicants for 100 vacancies. The regular admissions formula took into account Medical College Admissions

Test scores, transcripts, grade point averages, applicant-supplied descriptions of activities and work, and letters of recommendation. The admissions committee was required to sift through these credentials and extend personal interviews to selected candidates (38 percent of the applicants in 1973 were interviewed). From the credentials and the interview, candidates were given "benchmark scores." Since the practice was for candidates to apply to a number of schools, an alternates list was compiled of those not admitted but standing high in the process. Regular admissions filled 84 of the 100 vacancies.

A special admissions program, begun in 1972, was designed "to increase opportunities in medical education for disadvantaged citizens." Sixteen vacancies were filled from a list of minority applicants. The process was the same as with regular admissions, but grade point average was not considered. From this separate list 16 vacancies were filled.

In 1973, Bakke was interviewed by Dr. Theodore West of UCDMS. West found Bakke a very desirable candidate and recommended him for admission. In the rating process, Bakke scored 468 on a 500 scale. UCDMS earlier in the year had accepted some applicants with lower scores. But Bakke's application came late in the year, and a score of 470 was then being required for acceptance. In early May 1973, Bakke received the UCDMS rejection.

Bakke wrote to Dr. George Lowrey, the UCDMS admissions committee chairman, asking to be placed on a waiting list or to be allowed to audit classes until a vacancy occurred. Lowrey did not reply. Bakke wrote again in July 1973, questioning Lowrey on the justice of racial quotas in admissions. Bakke indicated that he would consider legal action.

Lowrey directed his assistant, Peter Storandt, to reply to Bakke's letters. Storandt had already expressed doubts about whether the UCDMS special admissions program was hurting qualified nonminority candidates. In his letter to Bakke, Storandt urged Bakke to apply early for the 1974 admissions process. He also encouraged Bakke to continue researching legal actions, noting a discrimination case, *DeFunis v. Odegaard* (1974), was then before the Supreme Court. In a series of letters, Bakke and Storandt discussed possible legal action, and Storandt offered advice about the best course to follow.

Bakke reapplied for admission to UCDMS in 1974. His preliminary scores were comparable to his 1973 application. In 1974, there were 3,737 applicants for 100 vacancies at UCDMS. A student member of the admissions committee interviewed Bakke. The interviewer gave Bakke a strong recommendation. Bakke was also interviewed by Lowrey, the admissions chairman and a strong supporter of special admissions. Lowrey's evaluation of Bakke was that he was self-centered and showed difficulty reaching independent conclusions. Lowrey devoted most of his written analysis to Bakke's views of special admissions. He concluded that Bakke was an acceptable, but not outstanding candidate. Bakke's overall benchmark score in 1974 was 549 on a 600 scale. Bakke's application was again rejected.

In April 1974, Bakke sued in California state court seeking admission to UCDMS. He contended the school's affirmative action program had unconstitutionally reduced the number of vacancies for which he was allowed to compete. If all 100 vacancies would have been open to him, would Bakke have been admitted? Bakke said yes, the UCDMS said no.

The UCDMS affirmative action program of 1974 was similar to many programs at colleges and universities nationwide. Its purpose was to compensate for past or present discrimination by giving special consideration to certain classes of individual applicants. Based on the alleged cultural bias of standardized tests, special standards for minority students were then being applied in most professional school admissions. Thus, minority inclusion occasionally meant majority exclusion. Some individuals, like Bakke, questioned whether affirmative action was going too far, becoming "reverse discrimination."

Shortly before *Bakke* went to trial, the U.S. Supreme Court heard an appeal from Marco DeFunis, a law student at the University of Washington Law School. DeFunis claimed to be a victim of reverse discrimination. The Supreme Court considered the case but did not rule on the merits of the affirmative action issue. The Court declared that since DeFunis was already attending the University of Washington Law School under a lower court order, and that law school officials testified that he would complete his legal degree soon, he had "nothing to lose." Thus, there was no live case or controversy.

Bakke had repeatedly maintained that he was not an antiaffirmative action crusader but that he just wanted to attend medical school. Regardless of his motives, Bakke's challenge to the UCDMS admissions policies presented a challenge to the constitutionality of affirmative action that could not be as easily avoided, as it had been in *DeFunis*.

Bakke was heard in rural Yolo County, California, before Judge F. Leslie Manker. The University of California was worried that the case would be settled without a definitive ruling on affirmative action. The university, therefore, filed a cross complaint requesting that the court declare the UCDMS special admissions program legal. Manker agreed with Bakke's attorney that UCDMS had a racial quota. He ruled that Bakke's rights were violated under the equal protection clause of the Fourteenth Amendment. He also felt that Title VI of the Civil Rights Act of 1964 applied. It reads: "No person in the United States shall, on the ground of race, color, or national origin, be excluded from participation in, be denied the benefits of, or be subjected to discrimination under any program or activity receiving Federal financial assistance."

UCDMS continued to maintain that Bakke would not have been accepted into the Davis Medical School even with all 100 vacancies available. Manker agreed, ruling that UCDMS could not be compelled to admit Bakke to its student body. In 1973, he noted, Bakke had applied to and was rejected by two medical schools. In 1974, he had applied to and was rejected by 11 schools. The burden of proof, Manker concluded, rested on Bakke to prove he would have been accepted by UCDMS if he had been eligible to compete for all 100 vacancies. Since Bakke had not fully documented that issue in his case, Manker would not command Bakke's admission to UCDMS.

A direct appeal was made to the California Supreme Court. That court in hearing the case had to select a standard of judicial review to weigh the merits of the issue. If a "rational basis

test" was selected, state action was permissible if a rational purpose was served. A "balancing test" had been proposed in a 1976 discrimination case in the New York courts. The balancing test required that: (1) a "substantial state interest" be present and (2) no nonracial classification could serve the same purpose. The California Supreme Court rejected both tests. The court relied on a form of judicial review called "strict scrutiny" that required: (1) a "compelling state interest" be served and (2) "no less onerous means" be available to fulfill the state's interest. The court found the UCDMS policy wanting on the basis of this test. Therefore, the California high court declared the Davis special admissions program unconstitutional under the equal protection clause of the Fourteenth Amendment. The court decision, rendered in September 1976, was by a 6–1 vote.

The California Supreme Court placed the burden of proof on the university. The Court ruled that UCDMS had not offered sufficient proof that Bakke should be denied a vacancy. It, therefore, ordered that Bakke be admitted. Finally, the court eliminated the consideration of race as a criterion for admissions. The court directed UCDMS to discontinue its present special admissions process.

The University of California appealed to the U.S. Supreme Court. Bakke was not admitted to medical school immediately. The university feared a repeat of *DeFunis*. If Bakke was admitted to UCDMS, could the Supreme Court rule the case moot?

Several minority organizations tried to stop the University of California from appealing. These organizations distrusted the sincerity of UCDMS and its affirmative action policy. Some minority organizations believed that *Bakke* was a "poor vehicle" to test affirmative action. The UCDMS special admissions was different from other affirmative action programs in that it used "disadvantaged citizens" in defining groups targeted for special consideration. Minority students who were not sufficiently "disadvantaged" would not be considered for special admissions. However, only nonwhite students were ever admitted as disadvantaged. There was also a question of discrimination against Asian students in the UCDMS admissions. Finally, experts questioned the use of test scores to give an accurate benchmark score. The standard-ized tests were designed with a statistical error margin that UCDMS did not consider in evaluating candidates.

The Supreme Court received 57 *amici curiae* ("friends of the court") briefs in *Bakke*. Constitutional experts cannot recall another Supreme Court case generating so many separate briefs. Some briefs came from friends of *Bakke*, but most were from foes. Some organizational constituencies were divided. For example, the National Education Association's brief was against Bakke, but the American Federation of Teachers' brief was for Bakke. The Justice Department's brief, which was the product of intense politics, condemned racial quotas but strongly supported affirmative action. Minority organizations, legal groups, labor unions, government agencies, professional groups, all were "friends of the court." On appeal, the University of California retained Archibald Cox, a former solicitor general of the United States and one victim of President Richard Nixon's "Saturday night massacre," to head its legal team.

The Supreme Court heard oral arguments on October 12, 1977. A steady stream of newspaper, magazine, radio, and television attention was directed at the *Bakke* case. When the Supreme Court ruled, confusion reigned. Six justices delivered opinions. The June 28, 1978 *New York Times* headline read "NO ONE LOST."

The Supreme Court ruled that Bakke should be admitted to UCDMS. Chief Justice Warren E. Burger, and Associate Justices John Paul Stevens, Potter Stewart, William H. Rehnquist, and Lewis F. Powell, Jr., voted to agree with the California Supreme Court. The U.S. Supreme Court also held that the university had the right to take race into account when setting admissions criteria. Associate Justices William J. Brennan, Jr., Byron R. White, Thurgood Marshall, Harry A. Blackmun, and Lewis F. Powell, Jr., voted to overturn the California Supreme Court ruling on admissions criteria. Thus, the Court held that Bakke's rights were violated by the consideration of race. But the university could continue to use race as an admissions criterion. This seeming contradiction came because of the mediating vote of Jus-

tice Powell. Powell voted with the "Stevens" group on the Bakke admission-to-school question. But he voted with the "Brennan" group on the admissions-criterion question.

The Stevens opinion (Burger, Stewart, and Rehnquist concurring) did not address the question of constitutionality. The Stevens group took a narrow view of the case. Stevens felt that Title VI of the Civil Rights Act had been violated. He ruled that Bakke must be admitted to UCDMS.

The Brennan opinion (White, Marshall, and Blackmun concurring) considered both Title VI of the Civil Rights Act and the equal protection clause of the Fourteenth Amendment. Brennan felt that broad remedial measures were possible: "We cannot let color-blindness become myopia which masks the reality that many 'created equal' have been treated within our lifetimes as inferior both by the law and by their fellow citizens."

The Brennan group rejected a strict scrutiny judicial review standard. The Brennan opinion proposed use of a standard review taken from sex discrimination cases: "[The classification] must serve important governmental objectives and must be substantially related to the achievement of those objectives." Brennan wrote that correcting past societal discrimination was a valuable objective. But no group or individual could be stigmatized as inferior by this process. In *Bakke*, no one claimed that whites were inferior. Since all the minority students admitted to UCDMS were qualified candidates, no stigma was being attached. Brennan viewed affirmative action as the only way to reduce underrepresentation of racial minorities in medical schools.

The Brennan group felt that displaced whites, such as Bakke, were not really "innocent victims" of racial preferences in admissions. Rather, these whites would not have won out in competition had the minorities not been handicapped by previous discrimination. The Brennan group seemed to view the equal protection clause of the Fourteenth Amendment as the protector of group rights.

Justices White, Marshall, and Blackmun all wrote additional opinions. White added that the enforcement of Title VI was the responsibility of the government. Marshall, in a strongly worded opinion, held that past discrimination required affirmative action. Blackmun emphasized that educators were the best qualified to determine admissions.

The opinion most analyzed was written by Justice Powell, the swing justice. It is ironic that his opinion was most consulted, since his view was not completely shared by any of the other justices. Powell agreed with the Brennan group that race was a permissible criterion in admissions. But Powell agreed with the Stevens group on admitting Bakke to UCDMS, basing his judgment on the equal protection clause of the Fourteenth Amendment (the Stevens group relied on Title VI). Thus, Powell created the majority, but disagreed in some form with both factions.

Powell rejected goals and quotas. He felt that both resulted in racial classifications based on race and ethnic status. He viewed the equal protection clause as the guarantor of individual rights. Powell felt that *Bakke* required a "strict judicial scrutiny." The UCDMS special admissions program supposedly was enacted to: (1) reduce the deficit of minority students in medical schools, (2) increase the number of physicians in minority communities by training minority doctors, (3) remediate past societal discriminations, and (4) obtain the educational benefits of a diverse student body. Powell rejected the first three as not substantial enough to merit a separate classification system. The Brennan group had based its judgment on the remediation of past societal discriminations, but Powell rejected that argument.

In Powell's mind, Bakke should not pay for society's past discriminations. Powell did offer an exception. If a specific institution was guilty of past discriminations, that institution could try to correct its own past shortcomings. Powell accepted the fourth goal, the attainment of a diverse student body, as being sufficiently important so as not to fall prey to the strict scrutiny requirements. He felt that the First Amendment has a special concern with academic freedom. Such academic freedom necessitated a diverse student body. However, in Powell's view, racial quotas were a constitutionally impermissible means of obtaining that diverse student body. Powell did hold that race could be used on an individual basis as one of the criteria

for admissions. He cited the Harvard College admissions process as an example of such a program. Harvard desired a diverse student body and viewed each applicant on an individual basis. It used a variety of criteria in its review, including race. Thus, Powell voted with the Brennan group to allow *consideration* of race in college admissions. He did so, however, for a different reason and to a lesser extent.

Powell continued his strict scrutiny review of the UCDMS admissions policy. Since Bakke could compete for only 84 vacancies, and minority students could compete for all 100 vacancies, Powell found that Bakke's rights had been violated. Thus, Powell voted with the Stevens group to admit Bakke to UCDMS. He did so on equal protection grounds.

What was the end result of *Regents of the University of California v. Bakke*? Bakke was admitted to UCDMS. The UCDMS special admissions policy was declared unconstitutional. The California Supreme Court's race-neutral admissions standard was overturned. Who was victorious?

Attorney General Griffin Bell called the decision "a great victory for affirmative action." The Reverend Jesse Jackson called it "a devastating blow to our civil-rights struggle." A. E. Howard of the University of the Virginia School of Law viewed the *Bakke* decision as a "Solomonic compromise." Lawrence Tribe of Harvard Law School called it an "act of statecraft." Eleanor Holmes Norton of the Equal Employment Opportunity Commission felt "that we are not compelled to do anything differently from the way we've done things in the past."

Good, bad, neutral, *Bakke* was a mixed decision. Some expert commentators saw the Court's decision as reflecting the larger society's split on how to resolve historic racial injustice with today's desire for equal opportunity. As society was split, so was the Supreme Court. Did *Bakke* have an impact? For Bakke most assuredly. He entered UCDMS amid protests, graduating in 1982. He interned at the Mayo Clinic in Rochester, Minnesota, where he later served as an anesthesiology resident.

In college admissions, *Bakke* has appeared to have had minimal impact. A 1982 survey of college admissions programs found that 83 percent had made no forced change in their programs as a result of it. Many experts saw a wide range of discretion possible for admissions officials. In reality, *Bakke* has not prohibited race-conscious admissions, but rather licensed such programs.

Later court cases did little to provide constitutional clarification for affirmative action. In *Kaiser Aluminum and Chemical Corporation v. Weber* (1979), a labor case involving minority quotas for entrance into a special training program, the Supreme Court held 5–2 that the use of quotas was permissible under the Civil Rights Act of 1964. In overruling the circuit court of appeals, the majority of opinion of Justice Brennan saw the equal protection clause of the Fourteenth Amendment as applying only to actions by states, not to private individuals or companies. However, when consenting parties to a labor agreement decide on private action to ameliorate past discrimination, those affirmative action measures are permissible.

Bakke, thus, provided a complex compromise to a vexing public policy concern. Subsequent Supreme Court decisions have not done much to clarify matters. As Bakke's medical career progresses, the courts continue to struggle with the issues he raised over 15 years earlier.

Selected Bibliography

Dreyfus, J., and C. Lawrence, III. *The* Bakke *Case: The Politics of Inequality*. New York: Harcourt Brace Jovanovich, 1979.

Eastland, T., and W.J. Bennett. *Counting by Race: Equality From the Founding Fathers to* Bakke *and* Weber. New York: Basic Books, Inc., 1979.

Schwartz, B. *Behind* Bakke: *Affirmative Action and the Supreme Court*. New York: New York University Press, 1988.

Simmons, R. *Affirmative Action: Conflict and Change in Higher Education After* Bakke. Cambridge, MA: Schenkman Publishing Co., Inc., 1982.

Sindler, A.P. Bakke, DeFunis, *and Minority Admissions: The Quest for Equal Opportunity*. New York: Longman, Inc., 1978.

Tribe, L.H. "Perspectives on *Bakke*: Equal Protection, Procedural Fairness, or Structural Justice?" *Harvard Law Review* 92 (Feb. 1979): 864–77.

Wilkenson, J.H. *From* Brown *to* Bakke: *The Supreme Court and School Integration: 1954–78*. New York: Oxford University Press, 1979.

E. Women

SHOULD A WOMAN BE ADMITTED TO THE BAR?

by Fara Y. Driver
Clemson, South Carolina

Bradwell v. Illinois, 18 U.S. 130 (1873) [U.S. Supreme Court]

In the past century women have taken significant steps toward legal recognition and legal independence: the right to vote, the right to own and control property, the right to make contracts, the right to control their own income, and the right to practice in a self-chosen profession. This latter right was hard won, and nowhere was it more resisted than within the legal profession itself.

Myra Colby Bradwell, the wife of practicing lawyer James Bradwell, was the chief editor and president of the *Chicago Legal News*, a weekly legal newspaper that soon became, according to one authority "the most important legal publication west of the Alleghenies." Mrs. Bradwell had been studying law under her husband. Through her work with her legal paper, charitable organizations, and the women's suffrage movement, she was very aware of the legal restrictions placed on women by her society. Her husband had already secured a special charter for her to be president of the law publication because Illinois law placed restrictions on the ability of a married woman to make contracts. Mrs. Bradwell herself was responsible for drafting legislation in Illinois to allow married women to control their own earnings.

In 1869, the same year that Arabella Mansfield was admitted to the bar in Iowa, Bradwell applied to practice law in Illinois. She passed the required examination but was denied the right to practice on the grounds that she was a married woman. This meant that she could not enter into the necessary contracts between an attorney and client. When she appealed the lower court decision to the Illinois Supreme Court, that court decided that the mere fact that she was a woman could prevent her from the practice of law. With this deci-

sion, Bradwell appealed to the U.S. Supreme Court.

The Supreme Court did not make a decision in her case until 1873. Coincidentally, the case was decided the same day as the more famous *Slaughterhouse Cases*. Distinguished attorney Matthew H. Carpenter argued both cases, the first two cases concerning the new Fourteenth Amendment heard by the Supreme Court. Carpenter attacked the Illinois law as an infringement on the privileges and immunities clause of the Fourteenth Amendment: "No State shall make or enforce any law which shall abridge the privileges or immunities of citizens of the United States." In contrast to his strategy in the *Slaughterhouse Cases*, Carpenter argued for a broad interpretation of this passage. In *Bradwell*, he stated in his brief that the Fourteenth Amendment "executes itself in every State of the Union." He carefully stayed away from the suffrage issue, going so far as to say that "the right to vote is not one of those privileges" protected by the amendment.

In presenting his case, Carpenter put great stress on a statement of Justice Stephen J. Field in *Cummings v. Missouri* (1867): "[I]n the pursuit of happiness all avocations, all honors, all positions, are alike open to everyone, and that in the protection of these rights all are equal before the law." Anticipating the Court's use of the Fourteenth Amendment for the protection of black people, Carpenter used the following arguments: "The legislature may say at what age candidates shall be admitted, may elevate or depress the standard of learning required. But a qualification, to which a whole class of citizens never can attain, is not a regulation of admission to the bar, but is, as to such citizens, a prohibition. . . . If the legislature may, under

461

the pretence of fixing qualifications, declare that no female citizen shall be permitted to practice law, it may as well declare that no colored citizen shall practice law; for the only provision in the Constitution of the United States which secured to colored male citizens the privilege of admission to the bar . . . is the provision that 'no State shall make or enforce any law which shall abridge the privileges or immunities of a citizen.' And if this provision does protect the colored citizen, then it protects every citizen, black or white, male or female."

Associate Justice Samuel F. Miller, writing the opinion, held that "there are privileges and immunities belonging to citizens of the United States . . . and that it is these and these alone which a State is forbidden to abridge. But the right to admission to practice in the courts of a State is not one of them." While Miller avoided discussion of the specifics of gender and the practice of law, the subject was covered in great detail in Justice Joseph P. Bradley's concurring opinion: "Man is, or should be, woman's protector and defender. The natural and proper timidity and delicacy which belongs to the female sex evidently unfits it for many of the occupations of civil life. The constitution of the family organization, which is founded in the divine ordinance, as well as in the nature of things, indicates the domestic sphere as that which properly belongs to the domain and functions of womanhood. The harmony, not to say identity, of interests and views which belong, or should belong, to the family institution is repugnant to the idea of a woman adopting a distinct and independent career from that of her husband. . . . The paramount destiny and mission of woman are to fulfill the noble and benign offices of wife and mother."

The Court's decision in *Bradwell* is significant in that it established a precedent for state regulation of women in occupations. Later decisions, especially the decision in *Minor v. Happersett* (1875) denying women the right to vote, reinforced the attitude of the U.S. majority in the late 1800s toward women and the role they should play in society.

In 1872, one year before the Court's *Bradwell* decision, the Illinois legislature passed a bill that made it illegal to prevent the entrance of anyone into any profession or employment (except the military) on the grounds of sex. Although Myra Bradwell did not reapply for admission to the Illinois bar, she was admitted, finally, in 1890 by a motion of the Illinois Supreme Court.

Selected Bibliography

Bredstein, B.J. *The Culture of Professionalism: The Middle Class and the Development of Higher Education in America*. New York: W.W. Norton & Co., Inc., 1976.

Harris, R.J. *The Quest for Equality*. Westport, CT: Greenwood Press Publishers, 1960.

Riley, G. *Inventing the American Woman: A Perspective on Women's History 1865 to the Present*. Arlington Heights, IL: Harlan Davidson, Inc., 1986.

Stevens, R. *Legal Education in America from the 1850's to the 1980's*. Chapel Hill, NC: University of North Carolina Press, 1983.

ABERRATION IN THE MOVEMENT TOWARD AN EIGHT-HOUR DAY

by Robert A. Waller
Department of History
Clemson University

Ritchie v. People, 155 Ill. 98 (1895) [Illinois Supreme Court]

Among the most celebrated state court cases impeding the movement toward an eight-hour day is *Ritchie v. People*. Here, reformers in Illinois sought to improve working conditions by using the state's police power to restrict property rights. The supporters of *laissez-faire* resisted such constraints by arguing for "freedom of contract" between employer and employee.

In 1893, the General Assembly of Illinois passed a law limiting women's hours in factories or workshops to no more than eight hours a day and 48 hours a week. This "Factory Act" established a system whereby inspectors were charged with the responsibility of enforcing the eight-hour clause for female workers. Among the inspectors was the noted social reformer, Florence Kelley. She and her colleagues successfully prosecuted several violators. In response, a number of factory owners formed the Illinois Manufacturers' Association (IMA) in order to resist the eight-hour provision. By January 1894, the IMA and the inspectors agreed to a test case in the state courts.

IMA counsel, Levy Mayer, argued that the clause was unconstitutional on two grounds. First, he argued that the law was discriminatory because it applied only to factories and workshops. Second, Levy used the conventional wisdom that the clause denied freedom of contract to both employer and employee. The attorney for the state, Alexander Bruce, responded that the eight-hour clause was a legitimate exercise of the state's police power for the protection of health and morals of women as childbearers and mothers. An estimated 30,000 women were affected.

On May 4, 1894, the Illinois Supreme Court heard the arguments of the attorneys. However, the court took almost a year to consider the case before rendering its opinion. In that interval, employers violated the law with impunity. Finally, on March 15, 1895 (one year after the famous Pullman strike), the state supreme court declared the clause unconstitutional because it impaired a woman's right to contract for her labor without due process of law. While conceding that the state's police power is extensive, the court declared that it must be directly related to the comfort, welfare, or safety of the society. In the opinion of the court, the law under consideration did meet this test. "It is not the nature of the things done," the opinion reads, "but the sex of the persons doing them, which is made the basis of the claim that the act is a measure for the promotion of the public health." *Ritchie v. People* became the model for how courts opposed to protective legislation would react.

The decision became one of the most celebrated of the late nineteenth century. Opponents of reform, such as the *Chicago Tribune*, announced that the decision meant "an end to the vexatious suits, begun by overzealous Inspectors to enforce a provision they must have known would be held illegal." The opposition newspaper, the *Chicago Times-Herald*, countered that the decision was "nothing but a setting back the hands of progress on the dial of time." In writing her third annual report, Kelley observed that the court had become "an insuperable obstacle to the protection of women and children." She hoped that this case would "be added to the reversed decisions in which the Supreme Court of Illinois is so rich." Ultimately, she proved to be correct.

The ramifications spread beyond the confines of the Prairie State. Supporters of *laissez-faire* found confirmation that a principal canon had been supported by the highest court of a major industrial state. Proponents of freedom of contract hailed the decision as anchoring the cornerstone of the free enterprise system. Agents of reform also believed that this opinion against protective legislation concerning hours of work also had a stultifying effect on child labor legislation, another progressive measure. The reformist press pilloried the decision for the obstacle that it represented to achieving an eight-hour day.

The conventional interpretation has held that *Ritchie v. People* was representative of the judicial opinion in the nation. Recent research, however, indicates that this much praised and maligned case rarely served as a precedent for other decisions. That investigation reveals that most state courts tended to reflect "the mildly reformist views of the country at large." The Progressives of the early twentieth century, in spite of the loud complaints, were making significant gains. *Ritchie* was an aberration. In *Muller v. Oregon* (1908), the U.S. Supreme Court affirmed the practice of women's hours legislation by upholding an Oregon law.

Interestingly, the Illinois Supreme Court had the opportunity to reconsider its position. In 1910, a second *Ritchie* case was considered, *Ritchie and Company v. Wayman*, in which the validity of the ten-hour law for women was revisited. The court reversed itself; Kelley was vindicated. Fifteen years later, the judges held that a limit to ten hours per day was a more reasonable rule than the previous proviso for eight. Conservatives now accepted the principle that inequalities existed between employers and employees and that the state had a role to play in placing limitations on the contractual powers of private parties. Two years later, the same bench favored another Illinois statute that expanded the coverage to women employed in hotels. The times, indeed, had changed. *Ritchie v. People* had been an exception rather than the rule.

Selected Bibliography

Baer, J.A. *The Chains of Protection: The Judicial Response to Women's Labor Legislation.* Westport, CT: Greenwood Press, 1978.

Goldmark, J. *Impatient Crusader: Florence Kelley's Life Story.* Urbana, IL: University of Illinois Press, 1953.

Harmon, S.D. "Florence Kelley in Illinois." *Journal of the Illinois State Historical Society* 74 (Autumn 1981): 162–78.

Urofsky, M.I. "State Courts and Protective Legislation During the Progressive Era: A Reevaluation." *Journal of American History* 72 (June 1985): 63–91.

THE LAW RECOGNIZES "WOMEN ARE DIFFERENT"

by Melvin I. Urofsky
Department of History
Virginia Commonwealth University

Muller v. Oregon, 208 U.S. 412 (1908) [U.S. Supreme Court]

Joseph H. Choate, a pillar of the New York bar, listened patiently and courteously as the two women explained their request. Florence Kelley, the Chief Factory Inspector of Illinois, and Josephine Goldmark of the National Consumers' League, wanted the eminent New York attorney to defend, in the U.S. Supreme Court, an Oregon law restricting the working hours of women to ten a day. "I can see no reason," he told them, "why a big husky Irishwoman should not work more than ten hours day in a laundry if she and her employer so desired."

The Oregon ten-hour law was part of the great spurt of reform activity that dominated American political life for the two decades prior to World War I; it has often been described as a "response to industrialism." Whether this characterization is true in all areas of Progressive reform, there is no doubt it marked various statutes known as protective legislation, which established maximum hours and minimum wages, restricted child labor, and created workmen's compensation plans. In the eyes of reformers, protective legislation would redress, in large measure, the perceived imbalance between the lords of big business and their ill-used workers.

These campaigns had begun in the latter part of the nineteenth century, as state after state passed some or all of the reformers' proposals. But in almost every state, conservatives challenged these measures as violating one or both of the great constitutional shibboleths: substantive due process and freedom of contract. The former rested on the due process clause of the Fourteenth Amendment and had been interpreted by state and federal courts to mean that certain property interests could not be diminished through regulation by the state acting under its police power. What these interests were, and how great their protection, depended on the particular courts, but the common thread of interpretation held property interests to be the backbone of society and progress and to be defended against wild-eyed reformers at all cost.

Freedom of contract, which derived from the pre-Civil War doctrine of free labor, was originally designed to distinguish northern industrial workers from southern slaves. Free workers could chose the terms of their employment, slaves could not; free workers could bargain with their employers, slaves could not; free workers could leave if they found other employment more to their liking or advantage, slaves could not. After the war, the free labor idea became converted into freedom of contract, in which nothing could be allowed to interfere with the voluntary bargaining between employer and employee. The fact that conditions had changed—that no actual bargaining took place between the owners of big factories and the thousands of workers they employed—did not penetrate the judicial consciousness; judges continued to decide cases as if each worker in a steel mill or coal mine had individually bargained out his employment contract with the owner.

As courts first began to hear constitutional challenges to protective legislation, conservative attorneys appealed to the doctrines of substantive due process and freedom of contract. Laws regulating factories, they claimed, interfered with the owners' free use of property, depriving them of that property without due process of law. Statutes controlling working conditions, on the other hand, deprived workers of their right to make any arrangement they wanted with their employers. Jurists unsympathetic to the goals of protective legislation could rely on either one or both of these arguments to find the statutes unconstitutional.

Not all judges and all lawyers opposed protective legislation. But courts are by nature conservative, and even if late-nineteenth century judges had been prescient about the direction of a rapidly changing society, it is unlikely they would have rushed to approve a wide spectrum of innovative laws, many of which ran counter to long-established common-law principles. The courts did eventually accept the need for protective legislation, and they did so under the rationale of the states' police powers.

As part of its sovereign powers, a state could employ its "police power" to override both property and individual rights so as to protect public order and maintain minimal standards of health, safety, and welfare for its citizens. Even property-conscious jurists, such as Justice Stephen J. Field, recognized the great range of the state's powers "to prescribe the regulations to promote the health, peace, morals, education and good order of the people, and to legislate so as to increase the industries of the state, develop its resources and add to the wealth and prosperity." In the famous Granger case, *Munn v. Illinois* (1877), one of the first cases involving the police power to reach the Supreme Court, the majority made clear that even the sanctity of contract and property rights, under proper circumstances, might be restricted for the public good, an idea that sent paroxysms of terror through conservative ranks.

The range of police powers, as well as the extent of property rights and freedom to contract, formed a central debate in American jurisprudence from the 1880s to the 1930s. Reformers applauded the statement by Justice Oliver Wendell Holmes, Jr., in 1911 that the police power "may be put forth in aid of what is sanctioned by usage, or held by the prevailing morality, or strong and preponderant opinion to be greatly and immediately necessary to the public welfare." By that reading, the police power could reach almost anything the legislature wished to regulate.

Conservatives, on the other hand, while conceding the existence of the police power, argued that it had only limited range, and the state could interfere only minimally with property and individual rights. Thomas M. Cooley, the leading law writer of the late nineteenth century, admitted the need for police regulations in any well-ordered society, but these rules "must have reference to the comfort, safety, or welfare of society . . . and they must not, under pretence of regulation, take from the corporation any of the essential rights and privileges which the charter confers." Rather than deny the existence of the police power and the state's authority to pass protective legislation, opponents argued that the power had been misused, that it had been extended in an illegitimate manner to matters beyond its reach. The states, on the other hand, would often preface their statutes with a claim that the ensuing legislation met a legitimate state interest. The preamble to an Oregon minimum wage law, for example, declared: "The welfare of the State of Oregon requires that women and minors should be protected from conditions of labor which have a pernicious effect on their health and morals, and inadequate wages . . . have such a pernicious effect."

The general perception of courts as a bastion of antireform sentiment is somewhat at variance with the facts. Although in well-known state cases such as New York's *In re Jacobs* (1885) and Illinois's *Ritchie v. People* (1895), state courts went out of their way to deny the applicability of the police power, the fact is that nearly all state courts approved protective legislation by the early years of the twentieth century. Moreover, in the U.S. Supreme Court a similar pattern emerged; with few exceptions, the Court rebuffed challenges to the states' police powers. One of the most famous—or infamous—of those exceptions, however, was *Lochner v. New York* (1905).

In that case, Justice Rufus W. Peckham, perhaps the most conservative member of the Court, spoke for a 5–4 majority in striking down a New York statute prescribing maximum hours for bakery workers. "Is this a fair, reasonable and appropriate exercise of the police power of the State," Peckham asked, "or is it an unreasonable, unnecessary and arbitrary interference with the rights of the individual?" Peckham's very phrasing of the question left no doubt as to his answer, and he went on to denounce the law, whose real object, he claimed, was "to regulate the hours of labor between the master and his employees . . . in a private business, not dangerous in any degree to morals or in any real and substantive degree, to the health of the employees."

The *Lochner* decision cheered conservatives, and it quickly became a classic statement of the defense of property and contract rights against the allegedly overweening power of the state. There is probably little doubt that the *Lochner* ruling led Curt Muller to appeal his conviction of the Oregon ten-hour law.

In 1903, Oregon had established a maximum of ten hours work a day for women employed in manufacturing, mechanical establishments, and laundries. On September 4, 1905, Joe Haselbock, the manager of Curt Muller's Grand Laundry in Portland required Mrs. Elmer Gotcher to work more than ten hours. She complained to the authorities, and two weeks later Muller was charged with violating the law, found guilty of a misdemeanor, and fined $10. He appealed to the Oregon Supreme Court, and when that body upheld the statute as a legitimate exercise of the state's police power, Muller appealed to the U.S. Supreme

Court. Reformers around the country noted the appeal with alarm, for if the Court struck down the Oregon statute, it might well mean the end of hours legislation. That is when Florence Kelley and Josephine Goldmark began seeking an eminent attorney to defend the statute; the day after Joseph Choate rebuffed them, the two women traveled to Boston to meet with Louis D. Brandeis.

By late 1907, Brandeis had already earned the title of "People's Attorney." After establishing a successful Boston practice, Brandeis had become interested in reform. He began, as did so many of the Progressives, on the local scene, fighting corrupt traction companies and opposing the giveaway of important municipal franchises. Brandeis then moved to the state level. In Massachusetts, he considered his most important reform contribution the establishment of savings bank life insurance. Following the great insurance scandals of 1905, Brandeis had condemned the insurance companies for their scabrous treatment of poor workers, who paid exorbitant premiums for so-called industrial life policies that provided very limited protection. As an alternative, Brandeis proposed and then secured approval of a plan in which low-cost life insurance would be sold through the state's savings banks.

The campaign for savings bank insurance illustrated a pattern Brandeis would employ not only in his career as a reformer and lawyer, but later as a member of the Supreme Court. First, identify the problem; second, gather all the facts available on that problem; and third, from those facts deduce an appropriate remedy. One of his favorite maxims was *ex facto jus oritur* ("out of facts springs the law"), and this would be the strategy he used in *Muller*.

Brandeis had, in fact, been the first choice of both Kelley and Goldmark; both knew him through a common network of reformers, and beyond that, he was married to Goldmark's sister. But an aide in the Consumers' League office had made the appointment with Choate while Kelley was out of town, so the two women felt bound at least to ask Choate to take on the case. When he refused, they gladly turned to Brandeis.

After listening to the two women, Brandeis agreed to take the case provided certain conditions could be met. First, Oregon would have to designate him as its official counsel; second, the Consumers' League would have to research certain areas for him very quickly and provide extensive documentation; third, he would accept no fee in the case. Although the conditions struck the two women as somewhat unusual, they agreed without any idea of how Brandeis would proceed.

Actually, the three conditions were not so unusual. Brandeis already had in mind a rather unorthodox strategy, and for it to be successful, he had to be in control of the litigation. The official counsel plans the brief and determines what form the main arguments will take, both in written and oral form. Had he been just an *amicus curiae* ("friend of the court"), he would have been allowed to submit a brief, but it would have been ancillary to the main arguments. He doubted whether the state's attorney general would be comfortable with the innovative strategy he had in mind, or if he would be willing to let Brandeis control the case. The state, as it turned out, was more than delighted not only to be spared the cost of the appeal, but also to let Brandeis and the Consumers' League act on its behalf.

Brandeis's refusal to take a fee was perhaps the most unusual of the demands. Early in his career as a reformer, Brandeis had accepted fees for his work, and then had turned them over to charity. But as long as he accepted payment for his work, he acted as an employee of a client, and thus his primary responsibility was to that client. He came to realize that in many cases, a difference existed between the specific interests of the client, even that of a reform group, and the larger interests of the public. By not accepting a fee, Brandeis could work for solutions that he believed were in the public interest, without being held accountable to a particular client. This policy helped garner for him the sobriquet "People's Attorney."

The request for data derived from Brandeis's belief that he had to know all the facts surrounding an issue before he could frame a workable solution. But in this particular case, the strategy, while certainly innovative, had in fact been suggested by Justice Peckham in his *Lochner* decision. The New York law, Brandeis claimed, exceeded the state's police power be-cause it had no relation to health or safety; merely because the state said it had a relation did not constitute proof. By implication, if a law could be shown to have a direct relation to health, safety, or public welfare, the courts would recognize it as a legitimate exercise of state power.

As Brandeis told Goldmark, he wanted "*facts*, published by anyone with expert knowledge of industry in its relation to women's hours of labor, such as factory inspectors, physicians, trade unions, economists [and] social workers" [emphasis in original]. Aided by ten readers, Goldmark scoured the holdings of the New York Public Library, Columbia University, and the Library of Congress. She enlisted a young medical student to research material on the hygiene of occupations. They had about two weeks to gather the material; Brandeis had agreed to take the case in mid-November 1907, and it would have to be argued before the Court in January 1908. After they presented the mass of data to him, he had to assimilate it, arrange it in an orderly and persuasive manner, and have the brief printed by the Court's deadline.

Brandeis recognized, as many people at the time did not, that *Lochner* represented a departure from the Supreme Court's earlier decisions on the police power. In *Holden v. Hardy* (1898), the Court had upheld a Utah law establishing an eight-hour day for miners; a few years later in *Atkin v. Kansas* (1903), the Court confirmed a state law mandating an eight-hour day on all public projects and for all private employers contracting to do state business. In response to the argument that the state had exceeded its authority, Justice John Marshall Harlan declared that "regulations on this subject suggest only considerations of public policy. And with such considerations the courts have no concern." Only a few months after its *Lochner* decision, the Court reaffirmed its *Holden* ruling with a *per curiam* ("by the court") decision upholding a similar Missouri statute and then, in 1907, extended *Atkin* by validating a federal eight-hour law for government laborers.

Brandeis had to get the majority of the Court to return to this earlier line of decisions, without asking it to overrule *Lochner*. He recognized, as a matter of strategy, that the Court would be unwilling to reverse itself so quickly (even though *Lochner* had been a 5–4 decision), and that even the justices who had voted to sustain earlier protective legislation still believed in freedom of contract and protection of property. So, instead of rebutting *Lochner*, he quoted selectively from it in the mere two pages he devoted to legal argument. Rather than deny the idea of freedom of contract, he acknowledged it, but then cited *Lochner* to claim that freedom of contract could be abridged to protect health, safety, and the public welfare.

Justice Peckham in his *Lochner* opinion had tried to show that the conservative majority was not placing its own social and economic views above the legislative judgment, and so had declared that "when the validity of a statute is questioned, the burden of proof" would be on the challenger rather than on the state. The Court itself, according to Peckham, would not strike down a statute unless it found no "fair ground, reasonable in and of itself, to say that there is material danger to the public health (or safety), or to the health (or safety) of the employees (or to the general welfare)." In *Lochner*, Peckham had claimed, the Court had been unable to find the connection between the statute and the public health and safety. The "Brandeis brief" attempted to demonstrate that connection.

After the two scant pages of legal citation, Brandeis set out to show the reasonableness and the factual basis for the Oregon law. He devoted 15 pages to showing that Oregon was not alone in believing that long hours of labor adversely affected women's health, and he cited the laws of other states as well as foreign countries to show that responsible people believed limiting hours a reasonable exercise of the state's power.

Then came a 95-page section entitled "The World's Experience upon which the Legislation Limiting the Hours of Labor for Women is Based," with various sections on "The Dangers of Long Hours" and "Laundries." Here Brandeis marshalled the facts that he had asked Goldmark and her researchers to find, and he used sources that, until then, had rarely been cited in legal briefs or judicial opinions—the British *Reports of Medical Commissioners on the Health of Factory Operatives* (1833), reports of the Massachusetts Bureau of Labor Statistics

and the Commissioners on the Hours of Labor, the *Journal of the Royal Sanitary Institute*, an 1892 treatise entitled *The Hygiene, Diseases, and Mortality of Occupations*, and many others. In fact, nearly all of this section consisted of lengthy quotations organized to prove the basic contention that contemporary knowledge justified restricting the hours that women worked in order to preserve their health.

The Court heard oral argument in *Muller v. Oregon* on January 15, 1908. William D. Fenton, counsel for the laundry owner, took the traditional view that freedom of contract should not be abridged, and that a law restricting hours only for women was unconstitutionally discriminatory. "Women equally with men," he declared, "are endowed with the fundamental and inalienable rights of liberty and property, and these rights cannot be impaired or destroyed by legislative action under the pretense of exercising the police power of the state. Difference in sex alone does not justify the destruction or impairment of these rights."

The gist of Brandeis's argument, however, and the whole point of nearly 100 pages of economic, medical, and sociological data had been to show that people outside the courts recognized that women in fact *were* different from men. By now Brandeis had completely mastered the voluminous data he had requested and, according to Goldmark's recollection, "slowly, deliberately, without seeming to refer to a note, he built up his case from the particular to the general, describing conditions authoritatively reported, turning the pages of history, country by country, state by state, weaving with artistic skill the human facts—all to prove the evil of long hours and the benefit that accrued when these were abolished by law." In his oral presentation as in the brief, he let the facts speak for themselves, and invited the justices to take judicial notice of them so they might understand the reasonableness of the state's action in passing the law.

The justices listened carefully and recognized that Brandeis had given them an opportunity to sidestep the *Lochner* decision (which had been overwhelmingly criticized by all but the most hidebound conservatives), without actually overruling it. Brandeis had proposed no radical jurisprudential doctrine, nor even an erosion of accepted principles. He merely asked the justices to recognize in law what everyone knew, the "common knowledge" that women differed from men.

Brandeis's innovative strategy worked. Justice David J. Brewer wrote the brief opinion for the Court upholding the Oregon ten-hour law, and in an unusual comment referred to counsel by name. "It may not be amiss, in the present case," he declared, "before examining the constitutional question, to notice the course of legislation as well as expressions of opinion from other than judicial sources. In the brief filed by Mr. Louis D. Brandeis . . . is a very copious collection of all these matters, an epitome of which is found in the margin." In a footnote, Brewer listed the state and foreign laws, and the fact that over 90 separate reports had been cited to justify this legislation. While constitutional issues could not be decided by "a consensus of present public opinion," the Court does "take judicial cognizance of all matters of general knowledge." The particular aspect of "general knowledge" referred to by Brewer was that "women's physical structure and the performance of maternal functions place her at a disadvantage in the struggle for existence."

The *Muller* decision, and especially Brandeis's strategy, received widespread praise in the contemporary press. *The Outlook* of March 7, 1908, called the decision "unquestionably one of the [most] momentous decision[s] of the Supreme Court . . . immeasurable in its consequences, laden with vast potential benefit to the entire country for generations to come." Similar puffery from reformers such as Goldmark and Felix Frankfurter have obscured the fact that in its holding, the Court did not hand down a revolutionary decision at all. If one looks at the long list of protective legislation cases that came before the High Court between 1897 and 1917, one finds that it is *Lochner* and not *Muller* that is the exception.

Lochner, with its extreme assertions of property rights, soon became the epitome of judicial activism, condemned by reformers for the next generation. But in terms of its actual holdings, the Court approved nearly all the hours laws cases that it heard; *Muller* fits into the pattern, and is noteworthy primarily for the Court's backtracking from *Lochner*. Many scholars, in

fact, thought that the Court would just bury *Lochner*, but in 1923 the reactionary bloc resurrected the case in *Adkins v. Children's Hospital*.

The "Brandeis brief," as it would henceforth be known, remains the most important legacy of the case. As long as courts insisted on reviewing the reasonableness of state police regulations, lawyers would be able to use nonlegal materials to secure judicial cognizance of the facts of real life. Before his own appointment to the Supreme Court in 1916, Brandeis, working with the National Consumers' League and Goldmark, defended a number of protective statutes in both state courts and the Supreme Court. In cases where Brandeis could not direct the litigation personally, the league gave local attorneys the factual data and suggestions on how to prepare a "Brandeis brief."

In the long run, the introduction of factual material became commonplace, and today many law schools offer courses on law and social sciences with the aim of using these disciplines in legal proceedings. Next to *Muller*, the most noteworthy case to employ the Brandeis brief was the great school desegregation decision *Brown v. Board of Education* (1954). In that case, the National Association for the Advancement of Colored People amassed as much factual data as it could to support its contention that discrimination wrought psychological damage on black children.

The Brandeis brief also epitomized what Roscoe Pound, Oliver Wendell Holmes, Jr., Ernst Freund, and others had been advocating for nearly a generation: that the law could not be divorced from facts. In his Lowell Institute lectures on the common law in 1881, Holmes had argued that "the life of the law has not been logic but experience." This assertion greatly impressed Brandeis, who was in the audience. In his own practice, Brandeis had made it a rule to know, as he put it, all the facts that surround a case. In his regular work as well as in the cases he argued for reform groups, Brandeis had always brought facts to bear in his arguments; the *Muller* brief may have been revolutionary to many attorneys, but it represented a logical culmination of Brandeis's own work.

In *Muller*, Brandeis opened a wide door for the entry of facts of all kinds into the courtroom. His strategy also affected how legislation would henceforth be written. Now, instead of merely declaring that a certain statute affected health or safety, the assembly could create a "legislative history," which litigants and judges could rely on for determining the reasons and the reasonableness of the laws. For better or for worse, the "felt necessities of the time," expressed in judicially cognizable facts, would henceforth be an essential component of American law.

Selected Bibliography

Brandeis, L.D., assisted by Josephine Goldmark. *Women in Industry*. New York: National Consumers' League, 1908.

Cahill, M.C. *Shorter Hours: A Study of the Movement Since the Civil War*. New York: Columbia University Press, 1932.

Goldmark, J.C. *Impatient Crusader: Florence Kelley's Life Story*. Urbana: University of Illinois Press, 1953.

Johnson, J.W. *American Legal Culture, 1908–40*. Westport, CT: Greenwood Press, 1981.

Semonche, J.E. *Charting the Future: The Supreme Court Responds to a Changing Society, 1890–1920*. Westport, CT: Greenwood Press, 1978.

Strum, P. *Louis D. Brandeis: Justice for the People*. Cambridge, MA: Harvard University Press, 1984.

Urofsky, M.I. "Myth and Reality: The Supreme Court and Protective Legislation in the Progressive Era." *Yearbook of the Supreme Court Historical Society* (1983): 53–72.

A SUPREME COURT "FIRST": EQUAL PROTECTION APPLIED TO WOMEN

by Nancy S. Erickson
Legal Department
City of New York

Reed v. Reed, 404 U.S. 71 (1971) [U.S. Supreme Court]

Most cases are brought to the U.S. Supreme Court because litigants believe that they have not received a correct decision from a lower court and want the Court to amend that error. However, there is another category of cases—sometimes called "test" cases—that are handpicked and specially groomed by organizations litigating for broad changes in the law and its application to society. The famous school desegregation case, *Brown v. Board of Education* (1954), was one of these cases. It was the culmination of 20 years of litigation strategy by the Legal Defense Fund for the National Association for the Advancement of Colored People, which carefully chose each case it would take to the Court, and in what order, to achieve its goals. *Reed v. Reed* was the result of a similar but more modest effort.

In 1970, the American Civil Liberties Union (ACLU) set up a Women's Rights Project (WRP), headed by Ruth Bader Ginsburg, then a professor at Rutgers Law School, to devise and implement a litigation strategy to pursue equality for women under the equal protection clause of the Fourteenth Amendment. In 1970, that clause had never been used by the U.S. Supreme Court to overturn a sex discriminatory law, although state courts and lower federal courts had begun to use it in that way. In fact, the existing Supreme Court precedent had consistently upheld sex-based laws on the ground that such laws were valid unless the challenger could show they were not rationally related to valid governmental objectives (the so-called rational basis text). The Court had heretofore never viewed a sex-based law as irrational.

The rational basis test was applied by the Court in almost all equal protection cases. One of the few exceptions to this general rule involved cases in which race-based statutes were challenged as violative of the equal protection clause. To such cases, because race was considered a "suspect classification," the Court applied a more rigorous standard—"strict scrutiny." Strict scrutiny meant that the burden was on the government to demonstrate that the race-based law was necessary (not just rationally related) to the achievement of a compelling (not just valid, but extremely important) governmental purpose. Desegregation laws and virtually all other race-based laws had failed to pass this test.

The WRP set out to convince the Court that sex discrimination, like race discrimination, should be judged by the strict scrutiny test. This appeared to be the only way for women to achieve equality under the Constitution, because the outcome of a particular case in the past had always depended on the test applied: if the rational basis test was used, the law would be upheld; if the strict scrutiny test was applied, the law would be invalidated.

The WRP also knew, however, that to convince the Court that race discrimination and sex discrimination are analogous would not be easy. After the civil rights movement, courts were prepared to see race discrimination for the evil that it was, but the women's movement had not progressed to the point where society, and the courts, saw sex discrimination in the same light. Treating women differently from men was viewed as "natural" or "normal," not as harmful or evil to women (or to men). Women's biological differences from men were seen as valid reasons for the attribution of different sex roles to men and women, and these stereotyped roles were the underpinnings of sex-based laws.

For these reasons, the WRP knew that it would have to choose very carefully the cases it would bring to the Court, starting with the most simple, blatant examples of sex discrimination in the law. *Reed* fit that bill perfectly. The case arose after the death in 1967 of Richard Reed, who was survived only by his estranged parents. He left no will and less than $1,000 in property. His mother, Sally Reed, petitioned an Idaho court for appointment as administrator of her son's estate, but then Richard's father Cecil filed a similar petition. The court ordered that Cecil be appointed. The court's order was based not on a finding that Cecil was better qualified than Sally, but rather on a section of the Idaho Code providing that, of persons related in the same manner to the deceased, "males must be preferred to females. . . ." Sally appealed, and the appellate court held that section of the Idaho Code to be in violation of the

equal protection clause. But Cecil appealed further, to the Idaho Supreme Court, which reinstated the original order. Sally then appealed to the U.S. Supreme Court.

It was the perfect case for the WRP to use to initiate its litigation campaign because there appeared no reasonable explanation for the statutory distinction between males and females. During the litigation, only two rationales for the law had been identified, and neither could withstand scrutiny. First, an Idaho court had indicated that the preference for males served the purpose of efficiency, because if two persons of the opposite sex related in the same degree to the deceased both applied to be administrator of the estate, the court could avoid the time and trouble of a hearing to determine who was better qualified by simply preferring the male over the female. This rationale clearly made no sense, because the court could just as easily use any other arbitrary measure, such as preferring the older one or the taller one. The second rationale was enunciated by Cecil in his briefs to the Idaho courts. He argued that giving preference to males was reasonable because "men [are] as a rule more conversant with business affairs than . . . women," and "it is a matter of common knowledge, that women still are not engaged in politics, the professions, business or industry to the extent that men are." This rationale was based on cultural notions of male and female sex roles and did not allow an individual woman to demonstrate that she did not fit the pattern.

The brief presented to the Supreme Court by the WRP was almost 70 pages, plus a 20-page appendix of laws similar to the Idaho law. Of the 70 pages, fewer than ten were devoted to the argument that the law could not pass the rational basis test. Most of the brief developed the argument that sex, like race, should be a "suspect classification" under the law. It supported this argument by offering historical, sociological, and economic data that documented both the traditionally inferior legal status of women in the United States and the modern legal trend away from that position. The brief quoted at length from a recent decision of the California Supreme Court, which had explicitly designated sex as a suspect classification and, on that basis, had held a sex-based California statute unconstitutional. The California Supreme Court clearly and eloquently explained its decision to hold sex a suspect classification: "Sex, like race and lineage, is an immutable trait, a status into which the class members are locked by the accident of birth. What differentiates sex from non-suspect statuses, such as intelligence or physical disability, and aligns it with the recognized suspect classifications is that the characteristic frequently bears no relation to ability to perform or contribute to society.... The result is that the whole class is relegated to an inferior legal status without regard to the capabilities or characteristics of its individual members....

"Another characteristic which underlies all suspect classifications is the stigma of inferiority and second class citizenship associated with them.... Women, like Negroes, aliens, and the poor have historically labored under severe legal and social disabilities. Like black citizens, they were, for many years, denied the right to vote and, until recently, the right to serve on juries in many states. They are excluded from or discriminated against in employment and educational opportunities."

In contrast to the voluminous brief submitted by the WRP, the Court's unanimous opinion is surprisingly short. And its failure to mention the suspect classification argument is striking. The Court declined to hold that sex is a suspect classification entitled to strict scrutiny, but nonetheless it held the statute violative of the equal protection clause under the rational basis standard. Ignoring Cecil Reed's argument that men are generally more well versed in business affairs, the Court addressed only the "efficiency" argument. While conceding that it was a valid legislative purpose, the Court held that the method of achieving that purpose did not pass muster. "To give a mandatory preference to members of either sex . . .

merely to accomplish the elimination of hearings on the merits, is to make the very kind of arbitrary legislative choice forbidden by the Equal Protection Clause of the Fourteenth Amendment. . . ."

The Court's conclusion—that the statute did not survive the rational basis test—was unexpected. Although not an ideal outcome, it was viewed by the WRP as a step in the right direction. In fact, some commentators believed that the *Reed* Court had formulated a new test, one more rigorous than the old rational basis test, but less strict than the strict scrutiny test. The WRP hoped that the next time the Court was presented with a sex discrimination case it would take one step further and declare sex a suspect classification.

Just two years later, a plurality of the Court did precisely that in *Frontiero v. Richardson* (1973), but a majority of the Court has never done so. In fact, the Court seems to have settled on a middle level of scrutiny for sex-based classifications since its 1976 decision in *Craig v. Boren.* It appears that the dream of the WRP—that sex, like race, would be declared a suspect classification—may not be achieved. Nonetheless, the Court's decisions from *Reed* to the present have laid down a general rule requiring formal legal equality between women and men. The exceptions to that general rule are problematic, but the establishment of the general rule is an enormous achievement for American women and men.

Selected Bibliography

Cowan, R. "Women's Rights Through Litigation: An Examination of the American Civil Liberties Union Women's Rights Project, 1971–76." *Columbia Human Rights Law Review* 8 (1976): 373–412.

Gunther, G. "The Supreme Court 1971 Term, Foreword: In Search of Evolving Doctrine on a Changing Court: A Model for a Newer Equal Protection." *Harvard Law Review* 86 (1972): 1–48.

SEX DISCRIMINATION: REASONABLE OR SUSPECT?

by *Elizabeth E. Traxler*
Department of Humanities
Greenville Technical College

Frontiero v. Richardson, 411 U.S. 677 (1973) [U.S. Supreme Court]

As a resurgent women's movement arose in the 1960s and 1970s, it was inevitable that challenges to the government's treatment of women would arise in the courts as well as in the other two branches. One of the more significant court challenges to discrimination based on gender was initiated by Sharron Frontiero, a lieutenant in the U.S. Air Force.

Consider the temerity displayed by a mere lieutenant breaking ranks to take the Secretary of Defense to court. At issue was a federal statute providing for additional quarters allowance and medical and dental care for dependents of members of the armed forces. The lieutenant's claim of her husband as a dependent for medical and dental benefits had been denied. Though the law allowed all service*men* to claim their wives as dependents without offering evidence of that fact, service*women* were required to prove that their spouses were dependent on them for over one-half of their expenses. Since Joseph Frontiero, as a full-time college student, received $205 a month in veteran's benefits to put toward his $354 expenses, he did not meet the test. Lieutenant Frontiero sued in federal district court, arguing discrimination on the basis of sex.

Previous legal challenges to gender-specific state laws were generally based on the Fourteenth Amendment's prohibition of a state denying equal protection of the laws to its residents. Since the statute in question in *Frontiero* was federal, this avenue was not open. Instead Lieutenant Frontiero's attorneys based her challenge on the due process clause of the Fifth Amendment. Though there is no explicit guarantee of equal protection under the laws in this amendment, previous Court opinions had interpreted due process to include equal protection. Both concepts are tied to the notion of fairness in the government's treatment of indi-

viduals. This interpretation was so widely accepted that the Court felt no need to rule on its applicability. Instead, the dispute arose over which test should be used to evaluate the constitutionality of legislation providing for classification based on sex.

This was only the second case claiming gender discrimination to be decided by the U.S. Supreme Court, but there existed a substantial body of opinions relating to other types of discrimination—the best known being race. As the courts had been confronted with a variety of claims of discrimination, they had developed two tests for evaluation purposes. The "rational basis" test found the legislation constitutional as long as the differing treatment served a reasonable purpose. The burden of proof here was on the plaintiff to demonstrate that no such purpose existed. This burden shifted to the government when the "strict scrutiny," or "compelling interest," test was imposed. In this case, the government had to demonstrate that the distinction made on the basis of sex was necessary to fulfill a compelling interest of government.

As the Supreme Court's rulings in other equal protection cases had demonstrated, the choice of test almost invariably determined the outcome of the constitutional challenge. If the Court chose the rational basis test, the statute in question would be upheld. Some reason could almost always be found for the different treatment. On the other hand, a statute subjected to strict scrutiny almost never survived. Therefore, the focus of argument in discrimination cases centered on the test to be used. The Court, over time, had identified two categories for which the more demanding test would be used. Classifications based on an immutable characteristic bearing little or no relationship to an individual's abilities were labeled "suspect" and subjected to strict scrutiny. At the time of *Frontiero*, the U.S. Supreme Court had identified several such classifications, including race, alienage, and national origin, but not gender. The other use of this test arose when "fundamental rights" were in question. Since economic rights were not so designated, Lieutenant Frontiero's challenge did not raise this issue, but it asked that sex be labeled a "suspect" classification. If successful in this, the odds were high that the law would be held unconstitutional. Even more significantly, a host of other laws that distinguished between the sexes would fall prey to similar equal protection law suits.

The district court, however, in ruling against Frontiero, argued that the issue was not one that turned on classification by sex. The district court judge noted that other sections of the statute ascribed dependency without relation to gender (e.g., minor children) and that, therefore, the treatment varied with relationship to the serviceperson, not in regard to the dependent's sex. Despite this holding, the judge added the opinion that if sex were the determining factor, the differing requirements had a rational basis in providing for administrative efficiency and saving money, and thus would still be constitutional. His choice of a test was clearly the less demanding rational basis one.

On appeal to the U.S. Supreme Court, Lieutenant Frontiero was more successful. In an 8–1 opinion, the Court ruled in her favor. On the paramount question of whether sex would be included as a suspect classification, the Court was less forthcoming. Justice William J. Brennan, Jr., joined by Justices William

O. Douglas, Byron R. White, and Thurgood Marshall, held sex to be "suspect" and found no compelling interest served by the different treatments mandated in this statute. The other four justices in the majority stopped short of this position and suggested that the issue was before the states with the pending ratification of the Equal Rights Amendment. Legal commentators in the case's aftermath found evidence of a third test evolving for use in sex discrimination cases—one that would demand more than the assumption of a rational basis, but less than a compelling interest. This intermediate standard would require the government to show that the distinction made between the sexes was, in fact, closely related to achieving the underlying goals of the statute. Lieutenant Frontiero's willingness to confront her superiors and the system initiated a period of successful court challenges to many classifications based on gender, albeit fewer than would have been the case if the strict scrutiny standard had been applied.

Selected Bibliography

Dixon, J. Case Note: "Constitutional Law—Due Process—United States Supreme Court in Plurality Opinion Names Sex a Suspect Classification Requiring Compelling Interest Test." *Creighton Law Review* 7 (Fall 1973): 69–91.

Walters, S.V. "Constitutional Law—*Frontiero v. Richardson*." *Loyola University Law Journal* 5 (Winter 1974): 295–313.

Wiesenberger, L.D. Recent Case: "Constitutional Law—Equal Protection—Discrimination Based on Sex in the Provision of Armed Service Dependents' Benefits." *Case Western Reserve Law Review* 24 (Summer 1973): 824–45.

"BENIGN" FAVORS TO THE "WEAKER SEX" ARE NOT DISCRIMINATORY TOWARD MEN

by Nancy S. Erickson
Legal Department
City of New York

Kahn v. Shevin, 416 U.S. 351 (1974) [U.S. Supreme Court]

In 1885, Florida put a provision in its state constitution giving a property tax exemption to every "widow dependent on her own exertions, that has a family dependent upon her for support" and to every disabled veteran. This provision was typical of many other laws of the period that gave women special favors on the assumption that their sex disabled them from making their own way in the world. Instead of permitting women to gain the wherewithal to support themselves and their families, the law and other institutions of society barred them from higher education, certain professions, and the most remunerative work. "Compensatory legislation," such as the Florida law, saved women a few dollars but could not begin to compensate them for the discrimination practiced against them in virtually all areas of life.

Many widows with children were even needier than other women because they did not expect nor were they prepared to work outside the home. And without child care they found it impossible to accept work even if it was available. Other mothers, such as unwed mothers or married women whose husbands had deserted them, were just as needy as many widows.

By 1971, revisions in the late nineteenth-century Florida law had extended the tax exemption to every widow, including those without children, along with the blind and disabled. Mel Kahn, a widower residing in Florida, thought the exemption should also apply to men whose wives had died as well as to women whose husbands had died. Therefore, he applied for the exemption. It was denied on the ground that he was not a widow.

The tax exemption was worth only a few dollars to Kahn, but the principle was important to him, so he brought a class action lawsuit, arguing that the law violated the equal protection clause of the Fourteenth Amendment and the "basic rights" provision of the Florida Constitution. The state court noted that the Florida legislature had recently enacted a law extending to women the liability for alimony and child support and that the Florida Supreme Court had held unconstitutional a common-law restriction allowing only husbands to bring actions for injuries to their spouses. On the basis of that precedent and the recent U.S. Supreme Court case *Reed v. Reed* (1971), the court held the tax exemption invalid. Thus, Kahn established the principle for which he was arguing, but lost the actual tax exemption for himself as well as for the widows who had previously received it.

Florida appealed, and the Florida Supreme Court reversed, upholding the constitutionality of the statute. The court noted that classifications on the basis of sex had been upheld in several prior cases, including a 1961 U.S. Supreme Court case, and a 1968 federal court case. Quoting *Reed*'s requirement that a classification must "rest upon some ground of difference having a fair and substantial relation to the object of the legislation," the court found such a "ground of difference" in the state's assertion that the objective was "to reduce to a limited extent the tax burden on widows who own property . . . and . . . thereby to 'reduce the disparity between the economic . . . capabilities of a man and a woman'. . . ." The court concluded: "[W]omen workers as a class do not earn as much as men. . . .

"We recognize that steps have been and are continuing to be taken toward the elimination of legal barriers to equality of the sexes. Among the significant steps toward this end is the legislative provision for alimony and child support payments by women as well as men. This provision, however, provides a means of taking into consideration the factual economic capability of each woman involved through judicial supervision and control.

"Significantly, the provisions of the statute under review do not provide any means for similar consideration. Therefore, until the steps taken toward legal equality result in equality in fact, a finding of identity between the sexes at this time would rest on fiction and not fact."

Kahn's attorney was being assisted by the Florida Civil Liberties Union, which filed an appeal to the U.S. Supreme court. When the American Civil Liberties Union (ACLU) was informed of this, its Women's Rights Project (WRP) was quite concerned.

The WRP, headed by Ruth Bader Ginsburg (then a professor at Rutgers Law School and later a federal judge), had devised a strategy to develop case law on sex discrimination. It had begun its litigation campaign with *Reed* because the facts of the case were so simple and the discrimination so clear and straightforward. Although the Supreme Court in *Reed* had failed to hold that sex was a "suspect classification" like race, it had seemed to use a higher standard of scrutiny in that case than it had in prior sex discrimination cases.

The ACLU tried to advance its position in the next case the WRP brought to the Court, *Frontiero v. Richardson* (1973). In *Frontiero*, a servicewoman challenged the Air Force rule that a serviceman could automatically get dependents' benefits for his wife, while a servicewoman had to prove her husband's dependency before she could get such benefits. Again the ACLU urged that sex should be viewed as a suspect classification, and this time four members of the Court agreed: Justices William O. Douglas, William J. Brennan, Jr., Thurgood Marshall, and Byron R. White. The ACLU seemed to be getting closer to a victory.

The next step in the strategy was to bring another easy case with compelling facts where the law clearly discriminated against women and to urge again that the Court should hold sex a suspect classification. Kahn's case, however, did not fit into the strategy. He was complaining of discrimination against men, not discrimination against women, and the challenged law was one that seemed on the surface to benefit women, not to hurt them. The argument that the WRP would have to make in Kahn's case—that even

laws that benefit women may ultimately harm them because "benign" laws embody pernicious stereotypes about women and men—was subtle and tenuous. However, the ACLU had little choice but to ratify the action of its affiliate and try to do the best it could with a bad case.

The case was argued before the U.S. Supreme Court in February 1974. Justice Douglas delivered the opinion of the Court, affirming the decision of the Florida Supreme Court, which had upheld the statute. He expanded on that court's theory that the "disparity between the economic capabilities of a man and a woman" was the reason for the statute, citing Labor Department statistics that confirmed the low median earnings of women as compared with those of men. This disparity in earnings, the Court asserted, would likely be worse for a widow, because when a woman dies, her husband continues working, but when a man dies, his wife must suddenly go to work. The law, stated the Court, was "reasonably designed to further the state policy of cushioning the financial impact of spousal loss upon the sex for which that loss imposes a disproportionately heavy burden." Douglas appeared to assume that widows had been housewives during their marriages, dependent on breadwinning husbands for their support, and that widowers had been self-supporting, not dependent on their wives' incomes.

Justices Brennan and Marshall dissented, adhering to their opinion in *Frontiero* that sex should be considered a suspect classification and that sex-based distinctions could be justified only by a showing of a compelling state interest. They agreed with the majority that "in providing special benefits for a needy segment of society long the victim of purposeful discrimination and neglect, the statute serves the compelling state interest of achieving equality for such groups." However, they found the statute overly inclusive, since wealthy, as well as poor, widows could benefit.

Justice White also dissented, finding that the tax exemption to widows served no purpose "other than to alleviate current economic necessity, but the State extends the exemption to widows who do not need the help and denies it to widowers who do." White pointed out that if the purpose of the law was to alleviate past discrimination against women, the law should have applied to all women, not just widows. Additionally, if the purpose was to alleviate past discrimination, the law should have applied to men who had been discriminated against on racial grounds.

One interpretation of the *Kahn* holding is that the Court saw a paternalistic statute as somewhat akin to an "affirmative action" statute. It is especially surprising that Douglas accepted this argument, because in *Frontiero* he appeared to recognize that unlike race discrimination, sex discrimination has been characterized more by paternalism than by cruelty. The racist says: Blacks are different (inferior), should work only at menial jobs, and should not mingle with whites. The sexist says: Women are different (inferior in some ways and superior in others) and should not work at all because if they go out into the hectic, dirty, rough, immoral world of men's activities they will be physically and morally endangered; their place is at home with the children. "Protective" labor laws—limiting women's hours of labor, prohibiting women from lifting more than a certain number of pounds, and excluding women from certain jobs—grew out of just such paternalism. This fact was recognized by the Equal Employment Opportunity Commission and the courts when such laws collided with Title VII of the Civil Rights Act of 1964, which prohibits race and sex discrimination in employment. The "good intentions" behind the statutes and the fact that they appeared to benefit women did not save them from invalidation.

The *Kahn* Court did not recognize the paternalistic assumptions behind the "*Kahn* statute," although these had been carefully presented in the appellant's briefs. Moreover, a look at the history of the Florida statute would have revealed that the statute's original purpose was not an ameliorative one in the sense of being designed to "rectify the effects of past discrimination" against women in the job market. When it was originally enacted in 1885, women did not even have the vote, and they were certainly not expected to work outside the home; what is now called employment discrimination against women was then considered valid, because the generally accepted view was that women should not be in the job market.

Now that society, including the legal system, has had more experience with the theory and practice of affirmative action, it is not difficult, in most instances, to distinguish affirmative action laws from paternalistic statutes. Affirmative action attacks the sources of discrimination rather than its effects. As one commentator has stated, "The widow's exemption statute in *Kahn* attempts to alleviate the symptom, income disparity, rather than its source, unequal employment opportunity." Yet the Court apparently had difficulty distinguishing the two concepts. Ginsburg has suggested that because *Kahn* was argued immediately before *DeFunis v. Odegaard* (1974), a true affirmative action case involving a law school's admissions policies, the two issues might have been confused.

Examined individually, paternalistic statutes may appear relatively innocuous. That is why courts and legislators must always bear in mind that each statute is part of a broad pattern of laws and practices that are premised on different societal roles for men and women. The whole cannot be destroyed without destroying each small part. Thus, the judicial validation of a statute such as that challenged in *Kahn* is harmful to all women in a very deep sense, and this harm to all women cannot be neutralized by the resultant financial benefit to a few.

Although *Kahn* was decided over 17 years ago, it has never been overruled. In fact, it was followed in 1975 by two Supreme Court cases: in *Schlesinger v. Ballard*, the Court upheld different promotion procedures for women and men naval officers; in *Califano v. Webster*, the Court upheld a provision in the social security law that treated women better than men. As the Court had done in *Kahn*, it treated these laws as though they were affirmative action statutes, although their histories did not support such a conclusion. The practical effects of the *Webster* decision were limited because Congress had already made the statute sex-neutral for future retirees, but the principle was preserved and can be used later as a precedent. The one advantage to this is that if a true affirmative action statute of real benefit to women were to be challenged, this precedent could be used to uphold it. On the other hand, until the Court clearly distinguishes between paternalism and affirmative action, statutes based on sex-stereotyped notions will also be upheld.

Selected Bibliography

Cole, D. "Strategies of Difference: Litigating for Women's Rights in a Man's World." *Law & Inequality* 2 (1984): 33–96.

Cowan, R. "Women's Rights Through Litigation: An Examination of the American Civil Liberties Union Women's Rights Project, 1971–76." *Columbia Human Rights Law Review* 8 (1976): 373–412.

Erickson, N.S. "*Kahn, Ballard*, and *Wiesenfeld*: A New Equal Protection Test in "Reverse" Sex Discrimination Cases?" *Brooklyn Law Review* 42 (1975): 1–54.

———. "Equality Between the Sexes in the 1980's." *Cleveland State Law Review* 28 (1979): 591–610.

Ginsburg, R.B. "Gender and the Constitution." *University of Cincinnati Law Review* 44 (1975): 1–42.

LAW UPHELD GUARANTEEING RIGHT TO RETURN TO WORK AFTER CHILDBIRTH LEAVE OF ABSENCE

by Nancy S. Erickson
Legal Department
City of New York

California Federal Savings and Loan Association v. Guerra, 479 U.S. 272 (1987) [U.S. Supreme Court]

Sex discrimination is a major problem in the United States. One type of sex discrimination—pregnancy discrimination—has proved to be especially difficult to eradicate. *California Federal* illustrates some of the complexities of the legal issues involved in pregnancy discrimination cases.

Lillian Garland, a receptionist at California Federal Savings and Loan (Cal-Fed) in Los Angeles, took a leave of absence in January 1982 to give birth. The child was delivered by Caesarean section. When her doctor certified that she was able to return to work in April, she requested reinstatement to her old job, but Cal-Fed informed her that her job had been filled and that there were no positions available for her.

A black, single mother, Garland was unable to pay her rent without an income, so she was evicted from her apartment. Then, with no home or resources to care for her child, she lost custody to the child's father. To further complicate matters, her subsequent job-hunting attempts were unsuccessful.

Finally, she contacted the California Department of Fair Employment and Housing. She was informed that part of the California Fair Employment and Housing Act required an employer to reinstate an employee returning from pregnancy leave of four months or less to the job she previously held, unless the job was no longer available, in which case the employer was obligated to make a good-faith effort to place the employee in a substantially similar job. The California reinstatement law had been enacted in 1978 as part of a larger statutory scheme designed to remedy pregnancy discrimination in employment, which was not, at that time, prohibited by Title VII of the Civil Rights Act of 1964. Title VII prohibited sex discrimination in employment, but in 1976 the U.S. Supreme Court ruled that an employer's disability insurance plan's failure to cover pregnancy-related disabilities did not violate Title VII. The Court relied on a 1975 case that upheld a similar plan against a Fourteenth Amendment attack. In that case, the Court had reasoned that discrimination against pregnant women is not sex discrimination. Not wanting to leave the women in its workforce unprotected against pregnancy discrimination, the California legislature enacted a pregnancy discrimination law, which included the reinstatement law. Later in 1978, Congress passed an amendment to Title VII, the Pregnancy Discrimination Act (PDA), thereby superseding much of the California statute, but the reinstatement provision remained.

Because Cal-Fed had failed to comply with the reinstatement law, the agency brought an action against the bank on Garland's behalf. Cal-Fed decided to turn its defensive posture into an offensive one by going into federal court (along with another large employer and the California Chamber of Commerce) to challenge the California law. Cal-Fed claimed that the California reinstatement statute conflicted with the PDA because the federal act required employers to treat men and women the same—not to give women preferential treatment. The bank argued that if two employees took leaves of absence—one a man to recover from a heart attack and the other a woman to recover from childbirth—the employer would be required to reinstate the woman but not the man. This would be discrimination against men and would violate Title VII's prohibition on sex discrimination. Thus, the California law must be held preempted by Title VII.

The federal district court agreed with Cal-Fed. However, in 1985 the court of appeals overturned that decision, reasoning that the PDA does not "demand that state law be blind to pregnancy's existence." In enacting the PDA, the court of appeals held, Congress intended "to construct a floor beneath which pregnancy disability benefits may not drop—not a ceiling above which they may not rise."

Cal-Fed appealed the case to the U.S. Supreme Court, which was presented with an unusual array of arguments. Cal-Fed argued that the California law was preempted by the federal law, and that the state law should therefore by nullified. The American Civil Liberties Union and some feminist lawyers and groups—including the National Organization for Women, the National Women's Law Center, and the Women's Legal Defense Fund—agreed with Cal-Fed that the state law was invalid the way it was written because Title VII prohibits preferential treatment based on sex or pregnancy and supersedes any inconsistent or conflicting state legislation. They based their arguments on what has become known as the "equal treatment" approach; that is, the most

effective way to prevent unfair treatment of pregnant workers is to treat them like others subject to temporary incapacities, not to segregate them for special treatment. Even well-intentioned protectionist legislation, they reasoned, pointing to nineteenth- and early twentieth-century "protective" labor legislation, has not served women's interests in equality. However, unlike Cal-Fed, these *amici curiae* ("friends of the court") argued that the Court should extend the state law to all disabled employees rather than take away the benefits from pregnant employees.

Other feminist groups—such as 9 to 5 (a national association of working women)—and several trade unions supported the California law, even though it applied only to women. Their "special treatment," or "treatment as equals," approach is that although both women and men suffer from most medical conditions, pregnancy and childbirth are additional medical conditions, suffered only by women, which harm women's job opportunities while they do not harm men's. Thus, special laws protecting job opportunities for pregnant women are as justifiable as, for example, laws requiring ramps for the use of individuals who need wheelchairs. As Marian Johnston, deputy attorney general of California, stated to the Court during oral argument in the *California Federal* case, "It's really irrelevant to male employees whether the employer provides pregnancy benefits. The male employee is going to keep his job when he has children."

Six members of the Supreme Court, in an opinion written by Justice Thurgood Marshall, held that the California reinstatement law was not preempted by federal law because it does not require or permit employers to violate Title VII, as amended by the PDA, and it is not inconsistent with the purposes of the federal statute. The PDA, they reasoned, was intended to "provide relief for working women and to end discrimination against pregnant workers. In contrast to the thorough account of discrimination against pregnant workers, the legislative history is devoid of any discussion of preferential treatment of pregnancy, beyond acknowledgments of the existence of state statutes providing for such preferential treatment." Thus, the Supreme Court agreed with the court of appeals that Congress intended the PDA to be "a floor . . . not a ceiling," and that the state law was not preempted by the PDA.

As a result of *California Federal*, women in California and the two other states with similar laws, Connecticut and Montana, have some limited protection against job loss attributable to pregnancy. However, such "special" laws for women may lead to backlash that could harm women workers. For example, male employees may become resentful of the benefits that pregnant women receive, and employers may be disinclined to hire women if they know they must provide pregnant women with reinstatement benefits.

The federal Family and Medical Leave Act of 1990, now pending in Congress, could have avoided these problems. Modeled on an equal treatment approach, the proposed act would have supplemented the PDA by giving limited reinstatement rights to employees who had to take disability leave of absence (up to 26 weeks), including women disabled by pregnancy and childbirth. The act would also have gone beyond disability leaves in granting a qualified right to an employee to be reinstated after a leave of absence (up to 18 weeks) for the purpose of caring for a newborn, adopted, or sick child or a seriously ill parent. Although the act passed Congress, it was vetoed by President George Bush in July 1990.

As an epilogue to *California Federal*: Garland was rehired by Cal-Fed, but only after she had been unemployed for seven months. "I don't want this to happen to another women," Garland said. "What are we supposed to do, have babies, stay home and go on welfare? That's not me."

Selected Bibliography

Krieger, L., and P. Cooney. "The Miller-Wohl Controversy: Equal Treatment, Positive Action and the Meaning of Women's Equality." *Golden Gate Law Review* 13 (1983): 513–72.

Rust, M. "Maternity Leave Caught in the Crossfire." *American Bar Association Journal* 72 (Aug. 1986): 52–55.

Williams, W. "Equality's Riddle: Pregnancy and the Equal Treatment/Special Treatment Debate." *New York University Review of Law and Social Change* 13 (1984–85): 325–80.

PART V: CIVIL LIBERTIES

PART V: CIVIL LIBERTIES

INTRODUCTION

One distinctive feature of the American legal system is the protection of the freedoms of individuals against encroachment by government. Individual freedoms—what are generally termed "civil liberties"—can be protected by government: after all, the very purpose of the criminal law is to safeguard the person and property of law-abiding individuals. But it is often the government—in its zeal for the enforcement of criminal laws and/or social policy—that may violate the freedoms of individuals. To guard against governmental infringement of the rights of individuals, such notable late eighteenth-century Americans as Thomas Jefferson, James Madison, and George Mason insisted on the passage of a "Bill of Rights" as a *quid pro quo* for the ratification of the U.S. Constitution.

For many years the Bill of Rights—the first ten amendments to the U.S. Constitution—lay dormant, seldom serving as the basis for challenges to governmental practices. That would change with World War I, which sparked a series of legal questions that brought the Bill of Rights out of forgotten appendices to textbooks and into the fabric of American life. The essays in Part V analyze some of the most important federal and state civil liberties decisions.

A. Freedom of Speech

The first essay in this section, "State Wrongs and the Bill of Rights," addresses the question of whether the Bill of Rights protects individuals against threats to civil liberties mounted by state governments as well as the national government. In the 1833 case examined, the U.S. Supreme Court held that the Bill of Rights did not apply to the states. For almost 100 years, this interpretation stood. It would be freedom of speech cases in the 1920s that would cause the Supreme Court to reconsider this nineteenth decision.

The first significant spate of freedom of expression cases reached the U.S. Supreme Court in the final stages of World War I. As discussed in "Defining Free Speech Protection in the World War I Era," the first efforts to challenge state and federal legislation restricting freedom of expression were upheld by the U.S. Supreme Court. The essay points out, however, that Justice Oliver Wendell Holmes enunciated his "clear and present danger test" in the World War I cases. This standard would be used, revised, and twisted in many directions over the years. "Agrarian Reforms and the Politics of Loyalty" provides an example of the Supreme Court siding with the government and not the individual in an early freedom of speech case.

With a case from New York discussed in "Expanding Free Speech to the States," the High Court noted that there exist "fundamental personal rights protected by the due process clause of the Fourteenth Amendment from impairment by the states." The rights the Court chose to identify were freedom of speech and of the press. Although the Supreme Court found in favor of the government in the case profiled, this was the beginning of what experts have called the selective "incorporation" of the Bill of Rights guarantees over and against state infringements. Thus, the 1833 opinion discussed in the first essay in this section was finally undercut.

Throughout the 1920s and 1930s, the Court generally found ways to uphold legislation restricting the speech of those on the left of the political spectrum. However, as discussed in "Silencing Critics: Guilty by Association in the 1920s" and "The California Red Flag Law and Freedom of Speech," strong dissenting voices from Justices Louis D. Brandeis and Oliver Wendell Holmes Jr., began to be raised in support of civil liberties.

Perhaps the case most clearly isolating polar positions on freedom of expression was *Dennis v. United States* (1951), a celebrated judicial action that concerned whether members of the American Communist party could be punished under federal legislation for advocating the doctrine of violent revolution. This case is examined in "Cold War, Communism, and Free Speech." Other cases involving free speech and membership in the Communist party can be found in Part VI.

This section is rounded out with an essay on the constitutionality of a "group libel" statute, "'Breach of Peace' and Group Libel," and an essay on the recent dispute over the constitutionality of legislation prohibiting flag burning, "Flag-Burning and the Constitution." Another essay on symbolic speech, "The Right of Children to Be Seen as Well as Heard," is included in Part VI as an example of a case that raises some of the controversial issues of the 1960s.

B. Freedom of the Press

The first essay in this section, "Myth and Reality: the Case of John Peter Zenger," deals with the well-known but often misunderstood libel trial of the colonial printer, John Peter Zenger. The next essay, "The Sedition Act and the Price of a Free Press," examines a freedom of the press case from the early national period involving a scurrilous journalist who blackened the reputation of several famous Americans.

In the landmark case *Near v. Minnesota* (1931), the Supreme Court held that freedom of the press was one of the "fundamental freedoms" that needed protection against state as well as national infringement; it is discussed in "The Limits of Prior Restraint."

The remaining five essays in this section probe Supreme Court decisions rendered since the mid-1960s involving "public figures": "Public Officials, Libel, and a Free Press" deals with the suit of a southern police officer who felt that his rights were violated by a civil rights news story; "Public Personalities and the Right to Privacy" and "Public Disclosure of Private Facts" concern stories that exacerbated the trauma of "unwilling" public figures; and "Did CBS Libel General Westmoreland?" and "The 'Preacher' and the 'Smut Merchant'" discuss

recent cases involving, respectively, a famous general and a controversial evangelist.

C. Freedom of Religion

Besides protecting speech and the press, the First Amendment to the U.S. Constitution also stipulates that "Congress shall make no law respecting an establishment of religion, or prohibiting the free exercise thereof." The "establishment" and "free exercise" clauses figure in some of the most interesting and controversial court decisions of the twentieth century.

The first essay in this section, "The Scopes Trial: A Collision of Cultures," delves into the famous 1925 evolution trial in Dayton, Tennessee. The second essay, "The Flag Salute Cases," considers whether the law can compel children to salute the flag even if such behavior violates personal religious beliefs; the Supreme Court struggled with this question during World War II and ended up reversing itself.

In "Religion in the Public School Day: The Released Time Cases," the issue of whether students can be released from public school classes to participate in religious instruction is examined. In "To Pray or Not to Pray: The Supreme Court Says No to Prayer in the Public Schools," the Supreme Court's still controversial decision to ban organized prayer in public schools is discussed. Whether a state's compulsory school attendance law violates the free exercise of religion of the Amish is considered in "Expanded Exercise: The Amish, Compulsory Education, and Religious Freedom." And whether a state-mandated "moment of silence" during the school day is an establishment of religion is discussed in "The Pieties of Silence."

D. Obscenity and Pornography

The final First Amendment issue addressed in Part V regards expression that may violate standards of good taste. American jurists have generally agreed that speech or expression that is "obscene" or "pornographic" is not deserving of First Amendment protection. But how should these concepts be defined? Courts have been groping, with little success, for such definitions for over a century. Justice Potter Stewart may have put it best in a mid-1960s decision when he lamented that he could not define obscenity but "I know it when I see it." The essay containing Stewart's famous pronouncement in the title, "Obscenity: 'I Know It When I See It!'" treats the Supreme Court's first modern attempt to set a standard for obscenity in *Roth v. United States* (1957). "A Book Named *Fanny Hill*" examines an extension of the *Roth* standard in a mid-1960s case. And "The Triumph of 'Community Standards'" delves into major modifications in standards for determining obscenity propounded by the Supreme Court under the leadership of Chief Justice Warren Burger in a set of 1973 cases.

E. Right to Counsel
The Sixth Amendment to the Constitution guarantees the right to an attorney in trials in federal court. It was not, however, until the 1963 case discussed in "'Incorporation' and the Right to Counsel" that this right was extended to individuals accused of serious crimes before state tribunals. The other essay included in this section, "Lawyer? You Want a Lawyer?" deals with when a lawyer should be provided to a person accused of a crime. An essay on the most famous right to counsel case of the modern era, "You Have the Right to Remain Silent," can be found in Part I.

F. Search and Seizure
The Fourth Amendment protects Americans against "unreasonable searches and seizures." But what is meant by "unreasonable"? "The Fruits of the Poisonous Tree" discusses the Supreme Court's 1914 decision that held that illegally seized evidence could not be used in a federal court against one accused of a crime. This was the birth of the so-called exclusionary rule. The second essay in this section, "Are Bootleggers Entitled to Privacy?" considers whether evidence obtained by wiretapping is admissible in federal court. The final essay, "The Exclusionary Rule Binds the States," as the title suggests, discusses the extension of the exclusionary rule to the states.

G. Privacy
The U.S. Constitution and its amendments do not contain the term "privacy." Yet Americans believe quite strongly in the principle of privacy. As early as 1890, Louis D. Brandeis and a collaborator wrote a famous law review essay defending the existence of a legal right to privacy. Constitutionally, the right to privacy was born in a 1965 decision, *Griswold v. Connecticut* in which Justice William O. Douglas, speaking for the Court, determined that a right of privacy grew out of the "penumbras" of the First, Third, Fourth, Fifth, and Ninth Amendments. Douglas's opinion has been described as "brilliantly creative" by some legal experts but "unduly sloppy" by others.

The leading right to privacy decision and, perhaps, the most controversial Supreme Court decision of the last quarter century is *Roe v. Wade* (1973). This decision upheld, subject to certain state restrictions, a woman's legal right to abortion. The *Roe* decision and a 1989 abortion decision seriously qualifying it are discussed in "Abortion: Who Shall Decide?" Also in this section is an essay, "When Consenting Adults Can't: Privacy, the Law, and Homosexual Conduct," on the constellation of privacy issues raised by homosexuality.

H. The Family
Not directly controlled by the Bill of Rights, but still related to individual freedoms, are issues concerning the family. They include marriage, divorce, sexuality, parenthood, and child custody. Essays dealing with a sample of such cases over the last two centuries are included in this final section of Part V.

"The Custody of Children" presents a brief discussion of an early nineteenth-century child custody case. "Religion, Cultural Pluralism, and the Constitution: Mormonism and Polygamy" examines what happens when a religious practice involving family life—the nineteenth-century Mormon custom of polygamy—violates secular public policy. "The Validity of Divorce During the Nineteenth Century" and "The Principle of Full Faith and Credit in Divorce Actions" discuss some of the complex legal issues raised in a series of nineteenth- and twentieth-century state divorce cases. The legality of state legislation forbidding marriage between members of different races is discussed in "A Case of Black and White: Removing Restrictions Against Interracial Marriages." And the recent legal controversy surrounding surrogate motherhood is examined in "Surrogacy Motherhood: Womb for Rent."

STATE WRONGS AND THE BILL OF RIGHTS

by Maxwell Bloomfield
Columbus School of Law
Catholic University of America

Barron v. Baltimore, 7 Peters 243 (1833) [U.S. Supreme Court]

Baltimore, Maryland, was a rapidly growing city in the early nineteenth century, with a severe shortage of municipal and public health services. To help meet these pressing needs, the city government launched an impressive public works program aimed in part at eliminating the health hazards associated with the old section of the harbor known as the Basin. As one contemporary reported, the slips between the docks in that area "often filled with stagnated water and every species of filth, which have not only been destructive to health but highly inconvenient in that part of the town to free mercantile intercourse." Between 1815 and 1821, the city council passed a series of ordinances that directed the extensive regrading and paving of streets near the Basin. In the process, embankments were built and neighboring streams diverted toward the harbor, causing soil and other debris to accumulate around the docks.

John Barron and John Craig owned one of the largest and most profitable wharves in the Basin. As the street construction progressed, they found that the surrounding water grew steadily shallower until no sizable vessel could use their facility. In 1822, Barron sued the city for compensatory damages, and thereby profoundly influenced the future of American civil rights.

Barron's lawyers argued that the city's acts had violated his property rights under state law. Alternatively, they contended that Barron, as a U.S. citizen, could claim protection under the Fifth Amendment to the U.S. Constitution, which prohibited the taking of private property for public use "without just compensation."

The attorneys for Baltimore denied all liability. Maryland law, they asserted, did not require payment to property owners who suffered incidental damage as a result of needed public improvements; and the federal Bill of Rights did not apply to the states.

Barron won his case in the Baltimore County Court, which awarded him $4,500 in damages. On appeal, however, the Maryland Court of Appeals ruled against him on all points; and from this decision of the state's highest tribunal Barron's lawyers carried the case to the U.S. Supreme Court on a writ of error.

For reasons that are not disclosed in the record, the Marshall Court did not hear the case until 1833, more than a decade after it began its progress through the state courts. By that time, federal-state relations had reached a crisis. During 1832, a defiant South Carolina had purported to "nullify" a congressional tariff law; while Georgia in *Worcester v. Georgia* had refused to enforce a Court decision affecting Indian rights. Although both controversies appeared to be heading toward a peaceful resolution, the justices must have been mindful of their potential consequences as they considered Barron's claims.

For a unanimous Court, Chief Justice John Marshall dismissed *Barron* for lack of jurisdiction. The compensation clause of the Fifth Amendment did not apply to the states, he ruled, and the case thus presented no federal question that the Court was empowered to decide.

In reaching this conclusion, Marshall relied in part on constitutional construction. He pointed particularly to the contrasting language used in Sections 9 and 10 of Article I. Section 9, whose restrictions clearly apply only to the federal government, sometimes just to "Congress." More often, however, the framers couched their provisions in general language, of the sort found in many of the later amendments. Section 10, which limits state power, contains no such general terminology. Instead, each paragraph begins with a specific reference to state action ("No State shall . . ."). The argument from analogy, while reasonable, was scarcely conclusive, since Marshall presented no evidence that those who framed the amendments intended to emulate the style of the main text.

More compelling was his appeal to history. The opponents of the new Constitution had pressed for amendments at the state ratifying conventions, he noted, out of fear of federal power: "These amendments demanded security against the apprehended encroachments of the general government—not against those of the local governments." Congress and the states later responded to these same pressures by adopting the first ten amendments. "These amendments contain no expression indicating an intention to apply them to the state governments," Marshall concluded. "This court cannot so apply them."

Barron was Marshall's last constitutional opinion, written when he was in failing health and despondent over the future of the Union. But it did not signal the Court's capitulation to the states' rights extremism of the time. Marshall's history, unfortunately, was quite accurate. The records of the ratifying conventions support his position, as do prior state-court decisions. Later courts extended the *Barron* holding by inevitable analogy to the rest of the Bill of Rights, and thus continued to prevent the federal government from interfering with state violations of civil rights.

Since the 1920s, however, successive Supreme Courts have found an indirect way of expanding federal power in this area through resort to the due process clause of the Fourteenth Amendment ("nor shall any State deprive any person of life, liberty, or property, without due process of law"). By defining specific guarantees of the Bill of Rights as fundamental rights implicit in the concept of due process, judges have gradually brought almost all of these guarantees under federal control. But the process of "selective incorporation" has been slow, erratic, controversial, and confusing. Had *Barron* been decided differently, these cumbersome maneuvers would have been unnecessary. But the Marshall Court could not have reached any other result without ignoring the founders' firm conviction that the basic rights of the individual could be more safely entrusted to local officials than to the agents of a distant, and potentially oppressive, central government.

Selected Bibliography

Currie, D.P. *The Constitution in the Supreme Court: The First Hundred Years, 1789–1888.* Chicago: University of Chicago Press, 1985.

White, G.E. *History of the Supreme Court of the United States. Vols. III–IV: The Marshall Court and Cultural Change, 1815–35.* New York: Macmillan Publishing Co., 1988.

DEFINING FREE SPEECH PROTECTION IN THE WORLD WAR I ERA

by *Carol E. Jenson*
Department of History
University of Wisconsin at La Crosse

Schenck v. United States, 249 U.S. 47 (1919); *Abrams v. United States*, 250 U.S. 616 (1919) [U.S. Supreme Court]

For over 125 years following the adoption of the Bill of Rights in 1791, the U.S. Supreme Court considered no First Amendment free speech cases based on federal law. Then, the advent of U.S. involvement in World War I and the passage of the Espionage Act of 1917 and its Sedition Act of 1918 supplement led to High Court interpretation of the extent to which political speech might be protected in times of war. In initiating development of that interpretation, Justice Oliver Wendell Holmes, Jr., introduced his "clear and present danger" doctrine in March 1919, in the unanimous opinion in *Schenck v. United States* and clarified it further in November 1919 when Justice Louis D. Brandeis joined him in the dissent in *Abrams v. United States.*

In June 1917, two months after the United States entered the war against Germany, Congress passed the Espionage Act. The act established three basic wartime offenses: (1) conveying false information intended to interfere with U.S. military operations, (2) causing insubordination in the military, and (3) obstructing recruiting. The statute also made it a criminal offense to use the U.S. mails for any of these purposes.

The Espionage Act did not satisfy some advocates of increased wartime zeal who concluded that the statute did little to restrict what they saw as disloyal speech and activity. Accordingly, the Senate Judiciary Committee responded to Attorney General Thomas Gregory's modest request for amending the wording of the 1917 act by including sweeping statements that added nine additional offenses to the original list of three.

After Congress passed the Sedition Act in May 1918, no one was to say or to write anything that might in any way intend to bring contempt or disrepute upon the U.S. government, flag, uniform, or Constitution or intend to promote resistance to U.S. policies in any way. These two pieces of legislation, the second an amendment and supplement to the first, were the statutes involved in the two most prominent free speech cases of the World War I period—*Schenck* and *Abrams.*

On August 13, 1917, two months after the passage of the Espionage Act, Charles Schenck and other members of the executive committee of the Socialist Party, meeting in Philadelphia, voted to print 15,000 copies of a pamphlet to be mailed to men who had passed the first phase of the conscription program. Within a few days, Schenck directed the printing of the pamphlets and purchased stamped envelopes for the mailing.

The pamphlet challenged the draft on grounds that it violated the U.S. Constitution's supremacy clause as well as the rights protected under the First and Ninth Amendments. The Socialists reasoned that officials who administered conscription contradicted the concept of the Constitution as the supreme law of the land, as well as the philosophy of individual rights, because "they refuse to recognize your right to assert your opposition to the draft." The pamphlet also argued that the draft interfered with freedom of religion, since it forced individuals to disregard the Old Testament commandment, "Thou shalt not kill." The law exempted only clergy and Quakers on religious grounds; others were subject to the conscription law and therefore suffered discrimination.

Socialists argued that it was a citizen's duty to assert individual rights and to seek the election of officials opposed to the draft policy. The pamphlet used the classic anticonscription argument made by some politicians during debate over passage of the 1917 draft law. The discussion pointed out that many immigrants settled in the United States because of opposition to European militarism and that President Woodrow Wilson had won reelection in 1916 on a theme of keeping the United States out of the European conflict.

The pamphlet advocated resistance to what it termed the "moloch of militarism" which, according to Socialist contentions, was leading U.S. policy to undermine the Constitution and presenting "jingoism masquerading under the guise of patriotism." The argument maintained that democracy could not be the result of war but only of education, thereby challenging President Wilson's theme of a "War to Make the World Safe for Democracy." Furthermore, the pamphlet challenged the draft as a violation of the Thirteenth Amendment ban on involuntary servitude.

The Socialist party pamphlet denounced what it termed the tactics of governmental intimidation and appealed for an adherence to constitutional principles of free speech, assembly, and petition, rather than a submission to the intimidating tactics of war zealots. Nowhere did the pamphlet mention overthrowing the government. Rather, it supported the Constitution and advocated a more intensive forum for discussion of issues using First Amendment rights of free speech and peaceful assembly and urging people to come to the headquarters to sign an anticonscription petition to be sent to Congress. The pamphlet pleaded: "Help us reestablish democracy in America. Remember, eternal vigilance is the price of liberty." These Socialists saw the U.S. Constitution as the principal protector of the rights they were attempting to exercise.

Several persons who received the pamphlet in the mail complained to Philadelphia postal inspectors, who contacted the U.S. attorney's office. The investigation led to a search of the Socialist party headquarters on August 28. Agents seized as evidence a file of newspaper clippings with lists of names of draft inductees, a pile of circulars, and the minutes book of the party's executive committee. The federal authorities questioned several men and arrested Schenck, the party's general secretary and the person in charge of the office. Later, police arrested four other members of the executive committee for violation of the Espionage Act.

After a September arraignment at which Schenck pleaded not guilty, the trial began on December 17, 1917, before Judge J. Whitaker Thompson in the U.S. District Court for the Eastern District of Pennsylvania. The government contended that Schenck and others had used the post office to send materials considered nonmailable under the Espionage Act. The prosecution presented testimony from postal inspectors and some young men who had received the pamphlet. In cross-examination by defense attorney Henry John Nelson, several of the young men testified that the pamphlet had not made them feel insubordinate to the United States. Several of them had not even read it. Others indicated they had not received letters addressed to them, which raised the possibility of post office intervention.

Attorney Nelson also raised objections that led to repeated discussion regarding the introduction of the minutes book as evidence. He contended that presentation of this material violated the constitutional protection of his clients' rights against self-incrimination. After some deliberation, Judge Thompson overruled the objection. Later, the court held that the prosecution could not introduce the minutes books because they constituted hearsay evidence, inadmissible in federal criminal conspiracy trials.

When Thompson made his charge to the jury, he asked for a directed verdict of not guilty for three defendants but pursued the charges against Schenck and Elizabeth Baer for conspiracy and willful use of the mails to commit an offense against the United States. The jury was not to determine the constitutionality of the law but to decide if the pamphlet "advocate[s] forcible resistance," which would make it nonmailable. The judge pointed out that committing a conspiracy required an agreement to do something, but conspiracy was not determined by whether the objective was successful. The jury agreed that advocacy had occurred and convicted Schenck and Baer on December 20. The court sentenced Schenck to six months and Baer to 90 days' imprisonment.

After the court denied a motion for a new trial in March 1918, attorneys for Schenck and Baer requested an assignment of errors to the U.S. Supreme Court. The subsequent brief, filed in December 1918 (just after Armistice Day), questioned the constitutionality of the Espionage Act in relation to First Amendment protection of freedom of speech and petition. Attorneys Nelson and Henry Gibbons saw the act as an infringement on necessary political discourse. "How can the citizens find out whether a war is just or unjust unless there is free and full discussion?" According to their analysis, the most critical statement in the Socialist pamphlet contended that a "conscript is little more than a convict," a statement attributed to Missouri Congressman Champ Clark in a speech on the floor of the House of Representatives. Such a statement hardly advocated interference with war aims.

Referring to the 1,200 cases that had arisen under the Espionage Act, they contended that the law was out of step with English and American legal developments. In this tradition, a distinction had been drawn between speech that involved sincere and honest communication of opinion and speech that involved incitement of a "forbidden action." In their view, the Espionage Act destroyed this distinction and made honest discussion an indictable offense. Therefore, the statute violated the First Amendment.

Gibbons and Nelson challenged the trial procedures, questioning the conspiracy evidence and the seizure of the papers from the Socialist headquarters. They argued that the acts had been committed before the Supreme Court held the draft law to be constitutional and that the evidence introduced was insufficient to support conviction. Furthermore, they said the government presented no evidence that Schenck and Baer had mailed the pamphlet, that the granting of the search warrant had not been based on probable cause, and that the seizure of private papers violated Fifth Amendment protection against self-incrimination because private written words were introduced as evidence. They concluded that the case involved a political issue in which the law attempted to restrict a small group of citizens "steadfastly standing for what they honestly, conscientiously believe."

John Lord O'Brian, special assistant to the attorney general for war work, and Alfred Bettman, special assistant to the attorney general, prepared the government's response. In their earlier careers, both men had subscribed to the concept of freedom of discussion and were knowledgeable about the content of left-wing literature. However, under the pressure of wartime circumstances, they came to view the Espionage and Sedition Acts as a way of calming the wartime hysteria that advocated far more drastic action against those with dissenting views. O'Brian and Bettman feared mob action and believed these laws would calm the public.

In their brief, O'Brian and Bettman argued that the case did not involve the First Amendment; therefore claims involving free speech violations were frivolous. Consequently, the Supreme Court should refuse to hear the case, since the issue had been settled in previous cases—particularly in the Selective Draft Law Cases in 1918. Apparently, O'Brian and Bettman saw no legal distinction between the refusal to comply with a draft summons and the discussion of the law as a matter of public policy and individual rights.

In the unanimous ruling of March 3, 1919, the Supreme Court presented Justice Oliver Wendell Holmes's clear and present danger test, a doctrine much discussed and evaluated in subsequent years. Holmes's analysis tied the act of political speech to the "circumstances in which it is done." He argued that the persons who sent the document intended it to have the ef-fect of obstructing persons from complying with the draft.

"The question in every case," Holmes wrote, "is whether the words used are used in such circumstances and are of such a nature as to create a clear and present danger that they will bring about the substantive evils that Congress has a right to prevent." According to Holmes, those arrested had been attempting to interfere with congressional conduct of war policy and therefore had committed "substantial evils." He went on to distinguish wartime circumstances from more peaceful contexts and argued that since the statute punished conspiracies as well as obstruction, it was not necessary for the action to be successful in order to violate the law.

Shortly after his introduction of the clear and present danger doctrine in *Schenck*, Holmes wrote two more unanimous opinions in Espionage Act cases. These discussions reveal a restricted view of the First Amendment and provide little clarification of the clear and present danger test. In *Frohwerk v. United States* (1919), the Court upheld the conviction of Jacob Frohwerk, who had published articles critical of the draft in a Missouri German-language newspaper. The justices determined that Frohwerk's words might "be enough to kindle a flame of resistance." This opinion presented a definite "bad tendency application," which meant that one could be found guilty of violating a statute if what a person said produced a tendency to bring about an evil effect. Such a tendency did not rely on any causal relationship.

In *Debs v. United States* (1919), the Court upheld the conviction of the prominent Socialist Eugene Debs for delivering a speech in Canton, Ohio, in which he had attacked capitalist wars. Also Debs had informed the trial jury that he abhorred war, and his 1917 Socialist party platform had advocated war opposition. On this basis, the Court held that Debs's speech intended to obstruct recruiting. However, Holmes did not apply a clear and present danger relationship analysis but relied entirely on the tendency of Debs's words.

In the years since 1919 much of the discussion generated by Holmes's famous doctrine has centered on just where he meant to draw the line between protected and unprotected speech. There is forceful scholarly argument that has concluded that in subsequent months Holmes honed his *Schenck* reasoning to develop the apparently more libertarian application written eight months later in his *Abrams* dissent, a case involving another group that challenged wartime restrictions on political expression.

Jacob Abrams, along with fellow anarchists Hyman Lachowsky, Jacob Schwartz, and Mollie Steimer and Socialist Samuel Lipman, were all Russian-born Jews struggling to make a new life in the traditional New York immigrant trades. The difficult working conditions and the resistance of employers to making any improvements brought Abrams and the others to consider anarchism and socialism as avenues in which to seek redress. The five became involved with a group that published the Yiddish-language anarchist paper *Der Shturm* ("The Storm"), which had a limited circulation in the Jewish neighborhoods of East Harlem. Members of Abrams group at times attended meetings of a no-conscription league organized by better-known anarchists Emma Goldman and Alexander Berkman, who at this time were supporters of the 1917 Russian Revolution.

During August 1918, the group reacted passionately to a U.S. decision to join the British and French allies in intervening on behalf of a contingent of Czechoslovakian troops trapped in the Ukraine when the Bolsheviks exited the war after the Treaty of Brest-Litovsk. In attempting to flee via Vladivostok, the Czechs had become involved in confrontations with the Red Army. President Woodrow Wilson responded to pressure that blamed German influence for the Russian withdrawal from the war. On a pretext of self-defense, Wilson dispatched 7,000 troops to aid the Czechs in Siberia.

The Abrams group viewed Wilson's action as a violation of the concept of the 1917 revolution. They reacted by purchasing their own printing press and preparing two protest statements—one in English and one in Yiddish—critical of U.S. intervention. On August 22 and 23, fellow anarchist sympathizers distributed the leaflets by scattering them from rooftops at several Manhattan locations. The English version

was entitled "The Hypocrisy of the United States and her Allies" and was fewer than 400 words. Author Lipman cautiously accused Wilson of deceiving the American people concerning the intervention. Lipman pointed to allied capitalism combined with German militarism as the enemy of the world and called on workers to "Awake!" He closed by denouncing German militarism and disavowing any alleged pro-German connections on the part of his group. Nowhere did the leaflet advocate a specific action.

Schwartz wrote the more militant Yiddish flyer entitled "Workers Wake Up!!" which was not translated into English until after the indictment. He accused the United States of hypocrisy in misleading people into support of the war and of using Russian immigrants to produce munitions to shoot Russian revolutionaries as well as Germans. He perceived the "barbaric intervention" as a betrayal of workers and an attempt to destroy the Bolshevik Revolution and called for a general strike, although he provided no organizational details. Subsequent translations of the leaflet have raised questions about the degree of militancy expressed in the version used at the trial. Some interpretations view the words as less harsh than the prosecution's version.

On August 23, New York police quickly traced the leaflets to Hyman Rosansky, one of the distributors and a fringe anarchist sympathizer. He confessed readily and agreed to serve as a police decoy when the members of the Abrams group made contact with him. By the end of the evening, police had arrested the major participants as well as Rosansky for violation of the 1918 Sedition Act.

Officers interrogated the group with assistance from the Military Intelligence Division (MID) of the U.S. Army, which had been integrated into the New York Police Department for the surveillance of radicals. Police successfully obtained a confession from each person arrested. Procedures to do so included beatings and other forms of mistreatment later implicated in the jailhouse death of Schwartz.

On September 12, a federal grand jury handed down a four-count indictment charging those arrested with conspiring to publish the leaflets, using "language intended to bring the government of the United States into contempt," and inciting resistance to the United States in the war. The fourth count charged that defendants attempted "to oppose the cause of the United States in said war." Francis Caffey, the U.S. attorney for the Southern District of New York and one who advocated "extermination" of war critics, revised the final count so that it included conspiracy "to urge . . . curtailment of things and products . . . necessary and essential to the prosecution of the war . . . with intent . . . to cripple and hinder the United States." According to Caffey's reasoning, opposition to intervention equaled a pro-Bolshevik position, which in turn was equivalent to a pro-German stand. He firmly believed all pro-Germans, and therefore all Bolsheviks, should be in prison. Caffey often relied on rumors, particularly those connecting the Abrams's group with well-known anarchist Goldman. Caffey was also in the habit of submitting the names of potential jurors in espionage and sedition cases to the Justice Department's newly created Bureau of Investigation. Consequently, he could rely on these background checks as a basis for preemptory challenges during jury selection.

The *Abrams* trial began on September 30, 1918, in the midst of an influenza epidemic which many New Yorkers blamed on German agents. Harry Weinberger, associated with earlier anarchist clients, defended Abrams and his colleagues before Judge Harry DeLamar Clayton, a patriarchal Alabamian temporarily assigned to relieve a heavy New York court docket. A former congressman and the author of the antitrust law that bears his name, Clayton harbored an intense hatred of Germany, which intensified when his younger brother was killed in the Great War. He saw the activities of radicals as a threat to a system of paternalism and 100 percent Americanism.

During the proceedings, prosecution attorneys John M. Ryan and Sanford Miller focused only on attempting to show that the defendants wrote, printed, and distributed the leaflets involved. They called a four-day parade of governmental witnesses, which included police officers as well as the man who had sold Abrams the printing press and the woman who had rented him the apartment where the meetings

and printing activity took place. Police testified they found partially burned copies of the leaflets there as well. The prosecution used this information as well as testimony that established Abrams's use of an alias at various times to support the government's claim that the group acted surreptitiously.

Prosecutors also used their questions to place into the record Mollie Steimer's earlier answer to a question indicating that she knew the leaflets were unlawful when she distributed them. With these trial tactics, prosecutors attempted to demonstrate that the defendants conspired with criminal intent. However, Ryan and Miller did not attempt to show that the leaflets specifically intended to interfere with the American intervention or that they affected U.S. policy. Essentially, the prosecution concentrated on depicting the Abrams group as dangerous, conniving radicals.

In conducting the defense, Weinberger cross-examined the government witnesses but for the most part did not challenge the testimony. However, he contended, very strongly at times, that the acts were not criminal. Furthermore, he claimed that the five principals were victims of police brutality, and he attempted to demonstrate this charge in his cross-examination of the officers. This tactic proved unsuccessful when Judge Clayton sustained several prosecution objections and later reprimanded Weinberger for overstepping his role as attorney. Several of the officers denied having engaged in improper behavior, and the judge accepted their denials at face value. Further demonstration of Clayton's disposition in the trial occurred when he ordered Weinberger to take his seat as the defense attorney attempted to question an undercover MID agent who had attended various radical meetings. Clayton then made an ethnic comment: "I have tried to out-talk an Irishman, and I never can do it, and the Lord knows I can not out-talk a Jew."

Weinberger also attempted to respond to prosecution's assumptions that pro-Bolsheviks equaled pro-Germans. He called to the witness stand social reformer Raymond Robins and journalist and Congregational minister Albert Rhys Williams, two vigorous opponents of Wilson's intervention policy. Both men had observed the 1917 revolution first-hand and maintained that the Bolsheviks, prior to their withdrawal from the war, had sought military and economic cooperation with the United States. A counter view based on information found in questionable documents released through the wartime Committee on Public Information maintained that the Germans dictated the 1917 revolution as well as subsequent Bolshevik policies. Weinberger's goal was to discredit the German-Bolshevik link. Although Clayton allowed Weinberger to question Robins and Williams, he forbade them to answer the questions.

During the proceedings, Clayton questioned witnesses, a rather common practice in federal trials in 1918. He interrogated the defendants in a hostile manner and inquired why they had not returned to Russia since they were so critical of the United States. He preached the virtues of an agrarian life to these New York workers and concluded verbally from the bench that they were not producers because they had never grown anything—not even a potato. While instructing the jury, Clayton delivered a long lecture on intent, emphasizing what he saw as the attempted secrecy of the defendants' actions. He rejected several points Weinberger had requested to be included in the charge, including a statement to the effect that the government had presented no evidence that the defendants had attempted to aid Germany. Instead, their objective had been to protest intervention in Russia. After deliberating just over an hour, the jury convicted all of the defendants. On October 25, after delivering a two-hour tirade on the evils of German and Bolshevik agents, Clayton sentenced Abrams, Lachowsky, and Lipman to 20 years and Steimer to 15 years.

While awaiting a direct appeal to the U.S. Supreme Court, Weinberger arranged bail financed by friends of the defendants, who ironically provided Liberty Bonds as the principal security. The defendants were under continued surveillance as the post-World War I Red Scare went into full gear. The Bureau of Investigation's J. Edgar Hoover proceeded with the early stages of establishing his master file of suspicious persons; and the government sought evidence of anarchist activity to serve as a basis for deportation—for the Abrams group as well as others.

In the midst of this Red Scare atmosphere, the U.S. Supreme Court heard oral argument in the *Abrams* case on October 21, 1919. Weinberger's brief argued that the evidence presented did not support a guilty verdict. His clients had been engaged in mere criticism involved with public discussion of a public policy, and according to his argument, such discussion enjoyed First Amendment immunity from governmental restriction. Since the United States was not at war with the Soviet Union, this discussion could not be interpreted as interference with the war effort in any way. Weinberger contended further that the Espionage Act of 1917 and its Sedition Act of 1918 amendment were both unconstitutional because they violated the natural right of liberty of discussion.

Originally, the defense's argument concerning the Sedition Act had been assigned to O'Brian and Bettman of the Justice Department's Emergency War Division. However, with the war's end, O'Brian and Bettman had resigned their jobs in May 1919, after having urged pardons for all those convicted under the Espionage and Sedition Acts—including the Abrams group. The task of presenting the government's case then fell to Assistant Attorney General Robert T. Stewart. He and his assistant W. C. Herron put together arguments not used at the earlier trial. They contended that the group had attempted to interfere with munitions production and had intended to overthrow the government by force. They argued a static constitutional view, which subscribed to the doctrine of seditious libel and which claimed that the First Amendment had been created merely to protect the press from prior restraint. Such a position reflected a narrow eighteenth-century English common-law view that provided no protection for public discussion and criticism of public policy.

On November 10, 1919, the Court in a 7–2 decision upheld the conviction of Abrams and his colleagues. Justice John H. Clarke's opinion rested on narrow, procedural grounds, which found the evidence sufficient to convict. He quoted the leaflets selectively and out of context to demonstrate the defendants' anarchist views and commented on their failure to apply for U.S. citizenship. Even though the trial prosecutors had not dealt with the issue of intent, Clarke concluded that "men must be held to have intended, and to be accountable for effects which their acts were likely to produce."

In applying this "bad tendency" test, Clarke reasoned that the Abrams group's plan for aiding the Soviet cause involved support for defeat of the U.S. war effort, since their leaflets advocated the tactic of a general strike. Bad tendency reasoning would argue that if such a strike had taken place, it could have interfered with munitions production, which could have affected the war effort. According to Clarke, the leaflets attempted to embarrass the U.S. government, to defeat U.S. war plans, and "to provoke and encourage resistance to the United States in the war." Such activity, regardless of outcome, violated the Sedition Act.

Justices Oliver Wendell Holmes, Jr., and Louis D. Brandeis dissented. Holmes centered his argument on the government's failure to demonstrate intent in the case. In his words, "a deed is not done with intent to produce a consequence unless that consequence is the aim of the deed." Holmes did not recant the line of reasoning he applied earlier in the year in the *Schenck*, *Frohwerk*, and *Debs* opinions, because he continued to acknowledge that dangers to the government were greater during wartime. However, he insisted in his dissent that a present danger must relate to an immediate evil, which in this case the defendants' words had not created because they had demonstrated no specific intent to damage the U.S. war effort. Their intention had been to aid Bolsheviks, not Germans. The key to creating clear and present danger was a relationship between specific intent and a specifically evil effect. According to Holmes, "[T]he defendants had as much right to publish [the leaflets] as the Government has to publish the Constitution of the United States."

Holmes went on in the final paragraph of the dissent to elaborate and clarify his ideas on freedom of speech, which he had wrestled with and developed in the months since his *Schenck* opinion. He granted that if a person was certain of his position, it was "logical" to try to "sweep away all opposition," since allowing discussion seemed to imply that the position is weak and fallible. But when men have realized that time has "upset many fighting faiths they may come to believe . . . that the ultimate good desired is better reached by free trade in ideas— that the best test of truth is the power of the thought to get itself accepted in the competition of the market and that truth is the only ground upon which their wishes safely can be carried out. That at any rate is the theory of our Constitution."

These words became the cornerstone of much subsequent clear and present danger doctrine application. For speech to be restricted, dangers must present an immediate evil and connect to a specific action. Unless those conditions exist, speech should be allowed to make its case against competing ideas.

Upon close examination, the reasoning in Holmes's *Abrams* dissent does not appear to follow from his *Schenck* opinion written eight months earlier, especially concerning the crucial relationship between intent and result. In *Schenck*, he had written that "it was not necessary for the action to be successful in order to violate the law." This consideration of intent is not consistent with his insistence in the *Abrams* dissent on the necessity to establish a connection between specific words and specific and immediate evil results. During the eight months between the two opinions, Holmes devoted considerable time to clarifying his First Amendment views for himself and his Court colleagues. After all, neither Holmes nor any other jurist had focused significant attention on this issue, since free speech interpretation was not yet a main body of constitutional interpretation.

During the summer of 1919, Holmes discussed the *Schenck* reasoning with other legal thinkers, including Judge Learned Hand and Harvard Law School professor Zechariah Chafee, Jr., both of whom shared libertarian views on the value of political discussion. Holmes also met with English socialist Harold Laski, often a visiting professor at Harvard. These discussions, together with Holmes's own thoughtful consideration focusing on questions of intent and effect, help to explain the difference between his *Schenck* and *Abrams* views, a fine-tuning in legal reasoning which makes the difference between restricting speech or allowing it to seek acceptance "in the competition of the market."

In his *Abrams* dissent, Holmes acknowledged one of the basic concepts in his legal philosophy, that the law, as well as life, is an experiment. Citizens should be "eternally vigilant" against silencing unpopular opinions unless the threat is so great and so imminent that "an immediate check is required to save the country." Holmes concluded that this emergency did not exist in *Abrams* and that the government had deprived the defendants of their First Amendment rights. As far as Holmes was concerned, the law of seditious libel reflected in the 1918 Sedition Act did not apply. Two years later, in 1921, Congress repealed the Sedition Act; the Espionage Act remained on the books to apply again in times of declared war.

The Holmes dissent caused a stir among legal scholars who, for the first time since the adoption of the Bill of Rights, began to analyze the First Amendment seriously in terms of the value of political discussion within a democratic society. In this sense, the World War I espionage and sedition cases helped to define a new area of constitutional development and discussion, which would lead eventually to a stronger

position for First Amendment freedoms as the clear and present danger approach developed in the *Abrams* dissent became the position of the Court majority in the 1930s.

Holmes's eloquent dissent, however, could not save the *Abrams* defendants, who endured prison sentences and then deportation to the Soviet Union in 1921. Eventually, their homeland also rejected each of them, and they were forced to go elsewhere to seek acceptance of their political views.

Selected Bibliography

Chafee, Z., Jr. "A Contemporary State Trial—the United States versus Jacob Abrams et al." *Harvard Law Review*. 33 (April 1920): 747–74.

————. *Free Speech in the United States*. Cambridge, MA: Harvard University Press, 1941.

Murphy, P.L. *World War I and the Origin of Civil Liberties in the United States*. New York: W.W. Norton & Co., Inc., 1979.

Polenberg, R. *Fighting Faiths: The* Abrams *Case, the Supreme Court, and Free Speech*. New York: Viking Press, 1987.

Ragan, F. "Justice Oliver Wendell Holmes, Jr., Zechariah Chafee, Jr., and the Clear and Present Danger Test for Free Speech: The First Year, 1919." *Journal of American History* 58 (June 1971): 24–45.

AGRARIAN REFORMS AND THE POLITICS OF LOYALTY

by Carol E. Jenson
Department of History
University of Wisconsin at La Crosse

Gilbert v. Minnesota, 254 U.S. 325 (1920) [U.S. Supreme Court]

When the Nonpartisan League (NPL) farmers' reform organization moved its campaign from North Dakota to Minnesota in 1917, the group encountered fierce opposition from incumbent politicians bent on using wartime loyalty issues to discredit any attempt to promote political change. The confrontation led to the arrest of Joseph Gilbert and others as the state's insistence on prevention of conflict clashed with the constitutional protection of the rights of

free speech and assembly. *Gilbert v. Minnesota* represented a series of Minnesota arrests of NPL leaders who fought early civil liberties battles at the state level while the more publicized confrontations involved the federal Espionage and Sedition Acts.

Organized in North Dakota in 1915 by ex-farmer A. C. Townley, the NPL won control of that state's government in the 1916 election. The chief goal of the farmers' organization was to increase farm income through improved marketing facilities, stricter regulation of elevators, lower interest rates, and use of state-owned facilities for the processing of agricultural products.

By the time the NPL attempted to extend its political successes to neighboring Minnesota, the United States had entered World War I, and Minnesota had preceded Congress in passing a sedition statue that vaguely outlawed any advocacy discouraging the war effort. The legislature also created the Commission of Public Safety (CPS), which was empowered to coordinate wartime programs down to the township level and designed to ensure statewide loyalty by stopping disloyalty before it erupted.

According to the CPS, much of the potential disloyalty centered in the ranks of the NPL, which sponsored a producers and consumers conference in St. Paul in September 1917. The conference attracted considerable attention when one featured speaker, war-entry opponent Senator Robert La Follette of Wisconsin, was misquoted by the Associated Press as stating that the United States had no grievances against Germany. Only verbatim transcripts produced by the U.S. attorney's office in Minnesota forced the Associated Press to change its story months later. The La Follette furor obscured the NPL's reaffirmation of its support of the war effort and Wilson administration policies and its criticism of "those who are making extortionate profits out of the necessities of the people in time of war."

The incident at the conference made the NPL the principal target of CPS suspicions, and Commission Vice-Chair Charles W. Ames wrote that "any movement which seeks to crystallize discontent" could not be dealt with tolerantly. As a result, the CPS proceeded to process 682 "sedition" cases during the war months and further exercised its broad arbitrary powers by sending field agents to check on NPL meetings. The spies reported back to a disappointed CPS that disloyal speeches had not occurred and that the NPL's organizers and members had endorsed the Wilson administration's war efforts and the sale of Liberty Bonds. After November 1, the CPS dispensed with the agents and thereafter relied on rumor and statements from frightened local officials as its main sources of information. As anti-NPL rumors spread, numerous communities denied the league access to speaking facilities and even forbade league meetings—eventually in 21 of Minnesota's 87 counties.

In early 1918, the NPL intensified its political campaign by focusing on precinct caucuses and the June primary. The state nominating convention selected former Congressman Charles A. Lindbergh, Sr., as the NPL gubernatorial candidate in the Republican primary, pitting him against incumbent J. A. A. Burnquist, a firm supporter of the CPS and an advocate of vigorous enforcement of the Sedition Act.

Throughout the campaign, Lindbergh had to battle charges of disloyalty. He had served in Congress for ten years; and prior to April 1917, he had opposed U.S. entry into the war, although his decision not to seek reelection in 1916 prevented him from casting his vote against interventionists. However, once the United States entered the conflict, he, like many other anti-interventions, supported the war effort. His 1918 campaign speeches revealed his firm support of Wilson administration policies, including the Liberty Bond and Red Cross campaigns.

Violence as well as denunciation plagued Lindbergh as he sought the gubernatorial nomination. Spies followed him, and more than once mobs pulled him from the speaker's platform. He was banned from Duluth and hanged in effigy in Red Wing. On one occasion, he emerged from a meeting to find a mob beating his driver. After considerable negotiation, Lindbergh persuaded the crowd to allow him to leave, only to be escorted by a shower of bullets. At this point, Lindbergh reportedly said to his driver, "We must not drive so fast. They will think we are afraid of them if we do."

At the height of the NPL's primary campaign, a Goodhue County grand jury, in the southeastern Minnesota community of Red Wing, indicted NPL Organization Manager Joseph Gilbert for violation of the state's sedition act. Gilbert was charged for remarks made in a speech on August 18, 1917, in the village of Kenyon, where he allegedly advocated "that men should not enlist" and that persons should not support the war effort.

Gilbert's May trial, held one month before the primary, reflected the anti-NPL political atmosphere in much of the state. Defense witness George Breidel was threatened and forcibly dragged from the St. James Hotel in Red Wing and later dumped and shot at in a rural area of the county. Local authorities made no attempt to apprehend or to arrest the kidnappers. The jury convicted Gilbert after six prosecution witnesses repeated verbatim ten sentences that appeared in the indictment, an incident that one of Gilbert's attorneys later described as "the only parrot chorus in the history of jurisprudence." The trial judge relied on a broad "bad tendency" application of the statute and instructed the jury that it was not necessary to show that Gilbert had advocated directly that men should not enlist or aid the war effort; Gilbert could be convicted "if the natural and reasonable effect of the words spoken" would lead to such advocacy.

The jury convicted Gilbert on May 10, and attorneys appealed to the Minnesota Supreme Court on the contention that Gilbert had not intended to interfere with the war effort. The appeal also cited the unusual testimony of the state's witnesses, reiterating in word-for-word fashion remarks Gilbert denied making. On December 20, 1918, the supreme court upheld the sedition statute on grounds of the state's power to protect the people's welfare. The court concluded that the "statute would be violated if the natural and reasonable effect of the words spoken is to teach or advocate that citizens should not aid or assist the United States," regardless of what Gilbert intended.

In late January 1919, Gilbert's lawyers approached the U.S. Supreme Court on a writ of error. They argued that the trial court in convicting Gilbert had not considered intent an element necessary under the Minnesota sedition law. The brief questioned the courtroom procedures involving the "parrot chorus," as well as the constitutionality of a state venturing into legislation involving wartime activities—normally an area reserved to the national government. Gilbert's lawyers emphasized the basic and natural rights involved in freedom of speech and argued that the state legislature had no power to curtail them.

Attorneys for Minnesota argued that the Supreme Court was without jurisdiction in the case because of lack of a federal question. They defended the statute as a police regulation that applied regardless of Gilbert's intent, and they maintained that the Constitution did not protect seditious speech of the type attributed to Gilbert.

When the High Court ruled in *Gilbert* in December 1920, it was the first time since the 1868 ratification of the Fourteenth Amendment that the justices had considered the issue of state sedition legislation. Seven members of the Court voted to uphold the Minnesota statute as part of a cooperative venture within the federal system, a "simple exertion of the police power to preserve the peace of the State."

In the opinion of the court, Gilbert's words had created disorder, and the state was justified in arresting him. Justice Joseph McKenna's majority opinion declared further that the World War I cases prosecuted under the federal Espionage and Sedition Acts had established that free speech was not an absolute and was subject to "restriction and limitation" especially during wartime. The opinion made no attempt to establish a relationship between Gilbert's words and their effect. In his brief dissent, Chief Justice Edward D. White accepted the contention of Gilbert's attorneys that the subject matter was "within the exclusive legislative power of Congress."

In contrast, Justice Louis D. Brandeis's dissent raised important new questions that would become part of a compelling body of constitutional development for the remainder of the twentieth century. In Brandeis's view, the Minnesota statute was unconstitutional because it provided no test to determine a relationship between ideas and action. More important, Brandeis also raised the issue of the application of the Fourteenth Amendment to circumstances involving possible state infringement on basic liberties. He saw Minnesota's sedition act as an attempt to "prevent not acts but beliefs," and in his analysis this restriction interfered with the privileges and immunities of a U.S. citizen. In his dissent, Brandeis supported vigorously the federal protection of freedom of speech and other Bill of Rights guarantees from state encroachment, a position the Court majority would accept in theory five years later in the better-known case, *Gitlow v. New York* (1925). This concept of the nationalization of the Bill of Rights, which has evolved since 1925, developed from Brandeis's *Gilbert* dissent when he linked the Fourteenth Amendment to the Bill of Rights, "I cannot believe that the liberty guaranteed by the Fourteenth Amendment includes only liberty to acquire and to enjoy property."

The NPL lost out in the 1918 Republican primaries in Minnesota. It attempted to regroup for the fall elections by forming a third party, but this campaign was also unsuccessful. The political disaster of several of these contests damaged the NPL organization in Minnesota, but the reform ideas lived on in the Farmer-Labor Party, which replaced the NPL in the agrarian protest tradition that eventually merged with Minnesota's Democratic party in the 1940s. Arthur LeSueur, one of Gilbert's attorneys, and A. B. Gilbert, editor of the *Nonpartisan Leader*, became active in the American Civil Liberties Union in the 1920s, contributing an often overlooked midwestern and agrarian element to that movement.

Selected Bibliography

Jenson, C.E. *Agrarian Pioneer in Civil Liberties.* New York: Garland Publishing, Inc., 1986.

———. "Loyalty as a Political Weapon: The 1918 Campaign in Minnesota." *Minnesota History* 43 (Summer 1972): 42–57.

Morlan, R. *Political Prairie Fire.* Minneapolis, MN: University of Minnesota, 1955.

EXPANDING FREE SPEECH TO THE STATES

by Harold Josephson
Department of History
University of North Carolina at Charlotte

Gitlow v. New York, 268 U.S. 652 (1925) [U.S. Supreme Court]

Prior to World War I, the U.S. Supreme Court treated the freedom of speech provision of the Constitution with benign neglect, saying nothing about when state legislatures could and could not limit expression. For the most part, Americans embraced freedom of speech as a theoretical principle and took it for granted. Unfortunately, neither Congress nor the Supreme Court transformed this First Amendment concept into a legal doctrine that would guarantee expression to all citizens.

Because almost no litigation relative to freedom of speech reached the Supreme Court, the limits of constitutional expression lacked definition. To make matters worse, the Court had held in *Barron v. Baltimore* (1833) that the federal restrictions and liberties guaranteed by the Bill of Rights did not apply to the states, thereby allowing them to abridge speech, as well as other liberties, at their discretion.

Restrictions on civil liberties increased at the turn of the century, as state governments and local communities sought to curtail the activities of the growing radical movement in the United States. Socialists, anarchists, and other radical critics of American society found little sympathy within the general community and faced sharp limitations during the Progressive Era. World War I carried repression even further. Federal laws, such as the Espionage Act of 1917 and the Sedition Act of 1918, put pacifists, conscientious objectors, radicals, and aliens on the defensive.

The end of World War I brought no decline in political repression. Instead, it led to increased anxiety in the face of political upheavals in Europe, unprovoked bombings, inflation, unemployment, and the outbreak of strikes throughout the country. Led by Attorney General A. Mitchell Palmer, federal, state, and local officials in the winter of 1919–20 rounded up and arrested labor radicals, Socialists, and Communists in a series of spectacular raids.

Because the Espionage and Sedition Acts had lost the force of law when the war ended, states replaced the federal government as the primary agency for prosecuting radicals. By 1920, some 35 states had passed repressive measures. In New York, one of the first Communists arrested was Benjamin Gitlow, a former Socialist assemblyman and founder of the Communist Labor Party, one of two Communists parties organized in 1919. Instead of passing a new antiradical statute after the war, New York chose to resurrect the 1902 Criminal Anarchy Act, enacted shortly after the assassination of President William McKinley. Rarely used before 1919, the law defined "criminal anarchy" as the doctrine that organized government should be overthrown by force or violence, by the assassination of executive officials, or by any other unlawful means. The specific charge against Gitlow and several other leading Communists was that they had violated the Criminal Anarchy Act by their association with the radical publications *Revolutionary Age* and the "Left Wing Manifesto." The manifesto, according to the indictment, was not only a broad critique of capitalism and a general defense of revolutionary socialism, but it was also an inflammatory call for immediate revolution.

Of the many Communists arrested in New York, Gitlow stood trial first. Assistant District Attorney Alexander Rorke reasoned that Gitlow's position as business manager of the *Revolutionary Age* made him more vulnerable than the others to the charge of publishing the paper. At the trial, Rorke argued that the "Left Wing Manifesto" clearly called for the violent, unlawful overthrow of the government and thereby came under the provisions of the Criminal Anarchy Act. According to Rorke, Gitlow's central objective in publishing the manifesto was "the destruction, the conquest and the annihilation of the government of the United States."

The defense team, lead by the renowned Clarence Darrow, admitted that Gitlow was a Communist, that he was the business manager of the paper, and that he had responsibility for its publication and circulation. Darrow denied, however, that the manifesto was a call for violent revolution or that it came within the prohibitions of the Criminal Anarchy Act. He also challenged the statute's constitutionality, declaring that it violated not only New York's guarantee of freedom of speech and press, but that it also violated the Fourteenth Amendment to the U.S. Constitution, which prohibited states from depriving persons of life, liberty, or property without the due process of law.

This final argument—that the due process clause of the Fourteenth Amendment held state governments to the same free speech standards as the First Amendment held Congress—was originally promulgated at Gitlow's preliminary hearing by Walter Nelles of the National Civil Liberties Bureau (the precursor of the American Civil Liberties Union (ACLU)). Both Nelles and Darrow hoped to use *Gitlow* to convince the U.S. Supreme Court that the Fourteenth Amendment reversed the legal doctrine promulgated in *Barron v. Baltimore* that the Bill of Rights did not apply to the states. They also wished to move Gitlow's defense from a narrow discussion of the contents of the manifesto to the broader issue of free speech and the repressive nature of laws like New York's Criminal Anarchy Act. Both attorneys emphasized that since, the law prohibited both actions and the promulgation of radical ideas, it threatened the constitutional guarantee of freedom of speech. In his trial summation, Darrow drove this point home. Communists, he declared, might be wrong, but they had to be given a chance to preach and to try to make the world a better place. The real danger to the nation was not in their ideas or publications, but in the government's attempt to curtail free expression. To send Gitlow to jail merely for holding unpopular views, he told the jurors, would be "to strike one blow which means the death of freedom in the United States."

Darrow's attempt to focus on the broader constitutional issues in the case was undermined by the presiding judge, Bartow S. Weeks. In his charge to the jury, Weeks declared that the New York Criminal Anarchy Act did not negate the right of free speech and that as far as he was concerned the constitutionality of the statute was not in question. The jury took only three hours to convict Gitlow and on February 11, 1920, six days after the trial ended, Weeks sentenced him to five to ten years in prison, the maximum penalty allowed by law.

During the next several months, other Communists faced Weeks and they, too, were found guilty of violating the New York statute and joined Gitlow in prison. New York officials had found an effective method for removing antiestablishment leaders from public activity. All of those who followed Gitlow to jail, however, gained their freedom by 1923, either by having their convictions overturned on technicalities by the New York Court of Appeals or by receiving a pardon from Governor Alfred E. Smith, who returned to the governor's office in January 1923 after a two-year absence. Governor Smith postponed issuing a pardon for Gitlow so that he and the ACLU could appeal his case to the Supreme Court and thus test the constitutionality of the state's criminal anarchy statute.

Both New York's appellate division and court of appeals upheld Gitlow's conviction. Moreover, both rejected his contention that the New York statute violated the First Amendment and the due process clause of the Fourteenth Amendment of the Constitution. Gitlow did find some support from the court of appeals, where two of the justices, Benjamin N. Cardozo and Cuthbert W. Pound, dissented. Pound, who wrote the dissent, defined "anarchy" very narrowly and argued that although the "Left Wing Manifesto" advocated the use of force and violence in overthrowing the government, it did not fall within the prohibitions of the New York statute. Gitlow had not sought to "establish" the Communist program, but rather to "teach" revolutionary doctrines and to "advocate" a fundamental change in the government. Strongly critical of Gitlow's aims, Pound pointed out that "although the defendant may be the worst of men; although left Wing socialism is a menace to organized government; the rights of the best of men are secure only as the rights of the vilest and most abhorrent are protected."

Both the ACLU and many radical organizations believed that a Supreme Court review of the case was important, for it would further clarify the rights of free speech and decide the extent to which Congress and state legislatures could suppress radical political dissent. Although the Supreme Court had offered little guidance as to the constitutional dimensions of the free speech guarantee of the First Amendment prior to World War I, after the war it heard several cases that led to the establishment of new standards by which to judge the constitutionality of free speech restrictions. In the first of these cases, *Schenck v. United States* (1919), Justice Oliver Wendell Holmes, Jr., writing a unanimous opinion, declared: "The question in every case is whether the words used are used in such circumstances and are of such a nature as to create a clear and present danger that they will bring about the substantive evils that Congress has a right to prevent."

Liberals and progressives cheered the "clear and present danger" test, for it seemed to limit the curtailment of speech only to those instances where a direct and immediate relationship between expressed ideas and alleged acts could be proven. Unfortunately, while all of the justices agreed on the principle, they applied it very restrictively. Schenck, a prominent Socialist indicted for writing and circulating a pamphlet counseling draft resistance in violation of the Espionage Act of 1917, found no relief as the Court upheld his conviction. One week later, the Court again unanimously upheld lower court convictions of violations of the Espionage Act in *Frohwerk v. United States* and *Debs v. United States*. Although the Court paid lip service to the clear and present danger test, in each specific case it embraced the idea that legitimate abridgements of freedom of expression could be based on the "bad tendency" of the words used, rather than on their direct relation to illegal actions.

After considering the liberalizing potential of the clear and present danger test, however, Justices Holmes and Louis D. Brandeis began to challenge the majority position. Eight months after the *Frohwerk* and *Debs* decisions, Brandeis and Holmes dissented in *Abrams v. United States* (1919), the first of several famous dissents rejecting the doctrine of bad tendency and advocating a broader interpretation of the clear and present danger test.

Although Gitlow's attorneys might have found some hope in the dissents of Holmes and Brandeis, they could find little encouragement in the Court decisions regarding challenges to state restrictions on individual rights. In *Gilbert v. Minnesota* (1920), the Court ruled that it had no authority to challenge a state's use of its police powers carried out in the public interest. Two years later, the Court formally rejected the concept that the Fourteenth Amendment prohibited states from abridging individual liberties.

Despite these rulings, the ACLU hoped to use *Gitlow* to move the Court majority toward the Holmes-Brandeis view of the First Amendment's guarantee of freedom of expression and toward an interpretation of the Fourteenth Amendment that would provide for federal protection against state abridgement of civil liberties. Unfortunately, on June 8, 1925, Justice Edward T. Sanford, writing for the Court's majority, found New York's Criminal Anarchy Act constitutional and upheld Gitlow's conviction. Sanford maintained that state legislatures, and not the courts, had responsibility for determining what kinds of utterances endangered society. They could not be required "to measure the danger from every such utterance in the nice balance of a jeweler's scale." States had a right and a duty to protect society from utterances that *might* lead to substantial danger, for "a single revolutionary spark may kindle a fire that, smoldering for a time, may burst into a sweeping and destructive conflagration." A state did not have to wait until that spark burst into a blaze before it could act.

On one issue only the Court supported the ACLU arguments on behalf of Gitlow. Without explanation of its support, it held for the first time that state laws restricting speech were to be judged by the standards of the First Amendment. "For present purposes," wrote Sanford, "we may and do assume that freedom of speech and of the press—which are protected by the First Amendment from abridgment by Congress—are among the fundamental personal rights and 'liberties' protected by the due process clause of the Fourteenth Amendment from impairment by the states." Despite this important new principle, Sanford and the Court majority did not think that New York's criminal anarchy statute crossed the line of unconstitutionality, nor that Gitlow's conviction should be overturned.

In dissent, Holmes and Brandeis further clarified their argument, begun in *Abrams*, that unless speech posed a clear and present danger to society there was more to be lost by its suppression than by its expression. Agreeing that the First Amendment should apply to the states, they stressed that no real threat was created by the distribution of the "Left Wing Manifesto." Holmes, writing the dissent, belittled the argument that the manifesto constituted an incitement. "Every idea," he argued, "is an incitement. It offers itself for belief, and, if believed, it is acted on unless some other belief outweighs it, or some failure of energy stifles the movement at its birth." Since the Court received no evidence that the manifesto would likely start an immediate conflagration, those responsible for its publication could not be prosecuted constitutionally. The dangers of suppression of speech far outweighed the state's desire to restrict expression that only remotely posed a threat to society. As in *Abrams*, however, Holmes and Brandeis could not move the Court majority to their position.

Reactions to the opinion were divided. Conservative newspapers and law journals found the majority opinion sound and appropriate. Radical and liberal commentators lamented the substitution of "bad tendency" for "clear and present danger" as the test for the constitutionality of legislative attempts to limit free speech. What few commentators perceived at the time, however, was how far the Court's new interpretation of the First and Fourteenth Amendments would move it in the area of civil liberties. By the late 1960s, the Court, using the concept of "selective incorporation," had expanded the meaning of the due process clause of the Fourteenth Amendment so that states had to provide most of the guarantees and abide by most of the restrictions imposed on the federal government in the Bill of Rights.

The Supreme Court's position on the proper limits of free speech also changed over time. As late as 1951, in *Dennis v. United States*, the High Court majority held that when the gravity of the evil was great enough, expression that tended toward eventual violent revolution may be punished by the government without violating the Constitution. But first in *Yates v. United States* (1957), and then in *Brandenburg v. Ohio* (1969), the Court rejected the concept that the dangerous tendency of expression was sufficient to permit its suppression. In *Brandenburg*, the Court unanimously reaffirmed the distinction between advocacy of ideas and advocacy of illegal action. For speech to be constitutionally restricted it had to pose a imminent danger that was real and not imaginary. The Court made clear that even threatening speech was protected unless it could be proved that the "advocacy is directed to inciting or producing imminent lawless action and is likely to incite or produce such action."

In 1925, when the Court issued the *Gitlow* decision, only Brandeis and Holmes called for a stronger defense of free speech, but not even they went so far as to advocate an incitement test for political expression. The Court majority, reflecting widespread popular opinion, believed that Communists and radicals should not be permitted to advocate ideas and policies that might eventually undermine public safety or the existing order. Gitlow returned to jail for a time, but was soon pardoned by Governor Smith and resumed active participation in the Communist party.

It would take many years for the Holmes-Brandeis dissent in the *Gitlow* decision to become the majority opinion or for selective incorporation to expand the Bill of Rights to the states. Until that time, the Court tended to embrace the principle that speech should be protected unless it posed a clear and present danger to society, but it applied that principle in a limited fashion. This gap between legal doctrine and its application enabled conservative politicians to severely restrict the influence of radical organizations like the Communist party by eliminating, through harassment and imprisonment, those who challenged American capitalism and the existing social structure. The *Gitlow* decision provided an opportunity for the future expansion of freedom, but in the context of the 1920s it represented another triumph for unwarranted repression.

Selected Bibliography

Chafee, Z., Jr. "Thirty-five Years With Freedom of Speech." *Kansas Law Review* 1 (Nov. 1952): 1–36.

Curtis, M.K. *No State Shall Abridge: The Fourteenth Amendment and the Bill of Rights*. Durham, NC: Duke University Press, 1986.

Josephson, H. "Political Justice During the Red Scare: The Trial of Benjamin Gitlow," in *American Political Trials*, M.R. Belknap, ed. Westport, CT: Greenwood Press, 1981.

Kalven, H., Jr. *A Worthy Tradition: Freedom of Speech in America*. New York: Harper & Row, 1988.

Murphy, P.L. *The Meaning of Freedom of Speech: First Amendment Freedoms from Wilson to FDR*. Westport, CT: Greenwood Press, 1979.

Warren, C. "The New 'Liberty' Under the Fourteenth Amendment." *Harvard Law Review* 39 (Feb. 1926): 431–65.

SILENCING CRITICS: GUILTY BY ASSOCIATION IN THE 1920s

by Carol E. Jenson
Department of History
University of Wisconsin at La Crosse

Whitney v. California, 274 U.S. 357 (1927) [U.S. Supreme Court]

Charlotte Anita Whitney's concern for the poor and downtrodden led her to leave the security of her wealthy and influential family to pursue a long and activist career in social work and an interest in left-wing politics. Her involvement in socialist activities made her the focus of the first significant and most publicized prosecution conducted under the California Criminal Syndicalism Act of 1919, which was designed to silence members of the Industrial Workers of the World (IWW), long active in California's agricultural fields and lumber camps.

The California statute, like a number of others passed by states in the early decades of the century, defined criminal syndicalism as "advocating, teaching or aiding . . . sabotage

... or unlawful acts of force and violence ... as a means of accomplishing a change in industrial ownership or control, or effecting any political change." Between 1919 and 1924, California used the statute to arrest 504 persons and to try 264, including Whitney.

For some years, Whitney had been active in the Socialist party in America and had participated in activities of the Oakland, California, branch. At a convention in Chicago during the summer of 1919, she joined other Oakland delegates to split from the main organization and form the Communist Labor Party (CLP). This group resolved to adhere to the principles of the Third International's manifesto to organize workers as a class movement. On November 9, Whitney and others held a convention in Oakland to organize a California branch of the CLP. Whitney was active in convention proceedings, including the Resolutions Committee which endorsed her views supporting traditional election procedures. This position clashed strongly with the views of the convention majority, which voted in favor of seizing power through industrial unions and strikes.

On November 28, nearly three weeks after the Oakland convention, Whitney delivered an address on the problems of American blacks. As she was leaving the meeting at the Oakland Center of the Civic League, authorities arrested her on a warrant that referred to her attendance at the CLP convention on November 9. Later, the five counts brought against her for violation of the Criminal Syndicalism Act would charge her with illegal activities on or about November 28, the day of the Civic League speech, an event that had no connection with her CLP membership. This discrepancy was one of many confusing and contradictory aspects of the case.

Since none of the five charges brought against Whitney under the Criminal Syndicalism Act referred to specific words or actions on her part, her attorney, J. E. Pemberton, filed a request for more precise and particular information. He contended that the charges were invalid, since nothing Whitney had done constituted an offense under the act. The Alameda County Superior Court denied the motion as well as another defense request asking the judge to instruct the jury to acquit on grounds that

the charges brought by the grand jury referred to the wrong date.

In the state's opening statement at the trial, which began in late January 1920, Deputy Alameda County District Attorney Myron Harris explained that it was his objective to make public the ideological positions of the CLP even though it was Whitney who was on trial—not the party. The guilt by association procedures had begun.

Whitney's other defense counsel, Thomas M. O'Connor, a well-known San Francisco labor attorney, conducted the courtroom questioning in the early days of the trial before his death from influenza on February 6. He objected repeatedly, and usually unsuccessfully, to a number of prosecution questions bearing no connection to Whitney and referring only to the CLP or the IWW. After O'Connor's death, Nathan Coghlan took over Whitney's courtroom defense. He unsuccessfully protested the introduction of a long parade of IWW literature, including renditions of Joe Hill songs and CLP history that predated the 1919 law. The court admitted these materials because the state presented evidence demonstrating that at one point the CLP briefly and generally had endorsed IWW objectives.

Whitney was the only defense witness; she attempted to discount her influence in the CLP by explaining that the convention majority had voted down her position on political action. She did not deny her membership in the CLP, and that association led to her February 20 conviction on count one, which referred to organizing and membership. The jury could not agree on the other four counts, and the state eventually dismissed them. Judge James Quinn sentenced Whitney to 14 years in San Quentin for doing nothing more than attending the organizational meeting of the CLP, which in its founding Chicago convention had referred in passing to the debt that it felt workers owed to the IWW. The prosecution had convinced the jury of Whitney's guilt by association.

In her appeals to higher California courts, Whitney argued that her actions were insufficient to constitute a public offense and that there was insufficient evidence to demonstrate that the activities of the CLP were covered by the Criminal Syndicalism Law. In April 1922, the

California Court of Appeals affirmed the trial court ruling, and, in June 1923, the California Supreme Court denied Whitney a hearing. This provided her an opportunity for an appeal to the U.S. Supreme Court.

When Whitney first appealed her case to the High Court, the justices denied jurisdiction for lack of a federal question. After attorneys demonstrated that in the California Court of Appeals they had raised constitutional questions regarding the possible conflict of the California law with the Fourteenth Amendment due process and equal protection clauses, the Court accepted the case on a writ of error.

Whitney's attorneys, who by this time included civil liberties advocates Walter Nelles and Walter Pollak, contended that California courts had denied Whitney equal protection of the law and numerous points of procedural due process because her accusation was not particularized and because of "subsequent acts of other persons—not her own acts." In the brief, they argued further that presumption of intent to conspiracy based on mere presence was also a denial of due process and that, without a definite test of criminality, the California statute required "prophetic qualities" in order to determine what a group and its members might do in the future. Attorneys also contended that the law violated First Amendment freedom of assembly and speech protections because it imposed "penal consequences for joining and participating in an organization still in its formative stage." In other words, this application of the law assumed guilt by association.

In defending the California law, the state attorney general's office argued that the law was comparable to other state statutes on the subject and, therefore, could not be criticized for being indefinite. The state also relied on World War I case precedents involving the federal Espionage Act of 1917 and Sedition Act of 1918 and accused the plaintiff of submitting a brief "devoted to political rather than legal argumentation."

On the contention involving the Fourteenth Amendment, California maintained that the case did not raise constitutional issues because the state's power to provide for the public safety outweighed any protection of individual rights. The state's attorneys argued that

under the law, membership alone was sufficient to convict those involved with the IWW. They claimed the state had demonstrated that the CLP recognized the "immense effect" of the IWW on the American labor movement, hence its effect on the CLP. According to this analysis, Whitney's continued membership in the CLP, even after her position was outvoted, constituted a violation of the law regardless of the fact that there was no evidence that she either advocated or committed violent action. This was clearly guilt by association. California's attorneys cited the Supreme Court's upholding of the conviction of CLP associate Benjamin Gitlow in 1925 as further argument against Whitney's position.

On May 16, 1927, the Supreme Court ruled. Technically, the decision was unanimous in upholding the California law. However, Justice Louis D. Brandeis joined by Justice Oliver Wendell Holmes, Jr., wrote a concurring opinion that raised crucial points of difference with the views of the majority. Justice Edward T. Sanford concluded for the Court that the California Criminal Syndicalism Law did not violate the Fourteenth Amendment due process clause on vagueness grounds; and he cited numerous precedents, none involving civil liberties issues. This line of reasoning concluded that the California law did not violate equal protection guarantees, since states had the power to classify their police laws. Finally, according to the majority, the state did not violate Fourteenth Amendment due process protection of free speech, since this right was not absolute.

In his oft-quoted concurring opinion, Brandeis contended that the First Amendment, linked with the Fourteenth Amendment, limited the state legislature's authority to restrict free speech and assembly. In his analysis, he extended the Fourteenth Amendment protection beyond the Court interpretation, which previously had involved only property rights. Brandeis advised that Whitney's attorneys should have argued for a clear and present danger test to distinguish between ideas and dangerous action. "There must be reasonable ground to believe that the danger apprehended is imminent. There must be reasonable ground to believe that the evil to be prevented is a serious one." Whitney had maintained that the California law violated the U.S. Constitution, "but she did not claim that it was void because there was no clear and present danger of serious evil." Had it not been for this technical point that the justices viewed as a mistake made by Whitney's lawyers, Brandeis and Holmes very likely would have dissented in the case.

Brandeis went on to explain the value of allowing political discussion with opportunity for various views to be expressed and challenged. He saw such debate as the essence of the American political system. He stated: "Those who won our independence by revolution were not cowards. They did not fear political change." If a group presented a challenge to the governmental system, it was important to discuss the differences of opinion; "the remedy to be applied is more speech, not forced silence." He concluded, "Only an emergency can justify repression." In Brandeis's view, freedom of assembly in a political party was protected from state regulation by the due process clause of the Fourteenth Amendment.

A few months after the Supreme Court decision, California Governor C. C. Young pardoned Whitney on grounds similar to those explained in Brandeis's reasoning. Young's action ended nearly eight years of a legal endurance contest that occurred because one prominent woman insisted on maintaining her political rights of speech and assembly despite a state's interference. Between 1924 and 1930, California prosecuted no one under its criminal syndicalism law. The publicity of *Whitney* brought left-wing political activity to a very low ebb. In 1969, the Supreme Court overturned the *Whitney* precedent in a unanimous *per curiam* decision, which declared a similar Ohio criminal syndicalism law unconstitutional. However, a modified California law still remains in force, presenting the risk of possible use of guilt by association tactics in the future.

Selected Bibliography

Chafee, Z., Jr. *Free Speech in the United States.* Cambridge, MA: Harvard University Press, 1967.

Dowell, E. *A History of Criminal Syndicalism Legislation in the United States.* New York: Da Capo Press, 1969.

Whitten, W. "Trial of Charlotte Anita Whitney." *Pacific Historical Review.* 15 (Sept. 1946): 284–94.

THE CALIFORNIA RED FLAG LAW AND FREEDOM OF SPEECH

by Carol E. Jenson
Department of History
University of Wisconsin at La Crosse

Stromberg v. California, 283 U.S. 359 (1931) [U.S. Supreme Court]

Events surrounding Yetta Stromberg's challenge of the California Red Flag Law reveal the conformist mentality of the 1920s and demonstrate the extent to which California state and local officials went in their attempts to impose political homogeneity on the community.

During the summer of 1929, Stromberg, a 19-year-old former political science student at the University of California, Los Angeles, and the U.S.-born daughter of Russian immigrant parents, became involved in the Pioneer Summer Camp Conference. A number of independent organizations, some Communist in ideology, others not, made up the group, which worked to make it possible for children of working-class parents to attend summer camp.

The selected campsite was part of a 60-acre farm, leased from the owner, near Yucaipa, California, in San Bernardino County. It was located in a secluded area, a distance from any town and one mile from a main highway. It was accessible only by a private road which passed through two gates. There, seven young women and one elderly male custodian maintained the camp facilities. Stromberg, a member of the Young Communist League, led the campers in a daily study of history and economics, presented from a Communist perspective. She also conducted a 6:30 a.m. flag-salute ceremony in the camp dormitory. Sleepy children emerged from their cots, observed the raising of a red flag with a hammer and sickle emblem, and recited a pledge acknowledging the red flag as a symbol of the freedom of the working class. During the remainder of the camp day, the children played baseball, hiked in the hills, and engaged in other typical summer activities.

Local organizations reacted negatively to the camp's presence—isolated as it was. The Better American Federation, a group determined to eliminate "dangerous" dissent from Southern California, teamed up with the American Legion and succeeded in convincing the county authorities to raid the camp. On August 3, the San Bernardino County Sheriff's Department conducted a surprise search of the premises, confiscated camp materials, including a small red flag, and jailed Stromberg and the other members of the camp's staff. County officials then had to determine what charges to bring against the group. After considering and later rejecting a criminal syndicalism charge, the authorities discovered the previously unenforced California Red Flag Law passed in 1919.

Under this statute, created to supplement the California Criminal Syndicalism Act adopted at the same time, using or displaying a red flag in a public place was considered a felony. The California legislature perceived the red fabric as a sign and emblem of opposition to organized government and an invitation to anarchy and sedition.

In addition to finding the flag at the camp, authorities had also discovered Communist-oriented books and other reading materials in the camp library, which was under the supervision of Stromberg. As a result, on August 26, Stromberg and the other members of the staff were charged not only with violating the Red Flag Law but also with conspiracy to display a red flag.

When the trial began on September 30, Judge Charles Allison instructed the jury that "it is only necessary for the prosecution to prove to you, beyond a reasonable doubt, that said flag was displayed for any one of the three purposes mentioned" in the charges. Those objectives included opposition to organized government, invitation to anarchistic action, or aid to seditious propaganda.

During the trial, the state presented some of the materials taken from the camp library. Despite defense objections, prosecutors read excerpts, some of which advocated the use of armed force, to the jury. Stromberg maintained that the library materials had not been presented to the children. However, the district attorney contended that the camp was "conducted as a school of armed revolutionary propaganda" and that the flag was displayed as a symbol of this teaching.

The defense argued that the camp was not a public place because of its limited clientele and its inaccessible location. Stromberg's attorneys contended that the California statute contradicted the Fourteenth Amendment protection of the First Amendment free speech privileges and immunities of U.S. citizens and that the law also conflicted with the California Constitution's protection of freedom of expression.

On October 23, 1929, the jury convicted Stromberg of violating the Red Flag Law and also convicted her and all except one of the other defendants on the conspiracy charge. The custodian committed suicide shortly after the verdict, and the charges against all except Stromberg were dropped after a California court of appeals, in June 1930, affirmed Stromberg's conviction. When the California Supreme Court declined to hear the case in July 1930, Stromberg's attorney John Beardsley, with help from the International Labor Defense and the American Civil Liberties Union, appealed to the U.S. Supreme Court on Fourteenth Amendment grounds.

The defense's Supreme Court brief discussed the judicial test of red flag laws, an area of civil liberties law not previously presented before the High Court. Beardsley distinguished Stromberg's situation from the Supreme Court opinions in *Gitlow v. New York* (1925) and *Whitney v. California* (1927), which had recently upheld convictions under criminal anarchy and criminal syndicalism statutes. He argued that the California Red Flag Law did not mention force or violence, "but is all inclusive in its condemnation of the display of a flag as an emblem of opposition to organized government." In other words, it could be interpreted to outlaw any form of opposition to government, including support of a candidate seeking to defeat an incumbent.

The brief went on to argue that the political teaching was only one aspect of the camp activities and that the state's evidence that the red flag at issue had stood for opposition to organized government came only from the Communist party literature confiscated from the camp library. That party, Beardsley pointed out, was on the presidential ballot in 1928 and had polled 50,000 votes. If the Communist party could legally field a presidential candidate, why could not Stromberg's camp display the party's red flag symbol?

Beardsley was able to draw on the experience of attorneys who had practiced in the newly developing field of civil liberties defense law in the years since World War I. Focusing on constitutionally based arguments, he cited the clear and present danger test developed by Justice Oliver Wendell Holmes, Jr., in the interpretation of the federal World War I Espionage and Sedition Acts. In his test, Holmes had maintained that the circumstances under which the alleged violation occurred had to be considered. Beardsley argued that this small camp in rural California could "scarcely be pictured as a menace to the stability and life of the Republic." The brief cited noted Harvard Law School professor Zechariah Chafee's scholarship that had concluded that the First Amendment free speech clause had abolished the crime of sedition. Beardsley repeated one of his brief's main points and concluded that the California statute was "arbitrary and vague" because it referred inclusively to outlawing a symbol of opposition to organized government, an opposition that included legitimate partisan activity.

California's attorneys countered by insisting that freedom of speech could not be interpreted to be unlimited but was subject to the restrictions of the state's police power to protect the public welfare. They maintained that the law was not uncertain and vague and that

the evidence found in the Communist party literature "overwhelmingly supports" the conviction. The state concluded that Stromberg was igniting in these children a spark that might at some time "burst into a great conflagration." According to this analysis, California was justified in restricting Stromberg's speech to prevent some possible future opposition to the government.

The justices responded on May 18, 1931, in a 7–2 decision with a Court opinion written by Chief Justice Charles E. Hughes. The majority overturned Stromberg's conviction on the ground that the California verdict was a general one based on all three points in the statute—including banning the red flag as a symbol of opposition to organized government. The Court majority concluded that such a ban was too vague, for it could be construed to refer to peaceful and legal political and partisan opposition to a party in power. Curbing such opposition would threaten "new thought and the development of original ideas." Hughes reasoned that since political change is based on the confrontation of ideas, "peaceful opposition is guaranteed to our people."

As a result of this line of reasoning, Hughes concluded that banning such political speech violated the liberty protected by the Fourteenth Amendment due process clause. Therefore, the Court declared the central portion of the California Red Flag Law unconstitutional. Hughes agreed with precedents that had determined the constitutional mechanism for Fourteenth Amendment protection of free speech but not as an absolute fashion, for he maintained that states could punish "abuse of this freedom."

Hughes's *Stromberg* opinion is often considered in tandem with another of his 1931 civil liberties commentaries, the 5–4 ruling in *Near v. Minnesota*. There, the Court discarded a Minnesota "gag law" as a violation of the First Amendment freedom of the press protections against the use of prior restraint. In each of these opinions, Hughes took the Court beyond using the Fourteenth Amendment simply as a vehicle for free speech protection. Hughes's opinions extended the concept of nationalization of the Bill of Rights—using the Fourteenth Amendment to protect basic rights against state encroachment—to protecting the substance of the symbolic speech of flag displays and to shielding freedom of the press from state-imposed restraint. Although Hughes did not directly discuss a clear and present test in *Stromberg*, his opinion vindicated the several dissents of Justices Holmes and Louis D. Brandeis, who throughout the 1920s had argued not only for applying the Fourteenth Amendment to protect basic liberties but also for extending the boundaries of protected speech. With the advent of Hughes's leadership, Holmes's and Brandeis's First Amendment views had become part of the opinion of the Court majority.

Selected Bibliography

Chafee, Z., Jr. *Free Speech in the United States*. Cambridge, MA: Harvard University Press, 1967.

Murphy, P.L. *The Meaning of Freedom of Speech*. Westport, CT: Greenwood Press, 1972.

COLD WAR, COMMUNISM, AND FREE SPEECH

by Michal R. Belknap
California Western School of Law

Dennis v. United States, 341 U.S. 494 (1951) [U.S. Supreme Court]

"We are fighting Communism with blood and money on both sides of the world; now the Supreme Court permits us to fight it at home," the *Los Angeles Times* editorialized on June 6, 1951. It was applauding the U.S. Supreme Court's decision two days earlier in *Dennis v. United States*, upholding the convictions of 11 top leaders of the Communist Party of the United States (CPUSA) for violation of a sedition statute known as the Smith Act. Such praise of *Dennis* was predictable. In June 1951, the United States was at war with Communist enemies in Korea, and the anti-Communist hysteria known as "McCarthyism" was sweeping the country. Unfortunately, while delivering a blow to communism, the Supreme Court had also injured free speech. Recognizing this, Justice Hugo L. Black, in a dissenting opinion, expressed the plaintive hope "that in calmer times, when present pressures, passions and fears subside, this or some later Court will restore the First Amendment liberties to the high preferred position where they belong in a free society."

Like *Dennis* itself, the statute whose constitutionality the Supreme Court upheld in that case was a product of times that were anything but calm. The Smith Act became law on June 28, 1940, just a few months after German aggression plunged Europe into World War II. It was an omnibus antialien and sedition measure, which, among other things, criminalized teaching and advocacy of the violent overthrow of the government and membership in any organization that engaged in such conduct. Opponents of the Communist party had introduced proposals similar to some of its provisions as early as 1935, but these had made little headway then. In 1939–40, with events in Europe inspiring fears of subversion by foreigners and foreign ideologies, the Smith Act marched relentlessly through Congress.

The target for those who promoted enactment of its sedition sections was the CPUSA, but eight years passed before the government used the new law against Communists. The reason was the World War II alliance between the United States and the Soviet Union. U.S. officials did not want to offend the Soviets by prosecuting their coadjutors in this country. As the joint Soviet-U.S. struggle against Nazi Germany approached a victorious conclusion, the two allies began to quarrel over the future of Eastern Europe. By 1948, their relationship had deteriorated into the bitter international confrontation known as the Cold War. That quarrel was essentially a conflict of interest between two powerful nation states. In trying to rally the American people behind a policy of containing Soviet expansionism, however, President Harry S Truman characterized the conflict between the United States and the Soviet

Union as an ideological struggle between democracy and communism.

Truman thereby created a serious political problem for his own Democratic party. At least since 1944, Republicans had been trying to discredit Democrats by linking them with communism. Until the onset of the Cold War, voters displayed little interest in such charges. When the president began insisting that the United States must spend millions of dollars to resist Communists abroad, however, the public started to take seriously the Republican party's allegations that Truman's administration was not doing enough to combat communism at home. Neither the president nor his attorney general, Tom C. Clark, considered domestic communism a serious problem. Nevertheless, after Clark received sharp criticism from the Republican-controlled House Un-American Activities Committee for not doing more about it, he decided to accept a recommendation made earlier by the director of the Federal Bureau of Investigation (FBI), J. Edgar Hoover, for a Smith Act prosecution of the CPUSA. The U.S. attorney for the Southern District of New York, John F. X. McGohey, was set to work preparing a case against the party's leaders, and on July 20, 1948, a federal grand jury in Manhattan indicted all 12 members of its national board.

The grand jury accused these radicals of conspiring with one another and with persons unknown to organize the CPUSA. The Communist party was, the indictment alleged, "a society, group and assembly of persons who teach and advocate the overthrow and destruction of the Government of the United States by force and violence." The grand jury also charged the defendants with conspiring to teach and advocate violent overthrow. Finally, it accused them of membership in an organization that engaged in such teaching and advocacy (a charge on which they were never tried). Contrary to what many people believed at the time, the indictment did not accuse the Communist leaders of conspiring to overthrow the government. There was a good reason for this: the Justice Department lawyer who reviewed the huge mass of evidence on the CPUSA assembled by the FBI concluded that prosecutors could not prove the defendants had committed that offense. Hence, the grand jury accused the party's leaders not of engaging in, or even plotting, revolutionary action, but merely of preparing to advocate revolutionary ideas.

Throughout most of 1949 all of the indicted Communists except National Secretary William Z. Foster (whose case was severed from those of his codefendants because of his severe heart condition), stood trial on this charge before Judge Harold Medina in the federal courthouse on New York's Foley Square. That tumultuous proceeding, which began on January 17 and did not stagger to a conclusion until October 14, was, according to *Newsweek*, "the longest, dreariest and most controversial" American criminal trial up to that time. The transcript of its tortuous progress stretched to over 20,000 pages.

Much of this record chronicled bitter wrangling between Medina and a battery of five defense attorneys. Those lawyers argued loudly, persistently, and with considerable justification that, particularly in his rulings on the admission and exclusion of evidence, Medina favored the prosecution. Their constant attacks convinced the judge that they were plotting to destroy his health and thus bring about a mistrial. Mutual distrust bred animosity, and the level of conflict between Medina and the defense attorneys rose as the trial progressed.

Their constant wrangling added fuel to fires ignited by the questionable tactics of the prosecution and defense. The Communists did not believe they could win this trial in any traditional sense; not even their lawyers thought the jury would acquit the defendants. Hence, rather than concentrating on rebutting the prosecution's case, the Communists adopted a "labor defense" strategy. The party organized demonstrations and correspondence campaigns designed to pressure the government into dropping the charges against its leaders. Meanwhile, with the assistance of their attorneys, the Communists sought to use the courtroom as a propaganda platform. Defense witnesses made political speeches and extolled the party's efforts on behalf of veterans, blacks, organized labor, and other interest groups in society. The Communists also sought to discredit the American government by, for example, attacking the system of jury selection used by the court, which they claimed discriminated against members of racial minorities, supporters of radical political parties, wage workers, and the poor. Medina's efforts to curtail this propagandizing triggered much of the conflict that disrupted the proceedings.

Another source of turmoil was a tactic that the government used repeatedly to discredit defense witnesses. Again and again, when cross-examining Communists, the government's lawyers asked them to identify as members of the CPUSA other persons having little or no connection with the case. As the defendants' attorneys pointed out many times, given the intense hostility toward communism that was gripping the country, anyone linked to it in this way was likely to suffer loss of governmental benefits, unemployment, and ostracism. Besides, like many persons associated with the American labor movement, Communists had a deep aversion to becoming "stool pigeons." They consistently refused to "name names." The prosecution went on demanding them anyhow. The results were a great deal of courtroom conflict and the jailing of defendants John Gates, Henry Winston, Gus Hall, and Carl Winter for contempt.

The government's case was as unimpressive as its methods were dubious. Most of the evidence that the prosecution produced had little or nothing to do with the nominal defendants. The prosecution devoted only about ten percent of its attention to proving the participation of General Secretary Eugene Dennis and the other members of the national board in the alleged conspiracy and about 90 percent to building a case against the CPUSA. Since the defendants were alleged to have violated the Smith Act by reconstituting the CPUSA in 1945, after it had dissolved itself temporarily during World War II, the character of the party was an issue. Only if it was an organization of the type prohibited by the Smith Act could the defendants be guilty of violating that law by conspiring to organize it. But the prosecution often acted as if the party itself were the defendant. The theory of its case was that the CPUSA was an instrument that a group of conspirators had created to accomplish its objective of teaching and advocating violent overthrow of the government. Yet much of its evidence was ad-

missible only if the party was itself the conspiracy.

That evidence consisted largely of articles, pamphlets, and books, many of which, as the defense pointed out, could be found on the shelves of university and public libraries. Most of these works had been written by Communists other than the defendants, and some of them, such as Marx's *The Communist Manifesto* (1848) and Lenin's *State and Revolution* (1917), had been published long before Congress passed the Smith Act. The government presented excerpts from these works that contained ominous-sounding references to violence. The defense sought to put those passages into what it insisted was a proper context by reading to the jury other parts of the same publications dealing with quite different subjects. Medina, convinced the Communists were stalling again and trying to exploit the trial for propaganda purposes, repeatedly thwarted the defense's efforts. What the jury heard was a disjointed and often incomprehensible collection of quotations that tended to overemphasize the importance of violent revolution in Communist ideology.

The witnesses called by the government were there mainly to identify the publications the government wished to use and to satisfy the legal requirements that had to be met to get these admitted into evidence. Some witnesses, such as Herbert Philbrick (an FBI informant who had spent nine years masquerading as a dedicated Communist), told stories that were as dramatic as a spy thriller. But the relevance of their accounts to the charges against the defendants was marginal, and such testimony was not nearly as common as dull recitations of what publications the teacher of some Communist class had assigned to the students. The literary evidence was the guts of the prosecution's case. It did not impress the *New Republic*, which observed that the government had "failed to make out the overwhelming case that many people anticipated when the trial began."

Although it failed to impress the *New Republic*, the prosecution's evidence proved sufficient to convict the defendants. After deliberating for seven and one-half hours, the jury returned guilty verdicts against all of them. What convicted the Communist leaders was not the strength of the government's case, but the intensity of public hostility toward communism. Politicians from both major parties applauded the verdicts, as did newspapers of almost every political persuasion throughout the country. Within a month after the trial ended, Medina received 50,000 congratulatory letters.

The judge, who was transformed by the Communist trial into a sort of folk hero, sentenced ten of the defendants to five years in prison. The only one toward whom Medina showed mercy was Robert Thompson, a World War II hero to whom he gave only three years. Besides sentencing the Communist leaders to prison, the judge jailed their lawyers. After the jury returned its verdicts, Medina castigated the defense attorneys for conspiring to disrupt the trial, adjudged all five (along with General Secretary Eugene Dennis, who had acted as his own attorney) guilty of multiple counts of contempt, and imprisoned them for periods ranging from 30 days to six months. The U.S. Court of Appeals for the Second Circuit affirmed contempt judgments against the defense attorneys; so did the U.S. Supreme Court.

Appeal proved equally futile for the defendants. The Communist leaders attempted to persuade the Second Circuit that Medina's bias and misconduct had deprived them of a fair trial. The judge had, they insisted, committed numerous reversible errors, particularly in his rulings on the admission and exclusion of evidence and in his instructions to the jury. The leaders of the CPUSA also claimed they had been deprived of an impartial jury and that the trial court had violated a number of their constitutional rights. They argued further that the Smith Act, both on its face and as Medina had construed and applied it, violated the First Amendment's guarantees of freedom of expression.

An *amicus curiae* ("friend of the court") brief filed by the American Civil Liberties Union (ACLU) supported that assertion, but the three judges who heard the Communists' appeal rejected it, along with all of their other contentions. Even before oral argument, two of these jurists expressed privately a distinct lack of sympathy for the defendants. The invasion of South Korea by its Communist neighbor, North Korea, while the case was being argued, and the United State's subsequent plunge into a shoot-

ing war with communism in Asia, destroyed whatever slight chance the leaders of the CPUSA had of persuading the Second Circuit to overturn the verdicts against them. On August 1, 1950, the court of appeals unanimously affirmed all of the convictions.

It also upheld the Smith Act, despite the substantial restrictions that law imposed on freedom of expression. In 1950, the generally accepted rule for determining whether speech or writing could be punished without violating the First Amendment was the "clear and present danger" test, formulated by Supreme Court Justice Oliver Wendell Holmes, Jr., just after World War I. Under that test, as it had come to be understood by the time of the *Dennis* trial, expression enjoyed constitutional protection unless it created an immediate danger of some serious evil that the authorities had a right to prohibit. The threat allegedly posed by Communist teaching and advocacy—violent revolution against the U.S. government—was certainly very serious. But the prosecution had failed to prove that such a rebellion was imminent, let alone that, at a time when most Americans would reject out of hand anything urged by the CPUSA, it had any chance of succeeding. To uphold the Smith Act, as applied to the *Dennis* defendants, Judge Learned Hand had to alter the clear and present danger test. In each case, he wrote in his opinion for the Second Circuit, courts "must ask whether the gravity of the 'evil,' discounted by its improbability, justifies such invasion of free speech as is necessary to avoid the danger." This reformulation eliminated the time element from the test. Under Hand's version, all that mattered was the gravity of the evil and the possibility that it could occur someday, however far in the future that day might be. As Hand saw it, the CPUSA was a rigidly disciplined band of zealots, committed to the eventual capture of all existing governments and acting in concert with a worldwide movement headed by the Soviet Union, which even then was agitating for control of various countries in Western Europe. "We do not understand how one could ask for a more probable danger, unless we must wait until the actual event of hostilities," he wrote. As far as Hand was concerned, with the United States and the Soviet Union locked in the Cold War, Communists constituted a clear and present danger. For that reason, restrictions on their speech did not violate the First Amendment.

The Supreme Court agreed. After the court of appeals ruled against them, Dennis and his comrades sought review of their convictions by the High Court. It refused even to consider most of the issues they had raised before the Second Circuit. The Communists obtained a hearing only on the question of the constitutionality of the Smith Act.

Before the Supreme Court they again argued that the Smith Act violated the First Amendment. Attorneys representing the Communist leaders insisted no one could make criminal advocating ideas or exercising the rights of speech, press, and assembly. According to them, even if advocacy were part of an effort to bring about a substantive evil, the First Amendment protected it unless there was a clear and present danger. The fact that the leaders of the CPUSA sympathized with the Soviet Union could not deprive them of the protection of that constitutional provision. Counsel for the Communists attacked Judge Hand for changing the meaning of the clear and present danger rule, which defense attorney Harry Sacher insisted during oral argument was that only an immediately threatening emergency could justify the government in abridging freedom of speech. Since no such danger existed, affirming the convictions of the Foley Square defendants would amount to "a confession of our unwillingness to take the risk of permitting political dissent to be heard," counsel for the Communists contended. That would amount to "suppression of the democratic process itself."

The Justice Department disputed the defense characterization of the case, strenuously denying that this litigation involved freedom of expression. Solicitor General Philip Perlman argued that because Communists would abolish free speech if they gained power, it was not an issue in *Dennis*. According to the Justice Department, what the Smith Act punished was not expression at all, but rather the formation of "fifth columns" serving the aggressive purpose of foreign powers. The government conceded that requiring prosecutors to establish the existence of an imminent and immediate danger, even after Congress had explicitly prohibited speech of a particular type, might be appropriate in dealing with unorganized and irresponsible agitators. "Applied to these petitioners and their Communist Party, it would mean that the First Amendment protects their preparations until they are ready to attempt a seizure of power, or to act as a fifth column in time of crisis."

That idea was as unacceptable to most members of the Supreme Court as it was to the Justice Department. On June 4, 1951, the Court ruled against the Foley Square defendants by a vote of 6–2 (with now-Justice Tom C. Clark excusing himself because of his previous involvement in the case). The High Court spoke through Chief Justice Fred M. Vinson, a man convinced that the government had to protect itself from Communists. Vinson entertained no doubts about how cases involving members of the CPUSA ought to be resolved. Having held several high-level administrative positions associated with the nation's economic mobilization for World War II, he appeared to have viewed *Dennis* as an opportunity to help mobilize America for the Cold War.

In formulating his opinion, Vinson followed the lead of Learned Hand, affirming Hand's conclusion that, as interpreted to the Foley Square jury by Medina, the Smith Act was constitutional. Free speech was not an unlimited and unqualified right, the chief justice asserted, and saving the government from violent overthrow was certainly an interest substantial enough to warrant restricting it. Vinson realized that the clear and present danger test controlled when this could be done, but as far as he was concerned, that rule could not mean that the authorities must wait "until the putsch is about to be executed, the laws have been laid and the signal is awaited." If government learned that a group bent on destroying it was indoctrinating members and committing them to act when the leaders of the combination thought the time was ripe, action was required. What the authorities might do should not depend on the immediacy of the threat or on the likelihood that the rebellion would succeed. Vinson endorsed as "succinct and inclusive" Hand's reformulation of the clear and present danger test. As far as the Chief Justice was concerned, the requirements of the new version had been met in this case; the formation by the leaders of the CPUSA of a "highly organized conspiracy with rigidly disciplined members" ready to act when they gave the word, together with the "inflammable nature of world conditions," and the tense state of relations between the United States and Communist countries had created the sort of danger it required.

Justice Felix Frankfurter agreed with Vinson that Dennis and his comrades had been "properly and constitutionally convicted for violation of the Smith Act," but he did not wish to associate himself with the chief justice's reasoning. As far as Frankfurter was concerned, suppressing advocacy of the overthrow of the government was an unwise policy. He believed, however, that judges should leave policy making to the legislative branch of the government. Congress had made a decision on this question, and while Frankfurter disagreed with what it had decided, he would defer to its judgment.

Like Frankfurter, Justice Robert H. Jackson wrote a separate concurring opinion. He thought that the clear and present danger test should not be used at all in cases involving conspiracies such as communism. Jackson maintained that what the Foley Square defendants had really been tried and convicted of was conspiring to overthrow the government. To him, conspiracy law seemed well-suited to dealing with defendants such as these.

Only Justices Hugo L. Black and William O. Douglas dissented. Black, who believed that the First Amendment prohibited all restrictions on freedom of expression, condemned the prosecution of the Communist leaders as "a virulent form of prior censorship of speech and press." Douglas did not endorse Black's absolutist position on freedom of expression, but he did believe that the First Amendment had been violated in this case, because the Foley Square jury had not been required to find the existence of a clear and present danger. Considering American Communists "the most beset and least thriving of any fifth column in history," Douglas denied that they posed a threat great enough to justify suppression of their speech. The Foley Square defendants had done nothing more than organize to teach and advocate doctrines that were themselves perfectly legal. They had been adjudged criminals not for what they had done

but rather because of who they were.

In 1951, there was general agreement that simply being a Communist was sufficient grounds for condemnation. Hence, the public viewed *Dennis* far more favorably than did Douglas and Black. "The American people in overwhelming majority will rejoice in this judicial affirmation of the nation's right and power," the *New Orleans Times-Picayune* predicted accurately. Few but close associates of the Communist party objected to the *Dennis* decision. The only independent groups to condemn it were the ACLU, the Trotskyist Socialist Workers Party, and the Congress of Industrial Organizations (CIO). In the entire country, only five major newspapers expressed opposition. Most editorial writers seemed unaware that freedom of speech had even been an issue in the case.

Among legal commentators, who more fully understood all of its implications, *Dennis* did not fare so well. Famed political scientist Edward S. Corwin endorsed the Court's ruling, but a number of other legal scholars, among them Robert McCloskey of Harvard and Eugene V. Rostow of Yale, criticized *Dennis* severely. To Rostow, the fact that the Supreme Court had abandoned the classic version of the clear and present danger test in order to uphold the Smith Act suggested that the country was in the midst of a grave civil liberties crisis.

Following the *Dennis* decision, the Justice Department launched an all-out war on the CPUSA, prosecuting 132 more Communists on Smith Act charges. By July 1956, it had tried "second string" party leaders in Los Angeles, Baltimore, Honolulu, Pittsburgh, Seattle, Detroit, St. Louis, Philadelphia, Cleveland, Denver, New Haven, and New York for conspiring to violate the 1940 sedition law. The government also secured conspiracy indictments against Communist functionaries in Boston and San Juan, Puerto Rico. In addition, it prosecuted seven party officials for membership in an organization that taught and advocated the violent overthrow of the government.

The Communists lost almost all of these post-*Dennis* cases. Of the 126 men and women indicted for conspiracy, only ten were acquitted. Eighteen were never brought to trial; and a hung jury, three severances because of ill health, and a death terminated five other cases without guilty verdicts. Of the Communists who had their fates decided by a trial court, just under 89 percent were convicted. Only once (in Cleveland) did a jury free any conspiracy defendants. Every Communist tried on membership charges suffered conviction. Smith Act defendants enjoyed even less success in appellate litigation. During the six years after *Dennis*, courts of appeals affirmed every conviction that came before them. Twice the Supreme Court refused even to review Smith Act cases.

Battered in the courts, the CPUSA also suffered from a loss of leadership. Believing that the United States was moving into a reactionary period during which the party would have to function both legally and illegally, its national committee decided that not all of the Foley Square defendants should go to prison. While seven of them reported to begin serving their sentences on July 2, 1951, Green, Thompson, Hall, and Winston went underground, forfeiting $80,000 in bail. Hall was captured by Mexican police and turned over to the FBI that October, and the bureau apprehended Thompson at a California mountain cabin in August 1952. Winston and Green managed to elude authorities until 1956 when, with their comrades emerging from prison, they surrendered voluntarily.

Neither in hiding nor serving their sentences were Smith Act defendants in a position to provide the CPUSA with guidance and direction. Dennis tried to continue running the party from his cell in the Atlanta penitentiary by passing instructions to his wife in correspondence and during her visits, but prison officials heavily censored his mail and managed to isolate the general secretary from his comrades on the outside. Other imprisoned party leaders experienced similar isolation. By 1953, the FBI considered the national committee "more or less inoperative."

Deprived of direction from much of its leadership, the CPUSA experienced a breakdown of internal discipline. While Thompson was in hiding and in jail, a "young Turk" movement within the New York state organization challenged his policies and plunged that segment of the party into a confrontation with the decimated national office. The ailing William Z. Foster could not control the dissident New

Yorkers. Nor could he keep California Communists from defying the national headquarters or a district organizer in Maryland from publicly advocating an unauthorized alteration of the party's "line."

The breakdown of discipline within the CPUSA grew worse as the Smith Act prosecutions spread and "second string" leaders followed the Foley Square defendants into prison or the underground. Members of the CPUSA who found themselves isolated from their associates in jail or in hiding had time to think, and many of them began to question for the first time the policies of an organization to which they had given blind allegiance for years. In 1956–57, the CPUSA figuratively blew apart and much of its membership walked away. While events abroad, such as Nikita Khrushchev's revelations concerning the crimes of Joseph Stalin and Russia's brutal suppression of the Hungarian Revolution, were the immediate causes of this collapse, they proved as destructive as they did only because *Dennis* and subsequent Smith Act prosecutions had badly undermined the party's organizational cohesion.

While the CPUSA was collapsing, the prosecutions that had disrupted it so badly were coming to an end. By 1956, Cold War tensions had eased. In the United States, too, the mood was changing. The most dramatic indication of this was the December 1954 vote by the U.S. Senate to censure Wisconsin's Senator Joseph R. McCarthy, a once-powerful demagogue whose name had become virtually synonymous with hysterical anticommunism and abuse of constitutional rights.

The Supreme Court shared the country's decreased fear of communism and increased concern for civil liberties. In 1956, it reversed the convictions of the Pittsburgh Smith Act defendants on grounds that these might have resulted from the use of perjured testimony against them. Then, in *Yates v. United States* (1957), the Court overturned the Los Angeles second-string convictions. It also interpreted the Smith Act in a way that severely limited the use of that law as a weapon against the CPUSA. Observing that the existing Communist party had come into being in 1945 and that the indictment in this case had not been returned until 1951, the Court held that the charge of conspiracy to organize the CPUSA on which the defendants had been convicted was barred by the three-year statute of limitations. It rejected the government's contention that "organization" was an ongoing process that included such actions as setting up new units. Its resolution of this issue ensured that no member of the CPUSA could likely be prosecuted for conspiring to organize. The Court also held that to be subject to punishment under the Smith Act, a person had to advocate not merely ideas but action. Those to whom the advocacy was addressed "must be urged to do something now or in the future, rather than merely to believe in something."

Because the government could not prove Communists did that, the *Yates* decision effectively blocked further legal assault on the CPUSA. Although offered by the Supreme Court the opportunity to retry nine of the 14 Los Angeles defendants, the Justice Department failed to do so because it lacked evidence of the kind of advocacy it now had to prove. Recognizing the government could not produce this, courts of appeals in four circuits ordered the release of all defendants in pending Smith Act cases. Appellate judges, who reversed convictions obtained in Detroit, St. Louis, Cleveland, Philadelphia, and Pittsburgh on the basis of *Yates*, did authorize the retrial of those cases. But the Justice Department itself terminated them because it could not produce the type of evidence the Supreme Court had demanded. Prosecutors did not even attempt to try the Boston and San Juan groups. Only in Denver were Communists again brought to trial on Smith Act conspiracy charges after *Yates*. The government obtained convictions there, but when the Court of Appeals for the Ninth Circuit reversed them because of errors in the conduct of the trial, the government dropped that case also. Ultimately, the *Yates* evidentiary standards even saved from prison all but one of the membership clause defendants.

While it halted the wave of prosecutions that *Dennis* had initiated, *Yates* did not reverse the 1951 ruling. It was not until the 1960s that the Court finally repaired the damage that *Dennis* had done to the First Amendment. In *Brandenburg v. Ohio* (1968), it adopted a new rule for defining the outer boundaries of constitutionally protected speech that was even more protective of freedom of expression than the classic version of the clear and present danger test. The *Brandenburg* Court declared that "the constitutional guarantees of free speech and free press do not permit [government] to forbid or proscribe advocacy of the use of force or law violation except where such advocacy is directed to inciting or producing imminent lawless action and is likely to incite or produce such action." The job of protecting the government from advocacy of anything but the most immediate attacks on it was left to counter speech.

Yet, while departing from the principles of *Dennis*, the *Brandenburg* Court did not actually overrule the 1951 decision. If passions as intense as those that gripped the United States during the early 1950s once more agitate the nation, the Supreme Court could resurrect its doctrine, and *Dennis v. United States* might become again something more than a legal relic of the Cold War.

Selected Bibliography

Belknap, M.R. "Cold War in the Courtroom," in *American Political Trials*, M.R. Belknap, ed. Westport, CT: Greenwood Press, 1981.

————. *Cold War Political Justice: The Smith Act, the Communist Party, and American Civil Liberties.* Westport, CT: Greenwood Press, 1977.

Boudin, L.B. "Seditious Doctrines and the 'Clear and Present Danger' Rule." *Virginia Law Review* 38 (Feb., April 1952): 143–86, 315–56.

Corwin, E.S. "Bowing Out Clear and Present Danger." *Notre Dame Lawyer* 27 (Spring 1952): 325–59.

Daniel, H. *Judge Medina: A Biography.* New York: Wilfred Funk, 1952.

Mendelson, W. "Clear and Present Danger from *Schenck* to *Dennis*." *Columbia Law Review* 52 (March 1952): 313–33.

Mollan, R. "Smith Act Prosecutions: The Effect of the *Dennis* and *Yates* Decisions." *University of Pittsburgh Law Review* 26 (June 1965): 705–48.

Nathanson, N.L. "The Communist Trial and the Clear and Present Danger Test." *Harvard Law Review* 63 (May 1950): 1167–75.

Rostow, E.V. "The Democratic Character of Judicial Review." *Harvard Law Review* 66 (Dec. 1952): 193–224.

Steinberg, P.L. *The Great Red Menace: United States Prosecution of American Communists 1947–52.* Westport, CT: Greenwood Press, 1984.

Wormuth, F. "Learned Legerdemain: A Grave But Implausible Hand." *Western Political Quarterly* 6 (Sept. 1953): 543–58.

"BREACH OF PEACE" AND GROUP LIBEL

by Susan Duffy
Speech Communication Department
California Polytechnic State University

Beauharnais v. Illinois, 343 U.S. 250 (1952) [U.S. Supreme Court]

On January 6, 1950, Joseph Beauharnais, president of the all-white activist group the White Circle League of America, met with his membership to distribute flyers (lithographs) and other materials to volunteers for subsequent distribution in Chicago the following day. Under an enlarged and boldfaced heading, the pamphlet proclaimed: "Preserve and Protect White Neighborhoods! From the Constant and Continuous Invasion, Harassment and Encroachment by the Negroes."

Beauharnais's flyer attempted to accomplish two things. First, it was to act as an organizing device for a petition to the mayor and alderman of Chicago to "halt the further encroachment, harassment and invasion of white people, their property, neighborhoods and persons, by the Negro—through the exercise of the Police Power; of the office of the Mayor of the City of Chicago, and the City Council." Second, it was to garner new members for the White Circle League, which saw itself as "the only articulate white voice in America being raised in protest against negro aggressions and infiltrations into all white neighborhoods . . ."

Beauharnais's position, and that of the White Circle League outlined in the lithograph, suffered from intolerance and undisguised prejudice, but it was an elaboration of the argument on the flyer that caused Beauharnais to be charged with violating a 1917 Illinois statute prohibiting group libel. In his call for racial unity, Beauharnais claimed in the flyer: "If persuasion and the need to prevent the White race from becoming mongrelized by the negro will not unite us, then the aggressions . . . rapes, robberies, knives, guns and marijuana of the negro, SURELY WILL."

Because of this claim, Beauharnais was charged with violating an Illinois criminal libel statute that provided: "It shall be unlawful for any person, form or corporation to manufacture, sell, or offer for sale, advertise or publish, present or exhibit in any public place . . . any lithograph, moving picture, play, drama or sketch, which publication or exhibition portrays depravity, criminality, unchastity, or lack of virtue of a class of citizens, of any race, color, creed or religion which said publication or exhibition exposes the citizens of any race, color, creed or religion to contempt, derision, or obloquy or which is productive of breach of the peace or riots."

Judge Joseph H. McGarry, of the Municipal Court of Chicago, found Beauharnais guilty. The defendant appealed to the Illinois Supreme Court, where his conviction was upheld on the basis that he did, in fact, "publish" the lithographs in question and that they exposed "citizens of Illinois of the Negro race and color to contempt, derision or obloquy." Beauharnais appealed this decision to the U.S. Supreme Court, claiming that he had been denied due process because he had not been permitted to defend the "truth" of his arguments or the "good motive" for their publication.

The Supreme Court upheld the Illinois courts' conviction by a vote of 5–4. Justice Felix Frankfurter's majority opinion reiterated the opinion of the municipal and state courts that Beauharnais's publication of the lithographs was in violation of the Illinois statute that prohibited portrayal of depravity, criminality, unchastity, or lack of virtue of a class of citizens of any race." Frankfurter elaborated further, claiming that Beauharnais's flyer fell under the "traditional justification for punishing libels criminally, namely their 'tendency to cause breach of the peace.'" The Court felt that given heated racial tensions in Chicago and in Illinois generally, that the language of the flyer fell readily into the "fighting words" class of speech that can be prevented and punished without violation of First Amendment rights. In short, the Court supported the position that the flyer could lead to civil disturbances and that it fit the "clear and present danger" test for libel convictions.

The dissenting opinions of Justices Hugo L. Black, William O. Douglas, Stanley F. Reed and Robert H. Jackson articulated clearly the areas that split the Court. Black's dissent, without condoning Beauharnais's racist statements, noted that Beauharnais and the White Circle League were making a genuine effort to petition their elected representatives and that it is illegal to prosecute such petitions. Black saw the decision against Beauharnais as one that curbed freedom of expression and dangerously expanded criminal libel laws.

In his dissent, Douglas lamented what he called an "alarming trend" in recent Court decisions that, like this one, placed "in the hands of the legislative branch the right to regulate 'within reasonable limits' the right of free speech." His position, like Black's, saw the expansion of the definition of individual libel to group libel ultimately expanding legislative control over speech. He claimed that "intemperate speech is a distinctive characteristic of man"—one readily known to the framers of the Constitution, who chose freedom of speech over restrained speech. It was this choice of liberty, he felt, that should be made no matter how distasteful the language of Beauharnais's flyer.

Jackson's dissent also raised interesting questions about the "concept of ordered liberty" over freedom of expression. He pointed out that "criminality of defamation is predicated upon power either to protect the private right to enjoy integrity of reputation or the public right to tranquility." Beauharnais's conviction was based largely on the potential of his flyer to incite a "breach of peace" in Illinois—though there was never evidence presented that it did, in fact, disturb state peace. There had been no actual violence caused by the flyer or specific injury. The conviction stood on what Jackson called the "likelihood of evil results." In his mind, this failed the clear and present danger test for suppression of speech.

Jackson also raised the crucial issue of due process, noting that the only defense in libel cases is the proof of the truth of the statements and that they were published with good motives for justifiable ends. In this case, the judges in the lower courts decided that the statements were criminally libelous and instructed the jury to convict on the basis of whether Beauharnais had published the flyer, a claim that was undisputed in the trial. The trial court refused Beauharnais's attempt to prove the truth of his statements as immaterial, to which Jackson argued, "If the court would not let him try to prove he spoke truth, how could he show that he spoke truth for good ends? . . . his evidence proffered for that purpose, was excluded instead of being received and evaluated."

Finally, the dissenting justices pointed to the all-encompassing language of the Illinois statute, which prohibited any printed matter, moving picture, play, drama, or sketch from portraying a class of citizens of any race, color, creed, or religion as being minimally "lacking in virtue." Black noted wryly that "the statute is broad enough to make criminal the publication, sale, presentation or exhibition of many of the world's great classics, both secular and religious."

Reactions by the press were quick and disapproving. The chilling effect of the ruling was not lost on the major publications of the day and the cry of censorship was loud.

Beauharnais v. Illinois was the first conviction under a group libel statute. It has served as a conservative litmus test by which First and Fourteenth Amendment rights have been measured ever since.

Selected Bibliography

Be Vier, L. "The First Amendment and Political Speech: An Inquiry Into the Substance and Limits of Principle." *Stanford Law Review* 30 (1979): 299–358.

Brennan, W.J., Jr. "The Supreme Court and the Meikeljohn Interpretation of the First Amendment." *Harvard Law Review* 79 (1965): 1–20.

FLAG-BURNING AND THE CONSTITUTION

by Paul Finkelman
Brooklyn Law School

Texas v. Johnson, 491 U.S.— (1989); *Eichman v. United States*, 496 U.S.— (1990)
[U.S. Supreme Court]

Texas v. Johnson ought to have been a relatively simple case involving freedom of expression. Instead, it sparked a highly emotional response that led to the adoption of a federal statute prohibiting the desecration of the flag and calls for a constitutional amendment on the subject.

During the 1984 Republican National Convention in Dallas, Texas, Gregory Lee Johnson was one of about one hundred demonstrators who participated in a march protesting policies of the Reagan administration and certain Dallas based-corporations. The march ended at city hall where Johnson burned an American flag in symbolic protest. No riot or violence occurred and no one was hurt during the demonstration, although some observers later testified that they "had been seriously offended by the flag-burning."

Johnson was the only person arrested after the demonstration. He was charged under a Texas law that made it a crime to desecrate "a venerated object." At trial, he was convicted and sentenced to one year in prison and fined $2,000. His conviction was later reversed by the Texas Court of Criminal Appeals, which found that this statue violated the right to freedom of expression found in the U.S. Constitution. The Texas court based part of its decision on the reasoning of *West Virginia Board of Education v. Barnette* (1943), where the U.S. Supreme Court had "recogniz[ed] that the right to differ is the centerpiece of our First Amendment freedoms." Further drawing from *Barnette*, the Texas court found that the burning of a single flag did not place the national flag in "grave and immediate danger" of losing its symbolic value. Indeed, although the Texas court did not make this point, the very fact that Johnson chose to burn the flag as an act of protest underscores the continuing viability of the flag as a national symbol, even to protesters.

Speaking for a sharply, and oddly, divided Court, Justice William J. Brennan, Jr. upheld the Texas court, which had overturned Johnson's conviction. That the Court split 5–4 on this case is not surprising, since many of the Court's important 1988–89 decisions were by that vote. For example, at about the time it announced this decision, the Court announced its decision in *County of Allegheny v. ACLU* (1989), an important establishment clause case involving the display of a Christmas tree, Menorah, and a cross on public buildings in Pittsburgh and Allegheny County. In that case, the Court was divided 4–1–4, with Justice Sandra Day O'Connor holding that one form of display was permissible, but that another form was not. What was surprising in all these cases was the alignment of the Court.

Siding with Justice Brennan were two consistent liberals, Harry A. Blackmun and Thurgood Marshall, and two consistent conservatives, Antonin Scalia and Anthony Kennedy. On the other hand, Justice John Paul Stevens, who is often a liberal on free speech matters, wrote an emotional dissent.

In the majority opinion, Brennan offered a straightforward liberal analysis, deeply rooted in First Amendment law. He acknowledged that the government had "a freer hand in restricting expressive conduct than it has in restricting the written or spoken word." But he also noted that any restriction of such symbolic speech turned on "the governmental interest at stake." Brennan asserted that the conviction could be sustained only if the state could show that "Johnson's conviction . . . is unrelated to the suppression of expression." But this was clearly impossible. There had been no violence or threat to the peace from Johnson's act. Therefore, the prosecution could only be interpreted as a judicial assault on the content of Johnson's expression. Indeed, in oral arguments the attorney for Texas argued that the state had an interest in protecting the flag as a symbol— which implies that it was the political content of burning the flag that Texas sought to prevent. Thus, Brennan concluded that "Johnson was not . . . prosecuted for the expression of just any idea; he was prosecuted for his expression of dissatisfaction with the policies of this country, expression situated at the core of our First Amendment values." All parties to the case agreed that Johnson burned the flag "because he knew that his politically charged expression would cause 'serious offense.'" But, Brennan noted, "If there is a bedrock principle underlying the First Amendment, it is that the Government may not prohibit the expression of an idea simply because society finds the idea itself offensive or disagreeable." To find for Texas, Brennan reasoned, the Court would have to hold "that the Government may ensure that a symbol be used to express only one view of that symbol or its referents." But such a conclusion would lead the Court "to enter territory having no discernible or defensible boundaries" and the justices would be "forced to consult our own political preferences, and impose them on the citizenry, in the very way that the First Amendment forbids us to do."

Brennan concluded by arguing that through this decision, "the flag's deservedly cherished place in our community will be strengthened, not weakened" because the decision is a "reaffirmation of the principles of freedom and inclusiveness that the flag best reflects, and of the conviction that our toleration of criticism such as Johnson's is a sign and source of our strength." He warned that "we do not consecrate the flag by punishing its desecration, for in doing so we dilute the freedom that this cherished emblem represents."

Kennedy, a conservative Republican and then the most recent appointee to the Court, concurred with Brennan, noting that "[t]he hard fact is that sometimes we must make decisions we do not like. We make them because they are right, right in the sense that the law and the Constitution, as we see them, compel the result" even when that result is one that is "painful."

In dissent, Chief Justice William H. Rehnquist quoted numerous poems, slogans, and songs about the flag. He mentioned images of soldiers dying in foreign wars and Iwo Jima, where "United States Marines fought hand-to-

hand against thousands of Japanese" and they "raised a piece of pipe upright and from one end fluttered a flag." He pointed out that the flag was on all cartons and containers involved in lend-lease during World War II, and that it is flown at half-mast at the death of a president. In a separate dissent, Stevens concluded, "The ideas of liberty and equality have been an irresistible force in motivating leaders like Patrick Henry, Susan B. Anthony, and Abraham Lincoln, schoolteachers like Nathan Hale and Booker T. Washington, the Philippine Scouts who fought at Bataan, and the soldiers who scaled the bluff at Omaha Beach. If those ideas are worth fighting for—and our history demonstrates that they are—it cannot be true that the flag that uniquely symbolizes their power is not itself worthy of protection from unnecessary desecration."

Although stirring paeans to patriotism and history, the two dissents did not confront the constitutional issue: the meaning of freedom of expression. Indeed, their very emotional content underscored the power of Brennan's analysis: precisely because a flag-burning generated such strong political feelings, it deserved the protection of the First Amendment. Significantly, conservatives like Scalia and Kennedy, as well as liberals like Marshall and Blackmun, joined Brennan.

Immediately after the decision, President George Bush called for a constitutional amendment to overturn the holding. Initially, there was great public support for Bush on this issue, but within months most opinion polls showed that a majority of Americans did not want to see an amendment to the Bill of Rights. Many newspapers, especially conservative papers in the South and Midwest, argued that however bad flag-burning might be, amending the Bill of Rights was worse.

In October 1989, Congress passed a law making it a federal crime to desecrate the U.S. flag. Some Republicans loyal to President Bush argued against a statute, on the grounds that it would violate the Constitution, as interpreted in *Texas v. Johnson*. These congressmen and senators also thought they could use the flag issue and the demand for a protective amendment as political weapons in future elections. Ultimately, though, most members of Congress supported the bill. President Bush allowed the bill to become law without his signature, because he was holding out for a constitutional amendment.

On October 19, 1989, the Senate voted 51–48 in favor of a constitutional amendment to restrict flag-burning. This was far short of the necessary two-thirds majority needed to send an amendment on to the states, and so the amendment died. Opponents of the amendment included over 11 Republicans, who broke with their president on this issue. Some had initially favored an amendment, but changed their minds as opposition to amending the Bill of Rights grew. By this time, national sentiment had shifted against an amendment to the Bill of Rights. Senator John Danforth, a Missouri Republican who had previously supported an amendment, now argued against it. He warned that those who voted for the amendment should not turn it into a political issue in a future election. They might castigate those who opposed the amendment for being "soft" on the flag, but, he warned, opponents of the amendment would successfully argue that they had in fact stuck up for the Constitution.

The initial political response to the flag-burning is significant for an understanding of the Bill of Rights and American culture. A popular president took a strong position in favor of amending the Bill of Rights because of his own emotional response to the decision. Many politicians initially hedged on the issue, but when brought to a vote nearly a majority of the Senate opposed any tinkering with America's basic freedoms. More significantly, most Americans rejected the simplistic patriotic appeal to the flag for the more intellectually and politically complex view that freedom of speech and the First Amendment are even more important than the symbol of the flag. Most Americans agreed that what Johnson did was reprehensible, but that freedom of expression was too valuable to risk, even for such an offensive act as burning the flag.

Instead of amending the Constitution, Congress wrote a new statute, designed to protect the flag from desecration. Immediately, a number of Americans challenged this law by actually burning the flag. In *United States v. Eichman* (1990), the Supreme Court reaffirmed its original flag-burning ruling by the same 5–4 vote. A new movement to amend the Constitution began. Opponents of an amendment immediately reconstituted the "Emergency Committee to Defend the First Amendment," which was led by an unusual coalition of civil libertarians and conservatives. The three co-chairs of the committee were New York University professor Norman Dorsen, president of the American Civil Liberties Union; Harvard Law School professor Charles Fried, who had been solicitor general under President Ronald Reagan; and President Richard Nixon's former solicitor general, Erwin Griswold. Other opponents of the amendment included three former presidents of the American Bar Association. After much heated debate, a majority of the House of Representatives voted for an amendment, but this majority was far short of the two-thirds needed to send the amendment on to the Senate and then to the states. Thus, as of June 1990, the flag-burning amendment was dead. With little public support for the amendment, and a great deal of opposition from the entire political spectrum, the amendment failed, despite attempts by President Bush and the Republican minority in the House to make this a litmus test of patriotism for members of Congress running for reelection. Particularly significant was the opposition to the amendment from a number of Democratic congressmen and senators who had served in the Vietnam War with great distinction, and had no doubt that the electorate understood the difference between flag-waving and what they conceived to be a patriotic duty to protect the basic fabric of liberty guaranteed by the Bill of Rights.

Selected Bibliography

Bloom, L.H., Jr. "*Barnette* and *Johnson*: A Tale of Two Opinions." *Iowa Law Review* 75 (Jan. 1990): 417–32.

Comment. "Flag Burning Yes, Loud Music No: What's the Catch?" *University of Miami Law Review* 44 (March 1990): 1033–74.

Kmiec, D.W. "In the Aftermath of *Johnson* and *Eichman*: The Constitution Need Not Be Mutilated to Preserve the Government's Speech and Property." *Brigham Young University Law Review* (1990): 577–638.

B. Freedom of the Press

MYTH AND REALITY: THE CASE OF JOHN PETER ZENGER

by William F. Steirer, Jr.
Department of History
Clemson University

New York v. Zenger (1735) [New York colonial court]

Few court proceedings have contributed more to the mythology of the American libertarian tradition than the case of John Peter Zenger in 1735. As recently as January 1989, a South Carolina assemblyman, Joe Wilder, justified his attack on the state's criminal libel law by referring to John Peter Zenger. Wilder noted that *Zenger* had established a principle that South Carolina was overdue in embracing.

Zenger, an interesting case with surprising twists and turns, involved a poorly educated and poorly trained printer whose role in the drama that unfolded in New York during 1734–35 was more coincidental than intentional. Political foes of Governor William Cosby had attracted Zenger to New York in 1733 to print the *New York Weekly Journal* for them. However, Zenger was "free" to publish only items that Cosby's foes wished published. These foes included James Alexander and William Smith, who would later serve as Zenger's first lawyers in the famous case.

The so-called Popular party had opposed Cosby's policies from the moment Cosby had landed in New York on August 1, 1732. One party member lamented, "If the Hand of Providence does not arrest and give us some relief very quickly, I cannot see that any one Man of Honor and Honesty can remain in this Province without falling a sacrifice to the basest and vilest of villains." Historians have universally accepted the Popular party's version of events during the three years of Cosby's administration, citing the governor's avariciousness and arbitrariness.

Prior to his position at the *New York Weekly Journal*, Zenger had done little to distinguish himself in the printing business. Born in Germany in 1697, he reached New York in 1710 and was an apprentice to William Bradford, Governor Cosby's printer. Finishing his apprenticeship in 1719, Zenger moved to Maryland, but in 1722 he returned to New York, where he was eventually hired to print the newspaper that would expose Cosby's "villainies." He was available, lacked better prospects and, apparently, was politically naive and unaware. It was Alexander who actually decided what to print of a politically sensitive nature.

The *New York Weekly Journal* added much spice to the political life of the colony, being filled with articles critical of Cosby and his supporters. Zenger's legal battle began with Chief Justice James Delancey opening court on January 15, 1734, by directing the grand jury to indict Zenger for seditious libel. This effort to indict failed, as did another grand jury charge on October 15, 1734. On October 17, the Governor's Council asked the Assembly to join with the council in having the common hangman burn Numbers 7, 47, 48, and 49 of Zenger's paper and in prosecuting the printer. After the Assembly refused, the Court of Quarter Sessions was asked to authorize burning the papers. On November 6, that court, filled with foes of Cosby, also refused to comply. Thus, the sheriff ordered his slave to burn the four "condemned" copies.

Zenger was arrested on November 17, 1734, by a council warrant that was probably illegal. In theory, the council could act with the governor only as a court for the correction of errors and appeals and should legally have extended to Zenger a prior opportunity to defend himself. Chief Justice Delancey refused to grant Zenger reasonable bail, so the hapless printer remained in jail for 260 days. Meanwhile, Alexander and Smith challenged the commissions of Judges Delancey and Philipse but succeeded only in getting themselves disbarred. Instead of using an inexperienced replacement who would have to deal with two implacable judicial enemies, Alexander hired the distinguished Philadelphia attorney, Andrew Hamilton, to take over Zenger's defense.

Together, Alexander and Hamilton produced the defense that eventually proved victorious at the trial on August 4, 1735. That defense was blessed with a jury that looked to be favorably disposed toward the Popular party. Furthermore, the prosecution had drawn a poorly worded charge that read, "printing and publishing a false, scandalous and seditious libel." The defense strategy was simple: admit that Zenger had printed the newspapers in question, but argue that a true statement could not be libelous and that the jury should decide the law as well as the facts in the case. The charge that Zenger had printed "a false . . . libel" made it easier to accomplish both tasks, since the jury seemed primed to believe that Zenger had printed only "true" stories.

Never did the attorney general deny that the newspaper stories were accurate. He relied on the common-law rule that mere publication constituted a libelous action and that a truthful story represented a greater threat to good order than did a false story. Why he included the superfluous word "false" in his charge, he never explained. Its inclusion was almost unheard of in the history of libel prosecutions and seems to have resulted from the incompetence of an officeholder chosen more for his loyalty to "friends" than for his legal skills.

The Alexander-Hamilton strategy worked precisely because the lawyers' argument that the jury should determine whether the statements were true met with the jury's approval. Hamilton noted that men are free to say anything about God without punishment, "I think it is pretty clear that in New York a man may make very free with his God, but he must take special care what he says of his governor." Hamilton questioned whether this law was appropriate for a free society.

Hamilton argued further that the notion that a true statement would provoke vengeance,

thereby breaching the peace, was absurd. That truth constituted an offense worse than falsehood harkened back to Star Chamber days and, said Hamilton, had no place in a free society. Today, for most Americans "Star Chamber" has little meaning, but for provincial New Yorkers in the 1730s, who revered the movement that had culminated in parliamentary sovereignty and the notion that law should be public and impartial, it possessed great meaning. Few charges that Hamilton hurled at the prosecution could have possessed more power.

After innumerable citations and pages filled with arguments, the King's attorney concluded his case by demanding that Zenger, having confessed to printing "two scandalous libels," must be found guilty. Delancey's charge to the jury emphasized that as a matter of law, it must declare Zenger guilty of libel. The jury rebuffed both men and quickly returned a verdict of not guilty.

Zenger was never cited seriously in an English court of law during the eighteenth century, and it was never a factor in the evolution of English law on seditious libel. As hard as it may be to believe in view of the *Zenger* trial's reputation, that is also the situation in American law.

The mythologizing process began almost immediately with the Corporation of the City of New York honoring Hamilton for "his learned and generous defense of the rights of mankind, and the liberty of the press." Between 1735–37, the news percolated slowly through the British Empire, with Hamilton receiving generally enthusiastic accolades. But nowhere did the case establish a legal precedent. In the Empire, people became aware of developing notions of free speech and free press, but that awareness did not translate into fundamental changes. The frequent arguments advanced to the effect that *Zenger* accomplished fundamental changes in thinking are done, as Leonard Levy so cogently put it, in "anticipation of the past." Too many scholars, even those as competent as Zechariah Chafee, instead of observing what did happen, have read back into the past what they wanted to have had happen. Levy observed further that "[t]he American contribution to libertarian theory on freedom of speech and press, so strikingly absent prior to the Zenger case of 1735, was inconspicuous for long after."

Myth-making must fill a need, and in this case the need was to find answers to the question, "how did the libertarian notion of a free press begin and develop?" To place the beginnings of that notion two generations before the Revolution and five generations before the principle became securely fixed in America law is clearly bad history.

Zenger represents another facet of American law—the careful designing of a strategy that relied on popular feelings rather than legal craft. What Alexander and Hamilton did was attack an unpopular governor who presented an oppressive, tyrannical face to the world and to appeal to the prejudices of a particular jury in order to gain sympathy for the unfortunate Zenger. All that the two successful lawyers proved, however, was that juries could be susceptible to prevailing prejudices—as readily swayed by emotion, interest, or ignorance as were judges.

Once *Zenger* was finished, three factors hampered its use as a precedent. One lay in the difficulty of relying on jury verdicts to provide definitions of law. The jury's verdict may represent one view of law. But what law? And how predictable? And who applies or interprets it? Since two separate groups of 12 people would not necessarily look at a situation in the same way, *Zenger* might have turned out differently if it had been argued before another jury. Law in such circumstances is whimsical and capricious. Precedents do not get established on such a basis.

A second difficulty arose from one of the strengths of the *Zenger* verdict. The fundamental premise of *Zenger* is that "truth" cannot be considered a libel—that truth marks how far men may go in writing, publishing, or speaking about authority. But truth, in many cases, cannot be proven or disproven. Truth is usually a matter of opinion, and one man's truth is not everyone's. Truth in *Zenger* depended on one jury's acquiescence in a definition of "truth" founded in a particular situation.

Third, Alexander and Hamilton were themselves acutely aware of the need for order, admitting that "to infuse into the minds of the people an ill opinion of a just administration, is a crime that deserves no mercy . . . ." This belief qualified their victory for "individual freedom" in *Zenger*. For eighteenth century Anglo-Americans, the value of order generally surpassed the value of justice.

For these reasons, *Zenger* had little practical effect in law. Following the *Zenger* decision, while governors no longer could get away with prosecuting printers for libel, popularly elected assemblies could and did. They did so throughout the remainder of the eighteenth century and into the nineteenth, not bothering to go into court after printers, but dragging errant printers before legislative assemblies where truth proved to be no defense.

Truth proved not to be a defense in libel cases until the passage of a New York sedition act and its interpretation in an 1864 New York case. Far less famous than *Zenger*, *People v. Croswell* nonetheless proved more significant in advancing the legal concept of a free press, for it was in the very next year that the New York legislature accepted the doctrine that truth is a defense in libel cases. Victory was not immediately complete, but the process that had begun haltingly and reluctantly in *Zenger* was on its triumphant way to final success.

Selected Bibliography

Alexander, J. *A Brief Narrative of the Case and Trial of John Peter Zenger*. S.N. Katz, ed. Cambridge, MA: Harvard University Press, 1963.

Levy, L.W. *Emergence of a Free Press*. New York: Oxford University Press, 1985.

———. *Freedom of Speech and Press in Early American History: Legacy of Suppression*. New York: Harper & Row, 1963.

Rutherford, L. *John Peter Zenger, His Press, His Trial and a Bibliography of Zenger Imprints*. New York: Peter Smith, 1941.

Salmon, L.M. *The Newspaper and Authority*. New York: Octagon Books, 1976.

THE SEDITION ACT AND THE PRICE OF A FREE PRESS

by Mary K. Bonsteel Tachau
Department of History
University of Louisville

United States v. Callender, 15 Federal Cases 239 (1800) [U.S. Federal District Court]

James Thomson Callender was a journalist whose scandalmongering made him notable even in an era of sensationalists. During his remarkable career, his wide swath humiliated Alexander Hamilton, infuriated John Adams, contributed to the impeachment of Samuel Chase, clouded the reputation of Thomas Jefferson, and led to his own conviction and imprisonment.

Callender's career as a critic of government and of governmental officials began in Scotland. In 1793, he ran afoul of the British law of seditious libel, which held that government was profoundly injured by criticism, especially if it was true. His book *The Political Progress of Great Britain*, published in 1792, led to his indictment. He fled to the United States to escape trial.

By 1796, Callender felt sufficiently knowledgeable about America that he published *History of the United States for 1796*, which brought him a well-deserved reputation as a muckraker. Among other revelations, the book disclosed that, in 1791, Alexander Hamilton had had an affair with the wife of James Reynolds, a well-known speculator in securities issued during the War for Independence. Hamilton responded by writing a book in which he admitted that charge but denied another Callender allegation that he had conspired with Reynolds to buy up certificates that, with his funding program, were redeemable at face value (which was probably also true). Callender also reported that as a bachelor, Thomas Jefferson had tried to seduce a married woman. Vice President Jefferson, too, confessed to his indiscretion. The acknowledged truth of Callender's assertions added to his stature.

By 1798, Callender had settled in Philadelphia, where he made common cause with Benjamin Franklin Bache and William Duane of the Republican newspaper *Aurora*. Callender soon joined in contributing to their anti-Federalist columns and sometimes edited the paper during Bache's absence.

Meanwhile, the wars of the French Revolution continued in Europe. Hoping to bring an end to French attacks on American shipping, President Adams had sent John Marshall and Elbridge Gerry to join Charles Cotesworth Pinckney to negotiate a treaty of amity and commerce with France. After some months, French envoys (called Messieurs X, Y, and, Z in the Americans' dispatches) agreed to meet only if the Americans met conditions that were unacceptable and humiliating. News of what was called "The XYZ Affair" set off a torrent of indignation throughout the United States.

The Federalist-controlled Congress responded by providing for a new standing army, a small navy, and the arming of American merchant ships. More ominously, it also moved against a perceived threat from within the nation by passing four measures directed at aliens and critics of the government. The three statutes affecting aliens tripled the time required for naturalization, gave the president authority in time of peace to deport aliens he believed dangerous, and in time of war to imprison them.

The fourth statute was the Sedition Act, which made it a high misdemeanor punishable by up to two years in prison and a fine of $2,000 to combine or conspire with intent to oppose any measures of the government. It also made it a crime for anyone to "write, print, utter or publish . . . any false, scandalous and malicious writing . . . against the government of the United States, or either house of the Congress . . . or the President . . . with intent to defame . . . or to bring them, or any of them, into contempt or disrepute." The vice president, against whom the statute was aimed, was conspicuously omitted from its proscriptions.

The Sedition Act violated the free speech and free press provisions of the First Amendment, whose unequivocal command was that "Congress shall make no law . . . abridging the freedom of speech, or of the press." Yet fewer than seven years after the amendment had been ratified, Congress passed just such a law. Its supporters noted that, unlike the common-law crime of seditious libel, it provided for truth as a defense and gave juries the right to determine the law as well as the facts. Nevertheless, it was clearly intended to silence domestic opponents and to cripple the opposition party: it was to expire on March 3, 1801, the day that the winner of the election of 1800 would take office. But when it was signed by Adams on July 14, 1798, it became the law of the land for two and one-half years. Presumed violators of the statute, passed by a Federalist Congress and signed by a Federalist president, would be tried in courts before Federalist judges. Critics of the government rightly feared its consequences. After a series of prosecutions and convictions of Republicans in Vermont, Massachusetts, New Jersey, Pennsylvania, and New York, the Sedition Act provided the occasion for a confrontation between Justice of the U.S. Supreme Court Samuel Chase and James Thomson Callender.

Chase, who had once championed the anti-Federalist cause in Maryland but who had since become an ultra-Federalist, had agreed to take the middle circuit for the spring of 1800. His progress through those states could be measured by the gasps of indignation that accompanied his management of their dockets. Chase was on the warpath against anyone whom he perceived to be a threat to Federalism and order. At the Sedition Act trial of Thomas Cooper in New York, he shifted the burden of proof to the defendant, requiring him to prove his innocence (instead of the prosecutor proving guilt). In Pennsylvania, he presided over the second treason trial of John Fries for his participation in the insurrection of the Northampton Insurgents (the so-called Fries Rebellion). There he issued the opinion of the court before the trial began; this led to the defense lawyers' refusal to continue in the case.

Chase then stormed into Delaware, and when neither the federal attorney nor the grand jury proffered victims, he referred them to Wilmington to get an indictment against a printer whom he believed to be seditious. Frustrated by their refusal to cooperate, Chase moved into Virginia, where, he promised, he would teach the lawyers the difference between liberty and licentiousness of the press—if a jury of honest men could be found there. He carried with him a copy of Callender's latest political pamphlet, *The Prospect Before Us*, with offensive passages carefully underlined.

By this time, Callender had become a citizen and, leaving his children behind, moved to Petersburg, Virginia. Believing that no judge in the Republican stronghold of Virginia would attempt to enforce the Sedition Act, he soon found compatible work on the Richmond *Examiner*. He had, however, underrated Secretary of State Timothy Pickering. Determined to silence the Republican press before the election of 1800, Pickering had instructed the federal attorney for the district to scrutinize the *Examiner* and to prosecute the perpetrators of "any libelous matter against the government or its officers."

The attorney had not only the newspaper as grist for his mill; he also had Callender's pamphlet, which gave the public, as its author had promised, "such a Tornado as no Govt ever got before." In it, Callender described the prospect before us as a choice between Jefferson ("that man whose life is unspotted by crime") and Adams ("that hoary headed incendiary . . . whose hands are reeking with . . . blood").

A grand jury, allegedly packed with Federalists, promptly responded to Chase's charge and brought a presentment against Callender as an offender against the sedition law, and the Federalist federal attorney drew up an indictment. Yet Callender was not without friends. The citizens of Caroline County contributed $100 for the support of his children, and three prominent Virginians contributed their services as defense counsel: the attorney general, the governor's son-in-law, and the clerk of the House of Delegates. They asked for a continuance until November to secure witnesses and documents, but Chase denied it on the ground that anyone who published an alleged libel ought always to have on hand the documents that would prove its truthfulness.

The trial, which began on June 3, 1800, was marked by what had become Chase's trademarks and would become charges in his later impeachment. Chase overruled defense counsel repeatedly and proclaimed that Callender's book was false and his intent obvious. He upheld the prosecution's assertions that Callender had to prove his own innocence and, despite the wording of the statute, that truth was not a defense. The judge admitted the book as evidence, although it was not mentioned in the indictment. He refused to let a defense witness testify on the ground that unless he could disprove all of the charges, his evidence on one was inadmissable. He denied the right of the jury to consider the constitutionality of the Sedition Act. He declared that it was his duty (not that of the executive branch) to execute the laws. Finally, his behavior caused Callender's attorneys, like Fries's, to withdraw from the case.

Whether the petit jury was packed cannot be proved, but all of its members were Federalists, and after only two hours, they returned a verdict of guilty. Chase congratulated them because they had shown that federal laws could be enforced in Virginia, "the principal object of this prosecution." He proceeded to lecture Callender for his "ungenerous" behavior as a foreigner who presumed to criticize the president and who disobeyed the laws of his adopted country. Callender was sentenced to nine months in prison, fined $200, and required to post a $1,200 bond guaranteeing his good behavior for two years.

Unrepentant and unsilenced, Callender wrote a second volume of The *Prospect Before Us* while in prison. To his list of despised Federalists, he added Chase: "the most detestable and detested rascal in the state of Maryland." Far from discrediting him, Callender's conviction brought him an even wider audience, and his writings and the accounts of his trial circu-

lated as campaign documents in the election of 1800.

Callender served out his sentence until Thomas Jefferson became president in March 1801. One of his first acts was to pardon Callender and the four others still imprisoned under the Sedition Act and to order compensation for the fines they had paid. That was not enough for Callender, who asked the president to appoint him postmaster in Richmond. When Jefferson refused, Callender fought back. In September 1802, as editor of the Federalist Richmond *Recorder*, he published the most sensational story of his notorious career, alleging that the president "for many years past has kept, as his concubine, one of his own slaves . . . [whose] name is SALLY" and by whom he had several children.

Although impossible to prove, the charge was also impossible to disprove. Nineteenth-century British travelers who were critics of the American experiment in democratic government spread and extended Callender's allegation: it suited their purposes to believe that the author of the Declaration of Independence was a hypocrite. Such a rumor about such a man has had a remarkable longevity. Two hundred years after they achieved notoriety, Chase, Callender, and even the Sedition Act are footnotes to history. But the Jefferson miscegenation myth lives on as an ironic reminder of the cost of a free press.

Selected Bibliography

Ellis, R.E. *The Jeffersonian Crisis: Courts and Politics in the Young Republic.* New York: W.W. Norton & Co., Inc., 1971.

Miller, J.C. *The Federalist Era, 1789–1801.* New York: Harper & Row, 1960.

Moss, S.P., and C. Moss. "The Jefferson Miscegenation Legend in British Travel Books." *Journal of the Early Republic* 7 (Fall 1987): 253–74.

Smith, J.M. *Freedom's Fetters: The Alien and Sedition Laws and American Civil Liberties.* Ithaca, NY: Cornell University Press, 1956.

THE LIMITS OF PRIOR RESTRAINT

by Paul L. Murphy
Department of History
University of Minnesota

Near v. Minnesota, 283 U.S. 697 (1931) [U.S. Supreme Court]

When the decision in *Near v. Minnesota* was handed down in June 1931, one legal expert promptly called it "the most important decision rendered since the adoption of the first amendment." Significantly, it was the first case in which the U.S. Supreme Court held that the freedom of the press provision of the First Amendment should be applied to the states. The case involved a Minneapolis scandal sheet and a state nuisance law passed to close down just such publications. In ruling that state law unconstitutional, Chief Justice Charles E. Hughes found, in the "general conception" of liberty of the press, as adapted by the federal constitution, the essential attribute of freedom from prior restraint, which the five-member majority was convinced the state had violated. Thus freedom from prior restraint, a concept embraced by William Blackstone in the eighteenth century, finally gained formal constitutional status in the fourth decade of the twentieth, opening a new area of permissible press expression and criticism.

The background of the case was legally and historically significant. In 1925, the Minnesota legislation had passed a public nuisance law, called a "gag law" by its critics, for one purpose—to close down John Morison's Duluth *Rip-Saw*, a newspaper notorious for its vicious attacks on public officials, both in that city and in the state. The law permitted a single judge, acting without a jury, to stop the publication by injunction of a newspaper or a magazine, if he found it "obscene, lewd, and lascivious . . . or malicious, scandalous and defamatory." More broadly at issue, however, was the question of how much the public, through the media, had a right to know about the actions of its governing officials, the policies they intended to follow, and the methods they planned to use in that pursuit, as well as the degree to which they indulged their own human venality. Questions were also raised as to the proper use of press

freedom and the responsibility of both government officials and media decision-makers to the public and to the general welfare of the nation. The steps leading up to the case's final adjudication tell an interesting story of attempts to answer such questions.

In 1927, Jay M. Near and Howard Guilford established the *Saturday Press* in Minneapolis. Near, an experienced journalist, was known for his bigotry against Catholics, blacks, Jews, and organized labor. Guilford had run scandal sheets in other cities that focused on exposing gambling, prostitution, and the sexual adventures of the local elite. Both Near and Guilford, however, specialized in reporting scandals in a sensational manner. From its first issue, the *Saturday Press* hammered away at supposed ties between gangsters and police. In a series of florid stories, the *Press* elicited not only verbal hostility and denunciation but also provoked a gangland attempt to kill Guilford (with assailants pumping four bullets into his car). Hit, he recovered and went on to expose city and county officials, attacking not only Minneapolis Police Chief Frank Brunskill, but also the future governor of Minnesota, then country prosecutor, Floyd B. Olson, for ties to the Minneapolis Jewish underworld. Near and Guilford wrote: "Practically every vendor of vile hooch, every owner of a moonshine still, every snake-faced gangster and embryonic yegg in the Twin Cities is a JEW." Specifically, the paper accused Olson of being a Jew-lover and dragging his feet in the investigation of gangland pursuits. Olson was enraged. On November 21, 1927, he filed a complaint under the state nuisance law with Hennepin County District Judge Mathias Baldwin, charging that the *Saturday Press* had defamed Mayor George Leach, Police Chief Brunskill, and Charles G. Davis, head of the Law Enforcement League, as well as the *Minneapolis Tribune*, the *Minneapolis Journal*, the Hennepin County grand jury, Olson himself, and the entire Jewish community. He went on to argue that continued publication of the paper was harmful to the community at large and that the public should be protected against it. The judge issued a temporary restraining order closing down the paper. Near and Guilford promptly demurred, arguing that the statute authorizing such a "padlock injunction" was unconstitutional. They in turn pointed to a clear statement in the Minnesota constitution that "the liberty of the press shall forever remain inviolate, and all persons may freely speak, write, and publish their sentiments on all subjects." The judge, conscious of this guarantee, certified an appeal in the case to the Minnesota Supreme Court, leaving to it the question of the law's constitutionality.

The removal of the *Saturday Press* from the streets was popular in the Twin Cities. Many people praised Olson's actions and those of the judge who had issued the restraining order. But its removal did little to hinder ongoing criminal action. In fact, shortly after the ban, a county grand jury began probing various charges of misconduct against Police Chief Brunskill, several having been first lodged against him in the *Saturday Press*. Olson called 17 witnesses (including Guilford), and the grand jury listened to charges ranging from political impropriety to allegations of covering up criminal behavior.

In the Minnesota Supreme Court, Near's attorney, Thomas Latimer, a talented Minneapolis lawyer who would later become mayor, raised the constitutional issue. The law, he contended, violated the state constitution. In addition, it was null, void, and invalid because it violated the Fourteenth Amendment of the U.S. Constitution. Latimer also stressed the denial of a jury trial, guaranteed by the Sixth Amendment, and contended that the entire concept of freedom of the press, guaranteed by the First Amendment, had been breached. He further argued that the due process clause of the Fifth Amendment, which he believed had been made applicable to the states by the passage of the Fourteenth, had been violated.

The Minnesota Supreme Court was unimpressed. Speaking through its chief justice, Samuel B. Wilson, it ruled unanimously to uphold the state law. Comparing the *Saturday Press* to houses of prostitution, noxious

weeds, itinerant carnivals, saloons, lotteries, and malicious fences, Wilson asserted that the legislature had the power to do away with such nuisances. In Minnesota, he argued, no one could stifle the truthful voice of the press, but the Constitution's drafters never intended for it to protect malice, scandal, and defamation.

By this time, the case had drawn national attention, in the legal community and more broadly. The law was seen as a model—a "wise and desirable remedy"—for the evils of yellow journalism. The national student debate topic for 1930 was: "Resolved: That the Minnesota Nuisance Law Should be Adopted by Every State in the Union." Other states were being urged to use their local police power in similar fashion.

Many were persuaded by arguments supporting the law. The complications of ordinary censorship, or of prior restraint, made such censorship impractical. It would be impossible for government censors to read every magazine and delete every falsehood, exaggeration, indecency, or obscenity. Censorship would require an enormous, highly trained staff and would, therefore, be expensive and unworkable. Legal actions against undesirable publications would also fail completely. Prosecutions under the criminal libel statutes would not result in effective repression of such literature. Further, civil actions for damages could not prevent the harm done and did not guarantee against a repetition of the offenses.

The publicity given to trials sometimes does more harm than good. In addition, the expense of trials and appeals puts these remedies out of the reach of all except the wealthy. Supporters argued that the Minnesota law could be applied promptly and could stop obscenity, indecency, falsehood, and defamation, as well as end the publication of scandal sheets completely. It could, in other words, make the journalistic profession responsible again, intimidate the criminal element among writers and publishers, and encourage reputable newspapers and magazines. Freedom of the press would not be impaired—it never meant a license to publish scandalous, malicious, obscene, or indecent matters. Finally, gag-law advocates contended that the First Amendment did not limit the power of the state governments; it merely limited Congress. Each state could properly regulate its own newspapers, magazines, and news agencies under its police power.

Clearly, the law established positive regulatory overtones. It sought to protect the property rights of certain individuals against blackmailers and scandalmongers who might damage their reputation and standing in the community and thus injure them financially. The purpose of the law placed the public welfare above any First Amendment rights that people might claim. To the extent that it protected "liberty," the law saw liberty as the citizen's freedom from the evil impacts of this new journalistic development; certainly it was not the liberty of members of the "fourth estate" to publish freely what they wanted.

But civil libertarians, including responsible publishers, were alarmed by this cavalier attitude toward a basic constitutional right. In New York and Chicago, the Minnesota gag order was being viewed with alarm. The American Civil Liberties Union (ACLU) sent money from New York for Near's legal defense, and ACLU lawyers focused on the doctrine of prior restraint. Before then, the only control of the press had been through prosecution for criminal or libelous matter after the material had been printed. "We see in this new device for previous restraint of publication a menace to the whole principle of the freedom of the press," the ACLU stated. It also saw the public nuisance law as a dangerous model: "If the Minnesota law is unconstitutional, then the Fourteenth Amendment and inferentially the First Amendment no longer protects the press against prior restraint."

Minnesota newspaper editors scoffed at the ACLU's fears. But the editor of the *Chicago Tribune* was not as myopic. Colonel Robert ("Bertie") Rutherford McCormick admired Near for his guts. Ultraconservative in his politics, McCormick disliked blacks, Jews, and other minorities, to say nothing of labor unions, and he had fought many legal battles over exposé-type articles published in his newspaper and particularly aimed at public officials. He agreed to provide extensive legal counsel in the case and ultimately succeeded in drawing the American Newspaper Publisher's Association behind Near's cause—that body contending that

Minnesota's action rendered all guarantees of free speech valueless in the state, and choked off thought and expression that should be constitutionally protected. The *New York Times* also editorially deplored the Minnesota statute as a "vicious law." Many other national newspapers did also.

The case was appealed to the U.S. Supreme Court, which for the first time heard a freedom of the press case involving the role of the states and the vital and venerable principle of prior restraint. It also returned to consideration of an ancient dilemma that had bothered James Madison, the leading "father" of the First Amendment.

Madison, in his concern for the potential abuse of governmental power, had been convinced the Constitution should forbid not only Congress but the executive and judiciary from limiting the guarantees to be placed in the First Amendment. And he had wanted more. Possibly anticipating a situation such as the one in *Near*, and clearly responding to the repressive behavior of some of the states during the confederation period, he advocated an amendment that he considered "the most valuable in the whole list." It stated that "no State shall violate the equal right of conscience, (or of the) freedom of the press . . . because it is proper that every Government should be disarmed of powers which trench upon those particular rights." "I cannot see any reason," he said, "against obtaining even a double security on these points. . . . It must be admitted, on all hands, that the State Governments are as liable to attack these invaluable privileges as is the General Government, and therefore ought to be as cautiously guarded against." Madison failed. Neither proposal was adopted. Only Congress was initially to be limited by the First Amendment and the states' role was left undesignated. This was done despite Madison's strong plea that the power of censorship should be exercised by the people over the government, and not by the government over the people.

In the argument before the Supreme Court, subsequent and recent history was on Near's side. Justice Louis D. Brandeis, the most eloquent justice on this issue, had been steering the Court for a decade toward protecting free speech and the press against state legislation by stressing the term "liberty" in the due process clause of the Fourteenth Amendment. "I cannot believe," he had argued in *Gilbert v. Minnesota* (1920), that "the liberty guaranteed by the Fourteenth Amendment includes only liberty to acquire and enjoy property." Further, he had strongly supported that Court's first steps in the mid-1920s to apply the First Amendment protections of speech and press against the states.

Brandeis had prepared himself assiduously for the *Near* appeal, even probing into the ousting of Police Chief Brunskill, an action that was not unrelated to the attacks on that official by the *Saturday Press* itself. Thus, when the *Chicago Tribune*'s attorney, Weymouth Kirkland, contended that the injunction closing the *Saturday Press* was a prior restraint violating the First and Fourteenth Amendments, Brandeis clearly agreed. The *Saturday Press*'s articles, Kirkland had argued, were defamatory. But "so long as men do evil, so long will newspapers publish defamation. Every person does have a constitutional right to publish malicious, scandalous, and defamatory materials, though untrue, and with bad motives, and for unjustifiable ends." Such persons could always be punished afterwards. But the remedy was not prior censorship of the offending newspaper. Rather, the state should bring specific criminal charges against such a newspaper after it has published the material.

The counsel for Minnesota was Deputy State Attorney General James F. Markham, along with William C. Larson, and Arthur I. Markve, representing the Hennepin County prosecutor's office, which had brought the original injunction. Markham argued that the law was constitutional and that the injunction was not a prior restraint. The public nuisance law was well within the police powers of the state. It was the responsibility of the state to interpret the provisions of the state constitution. The state court had done so, and it had done so properly.

Brandeis, in a questioning role, however, probed further. How, he asked Markham, can a community secure protection from combinations between criminals and public officials if people are not allowed to engage in free discussion of such matters? "You cannot disclose evil,"

he observed, "without naming the doers of evil. It is difficult to see how one can have a free press and the protection that it affords in the democratic community without the privilege this act seems to limit." This question, he went on, is of prime interest to every U.S. citizen and should be privileged communication. "Assuming it to be true . . .," Markham countered. "No," Brandeis snapped, "even if it was not true, a malicious and scandalous statement could not be restrained before publication. A newspaper cannot always wait until it gets the judgment of the court." Sometimes it must invite suits for criminal libel in order to inform the public.

In the secret conference among the justices that followed the oral arguments, Chief Justice Charles E. Hughes elicited from a majority of the conferees the view that the nuisance law was a suppression not just of defamatory material, but of any future publication and thereby a clear violation of the guarantee of no prior restraint. This view was strongly denounced by Justice Pierce Butler, the one Minnesota member of the Supreme Court, who could not understand how Justices Hughes, Brandeis, and Oliver Wendell Holmes, Jr., could give First Amendment protection to scoundrels such as Near and Guilford. The public nuisance law, he argued, was not suppression, but punishment for an injustice already committed.

But the Hughes view prevailed, and the chief justice assigned himself the task of writing the majority opinion. Setting the case in broad national context, he argued: "The administration of government has become more complex, the opportunities for malfeasance and corruption have multiplied, crime has grown to most serious proportions, and the danger of its protection by unfaithful officials and of the impairment of the fundamental security of life and property by criminal alliances and official neglect, emphasize the need of a vigilant and courageous press, especially in great cities. The fact that liberty of the press may be abused by miscreant purveyors of scandal does not make any less necessary the immunity of the press from prior restraint in dealing with official misconduct."

Regarding the limits of public criticism and exposure of officials, Hughes quoted Madison, pointing out that statesman's role as a leading spirit in the preparation of the First Amendment. Hughes stated: "Some degree of abuse is inseparable from the power use of everything, and in no instances is this more true than in that of the press. It has accordingly been decided by the practice of the states that it is better to leave a few of its noxious branches to this luxurious growth than, by pruning them away, to injure the vigour of those yielding the proper fruits." But Hughes also understood Madison in another way as well, and his *Near* opinion finally made concrete the Virginian's desired safeguard in protecting the press freedom from state encroachment. Thus, finding the Minnesota law to be an unconstitutional infringement of freedom of the press, safeguarded by the due process clause of the Fourteenth Amendment, was a latter-day vindication for the First Amendment's initial sponsor.

But there were limits to what the broad prohibition against prior restraint could protect. Minor exceptions did exist. The four suggested exceptions were (1) publication of critical war information ("no one would question but that a government might prevent actual obstruction to its recruiting service or the publication of the sailing dates of transports or the number and location of troops"); (2) publication of obscenity; (3) publications inciting acts of violence against the community or violent overthrow of the government; and (4) publications invading private rights. Contemporary commentators viewed the exceptions as insignificant and hypothetical. Ironically, however, *Near* was to become the doctrinal starting point for most defenses of prior restraint as the legitimacy of those exceptions was later developed. Contemporaneously, it was the broader implications of the majority opinion that gave the decision its historical significance as a turning point in American law and public policy.

Butler, speaking for four dissenters, deplored the ruling. Near and Guilford he was convinced, were threatening the morals, peace, and good order of the state. Their behavior was a nuisance. Any way that such a nuisance could be legally suppressed appeared to be condonable in his eyes.

The immediate reaction to the decision was overwhelmingly positive. The nation's press was generally gratified and relieved. Many newspapers quoted Colonel McCormick's statement that "the decision of Chief Justice Hughes will do down in history as one of the greatest triumphs for free thought." The irrepressible colonel even wrote a letter to Hughes stating: "I think your decision in the Gag Law case will forever remain one of the buttresses of free government." The *Chicago Times*, competitor to the *Tribune*, graciously praised the latter for performing "a public service of high order when it carried the Minnesota case to the Supreme Court." The *New York Times* called the decision "weighty and conclusive," although it added a note of caution: "Freedom of the press, now again happily vindicated and affirmed, is not freedom to be a 'chartered libertine.'" The *New York Herald Tribune* observed that "the very fact the exercise of liberty of the press in this momentous case came before the Supreme Court in the least favorable light adds a buttress of steel to the constitutional guarantee."

The long-range implications of the ruling were many. It brought to a significant new stage Brandeis's long crusade for redefining "liberty" in human rights terms rather than in property rights terms. By using that concept to strike down a state law, the decision logically extended the incorporation theory as it related to freedom of the press. It also shifted the presumptions regarding the constitutionality of state laws. Laws restricting personal liberties now demanded new and vigorous justification, while laws restricting property rights were to be given the judicial benefit of the doubt. Thus, the ruling culminated more than 60 years of struggle over the proper relationship among the federal government, the states, and the citizen regarding First Amendment issues. The press now joined speech in being protected not only from formal federal government restraint but from state restraint and more subtle forms of local restraint, such as those authorized by the Minnesota law.

The ruling was also a reflection of marketplace theory. It strongly stressed the importance in a democratic society of the press being free to carry out its proper function of informing the electorate, particularly about the behavior of public officials. The behavior of the editors of the *Saturday Press* obviously troubled the chief justice. For him, the type of exposé writing they pursued was clearly designed to arouse passions rather than to dispense information. His opinion, however, in some ways blurred this distinction, stressing instead the importance of editors being able to criticize public officials and downplaying any illicit motives the editors might have. Hughes focused on what was defensible rather than indefensible, about Near's operation. In this regard, the opinion came directly to terms with the changing and modernizing conditions that produced much of the new exposé journalism.

Near's subsequent history as a precedent is impressive. The list of cases in which it has been cited takes up two full pages of *Shepard's U.S. Citations* and includes Supreme Court cases, lower federal courts cases, and cases in the supreme courts of many states. Its most famous use came in *New York Times Company v. United States* (1971), the "Pentagon Papers" case involving the Nixon administration's effort to prevent publication of a 47-volume secret history of the Vietnam War and detailing aspects of the reasons behind U.S. involvement. There, attorneys for both sides, cited the decision: opponents of the government's injunction against publication, using the *Near* argument for prior restraint; attorneys for the government focusing on the *Near* exception and stressing the need for the government to restrain publication of information covering a broad range of national defense activities. The court victories of the *New York Times* and the *Washington Post*, was a latter-day victory for Hughes's view, and the view of federal Judge Murray I. Gurfein who, in following *Near*, stated, "[T]here is no greater safety valve for discontent and cynicism about the affairs of government than freedom of expression in any form." Thus, Jay M. Near, although clearly a "miscreant purveyor of scandal," was a catalyst for redefining and extending one of the most basic freedoms of the Bill of Rights.

Selected Bibliography

Blasi, V. "Toward a Theory of Prior Restraint: The Central Linkage." *Minnesota Law Review* 66 (1981): 11–93.

Emerson, T.I. "The Doctrine of Prior Restraint." *Law and Contemporary Problems* 20 (1955): 648–71.

———. *The System of Freedom of Expression.* New York: Random House, 1981.

Friendly, F.W. *Minnesota Rag: The Dramatic Story of the Landmark Supreme Court Case That Gave New Meaning to Freedom of the Press.* New York: Random House, 1981.

Haiman, F.S. *Speech and Law in a Free Society.* Chicago: University of Chicago Press, 1981.

Knoll, E. "National Security: The Ultimate Threat to the First Amendment." *Minnesota Law Review* 66 (1981): 161–70.

Linde, H.A. "Courts and Censorship." *Minnesota Law Review* 66 (1981): 171–208.

Murphy, P.L. "*Near v. Minnesota* in the Context of Historical Development." *Minnesota Law Review* 66 (1981): 95–160.

PUBLIC OFFICIALS, LIBEL, AND A FREE PRESS

by Susan Duffy
Speech Communication Department
California Polytechnic State University

New York Times Company v. Sullivan, 367 U.S. 254 (1964) [U.S. Supreme Court]

On Tuesday, March 29, 1960, as the civil rights movement was struggling for recognition, the *New York Times* ran a full-page advertisement, paid for by the Committee to Defend Martin Luther King and the Struggle for Freedom in the South. Over the names of 64 prominent Americans, with an addended list of 20 southern clergy and civil rights activists, the advertisement outlined a litany of abuses directed against blacks in the South. Racial incidents in Orangeburg, South Carolina, and in Montgomery, Alabama, were outlined specifically, while confrontations in Tallahassee, Atlanta, Nashville, Savannah, Greensboro, Memphis, Richmond, and Charlotte were alluded to in passing. It was the eight-line description of events in Montgomery that rankled L. B. Sullivan, a public official in that city, and prompted him to initiate litigation that would lead to this landmark decision supporting freedom of the press.

The offending lines in the advertisement read: "In Montgomery, Alabama after students sang 'My Country Tis of Thee' on the state capitol steps, their leaders were expelled from school, and truckloads of police armed with shot-guns and tear gas ringed the Alabama State College campus. When the entire student body protested to state authorities by refusing to re-register, their dining hall was padlocked in an attempt to starve them into submission." Three paragraphs later, the advertisement claimed: "Again and again the Southern violators have answered Dr. King's peaceful protest with intimidation and violence. They have bombed his home almost killing his wife and child. They have assaulted his person. They have arrested him seven times—for speeding, loitering and similar offenses."

More than being hyperbolic, these lines contained factual errors which, most probably, influenced the trial courts finding in favor of Sullivan. However, Sullivan's suit against the *New York Times* and four black Alabama clergymen whose names appeared in the advertisement published by the *Times* did not rest on the inaccuracy of the details. Sullivan claimed that he had been defamed in the advertisement through the explicit use of the word "police" and in the implied activity of the police in the arrests of Martin Luther King. Sullivan contended that, as the Montgomery commissioner who supervised the police department, he was considered directly responsible for the actions of that department. His claim essentially was that he, as commissioner, was synonymous with "police." He therefore claimed that he was the one accused for the "ringing" of Alabama State College's campus with police—an inaccurate statement, since the campus was not surrounded; and that the references to the seven (an inflated number) arrests of King, referred to him, since arrests were obviously made by the police. The fact that he was never mentioned by name in the advertisement did not seem to be a salient issue in the circuit court of Montgomery County. It found in favor of Sullivan and awarded him an unprecedented $500,000 in damages. This was one thousand times higher than the $500 penalty provided for under Alabama defamation law.

The Alabama Supreme Court upheld the decision. But when the case reached the U.S. Supreme Court in January 1964, the result was a striking and total repudiation of the lower court decisions. In a 9–0 vote, the Court reversed the decision and remanded it to the state courts for further proceedings. Justice William J. Brennan, Jr., delivered the opinion of the Court. In it he clearly outlined the constitutional deficiencies in the Alabama libel law, which empowered states to award damages to public officials when their official conduct had been the target of criticism. Comparing it to the notorious Sedition Act of 1798, which prohibited criticism of the government and elected officials, Brennan argued that the Alabama law directly threatened First Amendment freedoms by "raising . . . the possibility that a good-faith critic of government will be penalized for his criticism." Brennan continued: "[T]he Constitution delimits a State's power to award damages for libel in actions brought by public officials against their official conduct." He maintained that impersonal attacks on governmental operations could not be construed to be libelous statements directed maliciously against the individual official responsible for those operations.

The justices discounted Sullivan's claim that his personal reputation was damaged because of the advertisement even though he was not mentioned in it by name. Brennan noted that Sullivan made no effort to prove that he had suffered real financial loss as a result of the libelous statements. An interesting footnote to this charge in Brennan's opinion further undermines Sullivan's claim by noting that of the 650,000 copies of the *Times* distributed that day, only 394 copies containing the advertisement were circulated in Alabama, and only 35 of those in Montgomery County. The likelihood of Sullivan suffering great loss was substantially reduced when one considered how few people would have seen the advertisement, read it in its entirety, and then concluded that Sullivan was the one being singled out for blame. Brennan reiterated the position taken in earlier decisions that criticism of public officials is not merely a right but a duty that must not be stifled.

Justice Hugo L. Black, adding a separate opinion with which Justice William O. Douglas concurred, said that unlike the Court opinion that rested on a myriad of issues, his vote rested exclusively on the *Times* and the individual clergymen's "absolute, unconditional constitutional right" to publish criticism of the Montgomery agencies' and officials' handling of the incidents recounted. Black maintained that the "factual background" to this case underscored the enormous threat posed by state libel laws to a free press. As a native Alabamian, Black's assessment of the facts of the case came very close to leveling charges of bigotry at the decisions of his state's trial courts. He wrote that despite several decisions of the Supreme Court forbidding segregation in public schools, Montgomery had manifested "widespread hostility" toward desegregation and that this hostility had been extended to anyone in favor of desegregation—labeling them "outside agitators." This appellation, he pointed out, was one that could readily be applied to the *New York Times*. Black maintained that there was pre-

sented no proof that Sullivan had suffered any damages. In fact, Black commented that a realistic appraisal of the record could lead one to infer that Sullivan's "political, social and financial" prestige had been enhanced rather than hurt by the advertisement.

New York Times Company v. Sullivan reaffirmed the rights of citizens and the press to criticize the government. For Sullivan to have won, the Court required proof of "actual malice" on the part of the *New York Times*. The decision to reverse and remand was one that worked to eliminate the chilling effect that could potentially paralyze the nation's press in its coverage of political issues and figures. In spite of criticisms of the decision that claimed that the Court established two separate standards for libel—one for private citizens and one for public figures—the decision of the Court is one against which libel cases have been measured for the last 25 years.

Selected Bibliography

Del Russo, A.D. "Freedom of the Press and Defamation: Attacking the Bastion of *New York Times Co. v. Sullivan.*" *St. Louis University Law Journal* 25 (1981): 501–41.

Lewis, A. *Make No Law: The Sullivan Case and the First Amendment.* New York: Random House, 1941.

PUBLIC PERSONALITIES AND THE RIGHT TO PRIVACY

by Susan Duffy
Speech Communication Department
California Polytechnic State University

Time, Inc. v. Hill, 385 U.S. 374 (1967) [U.S. Supreme Court]

The experience of hostage-taking is not new in American history. Today, however, the exploitation of the hostage situation by the media arouses controversy. The lives of private citizens are dramatically altered when, as hostages, they, their families, and their friends become public personae. Even after the ordeal ends, public interest often persists and the victims are faced with living in the glare of media scru-

tiny for weeks, months, and even years. The issue of the private citizen becoming the unwilling target of public attention was central when James J. Hill sued Time, Inc. for invasion of privacy.

In 1952, Hill's family was held hostage for 19 hours by three escaped prisoners in their suburban Philadelphia home. When released unharmed on September 12, 1952, the family's ordeal was covered extensively by the national press. The Hills stressed that they had been treated courteously by the convicts, and that there had been no violence, molestation, or abuse directed toward members of the family. In an effort to regain normalcy in their lives, the Hills moved to Connecticut and subsequently rejected efforts by both the print and broadcast media to "tell" their story. They assiduously avoided the notoriety of becoming a public commodity.

The following year, Joseph Hayes wrote and published *The Desperate Hours*, a novel that depicted a family of four being held hostage in their suburban home. As a novelist, Hayes had an interest in writing about actual crimes. He had for years prior to the Hill's incident maintained a clippings file of articles about hostages. The Hills' ordeal ultimately proved the impetus for Hayes to write *The Desperate Hours*, but the novel was factually different. Still, the public associated the novel with the Hills' situation. There is no evidence to suggest that this was troublesome to James Hill. Hayes later adapted his novel to a script for a Broadway play and sold it as a screenplay: all bore the same title. With this too, the Hills were acquiescent.

The problem, and ultimately the legal action, came because of an article about the play in *Life Magazine* in February 1955. It was on the pages of *Life* that an overt reference to the Hills appeared in the text of an article showcasing the opening of *The Desperate Hours* in Philadelphia. *Life* included photographs of scenes from the play as well as photographs of actors at the former Hill home reenacting scenes of physical confrontation, something the Hills maintained never happened. These pictures, coupled with the text of the article, prompted James Hill to sue Time, Inc. because he believed the *Life* article portrayed the play falsely and irresponsibly as being a "reenactment of the Hills' experiences" and that statements made in the article were knowingly false.

The issue in the trial court focused on the "truth" of the article. A secondary issue was whether *Life*, in an attempt to increase circulation, exploited the Hills' situation by using the sensational headline, "True Crime Inspires Tense Play," and knowingly allowed the article

to run with factual errors. The trial court held *Life* liable. On appeal, the case eventually reached the U.S. Supreme Court, which considered it on the constitutional question of freedom of speech and press. Harold R. Medina, Jr., argued for Time, Inc.; former vice president and soon to be president Richard M. Nixon argued for Hill.

Reversing the judgment of the lower courts, the Supreme Court remanded the case for further proceedings consistent with the Court's ruling in *New York Times Company v. Sullivan* (1964). Justice William J. Brennan, Jr., wrote the opinion of the Court, but Justice William O. Douglas's concurring opinion explains the decision compactly: "[A] private person is catapulted into the news by events over which he has no control. He and his activities are then in the public domain as fully as the matters at issue in *New York Times Company v. Sullivan*." The Court's preservation of the rights of freedom of speech and press was the overriding concern.

Acknowledging that private citizens inadvertently may become individuals of public interest, and that reportage and debate about a situation of public interest may contain some error, the Court held the press still has a constitutional right to print such stories provided they do not contain maliciously calculated false statements or statements made with reckless disregard for the truth. Essentially, the Court held that once a citizen becomes the subject of public interest, the press has a right to print stories about the individual; "inevitably" these stories will contain some factual errors or distortions, but the citizen cannot claim a violation of his "right to privacy," stop publication, or receive damages for publication. To the Court, such actions would be tantamount to censorship, and the rights of the press outweighed the rights of the citizen to privacy.

The dissenting opinion, penned by Justice Abe Fortas with Chief Justice Earl Warren and Justice Tom C. Clark concurring, outlined several problems. They felt that private citizens do have a right to be protected from untrue printed statements and that the First Amendment does not preclude "effective protection of the right of privacy." They cited "The Right to Privacy," the landmark 1890 article by Samuel

Warren and Louis D. Brandeis, in which it is argued that "'excesses of the press in overstepping . . . the obvious bounds of propriety and decency' made it essential that the law recognize a right to privacy, distinct from traditional remedies of defamation, to protect private individuals against the unjustifiable infliction of mental pain and distress."

The justices in dissent noted that "political personalities" should be governed by the judgment of *New York Times Company v. Sullivan,* but that a distinction was called for concerning private citizens. Implicit in this line of reasoning is that public officials seek public office and are, therefore, rightfully subject to continuous public scrutiny and analysis in the press, while the private citizen, thrown involuntarily into the public arena should be protected from the

press. The dissenters felt that the decision of the Court totally "immunized the press."

Selected Bibliography

Becker, M.S. "Torts—Privacy—Actual Malice Required for Redress of False Reports of Matters of Public Interest—*Time Inc. v. Hill.*" *The American University Law Review* 16 (June 1967): 442–49.

Brandeis, L.D. and S.D. Warren. "The Right to Privacy." *Harvard Law Review* 5 (1890): 193–220.

Braun, R.A. "Discussion of Recent Decisions." *Chicago-Kent Law Review* 44 (Spring 1967): 58–63.

Carl, W.J. "Right of Privacy: Knowing or Reckless Falsity in Publication Required to Sustain Liability Under New York Right of Privacy Statute." *Montana Law Review* 28 (Spring 1967): 243–49.

Kellogg, P.L. "Constitutional Law—State Cannot Award Damages for Invasion of Privacy Without Proof of Malice." *North Carolina Law Review* 45 (April 1967): 740–47.

PUBLIC DISCLOSURE OF PRIVATE FACTS

by Susan Duffy
Speech Communication Department
California Polytechnic State University

Cox Broadcasting Corporation v. Cohn, 420 U.S. 469 (1975) [U.S. Supreme Court]

In August 1971, Cynthia Cohn, a 17-year-old high school student, was raped and murdered by six youths in Sandy Springs, Georgia. The trial, held in April 1972, was the source of intense media coverage. As part of this coverage, Tom Wassell, a reporter for WSB-TV, attended the trial. While preparing his story, he asked to see the rape and murder indictments, which were given to him freely by the clerk of courts. Wassell subsequently broadcast a report of the trial on the evening news in which he mentioned the name of the victim.

Martin Cohn, the victim's father, sued Cox Broadcasting for invasion of privacy. Under a Georgia statute, which made it a misdemeanor to publish or broadcast the name of a rape victim, Cohn won the case. The majority opinion of the Georgia Supreme Court asserted: "The surviving father . . . contends that the public disclosure of the identity and involvement of his daughter eight months after the fact invaded his right to privacy and intruded upon his right

to be left alone, free from and unconnected with the sad and unpleasant events that had previously occurred." Along with the Georgia law making it a misdemeanor to reveal the name of a rape victim, Cohn's arguments relied on the contention that the private matter disclosed must be one that would be "offensive and objectionable to a reasonable man of ordinary sensibilities."

Cox Broadcasting maintained that its reporter had obtained information from a public trial and a public document open to investigation by any interested citizen. The report aired contained no distortion of fact. Thus, Cox Broadcasting concluded that the Georgia statute under which the company was held liable was a violation of the First and Fourteenth Amendments. The Georgia Supreme Court upheld the state's "tort for public disclosure" in ruling for Cohn when it found "no public interest or general concern about the identity of the victim of such a crime . . . will make the right to disclose the identity of the victim rise to the level of First Amendment protection."

Cox Broadcasting appealed the decision. On appeal to the U.S. Supreme Court, the decision was overturned in favor of the rights of a free press. Justice Byron R. White delivered the opinion of the Court on behalf of himself, and Justices William J. Brennan, Jr., Potter Stewart, Thurgood Marshall, Harry A. Blackmun, and Lewis F. Powell, Jr. Chief Justice Warren E. Burger and Justice William O. Douglas concurred in the judgment, while Justice William H. Rehnquist filed the sole dissent. The heart of the issue rested on the clash between the individual's right to privacy and the press's right to print the truth.

The Court stepped carefully in its decision, recognizing the dilemma posed by the "collision between claims of privacy and those of the free press." White took three pages in the decision to outline the historical precedents and arguments. He noted that this issue was not unlike the issue central to the article "The Right of Privacy," written in 1890 by Samuel Warren and Louis D. Brandeis. And he acknowledged that in this century there is a "strong tide running in favor of the so-called right of privacy." However, White cited favorable language from a 1947 opinion of Justice Douglas: "A trial is a public event. What transpires in the court room is public property. If the transcript of the court proceedings had been published, we suppose none would claim that the judge could punish the publisher for contempt. . . . Those who see and hear what transpired can report it with impunity. There is no special perquisite of the judiciary which enables it, as distinguished from other institutions of democratic government, to suppress, edit, or censor events which transpire in proceedings before it." With this in mind, the Court voted to reverse the state court's decision, concluding, "Under these circumstances, the protection of freedom of the press provided by the First and Fourteenth Amendments bars the State of Georgia from making appellants' broadcast the basis of civil liability."

Most of the criticism leveled at this decision focused on the argument that the name or identity of the victim in no way served the public interest and that there was little, if anything,

to be gained from knowing the name of a rape victim. The fact that such a revelation would cause pain and emotional distress to a victim's family and that such a revelation would, indeed, be an invasion of privacy, were important in the counter arguments. These considerations were overridden, however, by the Court's position that the identity of the victim was already a matter of public record and that under the First Amendment this was information available to the public and press alike. The Court advised that to protect the right of privacy, states must move to keep names out of the public record.

White also noted that the Court's failure to decide the question would "leave the press in Georgia operating in the shadow of the civil and criminal sanctions of a rule of law and a statute the constitutionality of which is in serious doubt . . . ." The Court's decision to uphold the rights of a free press reinforced other landmark free press decisions in this century that allowed the rights of the press to outweigh those of the individual citizen. Yet as one law review article, written in the wake of the decision, noted, "In *Cox Broadcasting Corp. v. Cohn*, the Court encountered for the first time the tension between the First Amendment and a privacy action based on public disclosure of wholly accurate information." The *Cox* decision may have freed the press from certain censorious overtures by states, yet it placed on the press a greater responsibility for self-restraint.

Selected Bibliography

Baer, R.L. "Constitutional Law—Right to Report Judicial Records." *Washburn Law Journal* 15 (Winter 1976): 163–67.

Blackmun, S.A. "Constitutional Law—Right of Privacy Versus Freedom of the Press—The Press Cannot Be Restrained From Reporting Facts Contained in Official Court Records." *Emory Law Journal* 24 (Fall 1975): 1205–28.

Brandeis, L.D. and S.D. Warren. "The Right to Privacy." *Harvard Law Review* 5 (1890): 193–220.

Martin, J.C. "First Amendment Limitations on Public Disclosure Actions." *University of Chicago Law Review* 45 (Fall 1977): 180–217.

McGinnis, P.E. "Civil Procedure—New Insight on Finality of State Court Judgments." *Arizona State Law Journal* (1975): 627–45.

McKeever, J. Recent Decisions. *Duquesne Law Review.* 14 (Spring 1976): 507–20.

Recent Decisions. *Georgia Law Review* 9 (Summer 1975): 963–79.

DID CBS LIBEL GENERAL WESTMORELAND?

by Edwin E. Moise
Department of History
Clemson University

Westmoreland v. Columbia Broadcasting System, Inc., 596 F. Supp. 1170 (1984) [U.S. Federal District Court]

On January 23, 1982, the Columbia Broadcasting System (CBS) presented a documentary entitled *The Uncounted Enemy: A Vietnam Deception*. It argued that during 1967, U.S. intelligence estimates in Vietnam had been formulated with deliberate and knowing dishonesty. Intelligence officers at Military Assistance Command, Vietnam (MACV), under pressure from their superiors to show progress in the Vietnam War, had seriously underestimated enemy strength. These underestimates had left the United States unprepared for the strength of the Tet Offensive of January 1968. The program indicated that General William Westmoreland, U.S. commander in Vietnam from 1964 to 1968, was primarily responsible for this deception.

The United States had sent ground troops into Vietnam in 1965 without having adequate intelligence on the Communist forces the U.S. troops were to fight. When MACV began to issue monthly reports on the organization and strength of the Communists in South Vietnam, the so-called order of battle, the figures were at first very incomplete.

As intelligence improved during 1966, the figures for the Communists' regular combat units came to be reasonably accurate. The order-of-battle reports also, however, contained figures for three other types of Communist personnel: (1) combat support or administrative services (i.e., those who provided transport, medical care, etc., for the enemy forces); (2) political cadres or political infrastructure (most of those in this category were local administrative personnel—village administrators, tax collectors, police—of the areas of South Vietnam that were partially or wholly under Communist rule); and (3) irregulars or militia (guerrilla and militia organizations, of varying capabilities, of which two would eventually become the subject of particular attention in the

case, the self-defense militia in Communist-controlled villages, and the secret self-defense militia in government-controlled villages).

Most of the Communist personnel in South Vietnam fell into these three categories, but the figures in the order-of-battle reports had little foundation in fact. The officers responsible had no idea how many personnel were actually in these categories, but bureaucratic inertia dictated that, for lack of anything better, they repeat each month the unfounded estimate in the previous month's report.

By the first half of 1967, enough information was becoming available to make realistic estimates possible for all categories. This created a major problem. The new estimates, especially for the administrative services and irregulars, were enormously higher than the old ones. Since public support for the war was already becoming shaky in the United States, if the official estimate of total enemy personnel in South Vietnam suddenly increased, perhaps even doubled, there could be serious repercussions.

There followed a series of acrimonious conferences at which the Central Intelligence Agency (CIA) argued for comparatively high estimates of Communist personnel and MACV intelligence argued for much lower estimates. In September 1967, an agreement was worked out under which the definitions used in compiling the estimates were drastically changed. U.S. intelligence simply stopped estimating the number of people in the self-defense and secret self-defense militia. Estimates of the number of political cadres continued to be compiled but were no longer treated as part of the military order of battle. Having dropped these categories, MACV accepted higher estimates of some others (though not as high as CIA estimates) without any increase in the overall total.

Samuel Adams, a CIA analyst of order-of-battle issues, had been one of the CIA negotiators at the conferences of 1967. He believed that the estimates agreed on at the September conference were grossly dishonest—incomplete and inaccurate to an extent that would seriously interfere with the war effort against the Communists. He made his view public in May 1975 in an article in *Harper's Magazine* entitled "Vietnam Cover-Up: Playing War with Numbers." Years later, George Crile, the editor who had handled the article in *Harper's*, took a position at CBS, and he decided that the story would make a good television documentary.

Crile began work on the project late in 1980; the 90-minute program was ready for broadcast at the beginning of 1982. Despite rather melodramatic publicity, which used the word "conspiracy" far more than the actual documentary did and later formed part of the basis for Westmoreland's libel suit, very few people watched the show.

When Westmoreland began to consider legal action, the prospects for winning a suit seemed poor. But after *TV Guide* conspicuously labeled the program a "smear" against him, and Dan M. Burt, head of the Capitol Legal Foundation, offered to have the foundation represent him without charge, he filed suit for $120 million. The defendants were CBS, Samuel Adams, George Crile, Mike Wallace (chief correspondent for the program), and Van Gordon Sauter (president of CBS News).

Westmoreland and Burt began the case with a crucial error. They could have filed the suit in the city where Westmoreland lived—militarily oriented and politically conservative Charleston, South Carolina—where they would have had an excellent chance of victory. Instead they went 200 miles northwest and filed in Greenville, South Carolina. Possibly they were hoping to benefit from the support of the local CBS station, WSPA-TV. WSPA had not broadcast *The Uncounted Enemy*, had given Westmoreland 30 minutes of prime time to respond to the program it had not broadcast, and had taken his side against the network in a broadcast editorial.

The defendants failed to get the case dismissed on the jurisdictional ground that none of the actions of which the defendants were accused had occurred in South Carolina. The defendants, however, asked for a change of venue, either to New York or to Washington D.C., on the ground that Greenville was not a convenient location for the plaintiff, the defendants, or any important witness for either party. Westmoreland said: "It would be a great personal hardship to me to be forced to litigate this case away from home. The expense of hotels, travel and retaining local counsel elsewhere would be a serious burden." As an argument for trying the case in Charleston, this might have been decisive. But when it was presented as a reason the case should be tried in Greenville, it was less compelling. The case was transferred to New York, where it came before Federal District Judge Pierre N. Laval.

Just before the trial began, Westmoreland dropped from his suit claims that CBS had libeled him by broadcasting that he had conspired to deceive the press, Congress, and the public. He narrowed his suit to the claim that CBS had libeled him by accusing him of conspiring to deceive his superiors in the military chain of command.

Some variations from usual trial procedure were made to help the jury cope with the extraordinary complexity of the issues in the case. Judge Laval allowed attorneys for both sides to make summations to the jury at intervals during the case instead of reserving the summations for the end of the trial. Each side was allowed a total of two hours for interim summations. Laval also encouraged the jurors to take written notes during testimony. Some witnesses, who lived far from New York, were allowed to present testimony without being physically present in the court. Before the trial, all witnesses had been questioned under oath by attorneys for both sides. Laval, in some instances, permitted the transcripts of these interrogations to be read from the witness stand by attorneys for the two parties, and treated them as if the witnesses themselves had been on the stand presenting testimony.

Westmoreland's avowed primary concern was to maintain his reputation in the press and before the public. The libel suit, he maintained, was a means to make his case heard, not an effort to win money (which he said he would give away if he won the case). He did very well in the struggle for public opinion, at least up to the time the trial began in October 1984. CBS was forced to admit having made factual errors in *The Uncounted Enemy*, having violated proper journalistic procedures by failing to interview several crucial witnesses, having used excerpts from filmed interviews out of context, having filmed one interview twice when the first version proved unsatisfactory, and having allowed one subject to view the film of an interview with another subject before the filming of his own interview.

However, once the trial began on October 9, 1984, these issues became less relevant. Compliance with proper journalistic procedures is not a legal obligation. After the defense began presenting its case on January 8, 1985, CBS was able to show credible evidence for the central thesis of its program: that military intelligence officers under Westmoreland's command had been pressured by their superiors to report fewer Communist personnel in South Vietnam than they believed were actually there.

Westmoreland and his supporters have tended to describe the intelligence debate of 1967 as having pitted the CIA against MACV and having been fully reported to the White House. At the trial, however, another division was made visible, this one within MACV intelligence.

On one side there had been intelligence officers, mostly of higher rank, who did not regard order-of-battle work (i.e., the production of estimates of the overall structure and strength of the enemy forces) as interesting or important. They did such work on a part-time basis, if at all, and they felt little respect for the officers who worked on it full time. Several of them appeared as witnesses for Westmoreland. They supported the relatively low estimates of overall enemy strength that had represented the official MACV position in 1967.

On the other side were officers, mostly of lower rank, who had been assigned full time to order-of-battle work during 1967. Several of them testified, as witnesses for CBS, that they had been ordered by their superiors to issue estimates that they believed seriously understated the level of enemy strength.

Colonel Gains Hawkins, the person immediately responsible for MACV's overall esti-

mates of enemy strength, testified that under pressure from his own superiors, he had ordered his subordinates to lower their estimates in mid-1967. He was not aware of any evidence justifying lower estimates; he said that the evidence suggested that the estimates were already too low. On the witness stand, he described the estimates that MACV had presented to other intelligence agencies in August 1967 as "crap."

For the most part, Westmoreland had not been directly involved; his immediate subordinates had passed down the chain of command what they believed to be his wishes, without necessarily consulting him in detail. General Phillip Davidson, chief of intelligence for MACV from mid-1967 onward, once stated in a directive to his officers: "[I]n view of General Westmoreland's conversations, all of which you have heard, I am sure that this headquarters will not accept a figure in excess of the current strength figure carried by the press. . . . Let me make it clear that this is my view of General Westmoreland's sentiments. I have not discussed this directly with him but I am 100 percent sure of his reaction."

CBS, however, was able to present two witnesses—General Joseph McChristian, former chief of MACV intelligence, and Colonel Hawkins—who in May 1967 had presented directly to Westmoreland more accurate figures which they wanted to substitute for the underestimates in the order of battle.

Westmoreland had to convince the jury of two arguments: (1) that the accusations made in the CBS program had been false and (2) that they had been made in reckless disregard of the evidence available to CBS. The testimony of McChristian and Hawkins left him little chance to accomplish the second, and in serious danger of failing with the first. On February 18, 1985, it was announced that he was withdrawing his suit.

The terms, less favorable than those CBS had offered him a few months before, included carefully worded statements by CBS. CBS said that it stood by its broadcast, but also said that it "never intended to assert, and does not believe, that General Westmoreland was unpatriotic or disloyal in performing his duties as he saw them." Westmoreland has interpreted this as an apology; a more realistic interpretation would be that CBS was saying that Westmoreland had believed it was his duty to distort intelligence estimates in order to keep the American public from becoming discouraged about the war.

Selected Bibliography

Brewin, B. and S. Shaw. *Vietnam on Trial: Westmoreland vs. CBS*. New York: Atheneum, 1987.

THE "PREACHER" AND THE "SMUT MERCHANT"

by Donald E. Boles
Department of Political Science
Iowa State University

Hustler Magazine v. Falwell, 485 U.S. 46 (1988) [U.S. Supreme Court]

Seldom in U.S. Supreme Court history have representatives of two more diametrically opposed social forces collided as they did in this case: the Reverend Jerry Falwell, a leader in the right-wing evangelical movement, sued Larry Flynt, the publisher of *Hustler*, one of the more uncouth national publications of the "girlie magazine" genre. At issue was the question of whether political cartooning was to remain constitutionally protected and unfettered from legal constraints even if it was outrageous and was intended to cause emotional distress to the party being caricatured.

The magazine had published an advertisement "parody," which, among other things, portrayed Falwell as having engaged in a drunken incestuous rendezvous with his mother in an outhouse. Following the appearance of the issue carrying the advertisement, Falwell brought a damage action against the magazine for libel, invasion of privacy, and intentional infliction of emotional distress. To exacerbate matters, while the case was pending, the advertisement parody was published in *Hustler* magazine a second time.

Pivotal to an understanding of the case is the fact that, throughout the litigation, it was accepted by all parties that Falwell was a "public figure." It is much more difficult for a public figure to prove libel or damage to one's reputation than it is for the average person. The Supreme Court, since *New York Times Company v. Sullivan* (1964), has held that not all speech about public figures is immune from legal sanctions. But, to be successful in such litigation, the public figure must demonstrate that the offending statement was made "with knowledge that it was false or with reckless disregard of whether it was false or not."

Counsel for Falwell argued, however, that a different standard should apply in this case, because here the state sought to prevent not reputational damage, but rather severe emotional distress suffered by the person who is the subject of an offensive publication. According to this view, as long as the utterance that was intended to inflict emotional distress was outrageous and did in fact inflict serious emotional distress, it was of no constitutional importance whether the statement was a fact or an opinion, or, for that matter, whether it was true or false. The key, as they saw it, was the intent to cause injury. Moreover, Falwell's attorney argued, the state's interest in preventing emotional harm simply outweighed whatever interest a speaker might have in speech of this type.

At trial, the federal district court threw out the invasion of privacy claim. The jury also ruled against Falwell on the libel claim, specifically finding that the parody could not "reasonably be understood as describing actual facts about [Falwell] or actual events in which [he] participated." On the other hand, the jury found for Falwell on the intentional infliction of emotional distress claim and awarded him $100,000 in compensatory damages, as well as $50,000 in punitive damages.

Flynt appealed the decision to the U.S. Court of Appeals for the Fourth Circuit. This court not only affirmed the judgment against Flynt, but seemed to go further in forging an important exception to *Sullivan*'s "public figure" doctrine. The court here rejected Flynt's argument that the "actual malice" standard of *Sullivan* must be met before Falwell could recover for "emotional distress." It went on to reject the contention that because the jury found that the parody did not describe actual facts about Falwell, the advertisement was an opinion that is protected by the First Amendment. As the court of appeals put it, this was "irrelevant," because the real issue as it saw it was "whether [the advertisement's] publication was sufficiently outrageous to constitute intentional infliction of emotional distress."

The U.S. Supreme Court opinion in the case began by reviewing in detail the facts. It noted that the inside front cover of the November 1983 issue of *Hustler* featured a "parody" of an advertisement for Campari Liqueur that contained the name and picture of Falwell and was entitled "Jerry Falwell talks about his first time." This parody was modeled after actual Campari advertisements that included interviews with various celebrities about their "first times." In the Court's words, "Although it was apparent by the end of each interview that this meant the first time they sampled Campari, the ads clearly played on the sexual *double entendre* of the general subject of 'first times.'"

Copying the form and layout of these Campari advertisements, *Hustler*'s editors chose Falwell as the featured celebrity and drafted an alleged "interview" with him in which he stated that his "first time" was during a drunken incestuous rendezvous with his mother in an outhouse. As the Court explained it, "The *Hustler* parody portrays respondent and his mother as drunk and immoral and suggest[s] that [he] is a hypocrite who preaches only when he is drunk." In an attempt to protect the magazine from legal action, in small print, at the bottom of the page, the advertisement contained the disclaimer, "ad parody—not to be taken seriously."

The magazine's table of contents also listed the ad as "fiction; Ad and Personality Parody."

It was clear from the outset that the Court's majority recognized the issues of this case far transcended the immediate battle between Falwell and Flynt. The novel question in the case, as Chief Justice William H. Rehnquist saw it, was whether a public figure could recover damages for emotional harm caused by the publication of an advertisement parody offensive to him and "doubtless gross and repugnant in the eyes of most."

Moreover, in the Court's view, Falwell sought to have the Court find that a "State's interest in protecting public figures from emotional distress is sufficient to deny First Amendment protection to speech that is patently offensive and is intended to inflict emotional injury." The Court was asked to arrive at this conclusion even though "the speech could not reasonably have been interpreted as stating actual facts about the public figure involved."

Then, to the surprise of some Court watchers, Rehnquist, long the leader of right-wing forces on the Court, launched a ringing defense of freedom of speech, press, and expression. He noted: "At the heart of the First Amendment is the recognition of the fundamental importance of the free flow of ideas and opinions on matters of public interest . . . [and] 'is essential to the common quest for truth and the vitality of society as a whole.'"

He emphasized, "The First Amendment recognizes no such thing as a 'false' idea." To support this sometimes forgotten point, he quoted Justice Oliver Wendell Holmes's famous lines from his dissenting opinion in *Abrams v. United States* (1919) "[W]hen men have realized that time has upset many fighting faiths, they may come to believe even more than they believe the very foundations of their own conduct that the ultimate good desired is better reached by free trade in ideas—that the best test of truth is the power of the thought to get itself accepted in the competition of the market . . . ."

Furthermore, Rehnquist explained that in the real world, "robust political debate . . . is bound to produce speech that is critical of those who hold public office . . . ." Indeed, "[o]ne of the prerogatives of American citizenship is the right to criticize public men . . ." and some of such commentary will be "vehement, caustic and sometimes unpleasantly sharp. . . ." However, the chief justice emphasized, because of the critical importance of free expression to the maintenance of a free society, the Court has held a speaker can be held liable for damage to the reputation of a public figure only if the statement was made with "knowledge that it was false or with reckless disregard of whether it was false or not."

The Court summarily rejected Falwell's contention that a different standard should apply to this case, since the law seeks to prevent not reputational damage but severe emotional distress to the public figure. As Rehnquist drolly explained it, "Generally speaking the law does not regard the intent to inflict emotional distress as one which should receive much solicitude. . . ." The Court previously has recognized that in the world of political debate, "many things done with motives that are less than admirable are protected by the First Amendment." Indeed, in the arena of public affairs, the Court has held that "even when a speaker or writer is motivated by hatred or ill-will his expression was protected by the First Amendment."

Then, getting to the case's real significance in today's politics, Rehnquist noted that using bad motive as a criterion for limiting public debate would effectively subject political cartoonists and satirists to damage awards without any showing that their work falsely defamed their subject. After all, he explained, "The appeal of the political cartoon or caricature is often based on exploration of unfortunate physical traits or politically embarrassing event . . . often calculated to injure the feeling of the subject." The cartoonist's work, as the chief justice saw it, typically is not "reasoned or evenhanded, but slashing and one sided." After reviewing the role of the political cartoons in U.S. political history, however, Rehnquist stressed that U.S. "political discourse would have been considerably poorer without them."

Falwell contended, however, that the caricature in question was so outrageous as to distinguish it from more traditional political cartoons, and, thus, it should not receive the same First Amendment protections. Acknowledging that the *Hustler* parody in question was "at best

a distant cousin of the political cartoon," the Court recognized, nonetheless, that a workable legal standard distinguishing between the two did not exist. More important, Rehnquist emphasized, the "pejorative description 'outrageous' does not supply" such a standard. "Outrageousness" as a standard, would permit individual jurors to use their personal tastes or views to find a cartoonist guilty, simply because the cartoonist's views did not conform to those of the jurors.

To prevent any misconceptions as to the scope of this decision, Rehnquist went on to emphasize that previously imposed limitations by the Court on freedom of expression continued to apply. Speech that is "vulgar," "offensive," and "shocking" is "not entitled to absolute constitutional protection under all circumstances," he noted. Nor do First Amendment protections apply to "fighting words" (i.e., words whose very utterance inflict injury or tend to incite an immediate breach of peace), explained Rehnquist. But, he went on, the type of expression in the *Hustler* advertisement clearly was not governed by these exceptions to First Amendment rights.

Thus, the Court concluded that public figures may not recover damages for the "intentional infliction of emotional distress" in cartoons or advertisements such as this without showing that the publications contains a "false statement of fact which was made with actual malice, i.e., with knowledge that the statement was false or with reckless disregard to whether or not it was true." This standard, the Court argued, "is necessary to give adequate 'breathing space' to the freedoms protected by the First Amendment."

Political satirists and cartoonists, such as the author of "Doonesbury," and their devoted followers (as well as Larry Flynt), can heave a collective sigh of relief at this decision. The case also demonstrates an adage in civil liberties law; that is, the rights of U.S. citizens are frequently protected by litigants with whom one may not agree, or whom one we might not be comfortable having as next-door neighbors. It also demonstrates what careful Rehnquist-watchers already know. That is, the chief justice, although normally supporting the power of the government over individual rights, marches to a different drummer in the area of political speech or expression. On that subject, he frequently supports a broad application of First Amendment protections.

Selected Bibliography

Note. "Did Falwell Hustle *Hustler*: Allowing Public Figures to Recover Emotional Distress Damages for Nonlibellous Satire." *Washington and Lee Law Review* 44 (1987): 1381–1414.

Note. "Free Speech and Emotional Distress—*Hustler Magazine v. Falwell*." *Harvard Journal of Law and Public Policy* 11 (1988): 843–49.

Stone, R. "Intentional Contempt and Press Freedom." *New Law Journal* 138 (1988): 423–24.

Wright, R.G. "*Hustler Magazine v. Falwell*." *Law Review* 19 (1988): 19–42.

C. Freedom of Religion

THE SCOPES TRIAL: A COLLISION OF CULTURES

by Bernard K. Duffy
Speech Communication Department
California Polytechnic State University

Tennessee v. Scopes, (1925) [State court of Tennessee]

The *Scopes* trial was a small, white-hot fire that was fed by the swirling ethers of fundamentalism and science. It was ignited by partisans who wished to illuminate the unresolved differences of culture, religion, and faith that divided the technological North from the agrarian South. Dayton, Tennessee, where the *Scopes* trial took place, became the crucible of a controversy that led the nation to recognize the existence of two national cultures, one steeped in the small-town values and mores learned at the hearth and in the pew, and the other based on beliefs learned in the laboratory and lecture hall.

The antievolution Butler Act, approved by Tennessee's state legislature and the governor, was not intended to create controversy. As Ray Ginger observed: "The Butler Act was a stump speech; it was each legislator telling his constituents that he very much wanted to be re-elected." The Butler Act prohibited the teaching of evolution in the public schools, universities, and normal schools. Despite its far-reaching implications, public universities ignored the bill, and the governor, whom some expected would veto it, signed it into law but expressed the opinion that it would not be enforced. He understood it for what it was, a symbolic protest against the undermining of religion by science.

Opportunism brought the Butler Act to a test that neither its author, the state legislature, nor the governor had anticipated. The city of Chattanooga was first to attempt to arrange a test case. The American Civil Liberties Union (ACLU) stood ready to bankroll the defense, but Chattanooga's plans fell through. In Dayton, however, George Rappalyea, a local mining engineer originally from New York, was successful in putting a sleepy southern town on the map by setting events in motion that would lead to a trial. A drugstore discussion with John T. Scopes, the local physics teacher and an occasional substitute in the biology class, resulted in an agreement that would put Scopes on trial for teaching the pernicious doctrine of evolution. Scopes obligingly asked the biology class to copy a diagram from a biology text and was, accordingly, arrested for violating the Butler Act. Ironically, this text had been approved by the state—presumably before the passage of the Butler Act.

Rappalyea had presciently foreseen the possibility of bringing to Dayton well-known scientific experts and fundamentalist leaders. It was an occasion for civic pride that such gladiators as three-time presidential candidate and leading spokesman for fundamentalism, William Jennings Bryan, and the celebrated but controversial "attorney for the damned," Clarence Darrow, offered to meet in rhetorical combat. Bryan would serve as the state prosecutor *pro tempore* ("for the time being"), and Darrow would serve on the defense team. Other attorneys who represented Scopes were Arthur Garfield Hays (a leading ACLU attorney), John Randolph Neal (a Tennessean expert in constitutional law, who led the defense team), and Dudley Field Malone (a brilliant defense counsel, who delivered some of the most incisive and eloquent speeches in the trial). The ACLU, advised by such astute legal minds as Felix Frankfurter, was concerned that Malone, a divorced man, and Darrow, an agnostic, would handicap Scopes's defense before a jury comprising Dayton townsfolk.

Darrow proposed to stop the *Scopes* trial and challenge the constitutionality of the law in federal court; Scopes agreed. Neal vetoed Darrow's plan, much to the relief of Daytonians, who feared that their day in the sun would be denied them. Darrow was rightly concerned that the trial judge, John Raulston, would rule evidence of the statute's absurdity inadmissible. Indeed, Bryan had already noted that the prosecution could win its case quickly if the only issue became whether Scopes had taught evolution.

The days preceding the opening of the trial on July 10 were marked by an influx and milling about of reporters, newsreel camera crews, revivalists, rusticating urbanites, farmers gawking at the city slickers, and hucksters selling everything from biology texts and religious treatises to hot dogs and lemonade. There were a hundred or more newspapermen, and Western Union was kept busy even with the 21 operators who worked at telegraphs installed in a makeshift office. Among the reporters was H. L. Mencken, the sage of Baltimore, for whose caustic wit the prejudices of what he dubbed the "Bible Belt" were an easy target. It was an unpleasantly hot July, and the cast of characters tried to cool off from the suffocating heat as best they could. Bryan strolled around town wearing a short-sleeve pongee shirt and pith helmet, fanning himself with a palm frond and eating radishes. The national press described Dayton as if it were a stage set for a comic opera, and indeed the scene did belie the seriousness of the issues that were to be brought before the bar.

Judge Raulston set a tone for the proceedings by conferring on the attorneys present the honorific titles of general, colonel, or captain. Raulston also did not hide the fact that his sentiments lay with the God-fearing Tennesseans who would vote on his reelection the following year. The court proceedings were opened with a lengthy invocation, punctuated with "Amens." The atmosphere of the trial was an extension of the one that had been established outside the courthouse. Raulston and the trial's cast of characters were aware that they were on stage and what was said at the trial would shape a perception of fundamentalism and the rural South as much as it would reflect on northern urban industrialism, modernist religious views, and faith in science.

From the beginning, the defense and the prosecution, though they agreed on the dramatic potential of the trial, had quite different interpretations of the case. The prosecution insisted that the reasonableness of the law and the truth or falsehood of evolutionary theory were irrelevant. Tennessee had exercised its rights to regulate the nature of public education; the legislature and governor had spoken on behalf of the people; and it was not for science or the federal government to interfere. Essentially, the prosecution asserted the right of a state to cultural autonomy. It was for the legislature to decide what was good or bad for the students of Tennessee's public schools and colleges. The defense, on the other hand, wished to show that the law was not only unconstitutional, but flew in the face of accepted scientific knowledge. Therefore, the defense brought to Dayton a battery of witnesses who were to give testimony to the objective truth of evolutionary doctrine. The defense would also play heavily on the theme that religious prejudice and fear, rather than a concern for the welfare of the state's youth, underlay the passage of the Butler Act.

Neal argued for the defense that the statute violated the Fourteenth Amendment's protection against the establishment of religion. Ben McKenzie, one of the prosecuting attorneys, responded that the Butler Act protected the people from the establishment of religion, since it disallowed teaching a doctrine that was antithetical to religion. "We cannot teach any religion in the schools, therefore you cannot teach any evolution, or any doctrine that conflicts with the Bible." But why, Neal asked the prosecution's "General Stewart," did the act prefer the Bible to the Koran? Because "we are not living in a heathen country" came McKenzie's confident response.

When Darrow rose to speak it was to establish the philosophy of the defense with the verbal pyrotechnics for which he had become famous. Darrow quickly warmed to his task and concluded with an emotional peroration in which he predicted that the Butler Act would be followed by more "ignorance and fanaticism." He stated, "After a while, your Honor, it is the setting of man against man and creed against creed, until with flying banners and beating drums we are marching backward to the glorious ages of the sixteenth century, when bigots lighted fagots to burn the men who dared to bring any intelligence and enlightenment and culture to the human mind."

The defense had brought to Dayton an array of experts to affirm the validity of evolutionary doctrine. The prosecution was immediately opposed to the idea; it saw the damage it could do, if not to their case against Scopes, then certainly to the public perception of the broader contest between religion and science. Argued Bryan: "It is not a mock trial; this is not a convocation brought here to allow men to come and stand for a time in the limelight and to speak to the world from the platform at Dayton." Scientific fact, the prosecution maintained, could not overturn the legislature's judgment that evolutionary theory would adversely affect the piety of its youth. The belief in an inerrant bible belonged to an entirely different order of knowledge; more than a religious doctrine, it was a basis of cultural conservatism, communicated and supported by the families and communities of the rural South. If anyone doubted that a child's schooling might affect his moral judgment, Bryan reminded the jury of Darrow's recent defense of Leopold and Loeb, the Chicago youths responsible for the brutal and irrational murder of another youth in Chicago. In pleading that the convicted murders lives be spared, Darrow had argued that Leopold's study of Nietzsche's nihilistic philosophy had numbed his moral sensibilities. If education can so affect one, should not Tennessee have the right to legislate against education it believes will adversely affect its citizens?

From the defense's point of view, calling witnesses for the scientific validity of evolutionary fact and theory was crucial: for if evolution is a legitimate scientific finding, it should unquestionably be taught. This is, however, a very difficult position to defend in a court of law, unless there is some prior agreement on the role of science. Without such agreement, the defense needed to argue what was by the 1920s a foregone conclusion to most of the developed world: that the dissemination of scientific fact and theory is of the utmost cultural value. Malone articulated this value with an encomium of truth, which the audience rewarded with their sustained applause: "There is never a duel with the truth. The truth always wins and we are not afraid of it. The truth is no coward. The truth

does not need the law. The truth does not need the forces of government. The truth does not need Mr. Bryan. The truth is imperishable, eternal and immortal and needs no human agency to support it. We are ready to tell the truth as we understand it and we do not fear all the truth that they can present as facts. We are ready. We are ready. We feel we stand with progress. We feel we stand with science. We feel we stand with intelligence. We feel we stand with fundamental freedom in America." Despite Malone's impassioned appeal, the judge ruled against the defense, which nevertheless managed to persuade the prosecution to allow the written statements of its experts to be entered into the trial transcript so that they might be used on appeal.

The climax of the trial is well remembered, not only because of the reporting of journalists like Mencken, but also because of the trial's reenactment in *Inherit the Wind*, a successful Broadway play and movie about the trial. Frustrated that he could not introduce the witnesses he had assembled on behalf of evolution, Darrow cagily called Bryan to the stand. What followed was a humiliating exercise for Bryan, who was ill-prepared for Darrow's adroit cross-examination. The effect of the questioning was cumulative. To show the unreasonableness of Bryan's commitment to the idea that the Bible was the revealed word of God, Darrow challenged Bryan to defend the literal truth of one biblical parable after the next. Darrow questioned Bryan about the story of Jonah and the whale; about Joshua, who was said to have made the sun stand still; about the date of the great flood; about the Tower of Babel; about the story of creation, and about Adam and Eve. The cross-examination was frequently acrimonious on both sides. At one point, Darrow referred to Bryan's "fool religion" and later stated flatly that the purpose of the defense was to prevent "bigots and ignoramuses from controlling the education of the United States," while Bryan declared that his purpose was "to protect the Word of God against the greatest atheist or agnostic in the United States." On the next day, the judge expunged Bryan's testimony from the record; he concluded that, like the testimony of scientific experts to the truth of evolutionary theory, Bryan's testimony regarding the validity of the Bible was not relevant. Although Raulston's decision to expunge Bryan's testimony made it impossible for Bryan to question Darrow in court, as was originally planned, a brief but pointless cross-examination occurred after the trial for the benefit of the press. Bryan simply established for the record what everyone already knew: Darrow was an agnostic. Bryan did not succeed in reclaiming his lost pride. Shaken by his embarrassment at the trial, he died of apoplexy only a few days later.

The defense wished to see the case come before a Tennessee appellate court and, with luck, the U.S. Supreme Court, so there was no objection to the jury's guilty verdict. A year elapsed, briefs were filed, and finally Darrow and other defense lawyers presented oral arguments for the appeal before the Tennessee Supreme Court. The court decided to reverse the decision of the lower court on a technicality and proposed that the indictment be dropped. The result was that Scopes was not retried, and the defense lost the basis for a further appeal to the U.S. Supreme Court.

Dayton, Tennessee, was the site of Bryan's last hurrah and, despite his failure to win a victory for religious fundamentalism, it is probable that his performance, and indeed his suffering, helped to deepen the commitments of many fundamentalists. On the other hand, those who did not abide fundamentalism had been confirmed in their belief that the claims of Biblical literalists were irreconcilable with the scientific and technological culture that the government had tried to legislate out of existence.

Selected Bibliography

Ginger, R. *Six Days or Forever*. Boston: Beacon Press, 1958.

Gould, S.J. "A Visit to Dayton," in *Hen's Teeth and Horse's Toes*. New York: W.W. Norton, 1983.

Hofstadter, R. *Anti-Intellectualism in American Life*. New York: Alfred A. Knopf, 1962.

Weaver, R.M. "Rhetoric and Dialectic in Dayton, Tennessee," in *The Ethics of Rhetoric*. South Bend, IN: Gateway Editions, 1953.

THE FLAG SALUTE CASES

by Paul Finkelman
Brooklyn Law School

Minersville School District v. Gobitis, 310 U.S. 586 (1940); *West Virginia State Board of Education, v. Barnette* 319 U.S. 624 (1943) [U.S. Supreme Court]

These two cases, commonly referred to as the "Flag Salute Cases," are among the most peculiar in U.S. constitutional history. At issue in both cases was the right of a state to require public school students to salute the flag and to say the "Pledge of Allegiance." The plaintiffs in both cases were Jehovah's Witnesses who refused to participate in flag ceremonies because such acts violated their religious precepts. In the first case, *Minersville School District v. Gobitis*, the U.S. Supreme Court upheld the school district's attempt to force students to salute the flag. In *West Virginia State Board of Education v. Barnette*, the Court reversed course,

siding with the claims of religious freedom made by the Jehovah's Witnesses.

These cases must be understood in the light of the evolution of the Jehovah's Witness faith, the emergence of a Roosevelt Court, and the issues of patriotism and national unity surrounding the United States's entrance into World War II.

The origins of the Jehovah's Witnesses are found in the Adventist bodies and ideas of the mid-nineteenth century. The Jehovah's Witness movement (members of the faith are emphatic that it is not a "church") began in the 1870s under the leadership of Charles Taze

Russell, but did not become widespread until the 1920s and 1930s, when Joseph F. Rutherford became the head of the movement. Rutherford organized a proselytizing movement, which was aggressively millennial in outlook. The Jehovah's Witnesses publicly bear "witness" against what they believe are the three major allies of Satan: the "false" teachings of most other churches and the Catholic church in particular, human government, and capitalism and business.

The proselytizing of the Jehovah's Witnesses, and their anti-Catholic rhetoric, first brought members of the faith before the Supreme Court in *Cantwell v. Connecticut* (1940). There, the Court affirmed the right of the Jehovah's Witnesses to publicly proselytize, even though their actions bothered many people in a particular neighborhood. In subsequent cases, however, the Supreme Court upheld the right of localities to require permits and licenses for Witnesses who held public marches or distributed or sold religious literature.

In addition to denouncing "false" churches, members of the faith also denounce patriotic exercises. Starting in 1935, Jehovah's Witnesses in the United States refused to salute the flag, asserting that it violated the biblical injunction against worshiping graven images. This meant that the Jehovah's Witnesses' children refused to salute the flag in public schools.

Their aggressive proselytizing, heated denunciations of other faiths, and uncompromising stands on scriptural interpretation made the Jehovah's Witnesses one of the most unpopular religious minorities in the nation. Their hostility toward political authority and their refusal to salute the flag further alienated them from mainstream America and from political and police officials. This set the stage for the Flag Salute Cases.

The first Flag Salute Case, *Minersville School District v. Gobitis*, resulted from the refusal of 12-year-old Lillian Gobitis and her ten-year-old brother William to say the Pledge of Allegiance in the public schools of Minersville, Pennsylvania. The father of these children, Walter Gobitis, had grown up in Minersville, was raised in a Roman Catholic family, and had saluted the flag as a child. In 1931, Gobitis became a Jehovah's Witness. At the time, Lillian

was eight and William was six. The Gobitis children continued to salute the flag until November 1935. In 1935, Jehovah's Witnesses in Germany refused to salute the Nazi flag. Ultimately, more than 10,000 German Jehovah's Witnesses would be sent to concentration camps for their affront to Nazi authorities. In 1935, the leader of the Jehovah's Witnesses in America declared that followers of the faith "do not 'Heil Hitler' nor any other creature." After this speech, American Jehovah's Witnesses refused to take part in flag saluting ceremonies.

In a more cosmopolitan community, the refusal of the Gobitis children to salute the flag might have gone unnoticed. But neither Gobitis nor his faith was popular in Minersville, where 80 percent of the population was Roman Catholic. Rather than ignoring what was neither an act of defiance nor a disruption in the schools, the School Superintendent Charles E. Roudabush took actions that eventually brought the school board and the Gobitis family before the U.S. Supreme Court.

After consulting the State Department of Public Instruction, the school board adopted a regulation allowing for the expulsion of any students who would not salute the U.S. flag. Roudabush then immediately expelled the Gobitis children and one other sixth-grader who was a Jehovah's Witness. Gobitis then sent his children to a private Jehovah's Witness school.

Eighteen months later, Gobitis filed a suit against the school district in federal district court. The case was first heard by Judge Albert B. Maris, a recent Roosevelt appointee to the federal court. As a Quaker, Maris was probably more sympathetic to the Jehovah's Witnesses than most Americans. Although he had a distinguished military record during World War I, as a member of a faith long persecuted for its pacifism, Maris doubtless understood the nature of prejudice and religious persecution that the Jehovah's Witnesses faced.

During the trial, Roudabush was openly hostile toward the Gobitis children and the Jehovah's Witnesses. He asserted that the children were "indoctrinated," thereby implying that their actions were not based on sincerely held religions beliefs. Maris rejected Roudabush's contentions. He asserted that "[t]o permit public officers to determine whether the views of individuals sincerely held and their acts sincerely undertaken on religious grounds are in fact based on convictions religious in character would sound the death knell of religious liberty." Maris refused to sustain "such a pernicious and alien doctrine." He reminded the school officials that Pennsylvania itself had been founded "as a haven for all those persecuted for conscience' sake."

Maris believed that the acts of these children "could not in any way prejudice or imperil the safety, health or morals, or the property or personal rights" of the other students in Minersville. After Roudabush's hostile testimony, Maris found that "although undoubtedly adopted from patriotic motives," the flag salute requirement "appears to have become in this case a means for the persecution of children for conscience' sake." Such persecution, the judge stated, is not permissible in a free society.

Finally, Maris noted that "religious intolerance is again rearing its ugly head in other parts of the world" and thus it was of "utmost importance that the liberties guaranteed to our citizens by the fundamental law be preserved from all encroachment." While not central to his decision, Maris's point placed the controversy over the Jehovah's Witnesses in the context of the rise of Nazism, preparation for World War II, and eventually American involvement in the war. In part, the cases involving the Jehovah's Witnesses raised important questions about how much dissent a democracy can allow at a time of crisis and international conflict. Maris took the position that such dissent was vital to the democracy and part of its ultimate strength. The Minersville School Board took the position that national unity required submission to the will of the majority, especially on issues involving outward displays of patriotism. This argument would reemerge among the justices before the Supreme Court in both *Gobitis* and *Barnette*.

Having concluded that the flag salute requirement was motivated by a desire to provide "a means for the persecution of children for conscience' sake," Maris ordered the children readmitted to the public schools, but then stayed the order pending an appeal to the U.S. court of appeals. Eighteen months later, a unanimous

three-judge panel upheld Maris. By this time, many other states had also begun to prosecute Jehovah's Witnesses for their refusal to salute the flag. In his opinion, Court of Appeals Judge William S. Clark denounced the "eighteen big states" that "have seen fit to exert their power over a number (at least 120 nationwide) of little children" who sought to worship God in their own way and to also attend the public schools. Clark also tied the controversy to the war against Nazism in Europe by quoting in a footnote Adolf Hitler's 1935 declaration dissolving the Jehovah's Witnesses in Germany and confiscating their property. Clark also argued that refusing to salute the flag created no "clear and present danger" to the government, and thus the religious freedom of the children should be protected.

Initially, the Minersville school officials did not plan to appeal to the U.S. Supreme Court. Such an appeal cost more than this rural school district cared to spend. But patriotic groups, including the American Legion, stepped in to help finance the case. Before the Supreme Court, Harvard Law School professor George K. Gardner argued Gobitis's case on behalf of the American Civil Liberties Union. He was joined by the national leader of the Jehovah's Witnesses, Joseph Rutherford, who was also an attorney and had once been a judge in Missouri. Joseph W. Henderson, a Philadelphia lawyer, continued to represent the school board as he had in the lower courts.

In an 8–1 decision, the Supreme Court reversed the two lower court decisions and upheld the right of the Minersville School District to require that students salute the flag. Writing for the Court was Justice Felix Frankfurter, a former Harvard Law School professor and liberal activist recently appointed to the Court by President Roosevelt. Frankfurter was a Jewish immigrant from Austria. From his background, one might assume that he would have responded favorably to those who were persecuted for their religious beliefs and who, at that very moment, were facing death alongside the Jews in Germany, Austria, and elsewhere in Europe. However, when Frankfurter became a justice, he adopted the credo of a self-restrainer and put aside many of his liberal sympathies and sensitivities to the plight of minorities.

Frankfurter conceded that "the affirmative pursuit of one's convictions about the ultimate mystery of the universe and man's relation to it is placed beyond the reach of law. Government may not interfere with organized or individual expression of belief or disbelief." However, Frankfurter noted that there were no absolute guarantees of religious freedom. He found that the task of the Court was to "reconcile two rights in order to prevent either from destroying the other." He found that "conscientious scruples have not, in the course of the long struggle for religious toleration, relieved the individual from obedience to a general law not aimed at the promotion or restriction of religious beliefs. The mere possession of religious convictions which contradict the relevant concerns of a political society does not relieve the citizen from a discharge of political responsibilities." Put simply, Frankfurter was arguing that the First Amendment's guarantee of religious freedom extended only to protection from laws that were overtly religious in nature. Frankfurter rejected the findings of the lower court that the enforcement of the pledge was overt religious discrimination.

In an analogy, Frankfurter compared the dilemma of the Jehovah's Witnesses to that of Abraham Lincoln's query during the Civil War: "Must a government of necessity be too *strong* for the liberties of its people, or too *weak* to maintain its own existence?" [emphasis in original]. Frankfurter argued that the flag was a "symbol of national unity, transcending all internal differences" and, as such, he implied that failure to salute it somehow threatened the existence of the nation.

He further argued that the states should be given great latitude in determining how best to instill patriotism in children. He argued that the state was doing no more than "asserting . . . the right to awaken in the child's mind considerations as to the significance of the flag contrary to those implanted by the parent." This, he thought, was constitutionally permissible. He ended by noting that judicial review was "a limitation on popular government" that should be used sparingly. He urged that issues of liberty be fought out in the state legislatures

and "in the forum of public opinion" in order to "vindicate the self-confidence of a free people."

Justice Harlan Fiske Stone dissented, asserting that "by this law the state seeks to coerce these children to express a sentiment which, as they interpret it, they do not entertain, and which violates their deepest religious convictions." Stone dismissed Frankfurter's appeals to patriotism and his suggestion that the issue be decided "in the forum of public opinion" by appeals to the wisdom of the legislature. Stone pointed out that "[h]istory teaches us that there have been but few infringements of personal liberty by the state which have not been justified, as they are here, in the name of righteousness and the public good, and few which have not been directed, as they are now, at politically helpless minorities." Finally, Stone argued that the Constitution was more than just an outline for majoritarian government, it was "also an expression of faith and a command that freedom of mind and spirit must be preserved, which government must obey, if it is to adhere to that justice and moderation without which no free government can exist."

Stone understood the value of instilling patriotism in future citizens. He declared that the state might "require teaching by instruction and study of all in our history and in the structure and organization of our government, including the guarantee of civil liberty, which tend to inspire patriotism and love of country." But forcing children to violate their religious precepts was, in Stone's mind, not the way to teach patriotic values. He thought it far better that the schools find "some sensible adjustment of school discipline in order that the religious convictions of these children may be spared" than to approve "legislation which operates to repress the religious freedom of small minorities. . . ."

The *Gobitis* decision helped unleash a wave of political, legal, and physical attacks on Jehovah's Witnesses. Immediately following the decision, there were hundreds of assaults on Jehovah's Witnesses and their property. In Kennebunk, Maine, a Jehovah's Witnesses temple was burned; in Maryland, the police helped a mob break up a Jehovah's Witnesses meeting; in Illinois, Texas, Arkansas, West Virginia, Wyoming, Oregon, Kentucky, New Hampshire, New Jersey, Pennsylvania, Mississippi, Louisiana, and Nebraska, Jehovah's Witnesses were beaten, mobbed, and kidnapped. Their attackers often included police officials. In Odessa, Texas, for example, 70 Jehovah's Witnesses were arrested for their own "protection," held without charges when they refused to salute the flag, and then released to a mob of over 1,000 people, which chased them for five miles, throwing stones at them. In Wyoming, some Jehovah's Witnesses were tarred and feathered; in Arkansas, some were shot; and in Nebraska, one Jehovah's Witness was castrated.

Besides mob violence, the Jehovah's Witnesses faced official violence and persecution. Throughout the country, Jehovah's Witnesses were arrested and incarcerated without charges or on bogus charges. Sometimes the police tortured them. In Richwood, West Virginia, the police arrested a group of Jehovah's Witnesses who sought police protection, forced them to drink large amounts of castor oil, tied them up, and paraded them through the town.

The nation's legislatures and school boards responded to *Gobitis* by adopting strict flag salute requirements. By 1943, over 2,000 Jehovah's Witnesses had been expelled from schools in all 48 states. This was the nationwide answer to Frankfurter's suggestion that the Jehovah's Witnesses appeal to the state legislatures for relief.

The nation's intellectual community responded to *Gobitis* quite differently. Overwhelmingly, law review articles condemned the decision. The law reviews at Catholic universities—such as Fordham, Georgetown, and Notre Dame—were unanimous in their opposition to *Gobitis*, even though the Jehovah's Witnesses had traditionally vilified the Roman Catholic Church. But, the issue here was civil liberties, not theology as Catholic scholars clearly understood.

Members of the Supreme Court soon came to doubt the wisdom of *Gobitis*. In *Jones v. Opelika* (1942), the Court affirmed the convictions of Jehovah's Witnesses for distributing their pamphlets without proper licenses from various towns in Alabama, Arkansas, and Arizona. The laws in question were similar to other repressive laws passed in the wake of *Gobitis*.

Significantly, however, this decision was not decided by the overwhelming 8–1 vote of *Gobitis*. In this case, four justices dissented, arguing that the statutes' unconstitutionally restricted freedom of the press, freedom of speech, and the free exercise of religion. One of the dissenters was Stone, recently promoted to chief justice. Also dissenting were three members of the *Gobitis* majority, Justices Frank Murphy, William O. Douglas, and Hugo L. Black. They specifically concurred in Stone's dissent and in a longer dissent written by Murphy. Finally, they concurred in an exceedingly short dissent by Black, which was designed to make only one simple point. Black wrote: "Since we joined in the opinion in the *Gobitis* Case, we think this is an appropriate occasion to state that we now believe that it was also wrongly decided. Certainly our democratic form of government functioning under the historic Bill of Rights has a high responsibility to accommodate itself to the religious views of minorities however unpopular and unorthodox those views may be. The First Amendment does not put the right freely to exercise religion in a subordinate position. We fear, however, that the opinions in these [*Jones v. Opelika* and its two companion cases] and in the *Gobitis* Case do exactly that."

Equally important, the majority opinion in *Jones v. Opelika* conspicuously failed to rely on *Gobitis* for its result. This was probably because the recently appointed Justice Robert H. Jackson, one of the majority justices, did not disagree with the reasoning and result in *Gobitis*. Just as *Gobitis* has served as an invitation for the states to suppress the Jehovah's Witnesses, the dissents in *Jones v. Opelika*, combined with the failure of the majority to cite *Gobitis*, served as an invitation for a challenge to that recent precedent.

The final step before a reversal of *Gobitis* was a change in the membership of the Court. In October 1942, Justice James F. Byrnes, one of the majority in *Opelika*, resigned. In February 1943, District Judge Wiley B. Rutledge, a former dean of the Iowa Law School, joined the Court. On the district court, Rutledge had dissented in a case very similar to *Opelika*. His dissent there seemed to indicate that he would also favor overturning *Gobitis*. It now appeared that a majority of the Court—either five or six justices—wished to overturn *Gobitis*. All that was lacking was a test case to bring the issue back to the Supreme Court.

That case emerged quickly. In January 1942, the West Virginia State School Board adopted a strict flag salute requirement. The board's resolution, which had the authority of a statute, began with a long preamble which quoted at length portions of Frankfurter's *Gobitis* opinion. The resolution ended by declaring "that refusal to salute the Flag [shall] be regarded as an act of insubordination, and shall be dealt with accordingly." Shortly after the adoption of this resolution, school officials in Charleston expelled a number of Jehovah's Witnesses, including the children of Walter Barnette.

In August 1942, two months after the decision in *Jones v. Opelika*, attorneys for Barnette and other Jehovah's Witnesses asked the district court to convene a three-judge panel to permanently enjoin state school officials from requiring Jehovah's Witnesses to salute the flag.

Writing for a unanimous court, Judge John J. Parker, of the Court of Appeals for the Fourth Circuit, granted the injunction. Parker acknowledged that "ordinarily" the lower court would "feel constrained to follow an unreversed decision of the Supreme Court of the United States, whether we agreed with it or not." Indeed, not to do so threatened "the orderly administration of justice." However, in the light of the dissents in *Opelika*, Parker expressed doubt that *Gobitis* was still binding. He noted that three justices had explicitly announced their disagreement with *Gobitis* and also that the majority opinion "thought it worth while to distinguish the decision in the *Gobitis* case, instead of relying upon it as supporting authority." Because the three-judge panel believed that the West Virginia flag salute requirement was "violative of religious liberty when required of persons holding the religious views of the plaintiffs," Parker declared that the panel members would be "recreant to our duty as judges, if through a blind following of a decision which the Supreme Court itself has thus impaired as an authority, we should deny protection to rights which we regard as among the most sacred of those protected by constitutional guaranties."

In the rest of his opinion, Parker made three important points. First, he noted that the flag salute controversy had become another episode in the history of religious persecution, and those who defended it differed little from past persecutors. "There is not a religious persecution in history that was not justified in the eyes of those engaging in it on the ground that it was reasonable and right and that the persons whose practices were suppressed were guilty of stubborn folly hurtful of the general welfare."

Second, he noted that religious freedom had its limits. "He (who belongs to the minority religion) must render to Caesar the things that are Caesar's as well as to God the things that are God's. He may not refuse to bear arms or pay taxes because of religious scruples, nor may he engage in polygamy or any other practice directly hurtful to the safety, morals, health or general welfare of the community."

Finally, he answered Frankfurter's point in his *Gobitis* opinion that the courts should show deference to the state legislatures. He argued that the "suggestion that the courts are precluded by the action of state legislative authorities in deciding when rights of religious freedom must yield to the exercise of a police power would of course nullify the constitutional guarantee." Indeed, the guarantee of religious freedom "would not be worth the paper it is written on if no legislature or school board were bound to respect it except in so far as it might . . . choose" to respect it. If the courts were "to abdicate the most important duty which rests on them," the "tyranny of majorities over the rights of individuals or helpless minorities" would continue to be "one of the great dangers of popular government."

The court found that to "force" someone to salute the flag "is petty tyranny unworthy of the spirit of this Republic. . . ." It was a spirit the three-judge panel would not support. Thus, the judges granted the injunction, and for the most part, West Virginia authorities obeyed. No more Jehovah's Witnesses were expelled from the schools, and even Barnette's children returned to their classes. Meanwhile, the West Virginia State Board of Education voted to appeal the case over the advice of its attorney, Ira J. Partlow. By the time the case reached the U.S. Supreme Court, Partlow had become the state's acting attorney general. He refused to argue the appeal, and he could find no one in his office willing to take the case. Ultimately, Partlow brought in outside counsel.

Before the Supreme Court, the attorney for the board of education offered an unimaginative argument that relied almost entirely on *Gobitis*. His brief was supported by a weak *amicus curiae* ("friend of the court") brief from the American Legion. Attorneys for Barnette attacked *Gobitis*, comparing it to the *Dred Scott* decision (1857). *Amicus* briefs for Barnette came from the American Civil Liberties Union, written by Osmond K. Fraenkel and Arthur Garfield Hays, and the American Bar Association's Committee on the Bill of Rights, written by Harvard Law School professor Zechariah Chafee, Jr.

On June 14, 1943, Flag Day, the Court announced its opinion, upholding the lower court and reversing the precedent in *Gobitis*. Justice Robert H. Jackson wrote for the six-judge majority, while Justice Frankfurter wrote a bitter dissent.

While the Flag Salute Cases are generally seen as involving freedom of religion, that issue was virtually absent from Jackson's majority opinion. He accepted, without question, that the Jehovah's Witnesses sincerely held beliefs made it impossible for them to conscientiously salute the flag. But Jackson does not analyze the importance of that belief or even of the role of religious freedom in striking down the mandatory flag salute. Instead, he linked the freedom to worship with other Bill of Rights protections, noting that the "right to life, liberty, and property, to free speech, a free press, freedom of worship and assembly, and other fundamental rights may not be submitted to vote; they depend on the outcome of no elections." He found that the "freedoms of speech and of press, of assembly, and of worship may not be infringed" on "slender grounds."

Rather than grounding his opinion in freedom of religion, Jackson analyzed the case as one of freedom of speech and expression. Jackson argued that the flag salute—or the refusal to salute the flag—was "a form of utterance" and thus subject to standard free speech analysis. He noted that the flag was a political symbol, and naturally, saluting that symbol was sym-

bolic speech: "Symbolism is a primitive but effective way of communicating ideas. The use of an emblem or flag to symbolize some system, idea, institution, or personality, is a short cut from mind to mind. Causes and nations, political parties, lodges and ecclesiastical groups seek to knit the loyalty of their followings to a flag or banner, a color or design. The State announces rank, function, and authority through crowns and maces, uniforms and black robes; the church speaks through the Cross, the Crucifix, the altar and shrine, and clerical raiment. Symbols of the State often convey political ideas just as religious symbols come to convey theological ones."

The questions for Jackson were rather simple: Did the "speech" of the Jehovah's Witnesses threaten the rights of any individuals, or did it threaten the peace and stability of the government? If the answer to either question was yes, Jackson might have allowed the mandatory flag salute. But if they did not threaten the rights of others or threaten the government, there was no valid reason to suppress their expression.

Jackson noted that the conduct of the Jehovah's Witnesses "did not bring them into collision with rights asserted by any other individuals." The Court was not being asked "to determine where the rights of one end and another begin." It was, rather, a conflict "between [governmental] authority and rights of the individual."

Jackson compared the forced flag salute to *Stromberg v. California* (1931), a decision that had allowed protestors to raise a red flag. This case and others supported the "commonplace" standard in free speech cases "that censorship or suppression of expression of opinion is tolerated by our Constitution only when the expression presents a clear and present danger of action of a kind the state is empowered to prevent and publish. It would seem that involuntary affirmation could be commanded only on even more immediate and urgent grounds than silence." But were there such grounds? No one claimed that the silence of the children "during a flag salute ritual creates a clear and present danger that would justify an effort even to muffle expression." Jackson pointed out the irony of the flag salute requirement in light of the expanded freedom of speech found in recent decisions: "To sustain the compulsory flag salute we are required to say that a Bill of Rights which guards the individual's right to speak his own mind, left it open to public authorities to compel him to utter what is not in his mind."

Jackson's shrewd analysis had turned the case inside out. It was no longer one of freedom of religion, but one that in part took the form of an establishment of religion on the part of the government through its "flag salute ritual." Jackson correctly saw that the Jehovah's Witnesses were not trying to force their views on anyone else, but rather, that the government was trying to force its views and beliefs on the Jehovah's Witnesses. He noted that in *Gobitis* the Court had "only examined and rejected a claim based on religious beliefs of immunity from general rule." But, Jackson pointed out, this was not the correct question to ask. Indeed, Jackson noted that people who did not hold the religious views of the Jehovah's Witnesses might still find "such a compulsory rite to infringe constitutional liberty of the individual." For Jackson, the correct question was "whether such a ceremony so touching matters of opinion and political attitude may be imposed upon the individual by official authority . . . under the Constitution." In other words, did the government have the power to force anyone, regardless of his religious beliefs, to participate in any ceremony or "ritual." What Jackson might have asked was, did the Constitution allow for the establishment of a secular national religion with the flag as the chief icon? This led him to a discussion, and refutation, of various points in *Gobitis*.

In *Gobitis*, Frankfurter had Lincoln's "memorable dilemma" of choosing between civil liberties and maintaining a free society. Jackson had little patience for "such oversimplification, so handy in political debate." He "doubted whether Mr. Lincoln would have thought that the strength of government to maintain itself would be impressively vindicated by our confirming power of the state to expel a handful of children from school." Here, Jackson revealed the fundamental weakness of Frankfurter's assertion in *Gobitis*: that somehow the safety of the nation depended on whether Jehovah's Witnesses were forced to salute the flag in the public schools.

Along this line Jackson noted that even Congress had made the flag salute optional for soldiers who had religious scruples against such ceremonies. This act "respecting the conscience of the objector in a matter so vital as raising the Army" contrasted "sharply with these local regulations in matters relatively trivial to the welfare of the nation."

This led Jackson to the national security issue raised by Frankfurter in *Gobitis*. At the time of *Gobitis*, the nation was not at war, but war seemed imminent. By the time of *Barnette*, the nation had been at war for over a year. Jackson agreed that in wartime "national unity" was necessary and something the government should "foster by persuasion and example." But could the government gain national unity by force? Jackson made references to the suppression of the early Christians in Rome, the Inquisition, "the Siberian exiles as a means of Russian unity," and the "fast failing efforts of our present totalitarian enemies." He warned that "those who begin coercive elimination of dissent soon find themselves exterminating the dissenters. Compulsory unification of opinion achieves only the unanimity of the graveyard." During a war against Nazism, Jackson's opinion was a plea for the nation to avoid becoming like its enemies.

Jackson ended his opinion by reminding Americans that patriotism in a free county could not be instilled by force. Indeed, he argued that those who thought otherwise "make an unflattering estimate of the appeal of our institutions to free minds." The nation's strength, he argued, was found in diversity. The test of freedom was "the right to differ as to things that touch the heart of the existing order." This led Jackson to a ringing defense of individual liberty: "If there is any fixed star in our constitutional constellation, it is that no official, high or petty, can prescribe what shall be orthodox in politics, nationalism, religion, or other matters of opinion or force citizens to confess by word or act their faith therein."

Frankfurter was unmoved by Jackson's powerful defense of individual liberty and his condemnation of oppressive "village tyrants" who expelled small children from school because of their religious beliefs.

At a time when millions of Jews (and thousands of Jehovah's Witnesses) were perishing in German death camps, Frankfurter used his ethnicity to justify his support for the suppression of a religious minority in the United States. He began: "One who belongs to the most vilified and persecuted minority in history is not likely to be insensible to the freedoms guaranteed by our Constitution." But he argued that he could not bring his personal beliefs to the Court because, "as judges we are neither Jew nor Gentile, neither Catholic nor agnostic." He then defended judicial self-restraint and recapitulated and elaborated on his *Gobitis* opinion.

Frankfurter argued that "saluting the flag suppresses no belief nor curbs it" because those saluting it were still free to "believe what they please, avow their belief and practice it." In making this point Frankfurter failed to explain how one could "practice a belief" by doing what that belief prohibited. Nor did he explain how forcing children to say and do one thing, while encouraging them to secretly believe that what they were doing was a violation of God's commandments, would inspire patriotism in them.

Frankfurter conceded that the flag salute law "may be a foolish measure" and that "patriotism cannot be enforced by the flag salute." But he argued that the Court had no business interfering with laws made by democratically elected legislatures. Frankfurter argued that because 13 justices had found the flag-salute laws to be constitutional, the state laws "can not be deemed unreasonable." Because the state legislators had relied on the recent decision in *Gobitis*, Frankfurter felt it unfair to strike down their legislation.

Frankfurter condemned "our constant preoccupation with the constitutionality of legislation rather than with its wisdom. . . ." Yet he refused to strike down the West Virginia law, which he conceded was unwise, not because it passed all constitutional tests, but because of judicial restraint and respect for *stare decisis* ("let the decision stand"). He argued that the "most precious interests of civilization" were to be "found outside of their vindication in courts of law," thus he urged that the Court not interfere in the democratic process but wait for a "posi-

tive translation of the faith of a free society into the convictions and habits and actions of the community." What would happen to the Jehovah's Witnesses in the meantime seemed of little concern to Frankfurter.

There was minor resistance in a few localities to *Barnette*. The Supreme Court heard a few cases in which various local decisions were overturned. For instance, on the same day it handed down *Barnette*, the Court unanimously overturned a conviction for sedition in *Taylor v. Mississippi* (1943). The Jehovah's Witnesses in that case had been convicted for "violating a statute making it an offence to preach, teach or disseminate any doctrine which reasonably tends to create an attitude of stubborn refusal to salute, honor, or respect the Government of the United States or the State of Mississippi." The defendants had been sentenced to remain in jail until the end of the war or for ten years, whichever came first. The Court found the act abridged freedom of speech and press and was "so vague, indefinite, and uncertain as to furnish no reasonably ascertainable standard of guilt." The Mississippi law and the prosecutions under it illustrate the extent of official persecution of the Jehovah's Witnesses.

After 1946, the Court heard no more cases on the flag salute issue. *Barnette* became an important precedent for other free speech and freedom of religion cases. However, in 1988, the flag salute issue arose in a new way.

As governor of Massachusetts, Michael Dukakis had vetoed a mandatory flag salute law for public school teachers. In 1988, Dukakis was the Democratic nominee for president. His opponent, George Bush, raised Dukakis's flag salute veto throughout the campaign in an attempt to imply that Dukakis was not a true patriot. Initially, Dukakis did not respond to Bush's attack. When he did respond, Dukakis did not give a ringing defense of freedom of religion. Instead, he said that he vetoed the bill because the Supreme Judicial Court of Massachusetts, relying on *Barnette* in an advisory opinion, had said the law would be unconstitutional. This answer was legally precise but politically unsatisfactory. And the flag salute issue probably contributed to Dukakis's defeat. During the campaign, Bush and his running mate J. Danforth Quayle often started campaign rallies with the Pledge of Allegiance. Shortly after Bush and Quayle assumed office, they stopped saluting the flag at all public events.

Selected Bibliography

Irons, P. *The Courage of Their Convictions*. New York: The Free Press, 1988.

Manwaring, D. *Render Unto Caesar: The Flag Salute Controversy*. Chicago: University of Chicago Press, 1962.

Roenme, V.W., and G.F.F., Jr. "Recent Restrictions Upon Religious Liberty." *American Political Science Review* 36 (1942): 1053–68.

RELIGION IN THE PUBLIC SCHOOL DAY: THE RELEASED TIME CASES

by Frank J. Sorauf
Department of Political Science
University of Minnesota

McCollum v. Board of Education, 333 U.S. 203 (1948); *Zorach v. Clauson*, 343 U.S. 306 (1952) [U.S. Supreme Court]

The decisions of the U.S. Supreme Court often outlive the policies and controversies that give rise to them. The Court's decisions in the "Released Time Cases," for example, remain landmark precedents in the constitutional law of church-state relationships even though the released time programs themselves are far less common than they once were.

In many parts of the United States in the years between the two World Wars, released time programs seemed to many religious groups, primarily Protestants, the answer to an absence of religious training in the country's public schools. The Roman Catholics had their flourishing, full-time parish schools, a system that was the pride of the world's Catholics, but there were relatively few non-Catholic elementary or secondary schools in the United States. For most Protestant and Jewish groups, the Sunday or Sabbath schools were the major vehicles for teaching their young. Released time programs— also called weekday religious education— supplemented them; they also integrated religious teaching into the public school week as it was defined by compulsory school attendance laws. Students choosing religious classes were "released" during the regular school day of the public schools to go to religious classes; other students remained in the school.

In virtually all released time programs, the religious teaching was done by representatives of the religious groups participating. The religious classes generally lasted approximately an hour a week. Otherwise the programs varied greatly. Some were held in the public schools, others convened in nearby churches or other church buildings. In some, the programs were promoted, even urged, by the public school teachers or systems; in others, a scrupulous detachment prevailed. In some, the apparatus of the public schools administered the programs; in others, the religious groups bore the administrative expenses and burdens.

The variety within the released time movement doubtless reflected adaptation to local circumstances and expectations—and thereby helped assure its growth. By the early 1930s, released time programs enrolled some 250,000 students, but by the early 1940s enrollment had jumped, according to its supporters, to 1.5 million in at least 40 states.

Just as the released time movement reached its zenith in the 1940s, the U.S. Supreme Court was beginning its first extended attempt to define the constitutional law of church-state relationships. Under the long-standing doctrine that the Bill of Rights applied only to acts of Congress (a position set down in 1833 in *Barron v. Baltimore*), the Court had decided very few church-state cases. Most of the close relationships between church and state that occasioned objections involved state and local governments, and under *Barron*, only the state constitutions might limit them. But gradually in the twentieth century the Court began to interpret the due process clause of the Fourteenth Amendment to include the various protections of the Bill of Rights, thus applying them against actions by the states. That process of "incorporating" (or "nationalizing") the Bill of Rights reached the two freedom of religion clauses of the First Amendment in 1940 in *Cantwell v. Connecticut*, a case involving local attempts to control prosyletizing by the Jehovah's Witnesses.

Cantwell was a general invitation welcoming issues of the relationship between religion and government to the federal courts. Just seven years later, in *Everson v. Board of Education*, a case from New Jersey, the Court decided its first post-incorporation case involving the First Amendment clause forbidding any law "respecting the establishment of religion." Since it dealt with relationships of help and support for religion by government—rather than with restrictions on religious practices—the "no establishment" clause was the one on which the separation between church and state rested. *Everson* involved New Jersey legislation permitting local school boards to reimburse parents of children going to private schools, including religious schools, for the cost of bus transportation to and from their schools. Ewing Township chose to do so, and several plaintiffs challenged those reimbursements on the ground that they violated the separation between church and state mandated by the First and, now, the Fourteenth Amendments.

In a 5–4 decision, the *Everson* Court upheld the reimbursements for bus rides to religious schools in New Jersey, treating those bus rides as a public or social service, much like police or fire protection. The aid went not to religious groups or schools, the majority reasoned, but to the children and their parents. The distinction was quickly tabbed the "child benefit theory." But, while ruling in favor of the religious parents in the case, the majority spelled out a commitment to the separation of church and state couched in absolute language. Interpreting the "no establishment" clause for the first time in the Supreme Court's history, Justice Hugo L. Black wrote that the no establishment clause meant "at least this": "Neither a state nor [the] Federal Government can set up a church. Neither can pass laws which aid one religion, and all religions, or prefer one religion over another. . . . No tax in any amount, large or small, can be levied to support any religious activities or institutions, whatever they may be called, or whatever form they may adopt to teach or practice religion. . . . In the words of Jefferson, the clause against establishment of religion by law was intended to erect a 'wall of separation between church and state' . . . . That wall must be kept high and impregnable. We could not approve the slightest breach. New Jersey has not breached it here." The four-justice minority in the case rejected the distinction between aid to the child and aid to the religious school. Justice Robert H. Jackson, speaking for the dissenters, had only ridicule for the gulf between the rhetoric and the outcome in the case. The majority reminded him of Byron's feckless Julia, who "whispering 'I will ne'er consent'—consented."

Before the *Everson* decision, however, Vashti McCollum, a mother of no religious sympathies, rebelled against the released time program in the local schools of Champaign, Illinois—a released time program in which the cooperation between the public schools and the religious groups running the classes was particularly close. School teachers and other personnel administered a good deal of the program, and school buildings were used for the religious classes. Moreover, McCollum believed her son was under an assortment of pressures to participate in the program, pressures that ranged from a fourth grader's desire to conform, to a teacher's campaign to get 100 percent participation in her class. Her resolve to challenge the program, she has written, crystallized on the day her son was banished to the school hallway during the religious classes, the only student in his grade not attending them.

So, in June 1945—more than a year and one-half before the decision in the New Jersey bus case—McCollum brought suit to stop released time in the local schools of Champaign.

The popularity of released time programs was at an all-time high in the nation—about two million students were enrolled—and the beginnings of what became a post-war religious renaissance were increasingly evident. At the same time, the Supreme Court was confronting for the first time the task of giving systematic meaning to the no establishment clause of the First Amendment. The religious movement, an emerging juris prudence, and a determined individual came together to produce a momentous case and precedent.

Except for an attorney provided by several Chicago separationist groups and for the advice and support of the local Unitarian minister, McCollum's battle in the local community was a lonely, difficult, and trying one. Popular outcry and harassment of the McCollums reached a peak about the time of the trial before a three-judge panel in the local circuit court. It was a long trial, which included four hours of testimony by the fourth-grader in the case, James Terry McCollum, on the pressures and harassment he reported. In January 1946, the three judges upheld the released time program in Champaign. In so deciding, the court relied on a lower court decision in Chicago upholding that city's released time program, even though the schools' cooperation with religious groups there was less close than it was in Champaign.

After the initial loss, McCollum hired her own lawyer, Walter F. Dodd, a distinguished constitutional scholar and author and a former professor of law at Yale University. The appeal went to the Illinois Supreme Court, and that court, after first deciding in favor of the Chicago program, unanimously upheld the Champaign plan. This was in late January 1947. Just two weeks later, the U.S. Supreme Court announced its decision in *Everson*, the school bus case from New Jersey. Then, less than four months after the *Everson* opinion came down, the Supreme Court noted probable jurisdiction in the *McCollum* case. The new jurisprudence of church-state relations unfolded with unexpected rapidity.

In appealing her case to the Supreme Court, McCollum attracted support from many *amici curiae* ("friends of the Court"), among them Baptist groups, the Synagogue Council of America, the American Civil Liberties Union (ACLU), Seventh Day Adventists, the American Unitarian Association, and the American Ethical Union. After oral argument in late 1947, the Supreme Court handed down its decision on March 8, 1948. With only one justice dissenting, the Court held the released time program of Champaign county in violation of the no establishment clause as it was applied to the states under the Fourteenth Amendment. Justice Black again wrote for the majority. Even leaving aside the disputed facts, he concluded, the undisputed facts of the released time program in Champaign "show the use of tax-supported property for religious instruction and the close cooperation between the school authorities and the religious council in promoting religious education. The operation of the State's compulsory education system thus assists and is integrated with the program of religious instruction carried on by separate religious sects. Pupils compelled by law to go to school for secular education are released in part from their legal duty upon the condition that they attend religious classes. This is beyond all question a utilization of the tax-established and tax-supported public school system to aid religious groups to spread their faith. And it falls squarely under the ban of the First Amendment (made applicable to the states by the Fourteenth) . . . ." In concluding, the Court explicitly rejected the state's contention that the First Amendment banned only aid to one or a small number of religious groups and that, consequently, the program in Champaign was permissible because it assisted any and all religious faiths. In the words of the concurring opinion written by Justice Felix Frankfurter, "Separation is a requirement to abstain from fusing functions of Government and of religious sects, not to treat them all equally."

Justice Stanley F. Reed, the sole dissenter, rested his position primarily on the traditional and historic closeness between church and state in American history. After noting such long-established practices as chaplains in the Congress and the armed services, Bible reading in the schools of the District of Columbia, and religious activities at West Point and the Naval Academy, Reed concluded that "past practice shows cooperation between the schools and a

567

non-ecclesiastical body is not forbidden by the First Amendment." And in conclusion, the "prohibition of enactments respecting the establishment of religion do not bar every friendly gesture between church and state. It is not an absolute prohibition against every conceivable situation where the two may work together, any more than the other provisions of the First Amendment—free speech, free press—are absolutes."

The reaction to *McCollum* was both mixed and vocal. The decision realized the worst fears of some religious groups and leaders; what had been absolutist rhetoric in *Everson* was actual outcome in *McCollum*. Criticism of the Court surfaced quickly in the media and pulpits of the nation; the Court was variously accused of reading secularism or atheism into the Constitution or, worse, of being unwitting dupes of godless international communism. Indeed, in his dissent in *Zorach v. Clausen*, Black would take official, and unusual, note of the criticism: "I am aware that our *McCollum* decision on separation of Church and State has been subjected to a most searching examination throughout the country. Probably few opinions from this Court in recent years have attracted more attention or stirred wider debate." Above all it seemed ironic, perhaps even incredible, that a doctrine of seemingly absolute separation should emerge at the very time of the rising visibility and importance of religion in American life.

On just the question of released time programs, however, *McCollum* left unanswered the question whether all or only some released time programs were doomed. On one hand, the majority emphasized the use of the state's compulsory school attendance laws as an integral part of released time programs, and that observation pointed to the invalidation of all programs. On the other hand, as the concurring opinion of Frankfurter underscored, the Court had before it only one program presenting one set of facts, and its decision applied only to that and identical released time programs.

Indeed, the role of the compulsory school attendance laws—and the school day, school week, and school year they were defined and enforced—was at the very nub of the matter. The whole issue could have been put to rest with programs scheduled "after school" or, very

likely, with the slight accommodation of an early closing of schools one day in the week (the "dismissed time" option). But released time programs are defined by the fact they go on during the school day. Their advocates want it so for several reasons. They seek the legitimacy of including religious education in the regular school day and week. They prefer released time to dismissed time because it offers more flexible scheduling over different hours of the week. And—and a large "and" it is—they are not anxious to compete with students' leisure time pursuits after the end of the school day.

That same uncertainty about the scope of the *McCollum* decision explains at least part of its mixed impact on existing released time programs. Those in which the classes were held off school premises generally continued without change on the assumption that the use of public school classrooms was the salient characteristic of the unacceptable program in Champaign. In those with classes in the schools, the future was varied. In Champaign, released time became an after-school program and declined into collapse by 1950. Other similar programs shifted to off-premise classes or dismissed time programs, often resulting in a decline in participation. Still others continued in the public schools with few if any changes, either out of defiance and noncompliance or out of a conviction that differences from the Champaign program distinguished them. Overall, however, released time enrollments declined after *McCollum*. Just how much of a decline there was nationwide is unclear, but observers agree that released time never regained its pre-*McCollum* levels of support.

Support for the Court's decision in *McCollum* was active, if less visibly so than the opposition. Traditional separationist groups were pleased—the ACLU, Protestants and Other Americans United, the American Jewish Congress (AJC), various Baptist and Masonic groups among them. Some of them sought other test cases to clarify and extend the application of the *McCollum* precedent. One of those actions challenged the New York City program. It was not an easy target, for unlike the Champaign plan, the one in New York involved classes in private buildings, administration by the religious groups, and a stated policy by public school authorities to make no comments on the program and to handle none of its administration. In New York there was, in other words, little more public aid to the program than the excusing of students from classes during the regular school day—little more, that is, than the leverage of required student attendance during the school day.

Zorach v. Clauson was the second challenge to New York City's released time program. Joseph Lewis, an organizer and publicist for militant atheism, quickly brought suit unsuccessfully after *McCollum* to direct the state commissioner of education to stop released time programs in New York City and other cities of the state. Experienced litigating groups in the separationist camp, especially the ACLU and the AJC, viewed Lewis's suit with apprehension. Lewis was widely identified as an enemy of religion in any form, and he was not a resident of New York City; moreover, they thought, his suit was hastily prepared and bare of the facts of the city program as it actually operated. Their apprehension changed to distress when they found that Lewis had appealed his loss to the state's highest court, the court of appeals. Despite their reservations about bringing their own challenge in the heated aftermath of *McCollum*, the ACLU and AJC agreed to do so when negotiations with Lewis made it clear that he would drop his appeal only if they agreed to bring their own suit. Thus *Zorach v. Clauson* was born.

In a group-organized case such as *Zorach*, the plaintiffs played a far less active and prominent role than McCollum had played in hers. Tessim Zorach and Esta Gluck were in fact recruited by the groups as ideal plaintiffs—respected and religious members of the community who were willing to leave the decisions in the case to the sponsoring groups. Zorach, a food broker and son of the noted U.S. sculptor William Zorach, was an Episcopalian who lived in fashionable Brooklyn Heights. Gluck, president of the local public school Parent-Teachers' Association, belonged to a local synagogue and was the mother of children who went to it for religious instruction after the public school day was over. The major decisions in their case were in the hands of their lawyers: Kenneth Greenawalt for the ACLU and Leo Pfeffer for

the AJC. Greenawalt was a member of a prestigious New York law firm, and Pfeffer was both an AJC official and a distinguished scholar of church-state relations who had written articles on the subject and an authoritative book, *Church State and Freedom*.

The suit to replace Lewis's was filed in June 1948, a little more than three months after the Supreme Court's *McCollum* decision. Preliminary skirmishing occupied much of the next two years, in the course of it three defendants were specified: the Board of Education of the City of New York (Clauson *et al.*), the state Commissioner of Education, and the Greater New York Coordinating Committee on Released Time of Jews, Protestants, and Roman Catholics, the umbrella group organizing the released time classes. Finally, in 1950 a New York trial court held that the New York program was constitutional after denying an ACLU-AJC request for a trial on the facts. On appeal, the Appellate Division of the New York Supreme Court upheld the trial court by a 3–2 margin. Finally, on July 11, the state's highest court, the New York Court of Appeals, affirmed the lower court decisions by a 6–1 vote.

Within a short time, therefore, 13 New York state judges had wrestled with the constitutionality of the New York City released time program and, indirectly, with the question of whether *McCollum* had ended all released time programs. Of the 13, all five Catholics voted in favor of released time, and both Jews voted against it; the remaining six Protestants split 5–1, the one being a Congregationalist. Interestingly, all 13 took the same positions on the issue that their organized denominations had taken on released time legislation in the state.

The judicial reasons for the decisions in the New York courts were also symmetrical. The majority judges all cited the differences between the Champaign and New York City programs, and all argued for a separation that would not end all friendliness and accommodation between church and state. The dissenters all argued that released time's use of the state's compulsory education system to secure its pupils was its central fact and its fatal flaw.

In a significant way, the *Zorach* outcomes in the New York courts were foreordained by the facts they considered. The separationist

The two released time cases come from the first, tentative attempts of the Supreme Court to piece together a viable interpretation of the no establishment clause. In retrospect, the Court's position in *McCollum* (reflecting that in *Everson)* seems more separationist than the Court's subsequent position; its position in *Zorach* seems much less so. One may see the two cases as early and inexperienced attempts to spell out a doctrine of separation that would be both juridically defensible and socially and politically acceptable. Alternatively, one can see them as a two-part sequence of probing and testing by the Court—a staking out of a strong (even absolutist) position and then a retreating from it in recognition of specific criticism and of a more general context of growing religious enthusiasm in the country. Whatever the explanation, the Court settled down to a more consistent and predictable outlook on church-state separation only in the cases of the 1960s and 1970s.

And what of released time itself? Its proponents (and most optimistic estimators) reckoned that it made a comeback after the favorable *Zorach* decision and reached some three million public school pupils by the late 1950s. That was still a smaller percentage of the school population than released time had enrolled in the 1940s. Moreover, the movement was still plagued by widespread defiance of the Court's *McCollum* decision; about one-third of released time programs were still using public schools at the end of the 1950s. Philosophically, also, released time began to lose ground. Many public educators had never favored it, and the mainline Protestant religious groups increasingly turned away from it. Some saw its brief weekly classes as theologically compromised or pedagogically ineffective. Various groups moved on to other options—expanded religious schools, shared time programs, or teaching "about" religion or morality and ethics in the public school curricula.

Selected Bibliography

McCollum, V.C. *One Woman's Fight*. New York: Doubleday, 1951.

Patric, G. "The Impact of a Court Decision: Aftermath of the *McCollum* Case." *Journal of Public Law* 6 (Fall 1957): 455–64.

Pfeffer, L. *Church State and Freedom*. Rev. ed. Boston: Beacon Press, 1967.

Shaver, E.L. *The Week Day Church School*. Boston: Pilgrim Press, 1956.

Sorauf, F.J. "The Released Time Case," in *The Third Branch of Government*. C.H. Pritchett and A. Westin, eds. New York: Harcourt, Brace, 1963.

———. "*Zorach v. Clauson*: The Impact of a Supreme Court Decision." *American Political Science Review* 53 (Sept. 1959): 777–91.

TO PRAY OR NOT TO PRAY: THE SUPREME COURT SAYS NO TO PRAYER IN THE PUBLIC SCHOOLS

by Paul Murphy
Department of History
University of Minnesota

Engel v. Vitale, 370 U.S. 421 (1962) [U.S. Supreme Court]

One of the most controversial decisions by the U.S. Supreme Court was handed down in June 1962. In *Engel v. Vitale*, the Court banned the use of prayer as part of public school exercises as a violation of the establishment clause of the First Amendment. The *Engel* decision engendered a firestorm of public protest because prayer in the public schools had been a common practice in many parts of the nation for years. The outpouring of criticism of the Supreme Court after *Engel* was thought by some to exceed even the venomous attacks made on the Court after its famous desegregation decisions in 1954.

The controversy began when the Engels and other parents, representing a total of ten children enrolled in school district number nine of New Hyde Park, New York, brought suit against the school board and the state for the use of a prayer in the opening exercises of the schools. The prayer had been adopted by the school board following the recommendation of the New York State Board of Regents that the prayer should be read in the schools. The prayer was composed by the regents and was intended to be nondenominational. It read: "Almighty God, we acknowledge our dependence upon thee, and we beg thy blessings upon us, our parents, our teachers, and our country." The regent's prayer was to be optional both for the local school boards and for individual students. Although the prayer was supposed to be voluntary, the New Hyde Park school board initially had made no provision for excusing from the classroom students who did not wish to participate.

The parents who brought suit represented various creeds, including the Jewish religion, Unitarianism, atheism, and the Ethical Culture Society. They protested that the so-called nondenominational prayer violated their religious beliefs, that the school had coerced their children into participating in a religious exercise, and that the state's authorization of the prayer was a violation of the First Amendment. The parents lost their case in the trial court of Nassau County, New York. The judge decided that the parents had no valid constitutional objection as long as the prayer was voluntary and students could be excused from participating. The judge based his decision on the long history of prayer in the state's classrooms and argued that prayer "is an integral part of our national heritage." He did not believe that the establishment clause of the First Amendment was intended to outlaw prayer in the public schools.

The trial court's decision was affirmed by the intermediate appellate court of New York and went on appeal to the state's highest judicial body. In July 1961, the New York Court of Appeals upheld the two lower court decisions by a vote of 5–2. The opinion of the court was that prayer was neither a form of religious education nor the establishment of religion in any "reasonable meaning" of the First Amendment phrase. The court contended that the founding fathers had not meant to prohibit "mere professions of belief in God," but only any "official adoption of a religion by the government when they wrote the First Amendment." "To hold this prayer unconstitutional," the court said, "would destroy a part of the essential foundations of the American governmental structure," as well as going against American history. The dissenters pointed out that U.S. Supreme Court decisions of the past had shown that the line between church and state may not be overstepped and asserted that the prayer was a form of state-sponsored religious education. Moreover, the dissenters argued that even though the prayer was voluntary, a type of compulsion still existed because children felt pressure to conform to the activities of their classmates.

Engel v. Vitale was the first case dealing specifically with the issue of prayer in the public schools to reach the U.S. Supreme Court. However, there had been several earlier precedents pertaining to the establishment clause of the First Amendment, which gave some indication of the position the Court would take in *Engel*. In *Everson v. Board of Education* (1947), the Court upheld a state program providing for the reimbursement of both public and parochial school students for transportation costs to and from school on the basis that the purpose of the law was secular, not religious and it provided benefits for all students, not just some. In his opinion for the Court, Justice Hugo L. Black explained the requirements of the establishment clause as follows: "Neither a state nor the Federal Government can set up a church. Neither can pass laws which aid one religion, aid all religions, or prefer one religion over another. Neither can force nor influence a person to go to or to remain away from church against his will or force him to profess belief or disbelief in any religion. No person can be punished for entertaining or professing religious beliefs, for church attendance or non-attendance. No tax in any amount, large or small, can be levied to support any religious activities or institutions, whatever they may be called, or whatever form they may adopt to teach or practice religion. Neither a state nor the Federal Government can, openly or secretly, participate in the affairs of any religious organizations or groups and vice versa. In the words of Jefferson, the clause against establishment of religion by law was intended to erect 'a wall of separation between Church and State.'"

In *McCollum v. Board of Education* (1948), the Supreme Court struck down a state program of religious education that allowed for "released time" during the regular school day. The program provided public school classrooms for various denominations to teach students religion and required the instructors to take attendance. Eight of the Court's justices found this released time practice a clear violation of the separation of church and state. The establishment clause had been breached by the use of tax-supported public school buildings for religious instruction and by the fact that the state's compulsory school attendance law was being used to provide students for religious classes. In a 1952 case challenging another released time program, *Zorach v. Clauson*, the Court upheld the plan on the basis that students were allowed to leave the public school grounds to attend religious instruction elsewhere and therefore tax dollars were not being used to support religious instruction.

The *Engel* Court decided that the New York Board of Regent's prayer was unconstitutional by a majority of 6–1. Speaking for the Court, Justice Black said that using the public school system to encourage recitation of the prayer was "a practice wholly inconsistent with the Establishment Clause." Contrary to the ruling of the New York Court of Appeals, the Supreme Court said there could be no doubt that the New York program of daily prayer in the classroom was indeed a religious activity and therefore subject to the prohibitions of the First Amendment. The Court agreed with the parents that a prayer composed by government officials, in this case the Board of Regents, breached the "Constitutional wall of separation between Church and State." As Black put it, "[T]he constitutional prohibition against laws respecting an establishment of religion must at least mean that in this country it is no part of

the business of government to compose official prayers for any group of the American people to recite as part of a religious program carried on by government."

Black went on to point out that the fact that the prayer was both "nondenominational" and voluntary in nature was irrelevant to the Court's decision in *Engel*. Neither characteristic could "serve to free it from the limitations of the Establishment Clause." It was not necessary to show direct governmental compulsion. Black argued, in order to find that the establishment clause had been violated: "When the power, prestige and financial support of government is placed behind a particular religious belief, the indirect coercive pressure upon religious minorities to conform to the prevailing officially approved religion is plain. But the purposes underlying the Establishment Clause go much further than that. Its first and most immediate purpose rested on the belief that a union of government and religion tends to destroy government and to degrade religion. The history of governmentally established religion, both in England and this country, showed that whenever government had allied itself with one particular religion, the inevitable result had been that it had incurred the hatred, disrespect and even contempt of those who held contrary beliefs. That same history showed that many people had lost their respect for any religion that had relied upon support of government to spread its faith. The Establishment Clause thus stands as an expression of principle on the part of the Founders of our Constitution that religion is too personal, too sacred, too holy, to permit its 'unhallowed perversion' by a civil magistrate. Another purpose of the Establishment Clause rested upon awareness of the historical fact that governmentally established religions and religious persecutions go hand in hand."

Justice William O. Douglas, in a concurring opinion, argued that the primary factor making the New York prayer unconstitutional was the fact that it represented a governmentally financed religious exercise. He believed that the First Amendment requires that the government be neutral with regard to religion in order to better serve all religious interests. In Douglas's words: "The philosophy is that the atheist or agnostic the non-believer is entitled to go his own way. The philosophy is that if government interferes in matters spiritual, it will be a divisive force."

The lone dissenter from the Court's opinion in *Engel*, Justice Potter Stewart, contended that the recitation of the prayer in the public schools did not constitute an establishment of an official religion within the meaning of the First Amendment. Stewart felt that "to deny the wish of these school children to join in reciting this prayer" was "to deny them the opportunity of sharing the spiritual heritage of our Nation." He argued that because the prayer was so brief and nonsectarian, it could not be considered unconstitutional. Furthermore, Stewart maintained that Black's reliance on English history was irrelevant to the question of prayer in U.S. schools.

The practice of incorporating certain religious activities that were largely Christian in nature into public school programs had been widespread up to the time the *Engel* decision was announced. It was not surprising, therefore, that public reaction to the Supreme Court's decision was both vociferous and negative. Politicians, church leaders, and various celebrities immediately jumped on the bandwagon to decry the justices and their decision. Former President Herbert Hoover claimed that *Engel* represented "a disintegration of a sacred American heritage." Former President Dwight Eisenhower and former Vice President Richard Nixon also publicly criticized the decision, the latter calling for a constitutional amendment to reverse *Engel* and to allow nonsectarian prayers in the schools. Democratic politicians, unless they were southerners, tended at least to be supportive of the Supreme Court's authority to interpret the Constitution in this area, even if they were not enthusiastic about the decision itself. Former President Harry Truman stated that the Supreme Court was the best interpreter of the Constitution and President John F. Kennedy advocated obedience to *Engel*, pointing out that the church and the home were the proper places for prayer.

Southern Dixiecrats led the attack on the Supreme Court in Congress, but criticism of *Engel* was common among politicians in both the House and Senate. Southern Dixiecrats were most vicious in their censure because they had hated the Warren Court since its 1954 desegregation decision. The "Impeach Earl Warren" signs that had appeared on southern highways after *Brown v. Board of Education* were updated with the phrases "Save Prayer" and "Save America." Senator Strom Thurmond of South Carolina was the most long-winded critic in the *Congressional Record*, inserting negative comments about the Court and *Engel* for two and one-half months after the decision. Senator Eugene Talmadge of Georgia charged that "the Supreme Court had set up atheism as a new religion." Many southern politicians shared the view that the Fourteenth Amendment, which the Court had used to apply the First Amendment to state law (because the Bill of Rights, in and of itself, applies only to the federal government), had never been legally adopted and therefore the limitations of the First Amendment could not be imposed on the states. They charged the Supreme Court with the unconstitutional usurpation of state power. Congressman George Andrews (Democrat, Alabama) summed up the southern position with regard to the Warren Court in his criticism that the justices had "put the Negroes in the schools" and had "driven God out." Comments by other unhappy congressmen included the assertion by Representative Mendel Rivers (Democrat, South Carolina) that the decision provided "aid and comfort to Moscow" and Representative Alvin O'Konski's (Republican, Wisconsin) statement that "these men in robes are doing everything possible to help Khrushchev to bury us . . . . We ought to impeach these men in robes who put themselves above God." Congressman Frank Becker (Republican, New York) found *Engel* to be the most "tragic" decision ever made in U.S. history.

Several congressmen proposed legislative action in an attempt to circumvent the Court's ban on prayer in the public schools. Fifty-three representatives and 22 senators joined in introducing constitutional amendments to overturn *Engel* in their respective houses. The Senate Judiciary Committee held hearings in consideration of proposed amendments to allow nondenominational prayer in schools. One senator, Kenneth Keating of New York, appeared before the committee with a proposal to impeach the justices as well.

Although attempts to amend the Constitution continued for years after June 1962, none succeeded. This was due mainly to the vigorous defense of *Engel* by key northern congressional leaders and by the gradual dissipation of the emotional atmosphere that had inundated Congress and the nation when the decision was first announced. Eventually cooler heads prevailed in Congress and a reasonable assessment of the ruling led many congressmen to find *Engel* consistent with the precedent and the spirit of the First Amendment.

The Becker Amendment, introduced as House Joint Resolution 693 in September 1963, was, perhaps, the most notable failed attempt to contravene the Court. At the time the House Judicial Committee held hearings to consider the amendment, congressmen testified that they were receiving more negative mail about the *Engel* decision than had been produced as a result of the civil rights controversy. The Becker Amendment passed the House but was defeated in the Senate. The opposition of 37 senators denied the joint resolution the two-thirds majority required for the passage of a constitutional amendment. Much of the credit for the defeat of Becker's proposal went to several grassroots organizations representing civil libertarians, Jews, and some Protestant denominations which organized meetings, speakers, and a writing campaign to influence the vote of congressmen. The efforts of these groups resulted in the shift in the mail on the Becker Amendment from support to opposition. A few prominent theologians were joined by numerous constitutional lawyers and a variety of interest groups in testifying against the amendment at the committee hearings. A push for the passage of a similar amendment was mounted a few years later in the Senate under the leadership of Senator Everett Dirksen of Illinois, but it failed also, as did scores of other such proposals. Interest in prayer amendments in Congress waned significantly beginning in 1965, and subsequently such action has not proved to have significant support.

The response to *Engel* among religious leaders was mixed. Cardinal Francis Spellman attacked the decision vehemently and attempted to stir up Catholic opinion against the Court. Few prominent Catholics supported *Engel*, despite President Kennedy's position. The response from Protestant church leaders ran the gamut from the view of Episcopal Bishop James Pike, who asserted that the Court had "deconsecrated the nation," to vigorous support for the decision. In general, Unitarians, nonsouthern Baptists, and Presbyterians supported the Court, while Methodists were divided on the issue. Although it was slow to make an official response, the Federal Council of Churches, which represented many of the mainstream Protestant denominations, eventually voiced support of *Engel* as a protector of religious liberty.

Jews were the most outspoken in their support of the decision because they had worked for years to eradicate the promotion of Christianity in the public schools. Most Jews viewed *Engel* as a long-awaited legal victory in their fight against discriminatory religious practices. The American Jewish Congress, the American Jewish Committee, and the Anti-Defamation League of B'nai B'rith had all filed *amici curiae* ("friends of the court") briefs in *Engel* in support of the petitioners. The counsel of the American Jewish Congress, Leo Pfeffer, organized 132 law school deans and professors of law and political science of various religious faiths from colleges and universities throughout the nation. This group issued a defense of the *Engel* decision and sent it to the Senate Judiciary Committee as it sat to consider the proposed constitutional amendments to put prayer back in the schools. In their influential statement to the committee, these legal experts argued that "the intrusion of religion upon the public school system both threatens the separation of church and state and challenges the traditional integrity of the public schools. That intrusion, if permitted, will greatly endanger the institutions which have preserved religious and political freedom in the United States...."

Although thousands of negative telegrams and letters were delivered to the Supreme Court within 24 hours of the *Engel* decision, the Court had many supporters as well. Leading newspapers favored the decision, including the *New York Times*, the *New York Herald Tribune*, the *New York Post*, the *Washington Post*, the *St. Louis*

Post-Dispatch, and the *Christian Science Monitor*, as well as *Time* magazine. Positive editorials in these publications were influential in shifting public opinion toward support for the Court's decision by the autumn of 1962. *Engel* was also evaluated in over 24 legal periodicals. Slightly over one-half of the articles were unfavorable. Some of the legal critics argued, among other things, that the decision institutionalized agnosticism as the official public religion, that it discriminated against the majority, that it was not the role of the Supreme Court to decide religious controversies, and that the decision was based too much on history and ignored contemporary issues.

The reaction among educators was varied as well. A poll taken several months after the decision showed that 51 percent of public school administrators disagreed with the Court, while 46 percent viewed the decision positively. Another poll taken in 1963–64 revealed that only 38 percent of the nation's high school principals supported banning prayer from the schools. This survey also demonstrated a striking difference in opinions on the issue depending on regional location. Principals in southern and border states were the least likely to support the Court (only 29 percent and 27 percent), whereas principals in the Pacific and Mountain states were most likely to support the Court (52 percent and 41 percent).

Although *Engel* prohibited prayer in the public schools, surveys taken during the 1960s revealed that many schools and school administrators had chosen to ignore the law of the land by continuing to pray in school. A 1965 poll of school superintendents in the South showed that in 26 percent of the school districts, prayers were said in all of the schools and in 35 percent of the districts prayers were said in some of the schools. Nationwide, 10.7 percent of superintendents reported that prayers continued to be part of the program in some of their schools. A 1969 *New York Times* poll demonstrated that 13 percent of the nation's schools and 50 percent of southern schools used some type of religious reading in their school exercises. This was despite two 1963 Supreme Court rulings that had outlawed Bible reading and the use of the Lord's Prayer in the public schools. Many school officials chose to ignore the law

with regard to religion in the schools in order to avoid conflict with parents in their school districts. Since the Supreme Court relies on governmental officials to execute its decisions, compliance with *Engel* and related cases depends on the willingness of local officials to enforce the law.

Despite efforts to resist the *Engel* and related cases, these decisions still had a great impact on the nation's schools. A 1960 survey revealed that 42 percent of the school districts in the continental United States had Bible reading in their schools and 50 percent said prayers. A 1965 survey demonstrated that Bible reading was practiced in only 19.5 percent of the schools and prayers were said in only 14 percent. These figures clearly indicate that the Supreme Court's decisions were effective, albeit not completely. Another effect of the *Engel* decision was to void laws in 11 states that had actually required religious exercises in the public schools.

In the 1970s and 1980s, the question of prayer in the public schools was no longer an issue of much interest to most Americans, despite the efforts of a vocal and conservative religious minority, which continued to advocate putting prayer back in the schools. It is highly unlikely that the Supreme Court will change its stance on religion in public education. In the three decades since the *Engel* precedent was established, the Court has been fairly consistent in maintaining a strict separation of church and state in the schools. The Court has continued this trend most recently in *Edwards v. Aguillard* (1987), a case in which it struck down a Louisiana law requiring the teaching of creationism (a religious explanation of the creation of the world based on a literal reading of the Bible) in the state's schools.

Selected Bibliography

Blanshard, P. *Religion and the Schools*. Boston, MA: Beacon Press, 1963.

Boles, D. *The Two Swords*. Ames, IA: Iowa State University Press, 1967.

Dolbeare, K., and P. Hammond. *The School Prayer Decisions*. Chicago: University of Chicago press, 1971.

Duker, S. *The Public Schools and Religion*. New York: Harper & Row, 1966.

Freund, P., and R. Ulich. *Religion and the Public Schools*. Cambridge, MA: Harvard University Press, 1965.

Hudgins, H.C. *The Warren Court and the Public Schools*. Danville, IL: Interstate Printers & Publishers, 1970.

Johnson, R. *The Dynamics of Compliance*. Evanston, IL: Northwestern University Press, 1967.

Laubach, J. *School Prayers*. Washington, DC: Public Affairs Press, 1969.

McMillan, R. *Religion in the Public Schools*. Macon, GA: Mercer University Press, 1984.

Muir, W. *Prayer in the Public Schools*. Chicago: University of Chicago Press, 1967.

EXPANDED EXERCISE: THE AMISH, COMPULSORY EDUCATION, AND RELIGIOUS FREEDOM

by Steven D. Reschly
Iowa City, IA

Wisconsin v. Yoder, 406 U.S. 205 (1972) [U.S. Supreme Court]

In early 1966, Adin Yutzy, an adherent of the Old Order Amish religion, sold his farm in Iowa and moved his family to Green County, Wisconsin, "to get away from all the trouble." The "trouble" Yutzy tried to escape occurred in Buchanan County, Iowa, in 1965 and involved Amish resistance to state compulsory education laws. The dispute in Iowa produced a dramatic photograph of Amish children dashing into a cornfield to avoid a forced bus trip to high school, intervention by Governor Harold Hughes, and a statutory exemption to the state's minimum educational standards law granted by the Iowa legislature. Similar compromise solutions had been reached in Pennsylvania and Indiana, where Amish children attended Amish-run vocational schools between eighth grade and age 16.

Only two years later, Yutzy and two other Amish fathers were arrested near New Glarus, Wisconsin, for failing to enroll their three children in high school. Frieda Yoder and Barbara Miller, both aged 15, and Vernon Yutzy, aged 14, all had completed the eighth grade in public schools. On complaint of the local school administrator, Jonas Yoder, Wallace Miller, and Adin Yutzy were arrested in November 1968 for violating the Wisconsin compulsory attendance law, which required schooling until a child's sixteenth birthday. As with most state laws, parents were held responsible for their children's school attendance. The three parents were charged, tried, and convicted in Green

County Court and were fined $5 each. However, before the trial began in March 1969, Yutzy moved once again, to southern Missouri, still seeking relief from compulsory education laws.

Why did consolidated schools and compulsory education beyond eighth grade violate Amish religion? The Amish trace their historical and spiritual roots to the Radical Reformation of sixteenth-century Europe. The Amish branch of the Anabaptists separated from the main body of Swiss Brethren and Mennonites in Switzerland and Alsace in the 1690s. Led by Jacob Ammann, an elder in the Swiss Brethren congregation at Markirch in Alsace, the Amish emphasized keeping the church pure through strict discipline and visible separation from the world. Biblical texts such as "Be not conformed to this world" (Romans 12.1) and "Do not be unequally yoked with unbelievers" (II Corinthians 6:14), combined with the historical experience of intense persecution and isolation, contributed to strong Amish values of differentiation from mainstream society.

Amish migration to America began in the 1730s, and the Amish, along with other German minority religions, established viable communities in Pennsylvania. By the early nineteenth century, the increasing pace of industrialization and urbanization led to stronger efforts by Amish leaders to maintain separate and distinct communities. The Amish built a "spiritual fence" to protect themselves against the encroachments of the world by developing comprehensive regulation and guidance of life, such as clothing, hair styles, decoration of homes, retention of German, and many other aspects of behavior; this containment became known as *Ordnung,* or "order," and separation from "pride" and anything "worldly" became overriding principles in Amish life.

In the nineteenth century, Amish children attended local public schools and Amish parents often helped to establish schools and served on school boards. By the early twentieth century, consolidation and, especially, the high school movement, began to threaten the carefully constructed spiritual fence protecting the Amish community from external forces. Consolidation weakened parental authority over children, and expanding the horizons of adolescents in high school endangered their loyalty to the Amish community. Both imperiled the efforts of Amish parents to retain their children within an agrarian religious tradition. At the same time, compulsory education laws, often tied with child labor legislation, required parents to enroll their children in school until a certain age, often age 16 or about two years of high school. Conflict with public officials occurred when the Amish refused to honor compulsory attendance laws that required high school attendance.

An Amish writer and teacher summarized the essential conflict in 1965: "The public schools are not striving for the same goal Christian parents are. We are not interested in building missiles and jet aircraft. They are not interested in building Christians. We must go separate ways." The first recorded conflict occurred in Geauga County, Ohio, in 1914, coinciding with the reorganization of the Ohio public school system. Three Amishmen were fined because they kept their children out of school in violation of the new school statutes. Amish frequently suffered fines and jail sentences during the 1920s and 1930s but were slow to establish parochial schools, since the point of controversy was high school attendance. With the exception of one case in Pennsylvania in 1949, all court decisions went against the Amish. In 1966, the Kansas Supreme Court adopted a distinction between the right to believe and the right to act in upholding the Kansas compul-

sory education law against Amishman LeRoy Garber; the U.S. Supreme Court denied review of the case.

The Amish traditionally refuse to pursue litigation and are reluctant to allow others to litigate in their behalf, often preferring migration in pursuit of less restrictive conditions, the very solution attempted by Yutzy. The Supreme Court case that decided the Amish education controversy arose from an unlikely location: a tiny, recent Amish settlement in southern Wisconsin. Begun in 1963 and consisting of only 24 families in 1968, New Glarus took temporary priority over the larger and more visible Amish communities in Lancaster County, Pennsylvania; Holmes County, Ohio; and LaGrange County, Indiana. The National Committee for Amish Religious Freedom, organized by Lutheran pastor William C. Lindholm in 1966, took the lead in organizing the legal defense of the three Amish parents from New Glarus and succeeded in gaining their cooperation and consent in appealing the case to higher courts. Attorney William Ball of Harrisburg, Pennsylvania, represented the Amish all the way from Green County to the U.S. Supreme Court.

One defendant in the local trial, Wallace Miller, was a Conservative Amish Mennonite, while Jonas Yoder and Adin Yutzy were Old Order Amish. The county court took note of the difference, acknowledged that Miller belonged to a related Amish group and could take part in the defense, and thereafter all parties referred to the parents as, simply, "Amish." Ball used expert testimony from sociologist John A. Hostetler, educator Donald A. Erickson, and local law enforcement and welfare officials to establish the intimate ties of Amish faith with life, the critical and successful role of education in maintaining the Amish community, and the complete lack of any burden placed on local legal and welfare systems by Amish customs.

The state did not contest the severe restriction placed on Amish religious practice by compulsory high school attendance, but instead argued that "the state's compelling interest in an informed citizenry to support a democratic society" was sufficient to justify infringement of the free exercise clause of the First Amendment. At one point in the testimony, the state's prosecutor cross-examined Hostetler regarding education: "Now, Doctor, let's talk about education. What's the point of education? Isn't it to get ahead in the world?" Hostetler replied, "It all depends on which world," referring to the Amish view that education is preparation for salvation rather than secular success. Erickson testified that learning by doing represented an "ideal system of education," which fully prepared Amish children for productive membership in their community. Higher courts repeatedly turned to the testimony of Hostetler and Erickson for guidance.

Following the pattern of most court cases, dating as far back as 1927, the Green County and Wisconsin circuit courts ruled against the Amish. Despite the trial court's finding that the compulsory education law infringed upon the free exercise of religion by the defendants, the courts held that the state's compelling interest in educating its citizens must overcome any violation of the Amish religion. However, the Wisconsin Supreme Court, in an elegantly written opinion, reversed and ruled in favor of the Amish on January 8, 1971. The First Amendment, made applicable to the states by the Fourteenth Amendment, prevented Wisconsin from compelling Amish parents to enroll their children in public high school. Hallows wrote that beyond the danger of exterminating the Amish community, "There is another impact on the Amish children themselves if they are required to go to high school. They would experience a useless anguish of living in two worlds. Either the education they receive in the public school is irrelevant to their lives as members of the Old Order Amish or these secondary school values will make life as Amish impossible." Basing the decision on the religious liberty of Amish parents to rear their children in their religion, the court denied any harmful impact of an exception from compulsory education for the Amish, since such an exemption "will do no more to the ultimate goal of education than to dent the symmetry of the design of enforcement." Further, the court denied any use of a belief-action distinction despite the precedent of Mormon polygamy rulings. For the Amish, "Their life style is dictated rather than motivated by their religion."

In a move that surprised attorney Ball, Wisconsin decided to appeal its case to the U.S.

Supreme Court. Bearded Amish leaders ascended the Supreme Court steps on December 8, 1971, to observe oral argument in the case and to seek protection for their way of life. Assistant Attorney General John W. Calhoun argued the case for Wisconsin, while Ball represented the Amish. Briefs of *amici curiae* ("friends of the court") urging affirmance were submitted by such diverse groups as the Mennonite Central Committee, the Seventh-Day Adventists, the National Council of Churches, the National Jewish Commission on Law and Public Affairs, and the Synagogue Council of America.

In a 7–0 vote, delivered by Chief Justice Warren E. Burger on May 15, 1972, (Justices Lewis F. Powell, Jr., and William H. Rehnquist took no part in the case), the Supreme Court affirmed the Wisconsin decision and freed the Amish from compulsory high school attendance. The High Court followed the Wisconsin Supreme Court for the most part, with the critical conceptual addition of a "balancing process" to resolve the conflict of interest between state and parents. The Court recognized the high responsibility of the state for education of its citizens. However, Burger wrote, "[A] State's interest in universal education, however highly we rank it, is not totally free from a balancing process when it impinges on fundamental rights and interests, such as those specifically protected by the Free Exercise Clause of the First Amendment, and the traditional interest of parents with respect to the religious upbringing of their children." Burger used a two-part test for analyzing free exercise claims. For Wisconsin to require school attendance beyond the eighth grade, "it must appear either that the State does not deny the free exercise of religious belief by its requirement, or that there is a state interest of sufficient magnitude to override the interest claiming protection under the Free Exercise Clause." The Court proceeded to make proving sufficient state interest extremely difficult, since "only those interests of the highest order and those not otherwise served can overbalance legitimate claims to the free exercise of religion."

After confirming that compulsory high school education did indeed pose a genuine threat to Amish religious practice and articulating the principle of balancing state and parental interests, the Court proceeded to evaluate Wisconsin's claim to compelling interest. Wisconsin advanced Jeffersonian arguments that education prepares citizens for political participation and prepares individuals to be self-reliant and self-sufficient members of society. Wisconsin also argued that compulsory education is necessary to protect children from ignorance, to allow for the possibility that some Amish children will leave the community and must be prepared for secular life, and that the common-law doctrine of *parens patriae* ("in the place of the parents," i.e., the state as common guardian of the community) constituted a substantive right of the Amish child to a secondary education, since the state could extend that benefit to children regardless of the wishes of their parents.

The Court rejected each argument, noting that Amish children were exceptionally well prepared for life in Amish communities; that the Amish were not opposed to all education beyond the eighth grade, only to conventional formal education; and that Amish values of reliability, self-reliance, and dedication to work would hardly place an individual at a disadvantage if that person decided to leave the community. In fact, Jefferson's ideal of the "sturdy yeoman" who would serve as the basis for democratic society may find its most complete contemporary fulfillment in the Amish. The Court denied any sweeping power of the state to intervene on behalf of children at the expense of parents' wishes.

Wisconsin failed to prove that forcing Amish children to attend public high school for one or two years beyond the eighth grade would serve any compelling state interest. In fact, by inhibiting the adolescent's integration into the community, compulsory education imposed a severe burden on the parents' religious practices. Therefore, the U.S. Supreme Court affirmed the Wisconsin Supreme Court in holding that "the First and Fourteenth Amendments prevent the State from compelling respondents to cause their children to attend formal high school to age 16." However, the Court also carefully circumscribed the decision: "Nothing we hold is intended to undermine the general applicability of the State's compulsory school-attendance statutes or to limit the power of the State to promulgate reasonable standards that, while not impairing the free exercise of religion, provide for continuing agricultural vocational education under parental and church guidance by the Old Order Amish or others similarly situated."

The doctrine of balancing parental and state interests drew a partial dissent from Justice William O. Douglas. In assessing the threat to free exercise, the Court conflated the interests of Amish parent and child, on the grounds that the parents were the ones at risk of punishment. Douglas argued that the balancing process neglected the interests of children, who "themselves have constitutionally protectible interests." Douglas also expressed concern that the decision "opens the way to give organized religion a broader base than it has ever enjoyed." He seemed to miss the point, however, by proclaiming, "Religion is an individual experience." For the Amish, religion is a communal experience.

The landmark First Amendment ruling, *Wisconsin v. Yoder*, provided relief for Yutzy and other Amish parents. The opinion also expanded the free exercise clause of the First Amendment. However, attempts to apply *Yoder* to other arenas, such as home schooling and preservation of native American religious sites, have generally not met with success. Religious fundamentalists do not intend to isolate themselves entirely from the rest of society, and the "threshold tests" for evaluating free exercise claims have not transferred easily to non-Christian religions or to individual conscience. The chronically ambiguous relationship of church and state continues. In *Yoder*, free exercise seems to mean, above all, the right to be left alone in educational policy.

Schools play a critical role in the reproduction of an established social order, both in dominant and minority cultures. Wisconsin argued that uniform schooling is essential to preserve a democratic political system, to prevent individuals from becoming an economic burden on society, and to socialize children into a common value system acceptable to the majority. The Amish sought the right to direct a nonconformist process of social reproduction, to foster cultural values at variance with the dominant society. Cultural pluralism won out over standardization in *Wisconsin v. Yoder*.

On hearing that the Supreme Court had upheld the Amish, defendant Yoder choked with deep emotion, then remarked, "I'm not one for making words, but it is a miracle from God. It's wonderful that a small people like us can still make a law in Washington. Now I just want to go back to farming."

Selected Bibliography

Erickson, D.A., ed. *Public Controls for Nonpublic Schools*. Chicago: University of Chicago Press, 1969.

Hostetler, J.A. *Amish Society*. 2d ed. Baltimore: Johns Hopkins University Press.

Hostetler, J.A., and G.E. Huntington. *Children in Amish Society: Socialization and Community Education*. New York: Holt, Rinehart & Winston, 1971.

Keim, A.N., ed. *Compulsory Education and the Amish: The Right Not to Be Modern*. Boston: Beacon Press, 1975.

Kraybill, D.B. *The Riddle of Amish Culture*. Baltimore: Johns Hopkins University Press, 1989.

McVicker, D.D. "The Interest of the Child in the Home Education Question: *Wisconsin v. Yoder* Re-examined." *Indiana Law Review* 18 (Summer 1985): 711–29.

Riga, P.J. "Yoder and Free Exercise." *Journal of Law and Education* 6 (Oct. 1977): 449–72.

Sher, J.P., ed. *Education in Rural America: A Reassessment of Conventional Wisdom*. Boulder, CO: Westview Press, 1977.

THE PIETIES OF SILENCE

by Frank J. Sorauf
Department of Political Science
University of Minnesota

Wallace v. Jaffree, 472 U.S. 38 (1985) [U.S. Supreme Court]

When the U.S. Supreme Court suddenly ended prayer and Bible reading in the public schools in the early 1960s, there was bound to be a major reaction. In parts of the country, the religious practices went on as before, especially in smaller or homogeneous communities in which no one disapproved or no one was prepared to pay the price of disapproving. Other proponents of prayer framed a constitutional amendment to overturn the Court's decisions; it, however, never got the necessary two-thirds vote in the two houses of Congress. Simultaneously, some state legislatures and local school districts cast about for alternatives to prayer that the Court would accept—prayerful verses of *America*, Bible studies before and after school, and in about one-half of the states, a "moment of silence."

The Alabama legislature approached the problem in three stages, each increasingly hostile to the Court's rulings. In 1978, it authorized a one-minute period of silence in the schools "for meditation"; in 1981, it approved a period of silence for "meditation or voluntary prayer"; and a year later, it authorized teachers to lead "willing students" in a prescribed prayer. It was the second of the three statutes—silence for meditation or voluntary prayer—that was at issue in *Wallace v. Jaffree*. That statute provided that the moment of silence not exceed a minute, that it be held at the beginning of the day, and that no other activities be undertaken during the silent moment.

In 1982, Ishmael Jaffree, an agnostic and an attorney with the Legal Services Corporation, filed suit against the school board of Mobile County challenging both the second and the third of the Alabama statutes. His suit followed the complaints of his three children that their teachers led prayers in school. It was, as most such suits are, an unpopular one. Jaffree was quoted in the *New York Times* about the effects of the suit. He had become, he said, "sort of *persona non grata* in the black community now, but the black community doesn't understand: I was never opposed to religion." As for his youngsters: "I'm still sorry for my children. They have told me they wish I'd never filed the suit. They said they have lost friends over it." Jaffree's suit never challenged the first Alabama statute, the one simply authorizing a period of meditation; his attorney, in fact, freely conceded its constitutionality throughout the case.

The decision of the federal district court went against Jaffree in an opinion the U.S. Supreme Court was later to characterize as "remarkable." Judge William Hand upheld the two Alabama statutes by ruling that the First Amendment and its "no establishment" clause did not apply to the states, thus ignoring some 50 years of Supreme Court precedents and the entire process of incorporating the First Amendment into the due process clause of the Fourteenth Amendment. The Court of Appeals for the Eleventh Circuit overruled and held the statutes in violation of the Fourteenth Amendment's application of the separation of church and state to the states. On appeal, the U.S. Supreme Court upheld the court of appeals summarily on the question of the 1982 statute (the one permitting prayer) and scheduled full oral argument on the questions raised by the 1981 statute—the second one—authorizing the moment of silence for "meditation or prayer."

In a 6–3 decision, the Supreme Court invalidated that statute because of the legislature's religious purpose and intentions. The testimony of the bill's sponsor in district court was unequivocal; when asked if his bill had any purpose other than the encouragement of prayer in the schools, he replied "No, I did not have no other purpose in mind." Justice John Paul Stevens, writing for the majority, also relied on the logic of passing the 1981 statute, after having passed one in 1978, simply setting up time for meditation. One of the dissenters, however, observed that the words "meditation or prayer" in 1981 might only have been there to make clear that prayer was a legitimate activity during the silence.

By failing the "secular purpose" criterion, it was not necessary for the Supreme Court to apply the second and third criteria of the test then used by courts to determine if a state law violated the establishment clause of the First Amendment. These two standards are (1) that the law's "principal or primary effect must be

one that neither advances nor inhibits religion" and (2) that the statute must not foster "an excessive government entanglement with religion." The Supreme Court case that mandated that a statute must survive scrutiny by all three tests was *Lemon v. Kurtzman* (1971). Sometimes the establishment clause tests, thus, are referred to as the "Lemon prongs."

All three dissenters—Chief Justice Warren E. Burger and Justices Byron R. White and William H. Rehnquist—wrote opinions. It was Rehnquist's that was the most dramatic. Arguing for a completely new interpretation of the no establishment clause, he spurned both the "wall of separation" metaphor and the Court's contemporary three-part test for violations of the separation. Rehnquist's case for beginning anew on church-state relationships rested primarily on his conviction that the framers of the First Amendment had intended only to prevent the favoring of one religion or sect over others.

Only fellow dissenter White answered Rehnquist's call to arms. *Jaffree* thus extended the Court's commitment to a view of church-state separation that originated with *Everson v. Board of Education* (1947) some 38 years earlier. As such, it was a loss for conservatives generally, for the Republican party, and for the Reagan administration, all of whom had hoped that the Court would retreat from its insistence on strict separation. The administration had urged the Court to do so in a brief of *amicus curiae* ("friend of the court"), and the deputy solicitor general, Paul Bator, had supported the urging in oral argument.

In broad doctrinal terms, therefore, *Jaffree*'s importance rests, in part, on what the Court did *not* decide. The same could be said for the outcome on the facts of "silence." It was clearly a narrow decision that hinged on the intention of the Alabama legislature to encourage prayer in the public schools. While the Court did not rule specifically on moments of silence without encouragements to prayer, a number of the opinions in the case were at pains to indicate that moments without a religious agenda would pass muster.

So, moments of silence survive in the public schools. The Court's opinion in 1985 noted 25 states with moment of silence statutes, most or all of them surely without the damaging legislative history of Alabama's. Since all apparently only authorize or enable local school districts to adopt such moments, there is no indication how widespread the practice is. If such moments have declined in number, it is not for constitutional reasons, for none of those 25 state statutes have come to the Supreme Court.

Selected Bibliography

Dellinger, W. "The Sound of Silence: An Epistle on Prayer and the Constitution." *Yale Law Review* 95 (July 1986): 1631–46.

Note. "The Supreme Court: Leading Cases." *Harvard Law Review* 99 (Nov. 1985): 183–93.

D. Obscenity and Pornography

OBSCENITY: "I KNOW IT WHEN I SEE IT"

by Elizabeth E. Traxler
Department of Humanities
Greenville Technical College

Roth v. United States, 354 U.S. 476 (1957) [U.S. Supreme Court]

"Congress shall make no law . . . abridging the freedom of speech, or of the press. . . ." Of all the civil liberties given in the Bill of Rights, this grant of freedom of expression is one Americans hold most dear. And unlike other much litigated phrases of the Constitution, such as equal protection and due process, its meaning appears to be quite straightforward, in need of little interpretation. In fact, this First Amendment freedom could be understood as an absolute, allowing for no exceptions to the rule. It does not say, for instance, "Congress shall not make most laws" or "Congress shall only make acceptable laws," but says Congress shall make *no* law. Yet the courts have struggled with it through the years when confronted with situations seeming to require that exceptions be found to its apparently absolute prohibition. As Samuel Roth learned with his conviction for engaging in the distribution of obscene works and his subsequent loss on appeal, "obscenity" has been identified as one such exception. The Supreme Court decision in *Roth v. United States* stands today as the landmark case governing the relationship of obscenity to the protection offered speech by the U.S. Constitution.

Roth and the publications he sought to distribute were perhaps unlikely warriors to wage a defense of such a cherished civil liberty. A Polish immigrant, Roth had established a successful mail order business out of New York City dealing in erotica and obscene works. His first brush with obscenity statutes had come with his unsuccessful efforts in the 1930s to distribute James Joyce's *Ulysses*. But the publications that led to his arrest in 1955 were hardly works of such literary merit: *Photo and Body* and *American Aphrodite Number Thirteen* have not emerged as classics in the field of literature. It was over such works, rather than ones of clear literary merit, that the U.S. Supreme Court would be asked to decide whether obscenity statutes were unconstitutional restrictions on First Amendment freedoms.

Before his arrest by federal authorities in 1955, Roth had been using the U.S. Postal Service to mail circulars advertising his merchandise to unsuspecting individuals. Several of these individuals complained to the post office, leading postal authorities to establish fictitious names and addresses from which orders were placed in order to ensnare Roth. Indictments followed, charging Roth with 26 counts of violating the federal statute known as the Comstock Act. This act, dating back to 1872, provided for criminal prosecution of anyone mailing obscene works or advertisements for them. Conviction for such acts could bring a maximum of five years in prison and/or a fine of up to $5,000. Found guilty in 1956 on four counts by a jury in the U.S. district court in New York, Roth received the maximum sentence. Though he had been convicted of similar offenses on two previous occasions, this was by far the longest sentence he had received. Not surprisingly, an appeal followed. On appeal to the U.S. Court of Appeals for the Second Circuit, Roth's lawyers questioned the constitutionality of the statute.

Roth's attorneys did not argue that the First Amendment absolutely prohibited restrictions on freedom of speech and press. After all, the U.S. government is founded on the belief that individuals have certain rights or liberties that existed before the creation of governments. The duty of government is to provide the order necessary for its citizens to enjoy these liberties, until they come in conflict with others' rights. The difficulty is in determining the point at which government may step in to prevent one individual's liberties from infringing on others. The Supreme Court had grappled to demarcate this line in other First Amendment cases where obscenity was not at issue. The "clear and present danger" test as elaborated by Justice Oliver Wendell Holmes, Jr., was one result. At its most basic, this test held that the government could deny or restrict freedom of speech if it could be shown that such speech would likely result in illegal or antisocial acts shortly after the speech was uttered. By the time of *Roth*, this test had been revised to allow greater latitude for the government to restrict freedom of expression. However, suppression of freedom of speech still turned on the presence of unacceptable overt action, not mere thoughts, following the speech. It was on this basis—that there was no evidence of a clear and present danger (of an overt act) resulting from exposure to obscene works—that Roth's attorneys cast their appeal to the court of appeals.

The majority of the appeals court was not swayed by this line of reasoning; it upheld Roth's conviction. Though the U.S. Supreme Court had not yet squarely addressed the constitutionality of obscenity legislation, the court of appeals relied on opinions from that highest court and from lower courts in asserting that regulation of obscenity had been presumed constitutional. Thus, the appellate court opinion maintained that it was not up to a lower court, but to the U.S. Supreme Court to reopen the question. Though this absolved the appeals court from applying a clear and present danger test, the opinion suggested that evidence seemed to point to a link between juvenile delinquency and such works. If true, this would render obscenity statutes acceptable under the clear and present danger test.

The most interesting aspect of the circuit court's decision was the separate concurring opinion filed by Judge Jerome Frank. Despite voting with the majority to uphold Roth's conviction, Frank's opinion is better read as a dissent. He, too, maintained that it was up to the Supreme Court to rule on the constitutionality of the statute, but he attached an appendix to his opinion reviewing research evaluating the linkage between obscenity and antisocial conduct and found it insufficient to meet the clear and present danger test. Frank's effort, however, to provide the Supreme Court with the argument and evidence for use in rendering obscenity statutes unconstitutional proved unsuccessful.

Roth and his attorneys held out hope for a reversal of the appeals court when the Supreme Court agreed to hear the case and rule on the constitutionality of obscenity statutes. An earlier attempt by the Supreme Court in 1947 to issue such an opinion had fallen short. As a friend of the author whose work was in question, Justice Felix Frankfurter felt obliged to disqualify himself, and the remaining eight justices split evenly on the decision. With no majority, the Court could not issue an opinion in the case. In the following ten years, a number of lower court decisions treating this issue did not find obscenity statutes unconstitutional, but instead discussed the test to be used to determine whether a work fell into the obscene category.

When the Supreme Court read the briefs and heard oral arguments in April 1957, it was confronted with opposing views on the protection afforded obscenity by the First Amendment. That of Roth's attorneys and the *amici curiae* ("friends of the court") briefs filed by such organizations as the American Civil Liberties Union and Authors League of America relied on the clear and present danger test. Since there was no agreement that reading obscene works produced illegal or antisocial conduct, the only "evil" that could result would be thoughts, not actions. The government, they argued, had no business regulating thoughts and, therefore, the statutes must be held unconstitutional.

The government, on the other hand, argued that not all speech was equally protected by the First Amendment, that some expression, such as speech concerning political issues, was due the greatest protection, and that other types of expression, such as obscenity, should receive the least. They attempted to establish a continuum of protection with various categories of speech ranged along it. As one moved along the continuum toward obscenity, the evidence of dangerous acts resulting from the speech in question could be less specific and less documented.

The government's attorneys also sought to weaken the other side's contention that the banning of *American Aphrodite* might lead to the suppression of a literary masterpiece tomorrow. In an unusual departure from the norm, they provided the justices with a large sample of obscene works that had been seized by the Postal Service under the statute in question. The samples included only hardcore pornography of the worst variety and this, they argued, was typical of most materials covered by this law. Roth's attorneys were not permitted to view the samples and to this day the influence the exhibit may have had on the Court's decision is unknown.

What is certain is that the majority of the Court refused both Roth's and the government's arguments that relied on the degree to which this statute met the clear and present danger test. The ruling, which remains the core of the Court's position on obscenity, held that obscene works do not fall under the protection of the First Amendment. In his majority opinion, Justice William J. Brennan reviewed bills of rights in the states at the time of the Constitution's adoption, the history of state statutes governing obscenity, international agreements on obscenity, and various court cases. He concluded that not all speech, in particular not obscenity, is to be afforded First Amendment protection. He maintained that obscenity fell into the same category of speech as libel. Five years earlier in *Beauharnais v. Illinois* (1952), the Supreme Court had ruled that libel was not speech under the meaning of the First Amendment. If there was no First Amendment protection, whether suppression of obscenity met the clear and present danger test was irrelevant.

Brennan also ventured the opinion that unlike speech afforded constitutional protection, obscenity was "utterly without redeeming social importance." Thus, if an expression contained social value, it fell under the First Amendment; if without such value, it stood alone and thus could be restricted or suppressed. Though *Roth* is often cited as the case in which this element became part of the test for obscenity, in fact, it was not until the *Fanny Hill* decision several years later that Brennan specifically added this language to the standards for scrutinizing allegedly obscene works.

The case's continuing importance also stemmed from Brennan's efforts to define obscenity. If obscene utterances were not protected by the Constitution, a test would have to be devised to pinpoint obscenity. His test for obscenity found in *Roth* included several elements: "whether to the average person, applying contemporary community standards, the dominant theme of the material appeals to prurient interest." The Court wished to devise a test that, on one hand, would not permit a work such as the Bible to be labeled obscene and yet, on the other hand, would not open the floodgates to a tidal wave of hardcore pornography.

Roth, then, was not able to avoid conviction for mailing obscene works nor was he able to convince the Supreme Court of the unconstitutionality of such laws. He did, however, lend his name to a decision that governed the law of obscenity for 16 years. The fundamental difficulty underlying the issue remained unresolved. If the justices had accepted obscenity as within the protection of the First Amendment, they would have faced a dilemma of considerable magnitude. Without clear evidence that exposure to obscenity results in undesirable acts, how could its suppression be justified? If the relevant authorities agreed that obscenity could lead a person to engage in antisocial acts, the clear and present danger test could be met. Short of this, the Court seemed faced with either a wholesale acceptance of obscenity, as argued by Roth and other civil libertarians, or the decision it reached. Categorizing obscenity as utterances outside constitutional protection presented even more difficulty by requiring its definition (i.e., when is speech obscene and when is it not?). The definition of obscenity, despite Brennan's efforts in *Roth*, proved so elusive over the years that the justices eventually agreed each to follow his own. Ultimately, it came down to Justice Potter Stewart's famous admission in *Jacobellis v. Ohio* (1964): "I know it when I see it."

A Supreme Court with a number of new faces attempted to resolve this difficulty in 1973. Chief Justice Warren E. Burger, in *Miller v. California* (1973), devised yet another test for obscenity. Despite his revisions, no change occurred in the central holding of *Roth*—that certain speech, including obscenity, falls completely outside the protection afforded by the First Amendment. Given the composition of the present Supreme Court, one may expect this aspect of *Roth* to hold for many years to come.

Selected Bibliography

Doggett, R.I. "Recent Decisions Approve Decency Statutes." *University of Cincinnati Law Review* 27 (Winter 1958): 61–75.

Ernest, M.L. and A.U. Schwartz. *Censorship: The Search for the Obscene.* New York: Macmillan Co., 1964.

Fahringer, H.P., and M.J. Brown. "The Rise and Fall of *Roth*—A Critique of the Recent Supreme Court Obscenity Decisions." *Criminal Law Bulletin* 10 (Nov. 1974): 785–826.

Rembar, C. *The End of Obscenity.* New York: Random House, 1968.

Schauer, F.F. *The Law of Obscenity.* Washington, DC: Bureau of National Affairs, Inc., 1976.

Schmidt, G.P. "A Justification of Statutes Barring Pornography From the Mail." *Fordham Law Review* 26 (Spring 1957): 70–97.

A BOOK NAMED FANNY HILL

by William Lasser
Department of Political Science
Clemson University

Memoirs v. Massachusetts, 383 U.S. 413 (1966) [U.S. Supreme Court]

The first reported obscenity case in the United States was an 1821 Massachusetts decision involving John Cleland's book, circa 1750, entitled *Memoirs of a Woman of Pleasure* (commonly known as *Fanny Hill*). It was therefore fitting that the most important obscenity case of the 1960s should also involve *Fanny Hill* and should also arise out of Massachusetts.

The 1966 U.S. Supreme Court case, generally known as *Memoirs v. Massachusetts*, began when the attorney general of Massachusetts brought a civil suit asking the courts of Massachusetts to declare *Fanny Hill* legally obscene. The Massachusetts procedure was designed to allow the courts to determine the legal status of an allegedly obscene book without the risk of criminal penalties against any interested party.

The legal status of obscenity in the United States was completely unsettled in the mid-1960s. The Supreme Court in *Roth v. United States* (1957) had determined that obscenity was not protected under the First Amendment and had made a first stab at defining that term under the law. Material could be declared obscene under *Roth* only if "the average person, applying contemporary community standards" would find that "the dominant theme of the material taken as a whole appeals to the prurient inter-

est." The *Roth* formulation raised as many questions as it answered, and it sparked a rash of lawsuits and legal analyses.

Central to the *Roth* Court's classification of obscenity as unprotected speech was its finding that obscene speech was "utterly without redeeming social importance." "All ideas having even the slightest redeeming social importance—unorthodox ideas, controversial ideas, even ideas hateful to the prevailing climate of opinion—have the full protection of the guaranties" of the First Amendment, wrote Justice William J. Brennan for the *Roth* Court. Obscenity, however, lacked even the slightest social importance, and was, therefore, outside the protections of the Constitution.

One of the issues left unclear by *Roth* was whether the Court's comments about "redeeming social importance" constituted an independent test for determining whether material was obscene or whether they were directed simply toward establishing the underlying basis for leaving obscenity outside the confines of the First Amendment. Put another way, the question was whether allegedly obscene material had to be shown not only to appeal to the prurient interest but also to be without redeeming social value or, conversely, whether the showing of prurient interest carried with it the implication of a lack of social importance. The distinction was critical: if those who sought to ban publication of a book or to punish for its distribution had to show that the material appealed to the prurient interest *and* was "without redeeming social importance," their burden would be far greater than if they had to satisfy the prurient interest test alone.

Two years before, in *Jacobellis v. Ohio* (1964), Justices Brennan and Arthur J. Goldberg suggested that the "social value test" was indeed separate and independent. *Memoirs* thus presented a perfect opportunity to allow the Court to clarify the meaning of *Roth* and to try to convince the entire Court that the social value test should be given independent weight. *Fanny Hill* was admittedly an erotic novel; but, unlike much of the material challenged as obscene in American courts, it was also recognized as literature. At the trial, several university professors testified as to the book's status as a literary document, describing it as a minor "work of art" having "literary merit." It was placed squarely in the eighteenth-century English literary tradition of Richardson and Fielding.

In the Supreme Court, counsel for *Fanny Hill* made the social value test explicit. The record in this case, the justices were told, contains "an overwhelming demonstration of the kind of value that all counsel here today agree invokes the protection of the First Amendment." Relying on Brennan's argument in *Roth*, counsel urged that "under the decisions of this Court, if it has value, literary value or some other type of value, then it cannot be obscenity. Obscenity is worthless trash. That is its definition constitutionally."

The plurality decision in *Memoirs* accepted these contentions. Written by Brennan and joined by Justice Abe Fortas and Chief Justice Earl Warren, it formally split the legal test for obscenity into three parts. For a work to be declared obscene, wrote Brennan, "three elements must coalesce: it must be established that (a) the dominant theme of the material taken as a whole appeals to a prurient interest in sex; (b) the material is patently offensive because it affronts contemporary community standards relating to the description or representation of sexual matters; and (c) the material is utterly without redeeming social value." Moreover, each of these tests had to be "applied independently; the social value of the book can neither be weighed against nor canceled by its prurient appeal or patent offensiveness." Under such a test, *Memoirs of a Woman of Pleasure* could not be declared obscene, for even the Massachusetts court below conceded that the book has "a modicum of literary and historical value."

Although Brennan's opinion carried the votes of only three justices, the concurring opinions of Justices Hugo L. Black and William O. Douglas made it clear that a majority of the Court was behind at least the level of constitutional protection recognized by the plurality opinion. Justice Potter Stewart stuck by his view that the Constitution protects all but "hardcore" pornography, though he found it unnecessary to define that term. Justices Tom C. Clark, John M. Harlan, and Byron R. White dissented.

The *Memoirs* standard, never formally endorsed by a majority of the Court, lasted only seven years. In *Miller v. California* (1973), the Court modified it by refining the meaning of "community standards" and by removing the word "utterly" from the social value test. Henceforth, material could be classified as obscene if it lacked "serious literary, artistic, political or scientific value." Still, *Memoirs v. Massachusetts* remains a landmark on the Supreme Court's tortuous road toward developing a constitutional standard for obscenity.

Selected Bibliography

Fahringer, H.P., and M.J. Brown. "The Rise and Fall of *Roth*—A Critique of the Recent Supreme Court Obscenity Decision." *Criminal Law Bulletin* 10 (Nov. 1974): 785–826.

Rembar, C. *The End of Obscenity*. New York: Random House, 1968.

THE TRIUMPH OF "COMMUNITY STANDARDS"

by William Lasser
Department of Political Science
Clemson University

Miller v. California, 413 U.S. 15 (1973); *Paris Adult Theatre I v. Slaton,* 413 U.S. 49 (1973)
[U.S. Supreme Court]

The U.S. Supreme Court struggled to define "obscenity" in legal terms from the late 1950s to the early 1970s. In the 1960s, the Court became the butt of jokes and ridicule because of the justices' habit of viewing allegedly obscene films on a case-by-case basis to determine their legal status. Moreover, the legal definition of obscenity was broadened and narrowed over and over again. At last, in 1973, the justices handed down a pair of decisions intended, at least in part, to ease the burden that these countless obscenity cases were placing on the Court. To some extent, the Court succeeded.

To understand the significance of the *Miller* and *Paris* decisions, a brief review of the Court's struggles with the obscenity question is necessary. As early as 1942, the Court held in *dicta* that "[t]here are certain well-defined and narrowly limited classes of speech, the prevention and punishment of which have never been thought to raise any Constitutional problem. These include the lewd and obscene. . . ." In all the obscenity cases that followed, the Court has never once challenged this basic proposition; in fact, it has hardly even seen fit to defend or justify it. Instead, all of the Court's obscenity decisions have focused on the definition of obscenity. Given that obscenity is unprotected by the First Amendment, the question has been reduced to determining precisely what constitutes obscenity.

The Court's first attempt to deal with the definitional question was in *Roth v. United States* and *Alberts v. California,* decided together in 1957. Justice William J. Brennan, writing for the Court, held that "sex and obscenity are not synonymous. Obscenity is material which deals with sex in a manner appealing to prurient interest. The portrayal of sex— e.g., in art, literature and scientific works— is not itself sufficient reason to deny the material the constitutional protection of freedom of speech and press." Brennan went on to specify the first of many "tests" used by the Court to define obscenity: "whether to the average person, applying contemporary community standards, the dominant theme of the material taken as a whole appeals to the prurient interest." In doing so, Brennan rejected the so-called Hicklin test, which judged allegedly obscene material by the effect of an "isolated excerpt upon particularly sensitive persons." Brennan's requirements that the work be judged as a whole and that it be judged according to the standards of the average person, together with his specific exemption of works judged scientific, literary, or artistic, were a victory of sorts for free speech advocates.

The *Roth* standard soon proved difficult to apply in practice. While the Court held to the *Roth* standard, or to a variant of it, throughout the 1960s, it was readily apparent that agreement on such a theoretical standard did not translate into agreement on the merits of any particular case. The Court soon split into distinct camps: at one extreme, Justices Hugo L. Black and William O. Douglas seemed to reject any attempt by government to regulate obscenity; at the other, Justice John M. Harlan expressed the belief that the states could ban any material that treated sex "in a fundamentally offensive manner." Justice Potter Stewart would have limited the government's power to a ban on "hard-core" pornography, a standard that Harlan would have applied at the federal level. The Court's frustration in dealing with the obscenity problem is best symbolized by Stewart's oft-quoted remark, in *Jacobellis v. Ohio* (1964), that, while unable to define hard-core pornography, "I know it when I see it."

In the Court's center, a consensus view was being built. In *Memoirs v. Massachusetts* (1966), Brennan wrote for himself, Chief Justice Earl Warren, and Justice Abe Fortas, enunciating a three-part formula derived from *Roth*. The state or federal governments could ban allegedly obscene material only if it was established that "(a) the dominant theme of the material taken as a whole appeals to a prurient interest in sex; (b) the material is patently offensive because it affronts contemporary community standards relating to the description or representation of sexual matters; and (c) the material is utterly without redeeming social value." This standard, though more precise than previous formulations, still had its problems. For one thing, it did not command a majority of the Court. For another, it masked serious questions of emphasis and interpretation that would continue to haunt the Court in later years.

In the years after *Memoirs*, the Court fell back on the practice of deciding obscenity cases using short, *per curiam* opinions reversing convictions in cases where a majority of the Court believed the material in question to be protected under the Constitution. This type of apparently standardless jurisprudence (which, in fact, represented a number of different and unexpressed standards) was initiated in *Redrup v. New York* (1967) and was used, according to Brennan, no fewer that 31 times. This was clearly an untenable situation for a Court used to principled decisionmaking, and in 1973 the Court finally tried to find a way out of the difficulties it had made for itself.

The Court that decided *Miller* was different from the one that had struggled with the obscenity problem in the 1960s. At its head was Chief Justice Warren Burger, who had replaced Earl Warren in 1969. Also new to the Court were the three other Richard Nixon appointees: Harry A. Blackmun, Lewis F. Powell, and William H. Rehnquist. They replaced Fortas, Black, and Harlan. The only justices left from the *Memoirs* Court were Brennan, Douglas, White, and Stewart.

Miller, Burger began for the Court, called for "a re-examination of standards enunciated in earlier cases involving what Mr. Justice Harlan called 'the intractable obscenity problem.'" To make sense of this difficult question, Burger both recast the *Roth-Memoirs* test and greatly changed its emphasis. Under the new *Miller* standard, works could not be judged legally obscene unless "(a) 'the average person,

applying contemporary community standards' would find that the work, taken as a whole, appeals to the prurient interest . . .; (b) . . . the work depicts or describes, in a patently offensive way, sexual conduct specifically defined by the applicable state law; and (c) . . . the work, taken as a whole, lacks serious literary, artistic, political, or scientific value."

Burger's new formulation fine-tuned the *Memoirs* test in three ways. First, obscenity laws were now restricted to depictions or descriptions of sexual conduct as opposed to sexual expression. Second, state obscenity statutes were now required to be quite specific in their description of the sexual conduct banned. Finally, and perhaps most important, works no longer had to be "utterly" without redeeming social value to be judged obscene; they could be so judged if found to be without "serious" literary, artistic, political, or scientific value. No longer could "a quotation from Voltaire in the flyleaf of a book" protect "an otherwise obscene publication," Burger wrote.

Throughout his opinion, Burger held to his view that *Memoirs* never commanded the support of more than three justices. While only three joined Brennan's *Memoirs* opinion, however, two more—Black and Douglas—took an even more expansive view of the First Amendment. It is clear, at least, that the *Miller* formulation would have been unacceptable to a majority of the *Memoirs* Court.

What was even more significant than these tinkerings with the *Memoirs* approach was the Court's decision to shift the burden of responsibility for the determination of obscenity from the judges to the local communities—as represented by the juries in criminal obscenity cases. Moreover, Burger gave up on any attempt to develop or impose "national standards" by which to judge obscenity. Instead, jurors would be asked to determine how "the average person, applying contemporary community standards" would react to the material in question. As representatives of a cross-section of their community, jurors would seem particularly well-placed to make such a determination. "The adversary system, with lay jurors as the usual ultimate factfinders in criminal prosecutions, has historically permitted triers of fact to draw on the standards of their community, guided always by limiting instructions on the law," Burger wrote. In a nation as large and as vast as the United States, it would be "futile" to ask jurors to determine national standards; and besides, "it is neither realistic nor constitutionally sound to read the First Amendment as requiring that the people of Maine or Mississippi accept public depiction of conduct found tolerable in Las Vegas, or New York City."

In the companion case *Paris Adult Theatre I v. Slaton*, the Court rejected the argument that the right to privacy extends to the commercial exhibition of obscene material in a theater closed to the unconsenting public. An earlier case, *Stanley v. Georgia* (1969), had held that individuals have an absolute right to view obscene materials in the privacy of their homes, but Burger, again writing for the Court, held that there are "legitimate state interests at stake in stemming the tide of commercialized obscenity," including "the interest of the public in the quality of life and the total community environment, the tone of commerce in the great city centers, and, possibly, the public safety itself."

The majority in both *Miller* and *Paris* was the narrowest possible: 5–4. Douglas wrote a dissent to each case, as did Brennan, who was joined by Marshall and Stewart. Douglas repeated his long-held view that obscene speech is protected by the First Amendment, and argued that, in any event, no one should be convicted on an obscenity charge unless the material in question has already been declared obscene in a civil proceeding. Brennan, after a long review of the precedents, concluded that it was impossible to define obscenity with sufficient precision and predictability, and warned that the Court's decision would have a "chilling effect" on freedom of expression in the United States. Therefore, he concluded, "in the absence of distribution to juveniles or obtrusive exposure to unconsenting adults," the states

were prohibited from attempting wholly to suppress allegedly obscene material on the basis of content.

Miller has suffered from vociferous criticism in the almost two decades since it was handed down. The *Miller* standard, however difficult to apply at the margins, has at least narrowed the definition of obscenity to "hardcore" material. Properly applied, the *Miller* standard would probably have little if any effect on chilling serious literary, artistic, scientific, or political expression. However, the *Miller* test has failed to achieve its objectives in at least two ways. First, the Court has found it impossible to rely on juries for the determination of obscenity questions, because the question of whether specific material is obscene involves questions not only of fact but also of law, and because the facts themselves are subject to appellate review. In one case, for example, the Court had to intercede when a Georgia jury decided that the film *Carnal Knowledge* violated community standards; even so, wrote Rehnquist for the Court, that film could in no way be seen as depicting "sexual conduct in a patently offensive way." Second, the *Miller* test has done nothing to clarify the meaning of obscenity where there still exists great uncertainty. Thus, national publications or films may be judged by the standards of the most restrictive communities in the nation, and local communities have the latitude to make sweeping attacks on alleged obscenity—at times to the detriment of the free exchange of ideas.

Miller has fulfilled its major purpose, however. The Court may still sit as the final arbiter in obscenity cases, but it does it far less frequently, and with far less embarrassment to the Court and the justices.

Selected Bibliography

Schauer, F.F. *The Law of Obscenity*. Washington, DC: Bureau of National Affairs, Inc., 1976.

E. Right to Counsel

"INCORPORATION" AND THE RIGHT TO COUNSEL

by Tinsley E. Yarbrough
Department of Political Science
East Carolina University

Gideon v. Wainwright, 372 U.S. 335 (1963) [U.S. Supreme Court]

Clarence Earl Gideon was not one of God's nobler creatures. When he was haled into a Florida circuit court to be tried for breaking into Panama City, Florida's Bay Harbor Poolroom, his "rap sheet" already included three prior burglary convictions, one for possession of governmental property, and a 20-day jail term for public drunkenness. He was 50 years old, but looked at least 60. His voice and hands trembled; his face was wrinkled. "Anyone meeting him for the first time," journalist Anthony Lewis later wrote, "would be likely to regard him as the most wretched of men."

But Gideon was not drained of spirit. Since he had no funds for a lawyer, he asked Judge Robert L. McCrary, Jr., to appoint counsel for his defense. Although obviously sympathetic to Gideon's plight, McCrary denied the defendant's request: "Mr. Gideon, I am sorry, but I cannot appoint Counsel to represent you in this case. Under the laws of the State of Florida, the only time the Court can appoint Counsel to represent a Defendant is when that person is charged with a capital offense. I am sorry, but I will have to deny your request to appoint Counsel to defend you in this case."

Gideon was hardly persuaded. "The United States Supreme Court," he replied defiantly, if inaccurately, "says I am entitled to be represented by counsel." But the judge had made his ruling, and Gideon was obliged to defend himself before a six-member jury. He "conducted his defense," U.S. Supreme Court Justice Hugo L. Black would later conclude, "about as well as could be expected from a layman," making opening and closing statements, cross-examining prosecution witnesses, presenting witnesses in his own behalf, and declining to testify himself.

Gideon was a layperson, however, not a lawyer, and he made mistakes no reasonably competent attorney would have been expected to make. The principal witness for the prosecution testified, for example, that he had seen Gideon in and then leaving the poolroom at 5:30 on the morning the break-in was discovered. On cross-examination, Gideon asked the witness what he had been doing outside the poolroom at that hour, but the defendant did not pursue that potentially fruitful line of questioning. Nor did he probe the witness's reputation, relationship with the defendant, or related areas a lawyer surely would have explored. Apparently because the prosecution's chief witness had also testified that Gideon was carrying a pint of wine when he left the poolroom, the defendant did question witnesses closely in an effort to establish that he had been intoxicated on the fateful morning. Yet under Florida law—law with which any attorney would have been familiar—evidence of intoxication could have served as a defense to the crime with which Gideon was charged. Finally, Gideon did not ask the judge to define the elements of the crime for the jury and did not challenge numerous errors McCrary arguably committed during the trial.

Following Gideon's conviction, McCrary sentenced Gideon to five years in prison, the maximum sentence allowed under state law for the felony of breaking and entering with intent to commit a misdemeanor. From his cell in the Florida State Prison at Raiford, Gideon then filed a petition for a writ of *habeas corpus* with the state supreme court, contending that the trial judge's failure to appoint him defense counsel violated rights "guaranteed by the Constitution and the Bill of Rights by the United States

Government." When the Florida high court denied his petition without opinion, he turned to the U.S. Supreme Court, seeking review through an *in forma pauperis* petition, a procedure allowing indigents to petition a federal court for relief without complying with the rules, or meeting the expense, ordinarily connected with the filing of a case.

The law clerk who initially screened Gideon's petition for Chief Justice Earl Warren decided that it at least merited some response from the state. He had the Court's clerk request a reply to the petition from Florida authorities. Citing the Supreme Court's decision in *Betts v. Brady* (1942), Florida's attorney general urged the Court to deny Gideon a hearing. Under *Betts*, he argued, the Sixth Amendment did not guarantee the right to counsel in federal cases, and it was not *per se* binding on the states through the due process clause of the Fourteenth Amendment. Instead, indigent state defendants were entitled to appointed counsel only when "special circumstances" in a case, such as the gravity of the offense or the accused's limited mental capacity, required appointment of a lawyer to assure the defendant a "fair trial." Gideon, who apparently was unaware of *Betts*, had claimed no "special circumstances" and thus had no right to appointed counsel.

In his response to the state's reply, as in his original petition, Gideon continued to maintain that "a citizen . . . cannot get a just and fair trial without the aid of counsel," whatever the circumstances. "It makes no difference," he added in a slap at the *Betts* rationale, "how old I am or what color I am or what church I belong too [sic] if any." Ultimately, the Supreme Court determined that *Betts* should indeed be given further scrutiny. On June 4, 1962, the Court granted Gideon's motion to proceed *in forma pauperis* and petition for a writ of *certiorari*. In addition to other issues raised by the case, the Court's order stipulated that the parties were to discuss the following question in their briefs and oral argument: "Should this Court's holding in *Betts v. Brady* . . . be reconsidered?"

Since Gideon was a pauper, the Supreme Court also granted the petitioner what Florida had denied him, a court-appointed attorney, and a very distinguished counsel at that. No doubt in recognition of the tremendous significance of the *Betts* reconsideration and possible reversal, the Court appointed prominent Washington attorney Abe Fortas—close friend of several justices, confidant of presidents, and a future member of the Court—to represent the petitioner. Since his principal responsibility was to represent Gideon, not to battle with Supreme Court precedent, Fortas and his staff first reviewed the record of Gideon's case to determine whether he might be entitled to counsel under the *Betts* special circumstances doctrine. They quickly determined that no such claim could be made; rather Gideon's case was an ideal one in which to challenge what they considered the *Betts* myth—the assumption that any layperson can receive a fair trial when obliged to act as his own counsel, whatever his background or the circumstances of his case. In briefs and oral argument, Fortas pressed that position before the Court. The American Civil Liberties Union and the attorneys general of 22 states supported Fortas's stance in *amici curiae* ("friends of the court") briefs, while officials of only two, Alabama and North Carolina supported Florida's contentions.

Now the matter was before the Court, which rarely overturns its own precedents. But *Betts* had always rested on a fragile foundation, and the Court's post-*Betts* counsel rulings had steadily weakened the precedent's underpinnings. Ten years before *Betts* was decided, in *Powell v. Alabama* (1932), the first of the infamous "Scottsboro Cases" to reach the High Court, the Court had stopped short of requiring appointed counsel automatically for indigent state defendants. Instead, it had held merely that appointed counsel was necessary to assure the Scottsboro defendants a fair trial, given the gravity of their offense, the possible imposition of the death sentence, their youth and limited education, their isolation from friends and family, and the mob-like atmosphere in which they were tried. Justice George Sutherland's opinion for the *Powell* Court did include the *dictum*, however, that the provision of counsel was a "fundamental" right of the sort earlier cases had found implicit in the Fourteenth Amendment's due process clause. A *dictum* in Justice Benjamin N. Cardozo's opinion for the Court in *Palko v. Connecticut* (1937) assumed the same position, as did *dicta* in several other cases decided between *Powell* and *Betts*. Thus, when the *Betts* Court limited *Powell* strictly to its facts and rejected any *per se* right of appointed counsel for state defendants, it ignored a significant body of developing *dicta*.

In the years after *Betts*, the difficulty of applying its special circumstances formula in individual cases had also become increasingly apparent. In two 1948 cases in which the absence of counsel had allowed significant errors of the trial judge to go unchallenged, for example, the Supreme Court reversed one defendant's conviction, yet affirmed the other's, for reasons difficult if not impossible to fathom. Partly no doubt because of such difficulties, the Court by 1945 had begun distinguishing noncapital and capital cases, invariably requiring counsel in the latter. More significantly, after 1950, the Court had invariably found special circumstances requiring the appointment of a lawyer in all state criminal cases, capital or noncapital. All that appeared to remain, it seemed, was *Betts*'s formal reversal.

On March 18, 1963, the Supreme Court, speaking through Justice Hugo L. Black, took that final step. Black, who had registered a dissent in *Betts* and had long urged application of the Sixth Amendment right of counsel in all state cases, was a fitting choice to write the Court's opinion. As the Court's spokesman, however, he was unable to reiterate his long-stated view that the framers of the Fourteenth Amendment had intended its first section to embody all the guarantees of the Bill of Rights, including the right to counsel, a position that had never acquired majority support on the Court. Instead, he drew on *Palko v. Connecticut* and other earlier opinions to conclude that the Fourteenth Amendment embodied "fundamental" guarantees of the Bill of Rights and that the *Betts* majority had erred in refusing to include the right to counsel among safeguards of that character. Citing *Powell* and other pre-*Betts* cases characterizing the right to counsel as a fundamental guarantee, he concluded that "the Court in *Betts v. Brady* made an abrupt break with its own well-considered precedents," adding: "In returning to these old precedents, sounder we believe than the new, we but restore constitutional principles established to achieve a fair system of justice." Rejection of

Betts, Black asserted, was also compelled by "reason and reflection." He continued: "[I]n our adversary system of criminal justice, any person haled into court, who is too poor to hire a lawyer, cannot be assured a fair trial unless counsel is provided for him. This seems to us to be an obvious truth. Governments, both state and federal, quite properly spend vast sums of money to establish machinery to try defendants accused of crime. Lawyers to prosecute are everywhere deemed essential to protect the public's interest in an orderly society. Similarly there are few defendants charged with crime, few indeed, who fail to hire the best lawyers they can get to prepare and present their defenses. That government hires lawyers to prosecute and defendants who have the money hire lawyers to defend are the strongest indications of the widespread belief that lawyers in criminal courts are necessities, not luxuries. The right of one charged with crime to counsel may not be deemed fundamental and essential to fair trials in some countries, but it is in ours. . . . Twenty-two States, as friends of the Court, argue that *Betts* was 'an anachronism when handed down' and that it should now be overruled. We agree."

Although Black was unable to advance his "total incorporation" thesis regarding the relationship of the Bill of Rights to the Fourteenth Amendment, Justice William O. Douglas, who had also dissented in *Betts*, was not subject to such strictures. Douglas drafted a brief separate opinion in which he noted that ten justices over the years had expressed support for total incorporation. He then added: "Unfortunately [that view] has never commanded a Court. Yet, happily, all constitutional questions are always open. . . . And what we do today does not foreclose the matter." After circulating his draft to Black for his approval, Douglas filed the concurrence.

Two other justices also registered concurrences in the case. Justice Tom C. Clark, who typically favored a more flexible approach to the Fourteenth Amendment's meaning than some of his colleagues, declined to join Black's opinion because it suggested that incorporated rights were to have equal application in federal and state cases. In his brief *Gideon* concurrence, however, Clark observed that the Fourteenth Amendment's due process clause applied to the deprivation of "liberty" as well as "life." He then asserted that he could "find no acceptable rationalization" for the Court's continuing to require counsel in all state capital cases, as it had been for many years despite *Betts*, yet refuse to apply such a *per se* rule in noncapital state cases. To eliminate this incongruity, Clark joined the Court's decision.

While agreeing that *Betts* should be overruled, Justice John Marshall Harlan considered the precedent "entitled to a more respectful burial than has been accorded," adding, with a nod to Black and Douglas, "at least on the part of those of us who were not on the Court when the case was decided." *Betts*, Harlan contended, was not, as Black had argued, "an abrupt break" with the Court's precedents. In *Powell*, the Court had ordered counsel for the Scottsboro defendants because of "the particular facts there presented," not as a requirement for all state cases, or even all state capital cases. The *Betts* special circumstances rule was thus consistent, Harlan contended, with *Powell*, indeed modeled after the Court's approach in the earlier case. Over the years, however, *Betts* had been gradually undermined, first in capital cases and then in all state prosecutions involving serious offenses. Harlan stated, "The Court has come to recognize that the mere existence of a serious criminal charge constituted itself special circumstances requiring the services of counsel at trial." Overruling *Betts*, therefore, would do "no more than to make explicit something that has long been foreshadowed in our decisions." Failure to do so, on the other hand, would "in the long run . . . do disservice to the federal system," especially since many state courts had not yet fully grasped the reality of *Betts*'s erosion.

In his *Gideon* concurrence, Harlan also rejected the notion that Bill of Rights safeguards found to be "implicit in the concept of ordered liberty," and thus binding on the states through the Fourteenth Amendment due process guarantee, should be given the same force in federal and state cases. In his view, the Fourteenth Amendment did not "incorporate" the terms of the Sixth Amendment or other Bill of Rights safeguards "as such"; it only guarantees approxi-

mating Bill of Rights provisions. Considerations of federalism demanded greater judicial deference, moreover, to the states than to the federal government.

However, as additional Bill of Rights safeguards were applied to the states through the Fourteenth Amendment after *Gideon*, the Court rejected Harlan's position, embracing instead the view, as put by Douglas in his *Gideon* concurrence, that "rights protected against state invasion by the due process clause of the Fourteenth Amendment are not watered-down versions of what the Bill of Rights guarantees." With the exception of its decision in *Apodaca v. Oregon* (1972), permitting nonunanimous state jury verdicts while forbidding them in federal cases, the Court remained largely faithful to that approach to the incorporation question. In such cases as *Argersinger v. Hamlin* (1972), the Court also carried *Gideon* beyond felonies to all cases in which any prison or jail sentence is imposed. Using a variety of constitutional rationales in cases decided before and after *Gideon*, moreover, the justices extended the right of indigent defendants to counsel to all "critical stages" of a criminal case, including custodial police interrogation, postindictment lineups, preliminary hearings, arraignments, and obligatory appeals.

The constitutional ruling that Gideon's minor run-in with the law had spawned, however, was to remain the Court's most significant decision regarding the scope of the right to counsel. Certainly for Gideon it was. On August 5, 1963, he was retried, represented on this occasion by counsel. After a little more than an hour's deliberation, the jury returned an acquittal verdict. That evening, Gideon paid another visit to the Bay Harbor Poolroom.

Selected Bibliography

Beaney, W.M. *The Right to Counsel in American Courts.* Ann Arbor, MI: University of Michigan Press, 1955.

Carter, D.T. *Scottsboro: A Tragedy of the American South.* Baton Rouge, LA: Louisiana State University Press, 1969.

Lewis, A. *Gideon's Trumpet.* New York: Random House, 1964.

LAWYER? YOU WANT A LAWYER?

by Delane Ramsey
Taylors, SC

Escobedo v. Illinois, 378 U.S. 478 (1964) [U.S. Supreme Court]

"You're under arrest." "I want my lawyer." These phrases have a staccato rhythm and familiarity that popular entertainment has burned into the collective American conscious. However, the right to counsel has not always been an American tradition.

The right to counsel has evolved slowly within American jurisprudence. Many state constitutions did not even mention counsel. The Sixth Amendment to the U.S. Constitution states, "In all criminal prosecutions, the accused shall . . . have the assistance of counsel for his defense." Until 50 years ago, this was interpreted as allowing the defendant to provide his own counsel, not compelling provision of counsel by an outside agency. The Supreme Court found, in 1938, that the Sixth Amendment required all defendants in federal criminal cases to have an attorney (at the defendant's expense) or to intelligently waive that right. In 1963, Congress required that counsel be provided for indigent defendants in federal cases.

The Constitution originally protected civil rights only from federal intrusion, not from state interference. Because federal constitutional protections had not yet been applied to the state courts, the suspect's rights in state criminal cases were comparatively unprotected. Although the Scottsboro Cases in 1932 drew attention to state courts' denial of counsel, not until 1961 did the Supreme Court rule that states must allow or provide counsel to defendants in state capital cases. In *Gideon v. Wainwright* (1963), the High Court went one step further and required the states to allow or provide counsel if necessary in any state criminal case that could result in imprisonment or loss of freedom. Since life and liberty are fundamental human rights, counsel necessary to protect a defendant's life, in a criminal case, is equally necessary to protect a defendant's liberty in another criminal case. *Gideon* answered the question of why counsel should be provided in state criminal cases. The

remaining issue was when: At what point before the trial does counsel become necessary for the protection of a defendant's rights?

On January 20, 1960, Danny Escobedo, 22 years old and of Mexican background, was arrested in Chicago for the murder of his brother-in-law. Escobedo was interrogated, said nothing, and was released later that day on a writ of *habeas corpus*. Ten days later, Escobedo was again arrested and taken to police headquarters. He was told that someone had identified him as the murderer. Escobedo was then taken to interrogation. He asked for his lawyer, Warren Wolfson, repeatedly during interrogation, but he was told that his lawyer did not want to see him. In fact, Wolfson had arrived at the station house shortly after the police brought in Escobedo. He had asked to see Escobedo, but was told that the interrogation was under way. When told that he would have to wait until it was completed, Wolfson complained to the chief on duty, but was still not allowed to talk to Escobedo. Wolfson then "had a conversation with every police officer that I could find," trying to get to his client. Wolfson saw Escobedo only briefly through an open door, but the police prevented any communication.

Escobedo was interrogated in Spanish by an officer who knew his family. Escobedo denied any criminal knowledge of the crime. He was then confronted with his accuser. Escobedo told his accuser "You're lying. I didn't shoot Manuel, you did it." This remark showed complicity in the murder, which under Illinois state law was as serious as the violent act itself. Escobedo then made other statements that further incriminated him. A state's attorney was called in and took Escobedo's statement. The state's attorney did not tell Escobedo of his right to remain silent or that his statement could be used against him at the trial.

At his trial, Escobedo's statement was admitted into evidence over the objections of his counsel. Escobedo was convicted. He appealed to the Illinois Supreme Court to have his statement suppressed, but the state supreme court ultimately reaffirmed his conviction. Escobedo then appealed to the U.S. Supreme Court on the ground that his Sixth Amendment right to counsel had been violated. The appeal was argued before the Court on April 29, 1964.

On June 22, by a 5–4 majority, the Supreme Court reversed Escobedo's conviction. The Court cited two reasons for its ruling: (1) the suspect under interrogation had been denied his request to see counsel and (2) the police had not warned the suspect of his constitutional protection to remain silent during the interrogation. Under Illinois state law, admission of "mere" complicity in a murder was as damaging as active participation in the violent act. "The guiding hand of counsel was essential" in protecting the defendant's rights, particularly in this specific case. Deprived of this guiding hand, the defendant had effectively been denied his Sixth Amendment protection of access to counsel and his Fourteenth Amendment right of due process.

The Court held that a suspect must have the protective assistance of counsel whenever that suspect becomes the specific focus of an investigation; in practical terms, at the time of arrest. "Where a police investigation is no longer a general inquiry into an unsolved crime but has begun to focus on a particular suspect," right to counsel must be allowed or provided. Any lack of such counsel, the Court concluded, would result in the exclusion of evidence obtained from the unprotected interrogation.

The *Escobedo* decision was announced in June 1964. This was in the midst of a hot, tension-filled summer in America's largest cities. The civil rights movement was provoking extremists to violence. Serious racial riots erupted in several northern cities, while antiblack violence rose in the South. The first opposition to the Vietnam War appeared. The U.S. Supreme Court added to the heat with several emotional decisions. Reaction was shrill from groups offended by decisions on apportionment, obscenity, and racial desegregation. However, there was little general reaction to *Escobedo*, since it was almost lost among these more controversial rulings. Still, California spinsters circulated

petitions to overturn *Escobedo*. Legislation restricting the Court's jurisdiction was introduced in Congress, although it later died of neglect. The public seemed more concerned with bigger issues in 1964.

Escobedo left at least one major legal question unanswered. Implicit within its decision is a Fifth Amendment value involving protection from self-incrimination. For this Fifth Amendment protection to be operative, the Sixth Amendment right to counsel must be available. A defendant deprived of counsel would incriminate himself. The defendant had an additional right: the right to remain silent during his interrogation in order to avoid incriminating himself. But to exercise this right of silence, the defendant must be aware of it, and if not already aware of that right, he must be told about it. The question remained: Who would tell him? The police had denied Escobedo this information. Who would advise future suspects? The *Escobedo* Court did not specifically address this Fifth Amendment matter.

The Supreme Court's ruling in *Miranda v. Arizona* (1966) did address the matter. A suspect in custody or under arrest must be told that he has the right to remain silent and that anything he says can be used against him at his trial. In addition, he has the right to an attorney before questioning, and an appointed attorney will be provided if he cannot afford his own. The suspect can stop the interrogation at any time. It was now the responsibility of the police to advise the suspect of his rights. The prosecution must demonstrate in court that the suspect was advised of these rights, including any informed waivers of these rights to which the suspect had agreed.

Miranda finally changed the relationship between citizen and state, between suspect and police. The citizen/suspect now had the right to be told, in a way that he understood, that his rights and person were protected from the abuse of institutional power. A citizen/suspect standing alone could now tell the assembled police power of county, city, state, or nation that he had nothing to say—and make it stick.

The public is more familiar with *Miranda* than it is with *Escobedo*. But many experts in the legal fraternity consider *Escobedo* the more significant decision; it extends the range of constitutional protection further. *Miranda* was the ultimate extension of a citizen/suspect's rights. *Escobedo* was the penultimate step, the steppingstone to *Miranda*. *Miranda* merely stated who advised the suspect of his rights. *Escobedo* had already stated that these rights must be protected. *Miranda* can be considered the icing on *Escobedo*'s cake. *Escobedo* did the work, *Miranda* got the credit.

Escobedo and *Miranda* were criticized as "coddling criminals," as unnecessarily restricting the police in their effort to control a rising crime rate. The passage of 25 years has changed that earlier response. Recently, the chief of police in a major southern city remarked that these decisions have actually strengthened the police. The recent videotaped beating in Los Angeles not withstanding, the police have become more professional in the thoroughness and scope of their investigations. The police themselves seem pleased that convictions are now based on hard evidence, not questionable confessions.

Escobedo and *Miranda* produced paradoxical results. Suspects are better advised of their rights and consequently speak less freely now than before 1966. Police professionalism has made impressive advances since then. The public is better served by a more professional police and by the knowledge that the citizen/suspect has an "even break" in court. The final winner is the citizen. He knows that whenever he needs them, his Fifth and Sixth Amendment rights of silence and counsel are protected and available.

After his release in 1964, Escobedo had several scrapes with the Chicago police. By 1968, he was serving concurrent 20- and 22-year sentences at the Leavenworth Federal Penitentiary for multiple federal drug violations. Twenty years later, Escobedo was again incarcerated, this time for child molestation.

Selected Bibliography

Enken, A.N., and S.H. Elsen. "Counsel for the Suspect: *Massiah v. U.S.* and *Escobedo v. Illinois.*" *Minnesota Law Review* 49 (1964): 47–91.

Michaux, R.H. Jr. "Right to Retained Counsel at Time of Arrest." *North Carolina Law Review* 43 (1964): 187–99.

F. Search and Seizure

THE FRUITS OF THE POISONOUS TREE

by William Lasser
Department of Political Science
Clemson University

Weeks v. United States, 232 U.S. 383 (1914) [U.S. Supreme Court]

One of the most controversial rules ever laid down by the U.S. Supreme Court is the so-called exclusionary rule, which bans the use in a criminal trial of illegally seized evidence. Although most of the controversy surrounding the rule has been generated in the past 30 years, the rule dates back to 1914, and the case of *Weeks v. United States.*

Weeks (a man so obscure that the Supreme Court opinion does not indicate his first name) was arrested by the U.S. marshal and charged with the transportation of lottery tickets through the U.S. mails. His arrest was based on two searches of his house: the first by local police officials and the second by the federal marshal; neither search was authorized by a search warrant. The searches yielded a variety of incriminating papers and articles, including lottery tickets and documents pertaining to the lottery. They were seized by the U.S. marshal and held for use in Weeks's upcoming criminal trial in the U.S. district court.

At this point, the case took an interesting procedural twist. Before the trial, Weeks brought an action in federal court demanding that his property be returned to him on the ground that it had been obtained in violation of the Fourth and Fifth Amendments to the U.S. Constitution. However, if the incriminating material was returned to Weeks, it would effectively eliminate the government's case against him. Weeks's demand for a return of his property eventually reached the U.S. Supreme Court.

Justice William R. Day wrote the opinion of the Court. The meaning of the Fourth Amendment, he began, was made clear by the Supreme Court in *Boyd v. United States* (1886). That case involved a suit by the government to take possession of 35 cases of plate glass, alleg-

edly imported into the United States fraudulently in violation of federal customs revenue acts. As part of this action, the government requested that Boyd be ordered to produce certain papers tending to implicate him in this alleged fraud. Under the federal statute, Boyd's failure to produce such papers was to be taken by the court as "confessed, unless his failure or refusal to produce" the documents "shall be explained away to the satisfaction of the Court." The Supreme Court held that such a rule constituted an illegal search and seizure under the Fourth Amendment and a violation of the self-incrimination guarantees of the Fifth Amendment. In doing so, the Court held that "constitutional provisions for the security of person and property should be liberally construed. A close and literal construction deprives them of half their efficacy, and leads to gradual depreciation of the right as if it consisted more in sound than in substance. It is the duty of courts to be watchful for the constitutional rights of the citizen, and against any stealthy encroachments thereto."

The specific right guaranteed by the Fourth and Fifth Amendments—which, the *Boyd* Court said, "throw great light upon each other"—was the right of the citizen in a free society to be free from "the invasion of his indefeasible right of personal security, personal liberty, and private property, where that right has never been forfeited by his conviction of some public offense." Therefore, the *Boyd* Court said that the only searches permissible under the Constitution were those "founded on affidavits, and made under warrants which described the thing to be searched for, and the person and place to be seized." The federal statute authorizing the production of evidence "by a mere service of notice upon the party," the Court concluded, failed to meet that test, and the court below was not permitted to draw incriminating conclusions from Boyd's refusal to produce the material in question.

Under the standards of the Fourth Amendment, as interpreted in *Boyd*, it seemed clear that the seizure of evidence in *Weeks* was unconstitutional. The Supreme Court focused its attention on the second search of Weeks's home—the one by the U.S. marshal. Since the first search was performed by nonfederal officers, it was beyond the reach of the Fourth Amendment, the Court said, because that amendment reaches only "the Federal Government and its agencies." (The Fourth Amendment was not extended to the states until 1961 in *Mapp v. Ohio*.) The second search, however, was performed by a federal agent and was clearly unconstitutional. The marshal, the Court concluded, had acted "without authority of process," nor was it clear whether "such could have been legally issued."

The Court's determination that the search of Weeks's house and the seizure of his property were illegal did not resolve the case, however. The Court still needed to act on Weeks's motion that the evidence in question be returned to him in consequence of the illegal actions of the marshal. And here the problem facing the Court was trickier, since the Fourth Amendment provides no specific remedy to enforce its guarantees.

Nevertheless, the Court proceeded to decide the case. The Fourth Amendment, wrote Day, "puts the courts of the United States and federal officials, in the exercise of their power and authority, under limitations and restraints as to the exercise of such power and authority, and to forever secure the people, their persons, houses, papers and effects against all unreasonable searches and seizures under the guise of law." The "tendency of those who execute the criminal laws of the country to obtain convictions by means of unlawful seizures and enforced confessions," Day concluded, "should find no sanction in the judgments of the courts which are charged at all times with the support of the Constitution and to which people of all conditions have a right to appeal for the maintenance of such fundamental rights."

Weeks, therefore, turned on a very specific issue: "the right of the court in a criminal prosecution to retain for the purposes of evidence" the letters and papers illegally taken from Weeks's house. Could the Court, as an agency of the federal government, keep such documents in its possession? "If letters and private documents can thus be seized and held and used in evidence against a citizen accused of an offense," Day answered, "the protection of the Fourth Amendment declaring his right to be secure against such searches and seizures is of no value, and, so far as those thus placed are concerned, might as well be stricken from the Constitution." The evidence in question had to be turned back to the defendant, and therefore could not be used at trial.

In later years, as the exclusionary rule was expanded and modified and as the controversy surrounding it grew, a great deal of attention would be paid to the theoretical justification for this extraordinary remedy. On the current Supreme Court (1990), there are two polar positions. On one end of the spectrum, Chief Justice William H. Rehnquist and Justice Byron R. White believe that the exclusionary rule is simply a means to the end of enforcing the Fourth Amendment through deterrence of police misconduct. For them, it is derived from, but not a part of, the Fourth Amendment and can be discarded in circumstances where it is counterproductive or where other ways of enforcing the amendment exist. The other extreme is represented by Justice Thurgood Marshall, who argues that the exclusionary rule is a part of, and required by, the Fourth Amendment. The remaining justices fall somewhere between these poles.

Scholars have attempted to find support for both positions in the *Weeks* decision; and there is language to support both in Day's argument. On one hand, Day declared that the district court's order denying Weeks's application for the return of his possessions was itself "a denial of the constitutional rights of the accused." At other times, however, Day seemed to treat the exclusionary sanction as a means to an end—in other words, as a remedy: "If letters and private documents can thus be seized and held and used in evidence," he wrote, "the protection of the Fourth Amendment . . . is of no value."

It seems clear, however, that Day's opinion leaned toward the view that the Fourth Amendment directly required the suppression of the evidence in *Weeks*, at least given the particular circumstances involved. Early on in the opinion, he tipped his hand: "The case in the aspect in which we are dealing with it," he asserted, "involves *the right of the court* to retain the letters and correspondence of the accused, seized in his house in his absence and without his authority" (emphasis added). For a Court to "sanction such proceedings," Day concluded, "would be to affirm by judicial decision a manifest neglect if not an open defiance of the prohibitions of the Constitution." The Fourth Amendment, in other words, was directed toward the federal courts as well as to federal law enforcement officials.

Day's conclusion in *Weeks* was influenced by factors not usually present in modern exclusionary rule cases. First, he was asked to decide directly on a motion to the federal court to return the papers in question. Thus, the Court was not being asked to impose a rule on law enforcement officials, but on the judiciary it-self. This conclusion was reinforced by the *Boyd* decision, in which the Supreme Court specifically stated that a court's use of private books and papers produced by compulsion is "the equivalent of a search and seizure" under the Fourth Amendment. "Though the proceeding in question is divested of many of the aggravating incidents of actual search and seizure, yet . . . it contains their substance and essence, and effects their substantial purpose."

Whatever Day's motivation, *Weeks* remains a landmark among the Supreme Court's decisions explicating and enforcing the Fourth and Fifth Amendments. Its legacy, both in protecting constitutional rights and in generating controversy for the Supreme Court, is considerable.

Selected Bibliography

Kamisar, Y. "Does (Did) (Should) the Exclusionary Rule Rest on a 'Principled Basis' Rather Than an 'Empirical Proposition'?" *Creighton Law Review* 16 (1982–83): 565–667.

Schlesinger, S.R. *Exclusionary Injustice: The Problem of Illegally Seized Evidence.* New York: Marcel Dekker, 1975.

ARE BOOTLEGGERS ENTITLED TO PRIVACY?

by Philippa Strum
Department of Political Science
City University of New York

Olmstead v. United States, 277 U.S. 438 (1928) [U.S. Supreme Court]

In 1919, the states ratified the Eighteenth Amendment, prohibiting the manufacture, sale, transportation, and importation of intoxicating liquors. Acting under its mandate, Congress passed the National Prohibition Act, which set out criminal sanctions for trafficking in liquor. "Bootlegging," or importing and selling liquor illegally, quickly became a major industry in the United States as Americans apparently decided that they wanted alcoholic beverages to be readily available (a preference that was translated into the repeal of this amendment by the Twenty-First Amendment in 1933).

Roy Olmstead put together a bootlegging business that, according to the federal government, had three offices in Seattle, Washington, employed at least 50 people, and used two seagoing ships and several smaller boats to transport liquor to British Columbia and throughout Washington State. This illegal business exceeded $2 million in sales a year.

The federal government discovered what the High Court called this "conspiracy of amazing magnitude" by wiretapping the telephone line in one of the company's offices as well as the telephone lines leading into the homes of four of its employees. The taps continued for many months, during which stenographers took notes of the conversations they overheard. Eventually 75 people were indicted on the basis of this evidence. Olmstead and two others, who were among those convicted of conspiracy to violate the National Prohibition Act, appealed to the Supreme Court on the grounds (1) that the wiretaps violated the Fourth Amendment's provision that "[t]he right of the people to be secure in their persons, houses, papers, and effects, against unreasonable searches and seizures, shall not be violated" and (2) that such searches and seizures are unreasonable unless the law enforcement officials undertaking them have been granted warrants for "probable cause." He also relied on the Fifth Amendment's guarantee that "[n]o person . . . shall be compelled in any criminal case to be a witness against himself."

The case raised two major issues. One was the extent to which the Court would interpret the Fourth Amendment's search and seizure clause in light of technological developments. That is, would the amendment be held to prohibit government wiretapping, which obviously could not have been foreseen at the time the amendment was written? The second was whether the Court would follow in this case the doctrine it had established in *Weeks v. United States* (1914), in which the Court had held that illegally obtained evidence could not be used in federal courtrooms. The *Weeks* decision was based on the Court's belief that the most effective way to prevent the government from obtaining evidence illegally in violation of the people's rights was to render the evidence useless by preventing it from being introduced in court. One of the dissenting justices also raised the issue of privacy.

Chief Justice William H. Taft, writing for himself and four other justices, upheld the convictions. He agreed with the *Weeks* doctrine, but he did not believe that the evidence gathered had been gotten illegally. Distinguishing the case from others in which homes and offices had been entered and searched by law enforcement officers who had no warrant, Taft noted that in those cases there was "actual entrance" into private premises "and the taking away of something tangible." But in the *Olmstead* situation, Taft said, "[W]e have testimony only of voluntary conversations secretly overheard . . . . There was no searching. There was no seizure . . . . There was no entry of the houses

or offices of the defendants." It was "reasonable" to assume, said Taft, that "one who installs in his house a telephone instrument with connecting wires intends to project his voice to those quite outside, and that the wires beyond his house, and messages while passing over them" are not protected by the Fourth Amendment. Congress could, if it chose, pass a statute making evidence derived from wiretaps inadmissible in the courtroom, but the courts had no right to add such "an enlarged and unusual meaning to the Fourth Amendment," which had not been violated here. The chief justice also maintained that the Fifth Amendment's privilege against self-incrimination had not been breached. No one had made the defendants talk on the telephone, so they had not been forced to incriminate themselves. Responding to the argument that a Washington State law made it a crime to intercept telephone messages, Taft noted that the statute did not make the evidence obtained from such interceptions inadmissible in court, so there was no reason to overturn the convictions.

Justice Louis D. Brandeis dissented. Reiterating the extent of the wiretaps, which involved eight telephones, at least seven governmental agents, and 775-typewritten pages of conversations overheard, he challenged the government's contention that this was not an unreasonable search and seizure. Brandeis reminded the Court that its own decisions had permitted constitutional phrases regarding governmental powers to be "updated" so as to meet "modern conditions" and argued that no less could be done for "clauses guaranteeing to the individual protection against specific abuses of power." When the Fourth Amendment was written, the search and seizure clause could be violated only by the physical intrusion of governmental agents into a home. But the privacy that the clause was designed to protect could now be invaded by "subtler and more far-reaching means." They were subtler because no physical intrusion was necessary for wiretapping; and they were more far-reaching because wiretapping invaded the privacy of people at both ends of every telephone call made or received by the person being tapped, no matter what the subject of the conversation. This, Brandeis believed, violated the intention of the

Constitution's framers, who "sought to protect Americans in their beliefs, their thoughts, their emotions and their sensations. They conferred, as against the government, the right to be let [left?] alone—the most comprehensive of rights and the right most valued by civilized men." Brandeis added that, to protect the right of privacy, every "unjustifiable intrusion by the government . . . whatever the means employed" had to be seen as a violation of the Fourth Amendment and the use of evidence gathered during it as a violation of the Fifth.

Brandeis's impassioned defense of privacy was not surprising. In 1890, Brandeis and his law partner Samuel Warren had written "The Right to Privacy," an article published in the *Harvard Law Review*. That article has been credited with alerting the legal profession to the importance of the right to privacy and its necessity in a democratic society. It was in that article that Brandeis and Warren had first called privacy "the right to be let [left?] alone," and had written that public scrutiny of private lives was a deprivation of the dignity to which human beings are entitled. They warned against the dangers of technology, including "instantaneous photographs" and "numerous mechanical devices" that could be used to invade privacy. In *Olmstead*, Brandeis added that "[d]iscovery and invention have made it possible for the Government . . . to obtain disclosure in court of what is whispered in the closet . . . . The progress of science in furnishing the Government with means of espionage is not likely to stop with wire tapping." And he foresaw accurately that "[w]ays may some day be developed by which the Government, without removing papers from secret drawers, can reproduce them in court, and by which it will be enabled to expose to a jury the most intimate occurrences of the home." This was of major concern to Brandeis, who felt that democracy was impossible unless each member of the electorate was free to try out various ideas in order to decide what he believed would be the best possible governmental system and policies. "Freedom to think as you will and to speak as you think are means indispensable to the discovery and spread of political truth," Brandeis would write in *Whitney v. California* (1927). Thus, privacy and democracy were inextricably

linked. And so he viewed wiretaps, used to supply evidence in *Olmstead*, as a threat not only to the defendants but to the entire democratic process.

Brandeis saw Fifth Amendment difficulties as well because he believed that wiretaps violated the right against self-incrimination, initially meant to negate the use of torture, but the spirit of which had consistently been construed by the Court to be "as broad as the mischief against which it seeks to guard." The government's admirable purpose, which was to enforce the law, was no excuse for its violating the Constitution: "Experience should teach us to be most on our guard to protect liberty when the government's purposes are beneficent. . . . The greatest dangers to liberty lurk in insidious encroachment by men of zeal, well-meaning but without understanding."

Aside from the constitutional issue, the government had gathered the evidence in clear violation of the Washington law against wiretapping. The government itself had "[laid] bare the crimes committed by its officers on its behalf." By introducing the tainted evidence in court, the Justice Department had sanctioned the illegal behavior of the police officers, and the Court was now giving further sanction to governmental criminality. "A federal court should not permit such a prosecution to continue," Brandeis protested. Nothing in the Eighteenth Amendment was designed to give governmental officials the power to break the law. It was an established rule of law that courts would not hear plaintiffs who came with "unclean hands." The need for the Court to follow that rule was particularly important here, since the party that had appeared with unclean hands was the government. This was a threat because of the educational role played by the government. Brandeis submitted eloquently: "Our government is the potent, the omnipresent teacher. For good or for ill, it teaches the whole people by its example. . . . If the government becomes a lawbreaker, it breeds contempt for law; it invites every man to become a law unto himself; it invites anarchy." Accepting tainted evidence was tantamount to a declaration by the Court that "the end justified the means." "Against that pernicious doctrine," said

Brandeis, "this court should resolutely set its face."

Justices Oliver Wendell Holmes, Jr., and Harlan F. Stone agreed, with Holmes adding that it is a "less evil that some criminals should escape than that the government should play an ignoble part" in capturing them. Holmes shared Brandeis's distaste for the lesson being taught by the Court's acceptance of governmental criminality. While it was undoubtedly desirable for criminals to be detected, it was equally desirable for the government to use only methods that did not require the government itself to "foster and pay for other crimes, when they are the means by which the evidence is to be obtained."

Justice Pierce Butler dissented separately, stating that the case should be retried with the understanding that wiretapping violated the Fourth and Fifth Amendments. He, too, disagreed with the Court's statement that telephone calls were not to be treated as private, saying not only that people contracting for telephone service assume they will have "the private use of the facilities employed in the service" but that "the communications belong to the parties between whom they pass." Butler noted that many telephone conversations "includ[e] communications that are private and privileged—those between physician and patient, lawyer and client, parent and child, husband and wife." The invasion of privacy was sufficiently distressing for Butler, who was known for his insistence on construing the words of the Constitution literally when the government threatened to regulate business, to add in *Olmstead* that "[t]he direct operation or literal meaning of the [constitutional] words do not measure the purpose or scope of its provisions" and that the Fourth Amendment was clearly designed to safeguard the people "against all evils that are like and equivalent to those embraced within the ordinary meaning of its words."

Thus, in addition to the question of how the Court would construe the Fourth and Fifth Amendments in criminal cases, *Olmstead* involved the concept of "privacy." The word itself is not to be found in the Constitution, but defenders of a constitutional right to privacy have found it implied not only in the sections of the Fourth and Fifth Amendments discussed above but by the First Amendment's guarantee of free speech and association; the Third Amendment's provision that soldiers shall not be quartered in homes without the permission of the owners; the Fifth and Fourteenth Amendments' prohibition of the government's taking of a person's liberty without due process of law; and the Ninth Amendment, which states: "The enumeration in the Constitution, of certain rights shall not be construed to deny or disparage others retained by the people." The kind of privacy protected by the Constitution has remained a major issue in constitutional law, affecting such disparate areas as the right not to be inoculated and the right to abortion.

The case also involved two competing approaches to constitutional interpretation: that which tended to limit individuals' rights to those specifically mentioned by the framers, and the competing approach that emphasized enforcing the spirit of the framers' intentions. *Olmstead* was eventually overruled by the Supreme Court's 8–1 decision in *Katz v. United States* (1967), which adopted the second form of jurisprudence in holding that "unreasonable searches and seizures" had to be defined in light of the government's ability to use methods for searching that could not have been foreseen at the time the Constitution was written.

Selected Bibliography

Brandeis, L.D., and S.D. Warren. "The Right to Privacy." *Harvard Law Review* 4 (1890): 193–220.

Ernst, M.L. and A.U. Schwartz. *Privacy: The Right to Be Left Alone.* New York: Macmillan, 1962.

Landynski, J.W. *Search and Seizure and the Supreme Court.* Baltimore: The Johns Hopkins Press, 1966.

Murphy, W.F. *Wiretapping on Trial: A Case Study in the Judicial Process.* New York: Random House, 1965.

Westin, A.F. *Privacy and Freedom.* New York: Atheneum, 1967.

THE EXCLUSIONARY RULE BINDS THE STATES

by Stephen Lowe
Lexington, KY

Mapp v. Ohio, 367 U.S. 643 (1961) [U.S. Supreme Court]

When the U.S. Supreme Court decided *Mapp v. Ohio*, it reversed *Wolf v. Colorado* (1949), a decision made only twelve years earlier. The earlier Court had decided that the Fourth Amendment's prohibition against illegal search and seizure applied only to the federal government, not to the states. To a bare 5–4 majority of the Warren Court of 1961, however, it was imperative that the exclusionary rule should apply equally to the states as well as to the federal government if the law were to have an element of common sense. Not only is logic an important element in the law, said Justice Tom C. Clark, but so is common sense.

Dollree (Dolly) Mapp had been convicted following a 1957 arrest under an Ohio law that forbade the possession of lewd and lascivious material. The facts of her arrest are a perfect example of the extent to which state and local police forces could technically go, although many states adhered to the exclusionary rule of their own volition. On the afternoon of May 23, 1957, several Cleveland police officers, acting on a tip, demanded entrance to Mapp's home, where they hoped to find a suspect of a local bombing. After contacting her lawyer, Mapp denied admission to the police unless they could produce a search warrant. Since they did not have a warrant, the officers left and began to watch the house. About three hours later, the policemen, reinforced by a lieutenant carrying what he claimed was a valid warrant, again demanded entrance to the house. When Mapp once again refused, the officers forced open a side door and entered. Once inside, they produced a warrant, which Mapp grabbed and "placed . . . in her bosom." A struggle followed, during which the police handcuffed Mapp for her belligerence. They then began to search the house. During the search, the materials that were used to convict her were discovered. At the trial, the prosecution failed to produce the warrant, "nor was," according to the Ohio Su-

preme Court decision, "the failure to produce one explained or accounted for."

The Ohio Supreme Court admitted that the argument could very well be made that the evidence was unlawfully seized, but it still upheld Mapp's conviction on two grounds. First, the fact that the evidence was not seized violently was considered important, since the U.S. Supreme Court held in *Rochin v. California* (1952) that only evidence seized in a "shocking" manner fell under the exclusionary rule. Second, the court pointed to *Wolf v. Colorado*, stating that even if the search was unreasonable, states are not prevented from using evidence gained in such a manner in court.

The arguments of Mapp's attorneys did not address the issue of illegal search and seizure; instead, they sought to have the Ohio law forbidding possession of lewd material declared unconstitutional. The Ohio Supreme Court ruled by a vote of 4–3 that the statute was just that, but Ohio's constitution required at least a 6–1 ruling to strike down a state law. Also, Mapp's attorneys sought to invoke *Rochin v. California* by arguing that the search of Mapp's home was a "shocking" disregard for her rights.

The American Civil Liberties Union (ACLU) filed an *amicus curiae* ("friend of the court") brief in *Mapp* when the case reached the U.S. Supreme Court. The ACLU, however, did not address the issue of search and seizure until the final paragraph of its brief. Instead, the brief argued that the Ohio law was illogical and unreasonable, since it served no rational purpose. Also, the ACLU argued for an interpretation of the Fourth and Fourteenth Amendments to guarantee a right of privacy, and that certain aspects of the Ohio law violated the equal protection clause.

Finally, in the last paragraph of the ACLU brief, the Court was asked to "re-examine this issue and conclude that the ordered liberty concept guaranteed to persons by the due process clause of the Fourteenth Amendment necessarily requires that evidence illegally in violation thereof, not be admissible in state criminal proceedings."

In its decision, the U.S. Supreme Court stuck to the search and seizure issue and ignored the privacy matter. Justice Clark, writing for himself and four other justices, pointed out that many states already adhered to the exclusionary rule and did not allow illegally seized evidence to be admitted in their courts. "Moreover," said Clark, "our holding that the exclusionary rule is an essential part of both the Fourth and Fourteenth Amendments is not only the logical dictate . . ., but it also makes very good sense. There is no war between the Constitution and common sense."

The *Mapp* Court's decision was widely criticized and immediately assailed because of the Court's reliance on the search and seizure ground, an issue that had hardly been raised in the lower court or discussed in oral arguments.

The decision was seen as devastating to police power and an unreasonable restriction of state power, leaving many questions unanswered until subsequent cases clarified and restricted it.

The *Mapp* decision had far-reaching effects. States were henceforth bound by the exclusionary rule. As Justice John Marshall Harlan said in his concurring opinion in 1969, "[E]very change in Fourth Amendment law must now be obeyed by state officials facing widely different problems of local law enforcement."

Selected Bibliography

Graham, F. *The Due Process Revolution: The Warren Court's Impact on Criminal Law*. New York: Hayden Book Co., 1970.

Howard, A.E.D., Jr., ed. *Criminal Justice in Our Time*. Charlottesville, VA: University of Virginia Press, 1965.

Sowle, C.R., ed. *Police Power and Individual Freedom: The Quest for Balance*. Chicago: Aldine Publishing Co., 1962.

G. Privacy

ABORTION: WHO SHALL DECIDE?

by Mary K. Bonsteel Tachau
Department of History
University of Louisville

Roe v. Wade, 410 U.S. 113 (1973); *Webster v. Reproductive Health Services*, 492 U.S.— (1989)
[U.S. Supreme Court]

The experiences of Justice Harry A. Blackmun give pause to anyone who harbors an ambition to become a member of the U.S. Supreme Court. It was Blackmun's fate to write the majority opinion in *Roe v. Wade*. Although six other justices joined in that decision, it was Blackmun, who became the object of angry demonstrations over the last 20 years.

Roe v. Wade may be the most controversial decision of the Court since the 1857 *Dred Scott* decision. By sweeping away state laws that stringently limited or absolutely prohibited abortion, it evoked a vigorous and widespread protest movement. Calling themselves "pro-life," rather than "antiabortion," some of its members publicized their convictions by bombing abortion clinics and threatening Blackmun's life. Until *Webster v. Reproductive Health Services*, those who supported *Roe v. Wade* had been, by comparison, relatively quiet and politically inactive.

Yet opposition to *Roe v. Wade* in American society goes beyond the tactics of single-issue, antiabortion activists. It includes many religious conservatives, from fundamentalists to the Roman Catholic hierarchy. Among opponents are prominent national leaders, usually those identified with the conservative wings of the major political parties, especially the Republican party. During the Reagan administration, candidates for appointment by the executive branch often found that their position on *Roe v. Wade* was a major determinant of their success: an antiabortion stance was necessary to pass the administration's "litmus test." Interestingly, most members of the bar and bench who disagree with the decision of the Court nevertheless focus their criticism on the opinion written by Blackmun, both for its breadth and its specificity.

The case involved an unmarried pregnant woman who wanted to terminate her pregnancy by an abortion to be preformed by a competent, licensed physician, under safe, clinical conditions. In all of the proceedings, the woman was identified as "Jane Roe" to protect her anonymity, thus conforming with the traditional Anglo-American legal convention of using pseudonyms such as "John Doe" or "Richard Roe." However, the plaintiff has since been identified in newspapers and on television as Norma McCorvey. It was rare for a pregnant woman who wanted an abortion to be a plaintiff because during the time between initiating a suit and having it come to trial, the woman is usually likely to have given birth—thus presenting the court with an opportunity to declare the case "moot" and entirely avoid the issue.

Roe asserted that she was unable to get a legal abortion in Texas because her life did not appear to be threatened by the continuation of her pregnancy. This was a necessary condition under the Texas statutes, which prohibited procuring or attempting an abortion except on medical advice for the purpose of saving the mother's life. The Texas statute had not been substantively changed since its passage in 1854. Roe stated that she could not afford to travel to another state to secure a safe, legal abortion. She further claimed that the Texas criminal abortion statutes were unconstitutionally vague and that they abridged her right of personal privacy, which was protected by the First, Fourth, Fifth, Ninth, and Fourteenth Amendments.

The action was brought in 1970 against Henry Wade, district attorney for Dallas County, in the U.S. District Court for the

Northern District of Texas. Roe asked for a declaratory judgment that the Texas abortion statutes were unconstitutional and for an injunction restraining him from enforcing them. In an amendment to her original complaint, Roe sued on behalf of herself and all other women similarly situated. Thus, the litigation was a class action suit (i.e., a case in which a plaintiff sues on behalf of other people, who can be identified as members of the same group because they are affected by the same laws).

Two other parties joined in the suit. One was a physician who had been arrested earlier for violating the Texas abortion laws and had two prosecutions pending against him. The district court allowed him to intervene, but the Supreme Court did not, on the ground that a defendant in a pending state criminal case cannot challenge the statutes under which the state was prosecuting him in a federal court. The other party was a married, childless couple, who stated that if the wife became pregnant, they would want to terminate her pregnancy by abortion because of a permanent condition that rendered her health precarious. The district court denied their request on the ground that they did not have standing (i.e., the right to come before a court because of a personal stake in the outcome of the controversy). The Supreme Court agreed, saying that the allegation of a possible injury that had not yet occurred did not present an actual case or controversy, as is necessary for adjudication.

Roe v. Wade was only one of dozens of challenges to state abortion laws that had been raised since 1965, the year the Supreme Court's decision in *Griswold v. Connecticut* declared unconstitutional state laws that prohibited the use or sale of contraceptives, or advising or counseling on their use. Six justices held that such laws abridged the right to privacy. Justice William O. Douglas's majority opinion stated that the right to privacy could be inferred from the First, Third, Fourth, Fifth, and Ninth Amendments, although it was not specifically mentioned in them or in the Constitution. In Douglas's controversial analysis, the right to privacy exists because of "emanations" from the "penumbras" of various Bill of Rights guarantees. Supporters of Douglas's holding in *Griswold* cited his creative jurisprudence; critics attacked the opinion as indicative of the worst of modern judicial activism.

The *Griswold* opinion would be central to the efforts of those who wished to change restrictive state abortion laws. For 15 years, they had focused on state legislatures, with uneven results. As several writers pointed out in influential law review articles, the Court's assertion of a right to privacy suggested a litigation strategy that might be more successful in challenging abortion statutes than the legislative strategy pursued thus far.

The modern doctrine of privacy—the "right to be let alone"—was first enunciated by Louis D. Brandeis and Samuel D. Warren in an 1890 article in *Harvard Law Review*. As a Supreme Court justice, Brandeis developed the doctrine further in a dissenting opinion in *Olmstead v. United States* (1928). He based his disapproval of governmental invasion of privacy on the Fourth Amendment's guarantees against unreasonable searches and seizures and the Fifth Amendment's protection against self-incrimination. The Supreme Court had held in *Mapp v. Ohio* (1961) that those guarantees were applicable to state governments, as well as to the federal government, because of the Fourteenth Amendment's requirement that states could not deprive any person of liberty without due process of law. Douglas's *Griswold* opinion provided additional grounds for assertions of a constitutional right of privacy by also citing the Third and Ninth Amendments. Perhaps the most significant expansion was that suggested by the Ninth Amendment, which alludes to rights retained by the people that are not enumerated in the Constitution.

By 1970, when *Roe v. Wade* was heard in the federal district court in Dallas, legal actions against state abortion laws were pending in 13 states. The difficulties inherent in so controversial an issue as abortion were compounded by the nature of the litigative process. Since *Eric v. Tompkins* (1938), lower federal courts have been obliged to follow the decisional law of the states in which they are located; state courts, which make the decisions that constitute that decisional law, are generally expected to uphold state statutes (although that is an unproven assumption). Women who had abortions were seldom prosecuted; challenges to state abortion laws were typically brought by physicians who were in a relatively weak position from which to protest.

Given those circumstances and the generally conservative cast of Texas, the decision of its federal district court was unexpected. A three-judge panel held that the right to choose whether to have children was protected by the Ninth Amendment, made applicable to the states through the Fourteenth Amendment. It also said that the Texas criminal abortion statutes were void because they were unconstitutionally vague and constituted an overbroad infringement of the plaintiffs' Ninth Amendment rights. The court did deny Roe's request for an injunction that would have prohibited the district attorney from bringing other prosecutions under the law. That minor setback proved to be an advantage as the case proceeded.

The case was appealed to the U.S. Court of Appeals for the Fifth Circuit, which ordinarily would have been the proper body to hear the case next. In *Roe v. Wade*, however, a direct appeal to the Supreme Court was allowed because of the district court's denial of the injunction.

The Supreme Court had for years been reluctant to hear abortion cases, although the post-*Griswold* litigation had led to mixed decisions in both state and lower federal courts. Some courts declared abortion laws unconstitutional, other upheld them; some granted injunctions against continued enforcement, others did not. It was clear that a decision by the nation's highest court was needed to bring uniformity and predictability into this area of law. Yet the Court had dismissed or upheld lower court dismissals of six cases by the end of its 1970 Term, when it was presented with six more requests for review. It accepted two: the Texas case of *Roe v. Wade* and *Doe v. Bolton*, a challenge to the Georgia abortion law.

The Court first heard *Roe v. Wade* in December 1971. According to some reports, the initial vote was 5–2 to strike down the abortion laws. Justices John Marshall Harlan and Hugo L. Black had died the previous summer, and Justices Lewis F. Powell and William H. Rehnquist had not yet joined the Court. Usually the senior justice in the majority chooses whether to write the opinion or to assign it to someone else. In this case, however, Chief Justice Warren E. Burger is generally said to have voted with the minority, but nevertheless assigned the writing of the majority opinion to Blackmun. Because the internal proceedings of the Court are confidential, it is impossible to verify what went on in the justices' deliberations, and it should be noted that the chief justice voted with the majority when the decision was announced. In any event, the selection of Blackmun was consistent with the practice of assigning opinions to members of the Court with expertise in the subject. Blackmun, prior to his appellate judicial service, had been counsel to the Mayo Clinic and was conversant with medical matters.

For whatever reasons, no decision was announced during the Term. Instead, the case was set for reargument in October 1972, when the two new members of the Court were present. Afterward, the vote to declare the Texas statutes unconstitutional became 7–2. Only Justices Byron R. White and Rehnquist were in the minority.

The Court at last announced its decision on January 22, 1973. Blackmun's majority opinion addressed not only the legal issues involved, but also discussed in detail the history of abortion laws. He later told Roe's attorney that he had spent the entire previous summer doing research. His analysis of history, combined with his knowledge of modern medical practice, led to a formula for appropriate governmental intervention in abortions. Blackmun began by quoting Justice Oliver Wendell Holmes's statement in *Lochner v. New York* (1905): "[The Constitution] is made for people of fundamentally differing views, and the accident of our finding certain opinions natural and familiar or novel and even shocking ought not to conclude our judgment upon the question whether the statutes embodying them conflict with the Constitution of the United States."

Blackmun answered Wade's claim that the case must now be moot because neither Roe nor any other members of her class were still subject to a 1970 pregnancy by stating that "pregnancy provides a classic justification for a conclusion of nonmootness" because it is a condition capable of repetition. Roe had an actual case and controversy when she filed it, and, as a pregnant woman thwarted by Texas abortion statutes, she had standing to challenge those laws.

He continued by pointing out that laws restricting abortion are of very recent origin in human history. The proscription against abortion in the Hippocratic Oath reflected a minority view: abortions were generally accepted in the ancient world, and were not prohibited by religious precepts. Later English common law did not prohibit abortion before "quickening" (i.e., after the sixteenth week). Most authorities agree that abortion, even after quickening, was not established as a crime in common law. The first English criminal abortion statute in 1803 made abortion of a quick fetus a capital offense, but provided lesser penalties for the felony of abortion before quickening.

The American colonies, and later the states, followed the English model with an important exception: abortion necessary to save the life of the mother was not a crime. Although statutes varied from state to state, over the next 50 years they became more restrictive as the quickening distinction disappeared and penalties increased. In some jurisdictions, the emphasis changed from preserving the life of the mother to preserving that of the fetus. These trends continued until the 1950s, when about one-third of the states adopted less stringent laws based on the American Law Institute's Model Penal Code of 1959, which allowed abortion under some circumstances. The opinion noted that modern medical techniques, especially when performed early in pregnancy, made abortion far safer than it had once been.

Blackmun then discussed the line of court decisions regarding privacy. He concluded that the right to privacy was not absolute but did encompass the abortion decision, which he found met the Court's standard of a fundamental right "implicit in the concept of ordered liberty." Whether the right to privacy was grounded in the Fourteenth Amendment's concept of personal liberty and its restrictions on state action, as he believed it to be, or on the Ninth Amendment, as the district court had ruled, it was broad enough to encompass a woman's decision whether to terminate her pregnancy.

The justice thought it inadvisable for the judiciary to try to resolve the question of when life begins, and he found no constitutional basis for applying the Fourteenth Amendment's protection of persons to the unborn. But even a woman's fundamental right to abortion could be limited, he submitted, by "a compelling state interest" to protect her health. Medical evidence placed the "compelling point" to be at the end of the first trimester. Before then, the mortality rate for abortion performed under clinical conditions is lower than in normal childbirth, and the state had no interest in the termination of a pregnancy. During the second trimester, Blackmun ruled, the state might regulate abortion in ways that are reasonably related to maternal health. Because of its interest in promoting the potentiality of life, the state might regulate or even proscribe abortion during the third trimester, except where it is necessary to preserve the life or health of the mother. Until the point where a compelling state interest justifies governmental intervention, Blackmun concluded, the abortion decision is inherently and primarily a medical one. The Texas law, by failing to distinguish between early and late abortions and by providing only one ground for legal abortion swept too broadly and thus interfered with basic constitutional rights. Yet, in a cryptic footnote, Blackmun stated that the Court would not, in this decision, determine the constitutionality of state laws requiring written permission of spouses or of the parents of minors.

Justices Powell, William J. Brennan, and Thurgood Marshall supported the majority opinion without qualification; Justices Douglas and Potter Stewart and Chief Justice Burger supported it with concurring opinions. Justices Rehnquist and White dissented.

The chief justice emphasized that the decision did not support abortion on demand. Stewart's concurring opinion was an exegesis on personal liberty. Douglas expanded on the doctrine of privacy and continued with a philosophically organized grouping of the liberties already recognized as coming under constitutional protection in order to demonstrate that the right to choose abortion fit reasonably within their number.

Rehnquist and White joined in a dissent objecting to the "raw judicial power" in the majority's decision, which they believed gave greater protection to the life of the mother than to the life of the fetus. Rehnquist added his own dissent, protesting what he saw as "judicial legislation" in the trimester test to be applied to a determination of compelling state interests. To him, a century's experience with restrictions on abortion countered the assertion of the Court's majority that such limitations were not traditional. He further objected to placing the right to abortion within the scope of the Fourteenth Amendment because he considered that contrary to the intent of its drafters. Finally, he thought that it was unnecessary to strike down the entire Texas statute when it might be applicable to later stages of pregnancy.

The Court's decision brought immediate reaction from the public and further politicized the issues. Women's rights groups worked to see that poor women had access to abortions in public hospitals. Those who opposed abortion pressed the pro-life aspect of their position, opposed candidates who were pro-choice, and supported state laws that might come within the scope of the majority's footnote. A flood of state legislation was passed, but until 1989, most of it was found too restrictive and was declared unconstitutional by the courts.

The composition of the Supreme Court had changed dramatically by the late 1980s when it heard *Webster v. Reproductive Health Services*, a case concerning a Missouri law placing significant restrictions on the right to secure an abortion. The statute banned the use of public facilities or public employees in performing abortions and required physicians to determine viability of a fetus thought to be at least 20 weeks old.

A majority of five justices led by now Chief Justice Rehnquist upheld the ban on public facilities and public employees, but declined to address the constitutionality of a "finding" in the preamble of the statute declaring that life begins at conception. The chief justice and Justices White and Anthony Kennedy upheld the viability test, even though it would fall within the second trimester when, under *Roe*, regulations must be related to the health of the mother.

Justice Sandra Day O'Connor found it unnecessary to reexamine the trimester framework; and Justice Antonin Scalia preferred to repudiate *Roe* outright.

There was more unanimity among the dissenters. Justice John Paul Stevens emphasized his disapproval of the preamble's "finding," declaring that, as an endorsement of a Christian religious tenet, it violated the First Amendment's establishment clause. Blackmun, writing for Brennan and Marshall, reiterated his support for *Roe* and wrote a brief but eloquent conclusion: "For today, at least the law of abortion stands undisturbed. For today, the women of this Nation still retain the liberty to control their destinies. But the signs are evident and very ominous, and a chill wind blows."

The six opinions among nine justices in *Webster v. Reproductive Health Services* assure a continuation of the controversy over the right to abortion. It may be useful to recall that the desegregation of public education ceased to be an issue only when the Supreme Court reached an unshakable unanimity that endured until well after a supportive national consensus developed. In time, the Court and the public must find a similar degree of tolerance or acquiescence to establish an acceptable public policy regarding abortion. It is not likely to be found in a return to home remedies and back-alley abortions, with their tragically high human cost, or in laws that deny safe medical procedures to women who are poor.

Selected Bibliography

Emerson, T.I. "Nine Justices in Search of a Doctrine." *Michigan Law Review* 64 (Dec. 1965): 219–34.

Goodman, J., et al. "*Doe* and *Roe*: Where Do We Go From Here?" *Women's Rights Law Review* 1 (Spring 1973): 2–38.

Gordon, L. *Woman's Body, Woman's Right*. New York: Penguin Books, 1977.

Lucas, R. "Federal Constitutional Limitations on the Enforcement and Administration of State Abortion Statutes." *North Carolina Law Review* 46 (June 1968): 730–78.

Mohr, J.C. *Abortion in America: The Origins and Evolution of National Policy*. New York: Oxford University Press, 1978.

Rubin, E.R. *Abortion, Politics, and the Courts: Roe v. Wade and Its Aftermath*. Westport, CT: Greenwood Press, 1982.

WHEN CONSENTING ADULTS CAN'T: PRIVACY, THE LAW, AND HOMOSEXUAL CONDUCT

by Roger D. Hardaway
Department of History
Northwestern Oklahoma State University

Doe v. Commonwealth's Attorney 425 U.S. 901 (1976) [U.S. Supreme Court]

Since 1965, the U.S. Supreme Court has issued several landmark decisions enunciating that a constitutional right of privacy exists in matters of sex and intimacy. Together, these cases stand for the proposition that sexual activity is protected from governmental intrusion and regulation when the participants are consenting adults. But the Court has refused to extend that right of privacy to persons engaging in homosexual conduct: states are free to enact laws prohibiting homosexual behavior.

In 1975, Virginia had a statute that proscribed anal and oral sex, making the participants in such activity liable to conviction of a felony and subject to imprisonment of one to three years. Two male homosexuals filed suit against local and state authorities, asking for an injunction to prohibit the enforcement of the law and for a judgment that the statute was unconstitutional. The plaintiffs relied primarily on *Griswold v. Connecticut* (1965), a U.S. Supreme Court case which had first articulated the right of privacy. That case had struck down a state statute forbidding the use of contraceptives by married couples. Subsequent Supreme Court opinions on privacy had, among other things, voided laws aimed at punishing the viewing of pornographic materials at home in *Stanley v. Georgia* (1969), the sale of contraceptives to minors in *Eisenstadt v. Baird* (1972), and the performing of most abortions in *Roe v. Wade* (1973).

Many observers believed that the Supreme Court would also rule against laws prohibiting homosexual activity. But when given the opportunity to do so in 1976, the Court declined, opting to allow a decision of a three-judge federal panel in Virginia to stand as the Supreme Court's position on the matter.

Doe v. Commonwealth's Attorney was a 1975 decision of the U.S. District Court for the Eastern District of Virginia. The district court's 2–1 decision was written by Senior Circuit Judge Albert V. Bryan of the U.S. Court of Appeals for the Fourth Circuit. He could find nothing in the statute, he said, that offended the U.S. Constitution.

Griswold was not applicable, Bryan asserted, because that case dealt with privacy in a marital situation, and homosexuality "is obviously no portion of marriage, home or family life. . . . If a State determines that punishment [for homosexual activity], even when committed in the home, is appropriate in the promotion of morality and decency, it is not for the courts to say that the State is not free to do so." The Virginia statute in question was justified by the state's police power to pass laws to protect the health, safety, and welfare of its citizens because homosexual "conduct is likely to end in a contribution to moral delinquency."

In a well-reasoned dissent, District Judge Robert R. Merhige, Jr., traced the steps the Supreme Court had taken in outlining the privacy doctrine. "I view those [Supreme Court] cases," he declared, "as standing for the principle that every individual has a right to be free from unwarranted governmental intrusion into one's decisions on private matters of intimate concern. . . . Private consensual sex acts between adults are matters, absent evidence that they are harmful, in which the state has no legitimate interest. To say, as the majority does, that the right of privacy, which every citizen has, is limited to matters of marital, home or family life is unwarranted under the law."

Merhige would have held that homosexual conduct was protected under the Fourteenth Amendment's guarantee that the government will not deny citizens liberty without due process of law. The majority's opinion, he concluded, had "misinterpreted the issue—the issue centers not around morality or decency, but the constitutional right of privacy."

On appeal, the U.S. Supreme Court affirmed without comment the lower court's decision. Only Justices William J. Brennan, Thurgood Marshall, and John Paul Stevens wanted the Supreme Court to address the issue with its own opinion. Thus, in effect, the Supreme Court upheld the constitutionality of the Virginia statute by a 6–3 vote.

In 1986, the Supreme Court had the opportunity to overturn *Doe v. Commonwealth's Attorney*; it declined to do so, by a 5–4 vote, in *Bowers v. Hardwick*. Once again, the Supreme Court refused to grant constitutional protection to homosexual conduct. As Chief Justice Warren E. Burger stated succinctly in his concurring opinion: "In constitutional terms there is no such thing as a fundamental right to commit homosexual sodomy."

Justice Harry A. Blackmun, joined by Justices Brennan, Marshall, and Stevens (the three dissenters in *Doe*), objected to the majority's interpretation of the issue. "The Court claims," he wrote, "that its decision today merely refuses to recognize a fundamental right to engage in homosexual sodomy; what the Court really has refused to recognize is the fundamental interest all individuals have in controlling the nature of their intimate associations with others. . . . Indeed, the right of an individual to conduct intimate relationships in the intimacy of his or her own home seems to me to be the heart of the Constitution's protection of privacy."

Most commentators agree that homosexual activity will not be curtailed by laws proscribing such conduct. Nevertheless, states remain free to pass statutes that criminalize such behavior. Whether the Supreme Court will reconsider its decisions in *Doe* and *Bowers*, and extend the constitutional right of privacy to homosexual conduct, is at best uncertain. Given the Court's emphasis in recent years on restricting rather than expanding the meaning of certain constitutional provisions, the entire right of privacy concept—which is not specifically mentioned in the Constitution—could be dismantled in future decisions. Rather than being exceptions to the general rule, as they are now, *Doe* and *Bowers* might become part of a Supreme Court trend to strengthen the states' police power at the expense of individual liberty.

Selected Bibliography

O'Neill, T. "*Doe v. Commonwealth's Attorney*: A Setback for the Right of Privacy." *Kentucky Law Journal* 65 (1976–77): 748–63.

Richards, D.A.J. "Homosexuality and the Constitutional Right to Privacy." *New York University Review of Law and Social Change* 8 (1978–79): 311–16.

Sullens, J.K. "Thus Far and No Further: The Supreme Court Draws the Outer Boundary of the Right to Privacy." *Tulane Law Review* 61 (March 1987): 907–29.

H. The Family

THE CUSTODY OF CHILDREN

by James W. Ely, Jr.
School of Law
Vanderbilt University

Prather v. Prather, 4 De Saussure's Equity 33 (1809) [South Carolina court of equity]

English common law enshrined paternal power over children, and this view was largely followed by American judges and legislators in the colonial era. The father was deemed the natural guardian of his children, and divorce or separation did not interrupt his rights. Thus, a husband enjoyed a paramount right to custody in the event of marital dissolution, despite abusive conduct toward his wife or children. The troubled marriage of Jennet Prather, however, gave South Carolina courts an opportunity to take a fresh look at the question of child custody. The result was a challenge to the traditional common-law right of the husband to custody.

In February 1809, Chancellor Henry De Saussure heard Mrs. Prather's request for a separate maintenance from her husband. At that time, South Carolina did not permit absolute divorces. Mrs. Prather also demanded that her two sons be apprenticed and that she be awarded custody of the couple's infant daughter. She charged her husband with living in open adultery, denying her the company of her children, and mistreating the children.

At a preliminary hearing, De Saussure had little difficulty in granting Mrs. Prather's first request. Although in England suits for separate maintenance were handled by ecclesiastical courts, the absence of such tribunals in South Carolina caused the Court of Equity to assert jurisdiction over such cases. "I do therefore think," the chancellor declared, "that where a husband uses his wife ill, and turns her off unprovided without a just cause, she may . . . claim the protection of this Court, and have relief by a separate maintenance."

The matter of child custody proved more vexing. Adhering to the common-law view, the chancellor declined to remove the children from paternal custody. He ruled that a father "is the natural guardian, invested by God and the law of the country, with reasonable power over them. Unless his paternal power has been monstrously and cruelly abused, this Court would be very cautious in interfering in the exercise of it." The chancellor declared, however, that "the mother has her rights also," and consequently ordered that Mrs. Prather be permitted to visit her children at reasonable times.

At a hearing in June 1809, Chancellor Waddy Thompson heard testimony about the husband's dissolute behavior and evidence that Mrs. Prather was "a prudent, discreet, virtuous woman." Following the hearing, Thompson then rejected the paternal bias of traditional custody law. Although aware that the court was "treading new and dangerous grounds," Thompson granted custody of the infant daughter to Mrs. Prather. This break with the common law was only partial because the two older sons remained with their father. Thompson also confirmed an award of alimony to Mrs. Prather during the period of their separation.

This hesitant innovation marked a new trail for American courts in handling custody disputes between natural parents. Although *Prather* was never a particularly famous decision, it illustrated two emerging trends in custody matters. First, judges increasingly stressed the welfare of the children in awarding custody. To determine the best interest of the child, courts considered the fitness and behavior of each parent. Second, as suggested by *Prather*, courts tended to place younger children and female children with the mother. Legislators encouraged this practice by enacting statutes that gave broad discretion to judges in the awarding of custody. Such legislation abrogated the father's common-law rights, and the result was a sharp reduction in paternal power over children. Indeed, Joel Bishop's 1852 treatise *Commentaries on the Law of Marriage and Divorce* declared that a father's right "is not an absolute one, and it is usually made to yield when the good of the child, which, especially according to the modern American decisions, is the chief matter to be regarded, requires that it should."

This judicial refashioning of custody law reflected new social attitudes toward children and the role of women. As child nurturing became a central concern, nineteenth-century society came to regard women as having a unique capacity to rear infant children. Perhaps inevitably, judges and legislators adopted these new gender views and abandoned traditional paternal custody. By the late nineteenth century, a mother was generally viewed as the parent best suited for child rearing, and courts gave her preference in awarding custody.

Selected Bibliography

Bishop, J.P. *Commentaries on the Law of Marriage and Divorce*. Boston: Little, Brown & Co., 1952.

Grossberg, M. *Governing the Hearth: Law and the Family in Nineteenth-Century America*. Chapel Hill, NC: University of North Carolina Press, 1985.

RELIGION, CULTURAL PLURALISM, AND THE CONSTITUTION: MORMONISM AND POLYGAMY

by Gordon Morris Bakken
Department of History
California State University at Fullerton

Reynolds v. United States, 98 U.S. 145 (1879); *Davis v. Beason*, 133 U.S. 33 (1889)
[U.S. Supreme Court]

The national efforts to eradicate polygamy generated much constitutional law and political rhetoric in the period 1862–90. Lawmakers in Washington and in the territories attacked behaviors of members of the Church of the Latter Day Saints, generally known as Mormons, found odious to the general moral and political culture of the period. Mainstream American culture found the religious practice of polygamy to be immoral. In addition, the Mormon political behavior of bloc voting deeply upset local politicians. The legal assault to end polygamy in federal and territorial law included both criminal sanctions and limitations on the franchise.

In *Reynolds v. United States*, the U.S. Supreme Court decided that the First Amendment protections of religious liberty do not extend to religious practices that impaired the public interest. The issue before the Court was whether polygamy, declared by Mormon doctrine to be a religious practice but designated by federal law to be a crime, was protected liberty to the extent that a bigamy conviction should be overturned. Chief Justice Morrison R. Waite, for a unanimous Court, declared that a federal statute could constitutionally punish criminal activity regardless of religious belief. Although the government could not punish religious beliefs, the government could punish activities that were declared to be crimes. To hold otherwise would undermine the foundations of government and make religion superior to law.

The national effort to eradicate polygamy had antebellum roots but no statutory support until the passage of an antibigamy act in 1862. The Mormon hierarchy put George Reynolds forward to test the statute. Reynolds was secretary to Brigham Young, the spiritual leader of the Mormons. He was also a faithful polygamist. First convicted in the territorial district court, Reynolds had his conviction sustained in the Utah Supreme Court in 1876. He then appealed to the U.S. Supreme Court. Anti-Mormon forces welcomed the test case.

Several years prior to *Reynolds*, the Grant administration—believing that polygamy was a relic of barbarism—attacked the surviving practice with gusto. President Ulysses S. Grant appointed James B. McKean as territorial supreme court chief justice and General J. Wilson Shaffer as territorial governor to root out the vestiges of polygamy. McKean used U.S. marshals to round up polygamists and select juries. This resulted in numerous indictments, convictions, and imprisonments. The Mormons appealed these convictions, based on procedural error in the jury selection process, and won a favorable Supreme Court ruling in 1872, which quashed 130 indictments and released scores from incarceration.

In Congress, anti-Mormon forces threw their support to legislation known as the Cullom Bill, which enlarged the appointive powers of the territorial governor to include local judges and law enforcement personnel, limited the jurisdiction of Mormon-controlled probate courts, excluded polygamists from juries, and made polygamy convictions easier to obtain. The bill even authorized the president of the United States to use military force to enforce the statute. The Cullom Bill never reached the president's desk. But in 1874, the Poland Bill did become law. This statute revised the territorial court structure and jurisdictions to limit the probate courts. Further, the law revised the jury selection process to attempt to balance Mormon and gentile representation. Anti-Mormons thought the Poland Act to be insufficient and looked to *Reynolds* as a means of attacking the moral menace in Salt Lake City.

In reaching the nation's highest tribunal, anti-Mormon forces branded polygamy as socially destructive and characterized Mormons as enemy deviants. Mormons countered by submitting that religious freedom of belief was inviolate under the Constitution and that polygamy was not bigamy. Further, they argued that plural marriage as practiced by Mormons was not destructive of any social interest or the public peace. Quite the contrary, Mormons maintained that plural marriage was supportive of the family, family values, and spiritual growth. Polygamy was religious in nature and not harmful to society. The 1879 Supreme Court, however, did not see the social utility as did the Mormons.

In the aftermath of *Reynolds*, anti-Mormonism in Idaho territory produced yet another Supreme Court ruling on anti-Mormon legislation. Mormons settled in southeastern Idaho before the creation of the territory. Mormon affiliation with the Democratic party in 1872 marked the beginning of organized anti-Mormon activity. By 1882, anti-Mormonism had become a territorial political issue and a Republican party initiative. Idaho Republicans used the Mormon menace to elect a territorial delegate. But, once in Washington, national Republicans denied the Utah territorial delegate his seat and passed the Edmunds Anti-Polygamy Act of 1882. The Edmunds Act effectively disfranchised the Mormons in the Utah and Idaho territories. With the franchise denied, anti-Mormon forces imposed the requirement of a test oath to disqualify Mormon legislators from sitting in 1884 or from holding county offices. The territorial legislature subsequently amended the test oath statute to exclude Mormons from office, from voting, and from jury service if they had been Mormons on January 1, 1888. The governor signed the amendatory legislation despite constitutional doubts about its retroactivity. The doubts about the constitutionality of the Idaho test oath were resolved by the U.S. Supreme Court in *Davis v. Beason*.

The facts in *Davis* were fairly simple. In April 1889, Samuel D. Davis was indicted in the third judicial district of Idaho Territory in the county of Oneida for conspiracy to obstruct the administration of the law and unlawfully attempting to register to vote. The legal issue was the constitutionality of the test oath statute. Davis's attorney argued that Idaho could not refuse registration based solely on church membership because that membership had not been declared to be a crime. Further, he argued that the statute was unconstitutional because it prohibited the free exercise of religion. The statute, Davis's attorney argued, also violated the Fourteenth Amendment as well as Article 6 of the Constitution. The latter specifically stated that "no religious Test shall ever be required as a Qualification to any Office or Public Trust under the United States." Finally, the attorney urged that the Edmunds Act had preempted the field and that the Idaho Territorial Legislature was without authority to legislate on the subject matter. Justice Stephen J. Field wrote the opinion for a unanimous Court, rebutting every claim.

Field stressed the jurisdictional issues in his opinion, but he also used the case to condemn polygamy. The issue that required legal attention was the jurisdiction of the territorial court. Polygamy and bigamy were clearly criminal. "They tend to destroy the purity of the marriage relation, to disturb the peace of families, to degrade woman and to debase man," Field maintained. Further, "few crimes are more pernicious to the best interests of society and receive more general or more deserved punishment," he continued. Finally, "to extend exemption from punishment for such crimes would be to shock the moral judgment of the community." To meet the free exercise argument, Field observed that the "laws are made for the government of actions, and while they cannot interfere with mere religious belief and opinions, they may with practices." From this it was clear that the territory had authority to make law because the federal statute had not dealt with the teaching, advising, or counseling

of the practices of bigamy and polygamy, thereby leaving open the regulation of these elements of behavior for the territorial government.

Field's *Davis* opinion contained a footnote documenting the long-standing position of the nation on the extent of religious freedom. The centerpiece of the note was the New York Constitution of 1777, which declared that "liberty of conscience . . . shall not be so construed as to excuse acts of licentiousness, or justify practices inconsistent with the peace or safety of this state." The Court listed numerous other examples of state constitutional condemnation of Mormon practices, indicating that the constitutional door was now completely closed to pro-polygamy arguments.

Selected Bibliography

Firmage, E.B., and R.C. Mangrum. *Zion in the Courts: A Legal History of the Church of Jesus Christ of Latter-day Saints, 1830–1900.* Urbana, IL: University of Illinois Press, 1988.

Wells, M.W. *Anti-Mormonism in Idaho, 1872–92.* Provo, UT: Brigham Young University Press, 1978.

THE VALIDITY OF DIVORCE DURING THE NINETEENTH CENTURY

by Glenda Riley
Department of History
Ball State Univeristy

Schliemann v. Schliemann (1869) [Indiana state court]; *Irwin v. Irwin* (1893) [Oklahoma Territorial Supreme Court]

During the nineteenth century, many divorce-seekers obtained the much-desired divorce decrees but then found themselves embroiled in controversy over the validity of the decrees. One reason that a divorce decree might be considered invalid was because it was a migratory divorce. In other words, divorce-seekers migrated temporarily to states or territories with liberal divorce codes in order to free themselves from unwanted spouses. The news of such a divorce often came as a surprise to a husband or wife

who had not been informed of the divorce proceedings. In a number of cases, the divorced spouse opposed the action and attempted to reverse the divorce court's ruling. Another situation that occasioned a disputed decree was confusion in the divorce laws of the state or territory granting the divorce. What follows are examples of each problem.

In pre-Civil War America, one of the earliest centers of migratory divorce was Indiana. Because of unusually liberal divorce laws adopted in 1852, Indiana emerged as a divorce mecca. As early as 1824, the Indiana legislature had adopted an "omnibus clause," which empowered a court to grant a divorce for any cause it deemed proper. The omnibus clause not only remained in force in the Indiana Code of 1852, but was enhanced by a new residency provision requiring that the petitioner must be a resident of the county of filing only at the time of the action and that the resident's own testimony constituted adequate proof of that residency. In addition, the law provided that the defendant did not have to be served personally with notification of proceedings but could be served through publication. Specifically, notice of a divorce action had to be published for three weeks in any local weekly newspaper in the venue where the action was filed. In 1859, a modest reform bill extended residency to one year and demanded additional proof of residency, but neither provision was strictly enforced. Instead, Indiana continued to capture public attention as a divorce mill through the Civil War period.

Financier and amateur archaeologist Heinrich Schliemann was one of the most well-known divorce-seekers to use the Indiana divorce law. In April 1869, Schliemann established residence in an Indianapolis hotel and hired several attorneys to file a petition against his wife, Catherine. His lawyers began publication of a notice of proceedings in an Indianapolis newspaper; because Catherine lived in St. Petersburg, Russia, it seemed unlikely that she would learn of the action before the divorce was decreed. To hurry matters along, Schliemann enhanced his residency by purchasing a house and an interest in a local starch factory. He used these purchases to convince the Marion County court that he intended to stay in Indiana, thus he received his decree in far less than the required year. The much-coveted divorce decree was granted on July 11; one week later he left Indianapolis.

One factor that Schliemann did not foresee was Catherine's outrage. For years, she had refused to leave St. Petersburg to live with him elsewhere although his business and other interests demanded his presence in various parts of the world. He, perhaps, assumed that her recalcitrancy meant that she would not be loath to part with him, especially since he made reasonable financial provisions for their children. Instead of taking the news calmly, however, Catherine engaged attorneys to file a suit protesting the Indiana divorce.

Schliemann agonized over this unexpected development. Not only had he left his Indianapolis "home," but he had already found a wife-to-be in Greece. He immediately wrote to his Indianapolis attorneys to determine how Catherine's opposition might be thwarted. Schliemann gloated that he had obtained U.S. citizenship (also in less than the required residency period) in New York before coming to Indianapolis so that his citizenship would not be an issue. Although U.S. citizenship was not a requirement to obtaining an American divorce decree, Schliemann feared that his tenuous residency might be grounds for appeal, so he issued a complex series of instructions to his attorneys, telling them to "prove" his residency. He also claimed that he intended to return to Indiana to live with his new wife. But his residency was not questioned by his wife's suit any more than was his citizenship.

The two points of law involved in *Schliemann* were whether a divorce case could be reopened in Indiana and whether an Indiana divorce decree was recognized in other jurisdictions. Schliemann was vastly relieved to learn that the Indiana Code of 1852 stated that Indiana divorce decrees were irrevocable and that the 1859 revision allowed appeal in "notice by publication" cases only on matters of alimony, child custody, and property. Because Catherine was attempting to appeal the actual decree, the case did not reach the hearing stage. Whether the divorce would be recognized in Russia, however, was another matter. Although several German attorneys advised Schliemann that the divorce was legal throughout the world, this was questionable. Despite the "full faith and credit" clause in the U.S. Constitution, the states did not even regularly recognize divorce actions in other states. Fortunately for Schliemann, Catherine dropped her opposition for unexplained reasons and in 1871 obtained a Russian divorce.

The second case to be considered also tested the legality of a divorce decree, but for different reasons. Because of highly contradictory divorce laws adopted in haste, Oklahoma Territory provided fertile ground for conflicts regarding the legality of the divorces granted within its boundaries.

The divorce problem began in 1890 when the Oklahoma Territory was created. In one section, territorial statutes declared that district courts would have jurisdiction in divorce cases and that the necessary residency would be 90 days. But in another section, the law stated that both probate and district courts would have jurisdiction and that residency would be two years in the territory and six months in the county where the suit was filed. In addition, the law allowed notification of divorce proceedings by publication and the reopening of disputed divorce cases. This contradictory and permissive legislation created the potential for numerous counter-suits and appeals.

Realizing the potential problems, the Oklahoma territorial legislature attempted to clarify the divorce code in mid-1893. Jurisdiction for divorce cases was placed in the hands of the district courts after a residency of 90 days. Unfortunately, probate courts continued granting divorces. Furthermore, probate courts had been hearing, and continued to hear, divorce cases after only 90 days, although the law stipulated two years residency for probate divorces.

The extremely complex situation in Oklahoma Territory became the focus of the *Irwin v. Irwin* divorce case and its appeal. The case originated in January 1893, in the probate court of Payne County, when Eliza Jane Irwin sued Elonzo Irwin for a divorce on the grounds of cruelty and neglect. The plaintiff claimed two years residency in the territory and current residence in the county. Elonzo personally received the notice of proceedings, which indicated that he was not only being sued for divorce, but that alimony, child support, and a restraining order on his property were also involved. He immediately challenged the charges and protested that the court did not have the power to grant a divorce. The court overruled his complaints and, on February 20, 1893, granted Eliza Jane a divorce, custody of the children, and substantial alimony.

Incensed by this decision, Elonzo filed an appeal. Among other complaints, he charged that the probate court had not had jurisdiction

in divorce cases at the time his divorce was granted and that the particular probate court involved had already formally adjourned two days prior to granting the divorce decree. Elonzo's appeal came before Frank Dale, chief justice of the Oklahoma territorial supreme court, in 1894. Dale ruled that the Irwin divorce was valid because the probate court granting it still had jurisdiction in divorce cases at the time the proceeding began, but he held that the probate court had, in fact, adjourned and ordered a rehearing.

Dale then turned to an examination of the jurisdiction of probate courts in divorce proceedings after the 1893 revision. After a lengthy and complex discussion of the Organic Act of 1890 that created Oklahoma Territory and subsequent divorce legislation, Dale found that probate courts lost the power to declare divorces after August 14, 1893. By implication, all probate divorces granted after that date were invalid. In the only dissenting opinion, Associate Justice Henry W. Scott warned that Dale's decision would "make innocent people guilty of adultery and bigamy."

Widespread public consternation flared in the wake of Dale's ruling. *The Kingfisher Free Press* declared that "hundreds" of divorces were now null and void, while *The Daily Leader* (Guthrie) maintained that people who had obtained probate divorces after August 14, 1893, and then remarried were bigamists. As a consequence of the near-panic that ensued, the Oklahoma territorial legislature passed a special bill that validated divorces granted by probate courts before February 28, 1895.

In the meantime, the Irwin rehearing came before the Oklahoma territorial supreme court. After an involved discussion of early legislation, two justices ruled that the *Irwin* divorce case was invalid because the granting court had formally adjourned before issuing the decree. They added that the probate court had *not* had the power to issue such a decree. Dale agreed with the invalidation of the *Irwin* divorce, although he held to his prior stand that the court had the power to grant divorces prior to August 14, 1893, or in other words, when the *Irwin* divorce petition was heard. Scott again dissented to the entire judgment.

These cases were only two among many that challenged the legality of nineteenth-century divorce decrees. Reformers and others concerned about the climbing divorce rate in the United States and the growing corruption involved in the granting of divorces believed that the problem could be resolved by national uniform divorce laws that would prevail in every state and territory throughout the country. Although a conference was held in Washington, D.C., in 1906 to consider uniform divorce laws for the nation, its proposals were defeated in the face of strong expressions of autonomy and individualism on the part of the states and territories. Thus, questions about the legality of divorce raised in the nineteenth century were passed on to the twentieth.

Selected Bibliography

Lilly, E., ed. *Schliemann in Indianapolis*. Indianapolis: Indiana Historical Society, 1961.

Nolan, V., Jr. "Indiana: Birthplace of Migratory Divorce." *Indiana Law Journal* 26 (Summer 1951): 515–27.

Riley, G. *Divorce: An American Tradition*. New York: Oxford University Press, 1991.

Traill, D.A. "Schliemann's American Citizenship and Divorce." *The Classical Journal* 77 (April/May 1982): 336–42.

Wires, R. *The Divorce Issue and Reform in Nineteenth-Century Indiana*. Muncie, IN: Ball State University, 1967.

THE PRINCIPLE OF FULL FAITH AND CREDIT IN DIVORCE ACTIONS

by Glenda Riley
Department of History
Ball State University

Williams v. North Carolina, 317 U.S. 287 (1942) [U.S. Supreme Court]; *Lambert v. Lambert*, 41 N.Y.S. 2d (1943) [New York Court of Appeals]; *Williams v. North Carolina*, 325 U.S. 226 (1945) [U.S. Supreme Court]; *Crouch v. Crouch*, 169 P. 2d 897 (1946) [California Supreme Court]

According to the U.S. Constitution and an act of Congress adopted on May 26, 1790, each state is obligated to extend full faith and credit to "the public Acts, Records, and judicial Proceedings of every other state" in the union. If an action is valid in the jurisdiction where it is pronounced, it is theoretically valid everywhere in the United States; if it is questionable in its own jurisdiction, it is questionable elsewhere.

The full-faith and credit provision is crucial to the maintenance of legislative and judicial consistency in a nation of 50 disparate states. But in divorce actions, full faith and credit is often a difficult principle to apply. Because each state has the right to regulate the marital status of its citizens according to its own standards of morality and public policy, some states have established statutes concerning marriage and divorce that are incompatible with those of other states.

Being called on to grant full faith and credit to the marriage and divorce provisions of another state can force a state to compromise its own morals and policies. If, for example, a particular state mandates one strict ground such as adultery, for divorce, must that state give full faith and credit to a decree obtained by one of its citizens in another state offering a more lenient ground, such as mental cruelty? If a state has to accept the more permissive cruelty decree under the full-faith and credit doctrine, is it not being forced to expand its own limited grounds against its will and original intent?

On the other hand, if full faith and credit is not extended to divorce decrees obtained in other states, chaos can result. If a citizen of a state that does not recognize divorce obtained a divorce in another state and then remarried, that person would be a bigamist if the home state refused to give full faith and credit to the divorce decree. Such a refusal to recognize the validity of the divorce and remarriage would also make illegitimate the children of the second marriage and create two sets of claims on property held by the twice-married spouse.

The conflict between full faith and credit and a state's right to regulate the marital status of its own citizens has created much confusion and bitterness in divorce actions. A migratory divorce (i.e., one in which the plaintiff temporarily relocates to a state to exploit its lenient divorce laws and then returns to the home state) particularly exacerbates the conflict between the two principles. Occasionally, spouses who find themselves divorced by an action in another state challenge the validity of that decree. In other instances, one spouse has already filed a suit for divorce in the couple's home state, an action that calls the out-of-state decree into question. A court asked to give full faith and credit to the actions of another state must do so only when the jurisdiction of the other state is unimpeachable. But because divorce law encompasses so many contradictory concepts of jurisdiction, a divorce court's jurisdiction is almost always vulnerable to attack.

As the divorce rate spiraled upward during the late nineteenth and early twentieth centuries, friction between the principles of full faith and credit and that of a state's right to control the marital status of its citizens not only grew, but increasingly centered on the varied periods of residency required by states before a divorce-seeker could initiate a divorce action. Some judges ruled that if basic residency requirements had been met in the venue where the divorce was granted, the divorce decree deserved full faith and credit; others maintained that if the plaintiff appeared to have established a minimum residency in the jurisdiction granting the divorce only to obtain the decree, the decree did not deserve full faith and credit.

These conflicting interpretations were ruled on by the U.S. Supreme Court in *Williams v. North Carolina* in 1942. The problem began when a woman and a man left North Carolina to relocate to Las Vegas, Nevada, for six weeks. After establishing the basic residency requirement of 60 days in Nevada, they both applied for and were granted divorces from their respective spouses in North Carolina. The woman and man immediately wed each other and returned to North Carolina as a married couple. They were subsequently charged with bigamous cohabitation under North Carolina law and sentenced to two years' imprisonment. They submitted their Nevada divorce decrees in their defense.

After the North Carolina Supreme Court upheld the bigamy conviction, the case reached the U.S. Supreme Court. The Court ruled that because due process was observed in the granting of the Nevada divorce decrees, the decrees deserved full faith and credit in North Carolina. The bigamy conviction was thus overturned by the Court. But a second issue was also raised: did six weeks residency in the Alamo Auto Court in Las Vegas constitute residence? The majority opinion held that the residency met Nevada's requirement, but the minority opinion maintained that Nevada law intended petitioners to establish a true domicile rather than temporary residence in a motor court.

State courts attempted to follow the precedent established in this ruling. In 1943, the New York case *Lambert v. Lambert* raised the issue of the validity of a Nevada divorce decree in New York. The Lamberts had married in New York in 1920 and separated 21 years later. Shortly thereafter, John Lambert relocated to Nevada, petitioned for a divorce on the ground of mental cruelty, married another woman on the day the divorce was granted, and moved to Massachusetts. But Lambert's first wife, Beatrice, had filed a petition for divorce on the ground of adultery before Lambert left for Nevada, an action that called the validity of his decree into question. In following the *Williams v. North Carolina* decision, the Monroe County court in New York ruled that the Nevada divorce deserved full faith and credit because Lambert had met Nevada's legal requirements by establishing a residency of 60 days. The court, thus, denied Beatrice's attempt to obtain a New York divorce, which would have included a more favorable property settlement for her than did the Nevada decree.

The following year, a second hearing of the *Williams* case came before the U.S. Supreme Court. This hearing focused specifically on the issue of residency. In 1944, the Court questioned whether North Carolina had to give full faith and credit to a divorce when no bona fide domicile had been established in Nevada by the petitioners. In 1945, the Court ruled that because residency in this case was a sham, North Carolina was not compelled to give full faith and credit to the Nevada decrees. Consequently, North Carolina could now convict the couple for bigamy.

Thus, the principle was established that if a divorce-seeker took up residence in a state only to acquire a divorce, the decree was not entitled to full faith and credit by other states; but if the petitioner maintained a genuine residence in the sense of a real domicile, the divorce decree was entitled to full faith and credit in other jurisdictions. Although this ruling came too late for Beatrice Lambert, it did help many others.

In 1946, for example, *Crouch v. Crouch* came before the California Supreme Court. Edith M. Crouch challenged the validity of Ben E. Crouch's Nevada decree by entering her own divorce petition, which included a claim on their community property. The court found that Ben had not established true residence in Nevada because he had no intention of becoming a Nevada citizen except for the explicit purpose of securing a divorce that would grant him a more favorable property settlement than that offered under California law. The California court granted Edith the right to file a divorce petition, including a property claim, against Ben—whom the court considered her legal spouse despite his Nevada decree.

The application of the full-faith and credit provision in divorce actions may best be summarized as follows: according to the U.S. Constitution, congressional action of 1790, and subsequent judicial rulings, a valid divorce decree granted in one state is entitled to, but may not always receive, full faith and credit from other states. Although it is generally true that a decree that is valid in the jurisdiction where it was rendered is valid everywhere, that validity is not guaranteed because a home state's rule can also be used to determine validity.

In addition, it should also be noted that divorces granted by jurisdictions outside the United States do not fall under the full-faith and credit provision. No state is required to recognize the validity of a divorce granted by another country, although most states frequently do so on the principle of comity (i.e., deference to the laws of another jurisdiction).

It is fully within a state's right, however, to reject a decree that offends its moral standards or is contrary to its own public policy. Thus, it cannot be assumed that an overnight divorce decree obtained in a nearby country will hold in the courts of the petitioner's home state.

Although the principle of full faith and credit is important to judicial consistency in the United States, the right of states to regulate the marital status of their citizens limits its application in divorce actions. As Justice Frank Murphy argued in his dissenting opinion in the first Williams appeal, divorce actions involve not only constitutional principles, but the interaction of the Constitution and state policy. Although Murphy did not envision state courts as censors of public morals, he did argue that "marriage and the family have generally been regarded as basic components of our national life, and the solution of the problems engendered by the marital relation, the formulation of standards of public morality in connection therewith, and the supervision of domestic (in the sense of the family) affairs, have been left to the individual states," each of which have "the deepest concern for its citizens." He concluded that when a conflict arose between two states on matters of domestic policy, a court could not simply apply the constitutional principle of full faith and credit, but must also consider the moral values and public policy of the states involved. This view continues to underwrite the application of full faith and credit in divorce actions.

Selected Bibliography

"Full Faith and Credit and the Out of State Divorce." *DePaul Law Review* 4 (Autumn/Winter 1954): 73–9.

Miers, H.E. "Full Faith and Credit—Procedural Limitation Bars Sister State's Collateral Attack on Jurisdiction." *Southwestern Law Journal* 22 (Oct. 1968): 662–75.

Powell, T.R. "And Repent at Leisure: The Unhappy Lot of Those Whom Nevada Hath Joined Together and North Carolina Hath Put Asunder." *Harvard Law Review* 58 (Sept. 1945): 930–1017.

Riley, G. *Divorce: An American Tradition*. New York: Oxford University Press, 1991.

Rodman, K.M. "Bases of Divorce Jurisdiction." *Illinois Law Review* 39 (March/April 1945): 343–66.

Swisher, P.N. "Foreign Migratory Divorces: A Reappraisal." *Journal of Family Law* 21 (Nov. 1982): 9–52.

A CASE OF BLACK AND WHITE: REMOVING RESTRICTIONS AGAINST INTERRACIAL MARRIAGES

by Roger D. Hardaway
Department of History
Northwestern Oklahoma State University

Loving v. Virginia, 388 U.S. 1 (1967) [U.S. Supreme Court]

Richard Loving and Mildred Jeter committed a felony when they got married. Virginia considered the marriage illegal, but the District of Columbia recognized it as valid. Whether these two people could legally stay married and live wherever they chose had to be decided by the U.S. Supreme Court.

The "problem" with the Loving-Jeter marriage was that Loving was white and Jeter was black. In 1958, when they decided to wed, such interracial marriages were legal in only about one-half of the nation's states. The couple lived in Virginia, one of those jurisdictions with a restriction against interracial relationships. On June 2, 1958, Loving and Jeter went to Washington, D.C., where such marriages were sanctioned, and exchanged vows. They then returned to Virginia to live.

A general rule of law holds that a marriage that is legal where contracted is legal everywhere. In Virginia, however, a law was in effect creating an exception to that rule in the case of biracial marriages. If two people who lived in Virginia left the state with the intent of circumventing the ban on interracial marriages and returned to the state as a "married" couple, their marriage was illegal and they were guilty of felonious behavior as though they had participated in a marriage ceremony in the state. This was the exact conduct in which Loving and Jeter had participated.

The parties were arrested and appeared in the Caroline County circuit court on January 6, 1959. Both entered pleas of guilty to the state's charges and were duly convicted. The court could have confined them for five years each in the state penitentiary; however, the judge sentenced them each to only one year in jail, with their sentences to be suspended for a 25-year period provided they left Virginia and did not return together or separately at the same time during those 25 years.

While another Virginia statute made the Lovings' marriage "absolutely void without any decree of divorce or other legal process," the circuit court did not mention this law in its decision. Apparently, the court was content to allow the couple's marriage to continue as long as they moved out of Virginia. Not surprisingly, the Lovings decided to relocate. They moved to the District of Columbia to continue their lives together.

In 1963, the Lovings filed a motion with the sentencing court asking that the judgments against them be vacated and their sentences be set aside. Their theory was that the Virginia miscegenation laws under which they had been convicted violated both the due process and equal protection provisions of the Fourteenth Amendment of the U.S. Constitution. Judge Leon M. Bazile of the Caroline County circuit court denied the motion, whereupon the Lovings appealed to the state's highest court, the Supreme Court of Appeals.

The Virginia high court had upheld the validity of the state's ban on interracial marriages several times before. Thus, the attorneys for the Lovings had to construct a novel attack upon the miscegenation statutes to present to the court.

That argument began with the allegation that miscegenation laws were unconstitutional because of the U.S. Supreme Court's holding in its landmark decision *Brown v. Board of Education* (1954). The Lovings argued that *Brown*, in effect, struck down all statutes that were based on the "separate but equal" reasoning of segregation, including the ultimate statute—that prohibiting the sexual integration of the races. Consequently, the Lovings submitted, the Virginia Supreme Court should reverse its prior decisions on the issue and invalidate the law the Lovings had violated.

The Virginia court shrugged off such reasoning in a 7–0 decision handed down on March 7, 1966. Associate Justice Harry L. Carrico, writing for the unanimous court, noted that six months after the *Brown* decision, the U.S. Supreme Court had refused to consider an appeal filed by an Alabama woman who had been convicted of violating that state's miscegenation ban. Consequently, Carrico wrote, the Supreme Court had obviously not meant for *Brown* to "have the effect upon miscegenation statutes which the defendants claim for it."

Undaunted, the interracial couple appealed to the U.S. Supreme Court, which agreed to hear their case and decide the constitutionality of the Virginia statutes. The Japanese American Citizens League was allowed to file an *amicus curiae* ("friend of the court") brief in support of the Lovings, an indication of the fact that miscegenation laws in some states prohibited interracial sex and marriages between individuals of many different races, not just between blacks and whites.

The arguments presented to the Supreme Court by the Lovings' attorneys differed somewhat from the position they had taken in front of the Virginia court. The basis of that argument remained the same—that the laws denied due process and equal protection to those who were not allowed to marry because of their racial differences. But instead of trying to show that *Brown* had already outlawed all segregation laws, the Lovings simply asked the Court to state emphatically that miscegenation laws violated the Fourteenth Amendment and to outlaw those statutes with its decision. On June 12, 1967, the Court, in a unanimous opinion written by Chief Justice Earl Warren, did just that. In doing so, the Court overturned one of its prior cases and relied to some degree on another.

The rejected case was *Pace v. Alabama* (1883). This opinion had upheld an Alabama miscegenation law because the penalty provided for the offending black person was the same as for the white sexual partner. Thus, since the two violators were treated equally, the Court had said the law did not contravene the Fourteenth Amendment.

The decision the court followed was *McLaughlin v. Florida* (1964), which overturned a Florida miscegenation law dealing with cohabitation outside of marriage even though both offending parties were punished equally under the statute. Because the people involved in that case were not married, the Court had sidestepped the question of the constitutionality of statutes that prohibited interracial marriages. The decision in *Loving*, thus, extended the Court's distaste for antimiscegenation statutes. Now such statutes, whether they proscribed interracial cohabitation in or outside of marriage, were held to be unconstitutional.

The *McLaughlin* also Court enunciated a new test for the validity of statutes based on racial distinctions. Racial statutes would no longer be automatically constitutional just because the parties were punished equally. Rather, a state must show "some overriding statutory purpose" in prohibiting interracial conduct that would be legal if the parties were of the same race. Florida had no statute prohibiting two whites or two blacks of different sexes from habitually living in and occupying the same room at night. Thus, black-white couples in Florida were being singled out for special punishment to which other couples were not subjected. When Florida chose to punish one group of people (black-white couples) for conduct permitted by other groups (black-black and white-white couples), it was engaging in discrimination based solely on race, the Court said. The statute, therefore, "must be viewed in light of the historical fact that the central purpose of the Fourteenth Amendment was to eliminate racial discrimination emanating from official sources in the States." The Court could find no "overriding" purpose for the law and found that it was unconstitutional; McLaughlin's conviction was overturned.

In *Loving v. Virginia*, Warren maintained that states were free to regulate marriage without federal interference, but that such regulation could not violate the Fourteenth Amendment. The fact that the Virginia laws punished both parties in an interracial marriage equally was a hollow argument considering the Court's decision in *McLaughlin v. Florida*. The laws in question, Warren said, were designed merely to perpetuate white supremacy in Virginia, and there was no other purpose in their enactment. Such legislative intent could not be justified under the equal protection clause of the Fourteenth Amendment.

In straightforward and forceful language, the chief justice methodically attacked the Virginia statutes and interpreted the Constitution to outlaw rather than sanction racial discrimination in the marital relationship: "The Equal Protection Clause requires the consideration of whether the [racial] classifications drawn by any statute constitute an arbitrary and invidious discrimination. The clear and central purpose of the Fourteenth Amendment was to eliminate all official state sources of invidious racial discrimination in the States. . . . There can be no question but that Virginia's miscegenation statutes rest solely upon distinctions drawn according to race. The statutes proscribe generally accepted conduct if engaged in by members of different races. . . . If [laws drawing racial distinctions] are ever to be upheld, they must be shown to be necessary to the accomplishment of some permissible state objective. . . . There is patently no legitimate overriding purpose independent of invidious racial discrimination which justifies this classification."

Further, Warren held that the Virginia miscegenation laws violated the due process clause of the Fourteenth Amendment by depriving interracial couples of a "fundamental" liberty interest—"the freedom of choice to marry" whomever they wished. Such a decision, the chief justice concluded, "resides with the individual and cannot be infringed by the State." Thus, the convictions of the Lovings were overturned, and racial distinctions in laws governing the institution of marriage were removed from the statute books of the United States.

Loving v. Virginia struck a blow for individual freedom by limiting the authority of state governments to prohibit certain people from engaging in acts that are legal for most of the population. Its immediate impact was to outlaw miscegenation laws not only in Virginia but in 15 other (mostly southern) states. By extending the coverage of the due process and equal protection clauses to additional persons targeted by criminal laws because of their race, *Loving v. Virginia* was a logical and appropriate step in the civil rights movement of the 1950s and 1960s.

Selected Bibliography

Drinan, R.F. "The *Loving* Decision and the Freedom to Marry." *Ohio State Law Journal* 29 (1968): 358–98.

Greenberg, J. *Race Relations and American Law*. New York: Columbia University Press, 1959.

Reuter, E.R. *Race Mixture: Studies in Intermarriage and Miscegenation*. New York: McGraw-Hill Book Co., Inc., 1931.

Wadlington, W. "The *Loving* Case: Virginia's Anti-Miscegenation Statute in Historical Perspective." *Virginia Law Review* 52 (Oct. 1966): 1189–1223.

SURROGACY MOTHERHOOD: WOMB FOR RENT

by Elizabeth E. Traxler
Department of Humanities
Greenville Technical College

In re Baby M, 109 N.J. 396 (1988) [New Jersey Supreme Court]

The case *In re Baby M* garnered nationwide attention when its facts were made public in 1986. Included in the story were elements of a drama guaranteed to rival the hottest soap opera: a baby passed through a window to escape "the law," charges of alcoholism and sexual abuse, flights to other states, a nomadic existence in motels, and a six-week trial involving the testimony of 38 witnesses and generating $500,000 in legal fees.

The *Baby M* case involved a situation that was by no means the first use of surrogacy motherhood contracts, and the case was not the first legal challenge to such agreements. The history of surrogacy can be traced at least as far back as the story told in the Bible of Sarah urging Abraham to enlist her maid Hagar as a surrogate mother. No doubt through the years there were cases of friends and relatives who provided this service for couples unable to have children. The use of legal surrogacy contracts emerged in the mid-1970s, and several hundred children had been born as a result before the *Baby M* case arose. Yet, none of the previous contracts or challenges in court attained the notoriety of this one. The publicity accorded this case guaranteed extensive consideration of the unresolved issues raised by this method of procreation. The court's decision and resulting commentary generated legislation to address the issue, and provided a precedent for cases subject to future litigation. Initially, however, there appeared to be nothing particularly unusual with this contract or the circumstances surrounding its creation.

The agreement entered into by William Stern and Mary Beth Whitehead was a fairly typical formulation of a surrogacy contract. Whitehead agreed to be artificially inseminated by Stern's sperm and to surrender the baby and all parental rights to Stern at birth so that his wife could then adopt the child. Contact after that point with Whitehead was to be limited to an annual picture and progress report. In return, Stern agreed to pay all expenses of insemination, pregnancy, and childbirth, as well as a fee of $10,000 at the time of termination of parental rights by Whitehead. If the baby was born with abnormalities, Stern agreed to accept legal responsibility for the child after birth. The contract also included stipulations that Whitehead would undergo amniocentesis and leave to Stern any decision regarding abortion.

Nor were the circumstances surrounding the agreement out of the ordinary. The Sterns—he a biochemist, she a pediatrician—decided on surrogacy childbirth after they learned that Mrs. Stern had a mild case of multiple sclerosis. Fearful that pregnancy would exacerbate her condition, they decided against that route to parenthood. Their ages and differing religions, as well as Stern's desire to carry on his family bloodline after the death of his last living relative, led them to rule out adoption as an alternative. They turned to the Infertility Center of New York in search of a surrogate. There they came into contact with Whitehead who sought to provide such services. Whitehead maintained that she turned to surrogacy as a way to provide money for her two children's future education and out of a desire to provide happiness for a childless couple. She and her husband considered their family complete, and he, in fact, had had a vasectomy nine years earlier. Yet what began over a celebratory dinner at the time of conception had soured even before Whitehead gave birth to a baby girl on March 27, 1986.

Indications of second thoughts surfaced during the pregnancy as Whitehead resisted Stern's medical advice and insistence on amniocentesis. Whitehead signed the papers acknowledging Stern's paternity after much hesitation. The issue came to a head at "Baby M's" birth when Whitehead began to voice her uncertainty over giving up the baby. Contrary to provisions of the contract, she both named the baby and identified her husband as the father on the birth certificate. Though she did relinquish the baby to the Sterns the day of her release from the hospital, she successfully convinced them the following day to allow her to take the baby for a week's visit. Fearful for Whitehead's emotional state if they refused her request, the Sterns grudgingly consented. Unknown to the Sterns, Whitehead took the baby out of state during that time to visit her parents in Florida. After much ambivalence, Whitehead finally told the Sterns that she would not give up the child and would not terminate her parental rights by honoring the contract. The Sterns obtained a court order granting them temporary custody of the baby when it appeared that the Whiteheads were planning a move to Florida before the issue could be litigated. They arrived at the Whitehead home accompanied by the police to enforce the decree but were stymied in their efforts when the Whiteheads spirited the baby away from the residence through a window. Then began a lengthy period during which the Whiteheads, with the baby, moved constantly to evade the authorities' efforts to enforce the court order. Finally, after 87 days, the Florida police were able to take custody of the baby and returned her to the Sterns in New Jersey. The legal battle culminated in a nonjury trial in the Superior Court of New Jersey.

The trial resulted in a lengthy decision which touched on most of the major unresolved issues surrounding surrogacy motherhood contracts. Essentially, the case turned on whether the contract was valid, enforceable by the state, and if so, what remedies were available given Whitehead's breach. At the time, there existed no state or federal law regarding such arrangements in the United States. It was left, therefore, to the court to determine the legality of the contract. Though New Jersey statutory law was silent on surrogacy, other New Jersey statutes, especially those concerning adoption, child custody, and termination of parental rights, could have been construed to govern the matter. That, in fact, is what had occurred in a 1981 Michigan case when that state's adoption laws were used to declare the fee payment aspect of surrogacy contracts illegal. Five years later, in a Kentucky case, that state's supreme court accepted a fee payment as payment for services, thus avoiding the antibaby selling elements of its laws. However, the court applied the adoption statutes to allow the surrogate mother a five-day grace period after the baby's birth in which to change her mind concerning her surrender of the baby and parental rights.

The New Jersey court, however, argued that surrogacy had not been medically perfected at the time of these statutes' passage and rejected them as irrelevant to these proceedings. Sokrow applied only principles of common and constitutional law in his assessment of the contract's legality. He argued that contracts are protected under common law unless they are against public policy. After brief consideration of the major critiques of surrogacy, he held that such contracts were not void from a public policy standpoint. In so doing, he rejected the following public policy objections to surrogacy: (1) that it degraded women by treating them only as reproductive machines; (2) that it could lead to exploitation of women of lower socioeconomic status by women in a financial position to rent another's womb; and (3) that the fee payment provisions amounted to buying and

selling a child, an act illegal in all 50 states.

Sokrow also found support for surrogacy contracts in principles of constitutional law, most notably in the right to privacy grounded in the Fourteenth Amendment's due process clause and its equal protection clause. Tracing the case history affirming the existence of a right to privacy, the judge asserted that such a right included within it a right to procreate. If that were the case, he maintained, the chosen means of procreation must also be protected. From this, he argued that the state could not deny men and women the right to enter into surrogacy contracts for the purpose of procreation unless a compelling reason for restriction could be shown. He found none of the reasons advanced by others (essentially the same ones used to argue that these contracts were harmful to public policy) sufficiently compelling to justify state restrictions.

Sokrow further argued that the constitutionality of the surrogacy contract was grounded in the Fourteenth Amendment's equal protection clause. He maintained that a woman offering her services for pay as a surrogate was substantially the same as a man's being paid as a sperm donor. The U.S. Supreme Court case *Reed v. Reed* (1976), a gender discrimination case, was cited to support the proposition that the equal protection clause forbade differential treatment of the sexes unless a compelling reason could be offered. In the absence of such a reason, he insisted that women must be accorded the same rights as men. Since the various public policy arguments were not found convincing enough to void the contract on common-law principles, they were also not held to be sufficient justifications for state restriction of constitutional rights lodged in both clauses of the Fourteenth Amendment.

Since Sokrow found the contract valid and Whitehead to have breached it, a determination of the remedies available to Stern was next made. Generally, contract law allows for two remedies: (1) payment of monetary damages to the aggrieved party or (2) an order for specific performance of the terms of the contract (to be used when money cannot adequately compensate). Sokrow maintained that while contract law principles would seem to mandate specific performance, this could not be ordered unless it was also in the best interest of the child. At this point, he asserted the common-law principle of *parens patriae* whereby the state acts as a guardian to protect the interests of those with legal disabilities—in this case Baby M. After a review of the testimony from experts on the meaning of "best interests" as well as their evaluations of the relative abilities of each couple to fulfill those interests, Sokrow ordered that the terms of the contract be specifically performed, thereby terminating Whitehead's parental rights and lodging all such rights with the father, Stern. Stern then proceeded to an immediate hearing in which Elizabeth Stern became the baby's adopted mother.

Given the emotions of the parties to this case, it is not surprising that it did not end at that point. Ten days later, the New Jersey Supreme Court, pending outcome of the appeal, ordered visitation privileges for Whitehead. On February 3, 1988, the state's highest court handed down its opinion, in which much of the lower court's decision was reversed. Surrogacy contracts were found to be contrary to existing New Jersey statutes forbidding payment for babies and regulating termination of parental rights. They were also held to be against the public policy of protecting the best interests of the child, which included being raised by both of her natural parents. While the court acknowledged a constitutional right to procreate, it held that this only pertained to the right to conceive a child, not to the right to contract away parental custody and rights. On these bases, surrogacy contracts were declared illegal and unenforceable in New Jersey.

The court then proceeded to a determination of custody of Baby M using only the principle of the "best interests of that child." Drawing on the expert testimony at the trial and on an assessment of the child's previous year and one-half with the Sterns, the court awarded custody to the Sterns. The issue of visitation was remanded to the trial court with the admonition that some form of visitation be allowed Whitehead.

Absent any legislation or federal court decision to the contrary, surrogacy contracts of the variety used in this situation are illegal in New Jersey. Any use of surrogacy must be purely voluntary with no pay involved and must allow the mother to change her mind and retain her parental rights. Obviously, this legal understanding will most likely reduce the number of surrogacy births. Legally, the appellate decision applies only to New Jersey, though it could be viewed as offering a "persuasive" precedent for other courts confronted with similar cases.

In the decision's wake, numerous bills relating to this subject were introduced in state and federal legislatures. The lower court decision was the subject of considerable scholarly analysis in which public policy and constitutional law issues were explored in greater detail than in the court's decision. As the New Jersey Supreme Court asserted at the close of its decision, "The problem is how to enjoy the benefits of the technology—especially for infertile couples—while minimizing the risk of abuse. The problem can be addressed only when society decides what its values and objectives are in this troubling, yet promising area."

Selected Bibliography

Bacin, J.F. "A Matter for Solomon: Rights and Obligations of Surrogate Mothers After *Baby M.*" *Western State University Law Review* 15 (Fall 1987): 297–317.

Field, M.A. *Surrogate Motherhood.* Cambridge, MA: Harvard University Press, 1988.

Recht, S.M. "'M' is for Money: *Baby M* and the Surrogate Motherhood Controversy." *The American University Law Review* 37 (Spring 1988): 1013–50.

Stark, B. "Constitutional Analysis of the *Baby M* Decision." *Harvard Women's Law Journal* 11 (Spring 1988): 19–52.

PART VI: LAW IN CRITICAL PERIODS OF AMERICAN HISTORY

PART VI: LAW IN CRITICAL PERIODS OF AMERICAN HISTORY

INTRODUCTION

Most of the essays in this final part could well be included in other parts of the *Encyclopedia*. However, they are grouped here because they offer examples of how the law has operated in particularly violent or contentious times in the nation's past. The British writer and critic D. H. Lawrence once described the United States as a land of "Thou shalt nots." At decisive moments in the American past, this admonition rings out with great cacophony. As the essays on the cases in this part indicate, however, sometimes the call is greeted with cries for blood but other times with pleas for understanding.

A. The American Revolution

There are two essays in this section. The first, "The Writs of Assistance Cases," deals with a set of cases that arose in the 1760s concerning the practices of British customs officials under the authority of the English Crown. The abuses of the so-called writs of assistants moved American colonists closer to independence. The other essay, "The Boston Massacre Trials," examines the trials of the British soldiers who were charged with the 1770 killings of colonial protesters. These killings and the subsequent acquittals of the Redcoats also helped to spark the American Revolution.

B. The Civil War and Reconstruction

Certainly the gravest crisis in U.S. history was the Civil War of 1861–65. The founding fathers made no provision in the U.S. Constitution for secession. Consequently, they did not anticipate the difficult legal questions that would arise as a result of a civil war and the nation's arduous recovery from it. In fact, the Union went to great lengths to deny that a state of war existed. President Abraham Lincoln did not want to grant legitimacy to the Confederate cause because this would qualify the South for military assistance from abroad.

Even before the war ended, the nation was forced to confront the legality of the seizure of ships under the proclamation blockading Southern ports. The dubious resolution of this matter is discussed in "When Was a War a War, and What If It Was?" The powers of the president in wartime were challenged in several cases, with the Supreme Court providing support for the prosecution of war critics in some cases but not in others. Two of these early civil liberties cases are discussed in "The Constitution: A Law for Rulers in War and Peace?" The so-called Test Oath Cases, which had the potential of raising disruptive constitutional questions about congressional plans for Reconstruction are discussed in "More Than a Trojan Horse: The Test Oath Cases." The question of just what was the legal status of a Southern state during the war was addressed but essentially skirted in the Supreme Court case *Texas v. White* (1869); this case is discussed in "Indestructible Union, Indestructible States." The final essay in this section, "By a Semicolon Divided: The Pitfalls of Excessive Judicial Activism," concerns a Texas court decision that dealt with a seemingly trivial matter, but one that ended up having significant implications for Reconstruction in that southern state.

C. The Great Depression

The economic and social crisis of the 1930s known as the Great Depression had significant legal dimensions. As noted in the essay "The Chambermaid's Revenge" in Part III, two justices on the U.S. Supreme Court in the 1930s literally underwent conversion experiences. This allowed the High Court to vote to uphold the constitutionality of state and federal legislation designed to improve the economic health of the nation by means of selective government regulation.

However, the first set of Depression cases to reach the Supreme Court saw the justices, led by the "Four Horsemen"—Pierce Butler, James McReynolds, George Sutherland and Willis Van Devanter—turn a deaf ear to the plight of the nation. For example, as discussed in "The Iceman and the Public," a majority of the Court refused to take judicial notice of the traumatic economic facts of the Great Depression. The tension on a Court not sure how to regard the Depression was apparent in 1934 when the justices split over the constitutionality of a state law that set prices for dairy products; this case is treated in "Nine Cents a Quart."

The switch in voting patterns of the justices was clear by 1937 when the Court upheld the constitutionality of the critical National Labor Relations Act; this case is examined in "The Wagner Act and the Constitutional Crisis of 1937." One form of regulation that the Supreme Court of the Depression era did not permit was the attempt by some states to cordon themselves off from the economic problems of the rest of the country: "The 'Indigent' Migrant" examines the Court's 1941 refusal to allow California to close its border to indigents. Perhaps the case illustrating how completely the Court had been converted to the belief that Congress and the state legislatures should be allowed to enact reasonable measures to deal with the bleak economic conditions of the Depression was the 1942 case *Wickard v. Filburn*, discussed in "Two Hundred and Thirty-Nine Bushels of Wheat." In this case, the Court upheld a federal law setting the price of wheat, even if that wheat was consumed on the farm and never entered the stream of commerce.

D. The Cold War

As the United States drifted away from its World War II alliance with the Soviet Union in the late 1940s, fears about internal communist subversion began to accelerate. Joseph McCarthy, Richard Nixon, and other staunchly anticommunist crusaders took it upon themselves to keep the specter of domestic communist subversion before the American people. McCarthy, Nixon, and their ideological cohorts were assisted by world events between 1946 and 1950, which saw Eastern Europe and China fall to communism and the Soviet Union ex-

plode an atomic device. In this tension-ridden climate, the leaders of the American Communist Party were tried and convicted of advocating the violent overthrow of the American government; this case is discussed in Part V, "Cold War Communism, and Free Speech."

The essays in this section treat other important Cold War cases. The essay "Icons of the Cold War: The Hiss-Chambers Case" probes the perjury trial of former State Department official Alger Hiss, a man accused of lying about passing top secret governmental documents to communist couriers. "A Crime Worse Than Murder" examines the trial and appeal of Julius and Ethel Rosenberg, the so-called Atom Spies. "The Smith Act Narrowed" treats the trial and appeals of lower level members of the American Communist Party. "The Court and the Committee" and "The Court and the Committee: Part Two" delve into the practices of trial by publicity of the House Un-American Activities Committee. Finally, "The Right to Travel" presents a case from the 1960s in which the Supreme Court held that a passport could not be withheld from a U.S. citizen solely because of his affiliation with the American Communist party.

E. The 1960s

In the 1960s, the United States fought an undeclared and increasingly unpopular war in Southeast Asia. The country endured a massive civil rights movement that went from peaceful protest and incremental legal change to violent confrontation. And the nation witnessed an increase in violent crime that ran parallel to an unprecedented extension of rights to those accused of serious crimes. Given these momentous and disturbing events, it is not surprising that the courts became involved. The attempts of courts in the 1960s to address these problems provide illustrations of Alexis de Tocqueville's famous statement that, in America, every political question sooner or later leads to a legal settlement.

In this final section of Part VI, discussions of three characteristic 1960s cases are presented. "Conscientious Objection: A Right or a Privilege?" deals with an issue of great controversy during the Vietnam War years. "The Right of Children to Be Seen as Well as Heard" examines the rights of public school students to express their social passions symbolically. And, finally, "The Pentagon Papers" analyzes the government's attempt to deny newspaper publication of top secret reports on the conduct of the Vietnam War.

A. The American Revolution

THE WRITS OF ASSISTANCE CASES

by David Thomas Konig
Department of History
Washington University at St. Louis

Petition of Lechmere (1761) [Massachusetts colonial court]

On September 10, 1760, Chief Justice Stephen Sewall of the Massachusetts Superior Court of Judicature died in Boston. A little more than a month later, King George II died in London. Individually, each death left a gap—Sewall's as chief magistrate, George's as monarch of the world's greatest empire. Together, however, they produced a crisis in Massachusetts politics and provided the setting for a legal struggle that yielded one of the earliest expressions of an American formulation of constitutional thought. John Adams was doubtless exaggerating when, in 1817, he looked back on the episode and said, "Then and there the child Independence was born"; but he did not err in identifying it as a landmark on the route toward revolution.

Sewall's death produced a dilemma for Governor Francis Bernard. In office for only five weeks since his arrival in the province, Bernard learned that his predecessor, William Shirley, had promised to appoint Colonel James Otis, Sr., to the next opening on the province's highest court. An ambitious politician from the small Cape Cod town of Barnstable, Otis had been spurned in his attempt to gain election to the Governor's Council in 1757 and only reluctantly had returned to the House. Now that a Superior Court vacancy appeared—and the chief justiceship, at that—Otis looked to achieve the capstone of his political career.

Bernard had misgivings about honoring Shirley's pledge, however. As governor, his salary depended in part on moneys collected in the process of justice. By statute, he received one-third of all moneys collected from forfeitures of smuggled goods. Moreover, Otis's son James, Jr.—no less ambitious a politician—was serving as advocate-general of the Vice-Admiralty Court, where forfeitures were supposed to be handled. Eager to cultivate the support of Boston's mercantile community, young Otis was notoriously diffident in prosecuting forfeiture cases, and Bernard was justifiably suspicious of the problems Otis might create for his personal finances and political success.

The new governor, therefore, made what he believed to be the safest choice possible when he overlooked the elder Otis and turned instead to Thomas Hutchinson. Scion of one of the province's oldest families, Hutchinson was as different from his ancestor Anne—of Antinomian fame—as anyone in Massachusetts. A man who once described himself as "a quietist, being convinced that what is, is best," Hutchinson was viewed by Bernard as a "much prudenter man than I ever pretended to be." Reliably pro-British in mercantile matters and a stalwart upholder of the *status quo*, he had risen to the provincial lieutenant-governorship and was considered a leader in the Governor's Council, the upper house of the legislature. Enjoying the fact that the doctrine of separation of powers did not exist, the loyal Hutchinson thus stood as a sturdy political foundation upon which Bernard might build a prosperous and successful governorship.

Instead, the Hutchinson appointment was the rock upon which his administration foundered. Holding multiple posts was legal, but Hutchinson's occupying such powerful and lucrative posts as these—executive, legislative, and now judicial—was certain to arouse resentment in patronage-conscious Boston, where he already had the reputation of belonging to a clique that included a brother-in-law as province secretary. Such accumulation of offices spurred the anti-government faction to protest. Young Otis resigned from his vice-admiralty position even before Hutchinson took office as chief justice on December 30, 1760.

Only three days earlier, news of George II's death had reached Boston. Amid the mourning for a king who had ruled for more than three decades and the celebration for the succession of a young and vigorous King George III, a normally routine matter was ignored. Writs—the formal, written warrants that ran in the name of the monarch—had validity only during the life of the monarch whose name had legitimized them, and for six months thereafter. All writs in George's name, therefore, would shortly have to be reissued.

Ironically, the writ that would set Otis, Jr., against Hutchinson was not a very common writ. In fact, the Superior Court had issued it to only eight men in Massachusetts between 1755 and 1760. This was the customs writ of assistance, a warrant that authorized a customs official to command a local constable or justice of the peace, during daytime, to assist him in entering "any house, shop, cellar, warehouse or room or other place, and in case of resistance to break open doors, chests, trunks and other packages, there to seize, and from thence to bring, any kind of goods or merchandize whatsoever, prohibited and uncustomed." For this reason, the writ was also known as a "writ of assistants."

This authority was vital to customs enforcement in a seaport where the illegal importation of goods was a mainstay of mercantile success. By the Staple Act of 1663, nearly anything shipped to the colonies from the European continent, India, or the East had to pass through Great Britain, there to pay a tax and be retransported to North America. Boston traders detested this law as an infringement on their rights and a drain on their profits, and they evaded it through every species of subterfuge imaginable.

They also fought the Staple Act legally. One stratagem was to remove forfeiture cases from the Vice-Admiralty Court, which used no jury and relied on civil law principles, to the Superior Court, where common law procedural guarantees obtained and where sympathetic local jurors would acquit them. This required a writ of prohibition from Superior Court judges, taking the case to their jurisdiction. By the 1750s, judges on the Superior Court were less willing to grant writs of prohibition, and other techniques were needed.

Would-be evaders of the Staple Act might also hide their goods once on shore and move

them as soon as a customs officer applied for a search warrant. Aware of this ploy, customs officers retaliated with a writ that enabled them to search likely hiding places—a writ of assistance. This writ, as authorized by the Act of Frauds of 1662 and extended to the colonies by another Act of Frauds in 1696 had the potent advantage of being a general writ: as issued in Massachusetts by the governor, it did not have to specify place or the precise nature of the goods. Always ready, it enabled swift application and bolstered customs enforcement greatly.

But the writ, when issued by the governor, violated the law: by statute, it was to be issued by the Court of Exchequer, not *ex officio* ("from the office") by the governor. Ironically, it was Hutchinson who pointed this out to his friend Governor Shirley in 1755; unknowingly, he had taken upon himself a thorny problem. In Massachusetts, there was no exchequer court, and the Superior Court was the only forum comparably close to serve in that capacity for this purpose. Some question existed as to whether it was close enough in jurisdiction to serve the exchequer purpose of issuing a writ of assistance, and in *McNeal v. Brideoak* (1754), the Superior Court had refused to exercise exchequer jurisdiction. But in that case, it was the chancery side of exchequer that was declined, not the common law side pertaining to writs of assistance. The issue of the Superior Court's authority to issue a writ of assistance, therefore, was still not settled when, in 1761, Boston port officials applied to the Superior Court for a new writ of assistance under the name of King George III. The chief justice to whom they addressed their request was Hutchinson.

The need for new writs quickly attracted the attention and talents of partisans on both sides. On the Crown's side, no less a personage than the Surveyor-General of His Majesty's Customs for the Northern District of America, Thomas Lechmere, took over for the port officers in petitioning for the writs; opposing him, a group of merchants led by Thomas Greene challenged the request. Arguing for the former was Jeremiah Gridley, perhaps Boston's most eminent attorney and a teacher of many leaders of the Boston bar; opposing him were his former student James Otis, Jr., and Oxenbridge

Thacher (possibly he, too, had been a Gridley student).

Gridley and Thacher drew the issue neatly on the question of the Superior Court's exchequer jurisdiction. To the former, such authority rested securely on statute: Parliament had conferred such power on the Court of Exchequer, and by a province statute of 1699 the Superior Court had been given exchequer jurisdiction. Thacher denied any exchequer jurisdiction in Massachusetts by referring to the 1754 *Brideoak* case and pointing out other differences between the provincial court and exchequer. No court in Massachusetts, he argued, possessed the authority to issue writs of assistance.

Their arguments, though properly to the point, are now forgotten, buried by the fallout from Otis's pyrotechnics. As described by John Adams in 1817, "Otis was a flame of fire! With the promptitude of Clasical Allusions, a depth of Research, a rapid Summary of Historical Events and dates, a profusion of legal Authorities, a prophetic glare of his eyes into futurity, and a rapid Torrent of impetuous Eloquence, he hurried away all before him; American Independence was then and there born. . . . Then and there was the first scene of the first Act of Opposition to the arbitrary Claims of Great Britain. Then and there the child Independence was born." There is some reason to question this distant recollection: Adams was writing to William Tudor, then at work on a biography of Otis, and he was trying to supply Tudor with information that would elevate a Massachusetts patriot over that of Virginian Patrick Henry, whose biography was also then in progress.

That motivation aside, Adams was correct in singling Otis out for having set forth a vital Revolutionary principle. Rather than addressing the statutes or the common law for that matter, Otis had chosen to rest his case on a "higher law" argument. General writs were unconstitutional simply because they violated "the fundamental Principles of Law." Special writs, issued on probable cause for a specific location on sworn application, were legal as a matter of state necessity, but the general writs could not be so justified. "A Man, who is quiet, is as secure in his House, as a Prince in his Castle," said Otis, who maintained that general writs were an arbitrary exercise of state power

that permitted wanton abuses by unrestrained officers who did not even have to account for their actions by returning the writ to the issuing court for examination and trial. Statutory empowerment did not matter. In the most controversial statement of the case, Otis attacked the writs and the authority of the legislature that had created them: "An Act against the Constitution is void: and if an Act of Parliament should be made, in the very Words of this Petition, it would be void. The executive Courts must pass such Acts into disuse."

Otis's argument was as confused as it was radical, for it was not at all clear what he meant by the requirement to "pass such Acts into disuse." He probably meant no more than that principles of statutory interpretation be applied to interpret the law in such a way as to make it consistent with common-law procedures. For this he was drawing on the English Lord Coke's decision in the 1610 *Bonham's Case*, in which Coke had written, "When an Act of Parliament is against Common Right and Reason, or repugnant, or impossible to be performed, the Common Law will control it, and adjudge such Act to be Void." Otis, therefore, was attempting to impose a rule of interpretation to limit the power of Parliament by restricting the writ to that of a special, not general, warrant. Although he went further in his 1764 pamphlet, *The Rights of the British Colonies Asserted and Proved*, Otis in 1761 was nonetheless making a radical point by invoking a power to restrain Parliament within prescribed constitutional bounds. Unfortunately, by 1761 Coke's view of judicial control of the legislature had been eclipsed by Sir William Blackstone's elevation of Parliamentary omnipotence, which would overwhelm any argument for limitation.

So, too, would English practice. Convinced that the Superior Court did have exchequer jurisdiction, Chief Justice Hutchinson needed to know only if general writs were issued in England. He therefore asked the province agent, William Bollan, for information on English practice and continued the case until an answer arrived. When the Superior Court resumed in November, Bollan's answer settled the question: general writs were, in fact, issued in England. Unanimously, the Superior Court agreed that Lechmere's petition be approved, and that general warrants be issued when requested. When such were requested in 1762, Otis's argument had some effect, however: they were made out to named officers rather than to anyone bearing them.

Otis attempted to keep his constitutional argument—and his political career—alive through pamphlets, but a head injury suffered in a barroom fight with an English officer aggravated a mental instability already beginning to appear, and he steadily withdrew from politics. Hutchinson, later governor of the province, also withdrew from politics prematurely. He came to be a hated symbol of British rule amid the collapse of royal government brought on, or at least hastened, by the ferment that had impelled Otis to oppose general writs of assistance.

Selected Bibliography

Dickinson, O.M. "Writs of Assistance as a Cause of the American Revolution," in *The Era of the American Revolution*, R.B. Morris, ed. New York: Harper & Row, 1965.

Frese, J. "James Otis and Writs of Assistance." *New England Quarterly* 30 (1957): 496–508.

Konig, D.T. "The Theory and Practice of Constitutionalism in Pre-Revolutionary Massachusetts: James Otis on the Writs of Assistance," in *Law in a Colonial Society*, J.A. Yogis, ed. Toronto: Carswell, 1984.

Smith, M.H. *The Writs of Assistance Case*. Berkeley, CA: University of California Press, 1978.

Ubbelohde, C. *Vice-Admiralty Courts and the American Revolution*. Chapel Hill, NC: University of North Carolina Press, 1960.

Waters, J.J. *The Otis Family in Provincial and Revolutionary Massachusetts*. Chapel Hill, NC: University of North Carolina Press, 1968.

Wroth, L.K., and H.B. Zobel, eds. *The Legal Papers of John Adams*. 3 vols. Cambridge, MA: Harvard University Press, 1965.

THE BOSTON MASSACRE TRIALS

by Harold B. Wohl
Department of History
University of Northern Iowa

Rex v. Preston; Rex v. Weems; Rex v. Manwaring (1770) [Massachusetts colonial court]

While no single riot can make a revolution, people taking to the streets in the years after 1763 played an important part in the coming of the American Revolution. In almost every instance, the anger of the crowd was directed against British policy and the people who served it. One particular incident sent shock waves through the colonies, fanning the flames of anti-British sentiment. It was the climax of a season of violence.

In early 1770, British troops had been quartered in Boston for more than a year. Traditionally, Boston had no British garrison and many townspeople resented their presence and demanded their removal. On Monday evening, March 5, in the square before the Custom House, a mob of toughs armed with clubs began taunting Private Hugh White, who was on duty in the sentry box, and began hurling icicles and chunks of ice at him. Pushed to the breaking point by this goading, the soldier struck one of his tormentors with his musket. Soon a crowd of 50 or 60 gathered around the frightened soldier, prompting him to call for help. The officer of the day, Captain Thomas Preston, and seven British soldiers hurried to the Custom House to protect the sentry.

Upon arriving at the Custom House, Captain Preston must have sensed the precariousness of the soldiers' position. The crowd had swelled to several hundred, some anxious for a fight, others simply curiosity seekers. Still others had been called from their homes by the town's church bells, a traditional signal that a fire had broken out. Efforts by Preston and others to calm the crowd proved useless. And because the crowd had enveloped Preston and his men as it had the lone sentry, escape was nearly impossible. The riotous crowd began striking at the troops with sticks and stones and finally knocked Private Hugh Montgomery down. He rose to his feet and fired into the crowd. Others fired too, and when the smoke had cleared, five people lay dead or dying and eight more were wounded. Preston and his men quickly returned to their barracks, where they were placed under house arrest. They were later taken to jail and charged with murder.

The cause of resistance now had its first martyrs. Provocative encounters between British soldiers and civilians were a common source of irritation and the cause of an increasing number of incidents around town. This was the first time, however, that soldiers had killed civilians. Those killed were Crispus Attucks (an Indian or mulatto seaman in his forties, who also went by the name of Michael Johnson), James Caldwell (a sailor), Patrick Carr (an immigrant from Ireland who worked as a leather-breeches maker), Samuel Gray (a ropemaker), and Samuel Maverick (a 17-year old apprentice). Anti-British "Patriots" in Boston promptly referred to the killings as "the Boston Massacre." Colonel William Dalrymple, the English commander, preferred to call it a "scuffle."

The morning after the fatal shooting on King Street, John Adams was retained to defend Preston. Adams did not know that it was the acting governor, Thomas Hutchinson, who had recommended him to Preston, along with another young patriot lawyer, Josiah Quincy. Although Hutchinson was a leading Tory figure, he apparently believed Adams was the best lawyer for so important a case. Adams detested both the Boston mob and the sight of British troops on Boston Common. But he firmly believed in the right of an accused person with his life at stake to have the counsel of his choice. It was Adams's and Quincy's devotion to the law that led them to put the cause of justice above their politics and join the defense team, which also included the Tory attorney Richard Auchmuty.

Apparently Samuel Adams and the leading Sons of Liberty also influenced the selection of the defense team. They signaled their approval of their young friends' acceptance of the assignment. Despite the political benefits the patriots derived from the massacre, they had, in the past, supported orderly demonstrations and expressed distaste for uncontrolled mobs, of which the Boston Massacre was a prime example. Confident that local jurors would re-

turn a verdict of guilty, they were willing to let the military have the best available lawyers. That way no one could later claim the proceedings were unfair or make martyrs of the soldiers. The patriots failed to consider the possibility of an acquittal.

Samuel Quincy, Josiah's elder brother and a Tory, was appointed one of the Crown's prosecutors. However, fearing that the Tory leanings of the prosecutor might soften the prosecution, the selectmen of Boston engaged Robert Treat Paine, John Adams's long-time rival at the bar, as a kind of special prosecutor to represent the families of the murdered and to assist the King's attorney.

Meanwhile, as John Adams and the Quincy brothers were preparing their respective cases, publicity about the deaths on March 5 enshrined the "massacre" in Whig legend. The patriot leaders of Boston used the episode as proof to other colonists that their earlier reports of oppression by the troops were not exaggerated. The *Boston Gazette*'s account of the "massacre," with black border and featuring four coffins, circulated through the colonies and was widely copied. Within weeks, all of the colonies knew that "the streets of Boston have already been bathed with the BLOOD of innocent Americans! Shed by the execrable Hands of the diabolical Tools of Tyrants!" Pamphleteers whipped up the townspeople by writing incendiary newspaper articles as well as letters and pamphlets portraying the victims as martyrs and memorializing them in extravagant terms. In one eulogy, Joseph Warren of the Sons of Liberty addressed the dead men's widows and children, dramatically recreating the gruesome scene in King Street: "Behold thy murdered husband, gasping on the ground . . . take heed, ye orphan babes, lest whilst your streaming eyes are fixed upon the ghastly corpse, your feet slide on the stones bespattered with your father's brains." To propagandists like Warren it mattered little that the five civilians had been bachelors.

For most colonists the description of the massacre in the Boston newspapers was reinforced by Paul Revere's famous engraving of the scene. Inaccurate in many details but dramatic in its overall effect, the engraving was a masterful piece of propaganda. Appropriately splattered with blood, it became an instant bestseller. In Revere's representation, Preston, with his sword drawn, seems to be ordering the soldiers to fire on peaceful, unarmed, well-dressed men and women. The Custom House is labeled Butcher's Hall, and smoke drifts up from a gun barrel sticking out of a second-floor window. In subsequent editions, the blood spurting from the dying Americans is more conspicuous. To the propagandists, what happened mattered little; their job was to inflame emotions, and they performed their work well.

The grand jury indicted Preston and his men in five separate indictments of murder and, for good measure, indicted four Customs employees, accused of firing out of a window of the Custom House. Samuel Adams and the Sons of Liberty preferred that the trial begin promptly, while memories were fresh and emotions ran high. But the trials of Preston and the soldiers were postponed until the fall session of the Superior Court to allow time for the preparation of the defense and to permit the town's passions to cool. It was not until September, six months after the shooting, before Preston and his men were arraigned. Each pleaded not guilty. The court then adjourned and on October 24, 1770, Adams rose to defend Preston.

Legally, the massacre was interesting because of British legal constraints on the military. Everyone knew that the soldiers could not use lethal force against unarmed civilians unless ordered to do so by some civil, not military, authority. Everyone, including the Sons of Liberty, Hutchinson, and General Thomas Gage, commander-in-chief of all the British troops in North America, agreed that Preston had had no orders to fire from a civil magistrate. Yet a soldier, like anyone else, also retained the right of self-defense. Therefore, were the soldiers' lives in danger? Did they fire only as a last resort to save their own lives?

As the time for the trial approached, the defense realized it had a possible conflict of interest on its hands. If Preston was tried in the same proceeding as the other soldiers, mutual finger-pointing might well convince the jury to find all of the defendants guilty. If the defense failed to show that the killings were justifiable, Preston would have to argue that the men fired without his orders. The men, on the other hand,

would likely argue that they had only obeyed their officer's command to fire. To avoid this difficulty, the defense moved for separate trials. First they would prove that Preston gave no order to fire. Then they would consider the defense of his soldiers.

Rex v. Preston began at 8:00 a.m. on Wednesday, October 24, 1770. The first item was impaneling the jury. A murder case could not be heard by a judge alone. The Tories feared that the jury would be packed with Sons of Liberty. After 19 challenges, Preston's lawyers seated a jury of 12, only two from Boston, and five of Tory persuasion.

Samuel Quincy opened for the Crown and handled the evidence, while Adams did the same for Preston. Auchmuty and Paine closed for the defense and prosecution, respectively. It was usual practice for the junior counsel to open the case and examine the witnesses with the senior man closing the argument. Josiah Quincy, although active in the pretrial preparations, did not participate in the trial itself.

By the standard of the day, the trial was a long one. With a break for the Sabbath, the court was done in six days. The trial of Preston, thus, became the first criminal trial in Massachusetts history to run more than one day.

Opening the argument against Preston, Quincy set out to establish that even if Preston had not given the order to fire the first shot, he had sufficient time to call "Recover" before the volley began. One witness swore to that. But the testimony soon became as chaotic as the night itself. Adams set out to prove that Preston gave no order to fire. Since the law forbade the accused to take the stand, Preston did not speak in his own defense. His best witness was Richard Palmes, the merchant and Son of Liberty, who said that Preston had been facing him and that he had had his hand on Preston's shoulder when someone shouted "Fire!": it had not come from Preston. Three black witnesses also bolstered Preston's defense. Two slaves, one belonging to a Son of Liberty, and a freeman from the West Indies testified to the provocation of Crispus Attucks and the crowd, who were swinging their sticks at the soldiers. The case went to the jury at 5:00 p.m. on Monday, October 29. The jury took only three hours to reach its verdict: not guilty. The vast weight of the evidence exonerated the captain; the Crown had failed to prove that he ordered his men to shoot. The British officer was quickly packed off to England, where he received a pension of £200 per year from George III "to compensate him for his suffering."

With Preston freed, attention now turned to the trial of the soldiers, which began three weeks later on November 27. Preston's acquittal actually made the soldiers' defense more difficult. Even if Preston had not given the order to fire the first shot, there was no question that shots had been fired and that the soldiers had fired them. That being the case, the soldiers must have fired without orders. If they fired without orders, so the thought ran, they must be murderers and "blood required blood."

Robert Treat Paine and Samuel Quincy again conducted the prosecution; John Adams, Josiah Quincy, and Sampson Salter Blowers were the attorneys for the defense. For some unknown reason, Auchmuty had not been retained to defend the soldiers. Adams now stepped into the senior counsel's role, while Josiah Quincy assumed the task of cross-examining the Crown's witnesses and presenting the defense's case. With a touch of irony, Samuel Quincy, a staunch Tory, shaped the argument to help hang the soldiers, whereas his younger brother Josiah, a fiery Whig, attempted to save their lives.

The first move of the defense attorneys was to exercise their preemptory challenges in the selection of the jury. Every man on the jury panel who was from Boston or its immediate vicinity was excluded. The jury that was finally seated consisted of country men who would presumably be less apt to sympathize with the Boston mob or feel pressures to return a guilty verdict.

The prosecution's trial strategy was simple: it need prove only that the defendants had fired their weapons. The burden was on the defense to prove that the provocation the soldiers faced justified the killings. The prosecution paraded a string of witnesses who testified that the crowd was "standing orderly and making no outcry" when the soldiers fired upon them in cold blood. In its turn, the defense produced witnesses who gave a different version of the night's events, testifying to the violence of the mob's attack,

first against the sentry and then against the file of soldiers. The soldiers' best defense came from beyond the grave. Dr. John Jeffries, who treated Patrick Carr for his wounds until the Irish boy died four days after the shooting, testified that Carr had repeatedly told him that the soldiers would have been injured if they had not fired. Asked by Jeffries if he believed the soldiers had fired in self-defense or purposely to kill civilians, Carr replied: "[I]n self-defense."

It was all hearsay evidence, but when Josiah Quincy put the next question, "Was he apprehensive of his danger?," it became admissible. Massachusetts law permitted unsworn testimony from someone who knew he was dying; presumably no man facing the ultimate judgment would use his last breath to lie. Samuel Adams was heard to remark that since Carr, an Irishman, had probably died a Roman Catholic, Protestant Boston could discount the worth of his last words.

In his summation, Adams blamed the riot on "outside agitators" who invited their own deaths: "a motley rabble of saucy boys, Negroes and mulattoes, Irish teagues and outlandish jack tars. And why should we scruple to call such a set of people a mob . . . unless the name is too respectable for them. The sun is not about to stand still or go out, nor the rivers dry up, because there was a mob in Boston on the fifth of March that attacked a party of soldiers."

Rex v. Weems was an even longer trial than Preston's, lasting from November 27 to December 5: five days were devoted to impaneling and taking testimony, and two and one-half days were expended for argument and charges. But the jurors were out for only two and one-half hours. Corporal William Weems and Privates James Hartigan, William McCauley, Hugh White, William Warren, and John Carroll were found not guilty. However, the jury had also decided that the soldiers had fired before it was absolutely necessary to their defense. Since Kilroy and Montgomery were the two soldiers whom witnesses had seen firing, the verdict for them was "not guilty of murder, but guilty of manslaughter." Those two men were held for sentencing and the others were released.

One trial remained. Edward Manwaring, a Custom's officer, and three of his friends were charged with firing from the windows of the

Custom House. *Rex v. Manwaring* began on December 12. The case against the four civilians was so thin and so riddled by the witnesses for the defense that by noon the jurors "acquitted all the Prisoners, without going from their Seats." In fact, the prosecution's principal witness, Manwaring's 14-year-old French servant boy, was himself indicted for perjury, convicted, and sentenced to an hour in the pillory and 25 lashes at the whipping post.

On December 14, nine days after the *Weems* trial ended, Adams was back in court to hear Kilroy and Montgomery sentenced. They were asked whether there was a reason they should be spared the death penalty, manslaughter being a capital offense. Each man pleaded "benefit of clergy," a remnant of medieval law that removed those in holy orders from civil jurisdiction. Defendants who could prove they were clergymen might insist on being tried by an ecclesiastical tribunal as the church's punishments were far less severe than those of a secular court. Since the law dated from the time when the clergy were the only literate class, a man could establish his status merely by reading Psalm 51:1. It came to be called "the neck verse." By claiming the benefit, the two soldiers would escape the death penalty. They would be branded "by fire on the thumb," the necessary judicial price for ensuring that the life-saving plea could not be claimed a second time. Kilroy and Montgomery held out their hands and Sheriff Greenleaf seared their thumbs. The two prisoners were then released from custody, and so nine months after the shooting the Boston Massacre, legally speaking, passed into history.

Those acquainted with the modern courtroom would find the proceedings of these trials quite unusual. Witnesses were not sequestered, but remained in open court during the taking of other testimony. Witnesses were also called out of order: for example, Crown witnesses were called in the middle of the defense's case; rebuttal witnesses were called immediately to refute specific segments of testimony. And when addressing the jury, counsel not only argued law but read directly from law books. Today, a lawyer's closing speech concentrates exclusively on the facts, leaving the law to be summed up in the judge's charge. Throughout the *Weems*

trial, there is not even the sign of an objection to a question, or a motion to strike an answer. Many witnesses, apparently took the stand, were asked what they knew of the events on the night in question, and then stepped down without being cross-examined.

Popular feeling did not rejoice in the triumph of justice over prejudice. Samuel Adams was so pained by the outcome of the trials that he demagogically retried the case in a series of heated newspaper articles, continuing to call the shootings a massacre and claiming that justice had not been done. But John Adams considered his participation in the defense "one of the most gallant, generous, manly and disinterested Actions of my whole life, and one of the best Pieces of Service I ever rendered my Country." The death sentence, he wrote in 1773, "would have been as foul a Stain upon this Country as the Executions of the Quakers or Witches, anciently. As the evidence was, the Verdict of the Jury was exactly right."

Of all the incidents leading to the American Revolution, many stand out as important or significant. The Boston Massacre is one such event. However, one must be careful in assessing its importance. After all, the Redcoats were exonerated. The verdict was, in John Adams's words, "exactly right." And the colonists and the mother country did not finally resort to arms until five years after this dramatic event. By that time, only an inflated and inflamed rhetoric kept the incident from being forgotten.

Yet the massacre, taken together with other events, did help to shape the popular attitude that the British were heartless tyrants who terrorized a peaceful citizenry. As a symbol of British oppression, it bolstered what their political theory told them—that a standing army was the greatest danger a people's liberty could face. For the next 13 years, Bostonians would gather each March 5 to commemorate the event. Only when the Peace of Paris in 1783 brought the final guarantee of American independence would they begin celebrating July 4 instead.

The site of the Boston Massacre is now on a traffic island in the midst of the city's financial district. Every day thousands of Bostonians and tourists stand on this historic spot waiting for the traffic to abate.

Selected Bibliography

Bailyn, B. *The Ordeal of Thomas Hutchinson*. Cambridge, MA: Harvard University Press, 1974.

Butterfield, L.H., eds. *Diary and Autobiography of John Adams*. 4 vols. Cambridge, MA: Harvard University Press, 1961.

Countryman, E. *The American Revolution*. New York: Hill & Wang, 1985.

Maier, P. *From Resistance to Revolution*. New York: Alfred A. Knopf, 1972.

Middlekauff, R. *The Glorious Cause*. New York: Oxford University Press, 1982.

Smith, P. *John Adams*. 2 vols. Garden City, NY: Doubleday, 1962.

Wroth, L.K., and H.B. Zobel, eds. *Legal Papers of John Adams*. 3 vols. Cambridge, MA: Harvard University Press, 1965.

Zobel, H.B. *The Boston Massacre*. New York: W.W. Norton & Co., 1970.

B. The Civil War and Reconstruction

WHEN WAS A WAR A WAR, AND WHAT IF IT WAS?

by *Thomas D. Morris*
Department of History
Portland State University

Prize Cases, 2 Black 635 (1863) [U.S. Supreme Court]

Shortly after the shells exploded over Fort Sumter, President Lincoln issued a series of executive proclamations. On April 19, 1861, he declared a blockade of the ports of several of the seceded Southern states, and on April 27 he extended the blockade to Virginia and North Carolina. He claimed he acted under the laws of the United States, and "of the law of nations."

Shortly after, a number of ships were seized and condemned as lawful "prizes" under this blockade. Among others, two ships claimed by John and David Currie, Richmond merchants, were seized. These were the *Crenshaw* and the *Amy Warwick*. The *Crenshaw*, with tobacco aboard, was captured off Newport News, Virginia, on May 17, 1861, and the *Amy Warwick*, loaded with coffee from Rio de Janeiro, was captured on the high seas headed for Hampton Roads. Several others were taken as well, including the *Hiawatha*, which was taken on May 20 in Hampton Roads, and the *Brilliante*, captured in Biloxi Bay, June 23, 1861. The *Hiawatha* was a British ship which had taken on a cargo of tobacco and cotton. The *Brilliante*, owned by a Mexican mercantile firm, was loaded with flour it had taken on in New Orleans and was bound for Mexican ports. To successfully wage war, the Confederacy needed trade. It was not even self-sufficient in food. "We cannot eat cotton, nor dine off tobacco and sugar," one Southerner ruefully observed in 1862. If the Union could successfully blockade the South, it would be a tremendous blow to the Confederacy.

But, were the seizures and condemnations made under Lincoln's proclamations lawful? That would depend on the legal definition of the Civil War, and it would depend on the na-

ture of the war powers, especially the powers claimed by the president. Lincoln consistently said that the states could not withdraw from the Union. He was confronted with a "combination of persons engaged in . . . insurrection." Critics of Lincoln's proclamations insisted that the war powers did not cover internal uprisings, but that they related only to foreign enemies. There was nothing in the U.S. Constitution about a civil war. The dilemma for Lincoln was that if he accepted the argument, he would be forced to do one of two things. On the one hand, if he were to claim the broad range of war powers allowed by international law (and the imposition of a blockade that neutrals were obliged to respect was one), he would have to recognize the Confederacy as a foreign state. That would admit the constitutional validity of secession. The Confederate States of America would then be a lawful nation state, and that would carry with it a range of "rights" to the insurrectionists. It would also implicitly accept the proslavery view of the Constitution that Lincoln, as a nationalist, had firmly rejected. Lincoln's alternative would be to try to put down the rebellion without all of the powers that would exist if the war was against a foreign nation.

There was, thus, a great deal at stake in the decision of the *Prize Cases* when the Court heard the arguments in February 1863 and rendered a divided judgment on March 10, 1863. Eminent counsel appeared for the United States: Richard Henry Dana, Jr., author of *Two Years Before the Mast*, and an expert on maritime law, and William M. Evarts, a leading conservative member of the New York Bar. The principal attorney for the ship owners was a prominent Washington lawyer, James M. Carlisle.

Carlisle argued that only "the sovereign power of the United States" could declare or recognize a state of war and thereby bring into existence "belligerent rights." That was Congress, and Congress had not declared war. He was particularly appalled at a new constitutional view: it was the notion that the president was the "embodiment of the Nation, and vested in that behalf with a species of natural right." He possessed, so the argument went, "implied powers." The only limit on his powers was "necessity." This was a frightening prospect wholly contrary to U.S. constitutionalism. It would make the president a dictator, it would be to make him the sovereign, as Richard Nixon was later to claim. The president, Carlisle conceded, did have the power to see that the laws were faithfully executed, but he did not have the right to change the law. The fact was that because there was no war in a legal sense under the Constitution, the federal government could not claim belligerent rights under international law against the Southern people, or neutrals.

The most expansive argument for the government was that of Evarts. War, he noted, was a "question of actualities," and a civil war brought with it to the sovereign the rights of war against neutrals, and full power or dominion over the rebels. "The form and spirit of the political institutions of a people, the frame of its very Constitution, do not measure or shape the power or duties of a government, so defended against foreign or civil war. The warlike strength of the nation, and the warlike power brought against it, furnish the only measure and method of the conflict."

Dana's argument had a different tone. He hit at Carlisle's position on a declaration of war. A sovereign, he argued, "never, in form, declares war against a rebellion," and it may exercise belligerent powers against rebels. Lincoln had done so, and Congress had validated his action in July of 1861. Since both Congress and the president had acted, Dana claimed, the issue was a political question, and the judgment of the political branches was conclusive. Before the decision of the Court was handed down, Dana wrote to Charles Francis Adams with some concern. It was alarming that the war had been going on for months and only now was the Court going to decide whether the govern-

ment could use the war powers. If it decided against the blockade, he feared the war would end unfavorably for the Union and leave the country in an awful situation regarding neutrals.

Although the Court divided 5–4, Dana could put his deepest fears to rest. Justice Robert C. Grier took the view that war, which was not declared against rebels, was nonetheless "a fact in our domestic history." Congress could not constitutionally declare war against a state. The majority seemed determined to avoid a highly legalistic approach. The Queen of England had, through a proclamation of neutrality, recognized the hostilities. Neutrals then could not ask a court of law to "affect a technical ignorance of the existence of a war" and thereby "paralyze" the government "by subtle definitions and ingenious sophisms." The "President was bound to meet it in the shape it presented itself, without waiting for Congress to baptize it with a name. . . ." Moreover, the president possessed the whole executive power under Article II, and, as commander-in-chief, had the duty to suppress the insurrection. It was in his political discretion to determine whether the insurrectionists should be given the status of belligerents, such as by treating captured Confederate soldiers as lawful prisoners of war rather than as traitors. The government, Grier concluded, possessed belligerent rights toward neutrals, and the seizure of the foreign-owned vessels under the blockade order was legal. The seizure of the property of people like the Curries was also legal. Such persons had thrown off their allegiance to the government, and were therefore no less "enemies because they are traitors." The property of enemies was lawful prize.

Justice Samuel Nelson wrote for the four dissenters, who, including Roger B. Taney, wished to restrain the executive power. Nelson claimed that until Congress acted, there was no lawful war and no lawful exercise of belligerent rights under international law. The so-called war that existed in the Southern states was a "personal war, until Congress . . . acted. . . ." He admitted that war could exist, and be extremely threatening. However, that amounted only to an admission that it existed in a "material sense," but that was of no moment when the question was what was a war "in a legal

D. The Cold War

A CRIME WORSE THAN MURDER

by Joseph Glidewell
Elberton, Georgia

United States v. Rosenberg (1951) [U.S. Federal District Court]

At 12:00 noon on April 6, 1951, Federal Judge Irving Kaufman faced Julius and Ethel Rosenberg in the largest federal courtroom in the Southern District of New York. His purpose was to impose sentence. For the past month, the Rosenbergs, along with Morton Sobell, Anatolia Yakovlev, and David Greenglass, had been on trial, charged with conspiracy to commit espionage in wartime. However, Yakovlev, who had left the country years before, and Greenglass, who had pleaded guilty, were granted severances for purposes of the trial. Therefore, the main defendants were the Rosenbergs and Sobell.

What had transpired from March 6 through April 6, 1951, was the nation's first trial for the theft of atomic bomb secrets. Found guilty of the charge on March 29, the defendants waited to hear their fate. As they stood facing Kaufman, little could they know that their trial would spark worldwide demonstrations, protests, and a controversy that still rages 40 years later.

The "Rosenberg Trial" occurred during what has been called the "Second Red Scare" in U.S. history. The period has been characterized as a time of anti-Communist furor, which developed into a "Communist witch-hunt." Numerous organizations, as well as individuals, were publicly accused of being Communist sympathizers simply because of their associations with left-wing political beliefs. This hysteria occurred because of the ideological conflict that had arisen at the end of World War II between the Soviet Union and the United States. Labeled the "Cold War," this ideological confrontation had the United States in its grip, and it permeated into all areas of American life.

Following World War II, Americans had witnessed Communist military advances and success in Eastern Europe and in other areas of the world. These and the revelations of espionage within the U.S. government that surfaced during the Alger Hiss trial, threw the United States into a mood of fearful anticipation of what would occur next. The years 1949–50 saw the fall of China to the Communist forces of Mao-Tse-Tung and the explosion of an atomic device by the Soviet Union years ahead of the timetable that had been predicted by western scientists. Then, in June 1950, the Korean War erupted and the initial success of the North Koreans' invasion set the stage for a major "Red Scare." It was amid this atmosphere that the Rosenberg Trial took place.

The arrests of the Rosenbergs and the other defendants were the result of intensive investigation that had lasted over four years. The investigation had begun in 1945 when a Soviet consul named Govzenko, in Ottawa, Canada, defected to the West. His tales of espionage took the combined efforts of the Canadian Mounties, Scotland Yard, and the Federal Bureau of Investigation (FBI) four years to unravel. The key break occurred in early 1950 when British scientist Klaus Fuchs confessed his espionage activities to a Scotland Yard agent. His confession led the authorities to Harry Gold, a chemist from Philadelphia, who in turn confessed to the FBI. It was Gold's confession that led to David Greenglass, Ethel Rosenberg's brother.

The government's case rested on the alleged scenario that, during the 1930s, the Rosenbergs had become members of the Communist party in New York City and had been active party members up until their arrest. During the summer of 1944, Greenglass, while in the U.S. Army, began to work as a machinist at the atomic weapons center in Los Alamos, New Mexico. In January 1945, Greenglass, after being recruited by Julius to help the Soviet Union, gave the Rosenbergs sketches of the high-ex-

699

plosive lens that was used to detonate an atomic bomb. Later, Gold was sent to Los Alamos to obtain more information from Greenglass. Through this meeting and others, more sketches were passed on, including one of the atomic bomb.

When World War II ended in August 1945, the espionage activities of Greenglass ended. He was released from the army and returned to New York City, where he and Julius Rosenberg, along with Bernard Greenglass, opened a machine business. The next several years passed quietly for both the Greenglasses and the Rosenbergs. But unknown to them, the Soviet spy ring to which they had belonged had been unraveled by the combined efforts of British and U.S. intelligence.

According to the government, when Julius read of Gold's arrest, he immediately began to make plans for the Greenglasses to leave the country. However, Ruth Greenglass, David's wife, refused to leave and 11 days after Gold's arrest, on May 23, the FBI arrested David. Several days later, on July 17, Julius was arrested and one month later, on August 11, Ethel was taken into custody.

The U.S. attorney who was given the task of prosecuting the "Atom Spies" was Irving Saypol. Known as the nation's number one legal hunter of Communists, Saypol was assisted by Myles Lane, Roy Cohn, James Kilsheimer, and James Branigan, Jr.

The trial was presided over by Judge Irving Kaufman, who, at age 40, was the youngest judge on the federal bench. Kaufman had a distinguished record, having served as special assistant to the U.S. Attorney for the Southern District of New York and later as assistant U.S. attorney. After several years of private practice, he became special assistant to the attorney general of the United States. Following this position, he accepted an appointment as a federal judge.

For the defense, the Rosenbergs were represented by Alexander Bloch and his son Emmanuel, better known as Manny. Manny Bloch, though he liked to be portrayed as just a "people's lawyer," was an accomplished attorney who had handled several national cases involving Communist party leaders and had a reputation as a crusader for left-wing causes.

Ethel's attorney, Alexander Bloch, had legal experience in dealing with unions, but was on unfamiliar ground with the type of case he was being asked to handle. However, he remained Ethel's attorney until the end, and she never questioned this arrangement.

The first day and one-half of the trial was spent selecting a jury. Over 300 prospective jurors were called as the importance of the case made jury selection a "tedious business." Kaufman led the questioning and, eventually, a jury of eleven men and one woman was chosen. With this and other formalities out of the way, late in the second day of the trial, the U.S. attorney delivered his opening statement.

Prosecuting attorney Saypol immediately set the tone of the trial as he tied Julius and Ethel Rosenberg to their devotion to communism. Immediately, defense attorney Bloch objected, arguing that communism was not on trial, but Kaufman allowed the remarks to stand. Saypol then proceeded to equate conspiracy with treason by promising to show "evidence of the treasonable acts of these three defendants" and that "they have committed the most serious crime which can be committed against the people of this country." This point was important in the government's case, since it wanted a charge of treason against the defendants so that stiff penalties could be obtained, possibly the death penalty for Julius. Although treason would be almost impossible to prove, conspiracy would not. But because conspiracy did not carry penalties as stiff as those for treason, Saypol linked treason and conspiracy together, hoping to get both a conviction and severe punishment.

From the beginning, the trial had the aura of a historic event. The prosecution had hinted that possibly 123 witnesses would be called, including such notables as atomic scientist Robert J. Oppenheimer and General Leslie Groves, head of the atomic research at Los Alamos. However, only a handful of witnesses were called; none had "household names."

The government's first witness was Max Elitcher, a close friend of defendant Morton Sobell. Elitcher's testimony linked himself, Sobell, and Julius together as he testified to numerous attempts by Julius to get information about military equipment and of his constant desire for Elitcher to recruit engineering students who might be able to obtain military information. Elitcher further testified about a trip he made to Sobell's home in which Sobell told him about information in his home that was "too valuable to be destroyed and yet too dangerous to keep around." He then told how he and Sobell drove to meet Julius and to give him what Elitcher identified as a 35-millimeter film can.

The prosecution's second witness was David Greenglass, Ethel's brother and the main witness for the government. Greenglass told of how Julius and Ethel during the 1930s had told him how they preferred Russian socialism to capitalism, how Julius convinced David's wife Ruth to ask him to get information that would be of value to the Soviet Union, of the sketches he had made for Julius, of his meeting with Gold, and of how Ethel had typed the information he had given to the Rosenbergs.

Greenglass's testimony gave the jurors an insight into the ingenuity of the agents involved in espionage as he described the method used by Ruth to meet her contact. According to Greenglass, after an evening meal with the Rosenbergs, it was decided that Ruth would go to live in Albuquerque and would be used to pass information to a Soviet operative. To construct an identification code, Julius went into the kitchen with Ethel and Ruth and cut a Jell-O box into two irregular sections. Julius kept one section and gave Ruth the other to use in identifying her contact. With this testimony David Greenglass forever linked Julius and Ethel to physical evidence that, unlike implosion theories, high explosives lenses, and isotopes, the jury and public could understand. Greenglass went on to testify regarding a meeting in Albuquerque with Gold and plans made by Julius for his family to leave the country.

The testimony of the government's next witness, Greenglass's wife Ruth, corroborated most of her husband's story. However, she added two crucial pieces of evidence that her husband had not mentioned. The testimony that further threw suspicion on the Rosenbergs was Ruth's statements about money being paid to David by Julius and about a mahogany console table. Ethel said this table, a gift from Julius, was hollow underneath for photographic pur-

poses; Julius, Ruth stated, had said that the table was to be used to take pictures on microfilm of the typewritten notes. On cross-examination, Ruth repeated her story nearly word for word.

The Greenglasses were the government's main witnesses, and no doubt it was their testimonies that led to the Rosenbergs' conviction. However, five other minor witnesses were called to corroborate their testimonies. Dorothy Printz Abel, Ruth's sister, corroborated the story of the Rosenbergs' meeting with the Greenglasses at the Rosenbergs' home; Lorin Abel, Ruth's brother-in-law, held the money Julius gave to David Greenglass; George Berhardt, a doctor, confirmed that Julius called him about inoculations needed for a trip outside the country; John Landsdale, an army intelligence officer, confirmed that David Greenglass was accurate in his description of the security measures at Los Alamos; and Gold corroborated the trip to Albuquerque and his meeting with David Greenglass with the famous remark "Julius sent me."

After Gold's testimony, the prosecution called eight minor witnesses to prove that Sobell had taken "flight" to Mexico to avoid being captured by the authorities. The final witness was Elizabeth Bentley, the famous "Red Spy Queen." Bentley more than likely was called for her effect rather than her testimony. However, she did relate her past history as a Soviet courier and gave suspicious testimony when she testified to telephone calls she received after midnight "in the small wee hours" and how the conversation always started with the saying, "This is Julius." Shortly after her testimony, the prosecution rested.

The defense called Julius as its first witness. He was questioned about his youth, political beliefs, family relationships, dealings with the family business, and about the charges made by his brother-in-law and sister-in-law. He denied that he had anything to do with espionage. Throughout his entire questioning and cross-examination, he remained calm and cool.

After several minor witnesses testified, Ethel, the final defense witness was called. She also denied all allegations regarding espionage activity, and, after denying that she secured passport pictures, the defense rested its case. Sobell elected not to take the stand.

The prosecution then recalled several rebuttal witnesses. First, Evelyn Cox, a household domestic, testified regarding the console table and its removal from its usual place in the Rosenberg home. Then Ben Schneider, the owner of a small photographic shop, testified it was the Rosenbergs who came into his shop in May or June and ordered 36 passport-size pictures. Following his testimony, the lawyers made their final arguments, the judge delivered his charge, and the case went to the jury. The jury retired on Wednesday, March 28, at 4:30 p.m., and one day later it reached verdicts of guilty against all three defendants. One week later, the three convicted defendants faced Judge Kaufman to hear their fate.

The law under which the three had been found guilty, the Espionage Act of 1917, carried a maximum of 20 years' imprisonment with the exception of violation during wartime, where the punishment was death or imprisonment for not more than 30 years. With these guidelines, Kaufman proceeded. He began by explaining the reason for the sentence he was about to impose and his opening remarks left no doubt of his decision: "I consider your crime worse than murder." Kaufman then stated that he had no doubt about the couple's guilt, that their actions had directly led to the Korean War, and that their deed had adversely changed the history of the United States.

After stating that Julius was the "prime motivator" in the crime, and Ethel "a full-fledged partner," he told the Rosenbergs, "it is not in my power to forgive you. Only the Lord can find mercy for what you have done." He then imposed the sentence. "The sentence of this court is . . . the punishment of death." Later, Sobell received the 30-year maximum penalty with the judge's recommendation for no parole.

What followed for the next three years was one unsuccessful appeal after another. After a final refusal by the U.S. Supreme Court to hear the case, the only avenue left for the defendants to pursue was a presidential pardon. However, this was also denied amid worldwide protests to spare their lives. On June 18, 1953, almost three years after their arrest, the Rosenbergs died in the electric chair at New York's Sing Sing Prison.

The Rosenberg Trial is still controversial 40 years later. While many have supported the verdict of the case, numerous questions have been raised as to whether the penalty was just and the depth of involvement of the Rosenbergs in Soviet espionage. Many Americans have even maintained that the Rosenbergs were innocent, the victims of an elaborate government frame-up.

The reasons for the skepticism are many. This was a case that had no disinterested eye-witnesses, and the prosecution offered no clear evidence that could tie the defendants together. The sketches, the cut Jell-O box, and hotel receipts of supposed espionage travels did not link the Rosenbergs to Greenglass or to any other espionage agent. Much of the physical evidence—such as the console table, the sales ticket for its purchase, or the negatives of the purported passport photographs—were never found. For these reasons, many believe that the Rosenbergs were innocent and found guilty only because of the hysteria of the times.

Arguments that support the verdict emphasize that the defense offered no major witnesses other than the defendants. Furthermore, none of the defendants offered a fool-proof alibi to refute any of the charges. And no physical evidence or witness testimony was given on their behalf. Finally, following the sentencing, 112 judges heard the appeals of the case over a three-year period. While 16 disagreed with whether a stay of execution should be granted or further review allowed, none contended the Rosenbergs were denied due process or that they were innocent.

For some, Julius and Ethel Rosenberg represent an era of Red Scare hysteria in which the rights of many were violated. In their struggle to exert their rights as U.S. citizens, they became "Cold War casualties." To others, the Rosenberg Trial is a symbol of justice done to those who committed "a crime worse than murder."

Selected Bibliography

Latham, E. *The Communist Controversy in Washington.* New York: Atheneum, 1969.

Nizer, L. *The Implosion Conspiracy.* New York: Doubleday & Co., 1973.

Pilat, O. *The Atom Spies.* New York: G.P. Putnam Sons, 1952.

Radosh, R., and J. Milton. *The Rosenberg File: A Search for the Truth*. New York: Holt, Rinehart & Winston, 1983.

Root, J. *The Betrayers: The Rosenberg Case—A Reappraisal of an American Crisis*. New York: Coward-McMann, Inc., 1963.

Schneir, M., and W. Schneir. *Invitation to an Inquest: Reopening the Rosenberg "Atom Spy" Case*. Baltimore: Penguin Books, Inc., 1973.

ICONS OF THE COLD WAR: THE HISS-CHAMBERS CASE

by John W. Johnson
Department of History
University of Northern Iowa

United States v. Hiss (1950) [U.S. Federal District Court]

On a humid Washington, D.C., day in August 1948, Whittaker Chambers, a short heavy-set man, testified before the House Un-American Activities Committee (HUAC) about his radical activities and associations in the 1930s. Seldom has an explosive case involving crime, politics, espionage, and famous people had such an unimpressive beginning. Chambers wore a rumpled suit and spoke quietly and phlegmatically. He stated that he was a former member of the underground wing of the American Communist Party. At first, Chambers was a decidedly uninspiring witness (it would later be revealed that he had a history of mental instability). His accusations, however, spawned a singular legal, political, and ideological mystery that still baffles historians.

Few members of the HUAC attended the August 1948 hearing at which Chambers testified. The claims that the committee had been making since the end of World War II about Communists in the United States were beginning to sound stale and empty. President Harry Truman, a Democrat, had recently blasted the HUAC for its transparent attempts to besmirch the legacy of the New Deal by branding liberal Democrats as Communist-inspired. Near the end of the summer of 1948, most Americans were beginning to agree with the president that the HUAC's accusations were just "red herrings."

If the HUAC was going to convince the country that Communists posed a significant danger, it was going to have to find a credible witness and at least one sensational villain. Chambers would ultimately be that witness. Personal appearance notwithstanding, he was an accomplished writer, translator, and editor who was acquainted with many major figures in American arts and letters from the 1920s through the 1940s. At the time of his HUAC testimony, he was a senior editor for *Time* magazine. He also had an excellent memory for details. The villain that Chambers identified as a possible candidate for the anti-Communist opprobrium of the HUAC was Alger Hiss.

A man of impeccable intellectual and political credentials, Hiss had graduated with honors from Harvard Law School, had been selected as a legal assistant for the great Supreme Court justice, Oliver Wendell Holmes, Jr., had served as a staff member for an important congressional committee, had served with distinction for 10 years in the Department of State, and was currently the president of the Carnegie Endowment for International Peace. Notably, while in the Department of State Hiss had attended the Yalta Conference with President Franklin Roosevelt and had directed the arrangements for the foundation of the United Nations. Indeed, it would have been difficult for a U.S. citizen of age 44 to have a better resume of public service than the one Hiss had in 1948. Moreover, Hiss looked like a respected statesman: he was tall and handsome, wore tailored suits, was a polished public speaker, and was married to an attractive woman. He also had distinguished friends in the federal government. There were some in the 1940s who said that Hiss, this rising star of foreign policy, would someday become the Secretary of State. If Hiss was a Communist, there was something decidedly wrong in the country. If a person as accomplished and poised for greatness as Hiss was not a loyal U.S. citizen, who could be trusted?

Chambers's fingering of Hiss provided the HUAC not only with weeks of spectacular media headlines, it also helped to establish the climate of fear that would lend credence to the charges of political conservatives in the late 1940s and early 1950s that the country was being undermined by Communists and their unwitting sycophants. Chambers's testimony, in short, advanced the Cold War.

Hiss promptly rebutted Chambers's charges. He appeared before the HUAC a few days after Chambers's initial charges and vehemently denied being a Communist. He also denied knowing Chambers. Most of the reporters covering the hearing believed Hiss and branded Chambers a liar. Some HUAC members even began to doubt whether the committee had been wise to allow Chambers to testify publicly before investigating fully his accusations. One HUAC member who expressed second thoughts was Richard M. Nixon, a young congressman from California. But Nixon and the Republican leadership of the committee decided to press forward and arranged a confrontation before the HUAC of Hiss and Chambers.

At this public encounter, Hiss again denied knowing a man named Whittaker Chambers; but he acknowledged that the man calling himself Chambers looked like George Crosley, a man he had known in the mid-1930s. Hiss then made a bizarre request: he asked the HUAC's permission to closely examine "Crosley's" teeth because Crosley had had bad teeth. After the examination, he seemed satisfied that the man before him was Crosley. He acknowledged that he and his wife, Priscilla, had known Crosley in the 1930s but that neither he nor Priscilla had ever passed confidential State Department papers or documents to him. Hiss also testified that he had broken off his acquaintanceship with Crosley in early 1937. The matter might have died then if it had just

been Chambers's words versus Hiss's—the words of a disturbed, self-described former Communist opposed to that of the country's rising star in foreign policy. At that point, there would have been little question who should have been believed. When Chambers repeated his charges on the radio show *Meet the Press*, Hiss brought suit against Chambers for slander.

Claiming that being slapped with a libel suit prompted his memory, in November Chambers produced confidential State Department documents from the 1930s that he had kept hidden away for over ten years. They could have come only from someone who had had official access to them, someone like Hiss. Most were typewritten: Chambers claimed that they had been typed on the Woodstock-brand typewriter that belonged to the Hiss family. Among these documents were four confidential memoranda in Hiss's handwriting. Chambers alleged that these materials had been passed to him by Hiss in 1937 and 1938 and that copies had been sent to the Soviet Union by a Communist courier. These materials were turned over to the U.S. Department of Justice's Criminal Division because they incriminated Hiss in an elaborate espionage scheme.

In early December, Chambers gave to the HUAC several rolls of microfilm he had hidden in a hollowed-out pumpkin in a field on his Maryland farm. The "pumpkin papers"—more copies of confidential State Department documents from the 1930s bearing Hiss's name or allegedly typed on the Hiss Woodstock typewriter—further inflamed the passions of the defenders of Hiss and Chambers. Finally, the Department of Justice subpoenaed Hiss and Chambers to testify before a federal grand jury, during which they repeated essentially the same stories that they had told before the HUAC. The grand jury accepted the face validity of Chambers's testimony and found that there was probable cause that Hiss had lied when he had denied passing state secrets to Chambers. On December 15, 1948, Hiss was indicted on two counts of perjury.

The first count claimed that Hiss had lied when he testified under oath that he had not stolen State Department documents and passed them to Chambers. The second count claimed that Hiss had testified falsely when he swore that he had not seen Chambers since late 1936. Because the statute of limitations had not expired and several witnesses who might have corroborated Chambers's allegations were not available to testify, Hiss was not charged with espionage for the illegal release of State Department documents in the 1930s.

The trial took place in the Foley Square Courthouse in New York City in the summer of 1949. In the same building and at the same time the Hiss trial was taking place, 11 members of the "open" portion of the American Communist Party were being tried for allegedly violating the Smith Act, a federal law making it illegal to belong to an organization that advocated the violent overthrow of the U.S. government. The stormy trial of the Smith Act defendants was complete with angry harangues by lawyers and defendants and the issuing of numerous contempt citations by Judge Harold Medina. It later became one of the longest trials in U.S. history and, on appeal, resulted in the important Supreme Court decision of *Dennis v. United States* (1951), which upheld both the constitutionality of the Smith Act and the conviction of the defendants. The *Hiss* trial was not as turbulent as the *Dennis* trial. Nor would it raise constitutional issues as important as those presented in *Dennis*. But in U.S. history, it would be as large as the trial of Eugene Dennis and his codefendants.

To many politically informed liberals in 1949, Hiss was a victim of the scare tactics of the right wing of the Republican party. Many Democrats also felt that the hostility Hiss faced was because he was seen by conservative Republicans as a symbol of what was wrong with the Democratic reform of the 1930s. By attacking Hiss, Republicans were thought to be getting in their licks at Franklin Roosevelt's New Deal.

Hiss was represented at the federal court trial by a large legal team led by the flamboyant Lloyd Paul Stryker. Hiss, also an attorney, had many friends and associates with legal expertise who rendered advice and volunteered research assistance. At the trial, the Hiss defense team pursued four main arguments. First, they suggested that Chambers was mentally unstable and presented four witnesses to corroborate this argument. To advance this line of inquiry, Hiss's attorneys emphasized Chambers's admitted homosexuality, thus playing on the homophobic prejudices of the time. Second, Hiss's attorneys stressed that Hiss and Chambers barely knew each other and seldom met. Third, they maintained that Hiss's Woodstock typewriter had been given away long before Priscilla Hiss could have retyped the State Department documents. The defense attorneys even suggested that the FBI or other unknown parties could have typed the documents to frame Alger and Priscilla. Finally, the defense attorneys presented many distinguished friends of Hiss who testified that the defendant was a man of complete integrity and would not have associated with Communists. Among the character witnesses were Supreme Court Justices Felix Frankfurter and Stanley F. Reed.

The prosecution's strategy was essentially to allow Chambers's testimony and the allegedly stolen documents to speak for themselves. The prosecution, with forensic evidence, attempted to show that Priscilla had retyped the purloined State Department papers on the Hiss Woodstock. Throughout the trial, the prosecution objected to what it perceived as favoritism toward Hiss and the defense's case. For example, the prosecution was incensed that the trial judge, Stanley H. Kaufman, came down from the bench to shake hands with the two Supreme Court justices who testified on Hiss's behalf.

Six weeks later, the case went to the jury. After more than two days of deliberations, the jury reported it was hopelessly deadlocked and could not reach a verdict. Kaufman reluctantly dismissed them. Reporters querying the jurors found that they had favored conviction by a vote of eight to four. The four favoring acquittal were not convinced that Priscilla had typed the stolen documents.

Prosecutor Thomas Murphy and his superiors in the Justice Department elected to retry the case. With Murphy again leading the prosecution, a second trial took place in November. In the four-month interval between the two trials, the world had changed: the Soviet Union had exploded an atomic bomb, the Communist Chinese had taken over all of mainland China, the HUAC had begun investigating alleged Soviet espionage in the wartime Manhattan Project, and U.S. public opinion polls showed an increasing concern over the threat of domestic Communism. In short, the Cold War was heating up.

For the second trial, Hiss retained Claude B. Cross, who was much less flamboyant than Lloyd Stryker, the Hiss attorney in the first case. The judge this time was the tough, no-nonsense Henry W. Goddard, the circuit's second most senior jurist. The second trial was conducted more professionally than the first. Unlike Stryker, Cross did not goad the prosecution or play on the jurors' emotions. In fact, attorneys for both sides were consistently polite. The case went to the jury on January 20, 1950. After deliberating all night, the jury returned the next afternoon with a verdict of guilty on both perjury counts. Hiss was then sentenced to five years in federal prison.

On appeal, Hiss's sentence was upheld by the circuit court. In 1951 the U.S. Supreme Court voted 4–2 not to hear the case. Three Supreme Court justices—Felix Frankfurter, Stanley F. Reed, and Tom C. Clark—did not participate in the decision. Frankfurter and Reed disqualified themselves because they had testified on Hiss's behalf at the first trial, and Clark disqualified himself because he had been U.S. attorney general when the indictment against Hiss was brought. Hiss surrendered to the U.S. marshall on March 21, 1951, and began serving his sentence in the Lewisburg Penitentiary. Subsequent appeals for review of his conviction were denied.

Less than three weeks after Hiss's January 1950 conviction, Senator Joseph McCarthy (Republican, Wisconsin) delivered his Wheeling, West Virginia, speech, alleging personal knowledge of Communists in sensitive governmental positions. McCarthy stated: "The reason why we find ourselves in a position of impotency is . . . because of the traitorous actions of those who have been treated so well by this Nation . . . those who have had all the benefits that the wealthiest nation on earth has had to offer—the finest homes, the finest college education, and the finest jobs in Government we can give. This is glaringly true in the State Department. There the bright young men who are born with silver spoons in their mouths are the ones who have been the worst." Clearly, McCarthy had Hiss in mind. Comments such

as these were the springboard that launched the Wisconsin senator's four-year campaign of allegations and undocumented attacks that constituted McCarthyism. In fact, in one speech during the 1952 presidential campaign, McCarthy cleverly appeared to stumble and confuse Hiss with the Democratic candidate for the presidency, Adlai Stevenson: "Strangely Alger—I mean Adlai . . . ." The point was not lost on his sympathetic listeners: Stevenson, a liberal Democrat, was easily confused with the convicted perjurer Alger Hiss.

After serving three years and eight months of his five-year sentence, Hiss was released from prison in November 1954. Throughout his incarceration and in the more than 30 years since his release, Hiss has professed his innocence. In 1957, he published *In the Court of Public Opinion*, a lawyerly defense of his innocence, alleging fraud and forgery by the federal prosecutors and the FBI. After his release from prison, Hiss attempted unsuccessfully to work in a small business. He also spoke occasionally on the Cold War to academic audiences. For liberals, Hiss came to be seen as one the principal casualties of the Cold War—a bright, accomplished, ambitious man cut down in his prime by demagogues of the political right.

For conservatives, Hiss, an example of what was wrong with America, was vilified for decades. Richard Nixon, for example, in his book *Six Crises* and in other accounts of his life, cited his success in "getting Hiss" as one of his greatest political accomplishments. By contrast, for Nixon and other conservatives, Hiss's accuser Chambers became a hero, his Communist past notwithstanding. Chambers became a favorite of conservatives after he testified against Hiss. Chambers told his fascinating life story in a popular book *Witness*. A Book of the Month Club selection, his 800-page memoir was more personal and revealing than Hiss's *In the Court of Public Opinion*.

In the years since the 1948 HUAC hearings, there have been scores of books and articles on the Hiss-Chambers case. Ironically, just as the case began to fade from memory, it was resuscitated in the early 1970s by the Watergate scandal. Nixon, who began his national political career attacking Hiss, was now the object of a sensational investigation of his own alleged wrongdoings. In fact, Hiss wrote an article for the *New York Times* in 1973, entitled "My Six Parallels," an allusion to Nixon's *Six Crises*, which included a chapter on the *Hiss* case. Hiss's article drew comparisons between his case and the break-ins of the Nixon years, suggesting that the Watergate fiasco and similar "dirty tricks" had been foreshadowed by government tampering with evidence in his own case. Thus, as Nixon's stock sunk, Hiss's seemed to rise.

In 1975, however, as a result of a lawsuit under the Freedom of Information Act, Allen Weinstein, a liberal historian, was successful in forcing the FBI to release its voluminous files on the Hiss-Chambers case. Drawing on the FBI's materials, hundreds of interviews, and the files of Hiss's attorneys, Weinstein published *Perjury*, a book that concluded that Hiss was guilty of lying under oath and, by implication, had committed several counts of espionage. Weinstein's book was certainly not the last word on the Hiss-Chambers case, but it offered, at the time, the most complete and persuasive

treatment in print. The publication of Weinstein's best-selling book about a 30-year-old dispute suggests that the Hiss-Chambers case still makes good copy. No doubt, as the climate of opinion shifts and a new generation of historians becomes acquainted with Hiss and Chambers, there will be a good deal more written about what has been termed, with some justification, "the American Dreyfus Affair."

Selected Bibliography

Caute, D. *The Great Fear: The Anti-Communist Purge Under Truman and Eisenhower*. New York: Simon & Schuster, 1978.

Chambers, W. *Witness*. New York: Random House, Inc., 1952.

Cooke, A. *A Generation on Trial: U.S.A. v. Alger Hiss*. New York: Alfred A. Knopf, 1950.

Hiss, A. *In the Court of Public Opinion*. New York: Alfred A. Knopf, 1957.

Latham, E. *The Communist Controversy in Washington: From the New Deal to McCarthy*. New York: Atheneum, 1969.

Nixon, R. *Six Crises*. New York: Warner Books, 1962.

Weinstein, A. *Perjury: The Hiss-Chambers Case*. New York: Alfred A. Knopf, 1978.

THE SMITH ACT NARROWED

by Jerold L. Simmons and Karen Bruner
Department of History
University of Nebraska at Omaha

Yates v. United States, 354 U.S. 298 (1957) [U.S. Supreme Court]

Thursday, July 26, 1951, began inauspiciously for 37-year-old West Coast newspaper editor, Al Richmond. As usual for a Thursday, he was at his desk before 8:00 a.m., hurriedly finishing an editorial for the newspaper's expanded weekend edition. The column that Richmond was busily composing that day, however, he was not destined to complete, for a few minutes later the hum of activity in the small San Francisco office was abruptly interrupted by the rude arrival of a phalanx of agents from the Federal Bureau of Investigation (FBI), an event that Richmond had been fearfully anticipating for over a month. As he was handcuffed, arrested, and transported to FBI headquarters, Richmond

mused about the battle that he knew awaited him and wondered if he would have to face it alone. Little did he suspect that the happenings of that morning were just the beginning of a chain of events that would have extraordinary implications for him personally, and even more momentously for the nation.

Richmond was no ordinary journalist. Nor was he alone in his predicament. As editor of the U.S. Communist party's (CPUSA) West Coast organ, *The Peoples World*, he was one of 14 California Communists also arrested that day in San Francisco, Los Angeles, and New York. Among the others arrested were William Schneiderman, the California Communist party state chairman, and Oleta O'Connor Yates, the state secretary. At the arraignment that afternoon, most of the defendants were required to post bail of $75,000, a testament to the seriousness of their crime: violation of the Smith Act.

Adopted by Congress in 1940, the Smith Act made it a crime to knowingly advocate or teach the forcible overthrow of the U.S. government, to organize or become a member of any group dedicated to such purposes, or to conspire to do either. The measure was one of nearly 100 antiradical proposals considered by Congress in the two years preceding World War II. Like many of the others, its target was the subversive propaganda of both the Fascist right and the Communist left. Its vague wording, especially when set against the First Amendment, made prosecution uncertain, and Franklin Roosevelt's Justice Department proved reluctant to enforce the measure. The postwar atmosphere, however, gave the Smith Act new life. Mounting national frustration over Soviet expansion, coupled with the strident rhetoric of the political right, eventually convinced the Truman administration of the need to embark on its own anticommunist crusade. The Federal Loyalty Program and the infamous attorney general's list of subversive organizations quickly followed, and in July 1948, the Justice Department brought charges against key members of the Central Committee of the CPUSA.

A stormy nine-month trial in 1949 culminated in the conviction of the communist leaders, and nearly two years later the Supreme Court both affirmed those convictions and upheld the constitutionality of the Smith Act in *Dennis v. United States* (1951). Chief Justice Fred M. Vinson's majority opinion avoided discussion of the meaning of such words as "teach" and "advocacy," and concentrated on the conspiratorial nature of the Communist party. While paying homage to Justice Oliver Wendell Holmes, Jr.'s "clear and present danger" test, Vinson largely dismissed its relevance: "Obviously, the words cannot mean that before the Government may act, it must wait until the putsch is about to be executed, the plans have been laid and the signal is awaited." The "gravity of the evil" combined with the party's secrecy thus justified prosecution well before the advocacy became action.

Armed with this new license, the government pursued a strategy of emasculating the Communist party by incarcerating its leaders. *Dennis* led directly to a roundup of top party functionaries, including editor Richmond and his California colleagues. In the trial of the Californians, which ran from February 1 to August 5, 1952, the defendants chose a strategy markedly different from that used by the *Dennis* group. The latter had elected to challenge directly prosecution allegations that Communist party doctrine was seditious. The California Communist leaders chose instead to focus on the constitutional right to advocate abstract political doctrine, no matter what its content. Not only did this strategy produce a more decorous proceeding, but it would prove significant five years later when the Supreme Court passed on the convictions in *Yates v. United States*. But in the shortrun, the more restrained tactics notwithstanding, the *Yates* defendants were all found guilty and received the maximum allowable sentences of five years in prison and $10,000 fines.

With little optimism, Richmond, Yates, Schneiderman, and the others embarked on what would be a lengthy appeals process. Their lack of confidence in obtaining a reversal seemed well founded when, in January 1955, the Supreme Court denied petitions to review the convictions of their comrades in New York and Baltimore who had been arrested at the same time and prosecuted on approximately the same charges. Nonetheless, after the circuit court ruled against the *Yates* group the following March, their lawyers dutifully filed for a writ of *certiorari*. Surprisingly, the Court granted the writ in October and heard oral arguments one year later.

The years of waiting between initial conviction and the final Supreme Court decision were suspended time for the *Yates* group, with a prison term always a likely eventuality. The rest of the country, however, was undergoing profound changes, particularly with regard to the fear of Communist subversion. Stalin's death, the Korean armistice, the Geneva Summit, and Khrushchev's startling 1956 speech denouncing the crimes of the Stalin era all seemed to soften the image of communism abroad. At home, four years of Republican prosperity, the absence of new spy scares, and the Senate's censure of Joe McCarthy diminished the fear of internal subversion. The startling announcements from the Kremlin, coupled with internal doctrinal disputes within the CPUSA, accelerated the decline in the fortunes of U.S. communism. Not only had the party been deprived of much of its leadership by the Smith Act prosecutions, but squabbling among its current directors also undermined the cogency of its message. The party was in shambles.

It was this milieu that provided the setting for the four startling decisions announced on June 17, 1957. On what became known as "Red Monday," the Court attempted to limit the excesses of the anti-Communist crusade. These decisions circumscribed the procedures of congressional investigating committees (*Watkins v. United States*), limited the authority of state investigations (*Sweezy v. New Hampshire*), set restraints on executive branch loyalty dismissals (*Service v. Dulles*), and reversed the convictions of the *Yates* defendants.

The majority opinion in *Yates v. United States*, written by Justice John Marshall Harlan, carefully avoided a direct reversal of *Dennis* and focused on two largely semantic issues. Harlan explained that the framers of the Smith Act intended the proscription against organizing a group that advocated forcible overthrow of the government to apply only to the single original act of organizing; it did not apply to the ongoing addition of new units or to the continuing recruitment of new members. The CPUSA had been reorganized in 1945; since the three-year statute of limitations for prosecution had expired in 1948, the *Yates* convictions under the organizing clause of the act were void.

Harlan's second major foundation for reversal involved the implications of the term "advocacy." In *Dennis*, Vinson had accepted the government's contention that the Smith Act had been "directed at advocacy, not discussion." While the latter was protected by the First Amendment, the former fell within the limits of permissible governmental action. Although Harlan accepted that distinction, he rejected its fundamental premise—that all advocacy of Marxism represents an incitement to illegal action. Instead he drew another, even narrower, distinction "between advocacy of abstract doc-

trine and advocacy directed at promoting unlawful action." With that, the central question in *Yates* became "whether the Smith Act prohibits advocacy and teaching of forcible overthrow as an abstract principal, divorced from any effort to instigate action to that end." The Court held it did not. Since the trial judge failed to note this distinction in his charge to the jury, all of the convictions were flawed. Based on a reading of the trial evidence in light of the new standards, Harlan ordered five of the *Yates* defendants, including Richmond, released and the other nine retried.

Faced with having to prove that the Marxism taught by the CPUSA was directly aimed at promoting illegal action, the government ceased all further prosecution under the advocacy clause of the Smith Act. Charges against the remaining nine *Yates* defendants were dropped. Charges were also dropped or convictions reversed for another 81 Communists in various stages of prosecution. The Smith Act, for all intents and purposes, was dead.

As expected, the Red Monday decisions generated intense criticism. Conservative opinion was vocal and harsh. David Lawrence, writing in *U.S. News and World Report*, scornfully asserted that "treason as an 'abstract doctrine' has now been legalized by the Supreme Court." The New York *Daily Mirror* characterized June 17 as a "moment for weeping." *Life* declared that "the Court displays the most lamentable virginity about Communism." Leaders of the legal and law enforcement communities likewise criticized the decisions as "an appalling setback" in the maintenance of national security and assailed the national tribunal as too zealous in the protection of individual rights at the expense of national self-preservation.

The loudest protests arose in the halls of Congress. To many conservative congressmen, the Court not only seemed to be giving Communists free reign to subvert U.S. institutions, it was also deliberately seeking to undermine legislative authority. Most vitriolic of all was Republican Senator William Jenner of Indiana who, in a speech on the floor of the Senate on July 26, 1957, asserted: "No conceivable combination of votes in Congress could have done as much damage to our legislative barriers against communism and subversion as the Supreme Court of the United States. . . . There was a time when the Supreme Court conceived its function to be the interpretation of the law. For some time now, the Supreme Court has been making law—substituting its judgment for the judgment of the legislative branch."

Accordingly in 1957 and 1958 a number of anti-Court bills appeared on the floors of both the Senate and the House. Most were aimed at curtailing the High Court's appellate jurisdiction in the areas of antisubversive activities. Four were introduced to reverse the Court's narrow definition of the world "organize" so as to amend the Smith Act and allow prosecution for activities that expanded and enlarged organizations dedicated to the violent overthrow of the government. Not one of the bills was enacted, but each generated intense debate. Efforts aimed at clarifying congressional intent concerning "advocacy" also made little headway, largely because Harlan's ruling clearly suggested that any law designed to punish the advocacy of abstract doctrine would be ruled unconstitutional. The strong sentiment voiced in Congress did, however, attract the Court's attention. In several political offender cases decided subsequently, the Court abruptly stepped back from its libertarian stance. In *Barenblatt v. United States* (1959), for example, the High Court sustained the contempt conviction of a college professor who refused to answer questions of the House Un-American Activities Committee concerning his membership in the Communist party. In *Scales v. United States* (1961), it also upheld the portion of the Smith Act that made it a crime to be a member of an organization advocating the violent overthrow of the U.S. government.

In spite of this retrenchment, the *Yates* ruling did signal a new determination on the part of the Warren Court to stem the excesses of anti-Communism. By interpreting the organizing and advocacy clauses very narrowly, Harlan and his colleagues rendered the Smith Act virtually unenforceable and thereby removed a powerful weapon from the arsenal of those who sought to crush political radicalism.

Selected Bibliography

Belknap, M.R. *Cold War Political Justice: The Smith Act, the Communist Party, and American Civil Liberties.* Westport, CT: Greenwood Press, 1977.

Mollan, R. "Smith Act Prosecutions: The Effect of the *Dennis* and *Yates* Decisions." *University of Pittsburgh Law Review* 26 (1965): 705–48.

Murphy, W.F. *Congress and the Court: A Case Study in the American Political Process.* Chicago: University of Chicago Press, 1962.

Richmond, A. *A Long View From the Left: Memoirs of an American Revolutionary.* Boston: Houghton Mifflin Co., 1973.

Steinberg, P.L. *The Great "Red Menace": United States Prosecution of American Communists, 1947–52.* Westport, CT: Greenwood Press, 1984.

THE COURT AND THE COMMITTEE

by Jerold L. Simmons
Department of History
University of Nebraska at Omaha

Watkins v. United States, 354 U.S. 178 (1957) [U.S. Supreme Court]

On April 29, 1954, John T. Watkins, an organizer for the United Auto Workers, appeared before a subcommittee of the House Un-American Activities Committee (HUAC) investigating Communist activities in the Chicago area. It was one of the HUAC's many "road shows," designed to demonstrate to the locals the widespread influence of Communists in the union movement and, at the same time, garner headlines for committee members. Watkins proved a cooperative witness. While denying membership in the party, he spoke candidly of his past work for Communist causes and participation in Communist meetings.

When the HUAC's counsel began to read a list of names, however, Watkins balked. He turned to a statement prepared by his lawyer, Joseph Rauh, Jr., and, with the committee's indulgence, read it into the record: "I am not going to plead the Fifth Amendment, but I refuse to answer certain questions that I believe are outside the proper scope of your committee's activities. I will answer any questions which this committee puts to me about myself. I will also answer questions about those persons whom I knew to be members of the Communist Party and whom I believe still are. I will not, however, answer any questions with respect to others with whom I associated in the past. . . . I do not believe that such questions are relevant to the work of this committee nor do I believe that this committee has the right to undertake the public exposure of persons because of their past activities."

It was a principled statement carefully drafted by Rauh to convince both the HUAC and the public that Watkins was sincerely concerned about Communist infiltration of the labor movement but could not bring himself to subject "innocents" to the HUAC's brand of exposure. It was not a new tactic. Writer Lillian Hellman, also a Rauh client, had taken a similar position before the committee in 1952. Hellman, though, covered herself with frequent references to the Fifth Amendment, as had several witnesses in the famous Hollywood hearings of 1951. The committee had been inconsistent in citing those who took this stand, and Rauh hoped his client might escape the hearings without a citation for contempt of Congress and with his reputation and conscience unsullied.

It was a position that appealed to Rauh's sense of what was right. A cofounder of Americans for Democratic Action, Rauh supported vigorous measures to fight Communism, but, like most liberals, he resented the unprincipled tactics used by congressional inquisitors. He especially resented the "degradation ceremonies" in which ex-Communists and other leftists were forced to inform on associates, many of whom had long since left the party. To him, naming names was a dirty business, often forcing honorable men to inform on other honorable men who had made innocent mistakes in the past. And it seemed to serve no real purpose. Invariably, the individuals named were

known to the committee, so the procedure seemed little more than a pointless ritual, a rite designed to show whether a witness had fully rejected his political heresy.

Yet those degradation ceremonies had become the Committee's *raison d'être* in the 1950s; they served to justify the Committee's ever-growing appropriations and staff, to keep the files of blacklisting agencies filled, and to satisfy the public's desire for retribution. It was the HUAC's business to collect names, to use its power to expose as a form of punishment. Witnesses could "take the Fifth" and thereby avoid answering the committee's questions, but taking the Fifth implied an admission of guilt and carried serious consequences. Many employers, including the United Auto Workers, automatically discharged "Fifth Amendment Communists," and the label invited private harassment. To avoid the harsh alternatives of taking the Fifth or naming names, a number of mid-1950s witnesses began to search for other options. Several, like college instructor Lloyd Barenblatt, challenged HUAC's authority to inquire into their private political beliefs and associations under the First Amendment. Others, like John Watkins and playwright Arthur Miller (another Rauh client), simply refused to name the "innocents."

HUAC's chairman, Harold Velde, rejected Watkins's statement and the House of Representatives cited him for contempt of Congress. A federal district court found Watkins guilty, and the sentence—a $500 fine and one year in prison—was suspended. The case was appealed to the Court of Appeals for the District of Columbia where, initially, a three-judge panel reversed the ruling, but on rehearing the full bench upheld the conviction. In 1956, the U.S. Supreme Court granted *certiorari*.

Traditionally, the Court had shown a marked reluctance to tamper with the authority of congressional inquiries. Prior to *Watkins*, the only substantive limit on the power to investigate was in *Kilbourn v. Thompson* (1881), which required that investigations be directed at a "valid legislative purpose." During the late 1940s, the Vinson Court had denied *certiorari* to a series of petitions challenging HUAC's power to subpoena documents and compel testimony. By granting Watkins *certiorari* in 1956, the Warren Court seemed to indicate its determination to abandon this tradition of tolerance.

Rauh's Supreme Court brief concentrated on challenging the Committee's power to punish through exposure. He argued that because Congress may investigate only as an aid to legislation and because the exposure of the beliefs and associations of witnesses could not serve that purpose, the questions put to Watkins had exceeded the HUAC's authority. The brief also raised two subsidiary points: (1) that questions probing political beliefs intruded on areas protected by the First Amendment and (2) that the House resolution under which HUAC operated was unconstitutionally vague. On each of these secondary points, Rauh solicited assistance in the form of *amicus curiae* ("friend of the court") briefs.

The American Civil Liberties Union submitted a brief arguing that the HUAC's questions exceeded the bounds of legislative power under the First Amendment and that its conduct in general had a chilling effect on free expression. Telford Taylor, lawyer for Robert M. Metcalf, who had been convicted for taking a stand similar to that of Watkins, submitted an *amicus* brief arguing that the questions put to Watkins were beyond the scope of the committee's authority. The House resolution creating the HUAC authorized investigations into "the extent, character, and objects of un-American propaganda activities in the United States," but, Taylor argued, the questions put to Watkins had nothing to do with propaganda. Since the statute governing contempt provided that witnesses need only answer questions pertinent to the inquiry, Watkins should not have been required to answer. Ironically, none of the briefs questioned the power of Congress to authorize an investigation into the "propaganda activities" of private citizens.

On June 17, 1957, the Court reversed Watkins's conviction and, for the first time, attempted to deal with the difficult constitutional issues raised by congressional investigations of communism. Chief Justice Earl Warren's discursive majority opinion incorporated most of the arguments in the three briefs. He agreed that the HUAC's mandate from the House was dangerously vague, that the First Amendment did constitute a substantive limitation on the investigative power, and that the naming of names could have a chilling effect on free expression. The chief justice was obviously appalled at the HUAC's use of its public hearings to punish political dissidents, especially for past sins, and denied the existence of any "congressional power to expose for the sake of exposure."

Yet having said this, Warren backed away from the implications of his *obiter dicta*. Instead of reversing Watkins's conviction on these grounds, he merely asked Congress to exercise closer supervision of its probes and to establish a more judicious system of procedures for its committees. "A measure of added care on the part of the House and the Senate" was all that was necessary to resolve the problem.

The reversal of Watkins's conviction rested on a narrow procedural point raised only indirectly in the briefs. Both Rauh and Taylor claimed that the questions asked Watkins were not pertinent to any purpose within the committee's authority. The Court did not specifically agree with this assertion, but it did rule that a witness must be able to determine with certainty whether the questions were pertinent. Since the HUAC's mandate from the House was too vague to afford guidance and the comments of the subcommittee chair during the hearings failed to establish that pertinence, Watkins was not given sufficient information to make that determination. Consequently, he was deprived of due process of law under the Fifth Amendment.

It was a curiously confusing ruling. Warren had rambled on about the dangers of the investigative power for 25 pages and then resolved the case on a narrow procedural point having little to do with the substantive issues raised. Warren may have intended his expansive *dicta* as a warning to Congress, a threat of stronger, more restrictive rulings in the future if Congress failed to curb the excesses of its committees. The narrowness of the holding, however, suggests that the chief justice lacked the votes to issue a more substantive ruling. Warren may have wanted to go further and probably had the support of Justices Hugo L. Black, William O. Douglas, and William J. Brennan, Jr. But to hold the votes of Justices Felix Frankfurter and John Marshall Harlan, the ruling had to be narrow. The Court's two most consistent advocates of judicial restraint apparently agreed with the holding but must have had reservations about Warren's *dicta*. (Justices Harold H. Burton and Charles E. Whittaker did not participate.) In any event, Warren's opinion bred confusion. Frankfurter found it necessary to write a concurrence "to state what I understand to be the Court's holding." He omitted all references to the larger questions raised in Warren's *dicta* and summarized the ruling in three paragraphs. Justice Tom C. Clark wrote a stinging dissent denouncing Warren's opinion as "a trespass upon the fundamental American principle of separation of powers," and attacked the majority for having placed itself in the position of "grand inquisitor and supervisor of congressional investigations."

Predictably, public reaction was governed far more by the *dicta* than the holding. In this instance, the response was intensified by the fact that the ruling was delivered on the same day that the Court reversed the convictions of identified Communists in two other controversial cases, *Yates v. United States* (1957) and *Sweezy v. New Hampshire* (1957). These "Red Monday" decisions outraged conservatives like David Lawrence, who entitled a three-page editorial in *U.S. News and World Report* "Treason's Biggest Victory." Representative Harold Jackson, a member of the HUAC, charged that the Court had rendered both his committee and its counterpart in the Senate "innocuous as two kittens in a cageful of rabid dogs." Liberals, however, read *Watkins* as "a landmark" ruling. The *Washington Post* praised the Court for "action long overdue," and *The New York Times* called *Watkins* "an admirable opinion." John M. Coe told members of the National Lawyers Guild that while *Watkins* might not have "completely castrated" the House committee, "it has at least seriously impaired its virility."

Five weeks after the ruling, Senator William E. Jenner of Indiana introduced a bill designed to remove five types of cases from the appellate jurisdiction of the Supreme Court, including all cases involving contempt of Congress. The measure was soon tabled and the movement to curb the Court was eventually blocked by the congressional leadership. Ironically, though, the whole affair had little impact on the conduct of the HUAC. Its chairman recognized that the Court had demanded very little of his committee. It merely required that the HUAC include a statement of legislative purpose at the beginning of each hearing and explain the pertinence of individual questions when challenged by a witness. This the committee did. Beyond that, its procedures were not altered.

The promise of Warren's *dicta* never materialized. Two years later the Court once again confronted the HUAC question, but this time with the chief justice and his liberal supporters in the minority. In *Barenblatt v. United States* (1959), the Court stepped back from the implications of *Watkins* and confirmed the committee's powers almost without exception. So *Watkins* remained little more than a lecture, a promise unfulfilled, and the HUAC continued its harassment of the left without interruption.

Selected Bibliography

Alfange, D., Jr. "Congressional Investigations and the Fickle Court." *University of Cincinnati Law Review* 30 (Spring 1961): 113–71.

Beck, C. *Contempt of Congress: A Study of the Prosecutions Initiated by the Committee on Un-American Activities.* New Orleans: The Hauser Press, 1959.

Goodman, W. *The Committee: The Extraordinary Career of the House Committee on Un-American Activities.* New York: Farrar, Straus & Giroux, 1968.

Millikan, K.B. "Congressional Investigations: Imbroglio in the Court." *William and Mary Law Review* 8 (Spring 1967): 400–20.

Murphy, W.F. *Congress and the Courts: A Case Study in the American Political Process.* Chicago: University of Chicago Press, 1962.

Pritchett, C.H. *Congress Versus the Supreme Court, 1957–60.* Minneapolis: University of Minnesota Press, 1961.

THE COURT AND THE COMMITTEE: PART TWO

by Jerold L. Simmons
Department of History
University of Nebraska at Omaha

Barenblatt v. United States, 360 U.S. 109 (1959) [U.S. Supreme Court]

In *Watkins v. United States* (1957), Chief Justice Earl Warren delivered a stern lecture to Congress on the constitutional dangers implicit in legislative investigations of communism. He affirmed the First Amendment as a substantive limit on congressional inquiries and denied the existence of any congressional power "to expose for the sake of exposure." While the exact holding in *Watkins* turned on a narrow legal point (the fact that the House Un-American Activities Committee (HUAC) had failed to inform the witness of the pertinence of the questions he was required to answer), Warren's expansive *dicta* led to speculation that the U.S. Supreme Court would soon deal the HUAC a lethal blow. Security conscious conservatives blasted the ruling and introduced a succession of Court-curbing bills in Congress. The HUAC's opponents hailed the decision as a turning point, a signal that the Court had finally decided to place limits on the excesses of McCarthyism. Yet two years later, in *Barenblatt v. United States*, the *Watkins* majority splintered and the Warren Court stepped back from its confrontation with the HUAC.

Lloyd Barenblatt, a 31-year-old psychology instructor, recently dismissed from Vassar College, appeared before the HUAC in June 1954 during its hearings on Communist infiltration of education. While specifically rejecting the protections afforded by the Fifth Amendment, he refused to answer any questions concerning his past or present membership in the Communist party. Instead, he denied the HUAC's authority to conduct investigations into higher education or to inquire into his political affiliations. Unlike Watkins, Barenblatt failed to challenge the pertinence of the HUAC's questions, so his case rested largely on claims of academic freedom and the First Amendment. His conviction for contempt of Congress was upheld by the Court of Appeals for the District of Columbia in January 1957,

and a petition for review was remanded to that court for rehearing in light of *Watkins* the following June. When the court of appeals again upheld the conviction, the Supreme Court granted *certiorari*.

Barenblatt's case appeared quite strong. The 1954 hearings were clearly designed to punish radical teachers, and the HUAC made no effort to hide that fact. The HUAC's stated purpose in the hearings was to identify Communist educators and its annual report for 1954 noted with obvious approval that "most of the teachers called have been suspended or permanently removed from their positions." Given Warren's pronouncements against this kind of punishment by exposure in *Watkins*, critics of the HUAC hoped that the Court would use *Barenblatt* to place substantive limits on the HUAC's conduct.

The Supreme Court's ruling, handed down on June 8, 1959, dashed all such hopes. Justice John Marshall Harlan's opinion—joined by Justices Felix Frankfurter, Tom C. Clark, Charles E. Whittaker, and Potter Stewart—specifically rejected Barenblatt's claims and in the process dramatically reversed the thrust of the *Watkins* ruling. The plaintiff's brief, prepared by the American Civil Liberties Union, concentrated on three points: that the HUAC had called Barenblatt to testify strictly to punish him, that the forced disclosure of private political beliefs violated Barenblatt's First Amendment rights, and that the HUAC had no authority to harass teachers or to invade the sanctity of educational institutions.

Harlan dispatched each of these contentions. He rejected any notion that the Court could or should attempt to judge the HUAC's motives in calling Barenblatt. In other words, exposure might have been a consequence of the committee's actions, but the Court would not inquire into the workings of congressmen's minds. While admitting that the HUAC's activities might intrude on protected freedoms, Harlan also insisted that Barenblatt's right to silence under the First Amendment had to be balanced against the nation's right of self-preservation. Because the Communist party was part of a recognized international conspiracy, Barenblatt's rights had to give way to Congress's need to know the details of that conspiracy. Barenblatt's academic freedom argument was also summarily dismissed. Harlan conceded that freedom of the laboratory and lecture hall was a value important to U.S. society, but an educational institution was "not a constitutional sanctuary."

Harlan's opinion prompted a stinging dissent written by Justice Hugo L. Black and joined by Chief Justice Earl Warren and Justice William O. Douglas and, in part, by Justice William J. Brennan, Jr. Black criticized the majority for failing "to see what is here for all to see—that exposure and punishment is the aim of this committee and the reason for its existence." He added: "I cannot believe that the nature of our judicial office requires us to be so blind." Black also rejected the entire notion of balancing First Amendment rights, arguing that the Court virtually always used the balancing test to reject claims of individual freedoms.

The *Barenblatt* ruling pleased conservatives and puzzled Court observers. Most attributed the Court's retreat from *Watkins* as a clear case of judicial timidity, a tactical withdrawal in the face of mounting public and congressional pressures. The Court-curbing proposals in Congress had given the justices a scare, the story went, and to protect the institution, they stepped back from the confrontation. Obviously, this explanation cannot account for the actions of the four dissenters. In *Barenblatt*, Black, Warren, Douglas, and Brennan adopted a position that was impressively radical. Yet it may explain the nature of Harlan's ruling. All Harlan

had to do in *Barenblatt* was to distinguish the two cases on the basis of fact. Watkins had challenged the pertinence of the questions, Barenblatt had not. But the ruling went much further, in effect confirming the validity of the HUAC's mandate to inquire into "propaganda activities" and its power to compel testimony to that end. For the first time, the HUAC's activities received clear constitutional sanction. Harlan may have felt it necessary to draft his opinion in such a way as to reject the implications of Warren's ruling in *Watkins* and at the same time pacify the Court's congressional critics.

Whatever the reason, *Barenblatt* ended speculation about the legality of the HUAC, and thereafter the Court limited its consideration to matters of committee procedure. The confrontation between the Court and the committee continued through the 1960s, and in the more liberal atmosphere of that decade, the justices reversed a succession of contempt citations. But in every case, the ruling turned on a narrow procedural point. The Court never again seriously weighed the constitutionality of congressional investigations of communism.

Selected Bibliography

Kalven, H., Jr. "Mr. Alexander Meiklejohn and the *Barenblatt* Opinion." *University of Chicago Law Review* 27 (Winter 1960): 321–25.

Millikan, K.B. "Congressional Investigations: Imbroglio in the Courts." *William and Mary Law Review* 8 (Spring 1967): 400–20.

Murphy, W.F. *Congress and the Courts: A Case Study in the American Political Process.* Chicago: University of Chicago Press, 1962.

Pritchett, C.H. *Congress Versus the Supreme Court. 1957–60.* Minneapolis: University of Minnesota Press, 1961.

Slotnick, M.C. "The Congressional Investigating Power: Ramifications of the *Watkins-Barenblatt* Enigma." *University of Miami Law Review* 14 (Spring 1960): 381–411.

THE RIGHT TO TRAVEL

by Jerold L. Simmons
Department of History
University of Nebraska at Omaha

Aptheker v. Secretary of State, 378 U.S. 500 (1964) [U.S. Supreme Court]

For over five decades, Elizabeth Gurley Flynn defied established authority. As a teenager, she harangued street-corner crowds with socialist dogma and recruited mill workers for the Industrial Workers of the World. In her twenties, she helped orchestrate the violent textile strikes in Lawrence, Massachusetts, and Paterson, New Jersey, and led antiwar protests against the Wilson administration. Devoting her life to labor activism and political radicalism meant frequent disappointment and official harassment. Often jailed for her work with the "Wobblies" and later with the American Civil Liberties Union (ACLU), she learned to confront authority with an engaging smile and firm defiance. After Sacco and Vanzetti, the Passaic strike, and other lost causes of the 1920s, she dropped out of radical activities for a decade. Returning in 1937, Flynn joined the Communist party, an action that prompted her ouster from the ACLU three years later. She rose rapidly in the party's hierarchy and, by the early 1950s, was its most prominent female advocate. In 1961, she succeeded Eugene Dennis as chair of the party's central committee; a few months later her passport was revoked.

For more than a decade, the State Department had attempted to restrict the foreign travel of U.S. Communists. In February 1951, under pressure from Senator Joseph McCarthy and the "China Lobby," the department began denying passports to party members and anyone else considered under Communist influence. In *Kent v. Dulles* (1958), the U.S. Supreme Court instructed the department to abandon the policy. Justice William O. Douglas declared the right to travel to be one of the liberties protected by the due process clause of the Fifth Amendment, but he chose to base the ruling on much narrower grounds—on the fact that Congress had not authorized the Secretary of State to deny passports on political grounds.

Four years later, the policy was revived, this time with congressional sanction. The Internal Security Act of 1950, popularly known as the McCarran Act, made it a crime for any member of an organization under order to register with the Subversive Activities Control Board (SACB) to use or seek to obtain a passport. When the Supreme Court upheld an SACB order against the American Communist party in June 1961, the State Department again cancelled the passports of party leaders.

Flynn and Herbert Aptheker, noted historian and editor of one of the party's journals, brought suit for the return of their passports. A three-judge district court upheld the ban as a reasonable action against "the threat posed by the world Communist movement," and, in December 1963, the Supreme Court agreed to review the case. In the oral arguments, John J. Abt, counsel for Flynn and Aptheker, drew heavily on Justice William O. Douglas's comments in *Kent v. Dulles*. He maintained that the passport restriction denied his clients due process and that Section 6 of the Internal Security Act was unconstitutionally broad. Calling the provision "preventive detention," he argued that Congress lacked the authority "to confine people to this country unless they had done something illegal."

His arguments found instant support among the justices. Justice Hugo L. Black voiced his opinion, expressed on numerous occasions, that the entire McCarran Act was unconstitutional. Other justices concentrated on Section 6 and pressed the State Department's counsel, Abram Chaves, to explain why the act banned the travel of all Communists in all situations. Chaves defended the law as a rational expression of the government's right of self-preservation. All Communists were potential agents of a foreign power, he argued, and federal officials were in no position to determine which party members were most dangerous. Therefore, the only rational plan consistent with national security was to ban the travel of all.

By a vote of 6–3, the Court sided with Flynn and Aptheker. Justice Arthur J. Goldberg, writing for Chief Justice Earl Warren, and Justices Douglas, Black, William J. Brennan, Jr., and Potter Stewart, struck down Section 6 of the Internal Security Act on the ground that it "too broadly and indiscriminately restricts the right to travel and thereby abridges the liberty guaranteed by the Fifth Amendment." To Goldberg, the statute made irrelevant the degree of a member's involvement in the party and therefore condemned the innocent along with the guilty. Under the law's provisions, it was a crime for any Communist "to apply for a passport to travel abroad to visit a sick relative, to receive medical treatment, or for any other wholly innocent purpose." Goldberg then applied the principle that a governmental purpose may not be achieved by means which "invade the area of protected freedoms" if a less objectionable means exists to achieve the same purpose. Since Congress might have distinguished between active and passive members of the party and between those traveling for innocent purposes and those whose activities might harm the country, the statute was arbitrary, overly broad, and void on its face.

The dissenting justices, led by Justice Tom C. Clark, objected to the fact that the majority had ruled on the potential dangers of the law rather than on its application in this case. "We have no 'innocent members' before us," he claimed. Flynn and Aptheker were active party members and their stated purpose for going abroad was to lecture and attend meetings. Clark maintained that such activities could harm U.S. interests and that the government was justified in prohibiting their travel.

The decision prompted little comment in the press. On the same day the Court decided *Aptheker* (June 22, 1964), it handed down two more controversial rulings: *Jacobellis v. Ohio*, which limited state powers to censor movies, and *Escobedo v. Illinois*, which extended the right to counsel to pretrial questioning. These two cases drove *Aptheker v. Secretary of State* to the back pages of the nation's newspapers. Nevertheless, Flynn and her colleagues considered it a major victory for the party and for the right to travel freely. The passport ban was lifted and six weeks later Flynn journeyed to the Soviet Union, where she received a hero's welcome. The following month, she died in a Moscow hospital at age 74.

Selected Bibliography

Baxandall, R.F. *Words on Fire: The Life and Writing of Elizabeth Gurley Flynn.* New Brunswick, NJ: Rutgers University Press, 1987.

"The Future of American Passports as Restrictions on Travel." *Northwestern University Law Review* 60 (1965): 511–30.

"Limitations of the Right to Travel Abroad and the Implications on First Amendment Rights of the Individual." *Oklahoma City University Law Review* 8 (1983): 469–504.

E. The 1960s

CONSCIENTIOUS OBJECTION:
A RIGHT OR A PRIVILEGE?

by Delane Ramsey
Taylors, South Carolina

United States v. Seeger, 380 U.S. 163 (1965) [U.S. Supreme Court]

Teachers often have trouble defining "democracy." "Rule by the people" does not prevail because it ignores the dynamics, tensions, and compromises that are characteristic of democracy. A better definition mentions the balancing between competing interests that typifies democracy: "rule by the majority, while protecting the rights of minorities." Among the competing interests that give democracy its dynamic thrust is the power of the state and the rights of citizens. Competition between these two interests often leads to political and philosophical conflict within democratic societies. Controversies over zoning, discrimination, privacy, and expression are some examples of the conflict between state interests and citizen's rights.

The competition between state and citizen can reach its most extreme form when the deepest held values of each conflict. For the state, the greatest value is its survival; thus, war is a state's greatest threat. For many citizens, their strongest value is religion. One of the most serious philosophical and, therefore, political problems a state must solve is the conflict between these two strongest values. Can a state compel a citizen to fight in its defense if the citizen is conscientiously opposed to war on religious grounds?

Religious objection to war has a long history in the United States. The beliefs of the peace churches, including the Quakers, Mennonites, and Moravians, were well-known and generally respected during the colonial period. Colonial and early state legislatures allowed exemptions from militia duty on religious grounds. These religious exemptions were continued by the federal Militia and Draft Acts of 1863 and 1864. In addition to religious exemp-

tions, commutation and substitute provisions made it possible for a federal conscript to buy his way out of service if he did not qualify for a religious exemption.

The philosophical base for exempting conscientious objectors from military service was succinctly stated by Chief Justice Charles E. Hughes in 1931: "In the forum of conscience, duty to a moral power higher than the State has always been maintained." In the U.S. experience, this "higher moral power" had been consistently and explicitly predicated on religion, since only a religious objection to military service was permitted. The Draft Act of 1917 continued the religious requirement for exemption, which was offered to those from "a well-recognized religious sect . . . whose principles forbade participation in war." An executive order soon expanded the exemption to those with "personal scruples against war," because of problems in identifying these sects and their members. The executive order effectively postponed having to solve the problem of nonreligious objection to war. In 1919, Harlan Fiske Stone, later U.S. Supreme Court justice, recognized that conscience "may be disassociated from what is commonly recognized as religious." Most legal questions dealing with conflict between the religious and the nonreligious eventually became constitutional questions falling under the establishment and free exercise of religion clauses of the First Amendment. However, in *United States v. Macintosh* (1931), the Supreme Court ruled that conscientious objection was a privilege subject to congressional action, not a constitutional question, thus apparently ending the constitutional debate.

In the Draft Act of 1940, Congress again established a religious requirement. Conscientious objector status was granted to those whose opposition to war was based on "religious training and belief." The test was now a personal religious belief, not membership in a recognized sect. The Selective Service Act of 1948 further defined religious training and belief as an "individual's belief in a Supreme Being involving duties superior to those arising from any human relation." Exemption was specifically refused on the basis of political, sociological, or philosophical views; or on a mere personal moral code.

In 1958, three challenges to the religious requirement for conscientious objector status began working their way through the federal court system. Daniel Seeger wanted exemption because of his belief in "goodness and virtue for their own sakes, and a religious faith in a purely ethical creed" and admitted "skepticism in the existence of God." Another claimant, Arno Jakobson, claimed conscientious objector status on the basis of his belief in "Godness" and that his "most important religious law was that no man ought ever to willfully sacrifice another man's life as a means to any other end." The third, Forest Britt Peter, claimed conscientious objector status because the taking of human life violated his moral code. He explained: "You could call that a belief in a Supreme Being or God. These just do not happen to be the words I use." All three were convicted for failing to report for induction. The court of appeals reversed the Seeger and Jakobson convictions, and the U.S. attorney appealed then to the U.S. Supreme Court. Peter's conviction was upheld by the court of appeals; and he, too, appealed to the Supreme Court. Because of their similarity, the Court combined all three cases for argument in November 1964 and considered them together.

Court watchers expected the ruling to be on constitutional grounds, possibly reversing *Macintosh*. The constitutional questions were based on the establishment and free exercise of religion clause of the First Amendment and the Fifth Amendment's due process clause. The court of appeals had, in fact, reversed Seeger's conviction on the constitutional due process grounds that the religious requirement for exemption created an impermissible classification by treating religious and nonreligious citizens differently. The Supreme Court, however, moved in a different direction and sidestepped the constitutional questions.

The Court's decision in the three combined cases, decided collectively as *United States v. Seeger* (1965), followed the judicial practice of narrow construction. Rather than deciding the cases and resolving the issue on broad constitutional grounds, the Court treated the matter in statutory terms: it redefined "Supreme Being" in the 1948 law. In reducing a Solomonic legal question to a lexicographer's task, the Court ruled that "religious belief within the meaning of the exemption . . . is whether it is sincere and meaningful belief occupying in the life of its possessor a place parallel to that filled by the God of those admittedly qualified for the exemption." The Court went on to state that the exemption does not cover "political, sociological, or economic considerations rather than religious belief." In an additional attempt to avoid the constitutional issue of the establishment clause, the decision stated: "There is no issue here of atheistic beliefs and accordingly the decision does not deal with that question." By redefining "Supreme Being" as a sincere, meaningful substitute for religious feeling or belief, the Court effectively left sincerity as the only requirement for the conscientious objector exemption. The burden of proof remained on the claimant, but his proof no longer had to include a specific religious component.

The thrust of the *Seeger* decision had been expected, even if on unexpected grounds. Some criticism came from the legal community, taking the Court to task for avoiding the constitutional question. Popular reaction, however, was rather muted. The Court was already unpopular among conservatives; this decision was just additional grist for their mill.

Contrary to popular expectations, mainstream clergy supported both the concept and the decision. Several denominations had been counseling conscientious objector claimants before the decision was announced. Following the decision, clergymen now suggested additional activism, saying "[T]he churches should either cease producing such young men or cease neglecting them."

Throughout the Vietnam War, during the late 1960s and the early 1970s, the *Seeger* decision was a staple part of the litany of young men seeking to avoid military service in a war they felt was unjust. In 1966, for example, heavyweight boxing champion Muhammad Ali claimed the exemption as a Muslim. His Selective Service board denied his claim, leading to his arrest and conviction. The board questioned his sincerity, because he had only recently converted to Islam. The Supreme Court reversed his conviction in 1970.

The conscientious objector controversy abated with the end of the draft in 1973. And constitutional issues involving religious and quasi-religious exemptions in the Selective Service System remain unresolved.

Selected Bibliography

Brodie, A., and H.P. Southerland. "Conscience, the Constitution, and the Supreme Court: The Riddle of *United States v. Seeger.*" *Wisconsin Law Review* 1966 (Spring 1966): 306–29.

"Do Pacifists Embarrass the Churches?" *Christian Century* 82 (Nov. 17, 1965): 1404–05.

THE RIGHT OF CHILDREN TO BE SEEN AS WELL AS HEARD

by Joseph F. Wall
Department of History
Grinnell College

Tinker v. Des Moines Independent Community School District, 393 U.S. 503 (1969)
[U. S. Supreme Court]

In early December 1965, a small group of peace activists met in the home of Mr. and Mrs. William Eckhardt of Des Moines, Iowa. Mrs. Eckhardt was an officer in the Women's International League for Peace and Freedom, and it had been her initiative that called this meeting.

Among those present was the Tinker family. Leonard Tinker, an ordained Methodist minister, was employed by the American Friends Service Committee, which had a regional office in Des Moines. The group discussed ways of making their opposition to the Vietnam War more visible to the general public, for in December 1965, most Americans were still supportive of President Johnson's policies in Southeast Asia. It was suggested at this meeting that an effective way to attract attention to their antiwar protest movement would be the wearing of black armbands as a symbol of mourning for the Vietnam casualties and also for the loss of the nation's traditional ideals and moral values.

Several of the families present had brought their children with them, and some of the children were eager to take part in this demonstration by wearing black armbands to school.

Christopher Eckhardt, who was a junior in high school, volunteered, along with the four Tinker children, who were, among themselves, able to cover the spectrum of public education in Des Moines: Paul was in second grade, Hope in fifth grade, Mary Beth in junior high school, and John, who was a classmate of Christopher, in senior high. It was agreed that the Eckhardt boy and the four Tinker children would wear armbands to school for the few days remaining prior to the break for the Christmas holidays.

The school officials heard of these plans, and the superintendent of the Des Moines community school district hurriedly called together the school principals on December 14. A statement was issued to inform all pupils and teachers that the wearing of armbands to school and the refusal upon request to remove them would result in suspension until the students agreed to attend school without the offending symbols. The next day, the Eckhardt and Tinker children appeared in school with armbands. When they refused to remove them, they were sent home.

Since there were only four days of school remaining before the holiday break, this suspension was not a Draconian punishment. Nevertheless, the issue was of immense importance to the Tinkers, the Eckhardts, and to other peace activists in the city. It was also of concern to the Iowa Civil Liberties Union, which offered the services of its legal counsel, Dan Johnston, if the families involved wished to pursue the case in court. The Tinkers and the Eckhardts accepted the offer. In the federal district court for southern Iowa, their suit asking for a permanent injunction against the regulation and for nominal damages was denied by the judge.

Undaunted, the petitioners then appealed to the U.S. Court of Appeals for the Eighth Circuit. This court of eight judges considered the case *en banc*, and divided 4–4 in its judgment. With an equally divided court, the decision of the lower court was, in effect, affirmed. The appellants and the Civil Liberties Union then asked for and received a writ of *certiorari* from the U.S. Supreme Court. The case was argued before the High Court on November 12, 1968, and the Court delivered its opinion on February 24, 1969—more than three years after the original incident had occurred.

By a 7–2 decision, the Supreme Court reversed the lower courts and found for the appellants. Justice Abe Fortas delivered the opinion of the Court. He found precedent for deciding for the petitioners in a 1966 case of the Fifth Circuit in which the rights of a group of black students, who had worn Student Nonviolent Coordinating Committee (SNCC) buttons to school in defiance of an order by school officials prohibiting the wearing of those buttons, were upheld. This case had established a principle applicable only to the Fifth Circuit, which the Supreme Court would now, with *Tinker*, make applicable to the entire nation. Fortas also found support for the *Tinker* decision in *West Virginia School Board of Education v. Barnette* (1943), which, in denying the right of West Virginia schools to compel students to salute the flag, had ruled that the First Amendment was applicable to all units of state government, "Board of Education not excepted."

The *Tinker* decision went far beyond these earlier cases, however, in extending First Amendment rights to school children. Although the Court recognized that school officials have a particular responsibility to maintain order so that the school's educational program can function properly, it now placed the burden of proof on school officials to justify any school regulation that impinged on the rights of freedom of speech, assembly, and religion.

In doing so, the Court quite explicitly reintroduced "the rule of reason" principle, which in the nineteenth century had been used most effectively to support a substantive interpretation of due process in the defense of property rights. Any regulation by school authorities must now be a "reasonable" restriction of an activity, which, if performed, would most certainly disrupt the educational process. The Court emphasized the fact that the Des Moines school officials had been unable to offer any evidence that the wearing of armbands had caused disruption in the classroom. Nor was the school district's regulation justified by an apprehension that something might happen if armbands were worn. "But in our system, undifferentiated fear or apprehension of disturbance is not enough to overcome the right to freedom of expression," Fortas declared. "Any departure from absolute regimentation may cause trouble. Any variation from the majority's opinion may inspire fear. . . . In our system, state operated schools may not be enclaves of totalitarianism. School officials do not possess absolute authority over their students. Students in school as well as out of school are 'persons' under our Constitution."

There was another precedent-breaking judgment in his opinion that had a special meaning to constitutional lawyers and judges: the statement that the wearing of armbands is "closely akin to 'pure speech' which, we have repeatedly held, is entitled to comprehensive protection under the First Amendment." What, in effect, the Court was doing was to blur, if not erase, the sharp distinctions that previous Courts had tried to establish among four categories of possible behavior: (1) pure speech, which is precisely that and which has the fullest protection under the First Amendment; (2) symbolic speech, in which such artifacts as buttons, flags, or armbands stand as symbols for the spoken word, and which may have full protection of the First Amendment; (3) symbolic action, such as hanging an official in effigy, or burning a draft card, which is even less protected by the Bill of Rights; and (4) pure action, such as blowing up a court house or hanging an official, an expression of protest that has no protection under the Constitution. In *Tinker*, the Court seemed to say that it was no longer possible to differentiate between pure speech and symbolic speech. Wearing an armband is as much a part of free speech as is delivering a sermon against the war. There were some constitutional authorities who thought that the next step might be to identify symbolic action as well as symbolic speech with pure speech, leaving only pure action outside the pale of full constitutional protection.

There were two dissenting opinions in this case. Justice John Marshall Harlan's dissent was short. Although recognizing that "state public authorities in the discharge of their responsibilities are not wholly exempt from the requirements of the Fourteenth Amendment respecting the freedoms of expression and association," he nevertheless could not concur in the Court's judgment that the burden of proof for maintaining a restrictive regulation must lie with the official. "I would in cases like this cast upon those complaining the burden of showing that a particular school measure was motivated by other than legitimate school concerns. . . ."

The other dissenting opinion was that of Justice Hugo L. Black, which was not short: it was an impassioned, some would later say hysterical, response to the majority opinion. He spoke extemporaneously for over 20 minutes, predicting terrible consequences as a result of this decision: students running amok in the school halls, children determining their own curricula, and youngsters setting their own standards for evaluation. His opinion is replete with clichés, one of the more unfortunate being that "children should be seen not heard"—hardly appropriate to this case, since the issue was not children being heard but children being seen wearing armbands.

Black's opinion shocked civil libertarians, for he had been the great apostle of civil liberties. He was the one justice to insist that the First Amendment was absolute, that when the Constitution says Congress may pass no law restricting freedom of speech, press, or religion, it means precisely that—no law. How could one then explain this seeming reversal of position? Had the First Amendment suddenly become for him something no longer absolute but highly qualifiable, based on the age of the person whose rights had been restricted? These were questions that liberals were asking about their tarnished hero.

Black maintained that he had not reversed himself at all in respect to the First Amendment. He insisted that it was the majority on the Court that had, with this decision, destroyed an important category of distinctions that must be maintained in the consideration of civil liberties. Every free speech case, Black believed, involves three disparate considerations: (1) the content of the expression, (2) the vehicle for the expression, and (3) the forum for that expression. On the first consideration, Black was an absolutist. He would defend to death, as he always did, free speech in the abstract—the right to say or express any idea with no restriction placed on that right. But expression was never in the abstract: there is always an agent for that expression, and there is always a place in which it is made. As to agent or vehicle of expression, Black was not an absolutist. He would again defend to death any adult who wore a black armband in a public park or street, but a child was an entirely different agent and not responsible enough to wear the mantle of freedom. Finally, there is the forum, and here Black was the most restrictive of all. There were certain fora in which the First Amendment could not prevail. Free speech could not be supported in an arena that was not designed for a public forum. Black thought he had established this concept in *Adderley v. Florida* (1966), in which he had given the majority opinion that a group of college students had no right to assemble at a county jail to protest the arrest of fellow students. A jail yard was not a public forum for assembly and free speech.

Now, he found his colleagues retreating from that position. For Black, a school, like a jail yard, was not meant to be a public forum. The First Amendment did not apply in that setting. Many students might have found wry humor in Black's equating high schools with jails. Black's dissent in *Tinker* was one of the last opinions he was to deliver. And sadly, many liberal students of the Supreme Court lost some respect for him as a result of it.

In spite of the pique of Black, the Eckhardt and Tinker children had won their long, hard fought suit. The case was remanded to the lower court for whatever it deemed proper relief. The children's long past three-day suspension was expunged from their school record, and the Des Moines School District had to pay all costs of the litigation. Five children had reached to the very top of the judicial system and had earned a place in U.S. constitutional history by taking the Bill of Rights into the classroom.

Selected Bibliography

Aldrich, A. "Freedom of Expression in Secondary Schools." *Cleveland State Law Review* 19 (Jan. 1970): 165–76.

Note, "Symbolic Speech, High School Protest, and the First Amendment." *Journal of Family Law* 9 (1969): 119–25.

Denno, T.F. "Mary Beth Tinker Takes the Constitution to School." *Fordham Law Review* 38 (Oct. 1969): 35–62.

Nahmod, S.H. "Beyond *Tinker*: The High School as an Educational Public Forum." *Harvard Civil Rights Law Review* 5 (April 1970): 278–300.

———. "Black Arm Bands and Underground Newspapers: Freedom of Speech in the Public Schools." *Chicago Bar Record* 51 (Dec. 1969): 144–53.

THE PENTAGON PAPERS

by Edwin E. Moise
Department of History
Clemson University

New York Times Co. v. United States, 403 U.S. 713 (1971) [U.S. Supreme Court]

The United States's participation in the Vietnam War was winding down by 1971, but public debate over the war was escalating. It was in this situation that *The New York Times* began to publish excerpts and summaries from a heavily documented history of U.S. policy toward Vietnam, originally compiled within the Department of Defense. Formally entitled *United States–Vietnam Relations, 1945–67*, it is commonly referred to as "The Pentagon Papers."

The decision to compile such a history had been made by Secretary of Defense Robert McNamara on June 17, 1967. A "task force," headed by Leslie Gelb, was established within the International Security Affairs section of the Department of Defense. Members of the task force were recruited from both within and outside the Department of Defense. Few were able to remain on the task force for the entire duration of the project; Gelb estimated that the 36 professionals who worked on the project did so for an average of four months each.

The task force conducted no interviews; its work was based entirely on written materials, mostly governmental files. It collected documents on U.S. policy toward Vietnam not only from the files of the Department of Defense, but also from the Department of State and the Central Intelligence Agency. Some of its members had a limited and informal access to White House files. The task of synthesizing the documents to produce a history was carried out collectively; most chapters had more than one author, and the final version does not carry the authors' names.

The end product was a history accompanied by the original texts of many of the documents on which it had been based. Narrative and documents totaled over 7,000 pages, arranged in 47 volumes. The writing was declared complete on January 15, 1969; retyping and reproduction took additional time. Fifteen copies were finally available for distribution—seven within the Department of Defense and eight elsewhere—in June 1969.

Daniel Ellsberg, a researcher with the Rand Corporation (a "think tank" devoted to national defense issues), had been a minor participant in the writing of the Pentagon Papers. After the project was completed, however, he studied the whole manuscript carefully. Having developed doubts about the Vietnam War; reading the Pentagon Papers turned him strongly against the war. He decided that the U.S. involvement in Vietnam had been fundamentally immoral and should be ended immediately. He believed that the evidence that had convinced him of this should be made available to Congress and the public.

The Rand Corporation had been given two of the 15 complete sets of the Pentagon Papers. Ellsberg began systematically photocopying one of these late in 1969. He then searched for a way to get this material released to the public. In March 1971, after failing to persuade several U.S. senators to make the study public, he delivered a large portion of the Pentagon Papers to Neil Sheehan of *The New York Times. The New York Times* did not receive the four volumes of the study devoted to U.S. efforts, conducted through intermediaries, to negotiate an end to the war. Ellsberg later explained "I didn't want to get in the way of the diplomacy. . . ."

Sheehan and others at the *Times*, working in extreme secrecy, produced a series intended for publication on ten consecutive days. Each daily installment consisted of a long article, plus the original texts of some of the most important supporting documents. The articles were not abridged versions of the corresponding sections of the narrative that had been written by the task force in the Department of Defense; they were written by reporters of *The New York Times*, using information from both the narrative and the documents in the Department of Defense version. On the average, about one-half of each installment was narrative and one-half was composed of texts of original documents. The first installment was published Sunday, June 13, 1971.

On the evening of June 14, at which point two installments had been published and the third was about to go to press, Attorney General John Mitchell informed *The New York Times* that "publication of this information is directly prohibited by the provisions of the Espionage Law, Title 18, United States Code, Section 793. Moreover, further publication of information of this character will cause irreparable injury to the defense interests of the United States. Accordingly, I respectfully request that you pub-

lish no further information of this character and advise me that you have made arrangements for the return of these documents to the Department of Defense." The newspaper rejected Mitchell's request.

On June 15, the Justice Department asked for an injunction forbidding the publication of further installments. Judge Murray I. Gurfein, of the Southern District of New York, issued a restraining order, preventing the publication of any further installments for four days, to allow time for the case to be argued. This set an important precedent. It was the first time that a U.S. court had restrained a newspaper, in advance, from publishing a specific article.

The fact that there was no precedent for such an action helps to explain the extraordinary speed with which the case moved through the courts. The Justice Department had obtained the restraining order without first proving to Gurfein's satisfaction that such restraint was either necessary or legal. All of the courts that became involved in the case agreed that such a situation could not be allowed to persist for the length of time that is usually required for the U.S. court system to decide anything important.

Gurfein heard arguments from both sides June 18. The hearing included a closed session, during which classified information was considered; Gurfein excluded from the court all but two members of *Times'* defense team, over the objections of the its attorneys. On June 19, he handed down a decision in favor of the *Times*. He cited principles of freedom of the press and a lack of evidence that publication of the Pentagon Papers posed a serious danger to the nation. He extended his restraining order, however, to allow the Justice Department time to appeal.

Immediately after the first restraining order was issued against the *Times*, Ellsberg provided a substantial portion of the Pentagon Papers to the *Washington Post*. The *Post* decided not to publish the texts of original documents, as the *Times* had done, but published on June 18 in some editions of the *Post*, the first of a series of articles written by *Post* reporters based on the Pentagon Papers.

The Justice Department made the same legal moves as in the *Times* case, but more quickly. The attorney general's request that the newspaper cease publication of the series, the newspaper's refusal, and the filing of a suit in U.S. District Court for the District of Columbia all occurred on June 18. District Judge Gerhard A. Gesell asked the *Post* to withhold publication voluntarily, for a brief period, to allow time for consideration of the case. The *Post* refused. Gesell then ruled in favor of the newspaper, citing (1) the First Amendment principle of freedom of the press; (2) the fact that the Espionage Act, which the Justice Department had used as the legal foundation of its suit, contained no provision for restraint or censorship of the press; and (3) the fact that "the Court ha[d] before it no precise information suggesting in what respects, if any, the publication of this information will injure the United States. . . ."

The Justice Department proceeded immediately to the U.S. court of appeals, which voted 2–1 to reverse Gesell's decision. The court of appeals temporarily restrained publication of the series in the *Post* and ordered Gesell to hold a hearing June 21, at which the Justice Department would have a further opportunity to prove that publication of the series in the *Post* would cause such harm to the United States as to justify a prior restraint on publication.

At the June 21 hearing, as at the June 18 one before Gurfein, there were several hours of secret testimony from which the public was excluded. Gesell, however, allowed the Post's full defense team to remain in the courtroom during this testimony. At the end of the day, Gesell ruled that the government had provided no proof that publication of the Pentagon Papers would cause disastrous harm to the country. He concluded: "The First Amendment remains supreme."

The Justice Department appealed the rulings by Judges Gurfein and Gesell; the appeal in each case was heard June 22 and produced a decision June 23. The Court of Appeals for the Second Circuit ordered that the case against *The New York Times* be sent back to Gurfein for him to hold another hearing. At that time the Justice Department would have the opportunity to present additional evidence that publication of the Pentagon Papers would harm national security. The U.S. Court of Appeals for

the District of Columbia upheld Gesell's ruling in favor of the *Post*, but extended the restraining order against it to allow time for the Justice Department to appeal to the U.S. Supreme Court.

On June 24, the *Times* appealed to the Supreme Court against the ruling of the Second Circuit. The Department of Justice, after an unsuccessful effort to win another hearing before the District of Columbia Circuit, also appealed the decision of that court to the Supreme Court. Four justices voted to reject the appeal by the Department of Justice without a hearing and to allow the newspapers to proceed with publication. The majority, however, voted to combine the two cases and hear them on June 26.

When the Supreme Court agreed to hear the two cases, it also narrowed the restraining orders then in effect against the two newspapers to cover only a limited amount of material from the Pentagon Papers that the government had designated as exceptionally sensitive. The newspapers did not take immediate advantage of this, however; one reason being that the list of documents whose publication was forbidden was itself a secret document, which could not legally be shown to the editor of either newspaper. The government did not want to give the newspapers information they might not already have about highly sensitive documents.

The two newspapers had refused, as a matter of principle, to tell the government what information they intended to publish, or even what portions of the Pentagon Papers they had in their possession. This was a serious handicap to the newspapers in court. It allowed the Justice Department to search through all of the Pentagon Papers, not just the sections the newspapers were actually planning to publish, for material whose disclosure would harm the national interest.

The last four volumes of the original study, whose disclosure seemed to the government extremely undesirable, had never been given to either newspaper because Ellsberg shared the government's view in this instance. In regard to the material that Ellsberg did furnish, the *Times* exercised some restraint in avoiding the publication of information about which the newspaper felt there might be legitimate national security concerns. The *Post* exercised more restraint, avoiding the publication of the full texts of any of the documents from the Pentagon Papers. Had the newspapers been less secretive about their publication plans, court proceedings might have centered on the articles that the two newspapers were planning to publish rather than on the original text of the Pentagon Papers, and the Justice Department would less often have been able to cite specific passages whose publication might imperil national security.

The decision whether to publish such material had been hotly debated at both newspapers; in each case the publishers were caught between news personnel, who urged publication and a vigorous assertion of freedom of the press, and attorneys, who urged a much more conservative attitude. *The New York Times'* law firm, Lord, Day, and Lord, had strongly advised against publication. This advice having been rejected, Lord, Day, and Lord declined to represent the newspaper when its legal battle with the government began on June 15. Alexander M. Bickel agreed to represent *The New York Times* only a few hours before the first Court hearing on June 16.

The withdrawal of the firm that *The New York Times* had consulted before publication left all the parties in the ensuing battles—the Justice Department and both newspapers—represented in court by attorneys who knew nothing about the Pentagon Papers until *The New York Times* began publication of its series on June 13. They did not have adequate time to familiarize themselves with this mass of material before the case reached the Supreme Court.

The fact that the attorneys had not had adequate time to prepare may help to explain the frequency with which the government, when asked before lower courts to cite particular items in the Pentagon Papers whose disclosure would seriously harm national security, had picked items that the newspapers were able to prove had already been published elsewhere, long before the *Times* began its series.

The Supreme Court heard arguments June 26. The entire hearing was public; the Court had rejected, 6–3, a request by the Justice Department that there be a closed session for discussion of secret material. Such material was discussed in secret briefs filed by both sides.

The Justice Department, by this time, had shifted the legal basis of its case from the Espionage Act, under which its suits against the two newspapers had originally been brought, to the inherent powers of the presidency. Solicitor General Erwin Griswold argued that the president's responsibility for the conduct of foreign policy and his role as commander in chief of the armed forces required that he have the ability to forbid the publication of military secrets.

The Court handed down its decision June 30, finding for the newspapers 6–3. Justices Hugo L. Black, William J. Brennan, Jr., William O. Douglas, Thurgood Marshall, Potter Stewart, and Byron R. White were able to agree on a very short statement, the core of which was: "Any system of prior restraints of expression comes to this Court bearing a heavy presumption against its constitutional validity." The government "thus carries a heavy burden of showing justification for the enforcement of such a restraint. The District Court for the Southern District of New York in the *New York Times* case and the District Court for the District of Columbia and the Court of Appeals for the District of Columbia Circuit in the *Washington Post* case held that the Government had not met that burden. We agree."

Each of the six, however, wrote a separate concurring opinion; Black and Douglas each joined in the other's opinion, and Stewart and White likewise. No common thread unites all six concurring opinions. Themes touched on in some of the opinions include assertions that (1) a free press plays a vital role and must be protected; (2) Congress had passed no law, and indeed had repeatedly rejected proposed laws, under which the government could enjoin publication of government secrets by the press; and (3) the government had failed to prove that publication of the Pentagon Papers would cause such dire harm as to justify making an exception to the general principles of the First Amendment.

The key to the outcome lay with Stewart and White, the two justices who had not been willing to find for the newspapers on June 25 without a hearing, but who did find for them on June 30. They believed that Congress had not intended that the Espionage Act be used as a basis for restraints on the press. They said that publication of the Pentagon Papers would cause significant harm to the nation, but that the government had not proven that publication would cause such great harm as to justify prior restraint. They rejected Solicitor General Griswold's arguments for the inherent powers of the presidency. As White put it, with Stewart joining him, "The Government's position is simply stated: The responsibility of the Executive for the conduct of foreign affairs and for the security of the Nation is so basic that the President is entitled to an injunction against publication of a newspaper story whenever he can convince a court that the information to be revealed threatens 'grave and irreparable' injury to the public interest; and the injunction should issue whether or not the material to be published is classified, whether or not publication would be lawful under relevant criminal statutes enacted by Congress, and regardless of the circumstances by which the newspaper came into possession of the information. At least in the absence of legislation by Congress, based on its own investigations and findings, I am quite unable to agree that the inherent powers of the Executive and the courts reach so far as to authorize remedies having such sweeping potential for inhibiting publications by the press."

The minority—Chief Justice Warren Burger and Justices Harry L. Blackmun and John Marshall Harlan—produced three dissenting opinions, but the three were in close agreement; Burger and Blackmun both joined in Harlan's opinion. By and large, they discussed entirely different questions from those analyzed in the opinions of the majority, rather than taking opposite sides on the same questions. They did not believe that restraints on publication of government secrets had to be based on legislation passed by Congress, and in the realm of foreign affairs, they were willing to grant the executive branch almost unfettered authority to decide which government secrets the press should be forbidden to publish. Also, they did not claim that the government had proved that publication of the Pentagon Papers would cause such dire harm to the nation as would justify an

exception to the First Amendment; the closest any of them came was Blackmun's statement that the evidence provided "possible foundation" for such a claim. Finally, they did not feel that the government should have been required to provide such proof. Harlan, indeed, appeared to take seriously the possibility that it would be legal to enjoin publication of a top secret document the actual contents of which were innocuous, on the theory that "harm enough results simply from the demonstration of such a breach of secrecy."

Harlan, with Burger and Blackmun joining him, argued that the decision whether the Pentagon Papers could be published without harm to the national interest was a decision only the executive branch was qualified to make, and that it would be a violation of the separation of powers for the judiciary to inquire too closely about the rationale for the decision of the executive branch, before enforcing it upon the press: "[I]n performance of its duty to protect the values of the First Amendment against political pressures, the judiciary must review the initial Executive determination to the point of satisfying itself that the subject matter of the dispute does lie within the proper compass of the President's foreign relations power. Constitutional considerations forbid a complete abandonment of judicial control. . . . Moreover, the judiciary may properly insist that the determination that disclosure of the subject matter would irreparably impair the national security be made by the head of the Executive Department concerned—here the Secretary of State or the Secretary of Defense—after actual personal consideration by that officer. . . . But in my judgment the judiciary may not properly go beyond these two inquiries and redetermine for itself the probable impact of disclosure on national security."

The case did not seem, on its face, an overwhelming victory for freedom of the press. The barrier against prior restraint of publication had been breached, and attorneys for both the *Times* and the *Post* had conceded, in arguments before the Supreme Court, that the breach was to an important degree legitimate—that the government could legally forbid publication of an article if it could prove that publication would cause sufficient harm. Of the six justices making up the majority, three—Brennan, Stewart, and White—suggested that prior restraint of publication would be acceptable if the government proved that what Stewart called "direct, immediate, and irreparable damage" would follow from publication. They found in favor of the newspapers because the government had failed to make such a proof.

Furthermore, the precedent had been set that a temporary restraining order could be issued in anticipation of the government's proof that serious harm would result from publication. Only three justices—Black, Douglas, and Brennan—opposed the use of such restraining orders in their opinions. At the other extreme, the three justices in the minority argued that the government should be permitted to enjoin publication for an extended period, much longer than had been done in this case, to allow time for a proper evaluation of the Pentagon Papers. Chief Justice Burger suggested that something clearly warranting prior restraint of publication, analogous to Justice Oliver Wendell Holmes's famous example of shouting "fire" in a crowded theater, "may be lurking in these cases and would have been flushed had they been properly considered in the trial courts, free from unwarranted deadlines and frenetic pressures."

Neither of these precedents has had an important impact since 1971, however, because they apply only in cases where the issue is prior restraint. The government can seldom learn, in advance, that a particular newspaper is about to publish government secrets. The newspapers had won on several issues that potentially had broader implications.

First, the Justice Department had attempted to establish a theory that the fact that documents were classified "top secret" created a presumption that their disclosure would harm the nation seriously enough to justify prior restraint on publication. As the Justice Department's brief in the Court of Appeals for the Second Circuit had put it, "[T]he government does not have the burden of supporting a Top Secret classification." This theory had been rejected. Second, the courts had rejected the theory that the Espionage Act applied to publication of secret material in the U.S. press. Finally, the Court

had rejected the Justice Department's claim for the inherent powers of the presidency.

Although the Supreme Court had rejected prior restraint of publication in this case, Stewart and White, the swing votes, suggested that the appropriate way for the government to protect its secrets was the deterrent effect of criminal prosecution rather than prior restraint of publication. The Justice Department did not attempt criminal action against the newspapers, but it did obtain indictments of Daniel Ellsberg for conspiracy, theft of government property, and violation of the Espionage Act.

The trial of Ellsberg and an alleged co-conspirator, Anthony Russo, began January 3, 1973, in Los Angeles. Its verdict might have clarified some of the issues that had been left unresolved by the plethora of opinions in *New York Times v. United States*, but the judge dismissed the charges on May 11, citing a pattern of governmental misconduct including the facts that (1) the government had repeatedly failed to make timely disclosure of exculpatory information to the defense; (2) some of Ellsberg's telephone conversations had been overheard by a governmental wiretap, but the records of this wiretap (including both the authorizations for them and the logs that would have revealed what conversations had been overheard) were missing from Justice Department files; and (3) the White House "plumbers," whose activities were beginning to be revealed in connection with the Watergate Affair, had burglarized the office of Ellsberg's psychiatrist in search of evidence against Ellsberg.

Some of the issues in the Pentagon Papers case were revisited in August 1984, when *Jane's Defence Weekly* published U.S. satellite photographs of a Soviet aircraft carrier. *Jane's*, a British publication, was less committed to protecting its sources than a similar U.S. publication might have been, and it quickly furnished investigators proof that the photographs had come from Samuel L. Morison, an intelligence analyst working for the U.S. Navy. Morison was arrested October 1, 1984, and charged with espionage and theft of government property in regard to the photographs and also some other classified information he had given to *Jane's*.

From the government viewpoint, this was a perfect case to test the theory that giving classified information to the press can be a violation of the Espionage Act, since prosecutors could plausibly claim that Morison had been motivated by money. He had been hoping to obtain a full-time job with *Jane's*, and he had actually been paid a small amount for some of the information he had given to the magazine.

United States v. Morison moved through the courts at a more normal speed than the Pentagon Papers case. Morison was convicted in October 1985. He was given a two-year sentence, of which he eventually served slightly less than eight months before being paroled. His appeal was rejected by the Fourth Circuit Court of Appeals in April 1988. On October 17, 1988, the Supreme Court announced its refusal to hear the case.

Morison established a precedent that the Espionage Act can apply to governmental employees who give classified information to the press. It remains to be seen whether this will reopen the question of whether the Espionage Act can be used against the press itself in cases of publication of classified information.

Selected Bibliography

The Pentagon Papers, as Published by The New York Times. New York: Bantam Books, 1971.

The Pentagon Papers: The Defense Department History of United States Decisionmaking on Vietnam. 5 vols. Boston: Beacon Press, 1971–72.

Schrag, P. *Test of Loyalty: Daniel Ellsberg and the Rituals of Secret Government.* New York: Simon & Schuster, 1974.

Ungar, S.J. *The Papers & The Papers: An Account of the Legal and Political Battle Over the Pentagon Papers.* New York: E.P. Dutton, 1972.

United States-Vietnam Relations, 1945–67: Study Prepared by the Department of Defense. 12 vols. Washington: U.S. Government Printing Office, 1971.

INDEX OF CASES

Note: Cases featured in an essay are in bold face.

INDEX OF NAMES AND SUBJECTS